LONGMAN

Thesaurus of American English

Pearson Education Limited
Edinburgh Gate
Harlow
Essex CM20 2JE
England, UK
and Associated Companies throughout the world

Visit our website: http://www.longmandictionariesusa.com

First published 2013

Words that editors have reason to believe constitute trademarks have been described as such. However, neither the presence nor the absence of such a description should be regarded as affecting the legal status of any trademark.

ISBN 978 1 4082 7197 1
ISBN 978 1 4479 3895 8

Set in Whitney by Letterpart, UK
Printed in China (SWTC/01)

Acknowledgements

Editorial Director
Michael Mayor

Publishing Manager
Laurence Delacroix

Managing Editor
Chris Fox

Senior Editor
Karen Cleveland-Marwick

Editors
Elizabeth Beizai
Stephen Handorf
Lucy Hollingworth
Elizabeth Manning
Michael Murphy
Martin Stark
Karen Stern

Project Management
Alan Savill

Production
Susan Braund

Design
Matthew Dickin
Sally Lace

Production Editor
Paola Rocchetti

Proofreaders
Pat Dunn
Isabel Griffiths
Ruth Hillmore
Howard Sargeant
Nicky Thompson

Pronunciation Editor
Dinah Jackson

Writing Guide
Lynn Bonesteel

Writing Guide Editor
Robyn Brinks Lockwood

Computational Linguist
Allan Ørsnes

Online Thesaurus Developer and Project Manager
Andrew Roberts

Project and Database Administrator
Denise McKeough

Picture Research
Sandra Hilsdon
Louise Edgeworth

The Publishers would like to thank:

- their special consultant Dr Kate Kinsella, Teacher Educator and National Academic Language and Literacy Consultant, for her support and highly informed guidance on this project
- all the teachers who have helped with the development of this new Thesaurus:

Raul Hurtado Jr, Maritza Olguin, Cassandra Roberts, Johnny E Gonzalez, Susan Watson, Priscilla Owren, Donna Amador, John Rivera, Rebecca Trissell, Kati Tobler, Claudia Rivera, Andrea Cabrera, Frances Bou, Fernando Zaike, Amy Lee, Anatoliy Verbin, Lisa Pesce, Simona McCray, Laura Fleder, Enid Villafane, Errol Lewis, Johanna, Kurt, Cheryl Madrid, Ruth Moore, Charl Norloff, Dorothy Schepps, Elly White, Tonie Badillo, Mary Beth Haan, Myshie Pagel, Tracy von Maluski, Carolina Boet, Lee Brochu, Marcella Baez,Frau, Marcello, Edith Gonzalez, Keri Kauk, Chris Sperry, Kathy Zimbaldi, Marcel Deleon, Maria Del Rocio Vargas, Judith Levy, Elisa Reyes, Kelley Baxter, Ginny Evans, Sarah Guedry, Ronica Hutson, Samantha Leinwands, Danielle Oakley, Dan Rosendahl, Holly Spinks, Marla Wharton, Elizabeth Fourzan, Myra Looper, Andrea Ramirez, Jennifer DeGraaf, Norma De La Rosa, Mary Lou Parker, Malin Jonsson, Agatha Munu, Rebecca Alvarado, Barrie S Mullian, Cristin Hickey, Katie Kennedy, Iiona Hanson, Kia McDaniel, Elizabeth Chewlin, Belinda Campbell, Mamiko Nakata, Nancy Joy Allchin, Carolyn Behram, Karen Hibbert, Joan Mitchell, Brittney Carlson, Melissa Nankin, Sonja Norwood, Erin Kirkland, Mary Lynn Poirier, Kent Adams, Joseph Halabi, David Allan, Abdou Hannaoui, Felicia Rose, Adam Kokosinski, Janna Corn, Kristine L Nazzal, Paula Leguizomon, Silna Abbato, Chris Abbato, Sandra Nunes, Mary Fodera, Veronica Tapanes, Lisa Pesce, Susan Price, Patricia McHugh, Jaclyn Pitula, Nelson Chew, Anatoliy Verbin, Dennis Robinson, Laura Fleder, Shari Friedman, Elizabeth Neblett, Shannonine M. Caruana, Mahua Re, Howard Sage, Prathima Christdas, Michael Zucaro, Daniel Perez, Tracy Martinez, Natalie Comeau, Sima Ruchanskaya, Florence Kay.

- Averil Coxhead for permission to reproduce the Academic Word List (AWL, compiled 2000), in the back of this dictionary

Table of Contents

Introduction

Kate Kinsella, Ed.D.
San Francisco State University, Center for Teacher Efficacy

The new U.S. Common Core State Standards are aligned with college and work expectations, and include rigorous content, literacy, and communication skills. They were designed to ensure that all students, regardless of economic background or neighborhood school, are receiving what they need to graduate from secondary schooling ready to pursue a higher education degree or a career. Amongst the profound shifts in this new set of standards is the emphasis on engaging with complex informational texts and using evidence routinely to analyze, inform, and argue in constructed verbal and written responses. The standards call upon students to be adept at sharing information accurately in academic register while collaborating or formally presenting judgments and interpretations. Using an appropriate academic register to articulate text comprehension and justify claims, implies an agile command of complex sentence structures, precise vocabulary, and grammatical accuracy.

Ensuring that every scholar is well equipped with the linguistic resources to tackle grade-level curriculum and assessments in the Common Core era is the responsibility of schools and districts across our nation. Every student is AELL, an academic English language learner, including those from a professional home in which language usage maps more readily onto classroom contexts. Whether collaborating with an assigned partner on a written critique of an argument or contributing an example of a concept during a class discussion, most students' linguistic default is casual interactional English. Everyday conversation is characterized by brief phrases, incomplete sentences, and imprecise vocabulary. Shifting to a style of speaking and writing that is at once formal, precise, and analytical will be for many students tantamount to linguistic whiplash.

Teachers and writing tutors have unwittingly advocated that students avail themselves of a classic thesaurus to translate their casual prose into scholarly register. However, an aspiring writer foraying recklessly into an online or hard cover traditional thesaurus is likely to deliver a final essay or speech meriting a "VUI" citation for vocabulary under the influence. Workplace colleagues and fellow classmates are equally wary of peers who awkwardly deploy sophisticated words without knowledge or conviction. Any novice writer and thesaurus user knows from experience how daunting it can be to search for a more articulate and engaging synonym for a pedestrian word, only to find a litany of 25 possible choices devoid of meaning or context. A lesson learned by legions of unsuspecting thesaurus abusers is that it is wiser to revert to banal, familiar words than to risk being derided.

The new ***Longman Thesaurus of American English***, available in print and digital formats, is an invaluable resource for writers aiming for greater lexical precision in secondary school, college, or the professional workplace. Native English speakers and English learners alike will readily appreciate the easy navigation system, accessible definitions, and illustrative sentences with modeled usage.

Proficient users of the ***Longman Thesaurus of American English*** will make fewer mistakes in word choice and sentence structure, and will see their writing dramatically improve. Online access to this user-friendly resource is straightforward and fast; the online Study Center offers a wealth of practice materials that help students become competent users of this innovative thesaurus.

As an academic language and writing mentor, I intend to recommend that every one of my students purchase this practical and potent resource. I believe that equipping classrooms with this fantastic resource will encourage students to make more mindful and articulate word choices. The new ***Longman Thesaurus of American English*** will also help deliver the promise of access and equity for youths whose educational and professional aspirations hinge upon communicative competence in the language of school and the professional workplace.

Guide to the Dictionary

All the words listed under each key word are synonyms or words with a similar meaning. However, there are differences of meaning depending on the context, usage, and how formal or informal the synonym is. You need to read the entry for each synonym to choose the correct word and see how to use it.

dry /draɪ/ *adjective*

1 when there is no water in something
- ► **dry**
- ► **dehydrated**
- ► **bone dry** (*informal*)

ANTONYMS → see **wet**

2 when the weather is dry
- ► **dry**
- ► **arid**
- ► **parched**

ANTONYMS → see **rainy**

1 when there is no water in something

dry
something that is dry has no water in it or on it: *Do you have a dry towel? This one is soaked.* | *The soil was dry and cracked.*

dehydrated
if you are dehydrated, you do not have enough water in your body: *After four days in the desert, he was severely dehydrated.*

bone dry *also* **dry as a bone** (*informal*)
something that is bone dry is completely dry: *I can walk through snow and puddles in these boots, and my feet stay bone dry.* | *There had been no rain for weeks, and the ground was dry as a bone.*

2 when the weather is dry

dry
if the weather is dry, there is no rain: *Tomorrow should be dry and sunny.* | *We've had a three-week dry spell that is hurting the crops.*
→ If you want to talk about a long period of dry weather when there is not enough rain, use the noun **drought**: *The drought has lasted for two years.*

arid
an area of a country that is arid gets very little rain and is very dry: *The cactus grows in the arid regions of the Southwest.*

Key words that you already know are shown in a blue box.

The part of speech is shown in italics after the key word. All the synonyms in each entry have the same part of speech.

A menu shows a list of the synonyms that you can use instead of the key word. It helps you find a new word quickly. All the synonyms in the menu have an explanation and an example in the section below the menu box.

Each key word has a definition, and all the synonyms listed have a similar meaning to the key word.

Some key words have several meanings. Each meaning is numbered, and has its own definition The most common meaning is shown first.

Each synonym has its own definition that explains how similar or how different it is from the key word.

Example sentences show typical contexts and how each synonym is used.

Pronunciation of the key words is shown in the International Phonetic Alphabet. Go online to listen to the pronunciation of all the words.

daily /ˈdeɪli/ *adjective*

► daily
► everyday

daily
done or happening every day: *Keep a daily record of the food you eat.* | *Exercise becomes part of your daily routine.*

everyday
ordinary, usual, or happening every day: *He liked cooking and cleaning and other everyday activities.* | *The movie is about people's everyday lives.*
→ see **day**

Cross-references show where you can find other words that you might want to look at, for example because they have a similar meaning. Sometimes, one of the meanings of a key word is dealt with at a different key word, and a cross reference will tell you where to look.

GRAMMAR CHECK: daily

Daily and **everyday** are always used before a noun: *Do you know what's happening in your children's daily lives?* | *The students write about events in their everyday world.*

Grammar Check boxes help you choose the correct word, preposition, structure, or tense and avoid making mistakes.

day /deɪ/ *noun*

► day
► daytime
ANTONYMS → see **night**

A cross-reference shows where you can find antonyms for a key word.

day
the time when it is light between morning and night: *It was a cold windy day.* | *She only leaves her house during the day – she doesn't feel safe at night.*
→ **Day** can also mean "a period of 24 hours, which starts at 12 o'clock at night": *Which day is her birthday?*

Usage notes give you extra information about how a word is used.

daytime
daytime means the same as **day**: *He works the night shift, so he sleeps during the daytime.*
→ **GRAMMAR: Daytime** can be used before other nouns to talk about things that happen during the day: *She watches a lot of daytime television.* | *Daytime temperatures rarely go above freezing in the winter.*
→ see **daily**, **sunrise**

Grammar notes help you use a particular word correctly in a sentence.

Some common words that are not key words are listed in alphabetical order with a cross-reference to where you can find them. You will find the word's definition and synonyms for it under the key word in the cross-reference.

daydream[1] *verb* → see **dream**[2]

The Topic Vocabulary section shows all the vocabulary that you need to know to talk about topics such as People's Character, Food, The Environment, and Sports.

discovery *noun* → see Topic **Science and Technology**

The Function Words section gives synonyms or related words for common prepositions, adverbs, or conjunctions such as *above*, *after*, and *between*.

during *preposition* → see Function Words

definite /ˈdefɪnət/ *adjective*

- definite
- clear
- distinct

definite (AWL)
strong and noticeable: ***There was a definite feeling of relief after the exam was over.*** | ***The team has shown definite improvement in the last few games.***

Words in the Academic Word List are important words to learn so you can use them in academic writing.

thankful /ˈθæŋkfəl/ *adjective*

- thankful
- grateful
- appreciative (*formal*)

A label after the synonym shows if a word is formal or informal.

thankful
feeling glad about something, especially that something bad did not happen or is over: *We have so much to be **thankful for** – a house to live in, enough money, and our health.* | *I am so **thankful that** no one was hurt.*

grateful
wanting to thank someone who has been kind or helpful: *I am very **grateful for** all the help I have been given.* | *She was **grateful to** her parents for their support.* | *The doctor received a thank-you letter from a grateful patient.*

appreciative (*formal*)
showing that you are pleased and feel grateful for something that someone has done: *The teacher gives them a lot of help, and the students are very appreciative.*

SYNONYM CHECK
Thankful or grateful?
You use **grateful** to say that you want to thank someone, and you use **thankful** when you are pleased or relieved about something that has happened: *I am grateful to all the doctors who helped me.* | *I am thankful that the doctors were able to help me.*

Synonym Check boxes explain confusing words and help you choose the correct synonym.

ADVERBS
You can make the adjectives that mean **thankful** into adverbs by using an **-ly** ending: *Thankfully, I have a house, enough money, and my health.* | *She thanked us gratefully for all our help.* | *The students applauded appreciatively for their teachers.*

Adverbs boxes show which adjectives can be used to make adverbs by using an *-ly* ending.

Forty Overused Words

Look up basic words you already know well and start learning new words.

Some very common words such as good, bad, beautiful, and say have many different meanings and many synonyms; these entries are shown on special pages. A cross-reference will send you to the correct pages.

good *adjective* → *go to pages 272-273*

The words with an asterisk (*) in the list below are shown on special pages.

angry, *adjective*
***bad,** *adjective*
***beautiful** (*also* **pretty**), *adjective*
***big,** adjective
easy, *adjective*
fast, *adjective, adverb*
funny, *adjective*
get, *verb*
***give,** *verb*
go, *verb*
***good** (*also* **great, amazing**), *adjective*
group, *noun*
happy, *adjective*
***hard,** *adjective*
interesting, *adjective*
like, *verb*
little, *adjective*
look, *verb*
***move,** *verb*
new, *adjective*
nice, *adjective*
old, *adjective*
***piece,** *noun*
really, *adverb*
run, *verb*
sad, *adjective*
***say,** *verb*
scared, *adjective*
slow, *adjective*
small, *adjective*
smart, *adjective*
talk, *verb*
then, *adverb*
tired, *adjective*
touch, *verb*
very, *adjective*
***walk,** *verb*
weird, *adjective*

abandon *verb* → see **cancel**, **leave**, **stop**[1]

ability /əˈbɪləti/ *noun*

- ► ability
- ► skill
- ► capability (*formal*)
- ► capacity (*formal*)
- ► aptitude
- ► potential
- ► promise
- ► competence

ability
if someone has the ability to do something, he or she can do it: *Because of the disease, she lost the **ability to** speak. | The children are divided into groups according to their ability.*

skill
the level of ability someone has to do something, especially a level that can be improved by practicing: *Most of the kids in this class need to improve their math skills.*

capability (AWL) (*formal*)
the level of ability that a person, country, machine, etc. has to do something: *It is not clear whether the country has the **capability to** produce nuclear weapons. | The test should be within the capabilities of any student.*

capacity (AWL) (*formal*)
the ability to do, understand, or behave in a particular way: *Children have a great **capacity for** love.*

aptitude
a natural ability that makes you good at learning how to do something: *From an early age, Eric showed an **aptitude for** math, and he was doing multiplication by age four.*

potential (AWL)
if someone has potential, he or she could become good at doing something in the future: *She has the **potential to** be the best basketball player in the school's history.*

promise
the ability to become good at doing something when you are older: *When his parents realized he had promise as a musician, they bought him a guitar.*

competence
someone's ability to do something in a satisfactory way, based on his or her level of knowledge or skill: *You need a basic level of competence in English to do the job. | The engineer told us that he didn't have the technical competence needed to deal with the problem, and that he would have to ask someone else to fix it.*

→ see **can** for words meaning "to have the ability to do something," **skill** and **talent** for words meaning "an ability to do something well"

able /ˈeɪbəl/ *adjective*

- ► able
- ► capable
- ► competent

able
good at doing something, especially at doing things that need intelligence: *Lucia is an able student who is earning very good grades. | He is a smart man, and as a lawyer he is very able.*

capable (AWL)
very good at doing something, especially because you have the knowledge you need or are good at organizing things: *He is a very capable and experienced coach, and the team is winning a lot of games.*

competent
having enough skill or knowledge to do something fairly well: *He is a competent actor, but he is not as good as stars such as Robert De Niro or Dustin Hoffman.*

→ see **can** for words meaning "to be able to do something," **talented** for other words meaning "good at something"

ADVERBS

You can make the adjectives that mean **able** into adverbs by using an **-ly** ending: *Laura dealt with the problem very capably. | He carried out the task competently.*

abnormal *adjective* → see **strange**

about *adverb, preposition* → see Function Words

above *preposition, adverb* → see Function Words

abroad /əˈbrɔd/ *adverb*

- ► abroad
- ► overseas

abroad
in or to a foreign country: *She returned to the*

U.S. after living abroad for many years. | *Americans traveling abroad should have medical insurance.*

overseas (AWL)
in or to a country that is across the ocean: *Catarina plans to go overseas for several months when she finishes college.* | *Do you think it is right for couples to adopt a child from overseas?*
→ see **foreign** for words meaning "not from your own country"

GRAMMAR CHECK: abroad

Abroad is an adverb, and it is never used before a noun. **Overseas** can be used as an adverb or an adjective. You can say: *My brother is traveling abroad* or *My brother is traveling overseas.* Don't say: ~~*an abroad bank*~~. Say: *an overseas bank*. Don't say: ~~*go to abroad/overseas*~~. Say: *go abroad/overseas*.

absence *noun* → see **lack[1]**

absent /ˈæbsənt/ *adjective*

- absent
- truant
- missing

ANTONYMS → see **present[1] (1)**

absent
not at work or school when other people expect you to be there, for example because you are sick: *Two people were absent today.* | *Lupe has been **absent from** work for a week with a bad back.*

truant
not at school when you do not have permission to stay away and you are not sick: *He was often truant and got into a lot of trouble.*

missing
someone who is missing cannot be found, and no one knows whether he or she is alive or dead: *Two of the soldiers survived, but two are still missing.*

absolutely *adverb* → see **completely**, **extremely**

academic *adjective* → see Topic **Education**

accept /əkˈsept/ *verb*

- accept
- take

ANTONYMS → see **refuse (2)**

accept
to agree to something that someone offers you: *Are you going to accept their job offer?* | *They invited me to dinner and I accepted.*
→ **GRAMMAR:** Don't say: ~~*He accepted to work for them*~~. Say: *He agreed to work for them.*

take
take means the same as **accept** but is less formal: *He decided to take the job.* | *I hope you'll take my advice and see a doctor.*

SYNONYM CHECK
Accept or take?

Accept and **take** mean the same thing and can be used in many of the same sentences. However, you usually **accept** an offer, an invitation, an award, help, or an apology. You usually **take** a job, advice, an opportunity, or a bribe.

acceptable /əkˈseptəbəl/ *adjective*

- acceptable
- valid
- legitimate
- tolerable
- bearable

ANTONYMS → see **unacceptable (2)**

acceptable
something that is acceptable is good enough, so people are willing to agree to it or allow it: *The solution needs to be **acceptable to** both sides.* | *Swearing is not acceptable in the classroom.*

valid (AWL)
having a good reason for doing something, which people will accept: *If you have a valid reason for missing the test, for example being sick, you will be allowed to take it at a later time.*

legitimate
legitimate means the same as **valid**: *Voters have legitimate concerns about the economy.*

tolerable
something that is tolerable is not very good, but you are able to deal with it: *The conditions in the prison are tolerable, but not pleasant.*

bearable
if something is bearable, it is difficult or unpleasant, but you can deal with it: *The breeze made the heat bearable.*
→ see **satisfactory** for **acceptable** meaning "good enough"

ADVERBS

You can make the adjectives that mean **acceptable** into adverbs by using an **-ly** ending: *The hotel room was acceptably clean.* | *It was tolerably cool in the house, even though it was very hot outside.*

access *noun* → see **entrance**, Topic **Computers and the Internet**

accident /ˈæksədənt/ *noun*

1 when a vehicle is damaged
- ► **accident**
- ► **crash**
- ► **collision**
- ► **wreck** (*informal*)

2 something bad that happens by chance
- ► **accident**
- ► **mishap**

1 when a vehicle is damaged

accident
an event in which a car or other vehicle is damaged while traveling, and often someone is hurt: *When speed limits are lowered, there are fewer traffic accidents.* | *She was badly injured in a car accident.*

crash
an accident in which a vehicle hits something hard: *Ten passengers were injured **in the** bus **crash**.*

collision
an occasion when a car, train, or plane hits something else that is moving: *The school bus was involved **in a collision with** a delivery truck.*

wreck (*informal*)
an accident in which a vehicle is badly damaged: *Ice on the highway caused the 18-car wreck.*

2 something bad that happens by chance

accident
something bad that happens by chance and hurts someone or damages something: *Terry had an accident at work and had to go to the hospital.* | *I'm sorry I broke your phone – it was an accident.*

mishap
a small accident or mistake that does not have a very serious effect: *We had a few minor mishaps in the kitchen, but we managed to make a good meal.*

accidental /ˌæksəˈdentəl/ *adjective*

- ► **accidental**
- ► **unintentional** (*formal*)

ANTONYMS → see **deliberate**

accidental
happening because of chance and not planned to happen: *We do not know whether the damage was accidental or deliberate.*

unintentional (*formal*)
not planned to happen. If an action is **unintentional**, it sometimes looks as though you planned it, when you did not: *He said that the errors on his tax return were unintentional.*

accidentally /ˌæksəˈdentəli/ *adverb*

- ► **accidentally**
- ► **unintentionally**
- ► **by mistake**
- ► **by chance**

ANTONYMS → see **deliberately**

accidentally *also* **by accident**
if you do something accidentally or by accident, it happens because of chance, not because you want it to happen: *I locked myself in the bathroom accidentally.* | *The boys say the fire started by accident.*

→ **GRAMMAR: By accident** usually goes at the end of a sentence: *I broke it by accident.* **Accidentally** sounds slightly more formal and can go at the end of a sentence or before a verb: *I broke it accidentally.* | *I accidentally broke it.*

unintentionally
if you do something unintentionally, you do not plan to do it, but it seems like you did it deliberately: *In her speech, she unintentionally offended some people.* | *The movie is unintentionally funny.*

by mistake
if you do something by mistake, you intend to do one thing but you make a mistake and do something else instead: *I took Gary's keys by mistake when I left the house.*

by chance
in a way that you do not expect, or in a way that does not seem to have a reason: *The last time I saw him was completely by chance, on the subway.*

→ see **accidental**, **chance**

accommodations *noun* → see **hotel**

accompany *verb* → see **come**

accomplish *verb* → see **succeed**

accurate *adjective* → see **exact**, **right**[1], **true**

accurately *adverb* → see **exactly**

accusation /ˌækyəˈzeɪʃən/ *noun*

- accusation
- allegation (*formal*)
- charge
- indictment (*formal*)

accusation
a statement saying that someone has done something wrong, when this has not been proved but may be proved later: *The former mayor faces **accusations of** stealing money from the city.* | *She denied **accusations that** she had lied in court.*

allegation (*formal*)
a statement that says someone has done something illegal, when this has not been proved but may be proved later: *The **allegation that** he was a spy has never been proved.*

charge
an official statement made by the police, saying that someone may have done something illegal: *He has been arrested **on charges of** murder.*

indictment (*formal*)
an official written statement saying that someone may be guilty of a crime and should go to a court of law: *According to the indictment, the woman had stolen over $1 million from the government.*

accuse /əˈkyuz/ *verb*

- accuse
- allege

accuse
to say that someone has done something wrong or illegal, when this has not been proved and may or may not be true: *She got upset when Michael accused her of lying.* | *He **is accused of** murder.*

allege
to say that someone has done something wrong, although it has not been proved and may or may not be true: *He **alleges that** the other man hit him first.*
→ see **prosecute**

accustomed to *adjective* → see **used to**

ache[1] *verb* → see **hurt**

ache[2] *noun* → see **pain**

achieve *verb* → see **succeed**

achievement *noun* → see **success**

acquire *verb* → see **buy**, **get**

across *preposition, adverb* → see Function Words

act[1] /ækt/ *verb*

1 to be a character in a play, movie, or on TV
- act
- play
- portray
- perform (*formal*)

2 to behave as if something is true, when it is not
- act (*informal*)
- pretend
- fake

1 to be a character in a play, movie, or on TV

act
to pretend to be a character in a play, movie, or television show: *I acted in high school, but I haven't been in any plays since then.* | *She loved to act and dreamed of becoming a movie star.*

play
if you play a character, you pretend to be that person in a play, TV show, or movie: *She played the role of Ray's mother in the TV series.* | *Who played Rachel in the TV show "Friends"?*

portray
portray means the same as **play** but sounds slightly more formal: *In the movie, he portrays a lawyer who is arrested by mistake.*

GRAMMAR CHECK: act
Don't say: ~~*She portrayed the role of Ray's mother in the TV series.*~~ Say: *She portrayed Ray's mother in the TV series.*

perform (*formal*)
if someone performs a role or part, he or she acts in a play or musical: *The director saw him perform the role of Curly in a production of "Oklahoma."*
→ If a group of people **perform** a play, they act that play in front of an audience: *The Modern Playhouse will be performing a new play tonight.*
→ see **actor**, **perform (1)**

2 to behave as if something is true, when it is not

act (*informal*)
to behave as if something is true or real when it is not: *He **was acting like** he was upset to get his teacher's attention.*

pretend
to behave as if you are someone else. Children often **pretend** for fun: *Lily likes to dress up and pretend she is a princess.* | *Moore* ***pretended to*** *be a bank executive and stole all their money.*

fake
to pretend that something is true or real in order to trick someone: *He faked his own death to escape being arrested.*

act[2] *noun* → see **action**, **law**, Topic **Entertainment**

action /ˈækʃən/ *noun*

- action
- act
- activity
- step
- measure
- gesture
- deed

action
something that someone does: *Don't blame Tania for her brother's actions – she didn't do anything wrong.* | *The protesters' violent actions included breaking windows and throwing rocks.*
→ **Action** is also used to talk about things that are done in order to achieve something or deal with something: *Urgent action is needed to deal with this problem.*

act
an action that shows a particular quality or purpose: *Saving the boys from the river was* ***an act of*** *courage.* | *The men are wanted by the police for a variety of criminal acts.*

activity
things that people do in an organized way, especially in order to achieve something: *The company uses computers for most of its business activities.* | *Regular physical activity is important for your health.*
→ An **activity** can also be something you do because you enjoy it: *Rebecca has always loved hiking and other outdoor activities.*

step
one of a series of things that you do in order to achieve something: *The first step is to make sure you have all the things you need to make the cake.*

measure
an official action that someone does to deal with a problem: *Police are increasing the security measures at all the airports.*

gesture
something that you do to show your feelings toward someone, usually feelings of friendship: *Bringing flowers when you apologize to her is a nice gesture.*

deed
an action, especially if it is very good or very bad. **Deed** sounds fairly literary and is often used in stories: *He must be punished for his evil deeds.*
→ see **movement**

active *adjective* → see **energetic**

activity *noun* → see **action**

actor /ˈæktɚ/ *noun*

- actor
- actress
- star
- the lead
- understudy

actor
someone who performs in plays, movies, or television shows: *She went to New York to become an actor.* | *He has wanted to be a professional actor since he was in 6th grade.*

actress
a girl or woman who performs in plays, movies, or television shows. Many women now prefer to be called **actors**: *Katharine Hepburn was a famous Hollywood actress in the 1940s and 50s.*

star
a famous actor: *Many movie stars live in Los Angeles because a lot of movies are made there.*
→ The **star** of a play, movie, or television show is the person who plays the most important role: *Daniel Radcliffe is* ***the star of*** *the Harry Potter movies.*

the lead
the main actor or the main acting part in a play or movie: *Vaughn will play the lead in this summer's new romantic comedy.*

understudy
an actor who learns a part in a play so that he or she can act if the usual actor cannot perform: *The lead got sick, so the understudy had to perform.*
→ see **performer**, **theater**

actress *noun* → see **actor**

actual *adjective* → see **real**

actually *adverb* → see **really**

acute *adjective* → see **serious**, **strong**, Topic **Describing People's Emotions**

adapt *verb* → see **change[1]**

A

A

add /æd/ verb

- add
- extend
- supplement
- contribute to

ANTONYMS → see **subtract**

add
to put something with another thing or other things to make something larger: *The hotel added a 10% service charge.* | *I hate to* ***add to*** *the work you already have, but could I ask you to help me?* | *I think you should add another sentence at the beginning of the paragraph.*

extend
to make something bigger or longer, especially by adding something to it: *Jones plans to extend the main part of the building by 40 feet.*
→ You can also say that someone **extends** his or her power or influence to mean that he or she gets more power or influence: *The new government has now extended its control to all parts of the country.*

supplement (AWL)
to add something extra that makes something better or larger. Use **supplement** especially about money or types of healthy food: *Kia supplements her regular salary by tutoring in the evenings.*

contribute to
to help make something succeed, by working or giving money: *He thanked everyone who had contributed money to his political campaign.* | *Several reporters contributed to the newspaper article.*
→ see **increase**[1] for "to make an amount, number, or size larger," **say** for **add** meaning "to say more"

addiction *noun* → see **habit**

additional *adjective* → see **extra**[1], Function Word **more**

adequate *adjective* → see **satisfactory**, Function Word **enough**

adjust *verb* → see **change**[1]

administration *noun* → see **government**, **management**, Topic **Government and Politics**

admire /əd'maɪɚ/ verb

- admire
- respect
- look up to
- idolize

admire
to like someone very much because he or she is a good person, has good qualities, or does good things. You often **admire** someone who has qualities that you wish you had: ***I admire*** *my sister* ***for*** *all the effort she puts into her work.* | *I admire your courage.*

respect
to feel that someone has good qualities that are very important. You do not have to like someone to **respect** him or her: *He never gives up, and* ***I respect*** *him* ***for*** *that.*
→ You can also say that you **respect** someone's opinion when you feel that his or her ideas are important, interesting, or valuable: *I respect your opinion, but I don't agree with it.*

look up to
to like and respect someone who is older than you or who has authority over you: *Jesse looks up to his older brother and wants to become a soldier too.*

idolize
to admire and love someone so much that you think he or she is perfect: *The singer's fans idolize her and follow her from city to city.*

admit /əd'mɪt/ verb

1 to say that you have done something bad or wrong
- admit
- confess
- own up (*informal*)

2 to say that something that you do not like is true
- admit
- accept
- recognize
- acknowledge
- concede (*formal*)
- confess

1 to say that you have done something bad or wrong

admit
to say that you have done something wrong: *She kept asking questions until he* ***admitted that*** *he had lied about where he was.* | *The men say the police forced them to* ***admit to*** *the crime.*

confess
to tell someone that you have done something illegal or very wrong: *In court, he **confessed that** he had taken the money.*

own up (*informal*)
to admit that you did something wrong, especially something that was not illegal: *He finally **owned up to** the fact that his drinking was causing problems in his marriage.*

2 to say that something that you do not like is true

admit
to say that something is true or that someone else is right, even though you do not want to: *Admit it! I was right, wasn't I? | My boyfriend Paul **admitted** to me **that** he sometimes feels jealous of my ex-boyfriends.*

accept
to understand that a bad situation exists and that it may be difficult to change, even when you do not want to believe this is true: *I finally **accepted the fact that** she is never coming back, but it took a long time.*

recognize
to realize that something unpleasant happens or is true, and be willing to say that it happens or is true: *It is important to **recognize that** there is still a lot we don't know about the disease.*

acknowledge (AWL)
acknowledge means the same as **recognize** but sounds a little more formal: *Deb **acknowledges that** she sometimes gets angry too quickly.*

concede (*formal*)
to admit that something is true in a discussion or an argument, even though you really do not want to: *After the judge questioned him, the defense lawyer **conceded that** he had been wrong.*

confess
to admit something that you feel embarrassed about: *Roger **confessed that** he didn't like Susan when he first met her, even though she is now one of his best friends.*

adolescent *adjective* → see **young[1]**

adore *verb* → see **love[1]**

adult[1] /ə'dʌlt/ *noun*

- adult
- grown-up
- grown man/grown woman

ANTONYMS → see **child (1)**

adult (AWL)
a person who is not a child and is over 18 or 21 years of age: *The tickets are $20 for adults and $10 for children. | He lived most of his adult life in Chicago.*

grown-up
an adult. Children use the word **grown-up**, or you use it when you are talking to children: *Grown-ups are so boring - all they ever do is talk! | Remember - always ask a grown-up for help turning on the stove when you are cooking.*

grown man/grown woman
an adult. You use **grown man** or **grown woman** when an adult is behaving like a child: *He is a grown man - he should be able to wash his own clothes.*
→ see **old person**

adult[2] *adjective* → see **mature**

advance[1] *noun* → see **progress[1]**, Topic **Science and Technology**

advance[2] *verb* → see **improve**, **move**

advanced /əd'vænst/ *adjective*

- advanced
- sophisticated
- high tech
- state-of-the-art
- cutting-edge

advanced
using modern equipment, ideas, and methods: *China is an advanced industrial country, and most of our computers are produced there. | Advanced technology will soon make it possible for cars to be driven automatically.*

sophisticated
advanced and well designed, but also often complicated: *Cell phones are now so sophisticated that you can check email on your phone.*

high tech
using very advanced technology, especially electronic equipment and computers: *The refrigerator tells you when you need to buy more milk - it's all very high tech.*

state-of-the-art
using the most modern and advanced technology and equipment: *The studio has state-of-the-art digital recording equipment.*

cutting-edge
cutting-edge technology or research is the most advanced that there is at this time: *The Harvard Medical School is a world leader in cutting-edge medical research.*
→ see **skilled** for **advanced** meaning "having reached a high level in a subject you are studying"
→ see **modern**

A

advantage /əd'væntɪdʒ/ *noun*

1 something that helps you do something or be happy (nouns)
- advantage
- benefit
- asset
- merit
- privilege

ANTONYMS → see **disadvantage**

2 to treat someone in an unfair way in order to get an advantage (verbs)
- take advantage of
- use
- exploit
- abuse

1 something that helps you do something or be happy (nouns)

advantage
something that helps you to be successful or happy: *Being able to speak two languages is a big advantage when you are looking for a job. | One of the* ***advantages of*** *living in New York is that there are lots of exciting things to do.*

benefit (AWL)
an advantage or useful thing that you get from doing or having something: *Regular exercise has physical benefits, and it can also make you feel happier.*

asset
someone or something that helps you to be successful: *His speed makes him a valuable* ***asset to*** *the soccer team.*

merit
a good feature that something has compared with other things: *We talked about the merits of each school: one has newer buildings, but the other is much closer.*

privilege
a special advantage that only one person or group gets: *Rich young people are used to privileges like private schools, beautiful homes, and travel.*

2 to treat someone in an unfair way in order to get an advantage (verbs)

take advantage of
to treat someone in a way that is not fair in order to get what you want: *Don't let him take advantage of you. You are his roommate, not his cook, so you shouldn't have to make meals for him. | I worry that people might take advantage of him because he trusts everyone.*

use
to treat someone in a nice way, in order to get something that you want. If you **use** someone, you treat someone nicely but do not really have the kind feelings you show to the other person. **Use** is more informal than **take advantage of**: *He doesn't love you. He is just using you to get a free place to live.*

exploit (AWL)
to treat someone or something in an unfair way, in order to gain an advantage for yourself. **Exploit** sounds more formal than **take advantage of**: *Some businesses exploited their workers, making them work long hours in poor conditions. | The company exploits people's fear of crime to sell them products they do not need.*

abuse
to use your power or position in a wrong or harmful way, in order to gain an advantage for yourself: *Officials abused their power by giving jobs to their friends.*

adventure *noun* → see **experience[1]**

advertise /'ædvəˌtaɪz/ *verb*

- advertise
- promote
- publicize

advertise
to try to make people buy a product or use a service by telling them the good things about it: *The company advertises its products on national television. | I wanted to sell my car, so I advertised it in the local newspaper.*

promote (AWL)
to tell people about something such as a movie, book, or song so that they want to buy or see it: *The actor appeared on the talk show to promote his new movie.*

publicize
to give information about an event, movie, or product to the public so that they will know about it. You usually use **publicize** about the things organizations or companies do, rather than what one person does: *The library always publicizes its events on its website and in the local paper.*
→ see **sell**

advertisement /ˌædvɚˈtaɪzmənt/ *noun*

- ► advertisement
- ► commercial
- ► billboard
- ► poster
- ► flier
- ► junk mail
- ► pop-up
- ► spam
- ► preview

advertisement *also* **ad**
a picture, set of words, or short movie that tries to make people buy a product or use a service. **Advertisement** is more formal than **ad**: *Those new TV* ***advertisements for*** *cat food are really funny.* | *I like the perfume advertisement on the back cover of the magazine.*
→ GRAMMAR: Don't say: ~~*an advertisement about something*~~. Say: *an advertisement for something*.

commercial
an advertisement on television or radio: *There are lots of toy commercials during children's TV programs.*

billboard
a big sign next to a road, used for advertising something: *Turn right just after you pass the* ***billboard for*** *the Harper Motel.*

poster
a large printed notice or picture that advertises something: *Help me put up these* ***posters for*** *the school dance.*

flier
a single sheet of paper that is advertising something: *Someone was handing out* ***fliers for*** *a sale at the furniture store.*

junk mail
advertising that you receive by mail at your house but do not want: *She took the junk mail out of the mail box and threw it into the recycling bin.*

pop-up
a window, often containing an advertisement, that suddenly appears on a computer screen when you are looking at a website: *I'm always getting* ***pop-ups for*** *travel sites when I surf the Web.*

spam
email messages and advertisements that you receive but do not want to read: *My email account is always full of spam, and it's never for anything I want.*

preview *also* **trailer**
an advertisement for a movie or television program, showing short parts from it: *They show 15 minutes of* ***previews for*** *new movies before the movie starts.*

advertisement

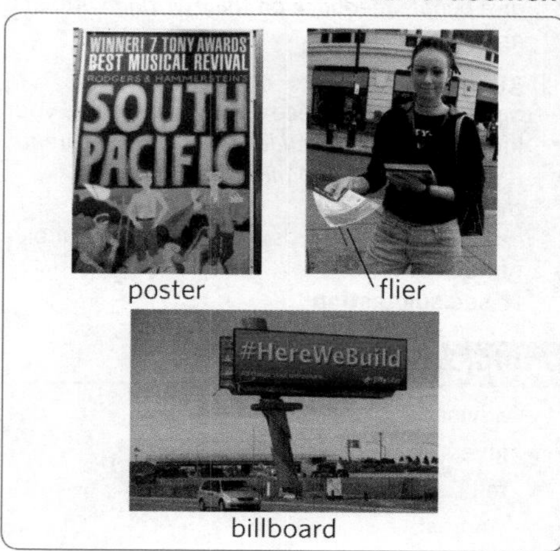

poster
flier
billboard

advice /ədˈvaɪs/ *noun*

- ► advice
- ► tip
- ► recommendation
- ► input
- ► feedback
- ► guidance

advice
ideas that other people give you, which help you to decide what you should do: *I need some* ***advice about*** *what kind of computer to buy.* | *If you had taken my advice, you wouldn't be having all these problems now.*
→ GRAMMAR: **Advice** cannot be used in the plural. Don't say: ~~*I need some advices*~~.

tip
a useful piece of advice about how to do something better: *She gave me a few* ***tips on*** *how to take more interesting pictures.*

recommendation
advice telling people what they should do, which someone gives when he or she has special knowledge of a subject or situation: *One of the report's recommendations is that class sizes should be smaller.*

input AWL
advice and ideas that you can use to help you make a decision or do something successfully. You often get **input** from several different people: *The teacher asked for* ***input from*** *the students about what topics they wanted to learn more about.*

feedback
remarks about how well someone has done something, and usually advice about how it can be improved: *These are a few ways that you can give people* ***feedback on*** *their writing without upsetting them.*

guidance
helpful general advice about how to live your life: *Children need guidance from their parents, but it's good for them to make decisions for themselves.*
→ see **hint[1]** for words meaning "a useful piece of advice"
→ see **suggestion**

advise /ədˈvaɪz/ *verb*

- ► advise
- ► give advice
- ► tell
- ► suggest
- ► recommend
- ► urge

advise
to tell someone what you think he or she should do. **Advise** sounds fairly formal and you often use it in situations where someone is giving official or legal opinions: *His lawyer* ***advised*** *him* ***to*** *talk to the police.* | *I* ***advise*** *you* ***to*** *think carefully before you make your decision.*

give advice
give advice means the same as **advise** but sounds less formal: *Marsha* ***gave*** *me some good* ***advice about*** *making new friends.*
→ **GRAMMAR:** Don't say: ~~*He gave advice me*~~ or ~~*He gave advice to me*~~. Say: *He gave me advice.*

tell
to say strongly that someone should do something, usually without allowing him or her to give an opinion: *My mom* ***told*** *me* ***that*** *I needed to get a job if I wanted to have any money this summer.*

suggest
to give someone your opinion about what he or she should do in a gentle way: *Teachers can suggest several things that might help a student, and the student can choose one.*
→ **GRAMMAR:** Don't say: ~~*She suggested him to take an English course*~~. Say: *She suggested that he take an English course* or *She suggested taking an English course.*

recommend
to say that someone should do something, especially when you have special knowledge about it or know it is good: *The mechanic strongly* ***recommended that*** *she replace her old tires before the trip.* | *One of my friends recommended this restaurant.*

urge
to try hard to persuade someone to do something by emphasizing or repeating how important it is: *My parents* ***urged*** *me* ***to*** *apply for the job, but I didn't want to.*
→ see **suggest**

affect /əˈfekt/ *verb*

- ► affect
- ► have an effect
- ► influence
- ► have an impact
- ► make a difference

affect (AWL)
to do something that produces a change in someone or something, often in a bad way: *The new fees will affect both current and new students.* | *Towns that are affected by the flooding will get help from the government.*

have an effect
have an effect means the same as **affect**, but you usually use it with an adjective to show the way in which something is affected: *The sun can* ***have*** *harmful* ***effects on*** *your skin, so always put sunscreen on your face.* | *The article* ***had a*** *huge* ***effect on*** *the way I view the fashion industry.*

influence
to affect the way someone behaves or thinks, or the way in which something develops: *His music influenced a lot of today's young musicians.* | *Does TV advertising influence what you buy?*

have an impact
to have an important or noticeable effect on someone or something: *My parents* ***have a*** *huge* ***impact on*** *my life – they help me in so many ways.*

make a difference
to change something in an important or noticeable way, especially in a way that is good: *Getting a job* ***made an*** *enormous* ***difference to*** *my confidence.*

afraid /əˈfreɪd/ *adjective*

- ► afraid
- ► scared
- ► frightened
- ► terrified
- ► petrified
- ► alarmed
- ► fearful
- ► intimidated

afraid
unhappy or worried because you think

something bad might happen: *My sister is **afraid of** flying.* | *Don't be afraid – it's just the wind making that noise.*

scared
scared means the same as **afraid** but is used in more informal or spoken language: *When he was little, he was **scared of** clowns.* | *We could hear the guns, and we were so scared.*

frightened
frightened means the same as **afraid** but sounds slightly more formal or literary: *The dog, **frightened by** the thunder, was found hiding in the barn.*

terrified
extremely afraid: *The little girl was terrified because she couldn't find her mother.*

petrified
petrified means the same as **terrified** but is used to emphasize that someone is completely terrified: *We hid in the dark closet together, **petrified that** the soldiers would find us.*

alarmed
suddenly very worried and frightened because you realize there is a problem or danger: *Her parents were alarmed when she didn't get home on time, but luckily everything was fine.*

fearful
afraid of something that could happen in the future. **Fearful** sounds slightly formal or literary: *Many people are **fearful of** losing their jobs in this bad economy.*

intimidated
feeling worried or afraid because you do not have enough confidence to deal with a situation: *Don't feel **intimidated by** the other team just because they're bigger.*
→ see Topic **Describing People's Emotions**

GRAMMAR CHECK: afraid

Afraid, **scared**, and **frightened** mean the same thing, but there are some differences in the ways you can use them.
You can say: *a scared/frightened child*, but don't say: *~~an afraid child~~*. You can say: *She was **frightened/scared by** the loud noise*, but don't say: *~~She was afraid by the loud noise~~*.
You can use all three adjectives before "of," "that," and "to": *He is **scared of** the dark.* | *I was **frightened that** no one would help me.* | *Women are **afraid to** walk alone at night.*

after *preposition, conjunction, adverb* → see Function Words

afterward *adverb* → see Function Word **after**

again *adverb* → see Function Words

against *preposition* → see **oppose**

age *noun* → see **time**

aggressive *adjective* → see **violent**, Topic **Describing People's Character**

ago *adverb* → see Function Word **for**

agree /əˈgri/ *verb*

1 to have the same opinion as someone
- ► agree
- ► share someone's view
- ► be in agreement
- ► concur (*formal*)

ANTONYMS → see **disagree**

2 to make a decision or plan after talking about it
- ► agree
- ► reach an agreement
- ► compromise

3 to say that you will do something or allow something to be done
- ► agree
- ► consent (*formal*)
- ► approve

ANTONYMS → see **refuse (1)**

1 to have the same opinion as someone

agree
to have the same opinion as someone else: *"I think blue is a good color for a bathroom." "I agree."* | *Brad said we should take a break and everyone **agreed with** him.* | *My sister and I **agree on** most things, but we have different tastes in music.*

share someone's view
to have the same opinion as another person about an important subject, especially in science, politics, or business: *There are many other scientists who share his views about the future of our planet.*

be in agreement
if people are in agreement, they have the same opinion, especially after discussing something: *I think we are all in agreement about what needs to be done.*

concur (*formal*)
to say that you have the same opinion as someone: *Three of the other Supreme Court Justices **concurred with** her decision.*

2 to make a decision or plan after talking about it

agree
to make a decision or plan after talking about it: *We **agreed to** meet later in the week.* | *Have you **agreed on** a name for the baby?*

reach an agreement
to agree about something, after discussing it until everyone is satisfied with the decision: *The two countries **reached an agreement to** end the fighting.*

compromise
to make an agreement by accepting something slightly different from what you wanted at the beginning: *Mom said I could invite six people to my party and I wanted ten, so we compromised and I invited eight people.*

3 to say that you will do something or allow something to be done

agree
to say that you will do something or allow something to be done: *My dad has **agreed to** lend me the money.*

consent (AWL) (*formal*)
to agree to do something or say that you will allow something to be done: *The actress rarely **consents to** do interviews.*

approve
to officially agree to a plan or idea: *Congress voted to approve the new law.*
→ see **match**[1] for **agree** meaning "to contain the same information"

agreement /əˈgrimənt/ *noun*

1 an arrangement or promise to do something
- ► agreement
- ► contract
- ► deal
- ► pact
- ► bargain (*informal*)
- ► compromise
- ► treaty
- ► truce
- ► alliance

2 a situation in which everyone in a group agrees
- ► agreement
- ► consensus (*formal*)

ANTONYMS → see **disagreement**

3 the act of saying yes to something
- ► agreement
- ► consent (*formal*)

ANTONYMS → see **refusal**

1 an arrangement or promise to do something

agreement
an arrangement or promise to do something, which two or more people, organizations, or countries make: *Our agreement is that if I cook dinner, he washes the dishes; if he cooks dinner, I wash the dishes.* | *The two countries have reached an **agreement to** end the war.*

contract (AWL)
a written legal agreement between two or more people, which says what each person will do: *The band signed a **contract with** a record company.*

deal
an agreement between two or more people, companies, or countries that helps both sides: *I made a **deal with** Jennifer **to** help her with math if she helps me with English.*

pact
an agreement between two people or countries, often a very serious or secret one: *We made a **pact to** keep it a secret and never tell anyone else.* | *The U.S. and Japan have a security pact that says the U.S. will help Japan if it is attacked.*

bargain (*informal*)
an agreement in which each side says exactly what it will do or give for the agreement to be complete: *I've kept my side of the bargain* (=I did what I said I would do), *now it's time for you to keep yours.*

compromise
an agreement in which both people or groups accept less than they really want: *We worked out a compromise – I'll do more chores and Mom will give me a bigger allowance.* | *There is no sign of a **compromise between** the company and the union.*

treaty
a formal written agreement between two or more countries or groups: *The war ended with the signing of a peace treaty.*

truce
an agreement between enemies to stop fighting or arguing for a short time: *The two sides agreed to a truce while the peace talks take place.*

alliance
an agreement between two or more groups to work together to try to change or achieve something: *During World War II, the U.S. had an **alliance with** the U.S.S.R. to defeat Germany.*

2 a situation in which everyone in a group agrees

agreement
a situation or feeling when everyone agrees about something: *There is agreement among*

most scientists that the Earth's climate is getting warmer.

consensus (AWL) *(formal)*
the situation when everyone agrees about something, especially when there is a lot of discussion before everyone agrees: *We need to reach a **consensus on** how to achieve our goal.*

3 the act of saying yes to something

agreement
the act of saying yes to a plan, idea, or suggestion: *The contract cannot be changed without the agreement of both people.*

consent (AWL) *(formal)*
the act of giving permission for someone to do something: *The patient must give his consent before we can do the operation.*

ahead *adverb* → see Function Word **forward, in front of**

aid¹ *noun* → see **help²**

aid² *verb* → see **help¹**

aim¹ *noun* → see **goal**

aim² *verb* → see **point²**

air /er/ *noun*

- ► air
- ► atmosphere
- ► oxygen
- ► breath

air
the gases around the Earth, which we breathe: *They decided to go outside and get some fresh air.*

atmosphere
the air around the Earth or another planet: *Cars send harmful gases into the Earth's atmosphere.*

oxygen
a gas in the air that all plants and animals need in order to live: *Fish take in oxygen from the water through their gills.*

breath
the air that you take in and let out when you breathe: *She took a deep breath before jumping into the water.*

→ see **sky** for words meaning "the air above the ground"

aircraft *noun* → see **airplane**

airplane /ˈerpleɪn/ *noun*

- ► airplane
- ► aircraft
- ► jet
- ► glider

airplane *also* **plane**
a vehicle with wings that flies through the air: *The passengers were waiting to get on the airplane to Lima.*

aircraft
an airplane or other vehicle that can fly, for example a helicopter: *The aircraft landed just after six o'clock.*

→ **GRAMMAR:** The plural of **aircraft** is **aircraft**, not "aircrafts."

jet
a fast airplane with a special type of engine that pushes out hot gases: *He is a millionaire and travels everywhere in his own private jet.*

glider
a light airplane that flies without an engine: *He is learning to fly a glider.*

airplane

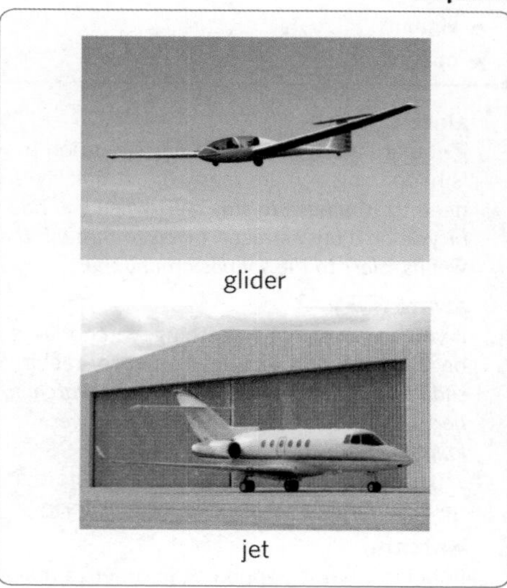

glider

jet

alarm /əˈlɑrm/ *noun*

- ► alarm
- ► warning
- ► siren

alarm
a piece of equipment that warns you about danger, especially by making a noise: *The car has an alarm to protect it from thieves.* | *The fire alarm*

woke them and they escaped from the burning house.

warning
something that tells you that something bad or dangerous might happen: *The weather report gave a warning of more snow later today.*

siren
a piece of equipment that makes a very loud warning sound, and is usually on a police car, fire engine, or ambulance: *I heard a siren, so I stopped the car at the side of the road so the ambulance could go past.*
→ see **fright** for **alarm** meaning "the feeling that something bad will happen"
→ see **fear**[1]

alarmed *adjective* → see **scared**, Topic **Describing People's Emotions**

alert /əˈlɚt/ *adjective*

- ► alert
- ► aware
- ► watchful
- ► vigilant
- ► observant

alert
if you are alert, you are paying attention to what is happening and are ready to act quickly if you need to: *You have to stay alert when you ride your bicycle on a busy street.* | *I walked through the woods,* ***alert to*** *the sounds around me.*

aware (AWL)
if you are aware of something, you notice it because you can see, hear, smell, or feel it: *She suddenly became* ***aware of*** *someone watching her.* | *I was* ***aware that*** *the other kids were laughing at me.*
→ **GRAMMAR:** Do not use **aware** before a noun. Do not say: ~~*She is an aware person*~~.

watchful
noticing what is happening in order to make sure that no one behaves badly or nothing bad happens: *Children were playing on the jungle gym under the watchful eyes of their parents.*

vigilant
paying careful attention to what is happening so that you are aware of any danger: *We are urging the public to remain* ***vigilant about*** *the possibility of terror attacks.*

observant
good at noticing things: *Police officers are trained to be observant so that they can prevent crimes.*

ADVERBS

You can make the adjectives **alert**, **vigilant**, and **observant** into adverbs by using an **-ly** ending: *The boy glanced at me alertly.* | *The little girl's parents watched vigilantly as she climbed higher.*

alien *noun* → see **foreigner**

alive /əˈlaɪv/ *adjective*

- ► alive
- ► living
- ► live

ANTONYMS → see **dead**[1]

alive
having life and not dead: *Are your grandparents still alive?*

living
having life and not dead: *All living things need food to give them energy.* | *He had no relatives still living.*

live
alive and not artificial. Use **live** in situations where you are comparing being alive or real with not being alive or with being artificial: *It was a recording on the phone, not a real live person.* | *They do experiments on live animals.*
→ **GRAMMAR: Live** is always used before a noun. Don't say: ~~These animals are live~~.
→ see **living**[2] for words meaning "people who are alive"

GRAMMAR CHECK: alive

Alive and **living** mean the same thing, but you cannot use **alive** before a noun. Don't say: ~~*Does he have any alive relatives*~~? Say: *Does he have any living relatives?*

You cannot use **living** after any verbs except "be." Don't say: ~~*They have just enough food to stay living*~~. Say: *They have just enough food to stay alive.*

all[1] *pronoun* → see **everyone**

all[2] *adjective* → see Function Word **every**

allow /əˈlaʊ/ *verb*

1 to say that someone can do something
- ► allow
- ► let
- ► permit (*formal*)
- ► give someone permission
- ► give your consent (*formal*)
- ► authorize (*formal*)
- ► sanction (*formal*)
- ► condone (*formal*)

ANTONYMS → see **forbid**, **refuse** (**3**)

2 to make it possible to do something or for something to happen
- ► allow
- ► let
- ► permit (*formal*)
- ► enable
- ► qualify
- ► entitle

ANTONYMS → see **prevent**

1 to say that someone can do something

allow
to say that someone can do something: *The school does not allow students to use cell phones in class.* | *I'm* ***allowed to*** *stay up later on weekends, but on school nights I have to be in bed by ten.*
→ GRAMMAR: Don't say: ~~*The teacher didn't allow to talk*~~ or ~~*The teacher didn't allow to us to talk*~~. Say: *The teacher didn't allow us to talk.*

let
let means the same as **allow** but is less formal: *Will your parents let you go to the party?*
→ GRAMMAR: Don't say: ~~*I let him to use my phone.*~~ Say: *I let him use my phone.*
Let is not used in the passive. Don't say: ~~*I was let to stay*~~ or ~~*I was let stay*~~. Say: *I was allowed to stay.*

permit (*formal*)
permit means the same as **allow**. **Permit** is often used on official signs: *The company permits people to smoke outside, but not inside the building.*

give someone permission
to allow someone to do something. You use **give someone permission** when a parent, teacher, or someone in an official position decides to allow you to do something: *The school gave him permission to leave early for a doctor's appointment.*

give your consent (*formal*)
give consent means the same as **give permission** but sounds very formal: *Her father gave his consent, saying that they could marry.*

authorize (*formal*)
to officially or legally say that someone can do something: *The UN authorized a peacekeeping mission in the country.*

sanction (*formal*)
to officially allow something or approve of doing it. You usually use **sanction** when the government or a large organization allows something, especially when some people think it is wrong: *In some states, the law sanctions the use of marijuana for medical reasons.*

condone (*formal*)
to accept or allow behavior that most people think is wrong: *I do not think our country should condone torture, even in a war.*
→ see **agree** (**3**), **permission**

2 to make it possible to do something or for something to happen

allow
to make it possible for someone to do something or for something to happen: *Loose clothes will* ***allow*** *you* ***to*** *move your body more easily during the exercise class.* | *The new system* ***allows*** *us* ***to*** *work more efficiently.*

let
let means the same as **allow** but is less formal: *The program lets you move text around the page really easily.*

permit (*formal*)
permit means the same as **allow**: *The bright moonlight* ***permitted*** *us* ***to*** *see a little way ahead.*

enable (AWL)
to make something possible, especially by giving someone the things he or she needs to do it: *The website* ***enables*** *customers* ***to*** *book tickets online.*

qualify
to make it possible for you to have or do something, because of something you have done or because you are in a particular situation: *This victory* ***qualifies*** *the team* ***for*** *the World Cup.*

entitle
to give someone the right to have or do something: *She was born in the U.S., which* ***entitles*** *her* ***to*** *citizenship.*

almost *adverb* → see Function Words

A

alone /əˈloʊn/ *adjective, adverb*

- alone
- on your own (*informal*)
- by yourself (*informal*)
- independently

alone
without any other people: *She lives alone.* | *You should never leave a child alone in the house.*
→ **GRAMMAR:** You cannot use **alone** before a noun. Don't say: ~~*an alone person*~~. Say: *He is alone.*

on your own (*informal*)
alone or without help from anyone else: *I can't move the bed on my own – it is too heavy.*

by yourself (*informal*)
alone or without help from anyone else: *See if you can figure out the answer by yourself.*
→ **On your own** and **by yourself** mean the same thing and can be used in the same way. They both sound less formal than **alone**.

independently
without help from anyone else, or without talking to anyone else: *The students worked independently on their science projects.*
→ see **lonely** for words meaning "unhappy because you are alone"

also *adverb* → see Function Words

alter *verb* → see **change**[1]

alteration *noun* → see **change**[2]

alternative *noun* → see **choice**, **replacement**

although *conjunction* → see Function Words

always /ˈɔlweɪz/ *adverb*

1 for all the time in the future
- always
- forever
- permanently
- for good (*informal*)

2 every time
- always
- whenever
- consistently
- constantly
- invariably (*formal*)

ANTONYMS → see **never**

1 for all the time in the future

always
for all the time in the future: *I will always love you.* | *Don't worry. Things won't always be this bad.*

forever
if something exists or continues forever, it remains or continues for all future time: *Nothing lasts forever.* | *I will remember this moment forever.*

permanently
for all future time or for the rest of your life. You use **permanently** when something has changed and will not change again: *They decided to move to New York permanently – they won't be returning to live in Chicago.* | *His eyesight might be permanently damaged.*

for good (*informal*)
for good means the same as **permanently**, but is only used at the end of a sentence or clause: *I thought that he was gone for good, and I'd never see him again.*

2 every time

always
every time, or at all times: *I always go to bed early.* | *Choir practice is always on a Thursday evening.*

whenever
every time that something happens: *I visit my brother whenever I'm in New York.* | *Try to take the bus whenever you can, instead of driving.*
→ **GRAMMAR: Whenever** is used to join two parts of a sentence together.

consistently
always doing something in the same way: *If you use the soap consistently, your acne should improve.* | *The food there is consistently good.*

constantly AWL
very often over a long period of time: *My sisters are constantly arguing.*

invariably AWL (*formal*)
if something invariably happens or is invariably true, it always happens or is always true: *The bus is invariably late.*
→ see **often**

amaze *verb* → see **surprise**[2]

amazed *adjective* → see **surprised**

amazing *adjective* → see **good**, **surprising**

ambiguous *adjective* → see **unclear**

ambition *noun* → see **determination**, **goal**

ambitious /æmˈbɪʃəs/ *adjective*

- ► ambitious
- ► aspiring
- ► competitive

ambitious
wanting very much to be successful, rich, or famous: *She is an ambitious politician who may someday be president.* | *He is good at his job, and very ambitious.*

aspiring
hoping to be successful at doing something in the future, for example as an actor, singer, or sports player: *Hollywood is full of aspiring young actors who want to get into movies or TV.*
→ GRAMMAR: **Aspiring** is always used before a noun. Don't say: ~~*These young actors are aspiring*~~.

competitive
always trying to be more successful than other people: *It should be an exciting game between these two very competitive players.*

ADVERBS

You can make the adjectives **ambitious** and **competitive** into adverbs by using an **-ly** ending: *She ambitiously attempted to increase sales by 20%.* | *The students work together and help each other, instead of working competitively.*

amend *verb* → see **change**[1]

amendment *noun* → see **change**[2]

among *preposition* → see Function Word **between**

amount /əˈmaʊnt/ *noun*

1 how much of something there is
- ► amount
- ► quantity (*formal*)
- ► number
- ► volume

2 an amount of money
- ► amount
- ► sum

1 how much of something there is

amount
how much of something there is: *There was a large* ***amount of*** *water on the floor.* | *Small* ***amounts of*** *iron are found in leafy green vegetables.*

quantity (*formal*)
quantity means the same as **amount**: *You may need to reduce* ***the quantity of*** *coffee you drink.*
→ Do not use **quantity** to talk about amounts of money or time, or about the amount of a quality.

number
an amount of something that you can count: *The* ***number of*** *students has increased from 28 to 30.*

volume AWL
the amount of something, especially sales, trade, or traffic: *The* ***volume of*** *sales increased by 6.5% last year.*
→ You also use **volume** to mean the amount of space that something takes up: *What is the volume of water in the fish tank?*
→ see **level**

GRAMMAR CHECK: amount

With a noun that has no plural, such as "milk" or "money," use **amount** or **quantity**: *Add a small amount of milk.* | *Add a small quantity of milk.*

With a noun in the plural form, use **number**: *A small number of cars were parked in the street.*

2 an amount of money

amount
an amount of money is how much money there is: *The amount you must pay is at the bottom of the bill.*

sum AWL
sum means the same as **amount**: *He borrowed a large sum from the bank.*

SYNONYM CHECK
Amount or sum?

Amount is the most usual word to use. You use it about the total on a bill, money that you are paid, or money in general.

You use **sum** especially with a word such as "large," "small," "huge," or "total." You can also say *a six-figure sum* to mean an amount of money that is between $100,000 and $999,000. You also use **sum** when talking about a particular amount of money. You say: *He received the sum of $50*, not ~~*He received the amount of $50*~~.

ample *adjective* → see **plentiful**

analysis *noun* → see **examination**, **research**[1]

analyze *verb* → see **examine**, **research**[2]

ancestor *noun* → see **family**

ancient *adjective* → see **old**

A

anger¹ /ˈæŋgɚ/ noun

1 the feeling you have when you are angry
- ► **anger**
- ► **rage**
- ► **fury**
- ► **outrage**
- ► **wrath** (*formal*)

2 the feeling you have when you are a little angry
- ► **annoyance**
- ► **irritation**
- ► **resentment**
- ► **frustration**
- ► **exasperation**
- ► **indignation** (*formal*)

1 the feeling you have when you are angry

anger
a strong feeling that you have when you think someone has behaved very badly or a situation seems bad or unfair: *She shouted at him **in anger**. | The governor lost the election because of the public's **anger over** the tax. | Ben wanted to hit him, but he tried to control his anger.*

rage
a very strong feeling of anger that often happens suddenly, is hard to control, and sometimes makes you feel violent: *Galloway came toward her **in a rage** and threatened her and her family.*

fury
a very strong feeling of anger: *"How dare you blame me for that!" she cried, shaking **with fury**.*

outrage
a strong feeling of anger and shock because you think something is unfair or wrong: *The decision to release the criminal from jail caused outrage.*

wrath (*formal*)
very strong anger. You use **wrath** about the anger of a powerful person such as a god or a king. **Wrath** is used in stories: *He left the city to escape the king's wrath.*

2 the feeling you have when you are a little angry

annoyance
the feeling of being a little angry: ***To her annoyance**, nobody had washed the dishes.*

irritation
the feeling of being a little angry, especially because something bad keeps happening or someone keeps saying something: *He had been interrupted four times, and his **irritation at** this was beginning to show.*

resentment
a feeling of anger about something that you think is unfair: *He was filled with resentment when his sister was invited to the party, but he wasn't.*

frustration
the feeling of being angry and upset because you cannot do what you want or you cannot change a bad situation: *He started crying **in frustration** because he couldn't solve the math problem.*

exasperation
the feeling of being angry and upset because something does not happen in the way you think it should: *"How can I help you when you won't tell me what's wrong?" she said **in exasperation**.*

indignation (*formal*)
a feeling of anger and surprise about an unfair situation: ***To his indignation**, he was made to wait for an hour.*

anger² /ˈæŋgɚ/ verb (formal)

1 to make someone feel angry
- ► **anger**
- ► **annoy**
- ► **irritate**
- ► **frustrate**
- ► **exasperate**
- ► **provoke**

2 to make someone very angry
- ► **outrage**
- ► **infuriate**
- ► **enrage** (*formal*)

1 to make someone feel angry

anger
to make someone angry: *She said something rude, which angered him. | Republicans were angered by the president's decision to raise taxes.*
→ **Anger** sounds fairly formal. It is more usual to say "make someone angry" than to say "anger someone": *She said something rude, which made him angry.*

annoy
to make someone feel a little angry: *It annoys me when he comes in late and doesn't even apologize.*

irritate
to make someone feel a little angry, especially because something bad keeps happening or someone keeps saying something: *After a while, the loud ticking of the clock began to irritate her.*

frustrate
to make someone feel angry and upset because he or she cannot do something or cannot change a bad situation: *It frustrates me that a lot of these children aren't getting the help they need.*

exasperate
to make someone feel angry and upset because something does not happen as it should, or someone does not do what he or she should: *He had obviously stopped listening, which exasperated his mother.*

provoke
to deliberately make someone angry: *He provoked the dog, and it attacked him.*
→ see **upset²**

2 to make someone very angry

outrage
to make someone feel very angry because something is unfair or wrong: *Customers were outraged by the price increases.*

infuriate
to make someone very angry: *Hikers are infuriated by mountain bikers who go too fast on narrow trails.*

enrage (*formal*)
to make someone very angry, in a way that is difficult to control and that seems to happen suddenly: *Her refusal to answer enraged him.*

angle *noun* → see see **be at an angle** at **lean**, **angled** at **slanted**

angry /ˈæŋgri/ *adjective*

1 feeling some anger
- ► angry
- ► mad (*informal*)
- ► annoyed
- ► irritated
- ► frustrated
- ► exasperated
- ► indignant

2 feeling a lot of anger
- ► furious
- ► outraged
- ► livid (*formal*)
- ► irate (*formal*)

3 to start feeling angry (verbs)
- ► get angry
- ► get mad
- ► lose your temper
- ► explode (*informal*)

1 feeling some anger

angry
feeling strong bad emotions, because you think someone has behaved very badly or a situation seems bad or unfair: *She was* ***angry with*** *him for being so late.* | *After the show, the TV station received hundreds of angry phone calls.* | *People were angry that no one had told them the school might close.*

mad (*informal*)
mad means the same as **angry**: *Mom was* ***mad at*** *me for not doing my homework.* | *Whenever he gets mad he turns red and starts shouting.*
→ **GRAMMAR: Mad** is not used before a noun. Don't say: ~~*a crowd of mad people*~~. Say: *a crowd of angry people*.

annoyed
a little angry: *My brother gets annoyed if anyone goes in his room.*
→ **GRAMMAR: Annoyed** is not used before a noun. Don't say: ~~*an annoyed man*~~. Say: *He is annoyed.*

irritated
a little angry because something keeps happening or someone keeps saying something: *Harris was irritated by all their questions.*
→ **GRAMMAR: Irritated** is not used before a noun. Don't say: ~~*an irritated woman*~~. Say: *She is irritated.*

frustrated
angry and upset because you cannot do what you want or because you cannot change a bad situation: *He gets so frustrated when people don't understand what he is trying to say.* | *About 100 frustrated fans couldn't get tickets for the concert.*

exasperated
feeling angry and upset because someone is continuing to do something he or she should not do: *Her exasperated mother told her to eat her breakfast and stop complaining.*

indignant
angry and surprised because a situation is unfair: *The boys were indignant: "We didn't do it! Why should we be punished?"*

2 feeling a lot of anger

furious
very angry: *She was* ***furious with*** *him for reading her diary.* | *They had a furious argument over money.*

outraged
very angry and shocked by something you think is unfair or wrong: *Outraged viewers complained about the bad language used on the TV show.*

livid (*formal*)
extremely angry: *She was livid that he had lied to her.*

irate (*formal*)
very angry: *Irate parents want to know why they weren't told about the problem.*
→ GRAMMAR: **Irate** is not used before a preposition. Don't say: ~~*Customers were irate with the store*~~. Say: *The store's customers were irate.*
→ see **grumpy** for words meaning "often becoming angry"
→ see **upset**[1], Topic **Describing People's Emotions**

ADVERBS

You can make the adjectives **angry**, **exasperated**, **indignant**, **furious**, **livid**, and **irate** into adverbs by using an **-ly** ending: *She shouted angrily at Sean.* | *"I didn't do it!" he said indignantly.* | *They argued furiously over money.*

3 to start feeling angry (verbs)

get angry *also* **become angry**
to start to feel a lot of anger because you think someone has behaved badly, or because a situation seems bad or unfair. **Become angry** is more formal than **get angry**: *He gets really angry if people keep him waiting.* | *Some children become very angry when they lose a game.*

get mad
get mad means the same as **get angry** but is more informal: *Don't get mad – I'm just teasing you a little.* | *Remy's mom* ***got really mad at*** *him for coming home so late.*

lose your temper
to suddenly become very angry, especially after you have been trying not to: *When the rehearsal went wrong, he lost his temper and began shouting at the dancers.*

explode *also* **blow up** (*informal*)
explode means the same as **lose your temper**. You use **explode** in everyday speech or in creative writing when you want to emphasize how angry someone is: *When he saw the damage to his new car, he exploded.* | *If I tell my parents what happened, they'll blow up and never let me go out again.*

SYNONYM CHECK

Get angry, become angry, or get mad?

Get angry and **become angry** are both more formal than **get mad**.

Become angry sounds the most formal and is the best choice in formal speech or writing.

Get mad is used in everyday speech and informal writing.

animal /ˈænəməl/ *noun*

1 a living thing
- ► animal
- ► creature
- ► beast (*formal*)
- ► pet
- ► livestock

2 types of animals
- ► mammal
- ► reptile
- ► amphibian

1 a living thing

animal
something that lives, breathes, and moves, for example a cat: *You can see lots of different animals at the zoo.*
→ **Animal** is usually used to mean only animals such as dogs, cows, or gorillas, and not birds, insects, fish, or people. In science, however, people are thought of as **animals**.

creature
an animal, bird, fish, or insect. You use **creature** when you are talking about all the different kinds of living things as a group, or when you are saying what quality a particular animal has: *Bears are dangerous wild creatures.* | *The reef is home to a wide variety of sea creatures.*

beast (*formal*)
an animal, especially one that is large, dangerous, or strange: *Tigers, leopards, and other dangerous beasts live in the jungle.*

pet
an animal that you keep in your home: *"Do you have any pets?" "Yes, a dog and a cat."*

livestock
animals that are kept on a farm: *They keep chickens but don't have any other livestock.*

GRAMMAR CHECK: animal

Livestock is a plural noun. Don't say: ~~*a livestock*~~.

2 types of animals

mammal
an animal that drinks its mother's milk when it is young, for example a cow, lion, or person. A **mammal** gives birth to baby animals, not eggs: *Humans live longer than any other type of mammal.*

reptile
an animal such as a snake or lizard whose body is covered in scales. **Reptiles** are cold-blooded

(=have a body temperature that changes depending on the surrounding temperature), and most reptiles lay eggs containing their babies: *Many types of reptiles live in the desert.*

amphibian
an animal, such as a frog, that starts its life living in water and later lives on land: *Most amphibians lay their eggs in water.*
→ see **group (3)** for words meaning "a group of animals"
→ see **cat**, **cow**, **dog**, **horse**, **pig**, **sheep**

announce *verb* → see **tell**

announcement *noun* → see **statement**

annoy /əˈnɔɪ/ *verb*

- annoy
- irritate
- bother
- pester
- harass

annoy
to make someone feel a little angry: *It annoys me when he comes in late and doesn't even apologize.*

irritate
to annoy someone, especially because something bad keeps happening or someone keeps saying something: *After a while, the loud ticking of the clock began to irritate her.*

bother
to annoy someone by interrupting him or her, or wanting his or her attention: *The sound of a fly or mosquito in the bedroom really bothers me.*

pester
to ask someone for something many times in an annoying way: *He pestered his dad to buy him a new cell phone.*

harass
to annoy someone by continuing to do things to get his or her attention: *The actress is often harassed by reporters who wait outside her house.*
→ see **anger**[2] for words meaning "to make someone angry"

annoyance /əˈnɔɪəns/ *noun*

- annoyance
- nuisance
- inconvenience
- pain (*informal*)

annoyance
something or someone that makes you feel slightly angry or annoyed. You usually use **annoyance** about things or situations: *It is such an annoyance to have to drive you everywhere.* | *You have to unlock the door each time you go through it, which is an annoyance.*

nuisance
someone or something that annoys you by causing problems: *The dogs next door are a real nuisance – they bark all the time.*

inconvenience
problems that annoy you and make a situation more difficult for you. **Inconvenience** sounds a little bit formal and it is often used in official language: *Your luggage will be arriving on a later flight – we are very sorry for the inconvenience.*

pain (*informal*)
pain means the same as **nuisance** but sounds informal. You use **pain** especially in spoken English: ***It is a pain** having to go to the post office to pick up a package.*
→ see **anger**[1], **annoy**

annoyed *adjective* → see **angry**, Topic **Describing People's Emotions**

annoying /əˈnɔɪ-ɪŋ/ *adjective*

- annoying
- irritating
- frustrating
- exasperating
- infuriating

annoying
making someone feel a little angry: *He kept pushing me, which was really annoying.* | *The annoying sound of dripping water kept me awake.*

irritating
making someone feel a little angry because something bad keeps happening or someone keeps saying something: *The report had an irritating number of mistakes in it.* | *Her voice is so irritating!*

frustrating
making someone feel angry and upset because he or she cannot do something he or she wants to do, or because he or she cannot change a bad situation: *It is frustrating when the team doesn't play as well as you know they can.*

exasperating
making someone feel angry and upset because something keeps happening when it should not happen: *It is so exasperating when the computer is slow.*

infuriating
making someone feel very annoyed: *He had the infuriating habit of giving you advice you didn't want.*

A

ADVERBS

You can make the adjectives that mean **annoying** into adverbs by using an **-ly** ending: *The camera is annoyingly difficult to use.* | *The game was frustratingly hard to play.* | *The lights flickered on and off irritatingly.*

annual *adjective* → see **yearly**

another /əˈnʌðɚ/ *adjective, pronoun*

- another
- spare
- substitute
- duplicate

another
one more person, thing, or amount of the same kind: *Do you want another cup of coffee?* | *If you buy two CDs, you can get another completely free.*

spare
another thing that is similar to the usual one, and that you can use if it is needed: *I always leave a set of spare keys with my neighbor.*

substitute
another person or thing that does what the usual person or thing does: *Our usual teacher was sick so we had a substitute teacher today.*

duplicate
another thing that is an exact copy and can be used in the same way: *You should keep a duplicate copy of the document.*
→ see **extra¹**

answer¹ /ˈænsɚ/ *verb*

- answer
- reply
- respond

answer
to say something after you have been asked a question: *"How was the movie?" "It was okay," she answered.* | *The witness answered the lawyer's questions with a quiet "yes" or "no."* | *I asked him why he hadn't told me, and he* ***answered that*** *he had not wanted to upset me.*

reply
to answer. You use **reply** more in writing than in speaking: *"I'm so sorry," he replied.* | *She* ***replied that*** *she did not need any help.* | *They did not* ***reply to*** *his cheerful "hello."*

respond (AWL)
to answer by saying or doing something: *His father* ***responded by*** *telling him to be quiet.* | *The congresswoman* ***responded that*** *she would look into the problem.* | *He paused to think before* ***responding to*** *my question.*

GRAMMAR CHECK: answer

Reply and **respond** are followed by "to," but **answer** is not.

Don't say: ~~*You haven't answered to my question*~~. Say: *You haven't answered my question.*

Don't say: ~~*You haven't replied my letter*~~. Say: *You haven't replied to my letter.*

answer² /ˈænsɚ/ *noun*

1 the answer to a question
- answer
- reply
- response

ANTONYMS → see **question¹**

2 the answer to a problem
- answer
- solution
- remedy

ANTONYMS → see **problem**

1 the answer to a question

answer
something that you say or write when someone asks you a question: *She refused to give me an* ***answer to*** *my question.* | *"What's 49 minus 23?" "26." "Yes, that's the right answer."*

reply
reply means the same as **answer**. You often use **reply** in written English to report what someone said: *When Katie asked how he was feeling, his reply was "awful."*
→ You also use **reply** when saying that someone sends you a letter or email after you have sent one to him or her: *I received a reply to my email the following day.*

response (AWL)
someone's reaction, after another person has said or done something: *The boy's first response was to deny that he knew anything about the money.* | *The government always gets an angry response when anyone mentions the idea of increasing taxes.*

2 the answer to a problem

answer
a way of dealing with a problem, especially one that has continued for a long time: *The crime rate keeps going up, but putting more people in prison is not the answer.* | *If you are worried about your weight, the answer is to exercise more.*

solution
a way of dealing with a problem: *They've been fighting a lot, and maybe the best solution is for them to separate.*

remedy
a successful way of dealing with a problem: *There are no easy remedies for the present economic situation.*

anticipate *verb* → see **expect**, **predict**

antique *adjective* → see **old**

antonym *noun* → see **opposite**

anxiety *noun* → see **nervousness**, **worry**[2]

anxious *adjective* → see **nervous**, **worried**, Topic **Describing People's Emotions**

anyway /ˈeniˌweɪ/ *adverb*

► anyway
► regardless

anyway
even though something else is true: *She wasn't sure that the book was the right one, but she bought it anyway.* | *I don't think anything's wrong, but I'll call him anyway.*

regardless
without being affected or influenced by something, even though that thing is true or important: *The law says that people should be treated equally,* ***regardless of*** *race, sex, or religion.*

apartment *noun* → see **house**

appalled *adjective* → see **shocked**

apparently /əˈpærəntli/ *adverb*

1 used when saying something that other people say is true
► apparently
► supposedly

2 used when saying what seems to be true
► apparently
► seemingly
► evidently

1 used when saying something that other people say is true

apparently
used when saying something that other people say is true, although you do not know whether it is really true: *I didn't see it, but apparently the movie was very good.* | *Apparently the puzzle is harder than it looks.*

supposedly
used when saying what other people say about someone or something, when you do not think they are right: *Supposedly everyone was scared of him, but I thought he was a nice man.*

2 used when saying what seems to be true

apparently
used when saying what seems to be true, although it may not be true: *He was lying on the couch, apparently asleep.*

seemingly
used to say that something seems to be true but is not really true: *These seemingly unrelated pieces of information helped the police solve the crime.*

evidently (AWL)
used to say that something is true in a way that is clear and easy to notice: *The room had been pretty once, but evidently no one had cleaned it in a long time.*

appear /əˈpɪr/ *verb*

► appear
► emerge
► come up
► surface

ANTONYMS → see **disappear (1)**

appear
to begin to be seen or to suddenly be seen: *An error message appeared on my screen when I tried to save the document.* | *The dog suddenly appeared, and I had to brake hard to avoid hitting it.*

emerge (AWL)
to appear, especially slowly, after being hidden: *A man* ***emerged from*** *behind the bushes.*

come up
to appear or be shown on a computer screen: *Click twice, and the image will come up on the screen.*

surface
if something surfaces, it rises from under the water, and you can see it: *Suddenly, a whale surfaced beside the boat.*

appearance /əˈpɪrəns/ *noun*

► appearance
► looks
► look
► image

appearance
the way someone or something seems to you

when you look at him, her, or it. For example, something's appearance would be what color it is, whether it looks new or old, etc.: *He changed his appearance by growing a mustache.* | *The mushrooms are similar **in appearance** to poisonous ones.*

A

looks
someone's appearance. You use **looks** especially when you are talking about how attractive someone is. **Looks** is more informal than **appearance**: *Do teenage girls worry too much about their looks?* | *At age forty, he still had his boyish good looks.*

look
the appearance of someone or something, especially when this has been carefully planned: *Her long straight hair and flowered top gave her a 1960s look.* | *The chair has an antique look, even though it is new.*

image (AWL)
the appearance that someone deliberately tries to have, by dressing or behaving in a particular way: *The singer and guitarist keeps his **image as** an ordinary working guy by wearing jeans and work boots.*

appetite *noun* → see **hunger**

application *noun* → see **request**, Topic **Computers and the Internet**, **Jobs and Work**

apply *verb* → see Topic **Education**, **Jobs and Work**

appoint *verb* → see **hire**

appointment *noun* → see **meeting**

appreciate *verb* → see **sympathize**, **understand**

appreciation *noun* → see **thanks**

approach[1] *verb* → see **move**

approach[2] *noun* → see **way**

appropriate /ə'proʊpriɪt/ *adjective*

- ► appropriate
- ► right
- ► suitable
- ► good
- ► fit

appropriate (AWL)
having the correct qualities for a person, situation, or time: *A suit is **appropriate for** a job interview.* | *She is too young to see an R-rated movie; it's not appropriate.*

right
best or most appropriate for a particular situation or purpose: *It is a nice house, but it isn't **right for** us.* | *It just felt like the right time to ask her to marry me.*

suitable
right for a person or situation: *Shorts are not **suitable for** a wedding.*

good
useful or appropriate: *Strong flours are **good for** making bread.* | *The park is a good place for a picnic.*

fit
appropriate or good enough for something. **Fit** is often used in negative sentences or questions: *His opponents say he is not **fit to** govern this state.*

ADVERBS
You can make the adjectives **appropriate** and **suitable** into adverbs by using an **-ly** ending: *She was appropriately dressed for the job interview.* | *Lupe's father was suitably impressed with her paintings.*

approval *noun* → see **permission**, **praise[2]**

approve /ə'pruv/ *verb*

1 to think someone or something is good or acceptable
- ► approve
- ► like
- ► applaud (*formal*)
- ► condone (*formal*)

ANTONYMS → see **disapprove**, **oppose**

2 to give official permission or support for something
- ► approve
- ► endorse

ANTONYMS → see **refuse (1)**

1 to think someone or something is good or acceptable

approve
to think that someone or something is good, right, or suitable. You usually use **approve** when you are talking about a parent, teacher, or someone in an official position approving of something: *Do your parents **approve of** you getting married so young?* | *She wants to get a tattoo, but she knows the teachers at her school wouldn't approve.*

like
to think that something is good or right. **Like** is more informal than **approve**: *I really like his ideas. I think they'll work really well.* | *My parents don't like me staying out late.*

applaud (*formal*)
to say that you strongly approve of something such as an idea or plan. **Applaud** sounds formal or literary: *The president applauds the groups' decision to hold peace talks.*

condone (*formal*)
to say that it is acceptable to do something that other people think is wrong: *We would all like to be rich, so does that mean our society condones greed?*

2 to give official permission or support for something

approve
if a person or group in an official position approves something, he, she, or it gives official permission for it to happen: *The Senate approved a bill that will strengthen immigration laws.* | *Once the city approves the plan, work will begin on the new building.*

endorse
to officially say that you support or approve of someone or something: *The governor endorsed the idea of building a new bridge.*
→ see **agree**, Topic **Government and Politics**

approximate /ə'prɒksəmət/ *adjective*

- ► approximate
- ► rough
- ► imprecise (*formal*)
- ► inexact (*formal*)

ANTONYMS → see **exact**

approximate (AWL)
an approximate number, amount, or time is close to the exact one, but could be a little more or a little less: *The approximate cost of the air ticket will be $150.* | *What is the approximate number of people who will be at the meeting?*

rough
not exact or not containing many details. **Rough** is less formal than **approximate**, and is used more often in everyday English: *Can you give me a rough idea of the time you will arrive?* | *He quickly made a rough translation of the letter before going over it again more carefully.*
→ GRAMMAR: **Rough** is used before a noun. Don't say: ~~*The guess was rough*~~. Say: *It was a rough guess.*

imprecise (AWL) (*formal*)
imprecise information is not exact, complete, or clear: *The description of the man was too vague and imprecise to help the police.*

inexact (*formal*)
not exact and not correct in every detail: *Predicting earthquakes is an inexact science, so we can never give an accurate warning of when one will occur.*

approximately *adverb* → see Function Word **about**

arch *noun* → see **curve[1]**

architect *noun* → see **designer**

area /'eriə/ *noun*

- ► area
- ► region
- ► neighborhood
- ► zone
- ► district
- ► vicinity (*formal*)

area (AWL)
a part of a place: *This area of the classroom has pillows so the children can sit and read.* | *We had just moved there, and I didn't know the area very well.*

region (AWL)
a large area of a country or of the world: *There was heavy snow throughout the whole region.*

neighborhood
a small area of a town or city where there are places to live: *The schools in this neighborhood are good.*

zone
an area where a particular thing happens or where there are special rules: *It was the first time the reporter had been in a war zone.*

district
an area of a town or city that has a particular quality or purpose, or an area that has been divided from other areas for official reasons: *Tourists to the city enjoy visiting the historic district.* | *There are over 600 schools in the Los Angeles Unified School District.*

vicinity (*formal*)
the area near a place: *The stolen car was found **in the vicinity of** the train station.*
→ see **place[1]**

argue /'argyu/ *verb*

- ► argue
- ► fight
- ► quarrel
- ► bicker

argue
if people argue, they disagree with each other and often shout or say angry things: *They **argued about** who would do the housework.* | *The girl had*

argued with her parents, because they had refused to let her go to a party. | The children were **arguing over** which TV show to watch.

fight
to argue in a very angry and noisy way. **Fight** is more informal than **argue**: *They're **fighting over** who should wash the dishes. | My parents **fought with** each other constantly while I was growing up.*

quarrel
to argue angrily: *He had **quarreled with** his wife **over** money.*

bicker
to argue about something that is not very important: *The kids were **bickering over** who would get to sit in the front seat of the car.*
→ see **claim¹** for **argue** meaning "to say that something is true"
→ see **disagree**, **say**

argument /'ɑrgyəmənt/ *noun*

- argument
- fight
- disagreement
- quarrel
- spat (*informal*)
- dispute (*formal*)
- confrontation (*formal*)
- feud

argument
if people have an argument, they shout or say angry things because they do not agree with each other: *My father and I had an **argument about** politics. | I could hear her on the phone, having an **argument with** someone from the bank.*

fight
a loud angry argument between two people who know each other well: *My parents got into a **fight over** money. | All teenagers have **fights with** their parents.*

disagreement
a situation in which people do not agree with each other, and sometimes say angry things. **Disagreements** are usually less angry than **arguments**: *He had a **disagreement with** his parents about staying out late on weekends.*

quarrel
an argument, especially one between family members or friends: *After a **quarrel with** his girlfriend, he left the apartment for an hour or more.*

spat (*informal*)
a short argument that is not important or serious: *She had a **spat with** her boyfriend, but they soon made up.*

dispute (*formal*)
a serious disagreement between two people, organizations, or countries, often about legal matters: *The two countries have had a **dispute over** the location of the border for many years.*

confrontation (*formal*)
a situation in which there is a lot of angry disagreement between two people or groups, which may develop into a fight: *A violent **confrontation** took place **between** the police and the protesters.*

feud
an argument that continues for a long time, especially between people or groups who know each other. A **feud** often involves saying or doing things that make the other person or group angry: *The **feud between** the Hatfield and the McCoy families lasted for 20 years.*

armchair *noun* → see **chair**

armed forces *noun* → see **military**

arms *noun* → see **weapon**

army /'ɑrmi/ *noun*

- army
- troops
- infantry

army
a large organized group of people trained to fight on land in a war: *They are very proud of their son, who is **in the army**. | I joined the army when I was 18.*

troops
soldiers, especially in large organized groups: *There are American troops in over one hundred countries all over the world.*

infantry
soldiers who fight on foot, and not from airplanes or tanks: *My great-grandfather was **in the infantry** in Europe during World War II.*
→ see **military**, **soldier**

aroma *noun* → see **smell¹**, Topic **Describing Food**

arrange *verb* → see **organize**

arrangement *noun* → see **order¹**

arrive *verb* → see **come**

arrogance *noun* → see **pride**

arrogant *adjective* → see **confident**, **proud**

art /ɑrt/ *noun*

- art
- painting
- drawing
- photography
- sculpture

art
the activity of making paintings, drawings, or other things for people to look at and enjoy: *She moved to New York last year to study art.* | *Art is a great way for kids to express themselves.*
→ A painting, drawing, sculpture, or other object that an artist makes can be called a **work of art**: *We saw drawings, paintings, and other works of art when we went to the museum.*

painting
the art or skill of making a picture with paint using special brushes: *Her style of painting is very modern and abstract.*

drawing
the art or skill of making pictures with a pen or pencil: *He enjoys drawing and takes his pencils everywhere he goes.*

photography
the art or skill of making pictures with a camera: *If you are interested in photography, you should get a better camera.*

sculpture
the art or skill of making objects out of stone, wood, clay, or metal: *The artist was trained as a painter, but later in life she became interested in sculpture.*
→ see **picture[1]** for "a drawing or a painting"
→ see **sculpture**

article *noun* → see **report**, **thing**

artificial /ˌɑrtəˈfɪʃəl/ *adjective*

- artificial
- man-made
- synthetic
- virtual

ANTONYMS → see **real**

artificial
not real or natural, but made by people to look or seem real: *I don't like artificial flowers - real ones are better.* | *There are no artificial colors or flavors in our ice cream.*

man-made
made by people, and not always looking like natural things. You use **man-made** especially about material or about things such as lakes, hills, or islands: *The apartments are being built next to a man-made lake.* | *Man-made fibers such as rayon are commonly used in clothing.*
→ **Man-made** is also used about problems that people have created, for example environmental problems: *Scientists agreed that man-made pollution had poisoned the water.*

synthetic
a synthetic substance is not natural, and is made in a factory using a chemical process: *Tires are made from synthetic rubber, not from rubber that comes from a rubber tree.*

virtual (AWL)
made by a computer or appearing on a computer, rather than in the real world: *In the virtual world of computer games, you can be anyone you want to be.*
→ see **fake[2]**

ADVERBS

You can make the adjectives **artificial** and **synthetic** into adverbs by using an **-ly** ending: *The candies are artificially colored and flavored.* | *Perfumes used to be made using a substance from whales, but now they are made synthetically.*

artist *noun* → see **performer**

artistic *adjective* → see **creative**, Topic **Describing People's Character**

ashamed *adjective* → see **guilty**, **sorry**, Topic **Describing People's Emotions**

ask *verb* → *go to pages 28-29*

asleep /əˈslip/ *adjective*

- asleep
- unconscious

ANTONYMS → see **awake**

asleep
sleeping: *Danilo was asleep on the couch.* | *It was the middle of the night and everyone else was asleep.*

unconscious
not awake, not dreaming, and not knowing what is happening around you, because you are very sick or badly injured: *The woman was found unconscious and had serious head injuries.*

aspect *noun* → see **part**

assault[1] *noun* → see **attack[1]**

assault[2] *verb* → see **attack[2]**

assembly *noun* → see **meeting**

assess *verb* → see **count**, **judge[2]**, **test[2]**

ask /æsk/ *verb*

1 to ask questions
- ask
- demand
- inquire (*formal*)
- question (*formal*)
- interrogate
- interview
- cross-examine

ANTONYMS → see **answer[1]**

2 to ask for something you want
- ask
- order
- demand
- request (*formal*)
- invite

ANTONYMS → see **refuse (3)**

3 to ask for something you want in an emotional way
- beg
- plead
- implore
- entreat (*formal*)

ANTONYMS → see **refuse (3)**

4 to ask what many people think about something
- poll
- survey

1 to ask questions

ask
to say something that is a question, for example in order to get information or help: *"How old are you?" she asked.* | *Several people asked questions at the end of the class.*
→ **GRAMMAR:** Don't say: ~~*I asked to him to help me*~~ or ~~*I asked to help me*~~. Say: *I asked him to help me.*

demand
to ask a question in a firm or angry way: *"Why are you so late?" he demanded.*

inquire (*formal*)
to ask someone for information: *She called the bank to **inquire about** any jobs that might be available.*

question (*formal*)
to ask someone questions so that you can get information about something. **Question** is often used when the police ask someone about a crime: *The police took the man to the station and questioned him for three hours.*

interrogate
if the police interrogate someone, they ask him or her a lot of questions for a long time in order to get information: *The men were interrogated for five hours because police believed they were involved in the bombing.*

interview
to ask a famous person questions on a television program or for a newspaper: *The singer was interviewed on television.*
→ You also use **interview** about asking someone questions when he or she wants a job or has applied to a college: *Mr. Nuñez **interviewed** me **for** a job at the store.*

cross-examine
to ask someone questions in a court of law after another lawyer has already asked that person questions: *The defense lawyer cross-examined the first witness.*

2 to ask for something you want

ask
to tell someone that you want something using a question: *If there's anything you need, just ask and I'll get it for you.* | *I **asked for** a glass of water.* | *Mrs. Ramos **asked to** see Juan's teacher.*

order
to ask for something that you are going to pay for. You use **order** when you ask for food or drinks in a restaurant, or when you ask a company to get a product for you: *I ordered spaghetti with meatballs.* | *You can **order** the book from the publisher online.*

demand
to ask for something in a firm or angry way: *The service at the restaurant was terrible, so she **demanded to** speak to the manager.* | *James **demanded that** Renee apologize to him.*

request (*formal*)
to ask for something officially or in a polite way: *You have to request permission if you want to take any photographs.*

invite
to ask someone to come to an event such as a party, wedding, or meal: *Who should we **invite to** the party?* | *I applied for a job, and now they have **invited** me **for** an interview.*

3 to ask for something you want in an emotional way

beg
to ask for something in a way that shows you want or need it very much: ***She begged and begged until finally her parents let her go to the party.***

→ **Beg** also means to ask people in the street for money because you do not have any: ***A man sitting outside of the store was begging for change.***

plead
to ask for something that you want very much, in a sincere and emotional way: ***"Please forgive me," she pleaded. "I'll never do it again."***

implore
implore means the same as **plead** but is more formal: ***She implored the soldiers to save her child.***

entreat *(formal)*
entreat means the same as **plead** and is used especially in literature: ***His friends entreated him not to go.***

4 to ask what many people think about something

poll
to ask a lot of people a set of questions to find out their opinions about something, especially politics: ***Only 36 percent of the people polled said they intended to vote for the Republican candidate.***

survey (AWL)
to ask a lot of people a set of questions about their opinions, the way they live, or what they like and dislike. **Surveys** are used to understand the way a large group of people think, and to make decisions about how to treat them or what to sell to them: ***Researchers surveyed 10,000 customers about which brands they buy most often.***

→ see **beg** for words meaning "to ask for something you want very much," **call (2)** for words meaning "to ask someone to come to you"

interview

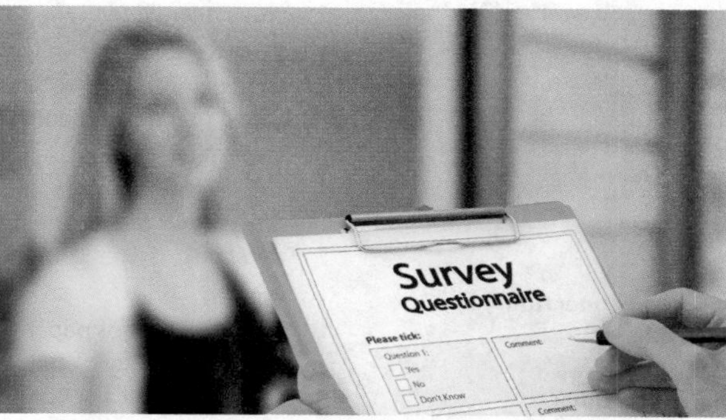

survey

assessment *noun* → see **measurement**

assign /əˈsaɪn/ *verb*

1 to give someone a particular job to do
- ► assign
- ► delegate

2 to give money or equipment to someone, or decide how it should be used
- ► assign
- ► allocate

A

1 to give someone a particular job to do

assign (AWL)
to give someone a job to do: *The soldiers were assigned to guard the bank.* | *The teacher assigned 25 math problems for homework.*

delegate
to give part of your work to someone else, especially someone whose position is not as important as yours: *When you delegate work, you expect that it will be done.*

2 to give money or equipment to someone, or decide how it should be used

assign (AWL)
to give something such as money or equipment to someone to use: *They assigned me a small room.*

allocate (AWL)
to decide to use something such as time or money for a purpose, or decide to give it to a particular person or group: *The city has allocated money to build a new swimming pool.*

assignment *noun* → see **job**, **work²** (**3**), Topic **Education**

assist *verb* → see **help¹**

assistance *noun* → see **help²**

assistant *noun* → see **helper**

association *noun* → see **connection**, **organization**, **relationship**

assume *verb* → see **expect**, **think**

assure *verb* → see **promise¹**

astonish *verb* → see **surprise²**

astonished *adjective* → see **surprised**

astonishing *adjective* → see **surprising**

astonishment *noun* → see **surprise¹**

astronomy *noun* → see Topic **Science and Technology**

athlete *noun* → see **player**, Topic **Sports and Exercise**

athletic *adjective* → see Topic **Sports and Exercise**

atlas *noun* → see Topic **Books and Literature**

atmosphere *noun* → see **air**, **mood**, **sky**

attach /əˈtætʃ/ *verb*

- ► attach
- ► fasten
- ► glue
- ► tape
- ► staple
- ► clip

attach (AWL)
to join something to another thing: *He **attached** the picture **to** the wall with a nail.* | *You need to **attach** a photo **to** the form.*

fasten
to join something onto another thing, especially in a way that makes it easy to separate them again: *She **fastened** the brooch **to** her dress.* | *Divers **fasten** weights **to** their belts, to help them stay under water.*

glue
to join something to another thing with glue: *I tried to **glue** the handle back **onto** the cup.*

tape (AWL)
to join something to another thing with tape: *She cut out the picture and taped it into her notebook.*

staple
to join pieces of paper together with a staple (=a small piece of thin metal that is pressed through paper using a special machine): *Can you **staple** the pages of your essay **together** so that you don't lose them?*

clip
to hold things together with a clip (=a small object that holds papers or other things together, but can be taken off easily): *He **clipped** the microphone **to** his tie.*
→ see **join** (**2**)

attack[1] /əˈtæk/ *noun*

1 an attack against a person
- ► **attack**
- ► **assault**
- ► **mugging**

2 a military attack
- ► **attack**
- ► **invasion**
- ► **strike**
- ► **raid**
- ► **ambush**
- ► **assault**
- ► **siege**

1 an attack against a person

attack
an attempt to hurt another person: *The attack took place as he was walking home.* | *You need to be careful when you are traveling in the area, because there have been recent* ***attacks on*** *tourists.*

assault
a physical attack on someone. You use **assault** when the attack is treated as a crime: *Reed is serving a five-year jail sentence for burglary and assault.*

mugging
an attack on someone in a public place such as a street, in order to steal something from him or her: *Her phone and wallet were taken in the mugging last night.*

2 a military attack

attack
an attempt to defeat enemy soldiers or damage a place in a war: *The enemy troops were planning an* ***attack on*** *the city.* | *More than 100 people were injured at the airport today in a terrorist attack.*

invasion
an occasion when an army enters a country in order to take control of it: *My parents left Czechoslovakia and came to the U.S. after the Russian invasion in 1968.*

strike
a sudden powerful attack by an army, especially an attack from the air that uses bombs: *Air strikes at the end of World War II destroyed over 50% of Tokyo.*

raid
a sudden attack on a place during a war: *They took prisoners during their* ***raids on*** *nearby villages.*

ambush
a sudden attack by someone who has been secretly waiting in a hidden place: *The soldiers moved into the area at night to prepare an ambush on enemy troops.*

assault
a military attack to take control of a place controlled by the enemy. **Assault** is more formal than **attack**: *During the American Revolutionary War, George Washington led many* ***assaults against*** *the British.*

siege
a situation in which the army or the police surround and attack a place and do not let anything go in or out of the place. They do this to get control of the place or force someone to come out of it: *The* ***siege of*** *the town lasted two months.*

attack[2] /əˈtæk/ *verb*

1 to attack a person
- ► **attack**
- ► **assault**
- ► **mug**
- ► **ambush**

2 to attack a place or country in a war
- ► **attack**
- ► **invade**
- ► **raid**
- ► **ambush**
- ► **storm**

1 to attack a person

attack
to use violence against someone and try to hurt him or her: *The man attacked her as she was walking home at night.* | *He was attacked by a group of men outside the bar.*

assault
to attack someone violently. You use **assault** when the attack is treated as a crime: *Angry fans ran onto the football field and assaulted the referee.*

mug
to attack someone and take money from him or her in a public place such as a street: *I was mugged on my way home last night – they took all of my jewelry.*

ambush
to suddenly attack someone after waiting in a hidden place: *The judge was ambushed by a gang of men as he drove to work at the courthouse.*

A

2 to attack a place or country in a war

attack
if an army or other group attacks a place, it fights the people in it and damages buildings: *The enemy attacked at night.* | *The village was attacked by enemy warplanes.*

invade
to enter a country with an army in order to take control of it: *World War II began when the Germans invaded Poland.*

raid
to attack a place suddenly, in a war: *Shortly after dawn, a small group of soldiers raided the enemy camp.*

ambush
to attack enemy soldiers after waiting in a hidden place: *The convoy of trucks was ambushed on the road to Kabul.*

storm
to attack a city or building using force, in order to take control of it: *Enemy soldiers stormed the city, and the people surrendered without a fight.*
→ see **criticize** for **attack** meaning "to say that someone or something is bad"

attain *verb* → see **succeed**

attempt¹ *noun* → see **try²**

attempt² *verb* → see **try¹**

attend *verb* → see **go**, Topic **Education**

attention /əˈtenʃən/ *noun*

1 the act of listening or looking at someone or something carefully (nouns)
- ► **attention**
- ► **interest**
- ► **concentration**
- ► **focus**

2 to listen or watch someone or something carefully (verbs)
- ► **pay attention**
- ► **concentrate**
- ► **focus**
- ► **keep your mind on something** (*informal*)
- ► **be absorbed in**
- ► **be engrossed in**

1 the act of listening or looking at someone or something carefully (nouns)

attention
the act of listening or looking at something or someone carefully, and thinking about it: *My brother gets a lot more attention from my parents than I do.* | *Can I please have your attention for an important announcement?*

interest
attention you give to something because you like it and want to know more about it: *The news story attracted a lot of public interest.* | *Parents need to* ***take*** *an* ***interest in*** *what their kids are doing at school* (=they need to show they are interested).

concentration (AWL)
the ability to think very carefully about something for a long time, without noticing or thinking about other things: *The work needs concentration, so it's best to not have the TV or radio on.*

focus (AWL)
concentration on only one idea, thing, or person: *When you are catching a ball, keep your* ***focus on*** *it and watch it come into your hands.*
→ **Focus** also means the person, thing, or situation that you pay special attention to: *The focus of the discussion will be the education of younger children.*
→ see **care²**

2 to listen or watch someone or something carefully (verbs)

pay attention
to listen to or watch something or someone carefully so that you know what to do, what is happening, or what someone is saying: *Kayla always pays attention in class – that's why she is doing so well.* | *The TV was on, but no one was really* ***paying attention to*** *it.*

concentrate (AWL)
to pay attention and think carefully about something without stopping for a period of time, without noticing or thinking about other things: *To do the job well, you must be able to concentrate for long periods of time.* | *I was tired, but I tried to* ***concentrate on*** *the road ahead.*

focus (AWL)
to pay careful attention to one thing, and not to other things: *You need to* ***focus on*** *getting better grades, and not play so many sports.*

keep your mind on something (*informal*)
to continue paying attention to something, even if you want to think about something else: *It is hard to keep your mind on school when summer vacation is about to start.*

be absorbed in
to be so interested in something that you pay attention only to it and not to other things: *The book has a really good story and I was completely absorbed in it.*

be engrossed in
be engrossed in means the same thing as **be absorbed in** but it is a little more formal: *He was so engrossed in watching the game on TV that he did not hear me go out.*

attitude *noun* → see **opinion**

attorney *noun* → see **lawyer**

attract /əˈtrækt/ *verb*

- ► attract
- ► draw
- ► bring in (*informal*)

attract
to make people feel interested in something, or want to take part in an activity: *The sport needs to attract more young people, both to watch it and to play.* | *Her concerts always attract a lot of media attention.*

draw
to make people notice something, or want to go to see something: *The fireworks display in the park drew a large crowd.*

bring in (*informal*)
to attract customers to a store so that they buy something: *To bring in customers, stores are having some great sales.*
→ see **interest**[1]

attractive *adjective* → see **beautiful**, Topic **Describing People's Looks**

atypical *adjective* → see **strange**

audience /ˈɔdiəns/ *noun*

1 the people who are watching or listening to a performance
- ► audience
- ► spectator
- ► crowd
- ► listener

2 the people who watch, listen to, or read something in newspapers, on television, etc.
- ► audience
- ► viewer
- ► reader
- ► listener
- ► readership, viewership, listenership

1 the people who are watching or listening to a performance

audience
the people who are watching or listening to a performance: *The audience clapped and cheered at the end of the concert.* | *There seemed to be a lot of young people **in the audience**.*
→ GRAMMAR: **Audience** is usually followed by a singular verb: *The audience was fascinated.*

spectator
someone who watches a sports event, especially with many other people: *More than 10,000 spectators came to see the football game.*

crowd
a large group of people. **Crowd** can be used about a large group who have gathered to see or listen to something: *A crowd of 43,000 cheered as the Giants won.*

listener
someone who listens to someone else give a speech: *The speaker made his listeners laugh many times.*

2 the people who watch, listen to, or read something in newspapers, on television, etc.

audience
the people who watch a television show, read a particular book, website, or magazine, or listen to a radio show: *The show attracts a regular audience of 20 million people.*

viewer
someone who watches a television show: *The Academy Awards are watched on television by millions of viewers around the world.*

reader
someone who reads a particular newspaper, magazine, or type of book: *The book was very popular with young readers.*

listener
someone who listens to a radio station or show: *Danny is one of the millions of listeners who hear our show every day.*

readership, viewership, listenership
the group or number of people who read a particular magazine or newspaper, who watch a particular television show, or who listen to a particular radio station or show. These words are used mainly in news reports or in business: *The newspaper has a readership of more than 500,000.* | *Fewer people are watching the news*

A

on television, and viewership is steadily decreasing.

audience

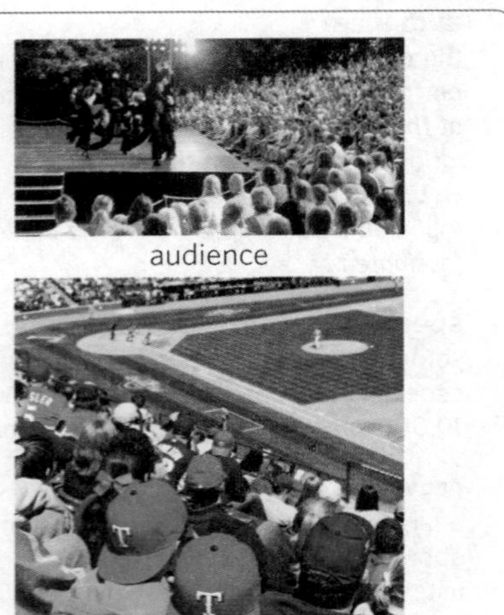
audience

spectators

authentic *adjective* → see **real**

author *noun* → see **writer**, Topic **Books and Literature**

authorities *noun* → see Topic **Government and Politics**

authority *noun* → see **expert**, **power**

automatic *adjective* → see **digital**

avenue *noun* → see **road**

average *adjective* → see **medium**, **ordinary**

avoid /əˈvɔɪd/ *verb*

- ► avoid
- ► get out of (*informal*)
- ► dodge (*informal*)
- ► evade (*formal*)

avoid
to deliberately not do or say something, especially something that you should do or say: *I didn't mention it, because I wanted to avoid an argument.* | *You can't avoid doing your homework forever!*
→ GRAMMAR: Don't say: ~~*They avoided to look at each other*~~. Say: *They avoided looking at each other.*

get out of (*informal*)
to find a way not to do something that you should do or that you have promised to do: *I'm supposed to stay at home with my little sister tonight, but I'll try to get out of it.*

dodge (*informal*)
to avoid talking about something or doing something that you do not want to do: *The senator dodged the reporter's question and started talking about something else.*

evade (*formal*)
to avoid talking about something or doing something, especially something you should do for legal or moral reasons: *The accountant was accused of helping his clients evade taxes.* | *Brady evaded the question of why it had happened, saying only that the problem was being dealt with.*
→ see **escape**, **miss**, **prevent**

awake /əˈweɪk/ *adjective*

- ► awake
- ► conscious

ANTONYMS → see **asleep**

awake
not sleeping. You use **awake** especially when you are describing someone who has just stopped sleeping or who is not sleeping at a time when he or she usually sleeps: *I stayed over at my friend's house last night, and we were awake all night.* | *Anna is awake, but she is still in bed.*
→ GRAMMAR: You cannot use **awake** before a noun. Don't say: ~~*an awake person*~~. Say: *She is awake.*

conscious
awake after being very sick or injured so badly that you did not know what was happening around you: *He was lying in his hospital bed, conscious but not able to talk.*
→ see **wake**

award[1] *noun* → see **prize**

award[2] *verb* → see **give**

aware /əˈwer/ *adjective*

- ► aware
- ► conscious of

ANTONYMS → see **unaware**

aware (AWL)
if you are aware of a fact or situation, you know or realize that it exists: *Are you **aware of** the risks involved in having surgery?* | *I wasn't **aware that** you needed help.*

conscious of
if you are conscious of something, you notice it and realize that it is important: *I was very conscious of the fact that I was wearing jeans and everyone else was dressed up.*
→ see **alert**

away *adverb* → see Function Words

awesome *adjective* → see **good**

awful *adjective* → see **bad**, Topic **Describing Food**, **The Weather**

awhile /əˈwaɪl/ *adverb*

► awhile
► for some time

awhile
used when you are not being definite about how long something lasts: *I stood at the bedroom door awhile, watching the kids sleeping.* | *We waited awhile at the restaurant until a table was ready for us.*

→ GRAMMAR: **Awhile** is an adverb and **a while** is a noun phrase, but they are similar in meaning. Use **awhile** after a verb: *Can you stay awhile?* Use **a while** after a preposition: *Can you stay for a while?*

for some time
used to say that something lasts for a fairly long time or longer than expected, without saying exactly how long: *I worked with Bill for some time before I left to set up my own business.*

awkward *adjective* → see **clumsy**, **embarrassed**

Bb

baby /ˈbeɪbi/ *noun*

1 a very young child (nouns)
- ► **baby**
- ► **newborn baby**
- ► **infant** (*formal*)
- ► **toddler**
- ► **fetus**
- ► **embryo**

2 to produce a baby from your body (verbs)
- ► **have a baby**
- ► **give birth**
- ► **in labor**

1 a very young child (nouns)

baby
a very young child who cannot talk or walk yet: *I could hear a baby crying upstairs.* | *They have a five-year-old boy and a baby girl.*

newborn baby *also* **newborn**
a baby that has just been born: *Newborn babies spend most of their time sleeping, feeding, and crying.*

infant (*formal*)
a very young baby who cannot talk or walk yet: *She held the infant in her arms until he fell asleep.*

toddler
a young child who is learning to walk. **Toddler** is usually used for children who are around 18 months to 3 years old: *A group of toddlers were playing with toy trucks in the sandbox.*

fetus
a baby that is developing in its mother's body. **Fetus** is used especially by doctors and in science: *By the end of the third month of pregnancy, the fetus begins to look like a human being.*

embryo
a baby that is in the earliest stages of development inside its mother's body. **Embryo** is mostly used in scientific and medical language: *When it is first formed, the embryo is only half a millimeter long.*

2 to produce a baby from your body (verbs)

have a baby
if a woman has a baby, it comes out of her body: *Marie had a baby last year.* | *The doctor couldn't be there when she had the baby, so the nurses helped her.*

give birth
give birth means the same as **have a baby**, but sounds more formal and puts more emphasis on the physical act: *She **gave birth to** a healthy baby girl.*

in labor
if a woman is in labor, she is pushing a baby out of her body: *She was in labor for over 16 hours with her first child.*

→ see **born**, **pregnant**

SYNONYM CHECK

Have a baby or give birth?

You only use **give birth** to talk about the physical act of having a child.

You use **have a baby** to talk about the physical act and also to talk about beginning to be a parent. Don't say: ~~*I'd like to give birth when I'm around 30 years old*~~. Say: *I'd like to have a baby when I'm around 30 years old.*

babysit *verb* → see **care[1] (3)**

back[1] /bæk/ *noun*

1 the part of your body
- ► **back**
- ► **spine**
- ► **backbone** (*informal*)

2 the part of something that is farthest from the front
- ► **back**
- ► **rear**
- ► **end**
- ► **stern**

ANTONYMS → see **front**

1 the part of your body

back
the part of your body between your neck and your waist, on the opposite side from your chest and stomach: *I hurt my back playing basketball with my son.* | *She lay **on** her **back**, staring at the sky.*

spine
the long set of bones that goes down the middle of your back: *He injured his spine in a motorcycle accident and had to spend months in bed.*

backbone (*informal*)
backbone means the same as **spine**: *The cow was so thin you could see her backbone and ribs.*

2 the part of something that is farthest from the front

back
the part of something that is farthest from the front: *The bus was crowded, but we found a few seats **in the back**. | The T-shirt has a picture of a snake **on the back**. | The sun had burned **the back of** my neck.*

rear
the back of an area. **Rear** sounds more formal than **back**: *There are more seats **in the rear of** the train. | The kitchen was **at the rear of** the house.*

end
the part of something that is farthest from the beginning. You use **end** about roads, hallways, lines, and other long narrow things: *Go to **the end of** the street and turn left. | We sat in silence at both **ends of** the long wooden table.*

stern
the back part of a boat or ship: *There was a rope attached to the stern of the boat, which he used to tie it to the dock.*

back² /bæk/ *verb*

1 to move backward
- ► back
- ► back up
- ► step back
- ► retreat

2 to make a vehicle go backward
- ► back
- ► back up
- ► put a car/truck, etc. in reverse

1 to move backward

back
to move backward in a particular direction, especially in order to leave a place or area: *We slowly **backed away** from the growling dog. | When she was sure the baby was asleep, she **backed** quietly **out of** the room.*

back up
to move backward: *Can you back up a little bit so that everyone can see?*

step back
to take one step or a few steps backward: *I stepped back to let the other people pass.*

retreat
to walk backward or away from the direction you were walking before. **Retreat** sounds fairly literary, and you use it when you want to show that someone is avoiding someone or something else: *He saw her and retreated up the stairs, because he was too shy to speak to her.*

2 to make a vehicle go backward

back
to drive a car or other vehicle backward: *He carefully **backed** the truck **into** the driveway. | **Back** the car **to** the end of the street and turn around.*
→ GRAMMAR: **Back** is always followed by a prepositional phrase, for example "back into something."

back up
back up means the same as **back**: *I couldn't back up because another car was parked very close behind me.*

put a car/truck, etc. in reverse
if you put a vehicle in reverse, you change the gear so that you can drive backward: *He started the car, put it in reverse, and then backed out of the parking space.*
→ see **invest** for **back** meaning "to invest in a project or business," **support** for **back** meaning "to agree with a person, group, or idea"

back³ /bæk/ *adjective*

- ► back
- ► rear
- ► backward

back
at the back of something: *We were sitting in the back row of the theater. | Kara walked around the house to the back door. | The back pocket of your jeans is ripped.*
→ GRAMMAR: **Back** is only used before a noun: *the back seat*.

rear
relating to the back part of a building, vehicle, ship, or airplane. **Rear** sounds more formal than **back**: *Passengers should exit through the rear door of the bus.*
→ GRAMMAR: **Rear** is only used before a noun: *the rear window of the car*

backward
toward the direction that is behind you: *I remember that she gave us a backward look and a little wave when she left.*
→ GRAMMAR: **Backward** is only used before a noun: *The gymnast did a backward somersault.*

background /ˈbækgraʊnd/ *noun*

1 someone's family, education, and past experience
- ► **background**
- ► **class**
- ► **upbringing**

2 events or information relating to something
- ► **background**
- ► **circumstances**
- ► **context**
- ► **history**

1 someone's family, education, and past experience

background
someone's family, education, and past experience: *It is always interesting to meet people who come from different backgrounds.* | *The interviewer asked me about my* ***background in*** *sales.*

class
a group of people in a society who have similar types of jobs, money, or education: *Nurses and teachers are part of the middle class in the U.S.* | *Her parents are rich, and they would not like her to marry someone from a lower social class.*

upbringing
the way that parents take care of their children and teach them to behave: *Because of my strict upbringing, I was not allowed to go to parties or go out with girls.*

2 events or information relating to something

background
information or past events that relate to something and explain why it happens: *One reason we study the history of Greece or Egypt is as a* ***background to*** *our own societies.*

circumstances
the things that are happening at the same time as a particular event: *The police are examining the circumstances surrounding the accident.*

context (AWL)
the situation, events, or information that are related to something and that help you to understand it: *I don't know the word, but when I read it* ***in context*** *I could figure out what it meant.* | *To understand his decision, you need to understand the context in which he was working.*

history
all the things that a particular person or group has done or experienced: *The man* ***has a history of*** *mental problems and has been arrested several times.*

back up *phrasal verb* → see **back²**, **prove**

backward *adverb* → see Function Word **back**

bad *adjective* → *go to pages 40-42*

badly /ˈbædli/ *adverb*

- ► **badly**
- ► **not well**
- ► **poorly**
- ► **terribly**

ANTONYMS → see **well**

badly
in a way that is not good: *The woman told her doctor she had been sleeping badly recently.* | *The essay was badly written.*

not well
not well means the same as **badly**, but you use it when **badly** seems too direct or too strong: *The team did not play well.* | *I didn't do well on my English test.*

poorly
in a way that is bad, especially in a way that does not show much skill or ability: *The clothing was poorly made.* | *The company designed the cars poorly, so they sometimes fell over when going around corners.*

terribly
very badly: *The hero of the movie suffers terribly, but eventually he wins.*

bad-tempered *adjective* → see **grumpy**

bag /bæg/ *noun*

1 a container for carrying things in
- ► **bag**
- ► **sack**
- ► **backpack**
- ► **briefcase**
- ► **suitcase**

2 a bag used to carry money and other things
- ► **handbag**
- ► **purse**
- ► **wallet**

1 a container for carrying things in

bag
a soft container that you carry things in, made

of paper, plastic, cloth, or leather: *Dan handed me a* ***bag of*** *groceries.* | *The store does not give customers plastic bags anymore, but asks customers to pay for them.*

sack
a large bag made of strong material, especially cloth: *The ships were carrying* ***sacks of*** *grain.*
→ In some parts of the U.S., paper and plastic bags are called **sacks**, for example bags from grocery stores: *She put a sack of groceries on the table.*

backpack
a bag for carrying things on your back, used especially for traveling, walking, or carrying books and other things to school: *The students were putting their books in their backpacks.*

briefcase
a flat bag with a handle, that business people, lawyers, etc. use for carrying papers: *There are two folders in my briefcase that I need for the meeting.*

suitcase
a large bag with a handle, in which you carry clothes when you travel: *The suitcase has wheels so that you can pull it.*
→ You can also use **bag** to mean **suitcase** in more informal English: *When we got to the airport, we had to go downstairs to pick up our bags.*

2 a bag used to carry money and other things

handbag *also* **bag**
a bag that women use to carry money, keys, and other things. **Handbag** and **bag** are used especially in advertising and at stores that sell these kinds of bags: *The website sells suitcases and handbags.* | *Someone stole my bag out of the car.*

purse
purse means the same as **handbag** but sounds a little old-fashioned: *I reached* ***into*** *my* ***purse*** *and pulled out my wallet.*

wallet
a small flat case that you keep money and credit cards in. Both men and women use **wallets**: *I have about $10* ***in my wallet.*** | *He took a credit card* ***out of*** *his* ***wallet.***

bag

baggage /ˈbægɪdʒ/ *noun*

- ► baggage
- ► luggage
- ► bags
- ► suitcase

baggage
all the bags and suitcases that belong to people who are traveling on a plane, bus, train, or boat: *They are loading the baggage onto the carts now and taking it to the plane.*

luggage
the bags and suitcases that you carry when you are traveling: *We didn't have a lot of luggage, just one suitcase each.*
→ GRAMMAR: **Baggage** and **luggage** cannot be used in the plural. Don't say: ~~*We didn't have a lot of luggages*~~.

bags
bags means the same as **luggage** but sounds slightly more informal: *Can you put the bags in the car, please?*

suitcase
a large bag with a handle, in which you carry clothes when you travel: *The suitcase has wheels so that you can pull it.*

baggy *adjective* → see **loose**, Topic **Describing Clothes**

bake *verb* → see **cook**[1]

bad /bæd/ *adjective*

1 describing an experience that is not nice or enjoyable
- ► bad
- ► awful
- ► terrible
- ► horrible
- ► nasty
- ► disgusting
- ► unpleasant
- ► negative
- ► mediocre

2 describing someone who is not good at doing something
- ► bad
- ► poor
- ► weak
- ► awful
- ► terrible
- ► incompetent

3 describing something that is not good quality
- ► bad (*informal*)
- ► poor
- ► badly made
- ► cheap

4 describing someone who behaves in a way that is bad
- ► bad
- ► mischievous
- ► disobedient
- ► naughty
- ► evil
- ► wicked
- ► wrong
- ► immoral
- ► improper (*formal*)

5 describing food that is not good to eat
- ► bad
- ► disgusting
- ► spoiled
- ► rotten
- ► moldy
- ► stale
- ► sour
- ► rancid
- ► off

ANTONYMS → see **good**

1 describing an experience that is not nice or enjoyable

bad
not nice or enjoyable, not at all what you want, and often upsetting: *I'm afraid I have some bad news – your sister is very sick.* | *The plane was delayed by bad weather.*

awful
very bad: *I had an awful day at work – everything went wrong.* | *The food was awful, and I couldn't eat it.*

terrible
terrible means the same as **awful** but sounds a little stronger: *The drive was terrible – it took us nine hours to get there because of the traffic.*

horrible
very bad and having a strong effect on your emotions so that you feel shocked, annoyed, or sick: *What is that horrible smell?* | *It was horrible just having to wait at the hospital to see if he would be all right.*

nasty
very bad, and shocking or painful: *I had a nasty experience on the subway – someone stole my purse.*

disgusting
very bad. **Disgusting** is a very strong word. You use it about a taste, smell, or habit that makes you feel sick: *Do you have to bite your nails? It's a disgusting habit.*

unpleasant
not nice or enjoyable. **Unpleasant** is more formal than **bad** but is not as strong: *There was an unpleasant smell coming from under the floorboards.* | *My sleeping bag was cold and damp, and it was unpleasant getting into it.*

negative (AWL)
bad or harmful: *Her illness was having a negative effect on her schoolwork, because she was often too sick to go to class.*

mediocre
not very good, but not really bad. You often use **mediocre** when something is not as good as it should be: *The team disappointed the fans with another mediocre performance.*

GRAMMAR CHECK: bad

Don't use "very" with adjectives that mean "very bad," such as **awful**, **terrible**, **horrible**, and **disgusting**. Don't say: ~~*It was very awful.*~~ Say: *It was awful* or *It was really awful.*

2 describing someone who is not good at doing something

bad
not good at doing something: *There are a lot*

of bad drivers on the roads. | *She is really bad at spelling.*

poor
not good at something, because you do not have the skills to do it. **Poor** is more formal than **bad**: *I was a poor student because reading was hard for me.*

→ GRAMMAR: **Poor** is only used before a noun. Don't say: ~~*She is poor at spelling*~~. Say: *She is a poor speller.*

weak
not successful or effective when you are trying to do an activity or something that takes skill: *The team's defense was weak, and the other team scored easily.* | *The company lost a lot of money because of its weak management.*

→ GRAMMAR: Don't say: ~~*The team is weak at defense*~~. Say: *The team had a weak defense* or *The defense was weak.*

awful
very bad at doing something: *My sister is an awful cook – she burns everything.*

terrible
terrible means the same as **awful** but sounds a little stronger: *I'm* ***terrible at*** *remembering people's names.*

incompetent
very bad at doing your job: *The company's problems were caused by incompetent management.*

3 describing something that is not good quality

bad (*informal*)
not good quality. **Bad** is used more in spoken English: *It was a really bad movie.* | *Her spelling is really bad.*

poor
not good quality, especially when something is not as good as it should be. **Poor** is used more in writing than **bad**: *There were complaints about the poor quality of the materials.* | *Her health has been poor for several years.*

badly made
if something is badly made, it has not been made in a skillful way and the quality is bad: *The shoes were badly made and they didn't last long.*

cheap
low in price and quality: *The furniture looked cheap, and one of the chairs broke when I sat down on it.*

4 describing someone who behaves in a way that is bad

bad
behaving in a way that is bad, for example by lying or doing unkind things to people. **Bad** is used mainly in spoken English: *Jones was a bad man, and I knew he could not be trusted.* | *My parents used to send me to my room when I was bad.*

mischievous
a **mischievous** child secretly behaves a little badly, especially in a way that makes people laugh rather than be angry: *My younger son is very mischievous and you always have to watch what he is doing.*

→ You also use **mischievous** about the look on someone's face, when he or she is secretly thinking about something a little bad: *"I'm not going to tell you," she said with a mischievous grin.*

disobedient
not doing what someone has told you to do: *If you train your dog well, it won't be disobedient. It will sit when you tell it to, and come back when you whistle.*

naughty
a naughty child behaves badly, for example by doing things that he or she should not do: *He knew he had done something naughty, but he didn't realize his mother would get so upset.*

evil
very cruel or bad: *He was an evil dictator who was responsible for the deaths of millions of people.*

wicked
very cruel or bad. **Wicked** sounds a little less strong than **evil**, and is often used in stories: *The wicked witch lived in the forest.*

wrong
not morally right. You use **wrong** when you think that something should not happen: *It's wrong that people have to sleep on the streets.*

immoral
not morally right. You use **immoral** when you strongly disapprove of something: *He believes that testing beauty products on animals is immoral.*

improper (*formal*)
improper behavior is behavior in which someone does something that he or she should not do, especially according to official rules: *The mayor had to resign after he was accused of improper behavior.*

5 describing food that is not good to eat

bad
not having a good taste: *The food in that restaurant is really bad.*

→ If food goes **bad**, it becomes rotten: *The meat had gone bad and we had to throw it out.*

disgusting
having a very bad taste, which makes you feel sick: *The stew was disgusting and I couldn't eat it.*

spoiled
if food is spoiled, it is no longer fresh or it is damaged, and it is not suitable to eat: *Several people became seriously ill after eating some spoiled food.* | *Some of the strawberries were spoiled.*

rotten
rotten food is old and starting to become soft because of natural chemical changes, and usually has a bad smell: *The apples were soft and rotten.*

moldy
covered in a soft green, gray, or black substance that grows on food which has been kept too long: *The only thing in the fridge was a piece of moldy cheese.*

stale
stale bread or cake is no longer fresh or good to eat, and is often too hard: *The cookies were hard and stale.*

sour
sour milk has a bad taste because it is no longer fresh: *The milk is sour. We'll have to throw it out.*

rancid
rancid butter, milk, or meat has a strong bad smell, because it is no longer fresh: *There was a horrible smell of rancid meat in the kitchen.*

off
if food is off, it is no longer fresh and it has a bad smell or taste: *The milk is off – it has a funny smell.*
→ GRAMMAR: You cannot use **off** before a noun. Don't say: ~~an off egg~~. Say: *The egg is off.*
→ see **serious (1)** for words used to describe a bad situation, problem, injury, etc.,
→ see **worse**, **get worse**

ADVERBS

You can make most of the adjectives that mean **bad** into adverbs by using an **-ly** ending, except for the words that describe food that is not good to eat: *The party went really badly – everything went wrong!* | *The kitchen was disgustingly dirty.* | *The shoes were poorly made.* | *"I put a frog in my sister's bed," said Joe, grinning mischievously.*

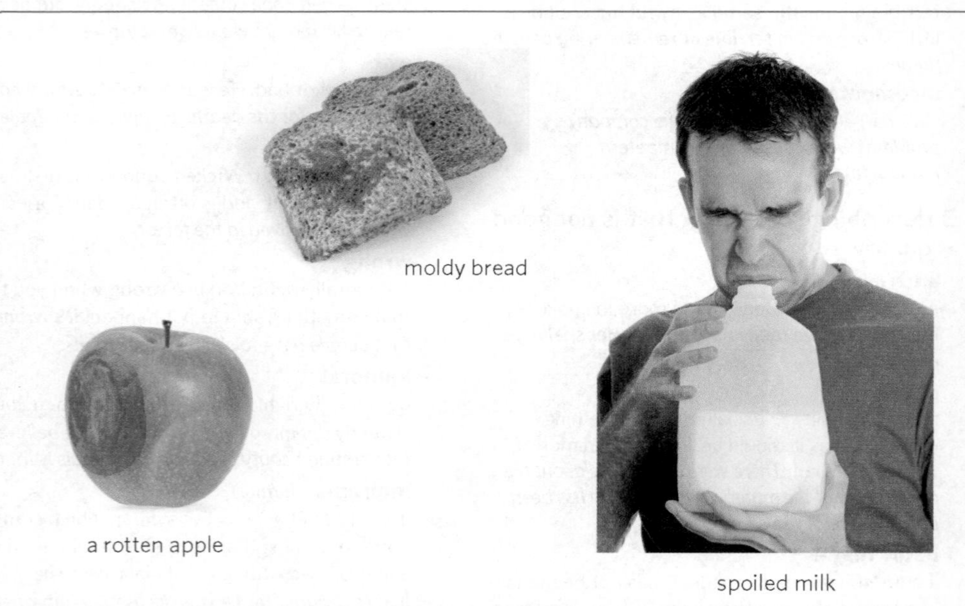

moldy bread

a rotten apple

spoiled milk

Online Thesaurus

Go to **www.longmandictionariesusa.com**
→ ***Longman Thesaurus of American English*** – with pronunciation of all the words
→ **Study Center** – interactive practice to help you learn synonyms, Academic Words, and Topic Vocabulary

bald *adjective* → see Topic **Describing People's Looks**

ballot *noun* → see **election**, **vote**[2]

ban *verb* → see **forbid**

band *noun* → see **group**, **stripe**

bang *verb* → see **hit**[1], Topic **To Make a Sound**

banned *adjective* → see **forbidden**

bar *noun* → see **piece**

bare *adjective* → see **empty**[1], **naked**, **plain**

barely *adverb* → see Function Word **almost**, **just**

bargain *noun* → see **agreement**

barrier *noun* → see **obstacle**, **wall**

base *noun* → see **bottom**

basic /ˈbeɪsɪk/ *adjective*

- basic
- fundamental
- essential
- elementary (*formal*)
- underlying
- inherent (*formal*)
- intrinsic (*formal*)

basic
simple and more important or necessary than anything else: *The army is bringing water and other basic supplies to the towns that were destroyed by the flood.* | *One basic rule of English grammar is that an adjective usually goes before a noun: a red car.*

fundamental (AWL)
relating to the most basic and important parts of something, which everything else depends on: *Reading is a fundamental skill that children must have in order to succeed in school.*

essential
relating to the most basic part or quality of something, which makes it what it is and makes it different from other things: *The essential difference between the human brain and a computer is the ability to feel emotions.*
→ GRAMMAR: When used with this meaning, **essential** is always used before a noun: *Helping children to talk about their feelings is an essential part of what we do.*

elementary (*formal*)
relating to the most basic ideas in a subject: *Using a computer has become an elementary skill in most jobs.* | *The class was in elementary biology.*

underlying (AWL)
an underlying cause or problem is the basic reason that something happens or exists: *When you are sick, doctors must find the underlying cause of your illness, for example being stressed or not eating well.*
→ GRAMMAR: **Underlying** is always used before a noun: *Engineers are working to fix the underlying problem.*

inherent (AWL) (*formal*)
a quality or feature that is inherent in something is a basic and permanent part of it so that it cannot be changed: *One of the dangers **inherent in** having only one political party is that there is likely to be corruption.*

intrinsic (AWL) (*formal*)
an intrinsic quality is part of someone or something's basic character: *Technology has become an intrinsic part of life in the Western world.*
→ see **simple**

basically /ˈbeɪsɪkli/ *adverb*

- basically
- essentially
- fundamentally

basically
in the most important or basic ways. You often use **basically** to introduce the most important or basic fact about something: *The lake is basically healthy for fish, but the water is not safe to drink.* | *Basically, a motorcycle is a bike with an engine.*

essentially
essentially means the same as **basically** but sounds more formal. You often use **essentially** when talking about the basic things that make one thing different from another: *The tunes of the two songs are essentially the same, but the words are different.*

fundamentally (AWL)
fundamentally means the same as **basically** but sounds more formal. You use **fundamentally** when talking about the most important parts of something that everything else about that thing depends on or develops from: *Schools and businesses are fundamentally different from one another, and they cannot be run in the same way.*

basis /ˈbeɪsɪs/ *noun*

- basis
- foundation

basis
an idea or reason that something develops from: *Ideas from the students' journals become the **basis for** classroom discussions.*

foundation (AWL)
an important idea or set of ideas that something develops from: *Love and respect form the foundation of a good marriage.*

bath *verb* → see **take a bath** at **wash**

bathe *verb* → see **wash**

bathroom /ˈbæθrum/ *noun*

- ► bathroom
- ► restroom
- ► ladies' room/men's room
- ► lavatory

bathroom
a room where there is a toilet and sink. In a house or apartment, there is also a bathtub or a shower: *The house has two bathrooms, but only one has a shower.*

restroom
a room with a toilet and sink, in a public place such as a restaurant or theater: *I could not find the restrooms in the airport.*

ladies' room/men's room
a restroom for women or men in a public place: *Excuse me, could you tell me where is the ladies' room?*

lavatory
a room with a toilet and sink on an airplane: *The sign says that smoking is not allowed in the lavatories.*
→ You can also talk about a **lavatory** in a public building such as a school, but this is very formal.

battle[1] *noun* → see **campaign[1]**, **fight[2]**, **war**

battle[2] *verb* → see **campaign[2]**, **fight[1]**, **try[1]**

bay *noun* → see **ocean**

beach *noun* → see **coast**

beam *verb* → see **smile[1]**

beast *noun* → see **animal**

beat /bit/ *verb*

- ► beat
- ► defeat
- ► conquer

beat
to get more points or votes than other people in a game, competition, or election: *We beat the other team 52–21. | Do you think the Republicans will beat the Democrats?*

defeat
to beat someone in a war, sport, or competition: *The Lions defeated the Bears in the final game of the season.*
→ **Defeat** is more formal than **beat**. You often use **defeat** when you are talking about winning a war against another country: *The American forces defeated the British at the Battle of Saratoga.*

conquer
to defeat people in a war and take their land: *The Aztecs conquered most of Mexico.*
→ see **hit[1]** for **beat** meaning "to hit someone or something," **stir** for **beat** meaning "to mix food"
→ see **win[1]**

beautiful *adjective* → *go to pages 46-47*

beauty /ˈbyuti/ *noun*

- ► beauty
- ► good looks
- ► attractiveness
- ► charm
- ► magnificence
- ► splendor

beauty
the quality of being beautiful to look at. You can use **beauty** about people, places, or things: *She was well-known for her beauty and talent as an actor. | In the mountains, you can see the beauty of the stars in the night sky because there aren't any lights.*

good looks
the quality that a person has of being attractive: *He is very popular, with his good looks and great sense of humor.*

attractiveness
the quality of being pleasant to look at. **Attractiveness** is used especially about people and does not sound as strong as **beauty**: *She worries too much about her physical attractiveness. | The soft colors add to the building's attractiveness.*

charm
a place that has charm has an attractive quality that pleases you and makes you like it: *The Italian landscape has beauty and charm, with its olive trees and gentle hills.*

magnificence
the fact that something is very beautiful and impressive or large: *Tourists come to see the magnificence of the huge waterfall.*

splendor
splendor is very similar in meaning to **magnificence**, but is used more about things made by people than about things in nature: *The palace has now been restored to its original splendor.*

because *conjunction* → see Function Words

become /bɪˈkʌm/ *verb*

- ► become
- ► get
- ► turn
- ► go
- ► grow
- ► develop into
- ► turn into

become
to begin to be something: *Ella became more and more angry as she listened to the woman talk.* | *He is trying to become a better person.*

get
get means the same as **become** but sounds more informal: *It was getting dark, and people began to leave.* | *I am getting very excited because my cousins are coming to visit.*

turn
to become different in color, or to change and become hotter, cooler, etc.: *Her face had turned white with anger.* | *The weather turned hot and humid.*
→ You also use **turn** when someone or something becomes **violent** or **nasty**: *Suddenly the conversation turned nasty.*

go
to become different in color, or to become dark or cold: *His hair is going gray.* | *The room suddenly went dark.* | *My body went cold with fear.*
→ You also use **go** when someone becomes **crazy**, **wild**, or **quiet**: *The crowd went wild when the Yankees won.*

grow
to slowly become different. **Grow** is used especially in stories and literature: *The sky grew dark and it started to rain.* | *He had grown very fond of her.*

develop into *also* **grow into**
to become something different over a very long time: *You have developed into a wonderful young woman these past few years.* | *The library has grown into a meeting place for the community.*

turn into
to become something completely different: *My great idea turned into a complete disaster.*
→ You also use **turn into** to show that something completely changes its shape or the way it looks, especially through magic: *The witch said a magic word and the prince turned into a frog.*

GRAMMAR CHECK: become

Become can be followed by an adjective or a noun: *He became upset.* | *The caterpillar became a butterfly.*

Get, **turn**, **go**, and **grow** can only be followed by an adjective: *He got upset.* | *The weather grew cold.*

Develop into, **grow into**, and **turn into** can only be followed by a noun: *The caterpillar turned into a butterfly.*

before *preposition, conjunction, adverb* → see Function Words

beforehand *adverb* → see Function Word **before**

beg /beg/ *verb*

- ► beg
- ► plead
- ► implore
- ► entreat (*formal*)

beg
to ask for something in a way that shows you want or need it very much: *She begged and begged until finally her parents let her go to the party.*
→ **Beg** also means to ask people in the street for money because you do not have any: *A man sitting outside of the store was* ***begging for*** *change.*

plead
to ask for something that you want very much, in a sincere and emotional way: *"Please forgive me," she pleaded. "I'll never do it again."*

implore
implore means the same as **plead** but is more formal: *She implored the soldiers to save her child.*

entreat (*formal*)
entreat means the same as **plead** and is used especially in literature: *His friends entreated him not to go.*
→ see **ask**

beautiful /'byutəfəl/ *adjective*

1 a person who is beautiful is very nice to look at
- ► beautiful
- ► pretty
- ► attractive
- ► good-looking
- ► handsome
- ► cute
- ► lovely
- ► elegant
- ► gorgeous
- ► stunning

2 a beautiful place or object is very nice to look at
- ► beautiful
- ► pretty
- ► attractive
- ► lovely
- ► magnificent
- ► breathtaking
- ► stunning
- ► exquisite (*formal*)
- ► scenic

3 something you hear that is beautiful is very nice to listen to
- ► beautiful
- ► pretty

ANTONYMS → see **ugly**

1 a person who is beautiful is very nice to look at

beautiful
very nice to look at. You use **beautiful** especially about women, girls, or babies: *She was a beautiful child with big dark eyes.*

pretty
nice to look at. **Pretty** is not as strong as **beautiful** and is used about women and girls: *His mother was a pretty woman with red hair.*

attractive
nice to look at. **Attractive** sounds slightly more formal than **pretty** and is used about adult men and women: *He is an attractive guy, but I don't think he is very interesting.*

good-looking *also* **nice-looking**
nice to look at. **Good-looking** is used slightly more often about men than women and is not as strong as **beautiful** or **handsome**: *Jordan is a very good-looking guy.*

handsome
nice to look at. You use **handsome** about men or boys, and it is stronger than **attractive** or **good-looking**: *Jill's boyfriend is very handsome.*

cute
a cute baby, small child, or animal is attractive to look at: *Your little sister is so cute!*
→ You can also use **cute** as an informal way to describe someone, especially a young woman or man, who is attractive: *Diana is smart and cute, and she makes me laugh.*

lovely
very pretty. You use **lovely** about women or older girls: *Lily had become a lovely young woman.*

elegant
beautiful and moving or dressing in a graceful way: *An elegant older couple, dressed in evening clothes, was seated at a nearby table.*

gorgeous
very beautiful or handsome. Women use the word **gorgeous** more often than men: *The new gym teacher is absolutely gorgeous.*

stunning
extremely beautiful. You use **stunning** about women: *Her face was stunning, and she moved like a model.*
→ see Topic **Describing People's Looks**

2 a beautiful place or object is very nice to look at

beautiful
very nice to look at: *We walked around the city looking at the beautiful old buildings.* | *His photographs are beautiful.*

pretty
nice to look at. **Pretty** is not as strong as **beautiful**: *We stopped in a pretty little town in the mountains to have dinner.*

attractive
attractive means the same as **pretty** but sounds slightly more formal: *The room was decorated in an attractive way.*

lovely
very pretty, in a way that pleases you: *Graz, in Austria, is a lovely 900-year-old city.*

magnificent
very beautiful, and very large or impressive: *The mountains looked magnificent in the late afternoon sunshine.*

breathtaking
beautiful in a way that excites or surprises you. You use **breathtaking** especially about a large area of land or water that you can see: *The views of the ocean from the cliffs were absolutely breathtaking.*

stunning
stunning means the same as **breathtaking** but is used less frequently: *The room has a stunning view of the city.*

exquisite *(formal)*
very beautiful. You use **exquisite** about things that have a lot of small details and have been made with a lot of care and skill: *The drawings are exquisite, with every tiny detail and color carefully done.*

scenic
surrounded by views of beautiful countryside: *We traveled to the coast by a very scenic route.*

3 something you hear that is beautiful is very nice to listen to

beautiful
very nice to listen to: *The music was so beautiful, it made me feel like crying.* | *She has a beautiful voice.*

pretty
nice to listen to. **Pretty** is not as strong as **beautiful**: *He was playing a pretty little tune on the piano.*

→ see Topic **The Weather**

ADVERBS

You can make the adjectives **beautiful**, **pretty**, **attractive**, **handsome**, **elegant**, **gorgeous**, **magnificent**, **breathtaking**, and **exquisite** into adverbs by using an **-ly** ending: *The woman sitting next to me was beautifully dressed.* | *He smiled attractively.* | *The mountains were breathtakingly beautiful.*

The mountains looked **magnificent** in the sunshine.

We traveled to the campsite by a very **scenic** route.

handsome

The room has a **stunning** view of the city.

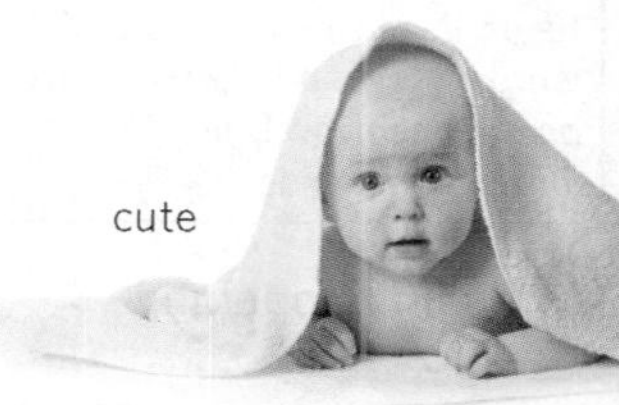

cute

begin /bɪˈɡɪn/ *verb*

1 to begin doing something
- ► **begin**
- ► **start**
- ► **launch**
- ► **take up**
- ► **initiate** (*formal*)

ANTONYMS → see **stop[1]**, **finish**

2 to begin happening
- ► **begin**
- ► **start**
- ► **commence** (*formal*)
- ► **break out**

ANTONYMS → see **end[2] (1)**

1 to begin doing something

begin
if you begin doing something, you were not doing it before but you are doing it now: *They slowly began to climb up the mountain.* | *The company plans to begin work on the bridge next year.* | *She began reading.*

start
start means the same as **begin** but is slightly less formal: *The clown fell down and the kids all started laughing.* | *When do you start your new job?* | *She tried to start a conversation with him.*

launch
to begin something new or important, such as an effort to do something or an attack: *The town launched a campaign to attract more tourists.*

take up
to become interested in a sport or activity, and start doing it regularly: *When did Bryan take up golf?*

initiate (AWL) (*formal*)
to start something, especially something important such as a new process, discussion, or plan: *Both sides have agreed to initiate peace talks in an effort to end the war.*

SYNONYM CHECK

Begin or start?

Start and **begin** both mean the same, but **begin** is a little more formal. With some words, you can only use **start**. You say *start an argument/war/fire*. You do not use **begin** with these words.

2 to begin happening

begin
if something begins happening, it was not happening before but is happening now: *The meeting begins at 10:30 a.m.* | *It began to snow.*

start
start means the same as **begin** but is slightly less formal: *What time does the movie start?* | *The rain started again.*

commence (AWL) (*formal*)
to begin. **Commence** is more formal than **start** and **begin**: *Work on the new building will commence immediately.*

break out
to begin happening. You use **break out** about unpleasant things such as wars, fires, or diseases: *The fire broke out on the top floor of the hotel.*

beginning /bɪˈɡɪnɪŋ/ *noun*

- ► **beginning**
- ► **start**
- ► **introduction**
- ► **origin**
- ► **birth**
- ► **outbreak**
- ► **outset**

ANTONYMS → see **end[1] (1)**

beginning
the first part of an event, period of time, story, etc., when something begins: ***At the beginning of** the movie, the two main characters hate each other.* | *We hope this is the beginning of a time of peace in our country.* | *The show lasts **from the beginning** until the end of August.*

start
the time or moment when something begins: ***At the start of** the second half of the basketball game, the score was 32 to 28.*

introduction
the part at the beginning of a book, report, or speech, which explains what it is about: *In the **introduction to** her book, Julia writes about how she first became interested in cooking.*

origin *also* origins
the beginning of something that started a long time ago: *Scientists still have many questions about **the origins of** language in humans.*

birth
the time when something starts to exist, especially something important that has a big effect on people's lives: *The website is about the singers and bands of the 1950s and **the birth of** rock 'n' roll.*

outbreak
a time when fighting or a disease starts: ***At the outbreak of** the war, he was living in Boston.* |

There was an **outbreak of** *food poisoning at the hotel.*

outset
the time when you start doing something or when something starts happening: *We knew* ***from the outset*** *that it was not going to be an easy task.*
→ **Outset** is only used in the phrases **from the outset** and **at the outset**: *They said at the outset that we would have to work hard.*

SYNONYM CHECK
Beginning or start?

Beginning and **start** mean the same thing. However, we think of the **beginning** of something as longer than the **start** of something. *Did you see the beginning of the game?* means the moment it started and a period of time after that. *Did you see the start of the game?* means only the moment it started.

You usually use **beginning** about stories or movies, or about long periods of time such as months. You usually use **start** about events, such as meetings or races.

behave /bɪˈheɪv/ *verb*

1 to do or say things in a particular way
- behave
- act
- conduct yourself (*formal*)
- react
- treat

2 to behave well
- behave well
- be well-behaved
- behave yourself
- be on your best behavior

ANTONYMS → see **misbehave**

1 to do or say things in a particular way

behave
to do or say things in a particular way: *The cat was behaving strangely, so we took her to the vet.* | *If there's a change in the way a child behaves, there may be something wrong.*

act
to behave in a particular way. **Act** is more informal than **behave**: *You are* ***acting like*** *a spoiled child!* | *The police asked me if my brother had been acting normally lately.*

conduct yourself (*formal*)
conduct yourself means the same as **behave** but is much more formal: *We expect all students to conduct themselves well when they are working in the community.*

react (AWL)
to behave in a particular way because something has happened: *The family* ***reacted*** *joyfully* ***to*** *the news that their son had been found.*

treat
to do or say things to someone else in a particular way, which has an effect on that person: *My mother still* ***treats*** *me* ***like*** *a child.* | *They treated me kindly.*

GRAMMAR CHECK: behave

All these words must be used with an adverb or a group of words that describes the behavior: *He is behaving oddly.* | *They treated me with kindness.*

2 to behave well

behave well
to behave in a way that is good in a particular situation, and that does not break rules or annoy people: *The players on the team behaved well after their loss in the playoffs.*

be well-behaved
to behave well. You use **be well-behaved** about a child: *She is very well-behaved for a three-year-old.*

behave yourself
to behave well in a particular situation. Parents and teachers say **behave yourself** to children when they want them to behave well: *Behave yourself when your grandparents come over.*
→ **GRAMMAR:** Don't say: ~~*I behaved myself well.*~~ Say: *I behaved myself.*

be on your best behavior
to behave in a way that is pleasant, polite, and exactly right for a particular situation: *All the young people were dressed up and on their best behavior at the meeting.*

behavior /bɪˈheɪvyɚ/ *noun*

- behavior
- conduct (*formal*)
- manner
- treatment

behavior
the way that a person behaves: *The prisoners can leave prison early if their behavior is good.* | *After taking the drug, the patients' behavior changed. They went from being calm to being anxious.*

conduct (AWL) (*formal*)
the way someone behaves, especially in a job or

at school. **Conduct** sounds more formal or official than **behavior**: *You will be graded on your work and your conduct in class.*

manner
the way someone talks to or deals with other people. **Manner** sounds fairly formal: *Her manner was always polite and professional.*

treatment
the things that a person or organization does that have an effect on people they have power over: *The **treatment of** prisoners at the women's prison has improved.*
→ see **misbehavior** for words meaning "bad behavior"

behind *preposition, adverb* → see Function Words

belief /bəˈlif/ *noun*

1 a strong feeling that something is true or right
- ► belief
- ► faith
- ► superstition
- ► conviction

2 something you think is true
- ► belief
- ► conclusion
- ► assumption
- ► suspicion
- ► inference
- ► deduction

1 a strong feeling that something is true or right

belief
a strong feeling that something is definitely true or right. You often use **belief** about someone believing that God exists: *She has a strong **belief in** God.*

faith
a strong belief that you can trust someone or something. You often use **faith** about someone's religious beliefs: *His faith helped him to deal with his son's illness.* | *He has great **faith in** her judgment, and asks for her advice about everything.*

superstition
a belief that some things are lucky and some are not: *There is a **superstition that** walking under a ladder is unlucky.*

conviction
a strong belief that makes you choose to do things or not do things. You use **conviction** especially about religious or political ideas: *Because of his religious convictions, he refused to fight in the war.*
→ see **religion**

2 something you think is true

belief
a strong opinion that information, an idea, or fact is definitely true: *It is my belief that hard work and determination are the keys to success.*

conclusion (AWL)
something that you decide is true after thinking about the information that you have: *Police reached the conclusion that the man had been poisoned.*

assumption (AWL)
something that you think is true, although you do not have definite proof: *The assumption is that children all over the world follow the same stages of development.*

suspicion
something that you think is likely to be true because you have a little information about it: *I had a suspicion that he was lying to me, because he had lied to me before.*

inference (AWL)
something that you think is true based on information that you have: *We used the surveys to draw inferences about what people liked and disliked about the presidential candidates.*

deduction (AWL)
something that you decide is probably true, after thinking carefully about the facts that you know. You use **deduction** about scientific or technical things: *The scientists examined cases of the disease, and made the deduction that mosquitoes were responsible for passing the disease from person to person.*
→ see **think (3)**

believe /bəˈliv/ *verb*

- ► believe
- ► accept
- ► take someone's word for it
- ► be taken in

ANTONYMS → see **disbelieve**

believe
to feel sure that something is true or that someone is telling the truth: *People used to **believe that** the Earth was flat.* | *Did the police believe his story?*

accept
to believe something because someone has told you it is true: *The teacher accepted his explanation for being late for class.*

take someone's word for it
to believe what someone tells you even though you have no proof that it is true: *When he told me he'd been in the army, I took his word for it.*

be taken in
to believe that what someone says is true, when he or she is lying: *More than 100 people were taken in by Hilson's promises and lost all their money.*
→ see **believe in** at **trust**[1]
→ see **think**

belong *verb* → see **belong to someone** at **own**[1]

belongings *noun* → see **possession**

below *preposition, adverb* → see Function Word **under**

bend[1] /bend/ *verb*

1 to move part of your body so that it is not straight
- bend
- bow
- stoop
- lean
- duck
- curl up

2 to change direction – used about roads, rivers, or paths
- bend
- curve
- twist
- wind

3 to push or turn something so that it is no longer straight or flat
- bend
- twist
- curl
- wind
- coil

1 to move part of your body so that it is not straight

bend
to move part of your body so that it is not straight, or so that you are not upright: *In this exercise you have to bend your knees, but keep your back straight.* | *She **bent down** to lift the box off the floor.* | *He **bent over** to pick up the coins.*

bow
to bend your head or the top part of your body forward, in order to thank an audience or show respect: *He bowed before the king.* | *At the end of the play, the actors bowed to the audience.*

stoop
to bend your head and shoulders forward and down, especially to go under something: *We had to stoop to go through the low doorway.*

lean
to bend your body forward, backward, or to the side: *She leaned forward so that she could hear him more clearly.*

duck
to lower your head or body very quickly, especially to avoid being seen or hit: *She ducked when the ball came toward her.*

curl up
to move so that you are sitting or lying with your arms and legs bent close to your body: *She curled up in the armchair with a book.*
→ see **kneel**

2 to change direction – used about roads, rivers, or paths

bend
if a road, river, or path bends, it changes direction to form a curve: *The road bends to the left.*

curve
if a road, river, or path curves, it changes direction smoothly over a long distance: *The beach gently curves around the bay.*

twist
if a road, river, or path twists, it changes direction suddenly many times: *The stream twisted through the rocks and trees.*

wind
if a road, river, or path winds somewhere, it changes direction smoothly many times over a long distance: *The trail **winds through** the forest.*

3 to push or turn something so that it is no longer straight or flat

bend
to push or press something so that it is no longer straight or flat: *The plumber used a special tool to bend the pipe.*

twist
to turn something several times, for example a piece of wire or cloth: *He twisted the rag to squeeze the water out of it.*

curl
to make something form a curved shape, especially hair: *She is curling her hair.*

wind
to turn or twist something several times around something else: *She started winding the scarf around her neck.*

coil
to turn or twist something long and thin so that

it looks like many circles on top of each other: *Coil the hose again once you have finished watering the plants.*

bend

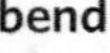

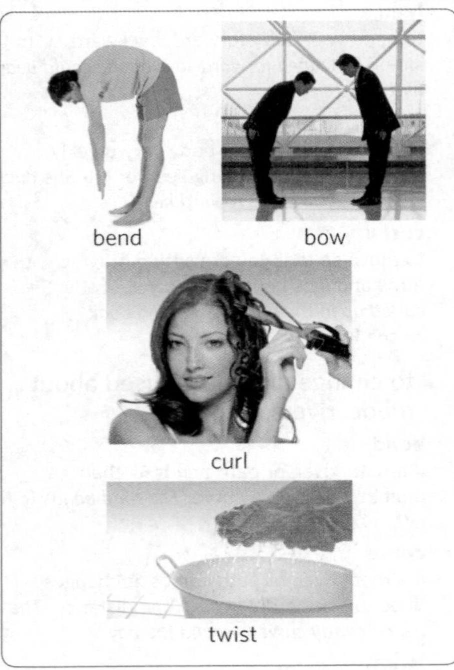

bend² /bend/ *noun*

- bend
- curve
- turn
- twists and turns
- zigzag

bend
a place on a road, river, or path where it turns to go in a different direction: *There are a lot of sharp bends on this road, so you have to drive carefully.*

curve
a **curve** is the same as a **bend**, but it does not change direction as much: *The road goes along the base of the hill in a long curve.*

turn
a place where roads join so that one of the roads goes in a different direction from the one you are on: *Take the second turn on the left.*

twists and turns
all the places on a road, river, or path where it suddenly turns to go in a different direction: *The path has a lot of twists and turns.*

zigzag
a place on a road, river, or path where it suddenly turns one way and then another to make a "Z" shape: *The trail goes up the mountainside in a series of zigzags.*

beneath *preposition, adverb* → see Function Word **under**

beneficial *adjective* → see **useful**

benefit *noun* → see **advantage**

bent /bent/ *adjective*

- bent
- twisted
- curved
- crooked
- warped
- wavy

bent
something bent is not straight because it has been pushed out of its usual shape: *The nail was bent and I couldn't make it go straight into the wood.*

twisted
having a bent shape that turns around. You often use **twisted** when something has been damaged: *After the crash, the truck was a pile of twisted metal.*

curved
having a smooth round bend, either naturally or because it has been made that way: *An airplane wing is curved on top and flat on the bottom.*

crooked
not straight and bending sharply in a way that is not usual: *A crooked path led to the house.*
→ You also use **crooked** about something that is placed in a way that is not straight: *That picture looks crooked – can you move it up on the left?* | *He has crooked teeth.*

warped
bent and no longer flat and straight. Things often become warped because they are too hot or wet, especially things made of wood: *The window frames are warped and you can't open the windows anymore.*

wavy
having smooth curved shapes in a regular

pattern. You use **wavy** to describe lines, patterns, and hair: *She has long wavy blonde hair.*

bent

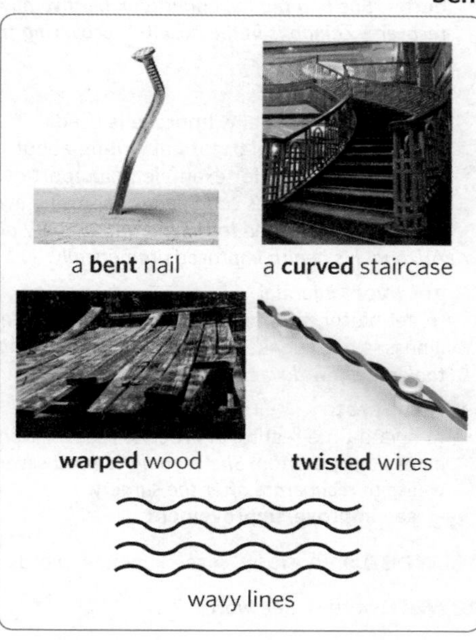

a **bent** nail a **curved** staircase

warped wood **twisted** wires

wavy lines

beside *preposition* → see Function Word **next to**

besides *adverb* → see Function Word **also**

best /best/ *adjective*

- ► best
- ► greatest
- ► finest
- ► top
- ► star

best
better than anyone or anything else: *She is the best student in our class – no one else gets such good grades.* | *That was the best vacation I've ever had.*

greatest
better than anyone or anything else in history or in the world: *Picasso was one of the greatest artists of the 20th century.*

finest
the best and most skillful, or the best and the highest quality. You use **finest** about things such as occasions, performances, achievements, and foods. **Finest** is more formal than **greatest**: *The actress gave one of the finest performances of her movie career.* | *We use only the finest ingredients in our food.*

top
the best or most successful. **Top** is more informal than **best**: *She is one of the top lawyers in the country.*
→ GRAMMAR: **Top** is only used before a noun: *He is a top student.*

star
star means the same as **top** and is used especially about sports people. **Star** is more informal than **best**: *He is the basketball team's star player.*
→ GRAMMAR: Don't say: ~~*She is star*~~. Say: *She is a star athlete* or *She is a star.*
→ see **better**

bet *verb* → see **gamble**

betrayal /bɪˈtreɪəl/ *noun*

- ► betrayal
- ► disloyalty
- ► treason
- ► treachery (*formal*)
- ► mutiny

betrayal
the act of not being loyal, which causes serious harm to someone who trusts you: *She had told my secrets to my parents, and I was shocked by the betrayal.*

disloyalty
the act of doing or saying things that do not support your friends or country: *If I did not obey him, my father saw this as disloyalty.*

treason
the crime of doing something that could harm your country, for example helping its enemies: *The soldier was charged with treason for giving war plans to the enemy.*

treachery (*formal*)
the actions of a person who secretly intends to harm people who trust him or her. **Treachery** is used mainly in books: *He became king by treachery – he killed his nephew, who should have become king instead of him.*

mutiny
a situation in which soldiers or sailors refuse to obey their leader or captain and take control for themselves: *One of the sailors led a mutiny against the captain.*

better /ˈbetɚ/ *adjective*

1 more useful or skilled than other people, or of a higher quality than other things (adjectives)
- ► **better**
- ► **superior**
- ► **preferable** (*formal*)

ANTONYMS → see **worse (1)**

2 to become healthy again after being sick (verbs)
- ► **get better**
- ► **get well**
- ► **recover**
- ► **improve**
- ► **get over** (*informal*)
- ► **recuperate**

ANTONYMS → see **worse (3)**

1 more useful or skilled than other people, or of a higher quality than other things (adjectives)

better
more useful, skilled, or of a higher quality than someone or something else: *My new camera is a lot **better than** my old one – the pictures are a lot sharper.* | *He is **better at** math than I am, but I'm better at English.*

superior
better than other people or things. You use **superior** about people's skills, or about products or services that you can buy: *Modern medicine is far **superior to** the medical treatments that were available in the past.*

preferable (*formal*)
better or more appropriate. Use **preferable** to say what you would choose: *I didn't want to go, but it was still **preferable to** staying here alone.*
→ see **best**

2 to become healthy again after being sick (verbs)

get better
to become healthy again after you have had an illness, injury, or operation. You can use **get better** about a person or a part of the body that is injured: *I hope you get better soon.* | *My knee still hurts, but it is getting better slowly.*

get well
to become healthy again after an illness. You only use **get well** about people, not about parts of their bodies that are injured. **Get well** is mostly used in the phrase **get well soon**, which you use to say that you hope someone becomes healthy again quickly: *I hope you get well soon.*

recover (AWL)
to become completely healthy after being sick or injured. **Recover** sounds more formal than **get better**: *She had the flu, and it took her five days to recover.* | *Zainab is in the hospital **recovering from** surgery.*

improve
to get better gradually. **Improve** is used especially in official or formal writing about someone's health, for example in a report by a doctor: *The patient's condition is improving every day.* | *After he moved to the warmth and dry air of Arizona, his health improved dramatically.*

get over (*informal*)
to get better after an illness, especially when the illness is not very serious: *I had a bad cold, and it took me a few days to get over it.*

recuperate
to spend time resting in order to recover from an illness or operation: *She is going to need several weeks to recuperate after the surgery.*
→ see **improve**, **improvement**

between *preposition* → see Function Words

beware *verb* → see **warn**

beyond *preposition* → see Function Word **above**

biased *adjective* → see **prejudiced**, **unfair**

bibliography *noun* → see **list**[1], Topic **Books and Literature**

big *adjective* → *go to pages 56-58*

bilingual *adjective* → see **fluent**

bill /bɪl/ *noun*
- ► **bill**
- ► **check**
- ► **tab**
- ► **invoice**

bill
a list of things that you have bought or that someone has done for you, which shows how much you have to pay for them: *Did you remember to pay the electric bill?* | *The **bill for** the repairs came to $450.*

check
a list of the food and drinks you have had in a restaurant, which shows how much you must pay: *At the end of the meal, I asked the waiter for the check.*

tab
a bill showing how much you need to pay for things that you have bought over a period of time, especially food or drinks. You add small

amounts to the **tab** and then pay for all of it later: *He ordered dinner at the hotel restaurant and asked for it to be put on his tab.*

invoice
a bill from a business that shows the things you have bought or the work they have done for you, and how much you must pay or have paid for them. You usually receive an **invoice** in the mail: *We received an* ***invoice for*** *$230 for the plumbing repairs.*
→ see **law** for **bill** meaning "a law"

biography *noun* → see **history**, **nonfiction**, Topic **Books and Literature**

biology *noun* → see Topic **Science and Technology**

birth *noun* → see **beginning**, **baby** (**2**) for "to give birth"

bit *noun* → see **piece**

bite /baɪt/ *verb*

1 to use your teeth, especially to eat food
- ► bite
- ► take a bite
- ► chew
- ► nibble
- ► gnaw
- ► peck

2 an insect, snake, etc. bites
- ► bite
- ► sting

1 to use your teeth, especially to eat food

bite
to cut or crush something with your teeth, or attack someone with your teeth: *The dog tried to bite the mailman.* | *He* ***bit into*** *the apple.*

take a bite
to bite off a piece of food and eat it: *She took a bite of her sandwich.*

chew
to bite food in your mouth several times. You **chew** food in order to make it softer and easier to swallow: *Don't eat so fast – slow down and chew your food so you don't choke.*

nibble
to eat food by taking a lot of small bites: *She didn't feel well and just* ***nibbled on*** *a cracker.* | *Rabbits had nibbled the lettuce growing in the garden.*

gnaw
if an animal gnaws something hard, it bites it many times: *The dog was in the yard* ***gnawing on*** *a bone.* | *They gnawed at the bones to get off all the meat.*

peck
if a bird pecks something, it quickly bites it with its beak: *Hens* ***pecked at*** *the corn scattered on the ground.*
→ If a person **pecks** at his or her food, he or she is not eating very much: *Polly just pecked at her dinner.*

2 an insect, snake, etc. bites

bite
if an insect or snake bites you, it hurts you by putting poison into your skin: *Many kinds of spiders bite, but only some spiders are dangerous.*

sting
if an insect, jellyfish, scorpion, etc. stings you, it hurts you by putting poison into your skin: *A wasp stung him on the arm.*

SYNONYM CHECK
Sting or bite?
You use **sting** for bees, wasps, jellyfish, and scorpions, and **bite** for mosquitoes, ants, spiders, and snakes.

bite

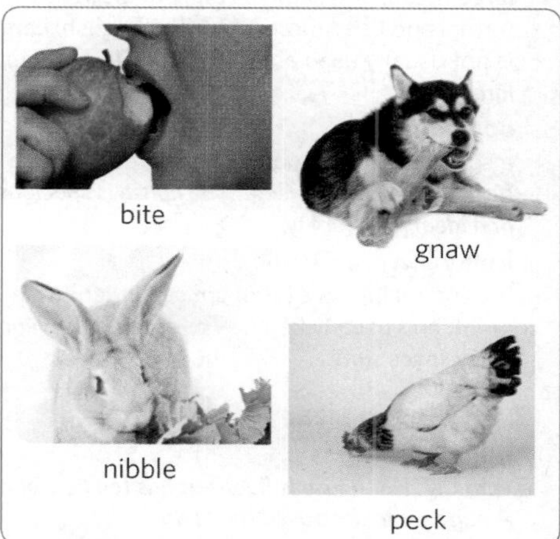

bitter *adjective* → see **cold**[1], **sour**, Topic **Describing Food**, **Describing People's Emotions**

bizarre *adjective* → see **strange**

big /bɪg/ *adjective*

1 big in size
► **big**
► **large**
► **spacious**
► **bulky**

2 very big in size
► **huge**
► **enormous**
► **gigantic**
► **giant**
► **massive**
► **immense** (*formal*)
► **colossal**
► **vast**
► **jumbo** (*informal*)

ANTONYMS → see **small (1)**

3 big in amount or number
► **big**
► **large**
► **high**
► **huge**
► **enormous**
► **vast**
► **massive**
► **immense** (*formal*)
► **tremendous**
► **substantial**
► **considerable** (*formal*)
► **sizable**

ANTONYMS → see **small (2)**

4 having a big effect
► **big** (*informal*)
► **huge**
► **enormous**
► **significant**
► **major**
► **massive**

ANTONYMS → see **small (3)**

1 big in size

big
more than the usual size: *They live in a big house in New York.* | *Canada is a big country.*

large
large means the same as **big**, but is slightly more formal and used more in written English. **Large** is not usually used about people: *She ordered a large pizza.*

spacious
a spacious room, apartment, car, etc. is large and has a lot of space inside: *The house is spacious and ideal for a family.*

bulky (AWL)
big and taking up a lot of space, difficult to move or lift, and usually heavy: *The astronauts wear bulky space suits.*

2 very big in size

huge
very big: *Her house is huge – it has ten bedrooms.* | *A huge wave destroyed the town.*

enormous (AWL)
enormous means the same as **huge** but sounds more formal: *The office is in an enormous 75-story building.*
→ You can use **huge** and **enormous** in many of the same situations, but **enormous** is the best choice for more formal writing or speech.

gigantic
extremely big or tall, and much bigger than other things of the same type, especially when they are strange or frightening: *Gigantic waves more than 40 feet high crashed against the boat.* | *Sequoia trees are gigantic and some are more than 1,500 years old.*

giant
giant means the same as **gigantic** but is more informal: *The old stories say that the forest is full of giant snakes and spiders.* | *It was once a small family-owned company, but now it is a giant corporation with stores in most countries.*
→ GRAMMAR: **Giant** is only used before a noun. Don't say: ~~*The spider is giant*~~. Say: *It's a giant spider.*

massive
very big and heavy: *The bell is massive and weighs more than 40 tons.*

immense (*formal*)
very big. **Immense** sounds fairly formal or literary: *Sixty million years ago, the whole area was an immense desert.*

colossal
extremely big. You usually use **colossal** about objects: *The soldiers seemed small next to the colossal antiaircraft gun.*

vast
very big. **Vast** is used about areas or distances: *The fire spread over a vast area.*

jumbo (*informal*)
larger than others of the same type. You use **jumbo** especially to describe the largest size of a

product you can buy: *He ordered a jumbo hot dog with fries.*

→ see **expand** for words meaning "to become bigger"

→ see **grow**

GRAMMAR CHECK: big

Don't use "very" with adjectives that mean "very big." Don't say: ~~*It was very huge*~~. Say: *It was huge* or *It was really huge.*

3 big in amount or number

big
more than the usual amount. **Big** is informal in this meaning and is not usually used to talk about numbers or amounts. It is better to use **large**: *She got a big raise at work.*

large
big in amount or number: *The computer can store large amounts of information.* | *New York City has the largest population of any city in the United States.*

high
a high price, rate, level, or measurement is bigger than usual or bigger than you want: *The price of gas is getting higher and higher.* | *High levels of mercury were found in the water.*

→ Don't say: ~~*The store has large/big prices*~~. Say: *The store has high prices.*

huge
very big in amount or number: *I have a huge amount of homework to do.* | *Huge numbers of people use the airport every year.*

enormous AWL
enormous means the same as **huge** but sounds more formal: *The government spends an enormous amount on defense.* | *She had an enormous sense of relief when she found out that he was all right.*

vast
very big in amount or number: *She spends a vast amount of money on clothes.*

massive
very big, and often having a serious effect: *There has been a massive increase in oil prices.* | *My phone bill was massive last month.*

immense (*formal*)
very big, and important or serious. **Immense** sounds fairly formal or literary, and it is often used about feelings or qualities: *The book contains an immense amount of information.* | *I was impressed by her immense enthusiasm for her work.*

tremendous
very large and having a big effect. You often use **tremendous** about something that is impressive or about emotions: *She has done a tremendous amount of work on her science project.* | *Andrea felt tremendous pressure to succeed.*

substantial
large enough to have an effect or be useful. You usually use **substantial** about amounts of things you can touch or see: *Mrs. Harrington gave a substantial amount of money to the charity when she died.* | *He ate a substantial breakfast.*

considerable AWL (*formal*)
fairly large. You often use **considerable** about things that people feel or the qualities they show, for example relief or interest: *There was considerable damage to the hospital in the bomb attack.* | *She read the book with considerable interest.*

sizable *also* **sizeable**
fairly large. You use **sizable** about amounts or numbers that can be measured: *Scientists believe there is a sizable quantity of oil in the area.*

→ see Topic **Describing Places**

GRAMMAR CHECK: big

Considerable and **sizable** both mean "fairly large." You use **considerable** with nouns that have no plural and with nouns that have a plural: *They have made considerable progress.* | *A considerable number of people came to the meeting.* You use **sizable** only with nouns that have a plural: *A sizable number of people came to the meeting.* Don't say: ~~*They have made sizable progress*~~.

SYNONYM CHECK

Huge, enormous, vast or massive?

All of these words have basically the same meaning and they can be used in many of the same sentences. You often use them when an amount or number is surprising or shocking: *A huge/enormous/vast/massive number of people do not even have enough food to eat.*

4 having a big effect

big (*informal*)
important and having a serious effect on the future. You use **big** about events, changes, and decisions: *I always ask for advice before making a big decision.* | *Our biggest problem is a lack of money.*

→ GRAMMAR: In this meaning, **big** is usually used before a noun. You can say: *The problem is very big*, but it is better to say: *It is a very big problem.*

→ Don't use **large** about problems, changes, difference, or effects. Use **big**: *There will be some big changes in the way the school is run.*

huge
very big, and very important or serious: *In the last 20 years, computers have had a huge effect on the way we work.*

enormous AWL
enormous means the same as **huge** but sounds more formal: *Enormous changes have taken place in our society.*

significant
important and having a strong effect on what happens in the future: *The new drug is a significant step forward in our fight against the disease.*

major
having a very large or important effect, especially when compared to other things: *There will probably be major changes in the earth's climate.*
→ GRAMMAR: **Major** is usually used before a noun: *We are having major problems with our computer.*

massive
unusually large, powerful, or damaging and having a big effect: *The area was hit by a massive earthquake yesterday.* | *The change to the welfare system will have a massive impact on people's lives.*
→ see **important**, **serious**

ADVERBS
You can make the adjectives **huge**, **enormous**, **gigantic**, **massive**, **immense**, **colossal**, **vast**, **tremendous**, **substantial**, **considerable**, **sizable**, and **significant** into adverbs by using an **-ly** ending: *The movie was enormously popular.* | *Gas prices have increased tremendously in the past few years.* | *The house was considerably bigger than I had expected.*

The **giant** heads of the presidents are in South Dakota.

Sequoia trees are **gigantic**.

gigantic waves

vast grasslands

Online Thesaurus
Go to **www.longmandictionariesusa.com**
→ ***Longman Thesaurus of American English*** – with pronunciation of all the words
→ **Study Center** – interactive practice to help you learn synonyms, Academic Words, and Topic Vocabulary

blame[1] /bleɪm/ *verb*

- blame
- put/place/lay the blame on
- accuse
- hold someone responsible

blame
to say or think that someone is responsible for something bad that has happened: *It was your fault! Don't blame me! | The driver of the truck was **blamed for** the accident. | Someone ate all the cake and she is **blaming** it **on** me.*

put/place/lay the blame on
to say who you think is responsible for something bad that has happened, sometimes unfairly or wrongly: *Richard puts all the blame for the divorce on his ex-wife. | The report placed the blame squarely on city officials. | It is easy to lay the blame for the recession on the mistakes the banks made.*

accuse
to say that someone is guilty of a crime or has done something very bad: *He **accused** her **of** lying to him. | She was **accused of** murder.*

hold someone responsible
to say who you think caused something bad when it was his or her duty to prevent it from happening. You use **hold someone responsible** when talking about a mistake, accident, or crime: *She **held** the hospital **responsible for** her husband's death.*
→ see **to blame** at **guilty**

blame[2] *noun* → see **fault**

bland *adjective* → see **tasteless**, Topic **Describing Food**

blank *adjective* → see **empty[1]**

blast *noun* → see **explosion**

blaze[1] *noun* → see **fire[1]**

blaze[2] *verb* → see **burn**, **shine**

bleak *adjective* → see **empty[1]**, **sad**

blend[1] *verb* → see **mix**, **stir**

blend[2] *noun* → see **mixture**

blind /blaɪnd/ *adjective*

- blind
- visually impaired (*formal*)

blind
not able to see: *The size of the coins helps blind people tell them apart. | At the age of 22, she went blind.*

visually impaired (*formal*)
not able to see, or only able to see a little: *There are special classes for visually impaired children.*

block[1] /blɑk/ *verb*

1 to prevent things from moving through something
- block
- obstruct (*formal*)
- bar
- clog
- plug

2 to prevent something from developing or making progress
- block
- disrupt
- hamper
- hinder
- impede (*formal*)

1 to prevent things from moving through something

block
to prevent things from moving through a space by putting something across it or in it: *Someone's car was blocking our driveway. | The kitchen sink is blocked.*

obstruct (*formal*)
to block a road, tube, or doorway so that nothing can get past: *Your equipment is obstructing the emergency exit, so you must move it.*

bar
to put a piece of wood or metal across a door or window in order to stop people from going in or out: *The windows were all barred to stop prisoners from escaping.*

clog
to block something from flowing through an area, especially with lots of small things that come together: *If you eat too much butter or cheese, your arteries can become **clogged with** fats. | Cars and buses clogged the streets.*

plug *also* **plug up**
to fill a hole in something so that nothing can get through: *When you're a teenager, too much oil plugs up the pores in your skin and causes acne.*

2 to prevent something from developing or making progress

block
to stop something from developing or making progress: *The government blocked the sale of*

weapons to the country. | *The senator said he would try to block the bill in Congress.*

disrupt
to cause problems that stop a situation or process from continuing in its usual way: *You will be sent to the principal's office if you keep disrupting the class.*

hamper
to make it more difficult for someone to do something so that progress is slower: *The rescue efforts were hampered by bad weather.*

hinder
hinder means the same as **hamper**: *A problem with getting supplies has hindered progress on building the new houses.*

impede (*formal*)
impede means the same as **hamper**: *Poor hearing may impede a child's learning.*
→ see **prevent**

SYNONYM CHECK
Hamper, hinder, or impede?

All these words mean the same thing, and they can be used in many of the same sentences. However, the emphasis is slightly different for each of these words.

Hamper comes from an old word that means "to tie someone or put handcuffs on him or her." So, when you use **hamper**, it carries the idea of someone not being able to achieve something because something is holding him or her back.

Hinder and **impede** carry the idea that something is in the way of making progress.

block² *noun* → see **piece**

blog *noun* → see **record**, Topic **Computers and the Internet**

blouse *noun* → see **shirt**

blow *noun* → see **hit²**

blow up /ˌbloʊ ˈʌp/ *phrasal verb*

- ► blow up
- ► inflate
- ► pump up

blow up
to fill something with air or gas, especially a balloon: *We blew up at least 50 balloons for the party.*

inflate
to fill something with air or gas. **Inflate** is more formal than **blow up**: *It took just a few minutes to inflate the air mattress.* | *The life jacket inflates automatically when you pull the cord.*

pump up
to fill something such as a tire or ball with air, using a tool called a pump: *I need to pump up my front tire before we go for a bike ride.*
→ see **explode** for **blow up** meaning "to explode"

blunt /blʌnt/ *adjective*

- ► blunt
- ► dull

ANTONYMS → see **sharp**

blunt
a blunt knife or object is not sharp or pointed: *The knife was too blunt to cut the rope.* | *Mr. Rodriguez was hit with a blunt object, possibly a rock, and robbed.*
→ In the formal language used in a court of law, **blunt** is often used with the word "instrument" to describe a heavy weapon that was used to hurt someone by hitting him or her: *Her injuries were caused by a blunt instrument.*

dull
a dull knife or blade is not sharp: *If the blade on the lawn mower is getting dull, take it somewhere to be sharpened.*

blurred /blɚd/ *adjective*

- ► blurred
- ► fuzzy
- ► hazy

ANTONYMS → see **clear (3)**

blurred *also* **blurry**
not clear, so that you can see only the general shape of something and not the small details: *Without my glasses, anything more than a few feet away looks blurred.* | *I only have a few letters and a blurry photograph to remind me of my grandfather.*

fuzzy
a photograph or television picture that is fuzzy is not clear so that you cannot see the details or edges of things: *Some of the photos were so fuzzy that it was difficult to tell who was who.*

hazy
if something you see is hazy, you cannot see it clearly because there is smoke, mist, or dust in the air, or you are very far away: *The mountains were only a hazy outline in the distance.*

blurred

the **hazy** shapes of the buildings

blush /blʌʃ/ *verb*

- ► blush
- ► turn red
- ► flush

blush
if you blush, your face becomes red, especially because you are embarrassed or nervous: *He looked at her and smiled, and she blushed.* | *Logan blushed as he said that his ambition was to be a doctor.*

turn red
if you turn red, your face becomes red because you are embarrassed, angry, ashamed, or proud: *His face turned bright red and he banged his fist down on the table.*

flush
flush means the same as **turn red** but is more formal: *The little boy's face flushed with shame, and he started to cry.*
→ see **embarrassed**

board *verb* → see **get on**, Topic **Travel and Vacations**

boast *verb* → see **brag**

boat /boʊt/ *noun*

- ► boat
- ► ship
- ► ferry
- ► sailboat
- ► yacht
- ► barge
- ► raft
- ► rowboat
- ► canoe
- ► submarine

boat
a vehicle that people travel across water in: *They crossed the lake* ***by boat****.* | *There were a few small fishing boats in the bay.*

ship
a large boat that carries people and things on the ocean: *The ship sails regularly across the Atlantic.*

ferry
a boat that regularly carries people and cars across a narrow area of water: *You could take the ferry from Manhattan to Staten Island.*

sailboat
a small boat with one or more sails: *They raced their sailboats across the lake.*

yacht
a large boat with a sail, used for sailing, racing, or traveling for pleasure: *The millionaire bought a 100-foot yacht.*

barge
a large boat with a flat bottom, used for carrying goods on a canal or river: *The barges carry coal up and down the river.*

raft
a small flat boat that is usually made by tying pieces of wood together: *They built a raft and floated down the river.*
→ A **raft** can also be a small rubber boat: *They rode a raft down the Colorado River.*

rowboat
a small boat that you move through the water using oars (=long sticks with flat ends): *They sat fishing from a rowboat on the lake.*

canoe
a light narrow boat that you move through the water using a paddle (=short stick with a flat end): *We paddled canoes along the lake shore and camped on the beach.*

submarine
a ship that travels underwater: *Submarines can stay deep underwater for weeks at a time.*

body /ˈbɑdi/ *noun*

- ► body
- ► physique
- ► figure
- ► build

body
the physical structure of a person or animal, including the head, arms, stomach, etc., or the shape of this: *There are over 1,000 muscles in the human body.* | *He lifts weights and has a great body.*
→ You often use **body** to talk about the main part of a person or animal, not including the

head, arms, or legs: *The spider has red spots all over its body.*

physique
the shape and size of someone's body, especially a man's body. **Physique** is used to talk about how strong someone looks: *He had the lean but strong physique of a runner.*

figure
the shape and size of someone's body, especially a woman's body. You usually use **figure** when a woman has an attractive shape: *She exercises a lot and has a nice figure.*

build
the shape and size of someone's body. You use **build** to talk about the structure of someone's body and whether their bones seem big or small: *Ballet dancers usually have a very slight build* (=they are small and thin). | *Police described the man as six feet tall with a medium build.*

→ see **physical** for words meaning "relating to your body"

boil *verb* → see **cook[1]**

boiling *adjective* → see **hot**

bold *adjective* → see **brave**, **bright**, **confident**

bond *noun* → see **relationship**

book[1] /bʊk/ *noun*

- ► book
- ► hardcover
- ► paperback
- ► publication (*formal*)
- ► text

book
something that you read that has a lot of pages inside a cover: *He is reading a* ***book by*** *Mark Twain.* | *This book is about cats.*

hardcover *also* **hardback**
a book that has a hard stiff cover: *The book is published as a hardback first, and then comes out in paperback about a year later.*

paperback
a book that has a paper cover: *I read a paperback on the plane.*

publication (AWL) (*formal*)
a book, magazine, or newspaper: *He has written articles for several scientific publications.*

text (AWL)
a piece of writing that is printed. You use **text** when you are talking about a piece of writing that you are studying: *Students sometimes find texts written before 1900 to be more difficult to understand.*

→ see **magazine**, Topic **Books and Literature**

book[2] *verb* → see **save**

boom[1] *noun* → see **increase[2]**

boom[2] *verb* → see Topic **To Make a Sound**

border /ˈbɔrdɚ/ *noun*

- ► border
- ► boundary
- ► line
- ► frontier

border
the line between two states or countries: *The town is close to the* ***border between*** *the U.S. and Mexico.* | *You need a passport to cross the border.*

boundary
the line that separates two areas of land: *The Mississippi River forms a natural* ***boundary between*** *Iowa and Illinois.* | *The boundary between the fields is marked by a fence.*

line
the border between two states or counties: *He drove across the state line into Nevada.*

frontier
the place where two countries meet: *Both India and Pakistan have troops stationed near the* ***frontier between*** *the two countries.*

→ see **edge** for **border** meaning "a narrow area around the edge of something"

border

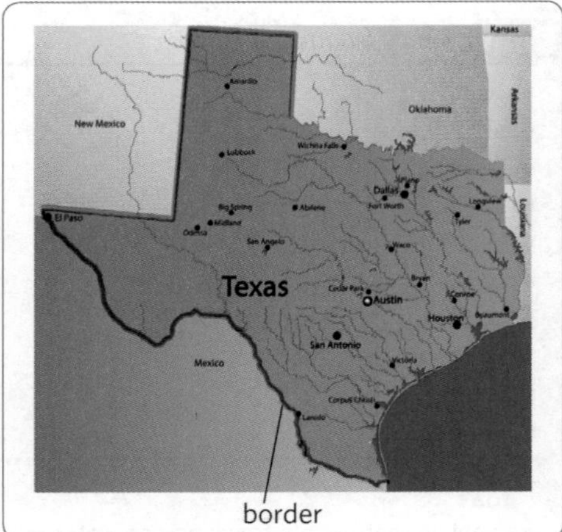

bore /bɔr/ verb

- bore
- find something boring
- be tired of

ANTONYMS → see **interest[1]**

bore
to make someone feel that something is not interesting so that he or she does not want to pay attention to it: *The movie will bore young children.* | *He is the kind of person who bores you with stories about his illnesses.*

find something boring
to not like something and not want to find out more about it: *I find golf really boring. I can't understand why anyone would watch it on TV.*

be tired of *also* **get tired of**
to be bored with doing something or with a subject, or to become bored: *They were tired of all their toys, and wanted something exciting to do.* | *Don't you get tired of eating the same thing for lunch every day?*

bored /bɔrd/ adjective

- bored
- tired of
- sick of

ANTONYMS → see **excited**, **interested**

bored
feeling that what you are doing is not interesting or exciting enough so that you do not want to pay attention to it: *I'm so bored! There's nothing to do.* | *The children were* ***bored by*** *the story and wanted one that was more exciting.* | *He got* ***bored with*** *the work and quit his job.*

tired of
feeling bored and annoyed with a situation that has continued for too long: *They were tired of eating the same thing for lunch every day.*

sick of
sick of means the same as **tired of** but is used more in spoken English: *I'm sick of telling you to clean up your room – go do it!*
→ see **uninterested**

SYNONYM CHECK

Bored or boring?

You use **bored** about a person who is not interested in something: *I was bored by the movie.*
You use **boring** about something that is not interesting: *The movie was boring.*

boring /ˈbɔrɪŋ/ adjective

- boring
- dull
- uninteresting
- tedious
- monotonous

ANTONYMS → see **interesting**, **exciting**

boring
not interesting, and making you feel impatient: *This book is so boring. I want an adventure story.* | *It was a boring party, so we left early.*

dull
boring because nothing different, interesting, or exciting happens: *The homework was dull, just circling the right answers on the paper.*

uninteresting
not making you feel interested in something. **Uninteresting** is slightly more formal than **boring**: *He gave a long uninteresting speech about economics.*

tedious
boring and continuing for a long time. **Tedious** is slightly more formal than **boring**: *Painting a house is a long tedious job.*

monotonous
boring and always the same. **Monotonous** is more formal than **boring**: *In prison, the days are monotonous and long.*

ADVERBS

You can make the adjectives **tedious** and **monotonous** into adverbs by using an **-ly** ending: *I tediously checked all the answers to the math homework.* | *Monotonously, he talked on and on without ever even looking at us.*

(be) born /bɔrn/ verb

- be born
- hatch

be born
to come out of your mother's body: *The baby was born three weeks early.* | *My grandmother was born in Nicaragua.*
→ **GRAMMAR:** Don't say: ~~*I borned in 1995*~~ or ~~*I born in 1995*~~. Say: *I was born in 1995.*

hatch
if a bird, fish, spider, etc. hatches, it comes out of an egg: *About 21 days after the hen lays the eggs, the chicks will hatch.*
→ see **to have a baby** at **baby** (**2**), **pregnant**

B

borrow /ˈbɑroʊ/ *verb*

- ► borrow
- ► take out a loan
- ► rent

ANTONYMS → see **lend**

borrow
to use something that belongs to someone else and that you must give back later: *Can I borrow your pen for a minute?* | *They* ***borrowed*** *money* ***from*** *the bank to buy a home.*

take out a loan
to borrow a large amount of money from a bank or company, which you pay back over a long period of time: *Many students need to take out loans to pay for college.*

rent
to pay money to use a car or piece of equipment for a short period of time: *We're going to rent a car at the airport.*

boss /bɔs/ *noun*

- ► boss
- ► manager
- ► head
- ► chief
- ► supervisor
- ► foreman
- ► employer

boss
someone who is in charge of a group of people at work and tells them what to do: *I asked my boss if I could have a day off next week.* | *There is a new guy at work who is always trying to impress the boss.*

manager
someone who is in charge of a store or part of an organization: *The service in the restaurant was terrible and I asked to speak to the manager.* | *He is a manager in the sales department, with ten employees under him.*

head
the person who is in charge of an organization or part of an organization: *She is the* ***head of*** *a small architecture company in St. Louis.* | *After teaching for many years, he became* ***head of*** *the English department.*

chief
the person who is in charge of an organization, especially the police or fire department, or some government jobs: *Scott has been the town's fire chief since 2005.* | *Rahm Emanuel was President Obama's chief of staff until 2010.*

supervisor
the person who is in charge of a group of workers, and who makes sure that they do the right things while they work: *Every year, I have a meeting with my supervisor to discuss my job performance.*

foreman
someone who is in charge of a group of factory workers or builders. A **foreman** makes sure that the workers do what the **manager** wants: *The foreman was showing a worker how to use one of the new machines.*

employer
a person, company, or organization that pays people to work for them: *She was a good employer and always treated me fairly.* | *The shoe factory is the largest employer in the area.*
→ see **chairman**, **leader**, Topic **Jobs and Work**

SYNONYM CHECK

Boss or manager?

Boss sounds more informal, and it is not an official job title. You use **boss** to talk about the person who tells you what to do at work. **Manager** is used in the names of people's jobs, and is often used with other words: *the sales manager* | *the store manager.*

both *adjective, pronoun* → see Function Words

bottom /ˈbɑtəm/ *noun*

1 the lowest part of something

- ► bottom
- ► base
- ► foot
- ► foundation

ANTONYMS → see **top**[1]

2 the ground under an ocean or river

- ► bottom
- ► floor
- ► bed

1 the lowest part of something

bottom
the lowest part or side of something: *We all ran down to the bottom of the hill.* | *The bottom of the box opened while I was carrying it and all the books fell out.* | *The page numbers are* ***at the bottom*** *of each page.*

base
the lowest part of something that is tall or thin, especially the part that supports it: *The lamp has a square base.* | *Place a small pillow at the* ***base of*** *your spine to support your back while you are driving.*

foot
the lowest part of something tall or high, such as a mountain, tree, or set of stairs: *She stood at **the foot of** the stairs and called the children down to dinner.*

foundation (AWL)
a solid base that is built below the ground to support the building that is on top of it: *The foundation of a building is usually constructed out of brick or concrete.*

2 the ground under an ocean or river

bottom
the ground under an ocean or river: *The bottom of the river is rocky. | The Titanic sank to **the bottom of** the ocean.*

floor
the wide area of ground at the bottom of the ocean: *It is very dark and cold **on the ocean floor**, but some fish do live there.*

bed
the flat ground at the bottom of a river, lake, or sea: *The water was clear, and we could see the rocks on the river bed.*

boulder *noun* → see **rock¹**

bounce *verb* → see **jump¹**, Topic **Computers and the Internet**

boundary *noun* → see **border**

bow *verb* → see **bend¹**

box¹ /bɑks/ *noun*

- box
- carton
- crate
- trunk
- case
- suitcase

box
a container shaped like a square or rectangle, usually made of thick stiff paper or wood: *The photos are in a box on the shelf. | The kids were playing in the big cardboard box that the computer came in.*

carton
a box made of stiff paper that is sometimes covered in wax or plastic. A **carton** usually contains liquids, eggs, or cigarettes: *A carton of orange juice was in the fridge.*

crate
a large wooden or plastic box used for carrying things, especially in a vehicle: *The tomatoes are shipped in wooden crates.*

trunk
a large box in which you store or carry things. A **trunk** is usually made of wood or metal: *I found some of my grandmother's dresses in an old trunk in the attic.*

case
a box or bag for storing something: *She took a pen out of her pencil case. | He took his violin out of its case.*

suitcase
a large box or bag with a handle, used for carrying clothes when you travel: *Have you packed your suitcase yet?*

box

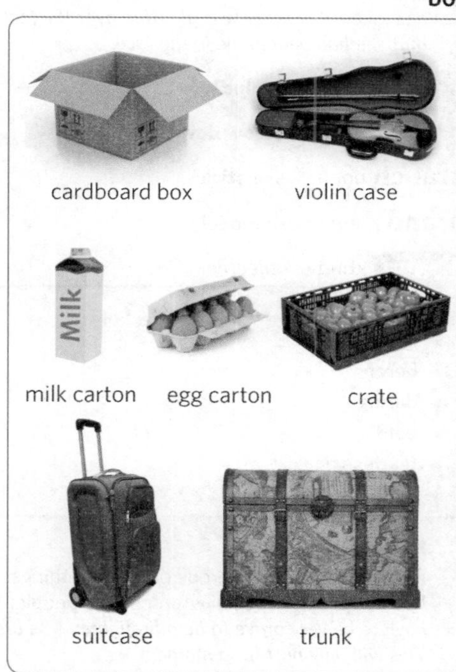

cardboard box, violin case, milk carton, egg carton, crate, suitcase, trunk

box² *verb* → see **fight¹**

boy *noun* → see **man**

boyfriend *noun* → see **friend**, Topic **Relationships and Marriage**

brag /bræg/ *verb*

- brag
- boast
- show off
- gloat

brag
to talk too much about good things you have done or things that you have, in a way that is

B

annoying and not polite: *I wish he would stop **bragging about** his perfect score on the test.*

boast
boast means the same as **brag** but is slightly more formal: *She is always **boasting about** how smart her children are.*

show off
to say or do things that you think will make people admire you. People use **show off** when this is annoying: *He is a good dancer, but he is always showing off.*

gloat
to behave in a way that shows you are happy that you have succeeded and that someone else has failed: *My sister was **gloating over** the fact that she had beaten me in the race.*

brain *noun* → see **mind**[1]

brake *verb* → see **slow down**

branch *noun* → see **stick**[2]

brand *noun* → see **model**

brave /breɪv/ *adjective*

- ► brave
- ► courageous
- ► heroic
- ► daring
- ► bold
- ► fearless
- ► valiant (*formal*)

brave
not afraid to do dangerous or difficult things. You use **brave** especially to describe people: *You have to be very brave to be a firefighter.* | *Be brave! This will only hurt for a moment.*

courageous
very brave, especially when you are fighting for something that you believe is right, or when you are fighting a disease. **Courageous** is more formal than **brave** and you can use it about people or actions: *Martin Luther King Jr. was a courageous leader who fought against injustice.*

heroic
a heroic action is very brave, and people admire the person who does it very much. You use **heroic** especially in situations when someone helps or saves another person even though there is a lot of danger: *His actions were truly heroic – he jumped into the water and rescued a drowning child.*

daring
willing to take a lot of risks or do difficult and dangerous things. You use **daring** especially with words like **escape**, **rescue**, and **attack**: *The soldiers made a daring raid on the enemy camp.*

bold
a bold action or plan shows that someone is willing to take risks and do something new and different: *With this new law the government has taken a bold step toward truly cutting harmful pollution.*
→ You can also use **bold** with the words **leader** or **leadership** to talk about someone in a powerful position who is not afraid to take risks to achieve things: *We need a leader who is bold enough to try new solutions.*

fearless
not afraid of anything or anyone, especially not afraid of physical danger: *Tyler was a fearless climber who would go to the very top branches of a tree.*

valiant (*formal*)
a valiant effort, struggle, or fight is usually not successful, even though it is brave: *The firefighters made a valiant effort to rescue the people in the burning building.*
→ see **courage**, Topic **Describing People's Character**

ADVERBS
You can make the adjectives that mean **brave** into adverbs by using an **-ly** ending: *He fought the fire bravely.* | *She climbed fearlessly to the very top of the tree.* | *Rosa Parks boldly and courageously refused to obey a law she thought was wrong.*

bravery *noun* → see **courage**

break[1] /breɪk/ *verb*

- ► break
- ► smash
- ► shatter
- ► crack
- ► split
- ► snap
- ► crumble
- ► burst
- ► pop
- ► fracture

ANTONYMS → see **fix**

break
if something breaks or you break it, it separates into pieces after being hit or dropped: *He dropped the glass and it broke.* | *I'm sorry, but I've broken one of your plates.* | *The first time she went skiing, she broke her leg.*

smash
to break into a lot of pieces after being hit with a lot of force or dropped: *The bowl smashed as it hit the floor.* | *All the mirrors in the room had been smashed.*
→ If you **smash** something, you break it deliberately: *He smashed a window to escape from the fire.*
If something **smashes**, it breaks accidentally, for example if you drop it: *The plate smashed when it hit the floor.*

shatter
if something such as a plate or glass shatters, it breaks into many small pieces, usually when something hits it: *The glass hit the floor and shattered.* | *The bomb blast shattered the windows of cars and buildings.*
→ If something **shatters**, it breaks accidentally, either because you drop it or because something hits it: *The window shattered when the ball hit it.* You do not usually say that a person **shatters** something.

crack
to break in a way that makes a line on the surface: *The window was cracked where a stone had hit it.* | *The ice cracked under our feet.*

split
to break into two pieces. You use **split** about something fairly large: *She picked up the ax and **split** the log **into** two pieces.* | *The melon split when it hit the floor.*

snap
to break into two pieces with a loud noise. You use **snap** about something long or thin: *One of the strings on his guitar snapped.*

crumble
if stone, brick, earth, paper, or a natural material such as a leaf crumbles, it gradually breaks into small pieces that are fairly round, especially because it is old or dry: *The old stone walls were crumbling.*
→ If you **crumble** food, you break it into small pieces that are fairly round: *Crumble the cheese onto the pasta.*

burst
if a tire, balloon, or pipe bursts, it gets a hole in it and air or liquid suddenly comes out of it: *One of the pipes in the basement burst and there was water everywhere.*

pop
if a bubble or balloon pops, it breaks with a short loud sound: *She stuck a pin in the balloon and it popped.*

fracture
to crack or break a bone in your body: *He fell and fractured his arm.*
→ see **broken**, **damage²**
→ see **break a rule/law** at **disobey**, **break off** at **pause¹**, **break up** at **divorce**

break

snap
split
smash
burst

break² /breɪk/ *noun*

- ► break
- ► crack
- ► chip
- ► fracture
- ► split

break
a place where something is broken. **Break** is used especially about bones: *The doctor said that the break would take two months to fully heal.*

crack
a thin line where something is slightly damaged: *I just noticed there is a **crack in** my guitar.*

chip
a place on a plate, cup, etc. where a small piece has broken off: *That cup has a **chip in** it – let me get you another one.*

fracture
a crack or break in a bone or rock: *X-rays revealed a small **fracture in** his right leg.*

split
a tear or crack in something made of cloth, plastic, or wood: *There was a **split in** the seam of*

his jeans and you could see his underwear.
→ see **broken**, **stop¹**, **take a break** at **rest²**

break a rule/law *verb phrase* → see **disobey**

breath /breθ/ *noun*

- ► breath
- ► sigh
- ► gasp

B

breath
the air that you let out and take in when you breathe: *It was so cold they could see their breath.* | *She took a deep breath and began explaining why she was angry.*

sigh
a loud breath that you take when you are disappointed or tired, or because you can begin to relax after worrying about something: *We all breathed a sigh of relief when he came home safely.*

gasp
a very loud sudden breath that you take when you are surprised or in pain: *Juanita jumped back with a gasp when the mouse ran right past her.*

breathe /brið/ *verb*

1 to breathe
- ► breathe
- ► take a breath
- ► inhale (*formal*)
- ► exhale (*formal*)

2 to breathe in a particular way
- ► be out of breath
- ► pant
- ► sigh
- ► snore
- ► gasp
- ► wheeze

1 to breathe

breathe
to take air into your body through your nose or mouth and let it out again: *I tried to relax and breathe more slowly.* | *It felt good to breathe the fresh air out in the countryside.*

take a breath
to breathe in once: *Alex took a deep breath and then jumped into the pool.*

inhale (*formal*)
to breathe in air, smoke, or gas: *Do not inhale the fumes from the paint, as it may make you feel dizzy.*

exhale (*formal*)
to breathe air or smoke out of your nose or mouth: *Hold your breath for five seconds, and then exhale slowly.*

2 to breathe in a particular way

be out of breath *also* **be short of breath**
to breathe with difficulty, for example because you have been exercising or because you are sick: *After swimming some laps in the pool, she was a little out of breath.* | *The lung disease means he always feels out of breath.*

pant
to breathe quickly with short breaths, especially because you have been exercising. Animals such as dogs often **pant**: *Matt was still panting several minutes after he stopped running.* | *The dog was panting in the heat.*

sigh
to breathe out loudly and slowly because you are disappointed or tired, or because you can begin to relax after worrying about something: *She sat down and sighed, closing her eyes for a moment.* | *I sighed with relief when he let me through the gate.*

snore
to breathe in a noisy way when you are sleeping: *My father was snoring so loudly that I could hear him from down the hall.*

gasp
to breathe in quickly and loudly, especially because you are surprised or in pain: *Trisha gasped with surprise when I told her that I had quit my job.* | *The runners bent over, gasping for air.*

wheeze
to breathe with difficulty, making a sound in your throat and chest because you are sick: *She is allergic to cats – they make her wheeze.*
→ see **choke** for words meaning "to prevent someone from breathing"

breeze *noun* → see **wind¹**, Topic **The Weather**

bride *noun* → see **wife**, Topic **Relationships and Marriage**

brief *adjective* → see **short**

briefly /ˈbrifli/ *adverb*

- ► briefly
- ► temporarily
- ► momentarily

briefly (AWL)
for a short time: *He worked briefly as a lawyer,*

but he did not enjoy the work. | *She looked at him briefly, but then went back to her work.*

temporarily
if something happens temporarily, it continues for only a short time, and will not be permanent: *The beach was temporarily closed because of the bad weather.*

momentarily
for a very short time. You usually use **momentarily** for something that only lasts a few seconds: *Kate looked momentarily surprised, but she laughed and quickly started speaking to the crowd again.*

bright /braɪt/ *adjective*

1 a bright light
- ► bright
- ► dazzling
- ► strong
- ► well-lit

2 a bright color
- ► bright
- ► brilliant
- ► vivid
- ► strong
- ► bold
- ► vibrant
- ► colorful

1 a bright light

bright
shining with a lot of light: *The sunshine was very bright.* | *We could see the bright lights of the city in the distance.*

dazzling
so bright that it hurts your eyes: *The snow was dazzling in the sunlight.*

strong
strong light is very bright: *Tomato plants need warmth and strong sunlight to grow properly.*

well-lit
bright because there are electric lights: *The desk was in a well-lit corner of the room.*
→ see **sunny**, Topic **The Weather**

2 a bright color

bright
a bright color is very easy to notice and does not have any white in it. Bright colors make you feel happy: *The fire engine is bright red.* | *Toys for babies are made in bright colors such as blue, red, and yellow.*

brilliant
very bright and easy to notice, and almost seeming to shine: *The sky was a brilliant blue.*

vivid
bright and easy to see in a way that looks good and lively: *The painting is dark, mainly blacks and blues, with one vivid splash of red paint.*

strong
bright and easy to see, and more noticeable than other colors: *Use a strong color such as red on a pillow to brighten your living room.*
→ **GRAMMAR:** Don't say: *~~a strong blue~~*. Say: *a strong blue color* or *a strong color*.

bold
very strong and noticeable: *The children used bold colors in their paintings.*

vibrant
bright and making something seem alive or exciting: *The flowers are vibrant shades of red and pink.*

colorful
having a lot of bright colors: *The dancers wore colorful clothes.*
→ see **smart** for **bright** meaning "intelligent"
→ see **light²**

ADVERBS

You can make the adjectives that mean **bright** into adverbs by using an **-ly** ending, except for **well-lit**: *The sun shone brightly in the sky.* | *The light was dazzlingly bright.* | *The walls were vividly painted in bright colors.*

brilliant *adjective* → see **bright**, **smart**

bring /brɪŋ/ *verb*

- ► bring
- ► take
- ► carry
- ► deliver
- ► transport (*formal*)

bring
to move someone or something with you to a place or person: *Can you bring me a pen?* | *Don't forget to bring your bike if you want to go riding with us.* | *I didn't expect Curtis to* **bring** *so many friends* **to** *the party.*

take
to move someone or something from one place to another: *I'm going to* **take** *my lunch* **to** *school tomorrow.* | *Would you mind taking Olivia home? We are not ready to leave yet.* | *I took Spencer one of the cookies.*

carry
to have something in your hands, arms or in your clothes as you go somewhere: *Ann carried the baby upstairs.* | *Could you help me **carry** these suitcases **to** the car?*
→ You can also say that a vehicle, pipe, or wire **carries** people or things when it takes them from one place to another: *The new plane can carry up to 600 passengers.* | *These wires carry electricity to the house.*

deliver
to take things such as letters, packages, and goods to a place or person: *Unfortunately, the package was **delivered to** the wrong address.*

transport (AWL) *(formal)*
to move things or people from one place to another in a vehicle: *The plane is used to transport military equipment.*
→ see **bring about** at **cause**[2]
→ see **bring down** at **reduce**
→ see **bring in** at **attract**
→ see **bring together** at **collect**

SYNONYM CHECK
Bring or take?
You use **bring** when you are moving things with you toward a place: *Don't forget to bring your umbrella* (=you should bring your umbrella with you when you come to where I am).
You use **take** when you are moving things away from a place: *Don't forget to take your umbrella* (=you should take your umbrella with you when you leave).

bring up /ˌbrɪŋ ˈʌp/ *phrasal verb*

- bring up
- raise
- nurture

bring up
to take care of a child until he or she is an adult: *I was born and brought up in Montana.* | *We **bring** our kids **up to** respect other people.*

raise
raise means the same as **bring up** but sounds a little more formal: *She was raised by her grandparents after her parents died.* | *I would like to get married and raise a family one day.*

nurture
to bring up a child and give him or her a lot of love and attention to help him or her develop well: *Parents nurture and guide their children so that the children know how to be loving parents when they grow up.*
→ see **mention** for **bring up** meaning "to mention something for the first time"

broad *adjective* → see **general**, **wide**, Topic **Describing Size**

broadband *noun* → see Topic **Computers and the Internet**

broadcast /ˈbrɔdˌkæst/ *verb*

- broadcast
- air
- televise
- transmit

broadcast
to send out a radio or television program so that it is received by radios and televisions in a particular area: *The show is going to be **broadcast on** several cable stations.* | *The awards show will be broadcast live in 17 countries.*

air
air means the same as **broadcast**: *He made the comment during an interview **aired on** the evening news.*

televise
to show a program on television: *The election debates will be televised nationally.*

transmit (AWL)
to send out signals containing information from one place to another. These signals may be radio or television signals, or they may carry other information: *The station began transmitting digital television signals back in 1998.* | *The Internet allows computers to transmit data at very high speeds.*
→ see Topic **Entertainment**

broken /ˈbroʊkən/ *adjective*

1 damaged or in pieces
- broken
- cracked
- chipped
- fractured *(formal)*
- torn

2 not working
- broken
- out of order
- faulty
- down

broken

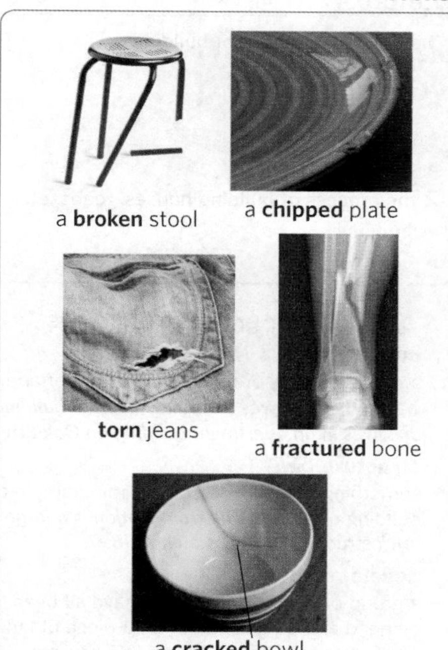
a **broken** stool
a **chipped** plate
torn jeans
a **fractured** bone
a **cracked** bowl

1 damaged or in pieces

broken
damaged or in pieces because of being hit, dropped, etc.: *After the car accident, there was broken glass everywhere.* | *Some of the chairs were broken and couldn't be used.* | *Her broken arm was in a sling.*

cracked
something cracked is damaged and has a thin line on its surface, where it could later break completely: *Throw that bowl away. It is cracked.* | *The car was dirty and had a cracked windshield.*

chipped
a cup, plate, etc. that is chipped has a small piece broken off the edge of it: *She gave me a cup of coffee in a chipped mug.*

fractured (*formal*)
a fractured bone is cracked or broken: *The X-ray showed that she had several fractured ribs.*

torn
torn paper, clothes, etc. have been damaged and have holes in them: *His jeans were torn at the knees.*
→ see **in bad condition**

2 not working

broken
not working correctly or not working at all: *The DVD player is broken, so we can't watch a movie.*

out of order
if a machine in a public place is out of order, it is not working: *One of the ticket machines was out of order.*

faulty
not working correctly or not made correctly: *The fire started because of faulty electrical wires.*

down
if a computer system is down, it is not working: *The computer system was down all afternoon, so we didn't get any work done.*

brother /ˈbrʌðɚ/ *noun*

- ► **brother**
- ► **sibling** (*formal*)

ANTONYMS → see **sister**

brother
a boy or man who has the same parents as you: *I have two younger brothers and an older sister.* | *My little brother is only ten.*

sibling (*formal*)
a brother or sister: *Older children sometimes take care of their younger siblings.*

browse *verb* → see **read**, Topic **Computers and the Internet**

bruise[1] *noun* → see **injury**, **mark**[1]

bruise[2] *verb* → see **hurt**

brush *verb* → see **sweep**, **touch**

brutal *adjective* → see **cruel**, **violent**

buffet *noun* → see **meal**, Topic **Eating in a Restaurant**

bug *noun* → see **insect**, Topic **Computers and the Internet**

build[1] /bɪld/ *verb*

- ► **build**
- ► **construct**
- ► **put up**
- ► **assemble**
- ► **erect** (*formal*)
- ► **pitch**

build
to make a building, bridge, or another structure: *Most of the houses in this neighborhood were built in the 1950s.* | *We want to build a fence around the backyard.*

construct (AWL)
to build something large such as a building, bridge, or road. **Construct** is more formal than **build**: *There are plans to construct a new bridge across the river.*

put up
to build something such as a building, wall, or fence. **Put up** sounds less formal than **build**: *They're planning to tear down these apartments and put up an office building.*

assemble (AWL)
to put the different parts of something together, such as a machine or piece of furniture: *The bookcase is easy to assemble.*

erect *(formal)*
to build a large important building or structure: *The first lighthouse was erected on the island in 1912.*

pitch
if you pitch a tent, you put it up so that it is ready to sleep in: *Make sure you pitch your tent somewhere flat and without too many rocks underneath it.*

build

build a wall

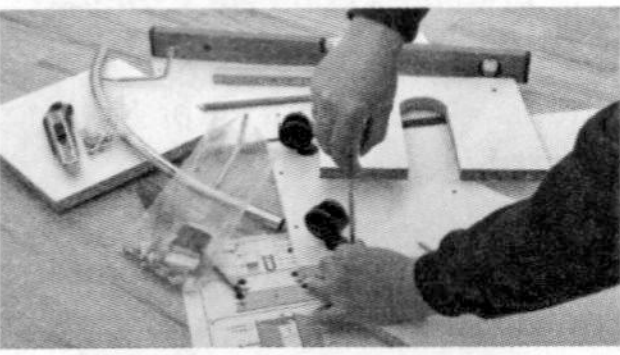

assemble furniture

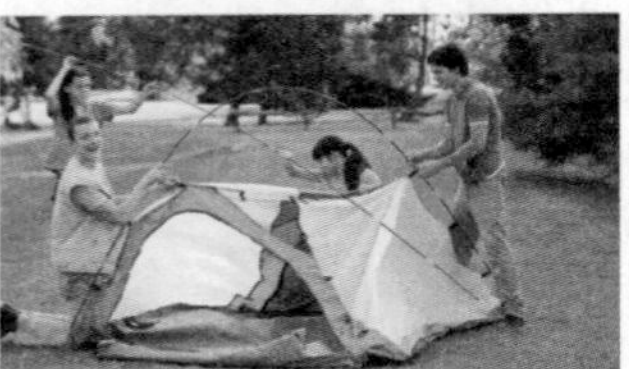

pitch a tent

build² *noun* → see **body**, Topic **Describing People's Looks**

building /ˈbɪldɪŋ/ *noun*

1 a building or group of buildings
► building
► structure
► development
► property

2 the process of building houses, roads, etc.
► building
► construction

1 a building or group of buildings

building
a house, school, or anything with a roof and walls: *The park was surrounded by tall buildings.* | *She lives in an apartment building on Oak Street.*

structure (AWL)
something that has been built, for example a building or bridge: *The train station is a large brick structure that was built in 1897.*

development
a group of new buildings that have all been planned and built together on a piece of land: *The farmland has been turned into housing developments and shopping malls.*

property
a building and the surrounding land. Use **property** to talk about buying or selling buildings or land: *A real estate agent showed us several properties that were for sale.*
→ see **castle**, **church**, **factory**, **hotel**, **house**

2 the process of building houses, roads, etc.

building
the process of building something, for example a house or school: *The **building of** the new factory took five years.*

construction (AWL)
the process of building large buildings, bridges, roads, etc.: *A new hotel is **under construction**.* | ***Construction of** the bridge will begin in April.*

bulb *noun* → see **light¹**

bull *noun* → see **cow**

bully /ˈbʊli/ *verb*

► bully
► harass
► torment

bully
to frighten or hurt someone who is smaller or weaker than you, especially many times over a long period: *The other girls bullied me. They made*

fun of me and sometimes even pushed me. | *Ben let his father* ***bully*** *him* ***into*** *studying law, which he disliked.*

harass
to keep doing things to someone that make him or her feel upset or threatened: *She quit her job, saying that her boss sexually harassed her by making comments and touching her.*

torment
to deliberately treat someone cruelly by annoying or hurting him or her: *He torments his younger brother by teasing and scaring him all the time.*

→ see **pick on**, **scare**

bullying /ˈbʊli-ɪŋ/ *noun*

- ► bullying
- ► harassment
- ► intimidation

bullying
the act of frightening or hurting someone who is smaller or weaker than you, especially many times over a long period: *The school has been praised for its effort to stop bullying.* | *Bullying can range from people saying mean things to hurting other people physically.*

harassment
behavior in which someone deliberately annoys or threatens someone else many times: *Many of the young black men we talked to complained about police harassment.*

intimidation
actions or behavior that threaten and frighten someone, in order to make him or her do something: *The people of my country lived with constant intimidation and violence from the government.*

bump[1] *verb* → see **hit**[1], **bump into** at **meet**

bump[2] *noun* → see **injury**, **lump**

bumpy *adjective* → see **rough**, Topic **Describing Texture**

bunch *noun* → see **group**

bundle *noun* → see **group**, **roll**[2]

burglar *noun* → see **thief**

burglarize *verb* → see **steal**

burglary *noun* → see **theft**

burn /bɚn/ *verb*

1 to produce flames and heat
- ► burn
- ► be on fire
- ► be in flames
- ► blaze
- ► flare
- ► smolder

2 to burn yourself
- ► burn
- ► scald

3 to make something burn
- ► burn
- ► burn down
- ► set fire to something
- ► light
- ► ignite (*formal*)
- ► scorch
- ► incinerate
- ► cremate

ANTONYMS → see **put out**

1 to produce flames and heat

burn
to produce flames and heat: *The fire was still burning.* | *A pile of branches was burning in the yard.*

be on fire
if a building, car, piece of clothing, etc. is on fire, it is burning and being damaged: *The house across the street was on fire, so I called 911.*

be in flames
if a building is in flames, it is burning with a lot of flames: *When the fire trucks arrived, the whole building was in flames.*

blaze
to burn very brightly with a lot of flames and heat. **Blaze** is used especially in writing: *A big log fire was blazing in the fireplace.*

flare *also* **flare up**
to suddenly begin to burn, or to burn more brightly for a short time: *He lit a match, which flared briefly.*

smolder
to burn slowly with smoke but no flames: *The fire in the factory was so intense that it was still smoldering a week later.*

2 to burn yourself

burn
to hurt your body with fire or something hot:

Don't touch the iron. You'll burn yourself. | *I* ***burned*** *my hand* ***on*** *a hot pan.*

scald
to burn yourself with hot liquid or steam: *The coffee was so hot it almost scalded his tongue.*

3 to make something burn

burn
to destroy or damage something with fire: *She lit a fire and burned his letters one by one.*

burn down
to completely destroy a building by burning it: *Rioters burned down several stores.* | *The theater burned down in 2009.*

set fire to something *also* **set something on fire**
to make something start burning so that it gets damaged: *One of the candles set fire to the curtains.* | *The criminals had overturned police cars and then set them on fire.*

light
to make something start to burn: *She lit a cigarette.*

ignite (*formal*)
to make something start to burn, especially something that burns easily such as a gas or chemical: *A spark ignited the gas and caused the explosion.*

scorch
to burn the surface of something and make a dark mark on it: *The iron was too hot and scorched the shirt.*

incinerate
to completely destroy something using fire: *Some of the garbage is incinerated after it has been collected.*

cremate
to burn the body of a dead person after a funeral ceremony: *He was cremated and his ashes were given to his family.*

→ see **fire**[1], **heat**[2]

burst *verb* → see **break**[1]

business /ˈbɪznɪs/ *noun*

- ► business
- ► trade
- ► industry
- ► commerce
- ► e-commerce

business
the work of buying and selling goods or providing services: *The hotel does a lot of business in the summer.* | *The company has been* ***in business*** *for over 30 years.* | *The ability to download music from the Internet is changing the music business.*

trade
the activity of buying and selling large quantities of goods, especially between one country and another: *There has been an increase in* ***trade between*** *the United States and South America.*

industry
all the companies that make a type of thing or provide a type of service: *In Detroit, many people still work in the the automobile industry.*

commerce
the activity of buying and selling goods and services. **Commerce** is used to talk about these activities in general: *When the economy is strong, there is usually a lot of growth in commerce.*

e-commerce
the practice of buying and selling things using the Internet: *E-commerce allows us to buy things without leaving our homes.*

→ see **company** for **business** meaning "a company"

businessman /ˈbɪznɪsˌmæn/ *noun*

- ► businessman
- ► executive
- ► entrepreneur (*formal*)

businessman *also* **businesswoman**
a man or woman who works in business: *Rodriguez is a successful businessman who owns several coffee shops.* | *Many businesswomen find good ways to balance work and family life.*

executive
a businessman or businesswoman in a company who helps make important decisions: *The newspaper's top executives are meeting to discuss the paper's future.*

entrepreneur (*formal*)
someone who makes money by starting a new business: *She is a successful entrepreneur who started a cosmetics company.*

busy /ˈbɪzi/ *adjective*

1 a busy person
- ► busy
- ► occupied (*formal*)

2 a busy time
- ► busy
- ► hectic
- ► eventful

3 a busy place
- ► busy
- ► bustling
- ► lively

1 a busy person

busy
if you are busy, you have a lot of things to do: *I'm busy right now – can we talk tomorrow? | She was busy working in the yard all afternoon. | He is a very busy person.*

occupied (*formal*)
busy doing something: *She is currently* ***occupied with*** *planning her wedding. | Some paper and crayons will keep him occupied.*

2 a busy time

busy
a busy time is one in which you have a lot of things to do: *Get a good sleep because tomorrow is going to be a busy day.*

hectic
very busy, with a lot of different things happening, and making you feel hurried: *It was really hectic at work today.*

eventful
full of interesting or important events: *It was an eventful weekend – we moved into our new apartment and had a party.*

3 a busy place

busy
if a place is busy, there are a lot of people there: *The supermarket is really busy on the weekends.*

bustling
a bustling place is very busy because a lot of people are there: *The souvenir stands were* ***bustling with*** *tourists.*

lively
full of activity or excitement, with a lot of different things happening: *Make sure you visit the lively outdoor market, which sells everything from jewelry to fresh fruit.*
→ see Topic **Describing Places**

but *conjunction* → see Function Words

button *verb* → see **fasten**

buy /baɪ/ *verb*

- **buy**
- **purchase** (*formal*)
- **get** (*informal*)
- **acquire** (*formal*)
- **go shopping**
- **stock up**

ANTONYMS → see **sell**

buy
to get something by paying money for it: *My dad says he wants to buy me a present. | I* ***bought*** *the books* ***from*** *the college bookstore.*

purchase (AWL) (*formal*)
purchase means the same as **buy**: *The company purchases all its office furniture online. | Tickets can be* ***purchased from*** *the box office.*

get (*informal*)
to buy something, be given it, or begin to have it: *I got a new dress when we went shopping. | What did you get for your birthday?*

acquire (AWL) (*formal*)
acquire means the same as **get**. You often use **acquire** when you do not know how someone gets something: *He* ***acquired*** *the painting* ***from*** *an art dealer.*

go shopping *also* **shop**
to go to stores to buy things, especially clothing: *If it's raining tomorrow, we could go shopping. | She and her mother were* ***shopping for*** *shoes.*

stock up
to buy a lot of something, especially food so that you can use it later: *We* ***stocked up on*** *snacks for the party.*

buzz *verb* → see **fly**, Topic **To Make a Sound**

by hand /baɪ 'hænd/ *adverb*

- **by hand**
- **manually**

by hand
using your hands instead of a machine: *Wash the sweater by hand, not in the washing machine.*

manually
manually means the same as **by hand**. **Manually** is often used when you do something that is usually done automatically by a machine or computer: *They did not have voting machines, so the votes were counted manually.*

Cc

café *noun* → see **restaurant**, Topic **Eating in a Restaurant**

C

cage /keɪdʒ/ *noun*

► cage
► coop
► pen
► corral
► enclosure
► pound

cage
a container made of wires or bars, used for keeping birds or animals in: *The cat was staring at the bird in the cage.* | *The cage for his pet hamster has a wheel that the hamster can run on.*

coop *also* **chicken coop**
an enclosed area for keeping chickens in: *We wanted to raise chickens in the backyard, so we built a coop.*

pen
an area with a fence around it for keeping farm animals in: *The pigs were in a large pen.*

corral
an area with a fence around it for keeping horses or cows in for a short time: *There was one horse in the corral.*

enclosure
a fairly large area that is surrounded by a fence to keep animals from getting out, especially at a zoo: *At the zoo, the lions are kept in a huge enclosure with rocks and trees.*

pound
a building where a city keeps lost pets and other animals without homes: *The animal control officer will catch the dogs and bring them to the pound.*

calculate *verb* → see **count**

calculation *noun* → see **measurement**

call /kɔl/ *verb*

1 to use a telephone to talk to someone
► call
► give someone a call
► phone
► telephone (*formal*)

2 to ask someone to come to you
► call
► invite
► summon
► send for

1 to use a telephone to talk to someone

call
to use the telephone to talk to someone: *Call your mom and ask her if you can go.* | *Don't forget to call when you get there.*
→ **GRAMMAR:** Don't say: ~~*call to someone*~~. Say: *call someone*.

give someone a call
give someone a call means the same as **call**: *If you want to ask her out, give her a call.*

phone
phone means the same as **call** but sounds more formal and old-fashioned: *She phoned to say that she would be late to work.*

telephone (*formal*)
telephone means the same as **call** but sounds very formal and old-fashioned: *The president telephoned the new prime minister to congratulate him.*

2 to ask someone to come to you

call
to ask or order someone to come to you: *The teacher called his students to come inside.* | *She* ***called for*** *an ambulance.*

invite
to ask someone politely to come to a place: *Mr. Beckman* ***invited*** *me* ***into*** *his office.* | *Are you* ***invited to*** *Ryan's birthday party?*

summon
to officially order someone to come to a place: *The judge summoned the lawyers to her office.*

send for
to tell someone to come to you by sending a message or sending someone else to get him or her: *The principal sent for the two boys who had started the fight.*
→ see **name²** for **call** meaning "to give someone or something a name"
→ see **shout¹**

calm[1] /kɑm/ *adjective*

1 a person who is calm
- ► calm
- ► relaxed
- ► mellow
- ► laid-back (*informal*)
- ► serene
- ► placid

ANTONYMS → see **excited**

2 calm weather, water, or a calm place
- ► calm
- ► serene
- ► placid

1 a person who is calm

calm
not angry, upset, or excited, even in a difficult situation: *I was scared, but I stayed calm.* | *Maria looked calm as she went up onto the stage.*

relaxed
feeling calm, not worried, and comfortable: *Sam looked really relaxed as he ran the second half of the 400 meter race.*

mellow
calm and not easily upset by things that annoy many people: *Most people become more mellow as they get older.*

laid-back (*informal*)
laid-back means the same as **mellow** but sounds more informal: *The coach is very laid-back – he never yells at the players.*

serene
calm, beautiful, and very peaceful: *She plays the piano with serene confidence.*

placid
a placid person seems very calm and does not easily get angry, excited, or nervous: *My father was a big placid man who never once yelled at me.*
→ see **patient[1]**, Topic **Describing People's Character**

2 calm weather, water, or a calm place

calm
weather that is calm is not windy, and an ocean or lake that is calm does not have waves caused by the wind: *It was stormy during the night, but the next day the weather was calmer.* | *The lake was calm and as smooth as glass.*

serene
an area of land or water that is serene looks calm, beautiful, and very peaceful: *The house looks out onto the serene beauty of the empty beach.*

placid
water that is placid has no waves: *The next morning the lake was placid, with mist rising from it into the gray sky.*
→ see **peaceful**, **quiet[1]**, **still**

ADVERBS

You can make the adjectives **calm**, **serene**, and **placid** into adverbs by adding **-ly**: *Maria walked calmly onto the stage.* | *The baby sat placidly on the floor and watched his mother.* The adverbs are used more often when a person is doing something **calmly**, but you can use them for calm weather or a calm place as well: *The sky was serenely blue and cloudless.*

C

calm[2] *noun* → see **peace**

calm down /ˌkɑm ˈdaʊn/ *phrasal verb*

- ► calm down
- ► cool off (*informal*)
- ► soothe
- ► settle down

calm down
to stop being angry or upset: *Please calm down. We can't solve the problem by yelling at each other.* | *She was really upset, and it took me a while to calm her down.*

cool off (*informal*)
to take time to make yourself less angry: *The teacher let the boys cool off, and then asked them to tell her what happened.*

soothe
to make someone feel less worried or upset: *She hugged the crying girl and tried to soothe her.*

settle down
to become quieter and less active. **Settle down** is used especially about groups of people: *All right, class. Settle down and start your math.*
→ see **comfort[2]**

camp *verb* → see **go camping** at **Travel and Vacations**

campaign[1] /kæmˈpeɪn/ *noun*

- ► campaign
- ► fight
- ► battle
- ► struggle
- ► movement
- ► drive

campaign
a carefully organized series of things that

someone does, in order to persuade people to do something: *The city government is starting an anti-drug campaign in the schools.*

→ **Campaign** is also used to talk about the time before an election when a politician tries to persuade people to vote for him or her: *She stopped in Des Moines several times during the presidential campaign.*

fight
the process of trying hard to achieve or change something: *The **fight for** women's right to vote began in the 1800s.*

battle
battle means the same as **fight** but is used especially in news reports: *More and more people are joining the **battle against** the poor treatment of farm animals.*

struggle
a long hard process in which people try to achieve or change something: *The **struggle for** democracy is not over, but the country will finally hold free elections.*

movement
a situation in which a large number of people work together to achieve or change something: *The local-food movement encourages people to buy food from farmers near them.*

drive
a carefully planned attempt to achieve a goal, especially one that a government or company does: *The company's **drive to** reduce waste has saved them a lot of money.*

campaign² /kæmˈpeɪn/ *verb*

- ► campaign
- ► work for/toward
- ► fight
- ► battle
- ► struggle
- ► lobby

campaign
to try to persuade politicians or other people in powerful positions to do or change something: *Human rights groups are **campaigning for** a change in the law.*

→ **Campaign** also means to make speeches and go to events in order to persuade people to vote for you in the time before an election: *The two leading candidates were campaigning today in California.*

work for/toward
to work in order to make something happen in society: *This is a great day for all of us who have been working so hard for peace in our country.* | *We are working toward raising $500,000 from our supporters.*

fight
to work very hard to persuade someone in government or in a powerful position to do something: *The group **fights for** the rights of women.*

battle
battle means the same as **fight** but is used especially in news reports: *The governor **battled with** state lawmakers for months over the budget.*

struggle
to try very hard to change something in politics, society, or the environment, when this is very difficult: *People who live on the island are **struggling to** protect the birds and fish from pollution.*

lobby
to try to persuade people who make laws to do something: *Insurance companies are **lobbying** Congress **to** change the law.*

can /kən, strong kæn/ *verb*

- ► can
- ► be able to
- ► have the ability to
- ► be capable of

ANTONYMS → see **cannot**

can
to be able to do something: *He can speak a little English and he knows words like "please" and "thank you."* | *Can everyone hear me, or do you want me to speak louder?*

→ **GRAMMAR:** Use **could** or **was/were able to** when talking about ability in the past: *She could ride a bike when she was three.* | *He was able to reach the top shelf.*

Use **will be able to** when talking about ability in the future: *When I get a job, I will be able to buy a car.*

be able to
be able to means the same as **can**. You use **be able to** especially when something is difficult or needs a lot of effort: *He is able to walk using a stick.* | *She was able to beat him in the first game, but she lost the second one.*

have the ability to
to be able to do something, especially something that most people cannot do: *Kirsten has the ability to make people feel relaxed and comfortable.*

be capable of
to have the skills, qualities, or equipment that you need to do something. You use **be capable**

of about people and machines: *He is an adult now and he should be capable of making his own decisions.* | *The plane is capable of flying at over 2,000 miles an hour.*
→ see **ability**, **possible (1)**

cancel /ˈkænsəl/ *verb*

- ► cancel
- ► call off
- ► abandon
- ► repeal

cancel
to stop an activity or event from happening before it starts: *We had to cancel the barbecue because of the rain.*

call off
call off means the same as **cancel** but sounds more informal: *My cousin called off her wedding because she had a big fight with her boyfriend.*

abandon (AWL)
to completely stop doing a project or activity that you have started, especially because there are problems that cannot be solved: *Government officials have abandoned the talks because they say there is no agreement possible.*

repeal
to officially end a law, by voting on it: *Congress is debating whether to repeal the health care law.*
→ see **stop**[1]

cannot /ˈkænɑt/ *verb*

- ► cannot
- ► can't
- ► be unable to do something
- ► be incapable of

ANTONYMS → see **can**

cannot
to not be able to do something: *I cannot remember the last time we met.* | *Louise cannot see anything without her glasses.*

can't
the short form of **cannot**: *I can't find my front door key.*

be unable to do something
to not be able to do something. You often use **be unable** when you cannot do something important that you want to do or need to do: *He lay awake all night, unable to sleep.* | *The surgery left her unable to walk for nearly three months.*

be incapable of
to not have the physical or mental ability to do something. You often use **be incapable of** when you are criticizing someone: *Matt seems to be incapable of keeping a job.*

can't *verb* → see **cannot**

cap *noun* → see **cover**[2]

capable *adjective* → see **able**, **be capable** at **can**

capacity *noun* → see **ability**, **size**, **space**

capital *noun* → see **money**, **town**

capture *verb* → see **catch**

care[1] /ker/ *verb*

1 to think something is important
- ► care
- ► mind

2 to think something is not important
- ► not care
- ► not mind
- ► indifferent
- ► unconcerned
- ► apathetic

3 to make sure that a person or animal is safe and has the things he or she needs
- ► care for
- ► take care of
- ► look after
- ► babysit

1 to think something is important

care
if you care about something, it is important to you. **Care** is usually used in phrases such as "I don't care" or "who cares?" to show that something is not important to you: *I don't care if we stay home or go out to eat.* | *It's not perfect, but who cares? It only cost $5.* | *I say I don't care when he teases me, but really I care a lot. It hurts my feelings.*

mind
to feel annoyed if someone does something. You say "would you mind..." when asking someone if you can do something, and "I don't mind" when allowing someone to do something: *Would you mind if I used your car tonight?* | *"Did it bother you that she got your name wrong?" "No, I didn't really mind."* | *Nobody minded that he was late.*

2 to think something is not important

not care
if you do not care about something, it is not important to you: *"You're making him angry." "I don't care!"* | *I like George, and I don't care what anyone else thinks about him.*

not mind
to not care because you will be happy with whatever happens: *Bill was just happy to be with her, and he didn't mind where they went.*

indifferent
not at all interested in something and not caring about what is happening, especially not caring about other people's problems or feelings: *He seemed **indifferent to** her problems and did nothing to help her.*

unconcerned
not worried or not caring about something, especially something important that you probably should be worried about. You use **unconcerned** especially in writing: *Many large companies seem completely **unconcerned about** the environment.*

apathetic
not caring about something and not willing to make any effort to change or improve things: *Many people have now become totally **apathetic about** politics.*

GRAMMAR CHECK: care

Not care and **not mind** are used in the verb phrases "do not care" and "do not mind." The other words in this entry are adjectives.

3 to make sure that a person or animal is safe and has the things he or she needs

care for
to make sure that someone who is old or sick has the things he or she needs. **Care for** sounds a little more formal than **take care of** or **look after**: *Louise has spent the last three years caring for her sick father.*

take care of
to make sure a person or animal is safe and has the things he or she needs: *Taking care of three small children all day is hard work.* | *When the old woman got sick, there was no one to take care of her.* | *You can have a dog if you are willing to take care of it.*
→ You can also **take care of** plants or objects by doing things to make sure they stay in good condition: *Who is taking care of the house while you're away?*

look after
to take care of a person or animal for a short time, especially a child: *Can you look after the kids for me this afternoon?* | *I usually look after my little brother after school before Mom gets home.*

babysit
to take care of a child while his or her parents are not at home, especially when you are paid to do this: *Amanda **babysits for** the neighbors to earn extra money.*
→ see **care about** at **love**[1]

care[2] /ker/ *noun*

- care
- caution
- diligence (*formal*)
- vigilance (*formal*)

care
careful attention so that you do not make a mistake or damage something: *David cleaned each musical instrument **with** great **care**.*

caution
if you do something with caution, you are careful because it could be dangerous or risky: *These chemicals are dangerous and need to be handled **with caution**.*

diligence (*formal*)
careful hard work that you do for every part of something: *The police officers investigated the case with diligence and attention to detail.*

vigilance (*formal*)
careful attention so that you are ready to stop something bad from happening: *Vigilance is important if we want to prevent another attack.*
→ see **worry**[2] for **care** meaning "something you are worried about"
→ see **take care of**

career *noun* → see **job**, Topic **Jobs and Work**

careful /ˈkerfəl/ *adjective*

- careful
- cautious
- thorough
- systematic
- meticulous
- conscientious
- painstaking

ANTONYMS → see **careless**

careful
trying to avoid mistakes, problems, or risks: *You need to be more careful with your spelling.* | *My sister is a very careful driver and she has never had an accident.*

cautious
careful to avoid danger or risks, because you are worried about what will happen: *I'm always cautious when I cross a busy street.* | *She was **cautious about** lending him money, because she wasn't sure that he could pay her back.*

thorough
careful to check everything, so that you do not miss anything important: *The mechanic gave the car a thorough examination and said that there was nothing wrong with it.*

systematic
using an organized and thorough plan in a careful way in order to do everything that you should. You can use **systematic** about the method you use or about the person who uses it: *We need a systematic way to grade students' work, so that we treat everyone the same.* | *Nurses who work in an operating room need to be very systematic about organizing the instruments.*

meticulous
very careful about every small detail in order to make sure everything is done correctly: *The teacher keeps meticulous records of the students' progress.*

conscientious
careful to do everything that you have been asked to do: *She's a conscientious student who always turns in her assignments on time.*

painstaking
very careful and using a lot of time and effort to do something: *The book is the result of ten years of painstaking research.*

→ see **organized**, **tactful**

> **ADVERBS**
>
> You can make the adjectives that mean **careful** into adverbs by using an **-ly** ending: *My sister drives carefully.* | *The mechanic examined the car thoroughly.* | *She is one of the students who conscientiously turns in her homework on time.*

careless /ˈkerləs/ *adjective*

- ► careless
- ► reckless
- ► irresponsible
- ► rash
- ► negligent
- ► clumsy

ANTONYMS → see **careful**

careless
not paying enough attention to what you are doing so that you make mistakes, damage things, or cause problems: *Her work is full of careless mistakes.* | *The company was **careless about** security before the computers were stolen.*

reckless
behaving in a dangerous way and not thinking about your safety or the safety of other people: *The police arrested him for reckless driving after he drove through several red lights at 60 miles per hour.*

irresponsible
careless because you do not think about the bad or dangerous effects that your actions may have on other people: *It was irresponsible of her to leave small children at home alone.*

rash
if you do something rash, you do not think carefully about the effect your action will have, and you wish later you had not done it. **Rash** is used more often to describe actions than to describe people: *Don't make any rash promises that you may regret later.*

negligent
careless because you do not do your job correctly. **Negligent** is used in legal language: *The court decided that the doctor was negligent because he used the wrong medicine.*

clumsy
often falling or dropping things, because you move in a careless way: *They have a large clumsy dog that is always knocking things off tables with his tail.*

> **ADVERBS**
>
> You can make the adjectives that mean **careless** into adverbs by using an **-ly** ending: *He threw his coat carelessly onto the couch instead of hanging it up.* | *Luke was arrested for driving recklessly.* | *She ran clumsily up the street, almost tripping over her own feet.*

cargo *noun* → see **load**

caring *adjective* → see **kind²**, **loving**, **sympathetic**

carnival *noun* → see **fair²**

carry /ˈkæri/ *verb*

- ► carry
- ► transport
- ► haul
- ► lug (*informal*)
- ► bear (*formal*)

carry
to have something in your hands or arms, or in your clothes as you go somewhere: *She was carrying a small child.* | *I always carry a couple of dollars in my pocket.*

transport (AWL)
to move things or people from one place to

C

another in a vehicle: *The company transports most of its products across the country by truck.*

haul
to pull or carry something heavy from one place to another: *They hauled the big man out of the water and laid him on the dock.*

lug (*informal*)
to carry something with difficulty because it is very heavy: *She was trying to run through the airport lugging two huge suitcases.*

bear (*formal*)
to bring or carry something. You only use **bear** in very formal or literary language: *Refugees walked along the road bearing everything they owned on their backs.*
→ see **hold**[1], **take**, **carry out** at **do**

C

cartoon *noun* → see **drawing**, Topic **Entertainment**

carve *verb* → see **cut**[1]

case *noun* → see **cover**[2], **example**, **patient**[2], **situation**, **trial**

cash *noun* → see **money**

cast *noun* → see **group**, Topic **Entertainment**

castle /ˈkæsəl/ *noun*

- ► castle
- ► palace
- ► fort
- ► fortress

castle
a large building with high walls to protect the people inside from attack, which was built a long time ago: *The castle sits on a hill looking over the river.*

palace
a large, expensive, and beautiful house where a king or queen lives: *We visited the palace of the French King, Louis XIV.*

fort
a strong building used by soldiers for defending an important place: *The army began to attack the fort with cannons.*

fortress
fortress is an older word that means the same as **fort**: *They believed that no army could destroy their fortress.*

castle

castle

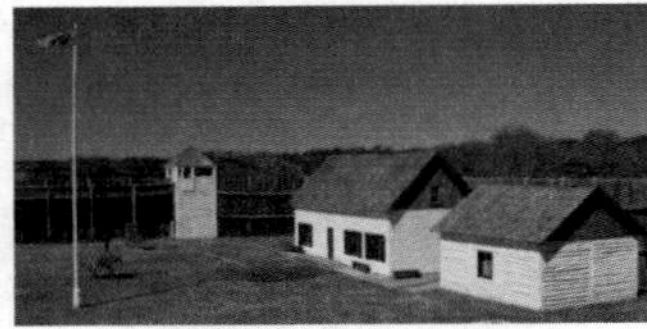
fort

palace

casual /ˈkæʒuəl/ *adjective*

- ► casual
- ► informal

ANTONYMS → see **dressy**

casual
casual clothes are not formal, and you usually wear them when you are not working: *The meeting was on a weekend, and most people were dressed in casual clothes.*

informal
informal means the same as **casual** when it is used about clothes. It is used especially in the phrase **informal dress** (=informal clothes) on an invitation, when people need to know what kind of clothes to wear: *Please note that dress for the party is informal.*
→ see **informal** for ways of describing informal words and situations
→ see Topic **Describing Clothes**

ADVERBS

You can make the adjectives that mean **casual** into adverbs by using an **-ly** ending: *He was not wearing a suit, but was casually dressed.* | *The wedding was on the beach, and guests were asked to dress informally.*

cat /kæt/ *noun*

► cat
► kitten

cat
a small animal with soft fur, pointed ears, and whiskers, which people often keep as a pet: *Our family has two cats, a dog, and lots of fish.*

kitten
a very young cat: *When our cat was a kitten, she liked to play with pieces of string.*

catch *verb* → see **get on**, Topic **Travel and Vacations**

categorize *verb* → see **sort**

category /ˈkætəˌgɔri/ *noun*

► category
► class
► style
► genre

category (AWL)
a group of things or people that are similar in some way: *The books were divided into two categories: fiction and nonfiction.*

class
a group of things that are considered together because they are similar. You use **class** when talking about scientific subjects: *Doctors realized that using this class of drugs increased the risk of infections.*

style (AWL)
a particular way of doing, performing, or playing something: *His style of singing is more like blues than jazz.* | *She is a tennis player with an aggressive playing style.*

genre
a type of writing, movie, art, or music. **Genre** is mainly used in academic writing: *The author is best known for his writing in the Fantasy and Science Fiction genres.*
→ see **kind**[1]

cattle *noun* → see **cow**

cause[1] /kɔz/ *noun*

► cause
► reason
► factor
► root
► source
► origins

cause
something that makes another thing happen: *Investigators are trying to find the **cause of** the fire.* | *Lack of money was the main **cause of** the problem.*

reason
the thing that makes you decide to do something, or makes something happen: *The reason I believe her is that she has always been honest before.* | *What was the **reason for** the flight delay?*
→ **GRAMMAR:** Don't say: *~~the reason of something~~*. Say: *the reason for something.*

factor (AWL)
one of the things that influence what will happen: *The value of a car depends on several factors, including how old it is and how many miles it has been driven.*

root
the most important cause of a problem or a bad situation: *We need to get to the **root of** the problem and find out why she is unhappy.*

source (AWL)
something that makes a feeling or problem begin and develop: *Her children are doing well in school, which is a **source of** pride for her.* | *The argument over who owns the land has been a **source of tension** in the region.*

origins
the situation in which something started to develop a long time ago: *The **origins of** the current war go back hundreds of years.*

cause[2] /kɔz/ *verb*

► cause
► make
► be responsible for
► lead to
► result in
► produce
► bring about
► trigger

cause
to make something happen, especially something bad: *Heavy traffic is causing long delays.* | *The problem was caused by a bug in the software.*

make
to cause someone to do something, or cause something to happen: *What made you decide to become a doctor?* | *The waves were making the boat go up and down.*
→ **GRAMMAR:** Don't say: *~~It makes me to feel uncomfortable~~*. Say: *It makes me feel uncomfortable.* But use "to" when using **make** in the passive: ***I was made to** feel uncomfortable.*

C

be responsible for
to be the person or thing that should be blamed for causing something bad to happen: *The person who is responsible for the damage will have to pay for the repairs.*

lead to
to cause something to happen later: *If children eat a lot of unhealthy food, this can lead to health problems when they are older.* | *The information the police received led to an arrest.*

result in
to cause something to happen. You use **result in** when talking about the effect or result of something: *The storm resulted in floods along the river.*

produce
to make something happen or have a particular effect, especially as part of a process: *Higher temperatures will produce a rise in sea levels.*

bring about
to cause something, especially a change that happens over a long period: *The Internet has brought about enormous changes in people's lives.*

trigger (AWL)
to cause a very bad event to suddenly happen: *The earthquake triggered a huge tidal wave.*

caution *noun* → see **care**[2]

cautious *adjective* → see **careful**

cease *verb* → see **stop**[1]

celebrate /ˈseləˌbreɪt/ *verb*

- ► celebrate
- ► commemorate
- ► mark
- ► honor

celebrate
to do something enjoyable because it is a special occasion: *We are going to have a party to celebrate your birthday this year.* | *People were celebrating in the streets after the team won.*

commemorate
to do something in order to remember an important person or event from the past: *The yearly parade commemorates all the soldiers who fought in past wars.*

mark
to do something special to show that an occasion is important: *A formal dinner is planned to mark the prime minister's visit.*

honor
to do something to show that someone is admired and respected, for example giving that person a prize: *The film director was recently honored with a lifetime achievement award.*
→ see **enjoy**

celebration *noun* → see **ceremony**, **party**

celebrity *noun* → see **star**

cell *noun* → see **prison**

cemetery /ˈseməˌteri/ *noun*

- ► cemetery
- ► graveyard
- ► burial ground

cemetery
an area of land where dead people are buried: *We go to the cemetery once a year to visit my grandmother's grave.* | *There was a special ceremony in the cemetery for soldiers who had died.*

graveyard
an area of land where dead people are buried. **Graveyard** is more old-fashioned than **cemetery** and is used especially in stories: *The headstones in the old graveyard were broken, and weeds grew on the graves.*

burial ground
an area of land where dead people are buried, especially a place that was used a very long time ago: *Native Americans used the island as a burial ground for their dead for hundreds of years.*

center /ˈsentɚ/ *noun*

- ► center
- ► middle
- ► heart
- ► core

center
the part of an area or object that is farthest from all the edges of that area or object. You use **center** especially about the part that is exactly at that point: *Draw a line through the center of the circle.* | *She placed the flowers **in the center of** the table.*

middle
middle means the same as **center**. You use **middle** especially about the part that is halfway between two sides: *Gary swam toward the **middle** of the lake.*
→ You can also use **middle** to talk about the part of something that is halfway between the beginning and the end: *I fell asleep in the middle of the movie.*

heart
the middle of an area, town, or city: *The hotel is located **in the heart of** Manhattan.*

core (AWL)
the central part of the Earth, or of an object: *The Earth has a solid inner core which is 2,500 kilometers in diameter.*

SYNONYM CHECK
Center or middle?

You usually use **center** when you mean an exact point: *The point where the lines cross is the center of the square.*

You usually use **middle** when thinking of a slightly larger area: *Put an X in the middle of the square.*

You can use both **middle** and **center** to talk about the center of a flat area or object, or about the point that is inside something and farthest from all the edges: *The donuts have jam in the center/middle.*

You usually use **middle** to talk about something that is inside something and halfway between two sides: *The cake has frosting in the middle.*

central /ˈsentrəl/ *adjective*

- ► central
- ► middle

central
in the center of an area or place: *Rwanda is a country in Central Africa.* | *The apartments all face onto a central courtyard.*

middle
closest to the center of something, or between the top and bottom, or between the left and right parts: *She was driving in the middle lane and cars were passing her on both sides.* | *The letter was in the middle drawer of her desk.*
→ see **main** for **central** meaning "with the most importance and influence"

ADVERBS
You can make **central** into an adverb by using an **-ly** ending: *The hotel is centrally located.*

century *noun* → see **time**

ceremony /ˈserəˌmoʊni/ *noun*

- ► ceremony
- ► service
- ► ritual
- ► celebration

ceremony
an important public or religious event that involves special words and actions: *The wedding ceremony will take place at the church.* | *The opening ceremony of the Olympic Games ended with the athletes walking into the stadium.*

service
a religious ceremony, especially in a church: *A memorial service was held for the disaster victims.*

ritual
a series of things that people always do in the same way in a ceremony: *Jewish women light candles as part of the Friday evening ritual.*

celebration
an event that happens because there is a special occasion: *The town is planning a big celebration of its 150th anniversary.*

certain /ˈsɚtn/ *adjective*

- ► certain
- ► sure to
- ► definite
- ► inevitable
- ► bound to

certain
if something is certain, you are completely sure that it will happen or is true: ***It** seemed **certain that** he would pass the test, because he had studied hard.* | *The movie is **certain to** surprise people.*

sure to
certain to happen. **Sure to** is more informal than **certain to**: *I didn't want to tell my mother, because the news was sure to upset her.*

definite (AWL)
completely certain, especially because someone has made a final decision: *I hope they will give me a definite answer soon.* | *The date for the wedding is finally definite: June 20.*

inevitable (AWL)
certain to happen and impossible to avoid. You use **inevitable** especially about bad things that you do not want to happen: ***It** was **inevitable that** her parents would find out what she had done.*

bound to
seeming very likely, because that is what you expect: *The boys haven't eaten since breakfast, so they are bound to be hungry.*
→ see **particular**, **sure**, **make certain** at **make sure**

C

ADVERBS

You can make **certain**, **definite**, and **inevitable** into adverbs by using an **-ly** ending: *It was certainly a difficult test.* | *Inevitably, her parents found out what she had done.* | *They are definitely getting married!*

certainly /ˈsɚtnli/ *adverb*

- ► certainly
- ► definitely
- ► undoubtedly
- ► surely

C

certainly
used when saying that you are sure that something is true: *I certainly couldn't move that big rock all by myself.* | *We don't know exactly when the house was built, but it's certainly over 200 years old.*

definitely (AWL)
certainly or without any doubt. **Definitely** in more common in spoken English than **certainly**: *I'm so sick of work – I definitely need a vacation.* | *"Are you going to invite Caitlin?" "Definitely."*

undoubtedly *also* **without a doubt**
used when saying that something is definitely true and that no one could disagree with it. **Undoubtedly** sounds a little more formal than **certainly**: *Alcohol undoubtedly played a part in the accident.* | *He is, without a doubt, the best baseball player I have seen.*

surely
used when saying that you are sure that something is true and you think other people would agree: *It is surely no coincidence that the man they decided to hire is the boss's nephew.*
→ **Surely** can also be used to show that you think something must be true, even if someone has said it is not: *Surely you knew that he was lying to you.*

certificate *noun* → see **license**

chair /tʃer/ *noun*

- ► chair
- ► seat
- ► stool
- ► throne
- ► highchair
- ► armchair
- ► couch

chair
a piece of furniture for one person to sit on: *He sat down on a chair at the desk.*

seat
something you can sit on. You use **seat** about places in cars, buses, planes, concert halls, etc. where you can sit: *Charlie was in the passenger seat of the car.* | *Did you get good seats at the concert?*

stool
a seat with three or four legs but no back or arms: *They sat on stools at the bar.*

throne
the special chair on which a king or queen sits: *The throne was covered in gold and jewels.*

highchair
a tall chair that a baby sits in to eat: *The baby was smearing yogurt over the tray of the highchair.*

armchair
a soft comfortable chair: *She was curled up in an armchair, reading a book.*

couch *also* **sofa**
a comfortable seat that is wide enough for two or three people: *They sat on the sofa watching TV.*

GRAMMAR CHECK: chair

A person sits **on** a hard or firm chair, a throne, or a couch, and **in** a soft comfortable chair or a highchair.

chairman /ˈtʃermən/ *noun*

- ► chairman
- ► chair
- ► director
- ► managing director
- ► chief executive
- ► president

chairman
the person who is in charge of an organization, committee, or meeting: *He started a software company and is now its chairman.* | *Chairwoman Nancy Jones began the meeting.* | *Who is the chairperson of the hiring committee?*
→ **Chairman** can be used for both men and women, but some women prefer to be called a **chairwoman**. You can also use **chairperson** for a man or woman.

chair
the person who is in charge of a university department, committee, or meeting: *Dr. Burns is the chair of the Political Science department at the university.*

director
the person who is in charge of a company or a

department in a company: *She is the director of advertising at a magazine.*

managing director
someone who is in charge of a large company or organization. A **managing director** controls the activities that happen every day: *He is the **managing director of** the Old Globe Theatre.*

chief executive *also* **chief executive officer** *or* **CEO**
the person who is in charge of a large company: *He is the chief executive officer of a Wall Street investment bank.* | *People expect the new CEO to make some changes at the company.*

president
the person who is in charge of a company or organization, for example a college or club: *The college president announced that fees would increase.*
→ see **boss**

challenge /ˈtʃæləndʒ/ *noun*

- ► challenge
- ► undertaking
- ► task

challenge (AWL)
something difficult that needs skill or effort to do well: *It's going to be a big challenge to get everything ready before the party, but we'll manage.* | *He is very ambitious and is always looking for new challenges at work.*

undertaking (AWL)
an important and difficult piece of work that you agree to do: *Directing a play is a major undertaking – are you sure you can handle it?*

task
something that must be done, especially something that is difficult or unpleasant: *I was given the task of cleaning out the garage.*

champion *noun* → see **winner**

championship *noun* → see **competition**, Topic **Sports and Exercise**

chance /tʃæns/ *noun*

1 a chance to do something
- ► chance
- ► opportunity

2 a chance that something may happen
- ► chance
- ► possibility
- ► probability
- ► prospect (*formal*)
- ► likelihood

1 a chance to do something

chance
a time or situation that you can use to do something that you want to do: *Alan was waiting for a **chance to** give his opinion.* | *If you get the chance, you should go biking around the island.*

opportunity
a chance to do something. **Opportunity** is slightly more formal than **chance**: *She was really excited about the **opportunity to** travel to India.*

2 a chance that something may happen

chance
if there is a chance that something will happen, it may happen, but you are not sure: *There is a **chance that** he will go to prison for life.* | *Eating well during pregnancy increases the **chances that** the baby will be healthy.* | *He has a good **chance of** winning.*

possibility
possibility means the same as **chance**. You usually use **possibility** in the phrase "there is a possibility (that)": *There is a **possibility that** she might lose her job.*

probability
the chance that something will happen, when it seems very likely that it will happen: *The probability is that small businesses will not have to pay the tax.*
→ **Probability** can also be used to mean how likely it is that something will happen: *The **probability of** winning the lottery is really low.*

prospect (AWL) (*formal*)
a possibility of something happening in the future: *Is there any **prospect of** her getting a job soon?*

likelihood
the chance that something will probably happen or is probably true: *Using a seat belt decreases the **likelihood that** you will be killed in a car accident.*
→ see **luck** for **chance** meaning "how things happen without planning"
→ see **risk**[1], **by chance** at **accidentally**

C

change¹ /tʃeɪndʒ/ *verb*

1 to become different
- ► change
- ► alter
- ► adapt
- ► evolve
- ► mutate
- ► fluctuate

2 to make something different
- ► change
- ► alter
- ► adjust
- ► modify
- ► amend
- ► convert
- ► reform
- ► revise
- ► reverse
- ► twist

3 to make something completely different
- ► transform
- ► revolutionize

C

1 to become different

change
to become different: *The town has changed a lot recently – there are a lot more houses.* | *The traffic lights* ***changed from*** *green* ***to*** *red.*

alter (AWL)
to become different, especially when something changes only a little bit. **Alter** sounds more formal than **change**: *His voice altered slightly and he became more serious.*

adapt
to change so that you can deal with a new situation: *My parents moved a lot, so I had to learn to* ***adapt to*** *new people and new schools.*

evolve (AWL)
if a species of animal or plant evolves, it gradually changes over a long period of time and develops into a different species: *Birds* ***evolved from*** *reptiles that lived millions of years ago.*
➔ You can also say that an idea or system **evolves** when it gradually develops: *The idea for the story took a long time to evolve in my mind.*

mutate
if a living thing mutates, it becomes different from others of the same kind because of a change in its gene: *The virus was found only in pigs, but it has now* ***mutated into*** *a form that will make humans sick.*

fluctuate (AWL)
if an amount, number, or temperature fluctuates, it goes up and down more than once: *The price of bread fluctuates depending on how good the wheat crop is.*

2 to make something different

change
to make something different: *You've changed your hairstyle – short hair looks good on you.* | *She* ***changed*** *her last name* ***to*** *Wilson when she got married.*

alter (AWL)
to make something different, especially by making small changes. **Alter** sounds more formal than **change**: *We decided to alter our plans and leave at an earlier time.*

adjust (AWL)
to change something so that it is a little bigger, higher, quieter, etc. because that is how you want it: *You can adjust the height of the chair to make it more comfortable.*

modify (AWL)
to make small changes to something, especially a design, plan, or structure: *They modified the car to use propane instead of gasoline.*

amend (AWL)
to make a change to a law or to an important document: *The date for finishing the project changed, so they had to amend his contract to show the new date.*

convert (AWL)
to change something so that it can be used for a different purpose: *The factory was* ***converted into*** *offices.* | *Plants* ***convert*** *light from the sun* ***into*** *energy, using a process called photosynthesis.*

reform
to change an organization, law, or system to improve it: *Reforming the health care system was important to the president.*

revise (AWL)
to change your plans, opinions, or a document, especially because something else has changed: *The map was revised to include recent changes in the names of some countries.* | *We revised our plans when we realized we didn't have enough money.*

reverse (AWL)
to change something so that it is the opposite, or so that it goes back to what it was before: *It will take years to reverse the damage done by pollution.*

twist *also* **distort**
to deliberately change facts or words, in a way that is not true: *He accused her of twisting the facts so that she wouldn't be blamed for the problems.* | *Opponents of the proposal have*

distorted the truth in order to make people vote against it.

3 to make something completely different

transform (AWL)
to make something completely different, especially so that it is much better: *The treatment has transformed his life, and he is now able to do things he couldn't do before.* | *The old factory was transformed into a busy shopping center.*

revolutionize (AWL)
to completely change the way people think or do something. You use **revolutionize** especially about a new idea or invention: *Einstein's theories revolutionized our understanding of the universe.*

→ see **undress** for **change** meaning "to change your clothes"

change² /tʃeɪndʒ/ *noun*

1 a change that someone makes
- ► change
- ► alteration
- ► adjustment
- ► modification
- ► conversion
- ► reform
- ► amendment

2 a situation in which something changes
- ► change
- ► fluctuation
- ► trend
- ► transition
- ► evolution

3 a big change
- ► revolution
- ► transformation

1 a change that someone makes

change
the action of making something different, or doing something in a different way: *The coach wants to make some big* ***changes to*** *the team, and bring in a lot of new players.* | *Congress has made* ***changes in*** *the immigration laws.*

alteration (AWL)
a small change that you make to something. **Alteration** sounds more formal than **change**: *She made some last-minute* ***alterations to*** *her speech.*

adjustment (AWL)
a small change you make to something such as a machine, system, or the way something looks. **Adjustment** sounds more formal than **change**: *He made a few* ***adjustments to*** *the machine and it was soon working again.*

modification (AWL)
a small change, especially to the design of something. **Modification** sounds more formal than **change**: *The car is the same as the old model, except for a few* ***modifications to*** *the engine.*

conversion (AWL)
the act of changing something so that it has a different form or purpose, or uses a different system: *The old warehouse is undergoing a* ***conversion into*** *apartments.*

reform
a set of changes that improve an organization, law, or system: *The president has introduced* ***reforms in*** *the health care system.*

amendment (AWL)
a change made to a law or to an important document: *The First* ***Amendment to*** *the U.S. Constitution protects your right to free speech, which means you can publicly give your opinion without being arrested.*

2 a situation in which something changes

change
a situation in which something becomes different: *I don't like change – I like things to stay the way they are.* | *There has been a big* ***change in*** *his behavior – he seems much more relaxed.* | *The children are healthier now because of* ***changes in*** *their diet.*

fluctuation (AWL)
a sudden change, when the price or level of something keeps going up and down: *Fish are sensitive to small* ***fluctuations in*** *water temperature.*

trend
a general change that happens in society over a period of time. You use **trend** especially when you are saying what you think is likely to happen in the future: *There is a* ***trend toward*** *buying cars that use less gasoline.*

transition (AWL)
the process of changing from one situation or system to another: *Some students find it hard to make the* ***transition from*** *middle school* ***to*** *high school.*

evolution (AWL)
the way in which something develops and changes over a long time. You use **evolution** about plants or animals that gradually develop into new types of plants or animals, or about ideas and systems that gradually develop over time: *Darwin's Theory of Evolution tries to show*

how species of animals and plants develop into new species. | *In her book, she traces the* ***evolution*** *of the justice system in the United States.*

3 a big change

revolution (AWL)
a complete change in the way people do or think about something, caused by new technology or new ideas: *The Internet started a* ***revolution in*** *the way we communicate with each other.* | *Louis Pasteur's work led to a* ***revolution in*** *medical science.*

transformation (AWL)
a complete change in a person or thing so that he, she, or it is improved a lot: *The* ***transformation*** *of a caterpillar* ***into*** *a butterfly takes several weeks.* | *Attitudes toward smoking have undergone a transformation, and now many countries have laws against smoking in public places.*
→ see **money** for **change** meaning "money in the form of coins"

changeable /ˈtʃeɪndʒəbəl/ *adjective*

- ► changeable
- ► variable
- ► inconsistent
- ► unstable
- ► precarious

ANTONYMS → see **same**

changeable
likely to change suddenly or often: *The weather is pretty changeable by the coast, especially during the winter.* | *His moods were changeable – I never knew how he was feeling from one minute to the next.*

variable (AWL)
likely to change a lot or to be different from others of the same type: *This tropical fish can be* ***variable in*** *color, ranging from light yellow to bright orange.* | *The rate of interest on the loan is variable, which means the bank can change the rate.*

inconsistent (AWL)
changing too often or too much so that you do not know what to expect: *The team has been inconsistent all season, sometimes playing very well and other times not.*

unstable (AWL)
likely to change suddenly and become worse: *The unstable political situation could lead to war.*

precarious
likely to change and quickly become worse: *There are concerns about the President's precarious state of health.*
→ see **flexible (1)**

ADVERBS

You can make **inconsistent** into an adverb by using an **-ly** ending: *The team has played inconsistently all season.*

channel *noun* → see **station**[1]

chapter *noun* → see **part**, Topic **Books and Literature**

character /ˈkærɪktɚ/ *noun*

1 the qualities that make someone a particular kind of person
- ► character
- ► personality
- ► nature
- ► temperament
- ► disposition (*formal*)

2 a person in a book, play, television show, or movie
- ► character
- ► hero
- ► heroine
- ► protagonist (*formal*)
- ► antagonist (*formal*)
- ► role
- ► part

1 the qualities that make someone a particular kind of person

character
the qualities that make you a particular kind of person. You use **character** when you are talking about someone's moral qualities, such as whether he or she is good, bad, or honest: *He is a man of good character and you can trust him completely.* | *It shows strength of character to not do what your friends are doing, if you think it's wrong.*

personality
the mixture of qualities that make you a particular kind of person. You use **personality** about how someone behaves with other people, for example whether he or she is usually friendly, confident, or shy: *Mike has a great personality – he is smart and funny, so everyone likes him.* | *My kids have very different personalities. Damon is happy and easy-going, but Evan is shy and worries a lot.*

nature
your character, and the usual way that you would behave. You often use **nature** when you are talking about the things someone would or would not do because of the kind of person he or she is: *He would never hurt anyone – it's not in his nature.*
→ **Nature** is used especially in the following phrases: *He **has a trusting nature**. | Humans are **by nature** hunters. | Everyone wants to be rich – **it's human nature*** (=it is what most people are like and is not surprising).

temperament
the type of character you have that you show in your emotions, for example whether you get angry easily or are usually relaxed: *My brother and I have different temperaments. He gets very excited about things, but I'm more relaxed and calm.*

disposition (*formal*)
disposition means the same as **temperament**. **Disposition** usually has an adjective before it: *She is a sweet child with a happy disposition.*
→ see Topic **Describing People's Character**

2 a person in a book, play, television show, or movie

character
a person in a book, play, television show, or movie: *The main character in the story is a young girl who is searching for her missing parents. | My favorite cartoon character is Donald Duck.*

hero
the man or boy who is the most important character in a book, play, television show, or movie: *At the end of the movie, the hero catches the bad guy and saves the girl.*

heroine
the woman or girl who is the most important character in a book, play, television show, or movie: *Like the heroine of the novel, the author was also married to a doctor.*

protagonist (*formal*)
the most important character in a book, play, television show, or movie: *The protagonist is a young woman who wants to be a dancer.*

antagonist (*formal*)
the main opponent of the protagonist: *In the Harry Potter stories, Voldemort is the main antagonist.*
→ You can also say that two characters who oppose each other are **antagonists**: *Wile E. Coyote and the Road Runner are antagonists in a cartoon, with the Coyote always trying to trap the Road Runner.*

role (AWL)
the character played by an actor in a play, television show, or movie: *Tom Cruise played **the role of** the young pilot in the movie "Top Gun."*

part
the words and actions of a character in a play, television show, or movie: *Have you learned your part yet? | I'm playing **the part of** Annie in the school play.*
→ see Topic **Books and Literature**, **Entertainment**

characteristic *noun* → see **quality**, **typical**

charge¹ *noun* → see **accusation**, **cost¹**, **manage** for **be in charge of something**

charge² *verb* → see **prosecute**

charity *noun* → see **help²**

charm /tʃɑrm/ *noun*

- ► charm
- ► charisma
- ► appeal

charm
a special quality that someone has that makes other people like him or her: *Joe has a boyish charm that all the girls seem to love.*
→ You can also use **charm** to talk about a quality that makes people like a place: *The book describes Savannah's old Southern charm perfectly.*

charisma
a strong special quality that makes a lot of people admire someone and be influenced by him or her: *He has the intelligence and charisma of a good leader.*

appeal
a quality that makes people like or be attracted to someone or something: *His books have a lot of appeal for younger readers. | We had already had pizza for lunch and the idea of eating another pizza for dinner had lost its appeal.*

charming *adjective* → see **nice**

chase¹ /tʃeɪs/ *noun*

- ► chase
- ► pursuit (*formal*)
- ► hunt

chase
the act of following someone or something quickly in order to catch him, her, or it: *After a short chase they caught the dog and returned it to its owner. | Robbers led police on a high-speed car chase through city streets.*

C

pursuit (AWL) *(formal)*
pursuit means the same as **chase**, and it is usually used in the phrase "in pursuit of": *She ran down the street **in pursuit of** the boy who had grabbed her bag.*

hunt
an attempt to find someone or something, especially one that takes a lot of effort and lasts a long time: *The 18-year **hunt for** the killer ended this week when police arrested a man living in Seattle.*

C

chase² *verb* → see **follow**

chat¹ *noun* → see **conversation**

chat² *verb* → see **talk¹**

chatter *verb* → see **talk¹**

cheap /tʃip/ *adjective*

1 not costing a lot of money
- ► cheap
- ► inexpensive
- ► low
- ► reasonable
- ► economical
- ► affordable
- ► budget

ANTONYMS → see **expensive**

2 not liking to spend money
- ► cheap
- ► stingy

1 not costing a lot of money

cheap
not costing a lot of money: *These shoes were really cheap – only $25. | It is cheaper to go by bus than by plane.*

inexpensive
inexpensive means the same as **cheap** but is more formal. You use **inexpensive** to describe things that are of good quality, even though they do not cost a lot: *The furniture is inexpensive, but it is well made. | It's a good store for inexpensive gifts.*

low
low prices, rents, or fees are not high: *They sell clothes at very low prices. | The rent for the apartment is very low – only $500 a month.*

reasonable
a reasonable price seems fair because it is not too high: *The restaurant serves good food at reasonable prices that most families can afford.*

economical (AWL)
cheap because you do not need to spend a lot of money or use a lot of fuel: *It's more economical to buy the big package – it's about five cents cheaper per pound. | The new car is more economical because it uses less gas.*

affordable
something affordable is cheap enough that most people are able to buy or pay for it: *There is a lack of affordable housing in the town. | The store sells designer clothes at affordable prices.*

budget
budget flights, airlines, hotels, etc. have very low prices: *I got a budget flight to Washington for less than $200.*
→ **GRAMMAR: Budget** is always used before a noun. Don't say: ~~*The hotel was budget*~~. Say: *It was a budget hotel.*

ADVERBS

You can make the adjectives **cheap**, **inexpensive**, **reasonable**, **economical**, and **affordable** into adverbs by using an **-ly** ending: *The goods can be made more cheaply overseas. | Email allows businesses to communicate easily and inexpensively. | The clothes are affordably priced.*

2 not liking to spend money

cheap
not liking to spend money so that you do not often buy expensive or good quality things: *He can afford to pay for my meal, but he won't because he's too cheap.*

stingy
not willing to spend money or give someone money: *Her stingy father won't give her money for new clothes, even though her old ones have holes in them.*
→ **Cheap** and **stingy** are both used when you think someone should be more willing to spend money.
→ see **thrifty**

cheat /tʃit/ *verb*

1 to do something dishonest to pass a test, win a game, etc.
- ► cheat
- ► copy
- ► plagiarize

2 to get something from someone by deceiving him or her
- ► cheat
- ► swindle
- ► defraud

1 to do something dishonest to pass a test, win a game, etc.

cheat
to do something that is not honest because you think it will help you succeed on a test or win a game: *Don't look at my answers – that's cheating!* | *If you are caught* ***cheating on*** *the test, you will receive a zero.*

copy
to cheat on a test or schoolwork by looking at someone else's work and writing the same thing as he or she has written: *If the teacher finds out that you copied Maya's homework, you'll get in trouble.*

plagiarize
to copy someone else's words or ideas and pretend they are your own: *In her essay, the student plagiarized an article she found on the Internet, and she was kicked out of college.*

2 to get something from someone by deceiving him or her

cheat
to get something from someone by deceiving him or her: *Some employers cheat illegal workers by not paying them what they've promised.* | *The singer's manager* ***cheated*** *him* ***out of*** *thousands of dollars.*

swindle
to trick someone in a clever way to get money from him or her: *He* ***swindled*** *investors* ***out of*** *millions of dollars by selling them worthless stock.*

defraud
to deceive someone in order to get money from him or her. **Defraud** is used to formally describe a crime: *Ogden is accused of attempting to defraud his business partner by putting the business's money in his own bank account.*

cheating *noun* → see **dishonesty**

check¹ /tʃek/ *verb*

1 to look at something to see if it is correct
- ► check
- ► examine
- ► inspect
- ► audit
- ► go through
- ► double-check

2 to find out if something is true or has happened
- ► check
- ► make sure
- ► make certain
- ► verify (*formal*)

1 to look at something to see if it is correct

check
to look at something to see if it is correct or the way it should be: *The man checked our passports before he let us through.* | ***Check*** *the plates* ***for*** *cracks before you buy them.*

examine
to check something carefully in order to find out or decide something: *Police* ***examined*** *the weapon* ***for*** *fingerprints.*

inspect AWL
to check something carefully as part of an official process: *Some insurance people have already been here to inspect the storm damage.*

audit
to officially examine a company's financial records to make sure they are correct: *An accounting firm was asked to audit the company's records.*

go through *also* **go over**
to check something such as a document or plan from beginning to end, to make sure that it is correct: *You should go through the contract before you sign.* | *I can go over your essay for you to check for mistakes.*

double-check
to check something again, so you are sure about it: *I'm sure this is the right address, but I'll double-check it.*

2 to find out if something is true or has happened

check
to find out if something is true or has happened: ***Check that*** *you have entered your password correctly.* | *I wanted to* ***check if*** *the company had received my order.*

make sure
to find out if what you want is true or has happened: *He called to* ***make sure that*** *we got home okay.* | *Can you* ***make sure that*** *I turned the oven off?*

make certain
to make completely sure that something is true or has happened. **Make certain** sounds a little more formal and a little more definite than **make sure**: *Before buying a sofa,* ***make certain that*** *it will fit in your living room.*

verify (*formal*)
to make sure officially that something is true: *They will need to* ***verify that*** *the letter was written by Abraham Lincoln – if it is, it could be worth a lot of money.*
→ see **examine**

C

check² /tʃek/ *noun*

- ► check
- ► examination
- ► inspection
- ► audit

check
a careful look at something to see if it is correct, safe, or good: *Do a quick check and make sure you filled out the whole form.* | *The company does checks on all its employees for any criminal record.*

examination
the process of looking at something carefully to find out more about it, especially when there is a problem: *The doctor's examination showed that Richard had broken his ankle.*

inspection (AWL)
a careful examination of something, to make sure that it is in good condition or that it has been done correctly. **Inspections** are usually done by someone in an official position: *There are regular inspections of the school by school board members.*

audit
an official examination of a company's financial records, to make sure that they are correct: *The IRS did an audit of the company's tax returns.*
→ see **bill** for **check** meaning "a bill in a restaurant"

C

check-up *noun* → see **examination**, Topic **Medical Treatment**

cheer¹ *verb* → see **clap**, **shout¹**

cheer² *noun* → see **shout²**

cheerful *adjective* → see **happy**, Topic **Describing People's Character**

cheer up /ˌtʃɪr ˈʌp/ *phrasal verb*

1 to feel happier
- ► cheer up
- ► feel happier
- ► brighten (*formal*)

2 to make someone happier or less worried
- ► cheer someone up
- ► make someone feel better
- ► console (*formal*)

ANTONYMS → see **sadden**

1 to feel happier

cheer up
to feel happier after feeling sad. You usually say **cheer up** to someone to tell them not to feel sad: *Cheer up, Sam. I'll only be gone one day.* | *He cheered up when he saw the cake.*

feel happier
to feel more pleased about your life, after feeling sad or worried: *Val's been feeling a lot happier since she quit her job.*

brighten (*formal*)
to become or look happier: *The little boy's face brightened when he saw his mother.*

2 to make someone happier or less worried

cheer someone up
to make someone feel happier: *Thanks for the card. It really cheered me up.*

make someone feel better
to make someone feel happier or less upset: *Why don't you tell me what's wrong? It might make you feel better.*

console (*formal*)
to help someone feel less sad or disappointed: *She tried to console him by reminding him that no one had done well on the test.*
→ see **comfort²**

chef *noun* → see **cook²**, Topic **Eating in a Restaurant**

chemistry *noun* → see Topic **Science and Technology**

chew *verb* → see **bite**

chicken /ˈtʃɪkən/ *noun*

- ► chicken
- ► rooster
- ► hen
- ► chick

chicken
a farm bird that is kept for its eggs and meat: *She scattered corn on the ground to feed the chickens.*

rooster
a male chicken: *The rooster started crowing at dawn.*

hen
a female chicken: *He reached under the hen to take the egg from her nest.*

chick
a baby chicken: *The little yellow chicks followed the mother hen around the farmyard.*

chief *noun* → see **boss**, **leader**, **main**, **top²**

chiefly *adverb* → see **mainly**

child /tʃaɪld/ *noun*

1 a young human
- ► **child**
- ► **kid** (*informal*)
- ► **little boy/little girl**
- ► **youngster**
- ► **teenager**
- ► **adolescent**
- ► **minor** (*formal*)

ANTONYMS → see **adult**[1], **old person**

2 young animals
- ► **offspring**
- ► **young**
- ► **litter**

1 a young human

child
a young person who is not yet fully grown. You do not usually use **child** about babies or teenagers: ***Many children are scared of the dark.*** | ***My grandfather lived in New York when he was a child.***

kid (*informal*)
a child: ***His kids are six and nine years old.***

little boy/little girl
a young male or female child: ***The little girl was holding her mother's hand.***

youngster
a child, or a young person who is not an adult. **Youngster** is used by adults, not by children: ***He runs a martial arts class for local youngsters.***

teenager
someone who is between 13 and 19 years old: ***The teenagers at the high school are washing cars to raise money.***

adolescent
a young person between 12 and 18 years old, when his or her body is changing to become more adult: ***When they are adolescents, boys' voices become lower.***

minor (*formal*)
someone who is younger than 18, and is not allowed by law to do things such as drink alcohol or vote: ***It's illegal to sell alcohol to minors.***
→ see **baby**, **teenager**

2 young animals

offspring
the young animals that an animal produces: ***All the bees in the hive are the offspring of the queen bee.***
→ When you use **offspring** about children, it sounds scientific or humorous.

young
a group of young animals from one mother or from one type of animal: ***The mother lion will fight to protect her young.***

litter
a group of baby animals born to one mother at the same time: ***There were two black puppies in the litter and the others were all brown.***

childhood /ˈtʃaɪldhʊd/ *noun*
- ► **childhood**
- ► **youth**
- ► **adolescence**
- ► **infancy**

childhood
the time when you are a child and a teenager: ***Kara says she had a very happy childhood.*** | ***It is fun to think back to those summers in my childhood.***

youth
the time when you are young, until you are in your twenties. You usually use **youth** about the time when you are a teenager or a little older. **Youth** sounds fairly formal or literary: ***In his youth, he was a great dancer.***

adolescence
the time in your life when your body is changing to become an adult, from about age 12 to 18. You use **adolescence** most often in scientific language: ***During adolescence, children become more independent, but they still need support from their parents.***

infancy
the period when someone is a baby. You use **infancy** especially in medical or scientific language: ***If children do not experience love in infancy, they can have problems with relationships later in life.***

childish /ˈtʃaɪldɪʃ/ *adjective*
- ► **childish**
- ► **immature**
- ► **juvenile** (*formal*)

ANTONYMS → see **mature**

childish
behaving in a silly way that makes you seem younger than you really are: ***"You can't make me go!" "Don't be so childish."*** | ***I knew it was childish of me, but the chocolate was mine and I didn't want to share it with her.***

immature (AWL)
behaving in a way that seems more like a younger person than people your own age. If someone is **immature**, he or she does not always make responsible decisions or cannot control his or her emotions as well as other people of the same age: *He's 18, but he is still very immature – I wouldn't lend him your car.*
→ You can also use **immature** to describe a child who is too young to have developed the control or understanding that older people have: *A three-year-old is still too immature to fully understand death.*

juvenile (*formal*)
silly and more like what a child would say, do, or enjoy than what an adult does: *The movie is full of juvenile humor – at one point the main character gets stuck in a toilet.*

ADVERBS

You can make the adjectives **childish** and **immature** into adverbs by using an **-ly** ending: *"You can't make me go," she shouted childishly.* | *She acted very immaturely.*

choice /tʃɔɪs/ *noun*

1 the things or people that you can choose from
- ► choice
- ► option
- ► alternative
- ► selection

2 a person or thing that you have chosen
- ► choice
- ► selection
- ► pick (*informal*)

3 the chance to choose, or the process of choosing someone or something
- ► choice
- ► selection

1 the things or people that you can choose from

choice
the things or people that you can choose from: *It's a small store, so there's not much choice.* | *These are your choices: you can have milk, tea, soda, or water.*

option (AWL)
one of the things that you can choose to do in a particular situation: *He has two options: he can have knee surgery, or he can give up running.*

alternative (AWL)
something you can choose to do or use instead of something else: *Joining a carpool is one* ***alternative to*** *taking the bus.*

selection (AWL)
a group of things that you can choose from: *The library has a wide selection of children's books.*

2 a person or thing that you have chosen

choice
the person or thing that someone has chosen: *I don't really like her choice of jewelry.* | *Pizza was a good choice for the kids' party.*

selection (AWL)
a small group of things that have been chosen from a larger group: *She showed me a selection of her drawings.*
→ **Selection** can also mean one person or thing that has been chosen from a group: *Sarah Palin was John McCain's selection as his running mate in the 2008 elections.*

pick (*informal*)
the person or thing that you have chosen from a group. You use **pick** in the phrase "my/your/her etc. pick": *I think they would all do a good job, but Mindy is my pick.*
→ see **choose**

3 the chance to choose, or the process of choosing someone or something

choice
the chance to choose, or the process of choosing: *I wasn't given a choice – Dad just said I had to help.* | *Many women feel they must make a choice between their families and their careers.*

selection (AWL)
the action of choosing someone or something carefully. **Selection** is more formal than **choice**: *Read the descriptions of the books before making a selection.*

choke /tʃoʊk/ *verb*

1 to prevent someone from breathing
- ► choke
- ► smother
- ► suffocate
- ► strangle

2 to be unable to breathe
- ► choke
- ► suffocate

1 to prevent someone from breathing

choke
to prevent someone from breathing, or make it impossible for someone to breathe: *Don't hold so*

tight – you're choking me. | The scarf was so tight that it was choking me.

smother
to put something over someone's face so that he or she cannot breathe, especially to kill him or her: *The woman tried to smother her husband with a pillow.*

suffocate
to kill someone by preventing him or her from getting air to breathe: *Never put a plastic bag over someone's head, because you could suffocate them.*

strangle
to kill someone by tightly pressing on his or her throat and preventing him or her from breathing: *It appears that the victim was strangled with a belt.*

2 to be unable to breathe

choke
to have difficulty breathing because your throat is blocked or there is not enough air: *Somebody help him – he's choking. | If someone is* ***choking on*** *a piece of food, press upward on their stomach, just under their ribs.*

suffocate
to die because there is not enough air to breathe: *Two of the birds had suffocated in the boxes.*

choose /tʃuz/ *verb*

1 to decide which thing or person you want
- ► **choose**
- ► **pick**
- ► **decide on**
- ► **select** (*formal*)
- ► **opt for**

2 to choose by voting
- ► **elect**
- ► **choose** (*informal*)
- ► **nominate**

1 to decide which thing or person you want

choose
to decide which one of a group of things or people you want: *I can't decide which dessert to get. You choose for me. | She was only 16 when the director* ***chose her to*** *be in the movie.*

pick
pick means the same as **choose**, but sounds more informal and is used more often in situations where the choice you are making is easy or quick: *Pick a number from one to five.*

decide on
to choose one thing from many possible choices, after thinking carefully about the choice: *Have you decided on a date for the wedding?*

select (AWL) (*formal*)
select means the same as **decide on** but sounds more formal: *It is important for parents to select the right school for a child with special needs.*
→ **Select** is also used in official or formal documents to mean the same as **choose**: *Select "privacy" from the pull-down menu if you would like to change your computer's settings.*

opt for
to choose to have one thing instead of another: *I think I would* ***opt for*** *the blue dress rather than the red one.*
→ see **decide (1)** for **choose** meaning "to choose to do something"
→ see **choice**

2 to choose by voting

elect
to choose someone for an official position by voting: *She was elected mayor. | Each class elects a representative to the student council.*

choose (*informal*)
choose means the same as **elect** but sounds informal: *Tomorrow the people will choose the person they want to be President.*

nominate
to officially suggest someone for an important job. Usually several people are **nominated**, and then there is an election to decide which person is chosen for the job: *Joe* ***nominated*** *Ella* ***to be*** *the club's chairwoman.*
→ see **vote**[1]

choosy /ˈtʃuzi/ *adjective*

- ► **choosy**
- ► **selective**
- ► **picky** (*informal*)
- ► **particular**

choosy
only willing to accept someone or something that you like or think is very good: *I get offered a lot of acting work, so I can be choosy. | She is very* ***choosy about*** *the books she will read.*

selective (AWL)
selective means the same as **choosy**, but sounds more formal and is the best choice when you are writing: *After winning an Oscar, he can afford to be more* ***selective about*** *the roles he takes.*

picky (*informal*)
someone who is picky will not accept many

things because there are a lot of things he or she does not like. It can sound slightly rude to say that someone is **picky**: *My daughter is a picky eater – the only vegetable she likes is corn.*

particular
very careful about what you think is good or acceptable, and wanting things to be done in the way you like. **Particular** is more formal than **picky** and is more polite: *As Joey has gotten older, he has become very **particular about** his clothes.*

chop *verb* → see **cut¹**

chore *noun* → see **job**

chubby *adjective* → see **fat**, Topic **Describing People's Looks**

church /tʃɚtʃ/ *noun*

- ► church
- ► cathedral
- ► chapel
- ► synagogue
- ► mosque
- ► temple

church
a building where Christians go to have religious services: *The Baptist church is the red-brick building with a steeple.*
→ **GRAMMAR:** When saying that someone goes to a religious service, don't use "a" or "the" with **church**. Say: *She goes to church every Sunday* or *She was in church this morning*.

cathedral
a big important church: *The president's funeral was held in the National Cathedral in Washington, D.C.*

chapel
a small church, or part of a church: *There's a small chapel in the hospital where family members of patients often go to pray.*

synagogue
a building where Jewish people go to have religious services: *Over the entrance to the synagogue is a large six-pointed star.*

mosque
a building where Muslims go to pray and have religious services: *Men gathered at the mosque for Friday evening prayers.*

temple
a building where Buddhists and other religions go to pray: *The Buddhist temple held several large golden statues of Buddha.*
→ see **religion**

circle¹ /ˈsɚkəl/ *noun*

- ► circle
- ► ring
- ► loop
- ► hoop
- ► oval
- ► disk

circle
a curved line or shape that forms a shape like the letter O: *Draw a circle around the correct answer. | We stood in a circle and took turns throwing the ball to each other. | The area where the red and blue circles overlap is purple.*

ring
an object, mark, or group of people or things that is shaped like the edge of a circle: *A ring of police officers surrounded the building. | There was a dirty ring around the bathtub.*

loop
a shape like a circle in a piece of string or wire: *Put the end of the string through the loop and pull it tight.*

hoop
a large piece of wood, metal, or plastic that is shaped like a ring: *The dog was trained to jump through the hoops.*

oval
a shape that is like a circle, but that is longer than it is wide: *A running track is an oval.*

disk
a flat round object: *The gold disk on the crown represents the sun.*
→ see **round¹**

circle

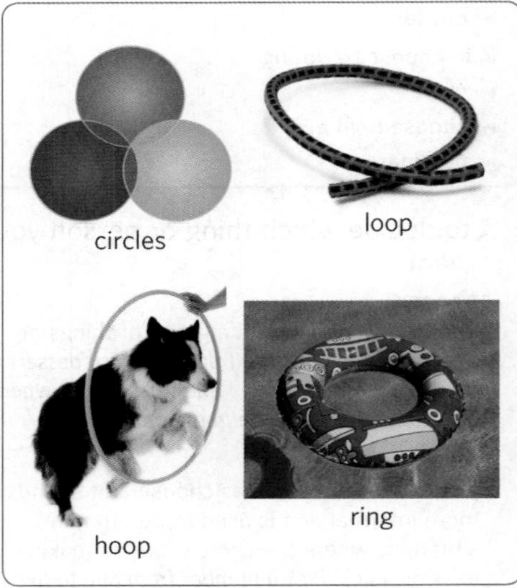

circle² /ˈsɚkəl/ *verb*

- ► circle
- ► orbit

circle
to move in the shape of a circle around something: *The plane circled the airport before landing.*

orbit
to move in a circle all the way around an object in space: *It takes a year for the Earth to orbit the Sun.*

circular *adjective* → see **round¹**

circumference /sɚˈkʌmfrəns/ *noun*

- ► circumference
- ► perimeter

circumference
the distance around the outside of a circle or a round object: *The island is only nine miles in circumference.*

perimeter
the total length of the sides of a shape such as a rectangle: *Measure the perimeter of the rectangle.*
→ You also use **perimeter** about the outside edge of a place or area: *Armed guards walk around the perimeter of the building.*

citizen /ˈsɪtəzən/ *noun*

- ► citizen
- ► taxpayer
- ► voter
- ► native
- ► resident
- ► patriot

citizen
someone who lives in a particular town, state, or country and has legal rights there: *She is now an American citizen.* | *The **citizens of** New Hampshire are the first to vote in the presidential primary elections.*

taxpayer
someone who pays taxes because he or she lives in an area: *The new government building will cost taxpayers $18 million.*

voter
someone who is allowed to vote in a particular city, state, or country. To have the right to vote, you have to be a citizen: *Younger voters preferred the Democratic candidate.*

native
someone who was born in a country: *He is a native of France and was born in Paris.*

resident (AWL)
someone who lives in a particular city, county, state, or country: *Local residents are complaining about the noise from the new road.*

patriot
someone who loves his or her country and is willing to defend it: *The monument honors the patriots who fought in World War II.*
→ see **person**, **population**

city *noun* → see **town**

civilization *noun* → see **society**

claim¹ /kleɪm/ *verb*

- ► claim
- ► allege
- ► insist
- ► argue

claim
to say that something is true, even though it might not be: *He **claims that** he didn't see anything.* | *The restaurant **claims to** use only organic vegetables in the soups it sells.*

allege
to say publicly that someone has done something wrong or illegal, although it has not been proved. **Allege** is often used in courts or in newspaper reports: *Harris **alleged that** Jones had tried to steal money from him.*

insist
to continue saying firmly that something is true, even when other people think you may not be telling the truth: *She **insists that** Tom was there, although he denies it.*

argue
to say that something is true and give clear reasons why you think this: *In the book, the author **argues that** women's most important job is to raise children.*
→ see **say**

claim² /kleɪm/ *noun*

- ► claim
- ► allegation

claim
a statement that something is true, even though it might not be: *Gould denied the **claim that** he had acted illegally.* | *The company has made **claims about** the health benefits of its products.*

allegation
a public statement that you think someone has done something wrong or illegal, which has not been proved: *There are **allegations that** the player was given $25,000 to deliberately lose the game.*

clap /klæp/ *verb*

- ► clap
- ► applaud (*formal*)
- ► cheer

clap
to make a noise by hitting your hands together, to show that you like something: *The audience clapped politely at the end of the concert.* | *"Hurray!" Bella cried, clapping her hands.*

applaud (*formal*)
if many people applaud, they clap to show that they like something: *When she finished speaking, the crowd applauded for a long time.*
→ You can also say that people **applaud** a decision or plan when they like it, but they do not actually clap: *The president's action was applauded by Congress.*

cheer
to shout as a way of showing that you support or like someone or something: *The crowd cheered when the team scored a goal.*

clap

clap

cheer

clash *noun* → see **fight²**

class /klæs/ *noun*

1 a group of students
- ► class
- ► grade

2 an occasion when someone teaches people
- ► class
- ► lesson
- ► period
- ► seminar

1 a group of students

class
a group of students who are taught together: *There are about 35 students **in the class**.*
→ You also use **class** about all the students in a particular year of school, in the phrases "freshman/junior etc. class" or "class of 2012/1995" etc.: *There were 2,225 students in the freshman class.* | *The class of 2001 had its ten-year reunion.*

grade (AWL)
one of the 12 years that students are in school in the U.S., or the students who are in that year: *My sister is **in tenth grade**.* | *The fifth and sixth grades worked together on the project.*
→ see Topic **Education**

2 an occasion when someone teaches people

class
an occasion when someone teaches a group of students: *What classes do you have this morning?* | ***In math class** the kids are learning about angles.*
→ You can also use **class** to talk about a series of lessons on a subject: *He is taking **a class in** photography at night school.*

lesson
an occasion when a teacher teaches a particular skill or subject, especially to only one person or to a small group: *She has piano lessons on Fridays.* | *The **lesson** was **on** multiplication.*

period (AWL)
one of the equal times that divide the school day, in which you have a class: *The students were taking a test **during first period**.*

seminar
a series of lessons in which a small group of students learn about a particular subject: *Students must take a seminar in their senior year.*
→ In a college or university, a **seminar** is similar to a normal class but is for a smaller group of people. In other situations people can take **seminars** that last only an hour or a day: *The one-day **seminar** is **on** planning your career.*
→ see **background** for **class** meaning "a group of people at a similar level in society"
→ see **category**, **subject**

GRAMMAR CHECK: class

Classes are usually **in** a subject: *They offer classes in ballet and tap.*

Lessons and **seminars** are usually **on** a subject: *The seminar was on Emily Dickinson's poetry.*

classic *adjective* → see **typical**, Topic **Books and Literature**

classify *verb* → see **sort**

clean¹ /klin/ *adjective*

- clean
- spotless
- immaculate (*formal*)
- pure
- sterile
- hygienic
- sanitary

ANTONYMS → see **dirty**

clean
not dirty: *She always keeps the house very clean.* | *He changed into some clean clothes.*

spotless
if a place or a piece of clothing is spotless, it is completely clean and has no dirty marks, especially because someone carefully cleans it: *Her kitchen is always spotless.*

immaculate (*formal*)
so clean and neat that something seems perfect: *The tables were covered with immaculate white tablecloths.* | *The house was immaculate.*

pure
pure air or water is clean and does not have anything harmful in it: *The water in the stream is pure and safe to drink.*

sterile
completely clean and having no bacteria so that something is safe to use in medicine or science: *The nurse put a sterile bandage on the wound.*

hygienic
clean so that people will not get diseases. **Hygienic** is used about keeping your body clean or keeping food, kitchens, and bathrooms clean: *The cows must be milked in hygienic conditions for the milk to be sold.*

sanitary
clean and not likely to cause diseases, especially diseases caused by body waste. **Sanitary** is used especially about keeping bathrooms clean and having clean systems for removing waste: *I keep the kitchen and bathroom sanitary, but otherwise I don't do much housework.* | *The campground has good sanitary facilities* (=bathrooms).

ADVERBS

You can make the adjectives **spotless** and **immaculate** into adverbs by using an **-ly** ending: *Her kitchen is spotlessly clean.* | *The house is beautifully decorated and immaculately clean.*

clean² /klin/ *verb*

1 to make something clean
- clean
- clean up
- wash
- wipe
- dust
- scrub
- mop

2 to make something completely clean so that it has no germs or bacteria
- cleanse
- disinfect
- sterilize
- purify

1 to make something clean

clean
to make something clean: *Your shoes need cleaning.* | *I clean the windows once a month.*

clean up
to make a place completely clean and neat, by putting things into the correct places and cleaning: *It took all morning to clean up the apartment.*

wash
to clean something using lots of water and usually soap. You use **wash** especially about clothes, dishes, parts of your body, and uncooked food: *Wash your hands before dinner.*

wipe
to remove dirt, water, etc. from something by moving a wet cloth or your hand across it: *Don't forget to wipe the countertops once you've finished washing the dishes.*

dust
to clean the dust (=very small pieces of dirt) off furniture and objects with a cloth: *Could you dust the living room, please?*

scrub
to clean something by rubbing it hard with a brush or cloth and soap and water: *She was on her knees scrubbing the kitchen floor.*

C

mop
to clean the floor with a wet mop. A **mop** is a tool with a long handle and a soft part that you put into water: *She was mopping the floor in the kitchen.*
→ see **sweep** for words meaning "to clean something with a brush"

2 to make something completely clean so that it has no germs or bacteria

cleanse
to make something completely clean, especially in order to get rid of germs or other things that are bad for you: *He cleansed the cut with soap and water.*

disinfect
to clean something with a chemical that kills bacteria: *Disinfect the toilet regularly.*

sterilize
to make something, for example a medical tool, completely clean and kill all bacteria in or on it. You usually use high temperatures or chemicals to **sterilize** things: *It is very important to sterilize baby bottles to keep your baby healthy.*

purify
to remove the dirty parts from something such as water or air, and usually to kill any bacteria in it: *To purify drinking water when you are camping, either boil the water or add a special tablet to it.*
→ see **wash**

clean

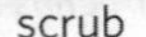
scrub

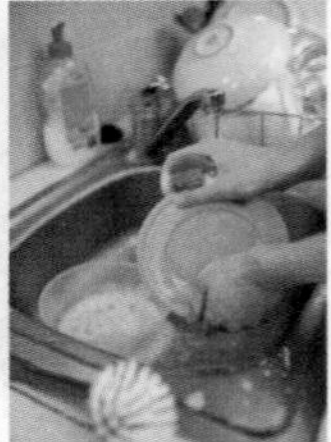
wash the dishes

mop

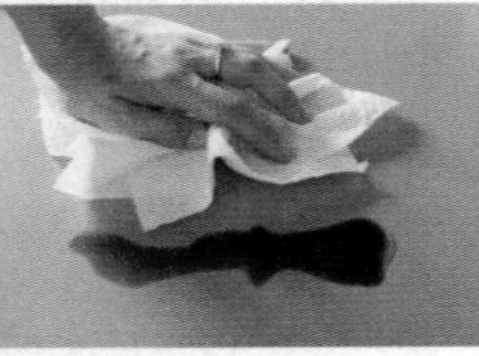
wipe

clear /klɪr/ *adjective*

1 if a substance is clear, you can see through it
► clear
► transparent
► see-through (*informal*)
► translucent (*formal*)
► sheer
2 easy to understand
► clear
► plain
► unambiguous (*formal*)
► explicit (*formal*)
► understandable
ANTONYMS → see **unclear**
3 easy to see
► clear
► distinct
► sharp
► legible

1 if a substance is clear, you can see through it

clear
easy to see through, and not colored or dirty: *The water was so clear that you could see the bottom of the lake.* | *The bottles were made of clear glass.*

transparent
if something is transparent, you can see through it. You use **transparent** about things that are solid, not about water: *The girls were wearing transparent plastic raincoats over their cheerleading uniforms.*

see-through (*informal*)
see-through means the same as **transparent** but sounds informal: *She was wearing a T-shirt under a black see-through top.*

translucent (*formal*)
not clear, but letting some light pass through. **Translucent** is often used about natural substances, such as paper, plastic, or skin, but it is not used about cloth or water: *The decorations were made of translucent paper and had little lights inside so that they glowed.*

sheer
a sheer material is very thin and fine so that it is almost transparent: *The stockings are made of sheer nylon.*

2 easy to understand

clear
easy to understand, hear, or read: *The*

instructions are clear and easy to follow. | *The doctor's advice was very clear: he must lose weight.*

plain
easy to understand, because of using simple words in a direct way: *She told him in plain language to sign the contract or leave.*

unambiguous (AWL) *(formal)*
completely clear because of having only one possible meaning: *His answer was unambiguous: "No, I won't let that happen."*

explicit (AWL) *(formal)*
said or written very clearly and including every detail so that no part of your meaning is hidden: *He gave explicit instructions that nobody should disturb him.*

understandable
possible for people to understand: *Politicians need to find ways to make the issues* ***understandable to*** *voters.*
→ see **obvious**

ADVERBS

You can make the adjectives that mean "easy to understand" into adverbs by using an **-ly** ending: *The instructions were clearly written.* | *He said explicitly that no one should disturb him.* | *Understandably, he didn't want to spend too much money.*

3 easy to see

clear
having details, edges, or lines that are easy to see, or shapes that are easy to recognize: *The TV has a very clear picture.* | *It was a beautiful day, and we had a clear view all the way to the Statue of Liberty.*

distinct (AWL)
an object, line, or shape that is distinct is very clear so that you can easily see that it is different or separate from the things around it: *The outline of the ship became more distinct as it approached the shore.*

sharp
if an image or photograph is sharp, you can see all the details and edges of objects very clearly: *I like my new printer – it prints sharp images with great color.*

legible
written or printed clearly enough for you to read: *Her handwriting is tiny, but it is legible.*
→ see **definite**, **obvious**, **sunny**

ADVERBS

You can make the adjectives that mean "easy to see" into adverbs by using an **-ly** ending: *From the top of the mountain, we could see clearly for miles.* | *You can see that the leaves from the two trees are distinctly different.* | *Please write legibly.*

clearly *adverb* → see **obviously**

clear out *phrasal verb* → see **empty²**

clever *adjective* → see **smart**

client *noun* → see **customer**

cliff *noun* → see **mountain**

climate *noun* → see **weather**, Topic **The Weather**

climax /ˈklaɪmæks/ *noun*

- ► climax
- ► high point

climax
the most exciting or important part of something, usually near the end: *The movie reaches its climax in the final scene.*

high point
a successful time or the best thing that happens in something such as someone's life: *Winning the award was a high point in the writer's career.*

climb¹ /klaɪm/ *verb*

- ► climb
- ► go up
- ► ascend *(formal)*
- ► scramble

climb
to go up toward the top of something, sometimes using your hands to help you: *Most kids love climbing trees.* | *Some boys had climbed onto the roof of the garage.* | *We climbed the steep mountain trail to a lake.*

go up
to walk up something such as a hill or stairs: *She went up the stairs.*

ascend *(formal)*
ascend means the same as **climb**: *Sir Edmund Hillary and Tenzing Norgay were the first men to ascend Mount Everest.*

scramble
to climb up or over something quickly, using your hands to help you: *He* ***scrambled over*** *the wall to get away from the dog.*

SYNONYM CHECK

Climb, go up, or ascend?

You **climb**, or **climb up**, trees, mountains, stairs, and ladders.

You can **ascend** mountains, stairs, and ladders, but not trees or other high things.

You can use both **climb** and **ascend** about airplanes or birds going upward into the sky: *The plane climbed to 10,000 feet.*

Go up is a general term and you can use it in all these situations: *The climbers went slowly up the mountain.* | *We watched the monkey go up the tree.* | *The plane went up into the sky.*

climb² /klaɪm/ *noun*

- ► climb
- ► ascent (*formal*)

climb
an act of going up toward the top of a tree, hill, or mountain. You use **climb** to show that you make a lot of effort: *It was a steep climb to the top of the hill.*

ascent (*formal*)
the act of going up to a high place. **Ascent** is often used about climbing mountains: *The climbers were preparing for the ascent of Mount Everest.*

clinic *noun* → see Topic **Medical Treatment**

clip *verb* → see **cut¹**

close¹ /kloʊz/ *verb*

- ► close
- ► shut
- ► slam
- ► seal
- ► fasten

ANTONYMS → see **open²**

close
to make something stop being open: *He closed the door.* | *Close your eyes and go to sleep.*
→ If a store **closes**, it stops letting customers in: *The store closes at 10 p.m.*

shut
shut means the same as **close**: *May I shut the window? I'm cold.*

slam
to shut a door, lid, etc. with a loud noise: *She left the room, angrily slamming the door behind her.*

seal *also* **seal up**
to close an entrance, container, or hole with something that stops things from going in or out: *The medicine bottle was sealed with plastic.* | *A large rock sealed up the entrance to the cave.*
→ You can also use **seal** about closing an envelope or package with something sticky like tape: *She sealed the envelope and put a stamp on it.*

fasten
to join together the two sides of something so that it is no longer open: *Have you fastened your seat belt?*
→ see **lock** for words meaning "to close something so that other people cannot open it"

SYNONYM CHECK

Close or shut?

You often use **close** and **shut** about your eyes, your mouth, a door, a window, or a container. **Shut** is sometimes used about closing something quickly and firmly: *He shut the door with a loud bang.*

Close sounds more careful: *She closed the door gently.*

close² *adverb, adjective* → see Function Words

close³ *noun* → see **end¹**

closed /kloʊzd/ *adjective*

- ► closed
- ► shut
- ► sealed

ANTONYMS → see **open¹**

closed
not open: *Her bedroom door was closed.* | *His eyes were closed and it looked like he was asleep.*

shut
shut means the same as **closed**: *Is the window shut?* | *She was sitting with her eyes shut.*

sealed
something that is sealed is completely closed so that nothing can get in or out: *Keep the fruit in a tightly sealed container so that it stays fresh.* | *He opened the sealed envelope and announced the winner of the award.*

SYNONYM CHECK

Closed or shut?

You can say that a door, gate, or someone's mouth or eyes are **closed** or **shut**.

If someone keeps his or her mouth **shut** or **closed**, that usually means that he or she is deliberately not saying anything.

You usually use **closed** about curtains or blinds.

GRAMMAR CHECK: closed

Closed is sometimes used before a noun. You can say: *He listened with closed eyes.*

You cannot use **shut** before a noun. Don't say: ~~*He listened with shut eyes.*~~ Say: *He listened with his eyes shut.*

closet /ˈklɑzɪt/ *noun*

- ► closet
- ► cabinet
- ► cupboard
- ► dresser
- ► bureau

closet
a place in a room where you hang your clothes. A **closet** is built into the wall of the room and has doors: *The closet is full of beautiful dresses.*

cabinet
a piece of furniture for keeping things in, which has a door and shelves and sometimes drawers: *She got the dog food out of the cabinet.*
→ **Cabinet** is sometimes used after a noun that shows what is in the cabinet: *He put the paper away in the file cabinet.* | *The vitamins are in the medicine cabinet in the bathroom.*

cupboard
cupboard means the same as **cabinet**, but **cupboards** are usually in a kitchen: *The sugar is in the cupboard next to the stove.*

dresser
a piece of furniture with drawers, used for keeping clothes in: *My socks and underwear are in the top drawer of the dresser.*

bureau
bureau means the same as **dresser**: *He shoved the T-shirts into his bureau drawer.*

cloth /klɔθ/ *noun*

- ► cloth
- ► fabric
- ► material
- ► textiles (*formal*)

cloth
something that is used for making clothes, sheets, curtains, and other things, which is made by weaving threads together: *His suit is made of dark gray cloth.*

fabric
fabric means the same as **cloth**: *I want to buy some fabric to make a skirt.*

material
material means the same as **cloth**: *She is helping me to choose the material for the bedroom curtains.*

textiles (*formal*)
different types of cloth. **Textiles** is usually plural, but you use **textile** when you are talking about the business of buying and selling cloth: *The museum has a collection of textiles ranging from an ancient linen sheet to rugs made in modern India.* | *The textile industry is important in Mexico.*

SYNONYM CHECK
Cloth, fabric, material, or textile?

If you are talking about cloth used to make things, you can use **cloth**, **fabric**, or **material**. People who sew a lot generally use the word **fabric**.

Cloth is used especially about material made from cotton or wool. If you are talking about the color of the cloth, you usually use **cloth** or **fabric**: *The dress is made of red cloth/fabric.*

If you are talking about the business of making or buying and selling cloth, you can say: *the textile/cloth industry* and *a textile manufacturer*. You cannot use **material** or **fabric** in either of these phrases.

clothes /kloʊðz/ *noun*

1 clothes
- ► clothes
- ► clothing
- ► outfit
- ► wardrobe
- ► uniform
- ► dress
- ► costume
- ► garment (*formal*)

2 words for clothes that are used in stores or in the business of making clothing
- ► garment (*formal*)
- ► apparel (*formal*)
- ► wear

1 clothes

clothes
the things that you wear, for example pants, dresses, underwear, and coats: *She always wears beautiful clothes.* | *I usually change my clothes as soon as I get home from work.*

clothing
clothing means the same as **clothes** but is more

formal: *They sell women's clothing.* | *It's cold here, so bring warm clothing with you.*

outfit
a set of clothes that you wear together, often for a special occasion: *I need a new outfit for the party.*

wardrobe
all the clothes that you own, or all the clothes that you wear at a particular time of year: *Jeans are an important part of anyone's wardrobe.* | *I need a new summer wardrobe.*

C

uniform
special clothes that people wear for some jobs, sports teams, or schools: *His baseball uniform was dirty and grass-stained.*

dress
clothes of a particular style or for a particular occasion: *The play was performed in modern dress.* | *Does the school have a dress code* (=rules about what kind of clothes you can wear)?
→ **GRAMMAR:** Don't use **dress** on its own. Say: *casual/formal/evening/national dress.*

costume
a set of clothes for acting in a play, or a set of clothes that you wear to make you look like someone or something else: *Who made the costumes for the play?* | *He wore a cowboy costume for Halloween.*

garment (*formal*)
one thing that you wear: *The princess wore garments made of silk and satin.*

SYNONYM CHECK
Clothes or clothing?

You **put on**, **take off**, or **change clothes**. **Clothing** is not usually used with these verbs. Don't say: ~~*put on clothing*~~. Say: *put on clothes.*

Clothing sounds more formal and is used to talk about clothes in general: *They need food and clothing.* You use **clothing** when talking about the business of making or selling clothes: *a clothing store.*

GRAMMAR CHECK: clothes

Clothes is a plural noun. Don't say: ~~*a clothe*~~. **Clothing** is a noun that has no plural and cannot be used with "a." Don't say: ~~*a clothing*~~ or ~~*clothings*~~. If you want to talk about one thing that you can wear, say **a piece of clothing, an article of clothing**, or **an item of clothing**: *He folded each piece of clothing neatly.*

2 words for clothes that are used in stores or in the business of making clothing

garment (*formal*)
one thing that you wear. **Garment** is often used when talking about the business of making clothes: *The garment industry employs about 14,000 people in San Francisco.*

apparel (*formal*)
clothes. **Apparel** is used in stores, and is used about the business of making clothes: *Women's apparel is on the first floor of the store.* | *She designs sportswear for a German apparel maker.*

wear
a particular kind of clothes, or clothes for a particular activity. You use **wear** when talking about types of clothes that are sold in stores: *The store specializes in outdoor wear.* | *Children's wear is on the first floor of the store.*
→ **GRAMMAR:** Don't use **wear** on its own. Say: *women's/men's/evening/casual etc. wear.* When another noun is put with **wear**, the combination is sometimes spelled as one word, for example "sportswear" or "footwear."
→ see **get dressed** for words meaning "to put clothes on your body"
→ see **coat**, **pants**, **shirt**

clothing *noun* → see **clothes**

cloud /klaʊd/ *noun*

- ► cloud
- ► fog
- ► mist
- ► haze
- ► smog

cloud
a white or gray thing in the sky that rain sometimes falls from. **Clouds** are made of many small drops of water: *There was a bright blue sky with a few white clouds.* | *The plane was flying above the clouds.*

fog
clouds that are near the ground and that are difficult to see through: *Traffic was moving slowly because of the thick fog.*

mist
cloudy air near the ground that is not as thick as fog: *A gray mist was hanging over the water.*

haze
smoke, mist, or dust in the air that is difficult to see through: *Winds blew away some of the haze caused by the fires.*

smog
dirty air caused by pollution from cars and

factories in cities: *The smog was so bad that you couldn't even see the mountains.*
→ see Topic **The Weather**

cloudy /ˈklaʊdi/ *adjective*

- ► cloudy
- ► gray
- ► overcast
- ► gloomy
- ► foggy
- ► misty
- ► hazy

cloudy
if it is cloudy, there are a lot of clouds in the sky: *It was cloudy and cold and looked like it might rain.*

gray
cloudy, so there is no blue sky and no sun showing: *The weather was cold and gray.*

overcast
if the sky is overcast, it is completely covered with clouds and makes the day seem dark, and it is likely to rain soon: *The day was overcast and it soon began to drizzle.*

gloomy
gloomy weather is dark and cloudy in a way that makes you feel sad: *The funeral took place under gloomy skies.*

foggy
if it is foggy, there is a lot of thick low cloud near the ground that is difficult to see through: *It was a foggy day in New York. | The accident took place on a foggy highway near Santa Cruz.*

misty
if it is misty, there is a lot of thin low cloud that is difficult to see through, but that is not as thick as fog: *It was a cool misty morning by the lake.*

hazy
if the sky is hazy, the air looks cloudy and it is difficult to see clearly, because there is smoke, dust, or mist in it: *The sun was a dull glow in the hazy sky.*
→ see Topic **The Weather**

club *noun* → see **organization**

clue *noun* → see **hint[1]**

clumsy /ˈklʌmzi/ *adjective*

- ► clumsy
- ► awkward
- ► uncoordinated

ANTONYMS → see **graceful**

clumsy
someone who is clumsy is likely to drop things or fall, and often moves in a way that is not graceful: *I felt clumsy on the dance floor – like my feet were three sizes too big. | Maria's clumsy boyfriend broke two plates while putting away the dishes!*

awkward
someone who is awkward feels uncomfortable and moves his or her body in a way that is not relaxed, usually because he or she is shy or embarrassed: *I remembered Tom as an awkward teenager who hardly spoke to anyone at the party.*

uncoordinated
not good at moving the different parts of your body in a controlled way. **Uncoordinated** people are not good at sports or other physical activities such as dancing: *I tried roller skating, but I am too uncoordinated and I kept tripping on my own skates.*

ADVERBS
You can make the adjectives **clumsy** and **awkward** into adverbs by using an **-ly** ending: *She ran clumsily up the street, almost tripping over her own feet. | He shook my hand awkwardly, seeming embarrassed.*

coach *noun* → see **teacher**

coarse *adjective* → see **rough**, Topic **Describing Texture**

coast /koʊst/ *noun*

- ► coast
- ► beach
- ► shore
- ► the seashore
- ► coastline

coast
the land next to the ocean: *The drive along the Pacific coast is really beautiful.*

beach
an area of sand or small stones at the edge of an ocean or lake: *In summer the beaches get very crowded.*

shore
the land along the edge of an ocean or lake: *The boat was about a mile from the shore.*

the seashore
the land along the edge of the ocean, where there is sand and rocks: *He walked with her along the seashore.*

coastline
the land at the edge of the ocean. You use **coastline** about a long area of land or the shape it makes, especially when seen from the air or the ocean: *The road follows the coastline for nearly 100 miles.*

C

coat /koʊt/ *noun*

- ► coat
- ► jacket
- ► raincoat
- ► overcoat

coat
something that you wear over other clothes to keep you warm outdoors: *He was wearing a long coat.*

jacket
a short coat: *He was dressed in jeans and a brown leather jacket.*

raincoat
a coat that keeps you dry in the rain: *People rushed through the rain in their raincoats.*

overcoat
a long warm coat: *It was a cold winter's day and he was wearing his overcoat.*

coat

coffin /ˈkɔfɪn/ *noun*

- ► coffin
- ► casket

coffin
the box in which a dead person is put in the ground or burned: *Four men were carrying the coffin to the grave.*

casket
casket means the same as **coffin**: *The dead man's body lay in an open casket.*

SYNONYM CHECK
Coffin or casket?

Coffin and **casket** mean the same thing, but a **coffin** is thought of as being flat on top and narrower at the foot. A **casket** sometimes has a rounded top and is rectangular.

coincidence *noun* → see **luck**

cold¹ /koʊld/ *adjective*

- ► cold
- ► cool
- ► chilly
- ► crisp
- ► freezing
- ► icy
- ► frosty
- ► bitter

ANTONYMS → see **hot (1)**

cold
having a low temperature: *It was a cold night in December.* | *I feel really cold – can we turn the heating on?*

cool
a little cold, especially in a way that feels pleasant: *He felt hot, so he poured himself a cool drink.*

chilly
a little cold, especially in a way that feels unpleasant: *Shut the window – it's getting chilly in here!*

crisp
cold, dry, and clear, in a way that seems pleasant: *The crisp mountain air is good for your health.*

freezing
very cold, especially in a way that makes you feel very uncomfortable: *You'll need your coat – it's freezing outside.* | *My feet were freezing.*

icy
very cold. You use **icy** when the temperature is below zero: *There was an icy wind, so she pulled her hat down over her ears.*

frosty
very cold so that the ground is covered in a frozen white powder: *It was a bright frosty morning.*

bitter
extremely cold in an unpleasant way: *A bitter wind was blowing from the east.*
→ see **cool²**, **unfriendly**

SYNONYM CHECK
Cold weather and feeling cold

You can use all of these words about the weather, the air, or the time of day: *It was a cold/freezing/frosty/bitter morning.*

You can use **cold**, **chilly**, and **freezing** to describe the way you feel or about a part of your body: *I'm so cold! | My hands are freezing. | I'm getting chilly.*

You cannot say: ~~*I am cool/icy*~~, but you can use **cool** or **icy** to talk about how someone's skin or a part of their body feels: *Her hands were cool/icy.*

You cannot use **crisp**, **frosty**, or **bitter** about the way you feel.

cold[2] /koʊld/ *noun*

- ► cold
- ► coldness
- ► chill

ANTONYMS → see **heat[1]**

cold
cold weather, or the feeling you have when you are cold: *Don't go out **in the cold** without your coat! | I was shivering **with cold**.*

coldness
the fact that something is cold - used especially about water or liquids: *The icy coldness of the water made him shiver.*

chill
a feeling of coldness in the air: *There was a slight chill in the air.*
→ see Topic **Medical Treatment** for **cold** meaning "a common illness that makes it difficult to breathe"
→ see **get cold** at **cool[2]**

collapse[1] *verb* → see **fall[1]**

collapse[2] *noun* → see **failure**

colleague *noun* → see **partner**, **worker**, Topic **Jobs and Work**

collect /kəˈlekt/ *verb*

- ► collect
- ► gather
- ► bring together
- ► accumulate (*formal*)

collect
to get things and put them together in one place so that the amount you have increases: *The teacher **collected** the homework **from** the students. | The information is **collected from** people across the nation.*
→ You can also use **collect** to mean "to get and keep objects of the same type because you think they are attractive, interesting, or valuable": *She collects stamps.*

gather *also* **gather up**
to get things from different places and bring them to one place: *He gathered up his books and put them in his bag. | The researchers have been gathering data about the effect of video games on children.*

bring together
to get people or things from different places and bring them to one place: *The university is going to bring together scientists from all over the world to work on the project.*

accumulate (AWL) (*formal*)
to gradually get more and more of something such as money, possessions, or knowledge: *Over his lifetime he accumulated a large number of paintings.*
→ see **raise** for "collecting money to help people"

SYNONYM CHECK
Collect or gather?

When you are talking about getting things, **gather** is used about things that are not very far apart, and **collect** is used about getting things from different people or places.

When you are talking about getting information, **collect** and **gather** have no difference in meaning.

collection *noun* → see **group**

college *noun* → see Topic **Education**

color[1] /ˈkʌlɚ/ *noun*

- ► color
- ► shade
- ► hue (*formal*)
- ► tint
- ► tone
- ► coloring
- ► pigment

color
red, blue, yellow, green, orange, etc.: *What color are his eyes? | The door was painted a bright blue color.*

shade
a particular type of a color: *The dress is a light shade of pink.*

hue (*formal*)
a color or shade of a color. **Hue** is used in literature and when talking about technical things: *The setting sun gave the rocks a golden hue.*

tint
a small amount of a color in something that is mostly another color: *The green leaves were beginning to show tints of orange and yellow.*

tone
one of the many different shades of a color. Each **tone** is slightly darker, lighter, or brighter than the next: *A lighter tone of yellow would look good in the kitchen.*

coloring
the color of something, especially someone's hair, skin, or eyes: *She has her mother's fair coloring.*

pigment
a natural substance that makes skin, hair, plants, rocks, etc. a particular color: *The artist uses natural pigments in her work.*

color² *verb* → see **dye**

colorful *adjective* → see **bright**

combat *noun* → see **fight²**, **war**

combination *noun* → see **mixture**

combine *verb* → see **mix**

come /kʌm/ *verb*

1 to arrive at a place
- ► come
- ► arrive
- ► get to
- ► reach
- ► land
- ► show up (*informal*)

ANTONYMS → see **go (1)**, **leave**

2 to go to a place with someone
- ► come with
- ► come along
- ► accompany
- ► escort
- ► join

3 to have been born in a place
- ► be born
- ► come from
- ► be from

4 to have developed from something
- ► come from
- ► be based on
- ► originate (*formal*)
- ► have its origins in
- ► be derived from (*formal*)
- ► be founded on
- ► go back to

1 to arrive at a place

come
to arrive at the place where you are now: *A letter came for you this morning.* | *What time is Dad coming home?* | *When the visitors come, send them up to my office.*

arrive
to get to the place you are going to: ***I arrived at** the party at around seven o'clock.* | *What time does the plane **arrive in** New York?*
→ **GRAMMAR:** Don't say: ~~*When did they arrive the hotel*~~? or ~~*When did they arrive to the hotel*~~? Say: *When did they arrive at the hotel?*

get to *also* **get home/get there/get here**
to arrive at a place. **Get to** is more informal than **arrive** and is used more often in everyday English: *What time do you usually **get to** work?* | *I'll call you when I get home.*

reach
to arrive somewhere, especially after a long trip, or after using a lot of effort: *When we finally reached the top of the mountain, we were all very tired.*
→ **GRAMMAR:** Don't say: ~~*We finally reached to the top*~~. Say: *We finally reached the top.*

land
if a plane or the passengers on a plane land, they arrive on the ground: *Our plane **landed at** about 10:30 in the morning.*

show up *also* **turn up** (*informal*)
to arrive somewhere, especially when someone is waiting for you: *She showed up an hour late for the meeting.* | *I had arranged to meet Tom, but he never turned up.*

2 to go to a place with someone

come with
if someone comes with you, he or she goes to a place with you: *Are you coming with us to the beach tomorrow?* | *My dad came to the United States with his brother in 1980.*

come along
to go somewhere with someone. **Come along** means the same thing as **come with**: *The party will be fun. Why don't you come along?*
→ **GRAMMAR:** You can say: *Come with us to the party* or *Come along to the party.*

accompany (AWL)
to go somewhere with someone, especially in order to give him or her help or protection: *Sylvia **accompanied** her grandmother **to** the doctor's office. | Children under 12 must **be accompanied by** an adult in the swimming pool.*

escort
to go somewhere with someone, especially in order to make sure that he or she gets there safely or does not escape: *Soldiers **escorted** the Secretary of State **to** the meeting.*

join
to go somewhere in order to be with someone or do something with someone: *I am still working, but I'll join you at the restaurant a little later.*

3 to have been born in a place

be born
if you were born in a place, you came out of your mother's body and began life in that place: *Carol was born in Texas and has lived there for her whole life.*
→ **GRAMMAR:** Don't say: ~~*She borned in Texas*~~ or ~~*She born in Texas*~~. Say: *She was born in Texas.*

come from
if you come from a place, you were born there: *Javier comes from Costa Rica.*
→ **GRAMMAR:** Don't say: ~~*Javier is coming from Costa Rica*~~.

be from
be from means the same as **come from**: *Her parents are from Thailand.*

4 to have developed from something

come from
to start somewhere, or to be first made or produced in a place, thing, or time: *A lot of medicines come from very common plants. | Many famous quotes come from Shakespeare's plays.*

be based on
if something is based on something else, that is where its basic ideas or facts come from: *Darwin's theory was based on his research in the Galapagos Islands.*
→ You often use **be based on** when saying that a movie, play, book, etc. gets its story from somewhere: *The movie is based on a popular novel.*

originate (*formal*)
to come from a particular place or start in a particular situation, especially a long time ago: *Yoga is a type of exercise that originated in India.*

have its origins in *also* **have its roots in**
to have developed from something and still be influenced by it: *Jazz has its roots in African music. | Chinese medicine has its origins in ancient philosophy.*

be derived from (AWL) (*formal*)
to be obtained from something else, especially using a special process: *Cheese is derived from milk.*
→ You often use **derive from** when saying where a word comes from: *Our word "science" derives from the Latin "scientia," meaning knowledge.*

be founded on
to have developed from an important basic idea, belief, etc.: *The U.S. Constitution was founded on the principles of liberty and freedom.*

go back to
to have developed from something that happened or existed a long time ago: *Our friendship goes back to our freshman year in college.*

→ see **come about** at **happen**,
→ see **come back** at **go back**
→ see **come down** at **rain²**, **snow²**
→ see **come forward** at **offer**
→ see **come in** at **enter**
→ see **come on** at **turn on/off**
→ see **come out** at **flow**
→ see **come over/by** at **visit**
→ see **come together** at **meet**
→ see **come up** at **appear**
→ see **come up with** at **think**

come before /ˌkʌm bɪˈfɔr/ *verb phrase*

- ► come before
- ► precede (*formal*)
- ► predate

come before
to exist or happen before an event or action or before something else in a series: *Our birthdays are both in April, but mine comes before my brother's. | His name comes before yours on the list. | It was a beautiful cool fall, which was a relief after the hot summer that came before it.*

precede (AWL) (*formal*)
precede means the same as **come before** but is used in formal writing and speech: *A flash of lightning preceded the thunder by a few seconds. | Prayers for the dead were preceded by songs praising God.*
→ When **precede** is used in the passive phrase "be preceded by," the first thing that happens is second in the sentence. So, in the sentence *The speeches were preceded by a dinner*, the dinner happened first, and the speeches happened after it.

predate
if one thing or event predates another, the first

thing happened or existed earlier in history than the other: *The ancient temple probably predates the Inca empire.*

comedy *noun* → see **humor**, Topic **Entertainment**

comfort¹ /ˈkʌmfɚt/ *noun*

1 a feeling of being relaxed
- comfort
- ease
- well-being
- relaxation

2 something that makes you feel calmer or happier
- comfort
- consolation
- reassurance

1 a feeling of being relaxed

comfort
the feeling of being physically relaxed and satisfied, for example because you have a nice soft chair, or the temperature is not too hot or cold: *It was nice to rest in comfort at the hotel after traveling all day.* | *Grandma sat on the porch, enjoying the **comfort of** a rocking chair.*

ease
a feeling of being relaxed, especially in a situation in which people might feel a little nervous: *The teacher tried to make the new students feel **at ease**.*

well-being
a feeling of being comfortable, healthy, and happy: *A good safe home is important for the child's sense of well-being.*

relaxation (AWL)
things that you do to make yourself feel relaxed in your mind and body: *At the end of the yoga class, we have five minutes for relaxation.*
→ see **luxury**

2 something that makes you feel calmer or happier

comfort
something that helps you feel less upset or worried: *Her religion has been a source of great comfort over the years.*

consolation
something that makes you feel less sad or disappointed, when what you wanted did not happen: *He lost the game but took some consolation in knowing he had done his best.*

reassurance
something that helps you feel calmer and less worried about something: *The doctor gave the patient reassurance that everything would be fine.*

comfort² /ˈkʌmfɚt/ *verb*

- comfort
- make someone feel better
- console
- reassure
- soothe

comfort
to make someone feel less worried or unhappy: *She put her arms around her crying child, to comfort her.*

make someone feel better
to make someone feel happier or less upset: *Why don't you tell me what's wrong? It might make you feel better.*

console
to help someone feel less sad or disappointed: *She tried to console him by reminding him that no one had done well on the test.*

reassure
to make someone feel less worried or frightened about something: *The doctor tried to reassure us that Mom would be okay.*

soothe
to make someone calmer when he or she is worried, angry, or upset: *Rocking the baby in your arms will help to soothe her.*

comfortable /ˈkʌmftəbəl/ *adjective*

1 feeling relaxed
- comfortable
- relaxed
- snug

2 making you feel relaxed
- comfortable
- relaxing
- pleasant
- cozy

1 feeling relaxed

comfortable
if you are comfortable, your body feels relaxed, for example because you are on a soft chair or bed, or you are not too hot or cold: *I was so comfortable and warm in bed I didn't want to get up.* | *Sit down and make yourself comfortable.*

relaxed
feeling calm and comfortable, and not worried: *Annie seemed relaxed and confident as she gave her speech.*

snug
comfortable because you are in a warm bed or room: *She lay warm and snug in bed, listening to the rain fall on the roof.*

ADVERBS

You can make the adjectives **comfortable** and **snug** into adverbs by using an **-ly** ending: *She sat comfortably in a large armchair. | She tucked her son snugly into bed.*

2 making you feel relaxed

comfortable
making your body feel relaxed, for example because you are on a soft chair or bed, and you are not too hot or cold: *I don't mind sleeping on the sofa – it's actually very comfortable. | Bring comfortable clothing for the camping trip.*

relaxing
making your mind feel relaxed and not excited or nervous: *I put on some relaxing music and sat down on the couch.*

pleasant
enjoyable and making you feel relaxed and happy: *It was pleasant to sit by the lake and watch the boats.*

cozy
a cozy room or place is small, warm, and comfortable: *The family gathered by the fireplace in the cozy living room.*
→ see **relaxed**

ADVERBS

You can make the adjectives **comfortable**, **pleasant**, and **cozy** into adverbs by using an **-ly** ending: *The bed was comfortably soft. | The room was pleasantly warm.*

command[1] *verb* → see **order**[2]

command[2] *noun* → see **order**[1]

comment[1] /ˈkament/ *noun*

- ► comment
- ► remark
- ► observation
- ► point
- ► statement

comment (AWL)
something that you say that shows your opinion about someone or something: *Jill made some interesting **comments about** the movie. | OK, does anyone have any comments or questions?*

remark
something that you say, for example about your opinion or something you have noticed: *He made a rude **remark about** my clothes. | Her **remarks on** the banking crisis were very interesting.*

observation
a comment on what you have noticed about something. **Observation** is more formal than **comment**: *Someone made the **observation that** Jenny has missed a lot of work lately.*

point
an idea or opinion that someone says in an argument or discussion: *Mrs. Woodall made a good **point about** the way bullying is dealt with at the school.*

statement
something that you say or write publicly and officially: *The president is expected to make a **statement about** the situation in the Middle East later today.*

comment[2] /ˈkament/ *verb*

- ► comment
- ► remark
- ► observe
- ► note (*formal*)

comment (AWL)
to say what you have noticed: *"The two boys seem very alike," she commented. | He **commented that** Ryan had grown a lot since he last saw him.*

remark
to say something, especially about something you have noticed: *"You look tired," he remarked. | Barbara **remarked that** she thought the movie was very good. | Her father **remarked on** how hard she had worked.*

observe
to say or write what you have noticed about something. **Observe** is slightly more formal than **remark** or **comment**: *"Tom and Rick argue a lot," she observed. | The doctor **observed that** some patients do not take their medications.*

note (*formal*)
to say or write that you have noticed that something is true, important, or interesting: *"Girls do just as well in math as boys," he noted. | The judge **noted that** Miller had never been arrested before.*

SYNONYM CHECK

Remark or comment?

Remark and **comment** can often be used in place of each other. However, you cannot use **remark** when you are asking for someone's opinion or saying that he or she will not give an opinion. Do not say: ~~*The president refused to remark on the progress of the talks*~~. Say: *The president refused to comment on the progress of the talks.*

commercial *noun* → see **advertisement**

committee *noun* → see **group**

common /ˈkɑmən/ *adjective*

1 happening often, or existing in many places
- ► **common**
- ► **widespread**
- ► **prevalent** (*formal*)
- ► **commonplace**
- ► **frequent**
- ► **typical**

ANTONYMS → see **rare**

2 shared by several people or things
- ► **common**
- ► **mutual**
- ► **shared**

1 happening often, or existing in many places

common
happening often, or existing in many places: *Maple trees are common in Canada.* | *García is a very common last name.* | *It is* ***common for*** *children* ***to*** *be afraid of the dark.*

widespread (AWL)
happening in a lot of places or done by a lot of people: *Many people are concerned about the widespread use of chemicals in farming.*

prevalent (*formal*)
common at a particular time, in a particular place, or among a particular group of people: *The flu is most prevalent in the winter months.*

commonplace
common in a particular place or time. You use **commonplace** to show that something that is unusual or surprising in one time or place is common in a different time or place. **Commonplace** is used in writing: *Having a computer in the home became commonplace within a very short time.*

frequent
happening very often: *It was hard to get my work done because there were frequent interruptions.*

typical
happening in the way that something usually happens: *Cool weather is* ***typical of*** *early April.*

ADVERBS

You can make the adjectives **common**, **prevalent**, **frequent**, and **typical** into adverbs by using an **-ly** ending: *Children are commonly afraid of the dark.* | *We were frequently interrupted by phone calls.* | *April is typically cool.*

2 shared by several people or things

common
if several people or things have common beliefs, ideas, or problems, they all have the same beliefs, ideas, or problems: *Students and teachers are working toward a common goal.* | *Problems such as poor housing and bad traffic are* ***common to*** *all big cities.*

mutual (AWL)
a feeling that is mutual is felt by two or more people for each other: *Our relationship has always been based on mutual respect.*
→ You can also use **mutual** to describe the word **friend** when you mean that you and another person are both friends with a particular person: *Ava and I met when a mutual friend introduced us at a party.*

shared
a shared interest, belief, emotion, or opinion is one that you and at least one other person have, feel, or believe: *The Amish community has a strong set of shared values and religious beliefs.* | *Raising a child is a shared experience like no other.*

communicate /kəˈmyunəˌkeɪt/ *verb*
- ► **communicate**
- ► **get in touch with**
- ► **contact**
- ► **reach**
- ► **correspond** (*formal*)
- ► **get a hold of** (*informal*)

communicate (AWL)
to speak or write to someone and tell him or her something: *Now that we live in different cities, we* ***communicate*** *mostly* ***by*** *email.* | *The students come from all over the world, but they* ***communicate with*** *each other in English.*

get in touch with
to telephone or write to someone: *If you want to*

get in touch with me, it's best to call me on my cell phone.

contact (AWL)
to telephone or write to someone, especially for the first time. **Contact** is more formal than **get in touch with**: *He was contacted by the company and invited to come for a job interview.*

reach
to be able to talk to someone on the telephone: *You can* ***reach*** *me* ***at*** *my work number until 5 p.m.*

correspond (AWL) (*formal*)
if two people correspond with each other, they write letters to each other: *The writer* ***corresponded with*** *many friends and relatives over her long life, and most of them kept her letters.*

get a hold of (*informal*)
to succeed in being able to talk to someone, especially on the telephone: *I kept trying to get a hold of Linda, but she wasn't answering her phone.*
→ see **express**, **talk**[1]

communication /kəˌmyunəˈkeɪʃən/ *noun*

- ► communication
- ► contact
- ► correspondence (*formal*)

communication
speaking or writing to people so that they know about your ideas and feelings: ***Communication between*** *parents and teachers is very important.* | *Salespeople need good communication skills because they talk to a lot of different people.*

contact (AWL)
if you are in contact with someone, you often talk or write to him or her: *Have you* ***stayed in contact with*** *any of your friends from high school?* | *After my parents got divorced, I had no contact with my dad at all.*

correspondence (AWL) (*formal*)
if you are in correspondence with someone, you send letters to that person and receive letters from him or her: *He was* ***in correspondence with*** *her for several years before they finally met.*
→ **Correspondence** also means the letters that someone sends and receives, especially business letters: *A secretary deals with his correspondence.*

community *noun* → see **society**

company /ˈkʌmpəni/ *noun*

- ► company
- ► business
- ► firm
- ► corporation
- ► enterprise (*formal*)
- ► establishment (*formal*)

company
an organization that makes or sells things or provides a service, in order to make money: *My father worked for the same company for 30 years.* | *I called the phone company about the bill.*

business
a company. A **business** can be big or small, but you usually use **business** about companies that employ only a small number of people: *She started a small business selling homemade cupcakes to restaurants.*

firm
a company that provides a service, rather than producing goods: *Carol is an attorney who works for a large law firm in Washington, D.C.*

corporation (AWL)
a large company that often includes several smaller companies: *Microsoft is one of the biggest corporations in the world.*

enterprise (*formal*)
a company. **Enterprise** is used especially in newspapers, and often shows that someone has had the idea for a business and started it: *The company began as a small family enterprise, but now employs thousands of people.*

establishment (AWL) (*formal*)
an organization, especially a store, restaurant, etc.: *The neighborhood has a mix of residential buildings and commercial establishments.*
→ **Establishment** is usually used in phrases such as "commercial establishment" (=any business that sells something) or "retail establishment" (=store).
→ see **guest** for **company** meaning "someone who is with you"
→ see **business**, Topic **Jobs and Work**

compare /kəm'per/ verb

- ► compare
- ► make a comparison
- ► contrast
- ► make a distinction between
- ► draw a parallel (*formal*)
- ► draw an analogy (*formal*)
- ► check against

C

compare
to think about how two or more people or things are similar or different: *When we got our tests back, my friend and I compared our grades.* | *He is an incredible basketball player and some people have **compared** him **to** Michael Jordan.*

make a comparison *also* **draw a comparison**
to compare two or more things or people, and often say that they are similar in some way: *Richards **drew a comparison between** America in the 1770s and what is happening now in the Middle East.* | *We **made a comparison of** the two paintings and decided they were by the same artist.*

contrast (AWL)
to say how two things or people are different: *In the novel, he contrasts the lives of two families living in New York, one of them rich and the other poor.*
→ Students are often asked to **compare and contrast** two things in essays. This means that they should find the similarities and the differences between them.

make a distinction between *also* **draw a distinction**
to say that you think two related things are very different: *It is important to make a distinction between scientific facts and things that people believe are true.*

draw a parallel (*formal*)
to say that things are similar in some ways: *It is possible to **draw a parallel between** the professions of acting and politics.*

draw an analogy *also* **make an analogy** (*formal*)
to say that two things are similar, even though they seem very different at first: *Some people have **drawn an analogy between** poetry and mathematics, saying that they both express complex ideas in a short form.* | *The artist explained the creative process by **making an analogy with** childbirth.*

check against
to compare something with something else to see if they are the same: *The teacher **checked** the names of the children who were present **against** her list of registered students.*

comparison /kəm'pærəsən/ noun

- ► comparison
- ► analogy (*formal*)
- ► parallel

comparison
the process of comparing two people or things: ***In comparison to** his brother, he is really shy.* | *New York City is so full of people that Atlanta seemed empty **by comparison**.*

analogy (AWL) (*formal*)
the process of saying that one thing is like another in some way, although the things may seem very different at first: *Dr. Wood explained the movement of light **by analogy with** the movement of water.*
→ An **analogy** is also a similarity between two things: *There are **analogies between** human and animal behavior.*

parallel (AWL)
if you draw a parallel between two things, you say that they are like each other in some way: *It is possible to draw a **parallel between** the professions of acting and politics.*
→ A **parallel** is also a similarity between two things: *There are many **parallels between** the political situation now and the situation in the 1930s.*
→ see **make a comparison** at **compare**

compete *verb* → see **play**[1], Topic **Sports and Exercise**

competition /ˌkɑmpə'tɪʃən/ noun

1 an event in which people try to be the best
- ► competition
- ► championship
- ► tournament
- ► contest

2 a situation in which people try to be more successful than other people
- ► competition
- ► rivalry

1 an event in which people try to be the best

competition
an organized event in which people or teams try to be the best at doing something: *He entered his*

photograph **in a competition** and won first prize. | We were watching the swimming competition on TV.*

championship
a competition to find the best player or team, especially in a sport: *Shannon Miller has won more world championships than any other American gymnast.*

tournament
a competition in which many players or teams compete against each other until there is one winner: *Our team is playing in the state basketball tournament in March.*
→ A **tournament** is usually not as important as a **championship**, and does not involve as many players or teams.

contest
a competition in which a person or team does an activity, and a group of judges decides which of them is the best: *The winner of the school essay contest will receive $100.*
→ see **game**, **sport**, Topic **Sports and Exercise**

2 a situation in which people try to be more successful than other people

competition
a situation in which people or organizations try to be more successful than other people or organizations: *There's a lot of* ***competition between*** *the big supermarkets.*

rivalry
a situation in which two or more people, teams, or companies try to do better than each other over a long period of time: *There was an intense* ***rivalry between*** *the American and Russian teams.*

complain /kəm'pleɪn/ *verb*

- ► complain
- ► grumble
- ► whine
- ► make a complaint
- ► protest
- ► object

complain
to say that you are annoyed about something or not happy with something: *My dad is always* ***complaining about*** *his job. | I* ***complained to*** *the manager of the restaurant because the food was so bad.*

grumble
to keep complaining about something, especially something that is not very important: *Larry was* ***grumbling about*** *having to wash all of the dishes.*

whine
to complain in a sad annoying voice about something. You use **whine** to describe what children do: *He cries and whines when he doesn't get what he wants.*

make a complaint
to tell someone in an official position that you are not satisfied with something that he or she is responsible for: *Parents* ***made a complaint to*** *the principal* ***about*** *bullying in the school.*

protest
to say that you think something is wrong and should not be allowed to happen. **Protest** is used especially about groups of people who meet in a public place to show that they do not approve of something: *Over a million people marched to* ***protest against*** *the war.*

object
to say that you do not like or approve of something: *She wanted to travel around Europe before starting college, but her parents* ***objected to*** *the idea because they thought she was too young.*

complaint /kəm'pleɪnt/ *noun*

- ► complaint
- ► objection
- ► protest
- ► grievance (*formal*)

complaint
a statement in which someone complains about something: *I called the police to* ***make a complaint about*** *the noise next door. | There were a lot of* ***complaints about*** *the food in the cafeteria.*

objection
a statement in which someone says that he or she opposes or disapproves of an idea or plan: *The mayor wants to close some schools, but there have been strong* ***objections from*** *the community.*

protest
something you say or do because you think something is wrong or unfair: *She ignored the children's protests and turned off the TV. | Students organized a* ***protest against*** *the school's new dress code.*

grievance (*formal*)
a complaint because you think you have been treated unfairly: *The meeting will give employees the opportunity to discuss problems and grievances.*
→ see **make a complaint** at **complain**

C

complete[1] /kəmˈplit/ *adjective*

- ► complete
- ► total
- ► absolute
- ► utter
- ► sheer
- ► pure
- ► downright (*informal*)

complete
in every way: *The news that she is getting married came as a complete surprise. | Doctors expect him to make a complete recovery following the surgery.*

total
total means the same as **complete**: *The job interview was a total disaster – I was not prepared for any of their questions.*

absolute
complete and without any doubt: *How can you know with absolute certainty that he is telling the truth? | The lawyer said he had absolute proof that Nicholls was guilty.*
→ You can also say that someone has "absolute power/control/authority" (=complete power, etc.): *In those days, the king had absolute power, and no one was allowed to disobey him.*

utter
complete or extreme. **Utter** is used especially to describe feelings and qualities: *She gave me a look of utter confusion, so I tried to explain the problem again.*

sheer
complete, without any other quality or feeling: *I fell asleep immediately from sheer exhaustion.*

pure
complete. **Pure** is used especially about strong feelings: *There was pure joy on the runner's face as he finished the race in first place.*

downright (*informal*)
complete – used when you strongly disapprove of something bad: *That's a downright lie! I never said that. | Some of his ideas are downright dangerous.*
→ see **done** for **complete** meaning "finished"

GRAMMAR CHECK: complete

All the words in this section are always used before a noun: *The apartment was a complete/total/absolute mess. | He had a look of utter/sheer/pure terror on his face.* However, **absolute** is sometimes used after "be": *The silence in the room was absolute.*

complete[2] *verb* → see **finish**

completely /kəmˈplitli/ *adverb*

- ► completely
- ► totally
- ► absolutely
- ► entirely
- ► utterly (*formal*)
- ► fully (*formal*)
- ► wholly (*formal*)

completely
in every way or to the greatest degree possible: *I completely forgot that it's his birthday today. | We took one wrong turn and got completely lost.*

totally
totally means the same as **completely** but sounds a little more informal: *She looks totally different with short hair. | He totally ignored my advice.*

absolutely
completely – used especially to emphasize something, or to show that you strongly agree with something: *The view was absolutely amazing. | You're absolutely right – we can't all fit in one car.*

entirely
completely and in every possible way: *I think that we need an entirely new approach to the problem.*
→ **Entirely** is often used after "not": *I am not entirely sure what he meant.*

utterly (*formal*)
completely or extremely. **Utterly** is used especially to say how bad or wrong something is: *With all of the noise, it was utterly impossible to work.*

fully (*formal*)
completely – used especially about understanding or explaining something: *Most people are fully aware of the dangers of smoking to their health.*

wholly (*formal*)
in every possible way: *Newborn babies are wholly dependent on their parents for all their needs.*

complicated /ˈkɑmpləˌkeɪtɪd/ *adjective*

- ► complicated
- ► complex
- ► elaborate
- ► involved
- ► intricate

ANTONYMS → see **simple**

complicated
having a lot of different parts, and difficult to

understand or deal with: *The rules of the game seem very complicated.* | *Many people want stricter laws about the environment, but it is a complicated issue.*

complex (AWL)
a complex process, relationship, etc. is difficult to understand because it has a lot of parts that are all connected in different ways: *Learning to read is a complex task, because you must link sounds with letters, join the sounds together, and understand the meaning.*

elaborate
having a lot of different parts or details and carefully planned or designed: *The actors wore elaborate costumes decorated with beads and feathers.*

involved
very long and complicated and difficult to understand. **Involved** is used especially about something that you think should be made simpler: *The story was so long and involved that I started to lose interest in it.*

intricate
containing many small parts or details. **Intricate** is used especially about something that you think is very well designed or made: *The women in the village weave baskets with intricate designs in them.*

ADVERBS
You can make the adjectives **elaborate** and **intricate** into adverbs by using an **-ly** ending: *The costumes were elaborately decorated.* | *The baskets have intricately woven designs on them.*

compliment[1] *noun* → see **praise**[2]

compliment[2] *verb* → see **praise**[1]

component *noun* → see **part**

compound *noun* → see **mixture**

compulsory *adjective* → see **necessary**

computer *noun* → see Topic **Computers and the Internet**

conceal *verb* → see **hide**

concentrate *verb* → see **pay attention**

concept *noun* → see **idea**, **theory**

concerning *preposition* → see Function Word **about**

conclude *verb* → see **decide**, **end**[2], **finish**, **think**

conclusion *noun* → see **decision**, **end**[1]

condition /kənˈdɪʃən/ *noun*

1 how something or someone is (nouns)
- ► condition
- ► state
- ► shape

2 words for describing something in good condition (adjectives)
- ► in good condition
- ► like new
- ► perfect

3 words for describing something in bad condition (adjectives)
- ► in bad condition
- ► shabby
- ► run-down
- ► battered
- ► derelict (*formal*)
- ► dilapidated (*formal*)
- ► decrepit (*formal*)
- ► worn
- ► threadbare

1 how something or someone is (nouns)

condition
how someone or something is, for example old or new, healthy or unhealthy, neat or messy: *Though the car was old, its condition was very good.* | *She keeps herself **in good physical condition** by exercising three times a week.*

state
the condition that someone or something is in, especially at a particular time. **State** is used especially when things are not in a good condition. **State** is not used when you are talking about someone's physical fitness: *When we bought the house, it was **in a terrible state**.* | *The accident happened so fast, and afterward we were all **in a state of** shock.* | *The president gave a speech on the state of the nation.*

shape
the condition that someone or something is in. **Shape** is usually used with words such as "good," "great," and "bad." **Shape** sounds less formal than **condition**: *The economy is **in** worse **shape** now than it was last year.* | *He is **in** great **shape** from working out in the gym.*
→ If someone is **in shape**, he or she is in good physical condition.

2 words for describing something in good condition (adjectives)

in good condition *also* **in good shape**
if something is in good condition or in good shape, it is the way it should be with little or no damage: *I'll only buy used clothes if they're in really good condition.*
→ You can use other adjectives besides **good** in this phrase: *Dad takes good care of his car, and it's still in great shape.*

like new *also* **as good as new**
in very good condition even though someone has used it: *His car was ten years old but still looked like new.* | *Your watch just needs cleaning and it'll be as good as new.*

perfect
in the best possible condition: *She wore braces for a couple of years and now her teeth are perfect.*
→ see **perfect (1)** and **strong (3)** for other words you can use to describe something that is in good condition

3 words for describing something in bad condition (adjectives)

in bad condition *also* **in bad shape**
broken or damaged because of being used a lot or because of being old. **In bad condition** is more formal than **in bad shape**: *The house is in bad shape, and it will need a lot of work before we can live in it.* | *After being left out in the rain, the old chair was in worse condition than it was before.*
→ You can use other adjectives besides **bad** in this phrase to show how bad the condition of something is. **Poor** and **terrible** are some of the most common adjectives: *The books were in terrible condition after the flood, so we threw most of them out.*

shabby
shabby clothes, places, or objects are in bad condition because they are old and have been used a lot: *Paul was wearing a shabby old suit with a hole in the sleeve.* | *The kitchen in the apartment was dark and shabby.*

run-down
a building or area that is run-down is in very bad condition, especially because the people who live there do not have very much money: *The movie takes place in a run-down section of Los Angeles.*

battered
something that is battered is in bad condition and looks old because it has been used a lot. You use **battered** about objects but not about places: *He arrived at our house with a battered old suitcase in his hand.*

derelict (*formal*)
a derelict building or piece of land is in very bad condition because no one has used it in a long time: *The warehouses by the dock are derelict and will probably be demolished.*

dilapidated (*formal*)
a building that is dilapidated is in very bad condition and has broken things that need to be repaired: *We stayed in an old dilapidated hotel with a leaky roof.*

decrepit (*formal*)
decrepit buildings, structures, or objects are old and in very bad condition and are likely to break or fall down: *The old bridge looked so decrepit that I was afraid to walk on it.*

worn
worn cloth is old and is thin or weak in some places: *There was some old furniture and a worn rug in the living room.*

threadbare
clothes, rugs, or pieces of cloth that are threadbare are very thin and almost have holes in them because they have been used so much: *It is his only coat, so he wears it even though it has become threadbare.*
→ see **sickness** for **condition** meaning "a medical problem"
→ see **situation**

conditions *noun* → see **situation**, **weather**

conference *noun* → see **meeting**

confess *verb* → see **admit**

confession /kən'feʃən/ *noun*

- ► confession
- ► admission
- ► acknowledgment (*formal*)

confession
a statement in which you admit that you committed a crime or did something wrong, especially an official statement to the police: *He made a confession to the police shortly after his arrest.* | *In his* ***confession****, Davis described how he had robbed the bank.*

admission
a statement in which you admit that you were wrong or that you have done something bad: *The Senator's* ***admission that*** *he had lied to Congress shocked Americans.*
→ **Admission** can also be used when someone does something that people think is a way of

admitting he or she has done something wrong: *The company agreed to settle the lawsuit without going to court, and people saw this as an* ***admission of guilt.***

acknowledgment (*formal*)
a statement that shows you accept that something has happened or is true: *The president offered an* ***acknowledgment that*** *mistakes had been made.*

confidence /ˈkɑnfədəns/ *noun*

- ► confidence
- ► self-confidence
- ► self-esteem
- ► morale

confidence
the feeling that you can do things well: *You need patience and confidence to be a good teacher.* | *I went into the test full of confidence, but it was more difficult than I had imagined.*

self-confidence
confidence in your abilities when you are dealing with other people: *Some teenage boys are shy and lacking in self-confidence.*

self-esteem
the feeling that you are a good person and that you deserve to be liked and respected: *Sports should build a child's self-esteem, not damage it.*

morale
the level of confidence, satisfaction, and hope that a group of people feels: *Morale among the soldiers is extremely low and many want to give up the fight.*
→ see **trust²**

confident /ˈkɑnfədənt/ *adjective*

- ► confident
- ► self-confident
- ► self-assured
- ► brash
- ► arrogant
- ► bold
- ► secure

confident
someone who is confident believes he or she can do something well and does not feel nervous: *You will feel more* ***confident about*** *riding when you have been on a horse a few times.* | *He began to read in a calm confident voice.*

self-confident
feeling sure about your ability to do things well and sure that people like or respect you. **Self-confident** people are not shy or nervous in social situations: *Mario is very self-confident. He won't be nervous about singing in front of the whole school.*

self-assured
self-assured means the same as **self-confident**: *She is a top student, relaxed and self-assured.*

brash
behaving and talking in a loud and confident way that annoys other people: *The brash young businessman has offended some people, but his business is growing.*

arrogant
behaving in a very confident and sometimes rude way that shows you think you are more important or more intelligent than other people: *He is a smart boy, but he can be very arrogant about it.*

bold
showing that you are confident and not afraid to offend people or do something dangerous or new: *He was a difficult man to work for, but no one was bold enough to complain about him.*

secure (AWL)
a secure person feels confident, safe, and happy: *The teachers at the school work hard to make the children feel secure.*
→ see Topic **Describing People's Character**

ADVERBS

You can make the adjectives **confident**, **brash**, **arrogant**, and **bold** into adverbs by using an **-ly** ending: *Jenny reads aloud confidently.* | *"The test was so easy," he said arrogantly.*

confirm *verb* → see **prove**, **say**

confirmation *noun* → see **proof**

confuse /kənˈfyuz/ *verb*

- ► confuse
- ► puzzle
- ► perplex (*formal*)
- ► baffle
- ► mystify

confuse
to make you feel that you do not understand something or do not know what to do: *I tried to explain the math problem in a different way, but it only confused him.* | *The new tax law is so complicated it has confused everyone.*

puzzle
if something puzzles you, it confuses you because you cannot understand it and it is different from what you expect: *The crash*

puzzled experts, as they believed the plane was safe to fly.

perplex (*formal*)
if a problem perplexes you, it confuses you and worries you, and it is difficult to understand: *The illness perplexed the doctors – they had never seen anything like this before.*

baffle
if something baffles you, you cannot understand it at all, even though you try very hard to: *The cause of the disease continues to baffle scientists.*

mystify
if something mystifies you, it is so strange or confusing that you cannot understand or explain it: *Her disappearance has mystified her friends and neighbors.*

C

confused /kən'fyuzd/ *adjective*

- confused
- puzzled
- bewildered
- perplexed (*formal*)
- baffled
- mystified

confused
not able to understand what someone is saying or what is happening: *I'm a little confused – could you explain it again? | She gave me a confused look.*

puzzled
confused because you cannot understand something, especially because it is different from what you expect: *"I thought the car was in the garage," she said with a puzzled expression on her face. | Mac was puzzled. "Why would she do that?" he said.*

bewildered
very confused and surprised when something happens that is unusual or that you do not expect: *He was bewildered to find three police officers at the front door.*

perplexed (*formal*)
confused and worried by an event or situation that you do not understand: *Her father was perplexed when she told him she did not want to get married.*

baffled
very confused and unable to understand something, even though you have tried hard for a long time: *The detectives are baffled. They have no idea how the painting was stolen.*

mystified
completely unable to understand something and very surprised, because it seems strange: *"How could you possibly have known that?" he asked, totally mystified.*

confusing /kən'fyuzɪŋ/ *adjective*

- confusing
- puzzling
- bewildering
- perplexing (*formal*)
- baffling

confusing
something that is confusing is difficult to understand because it is complicated and not clear: *The instructions on the box were so confusing that I could not put the table together.*

puzzling
making you feel unsure about why something happened, especially when it is different from what you expect: *Kara's behavior was puzzling. Why did she refuse to run in the race, when everyone expected her to win?*

bewildering
making you feel extremely confused and not sure what to do or think: *David's sudden anger was bewildering to his children. | There is a bewildering number of computers to choose from.*

perplexing (*formal*)
making you feel confused and worried, especially because something seems strange: *Scientists have found this problem perplexing, because there is no obvious explanation.*

baffling
very confusing, even though you have tried hard to understand something: *The detectives say that it is one of the most baffling cases they have ever dealt with.*

congratulate *verb* → see **praise**[1]

Congress *noun* → see Topic **Government and Politics**

connect /kə'nekt/ *verb*

- connect
- make a connection
- relate to
- associate (*formal*)
- link

connect
to notice or show that there is a relationship between two things, events, or people: *At the time I didn't connect the two events in my mind, but now I can see that one caused the other. | The evidence **connects** him **with** two other robberies.*

make a connection
to notice that two people or things are connected: *Most people do not* ***make a connection between*** *the energy they waste and environmental problems.*

relate to
to be involved with something else or to affect that thing: *The activities in the book relate to specific ideas in science.*

associate (*formal*)
to always think of two things together, because they often happen together: *I always* ***associate*** *the smell of baking* ***with*** *my grandmother's house.*

link (AWL)
to say or show that one thing causes or affects another. **Link** is often used in reports about science or medicine: *Scientists have recently* ***linked*** *the drug* ***to*** *heart disease.*
→ see **join** for **connect** meaning "join together"

connected /kəˈnektɪd/ *adjective*

- ► connected
- ► related
- ► associated (*formal*)
- ► linked
- ► relevant
- ► corresponding (*formal*)

connected
if two things, people, or events are connected, they are involved with each other or affect each other: *Both men died that day, but their deaths were not connected. | He was* ***connected to*** *a terrorist group.*

related
related means the same as **connected**: *The lawyers showed how the two events were related. | The cloud of smoke was not* ***related to*** *the fire downtown – it came from a factory outside of the city.*
→ When you are talking about information that is connected to something, or information about something, you can use **relating to**: *My family is looking for legal information relating to U.S. citizenship.*

associated (*formal*)
connected with someone or something, usually by happening or existing together, or because one thing causes the other: *There are some risks* ***associated with*** *playing football, such as neck injuries. | Was he ever* ***associated with*** *the Mafia?*

linked
if two things are linked, one causes or has an effect on the other. **Linked** is often used in reports about science or medicine: *These chemicals are* ***linked to*** *several forms of cancer.*

relevant (AWL)
directly connected to what you are talking about or doing: *Dr. Connelly's evidence is* ***relevant to*** *the case, because he believes the murderer is mentally ill.*

corresponding (AWL) (*formal*)
caused by or connected with an idea, fact, or number that you have already mentioned: *An increase in the number of cars on the road leads to a corresponding increase in the amount of pollution. | He accepted the job and its corresponding $600,000 salary.*

connection /kəˈnekʃən/ *noun*

- ► connection
- ► relationship
- ► link
- ► association (*formal*)
- ► correspondence

connection
something that makes things or people connected with each other: *There is a* ***connection between*** *how much you weigh and how healthy you are. | Eleven people were arrested* ***in connection with*** *the attack.*

relationship
relationship means the same as **connection**. You use **relationship** especially when the situation is complicated and there are several things involved: *There is a* ***relationship between*** *smoking and lung cancer, so people who smoke are more likely to get cancer.*

link (AWL)
a connection between two or more situations or events in which one causes or affects the other: *The experiment did not show a* ***link between*** *watching violence on TV and violent behavior.*

association (*formal*)
a connection in your mind that makes you think of two things together because they often happen together: *For me, the smell of suntan lotion has an* ***association with*** *a summer day at the pool.*

correspondence (AWL)
a connection between ideas, facts, or numbers. **Correspondence** is often used in writing about science and math: *In German there are no silent letters. There is a direct* ***correspondence between*** *the letters in a word and the sounds in the word.*
→ see **make a connection** at **connect**

conquer *verb* → see **beat**

conscience /ˈkɑnʃəns/ *noun*

- ► conscience
- ► morals
- ► principle
- ► scruples
- ► standards

conscience
the feeling inside you that tells you that you should not do something: *My conscience told me I shouldn't go with them, but it looked like so much fun!*
→ You can say that someone has a **good** or **clear conscience** when he or she has done something right, or a **bad** or **guilty conscience** when he or she has done something wrong: *I don't have a guilty conscience telling the teacher about him – he was bullying her.*

morals
the basic ideas that a person or society has about what is good and right behavior, especially in matters of sex: *Morals and attitudes changed in our society during the 1960s so that more people lived together without getting married.*

principle (AWL)
a moral rule or belief about what is right and wrong that helps you decide what you should or should not do: *My grandfather was a man who had very strong principles. He would never lie or cheat.*

scruples
beliefs about what is right and wrong that prevent you from doing something bad: *His scruples would not allow him to keep the money he had found.*

standards
personal rules of behavior, based on an idea of what is morally good and right: *I am the oldest child, and my parents expected me to set high standards of behavior for my younger brother.*
→ see **guilt**, **morality**

conscious *adjective* → see **awake**, **deliberate**

consequences *noun* → see **effect**, **result**

conservation *noun* → see **protection**, Topic **The Environment**

conservative /kənˈsɚvətɪv/ *adjective*

- ► conservative
- ► right-wing

ANTONYMS → see **liberal**

conservative
a conservative person believes that the government should not limit people's freedom, and wants lower taxes and fewer controls on business: *My father became more conservative as he got older.*

right-wing
being on the conservative side of politics, or showing very conservative political beliefs: *One of the party's right-wing ideas is that businesses should pay lower taxes because they create jobs.*
→ see **traditional**, Topic **Government and Politics**

consider *verb* → see **think**

consist of *phrasal verb* → see **include**

constant /ˈkɑnstənt/ *adjective*

1 happening a lot over a long period of time
- ► constant
- ► continual
- ► ongoing
- ► persistent
- ► chronic

2 continuing and never stopping
- ► constant
- ► continuous
- ► perpetual
- ► nonstop
- ► never-ending
- ► relentless

3 not changing and always the same
- ► constant
- ► steady
- ► stable
- ► consistent
- ► unchanging

1 happening a lot over a long period of time

constant (AWL)
happening very often over a long period of time: *The car is old and needs constant attention to keep it running.* | *He keeps in constant contact with his family in Costa Rica.*

continual
continual means the same as **constant**: *He has a medical condition that needs continual attention, so he cannot leave his house.*

ongoing (AWL)
happening now and continuing over a period of time: *Police say they cannot discuss the ongoing investigation into the murder.*

persistent (AWL)
continuing to happen, even though you try to get rid of it. You use **persistent** especially about illnesses or problems that are not very serious: *Smoking has given him a persistent cough.*

chronic
a chronic illness, condition, or problem is one that continues for a long time and cannot be cured: *She has chronic asthma and has to carry an inhaler everywhere.* | *When the factories closed, people in the area suffered from chronic unemployment.*
→ see **frequent**

ADVERBS

You can make the adjectives **constant**, **continual**, **persistent**, and **chronic** into adverbs by using an **-ly** ending: *The car constantly needs repairing.* | *Unemployment is persistently high, despite efforts to get people back to work.* | *She stopped working in order to take care of her chronically ill child.*

2 continuing and never stopping

constant (AWL)
continuing and never stopping: *I'm so tired of listening to your constant whining.* | *He suffered constant pain in the months before his death.*

continuous
continuous means the same as **constant** but sounds more formal: *There has been continuous fighting on the border for the past week.*

perpetual
continuing forever or for a long time. You use **perpetual** especially about bad situations or feelings that do not change: *The people live in a perpetual state of fear because of the war.*

nonstop
without stopping, or seeming not to stop: *The movie is 120 minutes of nonstop action.*
→ **GRAMMAR: Nonstop** can also be used as an adverb: *She was so excited that she was talking nonstop.*

never-ending
seeming to continue forever: *After the disaster, there was a never-ending flow of people coming to ask for help.*

relentless
if something bad is relentless, it never seems to stop or improve: *She was under relentless pressure from her parents to get good grades.*

ADVERBS

You can make the adjectives **constant**, **continuous**, **perpetual**, and **relentless** into adverbs by using an **-ly** ending: *She constantly complains about everything.* | *Have you lived continuously in the United States for more than five years?* | *It rained relentlessly for two whole weeks.*

3 not changing and always the same

constant (AWL)
always staying at the same level or amount. **Constant** is used especially about temperature and speed: *We keep the room at a constant temperature to protect the old books from damage.* | *The boat moved ahead at a fairly constant speed.*

steady
staying the same for a long time, especially when this is a good thing: *She listened to the steady rhythm of her son's breathing as he slept.*
→ You also use **steady** about things that change in the same way over a long period: *There has been steady growth in the economy for the past six months.*

stable (AWL)
a situation that is stable stays the same, with no big changes or problems: *The weather conditions should remain stable for the rest of the week.* | *She comes from a stable family.*

consistent (AWL)
always doing something or always happening in the same way: *When you go to bed and get up at the same time each day, this consistent pattern helps you to sleep better.*

unchanging
staying the same for a very long time. **Unchanging** is usually used in formal writing: *We drove for miles through the unchanging flat landscape.*
→ see **same**

ADVERBS

You can make the adjectives **steady**, and **consistent** into adverbs by using an **-ly** ending: *I could feel his heart beating steadily in his chest.* | *The White House consistently opposed the bill.* **Constantly** is not used as an adverb with this meaning.

constantly *adverb* → see **always**, **often**

construct *verb* → see **build**[1]

construction *noun* → see **building**

consult *verb* → see **discuss**

consumer *noun* → see **customer**

contact[1] *noun* → see **communication**

contact[2] *verb* → see **communicate**, **write**

contagious /kən'teɪdʒəs/ *adjective*

- ► contagious
- ► infectious

contagious
if a disease is contagious, it spreads easily and you can easily get it from another person: *This is the area of the hospital where people with highly contagious diseases stay.* | *The illness is contagious until the itchy spots go away.*

infectious
an infectious disease is spread from one person to another: *The group is raising money to fight AIDS and other infectious diseases.*

→ You can say that a person is **contagious**, but you cannot say that a person is **infectious**: *People with a cold are contagious for about a week.*

contain *verb* → see **include**

contemporary *adjective* → see **modern**

content *adjective* → see **happy**, Topic **Describing People's Emotions**

contest *noun* → see **competition**

context *noun* → see **background**

continue /kən'tɪnyu/ *verb*

1 to not stop doing something
- ► continue
- ► keep
- ► go on
- ► persist (*formal*)
- ► persevere (*formal*)
- ► stick to (*informal*)
- ► maintain (*formal*)
- ► sustain (*formal*)

ANTONYMS → see **stop[1]**

2 to happen without stopping
- ► continue
- ► keep
- ► last
- ► go on
- ► endure
- ► persist (*formal*)

ANTONYMS → see **end[2]**

1 to not stop doing something

continue
to not stop doing something: *Students who want to continue their education can go to college or community college.* | *She wants to continue working after she has had the baby.* | *The rain continued to fall.*

keep *also* **keep on doing something**
to continue to do something. **Keep** is a little more informal than **continue**. You use **keep** especially when someone uses a lot of effort, or when someone does something a lot in an annoying way: *The rescue workers kept on working through the night.* | *The coach keeps telling us to run faster, but we can't.*

go on
to continue doing something for a long time, or continue after stopping: *The two men went on arguing.* | *The old lady looked at me and then went on with her knitting.*

persist (AWL) (*formal*)
to continue to do something, especially in a determined or annoying way: *I didn't want to answer her question, but she* ***persisted in*** *asking me.*

persevere (*formal*)
to continue trying to do or practice something difficult: *He* ***persevered at*** *soccer and began to improve.*

stick to (*informal*)
stick to means the same as **persevere**: *If you stick to it, you will play the guitar really well one day.*

maintain (AWL) (*formal*)
to make something continue in the same way as before: *Though they now live in different cities, they have maintained close family ties.*

sustain (AWL) (*formal*)
to make something continue to exist or happen for a long time: *The company hopes the ads will help sustain its recent growth.*

2 to happen without stopping

continue
to happen without stopping: *The cheering continued even after the President asked everyone to sit down.*

keep *also* **keep on doing something**
to continue being in a particular situation or state, or continue developing in a particular way: *We were expecting warmer weather, but it keeps getting colder.*

last
to happen for a period of time: *The thunder* ***lasted for*** *more than 20 seconds.*

go on
if something goes on, it continues to happen for a long time: *The party will* ***go on for*** *hours.*

endure
if something good endures, it continues for a long time: *They've had some problems, but their marriage has endured.*

persist (AWL) (*formal*)
if something bad persists, it continues: *The pain persisted, so Manny went to the doctor.*

contract *noun* → see **agreement**

contrast[1] /kən'træst/ *verb*

- ► contrast
- ► conflict
- ► contradict

contrast (AWL)
if two things contrast, they are different in a way that is very easy to see and that may be surprising: *The crisp white snow on the mountains* ***contrasted*** *sharply* ***with*** *the clear blue sky.* | *Alicia's friendly personality* ***contrasts with*** *her twin brother's shyness.*

conflict (AWL)
if two ideas or pieces of information conflict, there are differences between them so that they cannot both be true or right: *The results of the tests* ***conflicted with*** *the results of previous experiments.*

contradict (AWL)
if one idea or piece of information contradicts another one, they are very different or opposite and cannot both be correct or true: *The evidence he gave in court contradicts the statements from the other witnesses.*
→ see **compare**

contrast[2] *noun* → see **difference**

contribute *verb* → see **give**, **take part**

control *verb* → see **manage**, **operate**

conversation /ˌkɑnvə'seɪʃən/ *noun*

- ► conversation
- ► chat (*informal*)
- ► talk
- ► discussion
- ► dialogue

conversation
if two or more people have a conversation, they talk about things in an informal way: *I had a great* ***conversation with*** *Mark at dinner last night.*

chat (*informal*)
a friendly conversation with someone you know well: *I called my friend Suzanna for a chat.*

talk
if people have a talk, they speak about things with each other. You use **talk** especially when one person is explaining something to someone or telling another person about something: *The professor* ***had a talk with*** *Joanna about her grades.*

discussion
if people have a discussion, they discuss or argue about their ideas and opinions: *My family had a* ***discussion about*** *where we might go on vacation.*

dialogue *also* **dialog**
a conversation in a movie, television program, book, or play, or these conversations in general: *Writing good dialogue will make your story seem more realistic and interesting.*
→ see **talk[1]** for "have a conversation"
→ see **discussion**

convince *verb* → see **persuade**

cook[1] /kʊk/ *verb*

1 to make food ready to eat
- ► cook
- ► make
- ► fix (*informal*)
- ► prepare

2 to cook food in a particular way
- ► fry
- ► bake
- ► roast
- ► boil
- ► steam
- ► broil
- ► grill

1 to make food ready to eat

cook
to make food ready to eat, usually by heating it: *Who is cooking dinner tonight?* | *Brendan likes to cook.*

make
to cook or prepare food so that it is ready to eat: *I'm making lunch. Do you want a sandwich?* | *Dad made a pasta dish for dinner.*

fix (*informal*)
fix means the same as **make**: *Dad was fixing breakfast for all of us.*

prepare
prepare means the same as **make** but sounds

C

more formal: *Tonight the chef has prepared roast pork and potatoes with local squash.*

2 to cook food in a particular way

fry
to cook something in hot oil or butter on top of the stove: *You only have to fry the fish for a few minutes.*

bake
to cook something such as bread or cake in an oven: *Put the cookies in the oven and bake them for ten minutes.* | *Antonio likes to bake his own bread.*

roast
to cook meat or vegetables in an oven: *For our dinner, I decided to roast the vegetables along with the beef.*

boil
to cook food in very hot water, or to cook a liquid until it is so hot it makes bubbles: *To make a soft-boiled egg, you boil the egg for three minutes.* | *Boil the sugar and water together until the sugar turns a golden brown.*

steam
to cook something using steam: *Steam the broccoli for about seven minutes.*

broil
to cook food by putting it directly over or under flames or heat. You usually broil meat: *Broil the pork chops for three minutes on each side before you serve them.*

grill
to cook food on a frame over a fire: *Dan was grilling in the backyard.* | *Grill the shrimp until they are pink.*

cook² /kʊk/ *noun*

- ► cook
- ► chef

cook
someone who makes food so that it is ready for people to eat: *One of the cooks at the diner accidentally started a fire in the kitchen.* | *My mother is a great cook.*

chef
someone who has had special training to cook and works in a restaurant: *The chef has decided to put lamb on the menu tonight.*

cooking *noun* → see **food**, Topic **Eating in a Restaurant**

cool¹ *adjective* → see **cold¹**, **light²**

cool² /kul/ *verb*

- ► cool
- ► get cold
- ► chill
- ► refrigerate
- ► freeze

cool *also* **cool down/off**
to become less hot, or make someone or something less hot: *Wait for the dish to cool before you try to pick it up.* | *Cool yourself down with some cold lemonade.*

get cold
to become cold: *When the oil in your engine gets cold, it becomes thicker.* | *The weather is getting colder, and soon the snow will fall.*

cook

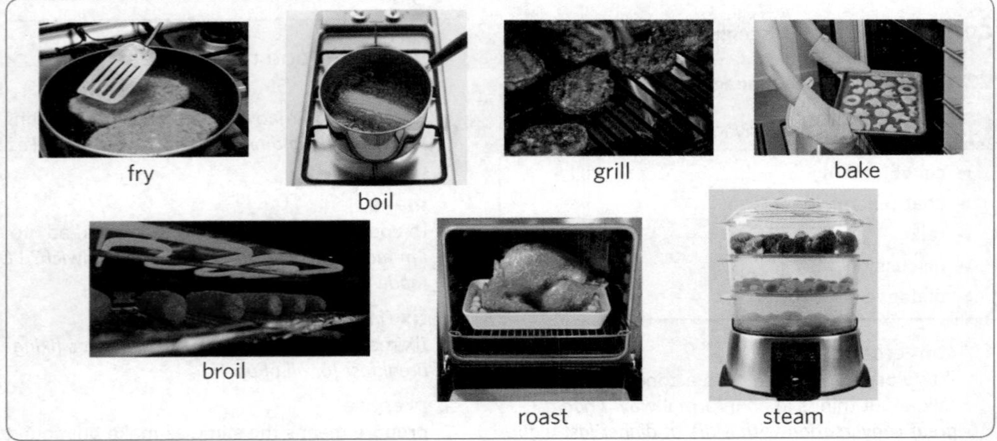

chill
to make something cold in a refrigerator: *Chill the dough for four hours before baking the cookies.*

refrigerate
to put food into a refrigerator to keep it cold and fresh: *Refrigerate the jam after opening the jar.*

freeze
if liquid freezes or something containing liquid freezes, it becomes solid and hard because it is so cold: *Freeze the meat that you do not use.* | *It was so cold that the water pipes in the house froze.*

cooperate /koʊ'ɑpəˌreɪt/ *verb*

- ► cooperate
- ► work together
- ► collaborate
- ► unite

cooperate (AWL)
to work with someone else in order to achieve something that you both want: *If we all cooperate, we will get this job done a lot faster.* | *Because lions **cooperate with** each other during a hunt, they can attack much larger prey.*

work together
if two or more people work together to do something, they do it as a group, not alone: *Many countries are **working together to** stop terrorism.* | *My sister and I started **working together on** this quilt about a month ago.*

collaborate
collaborate means the same as **work together** but sounds more formal: *Lennon and McCartney **collaborated on** writing many of The Beatles' songs.*

unite
to work together with other people to achieve something, even though everyone may have different ideas or opinions: *Democrats in Congress **united behind** the president.* | *The people of the town have **united against** the closing of their school.*

cooperation /koʊˌɑpə'reɪʃən/ *noun*

- ► cooperation
- ► teamwork
- ► collaboration

cooperation (AWL)
the act of working with someone or doing as he or she asks, without being forced or persuaded: ***Cooperation between** teachers and students is the key to our school's success.* | *The Dallas police force is working **in cooperation with** the FBI to catch the criminals.*

teamwork
the ability of a group of people to work well together: *By working on the task in groups, students learn the value of teamwork.*

collaboration
the act of working with another person or group in order to achieve or produce something: *He wrote the script **in collaboration with** a friend.* | *The project involves **collaboration between** schools and local businesses.*

cop *noun* → see **police officer**

cope *verb* → see **deal with**

copy[1] /'kɑpi/ *noun*

- ► copy
- ► duplicate
- ► photocopy
- ► model
- ► replica
- ► reproduction
- ► clone
- ► simulation

copy
something that is made to look exactly the same as something else: *Print out a **copy of** the letter to keep in the file.* | *Make a **copy of** the disk so that you do not lose the data.*
→ You can also use **copy** to talk about one book or magazine from the large number that were printed: *I picked up a paperback copy of the novel at the library.*

duplicate
an exact copy of something, which you can use in the same way. You use **duplicate** especially about documents and other printed things: *Several **duplicates of** the photograph had been printed.*

photocopy
a copy of a piece of writing or a picture that you make on a copy machine: *You can make **photocopies of** the page on the machine over there.*

model
a small copy of something such as a building or machine. **Models** can be used to show people what something looks like or what it does, either before it is built or when it is in a different place: *The museum has a four-foot **model of** the Statue of Liberty that you can look inside.*

replica
a copy of a famous machine, structure, or other object. A **replica** is often the same size as the

original: *The building is an exact **replica of** the original Globe Theatre.*

reproduction
a copy of an old or valuable work of art or a piece of furniture: *A **reproduction of** Van Gogh's painting "Sunflowers" was hanging on the wall.*

clone
an animal or plant that is an exact copy of another one, and that is produced by taking a cell from the original plant or animal and making it grow: *These plants are all **clones of** the same original plant.*

simulation (AWL)
something that uses machines or computers to make a situation seem real, especially in order to test something: *The company uses a computer simulation to train pilots.*

→ see **fake**[1], **make a copy** at **copy**[2]

C

copy² /ˈkɑpi/ *verb*

1 to copy an object or information
- ► **copy**
- ► **duplicate**
- ► **photocopy**
- ► **make a copy**
- ► **reproduce** (*formal*)
- ► **copy down** (*informal*)
- ► **trace**
- ► **clone**
- ► **simulate**

2 to copy what someone does or says
- ► **copy**
- ► **imitate**
- ► **mimic**
- ► **do an impression**
- ► **impersonate**
- ► **do what someone does**

3 to copy something when it is wrong or illegal to do this
- ► **copy**
- ► **plagiarize**
- ► **forge**

1 to copy an object or information

copy
to make or write something that is the same as something else or very similar to it: *Copy the disk and store it in a safe place.* | *The first people who designed airplanes tried to copy the way birds fly.*

duplicate
to make an exact copy of something: *It is hard to duplicate the colors exactly when you print the picture on a different printer.*

photocopy
to copy writing or a picture on a copy machine: *Carlos was photocopying his passport to send in with his application.*

make a copy
make a copy means the same as **photocopy** but sounds a little more informal: ***I made a copy of** the recipe for her.*

reproduce (*formal*)
to print a copy of a photograph, work of art, or document, especially in a book or newspaper: *Some of Adams' photographs are reproduced in his biography.*

copy down (*informal*)
to copy a short piece of information by writing it down: *I copied down her phone number and address.*

trace (AWL)
to copy a picture by putting thin paper over it and then drawing along the lines you can see through the paper: *The children traced the map of the United States and then wrote in the names of the places they had visited.*

clone
to make an exact copy of a plant or animal by taking a cell from it and developing it artificially: *Scientists successfully cloned a sheep called Dolly in 1996.*

simulate (AWL)
to produce something that is not real, but has the appearance or feeling of being real: *The machine simulates conditions in space and is used to train astronauts.*

2 to copy what someone does or says

copy
to behave, speak, or move in the exact same way as someone else: *Be careful what you say, because your little brother will copy you.* | *People who are listening to someone will often copy their movements.*

imitate
to copy the way someone behaves, speaks, or moves, especially to make other people laugh: *Julia was imitating Mom and the way she yells at us.*

mimic
mimic means the same as **imitate**, but it is used especially about the way someone speaks, and is often done in an unkind way: *"Be in my office in ten minutes!" Elaine said, mimicking the principal's voice.*

do an impression
to copy the way someone famous speaks or moves, especially to entertain people: *He does a great impression of the president.*

impersonate
to pretend to be someone by copying the way he or she speaks or looks, often in order to entertain or trick people: *She impersonates many Hollywood stars, such as Marilyn Monroe.* | *He was arrested for impersonating a police officer.*

do what someone does
to do the same things as someone else, especially in order to learn from him or her: *Watch the way I move my feet, and do what I do.*

3 to copy something when it is wrong or illegal to do this

copy
to make or write something that is the same as something else, when you should not do this or when it is illegal: *The teacher warned us not to copy our friends' work.* | *Their business competitors had copied their designs for the phone.*

plagiarize
to copy someone else's words or ideas and pretend they are your own: *If you use more than ten words from any article without saying where they are from, the teacher will say you have plagiarized.*

forge
to make or copy something in order to make people think it is real: *He is accused of forging paychecks by using his boss's signature.* | *The painting looked like a Picasso, but it was forged.*
→ see **cheat**

corner /ˈkɔrnɚ/ *noun*

- ► corner
- ► intersection
- ► turn

corner
the point at which two roads meet: *I saw the dog **on the corner of** Oak Street, but it ran away.* | *The car went around the corner onto Victory Avenue.*
→ You also use **corner** about the place where two walls, sides, or edges meet: *He was standing in the corner of the room.*

intersection
a place where two or more roads meet and cross each other, often where there is a traffic light: *The light was not working **at the intersection**.* | *Take a right at the **intersection of** routes 28 and 16.*

turn
a place where you turn from one road onto another, especially in a vehicle or on a bicycle: *Take the right turn after the red mailbox.*

corporation *noun* → see **company**

correct[1] *adjective* → see **right[1]**, **true**

correct[2] /kəˈrekt/ *verb*

- ► correct
- ► make a correction
- ► rectify (*formal*)
- ► proofread

correct
to change a piece of writing so that there are no mistakes, or explain the right way to say or write something: *There were some mistakes in the letter, but we corrected them before we sent it out.* | *"Me and Patrick are going outside," said Jack. "Patrick and I are going outside," his mother said, correcting him.*

make a correction
to correct a mistake in a piece of information or language: *I would like to **make a correction to** something I said earlier. I gave the man's name as Wright, but it is actually Wrightson.*

rectify (*formal*)
to correct a problem or mistake: *As soon as we saw the problem, we put measures in place to rectify it.*

proofread
to carefully check and correct spelling mistakes, grammar, and other details in a piece of written work: *Did you proofread your English paper?*
→ see **check[1]**, **improve**

correspond *verb* → see **communicate**, **match[1]**, **write**

correspondence *noun* → see **communication**, **connection**, **letter**

corridor *noun* → see **hall**

corrupt *adjective* → see **dishonest**

corruption *noun* → see **dishonesty**

cost[1] /kɔst/ *noun*

- ► cost
- ► price
- ► value
- ► rent
- ► fare
- ► charge
- ► fee
- ► expenses
- ► rate

cost
the amount of money you have to pay for something: *The stadium was built **at a cost of***

over $300 million. | *Does this include the cost of delivery?*

price
the amount of money that you must pay in order to buy something that is being sold: *Airline ticket prices have gone up again.*

value
the amount of money that something is worth: *A new kitchen can increase the value of your home.*

rent
the amount of money that you pay to live in a place or use something for a period of time: *How much is **rent on** a two-bedroom apartment in this part of town?*

fare
the amount of money you pay to travel by bus, plane, or train: *I didn't have enough money for the bus fare to get home!*

charge
the amount of money you have to pay to do or use something: *There's a small charge for Internet access at the hotel.*

fee (AWL)
an amount of money that you pay to do something, especially to enter a place, join a group, or get advice from a lawyer or doctor: *The gym membership fee is $100 a year.*

expenses
the amount of money that you have to spend on something: *He had to borrow money to pay for his legal expenses.* | *The insurance company will pay for all my medical expenses.*

rate
a charge that is different at different times, for different people, or for other reasons: *Some hotels offer special rates for senior citizens.* | *You may be able to get a lower rate in the winter.*

cost[2] /kɔst/ *verb*

- cost
- be
- sell for
- retail for
- be priced at
- come to

cost
to have a particular price: *A movie ticket costs $10.* | *I really liked the dress, but it cost too much.*

be
to cost a particular amount of money. **Be** is usually used with numbers: *These shoes were only $15.*

sell for *also* **go for**
to be sold at a particular price. **Go for** is more informal than **sell for**: *How much did your bike sell for in the end?* | *Houses in this area usually go for about $200,000.*

retail for
to be sold at a particular price in stores: *The new video game retails for $34.99.*

be priced at
to have a particular price. Use **be priced at** when giving the exact price that a store or company charges for something: *The downloads are priced at 99 cents per song.*

come to
to cost an amount when several prices are added together: *We ordered a lot of food and the bill came to $100!*

costly *adjective* → see **expensive**

costume *noun* → see **clothes**

count /kaʊnt/ *verb*

1 to find out an amount by using mathematics
- count
- add
- total
- figure out
- calculate (*formal*)
- estimate
- tally
- assess

2 to make a record of an increasing amount
- keep count
- keep score
- keep track
- keep a tally

1 to find out an amount by using mathematics

count *also* **count up**
to find the number of things in a group by saying or thinking numbers in order, usually starting with 1: *The teacher counted the students before they left the museum to make sure everyone was there.* | *We counted up the money, and there was $495.*

add *also* **add up**
to put numbers together to find the total: *When you add 4 and 28, the answer is 32.* | *Add up all the numbers in the first column and write the answer at the bottom.*

total *also* **total up**
to add up numbers to find a total, especially when you are adding lots of numbers or groups

of numbers that each have their own separate totals: *Once the scores have been totaled, we will announce the winner.*

→ You can also say that something **totals** an amount, after everything has been added together: *The cost of repairs totaled over $3,000.*

figure out
to find out a number or amount using mathematics in order to answer a question or solve a problem. **Figure out** is used more often than **calculate** in everyday English: *He needs to figure out how much the trip is going to cost.*

calculate (*formal*)
to find out an amount using mathematics. **Calculate** is more formal than **figure out**: *Sally **calculated that** she needed $600 to pay all of her bills.*

estimate (AWL)
to guess an amount as exactly as you can, based on the knowledge you have: *She didn't have a scale, but she **estimated that** the box weighed about 20 pounds.*

tally *also* **tally up**
to count something by recording each thing and then adding them to find the total number: *When the votes were tallied, 80% of the students voted against the idea.*

assess (AWL)
to find out the value or cost of something using mathematics: *The value of the home was assessed at $1.2 million.*

→ see **add**, **subtract**

2 to make a record of an increasing amount

keep count
to count and record the number of things in a group as it increases: *I haven't **kept count of** all the books I've read this summer, but it must be over 15.*

keep score
to count and record the number of points that each team or player has won in a game or competition: *Alan is keeping score – it's 22 to 18.*

keep track
to pay attention to or record an amount that increases over a period of time so that you always know the total: *Employees are required to **keep track of** the number of hours they work each week.*

keep a tally
to record each time a group increases so that you know how many people or things are in the group: *She **keeps a tally of** the people who call to complain.*

count on *phrasal verb* → see **trust[1]**

country /ˈkʌntri/ *noun*

1 a place with its own government
- ► country
- ► nation
- ► state
- ► land
- ► territory

2 land that is not near a city
- ► the country
- ► the countryside

1 a place with its own government

country
a separate independent area of land with its own government or ruler: *India is a fascinating country.* | *How many foreign countries have you been to?*

nation
a country, its people, and its government: *The U.S. is the most powerful nation in the world.*

state
a country with a government. You use **state** when you are talking about a country as a political organization: *Israel became an independent state in 1948.*

→ You also use **state** about the large area of the U.S. that has its own government: *Hawaii became the 50th state of the United States in 1959.*

land
a country. Use **land** especially when you are writing stories: *The old man had come from a distant land.*

territory
land that is owned or controlled by a country: *The plane was shot down over enemy territory.*

→ see **nationality**

2 land that is not near a city

the country
areas that are not near towns and cities: *She had always wanted to live in the country, away from the noise of the city.*

the countryside
areas that are not near towns and cities, with rivers, trees, hills, etc.: *The house has beautiful views of the surrounding countryside.*

SYNONYM CHECK

The country or the countryside?

You use **the country** to emphasize being away from towns. You use **the countryside** when you want to emphasize that there are trees, hills, etc.

couple *noun* → see **pair**, Function Word **some**, Topic **Relationships and Marriage**

courage /ˈkɚɪdʒ/ *noun*

- ► courage
- ► bravery
- ► heroism
- ► nerve

courage
the quality of not being afraid or showing your fear: *He finally found the courage to ask her for a date. | Standing up to the bullies took a lot of courage.*

bravery
courage and brave actions in a very dangerous or frightening situation, especially when you are fighting in a war: *He was given a medal for his bravery, after he risked his life to help an injured soldier.*

heroism
a lot of courage and very brave actions, especially to save other people: *The mayor praised the heroism of the firefighter who saved the little girl.*

nerve
courage or confidence to do something difficult or frightening. **Nerve** is more informal than **courage**: *I didn't agree with my boss, but I didn't have the nerve to tell him.*
→ see **dare (1)** for "have the courage to do something"
→ see **brave**

courageous *adjective* → see **brave**

course *noun* → see **direction**, Topic **Education**

court *noun* → see Topic **Sports and Exercise**

cover¹ /ˈkʌvɚ/ *verb*

- ► cover
- ► wrap
- ► coat
- ► envelop (*formal*)

cover *also* **cover up**
to put something over something, especially to protect it or hide it: *If it rains, we'll have to cover the hole in the roof with a sheet of plastic. | She wears make-up to cover up the scar on her cheek.*
→ You can also use **cover** when saying that something is all over a surface: *The ground was covered in snow.*

wrap
to put paper, plastic, or cloth tightly around something: *Help me wrap the Christmas presents.*

coat
to thinly cover the whole surface of something with something soft or liquid: *The nuts are coated in chocolate.*

envelop (*formal*)
if something, especially mist or smoke, envelops something else, it covers it completely: *Fog enveloped the top of the mountain.*

cover² /ˈkʌvɚ/ *noun*

1 something that protects a surface
- ► cover
- ► wrapper
- ► envelope
- ► case
- ► covering

2 something you put on a container to close it
- ► lid
- ► top
- ► cap

1 something that protects a surface

cover
something that you put over another thing to protect it: *A cover will keep the dust off your keyboard. | She took the card out of its plastic cover.*
→ You can also use **cover** to talk about the outside of a book or magazine:*His picture is on the back cover of the book.*

wrapper
the paper or plastic that covers something you buy: *There were empty candy wrappers all along the sidewalk.*

envelope
a paper cover that you put a letter in: *She tore open the envelope to see what was inside.*

case
a container or covering that is made to protect or hold something: *She took the DVD out of its case and put it in the player.*

covering
a layer of something that covers a surface: *Carpet and vinyl are common floor coverings.*

2 something you put on a container to close it

lid
a cover for a pot, box, or other container: *Put the lid on the pot, so the water will boil faster.*

top
the cover for a container or pen: *Who left the top off the toothpaste again?*

cap
a cover that closes a bottle or tube or goes on the end of a pen: *She was having trouble getting the cap off the pill bottle.*

cow /kaʊ/ *noun*

- ► **cow**
- ► **bull**
- ► **calf**
- ► **cattle**
- ► **steer**
- ► **ox**

cow
a large animal that lives on farms and is used for its milk or meat: *There were cows in the field.* | *We had milk and butter from our own cows, eggs from the chickens, and vegetables we grew ourselves.*
→ **Cow** can also mean only a female cow.

bull
a male cow: *There was a huge bull standing in the field behind a fence.*

calf
the baby of a cow. You use **calf** about both male and female babies: *The calf stayed close to its mother.*

cattle
male and female cows that are kept on a farm: *A herd of cattle is blocking the road over by the creek.*

steer
a young male cow that is raised for its meat: *The steers are fed on grass for a good quality meat.*

ox
an adult male cow that has its sexual organs removed and is used for work, for example pulling wagons or machinery, especially in past times: *Some of the wagons were pulled by oxen, and some by horses.*
→ **GRAMMAR:** The plural of **ox** is **oxen**.

cozy *adjective* → see **comfortable**

crack¹ *verb* → see **break¹**, **hit¹**, Topic **To Make a Sound**

crack² *noun* → see **break²**, **hole**

crash¹ *verb* → see **crash into** at **hit¹**, Topic **Computers and the Internet**, **To Make a Sound**

crash² *noun* → see **accident**, **recession**

crawl *verb* → see **walk¹**

crazy /ˈkreɪzi/ *adjective*

- ► **crazy** *(informal)*
- ► **insane** *(informal)*
- ► **nuts** *(informal)*

crazy *(informal)*
behaving in a way that is not sensible and seems strange: *It was crazy to try to drive all the way to Nashville in one day.*
→ Do not say: ~~*very crazy*~~. Say: *totally crazy*.

insane *(informal)*
behaving in a way that is very stupid and often dangerous: *You can't jump over the car with your bike – that's insane.*

nuts *(informal)*
behaving in a silly or strange way that is not sensible: *People think I'm nuts because I like to rock climb without using ropes, but I know what I'm doing.*

ADVERBS

You can make the adjectives **crazy** and **insane** into adjectives by using an **-ly** ending: *I saw Beth waving crazily to me and wondered what was going on.* | *A man was walking insanely through the rush-hour traffic.*

create /kriˈeɪt/ *verb*

- ► **create**
- ► **invent**
- ► **devise**
- ► **pioneer**
- ► **innovate**

ANTONYMS → see **destroy**

create (AWL)
to think of or make something that did not exist before: *The government wants to help businesses that create jobs.* | *The dish was created by the restaurant's new chef.*

invent
to think of something that is completely new and different. You usually use **invent** about machines or devices: *Thomas Edison invented the electric light bulb.*

devise
to plan or invent a new way of doing something. **Devise** is used especially about new methods or systems: *He **devised** a simple system **for** shipping goods to customers.*

pioneer
to be the first person to do, invent, or use something: *Dr. Janssen pioneered the surgical technique in the 1960s.*

innovate (AWL)
to invent or begin using new ideas, equipment, or ways of doing something: *In the electronics industry, companies need to innovate to stay in business.*
→ see **make**

creation /kri'eɪʃən/ *noun*

► creation
► making
► formation
► birth
ANTONYMS → see **destruction**

creation (AWL)
the act of making something new: *The project could result in* ***the creation of*** *5,000 jobs.* | *The Christian story of creation says that God made the world in seven days.*

making
the process of making or producing something: *No animals were harmed in* ***the making of*** *this movie.* | *Cheese making is a very old skill.*

formation
the process by which something develops into a particular thing or shape: ***The formation of*** *the planets started in huge clouds of gas and dust surrounding the Sun.*

birth
the time when something new starts: *Many Jewish people moved to Israel after the country's birth in 1948.*
→ see **invention**

creative /kri'eɪtɪv/ *adjective*

1 good at thinking of new ideas
► creative
► imaginative
► ingenious
► inventive
2 good at making art
► creative
► artistic
► imaginative

1 good at thinking of new ideas

creative
good at thinking of new ideas or making new things: *We need someone who is creative and enthusiastic to lead the project.*

imaginative
good at thinking of new and unusual ideas that surprise or please people: *Ben was an imaginative playmate who had us pretending to go in search of dragons.*

ingenious
very good at thinking of intelligent new ideas that solve problems: *We had an ingenious designer who figured out a way to add more storage space to our house.*

inventive
good at thinking of new, different, or interesting ideas: *She is an inventive teacher who always finds new ways to keep the students interested.*

SYNONYM CHECK
Creative, imaginative, etc.

These words can also be used to describe new things that people think of: *Alex is very good at coming up with creative solutions that no one else has thought of.* | *The imaginative design of the chairs looks very modern.*
Ingenious is especially used in this way: *This ingenious game teaches kids the times tables in a fun way.*

2 good at making art

creative
good at making art, music, or literature in new and interesting ways: *Set out all kinds of art materials and let the children be creative.* | *Davis was a very creative jazz musician.*

artistic
good at painting, drawing, or making beautiful things: *John is very artistic – in fact, he painted the picture on the wall.*

imaginative
good at making pictures in your mind and producing new and unusual art, music, or literature: *Sally is very imaginative and entertains the other children with her stories.*
→ see Topic **Describing People's Character**

SYNONYM CHECK
Creative, artistic, and imaginative

You can also use **creative**, **artistic**, and **imaginative** to describe things that someone makes or does: *The food was arranged on the plate in an artistic way.* | *He wrote a very imaginative story.*

ADVERBS

You can make the adjectives that mean **creative** into adverbs by using an **-ly** ending: *The company wants workers who can think creatively and solve problems.* | *The artist inventively mixes colored glass with his photographs to create unusual works of art.* | *He is artistically talented.*

creature *noun* → see **animal**

credit *noun* → see **loan**, **praise²**

creep *verb* → see **walk¹**

crew *noun* → see **group**

crime /kraɪm/ *noun*

- ► crime
- ► offense
- ► misdemeanor
- ► felony
- ► wrongdoing (*formal*)
- ► misconduct (*formal*)

crime
an action that the law does not allow: *The police are asking for the public's help to solve the crime.* | *He used a gun while committing the crime.*

offense
an action that the law does not allow. **Offense** sounds less serious than **crime**: *It was only her first offense, so the judge just gave her a warning.*
→ **Offense** is often used to describe crimes that are not very serious, such as speeding. However, **offense** is also used in courts or by the police about more serious crimes.

misdemeanor
a crime that is not very serious: *The boys who had painted the graffiti pleaded guilty to a misdemeanor and were fined.*

felony
a serious crime such as murder or robbery. **Felony** is used in courts and by the police, or in reports about crimes: *Deliberately starting a fire that damages property is a felony.*

wrongdoing (*formal*)
illegal actions or immoral behavior: *The investigation eventually cleared the accountant of any wrongdoing.*

misconduct (*formal*)
bad or dishonest behavior by someone in his or her job: *Stealing money from your workplace is very serious misconduct.*
→ see **illegal**, **murder**, **theft**

criminal /ˈkrɪmənəl/ *noun*

- ► criminal
- ► offender
- ► felon (*formal*)
- ► accomplice
- ► delinquent
- ► wrongdoer (*formal*)
- ► the culprit (*formal*)

criminal
someone who is guilty of a crime: *He is considered one of the most dangerous criminals in the country.* | *Violent criminals should stay in prison for a long time.*

offender
someone who has broken the law: *The new law increases prison sentences for violent offenders.*

felon (*formal*)
someone who is guilty of a serious crime: *The two felons had stolen the life savings of more than 20 people through their false investment scheme.*

accomplice
someone who helps a criminal do something wrong: *Police believe that the thief must have had an accomplice.*

delinquent
a child or young person who behaves very badly or does illegal things: *The program has reduced the number of juvenile delinquents who go on to commit more crimes.*

wrongdoer (*formal*)
someone who does something illegal or immoral: *The job of the police is to find wrongdoers and make sure they are punished.*

the culprit (*formal*)
the person who has done something wrong or illegal: *Police are looking for the **culprits behind** the robbery of a liquor store.*
→ see **illegal**, **prisoner**, **thief**

SYNONYM CHECK

Criminal or offender?

You use **criminal** about someone who has broken a law and will be punished by going to prison.

You can use **offender** about someone who has committed serious crimes, but an **offender** can also be someone who has broken a less serious law, such as a law about speeding. **Offender** is often used in courts, by the police, or in newspaper reports.

crisis *noun* → see **emergency**

critic *noun* → see **judge¹**

C

critical *adjective* → see **important**, **necessary**, **be critical of** at **criticize**, Topic **Describing People's Character**

criticize /ˈkrɪtəˌsaɪz/ *verb*

- ► criticize
- ► be critical of
- ► find fault with
- ► attack
- ► condemn (*formal*)

ANTONYMS → see **praise¹**

C

criticize
to say that someone or something is bad: *Many people have* ***criticized*** *the government* ***for*** *not being prepared for the flood.* | *The report has been* ***criticized for*** *not giving all the facts.*

be critical of
to criticize someone or something, especially by giving detailed reasons: *In his speech, Robinson was* ***critical of*** *the governor's plans.*

find fault with
to criticize someone or something, by deliberately trying to find mistakes. You often use **find fault with** when you think someone is being unfair: *No matter how hard I tried, he always found fault with my work.*

attack
to publicly criticize someone or something very strongly: *The health care plan was* ***attacked as*** *too expensive.*

condemn (*formal*)
to say publicly that you strongly disapprove of someone or something: *Politicians were quick to condemn the bombing.*
→ see **scold** for words meaning "to criticize someone in an angry way"

crop /krɑp/ *noun*

- ► crop
- ► harvest
- ► yield (*formal*)

crop
the amount of corn, vegetables, fruit, etc. that is produced and collected in one year: *We had a good crop of beans this year.*
→ **Crop** also means a plant that farmers grow for food: *Farmers plant their crops in spring.*

harvest
the work of collecting corn, wheat, vegetables, fruit, etc. that has grown, or the amount that is collected: *During the harvest, the whole family helps in the fields.* | *Farmers in the region are hoping for a good harvest this year.*

yield (*formal*)
the amount produced by the plants that the farmer has grown: *We get high yields because the soil is very rich here.*

cross /krɔs/ *verb*

- ► cross
- ► go across
- ► span

cross
to go from one side of something to the other, especially to go from one side of a road, river, or room to the other: *Julia crossed the street and went into the drugstore.* | *I crossed the room to open the window.*

go across
to cross something, especially something large: *Traffic was going slowly across the intersection.* | *He went across America on a motorcycle.*

span
if a bridge spans an area of water, it goes from one side to the other: *The bridge spans the Charles River, connecting Boston to Cambridge.*

crowd *noun* → see **group**

crude *adjective* → see **simple**

cruel /ˈkruəl/ *adjective*

- ► cruel
- ► vicious
- ► brutal
- ► abusive (*formal*)
- ► heartless
- ► inhumane (*formal*)
- ► ruthless

ANTONYMS → see **kind²**

cruel
very unkind and often deliberately hurting people or animals: *He was a cruel man who abused his wife and children.* | *It's cruel to leave the dog chained up in the snow like that all day.*

vicious
very cruel and violent, and intended to hurt someone: *The vicious attack on a brave young policewoman shocked the city.*
→ You can use **vicious** about words or actions that are cruel and are intended to upset someone: *Sarah made some vicious comments about Liz's weight.*

brutal
very cruel and violent, in a way that shows no human feelings: *The police are investigating a series of brutal murders.*

abusive (*formal*)
saying cruel things or using physical violence: *The woman became angry and abusive when she was not allowed into the hotel.*

heartless
very unkind and not caring at all about other people's feelings: *It was **heartless to** fire so many people right before Christmas.*

inhumane (*formal*)
very cruel and causing more suffering than is acceptable: *The inhumane treatment of prisoners must stop.*

ruthless
so determined to get what you want that you do not care if you have to hurt other people in order to do it: *These men are ruthless terrorists and will kill anyone who tries to stop them.*
→ see **evil¹**, **mean²**, Topic **Describing People's Character**

ADVERBS

You can make the adjectives that mean **cruel** into adverbs by using an **-ly** ending: *They laughed at him cruelly.* | *"You can't come," she said heartlessly.* | *He ruthlessly pushed aside anyone who got in his way.*

cruelty /ˈkruəlti/ *noun*

- cruelty
- brutality
- abuse
- persecution

ANTONYMS → see **kindness**

cruelty
behavior that deliberately causes pain to people or animals: *He was arrested for **cruelty to** animals after someone saw him beating his dog.*

brutality
very violent behavior that is intended to hurt people, for example by hitting them: *The demonstrators complained about police brutality.*

abuse
cruel treatment of someone you should take care of, or someone you know well: *The boy's parents were arrested and charged with child abuse.* | *Victims of abuse are often too scared to report the crime to the police.*

persecution
cruel and unfair treatment of a group of people, especially because of their religious or political beliefs: *Many people came to the U.S. to escape from religious persecution in Europe.*
→ see **bullying**, **violence**

crumple *verb* → see **fold¹**

crush *verb* → see **press**

cry¹ /kraɪ/ *verb*

- cry
- be in tears
- sob
- weep (*formal*)
- wail
- whimper

ANTONYMS → see **laugh¹**

cry
if you cry, tears come out of your eyes because you are unhappy or you feel pain: *Sad songs always make me cry.* | *The boy was crying because his mom wouldn't buy him a candy bar.*

be in tears
to be crying: *His wife was in tears as he was taken from the court room.*

sob
to cry with quick noisy breaths when you are very upset: *"Please don't leave me!" she sobbed.*

weep (*formal*)
to cry a lot for a long time, because you feel very unhappy. **Weep** is used mainly in written English: *The family wept when they heard the news about their son.*

wail
to shout or cry with a long high sound. **Wail** is mainly used about babies and children: *The child was wailing because he had lost one of his toys.*

whimper
to cry quietly and weakly: *A child lay in the hospital bed, whimpering with pain.*
→ see **shout¹** for **cry** meaning "to suddenly shout"

cry² *noun* → see **shout²**

cube *noun* → see **piece**

cuddle¹ *verb* → see **hug¹**

cuddle² *noun* → see **hug²**

cultural *adjective* → see **racial**

culture *noun* → see **society**

cure¹ /kyʊr/ *verb*

► cure
► relieve
► make someone/something feel better
► heal

cure
to make an illness better so that someone is completely healthy again: *The disease can be cured easily now, but in the past people died from it.* | *The doctors* ***cured*** *him* ***of*** *his illness.*

relieve *also* **ease**
to reduce the pain of an illness or injury: *The doctor gave me some medicine to relieve the pain.* | *The new drug could ease the suffering of millions of people with diabetes.*

make someone/something feel better
to make someone feel healthy again, or make someone stop feeling pain: *Drink this. It will make your throat feel better.* | *The medicine made me feel better for a while.*

heal
if a person heals someone, he or she makes the person healthy again: *He was able to heal the sick.*
→ **Heal** is also used to say that a wound gets better: *His wounds have all healed and he says he feels fine.*

cure² /kyʊr/ *noun*

► cure
► remedy

cure
a way of making an illness go away completely: *One day, scientists will find a* ***cure for*** *cancer.*

remedy
a cure for a small health problem: *A warm honey and lemon drink is a good* ***remedy for*** *a cold.*
→ see **medicine**, **treatment**

curious *adjective* → see **interested**

currency *noun* → see **money**

current *adjective* → see **modern**, **present¹**

curve¹ /kɚv/ *noun*

► curve
► arc
► arch
► crescent

curve
a line that bends like part of a circle: *The bay is*

curve

the **curve** of a bay

the **arc** of a rainbow

the **arches** of a bridge

a **crescent** moon

in the shape of a curve. | The car went around the curve too fast and almost crashed.

arc
a curved line, especially one that forms part of a circle: *The ball went up into the air and down again in a long arc.*

arch
a curved shape at the top of a door or window, or a supporting part of a building or bridge that forms this shape: *Water flows under the arches of the bridge.*

crescent
a curved shape that is wide in the middle and pointed at each end, like a thin moon: *Pakistan's flag has a white crescent and a star on a green background.*
→ see **bend²**, **circle¹**

curve² *verb* → see **bend¹**

custom *noun* → see **practice¹**, **tradition**

customer /ˈkʌstəmɚ/ *noun*

- customer
- client
- guest
- consumer
- shopper
- patron (*formal*)
- clientele (*formal*)
- patient

customer
someone who buys things from a store or company: *She is a regular customer at the store. | The company is well known for the excellent service it gives their customers.*

client
someone who pays to have work done by a professional person or company: *Andrew is a financial adviser with many wealthy clients.*

guest
someone who stays at a hotel or similar place: *The pool is for hotel guests only.*

consumer (AWL)
anyone who buys things or uses services. You use **consumer** when talking or writing about people in general: *The report studies the habits of consumers between the ages of 25 and 44.*

shopper
someone who goes into a store and looks for things to buy: *The store manager made an announcement to the shoppers about the sale.*

patron (*formal*)
someone who uses a store, restaurant, hotel, library, museum, etc.: *Many of our patrons come to the library to use the computers.*

clientele (*formal*)
all the people who use a business such as a store or restaurant: *The health club has a wealthy clientele.*

user
someone who uses a system or service: *Users complained that they were having problems downloading the software from the internet.*

cut¹ *verb* → *go to pages 142-143*

cut² /kʌt/ *noun*

- cut
- scratch
- gash
- wound

cut
an injury you get when something sharp cuts your skin: *The nurse cleaned the cut and put a bandage on it. | I got a small cut from the knife.*

scratch
a small cut on your skin that is not deep: *I climbed a tree and got a few scratches on my arms from the tree branches.*

gash
a deep cut: *His leg had a deep gash in it from the motorcycle accident.*

wound
a deep cut or hole in your skin, made by a weapon. **Wounds** are usually serious: *The soldiers were in the hospital recovering from bullet wounds.*
→ see **decrease¹** for **cut** meaning "a reduction"

cut down *phrasal verb* → see **reduce**

cute *adjective* → see **beautiful**, Topic **Describing People's Looks**

cut out *phrasal verb* → see **remove**

C

cut[1] /kʌt/ *verb*

1 to cut something with a knife, scissors, etc.
- ► cut
- ► snip
- ► slit
- ► slash
- ► hack
- ► amputate (*formal*)
- ► sever (*formal*)

2 to cut someone's skin
- ► cut
- ► scratch
- ► stab

3 to cut food
- ► cut
- ► chop
- ► slice
- ► carve
- ► peel
- ► dice
- ► grate

4 to cut wood, grass, or other plants
- ► cut
- ► mow
- ► clip
- ► trim
- ► cut down
- ► chop
- ► saw

5 to cut hair or fingernails
- ► cut
- ► shave
- ► trim
- ► shear

1 to cut something with a knife, scissors, etc.

cut
to divide or make a hole in something, using a knife, scissors, etc.: ***Cut** the cardboard **into** a triangle.* | *He cut a hole in the fence and escaped.*

snip
to cut something quickly with scissors: *Snip off the end of the string behind the knot.*

slit
to make a thin cut all the way through something: *Roberto **slit open** the envelope with a knife.*

slash
to cut something in a very violent way: *Someone had slashed a hole in our tent and taken my wallet.*

hack
to cut something in a very rough or violent way: *Mr. Powell was **hacking at** the base of the tree with an ax.*

amputate (*formal*)
to cut off someone's arm, leg, foot, etc. in a medical operation: *The soldier's wound was so bad that the doctors decided they had to amputate his leg.*

sever (*formal*)
to cut off a part of someone's body in an accident or attack: *Her hand was severed in the accident.*

2 to cut someone's skin

cut
to cut someone's skin: *The knife is very sharp – be careful you don't cut your finger.* | *I **cut myself** on some glass.*

scratch
to make a small cut that is not very deep: *The cat scratched him and ran away.*

stab
to push a knife or other sharp object into someone's body: *The attacker stabbed him, but his injuries are not serious.*

3 to cut food

cut
to divide food into pieces using a knife: *She cut the pizza in half.* | ***Cut** the carrots **into** long sticks.*

chop
to cut something into small pieces with quick movements of a knife: ***Chop** the garlic **into** little pieces and add them to the pan.*

slice
to cut flat pieces from a larger piece of food, especially bread or meat: *Slice the beef thinly.* | *She sliced a few pieces of bread to use for toast.*

carve
to cut a large piece of cooked meat into slices, in order to serve it: *My mother carved the turkey at the table.*

peel
to take the outside part off a fruit or vegetable: *I peeled the potatoes and put them in boiling water.*

dice
to cut vegetables or fruit into fairly small square pieces: *Dice the carrots and add them to the soup.*

grate
to cut food into small thin pieces by rubbing it

against a tool with lots of sharp holes called a grater: *Grate the cheese and sprinkle it on the top of the pasta.*

GRAMMAR CHECK: cut

Many of the verbs you use to talk about cutting food can be turned into adjectives by adding "**-ed**." You can say **chopped**, **sliced**, **peeled**, **diced**, and **grated**: *Mix the chopped nuts in with the other ingredients.* | *Put the diced onion into the pan with the olive oil.*

4 to cut wood, grass, or other plants

cut
to make grass or other plants shorter: *Now that spring is here, it's time to cut the grass again.* | *I cut back a few of the branches so that they didn't hang over the sidewalk.*

mow
to cut grass with a machine: *My brother was in the backyard mowing the lawn.*

clip
to cut small amounts of grass, a hedge, or a bush with a tool you hold in your hand, in order to make it shorter or smaller: *That hedge looks better now it has been clipped.*

trim
to cut a small amount off a bush or other plant, to make it look neater: *The roses need trimming.*

cut down *also* **chop down**
to completely remove a tree or other large plant by cutting it all the way through: *They cut down several old trees on our street.* | *Don't let them chop down that maple tree!*

chop
to cut wood into pieces with an ax: *My sister helped my dad chop wood for the fire.*

saw
to cut wood using a tool called a saw, which you push forward and back: *It takes a long time to **saw through** one of these big logs.*

5 to cut hair or fingernails

cut
to cut someone's hair or nails: *My mom usually cuts my hair for me.* | *How often do you cut your nails?*
→ When another person cuts your hair, say: *I'm having/getting my hair cut*. Don't say: ~~*I'm cutting my hair*~~.

shave
to cut off the hair on your face or body with a razor (=a tool with thin sharp blades on a handle): *He was shaving in the bathroom.* | *She shaves her legs every two days.*

trim
to cut off a small amount of hair, to make it look neater: *Can you trim about an inch off the ends of my hair?*

shear
to cut the wool off a sheep: *He grew up on a farm and knew how to shear sheep.*
→ see **reduce** for cut meaning "to reduce something such as prices or costs"
→ see **shorten**

chop dice carve slice grate peel

Online Thesaurus

Go to **www.longmandictionariesusa.com**
→ ***Longman Thesaurus of American English*** – with pronunciation of all the words
→ **Study Center** – interactive practice to help you learn synonyms, Academic Words, and Topic Vocabulary

Dd

dad *noun* → see **father**

daddy *noun* → see **father**

daily /ˈdeɪli/ *adjective*

- daily
- everyday

daily
done or happening every day: *Keep a daily record of the food you eat.* | *Exercise becomes part of your daily routine.*

everyday
ordinary, usual, or happening every day: *He liked cooking and cleaning and other everyday activities.* | *The movie is about people's everyday lives.*
→ see **day**

GRAMMAR CHECK: daily

Daily and **everyday** are always used before a noun: *Do you know what's happening in your children's daily lives?* | *The students write about events in their everyday world.*

damage[1] /ˈdæmɪdʒ/ *noun*

- damage
- harm
- destruction

damage
the fact of being broken or spoiled, especially because of an accident or event: *The storm caused a lot of* ***damage to*** *the roof.* | *Luckily there was no* ***damage to*** *the engine.*

harm
bad effects, serious problems, or injury: *These chemicals can cause* ***harm to*** *the environment.* | *No animals suffered any harm during the filming of this movie.*

destruction
a situation in which something is completely destroyed: *The story tells about the* ***destruction of*** *the city during the war.*
→ see **injury**

damage[2] /ˈdæmɪdʒ/ *verb*

- damage
- do/cause damage
- break
- harm
- be bad for
- scratch
- vandalize
- sabotage

damage
to make something be broken, spoiled, or in bad condition: *In winter, the salt on the roads damages cars.* | *The house was badly damaged by an earthquake.*

do/cause damage
to damage something. You use **do** or **cause damage** especially when saying how much something is damaged: *The storm caused a lot of damage in the old part of town.* | *Luckily the thieves didn't do much damage to the car.*

break
to damage something so that it separates into pieces or does not work: *Be careful, the dolls are old and they will break easily.* | *I'm not sure what I did, but I think I have broken the camera.*

harm
to have a bad effect on someone or something, especially over a period of time: *Farmers are worried that the hot weather will harm their crops.* | *Smoking harms your health.*

be bad for
be bad for means the same as **harm** but sounds more informal: *Too much sugar is bad for your teeth.*

scratch
to damage something by marking or cutting its surface: *When we moved the table we scratched the floor.*

vandalize
to deliberately damage a building, vehicle, or public place: *The boys broke windows and painted graffiti, but they were caught and arrested for vandalizing the school.*

sabotage
to damage something secretly and deliberately, especially in order to cause problems for your enemy: *They sabotaged trucks carrying weapons to the enemy.*
→ see **break[1]**, **destroy**, **harm[2]**

damp /dæmp/ *adjective*

- ► damp
- ► moist
- ► clammy
- ► humid

ANTONYMS → see **dry**

damp
a little wet: *The shirt was still damp, so I put it back in the dryer.* | *The grass is a little damp from the rain.*

moist
a little wet in a way that is good or pleasant. You use **moist** especially about cake, soil, or skin: *This cake is nice and moist!* | *The plant likes moist soil.*

clammy
wet, cold, and sticky, in a way that is unpleasant to touch. You use **clammy** about someone's hands or skin: *My whole body was clammy and I was shivering.*

humid
if the weather is humid, the air feels warm and wet: *It was a humid summer afternoon.*
→ see **rainy**, **wet**, Topic **The Weather**

dance /dæns/ *noun*

- ► dance
- ► prom
- ► ball

dance
an event like a party, at which people dance: *The teenagers were dressed up for the Halloween Dance at school.*

prom
a formal dance party for students in high school: *Did you buy a dress for the prom?*

ball
a very formal event at which people dance: *We watched the president and first lady dance together* ***at the ball****.*

danger /ˈdeɪndʒɚ/ *noun*

- ► danger
- ► risk
- ► threat
- ► hazard
- ► peril (*formal*)

ANTONYMS → see **safety**

danger
a situation in which someone or something might be harmed or something bad might happen: *Parents want to protect their children from danger.* | *There was a small fire, but no one in the building was* ***in serious danger****.*

risk
the possibility that something bad might happen: *There is a* ***risk that*** *the cancer will come back.*

threat
something very bad that people are worried might happen soon: *The workers face* ***the threat of*** *losing their jobs.* | *The oil spill poses a* ***threat to*** *many animals and birds.*

hazard
something that might cause accidents or be dangerous to your health. **Hazard** is used especially in official warnings: *Drive carefully – the ice on the roads this morning is a hazard.* | *Everyone knows about the hazards of smoking.*

peril (*formal*)
very serious danger: *We pray for our soldiers and others* ***in peril*** *because of the war.*

dangerous /ˈdeɪndʒərəs/ *adjective*

- ► dangerous
- ► unsafe
- ► risky
- ► hazardous (*formal*)
- ► treacherous (*formal*)

ANTONYMS → see **safe (2)**

dangerous
likely to cause death or serious harm. You can use **dangerous** about a situation, activity, thing, place, or person: *The ship was about to sink and we were in a very dangerous situation.* | *It is dangerous to play with fire.*

unsafe
not safe. You use **unsafe** about an activity or place: ***It is unsafe to*** *drink the water here.* | *The building is unsafe because it was damaged by an earthquake.*

risky
if an action is risky, something bad might happen if you do it: *The doctors decided that the operation was too risky.*

hazardous (*formal*)
likely to be dangerous. **Hazardous** is often used in official warnings: *The freezing temperatures are making driving hazardous.* | *There are strict rules about the use of hazardous chemicals.*

treacherous (*formal*)
very dangerous. **Treacherous** is used especially about a place where there are hidden dangers:

D

The ship sailed along the coast, trying to avoid the treacherous rocks and sandbanks.
→ see **harmful**

ADVERBS

You can make the adjectives **dangerous**, **unsafe**, and **treacherous** into adverbs by using an **-ly** ending: *Her blood pressure was dangerously high.* | *The streets were treacherously icy.* | *I was so tired that I may have been driving unsafely.*
Hazardous and **risky** can be made into adverbs, but they are not common.

dare /der/ *verb*

1 to have enough confidence to do something difficult or frightening
► dare
► have the courage
► be brave enough

2 to say that someone should do something to prove that he or she is brave, or the best at something
► dare
► challenge

1 to have enough confidence to do something difficult or frightening

dare
to have enough confidence to do something that is dangerous, frightening, or difficult. **Dare** is usually used with negative words such as "no," "not," or "never": *Nobody* ***dared to*** *go into the dark house alone.* | *I always wanted to ask Julia for a date, but I never dared.*

have the courage
to have enough confidence that you do not feel afraid of a difficult or dangerous situation: *He said that your dreams can come true if you* ***have the courage to*** *really work at making them come true.*

be brave enough
to have enough courage or confidence to deal with danger, pain, or a difficult situation: *Martin Luther King Jr. was* ***brave enough to*** *try to change America's treatment of black people.*

2 to say that someone should do something to prove that he or she is brave, or the best at something

dare
to say that someone should do something difficult or dangerous to show that he or she is not afraid: *Mike* ***dared*** *her* ***to*** *hold the spider in her hand for a whole minute.*

challenge (AWL)
to ask someone to do something, such as play a game or fight against you. You use **challenge** when each person is trying to be the best or to win: *The knight* ***challenged*** *him* ***to*** *a duel.* | *The teachers at this school* ***challenge*** *us* ***to*** *do our best.*

dark[1] /dark/ *adjective*

1 without any light, or with only a little light (adjectives)
► dark
► dim
► darkened
► shady
► gloomy

ANTONYMS → see **light[2] (1)**

2 not pale in color (adjectives)
► dark
► deep
► rich

ANTONYMS → see **light[2] (3)**

3 to become dark at night (verbs)
► get dark
► darken (*formal*)
► fall (*formal*)

1 without any light, or with only a little light (adjectives)

dark
with no light, or with very little light: *It is very dark in here – can I turn on the light?* | *There was no moon, and it was too dark to see where the trail went.*

dim
slightly dark and not bright: *I could just see her face in the dim light.* | *It was too dim to read.*

darkened
dark because someone has switched off the lights or closed the curtains: *The baby was sleeping peacefully in the darkened bedroom.*

shady
protected from the light of the sun, especially by trees, so that a place is less bright: *I found a shady place to sit, under an old oak tree.*

gloomy
not bright or cheerful, and seeming dark: *It was a gray and gloomy morning.*
→ see Topic **Describing Places**

ADVERBS
You can make the adjective **dim** into an adverb by using an **-ly** ending: *The room was dimly lit.*

2 not pale in color (adjectives)

dark
a dark color is not pale, and is closer to black than white: *She wears clothes in dark colors: black or brown or sometimes dark blue.* | *He had black hair and dark eyes.*
→ You can use **dark** about someone's skin: *He is very handsome, with curly hair and dark skin.*

deep
a deep color is dark and looks good: *Blueberries are a deep blue color when they are ripe.*

rich
a rich color is dark and makes you feel that something is special or expensive: *The paintings, with their rich colors, are some of the artist's most beautiful works.*

ADVERBS
You can make the adjectives **dark** and **rich** into adverbs by using an **-ly** ending, but these words are only used in some phrases.
You can say that a man is "darkly handsome," which means that he has dark skin, hair, or eyes and is attractive: *He was Italian and darkly handsome.*
You can say that something is "richly colored" or "richly red/blue/green": *The glass in the church windows is richly colored.*

3 to become dark at night (verbs)

get dark
if it gets dark, the sky becomes dark, usually because it is night: *It was getting dark, and we still had a long way to go.* | *My mom told me to be home before it gets dark.*

darken (*formal*)
if the sky darkens, it gradually becomes darker, usually because of bad weather and clouds: *As the storm approached, the sky darkened and the wind began to blow.*

fall (*formal*)
if night or darkness falls, night begins and the sky becomes dark. **Fall** sounds literary and is used especially in stories: *They arrived at the cabin just as night was falling.*

dark² *noun* → see **darkness**

darkness /ˈdɑrknəs/ *noun*

- ► darkness
- ► the dark
- ► the gloom

ANTONYMS → see **light¹** (**1**)

darkness
a situation in which there is no light: *The electricity went out, and the whole street was left* ***in darkness.*** | *A man suddenly appeared* ***out of the darkness.***

the dark
the darkness in a place at night: *When I was young, I was scared of the dark, and I had to sleep with the light on.* | *She was lying there* ***in the dark,*** *listening to the sounds of the house.*
→ **Dark** is also used in the phrases "before dark" and "after dark", which mean before and after nighttime: *They wanted to get home before dark.*

the gloom
a situation in which there is not much light and it is difficult to see clearly. **The gloom** is used especially in written descriptions in stories: *He was standing* ***in the gloom*** *of the hallway.*
→ see **shadow**

dash¹ *verb* → see **run¹**, **rush¹**

dash² *noun* → see **run²**

data *noun* → see **information**

database *noun* → see Topic **Computers and the Internet**

date *noun* → see Topic **Relationships and Marriage**

dawn /dɔn/ *noun*

- ► dawn
- ► sunrise
- ► daybreak
- ► sun-up
- ► first light

ANTONYMS → see **sunset**

dawn
the time of day when light first appears as the sun comes up: *The general had planned to attack* ***at dawn*** *the next day.*

sunrise
the sky when the sun first appears, or the time when this happens: *I got up early to see the sunrise.* | *She awoke* ***at sunrise.***

daybreak
daybreak means the same as **dawn** and is used

especially in writing: *His father left the house before daybreak.*

sun-up
sun-up means the same as **dawn** but is more informal: *I've been working since sun-up.*

first light
the time when light first appears in the sky in the morning. **First light** sounds more poetic than **sunrise**: *The hikers camped at the foot of the mountain for the night, and started up the trail at first light.*

day /deɪ/ *noun*

► day
► daytime
ANTONYMS → see **night**

D

day
the time when it is light between morning and night: *It was a cold windy day.* | *She only leaves her house during the day – she doesn't feel safe at night.*
→ **Day** can also mean "a period of 24 hours, which starts at 12 o'clock at night": *Which day is her birthday?*

daytime
daytime means the same as **day**: *He works the night shift, so he sleeps during the daytime.*
→ **GRAMMAR: Daytime** can be used before other nouns to talk about things that happen during the day: *She watches a lot of daytime television.* | *Daytime temperatures rarely go above freezing in the winter.*
→ see **daily**, **sunrise**

daybreak *noun* → see **sunrise**, Function Word **down**

daydream¹ *verb* → see **dream²**

daydream² *noun* → see **dream¹**

daytime *noun* → see **day**

dead¹ /ded/ *adjective*

► dead
► deceased (*formal*)
► late (*formal*)
► lifeless (*formal*)
► extinct
ANTONYMS → see **alive**

dead
no longer alive: *"I didn't know her grandfather was dead." "Yes, he died last year."* | *Police are trying to contact the family of the dead man.*
→ **GRAMMAR: Dead** is an adjective, not a verb. Don't say: ~~*He dead in 2002*~~ or ~~*He was dead in 2002*~~. Say: *He died in 2002.*

deceased (*formal*)
deceased means the same as **dead** but is used mainly in writing: *Her parents, who are now deceased, were very wealthy.*

late (*formal*)
dead. You use **late** as a polite way of talking about someone who has died, especially recently: *We were good friends of Mrs. Lambert's late husband.*
→ **GRAMMAR:** When used with this meaning, **late** is always used before a noun. Don't say: ~~*Her father is late*~~. Say: *Her father is dead* or *Her father died recently.*
Use **the late**, not just **late**, before someone's name: *The church was built by the late Roger Whitaker, who was one of the city's best architects.*

lifeless (*formal*)
dead or not moving in a way that is like being dead. **Lifeless** sounds fairly literary: *He found her cold lifeless body stretched across the bed.*

extinct
an extinct type of plant or animal no longer exists: *The tigers could become extinct if the forests they live in are not protected.*
→ see **death**

dead² /ded/ *noun*

► the dead
► body
► corpse
► remains
► ashes
► casualty
ANTONYMS → see **living³**

the dead
people who are dead: *After the battle, it took several days to bury the dead.* | *Because several offices were destroyed in the attack, a large number of the dead were office workers.*
→ **GRAMMAR:** In the phrase **the dead**, **dead** is a plural noun. Don't say: ~~*the deads*~~.

body
the body of someone who has died: *His body was found in the woods covered in leaves.*
→ You can also use **a dead body** to mean the same as **body**, especially when you do not know who the person is.

corpse
a dead human body. You use **corpse** in medical or technical language, or when you do not know who the person was: *The police caught the murderer the day after they found the corpse.*

remains
a person's body or body parts after he or she has died. Use **remains** especially if the person died a long time ago or if you are talking about what happened to the body: *In 1872 his remains were moved to a new cemetery from the original grave.*

ashes
the gray powder that is left when a dead person's body is burned as part of a funeral ceremony: *After the funeral, his ashes were scattered at sea.*

casualty
a person who has died or been injured in a war, attack, or accident: *The number of casualties after the bomb blast has risen to more than 300.*
→ **GRAMMAR: Casualty** is usually used in the plural.
→ see **death**

deadline *noun* → see **limit**[1]

deadly /ˈdedli/ *adjective*

- ► deadly
- ► fatal
- ► lethal

deadly
something that is deadly can kill you: *Terrorists planned to release a deadly gas in the train station.* | *Plutonium is* ***deadly to*** *humans, even in small doses.*

fatal
a fatal accident, disease, or injury causes someone to die: *The snake's bite could be* ***fatal to*** *young children or older people.* | *Her father suffered a fatal heart attack when he was 77 years old.*

lethal
a lethal weapon or substance can kill someone: *The river near the factory contains lethal amounts of the chemical.*
→ see **poisonous**

ADVERBS

You can make the adjectives **fatal** and **lethal** into adverbs by using an **-ly** ending: *He was fatally injured in the accident.* | *The diseases spread quickly and lethally.*

Deadly looks like an adverb but is an adjective. It cannot be used as an adverb.

deaf /def/ *adjective*

- ► deaf
- ► hard of hearing
- ► hearing impaired (*formal*)

deaf
not able to hear: *Many deaf people use sign language to communicate.* | *The ear infection was so severe that it left him completely deaf.*

hard of hearing
unable to hear well: *Grandma is getting hard of hearing and will probably get a hearing aid.*
→ **GRAMMAR:** You cannot use **hard of hearing** before a noun. Don't say: ~~*a hard of hearing person*~~. Say: *a person who is hard of hearing.*

hearing impaired (*formal*)
not able to hear, or only able to hear a little: *Some TV shows have words on the screen for people who are hearing impaired.*

deal *noun* → see **agreement**

deal with /ˈdil wɪθ/ *phrasal verb*

- ► deal with
- ► handle
- ► take care of
- ► tackle
- ► address (*formal*)
- ► see to
- ► face
- ► cope

deal with
to do what needs to be done in a situation, for example to help someone, solve a problem, or control a situation or emotion: *I spend most of my day dealing with customers.* | *We need to find a new way to deal with the problem of homelessness.* | *It is hard to deal with all the emotions you feel when someone dies.*

handle
handle means the same as **deal with.** You often use **handle** when you are talking about how well someone deals with something: *I don't think I handled the situation very well, because Mario is even more upset now.*

take care of
to deal with a situation or problem, especially when you do this for someone else so that he or she does not have to: *I'll take care of all the emails and phone calls while you're away.*

tackle
to deal with a difficult problem in a determined way: *The school is looking for new ways to tackle the problem of bullying among its students.*

D

address *(formal)*
to start to deal with a problem by thinking about it or trying new ways to solve it: *The police need to address the problem of street crime.*

see to
to deal with all the practical details of something that needs to be done or organized: *His son will see to all the funeral arrangements.*

face
to have to deal with a difficult situation: *We were facing the horrible job of cleaning up the house after the flood.*

cope
to be able to deal with a difficult situation, especially without becoming too upset: *She found it hard to* ***cope with*** *taking care of two young children on her own.*
→ see **treat**

D

dealer *noun* → see **seller**

death /deθ/ *noun*

1 the end of someone's life
- ► death
- ► loss
- ► passing

2 the event when someone dies
- ► death
- ► fatality *(formal)*
- ► casualty

1 the end of someone's life

death
the end of someone's life: *He lived in Florida from the time he stopped working until his death. | Heart disease is the leading cause of death among women.*

loss
someone's death. Use **loss** when you are talking about how someone's death affects his or her family or friends: *She must be feeling very lonely after* ***the loss of*** *her husband.*

passing
someone's death. **Passing** is used in order to avoid saying the word **death** directly: *We were saddened to hear the news of your father's passing.*

2 the event when someone dies

death
the event when someone dies. **Death** is used in this meaning especially in news reports or other official reports: *The number of deaths from cancer dropped last year. | All deaths must be reported to the state within 96 hours.*

fatality *(formal)*
a death in an accident or attack. **Fatality** is used in news reports and official or legal language: *It was a terrible accident with eight fatalities.*

casualty
a person who has died or been injured in a war, attack, or accident: *The number of casualties after the bomb blast has risen to more than 300.*
→ GRAMMAR: **Casualty** is usually used in the plural.
→ see **die**

death penalty /ˈdeθ ˌpenlti/ *noun*

- ► the death penalty
- ► capital punishment
- ► execution

the death penalty
the legal punishment of killing someone who is guilty of a serious crime: *If he is found guilty of murder, he could face the death penalty.*

capital punishment
the system of killing criminals as a legal punishment: *Is there any evidence that capital punishment reduces crime?*
→ GRAMMAR: **Capital punishment** cannot be used in the plural. Don't say: ~~*The country does not have capital punishments*~~.

execution
the act of killing someone as a punishment: *His execution finally took place several years after he was convicted of the murder.*

debate[1] *noun* → see **discussion**

debate[2] *verb* → see **discuss**

debt *noun* → see **loan**

decay /dɪˈkeɪ/ *verb*

- ► decay
- ► rot
- ► decompose
- ► spoil
- ► go bad *(informal)*

decay
if something decays, natural chemical processes slowly destroy it. You use **decay** especially about wood, plants, teeth, and dead bodies: *The leaves decay and make the soil richer. | Too much sweet food will cause your teeth to decay.*

rot
rot means the same as **decay** but sounds more informal. You use **rot** especially about food, teeth, and wood: *His teeth were rotting, and his breath smelled terrible.*

decompose
if a dead plant, animal, or person decomposes, it decays: *A human body starts to decompose very soon after death.*

spoil
if food spoils, it starts to decay so that it is no longer safe to eat: *Food that is left in the sun will quickly start to spoil.*

go bad (*informal*)
go bad means the same as **decay**: *I poured the milk down the drain because it was going bad.*
→ see **rotten**

deceit *noun* → see **dishonesty**

deceitful *adjective* → see **dishonest**

deceive *verb* → see **lie²**, **trick²**

decent *adjective* → see **good**, **satisfactory**

deception *noun* → see **dishonesty**, **trick¹**

decide /dɪˈsaɪd/ *verb*

1 to make a choice about doing something
- ► decide
- ► make up your mind (*informal*)
- ► make a decision
- ► choose
- ► opt
- ► come to a decision
- ► resolve (*formal*)

2 to decide that something is true
- ► decide
- ► conclude (*formal*)
- ► determine (*formal*)
- ► come to the conclusion
- ► infer (*formal*)
- ► deduce (*formal*)

1 to make a choice about doing something

decide
to make a choice about what you are going to do, after thinking about all the possibilities: ***I decided to** learn Spanish instead of French.* | *Have you decided what you're going to wear to the party?*

make up your mind (*informal*)
to decide what you are going to do and be unlikely to change your decision: *She **made up her mind to** look for a new job.*

make a decision
to decide what you are going to do after thinking carefully about something important: *They **made a decision not to** have children.*

choose
to decide to do something, especially when this is different from what people expect or tell you to do: *I told her not to go out with him, but she **chose to** ignore my advice.*

opt
to choose to do one thing instead of another: *Some people in the group **opted to** take the bus instead of a cab.*

come to a decision *also* **reach a decision**
to officially decide something important after discussing and thinking carefully about it. You use **come to a decision** and **reach a decision** about a decision that a group of people makes: *After several weeks of discussions, the committee still has not **come to a decision on** how to spend the money.*

resolve (AWL) (*formal*)
to decide that you will definitely do something: *After failing the test, she **resolved to** study harder.*
→ see **choose** for **decide on** meaning "to choose one thing from many possible choices"

2 to decide that something is true

decide
to make a judgment about something after thinking about all the information: *I can't decide whether he was serious or joking.* | *We **decided that** the trip to Hawaii would be too expensive.*

conclude (AWL) (*formal*)
to decide that something is true from the information you have: *The jury listened carefully to the evidence and **concluded that** the man was guilty.*

determine (*formal*)
to decide what is true by finding out the facts about something: *Experts have **determined that** the signature on the letter was a fake.*

come to the conclusion *also* **reach the conclusion**
to decide that something is true after thinking carefully about all the facts: *After talking to several people, **I came to the conclusion that** Joe was lying.* | *The committee **reached the conclusion that** the program was not achieving the results they wanted.*

infer (AWL) (*formal*)
to decide that something is probably true because of what you see or hear, but not because you are told something directly. **Infer** is most often used in scientific, literary, and formal writing: *We can **infer from** her letters **that** she was*

D

very unhappy at this time, even though she never really complains.

deduce (AWL) (*formal*)
to decide that something must be true by thinking carefully about the facts that you know. You use **deduce** to talk about scientific or technical decisions: *By looking at when and where people became infected, scientists **deduced that** mosquitoes were spreading the disease.*

decision /dɪˈsɪʒən/ *noun*

1 the action of choosing to do something
- ► decision
- ► choice

2 the action of deciding that something is true
- ► decision
- ► conclusion
- ► judgment

1 the action of choosing to do something

decision
the action of choosing to do something after you think about different possibilities: *His **decision to** quit school at age 15 was a big mistake.* | *Are you coming to the park or not? You need to make a decision.*

choice
a deliberate decision to do something, especially when this is different from what people expect or tell you to do: *I made the **choice to** stop eating meat when I was in high school because I didn't like the idea of animals being killed for food.*
→ see **choice**

2 the action of deciding that something is true

decision
the action of deciding that one thing is good, right, or true instead of something else: *Sandra won the competition, but I don't agree with the judges' decision.* | *They expect the jury to make a decision by the end of the week.*

conclusion (AWL)
a decision that something is true, which you make after thinking about the information that you have: *Police reached the **conclusion that** the man had been poisoned.*

judgment
a decision or opinion about something that you reach after thinking about it carefully: *We don't have enough information to make a **judgment about** how fair the test is.*
→ **Judgment** can also be used for an official decision made by a judge or court of law: *Thompson won $100,000 in a court **judgment against** the company.*
→ see **judgment**, **make a decision** at **decide**

declaration *noun* → see **statement**

declare *verb* → see **say**

decline[1] *noun* → see **decrease[1]**

decline[2] *verb* → see **decrease[2]**, **get worse**, **refuse**

decoration /ˌdekəˈreɪʃən/ *noun*

- ► decoration
- ► ornament

decoration
a pretty thing that you use to make something look more attractive: *A group of students put up decorations in the gym for the school dance.* | *Ribbon is used as a decoration on Christmas presents.*

ornament
a beautiful object that you show in your home or use to decorate something: *Help me hang the ornaments on the Christmas tree.*

decorative /ˈdekərеɪtɪv/ *adjective*

- ► decorative (*formal*)
- ► fancy
- ► ornamental

decorative (*formal*)
pretty and used to make something look more attractive, but not always useful or necessary: *She had placed a few decorative pillows at the end of the couch.* | *These wooden beams are just decorative – they don't support the roof.*

fancy
decorative and usually expensive: *We put out fancy soaps and towels when guests come to stay at our house.*

ornamental
designed to decorate a place, and usually without a useful purpose: *There is an ornamental pond in the backyard.*

ADVERBS

You can make the adjectives that mean **decorative** into adverbs by using an **-ly** ending: *Arrange the nuts decoratively over the top of the cake.* | *The sisters were fancily dressed.*

decrease¹ /ˈdikris/ *noun*

- decrease
- fall
- drop
- decline
- reduction
- cut

ANTONYMS → see **increase² (1)**

decrease
a situation in which an amount, price, or level becomes less: *The* ***decrease in*** *students' test scores is worrying the teachers.* | *There has been a significant* ***decrease in*** *the number of deaths from lung cancer.*

fall
a sudden or large decrease in the amount, price, or level of something: *The company is reporting a 12%* ***fall in*** *profits this year.*

drop
drop means the same as **fall** but sounds a little more informal: *The sudden* ***drop in*** *temperature killed some of my outdoor plants.*

decline (AWL)
a decrease in the number, amount, or quality of something, especially a gradual decrease. **Decline** is slightly formal and is used especially in news and official reports: *In the past two years, there has been a* ***decline in*** *the number of people using public transportation.*

reduction
a situation in which someone deliberately makes the amount, price, or level of something lower. **Reduction** is slightly formal and is used especially in news and official reports: *A small* ***reduction in*** *costs can result in a large increase in profits.*

cut
cut means the same as **reduction** but sounds more informal. You use **cut** especially about reductions made by a government or company: *Politicians are promising more tax cuts.*

decrease² /dɪˈkris/ *verb*

- decrease
- go down (*informal*)
- fall
- drop
- decline
- diminish (*formal*)
- plunge

ANTONYMS → see **increase¹ (1)**

decrease
to become less in number or amount. **Decrease** sounds slightly formal and is used especially in reports and official writing: *The average rainfall decreased by around 30% during the drought.* | *What can you do to decrease your risk of a heart attack?*

go down (*informal*)
go down means the same as **decrease**: *Unemployment has gone down slowly in the past few months, but more jobs are still needed.*

fall
to decrease, especially suddenly or by a large amount: *At night, the temperature* ***falls to*** *minus 20 degrees.* | *Housing prices are continuing to fall, with most houses costing about 15% less than at this time last year.*

drop
drop means the same as **fall** but is a little more informal: *At night, the temperature* ***drops to*** *minus 20 degrees.*

decline (AWL)
to decrease in amount, level, or quality, usually gradually. **Decline** is slightly formal and is used especially in news and official reports: *Support for the president has steadily declined since the election.*

diminish (AWL) (*formal*)
to become smaller or less important: *As the planet warms up, the ice in the Arctic is diminishing every year.* | *Her interest in soccer diminished as she became older.*

plunge *also* **plummet**
to decrease suddenly and by a very large amount. **Plunge** and **plummet** are used especially in news reports about numbers and levels: *The company's stock price has plummeted 30% because of the lawsuit against it.* | *Temperatures* ***plunged to*** *30 degrees below zero.*
→ see **reduce**

dedicated *adjective* → see **hard-working**

dedication *noun* → see **determination**

D

deep *adjective* → see **dark¹**, **low**, **strong**, Topic **Describing People's Emotions**, **Describing Size**, **Describing Sounds and Voices**

deeply *adverb* → see **very**

defeat¹ *noun* → see **loss**

defeat² *verb* → see **beat**

defect /ˈdifekt/ *noun*

- defect
- fault
- problem
- flaw
- bug
- glitch

defect
a problem with the way a product or machine is made so that it does not work correctly or it looks wrong: *Cars are tested for defects before they leave the factory.* | ***Defects in** the computer software caused a lot of problems.*

fault
something that is wrong with a part of a machine, which stops it from working well: *He corrected a fault in the wiring of the house.*

problem
something that is wrong, which you have to deal with. **Problem** is a very general word and you use it to talk about situations as well as machines: *There seems to be some kind of problem with the air conditioning system.*

flaw
a mark or weakness that makes something not perfect: *The price of the wine glasses was reduced because they had **flaws in** them.*
→ You also use **flaw** about a mistake in something such as an argument or plan: *His opponent quickly found a **flaw in** his argument.*

bug
a small problem in a computer program, which stops it from working well: *We need to fix a **bug** in the software.*

glitch
a small fault in a system, which stops it from working correctly: *There was a **glitch** in the computer system and the letter was sent to the wrong address.*

defend /dɪˈfend/ *verb*

- defend
- stand up for (*informal*)
- stick up for (*informal*)
- come to someone's defense (*formal*)

ANTONYMS → see **criticize**

defend
to say or do something to show you support a person or idea that is being criticized: *She defended her daughter's decision to leave college and travel for a year.* | *The local people said they were fighting to defend their freedom.*

stand up for (*informal*)
stand up for means the same as **defend**, but sounds more informal and is used especially about ideas: *We will stand up for our civil rights, and protest if the government tries to stop us.*

stick up for (*informal*)
to defend a person who is being criticized, especially when no one else will defend him or her: *My big sister stuck up for me when all the other kids were teasing me.*

come to someone's defense (*formal*)
come to someone's defense means the same as **stick up for** but sounds more formal: *She thought Tom would come to her defense, but he just watched while they all blamed her.*
→ see **protect**

defiant *adjective* → see **rebellious**

define *verb* → see **explain**

definite /ˈdefɪnət/ *adjective*

- definite
- clear
- distinct

definite (AWL)
strong and noticeable: *There was a definite feeling of relief after the exam was over.* | *The team has shown definite improvement in the last few games.*

clear
easy to notice, and impossible to doubt or make a mistake about: *It is **clear that** she is in love with him.* | *The teacher made it **clear that** she was ready to begin by clapping her hands.*

distinct (AWL)
a distinct feeling or possibility clearly exists and cannot be ignored, even though you are not completely certain that it is true or correct: *There is a distinct possibility that we will all lose*

our jobs. | *I had the distinct impression that someone was watching me.*
→ see **certain**

ADVERBS

You can make the adjectives that mean **definite** into adverbs by using an **-ly** ending: *The team has definitely improved this season.* | *She was clearly angry.* | *It is distinctly possible that she will lose her job.*

definitely *adverb* → see **certainly**

definition *noun* → see **meaning**

defy *verb* → see **disobey**, **rebel**[2]

degree *noun* → see **level**, Topic **Education**

delay[1] /dɪˈleɪ/ *noun*

- **delay**
- **holdup** (*informal*)
- **wait**
- **postponement** (*formal*)

delay
a situation when something happens later or more slowly than you planned or expected: *The plane finally took off after **a delay of** about an hour.* | *The work on the bridge is likely to cause long traffic delays, so plan ahead.*

holdup (*informal*)
a situation that is causing something to happen more slowly than you planned or expected: *We've been waiting in line for 45 minutes. What's the holdup?*

wait
a time when you have to wait for something to happen: *There will be a short wait before you can see the doctor.*

postponement (*formal*)
the act of changing the time or date of an event to a later time or date: *Ken asked for a **postponement of** the meeting so he could have another day to prepare.*

delay[2] /dɪˈleɪ/ *verb*

- **delay**
- **hold up** (*informal*)
- **postpone**
- **procrastinate**
- **put off** (*informal*)
- **stall** (*informal*)
- **defer** (*formal*)

delay
to make someone arrive late or make something happen late: *The meeting was delayed for ten minutes while we waited for Gina.* | *They delayed the flight because of fog.*

hold up (*informal*)
hold up means the same as **delay** but is informal: *The accident held up traffic for more than two hours on Route 1.* | *Sorry I'm late – I **got held up** at work.*

postpone
to change the time of an event to a later time or date: *We had to postpone the trip because of Dad's illness.*

procrastinate
to delay doing something that you should do, because you do not want to do it: *Stop procrastinating and get your homework done!*

put off (*informal*)
put off means the same as **procrastinate** but is informal: *I keep putting off doing my housework, because it's so boring.* | *Don't put it off any longer, or you won't have any time to see your friends.*
→ **GRAMMAR:** You say "put off something" or "put something off," not just ~~*put off*~~.

stall (*informal*)
to deliberately delay doing something until a later time, either because you are not ready or to give yourself an advantage: *You need to quit stalling and go out there and talk to him.*
→ If you **stall** someone, you try to prevent him or her from doing something until later: *Can you stall her for a few minutes while I keep looking for her keys?*

defer (*formal*)
to delay starting or doing something, usually so that something else can happen first: *The committee deferred the decision so that they could get more information on the subject.*

delayed *adjective* → see **late**

delegate *verb* → see **assign**

deliberate /dɪˈlɪbərət/ *adjective*

- **deliberate**
- **intentional**
- **conscious**

ANTONYMS → see **accidental**

deliberate
planned and intended: *It was no accident that he broke the bowl. It was deliberate.* | *The explosion was a deliberate attack on the local people.*

intentional
deliberate. You use **intentional** especially about actions that are wrong or illegal: *The referee said the push was intentional and called a foul.*

conscious
done deliberately after you have thought about what the results will be: *Valerie made a conscious effort to be friendly even though she was feeling very shy.*

deliberately /dɪˈlɪbərətli/ *adverb*

- ► deliberately
- ► on purpose (*informal*)
- ► intentionally
- ► consciously

ANTONYMS → see **accidentally**

deliberately
if you do something deliberately, you mean to do it and you hope it has a particular effect: *He deliberately slowed down to annoy the driver behind him.* | *I know she hurt your feelings, but I don't think she did it deliberately.*

on purpose (*informal*) *also* **purposely**
on purpose means the same as **deliberately**, but is informal and you use it especially in spoken language. **Purposely** is slightly more formal and is also used in writing: *Will always calls me the wrong name. Do you think he does it on purpose?* | *He caught the first ball, but purposely missed the second.*

intentionally
deliberately. You use **intentionally** especially about actions that are wrong or illegal: *He would never intentionally hurt her.*

consciously
if you do something consciously, you do it deliberately after thinking about what the results will be: *She consciously designed the room to make you feel like you are outside in nature.*

delicacy *noun* → see **food**

delicate *adjective* → see **weak**

delicious /dɪˈlɪʃəs/ *adjective*

- ► delicious
- ► good
- ► tasty (*informal*)
- ► flavorful
- ► appetizing (*formal*)
- ► mouth-watering
- ► scrumptious (*informal*)

delicious
delicious food tastes very good: *The soup is delicious! You'll have to give me the recipe.* | *He served a delicious chocolate dessert with a raspberry sauce.*

good
good food has a pleasant taste. **Good** is the usual word in everyday English to describe food when you enjoy its taste: *This tomato soup is really good - can I have some more?*

tasty (*informal*)
having a very good taste: *She makes a really tasty chicken and rice dish.*

flavorful
having a strong pleasant taste. You use **flavorful** especially in written descriptions: *This flavorful sauce comes from a recipe by Larry Forgione.*

appetizing (*formal*)
food that looks or smells appetizing makes you want to eat it: *The appetizing smell of baked apples filled the house.*

mouth-watering
very appetizing: *The mouth-watering smells from the kitchen were making my stomach feel very empty.*

scrumptious (*informal*)
tasting very good. **Scrumptious** is used about food, but not about drinks: *Karen's homemade brownies are really scrumptious.*
→ see Topic **Describing Food**

GRAMMAR CHECK: delicious

Don't use "very" with **delicious**, **mouth-watering**, or **scrumptious**. Say: *It was really/absolutely delicious.*

ADVERBS

You can make **delicious** into an adverb by using an **-ly** ending: *The food was deliciously spicy and satisfying.*

delight *noun* → see **happiness**, **pleasure**

delighted *adjective* → see **happy**, Topic **Describing People's Emotions**

delightful *adjective* → see **nice**

deliver *verb* → see **give**, **take**

delivery *noun* → see **mail[1]**

demand[1] *noun* → see **request**

demand[2] *verb* → see **ask**, **expect**, **insist**, **need[1]**

demonstrate *verb* → see **explain**, **protest[2]**, **show[1]**

demonstration *noun* → see **explanation**, **protest[1]**

denial *noun* → see **refusal**

dense *adjective* → see **heavy**, **thick**, Topic **Describing Places**

dentist *noun* → see **doctor**, Topic **Medical Treatment**

deny *verb* → see **refuse**, **say**

depart *verb* → see **leave**

dependence /dɪˈpendəns/ *noun*

- ► dependence
- ► reliance

ANTONYMS → see **freedom**

dependence
the state of needing someone or something else in order to exist, continue, or succeed: *The U.S. must reduce its **dependence on** foreign oil. | His **dependence on** pain medicine became a problem.*

reliance (AWL)
the state of needing someone or something in order to be able to do something: *Do you think our **reliance on** computers is a good thing or a bad thing?*

depend on /dɪˈpend/ *phrasal verb*

- ► depend on
- ► rely on
- ► count on
- ► be reliant on
- ► trust

depend on
to trust that someone or something will do something that you need or that you expect him or her to do: *You can depend on Jane – she always keeps her promises.*

rely on (AWL)
to trust that someone or something will do something that you need: *The city relies on the police to keep people safe.*
→ **Depend on** and **rely on** have very similar meanings and you can usually use either expression in a sentence: *I knew I could depend on you for help. | I knew I could rely on you for help.*

count on
to trust that someone or something will do something that you want. **Count on** is a little more informal than **depend on** or **rely on**: *I knew I could count on my older brother for protection.*
→ You can also use **count on** to say that you expect someone to do something, even if it is not a good thing: *You can always count on Jack to say the wrong thing.*

be reliant on
to rely on someone or something completely to do or provide something: *When she got older and could not drive, she **was reliant on** her family to take her to the supermarket, to church, and anywhere else she needed to go.*

trust
to feel sure that someone will do what he or she says or what is right: *David is one of my oldest friends – I trust him completely. | I wouldn't trust Tina to babysit – she is too immature.*
→ **Trust** can also mean "to feel sure that something is correct or will work correctly": *She needs a car she can trust.*

depressed *adjective* → see **sad**, Topic **Describing People's Emotions**

depressing *adjective* → see **sad**

depression *noun* → see **recession**, **sadness**

depth *noun* → see **thickness**, Topic **Describing Size**

derive *verb* → see **come**

descend *verb* → see **go down**

describe /dɪˈskraɪb/ *verb*

- ► describe
- ► tell someone about something
- ► write about
- ► give an account of
- ► portray (*formal*)
- ► characterize (*formal*)

describe
to say what someone or something is like: *She **described** the man **as** tall, with black hair and a mustache. | It is difficult to **describe how** I feel – excited but a little scared, I guess.*

tell someone about something
to talk to someone about something, and give him or her information about it: *So, tell me about your vacation!*

write about
to describe someone or something in a piece of writing: *In his book, he writes about his life in Mexico.*

give an account of
to describe what happened in a situation: *The judge asked the witness to give her account of the robbery.*

portray (*formal*)
to describe someone or something in a particular way, especially when this is wrong: *In the book she is **portrayed as** being a cruel woman, but that is far from the truth.*

characterize (*formal*)
to describe someone or something as a particular type of person or thing: *Sarah likes to*

D

***characterize** herself **as** an ordinary working mother.*

description /dɪˈskrɪpʃən/ *noun*

- ► description
- ► narration
- ► commentary

description
a piece of writing or speech that gives details about what someone or something is like: *Write a **description of** someone you know well.* | *Tom gave the police a **description of** the car.* | *The guidebook contains a good **description of** the church.*

narration
a spoken description of what is happening that you listen to while you are watching a movie or TV show, or the main description of what is happening in a story or novel: *Morgan Freeman provided the **narration for** the documentary "March of the Penguins."* | *The narration is done in the first person – the main character tells the story.*

commentary (AWL)
a spoken description of an event, such as a sports event or race, that is given while the event is happening, especially on television or radio: *He does radio **commentary for** all of the baseball games.*

deserted *adjective* → see **empty**[1]

deserve /dɪˈzɚv/ *verb*

- ► deserve
- ► earn
- ► merit (*formal*)
- ► have a right to
- ► be entitled to (*formal*)

deserve
if you deserve something, it is right that you should get it because of something good or bad you have done: *You've been working hard all morning – you deserve a break.* | *He **deserves to** be punished for his crimes.*

earn
to deserve something because you have worked for it: *I think Sofia should get the award – she has definitely earned it.*

merit (*formal*)
to deserve something, especially praise or attention: *It is a fascinating book that merits attention.*

have a right to
if you have a right to something, you should be allowed to have it or do it: *Ernesto has a right to know what happened to his father.*

be entitled to (*formal*)
if you are entitled to something, you should be allowed to have it: *Everyone is entitled to a fair trial under U.S. law.*

design /dɪˈzaɪn/ *noun*

- ► design
- ► layout
- ► format

design (AWL)
the way that something has been made and how it looks or works: *The engine has a new design that uses less gas.* | *The building has a very modern design with open spaces and huge glass windows.*

layout
the way that things are arranged. You use layout about the way things are placed in a building, book, magazine, or website: *They have changed the layout of the store – the bakery is near the entrance now.* | *The website's layout is very clean and readable, with links on the side.*

format (AWL)
the way in which something such as an article or page is printed: *A common newsletter format is to have two columns.* | *The interview was printed in a question-and-answer **format**.*

designed *adjective* → see **be designed to** at **supposed to**

designer /dɪˈzaɪnɚ/ *noun*

- ► designer
- ► architect
- ► engineer
- ► developer
- ► planner

designer
someone who decides how new things will look or how they will be made: *She works as a fashion designer.* | *He was the designer of the first jet plane.*

architect
someone whose job is to design buildings: *The town hall was designed by a famous architect.*

engineer
someone whose job is to design and build machines, roads, and bridges: *The engineers had to deal with a lot of problems when they were building the bridge.*

developer
someone who designs new software or

products: *Software developers are working on a new video game that you can use for learning languages.*

planner
someone who plans the way cities grow and develop: *Planners are looking at ways to improve the city's public transportation system.*

desire[1] *noun* → see **wish**

desire[2] *verb* → see **want**

desperate *adjective* → see **serious**

despise *verb* → see **hate**

despite *preposition* → see Function Word **although**

dessert *noun* → see Topic **Eating in a Restaurant**

destiny *noun* → see **future**

destroy /dɪˈstrɔɪ/ *verb*

- ► destroy
- ► demolish
- ► tear down
- ► wreck
- ► devastate
- ► wipe out (*informal*)
- ► level

ANTONYMS → see **create**

destroy
to damage something so badly that it no longer exists or cannot be fixed: *The hotel was destroyed by fire.* | *The explosion destroyed the building.*

demolish
to completely destroy a building or part of a building, often deliberately so that you can build something new: *They demolished the old houses and built an apartment building there.*

tear down *also* **knock down**
to deliberately destroy a building or part of a building. **Tear down** and **knock down** are more informal than **demolish**: *We decided to tear down the wall so that we could make the kitchen bigger.*

wreck
wreck is similar in meaning to **destroy**, but it is less formal, and you use it especially about vehicles: *He wrecked the car in a high-speed crash.*

devastate
to cause serious damage to a large area and destroy many things in it: *The earthquake devastated the city.*

wipe out (*informal*)
to destroy all of a group of people or things: *The flood wiped out the whole village.*

level
to destroy everything in an area so that nothing is standing above the ground: *Enemy planes dropped bombs that leveled a large part of the town.*
→ see **damage**[2]

destruction /dɪˈstrʌkʃən/ *noun*

- ► destruction
- ► devastation
- ► demolition

ANTONYMS → see **creation**

destruction
a situation in which something is destroyed: *We must save the rainforests from destruction.* | *The volcano caused the **destruction of** the city of Pompeii.*

devastation
a lot of damage to a large area: *The bombs caused widespread devastation – many parts of the city were completely destroyed.*

demolition
the act of completely destroying a building, especially to build a new one: *Demolition of the old factory will start tomorrow.*
→ see **damage**[1]

destructive *adjective* → see **harmful**

detach *verb* → see **remove**

detail /ˈditeɪl/ *noun*

- ► detail
- ► point
- ► thing (*informal*)

detail
one fact or piece of information about something: *I can't remember every **detail of** the story – it's very complicated.* | *Your report should include lots of details about what happened.*

point
a detail in a speech, piece of writing, plan, etc., especially one that you want to discuss: *I agreed with most of what you said, but there were a couple of points that I wanted to talk to you about.*

thing (*informal*)
thing means the same as **point**: *There is one thing I'm not sure about, and that is how we're going to get to the airport.*

D

detailed /dɪˈteɪld/ *adjective*

- ► detailed
- ► elaborate

ANTONYMS → see **general (1)**

detailed
including a lot of pieces of information: *Do you have a more detailed map of the area? | She gave the police a detailed description of the robbers, including the clothes they were wearing and their car license plate number.*

elaborate
complicated and having a lot of small details or parts that are connected with each other: *The cloth has an elaborate design of circles and squares. | They came up with an elaborate plan to kidnap the mayor.*
→ see **complicated**

ADVERBS
You can make the adjective **elaborate** into an adverb by using an **-ly** ending: *The cloth was elaborately patterned.*

details *noun* → see **information**

detect *verb* → see **find, notice**[1]

detective *noun* → see **police officer**

determination /dɪˌtɚməˈneɪʃən/ *noun*

- ► determination
- ► ambition
- ► drive
- ► persistence
- ► perseverance
- ► dedication
- ► commitment
- ► willpower

determination
a strong desire to do something so that you keep trying, even when it is difficult: *The team showed a lot of determination, and they eventually won the game 48-46. | The civil rights leaders had great courage and determination. They refused to give up.*

ambition
determination to be successful, rich, or famous: *He had both talent and ambition, and was likely to do well in politics.*

drive
the determination and energy that helps someone succeed, especially in business or work: *Do you think she has **the drive to** become a successful businesswoman?*

persistence (AWL)
determination that makes you keep trying to do something, even when you have problems or people say you cannot do it: *She kept applying for jobs, and her persistence was finally rewarded when she got an interview.*

perseverance
the ability to continue trying to achieve something over a long period in a patient way, even when this is difficult: *Learning a language takes a lot of patience and perseverance – you can't just learn it in a week.*

dedication
determination that makes you work hard because you care a lot about something: *Becoming a professional musician takes a lot of dedication, because you must practice for hours every day.*

commitment
determination to work hard at something until it is finished, because you believe it is good or important: *The teacher's **commitment to** her students is very obvious from the way she gives attention to each one.*

willpower
the ability to control your mind and body in order to achieve something you have decided to do: *It takes a lot of willpower to give up smoking.*
→ see **stubbornness** for words meaning "not changing your opinions or what you are doing"

determined /dɪˈtɚmɪnd/ *adjective*

- ► determined
- ► stubborn
- ► single-minded
- ► tough
- ► persistent
- ► tenacious (*formal*)
- ► resolute (*formal*)
- ► pushy (*informal*)

determined
having a strong desire to do something, even when it is difficult: *He was **determined to** go to medical school and become a doctor. | My mother was **determined that** we should stay in school and get a good education.*

stubborn
determined not to change your ideas or what you are doing, even when other people think you

are being unreasonable: *Some children are stubborn and refuse to do what you ask, so you'll need all your patience with them.*

single-minded
very determined to achieve one thing and ignoring everything else: *He has not married because he is too single-minded about his career.*

tough
having a strong character and determined to succeed, even in difficult situations: *To be a successful athlete, you need to be mentally tough as well as physically fit.*

persistent (AWL)
continuing to try to do something, even when you do not succeed for a long time: *If you want to get a job, you have to be persistent. Don't give up.*

tenacious (*formal*)
very determined to do something and refusing to stop trying: *Thanks to the firefighters' tenacious efforts, the building was saved.*

resolute (*formal*)
very determined to not change a decision or plan because you believe strongly that you are right: *The president remained resolute despite strong opposition from Congress.*

pushy (*informal*)
determined to get what you want, even though other people think you are being rude or annoying: *A pushy salesman was trying to sell me a phone I didn't want.*

ADVERBS

You can make the adjectives **stubborn**, **persistent**, **tenacious**, and **resolute** into adverbs by using an **-ly** ending: *"I won't go," he said stubbornly.* | *Reporters persistently questioned the mayor about the program.* | *The senator is resolutely opposed to raising taxes.*

detest *verb* → see **hate**

develop *verb* → see **become**, **grow**

development *noun* → see **building**, **progress**[1]

device *noun* → see **tool**

devise *verb* → see **create**

diagram *noun* → see **drawing**

dialect *noun* → see **language**

dialogue *noun* → see **conversation**, **discussion**, Topic **Books and Literature**

diary *noun* → see **record**

dictator *noun* → see Topic **Government and Politics**

dictionary *noun* → see Topic **Books and Literature**

die /daɪ/ *verb*

- ► die
- ► pass away (*formal*)
- ► be killed
- ► lose your life
- ► perish (*formal*)
- ► drop dead (*informal*)

ANTONYMS → see **live**

die
to stop living and become dead: *Her mother **died of cancer.*** | *The actor **died in a car accident.***
→ **GRAMMAR:** Don't say: ~~*He was died last year.*~~ Say: *He died last year.*

pass away (*formal*)
to die. You use **pass away** when you want to be polite and avoid using the word **die**: *His wife passed away last week.*

be killed
to die in an accident, war, or fight: *Over 2,800 people were killed when two planes flew into the World Trade Center in New York.*

lose your life
to die in a terrible event: *Hundreds of people lost their lives when the ship went down.*

perish (*formal*)
to die, especially in a sudden and terrible way. You use **perish** especially in stories and news reports: *Five children perished before firefighters could put out the fire.*

drop dead (*informal*)
to die suddenly when people do not expect you to: *He dropped dead of a heart attack when he was only 47.*
→ see **die down** at **quiet**[2], **die out** at **disappear**
→ see **dead**[1], **dead**[2]

diet *noun* → see **food**

differ *verb* → see **disagree**, **vary**

difference /ˈdɪfərəns/ *noun*

- ► difference
- ► contrast
- ► distinction
- ► gap
- ► contradiction (*formal*)

ANTONYMS → see **similarity**

difference
a way in which two things or people are not the same: *There is a small* ***difference in*** *price between the two phones – one costs $95 and the other costs $99.* | *One* ***difference between*** *African and Asian elephants is the size of their ears.*

contrast (AWL)
a very clear difference that you can easily see when you compare two things or people: *The* ***contrast between*** *the old buildings and the modern skyscrapers makes an interesting photograph.*

distinction (AWL)
a difference that exists between two things that seem similar: *There is a* ***distinction between*** *deliberately telling lies and lying so that you don't hurt someone's feelings.*

D

gap
a big difference between two amounts, ages, or groups of people: *There is a big* ***gap between*** *their ages – she is 22 and he is 39.* | *The* ***gap between*** *the rich and the poor is becoming wider every day.*

contradiction (AWL) (*formal*)
a difference between two things that someone says, which means they cannot both be true: *There is a* ***contradiction in*** *his argument – he says you must not kill people, but that all murderers should be killed.*
→ see **variety** for "a lot of different types of something" and "a situation in which there are a lot of different people or things"
→ see **make a difference** at **affect**

different /ˈdɪfərənt/ *adjective*

1 not the same
- ► different
- ► not like
- ► unlike
- ► distinct
- ► dissimilar (*formal*)
- ► contrasting
- ► contradictory
- ► incompatible
- ► inconsistent

ANTONYMS → see **same**

2 including many different things or people
- ► varied
- ► diverse
- ► varying

1 not the same

different
not the same: *The two brothers are very* ***different from*** *each other in looks and in personality.* | *You look different – have you had a haircut?* | *"Wait" and "weight" have different spellings, but the same pronunciation.*

not like
completely different from another person or thing: *The movie was not like the book. They changed just about everything.*

unlike
unlike means the same as **not like**, but is more formal and can be used at the beginning of a sentence: *He is unlike any other person I've ever met.* | *Unlike me, she is very good at art.*

distinct (AWL)
if two things are distinct, they are clearly different and separate from each other: *Spanish and Portuguese are two distinct languages.*

dissimilar (AWL) (*formal*)
very different and not like anyone or anything else: *They were both engineers, but otherwise were as dissimilar as steel and silk.*

contrasting (AWL)
two or more things that are contrasting are very different from each other and are almost opposites of each other: *The two judges have contrasting views on what the law means.* | *Choose a shirt in a contrasting color to make the outfit more exciting.*

contradictory (AWL)
if two things are contradictory, they are different and cannot both be true: *The two witnesses' descriptions of what happened are contradictory, so one of them must be lying.*

incompatible (AWL)
if two ideas or methods are incompatible, they are so different that they cannot be used or exist together: *Many doctors think that helping a dying patient to die is* ***incompatible with*** *their promise to save people from death.*
→ You can also use **incompatible** about people who are so different that they cannot have a good relationship or work well together: *Sara and Eduardo married very quickly, and after realizing they were incompatible, they got divorced.*

inconsistent (AWL)
dealing in different ways with situations or people that are the same: *It is* ***inconsistent to*** *send some people to jail and give other people a fine for the same crime.*
→ see **opposite**, **special**

ADVERBS

You can make the adjectives **different**, **distinct**, and **inconsistent** into adverbs by using an **-ly** ending: *"Wait" and "weight" sound the same, but they are spelled differently.* | *The two types of tree are similar, but their leaves are distinctly different.* | *The rules were applied inconsistently, so some students were allowed to do things that other students were punished for.*

2 including many different things or people

varied (AWL)
including many different things or people: *It is important to have a varied diet that includes many different foods.*

diverse (AWL)
including very different things or people: *A diverse group of people – from teenagers to the elderly – expressed their opinions of the plan.*

varying
having different levels or amounts of something: *The students have varying levels of ability, from beginners to advanced learners.*
→ **GRAMMAR: Varying** is always used before a noun: *The books are good for children of varying ages.*

difficult /ˈdɪfɪkəlt/ *adjective*

1 not easy to do, understand, or deal with
- ► difficult
- ► hard
- ► tough (*informal*)
- ► rough (*informal*)
- ► tricky
- ► challenging
- ► daunting (*formal*)
- ► formidable (*formal*)
- ► problematic

2 difficult and tiring
- ► difficult
- ► hard
- ► tough
- ► demanding
- ► strenuous
- ► grueling
- ► laborious

ANTONYMS → see **easy**

1 not easy to do, understand, or deal with

difficult
not easy to do, understand, or deal with: *The questions were difficult to answer.* | *The country is in a difficult economic situation.*

hard
hard means the same as **difficult** but is a little less formal: *The test was really hard.* | *I was having a hard time doing my math homework.*
→ You do not use **hard** with words like "problem," "situation," or "issue," but you can use **difficult** with these words. Don't say: ~~*This is a hard problem/situation/issue to deal with*~~. Say: *This is a difficult problem/situation/issue to deal with.*

tough (*informal*)
very difficult to do or deal with. You use **tough** especially about decisions, questions, or situations: *I like both colleges, so choosing one will be tough.* | *His parents just got divorced, so he has been having a tough time.*

rough (*informal*)
a rough time is one when you have a lot of problems in your life: *He had a rough time after his father died, and he got into a lot of trouble.*

tricky
difficult because you need to think carefully about how to deal with something: *The case has raised some tricky legal questions.*

challenging (AWL)
a challenging situation or problem is difficult in an interesting and enjoyable way. You must work hard to deal with a **challenging** situation: *The writing project is challenging, but most of our students learn a lot.*

daunting (*formal*)
if something is daunting, you are worried that it will be difficult and you do not feel confident that you can do it: *Cooking for 20 people sounded daunting, and I wasn't sure that I could do it on my own.*

formidable (*formal*)
seeming very difficult and needing a lot of effort or skill to do: *The new president will have to deal with some formidable economic problems.*

problematic
involving problems that are difficult to deal with: *Improving the college buildings is a problematic issue because of the high cost.*

ADVERBS

You can make the adjectives **daunting** and **formidable** into adverbs by using an **-ly** ending: *The wall that we had to climb over seemed dauntingly large.* | *The piece of music he had to learn looked formidably difficult.*

2 difficult and tiring

difficult
not easy to do because you have to use a lot of

D

effort: *The Tour de France is the most difficult bicycle race of the year.*

hard
hard means the same as **difficult**: *It was a long hard climb to the top of the mountain.*
→ If something is tiring and needs a lot of effort, you usually use **hard** rather than **difficult**: *It was a hard race.*

tough
very difficult because you have to use a lot of effort: *The other team has some good players, so it is going to be a tough game.*

demanding
difficult and tiring. You use **demanding** especially about jobs or activities: *Being a nurse is a demanding job.* | *Taking care of young children can be very demanding.*

strenuous
needing a lot of effort and strength: *Don't do any strenuous exercise until your back is completely better.*

grueling
very tiring and continuing for a long time: *The race is a grueling 24-hour run across the desert.*

laborious
taking a long time and needing to be done very slowly and carefully: *Making a movie is a laborious process involving a huge amount of work.*

ADVERBS

You can make the adjectives **strenuous** and **laborious** into adverbs by using an **-ly** ending: *She practiced strenuously before the game.* | *He laboriously began digging the holes for the fence posts.*

difficulty *noun* → see **problem**

dig /dɪɡ/ *verb*

- ► dig
- ► tunnel
- ► burrow
- ► shovel
- ► plow
- ► excavate (*formal*)
- ► scoop

dig
to make a hole in the ground, using your hands, a tool, or a machine: *The kids used shovels to dig in the sand.* | *She dug a hole in the ground and put some seeds in it.*

tunnel
to dig a long passage under the ground: *Worms eat dirt and **tunnel through** the earth.* | *The men had **tunneled** their way **out** of the prison.*

burrow
if an animal burrows, it makes a hole or tunnel in the ground by digging the earth with its feet, nose, or other part of its body: *The rabbits had **burrowed under** the fence.*

shovel
to lift and move soil or stones with a shovel. A **shovel** is a tool that has a long handle and a wide piece of metal at the bottom, and you use it for digging soil or moving snow: *Ricardo was **shoveling** snow **off** the sidewalk.*

plow
to turn over the earth in a field using a special tool or machine, in order to prepare it for planting seeds: *Farmers were plowing their land and planting cotton seeds.*

excavate (*formal*)
to dig a large hole in the ground, especially to prepare for building something: *The men began excavating the hole for the pool.*

scoop
to pick up or remove something using a spoon or your curved hand: *I **scooped up** some snow and packed it into a ball.*

dig

dig
excavate
plow

digital /ˈdɪdʒɪtl/ *adjective*

- ► digital
- ► electronic
- ► computerized
- ► automatic
- ► automated

digital
using a system in which sounds, writing, or pictures are stored as a set of the numbers 1 and 0. Computers, cameras, cell phones, and other equipment use digital systems: *A digital camera will quickly upload your pictures onto the computer.*

electronic
electronic equipment, such as a computer or television, has small parts inside it that control the electricity that the equipment uses to do complicated things: *The store sells various electronic devices, from cell phones to computers and digital cameras.*

computerized
using a computer to control the way something is done, or to store information: *A lot of banking work has been computerized.*

automatic (AWL)
an automatic machine works by itself, without people needing to operate it: *The automatic safety system shut down the nuclear reactor at the power plant.*

automated (AWL)
using machines to do a job, rather than people: *The factories are completely automated and need very few workers.*

ADVERBS

You can make the adjectives **digital**, **electronic**, and **automatic** into adverbs by using an **-ly** ending: *The information is stored digitally on the computer.* | *I sent her the picture electronically* (=I used electronic equipment to send the picture). | *The doors will shut automatically.*

dignity *noun* → see **pride**

dim *adjective* → see **dark¹**

dimensions *noun* → see **size**, Topic **Describing Size**

dine *verb* → see **eat**

dinner *noun* → see **meal**

diploma *noun* → see Topic **Education**

direct¹ *adjective* → see **honest**

direct² *verb* → see **manage**, **order²**, Topic **Entertainment**

direction /dəˈrekʃən/ *noun*

- ► direction
- ► way
- ► route
- ► course

direction
the area that someone or something is moving, looking, or pointing toward: *"Which direction did they go in?" "I think they were going south."* | *She looked* ***in the direction of*** *the river.*

way
a direction, road, or path that you take to get to a particular place: *Which way is north?* | *Could you tell me the* ***way to*** *the nearest gas station?* | *I couldn't find my way out of the woods and got really scared.*

route (AWL)
the way that you use to go from one place to another: *The most direct* ***route*** *from here* ***to*** *the school is through the park.*

course
the direction in which a boat or plane is moving: *The captain changed the ship's course to avoid the storm.*

directions *noun* → see **instructions**

directly *adverb* → see **straight¹**

director *noun* → see **chairman**, Topic **Entertainment**

dirt /dɚt/ *noun*

- ► dirt
- ► soil
- ► earth
- ► mud
- ► dust

dirt
the natural brown substance that the top layer of the ground is made of. You usually use **dirt** when nothing is growing in it or when it is loose and dry: *There was a pile of dirt next to the hole where the workmen had been digging.* | *You have some dirt on your jeans.*

soil
the top layer of dirt that plants grow in. **Soil** sounds more formal than **dirt**: *The soil in the garden was dry after three weeks without rain.*

earth
the natural substance that the ground is made of. **Earth** is more formal than **dirt**, and you often use it when saying what color it is, when talking about whether it is good for growing crops, or

D

when talking about earth that is deep under the surface: *The workers had to move hundreds of tons of earth and rock in order to build the tunnel.*

mud
wet dirt that is soft and sticky: *Take your shoes off – we don't want mud all over the carpet!*

dust
very small pieces of dirt that look like powder: *The car left a cloud of dust behind it as it drove along the dirt road.*
→ see **ground**

dirty /ˈdɚti/ *adjective*

1 not clean (adjectives)
- dirty
- filthy
- dusty
- muddy
- greasy
- grimy
- polluted
- contaminated (*formal*)

ANTONYMS → see **clean**[1]

2 to become dirty (verbs)
- get something dirty
- stain
- leave a stain
- smudge
- mark
- dirty (*formal*)

ANTONYMS → see **clean**[2] **(1)**

1 not clean (adjectives)

dirty
not clean: *How did you get your hands so dirty? Have you been digging in the mud? | I'm going to put these dirty clothes in the washing machine.*

filthy
very dirty: *The streets were filthy, covered in garbage and mud.*

dusty
covered with dust: *The room is dusty and clearly has not been cleaned for a very long time.*

muddy
covered with mud: *The children's shoes were muddy from playing outside.*

greasy
covered with oil or grease: *He had been working on the car and his hands were greasy.*

grimy
covered with a thin layer of oily dirt or dust that is hard to remove: *The grimy apartment windows looked out onto a street that was always full of traffic.*

polluted
polluted water or air has harmful chemicals or waste in it: *The city has the most polluted air in the U.S., because of all the factories and cars.*

contaminated (*formal*)
contaminated water, food, or land is not safe to use because it contains harmful chemicals or bacteria: *Several people became sick after drinking contaminated water.*

2 to become dirty (verbs)

get something dirty *also* **make something dirty**
to cause something to have dirt or marks on it so that it does not look clean: *Take off your shoes. You're getting the floor dirty. | If I touch it with my muddy fingers, I'll make it dirty.*
→ You can also say that someone or something **gets dirty**: *I dropped my sweatshirt on the ground and it got dirty.*

stain
to accidentally make a colored mark on something, that is difficult to remove: *Allie spilled some grape juice and stained the carpet.*

leave a stain *also* **leave a mark**
to stain or mark something, often without realizing you have done this: *The rubber soles of Joe's shoes left black marks on the kitchen floor. | The hair dye can leave stains on your skin if you're not careful.*

smudge
to make a substance spread in a messy way by rubbing it, especially a substance such as ink, paint, or makeup: *She wiped the tears from her eyes and smudged her makeup.*
→ You can also say that a surface or piece of material **is smudged** when there is something like ink, paint, or food rubbed on it: *The kids' clothes* ***were smudged with*** *blackberry jam.*

mark
to make a dirty or damaged area on something in a way that spoils it, often permanently: *Put the cap on the pen so it doesn't mark the tablecloth.*

dirty (*formal*)
to make something dirty: *We'll just reuse the same towels. We don't need to dirty any clean ones.*
→ see **pollute**

disabled /dɪsˈeɪbəld/ *adjective*

- ► **disabled**
- ► **special needs**
- ► **handicapped**
- ► **paralyzed**

disabled
someone who is disabled cannot use a part of his or her body, or has difficulty using it: *Her son is disabled, and he has to use a wheelchair.* | *Disabled people should have the same rights and choices as everyone else.*

special needs
if someone has special needs, he or she has mental or physical problems that make it difficult to do the things most people are able to do: *He goes to a school for children with special needs.*

handicapped
handicapped means the same as **disabled**, but it is old-fashioned and many people think it is offensive. It is better to say that someone is **disabled** or has **special needs**: *Polio is a disease that can leave people handicapped.*

paralyzed
completely unable to move part of your body: *A car accident left him paralyzed from the waist down.*
→ see **blind**, **deaf**

disadvantage /ˌdɪsədˈvæntɪdʒ/ *noun*

- ► **disadvantage**
- ► **drawback**
- ► **bad point**
- ► **the downside** (*informal*)

ANTONYMS → see **advantage**

disadvantage
something that causes problems, or that makes someone or something less likely to work correctly or be successful: *One of the disadvantages of getting older is that your eyesight gets worse.* | *The main disadvantage of this method is the cost – it's very expensive.*

drawback
a disadvantage that something has when it is good in other ways: *The big drawback of being famous is that you can't go anywhere without people noticing you.*

bad point
something that is bad about something: *One of the bad points about living here is the long winters.*

the downside (*informal*)
the disadvantage of a situation that in most other ways seems good or enjoyable: *It is a great job. The only downside is that I don't get much free time.*

disagree /ˌdɪsəˈgri/ *verb*

- ► **disagree**
- ► **differ** (*formal*)
- ► **be divided**
- ► **take issue with** (*formal*)
- ► **dispute** (*formal*)

ANTONYMS → see **agree**

disagree
to have a different opinion from someone else: *I understood what you said – I just* ***disagreed with*** *it.* | *Scientists* ***disagree about*** *the effects of global warming.*

differ (*formal*)
if two or more people differ about something, they have different opinions from each other about it: *Experts* ***differ on*** *the best way to solve the country's economic problems.*

be divided *also* **be split**
if a group of people are divided or split on something, some of them have one opinion and others have a completely different opinion: *People* ***are divided about*** *the war. Some people think it was the right thing to do, but other people think it was a big mistake.*

take issue with (*formal*)
to say that you strongly disagree with someone or something: *Many people took issue with the judge's decision to release the prisoners.*

dispute (*formal*)
to say that you think something is wrong, or to argue about something: *His claims are disputed by other scientists, who say that he does not have enough evidence.*
→ see **argue**

disagreement /ˌdɪsəˈgrimənt/ *noun*

- ► **disagreement**
- ► **difference of opinion**
- ► **controversy**
- ► **dissent**

ANTONYMS → see **agreement (1)**

disagreement
a situation in which people have different opinions about something and sometimes argue: *We have had a few disagreements, but we are still good friends.* | *There is* ***disagreement*** *among doctors* ***about*** *the best way to treat the disease.*

difference of opinion
a disagreement. You use **difference of opinion**

D

when you want to be polite and avoid more direct words like "argument" and "disagreement": *My sister and I had a* ***difference of opinion about*** *politics.*

controversy (AWL)
a serious disagreement among many people about a decision, plan, or action, which causes arguments for a long time: *There has been a lot of* ***controversy about*** *where to build the city's new sports stadium.*

dissent
the refusal by some people to accept an official opinion or an opinion that most people accept: *During Communist rule, all dissent against the government was severely punished.*
→ A **dissent** is also a statement that a judge writes to give the reasons why he or she disagrees with the opinion of other judges.
→ see **argument**, **objection**

D

disappear /ˌdɪsəˈpɪr/ *verb*

1 to become impossible to see any longer
- ► disappear
- ► vanish
- ► fade away

ANTONYMS → see **appear**

2 to be lost, or to be impossible to find
- ► disappear
- ► vanish
- ► disappear/vanish without a trace

3 to stop existing
- ► disappear
- ► die out
- ► become extinct
- ► cease to exist (*formal*)

1 to become impossible to see any longer

disappear
to become impossible to see any longer: *The sun disappeared behind a cloud.* | *I watched until the ship disappeared over the horizon.*

vanish
to disappear suddenly, in a way that you cannot explain: *When I looked again, the men had vanished into the crowd.*

fade away
to gradually become less clear, strong, or bright, and then disappear: *The last rays of the evening sun faded away.*

2 to be lost, or to be impossible to find

disappear
to be lost, or to be impossible to find: *My keys have disappeared again. I can't find them anywhere.* | *The dog disappeared when we were hiking in the mountains.*

vanish
to suddenly be impossible to find. You use **vanish** when this happens suddenly and you cannot explain why: *I put my bag on this chair a moment ago, and now it seems to have vanished.*

disappear/vanish without a trace
to disappear completely without leaving anything that shows what happened: *The boat vanished without a trace off the coast of Bermuda.*

3 to stop existing

disappear
to stop existing: *Fifty percent of the forest has disappeared over the last ten years.*

die out
to gradually stop existing. You use **die out** especially about a type of animal or plant, a disease, or a custom: *The disease has died out in most of the world, but it is still found in a few areas of Africa.* | *The old ways of farming are slowly dying out.*

become extinct
if a type of animal or plant becomes extinct, it stops existing completely: *If nothing is done to save the whales, they will become extinct.*

cease to exist (*formal*)
to stop existing completely: *The Soviet Union ceased to exist in 1991 and was divided into different countries.*

disappoint /ˌdɪsəˈpɔɪnt/ *verb*

- ► disappoint
- ► let someone down

disappoint
to make someone sad because something does not happen or is not as good as expected: *We realize this will disappoint a lot of people, but we have to cancel the game.* | *I felt that I would disappoint my parents if I didn't get good grades.*

let someone down
to not do what someone expects you to do, or not be as good as someone expects you to be: *I told my mother I would be there, and I don't want to let her down.*

disappointed /ˌdɪsəˈpɔɪntɪd/ *adjective*

- ► disappointed
- ► let down (*informal*)
- ► disillusioned (*formal*)
- ► disenchanted (*formal*)

disappointed
sad because something does not happen or is

not as good as you expected it to be: *I was **disappointed with** my grade on the test.* | *She was **disappointed that** she could not get a ticket for the concert.*

let down (*informal*)
disappointed because someone did not do what he or she promised, or because something is not as good as you expected it to be: *I felt so let down. He promised to help but never came.* | *Some people felt let down by the movie because it wasn't as good as the book.*
→ **GRAMMAR:** Do not use **let down** before a noun. You usually use it after the verb **feel**.

disillusioned (*formal*)
disappointed because you no longer believe that an idea is right or that something or someone is good: *People are becoming **disillusioned with** the president because he has not made the changes he promised to make.*

disenchanted (*formal*)
disappointed and no longer interested or excited by something so that you do not want to spend time doing it or supporting it: *Many Americans are becoming **disenchanted with** politics.*

disappointing /ˌdɪsəˈpɔɪntɪŋ/ *adjective*

- ► disappointing
- ► be a disappointment
- ► be a letdown (*informal*)
- ► not live up to your expectations

disappointing
not as good as you hoped or expected: *Her test scores were disappointing.* | *The team has had a disappointing season, with more losses than wins.*

be a disappointment
not happening in the way that you hoped it would, or not as good as you expected: ***It was a** great **disappointment to** his parents that he did not go to university.* | *The vacation was a disappointment. It rained the whole time.*

be a letdown (*informal*)
to not be as enjoyable as you hoped something would be: *The party was a real letdown. Not many people came.*

not live up to your expectations
to not be as good as someone expected: *I heard so many good things about the movie, but it didn't really live up to my expectations.*

ADVERBS
You can make the adjective **disappointing** into an adverb by using an **-ly** ending: *Her test score was disappointingly low.*

disappointment *noun* → see **failure**

disapprove /ˌdɪsəˈpruv/ *verb*

- ► disapprove
- ► think something is wrong
- ► frown on
- ► show/express/voice your disapproval (*formal*)
- ► condemn
- ► denounce

ANTONYMS → see **approve**

disapprove
to think that someone or something is bad or wrong: *More people today **disapprove of** smoking than in the past.* | *I wanted to be an actor but my parents disapproved.*

think something is wrong
to think that people should not do something: *I think it is wrong to hit children.*

frown on
to think that something is not the right way to behave. You use **frown on** when talking in general about what people think: *In those days, many people frowned on the idea of women working after they got married.*

show/express/voice your disapproval (*formal*)
to show or say publicly that you think someone or something is wrong: *Thousands of people marched through Washington in order to **express** their **disapproval of** the war.*

condemn
to say publicly that you strongly disapprove of someone or something: *The country's leaders condemned the bombings and asked local people to stay calm.*

denounce
denounce means the same as **condemn** but sounds more strongly disapproving: *The senator denounced the waste of public money.*

disaster /dɪˈzæstɚ/ *noun*

- ► disaster
- ► tragedy
- ► catastrophe

disaster
a sudden event such as a flood, storm, or accident that causes great damage or suffering: *Thousands of people lost their homes in the disaster.* | *Disaster struck when the bike rider was hit by a car.* | *Natural disasters such as fires and earthquakes are common in California.*

tragedy
a very sad event or situation in which people

suffer or die: *The plane crash was a terrible tragedy: at least 100 people were killed.*

catastrophe
a terrible event that causes a lot of deaths, damage, and destruction over a very large area: *Scientists say that the oil spill could be a catastrophe for the Gulf Coast.*
→ see **failure**

SYNONYM CHECK
Disaster or catastrophe?

You use **catastrophe** especially when you are talking about events that cause destruction to the environment: *Global warming could result in an environmental catastrophe.*

Disaster is a more common word than **catastrophe**. You use **disaster** when you are talking about a particular event: *Thousands of people were killed or injured in the Chernobyl nuclear disaster.*

D

disbelieve /ˌdɪsbəˈliv/ *verb*

- disbelieve (*formal*)
- distrust
- mistrust
- suspect
- be suspicious of

ANTONYMS → see **believe**

disbelieve (*formal*)
to not believe someone or something: *She was telling the truth, but her story was disbelieved at the time.* | *At first, the research that linked pollution to the dying of trees was widely disbelieved.*

distrust
to not trust someone or something, especially because you think you will be treated in a bad, unfair, or dishonest way: *She learned to distrust her father when she was very young, as he never kept his promises.*

mistrust
mistrust means the same as **distrust**: *He mistrusted lawyers, because he felt they cared more about money than about justice.*

suspect
to think that someone is probably guilty of something illegal or dishonest, but not be completely sure: *The teacher suspected the student **of** cheating on the exam.* | *Do you have any reason to **suspect that** he is lying?*

be suspicious of
if you are suspicious of someone, you think that he or she might be bad or dishonest: *It is a small town, so people are often suspicious of strangers.*

GRAMMAR CHECK: disbelieve

Don't use "be" with **disbelieve**, **distrust**, **mistrust**, or **suspect**. Don't say: ~~*I was disbelieving/distrusting him*~~. Say: *I disbelieved/distrusted him.*

SYNONYM CHECK
Distrust or mistrust?

Distrust and **mistrust** mean the same thing and can often be used in the same sentences. However, you often choose **distrust** when you are sure that you cannot trust someone, and **mistrust** when you think you cannot trust someone, but are not sure.

Both **distrust** and **mistrust** sound formal and are used especially in writing. In everyday English, people usually use **not trust**: ***I do not trust him**, because he never keeps his promises.*

discomfort *noun* → see **pain**

discontinue *verb* → see **stop**[1]

discount *noun* → see **sale**

discourage *verb* → see **persuade**

discouraged /dɪˈskɚɪdʒd/ *adjective*

- discouraged
- dismayed
- demoralized

discouraged
not confident that you can succeed, because you have had problems trying to do something: *Some players got discouraged and quit the team.* | *I felt **discouraged by** the bad grade I got on the test.*

dismayed
discouraged and very worried or disappointed: *He was dismayed when he could not find a job after graduating from college.*

demoralized
someone who is demoralized has lost all confidence and wants to give up: *After losing another game, the team felt completely demoralized.*

discover *verb* → see **find**, **find out**, Topic **Science and Technology**

discovery *noun* → see Topic **Science and Technology**

discrimination *noun* → see **prejudice**, **unfair**

discuss /dɪˈskʌs/ *verb*

- ► discuss
- ► talk something over
- ► debate
- ► confer (*formal*)
- ► consult (*formal*)
- ► negotiate
- ► bargain
- ► haggle (*informal*)

discuss
to talk about something with someone in order to make an agreement, understand it better, or make plans: *Parents at the school were discussing plans for the winter carnival.* | *In English class, we discussed the poem in small groups.* | *If you have any questions, you should **discuss** them **with** your doctor.*

talk something over
talk something over means the same as **discuss** but is more informal: *Before you accept the job, **talk it over with** your family.*

debate (AWL)
to discuss the possible choices of what to do before choosing the best one: *We are **debating whether to** go to the mountains or the beach for our vacation.*

confer (AWL) (*formal*)
to discuss something with someone else, in order to get his or her opinion: *The man **conferred** privately **with** his lawyer for a few minutes before answering the police officer's question.*

consult (AWL) (*formal*)
to discuss something with someone in order to get advice or information: *The president **consulted with** European leaders before taking action.*

negotiate
to discuss something in order to come to an agreement. Use **negotiate** especially when you are talking about politics and business: *You will need to **negotiate** a raise **with** your boss.* | *The teachers' union has **negotiated for** smaller class sizes.*

bargain
to discuss something with someone in order to come to an agreement in which each side gets something that it wants. Use **bargain** when you are trying to get a lower price or conditions that are better for you: *I **bargained with** the man in the shop – I told him I would buy two rugs if he would give me a lower price on both of them.*

haggle (*informal*)
to discuss something in order to persuade someone to reduce the price of something. Use **haggle** especially when someone is discussing a very small amount of money: *Women at the street market were **haggling over** the price of the fabric.*

discussion /dɪˈskʌʃən/ *noun*

- ► discussion
- ► debate
- ► talks
- ► negotiations
- ► dialogue (*formal*)

discussion
an occasion when people talk about their ideas about a subject: *After some discussion, we decided to go to an Italian restaurant for dinner.* | *There has been a lot of **discussion about** freedom of speech and the Internet.*

debate (AWL)
a formal discussion in which people make speeches giving different opinions about a subject. At the end of a **debate**, people often vote to say which opinion they agree with: *In class, the students had a **debate about** the advantages and disadvantages of nuclear power.*
→ You also use **debate** about a situation in which people have different opinions about an important subject: *There is some debate over whether increasing taxes is good for the economy.*

talks
official discussions between two groups of people, especially in order to reach an agreement about something: *Company managers will begin **talks with** union leaders to end the strike.*

negotiations
negotiations means the same as **talks** but sounds more formal: *Peace **negotiations between** the two countries started last week.*

dialogue *also* **dialog** (*formal*)
a discussion between two opposing groups, especially in order to end a disagreement or fighting: *The Secretary of State says she wants to begin a **dialogue with** the rebel leaders.*
→ see **conversation**, **meeting (1)**

disease *noun* → see **sickness**, Topic **Medical Treatment**

disguise¹ *verb* → see **hide**

disguise² *noun* → see **mask**

disguised *adjective* → see **hidden**

disgust /dɪsˈgʌst/ *verb*

1 to make someone feel sick to his or her stomach
- ► **disgust**
- ► **revolt**
- ► **nauseate**

2 to make someone feel shocked
- ► **disgust**
- ► **revolt**
- ► **repel**
- ► **appall**
- ► **sicken**

D

1 to make someone feel sick to his or her stomach

disgust
to make someone feel a little bit sick because something is very bad or unpleasant: *The idea of eating raw fish disgusts me.* | *She was disgusted by the feel of his cold damp hand on her shoulder.*

revolt
to make someone feel very sick. You use **revolt** especially about bad tastes and smells: *He was revolted by the smell of garbage in the kitchen.*

nauseate
to make someone feel as though he or she might vomit: *The thought of food nauseated Eddie.*

2 to make someone feel shocked

disgust
to make someone feel upset and offended because something is very bad or unpleasant: *Many parents were disgusted by the amount of violence in a movie for teenagers.*

revolt
to make someone feel shocked and offended because something is so bad or unpleasant: *The nation was revolted by the pictures from the war zone.*

repel
if someone or something repels you, you are upset or offended by it and want to stay away from it: *His attitudes toward women repel me.*

appall
to make someone feel very shocked and upset: *I was appalled by the terrible conditions of the bathrooms at the school.*

sicken
to make someone feel very shocked and upset. Use **sicken** especially about things that are very unpleasant and offensive: *We were sickened by more newspaper reports of child abuse.*

→ see **shock²**

GRAMMAR CHECK: disgust

All these verbs are often used in the passive.

disgusting *adjective* → see **bad**, Topic **Describing Food**

dish *noun* → see **food**, **pan**, **plate**, Topic **Eating in a Restaurant**

dishonest /dɪsˈɑnɪst/ *adjective*

- ► **dishonest**
- ► **untruthful** (*formal*)
- ► **deceitful** (*formal*)
- ► **corrupt**
- ► **crooked** (*informal*)
- ► **devious**
- ► **underhanded**
- ► **shady** (*informal*)

ANTONYMS → see **honest**

dishonest
a dishonest person tells lies, cheats, or steals things: *I don't trust him. I think he is dishonest.* | *She had gotten the money in a dishonest way, by using someone else's credit card.*

untruthful (*formal*)
not telling the truth about something: *The judge said that Carman had been deliberately untruthful to the court.*

deceitful (*formal*)
telling lies and trying to make people believe things that are not true: *He tricked me. He is a deceitful horrible person.*

corrupt
doing dishonest or illegal things in order to get money or power. You use **corrupt** about government officials and police officers: *Corrupt police officers took money from criminals in return for not arresting them.*

crooked (*informal*)
dishonest and doing illegal things, especially in order to get money: *A crooked judge let him go free.*

devious
dishonest in a clever way, and good at thinking of ways of secretly tricking people in order to get what you want: *Some companies use devious methods to get you to buy their goods.*

underhanded
dishonest because you secretly deceive people in order to get what you want: *An underhanded co-worker took the sales that should have been hers.*

shady (*informal*)
probably dishonest and illegal. You use **shady** especially about business deals: *Mills made his money from shady business deals with the Mafia.*
→ see **cheat** for words meaning "to do something dishonest"
→ see Topic **Describing People's Character**

ADVERBS

You can make the adjectives **dishonest**, **untruthful**, **deceitful**, and **devious** into adverbs by using an **-ly** ending: *He had gotten the money dishonestly.* | *"Yes, I've done the work," he said untruthfully.* | *If you never intended to pay the bill for the goods you received, then you acted deceitfully.*

dishonesty /dɪsˈɑnəsti/ *noun*

- ► dishonesty
- ► lying
- ► cheating
- ► corruption
- ► deception
- ► deceit

ANTONYMS → see **honesty**

dishonesty
behavior that is not honest, for example lying, cheating, or stealing: *If a lawyer is suspected of dishonesty, he risks losing his job.* | *Through bad luck and other people's dishonesty I lost all my money.*

lying
not telling the truth: *There are some cases where lying is a good thing, for example when someone says to you "How old do you think I am?"*

cheating
behaving dishonestly so that you can win a game or competition, or pass a test: *Don't look at my cards – that's cheating!*

corruption
the dishonest use of official power, in order to get money or advantages for yourself. You use **corruption** about government officials and police officers: *The newspaper report said that there was a lot of corruption in the police department.*

deception
dishonest behavior in which you make someone believe something that is not true, especially by hiding the facts about it: *His wife did not find out about his deception until much later, when she found a letter in his jacket pocket.*

deceit
very dishonest behavior and lies that are intended to trick people: *He had lied to me, and I could not forgive his deceit.*

dislike /dɪsˈlaɪk/ *verb*

- ► dislike
- ► not think much of
- ► not care for (*formal*)

ANTONYMS → see **like[1]**

dislike
to not like someone or something. **Dislike** sounds a little formal and is often used when you have strong feelings: *He disliked her because she was so selfish.* | *Most people dislike the idea of eating insects.*

not think much of
to not think that someone or something is very good: *I don't think much of that restaurant. It is expensive and the food isn't very good.*

not care for (*formal*)
to not like someone or something: *His mother didn't care much for New York and wanted to be back home in Italy.*
→ see **hate**

dismay *noun* → see **shock[1]**

dismayed *adjective* → see **discouraged**, **upset[1]**

dismiss *verb* → see **fire[2]**

disobedient *adjective* → see **bad**, **rebellious**

disobey /ˌdɪsəˈbeɪ/ *verb*

- ► disobey (*formal*)
- ► break
- ► violate (*formal*)
- ► stand up to
- ► defy

ANTONYMS → see **obey**

disobey (*formal*)
to not obey a person or rule: *He disobeyed the safety rules, and he got hurt.* | *I never dared to disobey my parents.* | *Two soldiers were punished for disobeying orders.*

break
to do something that a rule or law says you should not do: *When you drive over the speed limit, you are breaking the law.* | *Students who break the rules will have to leave the class.*

violate AWL (*formal*)
to break a law. **Violate** is used in official language: *Companies that violate the law must pay a $2,000 fine.*

stand up to
to disobey someone in a way that seems brave,

D

especially because the person you disobey has much more power than you do: *The Princess stood up to her father and refused to marry the Duke.*

defy
to choose to disobey, especially in order to prove that you do not care about someone's rules or power: *He defied his father's wishes and became a great dancer.* | *The country has defied pressure from other nations to give its people more freedom.*
→ If the person or rule you **defy** is bad, then it is brave for you to disobey them. If the person or rule is good, then people think it is wrong to **defy** them.
→ see **rebel²** for "to not obey your parents or someone in authority"

D

disorganized *adjective* → see **messy**

display¹ *noun* → see **show²**

display² *verb* → see **show¹ (1)**, **show¹ (3)**

dispute¹ *noun* → see **argument**

dispute² *verb* → see **disagree**

disrespect *noun* → see **scorn**

disrespectful *adjective* → see **rude**

disrupt *verb* → see **block¹ (2)**

distant *adjective* → see Function Word **far**

distinct *adjective* → see **clear**, **definite**, **different**

distinction *noun* → see **difference**

distinguish *verb* → see **recognize**

distract *verb* → see **interrupt**

distribute *verb* → see **give**

district *noun* → see **area**

distrust¹ *verb* → see **disbelieve**

distrust² /dɪsˈtrʌst/ *noun*

- ► distrust
- ► mistrust
- ► suspicion

ANTONYMS → see **trust²**

distrust
a feeling that you cannot trust someone or something: *Many people view politicians with distrust, because they think a politician will say anything to get elected.* | *His **distrust of** journalists means that he rarely gives interviews to the press.*

mistrust
a feeling of worry that you should not trust someone: *His bad experiences in court have left him with a deep **mistrust of** lawyers.*

suspicion
a feeling that you do not trust a person or idea. You have this feeling before you know what he, she, or it is really like: *They looked at us with suspicion because we were strangers.*

disturb *verb* → see **interrupt**, **upset²**, **wake**

disturbance *noun* → see **trouble**

disturbed *adjective* → see **upset¹**

disturbing *adjective* → see **upsetting**

ditch *noun* → see **hole**

dive *verb* → see **sink**

diverse *adjective* → see **different**

divide *verb* → see **separate²**, **share¹**

division *noun* → see **separation**

divorce /dɪˈvɔrs/ *verb*

- ► divorce
- ► separate
- ► break up
- ► split up (*informal*)

ANTONYMS → see **marry**

divorce *also* **get divorced**
to legally end a marriage: *Her parents divorced when she was six.* | *My mom and dad decided to get divorced.* | *He wants to divorce his wife.*

separate
to start to live apart from your husband or wife. When two people **separate**, it is usually because they intend to get divorced: *They separated for three months, but now they are trying to save their marriage.*

break up
if two people break up, they end their marriage or romantic relationship: *Their marriage broke up just before Christmas.* | *Did she just **break up with** her boyfriend?*
→ You usually say that someone **breaks up with** a girlfriend or boyfriend. You do not usually say that someone **breaks up with** his or her husband or wife.

split up (*informal*)
split up means the same as **break up**: *My wife and I split up two years ago.*
→ **GRAMMAR:** Don't say: *~~Their marriage split up~~*. Say: *They split up* or *He split up with his girlfriend/wife.*

divorced *adjective* → see **married**, Topic **Relationships and Marriage**

dizzy /ˈdɪzi/ *adjective*

- ► dizzy
- ► faint
- ► light-headed

dizzy
feeling as if you cannot stand up steadily, especially after turning around many times or because you feel sick: *I felt dizzy when I looked down at the street from the top of the tall building.* | *If you **get dizzy** or feel any pain, stop exercising immediately.*

faint
feeling weak and unsteady, as if you could become unconscious, because there is not enough blood going to your brain: *The intense heat made Cara feel faint.* | *I was **faint with** hunger.*

light-headed
if you are light-headed, you feel slightly faint and dizzy. Use **light-headed** especially about someone who has drunk too much alcohol or is sick: *Brendan had a fever and was feeling light-headed and weak.*

GRAMMAR CHECK: dizzy

Dizzy is not usually used before a noun, although you can say: *She had a dizzy spell/sensation* (=she felt dizzy).

Faint is not used before a noun. Don't say: ~~*She had a faint feeling*~~. Say: *She felt faint.*

ADVERBS

You can make the adjective **dizzy** into an adverb by using an **-ly** ending: *Her head seemed to be spinning and she swayed dizzily.*

do /du/ *verb*

- ► do
- ► commit
- ► carry out
- ► perform (*formal*)
- ► conduct (*formal*)
- ► implement (*formal*)

do
to work at an activity or deal with some work: *"What are you doing?" "I'm making a cake."* | *Are you going to do your homework now?* | *I have so much to do today!*

commit
to do something wrong or illegal. You only use **commit** with words such as "crime," "murder," "theft," "sin," etc.: *She was accused of committing a crime, but she was not found guilty.* | *These men have committed horrible acts of violence.*

carry out
to do something that has already been planned or that someone has told you to do. You use **carry out** with words such as "plan," "attack," and "orders": *The FBI is trying to find out who carried out the attack.* | *The soldier was just carrying out the general's orders.*

perform (*formal*)
to do something, especially something difficult or useful: *Computers can perform several tasks at the same time.* | *Which doctor will perform the operation?*

conduct (AWL) (*formal*)
to do something in an organized way: *The scientists have been conducting research into the causes of cancer.*

implement (AWL) (*formal*)
to do something or make changes that someone has officially decided should happen: *Stores must implement the new rules by October 1.*
→ see **succeed** for words meaning "to succeed in doing something"

SYNONYM CHECK

Do or perform?

You use **do** when talking about everyday tasks: *I need to do the ironing.*

Perform is formal and is used especially with "task" and "duties": *The soldier was sick and not able to perform his duties.* You can say: *What are you doing?* but you cannot say: ~~*What are you performing*~~?

do better *verb phrase* → see **improve**

doctor /ˈdɑktɚ/ *noun*

- ► doctor
- ► physician (*formal*)
- ► specialist
- ► surgeon
- ► pediatrician
- ► dentist
- ► psychiatrist
- ► veterinarian
- ► M.D.

doctor
someone whose job is treating people who are sick: *Josh went to the doctor because his stomach hurt.*

D

physician (*formal*)
physician means the same as **doctor**: *See your physician if the pain continues.*

specialist
a doctor who only treats people with problems in a particular part of the body or with a particular disease: *Dr. Vicks is a heart specialist.*

surgeon
a doctor who cuts open someone's body to fix or replace something inside: *The surgeon removed the tumor from the patient's brain.*

pediatrician
a doctor who treats children: *Call your pediatrician if your baby has a fever.*

dentist
someone whose job is to do work on people's teeth: *I went to the dentist to have my teeth cleaned and checked.*

psychiatrist
a doctor who treats people who have a mental illness: *She has been seeing a psychiatrist for several years.*

veterinarian *also* **vet** (*informal*)
a doctor for animals: *The veterinarian gave the dog a shot.*

M.D.
used after someone's name to show that someone is a doctor, because he or she has earned the degree of Doctor of Medicine: *The class will be taught by Dr. Gregory Hartmann, M.D.*
→ People sometimes use **M.D.** by itself, to mean the same as **doctor**: *He was treated by a local M.D., but he did not go to the hospital.*
→ see **patient²** for words meaning "someone who is being treated by a doctor"
→ see Topic **Medical Treatment**

document /ˈdɑkyəmənt/ *noun*

- ► **document**
- ► **file**
- ► **form**
- ► **papers**

document (AWL)
a piece of paper with official information on it: *Your birth certificate is a very important document because it proves when and where you were born.* | *You will have to sign a lot of legal documents when you sell your house.*
→ **Document** is also used about written information that is kept on a computer: *Go to the folder called "Money" and open the document called "Taxes."*

file (AWL)
a set of documents that contains information about a person or subject: *The doctor's office keeps **files on** each patient.*

form
a document with spaces where you write information, especially legal or official information about yourself. **Forms** are usually used by a government, company, or organization for their records: *I completed the job application form and gave it to the manager at the store.*

papers
official documents, such as a passport or identification card. You use **papers** about documents that give you permission to do something or that prove who you are: *We had to show our papers at the security desk in the airport.*
→ see Topic **Computers and the Internet**

dog /dɔg/ *noun*

- ► **dog**
- ► **puppy**
- ► **hound**

dog
an animal that people keep as a pet or use for work such as guarding buildings or helping blind people: *"What kind of dog do you have?" "A labrador."* | *A police dog was sniffing bags in the airport.*

puppy
a young dog: *The puppies were rolling around playing with each other.*

hound
a dog used for hunting: *The hounds were allowed to run free through the woods.*

donate *verb* → see **give**

donation *noun* → see **help²**, **present²**

done /dʌn/ *adjective*

- ► **done**
- ► **finished**
- ► **complete** (*formal*)
- ► **over** (*informal*)
- ► **through** (*informal*)

ANTONYMS → see **unfinished**

done
if you are done, you have come to the end of doing or using something: *Are you almost done mowing the lawn?* | *Can I borrow that pen when you **are done with** it?*

finished
finished means the same as **done** but sounds slightly more formal: *Put your plate in the dishwasher when you're finished.* | *I was very happy with the finished painting.* | *Are you* ***finished with*** *your homework?*

complete (*formal*)
if something such as a piece of work is complete, all the parts of it are done: *When the assignment is complete, staple the pages together and give it to your teacher.*

over (*informal*)
if an event or period of time is over, you have come to the end of it: *What time will the movie be over?*

through (*informal*)
if you are through with something, you have finished doing or using it: *Are you* ***through with*** *the dishes yet?*

> **GRAMMAR CHECK: done**
> **Done**, **complete**, **over**, and **through** cannot be used before a noun. Only **finished** can be used before a noun. Don't say: ~~*He showed the done model to his mother*~~. Say: *He showed the finished model to his mother.*

donor *noun* → see **sponsor**

doodle *noun* → see **drawing**

dose *noun* → see **medicine**

doubt /daʊt/ *noun*

- ► doubt
- ► uncertainty (*formal*)
- ► question
- ► reservations
- ► misgivings
- ► mixed feelings
- ► second thoughts

doubt
a feeling that something is not good, right, or true: *He said he trusted me, but I could see the doubt in his eyes.* | *Christina had some* ***doubts about*** *going to college; she wasn't sure it was the right thing for her.*

uncertainty (*formal*)
the feeling of not being sure what will happen, what is the best thing to do, or what is true: *My* ***uncertainty about*** *what to say in the job interview was making me feel very nervous.*
→ **GRAMMAR:** In this meaning, **uncertainty** cannot be used in the plural. Don't say: ~~*She was filled with uncertainties about college*~~. Say: *She was filled with uncertainty about college.*

question
if there is a question about a situation, people feel doubt about it and want to know more about the facts in the situation. You use **question** mostly in the phrases "There is some question about..." or "There are some questions about...": *There is some* ***question about*** *whether the report in the newspaper was true.*

reservations
if you have reservations about a situation, you are not sure that an action is the best thing to do, and worry that there may be problems: *They seem very happy together, but I have some* ***reservations about*** *them getting married so quickly.*

misgivings
if you have misgivings about something, you feel doubtful that it is the right thing to do: *Fifty-nine percent of voters say they have* ***misgivings about*** *entering the war.*

mixed feelings
if you have mixed feelings about a situation, you have some doubts and some positive feelings about it: *My parents had* ***mixed feelings about*** *me going so far away for college.*

second thoughts
the feeling that a decision or choice you made was the wrong one: *Kerry is having* ***second thoughts about*** *going on the trip – she says she can't afford it.*
→ see **distrust**[2]

> **GRAMMAR CHECK: doubt**
> **Reservations**, **misgivings**, **mixed feelings**, and **second thoughts** are always used in the plural. Don't say: ~~*I have a misgiving about this*~~. Say: *I have misgivings about this.*

doubtful *adjective* → see **unlikely**, **unsure**

down *adverb, preposition* → see Function Words

download *verb* → see Topic **Computers and the Internet**

downward *adverb* → see Function Word **down**

doze *verb* → see **sleep**[1]

drag *verb* → see **pull**[1]

drain *verb* → see **empty**[2]

drama *noun* → see **play**[2], Topic **Books and Literature**, **Entertainment**

dramatic *adjective* → see **exciting**, **sudden**

draw /drɔ/ *verb*

- draw
- sketch
- illustrate
- doodle
- trace
- scribble

draw
to use something such as a pen or pencil to make a picture of something: *The boy was drawing on colored paper.* | *Can you draw an elephant?*

sketch
to make a quick drawing that does not have a lot of details: *An artist was sketching people as they walked through the park.*

illustrate (AWL)
to draw or paint pictures to go in a book: *They asked ten famous artists to each illustrate one chapter of the book.*

doodle
to draw pictures, shapes, or patterns while you are thinking about something else: *A lot of people doodle while they're talking on the phone.*
→ **GRAMMAR:** You can say: *She doodled pictures on her notebooks*, but it is more usual to say: *She* ***doodled on*** *her notebooks.*

trace (AWL)
to copy a picture by drawing on a thin piece of paper that you put over it: *Kara traced the picture of the dog.*

scribble
to draw marks that have no meaning: *Little kids were* ***scribbling on*** *pieces of colored paper.*
→ **GRAMMAR:** Don't say: ~~*She scribbled a picture*~~. Say: *She* ***scribbled on*** *a piece of paper.*
→ see **attract** for **draw** meaning "to make people notice something," **pull**[1] for **draw** meaning "to pull something gently"
→ see **art**, **picture**[1]

draw

scribble draw trace doodle

drawing /ˈdrɔɪŋ/ *noun*

- drawing
- sketch
- doodle
- cartoon
- comic
- diagram

drawing
a picture you make with a pen or pencil: *I did a drawing of a spaceship.* | *The drawings help children to understand the story.*

sketch
a simple drawing that does not have a lot of detail, especially one you draw quickly: *I made a quick sketch of the boys playing soccer in the park.*

doodle
a picture, shape, or pattern that you draw while you are thinking about something else: *During the meeting, she covered the sheet of paper with doodles.*

cartoon
a funny drawing, especially in a newspaper or magazine: *The artist is famous for his political cartoons that make fun of the government.*

comic *also* **comic strip**
a series of pictures that tell a story, with each picture drawn inside a separate box. You usually use **comic** in the phrase **the comics** to mean a

page of comics in a newspaper: *He called his dog Snoopy after the character in the comic strip "Peanuts." | I like reading the comics in the Sunday paper.*

diagram
a simple drawing that shows a machine, structure, or object and how it works or is built: *The diagram shows what scientists think different parts of the brain are used for.*
→ see **picture[1]**

drawing

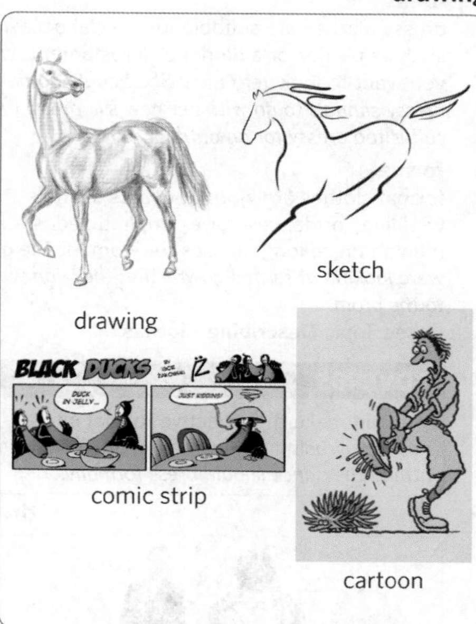

dream[1] /drim/ *noun*

► dream
► nightmare
► daydream
► fantasy

dream
the images that you see in your mind when you are asleep: *I had a good dream last night and woke up smiling.*
→ **Dream** is also used to mean "something you really want to achieve, especially when this is difficult or unlikely": *Maya's dream was to win an Olympic gold medal one day.*

nightmare
a very frightening dream: *I have the same nightmare again and again – I'm driving along and I fall off a bridge.*

daydream
thoughts about nice things that make you forget what you should be doing: *In her daydreams, she saw herself walking along the beach with Jack.*

fantasy
something that you imagine happening to you, especially something exciting or enjoyable that will probably never happen: *Every little kid has the **fantasy of** becoming rich and famous some day.*
→ see **hope[2]**

dream[2] /drim/ *verb*

1 to dream while you are asleep
► dream
► have a dream
► have a nightmare

2 to think about something that might happen
► dream
► daydream
► fantasize
► imagine

3 to see pictures in your mind while you are awake
► hallucinate (*formal*)
► see a vision

1 to dream while you are asleep

dream
to see images in your mind while you are asleep: *He **dreamed that** a monster became his friend. | Last night I **dreamed about** winning a dance contest, which is strange because I don't dance!*

have a dream
have a dream means the same as **dream**: *I **had a dream that** you all hated me. | She had a scary dream and woke up crying.*

have a nightmare
to have a frightening dream: *I **had** the worst **nightmare** last night **about** some guy chasing me.*

2 to think about something that might happen

dream
to think about something that you hope will happen: *Zach **dreamed that** one day he would play in a band. | Many scientists **dream of** winning a Nobel Prize for their work.*
→ **GRAMMAR:** Don't say: ~~*dream to do something*~~. Say: *dream of doing something*.

daydream
to think about nice things that make you forget what you should be doing: *In the winter we all **daydream about** hot summer days on the beach.*

fantasize
to think about doing or having something

exciting, even though it is very unlikely to happen: *Sometimes I **fantasize about** owning my own restaurant.*

imagine
to think about what something could be like or what it must have been like: *The teacher asked us to **imagine that** we were on an island with no other people. | Can you **imagine how** Jennifer feels, after you called her names like that?*

3 to see pictures in your mind while you are awake

hallucinate (*formal*)
to see things that are not really there because you are ill or have taken drugs: *After two days without food and water, Voss began to hallucinate.*

see a vision *also* **have a vision**
to see something as part of a powerful religious experience: *She had a vision in which Jesus appeared before her.*

D

dress[1] /dres/ *noun*

- ► dress
- ► gown

dress
a piece of clothing for a woman or girl, that covers her body and part of her legs: *She wore a pretty summer dress. | The dress was black, and had long sleeves and a skirt that came down to her knees.*

gown
a long dress worn by a woman on formal occasions: *The bride wore the wedding gown that had belonged to her mother.*
→ see **clothes**

dress[2] /dres/ *verb*

- ► dress (*formal*)
- ► get dressed
- ► put on
- ► try on

ANTONYMS → see **undress**

dress (*formal*)
to put clothes on your body: *Luis washed, dressed, and shaved before work.*

get dressed
get dressed means the same as **dress** but sounds less formal: *She woke up, got dressed, and ate breakfast.*

put on
to put a piece of clothing on your body: *He was putting on his shirt when it ripped. | I'll put a skirt on, and we can go out.*

try on
to put clothes on to see how they look or fit: *Try on this T-shirt – I think it will look good on you.*

dressed *adjective* → see **be dressed in** at **wear**

dressy /'dresi/ *adjective*

- ► dressy
- ► formal

ANTONYMS → see **casual**

dressy
dressy clothes are suitable for special occasions, such as parties or a dinner at a restaurant, when you want to look very nice: *She bought some dressy sandals to go with her new silk dress. | A suit is too dressy for an outdoor party.*

formal
formal clothes are worn at events such as weddings or dances, for example tuxedos for men and nice long dresses for women: *The girls were looking at formal gowns that they can wear to the prom.*
→ see Topic **Describing Clothes**

ADVERBS
You can make the adjective **formal** into an adverb by using an **-ly** ending: *Students who attend the dance should dress formally.*

dressy

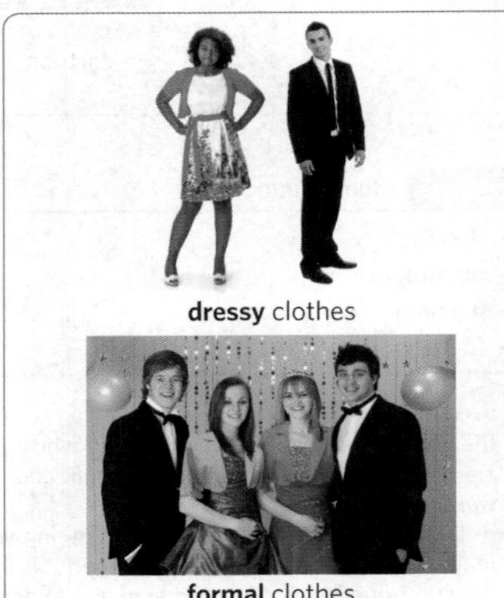

dressy clothes

formal clothes

drill *verb* → see **pierce**, **practice[2]**

drink[1] /drɪŋk/ *noun*

1 a liquid you can drink

- ► drink
- ► beverage (*formal*)

2 the action of taking an amount of liquid into your mouth and swallowing it
- drink
- sip
- gulp

1 a liquid you can drink

drink
a liquid that you can take into your mouth and swallow: *He asked for a **drink of** water.* | *The waiter dropped his tray of food and drinks.*

beverage (*formal*)
beverage means the same as **drink** but is used especially in restaurants on menus and signs, or in formal writing such as reports: *Beverages such as colas can cause tooth decay.*

2 the action of taking an amount of liquid into your mouth and swallowing it

drink
if you take a drink, you take an amount of liquid into your mouth and swallow it: *He took a **drink of** his lemonade.*

sip
if you take a sip, you take a small amount of a liquid into your mouth and swallow it: *She took a **sip of** the hot tea.*

gulp
if you take a gulp, you take a large amount of a liquid into your mouth and swallow it quickly: *She finished the drink in a single gulp.*

drink² /drɪŋk/ verb

- drink
- sip
- take a sip
- gulp (*informal*)
- take a gulp (*informal*)
- lap

drink
to take liquid into your mouth and swallow it: *Drink your milk; it's good for you.* | *My brother was drinking a glass of orange juice.*

sip
to drink something slowly in small amounts: *The coffee was hot, and she sipped it carefully.*

take a sip
to drink a small amount of something one time: *I handed Juanita the juice, and she took a sip.*

gulp *also* **gulp down** (*informal*)
to drink something in large amounts: *She ate fast, gulping her milk.* | *Andrei gulped down half a glass of water and ran back outside.*

take a gulp (*informal*)
to drink a large amount of something one time: *She **took a** big **gulp of** the chocolate shake and passed it to her brother.*

lap *also* **lap up**
if an animal laps a drink, it drinks by touching the liquid with its tongue: *The cat **lapped** milk **from** the bowl.* | *The kitten was lapping up as much of the milk as she could.*
→ see **thirsty** for words meaning "wanting to drink"

drink

drink lap

drip /drɪp/ verb

- drip
- splash
- spray

drip
if a liquid drips from something, it falls in drops: *All night we could hear the rain **dripping from** the roof.* | *Water began to **drip** from the leaves **onto** my head.*
→ If a faucet or hose **drips**, water falls in drops from it: *The bathroom faucet was dripping.*

splash
if a liquid splashes, a lot of drops of liquid fall into more liquid: *Water splashed in the fountain.*

spray
if a liquid sprays from a faucet or hose, it comes out in very small drops: *He put his thumb over the hose to make the water spray everywhere.*
→ see **splash¹** for words meaning "to make small drops of liquid fall"
→ see **flow**

D

drive /draɪv/ *verb*

- drive
- go by car
- steer
- maneuver
- be behind the wheel

drive
to control a vehicle and make it move somewhere: *I drive to work every day.* | *My Uncle Diego drives a pickup truck.*

go by car
to travel somewhere in a car: *We can take the bus, but it will be quicker if we go by car.*

steer
to control the direction a vehicle is going by turning a wheel: *He was steering with one hand instead of two, which made me nervous.* | *She steered the car into the garage.*

maneuver
to move or turn a vehicle skillfully: *I tried to **maneuver** the car **into** the parking space, but it was too small.*

be behind the wheel *also* **be at the wheel**
to be driving a vehicle: *Monica is a good driver, and I feel safe when she is behind the wheel.*

drop[1] /drɑp/ *verb*

- drop
- let go
- release (*formal*)
- fumble
- scatter
- litter

ANTONYMS → see **catch (1)**

drop
if you drop something you are holding, you let it fall, often by accident: *It is heavy – try not to drop it!* | *The player at second base dropped the ball.*

let go
to stop holding someone or something: *She **let go of** the rope and jumped to the ground.*

release (AWL) (*formal*)
release means the same as **let go** but sounds more formal: *Release the handle and allow the door to open.*

fumble
to drop a ball, especially in the sport of football: *The quarterback fumbled the ball, and the other team picked it up.*

scatter
to drop many things over a wide area: *Scatter the seeds over the soil.*

litter
to drop trash or other things where they do not belong: *Don't litter! Put your empty can in the recycling.*
→ see **drop in/by** at **visit**, **drop out** at **quit**
→ see **free[2]**

drop[2] *noun* → see **decrease[1]**

drug *noun* → see **medicine**

drunk /drʌŋk/ *adjective*

- drunk
- tipsy
- had too much to drink
- intoxicated (*formal*)
- under the influence

drunk
if someone is drunk, he or she has drunk too much alcohol and cannot think or act normally: *You are too drunk to drive – give me the keys.* | *The drunk driver was pulled over by the police officer.*

tipsy
slightly drunk, especially in a way that is funny: *I think she was a little tipsy because she kept giggling.*

had too much to drink
if someone has had too much to drink, he or she is drunk. You use **had too much to drink** when you do not want to say **drunk** directly: *I think Bob has had a little too much to drink. I'll take him home.*

intoxicated (*formal*)
intoxicated means the same as **drunk**: *Police said the breath test showed that the man was intoxicated.*

under the influence
drunk or feeling the effects of an illegal drug, especially when you are driving. **Under the influence** is used in official or legal language: *If you are caught driving under the influence, you can lose your license.*

dry /draɪ/ *adjective*

1 when there is no water in something

- dry
- dehydrated
- bone dry (*informal*)

ANTONYMS → see **wet**

2 when the weather is dry
► dry
► arid
► parched
ANTONYMS → see **rainy**

1 when there is no water in something

dry
something that is dry has no water in it or on it: *Do you have a dry towel? This one is soaked.* | *The soil was dry and cracked.*

dehydrated
if you are dehydrated, you do not have enough water in your body: *After four days in the desert, he was severely dehydrated.*

bone dry *also* **dry as a bone** (*informal*)
something that is bone dry is completely dry: *I can walk through snow and puddles in these boots, and my feet stay bone dry.* | *There had been no rain for weeks, and the ground was dry as a bone.*

2 when the weather is dry

dry
if the weather is dry, there is no rain: *Tomorrow should be dry and sunny.* | *We've had a three-week dry spell that is hurting the crops.*
→ If you want to talk about a long period of dry weather when there is not enough rain, use the noun **drought**: *The drought has lasted for two years.*

arid
an area of a country that is arid gets very little rain and is very dry: *The cactus grows in the arid regions of the Southwest.*

dry

arid desert

parched earth

parched
soil that is parched is extremely dry. **Parched** is used especially in literature and news reports: *Each night they prayed for rain to come and soak the parched earth.*
→ see Topic **Describing Places**

due to *preposition* → see Function Word **because**

dull *adjective* → see **blunt**, **boring**

dumb *adjective* → see **stupid**

dump *noun* → see **mess**, **put**

during *preposition* → see Function Words

dusk *noun* → see **evening**, **sunset**

dust¹ *noun* → see **dirt**

dust² *verb* → see **clean² (1)**

dusty *adjective* → see **dirty**

duties *noun* → see **work²**

duty /ˈduti/ *noun*

► duty
► responsibility
► job (*informal*)
► obligation

duty
something that you have to do because it is right or it is part of your job: *One of your duties is keeping records of what happens at every meeting.* | *As a police officer I have a* ***duty to*** *uphold the law.*

responsibility
something that you must do because it is part of your job and you are in charge of doing it: *My boss has given me more responsibility at work.* | *Parents have many responsibilities, from making sure their children are clean and fed to making sure they go to school.*

job (AWL) (*informal*)
something you do because someone in authority has asked you to do it: *Your job is to help your classmates with any math problems that they do not understand.*
→ **Job** is usually used in the phrases "it's my/your/his job to do something" or "my/your/his job is to do something."

obligation
something that you must do because it is the law or your duty: *If you are in a car accident, you have a legal* ***obligation to*** *stay at the place where the accident happened until the police come.*
→ see **tax** for **duty** meaning "a tax on things you bring into a country"

D

dye /daɪ/ *verb*

- ► dye
- ► color

dye
to change the color of something using a special substance: ***She started dyeing her hair as soon as the first gray hairs appeared. | We dyed T-shirts using natural things such as beets or onion skins.***

color
to make your hair a different color from its natural color: ***There has been an increase in the number of women who color their hair.***

D

Ee

eager /ˈigɚ/ *adjective*

- ► eager
- ► enthusiastic
- ► avid
- ► passionate
- ► zealous (*formal*)

eager
very excited about something that is going to happen or something that you want to do: *My brother is bringing his girlfriend home tonight, and we are all **eager to** meet her.* | *A crowd of eager customers were waiting to buy tickets for the movie.*

enthusiastic
showing a lot of interest and excitement about something: *Adam is **enthusiastic about** the new project and is looking forward to working on it.*

avid
eager to do something as much as possible, especially an activity that you do in your free time: *Sonia is an avid reader. She always seems to have a book in her hand.*

passionate
showing a very strong feeling of interest and excitement about someone or something: *He is **passionate about** painting, and he teaches free classes at the college.* | *Dana gave a passionate speech about saving the environment.*

zealous (*formal*)
very eager to achieve something, especially to achieve a particular religious or political aim. You often use **zealous** when you think someone is being too extreme: *She has became zealous in her religious faith and spends all her time at church.*
➔ see **excited**

ADVERBS

You can make the adjectives that mean **eager** into adverbs by using an **-ly** ending: *Fans waited eagerly to buy tickets for the concert.* | *The audience applauded enthusiastically.* | *The books were read avidly by children and parents alike.*

eagerness /ˈigɚnəs/ *noun*

- ► eagerness
- ► enthusiasm
- ► zeal

eagerness
a feeling of excitement about something that is going to happen or that you want to do: *We were looking forward to our vacation **with eagerness**.* | *People were pushing each other **in** their **eagerness to** be first in line.*

enthusiasm
a feeling of being very interested in something, and excited and eager to be involved in it: *Her **enthusiasm for** teaching has stayed strong through a 30-year career.*

zeal
a very strong feeling of eagerness and enthusiasm, which often seems too extreme. **Zeal** sounds a little more formal or literary than **eagerness**: *In her **zeal to** improve her vocabulary, she stayed up all night studying word lists.*
➔ see **excitement**

earlier *adverb* ➔ see Function Word **before**

early /ˈɚli/ *adjective*

- ► early
- ► ahead of schedule
- ► ahead of time
- ► premature
- ► untimely (*formal*)

ANTONYMS ➔ see **late**

early
before the usual or expected time: *The bus was a few minutes early.* | *We had an early lunch at about 11:30.*

ahead of schedule
earlier than the time when you have arranged to do something. You use **ahead of schedule** especially for situations when there is a planned schedule with a list of times, dates, and aims: *The building work was completed two months ahead of schedule.*

ahead of time
earlier than the time when you expect to do something or expect something to happen: *We were hoping to get to Austin by 6:00, but we got there a little ahead of time, at about 5:30.* | *You can make the dessert ahead of time so that you do not need to worry about it on the day of the party.*

premature
happening before the normal or natural time. **Premature** is used especially about medical

E

conditions: *Too much time in the sun causes premature aging of the skin.*

→ You say a baby is **premature** when he or she is born before the normal time: *Premature babies usually stay in the hospital for several weeks before coming home.*

untimely (*formal*)

an untimely death or end happens earlier than it should or earlier than you expected. **Untimely** sounds fairly formal or literary: *He was a friend of our family for many years, until his untimely death in a boating accident.*

→ see **on time**

ADVERBS

You can make the adjective **premature** into an adverb by using an **-ly** ending: *The baby was born prematurely.*

Early and **untimely** look like adverbs, but they are adjectives and cannot be used like adverbs.

E

earn /ɚn/ *verb*

- earn
- make
- get (*informal*)
- be paid

earn

to get money for the work you do: *Police officers in the city earn about $50,000 a year.* | *Kevin is looking for a job on the weekends to earn some extra money.*

make

to earn money by working or be paid money for something you sell: *I make about $35,000 a year.* | *Our neighbors made a lot of money when they sold the house.*

→ If a company **makes** a profit, it earns more than enough money to pay for the cost of running the business and producing its product or service: *The company made a profit of $2 million last year.*

get (*informal*)

to earn money. You use **get** especially when you are saying or asking how much someone earns: *"How much do you get per hour?" "I get $18."* | *I got $10 for washing the car.*

be paid *also* **get paid**

to be given money for doing a job: *We get paid every two weeks.* | *All the people who work at the restaurant are paid in cash.*

→ see **pay[1]**, Topic **Jobs and Work**

Earth /ɚθ/ *noun*

- Earth
- the world
- the planet
- the globe

Earth *also* **the Earth, earth**

the name of the planet that we live on: *The Earth revolves around the Sun.* | *In the story, Hercules is the strongest man* ***on earth.***

the world

the planet we live on, and its countries, people, mountains, oceans, etc.: *Athletes from* ***all over the world*** *compete in the Olympics.* | *What is the tallest building* ***in the world****?*

the planet

the large round object in space that we live on. You use **the planet** when you are talking about problems that affect the environment: *Global warming affects* ***the whole planet.***

→ A **planet** is a large round object that moves around a star. The Earth is one of eight planets that go around the Sun.

the globe (AWL)

the planet that we live on. You use **the globe** when you are thinking about how big the world is, the fact that it is round, and how far apart things are on it: *Water covers over half of* ***the globe.*** | *People* ***around the globe*** *watched the Olympic Games.*

→ see **dirt**, **ground**

SYNONYM CHECK

World or Earth?

Use **world** when you are thinking of the world as a place where there are people and countries: *In some parts of the world, people do not have enough food.*

Use **Earth** when you are thinking about the Earth as compared to things in space or to other planets: *The space shuttle returned to Earth safely.* You also use **Earth** when you are talking about scientific subjects such as geology: *Earthquakes happen when parts of the Earth's surface move.*

GRAMMAR CHECK: Earth

You say the biggest, smallest, best, etc. **in the world**, but you say the biggest, smallest, best, etc. **on earth**: *It's the highest mountain* ***in the world.*** | *It's the highest mountain* ***on earth.***

earthquake /ˈɚθkweɪk/ *noun*

- ► earthquake
- ► quake
- ► tremor
- ► aftershock
- ► temblor (*formal*)
- ► tsunami

earthquake
a sudden shaking of the ground, caused when parts of the earth's surface move: *Some old buildings were badly damaged when the earthquake struck.* | *In the United States, most earthquakes occur in California.*

quake
an earthquake. **Quake** is used especially in news reports: *More than 60,000 houses and apartments were damaged in the quake.*

tremor
a small earthquake in which the ground shakes slightly: *He woke up because of a series of tremors during the night.*

aftershock
an earthquake or tremor that comes after the first earthquake: *The earthquake was followed by an aftershock 40 minutes later.*

temblor (*formal*)
temblor means the same as **earthquake** but is more formal: *The temblor hit at 1:30 a.m., with a magnitude of 4.9.*

tsunami
a very large wave caused by an earthquake: *A tsunami struck the coast of Hawaii after a big earthquake in the Pacific Ocean.*

ease *verb* → see **reduce**

easily /ˈizəli/ *adverb*

- ► easily
- ► without difficulty
- ► effortlessly
- ► with ease
- ► simply

easily
without using much effort or energy: *Our team played really well, and we won easily.* | *She easily solved the first math problem and started on the next one.*

without difficulty *also* **with no difficulty**
without difficulty means the same as **easily** but sounds slightly more formal: *The door had been left open, so the robbers entered the building without difficulty.* | *When they speak slowly, I can understand them with no difficulty.*

effortlessly
if you do something effortlessly, you do it in a very skillful way that makes it seem easy: *The ballet dancer was effortlessly spinning around on one leg.*

with ease
if you do something with ease, you do it very easily. **With ease** sounds fairly literary: *The boy climbed over the fence with ease and ran through the field.*

simply
used to emphasize how easy it is to do something: *You simply mix the melted butter and chocolate together, pour it over the cornflakes, and stir it all together.*

easy /ˈizi/ *adjective*

- ► easy
- ► simple
- ► straightforward
- ► user-friendly
- ► effortless

ANTONYMS → see **difficult (1)**

easy
not difficult to do, and not needing much effort: *The questions on the test were really easy.* | *It is a great car, and it's very* ***easy to*** *drive.*

simple
easy to do and not having too many parts: *The recipe is very simple – you just mix the butter with the chocolate and pour it onto the cornflakes.*

straightforward (AWL)
simple, not confusing, and not likely to cause problems. You use **straightforward** especially about instructions or ways of doing things: *It sounds straightforward to me. You click on the file you want and press "enter."*

user-friendly
easy to operate, use, or understand. You use **user-friendly** especially about machines, systems, and ways of doing things: *The camera is very user-friendly and it is easy to take good pictures with it.*

effortless
an effortless performance or action is difficult to do but looks easy: *Her piano playing looks effortless, but she spends many hours practicing.*
→ see **easily**

eat /it/ *verb*

- ► eat
- ► have
- ► devour
- ► consume (*formal*)
- ► overeat
- ► feed on
- ► dine (*formal*)

eat
to put food in your mouth, chew it, and swallow it: *I was eating a sandwich.* | *Tom sat at the table eating breakfast.* | *I'm hungry – let's go get something to eat.*

have
to eat or drink a particular thing: *I think I'll have one more piece of cake.* | *What would you like to have for dinner?*

devour
to eat something very quickly because you are very hungry. **Devour** sounds literary and is often used in stories: *He had devoured the food on his plate, so we gave him more.*

consume (AWL) (*formal*)
to eat or drink something. **Consume** is used especially in nonfiction writing: *Coffee is consumed by millions of people every day.*

overeat
to eat too much, or eat more than is healthy: *People often overeat when they are feeling stressed.*

feed on
if an animal feeds on a particular type of food, that is the food it usually eats. **Feed on** is often used in scientific writing: *Foxes feed on mice, insects, and fruit.*

dine (*formal*)
to eat a meal, especially dinner. **Dine** is used only in very formal situations, for example on a formal invitation: *She received an invitation to dine with the mayor.*
→ see **hungry**

echo *noun* → see **repeat²**

ecology *noun* → see **environment**, Topic **The Environment**

economical *adjective* → see **cheap**

edge /edʒ/ *noun*

- ► edge
- ► side
- ► border
- ► rim
- ► margin

edge
the part of an object or area that is farthest from the center, where the object or area ends: *The plates have blue lines around the edges.* | *Don't put your glass so close to **the edge of** the table.* | *They live in a little house on **the edge of** town.*

side
the part of an object or area that is near an edge: *The car was parked by **the side of** the road.* | *If you don't want to eat it, just push it to **the side** of your plate.*

border
a narrow area that goes around the edge of something such as a picture or piece of material: *The plate has a bright orange border.*
→ **Border** is also used to mean "the official line that separates two countries, or the area of land near this line": *The southern parts of Arizona and Texas are **on the border with** Mexico.*

rim
the curved edge of something such as a cup or container: *I lifted the cup too quickly and tea spilled over the rim.*

margin (AWL)
the empty space at the side of a page of writing: *My teacher usually writes a lot of comments **in the margins** of our papers.*

edge

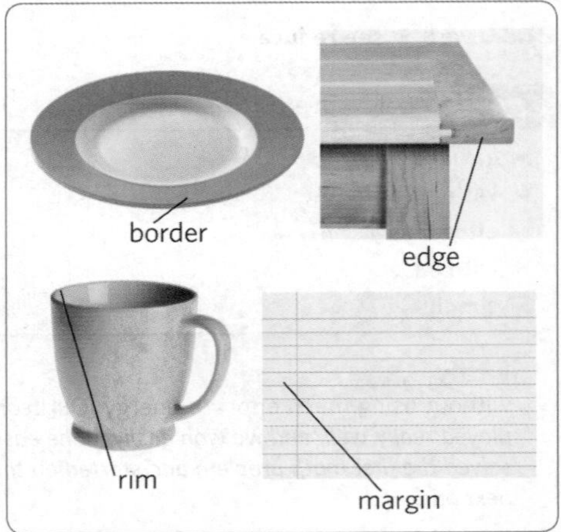

edit *verb* → see **rewrite**

educate *verb* → see **teach**

education /ˌedʒəˈkeɪʃən/ *noun*

- ► **education**
- ► **teaching**
- ► **instruction** (*formal*)
- ► **tuition** (*formal*)

education
the activities of teaching and learning, especially in schools or colleges: *All children should have the chance to get a good education.* | *Most students here continue their education after high school by going to college.*

teaching
the work that a teacher does, or the profession of being a teacher: *Sherry chose teaching as a career.* | *The best teachers can change their teaching style to help different types of learners.*

instruction AWL (*formal*)
teaching that you get in a particular skill or subject: *The children receive **instruction in** reading and math each day.*

tuition (*formal*)
the instruction that you get in a subject: *He is receiving tuition in math and English from a private tutor.* | *The cost of tuition at a private college is about $30,000 a year.*
→ **Tuition** can also be used to mean "the money you must pay for someone to teach you, especially at a school or college": *Tuition has increased by 7% at the state universities.*

educational *adjective* → see Topic **Education**

effect /ɪˈfekt/ *noun*

- ► **effect**
- ► **impact**
- ► **influence**
- ► **consequences**
- ► **side effect**

effect
a change that is the result of something: *It will take a while before the medicine has an effect.* | *Pollution has had a big **effect on** the lake – there are not many fish in it anymore.*

impact AWL
the big and important changes that happen as a result of something: *Computers have had a great **impact on** the way we work in the past 30 years.*

influence
the effect that something has on people's opinions or behavior, or on how something develops: *American television has had a big **influence on** popular culture all over the world.*

consequences
the things that happen directly as a result of an action or event: *Global warming will have serious **consequences for** the environment.*

side effect
an unwanted effect, especially of a drug or medical treatment: *The drug's side effects can include headaches and muscle pain.*
→ see **have an effect** at **result[1]**

effective *adjective* → see **successful**

efficient *adjective* → see **organized**

effort /ˈefɚt/ *noun*

- ► **effort**
- ► **energy**
- ► **work**
- ► **exertion** (*formal*)

effort
the physical or mental activity that you use to do something: *Kenny put a lot of effort into his research paper.* | *The coach praised the team for their great effort.*

energy AWL
the physical and mental strength that makes you able to do things: *He puts all his energy into his career.* | *I thought he was wrong, but I did not have the energy to argue.*

work
the things you do that take a lot of time and effort: *After many hours of hard work, we finally finished the project.* | *Raising children is a lot of work and takes patience and love.*

exertion (*formal*)
a lot of effort, especially hard physical effort: *He had been running fast, and his face was red from the exertion.*
→ see **try[2]**, **work[2]**, **make an effort** at **try[1]**

elderly[1] *adjective* → see **old**

elderly[2] *noun* → see **old person**

elect *verb* → see **choose**

election /ɪˈlekʃən/ *noun*

- ► **election**
- ► **primary**
- ► **race**
- ► **the polls**
- ► **ballot**

election
an occasion when people choose a government

E

official or leader by voting: *In a fair election every vote is counted.* | *Ronald Reagan won the U.S. presidential election of 1980.* | *Elections are held every four years.*

primary
an election in the U.S. in which people vote to decide who will be the person that their political party wants to be president, senator, etc. That person will then run against the other party's choice in a later election: *The primary in New Hampshire is often very important in deciding who will run for president for each party.*

race
a situation, for example an election, in which people are competing with each other to get a political position. **Race** is often used in news reports: *There are four strong candidates in the race for the presidency.*

the polls
the process of voting in a political election. **The polls** is used especially in news reports: *Voters will go to the polls on Tuesday.*

ballot
an occasion when people vote by choosing what they want on a piece of paper or computer, especially when this process is secret: *The results of the ballot showed that most workers were in favor of a strike.*
→ see **vote¹**, **vote²**, Topic **Government and Politics**

electric /ɪ'lektrɪk/ *adjective*

- ► electric
- ► electrical
- ► electronic

electric
needing electricity in order to work: *Mandy is learning how to play the electric guitar.* | *I use an electric lawn mower.*

electrical
relating to or using electricity: *Solar panels change sunlight into electrical power.*

electronic
electronic equipment, such as a computer or television, has small parts inside it that control the electricity that the equipment uses to do complicated things: *The store sells various electronic devices, from cell phones to computers and digital cameras.*

SYNONYM CHECK
Electric or electrical?

Electric is used before the names of things that need electricity in order to work: *I like to use an electric toothbrush.*

Electrical is used to talk about things that use or produce electricity: *The fire started because of a problem with the electrical wires.*

ADVERBS

You can make the adjectives **electrical** and **electronic** into adverbs by using an **-ly** ending: *The company sells electrically powered bicycles.* | *I sent the pictures electronically* (=using a piece of electronic equipment such as a computer).

electrical *adjective* → see **electric**

electronic *adjective* → see **electric**

elegance *noun* → see **style**

elegant *adjective* → see **beautiful**, **graceful**, **stylish**

element *noun* → see **part**

elementary *adjective* → see **basic**

elementary school *noun* → see Topic **Education**

email¹ *noun* → see **letter**, **mail¹**, **message**, Topic **Computers and the Internet**

email² *verb* → see **write**, Topic **Computers and the Internet**

embarrass /ɪm'bærəs/ *verb*

- ► embarrass
- ► humiliate
- ► shame

embarrass
to make someone feel ashamed, nervous, or uncomfortable, especially in front of other people: *She embarrassed her son by showing his girlfriend pictures of him when he was a little boy.* | *I told Maya that she would embarrass herself if she told that stupid joke.*

humiliate
to make someone feel weak or stupid, especially in front of other people: *Her boss humiliated her by criticizing her work in front of all her colleagues.*

shame
to make someone feel guilty and ashamed about something, often to get him or her to behave in

a different way: *Children should never be **shamed into** trying to lose weight.*

→ You can also use the phrase **it shames someone** to say that someone feels ashamed about something: ***It shamed her that** she still hadn't told her brother the truth.*

embarrassed /ɪmˈbærəst/ *adjective*

- embarrassed
- uncomfortable
- awkward
- self-conscious

embarrassed
feeling ashamed and nervous, and worrying about what people think of you: *Tony spilled grape juice all over the carpet. He was so embarrassed! | I felt **embarrassed about** how messy the house was.*

uncomfortable
feeling a little worried or embarrassed and not sure what to say or do: *The two of them started arguing, and everyone else at the table looked uncomfortable.*

awkward
feeling embarrassed because you are in a situation in which it is difficult to behave naturally: *Teenagers often feel awkward in formal social situations because they are not used to them.*

self-conscious
embarrassed about your body or the way you look or talk: *I always feel really self-conscious about dancing in front of people.*

→ see **blush** for words meaning "to become red because you are embarrassed"

→ see Topic **Describing People's Emotions**

ADVERBS

You can make the adjectives **uncomfortable**, **awkward**, and **self-conscious** into adverbs by using an **-ly** ending: *The rest of us listened uncomfortably as our friends argued. | He didn't know anyone at the party, and stood awkwardly near the kitchen door.*

embarrassment /ɪmˈbærəsmənt/ *noun*

- embarrassment
- humiliation
- shame

embarrassment
the feeling of being embarrassed and uncomfortable: *I looked down **in embarrassment** when the teacher read my poem out loud. | Marcus began to sing in front of the whole class, without any embarrassment at all.*

humiliation
a feeling of strong embarrassment because something makes you seem weak or stupid, especially in front of other people: *The biggest humiliation for me was being beaten in the first game of the competition.*

shame
the feeling of being guilty or embarrassed because you have done something that is wrong: *I felt a sense of deep shame for having lied to my mother.*

embrace[1] *verb* → see **hug[1]**

embrace[2] *noun* → see **hug[2]**

emergency /ɪˈmɚdʒənsi/ *noun*

- emergency
- crisis

emergency
a very serious and dangerous situation that you must deal with immediately: *Call 911 – this is an emergency! | Nurses are trained to deal with emergencies such as heart attacks or injuries.*

crisis
a bad situation with problems that can quickly get worse. You use **crisis** about political or economic situations, and sometimes about personal problems: *The country is facing an economic crisis, and millions of people could lose their jobs.*

emigrant *noun* → see **immigrant**

emigrate *verb* → see **leave**, **move**

emotion /ɪˈmoʊʃən/ *noun*

- emotion
- feeling
- a sense of
- sentiment (*formal*)
- expression

emotion
something you feel such as love, hate, or sadness: *When I saw my father again after five years, I was filled with emotion. | He did not want to show his emotions because he was afraid people would laugh at him.*

feeling
feeling means the same as **emotion** but sounds less formal: *It was a wonderful feeling to be home again. | For a few minutes she experienced **feelings of** real fear when she realized she was lost.*

E

a sense of
if you feel a sense of fear, joy, loss, etc., you feel that emotion. **A sense of** sounds slightly more formal than **a feeling of**: *He felt **a sense of** relief after he finished his last exam.*

sentiment (*formal*)
a feeling or opinion that you have about something: *One man said he was angry, and other people expressed similar sentiments.*
→ You can also use **sentiment** to mean "feelings of love, pity, sadness, etc. that people think are too strong or not appropriate for a situation": *There is no room for sentiment in business – if I need to fire someone, I'll do it even if I feel sorry for him.*

expression
a way of doing something that shows what you feel: *Crying is a healthy **expression of** grief.*

E

emotional *adjective* → see **moving**

emphasis /ˈemfəsɪs/ *noun*

1 special attention or importance that is given to something
► emphasis
► stress

2 the fact of saying part of a word or phrase with more force
► emphasis
► stress

1 special attention or importance that is given to something

emphasis (AWL)
special attention or importance that is given to something such as an idea or activity: *Our parents always put a strong **emphasis on** education.*

stress (AWL)
stress means the same as **emphasis**: *The school lays great **stress on** trying your best.*

2 the fact of saying part of a word or phrase with more force

emphasis (AWL)
the fact of saying part of a word or phrase louder or with more force, or by printing it in a special way: *In the sentence, "We **both** like ice cream," the word "both" is given emphasis.*

stress (AWL)
stress means the same as **emphasis** but is used in more technical language: *In the word "dessert," the main stress is on the second syllable, "-sert."*

emphasize /ˈemfəˌsaɪz/ *verb*

► emphasize
► stress
► highlight
► underline (*formal*)

emphasize (AWL)
to say or show that something is important: *My teacher emphasized the importance of grammar.* | *Scientists **emphasized that** more research needs to be done.*

stress (AWL)
stress means the same as **emphasize** but is slightly more informal: *I want to **stress that** there is no right or wrong answer here – we want students to think of new ideas.*

highlight (AWL)
to show that something is especially important so that people notice it compared to other things: *Your résumé should highlight your skills and experience.*
→ You also use **highlight** to talk about marking words on paper or on a computer using a color that is easy to see: *As I was reading, I highlighted the important parts of the paragraph.*

underline (*formal*)
to help to show clearly that a fact is true, especially a fact that is already known: *The report on children's weight underlines the need for more P.E. in schools.*
→ You also use **underline** to talk about drawing a line under a word or sentence to show that it is important: *In my history textbook, I underlined some of the important dates and events.*

employ *verb* → see **hire**, **use**[1], Topic **Jobs and Work**

employee *noun* → see **worker**, Topic **Jobs and Work**

employer *noun* → see **boss**, Topic **Jobs and Work**

empty[1] /ˈempti/ *adjective*

1 with nothing inside or on the surface
► empty
► blank
► bare
► hollow

2 without any people
► empty
► vacant
► free
► deserted
► uninhabited
► unoccupied (*formal*)

ANTONYMS → see **full**

3 without any buildings or other features
► empty
► bleak
► desolate
► barren

1 with nothing inside or on the surface

empty
having nothing inside: *Her glass was empty, so I offered her more lemonade.* | *There's an empty box under the stairs if you need it.*

blank
without any writing, print, or recorded sound: *She took out a blank sheet of paper and started drawing.* | *Here's a blank CD you can copy the data onto.*

bare
a room, building, or area that is bare has very little furniture or other things in it: *The room was completely bare except for a bed against the wall.*

hollow
having an empty space inside: *Sometimes small animals will make nests in a hollow tree.*

empty

an **empty** glass

a **bare** room

a **blank** sheet of paper

a **hollow** tree

2 without any people

empty
a place that is empty has no one in it or no one using it: *The house was dark and looked empty.* | *We went looking for them in the restaurant, but the place was empty.*

vacant
a vacant room, seat, building, or area of land is empty and available for someone to use: *Many people have moved out of Detroit, and there are a lot of vacant buildings there.* | *There are a few vacant seats in back.*

free
a seat, space, or room that is free is empty and available to use because no one else is using it right now: *Is this seat free?*

deserted
a place that is deserted is empty and quiet because there are no longer any people there: *At night the streets are deserted.*

uninhabited
an uninhabited place has no one living there: *There are some islands off the coast of Africa that are uninhabited.*

unoccupied (*formal*)
something such as a seat, house, or room that is unoccupied is not being lived in or used: *We had to look around to find an unoccupied bench in the gardens.*

empty

a **deserted** street

an **empty** restaurant

an **uninhabited** island

vacant seats

E

3 without any buildings or other features

empty
with no buildings, trees, mountains, or other things that you can look at: *The prairies seem like an empty landscape to people who are used to cities.*

bleak
a place that is bleak is empty and makes you feel sad and lonely: *The snow-covered coast looked bleak.*

desolate
a place that is desolate is empty and makes you feel very sad and lonely: *We looked out over a desolate landscape of bare trees and stony fields.*

barren
a place that is barren has no trees or plants growing in it: *Not many animals can survive in the hot barren desert.*

E

empty[2] /'empti/ *verb*

- ► empty
- ► drain
- ► clear out
- ► unload
- ► unpack
- ► evacuate

ANTONYMS → see **fill**

empty
to take out everything that is inside something: *He emptied his pockets, placing his keys and wallet on the desk.* | *My job was to* ***empty*** *all the trash* ***from*** *the trash cans around the park.*

drain
to take out all of the water or liquid that is inside something: *They drain and clean the swimming pool every winter.* | ***Drain*** *the water* ***from*** *the pot of pasta, and put the pasta in the bowls.*

clear out
to empty something such as a building, room, or cupboard because you no longer want the things that are in it: *I found a pile of old letters while I was clearing out my desk.* | *We had to* ***clear out*** *all the dead leaves* ***from*** *the sandbox before the kids could play there.*

unload
to take things out of a vehicle or large piece of equipment: *Help me* ***unload*** *the groceries* ***from*** *the trunk of the car.* | *Would you unload the dishwasher and put the dishes away please?*

unpack
to take everything out of a suitcase or box: *At the hotel, I unpacked the suitcase and put my clothes in the dresser.* | *I won't unpack anything until we have moved all the boxes from the other house.*

evacuate
to make people leave a place, because the place is dangerous: *The police evacuated people before the hurricane.* | *They had to evacuate a 20-mile area after the nuclear disaster.*

GRAMMAR CHECK: empty

You can **empty** a container or place: *He emptied the trash can.* You can also **empty** things that are in a container or place: *He emptied the trash from the trash can.*

The other words in this entry can be used in the same way: *I drained the bathtub.* | *I drained the water from the bathtub.*

encourage /ɪn'kɚɪdʒ/ *verb*

1 to help someone to do something
- ► encourage
- ► support
- ► inspire

2 to try to make someone want to do something
- ► encourage
- ► motivate
- ► promote
- ► drive

1 to help someone to do something

encourage
to help someone feel more hopeful and more confident so that he or she feels able to do something: *She is a wonderful teacher who is always encouraging her students.* | *Cooder's father* ***encouraged*** *him* ***to*** *play the guitar.*

support
to encourage and help someone during a difficult time: *Rick's friends supported him when he lost his job.*

inspire
to encourage someone so that he or she wants to do or produce something good: *We need a coach who can inspire the team.*

2 to try to make someone want to do something

encourage
to try to persuade someone to do something, because you think it will be good for him or her: *We want to **encourage** more children **to** use the library.*

motivate
to make someone want to achieve something and be willing to work hard in order to do this: *Teachers must be able to **motivate** students **to** work hard and learn.*

promote (AWL)
to try to persuade people to support or use something: *The city government should do more to promote recycling.*

drive
if a feeling drives someone, it makes him or her want to work hard to do something: *His embarrassment at being poor as a child drives him to earn money.*
→ see **persuade**

encouragement /ɪnˈkɚɪdʒmənt/ *noun*

- ► encouragement
- ► support
- ► inspiration

encouragement
things that you say that make someone feel more confident, and makes him or her want to do something: *Children need a lot of encouragement when they are learning new things.*

support
encouragement and help that you give to someone, especially in a difficult situation: *When the actor won the award, he thanked his family for all their support.*

inspiration
something or someone that encourages you and makes you want to do or produce something good: *Her courage was an inspiration to us all.*
→ see **persuasion**

encyclopedia *noun* → see Topic **Books and Literature**

end[1] /end/ *noun*

1 the last part of a period of time, event, activity, or story
- ► end
- ► conclusion (*formal*)
- ► ending
- ► close (*formal*)
- ► finish

ANTONYMS → see **beginning**, **start[2]**

2 the place where a long object ends
- ► end
- ► tip
- ► point

1 the last part of a period of time, event, activity, or story

end
the last part of something: *The **end of** the game was really exciting.* | *I'll know if I got the job **by the end of** the week.* | *There are study questions **at the end of** each chapter.*

conclusion (AWL) (*formal*)
the last part of something such as a play or book, or of an event, especially one that has continued for a long time: ***At the conclusion of** the meeting, we had finally reached an agreement.*
→ A **conclusion** is also the last paragraph of an essay. In a conclusion, you often repeat the main points you have written about: *In the **conclusion of** his essay, he again stated the reasons why the U.S. should use more solar power.*

ending
the end of a story, movie, or play: *I love those old Hollywood movies with happy endings.*

close (*formal*)
the end of an activity or period of time: *We were coming to **the close of** the school year, and students were preparing for their final exams.*

finish
the end of a race: *The finish was very exciting because three of the runners were very close together.*

2 the place where a long object ends

end
the place or part where a long object ends: *She was chewing on the **end of** her pencil.* | *There is a fence **at the end of** the path to stop you from going farther.*

tip
the end of something long, narrow, and pointed: *Dr. Gordon felt my neck with the **tips of** his fingers.*

point
the sharp end of something: *Ben carved his name in the tree trunk, using the **point of** his knife.*
→ see **back[1]**

end² /end/ *verb*

1 to stop happening
- ► end
- ► finish
- ► stop
- ► be over
- ► conclude
- ► expire (*formal*)
- ► run out (*informal*)

ANTONYMS → see **begin**

2 to make someone or something stop happening
- ► end
- ► stop
- ► put an end to
- ► terminate (*formal*)

ANTONYMS → see **start¹ (1)**

3 to stop – used about a road or other path
- ► end
- ► stop (*informal*)
- ► terminate (*formal*)

1 to stop happening

end
to come to the end of something and not happen anymore: *The American Civil War started in 1861 and ended in 1865.* | *The party ended about midnight.* | *The game **ended with** Johnson scoring a touchdown at the last minute.*

finish
to end. **Finish** is often used when saying what time something ends, especially an organized event such as a meeting, class, or party: *What time does your class finish?* | *The meeting will **finish at** 5:30.*

stop
to end. You use **stop** about things that may start happening again: *We waited for the rain to stop.*

be over
if an event, activity, or period of time is over, it has ended: *The long summer vacation was almost over.*

conclude (AWL)
to end. You use **conclude** when something happens at the end of an event, activity, etc.: *The Independence Day celebration **concluded with** fireworks.*
→ **GRAMMAR:** Use **conclude** followed by a preposition such as "with," "by," or "on." Don't say: ~~*The concert concluded*~~. Say: *The concert **concluded with** the music from "Star Wars."* | *The concert will **conclude at** about 9:30 p.m.*

expire (*formal*)
if an official document expires, the period of time during which you can use it has ended: *My driver's license **expires in** May, so I need to send in the form and get a new one.*

run out (*informal*)
if a legal agreement or document runs out, it ends or stops being effective: *My contract runs out in May, so I'm looking for another job.*

2 to make someone or something stop happening

end
to make a situation or something that is happening come to an end: *She told him she wanted to end their relationship.*

stop
to make someone or something end: *We need to stop the destruction of the rain forests.* | *I tried to stop him from running away.*

put an end to
to stop something, especially so that it never starts again: *The injury could put an end to her dancing career.*

terminate (AWL) (*formal*)
to end a legal agreement: *The management cannot terminate an employee's contract without talking to the union.*
→ see **prevent**, **stop¹ (4)**

3 to stop – used about a road or other path

end
if something long ends, especially a road, path, railroad, or something similar, it does not go any farther: *The paved road ends here, and the dirt road begins.* | *The stick **ends in** a point and can be used like a spear.*

stop (*informal*)
stop means the same as **end**: *The bike lane stops after about five miles.*

terminate (AWL) (*formal*)
terminate means the same as **end** but is used only in official language: *The railroad line **terminates in** Seattle.*
→ see **cancel** for words meaning "to stop an activity or event from happening"

endeavor *noun* → see **try²**

ending *noun* → see **end¹**, Topic **Books and Literature**

endless /'endləs/ *adjective*

- endless
- limitless
- infinite

endless
seeming to have no end or limit: *She spent endless hours on the tennis court as she worked on improving her skills.* | *The road seemed endless as it stretched out across the prairie.*

limitless
very large or without any limits: *The sun is a limitless source of energy, if we can only store it easily.* | *The store sells so much music – the choices are almost limitless.*

infinite (AWL)
without a limit or end, especially in number, space, or time. **Infinite** is used especially in science: *The colors of the rainbow can combine to form an infinite number of colors.* | *The universe is infinite.*
➔ see **limited**

ADVERBS
You can make the adjectives that mean **endless** into adverbs by using an **-ly** ending: *We would talk endlessly about our lives, our children, and our activities.* | *The universe is infinitely big.*

enemy /'enəmi/ *noun*

- enemy
- rival
- adversary (*formal*)
- foe (*formal*)

ANTONYMS ➔ see **friend**

enemy
the country or military group who are fighting against your country in a war: *On his first day in Iraq, he and the other soldiers in his squad were attacked by **the enemy**.* | *Enemy soldiers ambushed the supply trucks.*
➔ **GRAMMAR:** In this meaning, don't say: ~~*They were attacked by an enemy*~~. Say: *They were attacked by the enemy.*
➔ You can also use **enemy** to mean "someone who wants to harm you or prevent you from being successful": *We were friends once, but now we are enemies because she is always so mean.*

rival
if two people, companies, or teams are rivals, they are always trying hard to do better than the other one in business or sports: *When I played football in high school, Medford High School was our biggest rival* (=the team it was most important to win against).

adversary (*formal*)
someone you are fighting or competing against, especially in politics or sports. **Adversary** sounds slightly literary and is often used in writing: *The president's political adversaries are trying to make voters feel that he cannot be trusted.*

foe (*formal*)
foe means the same as **enemy** but sounds literary: *King Arthur was a great knight who easily defeated his foes in battle.*
➔ see **opponent**

energetic /ˌenəˈdʒetɪk/ *adjective*

1 having a lot of energy
- energetic
- active
- lively
- boisterous
- dynamic
- vigorous

2 involving using a lot of energy to do things
- energetic
- lively
- vigorous
- strenuous

1 having a lot of energy

energetic (AWL)
having a lot of energy and liking to move and do things: *If you're feeling energetic, we could go running.* | *My aunt is an energetic woman who always has several projects going at the same time.*

active
an active person does a lot of physical things and has a lot of energy: *The trip is for active older people and includes a lot of walking.*

lively
active, exciting, and full of energy. You use **lively** especially to describe someone's personality or way of talking: *Maggie is a lively storyteller who entertains kids with music as well as stories.*

boisterous
noisy and full of energy. You use **boisterous** especially about young people: *It is hard to control a classroom full of boisterous eight-year-olds.*

dynamic (AWL)
full of energy and ideas and wanting to do new

E

things: *He is a dynamic and ambitious young man who is expected to do well in politics.*

vigorous
strong, healthy, and full of physical energy: *My grandfather is a vigorous 75-year-old who still mows his own yard.*

2 involving using a lot of energy to do things

energetic (AWL)
involving using a lot of energy to do a physical activity: *Pete was resting on the couch after an energetic game of tennis.* | *I'm pretty tired – I don't want to do anything too energetic this evening.*

lively
if a discussion or place is lively, people are talking a lot and doing a lot of things and it is exciting: *They were having a lively discussion about politics at the dinner table.* | *Venice Beach has a lively atmosphere, with many street performers, tourists, and people skating.*

vigorous
using a lot of physical energy or effort, especially in a way that feels good: *Vigorous exercise raises your body temperature.*

strenuous
needing or using a lot of physical effort and strength, in a way that makes you tired: *The doctor told Ken to avoid strenuous activity for a few weeks after the surgery.*

ADVERBS

You can make the adjectives that mean **energetic** into adverbs by using an **-ly** ending: *They began waving energetically, trying to attract his attention.* | *The kids were bouncing boisterously around the room.* | *She shook her head vigorously, so there was no doubt that she disagreed.*

Lively looks like an adverb, but it is an adjective.

energy /ˈenɚdʒi/ *noun*

1 power that is used to make things work
- ► energy
- ► power
- ► fuel

2 a person's ability to do things
- ► energy
- ► vitality
- ► vigor
- ► life

1 power that is used to make things work

energy (AWL)
a physical force that can be used to move things, make machines work, or produce light or heat: *The water is heated using energy from the sun.* | *The problem with nuclear energy is how to deal with the waste.*

power
energy such as electricity that is used to make machines or equipment work: *There was not enough electrical power to run a computer.*
→ You can use **power** after adjectives and nouns such as "solar" or "wind" to show where the power comes from: *Solar and wind power are better for the environment than using oil or coal.*

fuel
a substance such as coal, gas, or oil that you can burn to make heat or power: *New cars use much less fuel than older ones.*

2 a person's ability to do things

energy (AWL)
the physical and mental strength that makes you able to do things: *Where do those kids get their energy from? They've been playing basketball all day.* | *She had been sick and did not have much energy.*

vitality
energy and eagerness to do things, which show that someone is healthy and happy: *At 80 years old, Elise is still full of vitality and is always looking for new challenges.*

vigor
strong physical energy. **Vigor** sounds fairly formal or literary: *He worked in the fields with a vigor that surprised even the younger men.*

life
a feeling of energy, activity, and excitement that you can feel in a person or place: *There is so much life in a kindergarten classroom, because little kids are full of enthusiasm.*
→ see **effort**, **strength**

engaged *adjective* → see **married**, Topic **Relationships and Marriage**

engagement *noun* → see **wedding**, Topic **Relationships and Marriage**

engine /ˈendʒɪn/ *noun*

- ► engine
- ► motor

engine
the part of a vehicle or machine that produces power to make the vehicle or machine move,

especially by burning a fuel: *He got in the car, started the engine, and drove away.* | *The plane's engines are extremely noisy.*

motor
the part of a machine that uses electricity to make the machine work or move: *The ceiling fan is powered by an electric motor.*

engineer *noun* → see **designer**, Topic **Science and Technology**

enjoy /ɪnˈdʒɔɪ/ *verb*

- enjoy
- like
- love
- have fun
- have a good/great/wonderful time
- relish
- revel in

ANTONYMS → see **dislike**, **hate**

enjoy
to get pleasure from doing something or watching something: *I really enjoyed the play – thanks for inviting me.* | *The kids love baking cookies, and they really enjoy eating them afterward.*
→ You can also say that you **enjoy yourself** when you get pleasure from doing something or being somewhere: *The party was great – I really enjoyed myself.*

like
to enjoy doing something, especially something you do regularly or for a long time: ***I like to** read books about vampires because they're scary and romantic.*

love
to enjoy doing something very much, especially something you do regularly or for a long time: *Cassie loves playing the guitar and she is getting really good at it.*

have fun
to enjoy yourself at an event or activity: *"Did you have fun at the party?" "Yeah, we had a lot of fun."*

have a good/great/wonderful time
to enjoy an event or activity very much: *We had a great time at the beach – you should have come.*

relish
to really enjoy doing something that is difficult or does not happen often: *Starting your own business is never easy, but Frank relished the challenge.*

revel in
to really enjoy or celebrate a situation, especially when this feeling does not last long. **Revel in** is used especially in literature: *The crowds poured into the streets after the team won, reveling in the moment of victory.*
→ see **pleasure**, **enjoy yourself** at **play**[1]

GRAMMAR CHECK: enjoy

Enjoy, **like**, **love**, and **relish** can all be followed by a word ending in "-ing" such as "cooking" or "singing": *I like cooking.*

Like and **love** can also be followed by "to" and an infinitive when you are talking about something that someone does regularly: *I like to cook.* Don't say: ~~*I enjoy to play soccer*~~. Say: *I enjoy playing soccer* or *I like to play soccer.*

enjoyable *adjective* → see **fun**[2], **nice**

enjoyment /ɪnˈdʒɔɪmənt/ *noun*

- enjoyment
- fun
- pleasure
- satisfaction
- delight

enjoyment
the feeling that you get when you enjoy doing something: *I get a lot of enjoyment out of playing the piano.* | *Many people hike on the mountain trails **for enjoyment** and exercise.*

fun
pleasure that you get from doing something: *She plays the guitar **for fun**.* | *We had lots of fun when we went skiing last winter.*

pleasure
a happy feeling because you like something very much: *Their music has brought pleasure to millions of people.* | *She ate her meal **with obvious pleasure**.*

satisfaction
the feeling that you have done something good or useful, or have gotten what you wanted: *As a teacher he got great satisfaction from helping people to learn.*

delight
a strong feeling of happiness and excitement, because something good has happened: *She screamed **with delight** when she found out that she had passed her driving test.*
→ see **fun**[1], **happiness**, **pleasure**

enormous *adjective* → see **big**, Topic **Describing Size**

enough *adjective, pronoun, adverb* → see Function Words

E

enter /ˈentɚ/ *verb*

- enter
- go in
- come in
- trespass (*formal*)

ANTONYMS → see **leave (1)**

enter
to walk or move into a place: *He took off his shoes when he entered the room.* | *The burglars entered the house through a back window.*
→ **GRAMMAR:** Don't say: ~~*A man entered in the room*~~ or ~~*A man entered to the room*~~. Say: *A man entered the room.*

go in *also* **go into something**
go in means the same as **enter** but sounds less formal: *Let's go in and find out how much the jacket costs.* | *The principal went into her office and closed the door.*

come in *also* **come into something**
to enter a room or building. You use **come in** or **come into** when you are already in the place that someone else is entering: *Please, come in and sit down.* | *She was all wet from the rain when she came into the house.*

trespass (*formal*)
to enter an area of land that belongs to someone else without permission: *Carlson was fined $1,000 for* ***trespassing on*** *government property.*
→ see **join** for **enter** meaning "to enter a company or organization," **play**[1] **(1)** for **enter** meaning "to enter a competition," **type** for **enter** meaning "to type words on a computer"
→ see **entrance**

entertainer *noun* → see **performer**

entertainment /ˌentɚˈteɪnmənt/ *noun*

- entertainment
- recreation
- play

entertainment
things for people to watch and do in order to enjoy themselves: *On a cruise ship there is plenty of entertainment. There are movies, dances, games, and even a swimming pool.*

recreation
activities people do for fun. **Recreation** is often used in formal or official language: *What do the local people do for recreation in the winter?*
→ **GRAMMAR:** **Recreation** is often used before another noun: *The state has decided to make the lake and the park around it a recreation area, with boating and horse riding.*

play
the things that children do for fun, such as using toys or playing games: *We watched all the kids at play in the park.* | *Children learn best through play.*
→ see **pleasure**

enthusiasm *noun* → see **eagerness**

enthusiastic *adjective* → see **eager**

entire *adjective* → see **whole**

entirely *adverb* → see **completely**

entrance /ˈentrəns/ *noun*

1 a place to enter a building or area
- entrance
- doorway
- way in
- entry
- access (*formal*)

ANTONYMS → see **exit**

2 the ability or right to enter a place
- entrance
- access

3 the act of entering a place
- entrance
- entry (*formal*)

1 a place to enter a building or area

entrance
the main door, gate, or other opening that you go through to enter a place: *We'll meet at the main* ***entrance of*** *the library at 1:00.* | *The* ***entrance to*** *the subway station is across the street.*

doorway
an opening into a room or building, where there is a door: *Don't stand in the doorway - come in.*

way in *also* **way into something**
a place or method you use to get into a place: *I was late for my appointment because I couldn't find the way into the building.* | *Going through the side door is the quickest way in.*

entry *also* **entryway**
an entrance or passage that you go through to enter a place or area, especially when the entrance or the place is large or impressive: *You get into the stadium through a huge marble entryway.* | *The* ***entry to*** *the market is a huge metal arch.*

access (AWL) (*formal*)
a way of getting into a place. **Access** is usually used in official writing or on signs: ***Access to*** *the restrooms is through the main hall.*

2 the ability or right to enter a place

entrance *also* **entry**
the ability or right to enter a place. **Entrance** and **entry** are used especially in official writing and in legal language: ***Entrance to** the museum is free.* | *The men became angry when they were not allowed **entry into** the bar.*

access (AWL)
the right or ability to enter a place or see something that most people cannot see: *Very few people have **access to** the President of the United States.* | *Nobody knows how the reporters gained **access to** the star's hotel room.*

3 the act of entering a place

entrance
the act of going into a place or room, especially in a way that people notice: *Bridget came late so that she could make an entrance in her bright red dress and heels.*

entry (*formal*)
the act of entering a place: *It was dark and their **entry into** the camp went unnoticed.*

entry *noun* → see **entrance**

envious *adjective* → see **jealous**, Topic **Describing People's Emotions**

environment /ɪnˈvaɪrə-nmənt/ *noun*

- ► the environment
- ► ecology
- ► ecosystem
- ► habitat
- ► biome
- ► the biosphere

the environment (AWL)
the natural world, including water, air, land, plants, and sometimes animals, which can be harmed by the way humans live: *Chemicals from the factory are dangerous to the environment.* | *What effect will the dam have on the environment?*

ecology
the relationship between the environment and all the plants, animals, and people living there: *The oil spill could affect **the ecology of** the sea shore.*
→ **Ecology** also means "the science that studies the environment": *He is a professor of ecology.*

ecosystem
the environment and all the plants and animals in a place, which are all connected with each other and have an effect on each other: *The decrease in the number of birds is affecting the island's ecosystem.*

habitat
the place in which a plant or animal lives: *The jungle is the tiger's natural habitat.*

biome
a type of environment with a particular type of weather and particular types of plants. **Biome** is used in scientific writing: *Some animals, such as camels, are found only in desert biomes.*

the biosphere
the Earth's surface and the air around it where animals and plants can live. **The biosphere** is used in scientific writing: *Changes in the biosphere can affect all life on the planet.*

envy *noun* → see **jealousy**

equal /ˈikwəl/ *adjective*

- ► equal
- ► even
- ► equivalent
- ► comparable
- ► corresponding

equal
the same in size, value, or amount: *The two cars are of equal value – each costs about $14,000.* | *What happens if they both receive an equal number of votes?*

even
if the score in a game is even, the two teams or players have the same number of points: *At the end of the first half, the score was even.*
→ You can also use **even** to say that two people or teams are equally good: *The two tennis players are about even in terms of their skill.*

equivalent (AWL)
the same in value, level, size, or importance as something of a different type: *The visa costs $25 or the equivalent amount in pesos.* | *People say that one year in the life of a dog is **equivalent to** seven human years.*

comparable
similar to something else in size, number, or quality so that you can easily compare the two things: *An apartment of comparable size costs much less in the suburbs than it costs in the city.*

corresponding (AWL)
relating to or similar to something else that existed in a different time or situation: *Sales in May were 10% higher than in the corresponding period last year.*
→ see **fair**[1]

E

ADVERBS

You can make the adjectives that mean **equal** into adverbs by using an **-ly** ending: *The two cars are equally expensive.* | *The players are evenly matched* (=they have the same level of skill). | *The soil is not very good, and the harvest is thus correspondingly poor.*

equality *noun* → see **fairness**

equally *adverb* → see **fairly**

equipment /ɪˈkwɪpmənt/ *noun*

- ► equipment
- ► tool
- ► tool kit
- ► gear
- ► materials

equipment (AWL)
the machines or objects that you need to do something or make something: *We're raising money to buy* ***equipment for*** *the baseball team.* | *The school has plenty of computer equipment for the students to use.*
→ **GRAMMAR: Equipment** cannot be used in the plural. Don't say: ~~*We need to buy equipments*~~.

tool
a piece of equipment, especially a simple object that you use to make something or do something useful: *The plumber went out to the van to get his tools.*

tool kit
a set of tools or equipment that you use to do something: *Can you bring me the hammer out of the tool kit?*

gear
special equipment and clothes that you need for an activity: *I have a sleeping bag, but I'm going to borrow some other camping gear from Bryan.*

materials
the things that you use in order to make something or do a job or activity: *They used very cheap materials to build the apartments.*
→ **GRAMMAR: Materials** is usually used in the plural, but if you are talking about information or books that you are using, you can say **material**: *Children should choose reading material that is right for their age.*
→ see **machine**, **tool**

equivalent *adjective* → see **equal**, **similar**

erase *verb* → see **remove**

erect *verb* → see **build**[1]

error *noun* → see **mistake**[1]

escape /ɪˈskeɪp/ *verb*

- ► escape
- ► get away
- ► run away
- ► flee (*formal*)
- ► evade (*formal*)

escape
to leave a place or person when it is dangerous, or when someone is trying to stop you from leaving or is chasing you: *Collins* ***escaped from*** *prison in October, and he is still missing.* | *Many people have moved across the border to escape the violence in their country.*

get away
get away means the same as **escape**, but sounds more informal and is used especially when someone is chasing you: *We chased the thief for three blocks, but he got away.*

run away
to escape from someone or something by running: *When the old man yelled at the kids, they ran away.*
→ **Run away** can also mean "to leave your home in order to escape from an unhappy situation." You use **run away** about children: *David ran away because he couldn't get along with his stepfather.*

flee (*formal*)
to leave a place very quickly in order to escape from a dangerous situation. You use **flee** especially about people who have to leave a place because of a war, an event such as a flood or storm, or a bad political situation: *Thousands of refugees had to flee their country when war broke out.*
→ **Flee** is also used in news reports to talk about a criminal who escapes: *The two bank robbers fled in a black car, and the police chased them across the city.*

evade (*formal*)
to avoid being caught by someone: *He managed to evade the security guards by hiding in a closet.*
→ see **leak**[1] for **escape** meaning "to leak in small amounts"

especially /ɪˈspeʃəli/ *adverb*

- ► especially
- ► particularly
- ► specifically
- ► above all

especially
more than at other times, or more than other

people or things: *It's really warm in this room, especially when the sun shines in the window.* | *Juan's family were especially kind to him.* | *The teacher seemed to be talking to me especially.* | *I especially like the artist's use of color.*

particularly *also* **in particular**
particularly means the same as **especially** but sounds a little more formal: *The surface is slippery, particularly when it has been raining.* | *The town gets a lot of tourists, particularly in the summer.* | *She likes all animals, but she likes dogs in particular.*

specifically (AWL)
for one person, thing, or purpose and not others: *Some advertisements are specifically aimed at children.* | *The tires are specifically designed for riding over rough ground.*

above all
most importantly, or more than anything else: *Get plenty of sleep, eat good food, and above all try to relax.*

essay /'eseɪ/ *noun*

- ► essay
- ► paper
- ► report
- ► composition
- ► thesis
- ► dissertation

essay
a piece of writing about a particular subject that someone writes for school or to be published. **Essays** are not stories: *The teacher told us to write a two-page* ***essay about*** *our family history.* | *My English essay is due tomorrow and I haven't started writing it yet!*

paper
a long piece of writing about something you have studied: *I have to write two research papers this semester.*

report
something written or spoken that tells about something you have read, experienced, or learned. You use **report** especially about pieces of writing for school and written or spoken news stories: *Every two weeks, each student reads a book and writes a book report.* | *The news report said that the plane landed safely after having some problems in the air.*

composition
composition means the same as **essay** but is a little more formal or old-fashioned: *We had to write a* ***composition about*** *our earliest memory.*

thesis (AWL)
a long piece of writing that you do in college, especially for a master's degree: *She wrote her master's* ***thesis on*** *the role of women in politics in the early 1900s.*

dissertation
a long piece of writing that you do at a university, especially in order to get a Ph.D.: *Adam needs to finish his research and write his dissertation before he can get his doctorate.*
→ see **report**, **story** (**1**), **work**[2] (**3**), Topic **Education**

essential *adjective* → see **basic**, **important**, **necessary**

essentials *noun* → see **need**[2]

establish *verb* → see **start**[1]

establishment *noun* → see **company**

estimate[1] *noun* → see **guess**[2]

estimate[2] *verb* → see **guess**[1]

ethical *adjective* → see **good**, **right**[1]

ethics *noun* → see **morality**

ethnic *adjective* → see **racial**

ethnic group *noun* → see **race**[1]

ethnicity *noun* → see **race**[1]

even *adjective* → see **equal**, **flat**

evening /'ivnɪŋ/ *noun*

- ► evening
- ► sunset
- ► sundown
- ► dusk
- ► twilight
- ► nightfall (*formal*)

evening
the end of the day and the early part of the night: *Do you want to have dinner together* ***this evening?*** | *Dad gets home from work about 6:30* ***in the evening.***

sunset
the time when the sun disappears at the end of the day, or the sky at this time: *There was a photograph of a beautiful pink and orange sunset on the wall.* | *The bats leave the caves* ***at sunset*** *each day.*

sundown
the time when the sun goes down in the sky at the end of the day: *We worked until sundown.* | *The two girls agreed to meet each other* ***at sundown*** *by the lake.*

E

dusk
the time when it starts to become dark at the end of the day: *The street lights come on **at dusk**.*

twilight
the time when it starts to become dark in the early evening, or the pale light at this time. **Twilight** sounds slightly literary: *They watched for the first stars to appear **at twilight**.*

nightfall (*formal*)
the time when it becomes dark in the evening and night begins. **Nightfall** sounds fairly literary: *We hurried to get back to camp before nightfall.*
→ see **night**

event /ɪˈvent/ *noun*

- ► event
- ► occasion
- ► incident
- ► affair
- ► occurrence (*formal*)
- ► phenomenon

event
something that happens, especially something important, interesting, or unusual: *We learned the dates of important historical events such as battles.* | *The Super Bowl is one of the most popular sporting events of the year.*

occasion
an important event or ceremony: *People dress in nice clothes on special occasions such as weddings.*

incident (AWL)
something that happens, especially something involving trouble or a crime: *He was injured **in a** violent **incident** outside a bar.*

affair
something that happens in politics or public life, especially something shocking or illegal, which is talked about in the newspapers and on television: *President Nixon was forced to resign after the Watergate affair.*

occurrence (AWL) (*formal*)
an event. You use **occurrence** especially to talk about how often something happens: *Storms like this are becoming a more common occurrence.*

phenomenon (AWL)
something that happens in society or nature, especially something that is difficult to understand: *Scientists cannot explain the strange **phenomenon of** so many birds dying at the same time.*

eventually *adverb* → see **finally**, **later**

every *adjective* → see Function Words

everyone /ˈevriˌwʌn/ *pronoun*

- ► everyone
- ► everybody
- ► all
- ► the whole world/city/family etc.

everyone
every person: *We can't leave until everyone is here.* | *I couldn't hear the teacher because everyone was talking.*

everybody
everybody means the same as **everyone** but is slightly more informal: *Everybody has a cell phone. I'm the only one who doesn't.*

all
every person in a particular group: *There was no one in the office – they were all at lunch.* | *All of the other kids are going – can't I go too?*

the whole world/city/family etc.
every person in a particular group: *The sound of the car's engine woke up the whole neighborhood.*

GRAMMAR CHECK: everyone

Everyone, **everybody**, and **the whole world/city/family** are followed by a singular verb: *Everyone was laughing.* | *Juan's whole family always eats dinner together.*

everywhere /ˈevriˌwer/ *adverb*

- ► everywhere
- ► everyplace
- ► throughout
- ► all over (*informal*)

everywhere
in every place or to every place: *Jack and his dog go everywhere together.* | *It's sunny everywhere else in the state, but it's raining here.*

everyplace
everyplace means the same as **everywhere** but sounds more informal: *I've been looking everyplace for you.*

throughout
in or to every part of a place or area. You use **throughout** only about fairly large areas: *He traveled throughout the Southwestern United States.* | *The house has wooden floors throughout.*

all over (*informal*)
everywhere on a surface or in a place: *There were stacks of newspapers all over the house.* | *He traveled all over the Southwestern United States.*

SYNONYM CHECK
Throughout or all over?

Throughout and **all over** are similar in meaning, but there are some important differences.

Throughout sounds more formal than **all over** and is only used about fairly large areas: *The news spread quickly throughout the city.*

Also, you do not use **throughout** about things on the surface of something, but you can use **all over** about a surface. Don't say: ~~*Her skin was red and itchy throughout*~~. Say: *Her skin was red and itchy all over.*

evidence *noun* → see **proof**

evil[1] /ˈivəl/ *adjective*

- evil
- wrong
- bad
- wicked
- sinister

ANTONYMS → see **good**, **right[1]**

evil
very cruel or bad: *The men do a dance to scare away evil spirits who would harm the tribe.* | *He was an evil dictator who was responsible for the death of thousands of people.*

wrong
if an action is wrong, it is not good and not acceptable by society: *You took your friend's MP3 player without telling him, and that was wrong.*
→ GRAMMAR: You cannot use **wrong** before a noun in this meaning. Don't say: ~~*You've done a wrong action*~~. Say: *You've done something wrong.*

bad
if a person or what a person does is bad, that person or action is morally wrong: *Yes, he lied to me once – does that mean he is a bad person?*

wicked
very cruel or bad. **Wicked** is often used in stories: *The princess was locked in a tower by her wicked uncle.*

sinister
frightening, and making you feel that something bad will happen. **Sinister** is also often used in stories: *He had discovered a sinister plan to kill the president.*
→ see **cruel**

SYNONYM CHECK
Evil or wicked?

Evil sounds stronger than **wicked**, and you use it about someone who is extremely cruel or bad, for example someone who kills or hurts a lot of people. Some people believe in **evil spirits**, which are spirits that harm people and can cause problems.

You use **wicked** in fairy tales, for example when talking about witches and stepmothers.

ADVERBS

You can make the adjectives **evil**, **wicked**, and **sinister** into adverbs by using an **-ly** ending: *He looked at her evilly.* | *They behaved wickedly and were punished.*

Wickedly is often used to show that something is funny but a little bit cruel: *The movie is a wickedly funny look at how actors behave off-screen.*

evil[2] /ˈivəl/ *noun*

- evil
- wickedness
- sin

evil
a power that makes people choose to do bad things, or behavior that is very cruel or bad: *The comic book is about superheroes who guard the world against evil.* | *Killing someone is pure evil.*

wickedness
behavior that is very cruel or bad. **Wickedness** is often used in stories: *In the story, the witch is going to eat the boy, but she is punished for her wickedness by being pushed into the oven.*

sin
behavior or an action that religious rules do not allow: *I have committed many sins, but I am not a thief!* | *Christians believe that Jesus died to save us from our sins.*

exact /ɪɡˈzækt/ *adjective*

- exact
- precise (*formal*)
- accurate

ANTONYMS → see **approximate**, **vague**

exact
completely correct in all the details: *"What is the exact time?" "It's 3:32 p.m."* | *The X marks the exact spot where the treasure is buried.*

precise (AWL) (*formal*)
completely correct and including every detail, especially because it is important that you make

E

no mistakes: *When making cakes, precise measurements are important.* | *What is the precise location of the ship?*

accurate (AWL)
completely correct because all the details are true or right. You use **accurate** about information, reports, descriptions, and numbers: *She gave an accurate description of the man she saw robbing the bank.* | *It is difficult to get an accurate count of the city's population.*
→ You can also say that a ball, weapon, or person is **accurate** when they hit the exact place that they aim at: *She made an accurate throw to first base.* | *The army says the weapons are very accurate.*
→ see **right[1] (1)**

SYNONYM CHECK
Exact, precise, or accurate?

Exact, **precise**, and **accurate** can often be used in the same sentences. When you use **exact**, you want to emphasize that the information is very detailed: *If you don't follow the exact instructions, you will get lost.*

When you use **precise**, you want to emphasize that the information is very clear: *The instructions were precise* (=the instructions were clear and detailed).

When you use **accurate**, you want to emphasize that the information is right: *The instructions were accurate* (=the instructions had the right information).

exactly /ɪɡˈzæktli/ *adverb*

- ► exactly
- ► precisely (*formal*)
- ► accurately

exactly
in a way that is completely correct or accurate: *The plane arrived exactly on time.* | *Craig and I got exactly the same answer on the first math question.*

precisely (AWL) (*formal*)
in a way that is completely correct or includes all the details, because it is important that you make no mistakes. **Precisely** can be used about actions as well as information: *The meeting will end precisely at 3:30 because we all have to leave.* | *I tried to aim precisely at the middle of the target.*

accurately
in a way that is completely correct because all the details are true or right: *In this experiment, you will need to weigh the substances accurately.*
→ You also use **accurately** when talking about throwing or aiming something so that it hits an exact place: *If you hit the spot in the center accurately, you get 50 points.*

exam *noun* → see **test[1]**

examination /ɪɡˌzæməˈneɪʃən/ *noun*

1 the process of looking at something to find out about it
- ► examination
- ► analysis
- ► inspection
- ► check (*informal*)
- ► evaluation

2 a medical examination
- ► examination (*formal*)
- ► check-up
- ► test
- ► scan

1 the process of looking at something to find out about it

examination
the process of looking at something carefully, especially so that you can find out more about it: *The **examination of** all the evidence took a long time.* | *A careful examination showed that the tree was 500 years old.*

analysis (AWL)
a careful examination of all the parts of something in order to understand it or to find out what it contains: ***Analysis of** the numbers showed that the company was in serious financial trouble.*

inspection (AWL)
a careful examination of something, to make sure that something is in good condition or that something has been done according to rules or laws. An **inspection** is usually done by someone with an official position: *The health inspector does an **inspection of** each restaurant to make sure they are clean and safe.*

check (*informal*)
check means the same as **inspection**: *We will do a **check of** all the alarm systems before we leave the building.*

evaluation (AWL)
an examination in which you judge how good, useful, or successful someone or something is: *Every year all employees have an evaluation to see how well they are working.*

2 a medical examination

examination (*formal*)
a medical check of all or part of your body: *The*

doctor will give you a complete medical examination before you enter the army. | *The* ***examination of*** *her chest showed that the infection was gone.*

check-up
a medical check that happens regularly to make sure you are healthy: *I went to the doctor for my yearly check-up, and she told me I needed to lose weight.*

test
an examination of part of your body: *Children should have an eye test every year.*

scan
a check of part of the inside of your body using a machine that can see inside your body: *The* ***scan of*** *his brain showed that there was a small tumor.*
→ see **check²**, **test¹** for **examination** meaning "test"

examine /ɪg'zæmɪn/ *verb*

- ► examine
- ► check
- ► inspect
- ► analyze
- ► evaluate
- ► look at
- ► study

examine
to look at something carefully in order to find out or decide something: *The little girl was examining the leaf she had pulled from the tree.* | *The researchers examined the connection between pre-school education and success in high school.*

check
to look carefully at something to see if it is correct or the way it should be: *I asked my friend to check my spelling and grammar after I finished the paper.*

inspect (AWL)
to carefully examine someone or something, to make sure that he, she, or it is in good condition or that something has been done according to rules or laws: *The sergeant inspected the soldiers and their equipment.*

analyze (AWL)
to examine the parts of something carefully in order to understand it or to find out what it contains: *They analyzed his blood and found that the levels of iron were very low.*

evaluate (AWL)
to examine someone or something so that you can judge how good, useful, or successful he, she, or it is: *At the end of the year, we will evaluate the program and decide whether it should continue.*

look at
look at means the same as **examine** but sounds more informal: *In this project we will look at how soil changes through the growing season.*

study
to spend time learning about something in detail: *Scientists have been studying the effects of climate change on the Earth for years.*
→ see **check¹**

example /ɪg'zæmpəl/ *noun*

- ► example
- ► case
- ► instance (*formal*)
- ► illustration

example
something that you mention to show the kind of thing you mean, or to show that something is true: *This painting is a good* ***example of*** *the artist's later work.* | *The computer is an* ***example of*** *technology that has changed our lives.*

case
an example of a situation, event, or thing, especially an example of something bad that has happened: *The company has two separate alarm systems, but* ***in this case*** *both systems failed.*

instance (AWL) (*formal*)
an example of a particular kind of situation or event, especially an example of something bad: *There have been many instances in which prisoners were badly injured in fights.*

illustration (AWL)
an example that shows how something is true. **Illustration** sounds formal or literary: *Brenna's story is a good* ***illustration of*** *how getting good grades can help you be successful.*
→ see **sample** for "a small amount of something that shows you what it is like"

exceed /ɪk'sid/ *verb*

- ► exceed (*formal*)
- ► be more than
- ► surpass (*formal*)

exceed (AWL) (*formal*)
to be more than a particular amount, or to be better than you expected: *The number of people who came to the meeting exceeded the number we expected.* | *I didn't think the movie would be very good, but it exceeded my expectations and I loved it.*

E

be more than
to be a larger number or amount than another amount: *Fifty is more than forty.* | *I enjoyed the party a lot more than I expected.*

surpass (*formal*)
to be bigger in amount or better in quality than someone or something else: *Sales of his new novel are expected to surpass his last book.* | *The quality of the café's food surpasses the food at the other restaurants in town.*

excellent *adjective* → see **good**

except *preposition* → see Function Words

exceptional *adjective* → see **good**

exceptionally *adverb* → see **extremely**

excessive *adjective* → see **wasteful**

exchange¹ *noun* → see **trade¹**

exchange² *verb* → see **trade²**

excite /ɪk'saɪt/ *verb*

- excite
- thrill
- exhilarate

excite
to make someone feel happy and eager or interested: *The idea of traveling to other countries excited me.*

thrill
to make someone feel great excitement and pleasure: *The band's music thrilled the crowd, who screamed and cheered.*

exhilarate
to make someone feel extremely excited and full of energy, because he or she is doing something unusual or dangerous: *I was very scared at first, but the parachute jump exhilarated me.*

excited /ɪk'saɪtɪd/ *adjective*

- excited
- thrilled
- exhilarated
- hysterical

ANTONYMS → see **bored**

excited
happy and eager or interested: *The boys were* ***excited about*** *seeing monkeys and lizards in the jungle.* | *I am* ***excited that*** *we have two great new teachers this year.* | *There were a lot of excited children at the birthday party.*

thrilled
extremely excited and pleased: *My grandmother is* ***thrilled that*** *we are coming to visit her.* | *He was* ***thrilled with*** *his birthday presents.*

exhilarated
feeling extremely excited and full of energy, especially because something is unusual or dangerous: *As she went faster and faster down the hill, she felt more and more exhilarated.*

hysterical
so excited or upset that you cannot control yourself: *Some of the fans became hysterical as the band walked on stage.*
→ see **eager**

ADVERBS
You can make the adjectives **excited** and **hysterical** into adverbs by using an **-ly** ending: *They began talking excitedly about their trip.* | *The fans began screaming hysterically as the band walked on stage.*

excitement /ɪk'saɪtmənt/ *noun*

- excitement
- thrill
- exhilaration
- hysteria

excitement
the feeling you have when you are excited: *The day we left on our trip, I was filled with excitement.* | *There is a feeling of great excitement here in the Olympic stadium.*

thrill
a strong feeling of excitement and a little nervousness: *I'll never forget the* ***thrill of*** *riding a horse for the first time.*

exhilaration
a feeling of being extremely excited and full of energy, especially because of something unusual or dangerous: *The feeling of exhilaration you get from being on a roller coaster is fantastic.*

hysteria
a feeling of strong excitement or a strong emotion that you cannot control. **Hysteria** can affect one person or it can affect a group of people: *There was hysteria in the city when the enemy attack began.*
→ see **eagerness**

exciting /ɪk'saɪtɪŋ/ *adjective*

► exciting
► thrilling
► exhilarating
► dramatic
► sensational

ANTONYMS → see **boring**

exciting
something that is exciting makes you feel excited: ***It was exciting to** see Niagara Falls!* | *The first time I flew in a plane was so exciting.*

thrilling
making you feel extremely excited and a little nervous: *We took a thrilling ride on the roller coaster.*
→ **GRAMMAR:** Don't use "very" with **thrilling**. Don't say: ~~*It was very thrilling*~~. Say: *It was thrilling.*

exhilarating
making you feel extremely excited and full of energy, especially because something is unusual or dangerous: *The water was moving fast, so the raft trip down the river was exhilarating.*

dramatic (AWL)
a dramatic story or situation has a lot of exciting things happening in it, especially because you do not know what will happen next: *I loved the dramatic ending to the movie, when they drive off the cliff in their car.*

sensational
a sensational story or situation is exciting in a way that makes people want to know more about it. **Sensational** stories often involve things like love, money, crime, sex, and death: *The newspaper printed a sensational story about the singer leaving her husband.*

ADVERBS

You can make the adjectives that mean **exciting** into adverbs by using an **-ly** ending: *Parker performed well, though not as excitingly as some of the other musicians.* | *"We're getting married!" Thomas announced dramatically.* | *The actress sensationally walked off stage in the middle of a performance.*

exclaim *verb* → see **say**

exclude *verb* → see **leave out**

excuse[1] /ɪk'skyuz/ *verb*

► excuse
► exempt (*formal*)
► waive
► pardon

excuse
to allow someone to leave a place when other people must stay, or to allow someone not to do something that other people must do: *He was **excused from** P.E. because he hurt his leg.* | *My parents would not **excuse** us **from** the table until everyone had finished eating.*

exempt (*formal*)
to officially allow someone not to do something that other people must do. **Exempt** is often used in official and legal documents to say that a group of people do not have to do something: *Families who do not have much money are **exempted from** paying the tax.*

waive
to state officially that someone does not have to follow a rule or pay something, or that you will not use a right that you have: *The lawyer agreed to waive his fee and defend the man.* | *The school waived a rule that said a girl could not play on the boy's soccer team.*

pardon
if a person in a powerful position pardons someone, he or she stops the punishment of someone who is guilty of a crime: *William Hayes expected to be in prison for 30 years for his crimes, but the governor pardoned him.*
→ see **forgive**

excuse[2] *noun* → see **reason**

execute *verb* → see **kill**

execution *noun* → see **death penalty**, **murder**

exercise[1] /'eksəˌsaɪz/ *noun*

► exercise
► workout
► warm-up
► training

exercise
physical activity that you do in order to stay strong and healthy: *I needed more exercise, so I started walking three miles every day.* | *The coach made us do lots of stretching exercises before we started running.*

workout
a series of physical exercises that use all the muscles in your body, especially in an exercise

class or gym (=place with special equipment for exercising): *Dan does a workout at the gym every morning.*

warm-up
a set of gentle exercises or practices that you do to prepare for playing a sport: *We ran around the gym and did stretching exercises as a warm-up.*

training
activities that you do to prepare for a sports competition, such as exercising and practicing skills again and again: *The baseball teams begin spring training in February.*
→ **GRAMMAR: Training** cannot be used with "a" or in the plural. Don't say: ~~*We have a training tomorrow*~~ or ~~*We have trainings next week*~~.
→ see Topic **Sports and Exercise**

exercise[2] /ˈeksəˌsaɪz/ *verb*

- ► exercise
- ► work out
- ► get in shape
- ► warm up
- ► train

exercise
to do physical activity so that you stay strong and healthy: *The doctor told him to exercise more and eat less.* | *I usually exercise before breakfast by running or swimming.*

work out
to exercise in a way that uses all the important muscles in your body, especially in an exercise class or gym (=place with special equipment for exercising): *I went running, and then I went to the gym to work out.*

get in shape
to make your body strong by exercising. You can also use **keep in shape** or **stay in shape** to talk about staying strong by exercising: *I didn't exercise all winter, and now I need to get in shape.* | *Mariana stays in shape by swimming three times a week.*

warm up
to prepare for an activity or sport by doing gentle exercises or practicing just before the activity or game starts: *Make sure you warm up with lots of stretches before you start playing.*

train
to prepare for a sports competition by exercising and practicing skills again and again: *She has been **training for** the marathon all year.*

exhausted *adjective* → see **tired**

exhausting *adjective* → see **tiring**

exhaustion *noun* → see **tiredness**

exhibition *noun* → see **museum**, **show[2]**

exist /ɪgˈzɪst/ *verb*

- ► exist
- ► there is/there are
- ► live
- ► be found
- ► occur *(formal)*

exist
to be present in the world: *The old road still exists, but it is not in good condition.* | *Dinosaurs no longer exist.*

there is/there are
used to say that something exists: *There are many animals that live in the desert.* | *There is a new restaurant on the corner of Main and Elm Streets.*
→ **GRAMMAR:** If you are saying that more than one thing exists, use "are" or "were." Don't say: ~~*There is many interesting places to visit*~~. Say: *There are many interesting places to visit.*

live
if a plant or animal lives in a place, it naturally exists there: *Groundhogs are common animals that live in many parts of the U.S.*

be found
to live or exist in a particular place. **Be found** can be used about living creatures or about something that is not living: *This tiny monkey is only found in the Pacific coast region.* | *The rock is only found near volcanoes.*

occur (AWL) *(formal)*
occur means the same as **be found**. **Occur** is used in scientific writing: *This mineral does not occur naturally in sandy soil.*

existence *noun* → see **life**, **presence**

exit /ˈegzɪt/ *noun*

1 a door or passage that leads outside
- ► exit
- ► way out

ANTONYMS → see **entrance (1)**

2 a way to leave a road
- ► exit
- ► off-ramp
- ► turn-off

1 a door or passage that leads outside

exit
a door or opening that you can use to leave a public place: *When the movie ended, we stood up and walked toward the exit.* | *The flight attendant pointed out all of the exits on the airplane.*

way out
a place or method that you can use to leave a building. You often use **way out** when there is a dangerous situation and people use any method or opening they can to get out of the building: *I got lost inside the museum and couldn't find the way out.* | *The building was on fire and people inside were looking for a way out.*

2 a way to leave a road

exit
a place where vehicles can leave a large road and join another road: *Take the Grove Street exit off the highway and go north.*

off-ramp
a short road that you use to drive off a highway or freeway: *I took the next off-ramp and drove to a gas station.*

turn-off
a smaller road that you can turn onto from a main road: *The turn-off to the shopping mall is just past Lake Street.*

expand /ɪk'spænd/ *verb*

- ► expand
- ► stretch
- ► swell
- ► enlarge
- ► blow up (*informal*)
- ► magnify

ANTONYMS → see **get smaller**

expand (AWL)
to become larger, or make something larger: *When you breathe in, your lungs expand.* | *The rebels are fighting to expand the area that they control.*

stretch *also* **stretch out**
to become bigger, longer, or looser, usually by pulling or pressing something: *The shoes will stretch out a little bit once you start wearing them.* | *She stretched the dough over the top of the apple pie.*

swell *also* **swell up**
if a part of your body swells, it becomes larger and rounder than normal because of an injury: *I fell and twisted my ankle and now it is starting to swell.*

enlarge
to make a photograph, picture, or document bigger: *I enlarged the map on my computer so that it covered the full screen.*

blow up (*informal*)
blow up means the same as **enlarge**: *That's a great picture – you should blow it up and frame it.*
→ **Blow up** also means "to fill something with air or gas so that it becomes bigger": *Come and help me blow up the balloons for the party.*

magnify
to make something look bigger than it really is by using a piece of equipment, for example a microscope or magnifying glass: *The bug is actually too small to see, but in this picture we have magnified it.*
→ see **increase[1]**, **lengthen**

expand

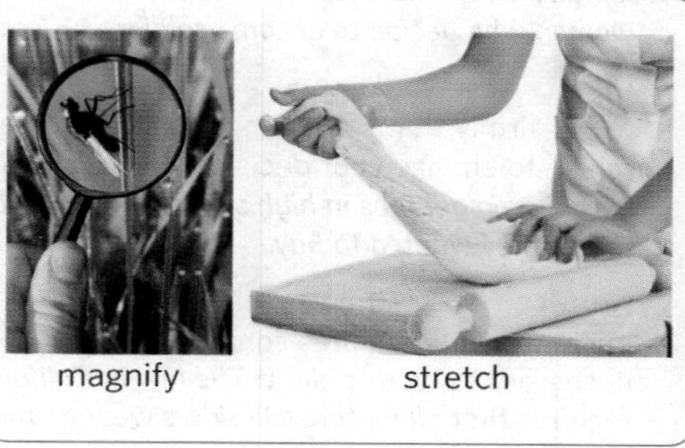

magnify stretch

expect /ɪk'spekt/ *verb*

1 to think that something will happen
- ► expect
- ► anticipate (*formal*)
- ► assume

2 to say that something is necessary or important
- ► expect
- ► demand
- ► insist
- ► require (*formal*)

1 to think that something will happen

expect
to think that something will happen: *Drivers can expect long delays on all roads out of the city today.* | *I* ***expected to*** *find him at home, but he wasn't there.*

anticipate (AWL) (*formal*)
to expect that something will happen, and be prepared for it: *I* ***anticipated that*** *I would have to wait at the airport, so I brought a book to read.*

assume (AWL)
to think that something is true, although you do not have definite proof. You often use **assume** in situations when you think something is true and then find out that it is not true: *The light in her room was on, so I* ***assumed that*** *she was still awake.*

E

2 to say that something is necessary or important

expect
to feel that it is necessary or important for someone to do something: *The boss is **expecting** everyone **to** be on time for the meeting.* | *The school **expects** hard work **from** all its students.*

demand
to feel very strongly that it is necessary or important for someone to do something: *The military **demands** loyalty **from** the men and women who decide to become soldiers.*

insist
to say firmly that something must happen and refuse to change your decision: *He **insisted that** his children get jobs in high school to pay for the things they wanted to buy.*

require (AWL) (*formal*)
if a law or rule requires something, it is necessary for you to do it: *The law in California **requires that** all motorcycle riders wear helmets.*

→ see **hope¹**

E

expel /ɪk'spel/ *verb*

- ► expel
- ► deport
- ► evict
- ► exile
- ► drive out

expel
to officially make someone leave a school, organization, or country: *The principal is **expelling** three boys **for** destroying school property.* | *During the war, all foreigners were **expelled from** the country.*

deport
to make someone leave a country and return to the country that he or she comes from: *Every year the United States deports thousands of illegal immigrants.*

evict
to legally force someone to leave the house or apartment that he or she is living in: *The landlord plans to **evict** the family **from** their apartment because they are not paying the rent.*

exile
to force someone to leave his or her own country, especially for political reasons: *The new government exiled the leader of the opposition and put many other people in prison.*

drive out
to force someone to leave a place, country, or organization: *When the French occupied Mexico in the 1860s, the Mexicans began fighting hard to drive them out again.*

expense *noun* → see **cost¹**

expensive /ɪk'spensɪv/ *adjective*

- ► expensive
- ► overpriced
- ► pricey (*informal*)
- ► costly
- ► high-priced

ANTONYMS → see **cheap (1)**

expensive
costing a lot of money: *She spends most of her money on expensive clothes.* | *Apartments in the city are very expensive.*

overpriced
more expensive than something should be: *Fifty dollars for a T-shirt seems very overpriced.*

pricey (*informal*)
expensive compared to other things of the same kind so that you are not sure if you should pay that much money for it: *The restaurant is a little bit pricey, but the food is good.*

costly
very expensive and often wasting money. **Costly** is usually used about activities and projects that governments or companies do, and not about buying things: *The company is involved in a costly legal battle over who owns the land.*

high-priced
expensive and usually used or owned by rich people. You use **high-priced** about expensive things or about people who are paid a lot of money for a service: *A high-priced lawyer will be representing the movie star in court.*

ADVERBS
You can make the adjective **expensive** into an adverb by using an **-ly** ending: *She was expensively dressed in designer clothes.*

experience¹ /ɪk'spɪriəns/ *noun*

- ► experience
- ► ordeal
- ► adventure

experience
something that happens to you: *Visiting Paris was a wonderful experience.* | *My brother and I went to the same high school, but our experiences were very different.*

ordeal
a very bad or difficult experience: *The police*

questioned me for hours, and I was thankful when the ordeal was finally over.

adventure
a situation in which exciting and sometimes dangerous things happen to you: *My grandfather was telling us about his adventures as a sea captain in the 1950s.*
→ see **knowledge** for **experience** meaning "the knowledge or skill you get by doing something"

experience² /ɪkˈspɪriəns/ *verb*

- ► experience
- ► have
- ► go through
- ► suffer (*formal*)
- ► face
- ► undergo (*formal*)

experience
if you experience a feeling or problem, you feel it or it happens to you. **Experience** sounds fairly formal and is used especially in writing and formal speech: *If you experience chest pain, call the doctor right away.* | *The counseling center offers help for students who are experiencing problems.*

have
have means the same as **experience**, but **have** is more common and you use it in everyday conversation and writing: *We are having a lot of problems with our new computer system.* | *I hope you have a good vacation.*

go through
to have a very upsetting or difficult experience, especially one that lasts a long time: *Kevin is going through a painful divorce.*

suffer (*formal*)
to have an unpleasant or difficult experience, for example illness, injury, damage, or defeat: *The team suffered its worst defeat in ten years.* | *If you have suffered the loss* (=death) *of a family member, you know how painful it is.*

face
if you face a difficult situation, you know it will affect you, and you must deal with it: *Many small businesses are facing problems because of the recession.*

undergo AWL (*formal*)
to experience a difficult situation or a change, especially a situation or change that you do not control: *Ireland has undergone many changes in the past 20 years.* | *Doctors say that he will have to undergo surgery.*
→ see **feel**

experienced /ɪkˈspɪriənst/ *adjective*

- ► experienced
- ► seasoned
- ► veteran

experienced
having skills or knowledge because you have done something for a long time: *Mrs. Ramirez is one of the most experienced teachers at our school.* | *The lawyer is* ***experienced in*** *handling many different kinds of cases.*

seasoned
very experienced and able to deal with difficult situations and problems easily: *We need a seasoned manager to run this project.*
→ **GRAMMAR: Seasoned** is always used before a noun: *She is a seasoned player.*

veteran
very experienced and respected by other people. You usually use **veteran** to describe people who have had long and successful careers: *He is a veteran journalist who has been reporting the news for 30 years.*
→ **GRAMMAR: Veteran** is always used before a noun: *He is a veteran coach.*
→ see **skilled**

experiment /ɪkˈsperəmənt/ *noun*

- ► experiment
- ► test
- ► trial
- ► study

experiment
a scientific process to find out what the effects of doing something are: *The students carried out an experiment to see whether heating the liquid made the chemical reaction faster.*

test
a process that is used to find out whether something works correctly or is of good quality: *New models of cars are put through careful tests before they can be sold.*

trial
a test in which a small group of people use something new, to find out if it is safe or if it works well. You use **trial** about products such as medicines, new methods, or machines: *The trial showed that the drug worked well for breast cancer patients.*

study
scientific research, usually over a long period, that is done to find out more about a particular subject or problem. A **study** usually includes a written report: *The study showed that children*

E

who eat a good breakfast every morning do better at school.
→ see **research**[1], **test**[1], Topic **Science and Technology**

expert /ˈekspɚt/ *noun*

- expert
- specialist
- connoisseur
- authority

expert (AWL)
someone with special skills or knowledge of a subject: *If you need help with the plumbing, it's best to ask an expert.* | *The new art history professor is an* ***expert on*** *Chinese pottery.*

specialist
someone who has studied something for a long time and has special skills or knowledge of a subject. **Specialist** is used especially about medical or technical subjects: *They need a lawyer who is a* ***specialist in*** *immigration law.* | *He will see a heart specialist on Monday at the hospital.*

connoisseur
someone who knows a lot about something such as art or food. A **connoisseur** knows when something is of good quality: *Ken said the table is valuable and I believe him – he is a* ***connoisseur of*** *antiques.*

authority (AWL)
someone who is very respected because he or she knows more about a subject than most people: *Dr. Hyde is a leading* ***authority on*** *skin diseases.*

GRAMMAR CHECK: expert
You can put a noun before **expert**, **specialist**, and **connoisseur** to show what subject that person knows about: *Wildlife experts say it is unusual for bears to behave like this.* | *a cancer specialist* | *a wine connoisseur*

explain /ɪkˈspleɪn/ *verb*

- explain
- show
- demonstrate
- go through
- clarify
- define
- illustrate

explain
to give someone the information he or she needs to understand something: *She explained how to use the new software.* | *The doctor* ***explained*** *the treatment* ***to*** *the patient.*
→ **GRAMMAR:** Don't say: ~~*She explained me what had happened.*~~ Say: *She explained what had happened* or *She explained to me what had happened.*

show
to explain to someone how to do something, especially by doing something while he or she watches you: *Ellen* ***showed*** *me* ***how to*** *use the camera.*

demonstrate (AWL)
demonstrate means the same as **show** but sounds more formal. You use **demonstrate** especially when you are explaining something as a part of your job: *The violin teacher* ***demonstrated how to*** *move the bow across the strings.*

go through *also* **run through** (*informal*)
to explain something carefully in the order that it happens, one part at a time: *I'll go through the instructions one more time in case you did not understand.* | *Could you run through the order of the program again, please?*

clarify (AWL)
to make something easier to understand, by explaining in a different way or adding more details: *Reporters asked the president to clarify his earlier statement, so he explained again in more detail.*

define (AWL)
to explain the exact meaning of a word or idea: *Please define the expression "social network" using a dictionary.*

illustrate (AWL)
to explain or make something clear by giving examples: *Test scores are higher this year, and this illustrates the fact that our school is improving.*
→ see **show**[1]

explanation /ˌekspləˈneɪʃən/ *noun*

- explanation
- demonstration
- clarification
- definition

explanation
something you say or write to help someone understand something: *Mr. Jackson is a great teacher who always gives clear explanations.* | *I'll try to give you a quick* ***explanation of*** *how the machine works.*

demonstration (AWL)
an act of showing how to do something or how something works: *The art teacher gave us a* ***demonstration of*** *how to make a clay bowl.*

clarification (AWL)
something you say to explain something in a different way or with more details: *We have asked for clarification of the rules about fund-raising for political candidates.*

definition (AWL)
an explanation of the exact meaning of a word or idea: *The judge asked for a clearer legal definition of terrorism.*
→ see **advice**, **reason**

explode /ɪk'sploʊd/ *verb*

- ► **explode**
- ► **blow up** (*informal*)
- ► **go off** (*informal*)
- ► **detonate** (*formal*)
- ► **erupt**

explode
to burst into small pieces, making a loud noise and causing damage: *Two soldiers were injured when the bomb exploded.* | *The car crashed and its fuel tank exploded a few seconds later.*

blow up (*informal*)
if a vehicle or other object blows up, it explodes and is destroyed: *The plane blew up in midair.*
→ You also use **blow up** when someone destroys something using a bomb: *Police have arrested a man who was planning to blow up a bridge.*

go off (*informal*)
if a bomb goes off, it explodes. **Go off** is less formal than **explode**: *Luckily the train was empty when the bomb went off.*

detonate (*formal*)
to make a bomb explode by using special equipment: *Army experts detonated the bomb safely in a nearby field.*

erupt
if a volcano erupts, it sends out smoke, fire, and rock into the sky: *When the volcano erupted, thousands of people had to leave the town.*

SYNONYM CHECK
Explode or blow up?
You use **blow up**, not **explode**, when saying that someone destroys something using a bomb. Don't say: ~~*Terrorists exploded the bridge*~~. Say: *Terrorists blew up the bridge.*

exploit *verb* → see **take advantage of**, **use[1]**

explore *verb* → see **travel[1]**

explorer /ɪk'splɔrə/ *noun*

- ► **explorer**
- ► **pioneer**
- ► **discoverer**

explorer
someone who travels to unknown places to learn about them: *The Spanish explorer Hernán Cortés reached Mexico in the year 1519.*

pioneer
one of the first people to go to a new place and start living there: *The "Little House on the Prairie" books describe the lives of pioneers in the American West.*

discoverer
someone who finds a place that other people did not know about before: *A man named Juan Ponce de León was* ***the discoverer of*** *the land that is now Florida.*

explosion /ɪk'sploʊʒən/ *noun*

- ► **explosion**
- ► **blast**
- ► **eruption**

explosion
the loud noise and violent force that is produced when something explodes: *The explosion could be heard three miles away.* | *A bomb went off in the hotel, and 11 people were hurt* ***in the explosion****.*

blast
blast means the same as **explosion** but is used mainly in news reports: *Every window in the building had been shattered by the force of the blast.*

eruption
an occasion when a volcano erupts: *During the* ***eruption of*** *the volcano, ash and dust filled the air.*
→ see **increase[2]** for **explosion** meaning "a sudden very large increase"

export[1] *noun* → see **product**

export[2] *verb* → see **sell**

express /ɪk'spres/ *verb*

- ► **express**
- ► **show**
- ► **communicate**
- ► **convey** (*formal*)
- ► **put your feelings/ideas into words**

E

express
to tell or show what you are feeling or thinking by using words, looks, or actions: *Sometimes it is hard to express my emotions.* | *Parents have expressed concerns about their children's safety.*
→ You can use **express yourself** to talk about how good someone is at using words or actions to explain something: *Young children cannot express themselves in words, so they cry or use actions instead.*

show
to let other people see what you are feeling or thinking through your words, looks, or actions: *When the police told him his son had been hurt, he showed no emotion.*

communicate (AWL)
to make someone understand what you mean or how you feel using words or actions. You use **communicate** especially when you are talking about expressing a message to many people: *The president is trying to communicate a message of hope.*

convey (*formal*)
to express what you are feeling or thinking, sometimes without stating it directly: *Ramón tried to convey his sympathy by touching her hand.*

put your feelings/ideas into words
to express your feelings or ideas clearly in words, especially when this is difficult to do: *When I try to put my feelings into words, everything I say sounds wrong.*
→ see **say**

expression /ɪk'spreʃən/ *noun*

- expression
- look

expression
the way your face appears and shows your thoughts and feelings: *His expression became serious as he listened to the news.* | *"I'm not eating that," Maria said, with an* ***expression of*** *disgust on her face.*

look
an expression on someone's face: *There was a confused look on his face, so I explained the problem again.*
→ see **phrase** for **expression** meaning "a group of words that have a particular meaning"
→ see **emotion**

SYNONYM CHECK

Expression or look?

You can talk about someone's **expression**, but you cannot talk about someone's **look**: *Suddenly, her expression changed.*

You can say **the look on someone's face**: *I could tell by the look on his face that things were bad.*

You can have an **expression** or a **look** on your face even when you do not realize it: *She had a strange expression on her face as she watched Tomás leave.* | *He had a sad look on his face.*

However, if you **give someone a look**, you deliberately look at someone with an expression that shows how you feel about him or her: *When my cell phone rang in class, the teacher gave me an angry look.*

extent *noun* → see **size**

exterior[1] *noun* → see **outside**[2]

exterior[2] *adjective* → see **outside**[1]

external *adjective* → see **outside**[1]

extinct *adjective* → see **dead**[1], Topic **The Environment**

extra[1] /'ekstrə/ *adjective*

- extra
- additional
- added
- spare
- superfluous (*formal*)

extra
more than the usual amount or number: *Could you get an extra loaf of bread when you are at the store?* | *Bring some extra clothes in case you decide to stay overnight.*

additional
more than the amount or number that was agreed or expected: *There will be an additional charge for any extra suitcases.*

added
more than usual, especially so that something is better or more effective: *I always use sunscreen, and on very hot days I wear a hat for added protection.*

spare
a spare key, room, tire, or other object is an extra one that you have in case you need it: *There is a spare tire in the trunk of the car in case of an emergency.*

E

superfluous (*formal*)
more than is needed or wanted: ***Your job is to remove any superfluous information so that the report is three pages shorter.***
→ see Function Word **more**

extra² /ˈekstrə/ *noun*

- extra
- supplement
- bonus

extra
something that is added to a basic product or service, which improves it and often costs more. An **extra** is usually something that you want but do not need: ***At the hotel, we had to pay for extras like bottled water and Internet access.*** | ***We can't afford extras like dance lessons for our daughters.***

supplement (AWL)
something that is added to something else in order to improve it or make it complete: ***I added a vitamin supplement to the juice.***

bonus
something that is added to something else, which makes it more or better than you were expecting. You use **bonus** especially about money that someone receives as a reward for good work: ***Each employee received a $1,000 bonus from the company at the end of the year.*** | ***The house is nicer than our old one, and being so close to the park is a bonus.***
→ **GRAMMAR:** You can also use **bonus** in front of another noun to show that an amount was more than expected: ***The customer will receive bonus air miles for using the card to buy tickets.***
→ see **surplus** for words meaning "an amount that is more than you need"

extraordinary *adjective* → see **good**

extravagant /ɪkˈstrævəgənt/ *adjective*

- extravagant
- wasteful
- lavish

extravagant
spending too much money or using too many things, in a way that seems wasteful: ***You spent $600 on a dress? That's extravagant!*** | ***The company paid for extravagant dinners and parties.***

wasteful
using more of something than you need or using it badly so that it is wasted: ***The government is trying to stop wasteful spending.***

lavish
large, impressive, or costing a lot of money: ***It was a lavish wedding, with 200 guests, dinner, dancing, and champagne.***
→ see **expensive**

ADVERBS

You can make the adjectives that mean **extravagant** into adverbs by using an **-ly** ending: ***She was extravagantly dressed.*** | ***They spent lavishly on the wedding.***

extreme /ɪkˈstrim/ *adjective*

- extreme
- severe
- drastic
- radical
- fierce
- harsh

extreme
to a much greater degree than usual so that something is more serious, more deeply felt, etc.: ***The pain was extreme, even though the doctors tried to lessen it.*** | ***The government used extreme violence against the protesters.***

severe
extreme or very strong. You use **severe** about things that have a bad effect, for example punishment, damage, problems, bad weather, and illness: ***The roads are closed because of severe weather conditions.*** | ***There was severe criticism of the way the president handled the problem.***

drastic
extreme, sudden, and having a big effect: ***There will be drastic cuts in programs this spring, because the school no longer has any money.***

radical (AWL)
a radical change or difference makes a situation completely different from the way it was before: ***Over the past 50 years, there have been radical changes in family life, with many more children living with a single parent.***

fierce
extremely strong. You use **fierce** about actions or emotions: ***There is fierce competition between the two teams.*** | ***She watched with fierce pride as her son accepted the award.***

harsh
harsh punishment or criticism seems very severe and extreme: ***He stole some food because he was hungry, so I think putting him in jail seems like a harsh punishment.*** | ***Don't be too harsh on her – she is only a child.***
→ You can also use **harsh** to describe weather that is extreme, especially cold weather: ***Many birds died during the harsh winter.***

extremely /ɪk'strimli/ *adverb*

- ► extremely
- ► unbelievably
- ► incredibly
- ► absolutely
- ► remarkably
- ► exceptionally
- ► enormously
- ► hugely

extremely
to a very great degree. **Extremely** is like **very** but stronger: *Earthquakes are extremely difficult to predict.* | *The test is extremely important for students who want to go to college.*

unbelievably
in a way that is very surprising or hard to believe: *He is unbelievably quick on the basketball court.*

incredibly
incredibly means the same as **unbelievably**: *Their house is incredibly cold – I don't think they heat it at all.*

absolutely
as much as it is possible to imagine. You use **absolutely** to emphasize a word that already has a strong meaning: *She was standing in the middle of the stage, looking absolutely terrified.*

remarkably
in a way that is very impressive and surprising: *The drugs worked remarkably well, and Kim was healthy again in a few weeks.*

exceptionally
in a way that is very unusual or very different from others: *The music teacher said that Natalie is an exceptionally talented singer.*

enormously (AWL)
extremely. You use **enormously** to emphasize how popular, successful, or powerful someone or something is: *The television show is enormously popular all over the world.*

hugely
hugely means the same as **enormously** but sounds more informal: *She started her own business and has become hugely successful.*
→ see **very**

E

fabric *noun* → see **cloth**

face¹ *noun* → see **side**

face² *verb* → see **deal with**, **experience²**

fact *noun* → see **truth**

factor *noun* → see **cause¹**, **part**

factory /ˈfæktəri/ *noun*

- factory
- plant
- workshop

factory
a building where goods are produced in large quantities, using machines: *She works **in a factory** that makes cars.* | *We went on a tour of a chocolate factory.* | *The clothing is made **at a factory** in the Philippines.*

plant
a factory that makes large machines or equipment: *The car company is going to build a manufacturing plant in Brazil.*
→ A **plant** can also mean "a factory where something such as energy or chemicals are produced": *There are over 100 nuclear power plants in the United States.*

workshop
a room or building where tools and machines are used for making or repairing things: *The carpenter was cutting wood with a saw **in his workshop**.*

facts *noun* → see **information**

fade *verb* → see **quiet²**

fail /feɪl/ *verb*

1 to not succeed in doing something
- fail
- go wrong
- not work
- backfire
- be a failure

ANTONYMS → see **succeed**

2 to not pass a test
- fail
- flunk (*informal*)

ANTONYMS → see **pass¹ (3)**

3 to be an unsuccessful business
- fail
- go out of business
- close down
- go bankrupt

4 to not do something that you should do
- fail to
- neglect to (*formal*)

1 to not succeed in doing something

fail
to not succeed in doing something: *The climbers **failed to** reach the top of the mountain.* | *We tried to make her change her mind, but we failed.*

go wrong
to not happen in the way you want: *The experiment went wrong and there was a big explosion.*

not work
if a method does not work, it fails and does not have the effect you want: *Maria tried to glue the pieces of the vase together, but that didn't work.*

backfire
if a plan backfires, it has the opposite effect to the one you intended: *He pretended he was too sick to go to school, but his plan backfired when his mom called the doctor.*

be a failure
to fail badly and have a very disappointing result: *I burned the pizza and the meal was a complete failure.*

2 to not pass a test

fail
to not pass a test or class: *I studied hard because I didn't want to fail my English class.* | *She failed her driving test.*

flunk (*informal*)
to fail a test or class: *He flunked the test because he didn't study.*

3 to be an unsuccessful business

fail
if a business fails, it is unsuccessful and cannot continue, because it does not make enough money: *Her father's business failed and they had to move out of their home.* | *The bank failed and a lot of people lost all their money.*

go out of business
to stop operating because of financial problems:

A lot of small stores have gone out of business because their prices were higher than prices in the big supermarkets.

close down
to stop operating permanently: *The factory closed down and 300 people lost their jobs.*

go bankrupt
if a company goes bankrupt, it cannot pay its debts and has to stop operating: *The company went bankrupt with debts of over $15 million.*

4 to not do something that you should do

fail to
to not do something that you should do: *He **failed to** follow the basic safety instructions.* | *The company **failed to** inform customers that there was a problem with the product.*

neglect to (*formal*)
to not do something because you forget or you do not pay enough attention: *He overslept and **neglected to** shave before leaving for work.*

F

failure /ˈfeɪlyɚ/ *noun*

1 something or someone that is not successful
- ► failure
- ► lack of success
- ► disaster
- ► fiasco
- ► catastrophe
- ► disappointment

ANTONYMS → see **success**

2 an occasion when a machine or system stops working
- ► failure
- ► breakdown
- ► collapse

1 something or someone that is not successful

failure
something or someone that is not successful: *Nobody came to see the show – it was a complete failure.* | *If you can't find a job, you feel like a failure.*
→ You can also use **failure** to mean "a lack of success in doing something": *The attempt to climb the mountain ended in failure.*

lack of success
a situation in which someone or something does not succeed in doing something: *Fans are disappointed by the team's lack of success.*

disaster
something that is extremely unsuccessful and makes people feel very disappointed: *The party was a disaster. I wish I had stayed at home.*

fiasco
an event that is not successful at all, in a way that is very embarrassing or disappointing: *The voting machines didn't work, which was a complete fiasco.*

catastrophe
a very bad event that causes a lot of problems: *The failure of the banks was an economic catastrophe.*

disappointment
someone or something that is not as good as you hoped or expected: *The movie was a real disappointment. I thought it was going to be much more exciting.*

2 an occasion when a machine or system stops working

failure
an occasion when a machine or part of your body stops working: *The plane crash was caused by engine failure.* | *She died of heart failure.*

breakdown
if a car or piece of machinery has a breakdown, it stops working: *There was a big traffic jam, because someone had a breakdown on the freeway.*

collapse (AWL)
the sudden failure of a business or system: *The collapse of the business was blamed on bad management.*

faint /feɪnt/ *verb*

- ► faint
- ► pass out (*informal*)
- ► lose consciousness

faint
to suddenly become unconscious for a short time, for example because of heat or shock or because you are sick: *Several people at the outdoor concert **fainted from** the heat.* | *I nearly fainted when I saw all the blood.*

pass out (*informal*)
pass out means the same as **faint**: *When I broke my arm, I **passed out from** the pain and shock.*
→ **Pass out** can also be used when someone stops being conscious because of drinking too much alcohol: *The old man had drunk too much and passed out on a park bench.*

lose consciousness
lose consciousness means the same as **pass out** but sounds more formal. You use **lose consciousness** especially in medical or scientific writing: *She collapsed and lost consciousness because her blood pressure was so low.*
→ see **dizzy**, **quiet**[1], **subtle**, **unconscious**

fair[1] /fer/ *adjective*

- ► fair
- ► reasonable
- ► just
- ► equal
- ► impartial
- ► unbiased

ANTONYMS → see **unfair**

fair
treating people in the same way, or in a way that most people think is right: *It is not **fair to** him if he has to do all the work by himself.* | *You have the right to a fair trial.*

reasonable
fair and sensible according to what most people think: *I don't think it's reasonable to ask people to work 60 hours a week.*

just
morally right and fair: *What do you think would be a just punishment for his crime?*

equal
having the same rights and opportunities as everyone else: *Our education system should provide equal opportunities for all children.* | *Women still don't always get equal pay for the same work as men.*

impartial
not supporting a particular person or group, because you are not involved in something. You use **impartial** about people: *The referee is supposed to be impartial and not help either of the two teams.*

unbiased (AWL)
not influenced by your own personal opinions, or by a connection to a particular company, political party, etc. You usually use **unbiased** about information: *The website provides unbiased information about new electronic products.*
→ see **light**[2] for **fair** meaning "light in color"
→ see **right**[1]

ADVERBS

You can make the adjectives **fair**, **reasonable**, **just**, **equal**, and **impartial** into adverbs by using an **-ly** ending: *The observers make sure the election is conducted fairly.* | *Our goal was that women should be treated equally to men.* | *The judges must examine the case impartially.*

fair[2] /fer/ *noun*

- ► fair
- ► carnival

fair
an outdoor event where you can do fun things, for example ride on special machines or play games to win prizes. Sometimes farmers also show their animals at a **fair** or people show things they have made: *The Ferris wheel at the fair was really big.* | *His pig won first prize at the county fair.*

carnival
an outdoor event where you can do fun things, for example ride on special machines, see special shows, or play games to win prizes. **Carnivals** usually move from place to place: *Did you see the show with the strong man and the lady with the beard at the carnival?*

fairly /ˈferli/ *adverb*

1 in a fair and equal way
- ► fairly
- ► equally
- ► impartially (*formal*)

2 more than "a little," but not as much as "very"
- ► fairly
- ► pretty (*informal*)
- ► quite
- ► rather
- ► reasonably
- ► somewhat (*formal*)
- ► moderately (*formal*)

1 in a fair and equal way

fairly
in a way that treats people the same, or in a way that most people think is right: *It is important that teachers treat all students fairly and give everyone a chance to speak.*

equally
in an equal way so that everyone is treated the same or receives the same amount of something: *We agreed to divide the money equally between everyone.*

F

impartially (*formal*)
in a way that does not support a particular person or group: *The judge will look at the evidence and make his decision impartially.*

2 more than "a little," but not as much as "very"

fairly
if something is fairly heavy, fairly easy, etc., it is more than a little heavy or easy but is not very heavy or easy: *The house has a fairly large yard.* | *The book is fairly easy to read.*

pretty (*informal*)
pretty means the same as **fairly**: *Her Spanish is pretty good and she can understand most of what people are saying.*

quite
fairly and more than you expected: *I thought the movie was quite good.* | *It was quite a long walk back to the car.*
→ **GRAMMAR:** When you use **quite** with an adjective before a singular noun, you must say **quite a/an**: *She is **quite a** tall woman.* | *It is **quite an** old building.*

rather
fairly but less than you expected: *Her eyes were brown and rather small.*

reasonably
fairly. You use **reasonably** especially when someone or something is satisfactory but not perfect: *The food is reasonably good.* | *I practiced until I could hit the ball reasonably well.*

somewhat (AWL) (*formal*)
a little, but not very. You use **somewhat** especially when comparing people or things: *He is older than I am, so his situation is somewhat different from mine.* | *I was somewhat surprised that he would do that.*

moderately (*formal*)
in the middle between a little and very: *The series was only moderately successful when it was first shown.*
→ see **very**

fairness /ˈfernəs/ *noun*

- ► fairness
- ► equality
- ► justice
- ► impartiality (*formal*)

ANTONYMS → see **unfairness**

fairness
treatment of people in a way that is fair and right: *Everyone has the right to be treated with fairness and dignity.* | *Children have a sense of fairness, and they will be upset if they are not treated equally.*

equality
fairness because everyone is treated in the same way and has the same rights and opportunities: *Women had to fight for **equality with** men in the job market.*

justice
treatment of people in a way that is fair and right according to the law: *She wants justice for her son and she wants his killers to be punished.*

impartiality (*formal*)
fairness because you do not show support for any of the people or groups who are involved in a situation: *Good journalists try to report events with impartiality.*

faith *noun* → see **belief**, **religion**, **trust[2]**

faithful *adjective* → see **loyal**, **religious**

fake[1] /feɪk/ *noun*

- ► fake
- ► forgery

fake
a copy of something that is intended to make people think it is real: *The museum thought it was an ancient pot, but it turned out to be a fake.* | *If you see an expensive watch being sold cheaply, it may be a fake.*

forgery
a copy of a document, painting, or piece of paper money, which is intended to make people think it is real: *The painting was a very clever forgery that fooled art experts for years.*

fake[2] /feɪk/ *adjective*

- ► fake
- ► false
- ► phony (*informal*)
- ► imitation
- ► forged
- ► counterfeit

ANTONYMS → see **real**

fake
not real, but made to look like something real in order to trick people. **Fake** is usually used about documents, especially documents that say who you are. **Fake** is also used about things that are made to look real, such as fur, blood, hair, nails, jewels, or snow: *The men entered the country using fake passports.* | *The actors use fake blood to make it look like they are hurt.*

false
not real. **False** is used about names and addresses, or about teeth or eyelashes that you wear in place of the real things: *The thief gave a false name to the police.* | *My grandmother wears false teeth.*

phony (*informal*)
phony means the same as **fake**: *She used a phony credit card to pay the hotel.*
→ You can also use **phony** about people, to mean that they are acting in a way that is not real or not natural: *She wiped away some phony tears.*

imitation
made to look like a more expensive material or object: *The shoes are made of imitation leather.*

forged
a forged document is made to look like a real one in order to trick people: *He was carrying a forged passport.*

counterfeit
counterfeit money or goods are made to look exactly like real ones in order to trick people: *The police found thousands of dollars of counterfeit money in his apartment.*
→ see **artificial**

fake[3] *verb* → see **act**[1]

fall[1] /fɔl/ *verb*

1 to go down to the ground
- ► fall
- ► drop
- ► tumble
- ► collapse

2 to fall or almost fall when you are walking
- ► slip
- ► trip
- ► stumble
- ► lose your balance

3 to fall quickly from a high place
- ► plunge
- ► plummet

1 to go down to the ground

fall
to go down onto the ground or toward the ground: *She loves to climb trees, but I worry that she will fall.* | *He fell down the stairs and hurt his leg.* | *The picture fell off the wall and broke.*

drop
to fall suddenly onto the ground or into something: *The apples are beginning to* ***drop from*** *the trees.*

tumble
to fall with a rolling movement: *The little boy* ***tumbled down*** *the steps and started crying.* | *T-shirts and shorts* ***tumbled out*** *of the broken drawer.*

collapse (AWL)
to fall suddenly onto the ground. If a person **collapses**, it is often because he or she is sick: *One of the runners collapsed halfway through the race.* | *The bridge collapsed into the river.*

2 to fall or almost fall when you are walking

slip
to accidentally slide on a smooth surface and fall down or almost fall down: *He walked carefully to avoid* ***slipping on*** *the ice.*

trip
to hit your foot against something so that you fall or almost fall: *He tripped and fell.* | *Pick up that box – someone might* ***trip over*** *it.*

stumble
to almost fall down while you are walking, especially because your foot hits something: *We kept* ***stumbling over*** *rocks in the dark.*

lose your balance
to become unsteady so that you start to fall: *She lost her balance on the first step and fell down the stairs.*

3 to fall quickly from a high place

plunge
to fall very quickly a long way down from a high

fall

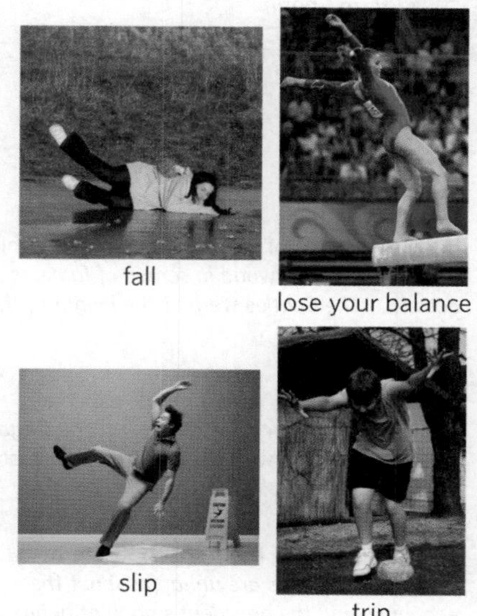
fall
lose your balance
slip
trip

F

place, especially into a liquid: *The car went off a cliff and **plunged into** the ocean.*

plummet
to fall very quickly a long way down from a high place: *The plane **plummeted toward** the Earth.*
→ see **drop¹** for words meaning "to let something fall"

fall² *noun* → see **decrease¹**, Topic **The Weather**

false /fɔls/ *adjective*

- ► false
- ► untrue

ANTONYMS → see true

false
not true or not correct: *On the test, you should mark each statement true or false.* | *He had given false information to the police, and was later arrested.*

untrue
not true: *The rumors that he had been fired were clearly untrue.*
→ You can also say that something is **not true**: *John did not take that money. That is just not true.*
→ see **fake²** for words meaning "not real," **wrong** for words meaning "not correct"

ADVERBS

You can make the adjective **false** into an adverb by using an **-ly** ending: *He was falsely accused of theft.*

fame /feɪm/ *noun*

- ► fame
- ► stardom
- ► popularity

fame
the state of being known about by a lot of people because of the things you have achieved: *She came to Hollywood in search of fame as an actress.* | *The Beatles were at the height of their fame in 1967.*

stardom
the state of being very famous, especially as an actor, musician, or sports player: *Lady Gaga achieved stardom with the release of her first album in 2008.*

popularity
the state of being liked or supported by a lot of people: *Americans are unhappy about the economy, and the president's popularity has gone down.*

F

familiar /fəˈmɪlyɚ/ *adjective*

- ► familiar
- ► recognizable

familiar
a familiar person, thing, feeling, etc. is one that you know, because you have seen or experienced it before: *The song was familiar, but I couldn't remember the name of it.* | *Children feel happier in familiar surroundings.*

recognizable
if someone or something is recognizable, it has qualities that help you know who or what it is because you have seen or experienced it before: *The actor's face is instantly recognizable.* | *In his uniform and with his new haircut, he was hardly recognizable as the boy I knew in high school.*
→ see **used to** for **familiar with** meaning "knowing something well"

ADVERBS

You can make the adjectives that mean **familiar** into adverbs by using an **-ly** ending. **Familiarly** is used when you do something in a way that shows you know a place, person, etc.: *They were chatting familiarly, so I guessed that they had met before.* | *The story is set in the future, but the problems are recognizably the same as the ones we face now.*

family /ˈfæməli/ *noun*

1 your parents, brothers, and sisters
- ► family
- ► folks (*informal*)
- ► next of kin
- ► immediate family (*formal*)
- ► nuclear family (*formal*)

2 your grandparents, aunts, uncles, and other family members
- ► relative
- ► relation
- ► extended family (*formal*)
- ► descendant
- ► ancestor

1 your parents, brothers, and sisters

family
a group of people who are related to each other, especially parents and their children: *He comes from a large family, and has seven brothers and sisters.* | *Children who eat dinner with their families tend to be happier and do better in school.*

folks (*informal*)
someone's parents: *I'm going to visit my folks on the weekend.*

next of kin
the closest living member of someone's family. If something bad happens to you, your **next of kin** is the first person who people tell: *The form asks for your next of kin, in case of an accident.*

immediate family (*formal*)
the people who are very closely related to you, such as your parents, children, brothers, or sisters: *Only members of the prisoner's immediate family are allowed to visit him.*

nuclear family (*formal*)
a type of family that consists of two parents and their children living together. **Nuclear family** is used when comparing this type of family with other types of families: *Many children do not live in a nuclear family, for example because their parents are divorced.*

2 your grandparents, aunts, uncles, and other family members

relative
a member of someone's family, such as a grandparent, aunt, uncle, or cousin: *She invited all her relatives to the wedding.*

relation
relation means the same as **relative** but sounds a little more formal: *Friends and relations attended the funeral.*

extended family (*formal*)
a family group that includes grandparents, aunts, and other family members, as well as parents and children: *Extended families rarely live together in this country, but they are still important.*

descendant
someone who belongs to the same family as a person who lived a long time ago: *The people on the island are the descendants of slaves who were brought over from Africa.*

ancestor
a member of someone's family who lived a long time ago: *Her ancestors originally came from Ireland.*

famous /ˈfeɪməs/ *adjective*

1 famous and admired
- ► **famous**
- ► **well-known**
- ► **legendary**
- ► **prominent** (*formal*)
- ► **eminent** (*formal*)
- ► **renowned** (*formal*)
- ► **celebrated**

2 famous for being bad
- ► **notorious**
- ► **infamous**

1 famous and admired

famous
known about and admired by a lot of people in many places: *Michael Jackson was a famous singer, with fans all over the world.* | *Hollywood is **famous for** the movie industry.*

well-known
known about by a lot of people: *He works for a well-known company in Seattle.* | *She is **well-known among** people who collect modern art.*

legendary
very famous and admired a lot for a long time. You use **legendary** especially about a performer, singer, or sports player: *Marlon Brando was a legendary Hollywood actor who appeared in many famous movies.*

prominent (*formal*)
well-known and important: *Her father is a church leader and a prominent member of the local community.*

eminent (*formal*)
famous, important, and respected for your knowledge. **Eminent** is used about scientists and people with a lot of knowledge about a subject: *She is an eminent biologist who has done a lot of important research.*

renowned (*formal*)
famous for a particular achievement or activity: *Stanford University is **renowned for** its academic research.*

celebrated
famous and often written about or talked about: *Frida Kahlo was one of Mexico's most celebrated artists.* | *Southern California is **celebrated for** its sunshine and its beautiful scenery.*

→ see **star** for words meaning "a famous person"
→ see **fame**

2 famous for being bad

notorious
well-known for being bad: *One of the country's most notorious criminals has escaped from prison.* | *The city is **notorious for** its smog.*

infamous
well-known for being extremely bad in a way that is very shocking: *September 11 is the day when the terrorists carried out their infamous attack on the World Trade Center.*

F

ADVERBS

You can make the adjectives **famous**, **notorious**, and **infamous** into adverbs by using an **-ly** ending. You use these adverbs about things, events, or the things that people do, not about the people themselves: *King famously remarked, "I have a dream!"* | *The violin is notoriously difficult to play well.*

fan /fæn/ noun

- ► fan
- ► lover
- ► admirer
- ► follower
- ► supporter
- ► enthusiast (*formal*)

fan
someone who likes a sport, team, or famous performer very much: *Are you a baseball fan?* | *Fans of Brad Pitt will love this movie.*

lover
someone who likes something very much, especially music, art, animals, or nature: *Every jazz lover dreams of visiting New Orleans.* | *Nature lovers will enjoy hiking through the forest of redwood trees.*

admirer
someone who thinks that a person or thing is very good, especially when this has a big influence on him or her: *She was a great* ***admirer of*** *Robert Frost's poems.*

follower
someone who believes in the ideas of a political or religious leader: *His followers believe that he is a messenger from God.*
→ **Follower** can also mean "someone who regularly pays attention to a blog or to Twitter messages."

supporter
someone who agrees with a person, group, or idea and wants to help it be successful: *The senator is one of the president's strongest supporters.* | ***Supporters of*** *women's rights are protesting against the court's decision.*

enthusiast (*formal*)
someone who likes doing something: *Golf enthusiasts will be able to see the tournament live on TV.*
→ see Topic **Sports and Exercise**

fancy *adjective* → see **decorative**

fantastic *adjective* → see **good**

fantasy *noun* → see **dream¹**, **illusion**, Topic **Books and Literature**

far *adverb* → see Function Words

fare *noun* → see **cost¹**, Topic **Travel and Vacations**

farm /fɑrm/ noun

- ► farm
- ► ranch
- ► orchard
- ► grove
- ► vineyard
- ► plantation

farm
a place where people grow crops or keep animals for food: *The farm grows hundreds of acres of wheat.* | *The whole family works* ***on the farm*** *in North Carolina.*

ranch
a large farm where people keep cows, horses, or sheep: *He owns a cattle ranch in Wyoming.*

orchard
an area of fruit trees, especially trees that produce fruit to sell: *They walked through the apple orchard.*

grove
an area of land with one type of tree growing on it, for example orange, lemon, or olive trees. The fruit from the trees is grown to be sold: *Orange County in California was once full of orange groves.*

vineyard
an area of land where people grow grapes for making wine: *The wine is from one of California's most famous vineyards.*

plantation
a large farm in a hot place, where people grow crops such as cotton, bananas, or coffee: *The slaves worked* ***on the cotton plantations.***

fascinate *verb* → see **interest¹**

fascinated *adjective* → see **interested**

fascinating *adjective* → see **interesting**

fashion /ˈfæʃən/ noun

1 something that is popular at a particular time
- ► fashion
- ► trend
- ► fad (*informal*)
- ► craze (*informal*)

2 clothes of a particular design
► fashions
► style

1 something that is popular at a particular time

fashion
a way of doing or making something that is popular at a particular time, especially a particular way of designing clothes or cutting your hair: *Pants with wide legs are back **in fashion**.* | ***It was the fashion** in the 1920s for women **to** cut their hair short.*

trend
a way of doing something that is becoming popular: *There is a general **trend toward** getting married at a later age.*

fad *(informal)*
something that is popular for a short time, especially something that you think is silly: *I have been reading about this **fad for** eating only raw food.*

craze *(informal)*
a thing or activity that is extremely popular for a short time: *The movie started a new dance craze.*

2 clothes of a particular design

fashions
clothes whose designs are popular at a particular time: *The store sells all the latest fashions for women.*
➔ **GRAMMAR: Fashions** is not used in the singular. Don't say: ~~*She's wearing a fashion*~~. You can use **fashion** to mean "the business of making and selling new styles of clothes": *I would love to have a career in fashion.*

style (AWL)
a particular design for a piece of clothing: *The newest styles for fall are being shown in New York and Paris.*

fashionable /ˈfæʃənəbəl/ *adjective*

► fashionable
► in fashion
► stylish
► trendy *(informal)*
ANTONYMS ➔ see **unfashionable**

fashionable
if something is fashionable, people think it looks good and it is popular at a particular time: *She likes wearing fashionable clothes.* | *Bright colors are very fashionable this year.*

in fashion *also* **in style**
if something is in fashion or in style, it is popular at a particular time. You use **in fashion** or **in style** especially about clothing or hair: *In the 1960s, long hair was in fashion for men.* | *Tight jackets are back in style.*

stylish (AWL)
attractive in a way that people admire, and popular now: *Monica was wearing a stylish blue dress.*

trendy *(informal)*
very popular and fashionable now. You use **trendy** about something that is not likely to remain popular for very long: *They went to a trendy new restaurant in Manhattan for dinner.*
➔ see **popular**

ADVERBS
You can make the adjectives **fashionable**, **stylish**, and **trendy** into adverbs by using an **-ly** ending: *She was very fashionably dressed.* | *His gray hair was stylishly cut.*

fast[1] /fæst/ *adjective*

1 moving with a lot of speed (adjectives)
► fast
► quick
► rapid
► swift *(formal)*
► brisk
► high-speed
ANTONYMS ➔ see **slow**

2 doing things in a very short time (adjectives)
► fast
► quick
► rapid
► swift *(formal)*
► speedy
ANTONYMS ➔ see **slow**

3 to move or do something faster (verbs)
► go faster
► speed up
► accelerate *(formal)*
► pick up speed
ANTONYMS ➔ see **slow down**

1 moving with a lot of speed (adjectives)

fast
moving with a lot of speed: *My dad likes driving fast cars.* | *José was the fastest runner in the race.*

quick
a quick movement is fast: *He took a quick step backward.*

F

rapid
rapid means the same as **quick** but sounds more formal: *During this period of sleep, people make rapid eye movements.*

swift (*formal*)
moving very fast: *The swift current makes the river dangerous for swimming.*

brisk
moving fast and with a lot of energy. You use **brisk** about walking, or about wind that moves quickly: *We went for a brisk walk in the fresh air.* | *The flag whipped back and forth in the brisk wind.*

high-speed
able to travel or do something very quickly. You use **high-speed** especially about trains and computer connections: *The trip only takes two hours on a high-speed train.* | *The company offers high-speed Internet access.*

2 doing things in a very short time (adjectives)

fast
doing something in a very short time: *She is a very fast reader – she finished that book in just two days.* | *The fast growth of the population has caused economic problems.*

quick
doing something in a short time: *I'll just have a quick shower before we go out.* | *You've finished already? That was quick!*

rapid
happening quickly or doing something very quickly. You use **rapid** especially about changes, increases, and improvements: *There has been a rapid increase in the number of people who have the disease.*

swift (*formal*)
doing something very quickly: *She gave him a swift hug goodbye.* | *My letter got a swift response.*

speedy
happening quickly in the way that you want: *She sent him a letter wishing him a speedy recovery from his illness.*

3 to move or do something faster (verbs)

go faster
to move or do something more quickly: *Can you go any faster? I don't want to be late!* | *It is not possible to go faster than the speed of light.*

speed up
to move faster: *The truck speeded up as it got on the freeway.*

accelerate (*formal*)
if a vehicle or its driver accelerates, the vehicle moves faster: *The car can accelerate from 0 to 60 miles per hour in less than 10 seconds.*

pick up speed *also* **gather speed**
to start to gradually move faster. You use **pick up speed** especially about cars or other vehicles. **Gather speed** is more formal than **pick up speed**: *The bike began to pick up speed as it rolled down the hill.* | *The train gathered speed as it left the station.*

fast² /fæst/ *adverb*

- ► **fast**
- ► **quickly**
- ► **rapidly**
- ► **swiftly** (*formal*)
- ► **briskly**
- ► **at high speed**

ANTONYMS → see **slowly**

fast
if you move or do something fast, you move or do it with a lot of speed: *You're driving too fast – slow down!* | *She can run much faster than I can.*

quickly
with a lot of speed, but slightly slower than **fast**: *He ate his lunch quickly.* | *Joanna walked quickly through the hall to her classroom.*

rapidly *also* **at a rapid rate**
moving, happening, or done very fast. You use **rapidly** especially about changes, increases, and improvements: *The population is growing rapidly.* | *Her heart was beating rapidly and she was short of breath.*

swiftly (*formal*)
moving or doing something very fast: *The river was flowing swiftly after the heavy rain.* | *The president swiftly took action.*

briskly
quickly and with a lot of energy. You use **briskly** especially to say how someone walks: *He walked briskly back along the path.*

at high speed
if something moves at high speed, it moves very fast. You use **at high speed** about vehicles: *The car was traveling at high speed.*
→ see **go faster**, **quickly**

fasten /ˈfæsən/ *verb*

- ► **fasten**
- ► **button**
- ► **zip**
- ► **tie**

ANTONYMS → see **undo (1)**

fasten
to join together the two sides of a coat, bag, belt, etc. so that it is closed: *She fastened her coat and went outside.* | *The pilot told us to fasten our seat belts.*

button *also* **button up**
to fasten buttons on clothes: *Button up your jacket – it's cold outside.*

zip *also* **zip up**
to close or fasten something with a zipper (=a thing that consists of two lines of small pieces of metal that slide together): *He got into his sleeping bag and zipped it up.*

tie
to fasten something by making a knot: *Tie your shoelaces before you trip on them!*
→ see **close[1]**, **join**

fat /fæt/ *adjective*

- ► fat
- ► overweight
- ► obese
- ► chubby
- ► plump
- ► flabby

ANTONYMS → see **thin**

fat
having too much flesh on your body: *The driver was a short fat man with glasses.* | *You'll get fat if you eat too many cookies.*
→ It is rude to say that someone is **fat**.

overweight
weighing more than you should: *I'm about five pounds overweight.*

obese
extremely fat in a way that is very unhealthy: *People who are obese often suffer from heart problems.*

chubby
a little fat in an attractive way. You use **chubby** especially about babies and children: *She was holding a chubby little baby boy.*

plump
large and round in an attractive way. **Plump** is used about a woman or child, especially in stories: *Her mother was a plump cheerful woman.*

flabby
if part of your body is flabby, it is too fat and has soft loose skin that looks unattractive: *Sit-ups will help get rid of that flabby stomach.*
→ see Topic **Describing People's Looks**

fatal *adjective* → see **deadly**, **incurable**

fate *noun* → see **future**, **luck**

father /ˈfɑðɚ/ *noun*

- ► father
- ► dad (*informal*)
- ► daddy
- ► father-in-law

ANTONYMS → see **mother**

father
a male parent: *His father is teaching him to drive.*

dad (*informal*)
father. You use **dad** in spoken English, when talking to your father or about someone's father: *Can I borrow your car, Dad?* | *My mom and dad are both retired.*

daddy
father. **Daddy** is used especially by young children, or when talking to young children: *Daddy, can we go to the park?* | *Where's your daddy?*

father-in-law
the father of someone's husband or wife: *Her father-in-law was in the army.*

fault /fɔlt/ *noun*

- ► fault
- ► responsibility
- ► blame

fault
if something bad is your fault, you caused it to happen: *She played well. It is not her fault we lost.* | *Johnny worried that his parents' divorce was his fault.*

responsibility
if something is your responsibility, you caused it to happen, or you should not have allowed it to happen. You often use **responsibility** when a person or organization caused an accident or let it happen: *The company that owns the mine admitted responsibility for the accident.*

blame
if you get the blame, people say that you caused something bad to happen and you should be punished for it: *The other kids ran away, and I got all the blame.*

SYNONYM CHECK

Fault, responsibility, or blame?

These words have similar meanings, but there are differences in the way they are used.

You usually say that something is **my/your/her fault**. You can also say that someone is **at fault** for doing something bad: *It was the other driver who was at fault.*

You usually say that someone **takes/accepts/admits responsibility** for something: *The other driver accepted responsibility for the accident.*

You say that someone **takes/accepts the blame** for something when that person admits that he or she has done something wrong: *The coach accepted the blame for the team's losing streak.*

If someone **puts/pins the blame on** someone else, that person says someone else did something wrong, even if he or she did not really do it: *My brother always tries to pin the blame on me, even if it isn't my fault.*

F

faulty *adjective* → see **broken**, **imperfect**

favorite[1] /ˈfeɪvərɪt/ *adjective*

- ► favorite
- ► best-loved
- ► preferred
- ► favored

favorite
your favorite person or thing is the one you like most: *Who is your favorite singer?* | *My favorite color is blue.*
→ **GRAMMAR:** Don't say: ~~*That's my most favorite song*~~. Say: *That's my favorite song.*

best-loved
liked most by many people. You use **best-loved** especially about books, songs, and paintings, and about writers, singers, and artists: *The band played some of their best-loved songs.*

preferred
the preferred method, plan, or choice is the one that people think is the best and would like to choose: *It will help the environment if bicycling becomes the preferred way to go to work or school.*

favored
liked more than others: *The guitar became the favored instrument for many rock musicians.*
→ **Favored** is also used about a person who gets special treatment because people like him or her more: *Her brother was the favored child and he got more attention from their parents.*
→ see **prefer**

GRAMMAR CHECK: favorite

Favorite, **best-loved**, **preferred**, and **favored** are always used before a noun. Don't say: ~~*This book is favorite*~~. Say: *This is my favorite book.* | *He is one of Hollywood's best-loved actors.*

favorite[2] /ˈfeɪvərɪt/ *noun*

- ► favorite
- ► preference

favorite
something that someone likes more than any others: *Chocolate cake is my favorite!* | *The sweaters all look good to me – which one is your favorite?*
→ You usually use **favorite** after "my," "your," "his," etc.

preference
if you have a preference for something, you like it better than another thing so that you are more likely to choose it: *Most customers have a strong* ***preference for*** *the smaller computer.* | *There are several colors available, and you can state your preference.*
→ see **prefer**

fear[1] /fɪr/ *noun*

- ► fear
- ► terror
- ► horror
- ► panic
- ► fright
- ► dread
- ► alarm
- ► phobia

fear
the feeling you have when you are afraid: *My* ***fear of*** *the dentist started when I was a child.* | *She was trembling* ***with fear*** *because of the sound of the thunder.*

terror
a very strong feeling of fear that you get when you think something very bad is going to happen to you soon: *The passengers screamed* ***in terror*** *as the bus drove off the road.*

horror
a very strong feeling of shock and fear when you see something very bad happen: *People watched* ***in horror*** *as he jumped from the roof of the building.*

panic
a sudden strong feeling of fear and worry that makes you do things without thinking carefully:

The fire caused a panic in the theater and everyone ran for the exit.

fright
a sudden strong feeling of fear: *The loud noise made her scream **with fright**.*

dread
a strong feeling of worry, fear, and unhappiness because of something bad that is going to happen or that might happen: *The thought of seeing her ex-husband again filled her with dread.*

alarm
a strong feeling of fear and worry because something bad or dangerous might happen soon: *She heard a loud noise outside and rushed to the window **in alarm** to see what was happening.*

phobia
a strong fear of something that you have even though it is not sensible to be afraid of that thing: *He has a **phobia about** riding in elevators so he always takes the stairs.*

→ see **nervousness**

fear² /fɪr/ *verb*

1 to feel afraid of someone or something
- ► **fear** (*formal*)
- ► **be afraid of**
- ► **be scared of**

2 to worry about something in the future
- ► **fear** (*formal*)
- ► **be afraid**
- ► **be scared**
- ► **dread**

1 to feel afraid of someone or something

fear (*formal*)
to feel frightened of someone or something that might hurt you or be dangerous: *I think children should respect their parents, not fear them.* | *They learned to fear the river after hearing stories of men drowning in it.*

be afraid of *also* **be frightened of**
to fear someone or something. **Be afraid of** and **be frightened of** are not as formal as **fear**: *I've always **been afraid of** flying and I hate getting on planes.*

be scared of
be scared of means the same as **be afraid of** but is a little more informal: *A dog bit Lisa last year, so now she is scared of dogs.*

→ see **scared**

2 to worry about something in the future

fear (*formal*)
to feel nervous or worried that something bad could happen: *The farmers **fear that** it may not rain for several months.*

be afraid
to worry that something bad could happen. **Be afraid** is less formal than **fear**: *I didn't want to ask you because I **was afraid that** you would say no.*

be scared
be scared means the same as **be afraid** but is a little more informal: *I **am scared that** the other kids will laugh at me when I give my speech.*

dread
to feel very worried about something that is going to happen, and not want it to happen: *He dreaded having to tell his parents that he had failed.*

fearful *adjective* → see **scared**

fearless *adjective* → see **brave**

feature *noun* → see **quality**, Topic **Describing People's Looks**

fee *noun* → see **cost¹**

feel /fil/ *verb*

- ► **feel**
- ► **be**
- ► **experience** (*formal*)
- ► **sense**

feel
to have a physical feeling such as hunger or pain, or an emotion such as sadness or happiness: *She put on a sweater, but she still felt cold.* | *I felt really embarrassed for forgetting her name.* | *Stop if you feel any pain.*

be
used to say what physical feeling or emotion someone has: *Tom was so sleepy he nearly fell asleep at dinner.* | *She just wanted to be happy.*

experience (*formal*)
experience means the same as **feel**, but you use it mostly about strong emotions or unusual physical feelings: *He experienced a great sadness when his father died.* | *Patients with the disease experience feelings of dizziness.*

sense
to feel or know that something is true without being told or having proof: *The fox sensed danger and ran into the woods.* | *I sensed that he wanted to be left alone.*

→ see **experience²**, **seem**, **think**, **touch**

GRAMMAR CHECK: feel

Feel can be followed by an adjective or a noun: *He felt sad.* | *She felt pain.*

Be can only be followed by an adjective: *He was sad.*

Experience and **sense** can only be followed by nouns: *You may experience some pain.* | *I sensed his presence before I saw him.*

feeling /ˈfiːlɪŋ/ *noun*

1 a feeling in your body
- ► feeling
- ► sensation

2 something such as love, hate, fear, happiness, etc.
- ► feeling
- ► emotion
- ► a sense of
- ► sentiment (*formal*)
- ► expression

3 a belief or opinion
- ► feeling
- ► impression
- ► hunch
- ► intuition
- ► instinct

1 a feeling in your body

feeling
something you feel in your body, such as pain or cold: *A sudden **feeling of** warmth came over my whole body.* | *He had a tight **feeling in** his chest and thought he was having a heart attack.*

sensation
a feeling that you get in your body, especially one that is hard to describe: *She had the tickling sensation that you get in your nose before you sneeze.*

2 something such as love, hate, fear, happiness, etc.

feeling
something you feel such as love, hate, or sadness: *It was a wonderful feeling to be home again.* | *For a few minutes she experienced **feelings of** real fear when she realized she was lost.*

emotion
emotion means the same as **feeling** but sounds more formal: *When I saw my father again after five years, I was filled with emotion.* | *He did not want to show his emotions because he was afraid people would laugh at him.*

a sense of
if you feel a sense of fear, joy, loss, etc., you feel that emotion. **A sense of** sounds slightly more formal than **a feeling of**: *He felt **a sense of** relief after he finished his last exam.*

sentiment (*formal*)
a feeling or opinion that you have about something: *One man said he was angry, and other people expressed similar sentiments.*
→ You can also use **sentiment** to mean "feelings of love, pity, sadness, etc. that people think are too strong or not appropriate for a situation": *There is no room for sentiment in business – if I need to fire someone, I'll do it even if I feel sorry for him.*

expression
a way of doing something that shows what you feel: *Crying is a healthy **expression of** grief.*

3 a belief or opinion

feeling
if you have or get the feeling that something is true, you think that something is probably true: *Leslie suddenly got the **feeling that** someone was watching her.*

impression
the opinion or feeling you have about someone or something because of what you see or hear: *I got the impression she wasn't very happy with her job because she kept criticizing the boss.*

hunch
a feeling that something is true or will happen, which is not based on any facts: *I have a **hunch that** Jodie may be planning a surprise party for her sister's birthday.*

intuition
an idea about what is true in a particular situation based on a feeling rather than facts. **Intuition** is more formal than **hunch**: *I had an **intuition that** something was not right, without knowing exactly why.*
→ **Intuition** can also mean "the ability to understand or know something because of a feeling rather than by considering the facts": *My intuition usually tells me when people are trying to trick me.*

instinct
a natural ability to know what you should do without having to learn it or be told it: *A cat's natural instinct is to chase birds.*

feelings *noun* → see **opinion**

female[1] /ˈfimeɪl/ *adjective*

- ► female
- ► feminine
- ► girlish
- ► ladylike

ANTONYMS → see **male[1]**

female
relating to being a woman or girl: *The president has a strong lead among female voters.*

feminine
having qualities that people think are typical of women: *The dress was light pink and looked soft and feminine.*

girlish
like a little girl: *I was surprised by the old woman's high girlish voice.*

ladylike
behaving in a polite and quiet way that some people think is how a woman should behave: *Grandma thinks that climbing trees isn't ladylike.*
→ see **woman**

ADVERBS

You can make the adjective **girlish** into an adverb by using an **-ly** ending: *She laughed girlishly.*

female[2] *noun* → see **woman**

feminine *adjective* → see **female[1]**

fence *noun* → see **wall**

few *adjective* → see Function Words

fiancé *noun* → see **husband**, Topic **Relationships and Marriage**

fiancée *noun* → see **wife**, Topic **Relationships and Marriage**

fiction *noun* → see **story**, Topic **Books and Literature**

field *noun* → see **land**, **park**, **subject**

fierce *adjective* → see **extreme**, **violent**

fight[1] /faɪt/ *verb*

- ► fight
- ► wrestle
- ► box
- ► struggle
- ► battle (*formal*)
- ► clash (*formal*)

fight
to use physical force or weapons to try to hurt someone: *The two boys were fighting and had to be pulled apart.* | *The soldiers **fought for** control of the city.*

wrestle
to fight by holding someone and trying to push him or her to the ground: *A security guard managed to wrestle the thief to the ground.*

box
to fight someone while wearing big leather gloves, as a sport: *He began to box as a boy and later competed in the Olympics.*

struggle
to fight someone who is holding you in order to get away: *"Let me go!" I shouted and began to struggle.*

battle (*formal*)
to keep fighting hard until one person or group wins: *Protesters battled police through the night.*

clash (*formal*)
if two armies or groups of people clash, they have a short fight: *Troops clashed near the border, and one soldier was injured.*
→ see **try[1]** and **campaign[2]** for **fight** meaning "to try hard to do something," **argue** for **fight** meaning "to argue with someone"

F

fight[2] /faɪt/ *noun*

- ► fight
- ► battle
- ► fighting
- ► combat
- ► brawl
- ► scuffle
- ► riot
- ► struggle
- ► clash (*formal*)
- ► duel

fight
a situation in which two people or groups attack each other and try to hurt each other: *She started a **fight with** another girl by pulling her hair.* | *Three young men were injured in the **fight between** the two gangs.*

battle
a fight between two armies or groups of people, especially during a war: *The first large battle of the Civil War was fought in Virginia.*

fighting
the things that happen when people or groups fight each other: *The **fighting between** the army and the rebels is continuing around the city.*

combat
fighting during a war: *Seven marines were wounded in combat on Sunday.*

brawl
a noisy fight among a group of people, especially in a public place: *Police had to come to the bar to stop the brawl.*

scuffle
a short fight that is not very serious: *He got a bloody nose in the scuffle.*

riot
violent behavior by a crowd of people, especially people who are protesting against something: *Many store windows were broken during the riots.*

struggle
a fight between two people to take hold of something, or an attempt by one person to get away from the other: *One of the men was hurt during the* ***struggle for*** *the gun.*

clash *(formal)*
a short fight between two armies or groups of people. **Clash** is usually used in news reports: *There have been violent* ***clashes between*** *the police and the gangs.*

duel
a fight with weapons between two people. In the past, **duels** were used to bring an end to an argument: *He was killed in a duel.*
→ see **argument** for **fight** meaning "an argument with someone," **campaign**[1] for **fight** meaning "an attempt to achieve something"

fight back /ˌfaɪt ˈbæk/ *phrasal verb*

- ► fight back
- ► retaliate
- ► strike back
- ► counterattack

fight back
to fight with someone who attacks you, instead of doing nothing: *She hit me, so I had to fight back.* | *The prisoner had his hands tied and could not even fight back.*

retaliate
to attack someone because he or she has attacked you first: *Government forces* ***retaliated against*** *the rebels by bombing their camp.*

strike back
to quickly attack a country or army that has attacked you first, especially to show that you are strong: *After the riots, the government* ***struck back at*** *the protesters.*

counterattack
to attack another army that has attacked you, especially in a planned and organized way: *Army forces counterattacked to take back the region.*

SYNONYM CHECK
Fight back, retaliate, and strike back

Fight back, **retaliate**, and **strike back** can also be used to talk about a situation when there is no physical fighting, but people do or say something when someone else has done something bad to them first: *She fought back by calling him a liar.* | *The U.S. put a tax on the goods, and China retaliated by raising prices.* | *The president struck back at his critics, saying that their argument was silly.*

Counterattack cannot be used in this way.

fighting *noun* → see **fight**[2], **war**

figure *noun* → see **body**, **person**, **shape**

figure out *phrasal verb* → see **count**, **solve**

file *noun* → see **document**, Topic **Computers and the Internet**

fill /fɪl/ *verb*

- ► fill
- ► refill
- ► load
- ► stuff
- ► cram
- ► jam

ANTONYMS → see **empty**[2]

fill *also* **fill up**
to put something in a container or space so that it becomes full: *We* ***filled*** *the baskets* ***with*** *cookies, nuts, and candy.* | *It is going to be a long trip, so fill up the gas tank.*

refill
to fill something again: *I want to refill my water bottle before we leave.*

load *also* **load up**
to put a lot of something inside a vehicle or container, especially so that you can do something with it or take it somewhere: *Help me load the dishwasher.* | *The car was* ***loaded up with*** *our camping equipment.*

stuff
to completely fill something, especially with something soft: ***Stuff** the peppers **with** the rice mixture and bake for 20 minutes.*
→ **Stuff** can also mean "to quickly push a lot of things into a small space": *He **stuffed** his gym clothes **in** a bag and ran out the door.*

cram
if a lot of people or things cram a place, they completely fill it so that there is no room left: *Shoppers crammed the store for the pre-Christmas sale.* | *The tiny room was **crammed with** furniture.*
→ **Cram** can also mean "to force a lot of things or people into a small space": *She **crammed** the boxes **in** the closet and closed the door.*

jam
if a lot of people or things jam a place, they completely fill it and it is difficult for them to move: *Thousands of runners jammed the streets on the day of the race.*
→ **Jam** can also mean "to push things or people into a small space using a lot of force so that they cannot move": *She **jammed** the suitcases **into** the trunk of the car.*
→ see **full**
→ see **blow up** for words meaning "to fill something with gas or air"
→ see **fill in** at **write**
→ see **fill out** at **write**

fill

He **filled** a glass with water.

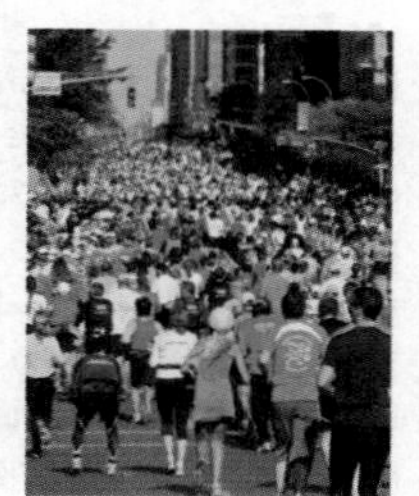
Thousands of runners **jammed** the streets.

She **was loading** the dishwasher.

Stuff the peppers with the rice mixture.

filled *adjective* → see **full**

film *noun* → see **layer**, **movie**

filthy *adjective* → see **dirty**

final[1] *adjective* → see **last[1]**

final[2] *noun* → see **game**, Topic **Sports and Exercise**

finally /ˈfaɪnl-i/ *adverb*

1 after a long time
- ► finally
- ► eventually
- ► in the end
- ► at last

2 at the end of a series of things
- ► finally
- ► lastly
- ► last but not least

ANTONYMS → see **first** (**2**)

1 after a long time

finally (AWL)
after a long time, especially when this is longer than you wanted or expected: *Robert has liked Megan for years, and he finally told her.* | *I can't believe the school year is finally over.*

eventually (AWL)
after a very long time or after a lot of things have happened: *Jana eventually realized that he had been lying to her the whole time.*

in the end
after thinking about something for a long time, or after a lot of other things have happened: *I really liked the car, but in the end I decided to buy a cheaper one.*

at last
after a long time. Use **at last** when something good happens after you have waited for it for a long time: *I'm glad that Dave found a job at last.*

2 at the end of a series of things

finally (AWL)
used before you say the last of a series of things: *Finally, I would like to thank everyone who helped make the conference a success.*

lastly
used when telling someone the last thing you want to say: *Firstly it's too big, secondly we can't afford it, and lastly we don't really need it.*

last but not least
used to say that the last person or thing in a list is as important as the others: *Last but not least, let me introduce Jane, our new team captain.*

F

find /faɪnd/ *verb*

- ► find
- ► discover
- ► detect (*formal*)
- ► locate
- ► trace
- ► track down

ANTONYMS → see **lose (1)**

find
to see or get something after looking for it, or by chance: *If you find a $10 bill on the sidewalk, can you keep it? | We found Donny hiding in the closet.*

discover
to find something hidden or something that was not known about before: *Marshall discovered gold in California in 1848.*

detect (AWL) (*formal*)
to find or notice something that is not easy to notice: *The disease can be cured if it is detected early.*

locate (AWL)
to find the place where someone or something is. **Locate** is more formal than **find**: *It took the airline several days to locate my luggage.*

trace (AWL)
to find someone or something that has disappeared by carefully looking for information about that person or thing: *The police are trying to trace the red van that was used in the robbery.*

track down
to find someone or something by looking carefully for that person or thing, or by asking questions. **Track down** is slightly informal: *I managed to track down my best friend from elementary school by searching on the Internet.*

find out /ˌfaɪnd ˈaʊt/ *phrasal verb*

- ► find out
- ► find
- ► discover
- ► see
- ► hear
- ► learn (*formal*)
- ► look into
- ► investigate

find out
to get information that you did not know before: *I don't know if she has children, but I can find out. | When we found out the price, we were shocked at how expensive it was! | The police are trying to find out what happened after Robinson left the house.*

find
to get new information as a result of tests or experience. **Find** is more formal than **find out**: *Researchers have* ***found that*** *the drug is more effective for women than for men.*

discover
to find out a fact, especially something that is surprising or difficult to find out. **Discover** is more formal than **find out**: *I was surprised to* ***discover that*** *Mrs. Tucker speaks perfect Spanish. | The scientists want to* ***discover whether*** *the gene makes someone more likely to get Alzheimer's disease.*

see
to find out information, especially because you see or read it: ***I saw*** *in the paper* ***that*** *Debbie Jones got married last week.*
→ **See** can also mean "to get information by going somewhere to look, or by doing something and noticing what happens": *Can you go and see who is at the door?*

hear
to find out information because someone tells you or you hear it on television or the radio: *I hear you're moving to Denver.*

learn (*formal*)
to find out information by hearing it from someone else or reading it: *Employees* ***learned*** *only yesterday* ***that*** *the company will be closing at the end of the month.*

look into
to try to find out more about a problem or crime: *Lawson said he had looked into the matter and no laws had been broken.*

investigate (AWL)
to try to find out the reasons why something happened, especially a crime. **Investigate** is more formal than **find out** or **look into**: *The police are investigating the explosion, but they do not yet know what caused it.*

fine *adjective* → see **good**, **narrow**, **sunny**, **thin**, Topic **The Weather**

finest *adjective* → see **best**

finish /ˈfɪnɪʃ/ *verb*

1 to do the last parts of something and then stop doing it

- ► finish
- ► complete
- ► conclude (*formal*)
- ► finalize
- ► bring to an end

ANTONYMS → see **start[1] (1)**

2 to stop happening
- ► finish
- ► end
- ► stop
- ► be over
- ► conclude
- ► expire (*formal*)
- ► run out (*informal*)

ANTONYMS → see **begin**

1 to do the last parts of something and then stop doing it

finish
to do or make the last part of something so that you have nothing more to do or make: *Have you finished cleaning your room? | We didn't finish dinner until 9:00.*

complete
to finish doing or making something that has taken a long time to finish: *They plan to complete the bridge in two years.*

conclude AWL (*formal*)
to officially finish something, such as a meeting, event, or process: *Police have concluded their investigations and written a report.*

finalize AWL
to finish the last details of a plan, business deal, etc.: *The agreement between the two countries was finalized last week.*

bring to an end *also* **bring to a close**
to be an event or action that finishes a long process: *The arrest brings to an end a year-long search for the killer.*

2 to stop happening

finish
to come to an end. **Finish** is often used when saying what time something ends, especially an organized event such as a meeting, class, or party: *What time does your class finish? | The meeting will **finish at** 5:30.*

end
to come to the end of something and not happen anymore: *The American Civil War started in 1861 and ended in 1865. | The party ended about midnight. | The game **ended with** Johnson scoring a touchdown at the last minute.*

stop
to finish. You use **stop** about things that may start happening again: *We waited for the rain to stop.*

be over
if an event, activity, or period of time is over, it has ended: *The long summer vacation was almost over.*

conclude AWL
to end. You use **conclude** when something happens at the end of an event, activity, etc.: *The Independence Day celebration **concluded with** fireworks.*
→ **GRAMMAR:** Use **conclude** followed by a preposition such as "with," "by," or "on." Don't say: ~~*The concert concluded*~~. Say: *The concert **concluded with** the music from "Star Wars." | The concert will **conclude at** about 9:30 p.m.*

expire (*formal*)
if an official document expires, the period of time during which you can use it has ended: *My driver's license **expires in** May, so I need to send in the form and get a new one.*

run out (*informal*)
if a legal agreement or document runs out, it ends or stops being effective: *My contract runs out in May, so I'm looking for another job.*
→ see **end**[2], **stop**[1]

finished *adjective* → see **done**

fire[1] /faɪɚ/ *noun*

1 a fire that is not controlled
- ► fire
- ► blaze
- ► flame
- ► spark

2 a controlled fire that is used for heat, cooking, or burning things
- ► fire
- ► campfire
- ► bonfire

1 a fire that is not controlled

fire
flames and heat that burn things: *The building was completely destroyed by fire. | Neighbors brought buckets of water to put out the fire.*

blaze
a big fire that spreads and is difficult to control: *Firefighters struggled to control the blaze.*

flame
the bright burning gas that you see coming from a fire: *Flames were coming out of the upstairs windows. | The candle flames flickered with an orange light.*

spark
a very small bright piece of burning material that comes from a fire: *The fire crackled and shot sparks into the air.*

F

2 a controlled fire that is used for heat, cooking, or burning things

fire
a pile of burning wood or coal that you use for heat or cooking: *The fire in the fireplace made the living room cozy.* | *Can you help me light the fire?*

campfire
a fire made outdoors by people who are camping: *They sat around the campfire, singing songs.*

bonfire
a large outdoor fire for burning things you do not need or for celebrating something: *We piled up all the leaves and branches to make a bonfire.*
→ see **put out** for words meaning "to make a fire stop burning"
→ see **burn**

fire[2] /faɪɚ/ *verb*

- fire
- dismiss (*formal*)
- lay someone off
- discharge

ANTONYMS → see **hire**

fire
if your employer fires you, you are told to leave your job, usually because you have done something wrong: *She was **fired for** stealing money from the company.* | *You need to work harder if you don't want to get fired.*

dismiss (*formal*)
to make someone leave his or her job, usually because he or she has done something wrong but sometimes for other reasons. **Dismiss** is usually used in official situations: *It is not easy to dismiss a teacher. Schools must have proof that the teacher cannot do the job correctly.*

lay someone off
to stop employing someone because there is not enough work for him or her to do: *The company will lay off 200 workers because it is not making enough money.*

discharge
to officially allow someone to leave his or her job in the army, navy, etc.: *He was discharged from the army after serving for six years.*
→ see **shoot** for **fire** meaning "to fire a weapon"

firm[1] *noun* → see **company**

firm[2] *adjective* → see **hard**, **tight**, Topic **Describing Texture**

firmly *adverb* → see **strictly**, **tightly**

first /fɚst/ *adjective, adverb*

1 before other things or people
- first
- original
- initial
- introductory
- earliest
- opening
- preliminary (*formal*)

ANTONYMS → see **last[1] (1)**

2 the first thing you want to say or ask
- first
- firstly (*formal*)
- first of all

ANTONYMS → see **finally (2)**

1 before other things or people

first
before any other times, people, or things: *Laurie's name was first on the list.* | *The first time I flew on a plane, I was really nervous.*

original
existing at the beginning, before anything was changed: *The house still has its original wood floors.*

initial (AWL)
happening at the beginning. You use **initial** to talk about what happens at the beginning of a process or activity, or about how someone feels at the beginning of something. **Initial** is used especially in writing and sounds more formal than **first**: *My initial reaction was anger, but then I felt sorry for him.* | *The country is taking the initial steps toward peace.*

introductory
said or written at the beginning of a book or speech in order to explain what it is about: *You should state your opinion in the introductory paragraph of your essay.*

earliest
happening or existing before similar things that came later: *Mozart's earliest symphony was written when he was just eight years old.*

opening
coming at the start of an event or period of time: *This Saturday is the opening day of the baseball season.*

preliminary (AWL) (*formal*)
happening just before a process or event, especially in order to prepare for the rest of it: *The architect's plans for the building are still in the preliminary stages.*

GRAMMAR CHECK: first

Original, **initial**, **introductory**, **opening**, and **preliminary** are always used before a noun: *His original idea was simple.* | *The initial reports did not have much information.*

2 the first thing you want to say or ask

first
used to say that the fact or reason that you are going to mention is the first one and will be followed by others: *First, I'll explain the problem, and then we can discuss possible solutions.*

firstly (*formal*)
firstly means the same as **first**. **Firstly** is used especially when you are giving the reasons for something: *They moved out of the city, firstly because of the crime, but also because there were no jobs.*

first of all
first of all is used in speaking rather than writing, when there are a lot of things you want to talk about: *First of all, I would like to thank all the fans for their support over the years.*

fit[1] /fɪt/ *verb*

- fit
- be the right size
- grow into

fit
if clothes fit you, they are the right size for your body: *The dress fit her perfectly.* | *Do these shoes still fit you, or have you grown out of them?*

be the right size
clothes that are the right size are not too big or too small: *I tried on the jeans to see if they were the right size.*

grow into
if a child grows into clothes, the clothes begin to fit correctly as he or she grows bigger: *The jacket is a little big for him now, but he'll soon grow into it.*

fit[2] *adjective* → see **healthy**

fit[3] *noun* → see **tantrum**

fix /fɪks/ *verb*

- fix
- repair
- mend
- patch
- renovate
- restore

ANTONYMS → see **break**[1]

fix
if you fix something that is broken or not working correctly, you do something to it so that it is in good condition again: *The radio is not working – can you fix it?* | *The repairman said it would cost more to fix the washing machine than it would to buy a new one.*

repair
repair means the same as **fix** but sounds more formal: *The builders are coming to repair the roof.* | *It will cost a lot of money to get the car repaired.*

mend
to fix a tear or hole in a piece of clothing: *Can you mend this sweater for me?*

patch
to quickly fix something that has a hole in it, by putting something over the hole: *He patched the holes in the knees of his jeans.*

renovate
to fix an old building so that it is in good condition again: *We decided to buy an old house and renovate it ourselves.*

restore (AWL)
to fix something old and valuable so that it looks the same as it did originally. You use **restore** especially about buildings, vehicles, and works of art: *Many paintings were damaged in the fire, but they have now been restored.*
→ see **join**

flabby *adjective* → see **fat**

flame *noun* → see **fire**[1]

flap *verb* → see **wave**

flash[1] *verb* → see **shine**

flash[2] *noun* → see **light**[1]

flat /flæt/ *adjective*

- flat
- level
- even
- horizontal
- smooth

flat
not sloping, and with no bumps or holes: *We sat down on a big flat rock.* | *The flat land in Kansas is good for farming.*

level
flat and having no part higher than any other part: *Make sure the shelves are level before you put the screws in the wall.*

F

even
completely flat and level. You use **even** especially about floors and roads, to emphasize that there are no bumps or holes at all: *The floor must be completely even before we lay the tiles.*

horizontal
flat and going straight across and not sloping: *His T-shirt had a horizontal stripe across the chest.*

smooth
without any rough or raised parts. **Smooth** is used especially when saying how something feels when you touch it: *The marble table felt smooth and cold against her arm.*
→ see **slanted** to describe surfaces or objects that are at an angle, **vertical** to describe surfaces or objects that are upright

ADVERBS

You can make the adjectives **even**, **horizontal**, and **smooth** into adverbs by using an **-ly** ending: *Spread the frosting evenly over the cake.* | *Hold your arms out horizontally in front of you.* | *The dress fit smoothly over her hips.*

F

flatten /ˈflætn/ *verb*

- ► flatten
- ► roll something flat
- ► smooth
- ► level

flatten *also* **flatten out**
to make something flat, or to become flat: *I flattened the empty milk carton and put it in the recycling bin.* | *The hills flatten out near the coast.*

roll something flat *also* **press something flat**
to make something flat by rolling or pressing it: *If you want to save this flower, you can press it flat inside a book.* | *She rolled the dough flat and then cut out two eight-inch circles.*

smooth
to make the surface of something such as cloth or hair completely flat and smooth: *Liz smoothed back her hair with her hand.*

level
to make a surface or piece of land flat and smooth: *It is important to level the soil before planting a vegetable garden.*

flatter *verb* → see **praise[1]**

flattery *noun* → see **praise[2]**

flavor *noun* → see **taste[1]**, Topic **Describing Food**

flaw /flɔ/ *noun*

- ► flaw
- ► fault
- ► weakness
- ► shortcomings

flaw
something that is bad about someone's character: *The witch's flaw was her pride.* | *Despite all his flaws, he was a great teacher.*

fault
fault means the same as **flaw** but sounds less serious: *Everyone has their faults – mine is that I put things off to do tomorrow instead of doing them today.*
→ **GRAMMAR: Fault** is often used in the plural in this meaning.

weakness
something that is bad about your character, which makes you less likely to be successful: *The personality test helps you to identify your strengths and weaknesses.* | *One of her weaknesses is that she is very lazy.*

shortcomings
parts of someone's character or abilities that are not as good as they should be: *He is aware of his shortcomings as a player, and has worked hard to get better.*
→ see **defect** for **flaw** meaning "a problem in the way something is made"

flawed *adjective* → see **imperfect**

flawless *adjective* → see **perfect**

flawlessly *adverb* → see **perfectly**

flexible /ˈfleksəbəl/ *adjective*

1 able to change or do different things
- ► flexible
- ► adaptable
- ► versatile
- ► variable

2 able to bend, move, or change position easily
- ► flexible
- ► elastic
- ► supple
- ► springy

1 able to change or do different things

flexible (AWL)
willing to change or deal with a situation that is changing. You use **flexible** especially when you are talking about changing times or dates: *We can meet anytime this weekend – I'm flexible.* |

Many women who have children want more flexible schedules at work.

adaptable (AWL)
able to change and be successful in new and different situations. **Adaptable** is usually used about people or other living things, but it can be used about other things: *Brian is outgoing and adaptable and quickly made friends when he moved to a new school.*

versatile
able to do a lot of different things or to be used in a lot of different ways: *Cotton is an extremely versatile material that can be used to make a wide variety of clothing.* | *She is a versatile performer who can sing, dance, and act.*

variable (AWL)
likely to change often or be different: *The color of the fish is variable – it changes throughout its lifetime.*

2 able to bend, move, or change position easily

flexible (AWL)
easy to bend or move easily: *My body has become a lot more flexible since I started doing yoga.* | *The plastic is flexible so that you can bend it into the right shape.*

elastic
a material that is elastic can stretch or bend and then returns to its original shape: *The pants have an elastic waistband, which stretches around your child's waist without being too tight.*

supple
able to bend and move easily and gracefully. You use **supple** especially to describe someone's body: *The dancers exercise every day to keep their bodies supple and strong.*

springy
something that is springy quickly moves back to its normal shape after you press it: *This mattress is too soft – I want one that is more springy.*

flight *noun* → see Topic **Travel and Vacations**

float /floʊt/ *verb*

- float
- drift
- hover
- hang

ANTONYMS → see **sink**

float
to stay up in the air or stay on the surface of the water: *The children were throwing sticks into the water and watching them float down the stream.* | *I looked up at the clouds floating in the sky.*

drift
to move along slowly in the air or water: *We stopped rowing for a while and just let the boat drift.*

hover
to stay in one place in the air. You use **hover** about things like helicopters, birds, and insects: *A police helicopter was* ***hovering over*** *the freeway.*

hang
to stay in the air in the same place for a long time. You use **hang** especially about clouds, smoke, and smells: *The smoke from the fire hung in the air.*

→ see **fly**

flood /flʌd/ *verb*

- flood
- submerge
- overflow

flood
to cover a place with water: *During the storm, water from the ocean flooded the village.* | *My basement floods whenever it rains.*

submerge
to cover something completely with water: *The rising river has submerged parts of the town.*

overflow
if a river, lake, or container overflows, it is so full that the liquid inside flows over its edges: *I left the water running into the tub while I answered the phone, and the water* ***overflowed onto*** *the floor.*

flooded *adjective* → see **underwater**

floor /flɔr/ *noun*

- floor
- story
- level
- deck

floor
the flat area in a building that you stand or walk on, and that often has more than one room on it. You can walk up stairs or take an elevator to get to another floor: *The apartment building has ten floors.* | *Our classroom is* ***on the second floor.***

story
a floor in a building. You use **story** especially when you are talking about how many floors there are in a building: *The hotel is a seven-story building facing the ocean.*

level
a floor, especially in a large public building or in

a place where people park their cars: *Women's clothing is **on Level** 2 of the department store.*

→ In a building where people work, shop, or leave their cars, the floor that is under the level of the ground is usually called the **lower level**: *There is more parking on the lower level.* In a house, the floor that is below the ground is called the **basement**.

deck
one of the floors on a ship, bus, or plane: *There is a nice restaurant **on the top deck** of the ship.*

→ see **bottom**, **ground**

flow /floʊ/ *verb*

1 to flow

flow
if a liquid flows, it moves in a steady stream from one place to another: *This is the place where the river **flows into** the ocean.* | *Her tears began to flow as we said goodbye.*

come out
if liquid comes out of a pipe or container, it flows out: *I turned on the faucet, but no water came out.*

drip
if a liquid drips from something, it falls in drops: *All night we could hear the rain **dripping from** the roof.*

→ If a faucet or hose **drips**, water falls in drops from it: *The bathroom faucet was dripping.*

leak
if a liquid leaks, it flows through a hole or crack when it should not: *Water is **leaking from** a pipe under the kitchen sink.*

→ You can also use **leak** about a container that has a hole or crack in it that liquid can flow through: *The roof is leaking – we have to get it fixed.*

spill
if you spill a liquid, it flows over the edge of a container by accident: *Katie knocked over her cup, and coffee **spilled** all **over** the table.*

overflow
if a liquid overflows, it goes over the edges of the container or place where it is: *The river overflowed its banks and began to flood the fields around it.*

→ You can also use **overflow** about a container that has liquid flowing out over the edge: *The glass was **overflowing with** water.*

2 to flow quickly

pour
to flow out quickly in large amounts: *When I run in the heat, the sweat **pours down** my face and back.*

run
if liquid runs somewhere, it flows quickly and smoothly: *A stream **runs along** the bottom of the field.* | *The water was **running out of** the sink.*

gush
to flow out quickly in large amounts, especially because there is pressure behind the liquid: *Oil*

flow

The bathroom faucet **is dripping**.

The stream **runs** through the woods.

Water **is leaking** from the pipe.

Coffee **spilled** onto the table.

The glass **is overflowing**.

Water **is gushing** out of the broken pipe.

was ***gushing out of*** *the broken pipeline into the ocean.*

stream
to flow quickly downward in large amounts: *They both had tears* ***streaming down*** *their faces.*

3 to flow slowly

trickle
if a liquid trickles somewhere, it flows there slowly in a thin line: *Blood* ***trickled down*** *his leg from the cut on his knee.*

seep
to flow slowly through very small holes or spaces: *If chemicals from the factory* ***seep into*** *the land, the crops will die.*

ooze
if a thick liquid or substance oozes out of something, it flows from it very slowly: *Melted cheese was* ***oozing out of*** *the sandwich.*
→ see **pour** for words meaning "to make a liquid flow"

flower /ˈflaʊɚ/ *noun*

- ► flower
- ► blossom
- ► bloom
- ► bud
- ► bouquet

flower
a pretty colored part on a plant or tree. A **flower** is often made up of many petals: *The plant has small white flowers.* | *She bent down and picked a flower in the garden.*

blossom
a flower on a tree or bush: *In spring, the lilac bushes have beautiful purple and white blossoms.*

bloom
a flower, especially one that is fully open. **Bloom** sounds more literary than **flower**: *The bush was covered with yellow blooms.*
→ You can say that a plant or tree with flowers on it is **in bloom** when the flowers are open: *It was June and the roses were all in bloom.*

bud
a young flower that is still tightly rolled up and has not yet opened: *The buds on the plant were beginning to open up into flowers.*

bouquet
a group of flowers given to someone as a present or carried at a formal occasion: *Someone in the audience gave the dancer a* ***bouquet of*** *flowers.* | *The bride wanted lilies in her bouquet.*
→ A group of flowers can also be called a **bunch of flowers/roses etc.** or simply **flowers**: *We gave Mom a big bunch of roses on Mother's Day.* | *On the last day of class, I brought flowers for my science teacher.*
→ see **plant**[1], **tree**

fluent /ˈfluənt/ *adjective*

- ► fluent
- ► able to speak
- ► proficient
- ► bilingual
- ► multilingual

fluent
very good at speaking a foreign language so that you can speak it quickly without stopping, and you understand it very well: *Our ESL teacher is* ***fluent in*** *both English and Spanish.*
→ You can also say that someone **speaks fluent Spanish/German/Urdu etc.**: *Jordan lived in Italy for many years, and he still speaks fluent Italian.*

able to speak
if you are able to speak a foreign language, you know that language or know some of that language: *Is anyone here able to speak Polish?*

proficient
good at speaking a foreign language, but not completely fluent: *She has lived in Tokyo for two years now, and she is gradually becoming more* ***proficient in*** *Japanese.*

bilingual
able to speak two languages very well: *The couple want their son to be* ***bilingual in*** *both Russian and English, so they use both languages with him.*

multilingual
able to speak several different languages: *Alberto is multilingual – he speaks Spanish, Portuguese, English, and Italian.*
→ **Multilingual** and **bilingual** can also be used about places where there are a lot of people who speak more than one language: *New York City is a multilingual city.* | *Our school has some bilingual classrooms where children learn in both Spanish and English.*

ADVERBS

You can make the adjectives **fluent**, **proficient**, and **bilingual** into adverbs by using an **-ly** ending: *He speaks Chinese fluently.* | *They both speak English and Spanish, so they decided to raise their child bilingually.*

fluid *noun* → see **liquid**

fly /flaɪ/ verb

- fly
- soar
- flutter
- glide
- float
- buzz

fly
to move through the air above the ground: *The planes fly right over our house.* | *A bee suddenly flew in through the open window.*

soar
to go quickly up, very high in the air. **Soar** sounds literary, and you use it in descriptions, stories, and poems: *The eagle soars high above the trees.*

flutter
if a small bird or an insect flutters somewhere, it flies there by moving its wings quickly and lightly. You use **flutter** especially in writing: *At night the moths flutter around the porch light.*

glide
to fly smoothly and quietly, in a way that looks easy: *Three huge birds were gliding gracefully over the tops of the waves.*

float
if something floats, it moves slowly through the air or stays up in the air: *A hot-air balloon floated above the fields.*

buzz
if an insect or plane buzzes, it makes a continuous sound when it is flying: *The bees were buzzing from flower to flower.* | *A police helicopter buzzed over our heads.*

fog /fɑg/ noun

- fog
- mist
- haze

fog
clouds that are near the ground and that are difficult to see through: *Traffic was moving slowly because of the thick fog.*

mist
cloudy air near the ground that is not as thick as fog: *A gray mist was hanging over the water.*

haze
smoke or dust in the air that is difficult to see through: *Winds blew away some of the haze caused by the fires.*
→ see **cloud**, Topic **The Weather**

foggy *adjective* → see **cloudy**, Topic **The Weather**

fold[1] /foʊld/ verb

- fold
- wrinkle
- crease
- crumple

fold
to bend a piece of paper or cloth so that one part covers another part: *Take the clothes out of the dryer and fold them.* | *Fold the square of paper in half* (=so that one half covers the other half).

wrinkle
to make messy folds and lines in a piece of clothing or cloth, usually accidentally: *My shirt was on the bed, and the cat sat on it and wrinkled it.*

crease
to make a line on a piece of clothing or paper by folding or pressing it, deliberately or accidentally: *She didn't sit down because she didn't want to crease her dress.*

crumple *also* **crumple up**
to crush a piece of paper into many small folds and make it smaller: *He crumpled the letter into a ball and threw it into the wastebasket.*

GRAMMAR CHECK: fold

These verbs can be made into adjectives – **wrinkled**, **creased**, and **crumpled**: *a wrinkled shirt* | *Her dress was creased.* | *He lay on the crumpled sheets.*

fold

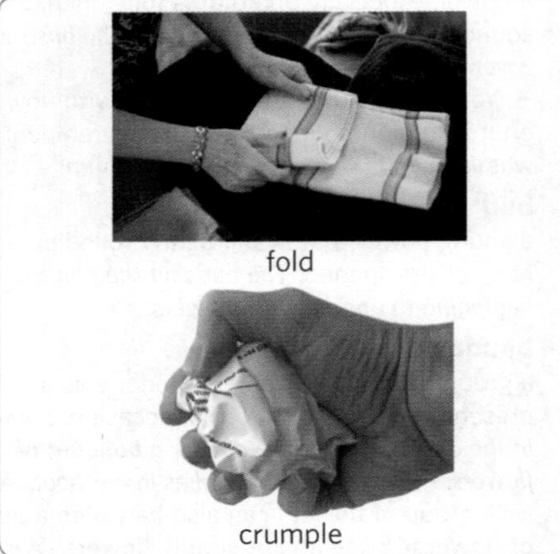

fold

crumple

F

fold² /foʊld/ *noun*

- ► fold
- ► wrinkle
- ► crease

fold
the place in paper or cloth where it has been folded, or the paper or material around this place: *Bend the cardboard in half and cut along the fold.* | *The boy hid his face in **the folds of** his mother's skirt.*

wrinkle
a small messy fold on a piece of clothing or paper. You do not usually want **wrinkles** on something: *You'll need an iron to get rid of the **wrinkles in** your shirt.*
→ If a piece of clothing has **wrinkles**, it is more usual to say: *My shirt is wrinkled.*

You can also use **wrinkles** to talk about lines on your face that you get when you are old: *I have gray hair and wrinkles now.*

crease
a deep line on a piece of clothing or paper, where it has been folded or pressed by an iron: *The pants have a sharp crease along the leg.*

folks *noun* → see **family**, **people**

follow /ˈfɑloʊ/ *verb*

- ► follow
- ► chase
- ► run after
- ► pursue
- ► stalk

ANTONYMS → see **lead¹**

follow
to walk, drive, or go behind or after someone else: *You drive on ahead, and I'll follow.* | *The detective looked over his shoulder, to make sure no one was following him.*

chase
to follow someone or something quickly, because you want to catch him, her, or it. You can **chase** someone on foot or in a vehicle: *A police officer chased the thief down the street.*

run after *also* **go after**
to quickly follow someone who is moving away from you, in order to catch or talk to him or her. You usually **run after** or **go after** someone on foot: *A group of kids ran after the baseball player to ask for his autograph.*

pursue (AWL)
pursue means the same as **chase** but sounds more formal. **Pursue** is often used in stories and news reports: *We ran faster, but the man continued to pursue us.*

stalk
to follow and watch someone very often, in a way that is very annoying or frightening: *Police have warned the man to stop stalking his ex-girlfriend.*
→ **Stalk** also means "to follow a person or animal slowly and quietly in order to attack or kill him, her, or it." You use **stalk** especially about cats and similar animals: *The cat was stalking a bird in the garden.*
→ see **obey** for **follow** meaning "to do what someone says"
→ see **understand**

follower *noun* → see **fan**, **supporter**

following¹ *preposition* → see Function Word **after**

following² *adjective* → see **next¹**

fond *adjective* → see **be fond of** at **like¹**

food /fud/ *noun*

1 something that you eat
- ► food
- ► meal
- ► snack
- ► refreshments
- ► take-out
- ► ration
- ► provisions (*formal*)

2 the type of food you eat or the way food is cooked
- ► diet
- ► nourishment (*formal*)
- ► dish
- ► cooking
- ► cuisine (*formal*)
- ► delicacy
- ► specialty

1 something that you eat

food
something that you eat: *Thank you for dinner – the food was delicious.* | *I love Italian food, especially pasta.* | *Do you think we have enough food for everyone?*

meal
the food that you eat at a particular time: *Dinner is the main meal of the day for most people.*

snack
a small amount of food that you eat between

meals: *The kids have a snack after school, usually cookies and a glass of milk.*

refreshments
small amounts of food and drinks that you can have at a meeting or other event: *Refreshments will be served at the art show.*

take-out *also* **takeout**
a meal that you buy at a restaurant to eat at home: *He likes to get take-out from the Thai restaurant down the street.*
→ **GRAMMAR:** Do not use "a" or "the" before **take-out**. Say: *I'm going to order takeout.*
You can also use **take-out** before a noun to describe a type of food that you bring home or a restaurant that serves this kind of food: *I picked up some take-out Chinese food on the way home.*

ration
an amount of food that people are allowed to have when there is not enough, for example during a war: *During World War II, each family was given a weekly meat ration.*
→ The food that soldiers carry when they are away from their bases is also called **rations**.

provisions (*formal*)
food, drinks, and other supplies, especially for a trip: *We had enough provisions for two weeks.*
→ see **hungry**, **meal**

2 the type of food you eat or the way food is cooked

diet
the type of food that someone eats each day. You use **diet** especially when you are talking about how healthy the food is: *A healthy diet includes plenty of fruits and vegetables.* | *Many of the children were unhealthy because of a poor diet.*

nourishment (*formal*)
the food or the substances in food that people need to live, grow, and be healthy: *People need the vitamins and minerals in food for nourishment.*

dish
food that is prepared or cooked in a particular way: *Spaghetti and meatballs is my favorite dish.*

cooking
food made in a particular way or by a particular person: *Herbs are used a lot in French cooking.*

cuisine (*formal*)
the types of food or type of cooking from a particular country, area, or restaurant: *When you travel, it is fun to try the local cuisine.*

delicacy
an unusual or expensive kind of food which people in a particular area think is very special: *Shark fins are considered a delicacy in many Asian countries.*

specialty
a kind of food that is always very good in a particular restaurant, country, or area: *The restaurant is famous for its seafood specialties.*

fool *verb* → see **joke²**, **trick²**

fool around *phrasal verb* → see **misbehave**

foolish *adjective* → see **stupid**

for *preposition* → see Function Words

forbid /fə'bɪd/ *verb*

- ► **forbid** (*formal*)
- ► **not allow**
- ► **not let**
- ► **not permit** (*formal*)
- ► **ban**
- ► **prohibit** (*formal*)
- ► **outlaw**
- ► **bar**
- ► **censor**

ANTONYMS → see **allow**

forbid (*formal*)
to tell someone in a very strong way that he or she must not do something: *As part of his punishment, he was* ***forbidden to*** *leave the house.* | *Both Islam and Judaism forbid the eating of pork.*

not allow
to say that someone must not do something, and stop him or her from doing it. **Not allow** is not as formal as **forbid** and is more common in everyday English: *The math teacher does* ***not allow*** *students* ***to*** *use calculators during math tests.*

not let
not let means the same as **not allow** but sounds a little more informal: *My parents won't let me stay out later than 11 p.m.*
→ **GRAMMAR:** **Not let** is never followed by "to" in the way that **not allow** and **forbid** are. Don't say: ~~*My dad won't let me to take the car*~~. Say: *My dad won't let me take the car.*

not permit (*formal*)
not permit means the same as **not allow**, but it is more formal and is used especially in official situations: *The police would* ***not permit*** *anyone* ***to*** *enter the area where the crime had occurred.*

ban
to say officially that people must not do or have something. **Ban** is used when something is not allowed because it is considered bad or harmful: *The government of Kenya banned the hunting of elephants.*

prohibit (AWL) (*formal*)
if a rule or law prohibits something, the rule or law says that it is not allowed: *The law prohibits smoking in all restaurants in the city.*

outlaw
to make a law that forbids something: *The new law outlaws the use of some types of chemicals on crops.*

bar
to officially stop someone from entering a place or doing something: *The government has **barred** foreign journalists **from** entering the country.*

censor
if people in authority censor newspapers, books, movies, or letters, they take out any parts that they do not want people to see: *The CIA reports were censored before being given to the press.*

forbidden /fɚˈbɪdn/ *adjective*

- ► **forbidden** (*formal*)
- ► **not allowed**
- ► **not permitted** (*formal*)
- ► **banned**
- ► **prohibited** (*formal*)
- ► **taboo**

forbidden (*formal*)
if something is forbidden, a person, rule, or law has said in a very strong way that you must not do it. **Forbidden** sounds formal or literary: *The use of cell phones in the library is forbidden.* | *Her parents are very strict and she is **forbidden to** go out on dates with boys.*

not allowed
if you are not allowed to do something, a person or rule says that you must not do it. **Not allowed** is not as strong as **forbidden** and is more common in everyday English: *I was **not allowed to** get my ears pierced until I was 15.*

not permitted (*formal*)
if something is not permitted, a rule or law says that you must not do it. **Not permitted** is more formal than **not allowed** and is used especially in official situations: *Parking is not permitted on this street after 3:00 p.m.*

banned
not allowed, because of an official rule or law. You use **banned** especially when things are not allowed because they are bad or harmful: *He was forced to leave the bicycle race because he used a banned drug.*

prohibited (*formal*)
not allowed because of a law. **Prohibited** is used especially on official notices and warnings: *Cars are prohibited on the island.*

taboo
if something is taboo, people do not do it because society thinks it is offensive: *Kissing in public is taboo in some Middle Eastern countries.*
→ see **illegal**

force /fɔrs/ *verb*

- ► **force**
- ► **make**
- ► **pressure**
- ► **put pressure on**
- ► **compel** (*formal*)
- ► **coerce** (*formal*)

force
to cause someone to do something that he or she does not want to do: *The thieves **forced us to** hand over all our money.* | *The knee injury **forced** him **to** miss the rest of the basketball season.*

make
make means the same as **force** but sounds less formal: *My mother tried to make me eat my vegetables.*
→ **GRAMMAR:** Don't say: ~~*She made me to eat it*~~. Say: *She made me eat it.*

pressure
to try to force someone to do something by using influence, arguments, or threats: *The salesman was trying to **pressure** me **into** buying a more expensive phone.*

put pressure on
to continuously try to persuade someone to do something: *Our parents are **putting pressure on** us **to** get married.*

compel (*formal*)
to force someone to do something by using official power or authority: *The law **compels** large companies **to** provide health insurance.*

coerce (*formal*)
to force someone to do something by threatening to hurt him or her: *The man says that the gang **coerced** him **into** helping them rob the bank.*
→ see **power**, **strength**, **violence**

forecast *noun* → see **prediction**

foreign /ˈfɑrɪn/ *adjective*

- ► **foreign**
- ► **imported**
- ► **exotic**
- ► **from abroad**

foreign
from or relating to a country that is not your own: *Everyone at our school must study a foreign*

F

language. | *He was in a foreign country, far away from home.*

imported
imported goods have been taken from a foreign country so they can be sold or used in your country: *A lot of people buy imported cars, but I want to buy a car that was made here in the United States.*

exotic
something that is exotic seems unusual and exciting, especially because it is related to a foreign country: *We saw some beautiful exotic birds when we were on vacation in Costa Rica.*

from abroad *also* **from overseas**
from a foreign country. You use **from overseas** when the foreign country is across an ocean or sea, and **from abroad** for any foreign country: *There are not enough doctors, so a lot of the doctors who work at the hospital are from abroad.* | *Many of the children have been adopted from overseas.*
→ **GRAMMAR:** You can also use **overseas** before a noun to show that someone or something happens or exists in another country: *A lot of the money comes from overseas investments.*
→ see **abroad** for words meaning "in or to a foreign country"

ADVERBS

You can make the adjective **exotic** into an adverb by using an **-ly** ending. **Exotically** is usually used when a person or thing looks like it comes from a place that is far away, such as Africa or South America: *She was tall, slender, and exotically beautiful.*

foreigner /ˈfɑrənɚ/ *noun*

- foreigner
- immigrant
- alien
- visitor
- newcomer

foreigner
someone who comes from another country: *About 40 million foreigners visited the U.S. last year.* | *Saleem felt that people were suspicious of him because he was a foreigner.*
→ **Foreigner** can sound negative and not very friendly. In everyday English, people often say **people from other countries** instead of **foreigners**: *I like meeting people from other countries.*

immigrant (AWL)
someone who comes to another country to live there permanently: *Many **immigrants from** China have settled in San Francisco.*

alien
someone who is not a legal citizen of the country that he or she is living or working in: *Many illegal aliens live and work in the United States.*
→ **Illegal alien** can sound disapproving. To avoid this, people sometimes use **undocumented worker/immigrant** to describe someone who is working in a country without the right legal documents.

visitor
someone who comes to visit another city, country, or area: *Many **visitors to** Quebec go skiing.*

newcomer
someone who has recently arrived in a foreign country or a place that is new to him or her: *The Level 1 class is perfect for **newcomers to** the United States who do not speak much English yet.*

forest /ˈfɔrɪst/ *noun*

- forest
- woods
- woodlands (*formal*)
- rainforest
- jungle

forest
a large area of land covered with trees: *The huge forest is made up mostly of pine trees.*

woods
an area of land covered with trees. You can use **woods** about a small or large area: *Diana's favorite activity is hiking **in the woods** near her home.*

woodlands (*formal*)
an area of land where trees grow. **Woodlands** is usually used when you are talking about the types of people or plants that live in areas with trees, or when you are comparing areas with trees to areas without trees: *The northeastern woodlands were the home of several native peoples, including the Huron and the Iroquois.*

rainforest
a thick forest in a part of the world that is hot and gets at least 100 inches of rain per year: *The medicine comes from a plant that grows in the Brazilian rainforest.*

jungle
a forest in a hot part of the world, that has many trees and large plants growing very close together: *As they move through the jungle, the men use large knives called machetes to cut a*

path. | *The monkeys live in the jungle of South America.*
→ see **tree**

forever *adverb* → see **always**

forget /fəˈget/ *verb*

1 to not be able to remember something
► forget
► have no recollection (*formal*)
ANTONYMS → see **remember**
2 to stop thinking or worrying about something
► forget
► put something out of your mind
► take your mind off something
3 to not bring something you had planned to bring
► forget
► leave

1 to not be able to remember something

forget
to not be able to remember a fact or something that happened: *I keep forgetting the name of the band who sing that song.*
→ **Forget** is also used to say that someone does not remember to do something he or she should do: *I'm sorry, I* ***forgot to*** *call you back.*

have no recollection (*formal*)
to not be able to remember something that happened at all: *He* ***had no recollection of*** *the accident.*

2 to stop thinking or worrying about something

forget
to stop thinking or worrying about someone or something: *Let's go to a movie and* ***forget about*** *school for a while.* | *"I'm really sorry about what I said." "Forget it!"*

put something out of your mind
to make an effort to stop worrying or thinking about something, especially when it is taking up too much of your time or energy: *The things he said to you were mean, but you have to try to put it out of your mind.*

take your mind off something *also* **keep your mind off something**
to help you stop worrying about someone or something. Usually, you do something that will help you **take your mind off** your problems: *I needed to take my mind off my exams, so I went for a run.* | *Working helps him to keep his mind off his other troubles.*

3 to not bring something you had planned to bring

forget
to not bring something with you when you go somewhere, when you had planned to bring it. **Forget** means the same as **leave**: *I forgot my math homework.*
→ **GRAMMAR: Forget** is followed only by an object. Don't say: ~~*I forgot my cell phone at home*~~. Say: *I forgot my cell phone.*

leave
leave means the same as **forget**: *Don't leave your passport at home when you go to the airport.* | *They drove away from the field, leaving all the soccer equipment behind.*
→ **GRAMMAR: Leave** is followed by an object, and an adverb or phrase. Don't say: ~~*I left my umbrella*~~. Say: *I left my umbrella behind/at school/in the desk etc.*

forgetful /fəˈgetfəl/ *adjective*

► forgetful
► absent-minded

forgetful
often forgetting things that you should remember: *She is becoming more forgetful as she gets older.*

absent-minded
often forgetting or not noticing things because you are thinking of something else: *He is a smart guy but he is very absent-minded. When he is working, he often forgets to eat!*

forgive /fəˈgɪv/ *verb*

► forgive
► excuse
► pardon

forgive
to stop being angry with someone who has done something wrong: *Talk to her about how upset you are, and then try to forgive her.*

excuse
to forgive someone for doing something wrong, especially something that is not very important, such as being late, messy, or careless: *The teacher does not excuse us for being late more than once.* | *Please excuse my messy handwriting.*

pardon
to allow someone who is guilty of a crime not to be punished for it: *The governor pardoned several prisoners who had spent years in prison for crimes that were not serious.*

F

forgiveness /fə'gɪvnəs/ *noun*

- ► forgiveness
- ► mercy
- ► pardon

forgiveness
the act of forgiving someone: *Santos apologized for the lie and asked for her forgiveness.*

mercy
kindness and a willingness to forgive people, especially when you have the power to punish people for bad things they have done: *The king showed mercy, only putting the man in jail for two weeks.*

pardon
an official order that allows someone who is guilty of a crime not to be punished for it: *The governor issued a pardon two hours before the man was to be executed.*

form *verb* → see **document**, **kind**[1], **make up**, **shape**

formal /'fɔrməl/ *adjective*

- ► formal
- ► stiff

ANTONYMS → see **informal (1)**

formal
formal language or behavior is used in important or official situations: *A business letter should be written in formal language, not as though you were writing to a friend.* | *Mr. Guthrie was very formal. He always called us by our last names.*

stiff
very formal and done in a way that is not relaxed and seems unfriendly: *Their goodbyes were stiff and formal.*
→ see **dressy** for "formal clothes", **official** for **formal** meaning "done in an officially agreed way"
→ see Topic **Describing Clothes**

ADVERBS
You can make the adjectives **formal** and **stiff** into adverbs by using an **-ly** ending: *The teacher addressed us formally, using our last names.* | *"Nice to meet you," he said stiffly but politely.*

former *adjective* → see **last**[1]

fortunate *adjective* → see **lucky**

fortunately *adverb* → see **luckily**

fortune *noun* → see **luck**, **money**

forward *adverb* → see Function Words

fraud *noun* → see **theft**

free[1] /fri/ *adjective*

1 not costing any money
- ► free
- ► free of charge
- ► for free
- ► at no extra cost
- ► complimentary (*formal*)

2 able to do what you want without being controlled by others
- ► free
- ► loose
- ► out
- ► at large

1 not costing any money

free
not costing any money: *The rides at the school fair are free.* | *They were giving away free samples of food.*

free of charge
free of charge means the same as **free** but is used mostly to advertise services that are free: *The first hour with the lawyer is free of charge, but his fee after that is $500 per hour.*

for free *also* **for nothing** (*informal*)
without paying or being paid: *Shane paid $10 for the CD, but I got mine for free.* | *I babysit for her, so she cuts my hair for nothing.*

at no extra cost
free. **At no extra cost** is used in advertising to say that if you are buying something, another thing is free: *When you buy this set of knives, we will give you the scissors at no extra cost.*

complimentary (*formal*)
free. You use **complimentary** about additional things that you get from a business such as a hotel or restaurant when you use their services: *Customers will receive a complimentary drink with their meal.*

2 able to do what you want without being controlled by others

free
able to do what you want without being controlled by someone else: *He left the prison, a free man again.* | *When you pay the entrance fee, you **are free to** go anywhere in the building and the gardens.*

loose
free to move around an area. You use **loose**

about an animal that escapes from a cage or rope, or that is able to move around an enclosed area: *The horses got loose and ran off into the woods.* | *The chickens are allowed to run loose in the yard.*

out
free. You use **out** about an animal or prisoner who is no longer in a prison, cage, or in another locked place: *I was in prison for ten years, but I have been out for five.* | *One of the puppies got out and crawled under the fence.*

at large
a criminal or prisoner who is at large has escaped from prison or the police and has not been caught: *The two men suspected in the shooting are still at large.*
→ see **empty**[1] for **free** meaning "not being used by another person"

free[2] /fri/ *verb*

- ► free
- ► set free
- ► release
- ► let go (*informal*)
- ► liberate
- ► emancipate (*formal*)

ANTONYMS → see **prison (2)**

free
to let someone leave prison or a place where he or she has been forced to stay, or to let someone stop being a slave: *The two men were **freed from** prison after five years.* | *The biggest reason for the Civil War was to free the slaves.*

set free
to let a person or animal leave a place where he, she, or it has been forced to stay: *I opened the trap and set the mouse free.* | *The pirates set their prisoners free when they received the payment from the king.*

release (AWL)
to let a person or an animal leave a place where he, she, or it has been forced to stay. **Release** is often used in official language: *Park rangers released the bear into the wild.* | *The crowd demanded that the woman be **released from** prison.*

let go (*informal*)
let go means the same as **release** but is more informal: *Please let her go – she is just a child.* | *We have to let the bird go – it's a wild animal and it doesn't belong with us.*

liberate (AWL)
to free people or a place from someone's control, especially control by a military government or a dictator (=ruler who uses force to stay in power): *We will never stop fighting until we liberate our country.*

emancipate (*formal*)
to make someone free and able to have the same rights as other people in society: *The group is working to emancipate women all over the world, to give them the same rights as men.*
→ see **drop**[1]

SYNONYM CHECK

Free, set free, release, or let go?

You use **free** especially when a decision has been made to free someone, or when someone is freed because of a rule. Do not use **free** about letting animals leave cages.

You use **set free, release**, and **let go** especially to show that something physically happens to allow the person or animal to leave a place, for example because someone has opened a door.

Set free sounds slightly literary, and **release** sounds official. **Let go** is the most informal, and is most likely to be used when you are speaking.

freedom /ˈfridəm/ *noun*

- ► freedom
- ► liberty
- ► independence
- ► liberation

freedom
the state of being free and allowed to do what you want: *Everyone should have the **freedom to** say what they think.* | *The slaves were given their freedom after the Civil War.*

liberty
the legal right to do what you want without too much control from a government or authority: *The protesters held signs that read "Liberty and Equality for all people."*

independence
freedom from control by another country: *The Americans fought for their **independence from** Britain in the 1770s.*
→ **Independence** also means "the freedom to do what you want and take care of yourself": *Her first job gave her a sense of independence.*

liberation
the act of giving people or a place freedom from the control of another country or group: *Crowds celebrated the **liberation of** Paris **from** the German army after World War II.*

F

freeze *verb* → see **cool²**, Topic **Computers and the Internet**

freezing *adjective* → see **cold¹**

frequent /ˈfrikwənt/ *adjective*

- frequent
- regular
- constant
- repeated
- habitual

ANTONYMS → see **rare**

frequent
happening very often: *My family made frequent visits to Florida, at least four times a year, to see my grandparents.*

regular
happening or doing something every day, every week, etc.: *Regular exercise keeps you healthy.* | *We keep our customers informed with regular email updates.*
→ **Regular** does not always mean that something happens often. If something happens at the same time every month, year, etc., it is still regular, even though there is a long time between events: *Regular visits to the dentist are important - you should go every six months.*

constant (AWL)
happening a lot or all the time, often in an annoying way: *The constant noise from the traffic was driving me crazy.*

repeated
done several or many times: *We made repeated calls to the store to try to speak to the manager, but he would not talk to us.*

habitual
often doing something because it is a habit: *Habitual smokers find it hard to quit smoking.*

ADVERBS

You can make the adjectives that mean **frequent** into adverbs by using an **-ly** ending: *We frequently visit my grandparents - at least once a week.* | *Do you exercise regularly?* | *He habitually wears a dirty old baseball cap.*

frequently *adverb* → see **often**

fresh *adjective* → see **new**, **raw**, Topic **Describing Food**

friend /frend/ *noun*

- friend
- acquaintance
- companion
- playmate
- girlfriend
- boyfriend

ANTONYMS → see **enemy**

friend
someone whom you like very much and enjoy spending time with: *Matt and Mark have been friends since second grade.* | *Carole is one of my best friends.*

acquaintance
someone you have met, but do not know well: *I saw an old acquaintance who I met when I was in military training.*

companion
someone you spend a lot of time with. **Companion** is fairly formal: *He and his companions began the walk up the mountain.*

playmate
a friend that a child plays with: *The two boys had been playmates when they were little.*

girlfriend
a girl or woman someone has a romantic relationship with: *Sam said he wanted us to meet his girlfriend.* | *Do you have a girlfriend?*
→ **Girlfriend** is sometimes used by women or girls to mean their female friends: *She went out with her girlfriends to celebrate her birthday.*

boyfriend
a boy or man someone has a romantic relationship with: *Marissa's boyfriend is really cute.*

friendly /ˈfrendli/ *adjective*

- friendly
- nice (*informal*)
- outgoing
- warm
- welcoming
- sociable
- hospitable

ANTONYMS → see **unfriendly**

friendly
wanting to talk to, help, and be nice to people, even if you do not know them: *When I first came to the school, Michaela was friendly and kind.* | *He is very **friendly to** all the other kids.*

nice (*informal*)
pleasant and easy to be with or talk to: *We talked for a long time at soccer practice – he was really nice.*

outgoing
liking to meet and talk to new people and not nervous in social situations: *Christina is an outgoing person who likes parties and other social events.*

warm
friendly and making other people feel happy and relaxed. **Warm** sounds slightly literary and you use it especially with words like "welcome," "smile," or "hug": *The audience gave him a warm welcome with lots of applause.* | *He glanced at her with a warm smile.*

welcoming
making you feel happy and relaxed when you arrive somewhere: *All the people in my new dorm were very welcoming.*

sociable
friendly and enjoying spending time with other people. **Sociable** sounds slightly formal or scientific: *The teacher said that he was a sociable child who got along well with everyone.*

hospitable
treating people who visit your home or country well: *The owners of the hotel were very hospitable and made us feel like we were at home.*
→ see **nice**, Topic **Describing People's Character**

ADVERBS

You can make the adjectives **nice**, **warm**, **sociable**, and **hospitable** into adverbs by using an **-ly** ending: *She smiled so nicely at us that we felt comfortable right away.* | *Jonathan greeted his guests warmly.* | *"Would you like a cup of coffee or something?" said Margo hospitably.*

friendship *noun* → see **relationship**

fright /fraɪt/ *noun*

- fright
- shock
- alarm
- scare

fright
a sudden strong feeling of fear: *Something moved in the darkness, and she gave a cry of fright.* | *The boy was shaking with fright.*

shock
the feeling when you are very surprised and upset by something: *The news of his death came as a **shock to** everyone.*

alarm
the feeling when you are worried something bad will happen: *When I said I could smell something burning, she looked at me **in alarm**.*

scare
a situation in which people feel frightened that something bad will happen, especially when it does not actually happen: *There was a health scare about cell phones – some people thought they gave you cancer.*
→ see **scare**, **scared**

frighten /ˈfraɪtn/ *verb*

- frighten
- scare
- terrify
- alarm
- startle
- intimidate
- terrorize

frighten
to make someone feel afraid and that something bad will happen to him or her. **Frighten** means the same as **scare** but is a little more formal: *The crazy look in his eyes frightened her.*

scare
scare means the same as **frighten** but is a little less formal: *There is no ghost – you're just trying to scare me!* | *Fireworks can scare dogs and other pets.*

terrify
to make someone feel very afraid: *The thought of making a speech to hundreds of people terrified her.*

alarm
to make someone feel worried or afraid: *I was alarmed by the strange noise the elevator was making.*

startle
to make someone feel a little afraid, because something happens very suddenly: *The doorbell suddenly rang, startling him.*

intimidate
to deliberately make someone feel afraid of you, especially to make him or her do what you want: *The criminals intimidated witnesses so that they would not give evidence in court.*

terrorize
to make people feel extremely afraid of you by attacking them and threatening to hurt them: *The gang had terrorized the neighborhood for years, and everyone was afraid of them.*

frightened /ˈfraɪtnd/ *adjective*

- ► **frightened**
- ► **afraid**
- ► **scared**
- ► **terrified**
- ► **petrified**
- ► **alarmed**
- ► **fearful**
- ► **intimidated**

frightened
unhappy or worried because you think something bad might happen. **Frightened** is more formal or literary than **afraid** or **scared**: *The dog, **frightened by** the thunder, was found hiding in the barn.*

afraid
afraid means the same as **frightened** but sounds slightly less formal: *My sister is **afraid of** flying. | Don't be afraid – it's just the wind making that noise.*

scared
scared means the same as **frightened** but is used in more informal or spoken language: *When he was little, he was **scared of** clowns. | We could hear the thunder, and we were so scared.*

terrified
extremely frightened: *The little girl was terrified because she couldn't find her mother.*

petrified
petrified means the same as **terrified** but is used to emphasize that someone is completely terrified: *We hid in the dark closet together, **petrified that** the soldiers would find us.*

alarmed
suddenly very worried and frightened because you realize there is a problem or danger: *Her parents were alarmed when she didn't get home on time, but luckily everything was fine.*

fearful
afraid of something that could happen in the future. **Fearful** sounds slightly formal or literary: *Many people are **fearful of** losing their jobs in this bad economy.*

intimidated
feeling worried or afraid because you do not have enough confidence to deal with a situation: *Don't feel **intimidated by** the other team just because they're bigger.*

GRAMMAR CHECK: frightened

Frightened, **scared**, and **afraid** mean the same thing, but there are some differences in the ways you can use them.

You can say: *a scared/frightened child*, but don't say: ~~*an afraid child*~~.

You can say: *She was **frightened/scared by** the loud noise*, but don't say: ~~*She was afraid by the loud noise*~~.

You can use all three adjectives before "of," "that," and "to": *He is **scared of** the dark. | I was **frightened that** no one would help me. | Women are **afraid to** walk alone at night.*

frightening /ˈfraɪtn-ɪŋ/ *adjective*

- ► **frightening**
- ► **scary**
- ► **terrifying**
- ► **alarming**
- ► **intimidating**
- ► **eerie**
- ► **spooky**
- ► **creepy**

frightening
making you feel frightened. **Frightening** sounds a little formal or literary: *It was frightening to realize that we were completely alone.*

scary
making you feel frightened. **Scary** is less formal than **frightening**: *I didn't want to watch the movie before I went to bed, because it was too scary.*

terrifying
making someone extremely frightened: *The bear ran toward us; it was absolutely terrifying.*

alarming
making you feel suddenly frightened and worried because you realize there is a problem or danger: *Bees are dying at an alarming rate, which is dangerous for farming.*

intimidating
making you feel worried or afraid because you feel you do not have enough confidence to deal with a situation: *He finds long books intimidating.*

eerie
strange and scary. You use **eerie** especially about sounds and things you see: *There was an eerie howling sound coming from the backyard. | The fire made an eerie glow on the man's face.*

spooky
scary because something reminds you of ghosts or similar things. You use **spooky** especially

about places, and sometimes about people: *The empty rooms upstairs were spooky in the dark.*

creepy
if something is creepy, it makes you feel frightened, and you feel slightly sick or uncomfortable when you think about it. You use **creepy** especially about people and places: *The way the old woman looked at me was really creepy.*

ADVERBS
You can make the adjectives that mean **frightening** into adverbs by using an **-ly** ending: *The story about a disease that kills most of the population was frighteningly real.* | *The future seems scarily uncertain.* | *The house was eerily quiet.*

front /frʌnt/ *noun*

- ► front
- ► head
- ► bow

ANTONYMS → see **back¹ (2)**

front
the part of something that is farthest forward: *The front of our car was damaged because we couldn't stop in time.*

head
the front of a line of people: *I wanted to be at the head of the line when the doors of the new store opened.*

bow
the front part of a ship or boat: *They stood in the bow of the ship and waved to the people waiting to welcome them.*
→ see Function Word **in front of**

frontier *noun* → see **border**

frost *noun* → see **snow¹**, Topic **The Weather**

frosty *adjective* → see **cold¹**

frown /fraʊn/ *verb*

- ► frown
- ► scowl
- ► glare
- ► grimace

ANTONYMS → see **smile¹**

frown
to move your eyebrows together and turn the corners of your mouth down when you are angry, unhappy, or thinking hard: *As she read the email, she began to frown.*

scowl
to frown at someone in an angry disapproving way: *"I asked you to stop talking," the teacher said,* ***scowling at*** *us.*

glare
to look at someone in a very angry way, often for a long time: *His sister* ***glared at*** *him, ran out of the room, and slammed the door.*

grimace
to show on your face that you feel pain or do not like something: *My father grimaced as he looked at the check at the end of dinner.*

GRAMMAR CHECK: frown
Frown, **scowl**, **glare**, and **grimace** can also be nouns that are used to talk about an angry expression on someone's face: *"Stop doing that!" he said with a frown.* | *Jenna has had a scowl on her face all day – what is she so mad about?*

frustrate *verb* → see **anger²**

frustrated *adjective* → see **angry**

frustrating *adjective* → see **annoying**

frustration *noun* → see **anger¹**

fuel *noun* → see **energy**

fulfilled *adjective* → see **satisfied**

full /fʊl/ *adjective*

- ► full
- ► filled with
- ► packed (*informal*)
- ► crammed (*informal*)
- ► overflowing
- ► overloaded
- ► stuffed (*informal*)
- ► teeming (*formal*)

ANTONYMS → see **empty¹**

full
containing so many things or people that no more will fit in: *The stadium was* ***full of*** *excited football fans.* | *If that box is full, I'll take it out to the car.*

filled with
filled with means the same as **full of**: *The bag was filled with candy.* | *The room was filled with teenagers waiting to sing for the judges.*

packed (*informal*)
full of people. You use **packed** especially about buildings or rooms that are as full as possible: *The auditorium was* ***packed with*** *parents waiting*

F

for the play to start. | We sold every ticket – the place was packed.*

crammed *(informal)*
so full of things or people that it is difficult to move: *On New Year's Eve the bar was crammed.* | *The tiny room was **crammed with** furniture.*

overflowing
a container or place that is overflowing has too many things or people in it so that they do not all fit: *The trash cans were overflowing.* | *The park is always **overflowing with** people on weekends.*

overloaded
having too many things or people inside something so that it is too heavy. You use **overloaded** about vehicles and machines: *The boat sank because it was **overloaded with** goods and people.*

stuffed *(informal)*
so full that there is no space left to put more in. You use **stuffed** about containers: *After Thanksgiving, the refrigerator is always **stuffed** with food.*

teeming *(formal)*
an area of land or water that is teeming is very full of people or animals that live in that area: *The ocean here is **teeming with** fish of all kinds.* | *We walked through the teeming streets of the city.*
→ see **fill**

F

full

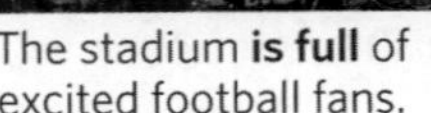
The stadium **is full** of excited football fans.

The trash can **is overflowing**.

The truck **is overloaded**.

The suitcase **is stuffed** with clothes.

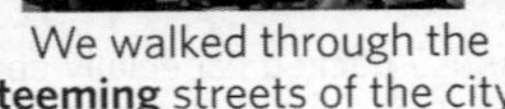
We walked through the **teeming** streets of the city.

The closet **is crammed** with all sorts of stuff.

fully *adverb* → see **completely**

fun[1] /fʌn/ *noun*

- fun
- enjoyment
- entertainment
- recreation
- leisure
- play

fun
pleasure that you get from doing something: *She plays the guitar **for fun**.* | *We had lots of fun when we went skiing last winter.*

enjoyment
enjoyment means the same as **fun** but sounds more formal: *Many people hike on the mountain trails **for enjoyment** and exercise.*

entertainment
things for people to watch and do in order to enjoy themselves: *On a cruise ship there is plenty of entertainment. There are movies, dances, games, and even a swimming pool.*

recreation
activities people do for fun. **Recreation** is often used in formal or official language: *What do the local people do for recreation in the winter?*
→ **GRAMMAR: Recreation** is often used before another noun: *The state has decided to make the lake and the park around it a recreation area, with boating and horse riding.*

leisure *also* **leisure time**
the time when you are not at school or working and can do things that you enjoy: *You need money and leisure to do some of these sports.*
→ **GRAMMAR: Leisure** is often used before another noun: *Playing video games is one of his favorite leisure activities.*

play
the things that children do for fun, such as using toys or playing games: *We watched all the kids **at play** in the park.* | *Children learn best through play.*
→ see **enjoy** and **play[1] (2)** for words meaning "to have fun"
→ see **pleasure**

fun[2] /fʌn/ *adjective*

- fun
- enjoyable

fun
if something is fun, you enjoy it because it is interesting or exciting: *Windsurfing is hard, but it's really fun.* | *It will be fun to see everyone again.*

enjoyable
pleasant and interesting. **Enjoyable** is more formal than **fun**, and you usually use it about activities: *I try to make math more enjoyable by using games.* | *We spent an enjoyable evening playing cards.*
→ see **nice**

function¹ *noun* → see **purpose**, **role**

function² *verb* → see **work¹**

fundamental *adjective* → see **basic**

fundamentally *adverb* → see **basically**

funds *noun* → see **money**

funny /ˈfʌni/ *adjective*

- ► funny
- ► hilarious
- ► humorous (*formal*)
- ► amusing
- ► witty
- ► comical

funny
making people laugh: *There are some very funny jokes in that movie.* | *Josh is so funny – he can always make me laugh.*

hilarious
very funny: *The ninth graders sang a hilarious song about a kid who loses his cell phone.*

humorous (*formal*)
funny. You use **humorous** about something someone writes or says rather than about the person: *Mark Twain wrote many humorous stories, on subjects from politics to frogs.*

amusing
funny and entertaining, but not in a way that makes you laugh out loud. **Amusing** sounds slightly formal or old-fashioned: *The speaker made a small but amusing mistake that made everyone smile.*

witty
good at talking in a funny way that is interesting or shows a lot of intelligence: *The film is full of witty conversation.*

comical
funny in a strange or silly way, especially without intending to be funny: *It was pretty comical watching my brother try to dance.*
→ see **strange** for **funny** meaning "strange"
→ see **humor**

ADVERBS
You can make the adjectives that mean **funny** into adverbs by using an **-ly** ending. The adverb **funnily** is not common, and the other words are used much more often: *The movie was hilariously funny.* | *He began dancing comically, trying to make the girls laugh.*

fur *noun* → see **hair**

furious *adjective* → see **angry**, Topic **Describing People's Emotions**

further *adjective* → see Function Word **more**

future /ˈfyutʃɚ/ *noun*

1 the time after now
- ► the future
- ► days/years to come

ANTONYMS → see **past¹**

2 the things that will happen in the future
- ► future
- ► fate
- ► destiny
- ► the outlook
- ► prospect

1 the time after now

the future
the time after now: *No one knows what will happen* ***in the future.*** | *What are your plans* ***for the future****? Will you go to college?*

days/years to come
the days, years, etc. that will happen in the future: ***In days to come,*** *you will look back at this experience and laugh.* | *The damage from the earthquake will affect people* ***for years to come.***
→ see **present²** (**2**)

2 the things that will happen in the future

future
the things that will happen to someone or something in the time after the present: *She is a very talented musician, and we think she has a great future.* | *The economy is bad, so we are concerned about the* ***future of*** *our country.*

fate
what will happen to someone or something in the future. You use **fate** when you are worried that something bad could happen, and when you do not have any choice about what

F

happens: *The city council meets today to decide the **fate of** the old library building.* | *The soldiers looked at each other. Was it going to be their fate to die here?*

destiny
the things that are going to happen to someone during his or her life, especially the important things. **Destiny** is literary and you use it when it seems like someone does not have a choice about what happens to him or her: *She felt that it was her destiny to work with poor people.*

the outlook
what people expect to happen in the future. **Outlook** is used especially to talk about the future of an economy, industry, or product: *The **outlook for** the U.S. economy is not good because unemployment is so high.*

prospect (AWL)
the idea or possibility that something will happen in the future: *The **prospect of** telling her parents she had failed made her feel like crying.*

→ see **next**[1]

F

gain[1] *verb* → see **get**

gain[2] *noun* → see **increase[2]**

gallery *noun* → see **museum**

gamble /ˈgæmbəl/ *verb*

- ► **gamble**
- ► **bet**
- ► **put $20/$50/$100 on something**
- ► **play the lottery**

gamble
to try to win money, for example by playing cards or guessing the result of a race or game: *They went to Las Vegas to gamble. | Even people who don't normally gamble will buy a lottery ticket. | He has lost a lot of money* ***gambling on*** *sports events.*

bet
to try to win money by guessing who will win a particular race, game, or competition: *Chris* ***bet*** *$50* ***on*** *the Patriots to win the Super Bowl.*

put $20/$50/$100 on something *also* **put/place a bet on something**
to bet an amount of money on a horse or team that you think will win: *We both* ***put $20 on a*** *horse called Troublemaker. | You can still* ***place a bet on*** *today's game.*

play the lottery
to gamble by buying a ticket with a set of numbers on it. If your numbers are picked during the game, you can win money or a prize. **Lotteries** are usually used to make money for a government or charity: *We play the lottery every week with the same numbers, but we've never won.*

game /geɪm/ *noun*

1 an activity with rules, in which you compete
- ► **game**
- ► **sport**

2 an occasion when you compete
- ► **game**
- ► **match**
- ► **set**
- ► **final**
- ► **round**

1 an activity with rules, in which you compete

game
an activity that you do for enjoyment, which has rules and which you play to win: *Chess is such a difficult game. | She likes playing computer games.*

sport
a physical activity in which players or teams compete against each other, for example by running or throwing a ball: *My favorite sports are basketball and tennis. | Which sports do you play at school?*

2 an occasion when you compete

game
an occasion when two people or teams compete against each other in a sport or other activity: *We won our first football game last night. | Let's play a* ***game of*** *cards.*

match
match means the same as **game**, but it is only used about some sports and games, such as tennis, chess, soccer, or boxing: *She won the tennis match in straight sets.*

set
one game in a group of games that you must play to win in some sports such as tennis or volleyball: *The Bruin volleyball team beat Pepperdine, three sets to two.*

final (AWL)
the last and most important game or race in a competition: *We have to play the Tigers in the final, and they're a very good team.*

round
one of the parts of a competition that you must win to get to the next part: *The second round of the NCAA championships starts tomorrow.*
→ see **competition**, **exercise[1]**, Topic **Sports and Exercise**

gap *noun* → see **difference**, **hole**

garbage /ˈgɑrbɪdʒ/ *noun*

- ► **garbage**
- ► **trash**
- ► **litter**
- ► **refuse** (*formal*)
- ► **waste** (*formal*)
- ► **junk**

garbage
things that you throw away. **Garbage** is used especially about food and containers for food: *We used paper plates for the party, so there was a lot of garbage afterward. | This garbage smells bad – let me take it out for you.*

trash
things that you throw away: *There was a pile of trash by the side of the road.* | *I cleaned up the backyard and took out three bags of trash.*
→ If you throw things **in the trash** or **in the garbage**, you put things in a bag or a can used for trash.

litter
pieces of paper, food containers, or other trash that people leave on the ground in public places: *I picked up the wrapper I dropped, so I wouldn't leave any litter on the street.*

refuse (*formal*)
garbage. You use **refuse** especially to talk about a lot of trash: *Each truck collects nine tons of refuse every day.*

waste (*formal*)
things that are left after you have used something. **Waste** is often used about the things that are left after an industrial process, for example making something in a factory: *Recycling is an important way to reduce waste.* | *Nuclear waste is stored deep underground for safety reasons.*

junk
old or unwanted things that have no use or value: *There was an old car without wheels, some broken garden tools, and lots of other junk in the backyard.*
→ see **nonsense**

G

gate *noun* → see Topic **Travel and Vacations**

gather *verb* → see **collect**, **meet**

gathering *noun* → see **meeting**, **party**

gaze[1] *verb* → see **look[1]**

gaze[2] *noun* → see **look[2]**

gear *noun* → see **equipment**

general /ˈdʒenərəl/ *adjective*

1 including all the main ideas, not the details
- ► general
- ► rough
- ► broad

2 involving many or most people
- ► general
- ► broad
- ► widespread
- ► universal

1 including all the main ideas, not the details

general
including the most basic information but not including all the details: *I have a general idea of what he wants me to do, but he'll give me more detailed instructions later.* | *The class is a general introduction to U.S. history.*

rough
not exact or complete, but with enough information for you to understand something: *I don't need to know everything, but give me a rough idea of what happened.*

broad
including the main ideas of something, and sometimes some things that are not as important. You often use **broad** with the words "category" or "outline," or with words such as "sense" or "definition": *We have a broad outline of the plan, but we still need to work out who is going to do each thing.* | *Sports, in a broad sense, includes everything from hopscotch to basketball.*

2 involving many or most people

general
relating to most people, or to most of the people in a group: *Email came into general use in the late 1990s and early 2000s* (=it was used by most people). | *The magazine covers topics of general interest, from fashion to sports.*

broad
including many different kinds of people: *The TV show is popular with a very broad audience, from children to senior citizens.*

widespread AWL
involving a lot of people in many places: *The president has widespread support among middle-class voters.*

universal
involving all the people in a group or in the world: *Not many people like the law, and there is almost universal agreement that it should be changed.*
→ see **common**

GRAMMAR CHECK: general

General and **broad** are usually used before a noun: *There is a broad market for the game.*

Widespread and **universal** do not have to be used before a noun: *The problem is widespread.*

generally /ˈdʒenərəli/ *adverb*

1 used when you are talking about the whole of something, and not particular parts of it
- generally
- in general
- mostly
- for the most part
- on the whole
- as a rule
- broadly

2 by many people
- generally
- broadly
- widely
- universally
- unanimously

1 used when you are talking about the whole of something, and not particular parts of it

generally
used when you are talking about most situations, and not the details of one situation: *I'm generally pleased with your work, but there are a few areas for improvement.* | *Generally, Americans eat too much fat and sugar.*

in general
in general means the same as **generally**: *In general, women live longer than men.*
→ GRAMMAR: You cannot use **in general** before a verb. Don't say: ~~I in general like science fiction~~. Say: *In general, I like science fiction.*

mostly
used when talking about most members of a group or most parts of something. **Mostly** is slightly more informal than **generally**: *The audience at the concert was mostly teenagers, but there were a few adults.*

for the most part
used when saying that something is true in most cases, but not in every case: *Raúl made a couple of small mistakes, but for the most part his English is very good.*

on the whole
used when something is true about the whole of something, even though it is not true about every part of it: *On the whole, I thought the movie was pretty good, but parts of it were kind of silly.*

as a rule *also* **as a general rule**
used when saying what happens in most situations. **As a rule** is sometimes used to give advice about what usually works best: *As a rule, roses grow best in full sunlight and shouldn't be planted in the shade.*

broadly
used when something is true in most ways, but not in every way: *The plot of the movie and the plot of the book are broadly the same, but some of the characters' names have been changed.*
→ see **mainly**, **usually**

2 by many people

generally
used when showing what most people think, or to show what most people can have or do: *Eating lots of junk food is generally considered unhealthy.* | *It could be five years before the medicine is generally available.*

broadly
broadly means the same as **generally**: *His ideas are broadly accepted by most scientists.*

widely
used to show that something is done by or available to many people in many places: *It used to be hard to find organic food in some places, but it is now widely available.*

universally
used to show that everyone in a group or the world does something: *"Huckleberry Finn" is universally accepted as a classic of American literature.*

unanimously
used to show that every person in a group has voted to do something: *The committee members unanimously approved the plan.*

generous *adjective* → see **kind²**, Topic **Describing People's Character**

gentle /ˈdʒentl/ *adjective*
- gentle
- light

gentle
not strong and without much force, in a pleasant way. Use **gentle** about wind or the way someone touches you: *A gentle breeze moved the tree tops.* | *He felt the gentle pressure of Jill's hand on his shoulder.*

G

light
without much force. Use **light** about wind or the way someone touches you: *He felt a light tap on his shoulder.*
→ see **kind²**

ADVERBS
You can make the adjectives that mean **gentle** into adverbs by using an **-ly** ending: *She gently stroked her son's hair.* | *David touched her lightly on her arm.*

gentleman *noun* → see **man**

genuine *adjective* → see **real**

get /get/ *verb*

1 to get something that someone gives to you
► get
► receive (*formal*)
► inherit
ANTONYMS → see **give**, **send (1)**
2 to get something by doing something
► get
► obtain (*formal*)
► acquire (*formal*)
► earn
► gain

1 to get something that someone gives to you

get
to be given something or be sent something: *I get about 50 emails every day.* | *Ben* ***got*** *a new computer* ***from*** *his parents* ***for*** *Christmas.*

receive (*formal*)
receive means the same as **get**: *Cecilia never received an invitation to the party.* | *She walked up to the stage to receive her award.*

inherit
to get something from someone after he or she has died: *Jim* ***inherited*** *a lot of money* ***from*** *his mother when she died.*

2 to get something by doing something

get
to start having something by finding it, asking for it, or paying for it: *She went to the bank to get some money.* | *How can I get more information about joining the club?* | *Where did you get those jeans?*

obtain (AWL) (*formal*)
obtain means the same as **get**: *Maps can be* ***obtained from*** *the tourist office.*

acquire (AWL) (*formal*)
to get or buy something expensive: *He acquired the land in 2003 and built a house on it.*
→ You can also use **acquire** to talk about getting knowledge or skills: *The course helps older people acquire computer skills.*

earn
to get money or something good for work you do, or for behaving well: *How much does Ann earn as a lawyer?* | *She* ***earned*** *the respect of her teammates* ***for*** *the way she played.* | *Class, you have* ***earned*** *some extra time outside* ***for*** *all the hard work you have done today.*

gain
to get something important or useful by trying hard or experiencing something: *He worked as an intern to gain experience.* | *The research helped us to gain a better understanding of how the brain works.*
→ see **go** for **get** meaning "to get to a place"
→ see **become**, **earn**
→ see **get away** at **escape**
→ see **get down** at **go down**
→ see **get in** at **get on**
→ see **get married** at **marry**
→ see **get out** at **avoid**, **get off**
→ see **get over** at **better (2)**
→ see **get soft** at **soften**
→ see **get to** at **come**
→ see **get up** at **stand**, **wake**

get back /ˌget ˈbæk/ *phrasal verb*

► get something back
► retrieve (*formal*)
► recover

get something back
to have something again after you have lost it or given it to someone: *Did you get your wallet back?* | *The airline lost my bags, and I hope that I will get them back.*

retrieve (*formal*)
to get something back after you have put or left it somewhere: *The lawyer left an important document at the office, so she had to go back to retrieve it.*
→ **Retrieve** is also used when a dog goes to get something and brings it back to its owner: *They teach the dogs to retrieve the birds that the hunters have shot.*

G

recover (AWL)
to get back something that was stolen or lost. **Recover** is used especially in official reports or news reports: *The police recovered two paintings that had been stolen from the museum.*

get off /ˌget ˈɔf/ *phrasal verb*

- ► get off
- ► get out
- ► leave (*formal*)

ANTONYMS → see **get on**

get off
to go out of a bus, train, or airplane: *We will get off at the next subway stop.* | *Everyone had to get off the bus when it broke down.*

get out
to go out of a car: *Stop the car. I want to get out.* | *He got out of the car to see what was going on.*

leave (*formal*)
to get off a bus, train, or airplane. **Leave** is used especially in official announcements and news reports: *Make sure to take all your belongings when you leave the aircraft.*

get on /ˌget ˈɔn/ *phrasal verb*

- ► get on
- ► get in
- ► catch
- ► board (*formal*)
- ► mount (*formal*)

ANTONYMS → see **get off**

get on
to go onto a bus, train, or plane: *We'll just get on and ask the bus driver where to get off.* | *I had trouble getting on the train with all my luggage.*

get in *also* **get into**
to go into a car: *Get in and put on your seat belt.* | *She got into a taxi and disappeared.*

catch
to manage to get on a bus, train, or plane and not miss it: *We need to catch the next bus to get to the meeting on time.*

board (*formal*)
board means the same as **get on** but is used especially in official language: *We will begin boarding the plane about 30 minutes before the flight.*

mount (*formal*)
to get onto a horse to ride it: *He mounted the horse and rode out toward the lake.*

get rid of /ˌget ˈrɪd ʌv/ *phrasal verb*

1 to remove or deal with something that is causing problems

- ► get rid of
- ► eliminate (*formal*)
- ► discard (*formal*)
- ► scrap
- ► abolish (*formal*)
- ► eradicate (*formal*)

2 to remove something you no longer want

- ► get rid of
- ► throw away
- ► throw out
- ► discard (*formal*)
- ► dispose of (*formal*)
- ► scrap

1 to remove or deal with something that is causing problems

get rid of
to remove or deal with something that is causing you trouble, such as an illness or problem: *He opened the window to get rid of the smell.* | *What can I do to get rid of this cough?*

eliminate (AWL) (*formal*)
to completely get rid of something that is unnecessary or unwanted: *The new treatment for this type of injury eliminates the need for surgery.*

discard (*formal*)
to get rid of ideas or suggestions because you do not think they are good: *We soon discarded that idea, as it was not practical.*

scrap
to decide not to use a plan or system because it is not working or not practical. **Scrap** is fairly informal: *The city has scrapped plans to build a new library because the cost is too high.*

abolish (*formal*)
to officially end a law or system, especially one that has existed for a long time: *Slavery was abolished in the U.S. after the Civil War.*

eradicate (*formal*)
to completely get rid of a disease or problem: *Modern medicine has eradicated the disease of smallpox.*

2 to remove something you no longer want

get rid of
to remove something that you no longer want, for example by giving it to someone or throwing it away: *It is time to get rid of these toys – you don't play with them anymore.*

throw away
to get rid of something that you do not want or need, usually by putting it in the garbage: *I threw away the empty box.* | *The cake tasted bad, so I threw it away.*

throw out
to get rid of something that you do not want in your house, usually by putting it in the garbage: *The orange was moldy, so I threw it out.* | *We threw out a lot of stuff when we moved.*

discard (*formal*)
to throw or leave something carelessly somewhere: *Empty bottles had been discarded on the beach.*

dispose of (*formal*)
to get rid of something that you do not need by putting it somewhere. You use **dispose of** especially about things that you must be careful with: *Dispose of cooking oil in the trash. Do not pour it down the drain.* | *The problem with nuclear energy is how to dispose of dangerous nuclear waste.*

scrap
to get rid of an old machine or vehicle so that the metal in it can be used for other things: *The old ship is being scrapped this year.*
→ see **remove**, **waste**

ghost /goʊst/ *noun*

- ghost
- spirit
- phantom
- specter

ghost
the spirit of a dead person that some people think they can see: *They say the captain's ghost still haunts the ship.* | *We sat around the campfire, telling ghost stories.*

spirit
the part of a dead person that continues to live after he or she dies: *They believe the spirits of their ancestors help to protect them.*
→ You can also use **spirit** about a creature without a physical body that has strange or magical powers: *My grandma wears a charm to protect herself against evil spirits.*

phantom
a frightening ghost: *The phantom appeared suddenly at the top of the staircase, dressed in a red robe.*

specter
specter means the same as **ghost** but is used mostly in literature and poems: *Some visitors to the theater say they have seen the **specter of** a murdered man.*

giant *adjective* → see **big**

gift *noun* → see **present**[2], **talent**

giggle *noun* → see **laugh**[2]

girl *noun* → see **woman**

girlfriend *noun* → see **friend**, Topic **Relationships and Marriage**

give *verb* → *go to pages 265-266*

give back /ˌgɪv ˈbæk/ *phrasal verb*

- give back
- hand back
- return (*formal*)
- restore (*formal*)

give back
to give something again to its owner or to the person who gave it to you: *You can use my pen, but please give it back.* | *She gave back all the money she had borrowed.*

hand back
to give something back to someone using your hand: *Alex read the letter and **handed it back to** her.*

return (*formal*)
to give something back to someone, especially after you have borrowed it: *She **returned** the notebook **to** him the next day.*

restore (AWL) (*formal*)
to give someone back something that was lost or taken from him or her: *The stolen paintings were **restored to** the museum.*

glad *adjective* → see **happy**

glamour *noun* → see **style**

glance[1] *verb* → see **look**[1]

glance[2] *noun* → see **look**[2]

global warming *noun* → see Topic **The Environment**

G

give /gɪv/ *verb*

1 to let someone have something
- ► give
- ► let someone have something
- ► share
- ► hand
- ► pass
- ► hand in
- ► submit (*formal*)
- ► dispense (*formal*)

ANTONYMS → see **take (2)**

2 to give something to all the members of a group
- ► give
- ► hand out
- ► distribute (*formal*)
- ► pass around

ANTONYMS → see **take (2)**

3 to give someone something that he or she needs or wants
- ► give
- ► provide (*formal*)
- ► serve
- ► deliver
- ► pass

ANTONYMS → see **get (1)**

4 to give someone an award
- ► give
- ► present
- ► award (*formal*)

ANTONYMS → see **get (1)**

5 to give money or things to help an organization do something
- ► give
- ► donate
- ► contribute

ANTONYMS → see **get (1)**

1 to let someone have something

give
to allow someone to have something, especially as a present: *Dad gave me his coat because I was cold.* | *The spy **gave** secret information **to** the enemy.* | *What did you **give** Angel **for** his birthday?*
→ Give can also mean "to put something in someone else's hand": *Give me your phone for a minute – I need to call my mom.* | *Please **give** this note **to** your mother.*

let someone have something
to give someone something that you have because he or she wants it or asks for it: *My cousin let me have his old bike when he got a new one.*

share
to let someone have part of something that belongs to you: *Will you **share** some of your chips **with** me?*

hand
to give something to someone else using your hand: *We **handed** our ticket **to** the woman at the door.*

pass
to take something from somewhere and put it into someone else's hand: *Could you pass me the ketchup?*

hand in
to give something such as a piece of work to a teacher or employer: *After you hand in your test, you may leave.*

submit (AWL) (*formal*)
to give an official document such as a plan or application to someone so that he or she can think about it and decide whether to accept it: *All applications must be submitted by the end of the month.*

dispense (*formal*)
to give something to someone, especially a particular amount of something. You use **dispense** especially about medicine: *Nurses dispense the medication at the same time every day.*

2 to give something to all the members of a group

give also **give out**
to let all the members of a group have something, especially when the thing you are

giving is free or is a gift: *Mrs. Roberts* ***gave*** *a piece of candy* ***to*** *each of the children.* | *The store is giving people free samples of the cookies.* | *The teacher gave out the workbooks.*

→ GRAMMAR: **Give** and **give out** mean the same thing, but you use them in different ways. You use **give** in the patterns "give someone something" or "give something to someone": *She gave the children candy.* | *She gave candy to the children.* You use **give out** in the patterns "give out something", "give something out" or "give something out to someone": *When you are all done, I'll give out the candy.* | *I'll give the candy out.* | *I'll give the candy out to the children.*

hand out *also* **pass out**
to give something to each person in a group by putting it in their hand: *There was a man outside the train station handing out newspapers.* | *The teacher asked me to pass out the tests to the class.*

distribute (AWL) *(formal)*
to give something to a large group of people, especially in an organized way: *The charity is* ***distributing*** *clothes and blankets* ***to*** *the refugees.*

pass around
to give something to one person, who then passes it to the next person in the group, so that everyone can see or use it: *We passed the pictures around the room so everyone could see.*

3 to give someone something that he or she needs or wants

give
to let someone have something that he or she needs: *The government is* ***giving*** *help* ***to*** *the flood victims.* | *My dad gave me a lot of advice when I was learning to ski.*

provide *(formal)*
to have something available for someone who needs it or wants it: *The hotel* ***provides*** *free parking* ***for*** *its guests.* | *Lunch will be provided at the meeting.*

serve
to give someone food or drinks as part of a meal: *The inn serves breakfast in the dining room until 10 a.m.*

deliver
to take a letter or package somewhere and give it to someone: *The mailman* ***delivered*** *the package* ***to*** *our house yesterday.*

pass
to give someone information that someone else has given to you: *The family stories have been* ***passed from*** *parents* ***to*** *children for several generations.*

4 to give someone an award

give
to decide which person should have an award and let him or her have it: *The school gave Ms. Gray the "teacher of the year" award.* | *They* ***give*** *the Nobel prize* ***to*** *people with outstanding achievements.*

present
to give something to someone in a formal or official way, for example at a ceremony: *The trophy will be* ***presented to*** *the winner by last year's winner.* | *He* ***presented*** *the winning team* ***with*** *a gold cup.*

award *(formal)*
to officially give someone an award, especially as a reward for something he or she has done: *The team members were* ***awarded*** *gold medals* ***for*** *their win.*

5 to give money or things to help an organization do something

give
to let an organization have money, food, or help that is needed to do something: *The school needs a lot of money, so please give generously.* | *After the earthquake, a lot of people* ***gave*** *money* ***to*** *the Red Cross.*

donate
to give money, food, or clothes to an organization that needs help or is helping other people: *Last year he* ***donated*** *$1,000* ***to*** *cancer research.*

contribute (AWL)
to give money or help to something that other people are also giving to: *The volunteers* ***contribute*** *their own time* ***to*** *the project.*

→ see **assign** for words meaning "to give someone a job to do"
→ see **give in** at **surrender**
→ see **give off** at **smell[2]**
→ see **give up** at **stop[1]**

hand out a test

present an award

globe *noun* → see **world**

gloomy *adjective* → see **cloudy**, **dark[1]**, **pessimistic**, **sad**

glow[1] *noun* → see **light[1]**

glow[2] *verb* → see **shine**

glue *verb* → see **stick[1]**

go /goʊ/ *verb*

1 to move to another place
- go
- come
- move
- get
- travel
- head
- make your way
- cross
- proceed (*formal*)

ANTONYMS → see **come (1)**

2 to go to a place with someone
- go with
- accompany
- escort
- join

3 to go to a place regularly
- go to
- attend (*formal*)
- be at
- be in

1 to move to another place

go
to walk, drive, run, etc. to another place: *Where are you going? | Every summer we* ***go to*** *see my grandparents in Iowa. | She leaves the office and goes home at about six o'clock.*

come
to move toward you or arrive at the place where you are: *Can you come here for a minute? I want to tell you something. | A huge truck was coming straight toward us.*

move
to go from one place or position to another: *Lily moved silently across the room.*
→ **Move** can also mean "to go to a new place to live": *He moved to New York to start a new job.*

get
to move or go somewhere quickly or with effort: *When we* ***got to*** *the other side of the river, we were very tired.*

travel
to go from one place to another, especially over long distances: *We traveled by train all over Europe.*

head
to go in a particular direction or toward a particular place: *The ship was* ***heading toward*** *Cuba.*

make your way
to go somewhere slowly or with difficulty: *The hikers slowly made their way through the snow.*

cross
to go from one side of something to another: *It is safest to cross the street at the corner.*

proceed (AWL) (*formal*)
to go in a particular direction. **Proceed** is used in formal and official announcements, for example at an airport: *Passengers flying to Miami should* ***proceed to*** *Gate 26.*

2 to go to a place with someone

go with
to go to a place with someone: *Are you going with them to the beach tomorrow? | My dad went to Canada with his brother in 1980.*

accompany (AWL)
to go somewhere with someone, especially in order to give him or her help or protection: *Sylvia* ***accompanied*** *her grandmother* ***to*** *the doctor's office. | Children under 12 must* ***be accompanied by*** *an adult in the swimming pool.*

escort
to go somewhere with someone, in order to make sure that he or she gets there safely or does not escape: *Soldiers* ***escorted*** *the Secretary of State* ***to*** *the meeting.*

join
to go somewhere in order to be with someone or do something with someone: *I am still working, but I'll join you at the restaurant a little later.*

3 to go to a place regularly

go to
to go regularly to a school, church, or other organization, especially because you belong to it: *I go to Milton Middle School. | She goes to Girl Scouts on Fridays. | We used to go to church a lot, but we don't go very much anymore.*

attend (*formal*)
to go to an event such as a meeting or class, or to go regularly to a school, church, or other organization: *I am the first child in my family to attend college. | Only twelve people attended the meeting.*

be at
to be studying at a particular school or college regularly: *Lars is at Indiana State University this year.*

be in
to be studying at a particular level of school or college: *I didn't know Rosa was already in college.*

→ see **become** for **go** meaning "to change in color or state"
→ see **leave**, **travel**[1]
→ see **go around** at **turn**[1]
→ see **go away** at **leave**
→ see **go back to** at **come**
→ see **go bad** at **decay**
→ see **go by** at **pass**[1]
→ see **go in** at **enter**
→ see **go off** at **explode**, **turn on/off**
→ see **go on** at **continue**
→ see **go out** at **turn on/off**
→ see **go through** at **check**[1], **experience**[2], **explain**, **suffer**

go across /ˌgoʊ əˈkrɔs/ *phrasal verb*

- go across
- cross
- span

go across
to start on one side of something and end on the other: *The bridge goes across the river.* | *Wide black stripes go across the fish's body.*

cross
cross means the same as **go across** but sounds slightly more formal: *Use the path that crosses the park – it's faster.*

span
if a bridge spans something, it reaches from one side of it to the other: *An old railroad bridge spans the river at the edge of town.*
→ see **cross**

goal /goʊl/ *noun*

- goal
- aim
- target
- objective (*formal*)
- ambition
- mission
- intention
- agenda

goal (AWL)
something that you hope to achieve in the future: *I've been exercising and my goal is to lose 20 pounds.* | *The company's long-term goal is to have the top-selling brand in the country.*

aim
something that you are trying to achieve: *In this game, the aim is to get your pieces to the other side of the board.*

target (AWL)
the amount or level that you are trying to get, make, do, etc.: *We wanted to raise $10,000, and we have almost reached our target.*

objective (AWL) (*formal*)
something that you are working hard to achieve, for example in business or in a war: *The soldiers had achieved their objective of destroying the ship.*

ambition
something that you personally want to achieve in the future in your work or life, although it may be difficult: *My ambition is to become a famous singer.*

mission
something important that an organization or person wants to achieve: *Our mission is to ensure that every child has enough to eat.*

intention
something that you are planning to do: *The senator has announced his* ***intention to*** *quit politics.* | *I have no* ***intention of*** *apologizing – he should apologize to me!*

agenda
a list of things that an organization is planning to do: *Protecting the environment is high on our agenda.*
→ see **purpose**

go back /ˌgoʊ ˈbæk/ *phrasal verb*

- go back
- come back
- return (*formal*)

go back
to go to a place where you were before: *I went to Florida when I was little, and I would love to go back.* | *We* ***go back to*** *school at the end of August.*

come back
to come to a place again after going somewhere else: *When are you going to come back and visit us again?*

return (*formal*)
to go or come back to a place where you were before. **Return** is more formal than **go back** or **come back**: *Val was studying in Mexico for a year, but she just returned.* | *He hoped that one day he would be able to* ***return to*** *London.*
→ **GRAMMAR: Return** is not followed by "back." Don't say: ~~She just returned back~~.

go down /ˌgoʊ ˈdaʊn/ *phrasal verb*

- ► go down
- ► get down
- ► descend (*formal*)
- ► set
- ► sink

ANTONYMS → see **go up**

go down
to move to a lower level: *We went down to the basement and waited for the storm to pass.* | *My ring went down the drain before I could catch it.*

get down
to move to a lower level using effort: *Get down from the roof before you hurt yourself!*

descend (*formal*)
to go down: *My ears popped as the plane started to descend.* | *She descended the staircase.*

set
when the sun or moon sets, it moves lower in the sky and disappears: *As the sun set, the sky turned orange and purple.*

sink
to move slowly downward. **Sink** sounds fairly literary: *Her chin sank onto her chest and she started to cry.*
→ **Sink** is also used in stories and descriptions to talk about the sun or moon as it sets: *As the sun sank lower, the sky turned orange and pink.*
→ see **decrease²**, **sink**

good *adjective* → *go to pages 272-273*

good-looking *adjective* → see **beautiful**, Topic **Describing People's Looks**

goods *noun* → see **product**

go up /ˌgoʊ ˈʌp/ *phrasal verb*

- ► go up
- ► climb
- ► ascend (*formal*)
- ► rise
- ► soar

ANTONYMS → see **go down**

go up
to move to a higher level or position: *Sandy went up to the top of the hill to look at the view.* | *Go up those stairs, and the bathroom is on the right.*

climb
if you climb a tree, a mountain, or some stairs, you go up toward the top: *Boys were climbing trees next to the river.*

ascend (*formal*)
ascend means the same as **go up**: *She ascended the narrow winding staircase.* | *The plane ascended to 30,000 feet above sea level.*

rise
to go up to a higher level, especially by floating in water or air: *The bubbles rise to the surface of the water and burst.*
→ When the sun or moon **rises**, it appears at the edge of the sky and moves upward in the sky: *The sun will rise at 7:00 in the morning tomorrow.*

soar
to go quickly up, very high in the air. **Soar** sounds literary, and you use it in descriptions, stories, and poems: *We watched the eagle soar high above the trees.*
→ see **climb¹**, **increase¹**

govern /ˈgʌvɚn/ *verb*

- ► govern
- ► run
- ► rule
- ► reign
- ► be in power
- ► hold office

govern
to legally control a country, state, or city and make all the decisions and laws: *Both political parties must work together to govern the state.* | *The military is governing the country until elections are held.*

run
run means the same as **govern** but sounds more informal: *If you don't like the way Congress is running the country, then vote for people in the other party.*

rule
to govern a country. You use **rule** when a king, queen, military leader, or foreign government has power over a country and the people in it: *India was ruled by the British until it became independent in 1947.*

reign
to be the king or queen of a country: *Pharaohs reigned over Egypt for centuries.*

be in power
to be the political leader or group that controls a country at a particular time: *Republicans plan to cut taxes when they are in power again.*

hold office
to have an important position in government, especially one that you are elected to. You can also use **hold office** about people who are chosen for a position by an elected official: *Senators hold office for six years between elections.*

government /ˈgʌvɚmənt/ *noun*

- ► the government
- ► administration
- ► regime
- ► leadership

the government
the group of people who govern a country or state: *No one wants the government to tell people what to do in their private lives. | The agreement was signed by the governments of several Latin American countries.*

administration (AWL)
the U.S. president and the people who work for him or her: *The new administration plans to change many of the last president's policies.*

regime (AWL)
a government, especially one that is strict or has not been elected: *Citizens protested against the military regime and demanded political change.*

leadership
the leader of a government and the other powerful or important people in that government: *"We are working with the leadership of several European countries to fix the problem," said the president.*
→ see **management**, Topic **Government and Politics**

graceful /ˈgreɪsfəl/ *adjective*

- ► graceful
- ► smooth
- ► elegant
- ► flowing

ANTONYMS → see **clumsy**

graceful
moving in a smooth and attractive way: *He is a very fast and graceful runner. | In the performance, dancers imitate the graceful movements of birds.*

smooth
with no sudden movements or changes in direction: *The plane made such a smooth landing that at first I didn't realize we were on the ground.*

elegant
very beautiful and graceful: *I love the elegant way she moves her arms when she dances.*

flowing *also* **fluid**
moving smoothly like water. You use **fluid** especially with the word "motion" or "movement": *You have to swing the golf club in one flowing motion. | The jaguar ran with fluid movements and amazing speed.*

ADVERBS
You can make the adjectives **graceful**, **smooth**, and **elegant** into adverbs by using an **-ly** ending: *The dancer lifted her arms gracefully over her head. | The curtain smoothly rose, showing a bare stage.*

grade[1] /greɪd/ *noun*

- ► grade
- ► score
- ► results
- ► grade point average

grade (AWL)
a letter or number that shows how good a student's work is: *Heidi works hard and gets good grades in all her classes. | "What* ***grade*** *did you get on your paper?" "I got a B."*

score
the number of points that you get on a test: *I only missed one question on the test, and I got the highest score in the class.*

results
the score or grade you get on a test, especially a test that many students in many schools take: *The students' test results were not as good as we had hoped.*

grade point average *also* **GPA**
a number that represents all of a student's grades. Each grade is worth points, and you add the points together and then divide them by the number of grades: *You need a high school GPA of at least 2.5 to be accepted at the university.*
→ see **quality**, Topic **Education**

grade[2] *verb* → see **judge[2]**, **rate**

gradual *adjective* → see **slow**

gradually *adverb* → see **slowly**

graduate *verb* → see **pass[1]**, Topic **Education**

grass *noun* → see **lawn**

grateful /ˈgreɪtfəl/ *adjective*

- grateful
- thankful
- appreciative (*formal*)

grateful
wanting to thank someone who has been kind or helpful: *I am very **grateful for** all the help I have been given.* | *She was **grateful to** her parents for their support.* | *The doctor received a thank-you letter from a grateful patient.*

thankful
feeling glad about something, especially that something bad did not happen or is over: *We have so much to be **thankful for** – a house to live in, enough money, and our health.* | *I am so **thankful that** no one was hurt.*

appreciative (*formal*)
showing that you are pleased and feel grateful for something that someone has done: *The teacher gives them a lot of help, and the students are very appreciative.*

SYNONYM CHECK

Grateful or thankful?

You use **grateful** to say that you want to thank someone, and you use **thankful** when you are pleased or relieved about something that has happened: *I am grateful to all the doctors who helped me.* | *I am thankful that the doctors were able to help me.*

ADVERBS

You can make the adjectives that mean **grateful** into adverbs by using an **-ly** ending: *"Thank you for your help," Lisa said gratefully.* | *Thankfully, Ben is recovering well from his operation.*

gray *adjective* → see **cloudy**, **rainy**, Topic **The Weather**

great *adjective* → see **good**

greatest *adjective* → see **best**

green *adjective* → see Topic **The Environment**

greenhouse effect *noun* → see Topic **The Environment**

greet *verb* → see **welcome**

grief *noun* → see **sadness**

grieve /griv/ *verb*

- grieve
- mourn

grieve
to feel very sad because someone you love has died: *She is still **grieving for** her husband, who died last year.*

mourn
to feel very sad because someone has died, or to show that you feel sad: *The nation is mourning the death of the former president.*

grill *verb* → see **cook**[1]

grimy *adjective* → see **dirty**

grin[1] *verb* → see **smile**[1]

grin[2] *noun* → see **smile**[2]

grip[1] *noun* → see **hold**[2]

grip[2] *verb* → see **hold**[1]

ground /graʊnd/ *noun*

- the ground
- land
- earth
- terrain
- floor

the ground
the solid surface of the earth that we stand on: *I found a dollar **on the ground** today.* | *The package slipped out of my hands and fell **to the ground**.*

land
the solid part of the earth's surface that is not covered by water: *Turtles live in the water, but they lay their eggs **on land**.*

earth
the surface of the planet that we live on. You use **earth** especially when talking about large areas of land: *The huge explosion made the earth shake.*

terrain
a particular type of land: *It is difficult to travel across Afghanistan's mountainous terrain.*

floor
the ground in an ocean, forest, or cave. You often put "ocean," "forest," or "cave" before the word **floor** in this meaning: *The forest floor was covered with pine needles.* | ***The floor of** the cave was covered with bones.*

→ **Floor** also means "the surface that you stand on in a building": *There weren't any chairs, so we had to sit **on the floor**.*

→ see **dirt**, **land**

G

good /gʊd/ *adjective*

1 of a high standard or quality
► good
► nice
► decent
► impressive
► fine

2 very good
► excellent
► great
► terrific
► wonderful
► fantastic
► incredible
► superb (*formal*)
► awesome (*informal*)

3 very good in a way that is unusual or surprising
► amazing
► outstanding
► exceptional
► extraordinary
► phenomenal
► spectacular

4 behaving well
► good
► polite
► well-behaved
► obedient

5 behaving in a way that shows you know the difference between right and wrong
► good
► decent
► respectable
► moral
► honorable
► ethical

ANTONYMS → see **bad, evil¹**

1 of a high standard or quality

good
of a high standard or quality: *I just read a good book – I think you would like it.* | *Your grades need to be really good to get into Harvard.*

nice
pleasant, attractive, and of good quality: *That's a nice dress. Where did you buy it?* | *They live in a nice house in the suburbs.*

decent
acceptable and good enough: *The restaurant is nice inside and the food is decent.* | *He makes a decent salary, but he isn't rich.*

impressive
if something is impressive, it is very good and you admire it: *The students studied really hard, and their test scores were impressive.* | *It's an impressive museum with lots to do for kids.*

fine
good and of a very high quality. **Fine** things are often valuable, rare, or skillfully made: *The restaurant is known for its excellent food and fine wines.*

2 very good

excellent
extremely good: *His English was excellent – he didn't make a single mistake.* | *The car is five years old, but it's still in excellent condition.*

great
very good or enjoyable, or of high quality: *The party was great – you should have come with us!* | *You did a great job decorating this room.*

terrific
extremely good or enjoyable: *That's a terrific idea! Let's get started!* | *Sharon, you look terrific in that dress.*

wonderful
very good and enjoyable in a way that makes you very pleased: *You're having a baby? That's wonderful news!*

fantastic
extremely good in a way that makes you excited and happy: *The view from the top of the mountain was fantastic!*

incredible
extremely good in a surprising and exciting way: *The trip was incredible – we saw so many interesting things.*

superb (*formal*)
extremely good and of the highest quality: *The food was superb, and everyone ate a lot.*

awesome (*informal*)
extremely good extremely good: *Have you heard her latest album? It's awesome.*

GRAMMAR CHECK: good

Don't use "very" with adjectives that mean "very good." Don't say: ~~*It was very wonderful*~~. Say: *It was wonderful* or *It was really/absolutely wonderful.*

3 very good in a way that is unusual or surprising

amazing
extremely good in a surprising way: *He is an amazing soccer player – I don't know how he scores so many goals.* | *You've done an amazing job of fixing up the house.*

outstanding
extremely good and better than most others: *She won an award for her outstanding essay.*

exceptional
very good in a way that is unusual: *There are a lot of smart kids in the class, but Tomaso is exceptional.*

extraordinary
better or more impressive than almost all others: *Helen of Troy was known for her extraordinary beauty.*

phenomenal AWL
unusually good or impressive because of a rare quality or ability: *George Harrison of the Beatles was a phenomenal guitar player.*

spectacular
something such as a view or performance that is spectacular is very impressive and exciting to look at: *The firework show was spectacular.*

ADVERBS

You can make the adjectives that mean "very good" into adverbs by using an **-ly** ending, except for the word **great**: *Peter was playing excellently.* | *The food was superbly cooked.* | *She is an amazingly fast runner.* | *In the mountains, the stars seem spectacularly bright.*

4 behaving well

good
a child or animal who is good behaves in the way he or she is expected to: *If you're good, we'll have ice cream for dessert.* | *She is such a good little girl; she always wants to help her mother.*

polite
a polite person behaves nicely and in a way that shows respect for other people: *Be polite and say "thank you."*

well-behaved
good and polite a well-behaved child is polite and does what he or she is expected to do: *The children were very well behaved at the restaurant.*

obedient
an obedient child or animal always does what a rule or someone in authority tells him or her to do: *The dog is obedient and very calm around children.*

ADVERBS

You can make the adjectives **polite** and **obedient** into adverbs by using an **-ly** ending. The adverb for **good** is **well**: *The children behaved very well.* | *"Thank you," she said politely.* | *The dog followed her obediently around the park.*

5 behaving in a way that shows you know the difference between right and wrong

good
behaving in the way society expects people to behave, and following society's rules about what is right and wrong. **Good** can be used about people or their actions: *John is a good guy – you can always count on him to help.* | ***It was good of** you **to** return the money.*

decent
decent people are good and honest: *Her husband is a decent dependable man.*

respectable
someone who is respectable behaves in a way that society respects and thinks is morally correct: *She comes from a respectable family, so her arrest was a surprise.*

moral
always doing what you know is right because you have strong ideas about what is right and wrong. **Moral** can be used about people or their actions: *Carol would never lie – she is very moral.*

honorable
deserving respect or praise for being good, fair, or honest. **Honorable** can be used about people or their actions: ***It was honorable of** him **to** say he made a mistake and not lie about it.*

ethical AWL
morally good or correct, and following the rules of society or a particular profession: *Is it ethical to give patients the drug without their permission?*

→ see **delicious** for good tasting, **satisfactory** for good enough, **skilled** for good at doing something and talented

→ see **appropriate**, **better**, **best**, **well**

ADVERBS

You can make the adjectives that mean "behaving in a good way" into adverbs by using an **-ly** ending. The adverb for **good** is **well**: *John offered to pay for the window he had broken, and his father said, "Well done."* | *Stealing is morally wrong.* | *The soldiers have served their country honorably.*

group /grup/ *noun*

1 a group of people
- ► group
- ► crowd
- ► committee
- ► team
- ► cast
- ► crew
- ► gang
- ► mob
- ► band
- ► party

2 a group of things
- ► group
- ► set
- ► collection
- ► bunch
- ► bundle
- ► cluster
- ► batch
- ► clump

3 a group of animals
- ► group
- ► herd
- ► flock
- ► pack
- ► school
- ► swarm
- ► litter

G

1 a group of people

group
several people that are together in the same place: *A **group of** children were playing a game.* | *The teacher asked the students to do the exercise in groups of four.* | *People were standing **in groups** on the dance floor.*

crowd
a large group of people, especially people who are close together: *People in the crowd started pushing forward to get near the stage.*

committee
a small group of people in an organization who have been chosen to make official decisions: *The finance committee will meet again next Wednesday.*

team (AWL)
a group of people who compete against another group in a sport or game: *There are 25 players on a baseball team, but only 9 play at one time.*
→ You also use **team** about a group of people who work together to achieve something: *The school has an excellent team of teachers.*

cast
all the people who act in a play or movie: *The cast includes some of the greatest actors of all time.*

crew
the people who work on an airplane or ship: *The flight crew served drinks to the passengers.*

gang
an organized group of young people in a city, who are involved in crime or violence: *Many of the neighborhood's young people join gangs and get in trouble with the police.*

mob
a large group of people who are noisy or angry and difficult to control: *The angry mob set fire to cars and buildings.*

band
a group of people who are together because

group

crowd

crew

cast

they have the same belief or purpose: *He was the leader of a **band of** rebels.*

→ **Band** also means "a group of people who play music together, especially popular music": *He plays drums in a band.*

party
a group of people who go somewhere together or do a job together: *A **party of** tourists was being shown around the church.* | *The search party is still looking for the boy who is lost in the woods.*

2 a group of things

group
several things that are together in the same place: *There is a small **group of** islands just off the coast.* | *A **group of** family photographs hangs on the wall.*

set
a group of similar things that belong together: *I bought a new **set of** towels for the bathroom.*

collection
a group of similar things that have been put together because they are interesting, valuable, or attractive: *Andrea has a **collection of** Japanese vases.* | *My brother's stamp collection is worth a lot of money.*

bunch
a group of things that grow together or are tied together, for example bananas, grapes, flowers, or keys: *She put a **bunch of** red grapes out for the party.*

→ In informal English, **bunch** is often used to mean a lot of similar things that are together: *There was a bunch of magazines on the table.*

bundle
a group of things that are usually tied together, especially papers, letters, clothes, or sticks: *They unloaded **bundles of** newspapers from the back of the truck.*

cluster
a group of things that are close together: *There was a **cluster of** buildings at one end of the park.*

batch
a group of similar things that are all dealt with together at the same time: *The next **batch of** cookies is ready to be baked.* | *The work is given to the employee in batches that must be completed by a deadline.*

clump
a group of trees or plants growing closely together: *The soldiers were hiding in a **clump of** trees.*

3 a group of animals

group
several animals that are together in the same place. You usually use one of the more specific words below to talk about groups of animals: *Dolphins travel in small groups called pods.*

herd
a group of cows, deer, or elephants that live together: *A **herd of** cows was blocking the road.*

flock
a group of sheep, goats, or birds: *The farmer has over 500 sheep in his flock.*

pack
a group of dogs, wolves, or similar animals that live and hunt together: *The deer was being chased by a **pack of** hungry wolves.*

school
a large group of fish that swim together: *A **school of** small fish swam around her feet.*

swarm
a large group of insects that move together: *In the evening **swarms of** mosquitoes started biting us.*

group

a **bunch** of grapes

a **bundle** of newspapers

a **group** of islands

a **set** of screwdrivers

a **cluster** of buildings

a stamp **collection**

litter
a group of baby animals born to one mother at the same time: *She chose the smallest puppy in the litter to take home.*

grow /groʊ/ *verb*

1 to become bigger and more developed
- ► **grow**
- ► **grow up**
- ► **develop**
- ► **mature** (*formal*)
- ► **get bigger**
- ► **get taller**
- ► **flourish** (*formal*)
- ► **thrive**
- ► **sprout**

2 to make plants grow
- ► **grow**
- ► **plant**
- ► **cultivate** (*formal*)
- ► **raise**

1 to become bigger and more developed

grow
to become bigger and change into a more adult form over a period of time: *Amy grew six inches last year.* | *The seeds will eventually grow into trees.*

grow up
if a person grows up, he or she gradually changes from being a child to being an adult. You often use **grow up** to talk about the place or situation in which someone becomes an adult: *Sylvia grew up in a small town, but she moved to the city after college.*

develop
if a child, animal, or plant develops, it gradually gets bigger and changes into a more adult form: *The baby develops very quickly during the first few months of pregnancy.*

mature (AWL) (*formal*)
to become fully grown or developed. **Mature** is used especially in scientific or medical language: *As the fish matures, its colors change.*

get bigger
to grow and become bigger or taller: *As the chickens get bigger, they will lay bigger eggs.*

get taller
to grow and become taller, especially in a short period of time: *Have you gotten taller? You look so grown-up.*

flourish (*formal*)
to grow well and be very healthy. **Flourish** sounds literary: *Most plants will flourish in the rich soil here.*

thrive
thrive means the same as **flourish**: *This particular tree thrives in the hot and damp conditions of the rainforest.*

sprout
if vegetables, seeds, or plants sprout, they start to grow out of the ground and produce their first leaves: *Move the pots outside when the seeds begin to sprout.*

2 to make plants grow

grow
to put plants or seeds in the ground and help them develop, for example by putting water on them: *We're trying to grow lettuce and tomatoes in the garden this year.* | *Small farmers in the region grow cotton to sell.*

plant
to put plants or seeds in the ground to grow: *Help me plant these flowers in front of the house.*

cultivate (*formal*)
to grow crops and plants by preparing the land for them. **Cultivate** is used especially in scientific language: *They have been cultivating grapes there for thousands of years.*

raise
to grow crops so they can be used as food: *Redding owns a 400-acre farm where he raises cotton.*
→ **Raise** can also mean "to look after animals as they grow so that they can be sold or used as food": *He raised cattle in Nebraska when he was young.*
→ see **become**, **increase**[1]

grown-up[1] *adjective* → see **mature**

grown-up[2] *noun* → see **adult**[1]

growth *noun* → see **increase**[2]

grumpy /'grʌmpi/ *adjective*

- ► **grumpy** (*informal*)
- ► **irritable**
- ► **crabby** (*informal*)
- ► **bad-tempered**
- ► **moody**
- ► **sullen**
- ► **sulky**

grumpy (*informal*) *also* **grouchy**
feeling unhappy or annoyed, and likely to become angry easily or to complain a lot: *Dad is grouchy this morning because he didn't get any*

sleep. | *When I'm feeling grumpy, I just stay in my room all day.*

irritable
irritable means the same as **grumpy**, but sounds more formal and is the best choice when you are writing: *Little children often get irritable and start crying when they are tired.*

crabby (*informal*)
crabby means the same as **grumpy**: *The crabby old man next door yells at us if we run onto his lawn.*

bad-tempered
often or always irritable or angry: *He complains about everything. I think he is getting more bad-tempered as he gets older.*

moody
someone who is moody feels very different at different times so that sometimes he or she is happy and at other times he or she is irritable: *Your sister has been moody lately. Do you know what's wrong?*

sullen
not saying anything and looking slightly angry: *She sat there looking sullen and refused to answer my questions.*

sulky
showing that you are angry or upset by being unfriendly and looking unhappy: *The boy stood there looking sulky as his parents scolded him.*

ADVERBS
You can make the adjectives **grumpy**, **irritable**, **moody**, **sullen**, and **sulky** into adverbs by using an **-ly** ending: *"I don't want breakfast," he said grumpily.* | *She wondered irritably why he wasn't helping her.* | *Carl stood sullenly by the truck, watching her.*

guard¹ *noun* → see **protection**

guard² *verb* → see **protect**

guess¹ /ges/ *verb*

- ► guess
- ► take a guess
- ► estimate
- ► underestimate
- ► overestimate
- ► speculate (*formal*)

guess
to answer a question or decide something when you are not sure if you are right: *I didn't know all the answers on the test, so I had to guess some of them.* | *Did Lena say she was pregnant, or are you just guessing?*

take a guess *also* **make a guess**
take a guess means the same as **guess** but sounds slightly more informal: *How old do you think I am? Take a guess.* | *I can't even* ***make a guess about*** *who will win the election.*

estimate (AWL)
to make a guess about a number or amount based on the information you know: *Police* ***estimate that*** *there were over 10,000 people at the march.*

underestimate (AWL)
to think that something is smaller, cheaper, less important, or easier than it really is: *We underestimated how long it would take to get there, so we were late.*

overestimate (AWL)
to think that something is bigger, longer, harder, or more important than it really is: *They overestimated the number of people who would come, so they had way too much food.* | *Are scientists overestimating the importance of climate change, or will it really have a big effect on our lives?*

speculate (*formal*)
to guess about the possible causes or effects of something, without knowing all the facts: *People are always* ***speculating about*** *what the president will do, but no one really knows.*

guess² /ges/ *noun*

- ► guess
- ► estimate
- ► speculation (*formal*)

guess
an attempt to answer a question or decide something when you are not sure if you are right: *She got my age right on the first guess.* | *Who do you think I saw today? I'll give you three guesses.*

estimate (AWL)
a guess about the number or amount of something that you make by using information that you know: *We need an* ***estimate of*** *the number of people who will come, even if it's not exact.* | *The estimate for the car repair was $650, but it actually cost a little more.*

speculation (*formal*)
the act of guessing about the possible causes or effects of something, without knowing all the facts: *There has been a lot of* ***speculation about*** *why the mayor resigned, but nobody really knows.*

G

guest /gest/ noun

- guest
- visitor
- company

guest
someone who you invite to stay in your home or invite to an event: *I put out some clean towels for our guests.* | *There were 200 guests at the wedding.*

visitor
someone who comes to visit a person or place: *I had an unexpected visitor the other day – my friend Lisa, who lives in Washington now.* | *Most **visitors to** the area enjoy the peace and quiet.*

company
if you have company, people are visiting you in your home: *We're having company this weekend – some friends of my dad's.*
→ see **customer**

guide *verb* → see **lead**[1]

guilt /gɪlt/ noun

- guilt
- shame
- remorse
- conscience

guilt
a sad feeling you have when you have done something that you know is wrong: *I felt a lot of **guilt about** being so mean to her.* | *After stealing the money, she felt so much guilt that she returned it.*

shame
a strong feeling of guilt and embarrassment that you have after doing something that is bad or wrong, especially something that other people know about: *She felt a sense of **shame for** lying to her husband.*

remorse
a feeling that you are sorry for doing something very bad: *If he really feels remorse for his crimes, then he would stop stealing.*

conscience
the feeling inside you that tells you whether it is right or wrong to do something: *Jana's guilty conscience finally made her give the money back.*
→ see **embarrassment**, **shame**

guilty /'gɪlti/ adjective

1 feeling bad about something you have done
- guilty
- embarrassed
- ashamed

2 responsible for something bad that has happened
- guilty
- responsible
- to blame
- at fault

ANTONYMS → see **innocent**

1 feeling bad about something you have done

guilty
feeling unhappy and sorry because you have done something that you know is wrong: *I feel really **guilty about** not inviting Dave to come with us.* | *Ann looked so guilty that we knew she had broken the window.*
→ You can also talk about someone having *a guilty feeling* or having *a guilty look*.

embarrassed
feeling silly and unhappy about something you have done wrong, and worried about what other people will think of you: *I was really embarrassed when I called Jason the wrong name.*

ashamed
feeling guilty and very embarrassed about something bad you have done, especially something other people know about: *She was feeling so **ashamed of** cheating on the test that she went to the teacher to tell her.*
→ You can also use **ashamed of yourself** with a similar meaning: *He was **ashamed of himself for** being rude to his grandmother.*
Don't say ~~an ashamed boy~~. Say: *The boy is ashamed.*
→ see **embarrassed**, **sorry**

ADVERBS
You can make **guilty** into an adverb by using an **-ly** ending: *"Did you break it?" his mother asked, and he nodded guiltily.*

2 responsible for something bad that has happened

guilty
if someone is guilty of a crime or doing something wrong, he or she did it: *The jury found Jones **guilty of** murder.* | *Edwards is **guilty of** breaking the rules and has been asked to leave the club.*

responsible
if someone or something is responsible for something bad, he, she, or it caused it to happen: *Police believe they know who is **responsible for** the burglary.*

to blame
if someone or something is to blame for something bad, he, she, or it caused it to happen and should be blamed: ***Some people say fast food is to blame for** many of the nation's health problems.*

at fault
if someone is at fault for something bad, he or she did something wrong that caused it to happen: *Maria was in a car accident, but the other driver **was at fault.***
→ see **blame**[1] for words meaning "to say that someone made something bad happen"
→ see Topic **Describing People's Emotions**

guy *noun* → see **man**

gym *noun* → see Topic **Sports and Exercise**

Hh

habit /ˈhæbɪt/ *noun*

1 something you do regularly
- ► **habit**
- ► **mannerism**
- ► **routine**
- ► **ritual**

2 something bad that you do regularly and cannot stop easily
- ► **habit**
- ► **addiction**
- ► **vice** (*formal*)

1 something you do regularly

habit
something that you do often or regularly, often without thinking about it: *Regular exercise is a good habit.* | *She has a habit of pausing for a second before she talks.*

mannerism
a way of speaking or moving that a person often uses: *The way she flips her hair and some of her other mannerisms are so annoying.*

routine
the usual things that someone does every day or every week: *Getting up, taking a shower, and going to school are all part of Antonio's daily routine.*

ritual
something that you do regularly and in the same way each time: *My son's bedtime ritual includes a bath, a story, and a song.*

2 something bad that you do regularly and cannot stop easily

habit *also* **bad habit**
something that you do often or regularly, even though you do not want to, because you cannot stop yourself: *I know that smoking is a bad habit, and I'm trying to quit.* | *She has a* ***habit of*** *biting her nails.*

addiction
a strong physical need to take a drug regularly, especially a drug that is harmful to you: *He lost his job because of his* ***addiction to*** *drugs.*

vice (*formal*)
something you do regularly that is bad for your health or that society thinks is wrong. **Vice** sounds fairly literary: *Drinking and gambling were two of her many vices.*

→ see **practice**[1]

hair /her/ *noun*

- ► **hair**
- ► **fur**
- ► **mane**

hair
the long thin things that grow from your head: *Jose has black hair and brown eyes.* | *She pulled her hair back from her face and tied it with a ribbon.*
→ **GRAMMAR: Hair** cannot be used in the plural with this meaning. Don't say: ~~*She has brown hairs*~~. Say: *She has brown hair.*

fur
the thick hair that covers an animal's body: *Rabbits have really soft fur.*

mane
the long hair on the neck of a horse or male lion: *You could tell it was a male lion because of its big mane.*

hair

hairdresser /ˈherˌdresɚ/ *noun*

- ► **hairdresser**
- ► **stylist**
- ► **barber**

hairdresser
someone whose job is to cut and arrange people's hair, especially women's hair: *I asked the hairdresser to give me a new hairstyle for the wedding.*

stylist
someone whose job is to cut and arrange people's hair. **Stylist** sounds a little more fashionable than **hairdresser**: *Renee is the top stylist at the salon, and she cuts a lot of famous people's hair.*

barber
a man whose job is to cut men's hair: *Joel goes to the barber every six weeks for a haircut.*

halfway /ˌhæfˈweɪ/ *adjective, adverb*

- ► halfway
- ► midway
- ► central

halfway
in the middle between two places or events: *We were **halfway to** the baseball game when it started raining, so we just kept going. | I left the theater **halfway through** the movie, so I don't know what happened at the end.*

midway
at the middle point between two places: *Wilmington, Delaware, is roughly **midway between** Washington, D.C., and New York City.*

central
in the center of an area: *The apartment is in a fairly central location, near subway stops and good restaurants.*

ADVERBS

You can make the adjective **central** into an adverb by using an **-ly** ending: *The hotel is centrally located in the downtown area.*

hall /hɔl/ *noun*

1 a long narrow area to walk along in a building
- ► hall
- ► hallway
- ► corridor
- ► aisle
- ► passageway

2 the area inside a building near the front door
- ► hall
- ► hallway
- ► entryway
- ► lobby

1 a long narrow area to walk along in a building

hall
a narrow area in a house or building, with doors that lead to other rooms: *The kitchen is at the end of the hall.*

hallway
hallway means the same as **hall**: *He led me down a long hallway toward his office.*

corridor
a long narrow hall in a building, with doors that lead to other rooms: *He walked down the hotel corridor to the elevators.*

aisle
a long narrow area you can walk along between rows of seats, or between rows of shelves in a store: *The choir walked down the aisle singing the first hymn. | Juice and soft drinks are in aisle 15.*

passageway *also* **passage**
a long narrow area that has walls and usually a roof, that connects one room or place with another: *A secret passageway led to a hiding place beneath the house. | There was an underground passage between the two buildings.*

SYNONYM CHECK

Hall, hallway, corridor, etc.

A **hall** or **hallway** can be in any kind of building, such as a house, school, or office building.

You use **corridor** about a hall in a building that many people use, such as a hotel or office building.

Aisle is used about the area between rows of seats in a plane, train, church, or theater, or about the area between shelves in a store.

Passageway is a more general word for any long narrow area that you can walk along, and it is also slightly formal. A **passageway** does not have to be inside a building: *We crawled through a narrow passageway in the cave.*

2 the area inside a building near the front door

hall
a small area near the front door inside a house or apartment building, with doors that lead to other rooms: *He tripped over a basketball Bryan had left in the hall.*
→ When you want it to be clear that **hall** means the area near the front door, use **entrance hall**.

hallway
hallway means the same as **hall**: *The mail was left on a table in the hallway by the door.*
→ Don't say ~~*entrance hallway*~~.

entryway
a small area near the entrance and inside a building: *He hung his coat on the rack in the entryway.*

lobby
a large hall inside the entrance of a large building that many people use: *We arranged to meet in the hotel lobby.*

hand in *phrasal verb* → see **give**

handle *verb* → see **deal with**, **treat**

hand out *phrasal verb* → see **give**

H

handsome *adjective* → see **beautiful**, Topic **Describing People's Looks**

handy *adjective* → see **useful**

hang /hæŋ/ *verb*

1 to hang down
- ► hang
- ► dangle
- ► droop
- ► sag

2 to put something somewhere so that it hangs down
- ► hang
- ► suspend (*formal*)
- ► drape

1 to hang down

hang
to be in a position where the top part is firmly fastened, but the bottom part is free to move: *A large chandelier **hangs from** the ceiling.* | *The keys are **hanging on** a nail by the door.*

dangle
to hang loosely and move slightly from side to side: *Two large earrings were **dangling from** her ears.*

droop
if something that is usually firm or upright droops, it hangs down: *These flowers are beginning to droop – they need watering.*

sag
if something sags, it hangs or bends down in the middle because it is old or has been used a lot: *Her old sofa sags in the middle where she always sits.*

2 to put something somewhere so that it hangs down

hang
to put something in a position where the top part is firmly fastened but the bottom part is free to move: *Where do you want me to hang this picture?* | ***Hang** your coat **on** the hook.*

suspend (AWL) (*formal*)
to attach something to a high place so that it hangs down: *At the circus, the acrobats swing on trapezes that are **suspended from** the ceiling.*
→ **GRAMMAR: Suspend** is usually used in the passive.

drape
to put something over or around something so that it hangs loosely: *He took off his jacket and draped it over a chair.*

hang

The flowers are beginning to **droop**.

A large chandelier **hangs** from the ceiling.

They **dangled** their feet over the edge of the water.

happen /ˈhæpən/ *verb*

- ► happen
- ► occur (*formal*)
- ► take place
- ► arise (*formal*)
- ► come up
- ► come about
- ► come true

happen
when something happens, there is an event. Often when things **happen** you do not plan or expect them: *When she didn't come home on time, I was worried that something had **happened to** her.* | *What happens when you pour the lemon juice over the baking soda?*

occur (AWL) (*formal*)
to happen. You often use **occur** about bad events that you do not expect: *The attack occurred in the early hours of October 26.*

take place
to happen. You use **take place** when the event has been planned: *The conference will take place on June 16.*

arise (*formal*)
to begin to happen. You often use **arise** when talking about problems, questions, and opportunities: *He is able to give medical help if the need arises.*

come up
come up means the same as **arise** but is less

formal: *I was planning to go, but something came up and I couldn't go after all.*

→ If an event or time is **coming up**, it is going to happen soon: *Abby's birthday is coming up in a couple of weeks.*

come about
to happen because of an event or decision that happened earlier. **Come about** is fairly formal and you use it to explain how something happened: *Scientists have some answers to how life came about on Earth, but they still do not know everything.*

come true
if a dream or wish comes true, it happens in the way you hoped it would: *He has always wanted to be a pilot, and now his dream has come true.*

happiness /ˈhæpinəs/ *noun*

1 the feeling of being happy
- ► happiness
- ► cheerfulness
- ► pleasure
- ► delight
- ► contentment

2 the feeling of being very happy
- ► joy
- ► ecstasy
- ► bliss
- ► euphoria (*formal*)
- ► elation (*formal*)

ANTONYMS → see **sadness**

1 the feeling of being happy

happiness
the feeling of being happy: *His grandchildren bring him great happiness.*

cheerfulness
happy feelings which you show by smiling, laughing, or talking in a happy way: *His usual cheerfulness was gone, and worry took its place.*

pleasure
the feeling you have when you enjoy something: *Her music brings pleasure to people across the world.*

delight
the feeling you have when you are very pleased and excited because something good has happened: *The baby splashed in the water and laughed* ***with delight****.*

contentment
the feeling of being quietly happy and satisfied. **Contentment** is fairly formal: *The bed was warm and comfortable, and she sighed* ***with contentment****.*

2 the feeling of being very happy

joy
a feeling of great happiness and pleasure: ***A new baby brings joy, but also a lot of responsibilities.***

ecstasy
a feeling of extreme happiness: *The fans were* ***in ecstasy*** *when their team scored a goal.*

bliss
a feeling of very great happiness and pleasure. You use **bliss** when you are happy because something makes you feel physically good: *Swimming in the warm ocean was bliss.*

euphoria (*formal*)
a feeling of extreme happiness and excitement, especially because you have achieved something or because of the effects of a drug. **Euphoria** lasts only a short time: *The country's problems were forgotten for a moment in the* ***euphoria over*** *winning the war.*

elation (*formal*)
a strong feeling of happiness, excitement, and pride because you have achieved something or something good has happened: *You could hear the elation in his voice as he talked about reaching the summit of the mountain.*

→ see **pleasure**

happy /ˈhæpi/ *adjective*

1 feeling happy
- ► happy
- ► glad
- ► pleased
- ► cheerful
- ► content
- ► satisfied

2 feeling very happy
- ► delighted
- ► thrilled
- ► ecstatic
- ► euphoric (*formal*)
- ► overjoyed
- ► elated (*formal*)

3 happy because you are celebrating something
- ► festive
- ► joyful

ANTONYMS → see **sad**

1 feeling happy

happy
feeling good and satisfied with your life, and often showing this by smiling or laughing: *Emily is a happy girl who hardly ever cries or gets*

angry. | *I'm so* ***happy to*** *see you! I missed you so much.* | *My wedding day was the happiest day of my life.*

glad
happy because something good has happened, and often feeling thankful about it: *He was* ***glad to*** *see someone that he knew.* | *I'm glad I was able to help.*
→ **GRAMMAR: Glad** is not used before a noun. Don't say: ~~*a glad man*~~. Say: *He is glad.*

pleased
happy because something good has happened or because someone has done something good. **Pleased** is a little more formal than **happy** or **glad**: *His parents are* ***pleased that*** *he has worked so hard and done well at school.*
→ When you meet someone for the first time, you can say "Pleased to meet you!". You can also say "Glad to meet you!", but this is more informal.

cheerful
happy, and showing this in your face or in the way you behave: *"It is great to see you!" he said in a cheerful voice.* | *She woke up feeling cheerful, and started singing as she got dressed.*

content *also* **contented**
feeling that you have all the things you want or need so that you are happy. You often use **content** when someone could have more things but is satisfied with what he or she has: *She has a good job and good friends and is* ***content with*** *her life.*

satisfied
feeling that something is as good as it should be, or that something has happened in the way that you want: *The teacher is* ***satisfied with*** *his progress.*

2 feeling very happy

delighted
very happy because something good has happened: *Kara was* ***delighted with*** *her birthday present.*

thrilled
very excited, pleased, or happy: *She was* ***thrilled at*** *the idea of traveling in Europe.*

ecstatic
feeling very happy and excited: *When the team won the tournament, the whole school was ecstatic.*

euphoric *(formal)*
feeling very happy and excited, especially because you have achieved something. You are usually **euphoric** for only a short time: *The scientists were* ***euphoric at*** *the results of the experiment.*

overjoyed
very happy because you have heard some good news. **Overjoyed** is more formal than **happy**: *She was overjoyed when she found out that her son was safe.*

elated *(formal)*
very happy and excited for a short time because you have achieved something that is important to you. You often use **elated** in written English: *He felt elated when he got accepted at Yale University.*

3 happy because you are celebrating something

festive
looking or feeling bright and cheerful in a way that seems suitable for a celebration: *The Christmas party was festive, with red and green decorations everywhere.*

joyful *also* **joyous**
very happy, especially because you are celebrating a happy event. **Joyful** is often used in literature: *Birthdays are joyful occasions in our house.* | *The soldiers got a joyous welcome when they returned from the war.*
→ **GRAMMAR:** Don't say: ~~*We are joyful*~~. **Joyful** is used more about the occasions when you feel joy.
→ see **cheer up** for words meaning "to feel happier," **please** for words meaning "to make someone feel happy"
→ see Topic **Describing People's Emotions**

ADVERBS

You can make the adjectives **happy**, **glad**, **cheerful**, **contented**, **ecstatic**, **euphoric**, **joyful**, and **joyous** into adverbs by using an **-ly** ending: *"We're home," he said happily.* | *She gladly helps anyone who asks.* | *We were ecstatically happy together.* | *Her family joyfully welcomed her home.*

harbor *noun* → see **port**

hard *adjective* → *go to pages 288-289*

harden /ˈhardn/ *verb*

- ► **harden**
- ► **set**
- ► **stiffen**

ANTONYMS → see **soften**

harden
to become hard or stiff: *The glue takes about an hour to harden.*

set
if a substance sets, it becomes solid instead of liquid: *Put the Jell-o in the fridge to set.*

stiffen
to make a material stiff so that it does not bend easily: *Starch will stiffen the fabric slightly.*

hardly *adverb* → see Function Word **almost**, **just**

hard-working /ˌhɑrd ˈwɚkɪŋ/ *adjective*

- ► **hard-working**
- ► **industrious** (*formal*)
- ► **dedicated**
- ► **diligent**
- ► **disciplined**
- ► **productive**

ANTONYMS → see **lazy**

hard-working
using a lot of effort and spending a lot of time on the work you do: *She is a very hard-working student who gets good grades.*

industrious (*formal*)
using a lot of energy and effort in your work, spending a lot of time working, and getting a lot of work done: *An industrious couple from Korea run the store by themselves.*

dedicated
working very hard at something because you care about it a lot: *The teachers here are very dedicated, and every one of them wants to help students do their best.*

diligent
working hard and being very careful to do your work correctly: *Be* ***diligent in*** *doing your exercises, and your muscles will become stronger.*

disciplined
organizing your time and making yourself work even when you do not really want to: *Disciplined students always turn their assignments in on time.*

productive
working hard and producing or achieving a lot: *The workers became more productive when they worked as a team.*
→ see Topic **Describing People's Character**

ADVERBS

You can make the adjectives **industrious**, **diligent**, and **productive** into adverbs by using an **-ly** ending: *The students were calmly and industriously getting on with their work.* | *Scientists worked diligently to find a cure for the disease.*

harm[1] /hɑrm/ *noun*

- ► **harm**
- ► **damage**
- ► **injury** (*formal*)

harm
a bad effect on someone or something: *Telling a child that he is stupid can do a lot of* ***harm to*** *his self-esteem.* | *The mistake did his political career a lot of harm, and he lost the election.*

damage
a very bad effect on something. **Damage** sounds more serious than **harm**: *Closing the factory will cause a lot of* ***damage to*** *the local economy.*

injury (AWL) (*formal*)
a bad effect on something, especially on the respect people have for someone. **Injury** is used in a court of law: *She said the newspaper article was false, and had caused* ***injury to*** *her reputation.*
→ see **damage[1]**, **injury**

harm[2] /hɑrm/ *verb*

- ► **harm**
- ► **damage**
- ► **be bad for**
- ► **hurt**
- ► **injure** (*formal*)
- ► **impair** (*formal*)

harm
to have a bad effect on someone or something: *The problems with the banks greatly harmed the economy.* | *The company doesn't want to harm its image by causing pollution.*

damage
to have a very bad effect on someone or something. **Damage** sounds more serious than **harm**: *Her mistake could damage her chances of getting a better job.*

be bad for
to be likely to have a bad effect on someone or something. **Be bad for** is more informal than **harm**: *The lack of rain is bad for the farming industry, because the crops need water.*

hurt
to have a bad effect on someone or something, especially by making him, her, or it less successful. **Hurt** sounds more informal than **harm** and does not sound as serious: *Changing the name of the store hurt the company's profits.* | *I'm sorry I said that. I didn't mean to hurt your feelings.*

injure (AWL) (*formal*)
to have a bad effect on the respect that

someone feels for himself or on the respect other people have for someone. You use **injure** especially in the phrases "injure someone's pride" or "injure someone's reputation": *The court agreed that the newspaper story had injured Mr. Smith's reputation.*

impair (*formal*)
to make something less able to be done easily: *The tax will impair the sale of food to foreign countries.*
→ see **damage²**, **hurt**

harmful /ˈhɑrmfəl/ *adjective*

- ► harmful
- ► damaging
- ► destructive

harmful
causing harm to someone or something: *Pollution in the air is* ***harmful to*** *our health.* | *Are there harmful effects on children from watching too much violence on television?*

damaging
causing serious harm to something: *Sunscreen protects your skin from the damaging effects of sunlight.*

destructive
causing a lot of damage: *The storm was very destructive and has caused $50 million worth of damage.*
→ see **dangerous**, **poisonous**

ADVERBS

You can make the adjectives **harmful** and **destructive** into adverbs by using an **-ly** ending. These adverbs are formal: *Smoking can affect the development of an unborn baby harmfully.*

harmless *adjective* → see **safe**

hate /heɪt/ *verb*

- ► hate
- ► cannot stand
- ► detest (*formal*)
- ► loathe (*formal*)
- ► despise

ANTONYMS → see **love¹**

hate
to dislike someone or something very much: *She hated her sister because she was jealous.* | *He made fun of her, and she* ***hated*** *him* ***for*** *it.* | *I hated P.E. when I was in school.*

cannot stand
to dislike someone or something very much, especially because he, she, or it upsets or annoys you. **Cannot stand** is more informal than **hate**, and you usually use it when you are speaking: *Her husband is so rude! I really can't stand him.* | *I like dogs, but I can't stand the way they smell.*

detest (*formal*)
to hate someone or something, especially for a particular reason. **Detest** is more formal than **hate**: *The men* ***detested*** *their captain* ***for*** *his lack of knowledge and his weakness.* | *I was forced to wear the sensible shoes that I detested.*

loathe (*formal*)
to hate someone or something very much, especially when you think he, she, or it is disgusting. **Loathe** is a stronger word than **hate**: *Her new boss was often mean and sarcastic, and she began to loathe him.* | *Many Republicans loathed the idea of a national system of health care.*

despise
to dislike someone or something very much and have no respect for that person or thing: *When he found out that she had cheated, he began to despise her.*
→ see **dislike**, **hatred**

SYNONYM CHECK

Hate, cannot stand, detest, etc.

People often use **hate**, **despise**, **loathe**, etc. about things that are not very important: *I hate carrots.* | *She loathes housework.* This means that they dislike these things very much. However, when you use these words about people, they show you feel a very strong emotion.

hatred /ˈheɪtrəd/ *noun*

- ► hatred
- ► hate
- ► loathing
- ► hostility
- ► contempt
- ► spite
- ► malice (*formal*)

hatred
a very strong feeling of dislike for someone or something: *He has a* ***hatred of*** *any kind of violence.* | *Her stepfather was cruel to her, and she felt nothing but* ***hatred for*** *him.*

hate
the angry feeling that someone has when he or

she strongly dislikes someone or something, and wants to harm him, her, or it: *The children grew up filled with hate and wanting revenge.*

loathing
a very strong feeling of hatred for someone or something: *After the horrible way he treated me, I feel only **loathing for** him.*

hostility
dislike of someone or something, which makes you behave in a very angry way toward him or her: *There has been a recent increase in **hostility toward** foreigners.*

contempt
a feeling of strong dislike toward someone or something you think does not deserve any respect at all: *She looked at him **with contempt** and said, "I don't care if I ever see you again."*

spite
a feeling of wanting to hurt or upset someone by saying or doing cruel things, especially because you feel jealous or think you have been unfairly treated: *Ignore what he said to you. He is angry and he said it **out of spite**.*

malice (*formal*)
the feeling of wanting to deliberately harm someone or hurt his or her feelings, because you hate him or her. **Malice** is used especially in literary writing and in legal language: *His eyes shone **with malice** as he told her about her husband's affair with another woman.*

SYNONYM CHECK

Hatred, hate, loathing, hostility, etc.

Hatred, **loathing**, **hostility**, and the other nouns in this entry are only used about serious feelings. You do not use these words to mean a strong dislike of something that is not important. You can say: *She hated carrots*, but don't say: ~~*She had a hatred of carrots*~~.

have *verb* → see **eat**, **experience[2]**, **own[1]**

have to /ˈhæftə, strong ˈhæftu/ *verb*

- have to
- must
- be required to (*formal*)
- be expected to (*formal*)
- be obliged to (*formal*)

have to
to need to do something because it is necessary or important: *I have to hurry because I'm late for class.* | *He has to return the books to the library.*

must
to have to do something because it is very important and because someone in authority or a rule says that you should do it. **Must** is stronger than **have to**, and it is more important that you obey: *Dad says we must be back home before 10 o'clock.* | *You must not smoke in here.*
→ **GRAMMAR:** Don't say: ~~*I must to do it*~~. Say: *I must do it.*

be required to (*formal*)
to have to do something, because there is a law or official rule that says you must: *Some travelers are required to have a visa before they enter the U.S.*

be expected to (*formal*)
to have to do something because it is right, or part of your job, or something you are responsible for: *You are expected to hand in your homework on time.*

be obliged to (*formal*)
to have to do something, especially because you feel it is the right thing to do or because the situation makes it necessary to do it: *Her husband lost his job, and she was obliged to work so that they could pay their bills.*
→ see **supposed to**

head *noun* → see **boss**, **leader**, **mind[1]**

headache /ˈhedeɪk/ *noun*

- headache
- migraine

headache
a pain in your head: *The neighbor's loud music was giving him a headache.*

migraine
a type of headache that is very bad and makes you feel sick: *When she has a migraine, she has to lie down in a dark room because the pain is so bad.*

heal *verb* → see **cure[1]**, **treat**, Topic **Medical Treatment**

health /helθ/ *noun*

- health
- well-being

health
your health is how well or sick you are most of the time: *Smoking damages your health.* | *He has a lot of health problems, including heart disease.*

well-being
the feeling of being healthy and happy, and that things in your life are going well: *A relaxing vacation can give you a feeling of well-being.*

hard /hɑrd/ *adjective*

1 not easy to do, understand, or deal with
- ► hard
- ► difficult
- ► tough (*informal*)
- ► rough (*informal*)
- ► tricky
- ► challenging
- ► daunting (*formal*)
- ► formidable (*formal*)
- ► problematic

2 difficult and tiring
- ► hard
- ► difficult
- ► tough
- ► demanding
- ► strenuous
- ► grueling
- ► laborious

ANTONYMS → see **easy**

3 not soft, and not bending, breaking, or cutting easily
- ► hard
- ► firm
- ► stiff
- ► rigid
- ► solid
- ► crisp
- ► stale

ANTONYMS → see **soft (2)**

1 not easy to do, understand, or deal with

hard
not easy to do, understand, or deal with: ***The test was really hard.*** | ***I was having a hard time doing my math homework.***
→ You do not use **hard** with words like "problem," "situation," or "issue," but you can use **difficult** with these words. Say: ***This is a difficult problem/situation/issue to deal with.***

difficult
difficult means the same as **hard** but is a little more formal: ***The questions were difficult to answer.*** | ***The country is in a difficult economic situation.***

tough (*informal*)
very difficult to do or deal with. You use **tough** especially about decisions, questions, or situations: ***I like both colleges, so choosing one will be tough.*** | ***His parents just got divorced, so he has been having a tough time.***

rough (*informal*)
a rough time is one when you have a lot of problems in your life: ***He had a rough time after his father died, and he got into a lot of trouble.***

tricky
difficult because you need to think carefully about how to deal with something: ***The case has raised some tricky legal questions.***

challenging (AWL)
a challenging situation or problem is difficult in an interesting and enjoyable way. You must work hard to deal with a **challenging** situation: ***The writing project is challenging, but most of our students learn a lot.***

daunting (*formal*)
if something is daunting, you are worried that it will be difficult and you do not feel confident that you can do it: ***Cooking for twenty people sounded daunting, and I wasn't sure that I could do it on my own.***

formidable (*formal*)
seeming very difficult and needing a lot of effort or skill to do: ***The new president will have to deal with some formidable economic problems.***

problematic
involving problems that are difficult to deal with: ***Improving the college buildings is a problematic issue because of the high cost.***

2 difficult and tiring

hard
not easy to do because you have to use a lot of effort: ***It was a long hard climb to the top of the mountain.***
→ If something is tiring and needs a lot of effort, you usually use **hard** rather than **difficult**: ***It was a hard race.***

difficult
difficult means the same as **hard** but sounds a little more formal: ***The Tour de France is the most difficult bicycle race of the year.***

tough
very difficult because you have to use a lot of effort: ***The other team has some good players, so it is going to be a tough game.***

demanding
difficult and tiring. You use **demanding** especially about jobs or activities: ***Being a nurse is a***

demanding job. | *Taking care of young children can be very demanding.*

strenuous
needing a lot of effort and strength: *Don't do any strenuous exercise until your back is completely better.*

grueling
very tiring and continuing for a long time: *The race is a grueling 24-hour run across the desert.*

laborious
taking a long time and needing to be done very slowly and carefully: *Making a movie is a laborious process involving a huge amount of work.*

ADVERBS
You can make the adjectives **strenuous** and **laborious** into adverbs by using an **-ly** ending: *The men worked strenuously to lay the railroad track.* | *I began laboriously copying my essay onto a clean sheet of paper.*

3 not soft, and not bending, breaking, or cutting easily

hard
not soft, and difficult to bend, break, or cut: *The workers wear hard hats to protect their heads.* | *I wish this chair wasn't so hard and uncomfortable.*

firm
not bending easily when you press it, but not completely hard either. You use **firm** to show that this is good: *It's best to buy pears when they are still firm.* | *A bed with a firm mattress is good for your back.*

stiff
something that is stiff keeps its shape and is not easy to bend. You use **stiff** about things that are harder than similar things: *His collar felt stiff and rubbed against his neck.*
→ You can say a part of your body is **stiff** when it hurts and is difficult to bend or move, especially after exercising: *I woke up with a stiff neck.*

rigid (AWL)
something rigid keeps its shape and is difficult or impossible to bend. You use **rigid** especially about structures that are made of things that do not bend: *The old tents were supported by rigid wood frames.*

solid
very hard and not bending or moving when you press on it, and usually not empty inside: *The walls of the castle were solid and thick, and the enemy could not easily break them down.*

crisp
slightly hard and making a pleasant noise when it breaks. You use **crisp** about food, dry leaves on the ground, and snow: *The cookies were crisp at the edges and chewy in the middle.*

stale
hard because no longer fresh – used about food bread or cake that is stale is no longer fresh and is hard and dry: *The sandwich was horrible because the bread was stale.*
→ see Topic **Describing Texture**

ADVERBS
You can make the adjectives **firm**, **stiff**, **rigid**, **solid**, and **crisp** into adverbs by using an **-ly** ending: *Add a cup of firmly packed brown sugar.* | *The furniture is solidly made.*
If a person is moving, sitting, or standing **stiffly** or **rigidly**, that person looks as though he or she cannot bend easily: *She walked stiffly to the door.* | *He sat rigidly in his chair.*

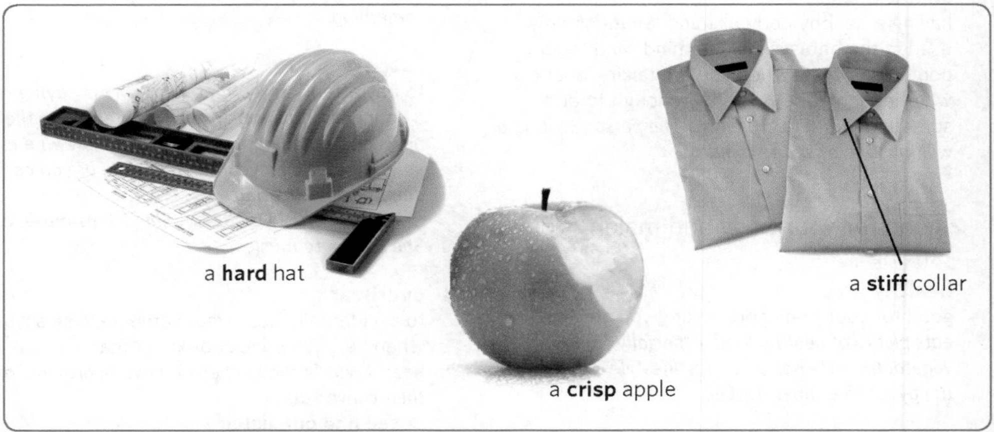
a **hard** hat

a **crisp** apple

a **stiff** collar

healthy /ˈhelθi/ *adjective*

1 physically strong and not likely to become sick or weak
- ► healthy
- ► well
- ► fit
- ► in shape
- ► sound (*formal*)

ANTONYMS → see **sick (1)**

2 good for your body and making you strong
- ► healthy
- ► nutritious
- ► nourishing
- ► healthful (*formal*)
- ► wholesome

1 physically strong and not likely to become sick or weak

healthy
physically strong and not likely to become sick or weak: *Exercise keeps you healthy.* | *She gave birth to a healthy baby boy.*

well
physically strong and not sick. You use **well** when describing or asking about how someone feels: *I don't feel well.* | *Jim hasn't been very well lately.*

fit *also* **physically fit**
having a body that is healthy and strong, especially because you exercise regularly: *She keeps fit by biking to work.*

in shape
in shape means the same as **fit** but is more informal: *Jogging keeps me in shape.*

sound (*formal*)
having a healthy body or mind. **Sound** is only used in the phrases "sound mind" and "sound body," especially when you are talking about whether someone is healthy enough to do something for legal reasons: *The person writing a will must be* ***of sound mind.***

2 good for your body and making you strong

healthy
good for your body and making you strong: *She eats plenty of healthy food, especially fruit and vegetables.* | *He has a healthy lifestyle and goes to the gym three times a week.*

nutritious
full of the natural substances that your body needs to stay healthy and grow well: *Eggs are a nutritious food, with lots of protein to help build strong muscles.*

nourishing
food that is nourishing helps your body to stay healthy and also gives you energy: *Chicken soup is both nourishing and delicious.*

healthful (*formal*)
healthful food or activities keep your body healthy: *Parents should encourage children to do healthful activities such as swimming.*

wholesome
wholesome food does not have things such as chemicals added to it: *Oatmeal cookies are a wholesome snack, but too many of them can still be bad for you.*
→ see Topic **Describing Food**

ADVERBS

You can make the adjectives **healthy**, **nutritious**, and **healthful** into adverbs by using an **-ly** ending: *We try to persuade people to eat more healthily.* | *Families who eat together tend to eat more nutritiously.*

hear /hɪr/ *verb*
- ► hear
- ► listen
- ► overhear

hear
to notice a sound with your ears: *Did you hear that noise? What is it?* | *You don't need to talk so loud – I can hear you.*
→ **GRAMMAR:** Don't say: *~~I am hearing something~~*. Say: *I hear something* or *I can hear something.*

listen
to pay attention to what someone is saying or to a sound such as music: *She is* ***listening to*** *the news on the radio.* | *Keep the sound low when you* ***listen to*** *music on your headphones, or you can damage your hearing.*
→ **GRAMMAR:** Don't say: *~~She listens music~~*. Say: *She* ***listens to*** *music.*

overhear
to accidentally hear what someone else says, when he or she does not know that you can hear: *I was in the kitchen and overheard part of their conversation.*
→ see **find out**, **listen**

H

SYNONYM CHECK

Hear or listen?

You **hear** sounds when they come to your ears, whether you want to hear them or not: *I heard music as the car passed me.*

You **listen** to sounds when you deliberately choose to hear those sounds: *I listened to music in the car.*

heart *noun* → see **center**

heat¹ /hit/ *noun*

- ► heat
- ► warmth

ANTONYMS → see **cold²**

heat
the quality that something hot has: *Fire fighters wear special clothes to protect them from the heat of a fire.* | *It was a hot day, and I could feel the heat from the sun on my shoulders.*

warmth
the quality of being warm. You use **warmth** about things that are not very hot: *It was cold out, and I was glad to go into the warmth of the house.* | *Put on an extra sweater for warmth.*

heat² /hit/ *verb*

- ► heat
- ► warm
- ► burn

ANTONYMS → see **cool²**

heat *also* **heat up**
to make something warm or hot: *Heat the milk until it boils.* | *The sun poured in, heating up the room.*

warm *also* **warm up**
to make someone or something warmer: *The cats lay warming themselves by the fire.* | *Have some soup – it will warm you up.*

burn
to destroy or damage something with fire or heat: *If the iron is too hot, it will burn the cloth.*

heavy /ˈhevi/ *adjective*

- ► heavy
- ► bulky
- ► dense
- ► weighty (*formal*)

ANTONYMS → see **light² (2)**

heavy
weighing a lot: *This suitcase is too heavy to carry.* | *The soldiers wore heavy black boots.*

bulky (AWL)
big and usually heavy, and taking up a lot of space: *The camera was old and bulky compared to today's digital cameras.*

dense
if something is dense, it is heavy in comparison to its size: *The cake is moist and dense, with a strong taste of chocolate.*

weighty (*formal*)
weighty books are large and heavy: *The encyclopedia consists of twelve weighty volumes.*
→ see Topic **Describing Clothes**, **Describing Food**

height /haɪt/ *noun*

- ► height
- ► altitude

height
how tall someone or something is, or how far above the floor or ground something is: *Stand up straight while I measure your height.* | *He changed the height of the microphone slightly.*

altitude
the height of something above sea level: *The plane was flying at an altitude of 30,000 feet.*
→ see **length**, **width**, Topic **Describing Size**

help¹ /help/ *verb*

- ► help
- ► assist
- ► aid (*formal*)
- ► give someone a hand (*informal*)
- ► support

help
to do something that makes it easier for another person to do something: *John helped his father clean up the garage.* | *She is really worried, but I don't know how I can help.*

assist (AWL)
to help someone, especially by doing less important things so that he or she can do the rest of the job: *Citizens have a duty to assist the police.* | *Workers at the wildlife center* ***assisted in*** *the efforts to rescue the whale.*

aid (AWL) (*formal*)
to help someone to do something, especially to achieve something: *The loans aid small businesses by allowing them to grow.* | *Four hundred people* ***aided in*** *the task of cleaning up the beaches.*

H

give someone a hand *also* **lend someone a hand** (*informal*)
to help someone, especially with jobs that involve physical work: *Will you **give me a hand with** the dishes? | The neighbors lent us a hand when we were moving.*

support
to help and encourage someone to achieve something or during a difficult time: *Her friends and family supported her after her husband died. | Parents can support their children's reading by enjoying books together.*
→ see **encourage**

help² /help/ *noun*

1 something you do to make things easier for another person
- help
- assistance
- support
- cooperation

2 money and other things that are given to help people
- help
- assistance
- aid
- relief
- donation
- charity
- handout

1 something you do to make things easier for another person

help
things you do that make it easier for another person to do something: *Do you want some help? I can carry your suitcase. | My brother needed some **help with** his math homework.*

assistance (AWL)
assistance means the same as **help** but is more formal: *The police are asking the public for their **assistance in** finding the missing women.*

support
help and encouragement that you give someone so that he or she can achieve something, or that you give to someone in a difficult time: *With my husband's support I was able to quit smoking. | The researchers received financial support from the U.S. government.*

cooperation (AWL)
a situation in which people work together to help achieve something that they all want to happen: *If we want to save the environment, we need cooperation from all the countries in the world. | I need your full cooperation.*
→ see **advice**

2 money and other things that are given to help people

help
money or other things that someone gives people who need them. **Help** is fairly informal in this meaning: *The college is able to give some students a little financial help.*

assistance (AWL)
money and other support that a government, university, or other official organization gives to help poor people. **Assistance** is used more often than **help** in this meaning: *The college gives financial assistance to students whose families have little money. | Families can sign up for the state's heat assistance program if they earn less than $30,000.*

aid (AWL)
money, food, medicine, or equipment that is sent to people in a difficult situation to help them: *The U.S. is sending aid to the victims of the earthquake.*

relief
aid that is sent to people because of an unexpected disaster such as a flood, earthquake, or famine (=situation in which people do not have enough food): *The government offered disaster relief to people affected by the hurricane.*
→ GRAMMAR: **Relief** is usually used after a noun that says what has happened: *All the money people give will go to the flood relief effort.*

donation
money, goods, or supplies that you give to help an organization, without expecting to receive anything for yourself: *I made a **donation to** the Save A Dog Foundation to help them find homes for dogs without families.*

charity
money and other things that people give to organizations who use them to help people: *He was proud and refused to accept charity.*

handout
money or other assistance that is given to people who are poor, especially by the government. You use **handout** only when you disapprove of this kind of help: *I think too many people sit around waiting for government handouts, instead of looking for a job!*

helper /ˈhelpɚ/ *noun*

- helper
- assistant
- aide

helper
someone who helps another person do

something: *There are a lot of books to hand out, and I'm going to need some helpers.*

assistant
someone whose job is to help a more important person with his or her work: *The assistant hands the dentist the instruments.*

aide
someone whose job is to help a more important person, especially a politician, nurse, or teacher: *He was an **aide to** President Clinton and gave him advice on his re-election campaign.*

helpful /ˈhelpfəl/ *adjective*

- ► helpful
- ► cooperative
- ► supportive

helpful
willing to help: *I couldn't find what I wanted at first, but the woman at the store was really helpful.*

cooperative AWL
doing what you are asked to do without causing any problems: *The police said that the witness was very cooperative and answered all their questions.*

supportive
giving you help and advice during a difficult time in your life: *It has been really hard, but my friends are all very supportive.*
→ see **kind[2]**, **useful**

ADVERBS
You can make the adjectives that mean **helpful** into adverbs by using an **-ly** ending: *Gina helpfully wrote down all the names of the students that were there.* | *The boy cooperatively opened his mouth for the dentist.*

helping /ˈhelpɪŋ/ *noun*

- ► helping
- ► serving
- ► portion (*formal*)

helping
an amount of food for one person, that you take from a dish or pot and put on a plate: *He took another helping of potatoes.*

serving
an amount of food that is enough for one person. **Serving** is used especially on packages of food or in recipes (=instructions on how to make food): *This recipe makes six servings.* | *One serving has 345 calories.*

portion AWL (*formal*)
an amount of food for one person: *The restaurant is known for serving huge portions.*
→ see Topic **Eating in a Restaurant**

hero /ˈhɪroʊ/ *noun*

- ► hero
- ► heroine
- ► idol

hero
a man who people admire for doing something very brave or good: *Dwight Eisenhower was a war hero before he became president.* | *When I was a kid, Michael Jordan was my hero. I wanted to play basketball just like him.*

heroine
a woman who people admire for doing something very brave or good: *She is a heroine who risked her own life to save a child.*

idol
a famous person, such as an actor, musician, or sportsperson, who you admire very much: *Beyoncé is a pop idol whom fans love for her music and her style.*
→ see **character**, Topic **Books and Literature**

hidden /ˈhɪdn/ *adjective*

- ► hidden
- ► concealed (*formal*)
- ► disguised
- ► secret

hidden
difficult to see or find, because someone has deliberately made this difficult: *She kept the letters hidden in a box in her closet.* | *A hidden camera in the bank filmed the robbery.*

concealed (*formal*)
concealed means the same as **hidden**: *The police found a concealed weapon in his car.*

disguised
made to seem like a different person or thing so that other people do not realize who or what it is: *They were caught by disguised FBI agents.*

secret
a secret place is a place that only you know about, and it is often hidden from other people: *The story says that pirates hid the money in a secret place, and no one has ever found it.*

hide /haɪd/ *verb*

- hide
- cover
- conceal (*formal*)
- disguise
- obscure (*formal*)

ANTONYMS → see **show[1] (1)**

hide
to deliberately make something difficult to see or find: *Where did you hide the kids' Christmas presents? | She put up her hand to **hide** her face **from** the cameras.*

cover
to hide something by putting something else over it: *She quickly **covered** herself **with** a towel.*

conceal (*formal*)
to hide something, often by covering it. **Conceal** is often used about hiding illegal things: *Illegal drugs were concealed in the trunk of the car. | Did the company deliberately conceal the fact that their product was dangerous?*

disguise
to make someone or something look different so that other people do not recognize the person or do not know what something is: *He escaped from the prison by **disguising** himself **as** a guard.*

obscure (*formal*)
to make it difficult to see something clearly. You often use **obscure** in written stories and descriptions: *The fog obscured our view of the mountain.*

H

high /haɪ/ *adjective*

1 near the top of the range of sounds people can hear
- high
- high-pitched
- shrill
- sharp
- squeaky

ANTONYMS → see **low**

2 bigger in height
- high
- tall
- towering

ANTONYMS → see **short (1)**

1 near the top of the range of sounds people can hear

high
near the top of the sounds that humans can hear. You use **high** especially about voices and musical notes: *He still has the high voice of a little boy. | Dogs can hear sounds that are too high for humans to hear.*

high-pitched
high and sometimes unpleasant. You use **high-pitched** about sounds and voices: *The lock made a high-pitched squeak as I turned the key. | People often use high-pitched voices when they talk to babies.*

shrill
very high and loud in a way that sounds unpleasant: *Her aunt's shrill voice could be heard from downstairs. | A shrill whistle stopped the game.*

sharp
high, sudden, and loud: *She gave a sharp cry of pain.*

squeaky
making short high sounds: *Put some oil on that squeaky door!*

2 bigger in height

high
bigger in height than most other things. **High** is used about things such as mountains and walls: *Mount Kilimanjaro is the highest mountain in Africa. | The prison was surrounded by a high wall.*

tall
bigger in height than most other people or things. **Tall** is used especially about things that are high and narrow, such as people, trees, and buildings: *Who is taller – Russ or me? | The Empire State Building used to be the tallest building in the world, but now there are many buildings that are taller. | Redwood trees are very tall.*

towering
very tall, in a way that seems impressive but also often a little frightening. **Towering** is used in books: *The storm sent towering waves over the deck of the ship.*

highest *adjective* → see **top[2]**

high school *noun* → see Topic **Education**

highway *noun* → see **road**

hill *noun* → see **mountain**

hint[1] /hɪnt/ *noun*

1 a useful piece of advice
- hint
- tip

2 something that helps someone find an answer
- ► **hint**
- ► **clue**

1 a useful piece of advice

hint
a useful piece of advice about how to do something: ***The magazine gave some helpful hints about** how to lose weight.*

tip
a useful piece of advice about how to do something more easily or how to do it better: *Here's a good tip. Pour boiling water over the tomatoes before peeling them, and the skins will slip off easily.*

2 something that helps someone find an answer

hint
something you say that helps someone guess something: *"I'll give you a hint: his name starts with J." "Jon?" | Has she given you any **hints about** what she wants for Christmas?*

clue
a piece of information that helps you find the right answer: *The airline is looking for **clues to** the cause of the crash.*

hint² *verb* → see **suggest**

hire /haɪɚ/ *verb*
- ► **hire**
- ► **employ**
- ► **appoint** (*formal*)
- ► **recruit**
- ► **take on**

ANTONYMS → see **fire²**

hire
to give someone a job: *The new store is hiring 15 sales people.*

employ
to have someone working for you and being paid for it: *The factory employs over 200 people.*

appoint (*formal*)
to choose someone for a job, especially an important job: *The President has **appointed** Jane Staller **as** Secretary of Health and Human Services.*

recruit
to find new people to work in a company or join an organization. You use **recruit** especially for teams or groups like the army: *Several colleges have tried to recruit Colley, who is one of the top high school players in the nation.*

take on
take on means the same as **hire** but is more informal: *The store will take on temporary employees at Christmas.*
→ see Topic **Jobs and Work**

history /ˈhɪstəri/ *noun*

1 all the things that happened in the past
- ► **history**
- ► **the past**
- ► **the old days** (*informal*)

2 a description of past events
- ► **history**
- ► **account**
- ► **biography**
- ► **memoir**

3 someone's personal or family history
- ► **background**
- ► **pedigree**
- ► **family tree**

1 all the things that happened in the past

history
all the things that happened in the past in a place: *This book is about the history of India.*

the past
the time that existed before the present: *The events of the past influence what happens in the future.*

the old days (*informal*)
a long time ago, when things were different from how they are now: *In the old days, we listened to the radio because there wasn't any TV.*

2 a description of past events

history
a description of past events: *He is writing a **history of** World War II.*

account
a spoken or written description that says what happens in an event: *The newspaper printed a detailed **account of** the trial.*

biography
a book about a person's life: *He has written a **biography of** George Washington.*

memoir
a book written by a famous person about his or her life and experiences: *The former president has just published his memoirs.*
→ **GRAMMAR: Memoir** is often used in the plural.
→ see **record**

H

3 someone's personal or family history

background
the type of home and family you come from, and its social class: *The school takes kids from all sorts of backgrounds.*

pedigree
a list of the parents and other past family members of an animal or person. You use **pedigree** especially to show that the person or animal comes from a good family: *People will pay a lot of money for a dog with a good pedigree.*

family tree
a diagram that shows how all the people in a family are related to each other over a long period of time: *Have you ever researched your own family tree?*

hit[1] /hɪt/ *verb*

1 to hit someone or something with your hand
- ► hit
- ► strike
- ► punch
- ► slap
- ► beat
- ► spank
- ► smack

2 to hit part of your body by accident
- ► hit
- ► bump
- ► bang
- ► crack
- ► stub

3 to hit something with a vehicle
- ► hit
- ► run into
- ► collide
- ► crash into
- ► ram

ANTONYMS → see **miss (3)**

4 to hit a door or window to get someone's attention
- ► knock
- ► rap
- ► tap
- ► pound
- ► hammer

1 to hit someone or something with your hand

hit
to move your hand onto someone or something with a lot of force: *The guy got mad and **hit** me **in** the face.* | *Mom yelled at my brothers to stop hitting each other.*

strike
strike means the same as **hit** but sounds more formal or literary: *Her mother struck her so hard that she fell backward.*

punch
to hit someone or something hard with your hand closed: *He made a fist and I thought he was going to **punch** me **in** the nose.*

slap
to hit someone with your hand open and flat: *As hard as she could, she slapped him across the face.*

beat
to hit someone many times so that he or she is injured: *A young man is in the hospital after being attacked and beaten.*

spank
to hit a child on the buttocks with your open hand as a punishment: *Her father spanked her for locking her brother in the closet.*

smack
smack means the same as **slap**, but you use it to emphasize that a short hard cracking sound is made: *She smacked her boyfriend on the side of his head and told him to shut up.*

2 to hit part of your body by accident

hit
to accidentally move part of your body against something and hurt yourself: *I **hit** my leg **on** the bed and bruised it.*

bump
to hit against something by accident. You use **bump** when you do not hit something with very much force: *It was dark, and she **bumped into** the table.* | *Grandma fell and bumped her head.*

bang
to hit a part of your body against something by accident. You use **bang** when you hit something with force and often make a noise: *One icy morning she slipped and **banged** her head **on** the sidewalk.*

crack
to hit a part of your body, especially your head, hard against something: *He fell down the stairs and **cracked** his head **on** the railing.*

stub
to hurt your toe by hitting it against something: *Ouch! I **stubbed** my toe **on** the leg of the chair.*

3 to hit something with a vehicle

hit
if a vehicle hits something, it travels into it with force: *The car hit the tree at 45 miles per hour.* |

I think I hit a squirrel when I was driving down Garden Street.

run into
to hit something, especially something large or something that can cause damage: *The garbage truck ran into the back of my mother's car.*

collide
if two vehicles or objects collide or one collides with another, they hit each other while they are moving: *There was thick fog and the two ferries collided in the ocean.*

crash into
to hit something hard when you are going fast, especially so that there is a loud noise and a lot of damage: *The train crashed into the back of another train that was stopped at a signal.*

ram
to hit something with a lot of force. **Ram** sometimes means that someone deliberately uses a vehicle to hit something: *The car **rammed into** the police car, and they both went off the road.* | *The environmental group tried to ram the whaling boat with their boat.*

4 to hit a door or window to get someone's attention

knock
to touch a door or window hard with your closed hand so that people inside will hear you: *Maya opened the door before I even knocked.* | *I **knocked on** the front door of the house.*

rap
to knock on something with force and a loud sound: *The officer **rapped on** the door and shouted "Police!"*

hit

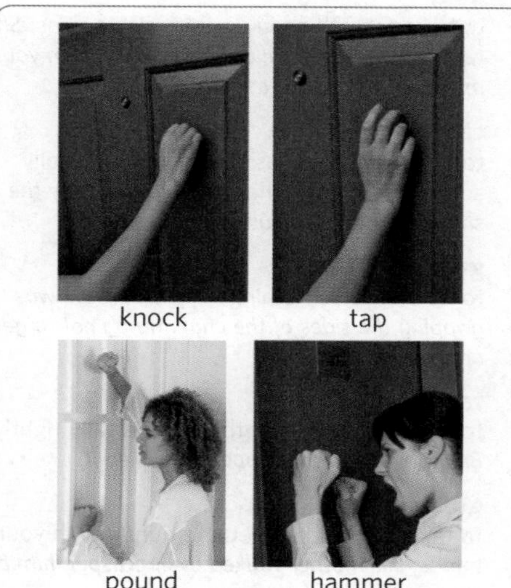

tap
to gently hit your fingers or knuckles against a door or window to get someone's attention: *I heard someone **tapping on** my door.*

pound
to knock on something many times with your fist: *He woke up to the sound of someone **pounding on** his door.*

hammer
to knock on a door or window many times, very hard and fast: *Someone was **hammering on** the door shouting, "Get everyone out!"*

hit² /hɪt/ *noun*

1 the act of hitting someone or something
- ► hit
- ► blow
- ► drive
- ► punch
- ► slap
- ► smack
- ► spanking
- ► tap

2 something that is popular and successful
- ► hit
- ► success
- ► bestseller
- ► blockbuster
- ► sell-out
- ► fad

1 the act of hitting someone or something

hit
an occasion when something that is aimed at something else touches it, reaches it, or damages it: *The ship took a direct hit and sank.*

blow
a hard hit with a hand, tool, or weapon: *He aimed a blow at Joe's head, but Joe ducked to avoid it.*

drive
an act of hitting a ball hard, especially in tennis, baseball, or golf: *Turner hit a long drive to center.*

punch
a hard hit with your hand closed: *He received a **punch in** the face and fell to the ground.*

slap
a quick hit with your hand held flat: *Julia gave Roy a **slap on** the cheek.*

smack
smack means the same as **slap**, but you use it

to say that a short hard cracking sound is made: *You're going to get a smack in a minute!*

spanking
the action of hitting a child on the buttocks with your open hand as a punishment: *If you don't stop that noise, you'll get a spanking.*

tap
an act of hitting something gently: *There was a **tap on** the door.* | *She felt a **tap on** her shoulder.*

2 something that is popular and successful

hit
a movie, song, or play that is very popular and successful: *The song "Poker Face" was one of Lady Gaga's early hits.*
→ **GRAMMAR: Hit** is often used before another noun such as "show" or "movie": *Sign up here to watch hit movies online any time.*

success
something that is successful and achieves a good result: *The new video game was a huge success.*

bestseller
a book that a lot of people buy: *Stephen King's horror novels have been bestsellers.*

blockbuster
a movie, computer game, or book that is very successful: *Harry Potter was a blockbuster both as a book and a movie.*

sell-out
an event for which all the tickets have been sold: *The first night of the play was a sell-out.*

fad
something that is popular for a short time: *There was a **fad** at school **for** colored bands in the shape of different animals.*

hobby /ˈhɑbi/ *noun*

- ► **hobby**
- ► **interest**
- ► **pursuit** (*formal*)
- ► **pastime**
- ► **passion**

hobby
an activity that you enjoy doing in your free time, for example a sport or making things: *Helena's hobbies are surfing, hiking, and reading.*

interest
an activity or subject that you enjoy and spend a lot of time doing or reading about: *Sharon has many interests, including reading, history, and traveling.*

pursuit (AWL) (*formal*)
pursuit means the same as **interest** but sounds more formal or literary: *Many people come to Arizona to enjoy their favorite pursuits, such as golfing, hiking, and enjoying the beauty of the desert.*

pastime
something that you do to relax or have fun when you are not working: *One of my mother's favorite pastimes is watching the birds in her backyard.*

passion
an activity that you feel a strong desire or need to do: *Poetry was her passion, and she wrote more than 1,700 poems in her short life.*

hold[1] /hoʊld/ *verb*

1 to hold something in your hands or arms
- ► **hold**
- ► **carry**
- ► **grip**
- ► **take hold of**
- ► **grasp**
- ► **clutch**
- ► **cling**
- ► **clasp**

2 to keep something in a position
- ► **hold**
- ► **support**
- ► **restrain**
- ► **secure** (*formal*)

1 to hold something in your hands or arms

hold
to have something in your hands or arms: *She was holding a picture of her mother.* | *Can you hold my books for me for a minute?*

carry
to hold something as you move, especially something large or heavy: *Help me carry the suitcases into the house.*

grip
to hold onto something very firmly: *He was gripping the sides of the chair, trying not to get angry.*

take hold of
to begin to hold something, especially tightly: *Ben took hold of the rope and pulled it.*

grasp
to take and hold something tightly with your hands: *His mother walked over, **grasped** him **by** the arm, and pulled him away.*

clutch
to hold something tightly, especially because you do not want to drop it or lose it: *The child was standing alone, clutching her teddy bear and crying.*

cling
to hold on to someone or something tightly, especially because you are frightened: *The little boy was **clinging to** his mother's skirt and crying.*

clasp
to hold one hand with another. You can also use **clasp** to talk about holding a part of someone else's body tightly: *She clasped her hands behind her back.* | *Sophia clasped his face in her hands and smiled at him.*

2 to keep something in a position

hold
to keep something in a position so that it does not move: *Use the pin to hold the cloth in place.* | *The stick was used to hold the window open.*

support
to hold something so that it does not fall: *The six pillars that support the porch roof are rotting.*

restrain (AWL)
to prevent someone from moving or doing something, especially by using physical force: *The boy wasn't strong enough to restrain the horse, and it ran away from him.*

secure (AWL) (*formal*)
to fasten or tie something firmly so that it stays in a position: *At the docks, thick ropes were used to secure the ship.*

→ see **hold on** at **wait**
→ see **hold on to** at **keep**
→ see **hold up** at **delay²**, **support**

hold² /hoʊld/ *noun*

- hold
- grip
- grasp

hold
an act of holding something: *The teacher did not release his **hold on** my arm.* | *I kept a tight hold on my bag in the crowd.*

grip
a strong hold on something: *Get a good grip and hold on tight to the rope.*

grasp
a strong hold on something, especially part of someone's body: *She pulled her hand from his grasp and walked away.*

hole /hoʊl/ *noun*

1 a hole that something can go through
- hole
- space
- gap
- opening
- crack
- slot
- leak
- puncture
- cavity (*formal*)

2 a space in the surface of the ground
- hole
- crater
- pothole
- pit

3 a long narrow hole in the surface of something
- ditch
- trench
- furrow
- rut
- groove

1 a hole that something can go through

hole
an empty place that goes through something, especially where it is broken or torn: *My sock has a **hole in** the toe.* | *The pencil was sharp and poked a **hole through** the paper.*

space
an empty place between two things or two parts of something: *I used to have a big **space between** my two front teeth, but then I got braces.* | *The book will fit in that space on the shelf.*

gap
gap means the same as **space**, but you use it especially when something is broken or missing: *There was a **gap between** the two fences that the boy could fit through.*

opening
a hole that someone or something can go through or see through, especially a hole that is an entrance to something: *The boxes are lowered down through an **opening in** the deck of the ship.*

crack
a small gap between two parts of something that has broken slightly: *There was a **crack in** the eggshell, and you could see the baby bird's beak.*

slot
a long narrow hole that you put something in: *Put the letter in the slot marked International Mail.*

H

leak
a hole that liquid or gas comes out of, where something has been broken or is damaged: *They say that a gas leak caused the explosion.*

puncture
a small round hole made by something sharp, especially one that gas or liquid comes out of: *Experts do not know what made the puncture in the side of the plane.*
→ GRAMMAR: **Puncture** is often used before another noun such as "mark" or "wound": *There were two small puncture marks where the snake had bitten her.*

cavity (*formal*)
a hole or space inside something such as a tooth or body part. **Cavity** is used in scientific and medical language: *The heart and lungs are located inside the chest cavity.*
→ see **pierce** and **tear²** for words meaning "to make a hole in something"

2 a space in the surface of the ground

hole
a space in the surface of the ground that has been dug out or formed naturally by wind, water, etc.: *The dog was digging a **hole in** the flower garden.* | *The action of the water has gradually made a **hole in** the rock.*

crater
a large round hole in the ground made by an explosion or a ball of rock that has fallen from space: *The craters on the Moon are caused by the impact of meteors* (=large pieces of rock traveling through space).

pothole
a hole in the surface of a road: *The street was full of potholes after the cold winter.*

pit
a hole that has been made for a particular purpose by digging: *We dug a pit about two feet deep so that we could start a big fire.*

3 a long narrow hole in the surface of something

ditch
a long narrow hole dug at the side of a field or road for water to flow away: *A ditch ran along the side of the field.* | *A system of ditches in the neighborhood helps to deal with the high ground water levels.*

trench
a long narrow hole that is dug in the ground. A **trench** can be used to carry a pipe or to give soldiers protection during a battle: *Workmen had dug a trench for an underground gas pipe.*

furrow
one of many long lines which have been dug in a field in order to plant crops: *The furrows were filled with snow.*

rut
a deep narrow hole in the ground made by a wheel: *The dirt road to the farm had deep ruts in it from all the trucks that drove down it.*

groove
a thin line that has been cut into a surface: *Then you cut a groove in the wood, so that the two pieces can be fitted together.*

hole

holiday *noun* → see **vacation**

holy *adjective* → see **religious**

home *noun* → see **house**

homework *noun* → see **work²**, Topic **Education**

honest /ˈɑnɪst/ *adjective*

1 being honest, especially in what you say
► honest
► sincere
► truthful

2 not hiding the truth or the facts about something
- ► honest
- ► straightforward
- ► direct
- ► frank
- ► blunt
- ► upfront
- ► outspoken
- ► candid

3 doing business in an honest way
- ► honest
- ► reputable
- ► above board (*informal*)

ANTONYMS → see **dishonest**

1 being honest, especially in what you say

honest
an honest person is good and does not lie or steal: *Do you trust your lawyer? Is he honest?* | *Maria is very honest. She would never cheat on a test.*

sincere
honest and meaning what you say: *When he praised her work, she felt he was being sincere.*

truthful
always giving the true facts about something: *Douglas said he didn't take the money, and I believe he is being truthful.*

ADVERBS

You can make the adjectives **sincere** and **truthful** into adverbs by using an **-ly** ending: *The teacher praised her work sincerely, saying that it was excellent.* | *"I never took the money," Doug said truthfully.*

2 not hiding the truth or the facts about something

honest
saying things in a way that is truthful and not hiding the facts about something: *Thank you for being* ***honest with*** *me – I need to know when I've made a mistake.* | *I want an honest answer – did you take the money?*

straightforward (AWL)
honest and saying something in a clear way that is easy to understand: *My mother gave me a straightforward explanation of how babies are made.* | *He is a good teacher. He is strict, but he is straightforward and fair.*

direct
saying exactly what you mean in an honest and clear way, even if this might upset people: *The doctor was very direct. "You are too heavy and you must lose weight," he said.*

frank
speaking honestly and directly about something, especially when it is something people do not like to talk about and you may upset them: *I have to* ***be frank with*** *you – I don't think you're being very nice.*

blunt
speaking very honestly and directly about something when it would be better to be more polite, so that what you say is likely to upset people: *Let me* ***be blunt*** *– you are behaving like a child, and you must stop.*

upfront
talking honestly about things that are usually private or secret: *He* ***was*** *completely* ***upfront with*** *me about his money problems.*

outspoken
an outspoken person says what he or she thinks, even when other people do not agree: *Lovett was an outspoken critic of the government's energy policy.*

candid
telling the truth, even when the truth may be unpleasant or embarrassing: *He has been* ***candid*** *with reporters* ***about*** *his mental health problems.*

SYNONYM CHECK

Being honest with people

Honest, **straightforward**, **upfront**, and **candid** can all be used to show that you respect or like the person who is telling the truth.

If someone is **direct**, **blunt**, or **outspoken**, he or she does not always say things in a polite way and people may get upset.

Frank is used when you want to show that something needs to be talked about in a clear and honest way, even if it upsets someone.

ADVERBS

You can make the adjectives **honest**, **straightforward**, **direct**, **frank**, **blunt**, and **candid** into adverbs by using an **-ly** ending: *I honestly don't know where he went; I'd tell you if I knew.* | *Frankly, I don't think you've done a very good job.* | *It is impolite to directly tell someone that he or she is fat.*

3 doing business in an honest way

honest
an honest businessperson does not lie to customers or try to cheat them: *Wright Motors are honest car salespeople. They won't sell a car that has something wrong with it.*

reputable
respected for being honest and doing good work: *They are an old and reputable jewelry store and they would never sell a fake diamond.*

above board (*informal*)
a business or deal that is above board is honest and does not break rules or laws: *My lawyer said that everything about the contract is above board, so I am going to sign it.*
→ see Topic **Describing People's Character**

honesty /ˈɑnɪsti/ *noun*

- ► honesty
- ► sincerity
- ► openness
- ► candor (*formal*)
- ► integrity

ANTONYMS → see **dishonesty**

honesty
the quality of being good and not lying or stealing: *He told me the truth about what happened, and I thanked him for his honesty.* | *She told us about her problems with honesty and courage.*

sincerity
the quality of being honest and really meaning the things you tell other people: *I knew he wasn't lying to me – I could see the sincerity in his eyes.*

openness
the quality of being honest and not keeping things secret: *Openness is important in a good marriage. Husbands and wives need to know they can trust each other.*

candor (*formal*)
the quality of talking honestly about things that are usually private or secret, especially things that are embarrassing. **Candor** sounds literary: *Mr. Andrews writes with candor about the pain and embarrassment he was feeling.*

integrity (AWL)
the quality of being honest and doing what you believe is right: *She has a lot of integrity and would not break the rules.*

honor[1] *noun* → see **prize**, **respect**
honor[2] *verb* → see **celebrate**
hop *verb* → see **jump[1]**

hope[1] /hoʊp/ *verb*

- ► hope
- ► wish
- ► expect

hope
to want something to happen or be true, and think it is possible: *I hope they pick me for the team!* | *It has been raining all week, but we are* ***hoping for*** *better weather tomorrow.*

wish
to want something to happen, even though it is unlikely: *I* ***wish that*** *I could afford a new car.* | *When she was young she* ***wished for*** *a big sister instead of a brother.*

expect
to think that something will happen or is very likely: *I have been working hard, so I* ***expect to*** *get an A.*

hope[2] /hoʊp/ *noun*

- ► hope
- ► optimism
- ► dream

hope
the feeling that something good can happen: *It seems that having hope helps patients get better.*
→ A **hope** can also be something good that you want to happen: *She told us about her hopes for the future.*

optimism
a way of thinking that shows you believe good things will happen: *The team had been playing well in practice, and they felt a sense of optimism as they started the game.*

dream
something you really want to happen or achieve, especially something that is very difficult to achieve: *Maya's dream was to win an Olympic gold medal one day.*

hopeful /ˈhoʊpfəl/ *adjective*

- ► hopeful
- ► optimistic
- ► positive
- ► upbeat

ANTONYMS → see **pessimistic**

hopeful
believing that what you want can happen: *Dario was* ***hopeful that*** *he would win the competition.*

optimistic
having an attitude that shows you have hope for the future: *Sales are good, and the company is very* ***optimistic about*** *its future.*

positive (AWL)
thinking about what is good in a situation rather than what is bad: *My teacher is always positive and encouraging, even when he wants us to do better.*

H

upbeat
cheerful and confident that good things will happen, even though the situation has been bad before: *The political situation is still difficult, but we are **upbeat about** the chances of reaching an agreement.*

ADVERBS

You can make the adjectives **hopeful**, **optimistic**, and **positive** into adverbs by using an **-ly** ending: *Danny looked up hopefully at his mother. "Can I go?" he asked.* | *Most people reacted positively to the idea.*

horrible *adjective* → see **bad**, Topic **Describing Food**

horror *noun* → see **fear**[1], **ordeal**, **shock**[1], Topic **Entertainment**

horse /hɔrs/ *noun*

- ► horse
- ► pony
- ► stallion
- ► mare
- ► foal
- ► colt
- ► filly
- ► steed

horse
a large animal that people ride: *The cowboy got on his horse and rode away.*

pony
a small horse: *They bought their daughter a pony to ride.*

stallion
a fully grown male horse: *Nobody could control the stallion.*

mare
a female horse: *The mare kept close to her foal.*

foal
a very young horse: *A foal takes its first steps very soon after birth.*

colt
a young male horse. **Colt** is used mostly by people who race horses: *The race was won by a three-year-old colt.*

filly
a young female horse. **Filly** is used mostly by people who race horses: *The race is for four-year-old fillies.*

steed
a horse that you ride. **Steed** is used mainly in stories, especially fairy tales or stories about knights: *He urged his steed forward into battle.*

hospital *noun* → see Topic **Medical Treatment**

hot /hɑt/ *adjective*

1 when something has or produces heat
- ► hot
- ► warm
- ► lukewarm
- ► scalding
- ► scorching
- ► blistering
- ► boiling (*informal*)
- ► humid

ANTONYMS → see **cold**[1]

2 when food is spicy
- ► hot
- ► spicy
- ► peppery

1 when something has or produces heat

hot
having or producing a lot of heat: *The pan on the stove was still hot, and I burned my fingers when I touched it.* | *Last summer was very hot and humid.*
→ You can also say that a person feels **hot**: *I was so hot! The pool felt great.*

warm
slightly hot: *The bread was still warm from the oven.* | *It was a warm spring day, and the flowers were beautiful.*
→ You can also say that a person feels **warm**: *She was warm and comfortable in bed.*

lukewarm
liquid or food that is lukewarm is slightly warm, usually when it should be hot: *The coffee was lukewarm, but I drank it anyway.*

scalding *also* **scalding hot**
if a liquid is scalding, it is hot enough to burn you: *A waiter spilled scalding hot coffee on her arm, leaving her with serious burns.*

scorching
if the temperature outdoors is scorching, it is extremely hot: *It was a scorching afternoon in July.*

blistering
blistering means the same as **scorching**: *The clothes dried quickly in the blistering sun.*

boiling (*informal*)
if the temperature indoors or outdoors is boiling, it is extremely hot: *Can we turn off the heat? It is boiling in here.*

humid
if the weather is humid, the air outside feels warm and wet: *The area is beautiful, but it's too humid in the summer for me.*
→ see Topic **Describing Places**, **heat¹**, **heat²**

2 when food is spicy

hot
hot food has a taste that burns your mouth: *The salsa was hot.* | *The ghost pepper is supposed to be the hottest chili pepper in the world.*

spicy
spicy means the same as **hot**: *The chicken dish is very spicy, but the pork is milder.*
→ It can be clearer to use **spicy** instead of **hot** when you are talking about food. If you use **hot**, people may not know if you are talking about the temperature of the food or the spice in the food.

peppery
having a spicy taste like pepper. You can use **peppery** to describe food that has pepper in it, or to describe food that tastes like pepper: *The cheese had a peppery taste that made it interesting.* | *The sausages were too peppery for me.*
→ see Topic **Describing Food**

hotel /hoʊˈtel/ *noun*

- ► hotel
- ► motel
- ► resort
- ► bed and breakfast
- ► inn
- ► hostel
- ► lodge
- ► accommodations

hotel
a building where you pay to stay when you are traveling or on vacation: *We stayed at a hotel right by the beach in Hawaii.* | *The hotels downtown are full of people who are here for the conference.*

motel
a hotel you stay in when you are traveling by car, with a place for your car near your room: *I walked over to the motel office to get the key.*

resort
a large hotel or group of hotels, which usually has swimming pools, tennis courts, golf courses, and other activities. **Resorts** are often by the ocean, in the mountains near a ski area, or in other similar areas: *It was a huge resort with its own golf course and a private beach.*

bed and breakfast *also* **B&B**
a house or a small hotel where the price of the room includes breakfast: *The B&B is run by a married couple who live on the ground floor.*

inn
a small hotel, usually not in a big city. **Inns** are often older houses that are now used as hotels: *The inn is an old farm about five miles from the ski area.*

hostel
a cheap place for young people to stay when they are traveling, often with big rooms that many people can sleep in: *The boys stayed for two nights in a hostel near Istanbul.*

lodge
a simple hotel in the countryside, especially in the mountains: *The lodge is built in the style of an old barn and has eight rooms and a breakfast area.*

accommodations
a place to stay or live. **Accommodations** sounds formal and is often used in written information about travel or vacations: *If you are a backpacker looking for cheap, clean accommodations in Thailand, this is the place for you.*
→ see Topic **Travel and Vacations**

SYNONYM CHECK

Hotel or motel?

The door to each room in a **motel** leads outside. In a **hotel**, the door to your room leads into a hallway that is inside the building. **Motels** are often less expensive to stay in than **hotels** because they do not always have restaurants and other shared indoor rooms.

house /haʊs/ *noun*

1 the place where someone lives
- ► house
- ► home
- ► residence (*formal*)
- ► housing
- ► shelter

2 types of houses
- ► house
- ► apartment
- ► condominium
- ► townhouse
- ► duplex
- ► mansion
- ► mobile home
- ► dorm
- ► cabin
- ► cottage
- ► hut
- ► shack

H

1 the place where someone lives

house
a building that people can live in. You use **house** especially about a building that is intended to be used by only one family, but you can use the phrase **my/your/his/her house** to talk about the place where someone lives, even if it is an apartment, condominium, etc.: *There are a lot of big houses on this street.* | *Do you want to have the party at my house?*

home
the place where you live. You can use **home** to mean a town, city, or building, but you use it especially about a place where you feel you belong: *I'm tired – I just want to go home.* | *He has lived in New York for three months now, but it still doesn't feel like home.*
→ Advertisers often use **home** instead of **house** to mean a building, because **home** suggests positive feelings, like being comfortable and in a familiar or safe place: *There are hundreds of new homes being built at the edge of town.*
→ **GRAMMAR:** Don't say: ~~*I went to home*~~ or ~~*I went back my home*~~. Say: *I went home.* Don't say: ~~*I arrived at home at 8:30*~~. Say: *I arrived home at 8:30.*

residence (AWL) (*formal*)
residence means the same as **house**, but is often used about the place where a person in an official position lives: *Reporters waited outside the governor's residence all night.*

housing
the houses and apartments within a particular area that people can live in: *The city is building more low-cost housing downtown.*

shelter
a place that gives you protection from bad weather or danger. You use **shelter** when you are talking about the basic needs of people to have somewhere to stay: *The refugees were given food, and tents were put up for shelter.*

2 types of houses

house
a building where someone lives, which is usually separate from others and is intended to be used by only one family: *They live in a two-story house in the suburbs.* | *Their house has three bedrooms and two bathrooms, and they have a pool in the backyard!*

apartment
a set of rooms where someone can live, in a large building that has many of these sets of rooms. You usually rent an apartment: *The family lives in a two-bedroom apartment in Brooklyn.* | *The apartment building has two empty apartments to rent.*

condominium *also* **condo** (*informal*)
an apartment that you can own rather than rent, which always has land outside it that the owner can use. You can also use **condominium** to talk about a large building that contains several **condominiums**: *My sister bought a condominium near the beach.* | *He lives in a two-story condo with a nice little garden.*

townhouse
a house in a group of houses that share one or more walls: *The couple bought the townhouse when their children went to college.*

duplex *also* **two-family**
a large house that is divided into two parts for two different families or people to live in: *This beautiful duplex was built in 1995 and has a large yard.* | *They bought a two-family in Dallas, and they rent out the upstairs.*

mansion
a very large, expensive house: *Hollywood's*

house

townhouses

apartments

cabin

cottage

duplex

hut

mansion

mobile homes

shack

H

biggest stars have mansions in the hills above Los Angeles.

mobile home *also* **trailer** (*informal*)
a house built in a factory, which a vehicle takes to the place where it will stay. **Mobile homes** are usually made of metal: *My family lived in a mobile home until I was nine.*
→ A neighborhood made up of **mobile homes** is called a "mobile home park" or a "trailer park": *The tornado destroyed a mobile home park on the west side of town.*

dorm *also* **dormitory** (*formal*)
a large building with many rooms for college students to live in while they are at college. Students often share their **dorm rooms** with one or more other students: *Jen was Kerry's roommate in the dorm for their freshman and sophomore years.*

cabin
a small house made of wood, usually in a forest or the mountains: *The early settlers built log cabins in the woods.*

cottage
a small house in the country. You use **cottage** especially about small country houses in Europe or about houses that are used for vacations in the U.S.: *The village was full of beautiful little stone cottages.* | *They have a cottage by the lake where they spend the summer.*

hut
a small simple house or building: *Most of the huts in the village were washed away in the floods.*

shack
a small house that has not been built very well: *The poorest people live in shacks made of pieces of wood, sheets of metal, and cardboard.*

how *adverb, conjunction* → see Function Words

however *adverb* → see Function Word **but**

hug[1] /hʌg/ *verb*

- hug
- hold
- embrace (*formal*)
- cuddle
- cradle

hug
to put your arms around someone to show love or friendship: *We hugged and said goodbye.* | *My mom hugged me and told me she was proud of me.*

hold
to hug someone for a long time, especially as a way to make him or her feel better: *She just held me and let me cry.*

embrace (*formal*)
embrace means the same as **hug** but sounds more literary: *Mr. Randall embraced each of his visitors as they arrived.*

cuddle
to hold someone you love close to you, especially a child or someone you love in a romantic way: *The young couple was cuddling in front of the TV.*

cradle
to hold someone or something gently in your hands or arms, especially a baby or someone who is injured: *Cradling Dan's head in her arms, Paula waited anxiously for the ambulance.*

hug[2] /hʌg/ *noun*

- hug
- embrace (*formal*)
- cuddle

hug
an act of hugging someone: *My aunt gave me a huge hug and a kiss.*

embrace (*formal*)
embrace means the same as **hug** but sounds more literary: *She held him in a long embrace.*

cuddle
an act of holding someone you love close to you, especially a child or someone you love in a romantic way: *The baby was enjoying a cuddle.*

huge *adjective* → see **big**, Topic **Describing Size**

human *noun* → see **person**

humble *adjective* → see **modest**

humid /ˈhyumɪd/ *adjective*

- humid
- muggy
- sticky (*informal*)

humid
if the weather is humid, the air feels warm and wet: *It was hot and so humid that we were sweating just sitting there.*

muggy
muggy means the same thing as **humid** but sounds more informal: *It was muggy, and we didn't feel like moving.*

sticky (*informal*)
sticky weather is very hot and the air feels wet: *In the summer, it's hot and sticky in Florida.*
→ see **damp**, **hot**, Topic **The Weather**

humor /ˈhyumɚ/ *noun*

- ► humor
- ► wit
- ► comedy

humor
funny things that someone says or writes: *The article uses humor to show what is wrong with our system of government in a funny way.*
→ Someone's **sense of humor** is their ability to say funny things or understand things that are funny: *Kelly has a different sense of humor and I don't always get her jokes.*

wit
the ability to say things that are funny and smart: *The author's wit and wonderful storytelling will keep you turning the pages.*

comedy
humor, especially in a performance on stage, on television, or in a movie: *There is both comedy and deep sadness in the play, so be ready for an emotional experience.*
→ A **comedy** is a funny play, TV show, or movie: *The movie is a romantic comedy that stars Hollywood's hottest couple.*

humorous *adjective* → see **funny**

hunger /ˈhʌŋgɚ/ *noun*

1 the feeling of wanting to eat
- ► hunger
- ► appetite
- ► craving

2 the state of needing to eat but not having enough food
- ► hunger
- ► starvation
- ► famine
- ► malnutrition

1 the feeling of wanting to eat

hunger
the feeling you have when you have eaten very little food and want to eat: *By the end of the day I was weak with hunger.* | *Pay attention to your feelings of hunger and only eat when you are really hungry.*

appetite
the feeling that you want to eat: *I felt really sick and completely lost my appetite.* | *After working outside all day, I had a really good appetite.*

craving
a very strong feeling that you want to eat or drink a particular thing: *I had a sudden* ***craving for*** *some ice cream, so I went down to the kitchen.*

2 the state of needing to eat but not having enough food

hunger
the state of needing to eat but not having enough food: *Many families are suffering from hunger because they cannot afford to buy food.*

starvation
a situation in which someone has little or no food to eat: *He got lost in the desert and almost died of starvation.*

famine
a very bad situation when a lot of people do not have enough food to eat: *Floods destroyed the crops and caused famine.*

malnutrition
illness that is caused by not having enough food to eat, or by not eating healthy food: *The boy was thin and weak and obviously suffering from malnutrition.*
→ see **thirst**

hungry /ˈhʌŋgri/ *adjective*

- ► hungry
- ► starving
- ► famished

hungry
needing to eat something: *We were hungry, so we stopped at a restaurant to eat.*

starving
someone who is starving is sick or dying because he or she has not had enough food for a long time: *War has torn the country apart, and people are starving.*
→ People often use **starving** in an informal way to mean that they are very hungry: *I'm starving! When do we eat?*

famished
very hungry. **Famished** sounds slightly old-fashioned: *We had been working outside all day, and we were famished.*
→ see **thirsty**

ADVERBS
You can make the adjective **hungry** into an adverb by using an **-ly** ending: *The children waited hungrily as their mother cooked dinner.*

hunt[1] *verb* → see **search[2]**

hunt[2] *noun* → see **search[1]**, **chase[1]**

H

hurried /ˈhɚid/ *adjective*

- ► **hurried**
- ► **rushed**
- ► **hasty**

hurried
done more quickly than usual: *Many workers now have a hurried lunch at their desks rather than going out for an hour. | She gave the papers a hurried glance before going into the meeting.*

rushed
done too quickly: *The plan should not be rushed – it has to be right.*
→ If a person is **rushed**, he or she feels pressure to get something done quickly: *The president refused to be rushed, saying that the plan would take time.*

hasty
done quickly or without thinking carefully enough: *When he realized he was in the wrong room, he made a hasty exit* (=left quickly). *| She advised him to think carefully and not make a hasty decision.*
→ You can also say that a person is being **hasty**: *Let's not be hasty – we don't want to make the wrong decision.*
→ see **fast**[1] **(2)**

ADVERBS
You can make the adjectives **hurried** and **hasty** into adverbs by using an **-ly** ending: *Worrying about being late for work, Alice swallowed her coffee hurriedly. | It was cold, so we hastily got dressed.*

hurry[1] /ˈhɚi/ *verb*

- ► **hurry**
- ► **rush**
- ► **dash**
- ► **hustle** (*informal*)
- ► **speed up**

hurry
to go somewhere or do something quickly, especially because you do not have much time: *You need to hurry, or you're going to be late for school! | He hurried across the street to the school.*

rush
to go somewhere or do something very quickly: *Everyone rushed out into the street to see what was happening. | When you are taking a test, it's best not to rush. Read the questions carefully.*

dash
to go somewhere quickly, especially by running or walking quickly: *He dashed into the store just as it was closing.*

hustle (*informal*)
to go somewhere or do sth quickly, because there is not much time: *You'll have to hustle or you'll miss the bus.*

speed up
to move or do something faster: *Come on, speed it up! You can walk faster than that. | We are looking for ways to speed up the children's progress in reading.*
→ see **fast**[1], **fast**[2]

hurry[2] /ˈhɚi/ *noun*

- ► **hurry**
- ► **rush**
- ► **haste** (*formal*)

hurry
a situation in which you have to do things very quickly, because you do not have much time. You usually use **hurry** in the phrase **in a hurry**: *I'm **in a hurry** – can we talk about this later? | Why did he leave **in such a hurry**?*

rush
rush means the same as **hurry**: *There was a rush to get everything ready for the party. | He did his homework **in a rush** just before school.*

haste (*formal*)
a lot of speed in doing something, especially so that you make mistakes: *In his **haste** to leave, he forgot his briefcase.*

hurt /hɚt/ *verb*

1 to damage someone's body or your own body

- ► **hurt**
- ► **injure**
- ► **harm**
- ► **wound**
- ► **bruise**
- ► **sprain**
- ► **twist**
- ► **strain**
- ► **pull**

2 if a part of your body hurts, you feel pain in it

- ► **hurt**
- ► **be sore**
- ► **ache**
- ► **burn**
- ► **sting**
- ► **be tender**

3 to upset someone by doing something unkind
- ► **hurt**
- ► **offend**
- ► **insult**
- ► **embarrass**
- ► **humiliate**
- ► **abuse**

1 to damage someone's body or your own body

hurt
to make someone feel pain, often by damaging a part of his or her body: *Was anyone hurt in the accident?* | *She hurt herself playing basketball.*

injure (AWL)
to damage a part of someone's body. **Injure** is slightly more formal than **hurt**, and you use it when the damage to the body seems more serious: *Carter injured his leg when he fell.* | *Nobody was killed in the accident, but several people were seriously injured.*

harm
harm means the same as **hurt** but sounds more formal: *No animals were harmed in the making of this film.*

wound
to injure someone, especially with a knife or gun: *The gunman wounded several people in the attack.*

bruise
to damage the skin or muscles so that there is a blue or purple mark on the skin: *I bruised my thumb when I hit it with the hammer.*

sprain
to injure a joint in your body by suddenly twisting it: *The tennis star had to stop playing after she sprained her wrist.*

twist
twist means the same as **sprain**, but is less formal and you use it when the injury is less serious: *I fell down the steps and twisted my ankle.*

strain
to injure a muscle by stretching it or using it too much: *Julio strained a muscle in his calf when he was hiking.*

pull
pull means the same as **strain**, but is less formal and you use it when the injury is less serious: *A good warm-up will help prevent you from pulling a muscle.*
→ see **injury**

2 if a part of your body hurts, you feel pain in it

hurt
if a part of your body hurts, you feel pain in it: *I ate too much – my stomach hurts.* | *His arm hurt where the doctor had given him the shots.*

be sore
if a muscle or part of your body is sore, you feel a dull pain in it because it has been injured or used more than usual: *When I woke up the next morning, my muscles were sore from running.*

ache
if part of your body aches, it hurts for a long time. You use **ache** especially about muscles, joints, and your head: *She had a fever and her head was aching.*

burn
if your skin or eyes burn, they hurt and feel hot: *All the smoke in the air was making my eyes burn.*

sting
sting means the same as **burn**, but if something **stings** it hurts less or for a shorter time: *Chopping onions can make your eyes sting.*

be tender
if a place on your body is tender, it feels slightly sore or painful when you touch it: *Her knee feels tender where she banged it.*

3 to upset someone by doing something unkind

hurt
to make someone feel very upset, especially by saying something that is not kind: *Words can hurt people, so be polite about what you say.* | *She hurt my feelings when she called me a liar.*

offend
to make someone angry and upset by doing or saying something that is rude or not kind: *His speech offended many Asian people, so he apologized the next day.*

insult
to say something unkind or rude to someone: *One of the boys insulted Jay's mother, saying that she was fat and stupid.*

embarrass
to say or do something that makes someone feel that other people will laugh at or lose respect for him or her: *Almost anything a parent says or does seems to embarrass teenage children.*

humiliate
to make someone feel stupid or weak, usually deliberately and often in front of other people: *Prisoners said that the guards humiliated them by making them stand in their underwear.*

abuse
to do or say cruel things that injure or humiliate someone: *He was reported for abusing his dogs after someone saw him hitting them.* | *For years he abused his wife, shouting and screaming at her constantly.*
→ see **upset²** for **hurt** meaning "to make someone feel sad"
→ see **harm²**, **upset¹**

husband /ˈhʌzbənd/ *noun*

- ► husband
- ► groom
- ► fiancé
- ► spouse (*formal*)
- ► widower
- ► partner

ANTONYMS → see **wife**

husband
the man that a woman is married to: *Tanya's husband is a lawyer.* | *Have you met my husband, Pete?*

groom
a man who is getting married at a wedding ceremony: *The groom waited at the altar as the bride came down the aisle.*

fiancé
the man that a woman has promised to marry: *Her fiancé bought her a beautiful engagement ring.*

spouse (*formal*)
someone's husband or wife. **Spouse** is used mostly on official forms: *The application asks for the name of your spouse.*

widower
a man whose wife is dead: *Mr. Johnson is a widower in his late sixties. He lost his wife last year.*

partner (AWL)
someone's husband, wife, girlfriend, or boyfriend. You often use **partner** when someone is in a relationship and living with someone else but they are not married: *He and his partner are going to New York for a week.*
→ see Topic **Relationships and Marriage**

H

Ii

idea /aɪˈdɪə/ *noun*

1 something that you think of
- ► **idea**
- ► **thought**
- ► **concept**
- ► **notion**

2 the image you have in your mind about what something is like
- ► **idea**
- ► **perception** *(formal)*
- ► **conception** *(formal)*
- ► **impression**

1 something that you think of

idea
something that you think of, especially a new plan or suggestion: *I have an idea – let's go swimming!* | *The Senator's **ideas about** cutting taxes are very popular.*

thought
something that you think in your mind: *The first thought I had when I woke up was, "I forgot to call Lena!"* | *What are your **thoughts about** what we should do for a vacation this year?*

concept (AWL)
an idea about how something is or how something should be done: *Democracy is a very important political concept in the U.S.*

notion (AWL)
an idea about life or society that seems old-fashioned or silly to the person speaking: *There is no evidence to support the **notion that** boys are better at math than girls.*
→ see **theory**

2 the image you have in your mind about what something is like

idea
an image in your mind of what something is like or should be like: *Chefs differ in their **idea of** what makes a good dessert.*

perception (AWL) *(formal)*
your belief or opinion about what someone or something is like: *There is a **perception that** philosophy is a very difficult subject to understand.*

conception (AWL) *(formal)*
the idea that one person has about something in his or her mind: *Families may have different **conceptions of** the roles of husband and wife in the marriage situation.*

impression
the opinion or feeling that you have about someone because of the way he or she seems: *What is your **impression of** Frank as a boss?*
→ see **theory**

ideal *adjective* → see **perfect**

identical *adjective* → see **same**

identify *verb* → see **recognize**

idiom *noun* → see **phrase**

if *conjunction* → see Function Words

ignorant /ˈɪgnərənt/ *adjective*

- ► **ignorant**
- ► **uninformed**
- ► **uneducated**
- ► **illiterate**
- ► **unaware**

ignorant (AWL)
not knowing something, especially something you should know: *Too many students are **ignorant of** world geography.*

uninformed
not having enough knowledge or information: *New immigrants are often **uninformed about** U.S. tax laws.*

uneducated
not having very much education, especially because you have not been able to go to school: *Many of the workers are uneducated and poor.*

illiterate
not knowing how to read or write: *Illiterate adults are often very embarrassed that they cannot read stories to their children.*

unaware (AWL)
not knowing or seeing what is happening: *I was **unaware that** the police were watching my house.*
→ see **stupid**

SYNONYM CHECK
Ignorant, uninformed, and uneducated

Be careful when using **ignorant**, **uninformed**, or **uneducated**. These words can mean simply that someone does not know something, but they can also sound as though you are saying that someone is stupid. It is often more polite to say that someone does not know something, or that someone does not have much education: *Too many students do not know very much about world geography.* | *Many of the workers do not have much education.*

ignore /ɪgˈnɔr/ *verb*

- ► ignore
- ► not pay attention to
- ► disregard
- ► not take any notice of

ignore (AWL)
to deliberately not look at or listen to someone or something: *We waved at the girls, but they walked by and completely ignored us.* | *Some people chose to ignore the hurricane warnings, and they lost their lives because of it.*

not pay attention to *also* **pay no attention to**
to not look at or listen to something, especially when you should do this or when something is hard to ignore: *He had the accident because he was talking on his cell phone and wasn't paying attention to the road.* | *Pay no attention to your sister – she is just being mean.*

disregard
to not do something you should do because you think it is not important or serious: *Students who disregard the dress code and wear skirts that are too short will be punished.*

not take any notice of *also* **take no notice of**
not take any notice of means the same as **not pay attention to** but sounds a little more formal or literary: *The older girls didn't take any notice of us, even though we tried to talk to them.* | *The teacher took no notice of the groans as he passed out the test.*

ill *adjective* → see **sick**

illegal /ɪˈligəl/ *adjective*

- ► illegal
- ► against the law
- ► unlawful (*formal*)
- ► unconstitutional
- ► criminal
- ► forbidden (*formal*)
- ► prohibited

ANTONYMS → see **legal**

illegal (AWL)
not allowed by the law: ***It is illegal to** drive without a license.* | *Police searched the house illegal weapons.*

against the law
against the law means the same as **illegal** but sounds slightly more informal: ***It is against the law to** drive past a stopped school bus.*

unlawful (*formal*)
not allowed by the law. **Unlawful** is used especially when the same thing would be legal in a different situation: *He was charged with making unlawful payments to an elected official.*

unconstitutional (AWL)
not allowed by the constitution (=set of laws, rules, or principles) of a country or organization: *The Supreme Court decided that it was unconstitutional to have separate schools for black and white children.*

criminal
relating to crime. **Criminal** is often used in phrases such as "criminal behavior" or "criminal activity," to mean that someone has done something that is a crime: *The police suspect her husband is involved in criminal behavior such as selling stolen goods.*

forbidden (*formal*)
not allowed by rules or laws: *Vehicles with more than two wheels are forbidden on the island.*

prohibited
prohibited means the same as **forbidden** and is used mostly on official signs and notices: *Drinking alcohol on campus is strictly prohibited.*
→ see **crime**

ADVERBS

You can make the adjectives **illegal**, **unlawful**, **unconstitutional**, and **criminal** into adverbs by using an **-ly** ending: *Did the police search the house illegally?* | *The Supreme Court said the the law unconstitutionally restricts freedom of speech.* | *Someone who is mentally ill is not always criminally responsible if he breaks the law.*

illness *noun* → see **sickness**, Topic **Medical Treatment**

illogical /ɪˈlɑdʒɪkəl/ *adjective*

- illogical (*formal*)
- irrational (*formal*)
- unreasonable
- senseless

ANTONYMS → see **sensible**

illogical AWL (*formal*)
an illogical idea or action is not based on sensible thinking: *It was illogical to shout for help when no one could hear us, but we shouted anyway.* | *Building a mall in such a small town seems completely illogical to me.*

irrational AWL (*formal*)
an irrational feeling, idea, or behavior is not based on sensible thinking or good reasons, but is based on your feelings: *He knows that his fear of cats is irrational, but that doesn't stop him from being frightened of them.*

unreasonable
not based on sensible or good reasons: *People are afraid of catching the disease from someone who has it, but this fear is unreasonable because you can't get this disease from other people.*

senseless
done for no good reason or with no purpose: *There was no reason for the rioting; it was just senseless violence.*

ADVERBS

You can make the adjectives that mean **illogical** into adverbs by using an **-ly** ending: *The characters in the book seem to act illogically, so the story wasn't believable.* | *He became unreasonably angry if I were even a minute late.*

illusion /ɪˈluʒən/ *noun*

- illusion
- hallucination
- vision
- fantasy

illusion
something that appears to be real or true but is not: *The road seems to slope downward but that's an optical illusion. It really slopes upward.* | *In a cartoon, each picture appears on the screen one after the other very quickly, creating the* ***illusion of*** *movement.*

hallucination
something that you think you can see or hear that is not really there. **Hallucinations** are usually caused by illness or drugs: *He had hallucinations in which his plants were talking to him.*

vision AWL
something you see that is like having a dream while you are awake. A **vision** is usually a religious experience: *Saint Bernadette had a vision in which the Virgin Mary appeared before her.*

fantasy
something exciting that you imagine happening, but that is not real: *When I was little, I used to have this fantasy that I would grow wings and fly.*

illustrate *verb* → see **draw**, **explain**, **show**[1]

illustration *noun* → see **example**, **picture**[1]

image *noun* → see **picture**[1], **reputation**

imaginary /ɪˈmædʒəˌneri/ *adjective*

- imaginary
- pretend (*informal*)

ANTONYMS → see **real**

imaginary
something that is imaginary is not real and only exists in your mind: *When Chelsea was a child, she had an imaginary friend that only she could talk to.* | *Let's take an imaginary trip into space, and think about what it might be like to travel to another planet.*

pretend *also* **make-believe** (*informal*)
relating to actions or play in which children imagine that something is really happening: *The girls sat at the table having a make-believe tea party with their dolls.* | *The box of clothes to dress up in is great for children's pretend play.*
→ see **fake**[2], **pretend**

imagination /ɪˌmædʒəˈneɪʃən/ *noun*

- imagination
- creativity

imagination
the ability to think of new things or form pictures in your mind: *Reading is a good way for kids to develop their imaginations.* | *I don't have any photographs of the island, so you'll have to use your imagination.*

creativity AWL
the ability to think of interesting new ideas or make new things: *I really admire people who have the* ***creativity to*** *design new machines that help people.*
→ see **illusion**

I

imagine /ɪˈmædʒɪn/ *verb*

- imagine
- picture
- visualize
- conceive of

imagine
to think about what something might be like: ***Imagine that** the house is made of candy and you can eat it!* | *Can you **imagine how** hard it must have been to cross the prairie in a covered wagon?*

picture
to think of a clear image of something in your mind: *I could picture him at home, pacing the floor and worrying because I was late.*

visualize (AWL)
to picture a situation, especially one that gives you a particular feeling or that helps you achieve something: *To calm yourself down, visualize blue waves breaking on a beautiful beach.* | *Good athletes will visualize themselves running every step of a race before the race begins.*

conceive of
to imagine a situation that is hard to believe could happen: *A hundred years ago, people could not conceive of space travel.*
→ see **dream² (2)**, **pretend**

imitation /ˌɪməˈteɪʃən/ *noun*

- imitation
- impression
- impersonation

imitation
the act of copying the way someone speaks or moves: *Parrots can do a good **imitation of** a human voice.* | *His **imitation of** his mother was funny but kind of mean.*

impression
the act of copying a famous person's voice or behavior in order to entertain people: *He is a comedian who does great impressions. His best one is of Justin Bieber.*

impersonation
the act of copying someone's voice and behavior in order to entertain or trick people: *His **impersonation of** George Clooney was funny.* | *The charges against him include **impersonation of** a police officer.*
→ see **copy¹**

immediate /ɪˈmidiət/ *adjective*

- immediate
- instant
- instantaneous
- prompt

immediate
happening or coming very soon after something: *I wrote them an email, and I got an immediate reply.* | *The decision will have an immediate impact on the size of classes in schools.*

instant
happening very quickly after something so that there is almost no time in between the two events. **Instant** is used especially to talk about success, a reply to a message, or not liking someone: *The movie was an instant success.* | *I took an instant dislike to his friend, who seemed stupid to me.*

instantaneous
happening immediately, without any delay at all: *Computer networks allow banks to make instantaneous transfers of money from one bank to another.*

prompt
done immediately, at the correct time: *If the firefighters hadn't taken prompt action, the man might not have survived.*

immediately /ɪˈmidiətli/ *adverb*

- immediately
- instantly
- at once
- right away
- promptly
- without delay

immediately
very quickly and without very much time in between: *I knew immediately that something was wrong when I saw her crying.* | *He drank a glass of water and immediately began to feel better.*

instantly
immediately after something else, with almost no time between: *It was years since I had seen him, but I recognized him instantly.*

at once
at once means the same as **immediately**: *Take this note to the principal at once, please.*

right away
immediately, because something is important or urgent. **Right away** is less formal than **immediately**: *When she got his message, she called him back right away.*

promptly
happening or done very quickly: *When questioned, she promptly denied that she had been near his house.*

without delay
very quickly and without waiting for anything else to happen. You use **without delay** when something has to be done as soon as possible: *If your credit card is lost or stolen, contact the bank without delay.*

immigrant /ˈɪməgrənt/ *noun*

- ► immigrant
- ► emigrant
- ► migrant

immigrant (AWL)
someone who goes to another country to live there permanently: *There are **immigrants from** all over the world in the United States.*

emigrant
someone who leaves his or her own country in order to live in another country: *Millions of **emigrants from** Eastern Europe settled in New York City in the early 1900s.*

migrant (AWL)
someone who goes to another area or country in order to find work: *Large numbers of migrants from the countryside were moving to the city to find work in factories.*
→ **GRAMMAR: Migrant** is often used before "workers" to talk about people who move around to do farm work, especially people who are from another country: *Many migrant workers from Mexico come to California and find work picking fruit.*

immigrate *verb* → see **move**

immigration *noun* → see Topic **Travel and Vacations**

impatient *adjective* → see Topic **Describing People's Character**

imperfect /ɪmˈpɚfɪkt/ *adjective*

- ► imperfect
- ► flawed
- ► defective
- ► faulty

ANTONYMS → see **perfect**

imperfect
not completely correct or perfect: *It is an imperfect plan, but it's the best one we have.* | *You have to accept that all people and relationships are imperfect in some ways.*

flawed
a flawed plan, idea, or system has weaknesses or bad parts that prevent it from working as well as it should: *The report is flawed, so we shouldn't base any decisions on it.*

defective
a defective machine or product is not made correctly, so it does not work correctly: *If the phone is defective, take it back to the store and get one that works.*

faulty
not made correctly or not working correctly: *The building collapsed because of faulty construction.*
→ **Faulty** can also be used to describe information or thoughts that contain mistakes: *He believes that the government relied on faulty information in making the decision about whether to go to war.*

ADVERBS

You can make the adjective **imperfect** into an adverb by using an **-ly** ending: *The bone had healed imperfectly, so it was weak.*

imply *verb* → see **suggest**

impolite *adjective* → see **rude**

import *noun* → see **product**

importance /ɪmˈpɔrtns/ *noun*

- ► importance
- ► significance
- ► value
- ► worth
- ► prominence

importance
the quality of having a strong effect on people's lives or on what happens: *The players understand the importance of this game, which they must win to stay in the tournament.* | *Americans believe in the importance of freedom of the press.*

significance
the importance that something has now and in the future: *The election of the first black American president was a moment of great historical significance.*

value
the importance or usefulness of something: *Close family relationships are of great value, because they help children grow up to care about other people.*

worth
worth means the same as **value**: *The new computer system has already proven its worth.*

prominence
the fact of being important and well known: *The prominence of the Daley family in Chicago has influenced political life in the city for years.*

important *adjective* → *go to pages 322-323*

impossible /ɪm'pɑsəbəl/ *adjective*

- ► **impossible**
- ► **impractical**
- ► **not feasible** (*formal*)

ANTONYMS → see **possible (1)**

impossible
if something is impossible, it cannot be done, happen, or be true: ***It is impossible** for dogs to talk.* | *The team was so far behind that winning seemed like an impossible task.*

impractical
an impractical plan or way of doing something is too difficult or expensive, or it will not work: *For most people, making bread at home is impractical because it takes too long.*

not feasible (*formal*)
if a plan, idea, or method is not feasible, it cannot be achieved or cannot work: *We cannot organize such a large event in two days – it just isn't feasible.*

ADVERBS
You can make the adjective **impossible** into an adverb by using an **-ly** ending: *He sets impossibly high standards for himself, and becomes frustrated when he cannot achieve them.*

impress /ɪm'pres/ *verb*

- ► **impress**
- ► **dazzle**
- ► **make an impression**

impress
to make someone think you are good or important: *He tried to impress me by taking me to a fancy restaurant.*

dazzle
to make someone admire you a lot. **Dazzle** is less formal than **impress**: *His intelligence and charm dazzled me, and it took me some time to notice that he was sometimes cruel.*

make an impression
to make someone remember you in a good or bad way: *She made a good impression at the interview and was offered the job.*

impression *noun* → see **feeling**, **idea**, **imitation**

impressive *adjective* → see **good**

improve /ɪm'pruv/ *verb*

1 to make something better

- ► **improve**
- ► **make something better**
- ► **perfect** (*formal*)
- ► **raise**
- ► **correct**
- ► **enhance**
- ► **upgrade**
- ► **advance** (*formal*)

ANTONYMS → see **worse (2)** for "to get worse"

2 to do better than before or better than other people

- ► **improve on/upon**
- ► **do better**
- ► **make progress**
- ► **outdo**
- ► **surpass** (*formal*)
- ► **excel**

1 to make something better

improve
to make something better: *He wants to improve his grades, so he has been studying very hard.*
→ You can also use **improve** to say that something becomes better: *If you do more exercise, your health will improve.*

make something better
to change something so that it is better than it was before: *Think about how you can make your report better. You could add a picture or graph, for example.*

perfect (*formal*)
to make something perfect: *The only way to perfect your tennis serve is to practice it over and over again.*

raise
to make the standard or quality of something better than it was before: *The new chef wants to raise the standard of food served in the restaurant.*

correct
to make something better or make it work in the right way: *He wears glasses to correct his vision.*

enhance (AWL)
to improve something by making a good quality in it even better: *The herbs will enhance the flavor of the meat.* | *The old movies have been enhanced using new computer technology so that their colors are more realistic and the picture sharper.*

upgrade
to make a computer, machine, or piece of equipment better than before, sometimes by changing it for a new one: *You will have to upgrade your computer if you want to use this software, because it uses a lot of memory.*

advance (*formal*)
if something advances scientific or technical knowledge, it makes it better: *She hopes that her research will advance medical science.*
→ see **better** (**2**) for "talking about when someone's health improves"

2 to do better than before or better than other people

improve on/upon
to do something better than before: *He came in fourth place in his last race, and he hopes to improve on that this time.* | *The cake was so good I don't see how anyone could improve upon it.*

do better
to reach a higher standard than you did before or than someone else: *He did better on the test than any of the other students in his class.*

make progress *also* **progress**
to continue to get better at doing something. **Progress** is more formal than **make progress**: *She has made good progress in English, and she now makes fewer mistakes.* | *The less experienced players are progressing well.*

outdo
to be better at doing something than someone else: *His younger brother is always trying to outdo him in sports.*

surpass (*formal*)
to be better or greater than someone or something else: *As a musician, he quickly surpassed his teacher.*

excel
to do something much better than most other people, especially because you have a natural ability to do it well: *Federico has always **excelled at** sports.*

improvement /ɪm'pruvmənt/ *noun*

- ► improvement
- ► recovery
- ► recuperation
- ► revival
- ► upturn

improvement
a situation in which something gets better: *His teacher says there has been a big improvement in his work, and he is getting good grades.* | *Her health is showing signs of improvement.*

recovery AWL
the process of getting better after an illness, operation, or injury, or after a bad situation: *We hope Maria will make a full **recovery from** her injuries.* | *There are signs of a recovery in the U.S. economy.*

recuperation
a period of resting and relaxing so that you get better after an illness, operation, or injury: *Menendez had a brain operation, and after a long period of recuperation, he went back to work.*

revival
a situation in which someone or something becomes successful or popular again: *Ten years later, the band had a revival and their latest record sold over a million copies.*

upturn
a time when business activity increases and the economy improves: *Homeowners are hoping for an upturn in the real estate market.*

impulsive /ɪm'pʌlsɪv/ *adjective*

- ► impulsive
- ► spontaneous
- ► rash
- ► hasty
- ► reckless

impulsive
an impulsive action or decision is done suddenly without thinking carefully about it. You use **impulsive** especially about things that one person does or decides, not a group. An **impulsive** action can be good or bad: *It was an impulsive decision to buy the bike, but I saw it and I just had to have it.* | *Part of growing up is learning to control your impulsive behavior.*

spontaneous
a spontaneous activity is something that one or more people suddenly do without planning it first. You use **spontaneous** especially about good things that someone does: *There was spontaneous applause when she made the statement about freedom of speech.*

rash
a rash decision, action, or statement is one that you make or do too quickly, without thinking about how serious the results could be. You use **rash** when you disapprove of what someone has said or done: *Many people began to worry after the senator made a series of rash statements about going to war.*

hasty
hasty means the same as **rash**, but you use it in situations where the results are bad but less serious: *Before you make any hasty decisions*

I

about quitting the team, discuss the situation with the coach.

reckless
a reckless action is dangerous and you have not thought about it carefully before doing it. You use **reckless** when you disapprove of someone's action: *He was arrested for reckless driving after almost hitting two people on the sidewalk.*
→ see **careless**

SYNONYM CHECK
Impulsive, spontaneous, rash, etc.
All these words can also be used to describe someone who does things without thinking or planning first: *Rosa is impulsive and sometimes later regrets what she has done.* | *I'm trying to be more spontaneous and not plan every minute of every day.* | *I think the manager was a little hasty in firing Ted without talking to him about the problem first.*

ADVERBS
You can make the adjectives that mean **impulsive** into adverbs by using an **-ly** ending: *Many children act impulsively, and they must learn to control themselves.* | *She rashly promised to help, before she knew what she would be helping with.* | *He was playing recklessly, not caring whether anyone else got hurt.*

in *preposition, adverb* → see Function Words

inaccurate *adjective* → see **wrong**

inadequate /ɪnˈædəkwət/ *adjective*
- ► inadequate (*formal*)
- ► insufficient (*formal*)
- ► deficient (*formal*)
- ► unsatisfactory (*formal*)

ANTONYMS → see Function Word **enough**

inadequate (AWL) (*formal*)
not enough or not good enough for a particular purpose: *Inadequate lighting made it difficult to read.* | *The parking lot is inadequate for a shopping center of this size.*

insufficient (AWL) (*formal*)
not enough to do what must be done. You use **insufficient** especially about resources such as information, money, and time: *The bank charged me a fee for having insufficient funds in my account.* | *The experiment did not have a clear result because the data was insufficient.*

deficient (*formal*)
not having or containing enough of something to be complete or good: *You can't stay healthy with a diet that is **deficient in** vitamins.*

unsatisfactory (*formal*)
not good enough or not acceptable: *If the situation is unsatisfactory, you should do something to change it.*

ADVERBS
You can make the adjectives that mean **inadequate** into adverbs by using an **-ly** ending, but only the adverbs **inadequately** and **insufficiently** are common: *The room was inadequately lit for reading.* | *Insufficiently trained workers have caused problems for the company.*

inappropriate *adjective* → see **unacceptable**

include /ɪnˈklud/ *verb*
- ► include
- ► contain
- ► come with
- ► incorporate (*formal*)
- ► consist of
- ► cover
- ► involve

ANTONYMS → see **leave out**

include
if one thing includes another, the second thing is part of the first: *The price includes two nights at a hotel.* | *There were 30 people there, including 7 children.*

contain
if a piece of writing, a movie, or a television program contains something, that thing is part of it: *The article contains a list of websites where you can get further information.*

come with
if a meal or product comes with something, that thing is included as part of it. **Come with** is less formal than **include**: *My laptop came with anti-virus software when I bought it.*

incorporate (AWL) (*formal*)
to deliberately include something as part of a larger thing: *I incorporated a quote from Martin Luther King, Jr. into the start of my essay.*

consist of (AWL)
to include or be made of a number of different things: *Your password should consist of at least ten letters and numbers.*

cover
to include or deal with a particular subject or thing: *The book covers the period in history from 1945 to 1968.*

involve (AWL)
if an activity or job involves something, that thing is included in the activity or job and is a necessary part of it: *Teaching involves planning and paperwork as well as dealing with children.*

income *noun* → see **pay²**

incomplete *adjective* → see **unfinished**

incorrect *adjective* → see **wrong**

increase¹ /ɪn'kris/ *verb*

1 to become bigger in size, number, degree, etc.
- increase
- go up
- rise
- grow
- expand

ANTONYMS → see **decrease²**

2 to increase a lot
- double
- triple
- shoot up
- soar

3 to make something increase
- increase
- raise
- expand
- step up
- boost
- maximize
- intensify
- heighten

ANTONYMS → see **reduce (1)**

1 to become bigger in size, number, degree, etc.

increase
if a number, amount, or the degree of something increases, it becomes bigger: *The number of students* ***increased from*** *800* ***to*** *almost 1,000.* | *Houses have continued to increase in value.* | *Studies say that children's self-esteem increases when they do something well and are praised for it.*

go up
to increase. **Go up** is less formal than **increase** and is often used about prices and taxes: *The price of gas has gone up a lot in the last few years.*

rise
to increase. **Rise** is more formal than **increase**: *The population* ***rose to*** *3.4 million.* | *The cost of a college education is rising rapidly.* | *His confidence rose as he made another basket.*

grow
to become bigger in size, number, amount, or degree, especially gradually: *Los Angeles* ***grew from*** *a small town* ***into*** *a huge city.* | *She started doing better in school, and her confidence grew.* | *The economy is expected to* ***grow by*** *3%.*

expand (AWL)
to become bigger in size: *The company is expanding and it needs to hire new workers.* | *Water expands when it is frozen.*

2 to increase a lot

double
to become twice as big: *Since 1950, the number of people who have the disease has almost doubled.*

triple
to become three times as big: *The company's profits tripled last year.*

shoot up
to increase very quickly and suddenly: *Prices* ***shot up by*** *over 50%.*

soar
to increase quickly to a high level: *The temperature* ***soared to*** *over 100 degrees Fahrenheit.*

3 to make something increase

increase
to make something bigger in number, amount, or degree: *They* ***increased*** *his salary* ***by*** *$200 a month.* | *Smoking increases the risk of getting cancer.* | *The attack has increased tension in the region.*

raise
to increase prices or taxes, or increase the level or standard of something: *Gas stations have raised the price of gas again.* | *The college wants to raise the standard of education for all students.*

expand (AWL)
to make something bigger in size: *They plan to expand the company and build a big new factory.*

step up
to increase your efforts or activities in order to try to do something. **Step up** is less formal than **increase**: *Police officers stepped up their efforts to find the missing girl.*

boost
to increase something so that it improves and becomes more successful: *The theme park has boosted tourism in the area.* | *Winning the game helped to boost the team's morale.*

maximize (AWL)
to increase something as much as possible: *The company is looking at ways of maximizing its profits.*

intensify (AWL)
to make something stronger, especially a feeling or your efforts to do something: *Spices help to intensify the flavor of food.* | *The fighters intensified their attacks on U.S. forces.*

heighten
to make something stronger, especially a feeling or effect: *The scary music helps to heighten the effect of the movie.* | *The program heightens awareness of the importance of healthy eating.*

increase² /ˈɪŋkris/ *noun*

1 a situation in which the number or amount gets bigger
- ► increase
- ► rise
- ► growth
- ► gain (*formal*)

2 a large increase
- ► surge
- ► hike (*informal*)
- ► boom
- ► explosion

ANTONYMS → see **decrease¹**

1 a situation in which the number or amount gets bigger

increase
a situation in which the number or amount of something gets bigger: *The company announced a small **increase in** profits.* | *Workers are not likely to get a pay increase this year.*

rise
an increase in the number, amount, or level of something: *There was a sudden **rise in** temperature.* | *The police have not been able to stop the **rise in** crime.*

growth
an increase in the size or amount of something over a period of time: *China has had a period of rapid economic growth.*

gain (*formal*)
a situation in which you get more of something: *The drug can cause weight gain.* | *The candidate has had a **gain in** popularity over the last few months.*

2 a large increase

surge
a sudden large increase in something: *The hot weather caused a **surge in** demand for electricity for air conditioners.*

hike (*informal*)
a large increase in prices, taxes, or wages. **Hike** is often used in news reports: *Will we get another **hike in** the price of gas?*

boom
a sudden large increase in the amount of sales or trade, or in the popularity of something: *The U.S. experienced an economic boom in the 1950s and 60s.* | *There has been a **boom in** sales of diet books.*

explosion
a sudden very large increase in the amount or number of something: *There has been an **explosion in** the number of people using the Internet.* | *The country has had a population explosion, so the number of people under 25 has greatly increased.*

incredible *adjective* → see **good**, **unbelievable**

incredibly *adverb* → see **extremely**

incurable /ɪnˈkyʊrəbəl/ *adjective*

- ► incurable
- ► chronic
- ► terminal
- ► fatal

incurable
an incurable disease cannot be cured: *She suffers from a rare incurable disease.*

chronic
chronic disease or pain continues for a long time and cannot be cured: *Older people are more likely than young people to have chronic illnesses such as heart disease or diabetes.* | *Many people have chronic back pain.*

terminal (AWL)
a terminal illness cannot be cured and causes death: *She developed terminal cancer and she died within a year.*

fatal
a fatal disease or injury causes someone to die: *The disease can be fatal if it is not treated quickly enough.*
→ see **cure**[1]

ADVERBS
You can make the adjectives that mean **incurable** into adverbs by using an **-ly** ending: *She takes care of her chronically ill child.* | *Two people were fatally injured in the accident.*

independence *noun* → see **freedom**

independent /ˌɪndəˈpendənt/ *adjective*

- independent
- self-sufficient
- liberated

independent
able to make your own decisions and take care of yourself, without other people telling you what to do: *She became more independent after she left college and started living on her own.*
→ You also use **independent** about a country or company that is not controlled by another country or company: *Mexico became an independent country in 1821.*

self-sufficient
able to get all the things you need without needing help from other people: *My job didn't pay much, but it was enough for me to be self-sufficient.* | *Some poor African countries are not* ***self-sufficient in*** *food.*

liberated (AWL)
free to do the things you want, and not controlled anymore by rules or by other people telling you what to do: *My marriage had not been happy, and when it ended I felt liberated rather than depressed.*

ADVERBS
You can make the adjective **independent** into an adverb by using an**-ly** ending: *She got advice from other people, but made the decision independently.*

index *noun* → see **list**[1], Topic **Books and Literature**

indirect /ˌɪndəˈrekt/ *adjective*

- indirect
- implicit

ANTONYMS → see **honest (2)**

indirect
not saying something in a direct and honest way: *"I guess you were right," he said, which I understood as an indirect apology for not listening to my warnings.*

implicit (AWL)
not said directly, but suggested in what someone says: *"We know where you live," he said, and his words contained an implicit threat.*

ADVERBS
You can make the adjectives that mean **indirect** into adverbs by using an **-ly** ending: *Angela apologized indirectly, saying that she guessed I was right after all.* | *By telling her that she could be a good student, he was implicitly suggesting that if she worked harder, she would do better in school.*

individual *noun* → see **person**

indoors *adverb* → see Function Word **in**

industry *noun* → see **business**

ineffective *adjective* → see **unsuccessful**, **weak**

inequality *noun* → see **unfairness**

inexpensive *adjective* → see **cheap**

infant *noun* → see **baby**

infect /ɪnˈfekt/ *verb*

- infect
- catch
- spread

infect
to make someone sick by giving him or her a disease or illness: *A sneeze or cough contains germs that can infect other people.* | *Cows that were* ***infected with*** *the disease were destroyed.*
→ Don't say: ~~My sister infected me with a cold~~. Say: *I got a cold from my sister* or *My sister gave me a cold.*

catch
to get an illness from someone else: *Children in school catch colds and other illnesses very easily.*

spread
to cause a disease to move from one person to another: *Mosquitoes spread the disease by biting people.*
→ see **sick**

influence[1] *noun* → see **effect**, **power**

influence[2] *verb* → see **affect**

I

important /ɪm'pɔrtnt/ *adjective*

1 having a lot of value and a big effect on the future
- ► important
- ► significant
- ► major
- ► big (*informal*)
- ► profound (*formal*)
- ► momentous (*formal*)

ANTONYMS → see **unimportant**

2 necessary and having a big effect
- ► important
- ► essential
- ► vital
- ► crucial
- ► critical
- ► key
- ► imperative (*formal*)
- ► instrumental (*formal*)

ANTONYMS → see **unnecessary**

3 having a lot of power or influence
- ► important
- ► powerful
- ► influential
- ► prominent (*formal*)
- ► dominant (*formal*)

1 having a lot of value and a big effect on the future

important
if something is important, it has a strong effect on a situation and people care about it: *Is money more important than happiness? | Becoming a doctor is very **important to** me.*

significant (AWL)
important and having a strong effect on what happens in the future: *The new drug is a significant step forward in our fight against the disease.*

major (AWL)
having a very large or important effect, especially when compared to other things: *Smoking is a major cause of lung disease.*

big (*informal*)
important and having a serious effect on the future. **Big** is less formal than **important**, and you use **big** about events, changes, and decisions: *I always ask for advice before making a big decision.*

profound (*formal*)
having a very strong influence or effect on a situation, especially so that major changes happen: *The writer's experience of war had a profound effect on his work.*

momentous (*formal*)
a momentous event, change, or decision has a much more important effect on the future than most events, changes, or decisions: *After she made the momentous decision to cancel the wedding, she then had to tell her parents.*

SYNONYM CHECK

Important or significant?

You can use **significant** when you are talking about numbers or amounts, but you cannot use **important** in this way. Don't say: ~~*There has been an important decrease in the number of bees in the wild*~~. Say: *There has been a significant decrease in the number of bees in the wild.*

2 necessary and having a big effect

important
necessary, because of having a big effect on you or on the future: *Eating healthy food is **important for** your health and makes you feel better about yourself. | **It's important to** read all the instructions before you start.*

essential
needed in order to do something or for something to happen: ***It's essential that** you work hard if you want to get good grades.*

vital
extremely important and necessary, and you will have serious problems if you do not have it or do it: ***It is vital that** you turn off the electricity before touching the wires.*

crucial (AWL)
important and necessary, because other things depend on it: *Our defense was great, and that was **crucial to** winning the game.*

critical
critical means the same as **crucial**: *Having a positive attitude is **critical to** achieving your goals.*

key
key people or things are very important and necessary in order for something to happen or be successful: *She has played a key role in the success of the company.*

imperative (*formal*)
extremely important and needing to be done or dealt with immediately: *It is **imperative that** the report is ready by tomorrow.*

instrumental (*formal*)
if someone is instrumental in doing something, he or she is the main reason why it happens: *He was **instrumental in** persuading two large companies to give money to the event.*

3 having a lot of power or influence

important
an important person or organization has a lot of power or influence: *She is an important senator who is on several committees.* | *All our customers are important.*

powerful
a powerful person, country, or organization has a lot of control over other people or over what happens: *China has become a very powerful country, especially economically.*

influential
having the power to affect the way something develops or how people think and behave: *This influential book is the source of many modern political ideas.*

prominent (*formal*)
well-known and having a lot of influence or power. You use **prominent** about people, not ideas or other things: *The Secretary of State is among a group of prominent politicians who oppose the bill.*

dominant AWL (*formal*)
more powerful than other things or people: *The United States is still the dominant economic and military power in the world.*

→ see **emphasize** for words meaning "to say or show that something is important"
→ see **main**

ADVERBS

You can make the adjectives **important**, **significant**, **profound**, **essential**, **vital**, **crucial**, **critical**, and **prominent** into adverbs by using an **-ly** ending: *You should exercise and, equally importantly, eat healthy food.* | *"I'm in charge," he said importantly.* | *The war profoundly influenced the writer's work.* | *The information was critically important to their decision.* | *These two teachers figured prominently in the development of his career as a dancer.*

informal /ɪnˈfɔrməl/ *adjective*

1 relating to words or clothes you use when you are relaxing
- ► informal
- ► casual

ANTONYMS → see **formal**

2 not done in an official way
- ► informal
- ► relaxed
- ► unofficial

ANTONYMS → see **official**

1 relating to words or clothes you use when you are relaxing

informal
informal words or clothes are used when you are with your friends, but are not suitable for an official situation: *You should not use informal words like "cool" in essays.*

casual
casual clothes are not formal, and you usually wear them when you are not working: *The students wear casual clothes such as jeans and T-shirts.*

2 not done in an official way

informal
not done in an official way or according to rules: *The interview was very informal – it was more like talking to a friend.*

relaxed
a situation that is relaxed is comfortable and informal, and you do not have to worry about obeying official rules: *The classroom was a relaxed place where students felt free to talk about their ideas.*

unofficial
not done according to official rules or ways of doing things, and not officially approved: *He met the Mexican president during an unofficial visit to the country. | According to an unofficial report, 50 people were injured during the riots.*

ADVERBS

You can make the adjectives **informal**, **casual**, and **unofficial** into adverbs by using an **-ly** ending: *The party will be at the park, so dress casually. | The evening was a chance to meet my children's teachers informally and ask questions about the school. | She was told unofficially that she got the job, and the official letter would come next week.*

information /ˌɪnfəˈmeɪʃən/ *noun*

- ► information
- ► fact
- ► detail
- ► data
- ► material

information
things that you know or can find out about a person, situation, event, etc.: *The website has a lot of useful **information about** visiting New York. | I'm looking for **information on** the Vikings for a history report.*
→ **GRAMMAR:** **Information** cannot be used in the plural. Don't say: ~~*a lot of informations*~~.

fact
a piece of information that you can show to be true: *Here is a weird fact – cats have 32 muscles in each ear. | Judges have to think about the facts of a case when they decide the punishment for a crime.*

detail
a small piece of information about something, which tells you exactly what it is like: *You can find more **details about** the program on the college website.*

data AWL
facts, numbers, and other information that have been collected and stored, especially on a computer. **Data** is used especially when writing about technical or scientific subjects: *Computers can store a lot of data.*
→ **GRAMMAR:** **Data** can be followed by a singular verb or a plural verb: *The data is correct* or *The data are correct*. **Datum** is the singular form of data and means "a piece of information," but it is only used in very technical writing.

material
information that you use when you write a book or report, or make a movie or program: *He is collecting **material for** a novel about life in Harlem in the 1920s.*
→ see **instructions**

in front of *preposition* → see Function Words

ingredient *noun* → see Topic **Eating in a Restaurant**

inherit *verb* → see **get**

inject *verb* → see Topic **Medical Treatment**

injure *verb* → see **harm²**, **hurt**

injury /ˈɪndʒəri/ *noun*

- ► injury
- ► wound
- ► cut
- ► scratch
- ► bruise
- ► bump
- ► sprain
- ► break
- ► fracture

injury AWL
damage to someone's body caused by an accident: *She can't play in the game, because she has a leg injury.* | *After the accident, José was taken to the hospital with serious injuries.*

wound
a deep cut or hole in someone's skin, caused by a weapon such as a knife, bullet, or bomb: *The congresswoman had a bullet* ***wound to*** *her head and she was lucky to survive the attack.*

cut
an injury caused when something sharp cuts someone's skin: *Cuts are always a risk when you are cooking, so be careful with the knives.*

scratch
a small cut on someone's skin, which is not deep: *I had a few* ***scratches on*** *my hand from playing with the kitten.*

bruise
a dark mark on someone's skin, where it has been hit by something: *The boxer was covered in bruises after the fight.*

bump
a raised area on someone's skin, where it has been hit by something: *"How did you get that* ***bump on*** *your head?" "I walked into a door."*

sprain
an injury from twisting your wrist, ankle, or knee, which is usually not serious: *It is just a sprain – you should rest your ankle for a week.*

break
the place where a bone has broken: *The doctor showed me the break on the X-ray.*

fracture
a crack or a broken part in a bone: *She suffered a hip fracture after falling down the steps.*
→ see **harm¹**, **hurt**

injury

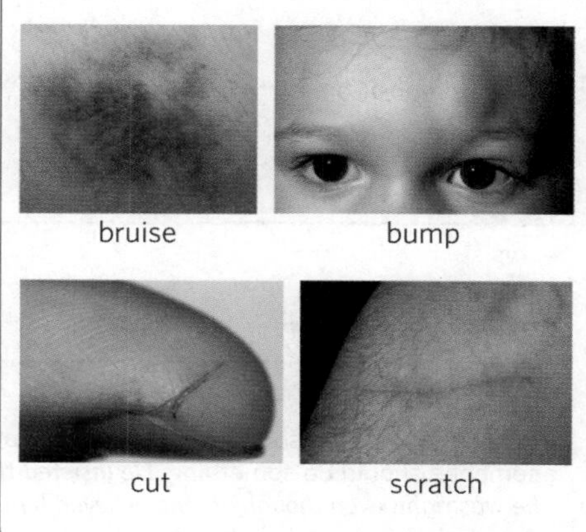

innocent /ˈɪnəsənt/ *adjective*

- ► innocent
- ► not guilty

ANTONYMS → see **guilty (2)**

innocent
if someone is innocent of a crime, he or she did not do it: *His friends say that he is innocent and that he was with them when the robbery took place.*

not guilty
innocent. You use **not guilty** especially when talking about a trial in a court of law: *Wilson pleaded not guilty to all the charges against him.* | *The court found her not guilty.*
→ A court of law does not say that someone is **innocent**. The court can only say that someone is **not guilty**.

in order to *conjunction* → see Function Words

inquire *verb* → see **ask**

inquiry *noun* → see **investigation**, **question¹**

insect /ˈɪnsekt/ *noun*

- ► insect
- ► bug (*informal*)
- ► pest

insect
a small creature with six legs, for example a bee, fly, or ant: *The air was filled with thousands of tiny insects.* | *I had an insect bite on my arm.*

bug (*informal*)
an insect: *The screen door keeps the bugs out of the house.*
→ In science, a **bug** is one type of insect, but most people use **bug** to mean any insect.

pest
an insect or animal that causes damage, for example by harming crops: *Farmers use chemicals to kill pests that destroy their crops.*

inside¹ /ɪnˈsaɪd/ *noun*

- ► the inside
- ► interior
- ► core

ANTONYMS → see **outside²**

the inside
the inner part of something, which is surrounded or hidden by the outer part: *The inside of the tree was hollow.* | *The door had been locked from the inside and I couldn't open it.*

interior
the inside of a building or car: *The interior of the apartment was dark.* | *The car has a leather interior.*

core (AWL)
the central part of something, especially of a planet or of fruits such as apples: *Remove the cores and bake the apples for 40 minutes.* | *The Earth's core was formed billions of years ago.*

inside

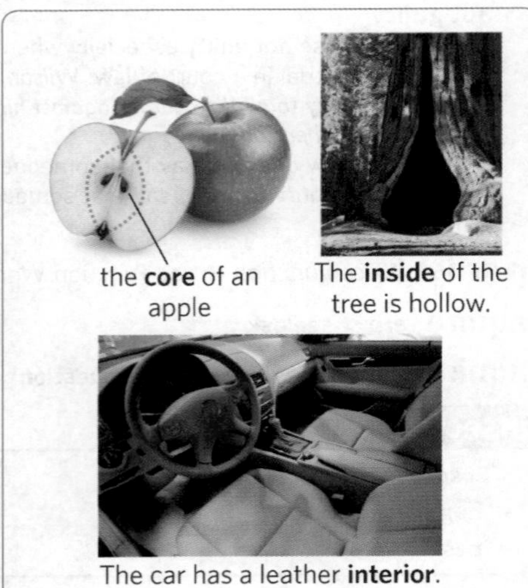

the **core** of an apple

The **inside** of the tree is hollow.

The car has a leather **interior**.

inside² /ɪnˈsaɪd/ *adjective*

- ► inside
- ► internal
- ► interior
- ► inner
- ► innermost (*formal*)

ANTONYMS → see **outside¹**

inside
in or on the part of something that is not the outside: *He keeps his money in the inside pocket of his jacket.*

internal (AWL)
inside someone's body or a building: *She suffered serious internal injuries as a result of the accident.* | *The internal walls are painted white.*

interior
inside a building: *Leave the interior doors open to allow air to move around the house.*

inner
close to the middle of something: *The inner part of this type of orange is a surprising red color.*

innermost (*formal*)
farthest inside: *They went down into the innermost depths of the cave.*

inside

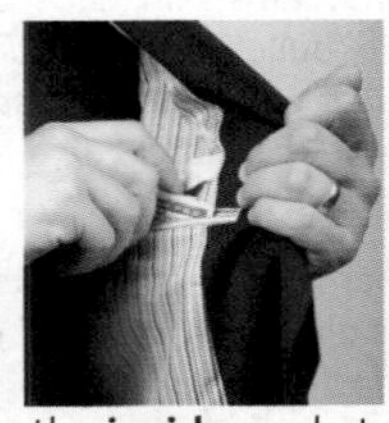

the **inside** pocket of his jacket

The **inner** part of the orange is red.

an **interior** door

The **internal** walls are painted blue.

inside³ *preposition, adverb* → see Function Word **in**

insist /ɪnˈsɪst/ *verb*

- ► insist
- ► demand
- ► be insistent (*formal*)

insist
to keep saying that something is true, or that someone should do something: *He **insisted that** he was right, even though no one believed him.* | *Amy **insisted on** coming along to help.*

demand
to say very firmly that you want something to happen: *The security guards **demanded to** see her ID.*

be insistent (*formal*)
to keep saying that someone should do something, especially when that person does not want to do it: *I didn't want to go to the party, but my friends were very **insistent that** I should go.*

inspect *verb* → see **check**[1], **examine**

inspection *noun* → see **check**[2], **examination**

inspiration *noun* → see **encouragement**

inspire *verb* → see **encourage**

instant *adjective* → see **immediate**

instantly *adverb* → see **immediately**

instead *adverb* → see Function Words

institution *noun* → see **organization**

instruct *verb* → see **order**[2]

instruction *noun* → see **education**

instructions /ɪn'strʌkʃənz/ *noun*

- instructions
- directions
- recipe
- guidelines
- manual
- handbook

instructions
information that tells you how to do something: *Always read the instructions carefully before you begin the test. | I followed the instructions that came with the model airplane to put it together.*

directions
information about how to go to a place: *She gave me **directions to** her house.*
→ In more formal English, **directions** also means "information that tells you how to do something": *The teacher told the students to follow the directions that were written on the board.*

recipe
a set of instructions that tells you how to cook something: *This is the best **recipe for** chocolate cake.*

guidelines (AWL)
official rules about the best way to do something: *The government has announced new **guidelines for** food safety.*

manual (AWL)
a book that gives instructions about how to use something or do something: *The camera comes with a manual.*

handbook
a small book with useful information about doing something: *The employee handbook tells you what to do if you are sick and cannot come to work.*
→ see **advice**

instructor *noun* → see **teacher**

instrument *noun* → see **tool**

insult *verb* → see **hurt**, **offend**

insulting *adjective* → see **offensive**

intelligence /ɪn'telədʒəns/ *noun*

- intelligence
- intellect (*formal*)
- brilliance
- wisdom
- common sense
- sense

intelligence (AWL)
the ability to learn and understand things: *How smart are you? These questions will test your intelligence. | In the animal world, dolphins and chimpanzees have about the same level of intelligence.*

intellect (*formal*)
the ability to think in an intelligent way and understand complicated ideas: *It was obvious from his speeches that the president was a man of great intellect.*

brilliance
a very high level of intelligence or ability: *Her brilliance as a scientist led to some important discoveries.*

wisdom
the ability to make good decisions and give good advice, because you have a lot of knowledge and experience: *We hope that our politicians will have the wisdom to make the right decisions.*

common sense
the ability to make good decisions when you are doing practical things: *Growing vegetables isn't difficult – you just need to use your common sense.*

sense
the ability to think about something in a sensible and practical way, and do what is best in a particular situation: *He should have had the sense to turn off the electricity first before trying to repair the lamp.*

intelligent /ɪnˈtelədʒənt/ *adjective*

1 intelligent – used about a person
- ► intelligent
- ► smart
- ► bright
- ► brilliant
- ► gifted
- ► wise
- ► quick
- ► sharp
- ► clever
- ► shrewd
- ► intellectual

ANTONYMS → see **stupid**

2 intelligent – used about ideas, actions, or things
- ► intelligent
- ► smart
- ► brilliant
- ► ingenious
- ► wise
- ► shrewd
- ► intellectual

1 intelligent – used about a person

intelligent (AWL)
able to learn and understand things quickly: *Dolphins are very intelligent animals that can be easily trained to do tricks.* | *Her son is highly intelligent.*

smart
smart means the same as **intelligent** but is less formal: *Diego is so smart. He'll probably become either a doctor or a lawyer.* | *She is a smart girl, and she works hard at school.*

bright
able to learn and understand things quickly. Use **bright** especially about children and young people: *Spencer is a bright kid – I'm sure he'll do well in kindergarten.*

brilliant
extremely intelligent and good at the work that you do: *The case was won by a brilliant young lawyer from Memphis.*

gifted
having a higher level of intelligence than most people, and likely to do well in school: *Some of the high school's gifted students also attend classes at the community college nearby.*

wise
able to make good decisions and give sensible advice, especially because you have a lot of experience: *As I became older and wiser, I realized that I had made many mistakes.*

quick
able to learn new things and react quickly: *Jen is so quick – she has a funny answer for everything!*

sharp
intelligent and able to notice and understand things quickly so that you are not easily tricked or confused: *A sharp salesman knows how to get you to buy the car at the right price.*

clever
smart and good at thinking of new ideas or ways of doing things. You often use **clever** about people who are good at thinking of new ways to do bad things: *The thief was clever enough to avoid being caught by the police for six years.*

shrewd
good at understanding situations or people and at making decisions to get what you want: *Sachs was a shrewd judge of character and chose his staff well.*

intellectual
intelligent and interested in thinking and talking about serious ideas: *Mark is very intellectual and prefers reading literature to watching TV.*

2 intelligent – used about ideas, actions, or things

intelligent (AWL)
an intelligent idea, question, decision, etc. is done by someone who has thought about the subject carefully and understands it well: *After the lecture, Amanda asked some intelligent questions.*

smart
a smart idea or action is good or sensible and shows that someone used his or her intelligence: *It was **smart to** call first to see if the store was open before driving all the way there.* | *She is a young businesswoman with a lot of smart ideas.*

brilliant
brilliant ideas are very good and show a lot of intelligence and imagination: *Sandra came up with a brilliant plan to raise money for the school.*

ingenious
an ingenious thing or method works very well or solves a problem that nothing else solves, and is usually designed in an intelligent way: *This ingenious gadget chops onions without making your eyes water.*

wise
a wise idea or action is sensible and shows that someone has learned from his or her experiences: *It was **wise to** leave when you did, because you avoided a fight.*

shrewd
a shrewd decision or choice is likely to be right because the person who makes it is good at understanding situations or people: *Charles made some shrewd investments when he was young, and now he has so much money that he doesn't have to work.*

intellectual
relating to serious ideas or subjects that interest intelligent people: *There aren't many TV shows on intellectual subjects, but this news and opinion show often makes me think more deeply about things.*

ADVERBS

You can make the adjectives that mean **intelligent**, and that are used about ideas, actions, and things, into adverbs by using an **-ly** ending: *He plays the game intelligently, not relying on luck.* | *They learned to spend their money wisely, and not on things they didn't need.* | *The class was intellectually challenging.*

intend *verb* → see **plan to**

intention *noun* → see **goal**

intentional *adjective* → see **deliberate**

intentionally *adverb* → see **deliberately**

interest[1] /ˈɪntrəst/ *verb*

- interest
- find something interesting
- fascinate
- intrigue
- appeal to

ANTONYMS → see **bore**

interest
if something interests you, it makes you want to know more about it: *Politics had always interested me and I decided to study it at university.* | *Your story will be better if you write about what interests you.*

find something interesting
if you find something interesting, you like it and want to know more about it: *I found the TV show about the Antarctic really interesting.*

fascinate
to interest you a lot so that you want to spend a lot of time learning about it: *Cars fascinate him, and he wants to be a mechanic when he is older.*

intrigue
to interest you because something seems unusual or mysterious: *The title of the book intrigued me. It was called "How to Talk to Your Pets."*

appeal to
to be the kind of thing that interests a particular person or group: *These stories appeal to boys because they contain lots of exciting adventures.*
→ see **attract**

interest[2] *noun* → see **attention**, **hobby**, **profit**

interested /ˈɪntrəstɪd/ *adjective*

- interested
- fascinated
- curious
- intrigued
- absorbed
- engrossed
- enthralled (*formal*)
- obsessed

ANTONYMS → see **bored**, **uninterested**

interested
giving a lot of attention to something because you want to find out more about it or because you enjoy it: *Are you **interested in** sports?* | *The kids suddenly became interested when I mentioned the word "cookies."*

fascinated
very interested in something: *I'm fascinated by the idea of time travel – wouldn't it be great to be able to go back to different time periods?*

curious
wanting to know or learn about something: *Small children are naturally curious and are always asking questions.*

intrigued
interested in something because it seems unusual or strange: *Scientists are intrigued by the rock, which they think may have come from outer space.*

absorbed
very interested in something and giving it all your attention: *The book has a really good story and I was completely **absorbed by** it.*

engrossed
engrossed means the same as **absorbed** but sounds a little more formal: *He was so **engrossed in** watching the game on TV that he did not hear me go out.*

enthralled (*formal*)
to feel very excited by something and enjoy it a lot, and give it all your attention. You use **enthralled** especially when people are interested in stories or entertainment: *From the beginning of the play, the audience was enthralled.*

obsessed
thinking or worrying about someone or something all the time and not being able to think about anything else: *Some people are so **obsessed with** losing weight that they hate their bodies.*

ADVERBS

You can make the adjective **curious** into an adverb by using an **-ly** ending: *"Why did he do that?" she asked curiously.*

interesting /ˈɪntrəstɪŋ/ *adjective*

- interesting
- fascinating
- intriguing
- engaging
- stimulating
- absorbing
- engrossing
- enthralling (*formal*)

ANTONYMS → see **boring**

interesting
keeping your attention and making you want to know more: *I saw an interesting show on TV about whales. | The novel was really interesting. I think I'll read more of his books.*

fascinating
very interesting: *New York is a fascinating city because there are so many places to visit and so many things to do.*

intriguing
interesting because something seems unusual or mysterious and you want to find out more: *The movie tells the intriguing story of a boy who was found in a forest, and nobody knows where he came from.*

engaging
making you feel interested and keeping your attention. You use **engaging** about people, books, movies, or games: *The story is engaging and perfect for young children. | She has an engaging personality.*

stimulating
giving you new ideas or experiences in a way that is interesting and enjoyable: *It was a good evening, full of stimulating conversation and excellent food.*

absorbing
very interesting so that you give something all your attention: *It is a brilliant and completely absorbing motion picture that has won several prizes.*

engrossing
engrossing means the same as **absorbing** but is more formal: *The reason the book is so engrossing is that all the characters seem real.*

enthralling (*formal*)
very interesting, exciting, and enjoyable. You usually use **enthralling** about stories or things you watch: *Visitors to the show will find it an enthralling experience.*

ADVERBS

You can make the adjectives **interesting**, **fascinating**, **intriguing**, and **engaging** into adverbs by using an **-ly** ending: *Interestingly, he is doing much better than expected in the election campaign. | The book is engagingly written.*

interfere /ˌɪntəˈfɪr/ *verb*

- interfere
- meddle

interfere
to get involved in a situation, when other people do not want you to: *I wish my parents would stop interfering and let me make my own decisions.*

meddle
meddle means the same as **interfere** but is less formal. You use **meddle** when you are very annoyed with someone for doing this: *China does not want the U.S. **meddling in** its political affairs.*
→ see **interrupt**

intermediate *adjective* → see **medium**

internal *adjective* → see **inside²**

international /ˌɪntəˈnæʃənəl/ *adjective*

- international
- global
- worldwide

ANTONYMS → see **national**

international
between two or more countries or involving more than one country: *More than 15 countries will sign an international agreement. | All international flights have been canceled.*

global
including or affecting the whole world: *Global warming will cause the level of the oceans to rise. | The global economy is experiencing great problems.*

worldwide
everywhere in the world: *The company had worldwide sales of $9.5 billion last year.*

ADVERBS
You can make the adjectives **international** and **global** into adverbs by using an **-ly** ending: *Their products sell internationally.* | *Globally, the company employs 750,000 people.*

Internet *noun* → see Topic **Computers and the Internet**

interrupt /ˌɪntəˈrʌpt/ *verb*

- ► **interrupt**
- ► **disturb**
- ► **bother**
- ► **distract**

interrupt
to do something that stops someone from continuing to do what he or she was doing: *I'm sorry to interrupt you while you're working, but there is someone here to see you.* | *My thoughts were interrupted when the phone started ringing.*

disturb
to interrupt what someone is doing in a way that is annoying: *Go take a nap, and I'll make sure no one disturbs you.*

bother
to interrupt and annoy someone by wanting attention when he or she is busy: *Mom, I'm trying to do my homework, but Chloe keeps bothering me!*

distract
to make someone stop paying attention to something by making him or her notice something else: *The girls' conversation was* ***distracting*** *the other students* ***from*** *what the teacher was saying.*
→ see **annoy**

interruption *noun* → see **pause²**

interval *noun* → see **time**

interview /ˈɪntɚˌvyu/ *noun*

- ► **interview**
- ► **interrogation**

interview
a meeting in which someone asks you questions to find out what you are like, for example to find out whether you are right for a job or to find out what your life is like: *My job interview went really well. They asked some hard questions, but I had good answers.* | *During the interview, Johnny Depp talked about his latest movie.*

interrogation
an occasion when someone is formally asked a lot of questions for a long time in order to get information. **Interrogations** are not friendly and are usually done by the police, the military, or the government: *The interrogation lasted for three hours, but the prisoner refused to answer any questions.*
→ see Topic **Jobs and Work**

introduce /ˌɪntrəˈdus/ *verb*

- ► **introduce**
- ► **present** (*formal*)

introduce
if you introduce someone, you tell people his or her name when they first meet: *Your friend is cute – can you* ***introduce*** *me* ***to*** *him?* | *After the lecture I went up to the speaker and* ***introduced myself.***

present (*formal*)
to formally introduce someone to another person. You only use **present** in very formal or official situations: *She was taken to the palace and presented to the queen.*

invade *verb* → see **attack²**

invasion *noun* → see **attack¹**

invent *verb* → see **create**, **lie²**, Topic **Science and Technology**

invention /ɪnˈvenʃən/ *noun*

- ► **invention**
- ► **creation**
- ► **innovation**

invention
something new that someone has designed or made for the first time: *The car was a German invention – the first car was made by Karl Benz in 1885.* | *Edison was responsible for the invention of the electric light bulb in 1879.*

creation (AWL)
something new that someone has thought of by using his or her imagination and has made, drawn, written, etc., for example a character in a book or a new type of fashion: *Mickey Mouse was the creation of Walt Disney.*

innovation (AWL)
something new that someone has thought of, especially a new way of doing something: *The Internet is a fairly recent innovation – it didn't exist in its current form much before the 1990s.*
→ see Topic **Science and Technology**

inventor *noun* → see Topic **Science and Technology**

invest /ɪnˈvest/ *verb*

- ► invest
- ► back
- ► put money into

invest (AWL)
to buy property, shares, or other things because you hope their value will increase and you will make a profit: *He **invested** $100,000 **in** his brother's business. | Why don't you invest the money on the stock market?*

back
to invest in a project or business, especially when doing this shows that you support the goals of the project or business: *The project aims to get teenagers into jobs, and is backed by several major companies.*

put money into
to give or lend money in order to help someone to be able to do something: *Every year the charity puts millions of dollars into research on finding ways to treat cancer.*

investigate *verb* → see **find out**, **research²**

investigation /ɪnˌvestəˈgeɪʃən/ *noun*

- ► investigation
- ► inquiry

investigation (AWL)
an official attempt to find out what happened, especially when there has been a crime or accident: *The police **investigation of** the murder led to two men being arrested. | NASA held a formal **investigation into** the failure of the equipment.*

inquiry
an official public investigation of something, usually by a committee of people: *There will be an **inquiry into** the crash, in which over 100 people died.*

invite *verb* → see **ask**, **call**

involve *verb* → see **include**

irony *noun* → see **sarcasm**, Topic **Books and Literature**

irritate *verb* → see **anger²**, **annoy**

irritated *adjective* → see **angry**

irritating *adjective* → see **annoying**

irritation *noun* → see **anger¹**

issue *noun* → see **subject**

item *noun* → see **thing**

I

Jj

jacket *noun* → see **coat**

jail *noun* → see **prison**

jam /dʒæm/ *noun*

- ► jam
- ► blockage
- ► obstruction
- ► hold-up (*informal*)

jam
a situation in which something is stuck in a machine and is preventing things from moving through it: *I think there is a jam in the photocopier.* → You also use **jam** or **traffic jam** when a line of vehicles cannot move along the road or can only move very slowly, because there are too many cars or something is blocking the road: *We arrived late because of a traffic jam.*

blockage
something that stops things from moving through a pipe or tube: *The water won't go down the sink – there must be a blockage in the pipe.*

obstruction
something that blocks something such as a tube, path, or road. **Obstruction** is more formal than **blockage**: *She had an operation to remove an obstruction from her throat.* | *The fallen tree has caused an obstruction in the road.*

hold-up (*informal*)
something that stops you from being able to continue doing something or going somewhere, especially when this only lasts a short time: *The work being done on the freeway is causing major traffic hold-ups.* | *The materials didn't come on time but, despite the hold-up, we finished the work by the deadline.*

jam

a traffic **jam**

There is a **blockage** in the pipe.

The fallen tree has caused an **obstruction** in the road.

jealous /ˈdʒeləs/ *adjective*

1 unhappy because someone has something that you want
- ► jealous
- ► envious

2 unhappy because you think someone loves another person
- ► jealous
- ► possessive

1 unhappy because someone has something that you want

jealous
feeling unhappy or angry because another person has something that you want to have: *I think he is jealous because I got the job and he didn't.* | *I was **jealous of** my sister because she was prettier than me.*

envious
wishing that you had something nice or special that someone else has: *I was not allowed to go to parties, and I was **envious of** the girls who did.*

SYNONYM CHECK

Jealous or envious?

Jealous and **envious** can often be used to mean the same thing, especially in spoken English. However, if you are **jealous**, you are angry or unhappy that another person has something and you don't. If you are **envious**, you want something that someone else has, but you do not always feel unhappy or angry about it.

2 unhappy because you think someone loves another person

jealous
feeling unhappy or angry because you think someone you love might love another person: *My husband gets jealous if he sees me talking to other men.* | *My brother got all my parents' attention, and I was very **jealous of** him.*

possessive
wanting to have all of someone's love and

attention, and not wanting him or her to spend time with other people: *My boyfriend was very possessive and always wanted to know where I was and who I was with.*
→ see Topic **Describing People's Emotions**

ADVERBS

You can make the adjectives that mean **jealous** into adverbs by using an **-ly** ending: *"Why were you talking to him?" her boyfriend asked jealously.* | *I looked enviously at his new bike.*

jealousy /ˈdʒeləsi/ *noun*

- **jealousy**
- **envy**

jealousy
a feeling of unhappiness or anger because someone else has something that you want: *Jealousy can cause huge problems in the office, especially when one person gets promoted and another one doesn't.*
→ **Jealousy** is also used about the angry and unhappy feeling you have when you think your husband, girlfriend, etc. loves someone else more than you: *When he saw her with her new boyfriend, he was filled with jealousy.*

envy
the feeling of wanting something nice or special that someone else has: *He stared with envy at Robert's new car.*

jet *noun* → see **airplane**

jewel /ˈdʒuəl/ *noun*

- **jewel**
- **gemstone**
- **precious stone**

J

jewel
a small and very valuable stone such as a diamond, especially one that has been cut into a shape and made shiny: *The thieves robbed the store of $250,000 worth of diamonds and other jewels.*

gemstone *also* **gem**
a valuable stone that is used to make jewelry: *South Africa produces much of the world's supply of gemstones.*

precious stone
precious stone means the same as **gemstone**: *The handle of the sword was decorated with precious stones.*
→ Valuable metals such as gold and silver are called **precious metals**.

job /dʒɑb/ *noun*

1 the work that you do to earn money
- **job**
- **work**
- **profession**
- **occupation** (*formal*)
- **career**
- **vocation** (*formal*)
- **trade**
- **employment**
- **livelihood** (*formal*)

2 a particular job in a company or organization
- **position** (*formal*)
- **post**

3 something that you have to do
- **job**
- **task**
- **chore**
- **assignment**
- **duty**

1 the work that you do to earn money

job (AWL)
the responsibility for doing a particular set of activities, for which you earn money: *My first job was in a fast-food restaurant.* | *When do you start your new job?* | *She got a job as a salesperson.*
→ When you are asking someone about his or her job, you usually say: *What do you do?* Don't say: ~~*What is your job?*~~

work
activities that people do to earn money: *He left college last month and he is still looking for work.* | *The work is interesting but the pay is not very good.*

profession
a job that needs special education and training, such as being a teacher, lawyer, or a doctor: *There are now more women in the legal profession.*

occupation (AWL) (*formal*)
the type of work that someone does. The word **occupation** is used especially on official documents: *Please give your name, age, and occupation.*

career
the job that you do for most of your life: *I'm interested in a **career in** teaching.*
→ You also use **career** about the time when you are doing a type of job: *During his career in soccer, he scored 180 goals.*

vocation (*formal*)
a job such as being a nurse, priest, or teacher

that you do because you have a strong feeling that you want to do it, especially because you want to help people: *Nursing is hard work and often low paid, but for many people it is a vocation.*

trade
a skilled job in which you use your hands to make or fix things: *Most of the men had worked in skilled trades such as carpentry and printing.*

employment
the situation of having a paid job. **Employment** is used especially in formal documents and news reports: *How many times were you promoted during your employment at the company?*

livelihood (*formal*)
the work that you do in order to earn enough money to live on: *Most of the people here depend on tourism for their livelihood.*

2 a particular job in a company or organization

position (*formal*)
a job at a particular level in a company or organization: *I am writing to apply for the position of technical support assistant.*

post
a position, especially an important one in a large organization: *She has held the post of managing director for two years.*

3 something that you have to do

job (AWL)
something that you have to do: *I sometimes do jobs for my dad, like washing the car.* | *Finding the house was not an easy job, because all the houses looked the same.*

task
task means the same as **job** but is more formal: *They began the task of clearing up after the earthquake.* | *There are many tasks that computers can do faster than humans.*

chore
a job that you have to do regularly in your home or on a farm, such as cleaning, washing clothes, feeding chickens, etc.: *I always help my mom with the chores and wash the dishes after meals.*
→ You also say that something is **a chore** when it seems boring and you do not want to have to do it: *I hate cutting up onions – it is such a chore.*

assignment (AWL)
something that you are asked to do for your studies or your work: *For our homework assignment, we had to write a poem.*

duty
something that you have to do as part of your job: *Her duties at the hotel include welcoming guests and showing them to their rooms.*
→ see **work²**, Topic **Jobs and Work**

jog *verb* → see **run¹**

join /dʒɔɪn/ *verb*

1 to become a member of an organization, club, or group
- ► join
- ► enter
- ► enlist (*formal*)
- ► enroll (*formal*)
- ► sign up

2 to connect or fasten things together
- ► join
- ► attach
- ► fasten
- ► fix
- ► connect
- ► link

ANTONYMS → see **separate²**

3 to come together and become connected at a particular point
- ► join
- ► meet
- ► merge
- ► converge (*formal*)

1 to become a member of an organization, club, or group

join
to become a member of an organization, club, or group: *Ethan wants to join the gym to get in shape.* | *He joined the army when he was 18 years old.*

enter
to start studying at a school or college, or start working for a company or organization: *Her daughter will enter high school next fall.*

enlist (*formal*)
to join the army, navy, etc.: *Adams **enlisted in** the air force and became a pilot.*

enroll (*formal*)
to join a class or college and put your name on the official list of students: *She did some volunteer work after high school, before **enrolling in** college.*

sign up
to put your name on the list of people who are doing a class or activity, because you want to take part in it. **Sign up** is more informal than **enroll**: *I'm thinking of **signing up for** a yoga class.*
→ see **take part** for words meaning "to do an

activity with other people," **unite** for words meaning "to join people or organizations together"

2 to connect or fasten things together

join
to make two things stay together permanently so that they form a single thing: *The doctors use a metal pin to join the two pieces of broken bone together.*

attach (AWL)
to join one thing to another, especially so that you can separate the two things later: *She* ***attached*** *the photo* ***to*** *the letter with a paper clip.*

fasten
to join together the two sides of a coat, shirt, bag, etc.: *"I'm going now," she said, fastening her coat.*

fix
to join one thing firmly to another, using screws, nails, or glue so that it stays there permanently: *The lamp was* ***fixed to*** *the wall with four screws.*

connect *also* **connect up**
to join pieces of equipment together, especially with a wire or pipe so that electricity, gas, water, etc. can pass from one to another: *Have you* ***connected*** *the microphone* ***to*** *the recorder?*

link (AWL) *also* **link up**
to connect different computers, machines, or systems so that electronic signals can pass from one to the other: *All the computers in the school are* ***linked to*** *the Internet.*
→ see **stick**[1] for words meaning "to join one thing to another using glue or tape"

3 to come together and become connected at a particular point

join
if two or more things join, they come together and become one single thing: *You can see on the map where the two rivers join.*

meet
if two things meet, they come together at a particular place: *The bottom of South America is where the Atlantic Ocean meets the Pacific Ocean.*

merge
to join together and become one. You use merge especially about roads: *The two freeways merge near downtown Los Angeles.*
→ If two companies **merge**, they join together and become one company: *The two electricity companies have recently merged.*

converge (*formal*)
if two or more lines, roads, rivers, etc. converge, they join together at a particular point: *The borders of three countries all converge at this point.*
→ see **join in** at **take part**

joke[1] /dʒoʊk/ *noun*

- ► joke
- ► gag
- ► one-liner
- ► punch line
- ► pun
- ► prank

joke
something funny that you say or do to make people laugh: *He was always telling jokes.* | *Do you want to hear an old joke? What's the difference between unlawful and illegal? One is against the law and the other is a sick bird.*
→ If you do something **as a joke**, you do it for fun, usually by tricking someone: *We moved my dad's car around the corner as a joke so that he would think someone had stolen it.*

gag
a short joke told by a professional entertainer: *He is a great comedian, with plenty of good gags.*

one-liner
a very short joke or funny remark: *There are some good one-liners in the movie.*

punch line
the last few words of a joke or story that make it funny: *I've heard that joke before, but I couldn't remember the punch line.*

pun
a joke using a word that has two very different meanings: *A pun about school that I like is: "Math teachers have a lot of problems."*

prank
a trick that you play on someone for fun: *Every year the older kids play pranks on the new students, like telling them that the principal's office is the bathroom.*

joke[2] /dʒoʊk/ *verb*

- ► joke
- ► tell jokes
- ► kid (*informal*)
- ► tease
- ► fool around

joke
to say something to make people laugh: *Tom was laughing and joking with his friends.* | *After Thanksgiving dinner, Dad joked that he would be hungry later.*

tell jokes
to tell funny stories: *She was always telling jokes and making people laugh.*

kid (*informal*)
to say something that is not true, as a joke: *Don't get mad. I was only kidding.* | *Are you kidding me? Are you really moving away?*
➔ You usually use **kid** in the phrase **be kidding**.

tease
to say things to someone for fun, in order to embarrass or annoy him or her: *The other kids at school used to tease him because he was overweight.*

fool around
to do or say silly things for fun: *Quit fooling around and get back to your work.*

journal *noun* ➔ see **magazine**, **record**

journalist *noun* ➔ see **reporter**, **writer**

journey[1] *noun* ➔ see **trip[1]**

journey[2] *verb* ➔ see **travel[1]**

joy *noun* ➔ see **happiness**

joyful *adjective* ➔ see **happy**

judge[1] /dʒʌdʒ/ *noun*

- judge
- critic

judge
someone who decides which person or thing is the best in a competition: *The judges gave Julio first prize for his essay.*

critic
someone whose job is writing about music, movies, books, etc. and saying whether they are good or bad: *The movie was praised by the critics when it first came out.*
➔ see **referee** for the judge in a sport

judge[2] /dʒʌdʒ/ *verb*

- judge
- assess
- evaluate
- grade
- review
- gauge

judge
to form an opinion, especially by deciding how good or bad someone or something is: *You should not judge other people by the way they look.* | *It is too early to* ***judge if*** *the operation was a success.*

assess (AWL)
to judge someone's level of skill or how good, bad, etc. something is: *Are tests the best way to assess students' progress?* | *The engineers are still assessing the damage to the plane.*

evaluate (AWL)
to judge something by carefully examining all the information: *The researchers are evaluating the effectiveness of the drug.*

grade (AWL)
to give a grade to a test or to a piece of school work: *Teachers spend a lot of time grading students' work in the evenings.*

review
to give your opinion about how good or bad something is, especially a new movie, book, play, etc., by writing a newspaper or magazine article: *He reviews movies for Time Magazine.*

gauge
to judge what will happen or how people feel about something: *It is difficult to* ***gauge what*** *the effect of these changes will be.*
➔ see **decide**

judgment /ˈdʒʌdʒmənt/ *noun*

- judgment
- decision
- ruling
- verdict
- sentence

judgment
an official opinion on a legal case that is formed by a judge or court after carefully thinking about all the evidence: *The company was fined $6 million following a recent court judgment.*
➔ You also use **judgment** about an ordinary person's opinion after he or she thinks carefully about something: *I trust my father's judgment, and he thinks it is not a good idea to lend her the money.*

decision
if a court or a judge makes a decision, they decide a legal case after discussing it and thinking carefully: *The decision of the Supreme Court in the Brown vs. Board of Education case allowed black students to attend the same schools as white students.*

ruling
an official decision, especially one made by a court or a judge: *The Supreme Court will give its ruling on the case later this week.*

verdict
a decision about whether someone is guilty or innocent, made by a jury in a court case: *At the*

end of the trial, the jury gave a verdict of "not guilty" and the men were released.

sentence
a punishment that a judge gives to someone who is guilty of a crime, especially a punishment of a period of time in prison: *Johnson received a sentence of 20 years in prison after he was found guilty of robbery.*
→ see **reason (2)** for **judge** meaning "the ability to make sensible decisions"
→ see **decision**

jump¹ /dʒʌmp/ *verb*

1 to push yourself up into the air or over something using your legs
- ► jump
- ► leap
- ► hop
- ► skip
- ► bounce
- ► pounce
- ► spring
- ► hurdle
- ► vault

2 to make a sudden quick movement because you are surprised or frightened
- ► jump
- ► jerk
- ► flinch
- ► cringe

1 to push yourself up into the air or over something using your legs

jump
to push yourself up into the air using your legs: *How high can you jump? | I don't want the dog* ***jumping up onto*** *the table.*
→ You can also jump from a high place to a low place: *She jumped off the fence into the yard.*

leap
to suddenly jump up high or a long way: *The boys* ***leaped over*** *the stream and ran away.*

hop
to jump or move around on one leg, or to jump on two legs but not high and only small distances: *She hurt her foot and had to hop to the car. | The children were hopping like bunny rabbits.*

skip
to move forward with little jumps between your steps, especially because you are feeling happy: *The little girl was skipping down the street.*

bounce
to jump up and down several times, especially on a surface that is soft and helps you to go up and down: *The kids were bouncing on the trampoline.*

pounce
to suddenly jump on a person or animal to try to catch him, her, or it, especially from a place where you have been hiding: *The cat, who had been sitting behind the bush, suddenly* ***pounced on*** *the bird.*

spring
to jump or move suddenly and quickly in a

jump

jump

hop

vault

hurdle

leap

pounce

bounce

J

particular direction. **Spring** is used especially in literature and writing: *She **sprang out of** her chair and ran to answer the door.*

hurdle
to jump over something while you are running: *He hurdled the fence and ran off down the road.*

vault
to jump over something in one movement, using your hands or a pole to help you go over it: *After vaulting the ticket gate in the metro station, he ran for the exit.*

2 to make a sudden quick movement because you are surprised or frightened

jump
to make a sudden quick movement because you are surprised or frightened: *Sorry! I didn't mean to make you jump! | I hadn't heard him come in, and I jumped when he said hello.*

jerk
to suddenly move part of your body: *She jerked her head up to see what was happening.*

flinch
to make a sudden small movement because you are frightened or in pain: *Brad flinched as he felt the needle go into his arm.*

cringe
to move back a little because you are frightened: *The little boy cringed when his father started shouting at him.*

jump² /dʒʌmp/ *noun*

- jump
- leap
- bound

jump
a movement in which you push yourself up into the air using your legs: *She gave a little jump of joy.*

leap
a big jump. **Leap** is more formal than **jump** and is used especially in stories: *With a huge leap he landed on the opposite bank of the river.*

bound
a sudden big jump. **Bound** is more formal than **jump** and is used especially in stories: *Superman has special powers and can jump on top of tall buildings **in a single bound**.*

jungle /ˈdʒʌŋgəl/ *noun*

- jungle
- rainforest

jungle
a forest in a hot part of the world, that has many trees and large plants growing very close together: *As they move through the jungle, the men use knives called machetes to cut a path.*

rainforest
a thick forest in a part of the world that is hot and gets at least 100 inches of rain per year: *The medicine comes from a plant that grows in the Brazilian rainforest.*
→ see **forest**

junk *noun* → see **trash**

just *adverb* → see Function Words

justice *noun* → see **fairness**

J

Kk

keep /kip/ *verb*

1 to continue to have something
- ► **keep**
- ► **hold on to** (*informal*)
- ► **store**
- ► **save**
- ► **hoard**
- ► **file**
- ► **retain** (*formal*)

ANTONYMS → see **throw away**

2 to keep a promise
- ► **keep**
- ► **fulfill** (*formal*)
- ► **deliver**
- ► **honor**
- ► **follow through**
- ► **carry out**

1 to continue to have something

keep
to continue to have something and not lose it, give it away, sell it, or throw it out: *We decided to keep our old car instead of selling it.* | *Even in difficult times, she kept her sense of humor.*
→ You also use **keep** when talking about where someone has put something until it is needed: *I keep all my winter clothes in a box in the attic.*

hold on to *also* **hang on to** (*informal*)
to keep something or make sure that you do not lose something, especially when this is difficult: *He had managed to hold on to his job while others lost theirs.* | *Hang on to those old comics – they might be worth a lot one day.*

store
to put things away and keep them until you need them: *Store potatoes in a cool dry place.*

save
to deliberately keep something, and not use it or throw it away so that you can use it in the future. **Save** is often used when talking about keeping money and not spending it: *She saved old jars to put rubber bands and paper clips in.* | *It is a good idea to save some money every month.*
→ You also use **save** when talking about making a computer keep the work that you have done on it: *It is important to save the file before you turn the computer off.*

hoard
to collect and keep a lot of something you will use in the future, especially because you are worried that something bad is going to happen: *During the war, people hoarded food in case they could not get any later.*

file (AWL)
to store papers or information in a particular place, and often in a particular order: *We file the letters we receive alphabetically.*

retain (AWL) (*formal*)
retain means the same as **keep**: *Retain a copy of the bill for your records.*

2 to keep a promise

keep
if you keep a promise or keep your word, you do what you promised to do: *He kept his promise to his mother and never stole anything again.* | *I said I would help you and I always keep my word.*

fulfill (*formal*)
to do what you have promised to do. You use **fulfill** especially about the promises made by politicians or other people in authority: *The governor has not fulfilled her campaign pledge to cut taxes.*

deliver
to do what you have promised to do, especially in politics or business: *Several countries have failed to **deliver on** promises of aid.*

honor
if you honor a formal promise, you do what you have agreed to do. You use **honor** about agreements, contracts, and commitments: *We expect the player to honor his contract.*

follow through
to do what you have said you will do in order to complete something or make it successful: *Will the government **follow through on** its promise to change the tax laws?*

carry out
to do something you have said you will do or that someone has told you to do: *The group threatened to carry out more attacks on Western military bases in the Middle East.*
→ see **continue**, **stay**

keyboard *noun* → see Topic **Computers and the Internet**

kick /kɪk/ *verb*
- ► **kick**
- ► **punt**

K

kick
to hit something with your foot: *Juan kicked the ball into the goal.* | *The boys were kicking each other under the table.*

punt
to kick a football a long way after dropping it from your hands: *Smith punted seven times with a 34.3-yard average.*

kid[1] *noun* → see **child**

kid[2] *verb* → see **joke[2]**

kidnap /ˈkɪdnæp/ *verb*

- kidnap
- abduct (*formal*)

kidnap
to take someone away using force, especially in order to keep him or her as a prisoner, and demand money or something else from that person's family or country: *The men kidnapped two tourists and demanded money for their safe return.* | *Police think the missing girl may have been kidnapped.*

abduct (*formal*)
to take someone away by force: *The boy was abducted from a bus stop on his way home from school.*

SYNONYM CHECK

Kidnap or abduct?

Kidnap and **abduct** are often used to mean the same thing. However, you usually use **kidnap** when someone takes someone away in order to get money or something else from that person's family or country.

You usually use **abduct** when someone is taken away, but no one asks for money for that person.

kill /kɪl/ *verb*

1 to make someone die
- kill
- murder
- execute
- assassinate
- take someone's life
- commit murder
- commit suicide
- put someone to death

2 to make an animal die
- kill
- slaughter
- put to sleep

3 to kill a lot of people or animals
- massacre
- slaughter
- exterminate

1 to make someone die

kill
to make a person die. A person or a thing can **kill** someone: *In World War I, soldiers could often see the enemy they were ordered to kill.* | *She was killed by a falling tree during a storm.*

murder
to kill someone deliberately: *He murdered his wife because he wanted to marry someone else.*

execute
to kill someone as an official punishment: *Should all murderers be executed, or should they spend the rest of their lives in prison?*

assassinate
to kill an important person: *President Kennedy was assassinated in 1963.*

take someone's life
to kill someone. You use **take someone's life** when you want to emphasize that life is important, or when the word **kill** sounds too direct: *I couldn't take the life of another human being.*
→ You can also say that someone **takes his/her own life**: *We were worried she might try to take her own life.*

commit murder
to murder someone: *The police have not yet found out who committed the murder.*

commit suicide
to kill yourself: *He thought about committing suicide when he lost all his money in the stock market crash.*

put someone to death
to kill someone as an official punishment, or when you have power over him or her: *The king had his wife put to death when he found out that she had betrayed him.*
→ see **choke**, **die**, **murder**, **shoot**

2 to make an animal die

kill
to make an animal die: *I can understand killing a deer for food, but I don't like hunting just as a sport.*

slaughter
to kill a farm animal for food: *The pigs are slaughtered when they are six months old.*

put to sleep
to kill a pet in a kind way by giving it a drug, for example because it is very sick: *I was very upset when our old dog had to be put to sleep.*

3 to kill a lot of people or animals

massacre
to kill a lot of people, especially people who cannot defend themselves: *The rebel soldiers have massacred hundreds of innocent people.*

slaughter
to kill a lot of people in a violent way, without caring at all: *Hundreds of people were slaughtered during the country's civil war.*

exterminate
to kill all of a particular group of living things: *Wolves had been exterminated almost everywhere in the United States, but now the wolf population is growing again.*

killer /ˈkɪlɚ/ *noun*

- ► killer
- ► murderer
- ► assassin

killer
a person, animal, or thing that kills: *She is hoping the police will find her son's killer.* | *The disease malaria is a major killer in hot countries.*

murderer
a person who deliberately kills someone: *The murderer was sentenced to life in prison.*

assassin
someone who kills an important person: *The president's assassin was immediately arrested.*

K

killing *noun* → see **murder**

kind[1] /kaɪnd/ *noun*

- ► kind
- ► type
- ► sort
- ► form (*formal*)
- ► of a scientific/practical/serious etc. nature (*formal*)
- ► species
- ► variety

kind
a group of things that are similar to each other in some way, or one of the things in the group: *"What **kind of** car did you buy?" "A Ford."* | *We like to eat at lots of different **kinds of** restaurants, especially Mexican and Thai ones.*

type
type means the same as **kind** but sounds a little more formal. You usually use **type** when you are writing about technical or scientific subjects: *The body of the car is made of two **types of** metal.* | *This **type of** monkey lives mostly in the highest branches.*

sort
sort means the same as **kind** but is not used as often: *What **sort of** job are you looking for?*

form (*formal*)
one type of something that has many different types. You use **form** especially when one type of something is physically different from the other types, or when it is organized in a different way: *The people want a new **form of** government – they want democracy, not dictatorship.* | *This **form of** skin cancer is very difficult to treat.*

of a scientific/practical/serious etc. nature (*formal*)
used to describe the particular kind that something is. You use this phrase especially to describe situations: *The people who have recently lost their jobs are given help **of a practical nature** – they are shown how to use the job website and given advice about going to interviews.* | *There have been seven fires this month, all **of a** similar **nature**, and the police think the same person started all of them.*

species
a group of animals or plants that are all similar and can breed together to produce young animals or plants of the same type. **Species** is used in scientific language: *There are more than 40 species of birds living on the island.*
→ **GRAMMAR:** The plural of **species** has the same spelling as the singular form: *one species – two species*

variety
a type of a thing, especially a plant or a food, that is slightly different from other things in the same group: *The Department of Agriculture is testing two more varieties of wheat for the disease.*
→ see **category**

kind² /kaɪnd/ *adjective*

- kind
- nice
- considerate
- thoughtful
- caring
- gentle
- helpful
- generous
- unselfish
- good-hearted
- humane (*formal*)

ANTONYMS → see **cruel**, **mean²**

kind
willing to help other people: *Our neighbors were very **kind to** us when we moved into our new house; they even made us dinner!* | *I could hardly lift my suitcase, but luckily a kind man helped me at the airport.*

nice
friendly and kind: *She is a really nice person who is always ready to help you.*

considerate
thinking about other people's feelings and what they want, and careful not to cause problems for them: ***It was considerate of** Sheila **to** call and tell us that she would be late.*

thoughtful
kind, and thinking about doing things that will please someone you know: *Jenny called to see if I was feeling better – that was really **thoughtful of** her.*

caring
kind, and wanting to help and take care of people: *She is lucky to have such a caring husband.*

gentle
nice and kind, and never angry or violent: *My father was always very gentle with us – he never hit us or even raised his voice.*

helpful
always willing to help people: *A helpful woman at the tourist office gave me some suggestions about places to visit.*

generous
always giving a lot of money, presents, or help to other people, without expecting anything back from them: *My dad offered to pay for my plane ticket, which was very **generous of** him.*

unselfish
caring about other people and thinking about their needs and wishes before your own: *Mothers are expected to be unselfish, but they need to take care of themselves too.*

good-hearted
kind and generous and wanting to do nice things for people: *She was a good-hearted woman who loved children.*

humane (*formal*)
treating people or animals in a way that is not cruel and causes them as little pain or suffering as possible: *According to the law, farm animals must be kept in humane conditions.*
→ see **nice**, Topic **Describing People's Character**

ADVERBS

You can make the adjectives **kind**, **nice**, **considerate**, **thoughtful**, **gentle**, **helpful**, **generous**, **unselfish**, and **humane** into adverbs by using an **-ly** ending: *"Here, let me help you," she said kindly.* | *Her uncle generously offered to pay for the meal.* | *All the animals used in the movie were treated humanely.*

kindness /ˈkaɪndnəs/ *noun*

- kindness
- thoughtfulness
- consideration
- generosity
- hospitality
- goodwill

ANTONYMS → see **cruelty**

kindness
behavior in which you treat other people in a way that is nice and helpful: *Martha's kindness made me feel welcome.* | *One of his many acts of kindness was to bring food to homeless people.*

thoughtfulness
behavior that shows that you think about what other people need and how to make them happy or comfortable: *The letter Dean wrote me after my dog died showed a lot of thoughtfulness.*

consideration
behavior that shows that you think about other people's feelings and are careful not to upset them: *Please show some consideration and turn the music down. We are trying to sleep.*

generosity
behavior that shows you are willing to give money or spend time to help other people or make them happy: *Mr. Norris paid for our meal, so we thanked him for his generosity.*

hospitality
friendly behavior toward people who visit you: *Visitors to their house can expect warm hospitality.*

goodwill
kind feelings between people and a feeling of wanting to be helpful to each other, especially because they have helped each other before: *When the country was hit by an earthquake, our government sent money as a gesture of goodwill.*

king /kɪŋ/ *noun*

- king
- queen
- ruler
- emperor
- pharaoh
- monarch

king
a man who is in charge of a country because he is from a royal family: *The prince will become king of Spain when his father dies.*

queen
a woman from a royal family who is in charge of a country, or the wife of a king: *Queen Victoria reigned for more than 63 years.*

ruler
someone who controls a country but has usually not been chosen by the people in an election: *The country's current ruler seized power last year.*

emperor
a man, usually from a royal family, who is in charge of a group of countries or a country such as China or Japan: *This is a statue of the Roman emperor Claudius.*

pharaoh
a ruler of ancient Egypt: *The pharaoh ordered a pyramid to be built.*

monarch
a king or queen: *King George VI was the first British monarch to visit the United States.*

→ see **leader**

kneel /nil/ *verb*

- kneel
- squat
- crouch

kneel *also* **kneel down**
to put your knees on the ground so that they are supporting your body: *She kneeled down to pray. | He was kneeling by the tub and giving the baby a bath.*

squat *also* **squat down**
to bend your knees so that your body is near the ground, supported on the backs of your legs: *I squatted by the stream and washed my hands.*

crouch *also* **crouch down**
to bend your knees with one foot slightly in front of the other foot and lean forward, so your body is close to the ground: *The girl crouched down behind a parked car to avoid being hit by the snowballs.*

→ see **bend**[1]

kneel

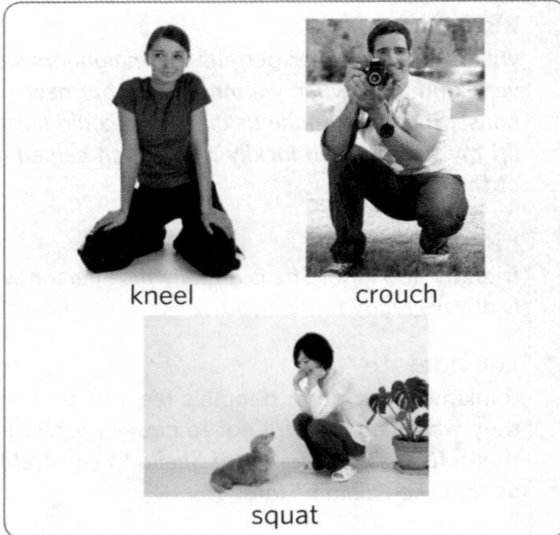
kneel
crouch
squat

knife /naɪf/ *noun*

- knife
- dagger
- sword
- scalpel
- jackknife

knife
a tool with a sharp blade which is used to cut things or used as a weapon: *Could you pass me a knife to chop the onions with? | Use a carving knife to cut the turkey.*

dagger
a short knife used as a weapon in past times: *A bronze dagger and a spear were found in the ancient grave of a warrior.*

sword
a weapon with a long sharp blade, which was used for fighting in past times: *Each knight drew his sword and prepared to fight.*

scalpel
a small sharp knife that a doctor uses for doing an operation: *The surgeon took the scalpel and made a cut in the patient's chest.*

jackknife
a knife with a blade that folds into its handle: *He took his jackknife out of his pocket and cut the apple into pieces.*

knife

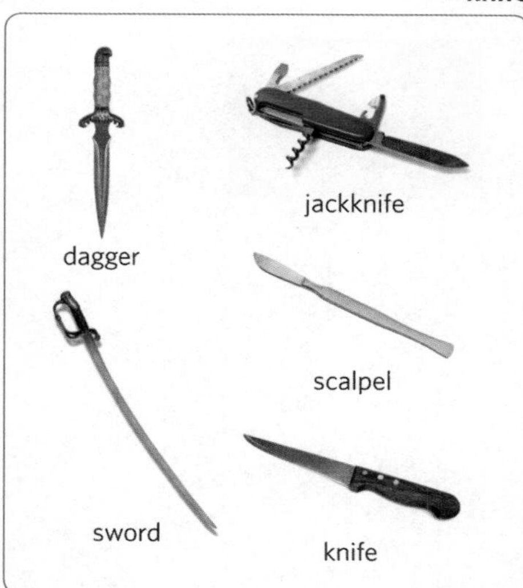

knock /nɑk/ verb

- knock
- rap
- tap
- pound
- hammer

knock
to touch a door or window hard with your closed hand so that people inside will hear you: *Maya opened the door before I even knocked.* | *I **knocked on** the front door of the house.*

rap
to knock on something with force and a loud sound: *The officer **rapped on** the door and shouted "Police!"*

tap
to gently hit your fingers or knuckles against a door or window to get someone's attention: *I heard someone **tapping on** my door.*

pound
to knock on something many times with your fist: *He woke up to the sound of someone **pounding on** his door.*

hammer
to knock on a door or window many times, very hard and fast: *Someone was **hammering on** the door shouting "Get everyone out!"*
→ see **knock down** at **destroy**, **knock on** at **hit¹**
→ see **rattle**, Topic **To Make a Sound**

know /noʊ/ verb

- know
- realize
- be aware

know
to have information or a fact about something in your mind: *Do you **know what** the capital of Japan is?* | *My kids **know that** I love them because I tell them every day.*

realize
to know and understand something, or to suddenly know something you did not know before: *Nobody **realized how** unhappy she was.* | *I suddenly **realized that** I had my T-shirt on inside out.*

be aware
to know about a fact or situation: *We have been **aware of** this problem for some time.* | *Everyone is **aware that** smoking is bad for you.*
→ see **understand**

knowledge /ˈnɑlɪdʒ/ noun

- knowledge
- experience
- expertise
- wisdom
- learning
- know-how (*informal*)

knowledge
all the information you have learned about something: *Her **knowledge of** what it is like to work in the business world will help her teach business students.* | *He has a good **knowledge of** Japanese.*

experience
the knowledge and skill you get from doing something, especially for a long time: *She has a lot of **experience in** teaching.*

expertise AWL
special skills, knowledge, and experience in a particular subject: *The oil company is hiring people with **expertise in** engineering and geology.*

K

wisdom
good judgment and sensible ideas that come from having a lot of experience: *The older people in the church are always willing to share their wisdom with young couples.*

learning
the process of getting knowledge or skills: *We want to make sure that the learning students do in school is connected with the skills they need in a real job.*

know-how (*informal*)
the knowledge or ability you need to do something, especially a practical or physical skill: *Our experts have the know-how to solve all your Internet security problems.* | *The country is trying to get the know-how to build nuclear weapons.*

Ll

lack¹ /læk/ *noun*

- ► lack
- ► shortage
- ► scarcity (*formal*)
- ► absence (*formal*)
- ► deficiency (*formal*)
- ► shortfall

lack
a situation in which there is not enough of something: *The project was canceled due to a **lack of** money. | Her work is good, but her **lack of** confidence makes her not want to speak in class.*

shortage
a situation in which there is not enough of something important that people need, or not enough of a type of person: *The hot dry weather has caused water shortages in some areas. | There is a **shortage of** skilled workers.*

scarcity (*formal*)
a situation in which there is very little of something, especially much less than people need: *In the desert there is a **scarcity of** places where you can shelter from the sun.*

absence (*formal*)
a situation in which there is none of something at all: *There is an **absence of** scientific evidence that the treatment actually works.*

deficiency (*formal*)
a lack of a substance that you need, especially to make your body healthy: *The scientists found that the illness was caused by vitamin C deficiency.*

shortfall
the difference between the amount you expect to get and the amount that you actually get: *There was a **shortfall in** oil production and the country was forced to import oil for six months.*

lack² /læk/ *verb*

- ► lack
- ► be short of
- ► be without
- ► be deficient (*formal*)

lack
to not have something you need, or to not have enough of it: *It has been difficult for her to find a job because she lacks experience. | The team isn't playing well – they seem to lack the desire to win.*

be short of
to not have enough of something, especially money: *Could you lend me ten dollars? I'm a little short of cash.*

label /ˈleɪbəl/ *noun*

- ► label
- ► tag
- ► sticker

label (AWL)
a notice on a product that gives information about it: *The label says that you should wash the sweater in warm water. | The handwritten label on the jar said "Plum Jam."*

tag
a small piece of paper, plastic, or cloth that is attached to something and gives information about it: *The shirt still has the price tag on it. | I wrote my name and address on the tag and attached it to my suitcase.*

sticker
a small piece of paper or plastic with a picture or writing on one side and a kind of glue on the back, that you can stick onto things: *She had put stickers with butterflies on them all over the front cover of her notebook.*

label

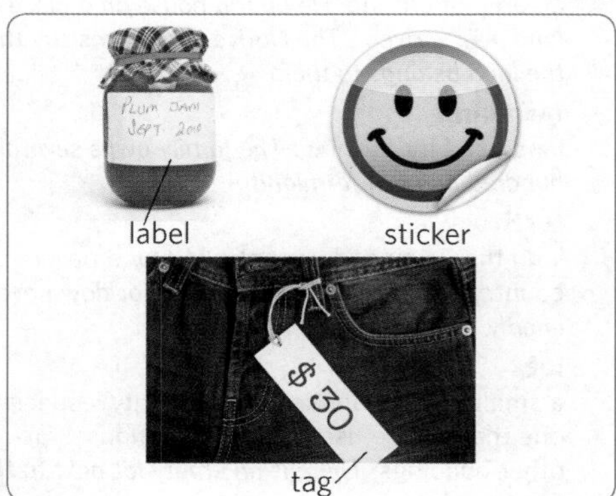

labor *noun* → see **work²**

laboratory *noun* → see Topic **Science and Technology**

L

be without
to not have something important that you need, for example water, food, or electricity: *Some towns are still without electricity after storms damaged power lines.* | *The team is without its star player after his injury in last night's game.*

be deficient (*formal*)
to not have enough of a substance, especially one that your body needs to be healthy: *If your diet **is deficient in** vitamin C, you can get a disease called scurvy.*

lady *noun* → see **woman**

lake /leɪk/ *noun*

- lake
- reservoir
- pond
- pool
- puddle
- waterhole

lake
a large area of water with land all around it: *We rowed across the lake.* | *Lake Tahoe is a popular place for a vacation.*

reservoir
a lake used for storing water, especially a lake that people have made: *The reservoir supplies water to the city.*

pond
an area of water that is smaller than a lake. A **pond** can be natural or made by people: *A frog jumped into the pond.*

pool
a small area of water or another liquid. A **pool** is often an area of still water that is left by or surrounded by moving water: *At the foot of the waterfall is a deep natural pool.*
→ You also use **pool** or **swimming pool** about a place where people can swim: *Does the hotel have a pool?*

puddle
a very small area of water on the ground, especially after it has been raining: *There were puddles on the sidewalk after the rain.*

waterhole
a small area of water in a country that does not get much rain, where wild animals go to drink: *The waterhole is used by elephants.*

lake

pond
pool
puddle
waterhole

lamp *noun* → see **light¹**

land /lænd/ *noun*

- land
- farmland
- territory
- lot
- field
- the ground

land
an area of ground: *He built a house on a piece of land near a river.* | *The Native Americans say that the land belongs to them.*

farmland
land used for farming: *The family owns several hundred acres of farmland.*

territory
land that is owned or controlled by a particular country or group: *His plane was shot down over enemy territory.*

lot
a small area of land in a town or city, especially one that will be used for building houses or other buildings: *There is an empty lot next to the supermarket.*

field
an area of land in the country, especially one where crops are grown or where animals eat grass: *There were cows in the field.*

the ground
the land below someone or something that is high in the air: *The plane was 30,000 feet **above the ground**.*
→ see **come**

landscape /ˈlændskeɪp/ *noun*

- ► landscape
- ► scenery

landscape
the land and things you can see in an area, for example trees, mountains, rivers, or buildings: *The desert landscape is bare and rocky.* | *In the fall, the landscape is beautiful with the trees changing color.*

scenery
the natural things you can see in a place, such as mountains, forests, lakes, and fields, especially when these are beautiful: *The scenery was breathtaking – high snow-capped mountains and clear blue water.*
→ see **nature**

land/touch down *verb* → see Topic **Travel and Vacations**

lane *noun* → see **road**

language /ˈlæŋgwɪdʒ/ *noun*

1 the words and grammar that people use
- ► language
- ► dialect
- ► native tongue (*formal*)
- ► vocabulary

2 a type of words
- ► language
- ► slang
- ► jargon
- ► wording

1 the words and grammar that people use

language
a system of words and grammar that people living in a country use: *"What languages do they speak in Morocco?" "Arabic, Berber, and French."* | *She speaks two languages very well.*

dialect
a type of a language that is spoken in one part of a country or by one group, and that includes words that are different from the words used by other people who speak the same language: *In the U.S., a Southern dialect is not very different from a Northern one, though a Southerner would say "spigot" rather than "faucet," and "bucket" rather than "pail."*

native tongue *also* **mother tongue** (*formal*)
the first language you learn as a child from your parents: *Her native tongue is French, but she is learning English.*

vocabulary
all the words that you know and use: *Her English vocabulary is good, but she needs to work on her grammar.*
→ **Vocabulary** also means "a list of words and meanings, especially ones that you learn when studying a foreign language": *There is a list of useful vocabulary at the back of the book.*

2 a type of words

language
a type of words: *You must not use that kind of language in class. Swearing is not allowed.* | *The science book is full of technical language.*

slang
very informal spoken words, especially words that are used by a particular group of people, for example young people: *"Sick" is **slang for** "good" or "cool."* | *You should not use slang in essays – it's too informal.*

jargon
technical words and phrases used by people who know a lot about a subject. **Jargon** can be difficult for ordinary people to understand: *The document was full of legal jargon, and I had to ask a lawyer to explain it to me.*

wording
the words someone uses when he or she is writing or talking about something: *I changed the wording from "let out of prison" to "freed from prison," so it would sound more formal.*
→ see **word**

lap /læp/ *noun*

- ► lap
- ► circuit

lap
a single trip around a track used for racing, or to one end of a pool and back: *The cars are now in the final lap of the Indianapolis 500!* | *She swims 15 laps every morning.*

circuit
one trip around a path that forms a circle around something, or the path itself: *We did a full circuit around the city in one afternoon.* | *When the circuit is complete, the electricity travels around the wire and lights up the bulb.*

laptop *noun* → see Topic **Computers and the Internet**

large /lɑrdʒ/ *adjective*

1 large in amount or number
- ► large
- ► big
- ► high
- ► huge
- ► enormous
- ► vast
- ► massive
- ► immense (*formal*)
- ► tremendous
- ► substantial
- ► considerable (*formal*)
- ► sizable

ANTONYMS → see **small (2)**

2 large in size
- ► large
- ► big
- ► spacious
- ► bulky

3 very large in size
- ► huge
- ► enormous
- ► gigantic
- ► giant
- ► massive
- ► immense (*formal*)
- ► colossal
- ► vast
- ► jumbo (*informal*)

ANTONYMS → see **small (1)**

1 large in amount or number

large
more than the usual amount or number: *The computer can store large amounts of information.* | *New York City has the largest population of any city in the United States.*

big
more than the usual amount. **Big** is informal in this meaning and is not usually used to talk about numbers or amounts. It is better to use **large**: *She got a big raise at work.*

high
a high price, rate, level, or measurement is bigger than usual or bigger than you want: *The price of gas is getting higher and higher.* | *High levels of mercury were found in the water.*
→ Don't say: ~~*The store has large/big prices*~~. Say: *The store has high prices.*

huge
very big in amount or number: *I have a huge amount of homework to do.* | *Huge numbers of people use the airport every year.*

enormous (AWL)
enormous means the same as **huge** but sounds more formal: *The government spends an enormous amount on defense.* | *She had an enormous sense of relief when she found out that he was all right.*

vast
very big in amount or number: *She spends a vast amount of money on clothes.*

massive
very big, and often having a serious effect: *There has been a massive increase in oil prices.* | *My phone bill was massive last month.*

immense (*formal*)
very big, and important or serious. **Immense** sounds fairly formal or literary, and it is often used about feelings or qualities: *The book contains an immense amount of information.* | *I was impressed by her immense enthusiasm for her work.*

tremendous
very large and having a big effect. You often use **tremendous** about something that is impressive or about emotions: *She has done a tremendous amount of work on her science project.* | *Andrea felt tremendous pressure to succeed.*

substantial
large enough to have an effect or be useful. You usually use **substantial** about amounts of things you can touch or see: *Mrs. Harrington gave a substantial amount of money to the charity when she died.* | *He ate a substantial breakfast.*

considerable (AWL) (*formal*)
fairly large. **Considerable** is used about amounts or numbers, but you also use **considerable** about things that people feel or the qualities they show, for example relief or interest: *There was considerable damage to the hospital in the bomb attack.* | *She read the book with considerable interest.*

sizable *also* sizeable
fairly large. You use **sizable** about amounts or numbers that can be measured: *Scientists believe there is a sizeable quantity of oil in the area.*
→ see Topic **Describing Places**

L

GRAMMAR CHECK: large

Considerable and **sizable** both mean "fairly large."

You use **considerable** with nouns that have no plural and with nouns that can have a plural: *They have made considerable progress.* | *A considerable number of people came to the meeting.*

You use **sizable** only with nouns that can have a plural: *A sizable number of people came to the meeting.* Don't say: ~~*They have made sizable progress.*~~

SYNONYM CHECK

Huge, enormous, vast, or massive?

All of these words have basically the same meaning and they can be used in many of the same sentences. You often use them when an amount or number is surprising or shocking: *A huge/enormous/vast/massive number of people do not even have enough food to eat.*

2 large in size

large
more than the usual size. **Large** is slightly more formal than **big** and is used more in written English. **Large** is not usually used about people: *She ordered a large pizza.* | *Their new car is fairly large – five people can sit in it comfortably.*

big
big means the same as **large** but is less formal: *They live in a big house in New York.* | *Canada is a big country.*

spacious
a spacious room, apartment, car, etc. is large and has a lot of space inside: *The house is spacious and ideal for a family.*

bulky (AWL)
big and taking up a lot of space, difficult to move or lift, and usually heavy: *The astronauts wear bulky space suits.*

3 very large in size

huge
very big: *Her house is huge – it has ten bedrooms.* | *A huge wave destroyed the town.*

enormous (AWL)
enormous means the same as **huge** but sounds more formal: *The office is in an enormous 75-story building.*
→ You can use **huge** and **enormous** in many of the same situations, but **enormous** is the best choice for more formal writing or speech.

gigantic
extremely big, and much bigger than other things of the same type, especially when they are strange or frightening: *Gigantic waves more than 40 feet high crashed against the boat.* | *Sequoia trees are gigantic and some are more than 1500 years old.*

giant
giant means the same as **gigantic** but is more informal: *The old stories say that the forest is full of giant snakes and spiders.* | *It was once a family-owned company, but now it is a giant corporation with stores in most countries.*

GRAMMAR CHECK: large

Giant is only used before a noun. Don't say: ~~*The spider is giant*~~. Say: *It is a giant spider.*

massive
very big and heavy: *The bell is massive and weighs more than 40 tons.*

immense (*formal*)
very big. **Immense** sounds fairly formal or literary: *Sixty million years ago, the whole area was an immense desert.*

colossal
extremely big. You usually use **colossal** about objects: *The soldiers seemed small next to the colossal antiaircraft gun.*

vast
very big. **Vast** is used about areas or distances: *The fire spread over a vast area.*

jumbo (*informal*)
larger than others of the same type. You use **jumbo** especially to describe the largest size of a product you can buy: *He ordered a jumbo hot dog with fries.*
→ see **expand** for words meaning "to become bigger"

GRAMMAR CHECK: large

Don't use "very" with adjectives that mean "very big." Don't say: ~~*It was very huge*~~. Say: *It was huge* or *It was really huge.*

ADVERBS

You can make the adjectives **huge**, **enormous**, **gigantic**, **massive**, **immense**, **colossal**, **vast**, **tremendous**, **substantial**, **considerable** and **sizable** into adverbs by using an **-ly** ending, especially when the word means "large in amount or number" or "very large in size": *The movie was enormously popular.* | *Gas prices have increased tremendously in the past few years.* | *The house was considerably bigger than I had expected.* | *The statue was immensely tall.*

last[1] /læst/ *adjective*

1 coming at the end
- ► last
- ► final
- ► ultimate
- ► closing
- ► concluding
- ► latter

ANTONYMS → see **first (1)**

2 happening before
- ► last
- ► past
- ► previous
- ► preceding (*formal*)
- ► former
- ► old (*informal*)

ANTONYMS → see **next[1]**

1 coming at the end

last
coming at the very end of something: ***She was the last one in the competition to sing.*** | ***The last movie was the best one of the three.***
→ **GRAMMAR:** **Last** can also be an adverb: ***I didn't know which book in the series was written first and which one came last.***

final (AWL)
final means the same as **last**, but is used to emphasize that something really is the last: ***The professor gave his final speech before retiring at graduation.***

ultimate (AWL)
last and most important in a process or series: ***Our ultimate aim is to build six new schools.***

closing
used to talk about the last part of a period of time, event, speech, book, or movie: ***She was passed in the closing stages of the race.*** | ***In the closing chapters of the book, the hero and heroine realize they love each other.***

concluding (AWL)
used about the words that come at the end of a speech or piece of writing and finish it: ***The lawyers made their concluding statements to the jury.*** | ***The concluding paragraph is too short.***

latter
used to talk about the last of two or more things: ***The children learn patience, kindness, and respect – and the latter quality, respect, is most important to us.***

2 happening before

last
relating to the most recent time before the present time: ***Last night we went to the movies.*** | ***The last time I saw you, you were only eight years old.***
→ **GRAMMAR:** Don't say: ***~~It happened in last week/month/year~~***. Say: ***It happened last week/month/year.***

past
the past week, year, few days, etc. is the period of time up until now: ***The past few months have been very difficult for our family.***
→ **GRAMMAR:** Don't say: ***~~Past week has been tiring~~***. Say: ***The past week has been tiring.***
→ Don't use **past** when talking about something that happened in the period of time before now, but that did not continue happening until now. Don't say: ***~~I saw him the past week~~***. Say: ***I saw him last week.***

previous (AWL)
the previous time, event, or thing is the one before the one you are talking about now. **Previous** sounds more formal than **last**: ***The dog's previous owner did not take good care of it.*** | ***The economic problems we are having now are worse than the previous troubles we had.***

preceding (AWL) (*formal*)
coming before the time you have just mentioned, or coming before the part of the piece of writing that you are reading now: ***After you have read the last paragraph, read through the preceding paragraphs again.***
→ Don't use **preceding** about activities or relationships. Don't say: ***~~She had two children from her preceding marriage~~***. Say: ***She had two children from her previous marriage.***

former
having a particular job or position in the past, but not now: ***The former president has written a book about his time in office.***

old (*informal*)
relating to people you knew or things you had in the past but do not know or have now, especially because they have been replaced by other people or things: ***My old teacher from last year was really nice.*** | ***Our old TV stopped working, and we had to get a new one.***

GRAMMAR CHECK: last

All the words meaning **last** must be used before a noun. Don't say: ***~~the president that was former/previous/last etc~~***. Say: ***the previous/former/last etc. president.***

last² *verb* → see **continue**

lasting /ˈlæstɪŋ/ *adjective*

- ► lasting
- ► enduring (*formal*)
- ► continuing
- ► everlasting

ANTONYMS → see **temporary**

lasting
happening for a long time, even when there are problems or when other things have ended: *The two sides have stopped fighting and are working toward a lasting peace.* | *The doctor told him that playing on his injured knee could cause lasting damage.*

enduring (*formal*)
enduring means the same as **lasting** but sounds more formal. You use **enduring** about good things that last: *The article tries to explain the enduring popularity of soccer.*

continuing
something that is continuing was happening before and is still happening now: *The continuing violence has made people in the city nervous.*

everlasting
continuing forever: *When we got married, we promised each other everlasting love.*
→ see **permanent**

lastly *adverb* → see **finally**

late /leɪt/ *adjective, adverb*

- ► late
- ► overdue
- ► tardy
- ► delayed
- ► behind

ANTONYMS → see **early**

late
after the usual or expected time: *I want you to be home at 5:00. Don't be late!* | *Hurry or we'll be* ***late for*** *the party.* | *We apologize for the late departure of Flight 839.*

overdue
done late or arriving late. You use **overdue** about things such as a payment or a piece of work that is late: *You could lose your apartment if your rent payment is overdue.* | *I have three overdue library books.*

tardy
late arriving to school or work: *Jack was tardy three days this week, so the teacher made him stay after school.*

delayed
not able to arrive at the correct time because of problems. You use **delayed** especially about planes and trains that are late: *The plane was delayed because of the storm.*

behind
late in doing work that you have to do by a particular time: *I had problems with my computer, and now I'm running* ***behind with*** *work.*
→ **GRAMMAR:** Don't say: ~~*My work is behind*~~. Say: *I am getting/falling/running etc. behind with work.*
→ You can say that something is **behind schedule**: *The work on the roads is behind schedule because of the rain.*
→ see **on time**

later /ˈleɪtɚ/ *adverb*

- ► later
- ► eventually
- ► subsequently (*formal*)

later
after the present time, or after the time you are talking about: *We called the ambulance at 9:20 and it arrived three minutes later.* | *I'll see you later at home.*

eventually (AWL)
after a long time, or after a lot of things have happened: *Eventually, the doctor called me back to say that everything was fine.* | *During the fire drill we stood outside for a long time, until eventually we were allowed to go back inside.*

subsequently (AWL) (*formal*)
after something else has happened in the past: *Two men were subsequently arrested for the robbery.*

latest¹ *adjective* → see **modern**, **new**, **recent**

latest² *noun* → see **news**

latter *adjective* → see **last¹**

laugh¹ /læf/ *verb*

- ► laugh
- ► giggle
- ► chuckle
- ► snicker
- ► roar with laughter
- ► get the giggles

ANTONYMS → see **cry¹**

laugh
to make a sound with your voice because you think something is funny: *That show is so funny –*

it always makes me laugh. | *We all* ***laughed at*** *Kevin's joke.*

giggle
to laugh quickly and in a high voice. You usually use **giggle** about girls or young children laughing: *She asked Shane to dance and giggled nervously when he said "yes."*

chuckle
to laugh quietly in a low voice: *Glen* ***chuckled at*** *the look on his sister's face when she realized she had been tricked.*

snicker
to laugh quietly in a way that is not nice: *A few people in the audience snickered when the actor forgot what he was supposed to say.*

roar with laughter *also* **shriek/howl with laughter**
to laugh very loudly. You often use **roar/shriek/howl with laughter** about groups of people laughing loudly: *The crowd roared with laughter when the performers got splashed with water.*

get the giggles *also* **have the giggles**
to be unable to stop yourself from giggling, especially in a situation when you should be quiet. You usually use **get the giggles** about children laughing: *Two of the boys got the giggles, and the teacher stopped talking until they were quiet.* | *We were supposed to be going to sleep, but we had the giggles.*

laugh[2] /læf/ *noun*

- laugh
- giggle
- chuckle
- snicker

laugh
the sound you make with your voice when something is funny: *"You don't want to see me dance!" he said* ***with a laugh.*** | *She threw back her head and gave a loud laugh.*

giggle
a quick high laugh. You usually use **giggle** about the way girls or young children laugh: *I heard giggles coming from behind the door to my daughter's room.*

chuckle
a low quiet laugh: *"You would make a great lawyer," she said* ***with a chuckle.***

snicker
a quiet laugh that is not very nice: *There were snickers from the back of the classroom when Terry got the answer wrong.*

laugh at /ˈlæf æt/ *phrasal verb*

- laugh at
- make fun of
- tease
- jeer
- ridicule (*formal*)
- mock

laugh at
to laugh in an unkind way that makes someone feel bad about himself or herself: *One boy started to cry, and some of the others laughed at him, calling him a crybaby.* | *They never said anything to her, but she knew they laughed at her behind her back.*

make fun of
to laugh at someone and make unkind jokes about him or her: *People sometimes make fun of me because I'm different, but I don't let it bother me.*

tease
to make jokes about someone in a way that is not very insulting but that is annoying: *My brothers* ***teased*** *me constantly* ***about*** *being so tall, asking me how the weather was up there or calling me "Stretch."*
→ People often **tease** in a way that is deliberately unkind, but sometimes you can **tease** people in a funny way that is not meant to hurt their feelings: *"It's my birthday today!" said the little girl. "Oh! Let's see, you must be 52 this year, right?" said her dad, teasing her.*

jeer
to laugh and shout rude things at someone in order to show that you do not respect him or her: *As the politician spoke, people in the crowd began to jeer at him.*

ridicule (*formal*)
to make jokes about someone or something in a way that makes him, her, or it seem stupid: *Doctors have ridiculed the treatment, saying that it won't work and that patients might as well try magic.*

mock
to make fun of someone unkindly by copying the way he or she speaks or behaves: *She was from the South, and when she moved to New York some of the kids mocked her accent.*

laughter /ˈlæftɚ/ *noun*

- laughter
- giggling
- chuckling
- mirth (*formal*)

laughter
the sound of people laughing: *It was an evening full of laughter, singing, and dancing.* | *The audience burst into laughter at the joke.*

giggling
the quick high sound of laughter. **Giggling** is usually done by young children or girls: *There was a lot of giggling and whispering coming from my daughter's room.*

chuckling
the low quiet sound of laughter: *I heard chuckling coming from under the bed, and I realized she had been hiding there the whole time.*

mirth (*formal*)
happiness and laughter. **Mirth** is a literary word: *They laughed and laughed, not even trying to control their mirth.*

law /lɔ/ *noun*

- law
- regulation
- bill
- legislation
- act
- initiative

law
a rule that everyone in a country or state must obey. **Laws** are made by the government of a country or state: *The **laws against** driving while drunk are very strict.* | *The new state law makes it illegal to smoke in public buildings.*

regulation (AWL)
an official rule that is part of a set of rules about how people should do something. A **regulation** supports a law by showing how you do things to follow the law: *The men ignored safety regulations and worked without protective clothing.*

bill
a suggestion for a law that must be voted on in order to become a law: *The bill has passed the House and now goes to the Senate to be voted on.*

legislation
a law or set of laws that is being made or that has already been made: *There is new legislation in the House that would limit the amount of money a politician can spend on an election campaign.*

act
a law that has been voted on and is now officially legal. In many English-speaking countries **act** is used in the name of the law: *The law is called the Official Secrets Act.*

initiative (AWL)
a suggested change to a law. Voters ask for the change by signing their names on a document. If there are enough names, then all citizens can vote on the change: *We did not get enough signatures to have a vote on the initiative.*
→ Twenty-four U.S. states use the **initiative**, but in some states they are called **propositions** or **ballot measures**.
→ see **legal**, **illegal**, **rule**[1], **vote**[2]

lawn /lɔn/ *noun*

- lawn
- yard
- grass

lawn
an area of grass around a house or building: *All the houses have beautiful lawns and gardens.* | *Will you mow the lawn this Saturday, please?*

yard
the land around a house, which is usually covered with grass: *Maria was out **in the yard**, raking leaves.*

grass
a plant with thin green leaves that covers the ground in yards, parks, and fields: *The grass is growing fast – we'll need to cut it soon.*

lawyer /ˈlɔyɚ/ *noun*

- lawyer
- attorney
- legal representative
- prosecutor
- defense attorney

lawyer
someone whose job is to advise people about the law, and speak for them in court: *Noah is a lawyer for a big firm in Boston.* | *She had a good divorce lawyer who helped make sure that she and the children would have enough money to live on.*

attorney
attorney means the same as **lawyer**: *My attorney advised me not to sign the contract.* | *The defense attorney is a smart woman who is very good in court.*

legal representative
legal representative means the same as **lawyer** but is used in formal or legal language, for example in contracts or court cases: *Mr. Valdez is acting as my legal representative in this case.*

prosecutor
the lawyer in a court who is trying to show that someone is guilty of a crime: *The prosecutor asked to speak with the judge in private.*

defense attorney
the lawyer in a court who is trying to show that someone is not guilty of a crime: *The defense attorney asked the witness several questions.*

lay *verb* → see **put**

layer /ˈleɪɚ/ *noun*

- ► layer
- ► coat
- ► sheet
- ► film

layer (AWL)
a thin covering of something over a surface: *We scraped several **layers of** paint from the walls.* | *The cake was covered with a **layer of** chocolate frosting.*

coat
a layer of paint or a similar substance: *Put one more **coat of** varnish on the table.*

sheet
a layer of ice or water: *The car was covered with a **sheet of** ice.*

film
a very thin clear layer, especially of something liquid, that has formed on a surface: *She was nervous, and a light **film of** sweat covered her face.*

lay off *phrasal verb* → see **fire²**, Topic **Jobs and Work**

lay out *phrasal verb* → see **spread**

lazy /ˈleɪzi/ *adjective*

- ► lazy
- ► unmotivated
- ► idle

ANTONYMS → see **hard-working**

lazy
not wanting to work or make any effort. Saying that someone is **lazy** is insulting, so it is important to be careful when you use it: *Stop being so lazy! Get off the couch and help me.* | *That lazy jerk never bothers to hang up his clothes.*
→ A **lazy** day or period of time is a time when you relax and do not do very much. This use of **lazy** is not insulting: *We spent long lazy summer days by the pool.*

unmotivated
not having a reason that makes you want to work: *Unmotivated students need extra attention from the teacher to help them feel they can succeed.*

idle
not working. **Idle** sounds fairly literary: *Two of the workers were sitting at one side, idle, while other workers helped to dig the hole.*
→ see Topic **Describing People's Character**

ADVERBS

You can make the adjectives **lazy** and **idle** into adverbs by using an **-ly** ending: *She was lazily stretched out beside the pool.* | *He stood there, idly watching the men working on the road.*

lead¹ /lid/ *verb*

- ► lead
- ► show
- ► guide
- ► escort
- ► usher

ANTONYMS → see **follow**

lead
to walk with or in front of someone to help him or her find the way to a place: *The forest ranger **led** us along the trail **to** the lake.* | *She was leading her little sister by the hand.*

show
to go with someone to help him or her find a place: *Come with me – I'll **show** you **where** you will be sleeping tonight.*

guide
to help someone to go to a place, often by leading him or her or by holding a hand or arm as you show him or her where to go: *My brother guided my mother through the crowd with a hand on her shoulder.*

escort
to go to a place with someone, in order to make sure that he or she gets there safely or does not escape: *Most parents escorted their children to and from the dance.*

usher
to politely or gently show someone where to go, by going with him or her: *The waiter **ushered** the two men **into** the dining room.*
→ see **manage** for **lead** meaning "to be in charge of a group or activity,"
→ see **lead to** at **cause²**

lead² *noun* → see **actor**

leader /ˈlidɚ/ *noun*

- ► leader
- ► ruler
- ► president
- ► head
- ► chief

leader
the person who is in charge of a country or group of people: *The country needs a strong leader.* | *Several important community leaders attended the meeting, including the imam from the local mosque.* | *Mrs. García is one of the* ***leaders of*** *the Girl Scout troop.*

ruler
someone who controls a country: *The military helped the ruler to stay in power for many years.*

president
the leader of the government of some countries, or the leader of a business, bank, club, or college: *The Secretary of State met with the French president to discuss the issue.* | *She was elected Student Body President.*

head
the person who is in charge of an organization or part of an organization: *After teaching for many years, he became* ***head of*** *the English department.*

chief
the leader of a group or organization, especially the police or fire department: *Scott has been the town's fire chief since 2005.*
→ **Chief** is also used when talking about the leader of a tribe: *Red Cloud and other Native American chiefs had signed the treaty.*
→ see **boss**, Topic **Government and Politics**

leadership *noun* → see **government**, **management**

leaf /lif/ *noun*

- ► leaf
- ► petal
- ► foliage
- ► greenery

leaf
one of the flat green parts of a plant or tree. **Leaves** grow from the plant's stem or the tree's branches: *The shape of this leaf tells us that it comes from an oak tree.* | *It was early spring and new leaves were appearing on the trees.*

petal
one of the parts of a flower that grows out from the center, and is often brightly colored: *The rose petals were soft and a beautiful pink color.*

foliage
the leaves of a plant or tree: *The plant has beautiful dark green foliage and white flowers in the spring.*

greenery
green leaves and plants, either growing or used for decoration: *We rode the horses past waterfalls and mountain greenery, until we were above the tree line.*

league *noun* → see Topic **Sports and Exercise**

leak[1] /lik/ *verb*

- ► leak
- ► escape

leak
if something leaks, liquid or gas comes out of a hole in it where it is broken or damaged: *The pipe under the sink was leaking, and there was water all over the bathroom floor.* | *Gas was* ***leaking from*** *the pipes under the building.*
→ **GRAMMAR:** The subject of the verb **leak** can be the container that has a hole in it, or the liquid or gas that comes out: *My water bottle leaks.* | *Water leaked from my bottle.*

escape
if gas or liquid escapes from a container, it comes out by accident: *A cloud of toxic gas* ***escaped from*** *the factory.*
→ **GRAMMAR:** The subject of the verb **escape** is always the gas or liquid that comes out. Don't say: ~~*The factory escaped gas*~~. Say: *Gas escaped from the factory.*
→ see **flow**

leak[2] /lik/ *noun*

- ► leak
- ► puncture

leak
a hole that liquid or gas comes out of, where something has been broken or is damaged: *They say that a gas leak caused the explosion.*

puncture
a small round hole made by something sharp, especially one that gas or liquid comes out of: *Experts do not know what made the puncture in the side of the plane.*
→ **GRAMMAR:** **Puncture** is often used before another noun such as "mark" or "wound": *There were two small puncture marks where the snake had bitten her.*
→ see **hole**

lean /lin/ *verb*

1 to lean something against something for support
- ► **lean**
- ► **rest**
- ► **prop**
- ► **stand**

2 to stand at an angle, not upright
- ► **lean**
- ► **be at an angle**
- ► **slope**
- ► **slant**
- ► **angle**
- ► **tilt**

1 to lean something against something for support

lean
to put something in a sloping position against something else in order to support it: *Derek **leaned** his bike **against** the wall.*
→ You can also say that a person **leans on** or **leans against** something, when he or she stands or sits in a sloping position with part of the body supported by something: *Miguel leaned on the fence.*

rest
to put something on or against something that supports it: *The boy **rested** his head **on** his mother's shoulder.*
→ You can also say that a person **rests on** or **rests against** something, when he or she is supported by it: *She sat down, resting against the trunk of the tree.*

prop *also* **prop sth up**
to make something stay upright by using something to support it: *She **propped** the cookbook **against** the wall so that she could look at it while she was cooking. | He was sitting **propped up** in bed with pillows.*

stand *also* **stand sth up**
stand means the same as **lean**: *He **stood** his bike **against** the fence.*

2 to stand at an angle, not upright

lean
if a structure or surface leans, it is not upright but stands so that the top is not directly above the bottom: *The tower **leans to** the right slightly.*

be at an angle
to be in a position in which one side of something is higher than the other side: *The plane came down at an angle, its nose lower than its tail.*

slope
if a line, surface, or piece of ground slopes, it is higher at one end than the other: *The lawn sloped down toward the swimming pool.*

slant
slant means the same as **slope**, but you do not use it about the ground: *The floor slanted slightly, so the balls would always roll toward the right.*

angle
to turn or move something so that it is pointing in a different direction, especially one that is not straight: ***Angle** the web camera **toward** you a little more – I can't see your whole face.*

tilt *also* **tip**
to move something so that its position is not straight or upright: *I **tilted** my head **back** to face the sun. | As the sail caught the wind, the boat **tipped to** the side.*
→ see **bend[1]** (**1**) for **lean** meaning "to bend your body forward, backward, or to the side"

lean

The tower **leans** to the right slightly.

The plane came down **at an angle.**

As the sails caught the wind, the boats **tipped** to the side.

The field **slopes** down to the river.

learn /lɚn/ *verb*

- ► **learn**
- ► **study**
- ► **master**
- ► **memorize**
- ► **rehearse**
- ► **become familiar with**

ANTONYMS → see **teach**

L

learn
to read about, hear about, or practice a subject or activity so that you know about it or know how to do it: *The students are learning English.* | *We **learned about** the Revolutionary War this week.*

study
to spend time learning about a subject: *I need to **study for** the test.* | *He wants to study law in college.* | *Anna is **studying to be** a veterinarian.*

master
to learn a skill or language so well that you can do it easily: *It takes years to master the art of Kung Fu.*

memorize
to learn words, music, or facts so that you can remember them: *The actors memorize all their lines in a few days.*

rehearse
to practice for a play, show, or concert before people come to see it so that you know what you need to do: *We will be rehearsing every day for two weeks before the performance.*

become familiar with *also* **familiarize yourself with**
to begin to learn about a subject or how to do something: *Take a few minutes to become familiar with the way the computer is set up.* | *The sales people familiarized themselves with the information before the meeting started.*
→ see **find out** for **learn** meaning "to find out about something"
→ see **learn by heart** at **memorize**

learner *noun* → see **student**

learning *noun* → see **knowledge**, Topic **Education**

least *adjective, pronoun* → see Function Words

leave /liv/ *verb*

1 to leave a place
- ► leave
- ► depart (*formal*)
- ► go
- ► set off
- ► go away
- ► take off (*informal*)
- ► emigrate

ANTONYMS → see **enter**, **come (1)**

2 to leave someone and not come back
- ► leave
- ► abandon
- ► desert

3 to forget something
- ► leave
- ► forget

1 to leave a place

leave
to go away from a place: *What time did you leave home this morning?* | *We **left at** 10:00.*

depart (*formal*)
depart means the same as **leave**. **Depart** is used especially about buses, trains, or planes: *The 9:16 bus from New York to Philadelphia is now ready to depart.* | *The flight will **depart at** 4:45 p.m.*

go
go means the same as **leave** but sounds slightly more informal: *We have to go soon, or we'll be late.*
→ **GRAMMAR: Go** is not used in the past tense with this meaning. Don't say: ~~*My family went at 10:00 this morning*~~. Say: *My family left at 10:00 this morning.*

set off
to leave, especially on a long trip. **Set off** sounds more literary or old-fashioned than **leave**: *Crowds watched the first train to California **set off from** New York City.*

go away
to leave home to go on vacation: *His family always goes away for two weeks in August.*

take off (*informal*)
to leave a place quickly: *Claire took off without saying goodbye to anybody.*

emigrate
to leave your own country in order to live in another: *Many Irish people **emigrated to** the U.S. in the 1900s.*

2 to leave someone and not come back

leave
to stop living with your husband, wife, or partner because you no longer love him or her: *Do you think she'll leave him?* | *He left his wife and went to live in Texas.*

abandon (AWL)
to leave a person, especially someone you take care of such as your child, and not come back: *She abandoned the baby outside the hospital.*

desert
to leave a person, especially someone you are responsible for and support with money, and not come back: *Jason deserted his family when they were very young.*
→ see Topic **Relationships and Marriage**

L

3 to forget something

leave
to not bring something with you when you go somewhere, when you had planned to bring it: ***Don't leave your passport at home when you go to the airport.*** | ***They drove away from the field, leaving all the soccer equipment behind.***
→ **GRAMMAR: Leave** is followed by an object and an adverb or phrase. Don't say: ~~*I left my umbrella*~~. Say: *I left my umbrella behind/at school/in the desk etc.*

forget
forget means the same as **leave**: *I forgot my math homework.*
→ **GRAMMAR: Forget** is followed only by an object. Don't say: ~~*I forgot my cell phone at home*~~. Say: *I forgot my cell phone.*
→ see **get off** for words meaning "to leave a bus, train, or plane," **quit** for words meaning "to leave a job," **expel** for words meaning "to make someone leave a place"

leave out /ˌliv ˈaʊt/ *phrasal verb*

- leave out
- exclude (*formal*)
- omit (*formal*)
- skip

ANTONYMS → see **include**

leave out
to not include something. You can **leave something out** deliberately or by accident: *I'll leave the chili **out of** the meat. I know you don't like it.* | *I was copying the paragraph, and I accidentally left out the last sentence.*

exclude (AWL) (*formal*)
to deliberately leave something out: *The government report excluded some of the most important information.*

omit (*formal*)
omit means the same as **leave out**: *The person who organized the party **omitted** several names from the guest list.*

skip
to not do something you usually do or are expected to do, especially deliberately: *She skipped the first two questions on the test, because she didn't know the answers.*

lecture¹ *noun* → see **speech**, Topic **Education**

lecture² *verb* → see **speech (2)**

left /left/ *adjective*

- left
- remaining (*formal*)
- left over

left
still there after everything or everyone else has gone or been used: *There's one piece of apple pie left.* | *Do you have any of these sweaters left in my size?*
→ **GRAMMAR:** You cannot use **left** before a noun in this meaning. Don't say: ~~*There's some left food*~~. Say: *There's some food left.*

remaining (*formal*)
remaining means the same as **left**: *She is making curtains, and she will make pillows out of the remaining material.* | *The yard sale was successful and there were only a few things remaining at the end of the day.*

left over
still there when you have used everything you need. You use **left over** especially about food or money: *There was a lot of food left over after the party, so we're eating it tonight.*

leg /leg/ *noun*

- leg
- limb (*formal*)

leg
one of the two long parts of your body that you use for standing and walking: *His legs and arms were dark brown from working in the sun.* | *The cat's right front leg was broken.*

limb (*formal*)
an arm or leg: *There were several soldiers with missing limbs in the army hospital.*

legal /ˈligəl/ *adjective*

- legal
- lawful (*formal*)
- legitimate
- permitted
- constitutional
- statutory
- valid

ANTONYMS → see **illegal**

legal (AWL)
allowed by law: ***Is it legal to** smoke inside public buildings here?* | *Fireworks are legal in this state.*

lawful (*formal*)
lawful means the same as **legal** but is used in official language. You use **lawful** when another

action that is similar would not be legal: *The bill would limit lawful immigration.*

legitimate
allowed by law or done in a legal way. You use **legitimate** especially about financial activities or products that are legal: *Robinson said that the money was used for legitimate business purposes.*

permitted
allowed by a rule or law: *Smoking is only permitted in two rooms in the building.*

constitutional (AWL)
legal according to the constitution (=set of rules) of a country or organization: *The Supreme Court decided that the law is constitutional.*

statutory
controlled by what a law says: *The city council has the statutory right to close the businesses down.* | *The statutory fine for this offense is $250.*

valid (AWL)
if a ticket or official document is valid, you can use it according to official rules or laws: *The tickets are valid for six months.*

ADVERBS

You can make the adjectives **legal**, **lawful**, **legitimate**, and **constitutional** into adverbs by using an **-ly** ending: *At what age can you legally get married?* | *The lawyer said that his client was not guilty and had acted lawfully.*

legislation *noun* → see **law**

leisure *noun* → see **fun**[1]

lend /lend/ *verb*

- ► lend
- ► loan (*informal*)

ANTONYMS → see **borrow**

lend
to let someone have some money, or something that belongs to you, for a short time: *Could you lend me $10? I'll pay you back tomorrow.* | *My dad lent me a suit and tie for the interview.*

loan (*informal*)
loan means the same as **lend**: *My best friend loaned me her car.*
→ In formal writing it is better to use **lend** as some teachers may consider **loan** to be wrong.

length /leŋkθ/ *noun*

- ► length
- ► height

length
the distance from one end of something to the other end: *The wall was about 60 feet **in length** and eight feet high.* | *Measure the length of the car.*

height
the distance from the top to the bottom of something: *Some of the redwood trees reach a height of more than 360 feet.*
→ see **height**, **measurement**, **width**, Topic **Describing Size**

lengthen /ˈleŋθən/ *verb*

- ► lengthen
- ► get longer
- ► extend (*formal*)
- ► prolong
- ► stretch

ANTONYMS → see **shorten**

lengthen
to make something longer. You use **lengthen** to talk about making something physically longer, or about making something take a longer period of time: *To build a new room, we will have to **lengthen** this wall **by** eight feet.* | *The time that the teacher spends with each student will be lengthened.*

get longer
to become longer. You use **get longer** to talk about something becoming physically longer, or about taking a longer period of time: *Your hair is getting longer – you need a haircut.* | *The meetings are getting longer and longer. They should last no more than an hour.*

extend (*formal*)
extend means the same as **lengthen**: *The hose extends so that it can reach the backyard.* | *The professor extended the deadline for the paper so we'd have more time to work on it.*

prolong
to make something continue for a longer period of time: *Let's make a decision instead of prolonging the discussion any more.*

stretch *also* **stretch out**
to make something longer by pulling: *He stretched the rubber band until it almost broke.* | *If you stretch out the rope, it might reach the boat.*

less *adjective, pronoun* → see Function Words

lesson *noun* → see **class**, Topic **Education**

L

let /let/ *verb*

- ► let
- ► allow
- ► permit (*formal*)
- ► give someone permission
- ► give your consent (*formal*)
- ► authorize (*formal*)
- ► sanction (*formal*)
- ► condone (*formal*)

ANTONYMS → see **refuse (3)**, **forbid**

let
to say that someone can do something, or say that something can happen: *Please let me help you carry that.* | *The teacher wouldn't let us go outside.*
→ **GRAMMAR:** Don't say: ~~*I let him to use my phone*~~. Say: *I let him use my phone.*

Let is not used in the passive. Don't say: ~~*I was let to stay*~~ or ~~*I was let stay*~~. Say: *I was allowed to stay.*

allow
allow means the same as **let** but is slightly more formal. You usually use **allow** about what a parent, teacher, or someone in authority lets someone do because of the rules they have made: *The school does not allow students to use cell phones in class.* | *I'm **allowed to** stay up later on weekends, but on school nights I have to be in bed by ten.*
→ **GRAMMAR:** Don't say: ~~*The teacher didn't allow to talk*~~ or ~~*The teacher didn't allow to us to talk*~~. Say: *The teacher didn't allow us to talk.*

permit (*formal*)
permit means the same as **let**. **Permit** is used especially in official or legal language about rules that allow people to do things: *The company **permits** people **to** smoke outside, but not inside the building.* | *Students are only **permitted to** use their phones at lunch and after school.*

give someone permission
to allow someone to do something. You use **give someone permission** when a parent, teacher, or someone in an official position decides to allow you to do something: *The school gave him permission to leave early for a doctor's appointment.*

L

give your consent (*formal*)
give consent means the same as **give permission** but sounds very formal: *Pascual gave his consent, saying that Benito could marry his daughter.*

authorize (*formal*)
to officially or legally say that someone can do something: *The UN authorized a peacekeeping mission in the country.*

sanction (*formal*)
to officially allow something or approve of doing it. You usually use **sanction** when the government or a large organization allows something, especially when some people think it is wrong: *In some states, the law sanctions the use of marijuana for medical reasons.*

condone (*formal*)
to accept or allow behavior that most people think is wrong: *I do not think our country should condone torture, even in a war.*
→ see **let down** at **disappoint**

letter /ˈletɚ/ *noun*

- ► letter
- ► note
- ► email
- ► correspondence

letter
a written message that you put into an envelope and send to someone by mail: *I got a letter from Mom today.* | *I wrote a **letter to** my Congresswoman to ask her to vote for the bill.*

note
a very short letter or message on paper: *I left a note for Jon on the kitchen table, asking him to feed the cats.*

email
a written message that is sent from one computer to another: *There were 50 new emails in my inbox this morning.*

correspondence (AWL)
a series of letters or messages between two people or groups: *We keep a record of all the correspondence with our clients.*
→ see **mail[1]**, **message**

level /ˈlevəl/ *noun*

1 the amount of something, when this changes
- ► level
- ► degree
- ► scale
- ► rate

2 how good something is, when this changes
- ► level
- ► standard
- ► grade

1 the amount of something, when this changes

level
the amount of something at one time, when the

amount may go up or down at other times: ***Levels of** pollution around the city have risen in the past six months.* | *The company's products are of a high **level of** quality.*

degree
degree means the same as **level** but is only used to talk about qualities, not things that can be seen or measured: *Children in the 1950s had a greater **degree of** freedom to play outside.*

scale
how big or important something such as a problem or change is, when other similar problems or changes are of different sizes: *It was hard to understand the **scale of** the disaster until we saw pictures taken from the air.*

rate
the speed at which something happens or develops, when this can change: *Sunlight increases the plant's **rate of** growth.*

2 how good something is, when this changes

level
how good someone or something is compared to other people or other things of the same type: *At the beginner's level, people start with how to hold a tennis racket and learning how to hit the ball.* | *I've reached the fifth level of the computer game.*

standard
a level that people think is the correct or acceptable level: *The school expects a high standard of behavior from all students.*

grade (AWL)
a level of quality that a product, material, etc. has: *The best grades of meat are expensive.*
→ see **amount**, **rank**

liberal /ˈlɪbərəl/ *adjective*

- ► liberal
- ► left-wing

ANTONYMS → see **conservative**

liberal (AWL)
a liberal person believes that the government should spend money to help people and make their lives better, and wants more controls on businesses: *Liberal groups were pushing the President to act more quickly on environmental problems.*

left-wing
being on the liberal side of politics, or showing liberal political beliefs: *Some left-wing groups want to have health care provided by the government.*
→ see **tolerant** for **liberal** meaning "respecting other people's ideas and behavior"

liberty *noun* → see **freedom**

license /ˈlaɪsəns/ *noun*

- ► license
- ► permit
- ► pass
- ► certificate

license
an official document from the government that allows you to do something or own something: *You need a driving license before you can drive.* | *Most states say you must have a license for any guns you own.*

permit
a type of **license**. A **permit** often allows you to do something for a shorter time, or only if you follow a set of rules: *We applied for a building permit when we decided to build our own house.* | *When he was 15, he got a learner's permit that allows him to drive if he has an adult in the car with him.*

pass
an official piece of paper from a business or organization that allows you to do something for a period of time: *The teacher gave him a hall pass so he could go to the principal's office.* | *The annual pass allows you to visit the amusement park as many times as you want in a year.*

certificate
an official document showing that something has happened or is acceptable: *She went back to college to earn a teaching certificate.* | *I need my birth certificate to apply for college.*

lick /lɪk/ *verb*

- ► lick
- ► suck

lick
to move your tongue across the surface of something: *The little boy was licking an ice cream cone.* | *The dog licked my face.*

suck
to hold something in your mouth and pull on it with your lips and tongue: *She **sucked** happily **on** her lollipop.*

lid *noun* → see **cover²**

L

lie¹ /laɪ/ *verb*

- ► lie
- ► stretch out (*informal*)
- ► sprawl

lie *also* **lie down**
to be or get in a position in which your body is flat on something: *I think I'll just lie down on the couch for a few minutes.* | *We lay down on the grass looking up at the stars.*
→ **GRAMMAR:** The past tense of **lie** is **lay**, not ~~lied~~.

stretch out (*informal*)
to lie down with your legs flat, usually in order to sleep: *He stretched out on the bed and yawned.*

sprawl
to lie or sit with your arms and legs spread out in a very relaxed way: *There were teenagers sprawled all over the living room, playing video games.*
→ see **lie down** at **rest²**

lie² /laɪ/ *verb*

- ► lie
- ► tell a lie
- ► make something up
- ► fib (*informal*)
- ► invent
- ► deceive
- ► mislead
- ► bluff
- ► falsify (*formal*)

lie
to deliberately say something that is not true: *If you* **lie to** *people, they will never believe you in the future.* | *She is 16, but she* **lied about** *her age and said she was 14 to get a cheaper ticket.*

tell a lie
tell a lie means the same as **lie**: *Children sometimes tell lies if they're afraid they will get in trouble for something.*
→ **GRAMMAR: Tell a lie** is not followed by "to." Don't say: ~~*You have been telling lies to me for years*~~. Say: *You have been telling me lies for years.*

make something up
to think of and tell someone a story that is not true, often as an excuse: *I made up an excuse, so I wouldn't have to go.* | *Daniel made the whole story about the dog up – he never owned a dog.*

fib (*informal*)
to tell a small lie that is not very important. **Fib** is used especially by children or when you are talking to children: *Jim is fibbing. I didn't hit him.*

invent
invent means the same as **make something up** but sounds more formal: *She invented the story about her mother being sick so that we would feel sorry for her.*

deceive
to make someone believe something that is not true, especially in order to trick him or her. **Deceive** sounds fairly formal: *The fake documents were made to deceive investors.*

mislead
to make someone believe something that is not true, by giving him or her information that is not complete or not completely true: *The company misled its customers by letting them think they would get their money back.*

bluff
to behave as if something is true when it is not true, in order to scare someone into doing something you want them to do: *"I'll tell your mother that you lied to her." "You're bluffing – you wouldn't tell her!"*

falsify (*formal*)
to dishonestly change official documents or records so that they contain false information: *She was found guilty of falsifying the company's financial accounts.*
→ see **trick²**

lie³ /laɪ/ *noun*

- ► lie
- ► falsehood (*formal*)
- ► fib (*informal*)
- ► libel
- ► slander
- ► perjury

lie
something that you say which you know is not true: *You said Mia broke the cup when it was you. That was a lie.* | *If you tell lies all the time, people will stop believing everything you say.*

falsehood (*formal*)
falsehood means the same as **lie** but sounds much more formal or literary: *The book is full of falsehoods and rumors, even though the author claims everything is true.*

fib (*informal*)
a lie, especially about something that is not very important. **Fib** is used especially by children or when you are talking to children: *Have you been telling fibs? Julio didn't really push you, did he?*

libel
the crime of writing or printing things about someone that are not true: *The actor will sue you*

for libel if you write that he took drugs when you have no proof!

slander
the crime of saying something that is bad and not true about someone, which could make people have a bad opinion of that person: *I have never had an affair. I could take you to court for slander!*

perjury
the crime of telling a lie in a court of law when you have promised to tell the truth: *If you say in court that you were not involved in the crime, when there is proof that you were involved, you will be guilty of perjury.*
→ see **trick**[1]

life /laɪf/ *noun*

1 the time between birth and death
- ► life
- ► lifetime

2 the way someone lives
- ► life
- ► lifestyle
- ► way of life
- ► existence (*formal*)

1 the time between birth and death

life
the period of time between someone's birth and death, and the things that happen to someone in that time: *My grandfather lived a long and happy life.* | *During her adult life she worked as a nurse in a hospital.*

lifetime
the time someone is alive. You use **lifetime** to talk about events that happen during someone's life, especially events that affect all of society: *She made more than 700 movies **during** her **lifetime**.* | *This is a once in a lifetime chance to do something really important.*

2 the way someone lives

life
all of the experiences and activities that are typical of a particular place, job, or society: *Life on the farm is not easy – there's a lot of hard work to do.* | *Having a baby completely changes your life.*

lifestyle
the way a person or family lives their life, including the kind of activities they do, where they live, and how much money they have: *The family has an active lifestyle with few health problems.*

way of life
the way a group of people lives, and the type of things they do and have: *The tribe's way of life changed as settlers took over the land.*

existence (*formal*)
life and the things that happen in it. **Existence** is most often used to talk about life when it is difficult or boring: *In books people's lives always seem more exciting than everyday existence.*

lift /lɪft/ *verb*

- ► lift
- ► raise
- ► pick up
- ► hoist
- ► boost

lift *also* **lift up**
to move a person or thing higher up into the air: *He lifted the lid on the pot of soup.* | *The little boy's father lifted him up, so he could throw the ball into the basket.*

raise
to move something to a higher position: *Raise your hand if you know the answer.* | *A school custodian raises the flag every morning.*

pick up
to lift something up from the ground, from a table, etc, especially something small or light: *Jane picked up her bag and left the room.*

lift

He is **lifting** the little boy.

The crane is **hoisting** the cargo.

He **is boosting** him up the tree.

The custodian **is raising** the flag.

hoist
to lift something, especially something which is heavy and difficult to carry, often using ropes: *The crane hoists the cargo onto the ship.*

boost
to help someone reach a high place by lifting or pushing him or her, especially by lifting with your hands under one of his or her feet: *I boosted her up so she could reach the first branch of the tree.*

light¹ /laɪt/ *noun*

1 brightness
► light
► flash
► glow
► glare
► beam
► ray
► sparkle

ANTONYMS → see **darkness**

2 something that produces light
► light
► lamp
► flashlight
► bulb
► candle
► lantern
► lighting

1 brightness

light
the brightness from the sun, a lamp, or a flame, that allows you to see things: *The light from the lamps gave the room a warm feeling.* | *The sun had gone down, and there wasn't enough light to see.*

flash
a sudden quick bright light: *The flashes from the cameras blinded him as he walked toward the courthouse.*

glow
a soft steady light: *I could see the glow of a small fire near the campsite.*

glare
a strong bright light that hurts your eyes: *The deer froze in the glare of the car's headlights.*

beam
a line of light or energy: *The beam from the flashlight lit up the dark stairs.*

ray
a narrow beam of light, especially from the sun: *Rays of sunlight came through the trees.*

sparkle
a small quick flash of light, especially one of many: *It was bright and sunny, and the sparkles from the snow almost blinded us.*
→ You can also say that someone has a **sparkle** in his or her eyes, when he or she looks happy or excited: *"The whole family will be together at Thanksgiving!" she said, with a sparkle in her eyes.*

2 something that produces light

light
something that produces light, for example an electric lamp: *Can you turn on the light, please? I can't see.*

lamp
a type of light that you can put on a table or stand on the floor: *It was fairly dark because there was only one lamp in the room.*

flashlight
a small electric light that you carry in your hand, that gets power from batteries: *I keep a flashlight in my backpack when I go hiking.*

bulb *also* **light bulb**
the glass part of an electric light, where the light shines from: *Two of the bulbs in the kitchen have burned out.*

candle
a thing that you burn to produce light, made of a piece of wax with string through the middle: *Put the two tall candles in the middle of the table and light them.*

lantern
a type of lamp you can carry, that has a metal frame and glass sides. **Lanterns** are usually old-fashioned, but people today use them when camping: *We lit the lantern and put it on the picnic table outside the tent.*

lighting
all the lights in a building or street. You often use **lighting** when talking about how bright or dim (=not bright) the lights are: *The low lighting in the restaurant made it feel warm and cozy.*
→ see **shine**

light² /laɪt/ *adjective*

1 not dark
► light
► bright
► well lit

ANTONYMS → see **dark¹ (1)**

2 not heavy
► light
► lightweight
► thin
► weightless

ANTONYMS → see **heavy**

3 light in color
- ► light
- ► pale
- ► pastel
- ► soft
- ► cool
- ► fair
- ► faded

ANTONYMS → see **dark¹ (2)**

1 not dark

light
if it is light, the sky or a place is not dark and there is brightness from the sun or a lamp: *The room was light and sunny because of all the windows.* | *It is getting light outside and the birds are starting to sing.*

bright
having or producing a lot of light: *The sun was bright and hot, so we sat down in the shade.*

well lit
a room or place that is well lit has the right amount of light and is pleasant or comfortable to be in: *The restaurant was beautifully decorated and well lit.*
→ If you use **well lit** before a noun, you should spell it as **well-lit**: *a well-lit room.* If **well lit** is not used before a noun, it is spelled as two words: *the room is well lit.*

ADVERBS
You can make the adjective **bright** into an adverb by using an **-ly** ending: *The sun shone brightly in the sky.*

2 not heavy

light
not weighing very much: *I gave my sister the lightest suitcase to carry.* | *This camera is so small and light compared to the one my parents have.*
→ You use **light** about things, not about people. Don't say: ~~*My sister is light*~~. Say: *My sister does not weigh much.*

lightweight
weighing less than other things of the same type: *The boots are lightweight and good for summer hiking.*

thin
thin cloth or clothes are not warm and and do not weigh very much: *It was cold, and she was wearing only a thin T-shirt.*

weightless
having no weight, especially when you are floating in space: *The astronauts have to practice being weightless before going to the space station.*
→ see **thin (1)** for words to describe people who are not heavy

3 light in color

light
a light color is closer to white than to black: *Clothes for baby boys always seem to be light blue!* | *The words were written in yellow, which was too light to see easily.*
→ You can say **light blue**, **light green**, **light purple**, etc., but you cannot say ~~*light red*~~.
You can also use **light** about the color of someone's skin: *Her light skin burns quickly in the sun.*

pale
very light, with a lot of white in it: *The little girl wore a pale pink dress.*
→ You can also use **pale** about the color of someone's skin, especially when he or she is sick or frightened: *She was still pale, even though she felt better.*

pastel
light and not at all bright. You use **pastel** especially about pink, yellow, green, or blue: *Her grandmother was knitting a baby's blanket in pastel colors.*

soft
light and not at all bright, and seeming pleasant and relaxing: *The bedroom was painted a soft shade of yellow.*

cool
fairly light and making you think of cool things. Blue and green are **cool** colors: *Cool colors on the walls will have a calming effect.*

fair
if someone's skin or hair is fair, it is light in color. For example, a white person with blond hair is **fair**: *She is a tall fair woman with blue eyes.*

faded
if something is faded, it is a lighter color than it was at first, because it has been changed by the sun, washing, or age: *She was wearing faded old jeans.*
→ see **gentle** for **light** meaning "not using a lot of force"

light³ /laɪt/ *verb*

- ► light
- ► brighten
- ► light up
- ► illuminate (*formal*)
- ► lighten

ANTONYMS → see **get dark**

light
to make something start producing light, or to

give light to a place: *Light the candles in the living room.* | *One spotlight lit the center of the stage.*
→ You do not usually use **light** about electric lights. Don't say: ~~*Light the lamp by the bed*~~. Say: *Turn on the lamp by the bed.*

brighten *also* **brighten up**
to become brighter or lighter: *The sky was brightening in the east as the sun rose.* | *You can brighten up the room by removing the heavy curtains.*

light up
to make something become bright: *They turned on the underwater lights to light up the swimming pool.* | *The sky lit up as the space shuttle took off.*

illuminate (*formal*)
illuminate means the same as **light up** but sounds more formal or literary: *He moved the flashlight so that it illuminated each of the kids' faces.* | *The workshop was illuminated by bright fluorescent lights.*

lighten
if the sky lightens, it becomes brighter: *The rain clouds disappeared and the sky lightened.*
→ see **burn**, **shine**

like[1] /laɪk/ *verb*

1 to like a person
- ► like
- ► be fond of
- ► care
- ► be attached to

2 to like doing something, and get pleasure from it
- ► like
- ► enjoy
- ► love
- ► have fun
- ► have a good/great/wonderful time
- ► relish
- ► revel in

ANTONYMS → see **dislike**, **hate**

1 to like a person

like
to think that someone is nice and friendly: *I really like your sister – she is such a friendly person.* | *Linda likes her boss, and they work well together.*

be fond of
to like someone very much, especially when you know him or her well. **Be fond of** sounds more formal than **like**: *We had all grown fond of Ann and were sad that she was moving.*

care
if you care about someone, you want that person to be well and happy: ***I care about** him, and I hate to see him so sad.*

be attached to
if you are attached to someone, you like that person a lot and are happy to be with him or her: *The kids had become very attached to their teacher during the school year.*

2 to like doing something, and get pleasure from it

like
to get pleasure from doing something, especially something you do regularly or for a long time: ***I like to** read books about vampires because they're scary and romantic.*

enjoy
to get pleasure from doing something or watching something: *I really enjoyed the play – thanks for inviting me.* | *The kids love baking cookies, and they really enjoy eating them afterward.*
→ You can also say that you **enjoy yourself** when you get pleasure from doing something or being somewhere: *The party was great – I really enjoyed myself.*

love
to like doing something very much, especially something you do regularly or for a long time: *Cassie loves playing the guitar and she is getting really good at it.*

have fun
to enjoy yourself at an event or activity: *"Did you have fun at the party?" "Yeah, we had a lot of fun."*

have a good/great/wonderful time
to enjoy an event or activity very much: *We had a great time at the beach – you should have come.*

relish
to really enjoy doing something that is difficult or does not happen often: *Starting your own business is never easy, but Frank relished the challenge.*

revel in
to really enjoy or celebrate a situation, especially when this feeling does not last long. **Revel in** is used especially in literature: *The crowds poured into the streets after the team won, reveling in the moment of victory.*
→ see **approve**, **love[1]**, **pleasure**

GRAMMAR CHECK: like

Like, **enjoy**, **love**, and **relish** can all be followed by a word ending in "-ing," such as "cooking" or "singing": *I like cooking.*

Like and **love** can also be followed by "to" and an infinitive when you are talking about something you do often: *I like to cook.*

Don't say: ~~*I enjoy to play soccer*~~. Say: *I enjoy playing soccer, I like playing soccer*, or *I like to play soccer.*

like² /laɪk/ *preposition*

- ► like
- ► similar to

ANTONYMS → see **different**

like
almost the same as someone or something else, or in almost the same way: *Jennifer is like her mother – they're both always late for things.* | *He opened and closed his mouth like a fish.*
→ **GRAMMAR: Like** is a preposition and must be followed by a noun or pronoun. Don't say: ~~*The two necklaces are like*~~. Say: *The two necklaces are similar/alike* or *This necklace is like that one.*

similar to
similar to means the same as **like** but is more formal: *This birthday card is similar to the one I gave my mom.*
→ see **look like**, **similar**

SYNONYM CHECK
Like or similar to?

You can use **just like** and **exactly like** to mean "the same as": *His car is just like mine – it's the same type, the same color, and the same age.* You cannot use **similar to** to mean "the same as."

like³ *conjunction* → see Function Words

likeable *adjective* → see **nice**

likely /ˈlaɪkli/ *adjective*

- ► likely
- ► probable
- ► liable
- ► prone
- ► inclined (*formal*)

ANTONYMS → see **unlikely**

likely
if something is likely, you expect that it will happen or be true: *Snow is likely later tonight.* | *Young drivers are more **likely to** have accidents than older drivers.*

probable
probable means the same as **likely**, but is more formal and is used especially in writing or in scientific language: *It is **probable that** global warming will cause higher sea levels.*

liable
likely to behave or do something in a way that results in something bad: *We didn't talk about politics because we knew that we were **liable to** get into an argument.* | *My car is **liable to** overheat on long trips.*

prone
likely to do something or suffer from something, especially something bad or harmful: *The area by the river is **prone to** flooding.* | *As a child I was **prone to** cry easily.*

inclined (*formal*)
likely to do something because you have a particular type of character: *Victor is **inclined to** get upset if he thinks people are ignoring him.*

limit¹ /ˈlɪmɪt/ *noun*

- ► limit
- ► restriction
- ► deadline
- ► maximum
- ► minimum
- ► parameter (*formal*)
- ► quota (*formal*)

limit
the largest amount, number, or distance that is possible or that is allowed by a law or rule: *The speed limit on this road is 35 miles per hour.* | *We decided to put a **limit on** how much we would spend at Christmas.* | *Is there **a limit to** how much information your brain can store?*

restriction (AWL)
a rule or law that controls an activity or the size of something: *Many people want more **restrictions on** the sale of guns.*

deadline
the date or time when something must be finished or done: *The **deadline for** the research paper is April 30, but please turn it in earlier if you can.*

maximum (AWL)
the largest number or amount that is possible or allowed: *He faces a **maximum of** seven years in prison.*

minimum (AWL)
the smallest number or amount that is possible

or allowed: *You have to stay at the hotel for a* ***minimum of*** *three nights to receive the discount.*

parameter (AWL) *(formal)*
a rule that controls the way that something should be done and that stops you from doing some things: *Animals can be used in tests by scientists, but only* ***within*** *strict* ***parameters****.*

quota *(formal)*
an official limit on the amount or number of something that can be bought, sold, or used, or on the number of times something can be done: *A new* ***quota on*** *the number of cars that can be imported will be introduced next month.*

limit² /ˈlɪmɪt/ *verb*

- ► limit
- ► set a limit
- ► restrict
- ► restrain *(formal)*
- ► ration

limit
to control something so that an amount or number does not get too big: *I am trying to limit the amount of salt in my diet. | Let's* ***limit*** *our discussion* ***to*** *the facts in the report.*
→ **Limit** can also mean "to keep the things that are possible in a situation to a small number": *If you don't have a high school diploma, that will limit the kinds of jobs you can get.*

set a limit
to control the size or amount of something, by deciding what the limit will be: *We* ***set a limit on*** *how much money we will spend on vacation.*

restrict (AWL)
to strictly control and limit an activity. **Restrict** sounds a little more formal than **limit**: *The law restricts the sale of guns.*

restrain (AWL) *(formal)*
to control or limit something that is increasing too much. You use **restrain** especially about money that a country or large organization is spending: *The president has promised to balance the budget and restrain government spending.*

ration
to control how much someone is allowed to have of something, especially because there is not enough of it: *In many countries, food was rationed during World War II.*

limited /ˈlɪmətɪd/ *adjective*

- ► limited
- ► finite
- ► restricted
- ► narrow

limited
not very large in amount or number. **Limited** is used to talk about how much of something is available or allowed: *We only have a limited amount of time in which to finish the work. | Each tour is* ***limited to*** *ten people.*

finite (AWL)
an amount or number that is finite has a clear end or limit. You use **finite** especially in scientific language: *Our planet has a finite amount of oil, and eventually there will be none left.*

restricted (AWL)
limited or controlled by a law or rule: *In the United States, the sale of alcohol is* ***restricted to*** *people over the age of 21.*

narrow
limited in range or variety. You use **narrow** when something is too limited, and you wish there were more choices or variety: *The students in this class are beginners, so they can only talk about a narrow range of topics.*
→ **Narrow** can also be used to describe a way of thinking that is too limited because someone does not think about a variety of opinions: *He has a very narrow view of life, so he finds it hard to accept other people's ideas about what is right.*

limp *verb* → see **walk¹**

line¹ *noun* → *go to pages 371-372*

line² /laɪn/ *verb*

- ► line
- ► line up
- ► get in line

line
if people line a street, they stand next to each other in lines along the sides of it, especially for an important event: *Hundreds of fans lined the streets to celebrate their team's victory. | The roads* ***were lined with*** *crowds of people waving American flags.*

line up
to form a line of people or things: *The runners lined up for the start of the race. | Cans were lined up neatly on the kitchen shelves.*

get in line *also* **form a line**
if people get in line, they move so that they are standing next to each other, or one behind the other. You use **get in line** in everyday English, and **form a line** sounds more formal: *The teacher asked the class to quietly get in line to go to lunch. | At the end of the performance, the dancers formed a line and bowed.*

link *verb* → see **connect**

L

line /laɪn/ *noun*

1 a line of people
► line
► row
► in single file

2 a line on paper
► line
► outline

3 a line on the ground or other surface
► line
► stripe
► wrinkle
► crease
► tracks

4 a deep line in the ground
► rut
► groove
► furrow

5 a line on someone's skin
► line
► wrinkle
► crease
► furrow

1 a line of people

line
several people or things who are standing next to each other, or standing one behind the other: *The teacher asked us to stand* ***in a line****.* | *There was a* ***line of*** *tables across the back wall, full of food.*
→ Sometimes people **stand in line** or **wait in line** while they are waiting in a line of people to do something: *I had to wait in line at the bank.* | *A lot of people were standing in line outside the movie theater.*

row
one of several lines of people or things: *I was sitting in the back* ***row of*** *seats in the classroom.* | *The corn is planted* ***in*** *long* ***rows*** *across the field.*

in single file
in a line with one person behind the other: *The path was so narrow that we had to walk in single file.*
→ **GRAMMAR:** You can also say that people walk or move **single file**, without the word "in": *Bicyclists should ride single file so that cars can pass.*

2 a line on paper

line
a long thin mark on paper or on another surface: *Draw a straight line across the top of the page.*

outline
a line around the edge of something which shows its shape: *The children all drew* ***outlines of*** *their feet on one big sheet of paper.*

3 a line on the ground or other surface

line
a long thin mark on the ground or on another surface: *If the ball goes over this line, it's out of play.* | *When you park the car, try to keep the car between the two yellow lines.*

stripe
a long narrow line of color, usually part of a pattern where the line is repeated many time: *The American flag has red and white stripes.*

wrinkle
a line in a piece of clothing that is caused when it has not been folded or hung correctly: *You should iron that shirt – it has a lot of wrinkles.*

crease
a line on a piece of clothing or material where it has been folded or pressed with an iron: *When you iron the pants, can you put a sharp crease in the leg?*

tracks
lines or marks on the ground that were made by someone or something that was moving: *The car left tracks in the mud on the dirt road.*
→ see **fold**[2]

4 a deep line in the ground

rut
a deep narrow line in the ground, made by a wheel: *There was a rut in the dirt road where the mud had become hard in the sun.*

groove
a thin line that has been cut into a hard surface: *You cut a groove into both pieces of wood, and then join them together.*

furrow
a wide deep line made in the the ground for planting seeds in: *The farmer used a plow to make furrows in the field, and then he planted the seeds.*

5 a line on someone's skin

line
a line on the skin of someone's face, for example a line that appears when you get older or when you frown: *She frowned, and lines appeared between her eyebrows.*

wrinkle
a line on someone's face or skin, which is caused by growing old: *The old woman's face was covered with wrinkles.*

crease
a deep line on someone's face or skin: *There were creases at the corners of his eyes.*

furrow
a deep line in the skin of someone's face, especially on the forehead (=part above your eyes): *A deep furrow appeared between his eyebrows.*

→ see **border** for words meaning "a line between two states or countries," **rope** for line meaning "a line you use for hanging or catching things," **stripe** for a colored line on something

furrows

tracks

groove

rut

a **row** of seats

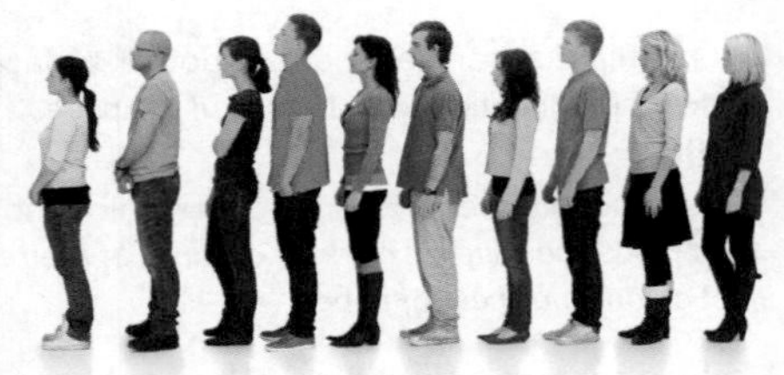
in a **line**

Online Thesaurus

Go to **www.longmandictionariesusa.com**
→ ***Longman Thesaurus of American English*** – with pronunciation of all the words
→ **Study Center** – interactive practice to help you learn synonyms, Academic Words, and Topic Vocabulary

liquid /ˈlɪkwɪd/ *noun*

- ► liquid
- ► fluid
- ► solution

liquid
a substance that is not a solid or a gas, for example water or milk: *Add a little more liquid to the sauce.* | *You can buy the laundry detergent as a powder or as a liquid.*

fluid
a liquid that is used by your body or a machine. **Fluid** is used especially in medical or technical language: *During exercise, the body loses fluids and salt.* | *We need to add more windshield wiper fluid to the car.*

solution
a liquid that has a solid, gas, or another liquid mixed completely into it: *I washed the refrigerator with a **solution of** 2 tablespoons baking soda in 1 quart of water.*

list¹ /lɪst/ *noun*

1 a list of things or places
- ► list
- ► checklist
- ► schedule
- ► agenda
- ► inventory
- ► outline
- ► table

2 a list of people
- ► list
- ► roll
- ► roster
- ► directory
- ► register
- ► short list

3 a list in a book
- ► table of contents
- ► glossary
- ► index
- ► bibliography

1 a list of things or places

list
a set of things or places that is written down. People usually write **lists** with one thing written underneath another: *I made a list before going to the grocery store.* | *The teacher gave us a **list of** words that we have to learn.*

checklist
a list of things you need or things you have to remember to do: *The school sends parents a **checklist of** things that the kids will need on their trip.*

schedule (AWL)
a list that shows the times that buses, trains, planes, etc. leave or arrive at a particular place: *The schedule says that the train should be here in about five minutes.*

agenda
a list of the subjects that the people at a meeting will discuss: *We only have a few minutes left, so let's move to the last item **on the agenda**.*

inventory
a list of all the things in a place, especially in a store or other business: *The librarian is taking an **inventory of** all of the maps currently in the collection* (=she is making a list of them).

outline
a list that shows the main ideas of a long piece of writing, but that does not show the details. An **outline** is a way of showing how a piece of writing is organized, and you use numbers and letters for each of the parts: *Before you write your history report, plan the report using an outline that shows the different sections.*

table
a set of numbers or other information, arranged in rows on a page: *The results of the experiment are shown in Table 5.*

→ see **bill** for words meaning "a list of things you have bought"

2 a list of people

list
a set of the names of people in a particular place or doing a particular activity. A **list** is usually written with one name below another, and it can be used as a record: *The coach will put up a **list of** the players he has chosen for the team.* | *The English class is full, but I am **on the waiting list**.*

roll
a list of the names of everyone in a class or at a meeting: *As the teacher called the roll, each student said "here" or "present."*

roster
a list of the names of people who are expected to take part in a class, activity, or sports event: *The regular pitcher is injured, so Manuel is **on the roster** for tomorrow's baseball game.*

directory
a list of the names, telephone numbers, and addresses of people who are a part of an organization: *The directory lists companies that will take you rafting on the river.*

register (AWL)
an official list or record of something: *We ask everyone who comes to the funeral service to sign the register.*

short list
a list of the best people for a job or a prize, chosen from all the people who were possible: *I was* ***on the short list*** *with five other people, but I didn't get the job.*

3 a list in a book

table of contents
the list at the beginning of a book that tells you the name of each part of the book: *I looked at the table of contents and saw that there were four short stories in the book.*

glossary
a list of words with an explanation of their meaning, usually printed at the end of a book in alphabetical order: *Some of the difficult words are in the* ***glossary*** *at the back of the book.*

index (AWL)
a list at the end of a book that tells you where each person or subject in the book is mentioned, by giving you the page numbers. In an **index**, the names and subjects are in alphabetical order: *Look under L in the index to see which pages talk about Abraham Lincoln.*

bibliography
a list of all the books and articles that someone used when he or she wrote something: *There is a short bibliography at the end of the article.*

list[2] /lɪst/ *verb*

- ► list
- ► outline

list
to write or say a list of things or people: *The teacher asked us to list three things we had learned on the field trip.* | *There were so many desserts listed on the menu – it was hard to choose just one.*

outline
to list the main ideas or facts about something, but not give all the details: *In his speech, the president outlined his new plan to improve the nation's schools.*

listen /ˈlɪsən/ *verb*

- ► listen
- ► pay attention
- ► eavesdrop

listen
to use your ears so that you can hear a sound or what someone is saying, and give your attention to it: *They all listened carefully while she was telling them the story.* | *Gordon was lying on his bed,* ***listening to*** *music.*
→ **GRAMMAR:** Don't say: ~~*She listens music*~~. Say: *She listens to music.*

pay attention
to carefully listen to what someone is saying: *I have some important information about the test, so please pay attention.*

eavesdrop
to listen secretly to other people's conversation: *Sue* ***eavesdropped on*** *their conversation through the open window.*
→ see **hear**

listeners *noun* → see **audience**

literature *noun* → see Topic **Books and Literature**

little[1] *pronoun* → see Function Words

little[2] /ˈlɪtl/ *adjective*

1 not large in size
- ► little
- ► small
- ► tiny
- ► low
- ► miniature
- ► compact
- ► minute
- ► microscopic
- ► minuscule

ANTONYMS → see **big (1)**, **big (2)**

2 not important or not having a large effect
- ► little
- ► small
- ► slight
- ► minor
- ► superficial

ANTONYMS → see **big (4)**, **important (1)**

1 not large in size

little
not large in size: *The little boy was walking home from school.* | *The cake was decorated with little flowers.*
→ **Little** is often used with other adjectives to show how you feel about someone or something small: *What a cute little kitten!* | *They bought a nice little house near the beach.*

small
small means the same as **little** but sounds slightly more formal: *It is easier to drive a small*

L

car in the city. | *These shoes are too small for me.* | *A small woman with straight dark hair was in the kitchen.*

tiny
very small: *Have you seen her apartment? It is tiny.* | *He touched the tiny fingers of the baby.*

low
not high, or not far above the ground. You use **low** about things such as mountains or walls: *The kids built a low wall around the sandcastle.*

miniature
much smaller than the usual size. You use **miniature** especially about things that are made to look just like something larger: *The children made miniature houses out of cardboard.*

compact
small, but comfortable, convenient, or easy to carry: *The kitchen in the apartment was perfect – compact but with everything we needed.* | *I want a compact camera that will fit easily in my pocket.*

minute
very small and difficult to see: *Many larger fish eat these minute shrimp.*

microscopic
extremely small and impossible to see without a scientific tool called a microscope: *The microscopic cells in your body that absorb food are called microvilli.*

minuscule
extremely small, especially in a way that seems surprising: *Compared to its adult size, a newborn kangaroo is minuscule.*

2 not important or not having a large effect

little
not very important or noticeable: *Nick gave a little nod of his head.* | *The program has had little effect on poverty in the area.*
→ **GRAMMAR: Little** is only used before a noun. Don't say: ~~*The difference between them was little.*~~ Say: *There was little difference between them.*

small
not important or not having a large effect: *We may have to make a few small changes.* | *The difference between the two prices is fairly small.*

slight
slight means the same as **little** but is more formal: *The doctor says there has been a slight improvement in her condition.* | *There was a slight smile on his face.*

minor (AWL)
not important enough or serious enough to worry about: *We have made some minor changes to the program.*

superficial
not serious or important and not having much effect on the way something works: *Fortunately her injuries were not serious – they were just superficial cuts and bruises.*
→ see Function Word **some**

little

a **compact** video camera — a **miniature** house

live /lɪv/ *verb*

1 to be alive
- ► **live**
- ► **survive**
- ► **thrive** (*formal*)

ANTONYMS → see **die**

2 to live in a place
- ► **live**
- ► **reside** (*formal*)
- ► **stay**
- ► **occupy** (*formal*)
- ► **inhabit**
- ► **dwell**

1 to be alive

live
to be alive or stay alive: *Dinosaurs lived 200 million years ago.* | *My grandmother* ***lived to be*** *85 years old.* | *Jackie Robinson was one of the greatest baseball players who ever lived.*

survive (AWL)
to continue to live after an accident, illness, or war: *When the ship sank, about 700 people got on lifeboats and survived.*

thrive (*formal*)
to live in a very strong and healthy way: *Cactuses thrive in dry environments.*
→ In everyday English, people usually say **do well** rather than **thrive**: *The whole family seems to be doing very well.*

2 to live in a place

live
to have your home in a particular place: *Michelle*

***lives in** France.* | *Do you **live in** an apartment or a house?* | ***I lived with** my parents until I went away to college.*

reside AWL *(formal)*
reside means the same as **live** but sounds formal: *A large number of Asian Americans **reside in** California.*

stay
to live in a place for a short time: *We **stayed with** my grandparents for two weeks.* | *Will you **stay in** a hotel when you're in New York?*

occupy AWL *(formal)*
to live in or use a building. **Occupy** sounds fairly formal and is used especially in legal or official language: *The company now owns the building and plans to occupy it next month.*

inhabit
if a plant or animal inhabits a place, it lives there. **Inhabit** is used especially in scientific writing: *Alligators inhabit the southeastern United States.*

dwell
to live in a particular place. **Dwell** is used especially in literary writing and poetry: *The story says that fairies **dwell in** the garden of the castle.*
→ see **exist**

lively *adjective* → see **busy**, **energetic**

living[1] *adjective* → see **alive**

living² /ˈlɪvɪŋ/ *noun*

- ► the living
- ► survivor

ANTONYMS → see **dead²**

the living
people who are living. You use **the living** when you are comparing people who are alive to people who have died: *The story is about ghosts of the dead who come back to visit the living.*
→ **GRAMMAR:** When used in the phrase **the living**, **living** is a plural noun. Don't say: ~~*the livings*~~.

survivor AWL
someone who is still alive after being in a war, an attack, or an accident: *The ship was carrying 500 passengers when it sank, and there were only 25 survivors.*

load /loʊd/ *noun*

- ► load
- ► shipment
- ► freight
- ► cargo

load
a large amount of something that is carried by a vehicle or a person: *The ship was carrying a full **load of** fuel and supplies.* | *Dad came back to the cabin with a **load of** wood for the fireplace.*

shipment
a load of goods that a business has ordered, which are sent to it: *The shop just received a **shipment of** fresh flowers from Holland.*

freight
the goods that are sent from place to place in trucks, trains, or planes: *The train delivers freight to the Northeast from Florida.*
→ You also use **freight** to talk about the system of carrying things by vehicles: *International mail is usually shipped by air freight.*

cargo
the goods that are being carried in a particular vehicle, especially a ship or plane: *The ship was carrying a **cargo of** sugar to Spain.*
→ **GRAMMAR:** **Cargo** can be used before a noun when talking about ships or planes that carry things: *Cargo planes brought food and water to the island after the earthquake.*
→ see **fill**

loan /loʊn/ *noun*

- ► loan
- ► mortgage
- ► credit
- ► debt

loan
an amount of money that you borrow from a bank: *They took out a loan to start their own business.* | *I will be paying off the loan for at least five years.*
→ A **student loan** is money that a student borrows to pay for college: *If you need money for college, you can apply for a student loan.*

mortgage
money that you borrow from a bank to buy a house or apartment. **Mortgages** are usually paid back by regular payments over a long period of time: *It took us thirty years to pay off the **mortgage on** our house.*

credit AWL
an arrangement with a bank or store that allows you to buy something and pay for it later: *They*

L

bought all their furniture ***on credit****, and are making monthly payments to the store.*

→ A **credit card** is a small plastic card that you use to buy things and pay for them later: *I paid for the meal with my credit card.*

debt
money that you owe: *He got a good job and finally paid off all his debts.*

→ If you are **in debt**, you owe a lot of money to the bank or credit card company: *They used the credit card too much, and now they are in debt.*

→ see **borrow**, **lend**

local /ˈloʊkəl/ *adjective*

- ► local
- ► neighborhood
- ► nearby

local
relating to the area near where someone lives: *He was taken to a local hospital after the car accident.* | *Both tourists and local residents enjoy the area's beaches.*

neighborhood
relating to places or people that are very close to where you live, especially when you can walk to them: *There are few children living in the area, and neighborhood schools are closing.*

nearby
not far away: *At the airport there is a free bus to nearby hotels.*

→ see **international**, **national**

ADVERBS

You can make the adjective **local** into an adverb by using an **-ly** ending: *I have my own apartment, but my family lives locally.*

located /ˈloʊkeɪtɪd/ *adjective*

- ► be located
- ► be in
- ► be situated (*formal*)

be located
to be in a particular place: *The movie theater* ***is located in*** *the center of town.* | *The park* ***is located on*** *the northern coast of Maine.*

be in *also* **be on**
be in means the same as **be located**, but it is more common, especially in spoken English: *Egypt is in North Africa.* | *The library is on the next street.*

be situated (*formal*)
to be in a particular place. **Be situated** is usually used in writing: *The farm* ***is situated in*** *a beautiful valley.*

lock /lɑk/ *verb*

- ► lock
- ► bolt
- ► bar

lock
to close something with a lock (=metal object that keeps things closed) so that other people cannot open it: *She took the key out of her bag and locked the door.* | *Did you remember to lock the car?*

bolt
to lock a door or window with a metal bar that you slide across a door or window, which is called a **bolt**: *I bolted the back door and closed the shutters before going to sleep.*

bar
to put something very heavy in front of a door or window so that people cannot go in or out: *After they were safe inside the house, they barred the door so enemy soldiers could not get in.*

→ see **lock up** at **prison** (**2**)

lock

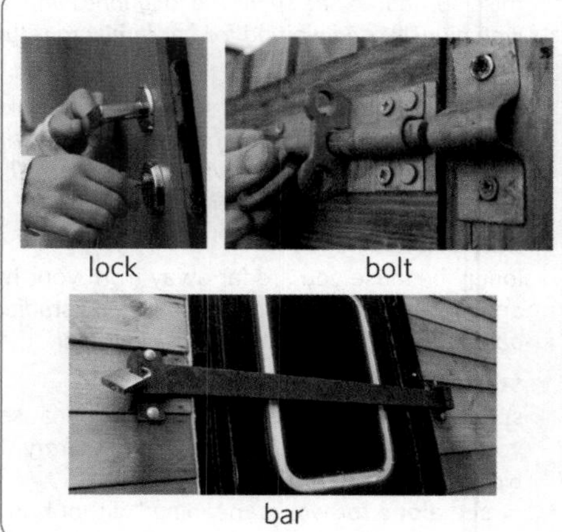

loneliness /ˈloʊnlinəs/ *noun*

- ► loneliness
- ► solitude
- ► isolation

loneliness
the feeling you have when you are unhappy because you are alone: *When she first moved to Seattle she complained of loneliness, but she soon made some friends.* | *Some of the first settlers on*

the plains almost went crazy with loneliness, because there were no neighbors close by.

solitude
the state of being alone, especially when you want to be alone: *I need solitude in order to create my art.*

isolation (AWL)
the state of being completely alone: *The prisoner was held* ***in isolation*** *because he was a danger to the other prisoners.* | *Older people can have a sense of isolation if no one visits them.*

lonely /ˈloʊnli/ *adjective*

- ► lonely
- ► lonesome
- ► isolated
- ► homesick
- ► solitary

lonely
unhappy because you are alone: *She felt lonely when her husband died.* | *I feel sorry for my neighbor – he never talks to anyone and seems like a very lonely man.*

lonesome
lonesome means the same as **lonely** but sounds more literary. You often use **lonesome** when you miss someone: *She spent the long lonesome days watching TV and waiting for her family to return.*

isolated (AWL)
completely alone and in a situation that makes it difficult to see or talk to anyone else: *Sometimes new mothers feel isolated when they spend all of their time at home with their babies.*

homesick
lonely because you are far away from your home and the people you know well: *When I studied abroad in Italy, I felt very homesick at first.*

solitary
spending a lot of time alone, usually because you like being alone: *She was a very solitary woman who didn't make friends easily.*
→ see **alone** for words meaning "without any other people"

long[1] /lɔŋ/ *adjective*

- ► long
- ► lengthy (*formal*)
- ► lasting
- ► extended
- ► prolonged

ANTONYMS → see **short (2)**

long
taking a large amount of time: *We drove to Florida from New York – it was a really long trip.* | *The movie was good, but it was too long.*
→ You also use **long** to describe something that measures a large distance from one end to the other: *Her hair was long and curly.*

lengthy (*formal*)
long, and often lasting for longer than you want or expect: *An accident on the highway has caused lengthy delays.*

lasting
continuing for a long time because of being strong or good enough: *The two governments are working to create a lasting peace after years of war.*

extended
an extended visit, trip, or break lasts longer than you planned: *He took an extended break from work after his father died.*

prolonged
continuing for longer than expected. You use **prolonged** especially before words that mean something bad or unwanted, like "illness," "absence," and "struggle": *She died after a prolonged illness.* | *The country has suffered through prolonged periods without rain.*
→ see **lengthen**

long[2] *verb* → see **want**

look[1] /lʊk/ *verb*

1 to use your eyes to see someone or something
- ► look
- ► take a look at
- ► stare
- ► gaze
- ► glance
- ► peek
- ► peep
- ► squint
- ► peer
- ► view (*formal*)

2 to try to find someone or something by looking
- ► look for
- ► search
- ► hunt
- ► raid

3 to have an appearance that is similar to someone or something else
- ► look like
- ► resemble (*formal*)
- ► remind you of

L

1 to use your eyes to see someone or something

look
to move your eyes toward something or someone so that you can see that thing or person: *Look, there are swans on the river.* | *He kept* ***looking at*** *his watch.* | *The teacher* ***looked around*** *to see if there were any questions.*

take a look at
to look carefully at someone or something in order to find out what is wrong with it or to find out something about it: *I asked Roberto to take a look at the car because the engine is making strange noises.*

stare
to look at someone or something for a long time without moving your eyes away: *The guy was* ***staring at*** *me, and it was making me nervous.*

gaze
to look at someone or something for a long time, giving all your attention to the person or thing you are looking at. **Gaze** sounds fairly literary and is used especially in stories and descriptions: *I lay back on the sand and* ***gazed at*** *the stars above.*

glance
to look at someone or something quickly and then look away: *I saw the two girls* ***glance at*** *each other as if they shared a secret.*

peek
to look at someone or something quickly, especially in a secret or shy way: *The little girl* ***peeked at*** *us from behind her grandmother's skirt.*

peep
to look at someone or something secretly, through a hole or opening where you cannot be seen. **Peep** sounds literary and is often used in stories: *We* ***peeped through*** *a crack in the fence and saw Mrs. Finley talking to a strange-looking man.*

squint
to look at someone or something with your eyes partly closed, usually in order to see better or because there is too much light: *She was* ***squinting at*** *the blackboard because she had forgotten her glasses.*

peer
to look using a lot of effort because it is dark or you cannot see well: *He* ***peered into*** *the dark yard to see what was making the noise.*

view (*formal*)
to look at something because it is beautiful or interesting: *Thousands of tourists come to view the gardens every year.*
→ see **see**, **watch**

2 to try to find someone or something by looking

look for
to try to find someone or something: *Could you help me look for my keys? I can't remember where I put them.*

search
to try to find someone or something by looking very carefully: *She began* ***searching through*** *the trash in case the letter had been thrown away.* | *Rescue workers are* ***searching*** *the buildings* ***for*** *survivors after the earthquake.*

hunt
to look for someone or something in many places. You do not usually use **hunt** about people unless they have done something wrong: *The police are* ***hunting for*** *more clues.*
→ **Hunt** also means "to look for and kill wild animals": *He uses the gun for hunting rabbits.*

raid
if the police raid a place, they go there suddenly to look for something illegal or to catch a criminal: *The police raided his house and found a large amount of stolen jewelry.*
→ see **find**

3 to have an appearance that is similar to someone or something else

look like
to have an appearance that is similar to someone or something: *Rick really looks like his brother – they have the same eyes and hair, and their smiles are the same.* | *From the outside the building looks like an old castle, but inside it's very modern.*

resemble (*formal*)
resemble means the same as **look like**: *As he got older, he resembled his father more and more.*

remind you of
if a person or thing reminds you of another person or thing you think of them because they are similar: *Clayton really reminds me of his grandfather – they have the same sense of humor.* | *The sandwich shop reminded me of a place I used to eat at in New York, because it smelled the same.*
→ see **seem** for **look** meaning "to look like someone or something"
→ see **look after** at **take care of**
→ see **look at** at **examine**, **see**
→ see **look for** at **search**[2]
→ see **look into** at **find out**
→ see **look through** at **read**
→ see **look up to** at **admire**

look² /lʊk/ noun

- ► look
- ► glance
- ► glimpse
- ► peek
- ► gaze
- ► stare
- ► glare

look
an act of looking at someone or something: *I think we are lost – let me take a **look at** the map again.* | *I think it's a skunk – take a look for yourself.*

glance
an act of looking at someone or something quickly and then looking away: *Tammy gave her sister a glance, and the two of them started to laugh.*

glimpse
if you catch or get a glimpse of someone or something, you are only able to see that person or thing for a very short time: *People had been waiting for hours for a **glimpse of** the princess.*

peek
an act of looking at someone or something quickly, especially in a secret or shy way: *The little boy took a peek inside the gift bag when no one was looking.*

gaze
an act of looking at someone or something for a long time, giving all your attention to the person or thing you are looking at. **Gaze** sounds fairly literary and is used especially when you are writing stories: *She felt embarrassed by his steady gaze, and looked away.*

stare
an act of looking at someone or something for a long time without moving your eyes: *Dave ignored the curious stares of the people on the bus.*

glare
an act of looking at someone or something for a long time in an angry way: *His mother looked him straight in the eye with a stern glare.*
→ see **expression**

loose /lus/ adjective

- ► loose
- ► baggy
- ► slack

ANTONYMS → see **tight**

loose
not fitting, tied, or stretched tightly. You use **loose** especially about clothing, ropes, knots, or skin: *It is best to wear loose comfortable clothes to the exercise class.*
→ You also use **loose** about things such as teeth, screws, or nails that do not fit into a hole correctly: *One of the screws was loose and needed to be tightened.* | *The boy was wiggling his loose tooth with his tongue.*

baggy
baggy clothes are big and loose: *He was working in the yard, wearing an old baggy sweatshirt and shorts.*

slack
a slack rope is loose and not pulled tight: *Keep the rope slack until I tell you to pull it.*
→ see **free¹** for **loose** meaning "free to move around instead of being held"
→ see Topic **Describing Clothes**

ADVERBS
You can make the adjectives **loose** and **slack** into adverbs by using an **-ly** ending: *She had a sweater loosely tied around her waist.* | *The clothesline hung slackly between two poles.*

loose

The tie is **loose**.

The rope is **slack**.

lose /luz/ verb

1 to become unable to find someone or something

- ► lose
- ► misplace (*formal*)

ANTONYMS → see **find**

2 to not win something

- ► lose
- ► be beaten
- ► be defeated (*formal*)

ANTONYMS → see **win¹**

L

3 to stop having your job
► lose your job
► be laid off
► be fired

1 to become unable to find someone or something

lose
to become unable to find someone or something: *I lost my keys and couldn't get back into the house. | If you lose your credit card, you should call your credit card company right away.*

misplace (*formal*)
to lose something because you have put it in the wrong place or forgotten where you put it. If you **misplace** something, you usually find it after a short time: *I misplaced my cell phone, and I had to get my mom to call it so I could find where it was.*

2 to not win something

lose
to not win a game, war, election, or competition: *Our team didn't play very well, and we* ***lost by*** *20 points. | He lost the election for student body president.*

be beaten
to lose to another person or team. **Be beaten** is not usually used about wars: *Brazil was beaten by France in the World Cup finals, 5-2.*

be defeated (*formal*)
to lose to someone else in a game, war, election, or competition: *The soldiers fought hard, but they were defeated by the larger army.*

3 to stop having your job

lose your job
to stop having your job because your employer tells you to leave, either because there is not enough work or because you have done something wrong: *The company is not doing well, and Marta is afraid she might lose her job there. | My dad lost his job in December and he is still unemployed.*

be laid off *also* **get laid off**
to lose your job because there is not enough work for you to do: *About half of the company's employees were laid off because of the economy.*

be fired *also* **get fired**
to lose your job, especially because you have done something wrong: *Adam got fired for missing too many days of work.*
→ see **fire²**

loser /ˈluzɚ/ *noun*

► loser
► runner-up
ANTONYMS → see **winner**

loser
someone who loses a competition, game, race, or election: *The loser of this game will go out of the competition.*

runner-up
the person or team that finishes second in a competition, game, race, or election: *The winner of the competition will get $100, and the runner-up will get $50.*

loss /lɔs/ *noun*

► loss
► defeat (*formal*)
ANTONYMS → see **win²**

loss
an occasion when you do not win a game, election, or competition: *The Bears have had three losses and only one win so far this season. | The senator expected to win, so his election loss surprised everyone.*

defeat (*formal*)
a time when someone beats you in a war, competition, or game, especially badly: *The coach blamed the team's 36-7 defeat on the bad weather.*

SYNONYM CHECK
Loss or defeat?
Loss and **defeat** mean the same thing, but you cannot say: *~~The team has had three defeats this season~~*. Say: *The team has had three losses this season.*

lot *noun* → see **land**

loud /laʊd/ *adjective*

► loud
► noisy
► deafening (*formal*)
► piercing
ANTONYMS → see **quiet¹**

loud
making a lot of noise. Use **loud** about sounds, voices, or music: *Sandra has such a loud voice that you can hear her talking in the next room. | The music is too loud – can you turn it down?*

L

noisy
a noisy person or machine makes a lot of noise, especially in an annoying way, and a noisy place has a lot of noise: *Don't be so noisy – you'll wake up the baby.* | *The restaurant was too noisy, so we went somewhere else.*

deafening (*formal*)
so loud that you cannot hear anything else: *The noise from the plane's engines was deafening.*

piercing
a piercing sound is loud and high, and hurts your ears: *The girl let out a piercing scream as the car drove toward her.*

ADVERBS

You can make the adjectives that mean **loud** into adverbs by using an **-ly** ending: *Lisa suddenly laughed loudly.* | *The students streamed noisily down the hall toward their next classes.* | *The music was deafeningly loud.*

love[1] /lʌv/ *verb*

- love
- care about
- adore
- be in love
- have a crush on
- be infatuated with
- be devoted to

ANTONYMS → see **hate**

love
to like a member of your family or a close friend very much and be concerned about what happens to him or her, or to like someone very much in a romantic way: *It is clear that José and his wife love each other very much.* | *I love my sister – we do everything together.*

care about
to be concerned about what happens to someone because you like or love him or her: *Most teachers work hard and care about the children they teach.* | *She married a nice man who really cares about her and her son.*

adore
to love someone or something so much that you do not think there is anything wrong with him or her: *As a little girl, she adored her father.*

be in love
to feel strongly that you love someone and want to have a romantic relationship with him or her: *If Rick **is in love with** Kim, he should ask her to marry him.*

have a crush on
to have a strong romantic feeling of love for someone that you are not having a relationship with, especially when you are young: *"Cathy always acts so strange around Eddie." "That's because she has a crush on him."*

be infatuated with
to have a romantic feeling of love for someone, in a way that is too strong or not sensible. This feeling often does not last very long. **Be infatuated with** sounds fairly formal: *Rob is infatuated with a girl he met last week, and he won't stop talking about her.*

be devoted to
to love someone so much that you want to give him or her a lot of attention and care. You usually use **be devoted to** about people in your family: *She is devoted to her husband and children, but her work is also important to her.*

→ see **enjoy**, **like[1]**

love[2] /lʌv/ *noun*

- love
- affection
- passion
- devotion
- infatuation

love
a strong feeling of liking and caring very much about a member of your family, a close friend, or someone you like in a romantic way: *Children need love and attention to be happy.* | *After 25 years of marriage, their **love for** each other is still strong.*

affection
a feeling that you like or love someone you know well: *Johnny showed his **affection for** his grandmother with hugs and kisses.*

passion
very strong and exciting romantic love. You often use **passion** to talk about the sexual feelings that come with romantic love: *They still love each other, but after 12 years they don't have as much passion as they used to.*

devotion (AWL)
a strong feeling of love that makes you want to do things for that person and give him or her a lot of attention: *His wife's devotion helped him through the difficult experience.*

infatuation
a feeling of love for someone that is strong but not sensible, and that often does not last very long: *He thinks he is in love with Julie, but it's just an infatuation that will pass in a few weeks.*

lovely *adjective* → see **beautiful**

L

lover *noun* → see **fan**, Topic **Relationships and Marriage**

loving /ˈlʌvɪŋ/ *adjective*

- ► loving
- ► caring
- ► affectionate
- ► devoted
- ► tender
- ► romantic
- ► passionate

loving
behaving in a gentle and kind way toward people you love: *You're lucky to have such loving supportive parents.* | *Her little boy is very loving – he is always giving her kisses and hugs.*

caring
a caring person is kind to other people and tries to help them: *Mrs. Peters was a kind and caring woman who was like a second mother to me.*

affectionate
showing your feelings to the people you love, especially by touching them or saying loving things: *He gave me an affectionate hug before getting in the car.*

devoted (AWL)
loving someone so much that you want to give him or her lots of attention and care: *Mark is a devoted father and husband.*

tender
gentle and loving. You use **tender** especially about someone's actions: *She used a tender voice to calm the crying child.*

romantic
showing strong feelings of love for a boyfriend, girlfriend, husband, or wife: *I want a romantic boyfriend who surprises me with love notes and flowers.*

passionate
showing a very strong romantic love and the sexual feelings that come with romantic love: *He pulled her to him and gave her a long passionate kiss.*

ADVERBS

You can make the adjectives that mean **loving** into adverbs by using an **-ly** ending. **Caringly** is an adverb but is not common: *He looked lovingly at his daughter's face.* | *Tenderly, she wiped his tears away.* | *They kissed passionately.*

low /loʊ/ *adjective*

1 near the bottom of the sounds that you can hear
- ► low
- ► deep

ANTONYMS → see **high**

2 a quiet voice or sound
- ► low
- ► quiet
- ► soft
- ► hushed

ANTONYMS → see **loud**

3 not costing a lot of money
- ► low
- ► cheap
- ► inexpensive
- ► reasonable
- ► affordable
- ► budget

ANTONYMS → see **expensive**

4 not tall, or not high above the ground
- ► low
- ► short
- ► little

ANTONYMS → see **tall**

1 near the bottom of the sounds that you can hear

low
a low voice or sound is near the bottom of the sounds that human ears can hear: *Boys' voices usually become much lower as they get older.* | *Suddenly we heard the long low blast of a ship's horn.*

deep
a deep voice or sound is very low, strong, and pleasant: *He is a big man with a very deep voice.*

2 a quiet voice or sound

low
not making a lot of sound so that you do not annoy or interrupt people: *"Don't wake him up," said Ben in a low voice.* | *I turned the volume of the TV down low.*

quiet
not making a lot of sound: *"What about me?" Ahmed asked in a quiet voice.* | *Listening to quiet music can help you fall asleep.*

soft
quiet and pleasant. You use **soft** especially about voices, music, and similar sounds: *Ellie's*

voice was soft and calming. | *It was a romantic dinner, with soft music and candlelight.*

hushed
if people talk in hushed voices or hushed tones, they talk quietly so that other people cannot hear: *Everyone in the library was speaking in hushed voices.*
→ see Topic **Describing Sounds and Voices**

ADVERBS

You can make the adjectives **quiet** and **soft** into adverbs by using an **-ly** ending: *"Don't wake her up," he said quietly.* | *There was music playing softly in the background.*

3 not costing a lot of money

low
low prices, rents, or fees are not high: *They sell clothes at very low prices.* | *The rent is very low – only $500 a month.*

cheap
not costing a lot of money: *These shoes were really cheap – only $25.* | *It is cheaper to go by bus than by plane.*

inexpensive
inexpensive means the same as **cheap** but is more formal. You use **inexpensive** to describe things that are of good quality, even though they do not cost a lot: *The furniture is inexpensive, but it is well made.* | *It is a good store for inexpensive gifts.*

reasonable
a reasonable price seems fair because it is not too high: *The restaurant serves good food at reasonable prices that most families can afford.*

affordable
something affordable is cheap enough that most people are able to buy or pay for it: *There is a lack of affordable housing in the town.* | *The store sells designer clothes at affordable prices.*

budget
budget flights, airlines, hotels, etc. have very low prices: *I got a budget flight to Washington for less than $200.*
→ **GRAMMAR: Budget** is always used before a noun. Don't say: ~~*The hotel was budget*~~. Say: *It was a budget hotel.*

ADVERBS

You can make the adjectives **cheap**, **inexpensive**, **reasonable**, and **affordable** into adverbs by using an **-ly** ending: *The goods can be made more cheaply overseas.* | *Email allows businesses to communicate easily and inexpensively.* | *The clothes are affordably priced.*

4 not tall, or not high above the ground

low
not high, or not far above the ground: *The kids built a low wall around the sandcastle.* | *I picked an apple that was hanging from a low branch.*

short
not as tall as most people: *Her father is a short man – only five foot four inches tall.* | *I am a little bit shorter than my sister.* | *The gymnast was short and strong.*

little
small in size: *We saw a little old lady with a walking stick.* | *A little Christmas tree stood by the fireplace.*

SYNONYM CHECK
Short or low?

You use **low** about things such as mountains and walls, and **short** about people. Don't say: ~~*There was a short wall around the yard.*~~
Say: *There was a low wall around the yard.*

lower[1] *adjective* → see Function Word **less**

lower[2] *verb* → see **reduce**

loyal /ˈlɔɪəl/ *adjective*

- ► loyal
- ► faithful
- ► devoted
- ► patriotic

loyal
always supporting a person, group, country, or idea so that you can be trusted: *He is very loyal to his friends – he'll always be there to help you.* | *The army has stayed **loyal to** the president in the civil war.*

faithful
continuing to support a person, group, country, or idea for a long time: *When Alice fell, her faithful dog stayed beside her until help arrived.*

devoted (AWL)
strongly loyal to someone or something because you admire or love that person or thing: *Devoted fans showed up for the concert despite the rain.*

patriotic
someone who is patriotic loves and is very loyal to his or her country: *Dan is very patriotic, and he plans to join the army after high school.*
→ see Topic **Describing People's Character**

L

ADVERBS

You can make the adjectives that mean **loyal** into adverbs by using an **-ly** ending: *An old friend loyally visits him every day.* | *They faithfully attend church every week.*

luck /lʌk/ *noun*

1 the way things happen without being planned
- ► luck
- ► chance
- ► fate
- ► fortune
- ► coincidence

2 how bad things happen by chance
- ► bad luck
- ► misfortune (*formal*)

1 the way things happen without being planned

luck
the way things happen to people when they are not planned and no one expects them. You use **luck** especially about good things that happen: *Some board games are games of luck, with no skill involved.* | *We had good luck in finding a parking spot near the theater.*

chance
the way that something happens without anyone planning it, often something surprising: ***By chance**, I ran into an old friend from college at the airport.* | *It was pure chance that he rolled the dice and got two sixes when he needed them.*

fate
the power that some people believe controls people's lives and the things that happen to them: *He believes it was fate that made him late that day so that he wasn't in the office when the fire started.*

fortune
luck and the influence it has on your life: *I had the good fortune to go to one of the best schools in the city.*

coincidence
a surprising situation in which two things happen that seem similar or connected, but no one planned or intended this to happen: *My mother is called Anna, and **by coincidence** my wife's mother is called Anna too.* | *The same red car has parked next to me in three different places today, but it has to be just a coincidence.*
→ see **future** (**2**)

2 how bad things happen by chance

bad luck
the way that bad things happen to people by chance, not because of something they have done: *It was just bad luck that it rained the day of the picnic.*

misfortune (*formal*)
bad luck or something that happens as a result of bad luck: *He had the misfortune to be in the area when the riots began.*
→ see **accident** (**2**)

luckily /ˈlʌkəli/ *adverb*

- ► luckily
- ► fortunately
- ► thankfully

ANTONYMS → see **unfortunately**

luckily
used when something happens because of good luck: *I forgot my key, but luckily Ahmed was there to let me in.* | *Luckily the museum was not damaged in the earthquake.*

fortunately
fortunately means the same as **luckily** but is a little more formal: *Fortunately there was no one in the building when the fire started.*

thankfully
used for saying that you are glad about something that has happened, especially something you were worried about: *Thankfully, we got to the station just in time for the last train.*

lucky /ˈlʌki/ *adjective*

1 a lucky situation
- ► lucky
- ► fortunate (*formal*)
- ► miraculous

ANTONYMS → see **unlucky**

2 a lucky person
- ► lucky
- ► fortunate (*formal*)

ANTONYMS → see **unlucky**

1 a lucky situation

lucky
happening because of good luck: *It is **lucky** that you saw that sign or we would have gone the wrong way.* | *"How did you know I would be here?" "It was a lucky guess."*

fortunate (*formal*)
happening because of good luck, in a way that lets you avoid serious problems: *It is fortunate I had my cell phone with me, or I would have missed your call.*

miraculous
avoiding a bad situation in a way that seems very lucky and almost unbelievable: *The woman made a miraculous escape from the burning car and was not hurt at all.*

2 a lucky person

lucky
someone who is lucky has good things happen to him or her because of good luck: *I feel* ***lucky*** *to be alive after falling off the roof.* | *She is so lucky – she always wins!*
→ You can also use **lucky** to describe something that brings you good luck: *This is my lucky shirt; every time I wear it, the team wins.*

fortunate (*formal*)
in a good situation because of good luck: *She is* ***fortunate to*** *have a job she really loves.*

luggage *noun* → see **baggage**

lump /lʌmp/ *noun*

- ► lump
- ► bump
- ► swelling

lump
a small hard swollen area under the surface of the skin, caused by an injury or infection: *She was worried that the lump in her armpit might be cancer.* | *The lump on his wrist was the size of a golf ball.*

bump
a lump caused by hitting part of your body on something: *I have a bump where I hit my head on the door.*

swelling
the condition in which an area on your body becomes larger than usual because of an injury or infection: *After the fight, George had swelling around his nose and bruises around both eyes.*
→ see **piece** for **lump** meaning "a piece that does not have a regular shape"

lunch *noun* → see **meal**

luxury /ˈlʌkʃəri/ *noun*

1 comfort and pleasure from expensive places and things
- ► luxury
- ► splendor
- ► comfort

2 something special or expensive
- ► luxury
- ► treat
- ► extravagance (*formal*)

ANTONYMS → see **need²**

1 comfort and pleasure from expensive places and things

luxury
a situation in which you have expensive, beautiful, and good quality things, and get pleasure from them: *Marissa was used to a life of luxury, with beautiful homes and fancy cars.* | *You can expect luxury from an expensive five-star hotel.*

splendor
the impressive beauty and luxury of a large building or large place. **Splendor** can be used about things or places made by people, and also about things in nature: *The palace has now been restored to its original splendor.*

comfort
a quality that makes you feel physically relaxed in a place, and not in pain or not too hot or cold: *The bed felt lumpy and hard, and he missed the* ***comfort of*** *his own bed in his own room.*

2 something special or expensive

luxury
something expensive that you want but do not need: *Right now a new computer is a luxury we can't afford.* | *Kendra wasted her money on luxuries like jewelry and expensive perfume.*

treat
a nice gift or activity that is special or unusual so that you do not have or do it often: *Uncle Jack took us all out for an expensive dinner as a special treat.*

extravagance (*formal*)
something you want but do not need, that costs much more than is necessary or much more than you can afford: *They went deeply into debt because of extravagances like new cars and expensive clothes and jewelry.*

lying *noun* → see **dishonesty**

L

Mm

machine /məˈʃin/ *noun*

- ► machine
- ► appliance
- ► machinery
- ► mechanism
- ► unit
- ► robot

machine
a piece of equipment that is used to do a particular job, and that uses power to make it work: *I called you and left a message on the answering machine.* | *The city uses machines to sort the garbage.*

appliance
a machine that is used in someone's home, such as a refrigerator or dishwasher: *We painted the kitchen, and we're buying new appliances.*

machinery
machines in general, especially large machines in factories or on farms: *Farmers use the machinery to harvest their crops.*

mechanism (AWL)
a part inside a machine that does a particular job: *The mechanism that raises the bridge wasn't working, and the ships couldn't go through.*

unit
a separate piece of equipment that is part of a larger machine: *The computer's hard drive is fine, but you'll have to replace the display unit.*

robot
a machine that can move and do some of the work of a person on its own: *Most factories use robots to do a lot of the work that people used to do.*
→ People usually think of **robots** as looking a little bit like a human being, but a robot is any machine that can do work without a person controlling it all the time.
→ see **equipment**, **tool**

mad *adjective* → see **angry**

magazine /ˈmægəˌzin/ *noun*

- ► magazine
- ► journal
- ► periodical (*formal*)
- ► comic book

magazine
a thing like a thin book with a paper cover that has photographs or pictures on it, which is published every week or every month. **Magazines** are about popular subjects such as sports, news, or fashion: *She is the fashion editor of a popular women's magazine.* | *The hiking magazine had some great pictures of trails in the Sierra Nevada.*

journal (AWL)
a magazine with articles about academic or technical subjects, written for professional people such as doctors, lawyers, or professors. **Journals** are usually published every month or every three months: *The results of the study were reported in the "New England Journal of Medicine."*

periodical (AWL) (*formal*)
any magazine or journal that is published regularly: *The newspapers and periodicals are in a separate area of the library.*

comic book *also* **comic**
a magazine that tells a story using a series of drawings: *Sam has a big stack of "Batman" comic books in his bedroom.*

magic /ˈmædʒɪk/ *noun*

- ► magic
- ► witchcraft
- ► sorcery
- ► the occult
- ► voodoo

magic
a special power that makes strange or impossible things happen: *In the story, the witch uses magic to turn the prince into a frog.* | *Local people believe that he can heal injuries using magic.*

witchcraft
the use of magic powers, especially by a woman, and usually to do bad things: *The old woman's neighbors accused her of using witchcraft to make the cow stop giving milk.*

sorcery
the use of magic powers to do bad things. **Sorcery** is usually done by a man, and the word is used especially in older literature: *The king*

was afraid that his kingdom would be taken from him by sorcery.

the occult
magical beliefs and practices that involve communicating with spirits: *After his wife died, he became interested in the occult and hoped to get a message from his wife.*

voodoo
magical beliefs and practices used as a form of religion, especially in parts of Africa, Latin America, and the Caribbean: *The priest killed a chicken as part of the voodoo ritual.*
→ see **spell** for "words used to make magic things happen"

magician /məˈdʒɪʃən/ *noun*

- ► magician
- ► witch
- ► wizard
- ► sorcerer

magician
a man in stories who can use magic: *The magician waved his wand and turned the princess into a bird.*
→ You can also use **magician** to talk about someone who does tricks that look like magic in order to entertain people: *Everyone clapped when the magician made the flowers disappear.*

witch
a woman in stories who has magic powers: *The apple that the witch gave Snow White made her seem like she was dead.*

wizard
a man in stories who has magic powers: *Harry Potter learns that all the strange things he can do are because he is a wizard.*

sorcerer
a man in stories who uses magic to do bad things: *The sky got dark as the evil sorcerer read the magic words.*

magnificent *adjective* → see **beautiful**

mail[1] /meɪl/ *noun*

- ► mail
- ► email
- ► delivery

mail
the system of sending, collecting, and delivering letters and packages: *I'll put the check* **in the mail** *tomorrow. | The mail here is pretty slow and unreliable – it can take two weeks for a letter to arrive.*

email
a system that allows you to send and receive messages by computer: *Can you send me the job application* **by email***?*

delivery
the act of bringing something, such as a package or food, to a place or person: *Most of the neighborhood restaurants offer free delivery to the businesses in the area.*
→ see **letter**, **message**

mail[2] *verb* → see **send**

main /meɪn/ *adjective*

- ► main
- ► major
- ► chief
- ► principal
- ► key
- ► primary
- ► prime
- ► core
- ► central
- ► predominant

main
bigger or more important than other things of the same kind: *I'll meet you at the main entrance of the building. | It is good to state your main idea at the beginning of your essay.*

major (AWL)
very large, serious, or important: *Democrats and Republicans are the two major political parties in the U.S. | When the stock market crashed, many businesses had major losses.*

chief
most important. **Chief** is more formal than **main** and is often used in written English: *Saudi Arabia's chief export is oil.*

principal (AWL)
principal means the same as **chief**: *Our principal reason for taking the trip is to visit family, but we'll do some sightseeing too.*

key
very important and needed for success: *The woman is a key witness in the trial, because she is the only one who saw the crime happen.*

primary (AWL)
most important or most basic. You use **primary** especially about the goal, role, cause, or concern that is most important: *As always, the children's safety is our primary concern.*

prime (AWL)
most important or most likely. You often use **prime** about someone who is important in a

particular situation: *Police consider Lewis the prime suspect because he knew the victim and was in the area at the time of the murder.* | *The Prime Minister of Britain is the politician who runs the government.*

core (AWL)
most important, basic, and necessary: *The school concentrates on teaching the core skills of reading, writing, and math.*

central
most important and having more influence than anything else: *My grandfather played a central role in my life after my parents died.*

predominant (AWL)
most common, most noticeable, or most important: *Anna was a little angry and confused, but her predominant feeling was surprise.*
→ see **important**

GRAMMAR CHECK: main

Most of the words meaning **main** can only be used before a noun. Don't say: ~~*This issue is main*~~. Say: *This is the main issue.*

However, you can say that something is **key**, or that something is **central to** something: *This idea is **key to** his success.* | *This issue is **key**.* | *This idea is **central to** his success.*

mainly /ˈmeɪnli/ *adverb*

- ► mainly
- ► mostly
- ► chiefly
- ► principally
- ► largely
- ► primarily
- ► predominantly

mainly
used to say that something is true about most situations, or to give the main reason for something: *The softball team has mainly boys on it, but a few girls play.* | *Her illness was caused mainly by stress.*

mostly
used to say that something is true about most situations or about most people or things: *We went hiking one morning, but mostly we just relaxed on the beach.*

chiefly
mainly. **Chiefly** is a little more formal than **mainly** or **mostly**: *The band's music is chiefly rock, with a little country and western.*

principally (AWL)
mainly. **Principally** is a little more formal than **mainly** or **mostly**: *As a receptionist, your job is principally to greet visitors and answer the phone.*

largely
used to say that something is true more often than it is not true, but not all of the time. **Largely** is a little more formal than **mainly** or **mostly**: *I largely agree with what he said, even though a couple of his ideas were a little strange.*

primarily (AWL)
mainly or in the most basic way: *Many adults enjoy the water park even though it is primarily for kids.*

predominantly (AWL)
mainly, most commonly, or most noticeably: *She is Hispanic, but she grew up in a predominantly white neighborhood.*
→ see **generally (1)**

GRAMMAR CHECK: mainly

None of these adverbs, except **mostly**, are commonly used at the beginning of a sentence. Don't say: ~~*Mainly they play on Saturdays*~~. Say: *They play mainly on Saturdays.*

major[1] *adjective* → see **important**, **main**

major[2] *noun* → see **subject**

major[3] *verb* → see Topic **Education**

majority *noun* → see Function Word **most**

make /meɪk/ *verb*

- ► make
- ► produce
- ► create
- ► manufacture
- ► form
- ► generate

make
to put things together or change something so that something new exists: *Diane makes all her own clothes.* | *Where was your computer made?* | *The actors first met when they were making a movie together.*

produce
to make something in large amounts to sell: *The factory produces high-quality steel.*
→ **Produce** also means "to make something as part of a natural process": *Our bodies produce carbon dioxide when we breathe.*

create (AWL)
to make or invent something new, especially something that has not existed before: *The software lets you create beautiful works of art.*

M

manufacture
to use machines to make things in large amounts in a factory: *Many cars are designed in the U.S. and manufactured in Mexico.*

form
to make something by combining two or more parts, often as part of a natural process: *Hydrogen and oxygen combine to form water.*

generate (AWL)
to make something such as heat or electricity: *Wind can be used to generate electricity.*

→ see **cause²** for **make** meaning "make something happen," **force** for **make** meaning "make someone do something"

→ see **build¹**, **cook¹**

make fun of *verb phrase* → see **laugh at**

maker /ˈmeɪkɚ/ *noun*

► maker
► producer
► manufacturer

maker
a person, company, or machine that makes something or does something: *This coffee maker makes one cup at a time.* | *The company is the country's leading computer chip maker.*

producer
a person, company, or country that makes or grows something to sell: *OPEC is an international organization made up of 13 oil producers.*

manufacturer
a company that makes things with machines in a factory to sell: *The clothing manufacturer had to close one of its factories because of poor sales.*

make sure /ˌmeɪk ˈʃʊr/ *verb phrase*

1 to do what is necessary so that something definitely happens
► make sure
► make certain
► ensure (*formal*)
► guarantee

2 to find out if something is true or has happened
► make sure
► make certain
► check
► verify (*formal*)

1 to do what is necessary so that something definitely happens

make sure
to do what is necessary so that something definitely happens, because this is important: *Make sure you get to the airport on time – we don't want to miss our plane.* | *You must **make sure that** you put your name at the top of the test paper.*

make certain
to make completely sure that something will happen. **Make certain** sounds a little more formal and a little more definite than **make sure**: *She bought a large turkey, just to **make certain that** there would be enough for everyone.*

ensure (AWL) (*formal*)
to make sure that something happens. You use **ensure** especially in official situations: *Please **ensure that** you have your passport with you.*

guarantee (AWL)
to make completely sure that something will happen or exist: *The team need to win this game in order to guarantee that they will stay in the competition.* | *The constitution guarantees the right to freedom of speech.*

2 to find out if something is true or has happened

make sure
to find out if what you want is true or has happened: *He called to **make sure that** we got home okay.* | *Can you **make sure that** I turned the oven off?*

make certain
to make completely sure that something is true or has happened. **Make certain** sounds a little more formal and a little more definite than **make sure**: *Before buying a sofa, **make certain that** it will fit in your living room.*

check
to find out if something is true or has happened: ***Check that** you have entered your password correctly.* | *I wanted to **check if** the company had received my order.*

verify (*formal*)
to make sure officially that something is true: *They will need to **verify that** the letter was written by Abraham Lincoln – if it is, it could be worth a lot of money.*

makeup /ˈmeɪkʌp/ *noun*

► makeup
► cosmetics (*formal*)

makeup
colored powders, creams, and other substances that women put on their faces to look prettier: *Julia is so beautiful that she doesn't even need to wear makeup.*

cosmetics (*formal*)
cosmetics means the same as **makeup**. You use

cosmetics when you are talking about the business of making, buying, and selling these products: *The company manufactures cosmetics and other skincare products.*

make up /ˌmeɪk ˈʌp/ *phrasal verb*

- ► make up
- ► constitute (*formal*)
- ► form
- ► comprise (*formal*)

make up
if several people or things make up something, they are the parts that make it what it is: *Rocks and minerals make up the Earth's outer layer.* | *The student council* ***is made up of*** *four representatives from every grade.*

constitute (AWL) (*formal*)
constitute means the same as **make up**: *Alaska is the largest of the 50 states that constitute the U.S.A.*

form
to be the thing that makes or is something. **Form** sounds fairly formal, and it is used especially in writing: *The river forms a natural boundary between the two countries.* | *Rice forms a basic part of their diet.*

comprise (AWL) (*formal*)
to form part of a larger group of people or things: *Women comprise a high proportion of part-time workers.*

→ see **make**
→ see **make up your mind** at **decide**, **make something up** at **lie²**

make up for /ˌmeɪk ˈʌp fɔr/ *phrasal verb*

- ► make up for
- ► compensate for
- ► counteract (*formal*)
- ► offset (*formal*)

make up for
to make a bad situation better by doing or providing something good: *Bryan took me out for dinner to make up for forgetting my birthday.* | *The boys paid for the window to make up for the damage they had caused.*

compensate for
to do or give something good, in order to reduce the bad effect of something: *Emiko's enthusiasm for the work helps to compensate for her lack of experience.*

counteract (*formal*)
to stop the bad effect of something, by having the opposite effect: *Doing math puzzles can help to counteract some of the effects of aging on your brain.*

offset (AWL) (*formal*)
if something offsets another thing, it has an opposite effect. You use **offset** especially about money and numbers: *The money I save on rent in my new apartment is offset by the increased cost of traveling to work.*

making *noun* → see **creation**, **production**

male¹ /meɪl/ *adjective*

- ► male
- ► masculine
- ► macho

ANTONYMS → see **female¹**

male
for men or typical of men. **Male** is used about jobs or activities that men do, or about behavior that is typical of men: *More women are entering traditionally male jobs like engineering.*
→ You also use **male** to show that a person is a man or boy, or to show that an animal is of the type that does not have babies or lay eggs: *A male nurse took her temperature.* | *A male goat can be called a billy goat.*

masculine
behavior or attitudes that are masculine are more typical of a man than a woman: *He wanted to say he was sorry, but his masculine pride wouldn't let him.*

macho
a man who is macho wants to show people that he is strong and brave, and does not show his feelings. **Macho** is sometimes used to show disapproval: *He is too macho to put a sweater on, even when it's really cold.*

male² *noun* → see **man**

mall *noun* → see **store**

man /mæn/ *noun*

- ► man
- ► boy
- ► guy
- ► gentleman
- ► male (*formal*)
- ► youth

ANTONYMS → see **woman**

man
an adult male person: *There were two men and a woman in the car.* | *Her father is a very rich man.* | *A man was sitting at a small table in the corner.*

boy
a male child or teenager: *I lived on a farm when I was a boy.* | *A group of boys were playing baseball in the field.*

guy
guy means the same as **man**, but sounds more informal and is used especially in spoken English: *Dave is a really nice guy.* | *One of the guys at work is from Mexico.*

gentleman
a polite word for a man, used when you do not know his name or when you are speaking to a group of people: *An elderly gentleman was asleep next to the fire.*

male (*formal*)
a man. **Male** is used especially by the police, doctors, or scientists: *Some medical conditions are found only in males.*

youth
a male teenager, especially one involved in violent or criminal activities: *There are reports that a gang of youths is robbing people in the park.*
➔ see **mankind**

manage /ˈmænɪdʒ/ *verb*

- manage
- run
- be in charge of
- be responsible for
- lead
- head
- direct
- control

manage
to organize and control the work of a company, organization, or group of people: *Katie agreed to manage a new department in the company.* | *The hotel has been owned and managed by the same family for over 100 years.*

run
to be the person who makes the important decisions about what will happen in a business or other organization: *He runs a software company in New York.*

be in charge of
to be the person who has the power to control an activity and to tell other people what to do: *The senior supervisor is in charge of training new employees.*

be responsible for
if you are responsible for something, you are in charge of it and have to make sure that problems are dealt with: *The Forest Service is responsible for fighting fires in national forests.*

lead
to be in charge of an activity or group of people working together on an important activity or project: *Dr. Hoffman will lead a team of researchers from the University of Chicago.*

head
to lead a group or activity, especially a department in an organization or a committee: *She has been picked to head the Department of Education because she is an experienced teacher and researcher.*

direct
to be in charge of an activity: *Mrs. Robertson has been hired to direct the company's marketing and development.*

control
to have power over a country, place, company, or group and decide what happens there: *The Republicans now control the U.S. Congress.*
➔ see **succeed** for **manage** meaning "to succeed after almost failing"
➔ see **supervise**

management /ˈmænɪdʒmənt/ *noun*

- management
- leadership
- administration
- government

management
the job of controlling a company or organizing a group of people and the work they do: *Under Angie's management, the whole project ran very smoothly.* | *Phil is now responsible for the management of the whole IT department.*
➔ You can also use **management** to mean the people who do this job: *Employees and management need to work together to find a solution.*

leadership
the job of being the leader of a group, organization, or country: *We cannot win the soccer tournament without leadership from our team captain.*

administration (AWL)
the job of controlling and organizing the everyday work of a company, organization, or project: *The federal government pays for the program, but state governments are responsible for its administration.*

government
the process or system of controlling a country, state, or city and making all the decisions and laws: *Good government means that you have to listen to the needs of the people.*
➔ see **government** for words meaning "the people who control organizations or countries"

manager /ˈmænɪdʒɚ/ *noun*

- ► manager
- ► boss
- ► head
- ► chief
- ► supervisor
- ► foreman
- ► employer

manager
someone who is in charge of a store or part of an organization: *The service in the restaurant was terrible and I asked to speak to the manager.* | *He is a manager in the sales department, with ten employees under him.*

boss
someone who is in charge of a group of people at work and tells them what to do: *I asked my boss if I could have a day off next week.* | *There is a new guy at work who is always trying to impress the boss.*

head
the person who is in charge of an organization or part of an organization: *She is the **head of** a small architecture company in St. Louis.* | *After teaching for many years, he became **head of** the English department.*

chief
the person who is in charge of an organization, especially the police or fire department, or some government jobs: *Scott has been the town's fire chief since 2005.* | *Rahm Emanuel was President Obama's chief of staff until 2010.*

supervisor
the person who is in charge of a group of workers, and who makes sure that they do the right things while they work: *Every year, I have a meeting with my supervisor to discuss my job performance.*

foreman
someone who is in charge of a group of factory workers or builders. A **foreman** makes sure that the workers do what the **manager** wants: *The foreman was showing a worker how to use one of the new machines.*

employer
a person, company, or organization that pays people to work for them: *She was a good employer and always treated me fairly.* | *The shoe factory is the largest employer in the area.*
→ see **chairman**, **leader**, Topic **Jobs and Work**

SYNONYM CHECK
Boss or manager?

Boss sounds more informal, and it is not an official job title. You use **boss** to talk about the person who tells you what to do at work: *My boss asked me to work for a few extra hours.*

Manager is used in the names of people's jobs, and is often used with other words: *the sales manager* | *the store manager*

maneuver *verb* → see **move**

mankind /ˌmænˈkaɪnd/ *noun*

- ► mankind
- ► man
- ► the human race
- ► humanity

mankind *also* **humankind**
all people, considered together as one group. **Mankind** is used especially when talking about the history of people and their development: *Landing on the moon was a great achievement in the history of mankind.* | *What will the future be like for humankind?*

man
human beings as one group or from a particular period of history: *Diamonds are the hardest substance known to man.* | *Prehistoric man hunted wild animals for food.*

the human race
all the people who have existed or will exist, thought of as different from other living things: *Pollution is a serious problem for the whole human race.*

humanity
humanity means the same as **mankind** but sounds more literary. You use **humanity** especially when you are talking about ways in which people suffer or have their rights taken away: *At least a fifth of humanity lives in poverty.*

SYNONYM CHECK
Mankind, man, or humankind?

Some people think that using **man** and **mankind** sounds like it does not include women. To avoid this problem, you can use **people** or **humankind**. For example, say: *People have always tried to understand the stars* instead of: *Man has always tried to understand the stars.* Instead of saying: *the history of mankind*, say: *the history of humankind.*

man-made *adjective* → see **artificial**

M

manner *noun* → see **behavior**, **way**

manners /ˈmænɚz/ *noun*

- ► manners
- ► courtesy
- ► politeness
- ► etiquette

manners
polite ways of behaving and speaking in social situations, such as polite ways of eating, meeting people, or asking for something: *Most parents try to teach their children good manners.* | *He has no manners! He kept talking on his cell phone during dinner.*

courtesy
polite behavior that shows respect for other people: *At least she had the courtesy to let us know she would be coming late.*

politeness
politeness means the same as **courtesy**: *I ate the food out of politeness* (=to be polite), *but I was not really hungry.*

etiquette
the rules for polite behavior in society or in a particular group: *Etiquette on the Internet says that you do not write in all capital letters, because that is like shouting at someone.*

mansion *noun* → see **house**

manual *noun* → see **instructions**

manufacture *verb* → see **make**

manufacturer *noun* → see **maker**

manufacturing *noun* → see **production**

many *adjective, pronoun* → see Function Words

march[1] *verb* → see **protest[2]**, **walk[1]**

march[2] *noun* → see **protest[1]**

mark[1] /mɑrk/ *noun*

1 a mark on something that spoils its appearance

- ► mark
- ► spot
- ► stain
- ► smudge
- ► smear
- ► track

2 a mark on someone's skin

- ► freckle
- ► mole
- ► scar
- ► bruise
- ► wart
- ► pimple
- ► blemish

1 a mark on something that spoils its appearance

mark
a dirty area on something that makes it look bad: *His shoes left dirty marks all over the floor.* | *What is that black mark on your T-shirt?*

spot
a small round mark on a surface, especially one that is made by a liquid: *There were a few **spots of** blood on his shirt.*

stain
a mark that is difficult to remove: *There was a dark red stain on the carpet, where someone had spilled a glass of wine.* | *You should wash the shirt right away or the tea will leave a stain.*

smudge
a dirty mark that is made when something soft or a liquid is rubbed against a surface: *There were smudges on his homework paper where his hand had rubbed the ink.*

smear
a mark that is made by a small amount of something that is spread across a surface: *The table had a **smear of** paint on the top.*

track
a mark left on the ground or another surface by a moving person, animal, or vehicle: *When the dog ran away, he left wet tracks on the sidewalk.* | *There were tire tracks in the sand leading to the water.*

2 a mark on someone's skin

freckle
one of several small light brown marks on someone's skin, usually on the face and arms. Some light-skinned people get **freckles** when they spend time in the sun: *She is a cute little girl with freckles across her nose and cheeks.*

mole
a small dark brown mark on someone's skin that is slightly higher than the skin around it: *She has a small mole above her eyebrow.*

scar
a permanent mark on your skin, caused by a cut or by something that burns you: *He has a bad* ***scar on*** *his ear where a dog once bit him.*

bruise
a purple or brown mark on your skin that you get because you have fallen or been hit. **Bruises** usually go away in a few days or weeks: *She came home from soccer practice with a big* ***bruise on*** *her knee.*

wart
a small hard raised mark on your skin that is not nice to look at. A **wart** is caused by a virus (=a living thing that causes an illness): *She went to the doctor to have a wart on her hand removed.*

pimple *also* **zit** (*informal*)
a small raised red mark on your skin that teenagers often have. **Zit** is more common in everyday English, and **pimple** sounds slightly more formal: *He looked in the mirror and saw he had a pimple on his face.* | *I always get zits just before I go to a party.*

blemish
a mark on your skin that spoils the way it looks. **Blemish** sounds fairly formal: *The makeup will hide any blemishes on your face.*

mark

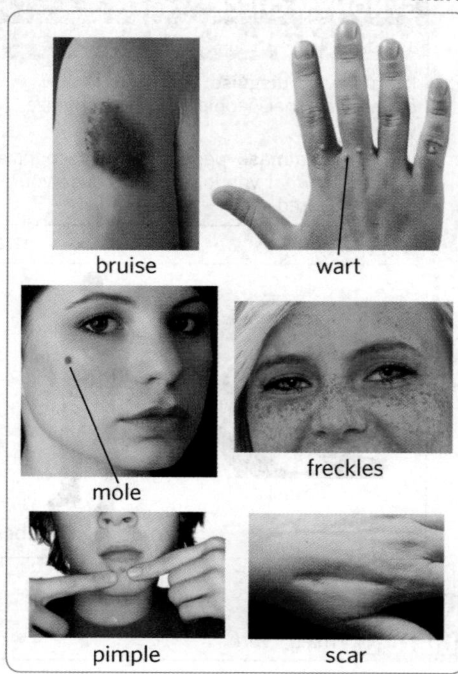

mark² *verb* → see **celebrate**, **dirty (2)**

marriage /ˈmærɪdʒ/ *noun*

- ► marriage
- ► relationship
- ► romance
- ► partnership

ANTONYMS → see **divorce**

marriage
the situation in which two people are married, or the time that they are married: *My grandparents had a long and happy marriage.* | *They love each other, and they have decided they are ready for marriage.* | *Is it true that almost half of all marriages end in divorce?*

relationship
a situation in which two people are together because they love each other: *He is much happier now that he is* ***in a relationship.***

romance
an exciting and often short relationship between two people who love each other: *Sometimes a summer romance turns into a serious relationship.*

partnership (AWL)
a relationship in which two people work together and help each other to achieve something: *Their marriage is a partnership that has remained strong despite hard times.*
→ see **wedding**, Topic **Relationships and Marriage**

married /ˈmærid/ *adjective*

- ► married
- ► single
- ► engaged
- ► separated
- ► divorced
- ► widowed

married
if you are married, you have a husband or a wife: *How long have you been married?* | *My brother is* ***married to*** *an Italian woman.* | *He is a married man with three children.*
→ **GRAMMAR:** Don't say: ~~*She is married with a nice man*~~. Say: *She is* ***married to*** *a nice man.*

single
someone who is single is not married: *When I was single, I went out with my friends every Friday and Saturday night.*

engaged
if someone is engaged, he or she has agreed to marry someone: *Sharon just got engaged – have you seen her ring?*
→ **GRAMMAR:** Don't say: ~~*He is engaged with a nice girl*~~. Say: *He is* ***engaged to*** *a nice girl.*

separated
if a husband and wife are separated, they are living apart because they are having problems in their marriage: *They were separated for six months, and in the end they got a divorce.*

divorced
no longer married because you have legally ended your marriage: *It has become common for children to grow up with divorced parents.*

widowed
no longer married because your husband or wife has died: *He is a widowed father of two young children.*

marry /ˈmæri/ *verb*

- marry
- get married
- remarry
- elope

marry
to become someone's husband or wife: *Will you marry me? | Alicia was 30 years old when she married Bryan.*
→ **GRAMMAR:** Don't say: ~~*He married to/with a Russian woman*~~. Say: *He married a Russian woman.*

get married
get married means the same as **marry** but is more common in everyday English: *We are getting married next month. | My parents got married in 1986. | Alicia was 30 years old when she **got married to** Bryan.*
→ **GRAMMAR:** Don't say: ~~*He got married with a Russian woman*~~. Say: *He **got married to** a Russian woman.*

remarry
to get married again: *He remarried three years after his wife died.*

elope
if two people elope, they go away secretly to get married: *My parents did not approve of the marriage, so we eloped.*
→ see Topic **Relationships and Marriage**

SYNONYM CHECK
Marry or get married?

When talking about two people, **get married** is more common and less formal than **marry**: *We're getting married soon.*

Marry is most common when you are saying who someone marries: *Cecilia married a boy from the neighborhood.*

masculine *adjective* → see **male[1]**

mask /mæsk/ *noun*

- mask
- disguise
- camouflage

mask
something that covers and hides all or part of your face: *The bank robbers were wearing masks, so we could not see their faces. | The boy had a Halloween mask on his face to make him look like a vampire.*

disguise
something you wear to change your appearance and hide who you really are: *He wore a fake beard as a disguise. | The poor woman in the market was actually the queen **in disguise**.*

camouflage
fur, skin, or feathers that make an animal difficult to see because the colors look like the natural background: *The polar bear's white fur is an excellent camouflage in the snow.*
→ **Camouflage** is also the patterns on military equipment or on soldiers' clothing that make them more difficult to see: *The soldiers were dressed **in camouflage** and were carrying weapons.*

SYNONYM CHECK
Mask or disguise?

If you wear a **disguise**, you try to look different so that people will not recognize you.

If you wear a **mask**, people cannot recognize you or see what you look like because your face is covered.

mask

mask
camouflage clothes

massive *adjective* → see **big**

match[1] /mætʃ/ *verb*

- match
- agree
- correspond
- mirror (*formal*)

match
if two things match, they look the same or have the same qualities or features: *Her red hat matches her red shoes.* | *The president's actions do not always match the promises he made before he was elected.* | *The police* ***matched*** *his fingerprints* ***to*** *the ones at the store where the robbery happened.*

agree
if two pieces of information agree with each other, they match or are the same: *Your story does not* ***agree with*** *what the police have told us.*

correspond (AWL)
if two things correspond, they are the same as each other or relate to each other: *The teacher was able to help students select books that* ***correspond to*** *their reading level.*

mirror (*formal*)
if one thing mirrors another, it is very similar to it in the way it looks or in the qualities it has. **Mirror** is used especially in writing: *Henry's sad face mirrored his son's unhappy expression.*

match[2] *noun* → see **game**, Topic **Sports and Exercise**

material *noun* → see **cloth**, **equipment**, **information**, **substance**

matter *noun* → see **subject**, **substance**

mature /mə'tʃʊr/ *adjective*

- mature
- adult
- grown-up

ANTONYMS → see **childish**

mature (AWL)
behaving in a sensible and responsible way, like an adult. You use **mature** especially about a child or a young person: *Lisa is only 13, but she is very mature for her age.* | *They should stop fighting and behave in a more mature way.*

adult (AWL)
behaving in a sensible, serious, and calm way, like an adult should behave: *I think it's best to sit down and discuss things in an adult way, without blaming each other.*

grown-up
grown-up means the same as **adult** but is more informal: *I expected more grown-up behavior from her.*
→ see **sensible**, Topic **Describing People's Character**

ADVERBS
You can make the adjective **mature** into an adverb by using an **-ly** ending: *When you show us you can act maturely, you can have a dog.*

maximum *adjective, pronoun* → see **limit[1]**, Function Word **most**

maybe /'meɪbi/ *adverb*

- maybe
- perhaps (*formal*)
- probably
- possibly
- conceivably (*formal*)

maybe
used for saying that something may be true or may happen, but you are not sure: *I wonder why she is late. Maybe she got stuck in traffic.* | *"Are you going to the party?" "Maybe."* | *Maybe you are right, but maybe not.*

perhaps (*formal*)
perhaps means the same as **maybe**. **Perhaps** is used especially in writing: *It was difficult to open the wooden door, perhaps because of the humidity.* | *The footprints belonged to a large cat – a tiger, perhaps.*

probably
used when saying that you are fairly sure something is true or will happen, although it is not completely definite. When you use **probably** you are more sure about something than when you say **maybe** or **perhaps**: *It is past six o'clock, so he has probably gone home.* | *We will probably come to the party, but I'll tell you definitely by tomorrow.*

possibly
used when saying that something may be true, but you do not have enough information to be sure: *The swimmer is competing in the Olympics, possibly for the last time.*

conceivably (*formal*)
if something may conceivably happen or be true, you think that it is possible, but it seems unlikely: *You might conceivably get a room when you arrive, but you should make a reservation to be sure.*
→ see **sure**

GRAMMAR CHECK: maybe
Maybe and **perhaps** are often used at the beginning of a sentence, but **probably**, **possibly**, and **conceivably** are not usually used to begin a sentence.

M

mayor *noun* → see Topic **Government and Politics**

meal /mil/ *noun*

1 meals during the day
- ► breakfast
- ► brunch
- ► lunch
- ► dinner
- ► supper

2 types of meals
- ► meal
- ► snack
- ► a bite to eat (*informal*)
- ► picnic
- ► barbecue
- ► buffet
- ► feast
- ► banquet

1 meals during the day

breakfast
the meal you eat when you get up in the morning: *What do you want **for breakfast** – eggs or pancakes? | Make sure you eat a good breakfast on the day of the test.*

brunch
a meal that you eat in the late morning, as a combination of breakfast and lunch: *We like to go out to a restaurant for brunch on Sunday.*

lunch
a meal that you eat in the middle of the day: *Have you had lunch yet? | I usually eat lunch at my desk.*

dinner
the meal that you eat in the evening: *We had fish and rice **for dinner**. | After dinner, we went for a walk in the neighborhood.*

supper
supper means the same as **dinner**, but it is used especially for an informal meal: *The kids had supper and went to bed early.*

2 types of meals

meal
the food that you eat for breakfast, lunch, or dinner: *Jeff cooked us a nice meal last night. | You shouldn't go swimming after a big meal. | We sat and ate our meal in silence.*

snack
something that you eat between meals: *The children have a snack at eleven o'clock – usually fruit and crackers.*

a bite to eat (*informal*)
a small meal that you eat quickly: *Let's get a bite to eat before the movie.*

picnic
a meal that you take with you to eat outside in a park or in the country: *It was a beautiful day – we had a picnic by the river.*

barbecue
a meal that you cook and eat outside: *If the weather is nice, we'll have a barbecue with hamburgers.*

buffet
a meal in which food is put on a table and you go and take what you want: *The lunch buffet at the Indian restaurant is delicious and it's only $10.*

feast
a very large meal for many people, to celebrate a special occasion. **Feast** is used in stories or in articles about food for special occasions: *The king promised to hold a great feast for all his people. | The turkey for the Thanksgiving feast is ready to go into the oven.*

banquet
a formal meal for many people on an important occasion: *A huge banquet was served to the winning team and its owners.*
→ see **food**, Topic **Eating in a Restaurant**

mean[1] /min/ *verb*

- ► mean
- ► represent
- ► signify
- ► symbolize
- ► stand for

mean
to have a particular meaning. **Mean** is used about words, symbols, or statements: *What does "abandon" mean? | The light means you are running out of gas. | It says "not suitable for children," which means anyone under 16 years old.*

represent
if a shape, letter, object, etc. represents something, it is used as a sign (=picture or shape) or mark for that thing: *The brown areas on the map represent deserts. | The letter "a" represents several different sounds in the English language.*

signify (AWL)
to mean or represent something. **Signify** sounds more formal than **mean** or **represent**: *The eagle in the flag signifies freedom and power.*

symbolize (AWL)
if something symbolizes a quality or feeling, it

represents it: *A wedding ring symbolizes a couple's promises to each other.*

stand for
if a letter or group of letters stands for something, it is a short way of saying or writing it: *NATO stands for North Atlantic Treaty Organization.*
→ see **mean to** at **plan to**

mean² /min/ *adjective*

- ► mean
- ► unkind
- ► hurtful
- ► nasty
- ► cruel
- ► malicious
- ► spiteful
- ► vindictive

ANTONYMS → see **kind²**, **nice (1)**

mean
treating people in a way that is not nice and makes them unhappy: *Don't be so **mean to** your little sister – give her the toy back.* | *Why does she say such mean things?* | ***It was mean of** you to laugh at his mistake.*

unkind
unkind means the same as **mean** but sounds a little more formal: *I started to shout, but then I realized I was being **unkind to** her. After all, she was only trying to help.*

hurtful
mean and making someone feel upset. You use **hurtful** about things that someone says or does: *During the argument he said some hurtful things which he later regretted.*

nasty
mean and seeming to enjoy making people unhappy: *He made a nasty comment about her weight.*

cruel
very mean and deliberately making someone suffer or feel unhappy: *He was **cruel to** his family, often saying terrible things or even hitting them.*

malicious
mean to someone because you want to upset, hurt, or cause problems for him or her. You often use **malicious** about things that people say or write: *Elena has never stolen anything – that is a malicious lie!*

spiteful
mean to someone, especially because you are jealous or angry: *The other women were spiteful and gave her the hardest work to do.*

vindictive
very mean and unfair because you want to harm someone who has harmed you: *She became bitter and vindictive after her husband left her, and she refused to let him see the children.*
→ see Topic **Describing People's Character**

ADVERBS

You can make the adjectives that mean **mean** into adverbs by using an **-ly** ending: *Mitchell laughed at her unkindly.* | *She had been treated cruelly by her first husband.* | *"I wouldn't go out with you for anything," she said spitefully.*

meaning /ˈminɪŋ/ *noun*

- ► meaning
- ► significance
- ► sense
- ► definition
- ► connotation (*formal*)
- ► nuance (*formal*)

meaning
the thing or idea that a word, picture, shape, or statement represents: *The word "spring" has several different meanings – the season, a curly piece of metal, and the place where water comes out of the ground.* | *There is a chart that explains the **meaning of** all the symbols on the map.*

significance
the meaning and importance of something. **Significance** sounds more formal than **meaning**: *It took us a little while to realize the full **significance of** what he had said – that his new job meant we would have to move.*

sense
one of the meanings of a word or phrase, when there are different possible meanings: *We are going to be talking about "power" in the military **sense of** the word.*

definition (AWL)
a phrase or sentence that says exactly what a word, phrase, or idea means: *Could someone in the class give me a **definition of** the term "global warming"?*

connotation (*formal*)
an idea or feeling that a word makes you think of, in addition to its basic meaning: *The word "professional" has connotations of skill and excellence.*

nuance (*formal*)
a meaning that is very slightly different from the basic meaning of a word or piece of writing: *The story has the nuances of a fable: it seems to say that if you work hard, you will succeed.*

meanwhile *adverb* → see Function Word **while**

measure /ˈmeʒɚ/ *verb*

- ► measure
- ► weigh
- ► time
- ► take
- ► gauge
- ► quantify (*formal*)

measure
to find out the size or amount of something, using a piece of equipment: *We need to measure the wall to see if the bookshelves will fit.* | *I measured the air pressure in the car tires at the gas station.*
→ You can also use **measure** to say that something is a particular size, length, or amount: *The table measures four feet by eight feet.*

weigh
to find out how heavy something is by measuring its weight with special equipment: *The nurse weighed the baby on a scale.*
→ You can also use **weigh** to say that someone or something has a particular weight: *She weighs 135 pounds.*

time
to measure how long it takes for someone to do something or for something to happen: *The coach timed the girls to see how long it took them to run a mile.*

take
to measure how hot someone is, or how fast his or her heart is beating, or to find another measurement as part of a medical examination: *The nurse came into the room and took my blood pressure.*

gauge
to measure or calculate something, especially when this is not completely accurate. **Gauge** sounds more technical than **measure**: *The research program will gauge the whale population in this part of the Pacific Ocean.*

quantify (*formal*)
to measure something and express it as a number: *It is difficult to quantify the damage that the hurricane has caused to the tourist industry.*
→ see **size**

measurement /ˈmeʒɚmənt/ *noun*

- ► measurement
- ► calculation
- ► assessment
- ► reading

measurement
the length, width, height, or amount of something: *Let's take measurements to make sure that the table will fit through the doorway.* | *I can make the dress fit you, but I will need your exact measurements.*
→ You can also use **measurement** to mean "the act of measuring something": *A physical exam in a doctor's office usually includes the measurement of height and weight.*

calculation
if you do a calculation, you use mathematics to find a number or amount: *Deb looked at the bill and made a few quick calculations to see how much money each person owed.*

assessment (AWL)
a measurement of the quality, amount, or value of something: *The bank will make an assessment of the house before giving you the loan.*

reading
a number that a piece of equipment shows when you are measuring something: *The scientists were taking temperature readings of the water in the Black Sea.*
→ see **height**, **length**, **size**, **width**

mechanical *adjective* → see **technical**

medal *noun* → see **prize**

media /ˈmidiə/ *noun*

- ► the media
- ► the press
- ► newspaper

the media (AWL)
newspapers, magazines, television, radio, and the Internet, and the reporters who work for them. You use **the media** when you think of these as a single group that provides news and information: *Crime in the city has received a lot of attention **in the media**.* | *The media has shown soldiers as brave men and women doing an important job.*
→ **GRAMMAR: The media** can be followed by a singular or plural verb. You usually use a singular verb: *The media is reporting on the election.* You can use a plural verb when you are thinking about **the media** as many separate newspapers, TV, magazines, etc.: *The media are very interested in her story.*

the press
newspapers and magazines, and the people who work for them. **The press** can mean the same as **the media**, but people think more of printed news when you use **the press**: *The president will be speaking to the press tomorrow about a new*

jobs program. | *The problems have been reported **in the press**.*
→ **GRAMMAR: The press** is followed by a singular verb.

newspaper
a set of large folded sheets of paper containing news, articles, and pictures, which is printed and sold every day or every week: *There was an article about the governor **in the newspaper**.* | *"The New York Times" is one of the nation's most respected newspapers.*
→ see **news**

medical *adjective* → see Topic **Medical Treatment**

medication *noun* → see **medicine**

medicine /ˈmedəsən/ *noun*

- ► medicine
- ► drug
- ► medication
- ► remedy
- ► dose
- ► prescription

medicine
a substance used for treating illness, for example in the form of a pill or liquid: *You have to take the medicine twice a day.* | *It is very important to keep all bottles of medicine away from children.*
→ **Medicine** also means "the treatment and study of illnesses and injuries": *Dr. Thompson has practiced medicine for 30 years.*

drug
a medicine, or a substance for making medicines: *There are many different drugs that are used in the treatment of cancer.*
→ **Drug** also means an illegal substance that some people take: *It is against the law to sell or use drugs such as heroin and cocaine.*

medication
medicine that a person takes over a period of time for a particular illness: *My grandmother is **on medication** for high blood pressure.*

remedy
a medicine or treatment for an illness or pain that is not very serious: *Hot lemon and honey tea is a good **remedy for** a sore throat.*

dose
a measured amount of medicine: *One **dose of** the medicine is a 5 ml spoonful.*

prescription
the medicine that a doctor says a sick person needs: *Will there be any side effects from this prescription?*
→ You can also use **prescription** when you are talking about the piece of paper on which a doctor writes what medicine a sick person should have: *I took the prescription to a pharmacy.*

SYNONYM CHECK
Medicine, medication, or drug?

If you are talking about the substances that people take to treat their illnesses, you use **medicine** or **medication**. Don't say: ~~*He takes drugs for his heart problems*~~. Say: *He takes medication for his heart problems.* | *He took some medicine for his cough.*

You use **drug** especially when you are talking about companies making substances for medical treatment: *The company has developed a new drug that is useful in treating heart problems.*

medium /ˈmidiəm/ *adjective*

- ► medium
- ► average
- ► intermediate
- ► moderate

medium (AWL)
in the middle of a range of sizes, levels, or amounts: *What size shirt does he wear – small, medium, or large?* | *Cook the potatoes over medium heat for ten minutes.*

average
around the usual level or amount: *He was in his late twenties and of average height.*
→ Use **average**, not **medium**, when you want to say that someone's level of skill or ability is neither high nor low. Don't say: ~~*The students are of medium ability*~~. Say: *The students are of average ability.*

intermediate (AWL)
between the basic level and the high level of a skill: *If I pass the intermediate Spanish class, I will take the advanced class next.*

moderate
not extreme so that something is not too much nor too little: *The doctor recommended moderate exercise after my surgery.*
→ see **large**, **small**

ADVERBS

You can make the adjective **moderate** into an adverb by using an **-ly** ending: *Most children are moderately active, but some don't do any exercise at all.*

M

M

meet /mit/ *verb*

1 to meet someone because you have planned to do this
- ► meet
- ► get together
- ► gather
- ► assemble

2 to meet someone without planning to do this
- ► meet
- ► run into (*informal*)
- ► bump into (*informal*)

1 to meet someone because you have planned to do this

meet
to go to the same place as someone else to see that person or do something together, when you have planned to do this: *I will meet you at the restaurant at seven.* | *We arranged to meet outside the movie theater.*

get together
to meet someone so that you can spend time with each other, especially with your friends or family. **Get together** sounds more informal than **meet**: *At Thanksgiving, the whole family gets together for a big meal.*

gather
if a crowd of people gathers somewhere, they go to the same place in order to do something or see something: *Fans started to gather outside the stadium an hour before the game began.*

assemble (AWL)
if people assemble somewhere, they go to the same place and stand together, especially in an organized way: *When the fire alarm rings, the students have to assemble outside on the field.*

2 to meet someone without planning to do this

meet
to see and talk to someone without planning to do this, or to see and talk to someone for the first time: *I met an old friend in the street.* | *We met on the first day of school and have been friends ever since.*

run into (*informal*)
to meet someone you know when you are doing something else: *Guess who I ran into at the post office today?*

bump into (*informal*)
bump into means the same as **run into** but is even more informal: *She bumped into Jorge at the grocery store.*
→ see **satisfy** (**2**) for **meet** meaning "to be good enough for what people need or want"

meeting /ˈmitɪŋ/ *noun*

1 an occasion when people meet to discuss something
- ► meeting
- ► conference
- ► convention
- ► assembly
- ► gathering
- ► summit
- ► interview

2 an occasion when you have arranged to meet someone
- ► appointment
- ► consultation (*formal*)
- ► date

1 an occasion when people meet to discuss something

meeting
an event at which people meet to discuss something: *Mr. Katz is **in a meeting** now, but he'll be free this afternoon.* | *She had a **meeting with** the principal yesterday to talk about the changes.*

conference (AWL)
a big meeting that lasts for several days, where people listen to talks about a subject and discuss it: *The professor gave a speech **at a conference on** climate change.*

convention (AWL)
a large meeting of people who belong to the same organization, do the same work, or are interested in the same thing: ***At the** Republican Party **convention**, the delegates clapped for her speech.* | *Fans go to the convention to see their favorite stars from the TV series.*

assembly (AWL)
a meeting of all the students and teachers at a school: ***At the assembly**, the people who were running for student government made speeches.*

gathering
an informal meeting, especially of family or friends: *We usually have a big family gathering at my grandparents' house at Thanksgiving.*

summit
an important meeting between leaders of different countries to discuss something: *World leaders are getting ready for a **summit on** global economic problems.*

interview
a formal meeting at which someone is asked questions to find out if he or she is suitable for something such as a job or course of study: *I need to buy a new suit for a job interview.*

2 an occasion when you have arranged to meet someone

appointment
an arrangement to meet someone such as a doctor, lawyer, or business person at a particular time and place: *I'd like to make an* ***appointment with*** *Dr. Hanson on Tuesday.* | *I have an* ***appointment with*** *the manager.*

consultation (AWL) *(formal)*
a meeting with someone such as a doctor, lawyer, etc. so that you can get advice or information: *The professors have office hours for* ***consultations with*** *students.*

date
an arrangement to meet someone, especially your boyfriend or girlfriend, and do something together such as see a movie or go to a restaurant: *I'm going on a* ***date with*** *Angela on Friday night.*

melt /melt/ *verb*

- ► melt
- ► thaw
- ► defrost
- ► dissolve

melt
if something solid melts, it changes to a liquid when it becomes warmer: *In the spring the snow starts to melt.* | *Melt two tablespoons of butter in a frying pan.*

thaw
if something frozen thaws, it becomes warmer until all the ice is gone: *The lake thawed in March.* | *Thaw frozen meat in its packaging and then cook as soon as possible.*

defrost
if frozen food defrosts, it gets warmer until it is not frozen anymore: *The turkey needs to defrost overnight.* | *You can defrost the meat in the microwave – it's quicker.*

dissolve
if a solid dissolves in a liquid, it mixes with it and becomes part of it: *Stir the water until all the sugar dissolves.* | *Dissolve the aspirin tablet in a glass of water.*

melt

melt dissolve

memorable /ˈmemərəbəl/ *adjective*

- ► memorable
- ► unforgettable

memorable
a memorable event or time is so good that you remember it for a long time: *Our wedding day was a truly memorable occasion.*

unforgettable
an unforgettable experience or sight has such a strong effect on you that you will never be able to forget it: *The trip had been an unforgettable experience for both of them.*

ADVERBS
You can make the adjectives **memorable** and **unforgettable** into adverbs by using an **-ly** ending: *Martin Luther King Jr. memorably said, "I have a dream!"* | *The ceremony was an unforgettably emotional experience.*

memorize /ˈmeməˌraɪz/ *verb*

- ► memorize
- ► learn something by heart

memorize
to learn words, music, or facts so that you can remember them: *Don't write down your PIN number, memorize it.*

learn something by heart
to memorize something, for example a poem or piece of music, especially so that you can say it or play it without any mistakes: *It is useful to learn your times tables by heart.*
→ see **remember**

memory /ˈeməri/ *noun*

- ► memory
- ► recollection *(formal)*
- ► reminiscences *(formal)*

memory
something in the past that you remember: *He left school with happy* ***memories of*** *his time there.* | *My earliest* ***memory*** *is* ***of*** *standing in my crib and crying for my mother.*
→ You also use **memory** about your ability to remember things: *I have a terrible memory for names – I can never remember them.*

recollection *(formal)*
a memory of something that happened: *She says she has no* ***recollection of*** *the accident.*

reminiscences (*formal*)
stories that you tell people about things you remember: ***We listened to his reminiscences about** his college days.*
→ see **remember**

M

mend *verb* → see fix

mental /ˈmentl/ *adjective*

- ► mental
- ► intellectual
- ► cognitive (*formal*)

ANTONYMS → see **physical**

mental (AWL)
relating to your mind and your thoughts: *The center provides help for people who are suffering from mental illness.* | *I had never met Jane's boyfriend, but I had a clear mental picture of what he looked like.*

intellectual
relating to your ability to think in an intelligent way and understand ideas and information: *The class appealed to her intellectual curiosity, and she wanted to find out more.*

cognitive (*formal*)
relating to people's ability to think and understand things. You use **cognitive** especially about the scientific study of people's thinking abilities: *She is researching the cognitive development of young children for her Ph.D.*
→ see **mind**[1]

ADVERBS
You can make the adjectives that mean **mental** into adverbs by using an **-ly** ending: *I added the numbers together mentally, then wrote the total on the bill.* | *The class is intellectually challenging.*

mentally ill /ˌmentl-i ˈɪl/ *adjective*

- ► mentally ill
- ► insane
- ► paranoid
- ► unstable
- ► crazy (*informal*)

mentally ill
having an illness of the mind that affects the way you behave: *Many people who are mentally ill have trouble keeping a job.*

insane
having a serious illness of the mind that affects the way you behave. You use **insane** especially about people who are accused of crimes: *The court ruled that the killer was criminally insane.*

paranoid
believing that you cannot trust other people, or that they are trying to harm you, because you have a mental illness: *The illness made him paranoid, and he thought his mother was trying to poison him.*
→ You can also use **paranoid** informally when someone does not have a mental illness: *Maybe I'm being paranoid, but I don't think he likes me.*

unstable (AWL)
not always able to think or behave in a normal controlled way: *He was a troubled and unstable man who would start shouting at us for no reason.*

crazy (*informal*)
behaving in a way that is not sensible and seems strange: *The old man seemed crazy, and I avoided him.*
→ It is impolite and not acceptable to use **crazy** about someone who is mentally ill.
→ see **crazy** for informal words meaning "stupid and not sensible"

ADVERBS
You can make the adjectives **insane** and **crazy** into adverbs by using an **-ly** ending: *The Queen was insanely jealous of Snow White's beauty.* | *The man was behaving crazily, and I avoided him.*

mention /ˈmenʃən/ *verb*

- ► mention
- ► refer to
- ► touch on
- ► raise
- ► bring up

mention
to talk or write about someone or something, usually quickly and without saying very much or giving details: *I **mentioned** the idea **to** Jim, and he seemed to like it.* | *Some of these problems were mentioned in his report.*
→ **GRAMMAR:** Don't say: ~~*I mentioned about the party*~~. Say: *I mentioned the party.*

refer to
refer to means the same as **mention** but is more formal: *He refers to the incident in his book.*

touch on
to say a little about a subject while you are talking or writing about something else. **Touch on** sounds a little informal: *This problem has already been touched on in Chapter 4.*

raise
to mention a subject for the first time so that it can be discussed: *He promised to **raise** the issue **with** the president.*

bring up
bring up means the same as **raise** but is a little more informal: *I didn't think it was a good time to bring up the subject of money.*

→ see **say**

menu *noun* → see Topic **Eating in a Restaurant**

merit *verb* → see **deserve**

mess /mes/ *noun*

- mess
- clutter
- jumble
- dump (*informal*)
- disorder (*formal*)
- chaos

mess
an area where things are not neat or clean: *We spent the morning cleaning up the mess after the party.* | *You can play in here, but try not to make a mess.*

clutter
a lot of things that fill a place and make it messy: *How can you work with all that clutter on your desk?*

jumble
a group of things that are mixed together in a messy way: *There was a **jumble of** old toys in the box.*

dump (*informal*)
a very messy or dirty place: *My brother's room is a dump – he never cleans it.*

disorder (*formal*)
a situation in which things are disorganized and messy: *The house was **in total disorder**, as if someone had thrown everything up in the air and left it where it fell.*

chaos
a confusing and completely disorganized situation: *The accident caused traffic chaos on the freeways.*

message /ˈmesɪdʒ/ *noun*

- message
- note
- memo
- text
- email

message
something that you say or write to tell someone about something, when you cannot speak to him or her yourself: *Jim, I have a **message for** you from your brother.* | *She is in a meeting right now, but I'll give her the message.*

note
a short written message: *He left a note on my desk saying he would be back in five minutes.*

memo
a short official written message to another person in the same organization: *I sent him a memo reminding him about the meeting.*

text *also* **text message**
a written message that you send using a cell phone: *Greg sent me a text to warn me that he would be late.*

email
a written message that is sent from one computer to another: *I get lots of emails every day, but most of them are about work.*

messy /ˈmesi/ *adjective*

- messy
- untidy
- cluttered
- sloppy
- disorganized
- chaotic (*formal*)

ANTONYMS → see **neat**, **organized**

messy
not neat or not clean: *He only cleans up his room when it gets really messy.* | *How can you work on such a messy desk?*

untidy
untidy means the same as **messy** but sounds more formal: *His office was untidy, with piles of books and papers everywhere.*

cluttered
messy because there are too many things in a place: *It is difficult to work when your desk is cluttered with books and pieces of paper.*

sloppy
doing something in a way that is not neat or careful. **Sloppy** sounds a little informal: *How can you expect a good grade for this class if you turn in such a sloppy paper?*

disorganized
not arranged or organized in a clear order: *The files on her computer were completely disorganized, so she could never find anything she wanted.*

chaotic (*formal*)
a chaotic situation is one in which no one knows what to do or where things are, and people get

confused: *The situation at the airport was chaotic. No one seemed to be in charge.*

ADVERBS

You can make the adjectives **messy**, **untidy**, and **sloppy** into adverbs by using an **-ly** ending: *The kids were messily making a cake in the kitchen.* | *Some of the guests were sloppily dressed.*

method *noun* → see **way**

middle¹ /'mɪdl/ *adjective*

- middle
- central

middle
closest to the center of something, or between the top and bottom, or between the left and right parts: *She was driving in the middle lane and cars were passing her on both sides.* | *The letter was in the middle drawer of her desk.*

central
in the center of an area or place: *Rwanda is a country in central Africa.* | *The apartments all face onto a central courtyard.*

ADVERBS

You can make **central** into an adverb by using an **-ly** ending: *The hotel is centrally located.*

middle² /'mɪdl/ *noun*

- middle
- center
- heart
- core

middle
the part of something that is farthest from all the edges of an area or object. You use **middle** especially about the part that is halfway between two sides: *Gary swam toward the **middle** of the lake.* | *She placed the flowers **in the middle** of the table.*
→ You can also use **middle** to talk about the part of something that is halfway between the beginning and the end: *I fell asleep in the middle of the movie.*

center
center means the same as **middle**. You use **center** especially about the part that is exactly in the middle: *Draw a line through the **center** of the circle.* | *She placed the flowers **in the center** of the table.*

heart
the middle of an area, town, or city: *The hotel is located **in the heart of** Manhattan.*

core (AWL)
the central part of the Earth, or of an object: *The Earth has a solid inner core which is 2,500 kilometers in diameter.*

SYNONYM CHECK
Middle or center?

You usually use **center** when you mean an exact point: *The point where the lines cross is the center of the square.*

You usually use **middle** when thinking of a slightly larger area: *Put an X in the middle of the square.*

You can use both **middle** and **center** to talk about the center of a flat area or object, or about the point that is inside something and farthest from all the edges: *The donuts have jam in the center/middle.*

You usually use **middle** to talk about something that is between the top and bottom of something: *The cake has a layer of frosting in the middle.*

middle-aged *adjective* → see Topic **Describing People's Looks**

mild *adjective* → see **tasteless**

military /'mɪləˌteri/ *noun*

- military
- armed forces
- the service
- troops

military (AWL)
the army, navy, and air force of a country: *We need a strong military to defend our country.*

armed forces
armed forces means the same as **military**: *The President is the commander of the armed forces.*

the service
the army, navy, or air force. You use **the service** especially when you want to emphasize that being in the military is someone's job: *She has two sons in the service – one in the army and one in the navy.* | *Women in all the services are flying planes.*

troops
people in the military. You use **troops** especially when talking about soldiers in a large organized

group: *The troops marched north to attack the enemy forces.*
→ see **army**, **soldier**

mind[1] /maɪnd/ *noun*

- ► mind
- ► brain
- ► head

mind
the part of you that you use for thinking and imagining things: *I never know what's going on in her mind.* | *There was no doubt in my mind that it was the right decision.*

brain
the part of your body that you use for thinking and feeling, and which controls the other parts of your body: *Come on, John, use your brain!* | *The brain sends a signal to your leg to move.*

head
head means the same as **mind** but is more informal: *Use your head and I'm sure you'll think of the right answer.*
→ see **mental**

mind[2] *verb* → see **care[1]**

minimize *verb* → see **reduce**

minimum *adjective, noun* → see **limit[1]**, Function Word **least**

minister /ˈmɪnəstɚ/ *noun*

- ► minister
- ► priest
- ► pastor
- ► preacher
- ► reverend
- ► chaplain
- ► rabbi
- ► imam
- ► the clergy

minister
a religious leader who is in charge of ceremonies in some Christian churches: *The minister's sermon was 20 minutes long.* | *I'd rather have a church wedding with a minister and music than get married at City Hall.*

priest
a religious leader in some Christian churches, especially the Catholic church, and in some other religions, for example the Buddhist religion: *The priest was saying Mass.* | *The Buddhist priests were wearing orange robes.*

pastor
a religious leader in some Christian churches, especially Protestant churches: *She asked her pastor to pray for her.*

preacher
someone who gives speeches about religious subjects, especially in a church: *The preacher was talking about the meaning of Christmas.*

reverend
used before someone's name to show that he or she is a minister in a Christian church: *The Reverend Jesse Jackson was born in Greenville, South Carolina.*

chaplain
someone who takes care of the religious needs of people in a prison, college, hospital, or the army: *He was a chaplain at Yale University for many years.*

rabbi
a Jewish religious leader and teacher who is in charge of prayers and ceremonies: *The traditional Jewish funeral prayers were said by Rabbi Mark Solomon.*

imam
a Muslim religious leader: *He asked the imam at his local mosque for advice.*

the clergy
religious leaders considered as a group: *Some members of the clergy are against the idea.*
→ see Topic **Government and Politics**

minor *adjective* → see **small**, **unimportant**

minority *noun* → see **race[1]**, Function Word **few**

minute[1] *noun* → see **moment**

minute[2] *adjective* → see **small**

misbehave /ˌmɪsbɪˈheɪv/ *verb*

- ► misbehave (*formal*)
- ► act up (*informal*)
- ► mess around (*informal*)
- ► be bad (*informal*)
- ► be naughty

ANTONYMS → see **behave (2)**

misbehave (*formal*)
if children misbehave, they behave in a way that breaks rules, causes trouble, or annoys people: *Kids often misbehave when they are bored or tired.* | *Students who misbehave in class will be sent to the principal.*

act up (*informal*)
if children act up, they behave badly by being very active and noisy in a situation that

interrupts or causes problems for other people: *A little boy started acting up in church and his mother took him outside.*

mess around *also* **fool around** (*informal*)
to behave in a silly way for fun, especially when you should be working or studying: *Stop messing around and pay attention!* | *Two of the kids were **fooling around with** firecrackers, and one got burned.*

be bad (*informal*)
to misbehave. You use **be bad** to talk about a child or animal who has misbehaved: *My parents used to send me to my room when I was bad.*

be naughty
to misbehave. **Be naughty** sounds old-fashioned or literary and is only used about children: *When we were naughty, my father would give us extra work to do.*
→ see **bad** (**4**)

misbehavior /ˌmɪsbɪˈheɪvyɚ/ *noun*

- ► misbehavior
- ► wrongdoing
- ► misconduct (*formal*)

misbehavior
behavior that breaks rules, causes trouble, or annoys people: *The soldiers will be punished for their misbehavior.* | *The best way of dealing with your child's misbehavior is to stay calm.*

wrongdoing
behavior that is illegal or morally bad: *The museum has been accused of showing stolen artworks, but it denies any wrongdoing.*

misconduct (*formal*)
very bad behavior when doing a job, especially bad behavior by someone who has important responsibilities: *The police officer was fired for misconduct, after it was found that he was drinking while on duty.*

miserable *adjective* → see **sad**, Topic **Describing People's Emotions**

misery *noun* → see **sadness**

miss /mɪs/ *verb*

1 to not do something or go to something
- ► miss
- ► pass up
- ► skip (*informal*)

2 to not see, hear, or notice something
- ► miss
- ► overlook

3 to not hit something
- ► miss
- ► avoid
- ► dodge

ANTONYMS → see **hit[1]** (**3**)

4 to feel sad because someone is not with you, or because you are not in a place
- ► miss
- ► be homesick

1 to not do something or go to something

miss
to not do something or not go to something, especially something you should have done or gone to: *I was late and I missed my first class.* | *He didn't want to miss the chance to earn some extra money.*
→ You also use **miss** when you are too late to get on a plane, bus, or train: *We need to hurry or we'll miss our plane.*

pass up
to decide not to use the chance to do something: *I don't think you should pass up the opportunity to go to university.*

skip (*informal*)
to not do something that you usually do, or that you should do. **Skip** is often used about classes and meals, or part of a book or movie: *Don't skip breakfast; it's the most important meal of the day.* | *I skipped a few paragraphs because they were boring.*

2 to not see, hear, or notice something

miss
to not see, hear, or notice something: *I missed the sign for the school and we drove straight past.* | *Make sure that you read the question carefully - it's easy to miss things and make silly mistakes.*

overlook
to not notice something important: *The police had overlooked an important piece of evidence that showed that the man was not guilty of the murder.*

3 to not hit something

miss
to not hit something: *The hitter completely missed the ball.* | *The ball narrowly missed her head.*

avoid
to move so that you do not hit something or get hit by it: *I had to drive onto the sidewalk to avoid the truck.*

dodge
to move quickly sideways in order to avoid someone or something: *They ran across the road, dodging the traffic.*

4 to feel sad because someone is not with you, or because you are not in a place

miss
to feel sad because someone is not with you, or because you are not in a place: *When we moved to Chicago, the children really missed their old friends.* | *I will miss New York when we move - it's a great place to live.*

be homesick
to feel sad because you are a long way away from your home, your family, and your friends, and you wish you were back there: *My sister was very homesick when she first went to college.*

missing *adjective* → see **absent**

mist *noun* → see **cloud**, Topic **The Weather**

mistake¹ /mɪˈsteɪk/ *noun*

- ► mistake
- ► error
- ► blunder
- ► inaccuracy (*formal*)
- ► mix-up
- ► oversight (*formal*)
- ► slip

mistake
something that is not correct: *I have made a mistake - it should say $230, not $320.* | *Her essay is full of spelling mistakes - she can't spell "success" or "beginning."*
→ You also use **mistake** when saying that you did something accidentally: *I picked up someone else's bag **by mistake**.*

error (AWL)
error means the same as **mistake** but is more formal: *There must be an **error in** your addition.* | *He makes some simple grammatical errors - for example he says "I is" when he should say "I am."*

blunder
a stupid careless mistake, especially one that has serious results: *In a serious blunder by the hospital, two babies were sent home with the wrong parents.*

inaccuracy (AWL) (*formal*)
a piece of information that is not completely correct: *The report contains several inaccuracies and some of the amounts are clearly wrong.*

mix-up
a mistake in which someone confuses one thing or person with another. **Mix-up** sounds a little informal: *There was a **mix-up over** the dates and I thought the meeting was this Thursday, when it is actually next Thursday.*

oversight (*formal*)
a mistake in which you forget to do something or do not notice something: *Due to an oversight, Sam's name was not included on the list.*

slip
a small unimportant mistake that is easy to make: *If you make a slip when you're painting, you can go back and paint over it.* | *I should have said 50, not 15 - it was a slip of the tongue* (=a mistake when speaking).
→ see **accidentally** for ways of saying that you did not intend something to happen, **defect** for words meaning "a mistake in the way something was made"

SYNONYM CHECK
Mistake or error?
In some phrases, you must use **error**, not **mistake**. Don't say: ~~*a computer mistake*~~. Say: *a computer error*. Don't say: ~~*The accident was caused by human mistake*~~. Say: *The accident was caused by human error.* However, you cannot say that you did something ~~*by error*~~. Say: *I did it **by mistake**.*

mistake² *verb* → see **misunderstand**

mistrust¹ *noun* → see **distrust²**

mistrust² *verb* → see **disbelieve**

misty *adjective* → see **cloudy**, Topic **The Weather**

misunderstand /ˌmɪsʌndəˈstænd/ *verb*

- ► misunderstand
- ► mistake
- ► misjudge
- ► misinterpret

ANTONYMS → see **understand**

misunderstand
to think that someone means one thing, when in fact he or she means a different thing: *When I asked where the bank was, the man misunderstood my question and said it was 10:30.* | *He said that his comments had been misunderstood, and that he had never meant to insult her.*

mistake
to misunderstand something and react in the

wrong way, especially to misunderstand the way someone behaves or what he or she intends to do: *She was very shy and didn't say much, and some people* ***mistook*** *this* ***for*** *unfriendliness.*

misjudge
to have a wrong or unfair opinion about a person or situation: *He began to help me when I didn't expect it, and I realized I had misjudged him.*

misinterpret (AWL)
to think that what someone says or does means something different from what it really means: *The president said that other people had misinterpreted his words. He had not said there would be no more tax increases.*

mix /mɪks/ verb

1 to put different substances together to make something new
- mix
- combine
- blend

2 to use different styles, ideas, or other things together
- mix
- combine
- fuse
- blend

1 to put different substances together to make something new

mix
to put different substances together to make something new: *If you mix yellow and blue paint together, you get green.* | *Mix the oil and the vinegar together with a spoon.*

combine
to mix things together completely. **Combine** is more formal than **mix**: *Combine the flour and the eggs.*

blend
to mix liquids or soft substances together, especially foods, to form a single smooth substance: ***Blend*** *the yogurt* ***with*** *fresh fruit for a great drink.*

2 to use different styles, ideas, or other things together

mix
to use different styles, ideas, or other things together: *His music mixes blues and jazz.* | *My pleasure was* ***mixed with*** *a sad feeling that this would all soon come to an end.*

combine
combine means the same as **mix** but is more formal: *Diets are most effective when they are* ***combined with*** *exercise.*

fuse
to mix different styles together to make a completely new style: *The band* ***fuses*** *traditional African rhythms* ***with*** *hip hop music.*

blend
to mix parts of different things together, especially in a successful and effective way: *He blended the pictures of the monkey and the baby together, and the final picture is really surprising.*

mixture /ˈmɪkstʃɚ/ noun

- mixture
- combination
- blend
- cross
- hybrid
- solution
- compound

mixture
several different things, ideas, or feelings that are mixed together: *Pour the mixture into the cake pan and bake for 50 minutes.* | *She felt a strange mixture of fear and excitement.*

combination
two or more different things that are used together or that happen together: *Doctors use a combination of three drugs to fight the disease.* | *The combination of hot weather and lack of rain was very bad for the crops.*

blend
a mixture that contains different types of the same thing, especially types that go together well: *Their music is a blend of different styles of jazz.* | *The coffee is a blend of Arabian and South American coffee beans.*

cross
a mixture of very different things. You use **cross** especially when you are describing what something looks or sounds like: *The building looked like a* ***cross between*** *a museum* ***and*** *a spaceship.*

hybrid
something that is produced from a mixture of things, especially a plant or animal: *The plant is a hybrid of wheat and rye.*
→ You also use **hybrid** about something that uses a mixture of different styles or methods: *The car is a hybrid – it gets its power from gas and batteries.*

solution
a liquid mixed with a solid substance or a gas: *You can use a salt solution to clean the wound.*

→ In science, a **solution** is a substance mixed with another substance so that both substances are evenly spread through the whole of the mixture. Usually people talk about **solutions** made from liquids and solids, such as sugar in water, but a solution can be gases mixed with gases, or liquids mixed with liquids.

compound (AWL)
a chemical substance that contains atoms of two or more elements: *Water is a compound that consists of hydrogen and oxygen.*

mix up /ˌmɪks ˈʌp/ *phrasal verb*

- ► mix up
- ► confuse
- ► mistake

mix up
to make the mistake of thinking that someone or something is another person or thing: *One of the students had mixed up the dates and thought the test was next week.* | *There are two keys for the front door and I sometimes get them mixed up.*

confuse
confuse means the same as **mix up** but is a little more formal: *Students often confuse words like "affect" and "effect."* | *Black bears are sometimes* ***confused with*** *brown bears, because black bears can actually have brown fur.*

mistake
mistake means the same as **mix up**: *A woman* ***mistook*** *him* ***for*** *a well-known actor and asked him for his autograph.*

GRAMMAR CHECK: mix up

Mistake and **confuse** mean the same but they are followed by different prepositions.

You **mistake** one thing or person **for** another: *I sometimes* ***mistake*** *her* ***for*** *her twin sister.*

You **confuse** one thing or person **with** another: *The teacher* ***confused*** *her* ***with*** *her twin sister.*

mobile /ˈmoʊbəl/ *adjective*

- ► mobile
- ► portable
- ► movable

mobile
easy to move and use in different places: *The store sells cell phones, laptops, and other mobile electronic devices.* | *After the hurricane, people lived in mobile homes until their houses could be rebuilt.*

portable
able to be carried or moved easily, and usually not weighing very much: *We took a portable radio with us so that we could listen to music at the beach.*

movable
able to be moved, and not staying only in one place or position: *The toy has movable arms that spin around and bend.*

model /ˈmɑdl/ *noun*

- ► model
- ► brand
- ► make

model
one of several types of a product that a company makes: *This car is the sports model, which can go from 0 to 70 miles an hour in less than 4 seconds.* | *Computers change so fast that new models come out all the time.*

brand
the name of a product made by a company, or the name of the company that makes it. **Brand** is used about names of everyday products such as food, drinks, and clothes: *The advertisement is for a well-known brand of soft drink.*

make
the name of the company that makes a product, especially a car, computer, or machine: *"What make of car does she drive?" "A Ford."*
→ see **copy**[1], **pose**

moderate *adjective* → see **medium**

moderately *adverb* → see **fairly**

modern /ˈmɑdə·n/ *adjective*

- ► modern
- ► contemporary
- ► current
- ► latest
- ► up-to-date

ANTONYMS → see **old-fashioned**

modern
relating to the time we live in now: *Computers are an important part of modern life.* | *In the modern world, traveling is much easier than it was in the past.*
→ You also use **modern** about things that use the latest methods, designs, and technology: *Modern buildings use much less energy for heating and lighting.*

contemporary (AWL)
contemporary art, music, literature, etc. was

produced recently: *The museum has an excellent collection of contemporary art.*

current
happening or existing now. You use **current** especially when you think a situation will change: *In the current economic situation, it is difficult to know what will happen.*

latest
most recent: *His latest movie is the best he has ever made.*

up-to-date
including all the most recent information: *See our website for the most up-to-date information about the weather.*
→ see **advanced** for **modern** meaning "using new methods, designs, or equipment"

ADVERBS
You can make **current** into an adverb by using an **-ly** ending: *The company currently employs 113 people.*

modest /ˈmɑdɪst/ *adjective*

- ► modest
- ► humble
- ► unassuming (*formal*)

ANTONYMS → see **proud (2)**

modest
not talking proudly about the things you do well: *She was **modest about** her own achievements as a tennis player. | Despite his fame, he is a modest man.*

humble
showing by your behavior that you do not think that you are better or more important than other people: *He is a gentle humble man who is surprised that people are interested in his life.*

unassuming (*formal*)
not wanting to make other people notice you or treat you in a special way: *This quiet unassuming woman is one of the world's most brilliant scientists.*

ADVERBS
You can make the adjectives that mean **modest** into adverbs by using an **-ly** ending: *"I had a lot of help on the project," Paul said modestly. | She was humbly grateful to have a job, when so many other people did not. | The hotel blends unassumingly into the natural environment.*

modesty /ˈmɑdəsti/ *noun*

- ► modesty
- ► humility

ANTONYMS → see **pride**

modesty
behavior in which you do not talk a lot about the things you do well, or try to make people admire you: *Her modesty is surprising, but she really does not believe that she should get any special treatment. | "We achieved a lot," he said, without modesty.*

humility
behavior that shows you are not too proud of yourself and do not think you are better than other people: *She remained a woman of great humility, despite all the attention and praise her work received.*

modify *verb* → see **change**[1]

mom *noun* → see **mother**

moment /ˈmoʊmənt/ *noun*

- ► moment
- ► minute
- ► instant

moment
a very short period of time: *After a moment, Ted came back into the room. | For a moment he seemed confused by my question.*

minute
minute means the same as **moment**: *Sam thought for a minute and then smiled at his brother. | I'll be with you in a minute.*

instant
an extremely short period of time. You use **instant** when something happens very quickly: *The thief was gone in an instant.*

money /ˈmʌni/ *noun*

1 what you use to pay for things

- ► money
- ► cash
- ► change
- ► currency
- ► funds
- ► capital
- ► revenue

2 the money that someone has

- ► money
- ► wealth
- ► fortune
- ► riches

1 what you use to pay for things

money
the coins and bills you use to pay for things: *I wish I had enough money to buy a new dress.* | *Beth wanted to get a job and earn some money.*

cash
coins and paper money, rather than checks or credit cards, which you use when you buy something: *I usually pay **in cash** if something only costs a few dollars.* | *He got some cash out of the ATM at the bank.*

change
money in the form of coins, not paper money: *I need some change for the parking meter.*
→ You also use **change** about the money you get back in a store, when you give more money than something costs: *He handed the clerk a $20 bill and she gave him $3 change.*

currency (AWL)
the type of money that a country uses: *"What's the currency in Japan?" "The yen."*

funds
the money that someone has available to buy things. You use **funds** especially when talking about the money that an organization has available for doing something: *They are selling chocolate to raise **funds for** the school.*

capital
money that you use to start a business, or that you invest in a business: *How did you get the capital to start your own company?*

revenue (AWL)
money that a company receives from business activities, or that the government receives from taxes: *The company's revenue has increased by 5% over the last six months.*

2 the money that someone has

money
the money that someone has: *Morgan made his money in the oil industry.* | *The business went bankrupt and they lost all their money.*

wealth
a large amount of money that someone has: *Her father was a man of great wealth.* | *Wealth doesn't bring happiness, and some very rich people are also very unhappy.*

fortune
a very large amount of money: *Gates wants to use his fortune to help people in poor countries.*

riches
large amounts of money and other valuable things: *People came to California hoping to find riches during the Gold Rush of the 1840s.*
→ see **payment**, **tax**

monster /ˈmɑnstɚ/ *noun*

- ► monster
- ► giant
- ► ogre
- ► beast

monster
a large frightening imaginary creature, especially in a story or movie: *In the movie, the Earth is taken over by monsters from outer space.* | *He dressed up as Frankenstein's monster for Halloween.*

giant
an extremely tall strong man. In children's stories, **giants** are often frightening and evil: *Jack waited for the giant to fall asleep and then climbed down the beanstalk.*

ogre
a large frightening ugly creature in children's stories, who eats people: *The story is about an ogre who lives in a castle in the mountains.*

beast
an animal, especially a dangerous or frightening one: *The jungle is full of tigers and leopards and other wild beasts.*

mood /mud/ *noun*

1 the way you feel at a particular time
- ► mood
- ► state of mind
- ► frame of mind

2 the feeling that a place, story, movie, etc. seems to have
- ► mood
- ► atmosphere
- ► ambience (*formal*)

1 the way you feel at a particular time

mood
the way you feel at a particular time, for example whether you are happy or angry: *She was **in a good mood** because she did well on the test.* | *His moods change quickly, so we never know whether he'll be happy or angry at us.*

state of mind
the way you feel at a particular time, which affects your decisions and your actions. **State of mind** is often used when discussing the reasons for someone's bad or unusual behavior: *What was Smith's state of mind at the time when he committed the crime?*

frame of mind
the way you feel at a particular time, which affects your attitude to what you are doing: *He was **in a positive frame of mind** and was looking forward to starting his new job.*

2 the feeling that a place, story, movie, etc. seems to have

mood
the feeling that something seems to have, for example a place, story, movie, or piece of music: *The scary music at the beginning sets the mood for the rest of the movie. | The political mood of the country improved as the economy got better.*

atmosphere
the feeling that a place or situation seems to have: *It is a good school and it has a happy atmosphere. | There is an atmosphere of tension on the city streets.*

ambience (*formal*)
the feeling that a place such as a restaurant or hotel seems to have: *The restaurant's new owners have created a welcoming ambience. | The area has a small-town ambience, with its tree-lined small shopping district.*

moody /ˈmudi/ *adjective*

- ► moody
- ► temperamental
- ► unpredictable

ANTONYMS → see **calm**[1] **(1)**

moody
often becoming angry or unhappy, especially without any reason: *My sister became moody and unhappy, and I wondered if something was worrying her. | He was a moody man, which was hard on his wife and kids.*

temperamental
quickly changing mood and suddenly becoming angry or excited: *Some people are very temperamental and this can make them difficult to work with.*

unpredictable (AWL)
if someone is unpredictable, you never know how he or she will behave or react to something, or what his or her opinion will be: *Her father was a violent and unpredictable man. The smallest thing could make him lose his temper.*
→ see **grumpy**, Topic **Describing People's Character**

ADVERBS

You can make the adjectives **moody** and **unpredictable** into adverbs by using an **-ly** ending: *Danny went moodily back to his room. | She has a type of mental illness that makes her behave unpredictably.*

moral *adjective* → see **good**, **right**[1]

morality /məˈræləti/ *noun*

- ► morality
- ► morals
- ► principles
- ► ethics
- ► values
- ► integrity

morality
ideas about whether behavior is right or wrong: *In class we discussed the **morality of** killing someone as a punishment for killing another person. | What parents do in difficult situations teaches children about morality.*

morals
a person or group's ideas about what is right or wrong: *The man has no morals and he does not care if he hurts people. | Society's morals are getting worse, and you see it in more violence and drug-taking.*

principles
a system of moral rules that you try to follow in everything you do: *It is **against** their **principles** to kill any living thing.*

ethics
a system of moral rules that people follow when they are deciding what is the right or wrong thing to do. You use **ethics** especially when talking about the rules followed by doctors, lawyers, or people working in business: *Medical ethics prevent doctors from discussing their patients with other people.*
→ **Ethics** is also used about the study of what people think is right or wrong: *Jordan teaches ethics classes at the University of Texas.*

values
people's beliefs about what is important in life, which affect their behavior: *His speech to the team was about the values of teamwork and cooperation. | A marriage works better when you share the same values.*

integrity (AWL)
the idea that you are an honest person who people respect because you always do what you believe is right: *She is a woman **of integrity** who always treats the people who work for her fairly.*

morals *noun* → see **conscience**, **morality**

more *adjective, pronoun* → see Function Words

most *adjective, pronoun* → see Function Words

mostly *adverb* → see **generally**, **mainly**

motel *noun* → see **hotel**, Topic **Travel and Vacations**

mother /ˈmʌðɚ/ *noun*

- mother
- mom (*informal*)
- mommy
- mother-in-law

ANTONYMS → see **father**

mother
a female parent: *Angelina looked like her mother. They both had the same color hair.*

mom (*informal*)
mother. You use **mom** in spoken English when talking to your mother, or when talking about someone's mother: *I love you, Mom!* | *I decided to call my mom and talk about it with her.*

mommy
mother. **Mommy** is used by young children, or when you are talking to young children: *Mommy, can I have a drink, please?*

mother-in-law
the mother of someone's husband or wife: *Her mother-in-law makes excellent cakes.*

motion *noun* → see **movement**

motivate *verb* → see **encourage**

motive *noun* → see **reason**

motor *noun* → see **engine**

mountain /ˈmaʊntən/ *noun*

1 a mountain
- mountain
- hill
- volcano
- cliff

2 the top of a mountain
- peak
- summit
- mountaintop

3 a group of mountains
- range
- foothills
- ridge

1 a mountain

mountain
a very high area of land that is much higher than the land around it, and that usually has a pointed or round top: *The mountains in the distance had clouds around their tops.* | *Mount Whitney is the highest mountain in the U.S. outside Alaska.*

hill
a small mountain: *From the top of the hill, we could see the city in the distance.*

volcano
a mountain with an opening at the top through which lava (=hot liquid rock) and hot ash (=gray powder) sometimes come out: *Since erupting last week, the volcano has been sending a cloud of ash into the sky.*

cliff
a high area of land with a very steep rocky side, especially by the ocean or a river: *The birds make their nests high on the rocky cliffs above the beach.*

2 the top of a mountain

peak
the pointed top of a mountain: *In winter, the peaks of the mountains are covered in snow.*

summit
the top of a mountain, used especially when people are trying to climb or walk to this part: *They were the first men to reach the summit of Mount Everest.*

mountaintop
the top part of a mountain: *The mountaintops were covered by clouds.*

3 a group of mountains

range (AWL)
a group of mountains or hills that are in a line: *The Alps are the biggest mountain range in Europe.*

foothills
the large hills below a group of high mountains: *The Blackfeet Indian Reservation is on the plains near the foothills of the Rocky Mountains in Montana.*

ridge
a long narrow area of high land along the top of hills or mountains: *The trail goes along the ridge for about three miles.*

mourn *verb* → see **grieve**

move *verb* → *go to pages 416-417*

move /muv/ verb

1 to move your body
- ► move
- ► fidget
- ► squirm
- ► wriggle
- ► wiggle
- ► stir
- ► jump
- ► twitch
- ► lunge
- ► lurch

2 to move from one place or position to another
- ► move
- ► advance
- ► progress (*formal*)
- ► approach
- ► surge

3 to move something from one place to another place
- ► move
- ► transport
- ► transplant
- ► transfer
- ► maneuver

4 to move somewhere as a group
- ► move
- ► stream
- ► pour
- ► swarm

5 to go to live or work in a different place
- ► move
- ► relocate
- ► immigrate
- ► emigrate
- ► migrate

6 to move part of an object
- ► move
- ► manipulate (*formal*)

1 to move your body

move
to change the position of your body: *Every time I move, my arm hurts. | My fingers were so cold that I couldn't move them.*

fidget
to keep moving a little bit because you are bored or nervous. You often use **fidget** about someone moving their feet or hands: *The kids were bored, so they kept fidgeting in their seats. | Stop **fidgeting** with your hair!*

squirm
to twist your body from side to side because you are uncomfortable, or to get away from someone who is holding you: *The baby was crying and squirming so much I nearly dropped her.*

wriggle
to move and twist your body or part of your body from side to side: *I managed to **wriggle through** the hole in the fence.*

wiggle
to move your toes, fingers, bottom, etc. with a series of small movements: *She took off her shoes and wiggled her toes in the sand.*

stir
to move slightly or change your position: *She stirred in her sleep but didn't wake up.*

jump
to make a sudden movement because you are frightened or surprised: *I'm sorry if I startled you – I didn't mean to make you jump.*

twitch
if a part of your body twitches, it makes a sudden small movement that you cannot control: *He was tired, and the muscle in his eye began to twitch.*

lunge
to make a sudden strong movement toward someone or something, especially to attack him or her: *The man lunged forward and grabbed John's arm.*

lurch
to move or walk very unsteadily, moving forward or from side to side with sudden irregular movements: *Paul lurched sideways as the boat rolled suddenly.*

→ see **fly**, **go**, **jump[1]**, **pass[1]**, **rock[2]**, **run[1]**, **slide**, **walk[1]**, **wave** for other words about moving

2 to move from one place or position to another

move
to go from one place or position to another: *She got up and moved closer to the fire. | The Marines moved slowly toward the enemy position. | It was a stormy day, and the clouds were moving quickly across the sky.*

advance
to move forward, especially in a slow and determined way: *The soldiers were unable to stop the enemy troops* ***advancing on*** *the city.*

progress (*formal*)
to move forward slowly: *The pain in his leg forced him stop before he had progressed more than a few steps.*

approach (AWL)
to move toward or nearer to someone or something: *The train slowed down as it approached the station.*

surge
to move forward very suddenly and quickly: *He hit the gas pedal and the car* ***surged forward.***

3 to move something from one place to another place

move
to take something from one place and put it in another place: *I moved the chair out of the way.* | *When the river started to flood, we moved everything we could carry to higher ground.*

transport (AWL)
to take goods, objects, or people from one place to another in a vehicle: *The fruit is* ***transported*** *by air* ***from*** *Costa Rica* ***to*** *the U.S.*

transplant
to remove an organ from someone's body and put it in the body of a sick person who needs it: *The doctors* ***transplanted*** *one of his kidneys* ***into*** *his daughter during the 5-hour operation.*

transfer (AWL)
to move someone or something from one place to another: *Dad's company is* ***transferring*** *him* ***from*** *San Francisco* ***to*** *New York.* | *During the magic trick, she quickly* ***transfers*** *the coin* ***into*** *her other hand.*

maneuver
to move something into a different position, when this is difficult and you must use skill: *We managed to maneuver the piano through the doorway.*

4 to move somewhere as a group

move
to go somewhere with a group of other people or animals: *Herds of buffalo used to move freely across the great plains.*

stream
to move somewhere quickly and steadily, in large numbers or amounts: *People began* ***streaming out of*** *the movie theater after the show.*

pour
pour means the same as **stream**: *People from all over the U.S.* ***poured into*** *Washington to see the new president take office.*

swarm
if a large group of people swarm somewhere, they go there quickly: *Shoppers began* ***swarming into*** *the mall as soon as it opened.*

5 to go to live or work in a different place

move
to go to live or work in a different place: *I* ***moved to*** *Texas with my parents when I was 11.*

relocate (AWL)
to move to a new place. You use **relocate** especially when people or things are moved for official or business reasons: *If the company* ***relocates to*** *Florida, will you leave your job or move there too?*

immigrate (AWL)
to come to a country in order to live there permanently: *His father* ***immigrated to*** *the United States* ***from*** *Poland.*

emigrate
to leave your own country in order to live in another country: *Yatsu* ***emigrated from*** *Japan* ***to*** *the United States at the age of 25.*

migrate (AWL)
if birds or animals migrate, they travel to a warmer part of the world in winter and return in spring: *The birds have started migrating south for the winter.*

6 to move part of an object

move
to make part of an object change position: *Look, you can move the toy's arms and legs so it looks like it's walking.*

manipulate (AWL) (*formal*)
to make something move or turn in the way that you want, using your hands: *Babies quickly learn how to hold and manipulate objects with their hands.*

Online Thesaurus

Go to www.longmandictionariesusa.com
→ ***Longman Thesaurus of American English*** – with pronunciation of all the words
→ **Study Center** – interactive practice to help you learn synonyms, Academic Words, and Topic Vocabulary

M

movement /ˈmuvmənt/ *noun*

- ▶ movement
- ▶ motion
- ▶ move
- ▶ action (*formal*)
- ▶ maneuver

movement
the action of moving from one place or position to another: *Try not to make any sudden movements that could frighten the deer.* | *The movement of the water pushed the boat down the river.*

motion
the process of moving, or the way in which someone or something moves: *The rocking motion of the boat made me feel seasick.* | *On the roller coaster, keep your hands and arms inside the car while the ride is in motion.*

move
a movement that someone makes: *We practiced some of the dance moves we had seen on the video.*

action (*formal*)
the way in which something moves: *The rocks had been worn down over the years by the action of the waves.*

maneuver
a skillful or complicated movement that someone or something makes, for example to avoid hitting something or to go through a narrow space: *The pilot tests the aircraft by putting it through a series of maneuvers.*
→ see **campaign**[1] for **movement** meaning "a large number of people working to achieve something"

movie /ˈmuvi/ *noun*

- ▶ movie
- ▶ film
- ▶ motion picture
- ▶ feature film
- ▶ flick (*informal*)

movie
a story that is told using moving pictures and sound. A **movie** is shown at a theater or on television: *We went to see a movie last night.* | *My favorite movie is "Star Wars."*

film
a movie, especially one that has a serious subject or has been made in a foreign country: *It should win the Oscar for best foreign film.*

motion picture *also* **picture**
a movie that is shown in a theater: *The novel was made into a motion picture starring Tommy Lee Jones.*

feature film
a full-length movie that people usually go to see in a theater: *He appeared in over 50 feature films during his long and successful career.*

flick (*informal*)
a movie, especially a particular type of movie: *There's nothing on, unless you want to go and see an action flick.*
→ see Topic **Entertainment**

moving /ˈmuvɪŋ/ *adjective*

- ▶ moving
- ▶ emotional
- ▶ touching
- ▶ poignant
- ▶ heartwarming
- ▶ uplifting

moving
making you feel a strong emotion, especially sadness or sympathy: *The novel tells the moving story of a child's battle with cancer.*

emotional
showing strong feelings, or making you have strong feelings: *Having a baby is a very emotional experience.* | *It was an emotional reunion for the two brothers after so many years apart.*

touching
making you feel sympathy or sadness: *In one very touching scene, the child refuses to leave his mother's grave.*

poignant
making you feel sad: *The photograph brought back poignant memories of his mother.*

heartwarming
making you feel happy and hopeful, because you see people being kind to each other: *It was heartwarming to see so many people volunteering to help.*

uplifting
making you feel happier and more hopeful: *Going to a church service where people sang so joyfully was a truly uplifting experience.*

ADVERBS

You can make the adjectives that mean **moving** into adverbs by using an **-ly** ending: *She spoke movingly of her experiences in India.* | *He was afraid of becoming emotionally involved with anyone.* | *Ashe poignantly describes the impact of racism on young people.*

mow *verb* → see **cut¹**

mud *noun* → see **dirt**

muddy *adjective* → see **dirty**

mumble /ˈmʌmbəl/ *verb*

► mumble
► murmur
► mutter
► stutter
► slur
► grunt

mumble
to say something quietly, in a way that is not clear: *"Who were you with?" his mother asked. "Nobody," Rob mumbled.* | *He looked down at his feet and mumbled an apology.*

murmur
to say something in a quiet gentle voice: *"It is all right," she murmured.* | *He held her hand and murmured her name.*

mutter
to say something quietly because you are annoyed or do not want people to hear: *"I don't like you," Sofia muttered.* | *Neil angrily muttered something about Sam being late.*

stutter *also* **stammer**
to say something with a lot of pauses and repeated sounds: *"N-n-no, it wasn't m-m-me!" he stuttered.* | *"I, uh, don't know," I stammered.* | *He stammered out an answer, his face flushing red.*
→ **Stutter** and **stammer** mean the same thing. However, **stutter** is usually used when there is a medical reason why someone stutters. **Stammer** is usually used when someone is stammering because he or she is upset or nervous.

slur
to speak in a way that is not clear because you are drunk or sick: *He has had a stroke, so his words are slurred.* | *Her speech was slightly slurred, and I wondered if she had been drinking.*
→ Don't use **slur** to show what someone said. Don't say: ~~*"I won't," he slurred.*~~

grunt
to say something using a short low sound that is difficult to understand: *"Yeah," the guard grunted.* | *He grunted a hello when Sylvia walked in.*
→ **Grunt** can also mean to "make a low noise instead of speaking": *I woke him up, but he just grunted and went back to sleep.*
→ see **whisper**

murder /ˈmɚdɚ/ *noun*

1 the crime of deliberately killing someone
► murder
► homicide
► manslaughter
► killing
► slaying
► assassination
► suicide
► execution

2 the act of deliberately killing a large group of people
► genocide
► massacre
► slaughter
► extermination

1 the crime of deliberately killing someone

murder
the crime of deliberately killing someone: *Two gang members were arrested and charged with murder.* | *If he committed the murder, he should go to jail for the rest of his life.*

homicide
the crime of killing someone. **Homicide** is used especially by people who work in the legal system, such as lawyers and police officers: *The police are treating her death as a homicide.* | *He faces charges of homicide if the driver of the other car dies.*

manslaughter
the crime of killing someone when you did not plan to kill him or her: *Jones was jailed for manslaughter after he caused an accident in which three of his coworkers died.*

killing
an act of murdering someone. **Killing** is used especially in newspapers: *The police think the killings are linked to gang crime.*

slaying
slaying means the same as **killing**. **Slaying** is used especially in newspapers: *He later confessed to the slaying of the actress and her family.*

assassination
the act of killing an important or famous person, especially for political reasons: *He is still in jail for the assassination of Rev. Martin Luther King Jr.*

suicide
the act of deliberately killing yourself: *He committed suicide by taking poison.*

execution
the act of killing someone as an official punishment for committing a crime: *The execution took place inside the prison.*

M

2 the act of deliberately killing a large group of people

genocide
the process of deliberately killing a lot of people who belong to a particular race or group: *The leader was charged with acts of genocide after the war in the 1990s.*

massacre
the act of killing a lot of people, especially people who cannot defend themselves: *The army was responsible for the massacre of hundreds of innocent women and children.*

slaughter
the act of killing a large number of people in a very cruel and violent way: *Should the United Nations try to stop the slaughter in the country's Civil War?*

extermination
the process of killing a whole group of people so that they no longer exist: *Diseases such as smallpox resulted in the extermination of whole villages.*
→ see **kill**

murderer *noun* → see **killer**

museum /myu'ziəm/ *noun*

- ► museum
- ► gallery
- ► exhibition

museum
a building where people can go and see important paintings and objects: *The Roman jewelry will be on display at the museum until September.* | *I have always wanted to go to the Museum of Modern Art in New York.*

gallery
a room or building where people can look at or buy art: *He sells his paintings at small galleries in Arizona and New Mexico.*

exhibition (AWL)
a show where people can go to see paintings, photographs, or other objects: *The museum is holding an exhibition of paintings by the French artist Monet.*
→ see **show²** (**2**) for words meaning "an event where people can see special things or art"

music /'myuzɪk/ *noun*

1 the sounds made when playing an instrument or singing
- ► music
- ► tune
- ► melody
- ► harmony

2 music that has been created or written down
- ► piece
- ► composition (*formal*)
- ► score

1 the sounds made when playing an instrument or singing

music
the sounds that people make when they play an instrument or sing: *I enjoy listening to music when I am driving.* | *What kind of music do you like?*
→ **GRAMMAR: Music** cannot be used in the plural. Don't say: ~~*I enjoy listening to musics.*~~

tune
a series of musical notes that are pleasant to listen to: *She hummed a tune to herself as she showered.*

melody
the main set of musical notes in a song or piece of music: *I really like the song's simple melody, but the words are so sad.*

harmony
a set of musical notes that sound good when they are played or sung with other notes: *Juanita sang the melody and her sisters sang the harmony.*

2 music that has been created or written down

piece
music that someone has created, written, or recorded: *The hymn is one of my favorite pieces of music.* | *The orchestra played pieces by Mozart and Brahms.*

composition (*formal*)
a piece of music that someone has written: *The album is a mixture of new compositions and old hits.*

score
a long piece of music written for a movie, television show, or play: *Do you know who composed the score for the movie?*
→ see **song**

M

musician /myuˈzɪʃən/ *noun*

- ► musician
- ► player
- ► performer
- ► singer
- ► vocalist
- ► soloist
- ► accompanist

musician
someone who plays an instrument or sings as a job: *The musicians in the band are all very talented.* | *She wants to be a musician and play in an orchestra.*

player
someone who plays a musical instrument: *The piano player was playing my favorite song.*
→ **Player** is always used after the name of the musical instrument being played: *The band has a good bass player.*

performer
someone who plays music, sings, or dances in order to entertain people: *Everyone cheered as the performers came on stage.*

singer
someone who sings, especially as a job or with a group: *The singer has just produced a new album of country songs.* | *She is a singer in the choir.*

vocalist
someone who sings popular songs, especially with a band: *He joined the group as the lead vocalist.*

soloist
a musician or singer who performs alone: *This world famous violinist has performed as a soloist with several orchestras.*

accompanist
someone who plays a musical instrument while another person sings or plays the main tune: *The singer's piano accompanist joined her on stage to perform the song.*

must /məst, strong mʌst/ *verb*

- ► must
- ► have to
- ► be required to (*formal*)
- ► be expected to (*formal*)
- ► be obliged to (*formal*)

must
to need to do something because it is very important, especially because someone in authority or a rule says that you should do it. **Must** is stronger than **have to**, and it is more important that you obey: *Dad says we must be back home before ten o'clock.* | *You must not smoke in here.*
→ **GRAMMAR:** Don't say: ~~*I must to do it*~~. Say: *I must do it.*

have to
to need to do something because it is necessary or important: *I have to hurry because I'm late for class.* | *He has to return the books to the library.*

be required to (*formal*)
to have to do something, because there is a law or official rule that says you must: *Some travelers are required to have a visa before they enter the U.S.*

be expected to (*formal*)
to have to do something because it is right, part of your job, or something you are responsible for: *You are expected to hand in your homework on time.*

be obliged to (*formal*)
to have to do something, especially because you feel it is the right thing to do or because the situation makes it necessary to do it: *Her husband lost his job, and she was obliged to work so that they could pay their bills.*

mysterious /mɪˈstɪriəs/ *adjective*

- ► mysterious
- ► strange
- ► mystifying

mysterious
a mysterious event or situation is very difficult to understand or explain because very little is known about it: *No one knows why the plane disappeared – it's all very mysterious.* | *People said they saw mysterious lights in the sky.*

strange
different from usual, in a way that makes you a little frightened or surprised: *Strange things began to happen, like things would be moved overnight and lights would turn on by themselves.*

mystifying
strange and confusing, and impossible to understand or explain: *Many parents find online games mystifying, and do not really know what their children are doing.*
→ see **confusing**

ADVERBS

You can make the adjectives that mean **mysterious** into adverbs by using an **-ly** ending: *The plane mysteriously disappeared near the island of Bermuda.* | *The street outside was strangely quiet.* | *The towel was not where I had left it, though no one else had gone into the room.*

M

mystery /ˈmɪstəri/ *noun*

- ► mystery
- ► riddle
- ► puzzle
- ► enigma

mystery
something that is very difficult to explain or understand, and may never be explained: *It is a mystery how he managed to escape from the prison cell. | The paintings were never found again, and what happened to them is still a mystery.*

riddle
a mysterious action, event, or situation that you do not completely understand or cannot fully explain: *These fossils may give scientists a clue to the riddle of why the creature became extinct.*

puzzle
something that is difficult to understand, and which can only be solved by thinking carefully about it: *The police have not yet solved the puzzle of her disappearance.*

enigma
someone or something that can never be fully understood or explained: *The purpose of the Mayan object is an enigma, and scientists can only make guesses.*

SYNONYM CHECK

Mystery, riddle, puzzle, or enigma?

If you think very carefully about a **riddle** or **puzzle**, you might be able to solve it.

A **mystery** can sometimes be explained if you find the right information.

An **enigma** can never be fully explained or understood.

Nn

ADVERBS

You can make the adjectives **naive**, **innocent**, and **gullible** into adverbs by using an **-ly** ending: *Perhaps naively, she believed that her own children would not do anything illegal.* | *Innocently, they thought that they could trust the people traveling with them.*

naive /nɑˈiv/ *adjective*

- **naive**
- **innocent**
- **inexperienced**
- **unsophisticated**
- **gullible**
- **impressionable**

ANTONYMS → see **sophisticated**

naive
believing that people are nicer and things are easier than they really are, because you do not have much experience of life: *It was naive of you to give your phone number to someone you had just met.*

innocent
not having much knowledge or experience of the bad things that can happen to you in life, and believing that most people are good: *Alfredo was young and innocent, and he trusted people without question.*

inexperienced
not having much experience of a situation, or not having enough experience to do something well: *Inexperienced players cannot handle the pressure of pro basketball as well as the older, more experienced players do.* | *You don't want an inexperienced doctor to do the surgery.*

unsophisticated
not having much experience of life in cities among educated and fashionable people, and showing this by the way you talk or behave: *She may be an unsophisticated girl from a farm in Nebraska, but she is not stupid!*

gullible
a gullible person is easy to trick because he or she is always ready to believe what other people say: *The criminals trick gullible people into giving them money to invest in a company that does not exist.*

impressionable
young and easy to influence: *The movie gives the wrong message to impressionable young girls – it isn't cool to smoke or take drugs.*

naked /ˈneɪkɪd/ *adjective*

- **naked**
- **nude**
- **bare**
- **undressed**

naked
not wearing any clothes: *Two small children were running around the yard naked, having fun in the water.*

nude
not wearing any clothes, or showing someone without any clothes: *There are several nude scenes in the movie.* | *He was nude except for the towel around his waist.*
→ You also use **nude** when you are talking about someone who is not wearing clothes in a piece of art: *The painting shows a nude woman sitting in front of a mirror.*

bare
not covered by clothes: *I love walking on wet sand in bare feet.*
→ **Bare** is usually used about a part of the body, not the whole body: *She wore a summer dress and her arms were bare.*

undressed
having taken off all your clothes: *He was completely undressed except for his socks.*

name[1] /neɪm/ *noun*

- **name**
- **pseudonym**
- **pen name**
- **nickname**
- **alias**
- **title**

name
the word that someone or something is called: *"What's your last name, Roberto?" "It's Bolano, Roberto Bolano."* | *What was the name of the hotel in Miami that we stayed in?*

pseudonym
a name that a writer or artist uses instead of his

or her real name: *Mary Ann Evans wrote under the pseudonym George Eliot.*

pen name
a pseudonym that a writer uses. **Pen name** is more informal than **pseudonym**: *Mark Twain was the author's pen name – his real name was Samuel Clemens.*

nickname
a name that people, especially your friends and family, call you instead of your real name. **Nicknames** are sometimes funny or silly: *He is really tall, so his nickname is "Shorty."*

alias
a name that is not your real name, especially a name that is used by a criminal instead of his or her real name: *The famous Western outlaw Jesse James used the alias "Mr. Howard."*

title
the name given to a book, painting, play, etc.: *"What is the title of the book?" "It is called 'To Kill a Mockingbird.'"*
→ Words such as Mr., Mrs., Jr., Sr., or Dr. that go before or after your name are also called **titles**.

name² /neɪm/ *verb*

- ► **name**
- ► **call**
- ► **be entitled** (*formal*)
- ► **nickname**
- ► **dub**
- ► **term**

name
to give someone or something a particular name: *We named our daughter Carol, after my mom.* | *The King School is* **named for** *Martin Luther King.*

call
to give someone or something a name, or use a particular name for someone or something: *New York is sometimes called The Big Apple.* | *His name is Danilo, but everyone calls him Dan.*

be entitled (*formal*)
if a book, poem, song, etc. is entitled something, it has that particular title: *The book is entitled "Charlie and the Chocolate Factory."*

nickname
to give someone another name that friends and family members use instead of that person's real name. These names are often funny or silly: *Butler was nicknamed "Bugsy" by his teammates.*

dub
to give someone or something a funny name that describes him, her, or it: *We dubbed the project "Titanic 2" because it seemed likely to fail.*

term
to use a particular word or expression to name or describe something: *Making small repeated movements can cause pain, and this condition is termed RSI, or repetitive strain injury.*

nap¹ *noun* → see **sleep²**

nap² *verb* → see **sleep¹**

narrate *verb* → see **tell**

narration *noun* → see **description**

narrative *noun* → see **story**, Topic **Books and Literature**

narrow /ˈnæroʊ/ *adjective*

1 measuring only a small distance from one side to the other
- ► **narrow**
- ► **thin**
- ► **fine**

ANTONYMS → see **wide (1)**, **thick (1)**

2 happening by only a small amount
- ► **narrow**
- ► **slim** (*informal*)

1 measuring only a small distance from one side to the other

narrow
measuring only a small distance from one side to the other: *The city's narrow roads were jammed with traffic.* | *The space between the rocks was very narrow, and we could barely squeeze through it.*

thin
having a small distance through something, between one of its sides and the other: *The ice was covered by a thin layer of snow, making it even more dangerous.*

fine
very thin or delicate. **Fine** is used about things that are long or flat and thin, for example hair or cloth: *It was getting colder and the fine hairs on my arms began to rise.*
→ see Topic **Describing Size**

ADVERBS
You can make the adjectives **thin** and **fine** into adverbs by using an **-ly** ending: *Slice the potatoes thinly.* | *Add two finely chopped onions.*

2 happening by only a small amount

narrow
a narrow victory, defeat, margin, or majority is

achieved or happens by only a small amount: *The law was passed by a narrow margin, with 158 votes in favor and 151 votes against.*

slim (*informal*)
very small in amount: *The other basketball team is much taller than us, so we have only a slim chance of winning this game.*

→ see **limited**

ADVERBS

You can make the adjective **narrow** into an adverb by using an **-ly** ending: *The candidate narrowly lost the election by fewer than 100 votes.*

narrow

a **narrow** trail

a **thin** layer of ice

nasty *adjective* → see **bad**, **mean²**

nation *noun* → see **country**

national /ˈnæʃənəl/ *adjective*

- ► national
- ► nationwide
- ► domestic
- ► civil

ANTONYMS → see **international**

national
relating to one particular country. You often use **national** when talking about an organization that represents a country or an event that happens across all of a country: *The president's speech was shown on national television.* | *The American national soccer team reached the final of the Women's World Cup, but lost to Japan.*

nationwide
happening or existing in every part of a country. A **nationwide** activity or event is one in which people from all over a country take part: *The nationwide survey found that 63% of all American women had trouble sleeping sometimes.*

domestic (AWL)
relating to things that happen inside one particular country, rather than things that happen in other countries: *You now have to pay for your suitcase on domestic flights from Los Angeles to New York.*

civil (AWL)
relating to the people who live in a particular country, or relating to that country's government: *The country has been torn apart by ten years of civil war.*

ADVERBS

You can make the adjectives **national** and **domestic** into adverbs by using an **-ly** ending: *The candidates took part in a nationally televised debate.* | *The movie was popular both domestically and overseas.*

nationality /ˌnæʃəˈnæləti/ *noun*

- ► nationality
- ► citizenship
- ► native

nationality
the fact that you are a citizen of a particular country: *"What nationality are you?" "I'm Canadian."* | *People of all nationalities have come to America to live.*

citizenship
the legal right to be a citizen of a particular country: *After marrying a French woman, Mr. Gomez applied for French citizenship.*

native
someone who was born in a particular place or country: *Juan is a native of Mexico who now lives in California with his parents.*

natural /ˈnætʃərəl/ *adjective*

1 existing in nature, and not made by people
- ► natural
- ► organic
- ► wild
- ► pure

2 relating to an ability or quality you are born with rather than learn
- ► natural
- ► innate (*formal*)
- ► instinctive

N

N

1 existing in nature, and not made by people

natural
existing in nature, and not made by people: *Wool is a natural material because it comes from sheep.* | *The hurricane was one of the worst natural disasters to hit the United States.*

organic
organic food is grown or produced naturally, without using chemicals: *The restaurant uses only organic meat and vegetables.*

wild
wild animals or plants are found in natural places and are not owned or grown by people: *Yellowstone National Park is the home of many wild animals, including wolves and bears.*

pure
pure water or air does not contain any harmful chemicals: *We drank pure water from mountain streams.*

→ see **wild**

ADVERBS

You can make the adjectives **natural** and **organic** into adverbs by using an **-ly** ending: *Glycerin is a chemical compound that is found naturally in animal fats.* | *The vegetables are organically grown.*

2 relating to an ability or quality you are born with rather than learn

natural
relating to an ability or quality that you are born with, rather than one that you learn: *He was a natural athlete and was good at most sports.* | *Hunting is a natural activity for cats.*

innate (*formal*)
an innate ability or quality is one that you have from the time you were born. You use **innate** especially in science writing: *Children have an innate ability to learn a language.*

instinctive
instinctive behavior is something you do naturally, without thinking about it or learning how to do it: *An animal's instinctive reaction is to run away from fire.*

SYNONYM CHECK

Natural or innate?

Natural and **innate** mean the same thing, but **natural** is the more common word to use. Don't say: ~~*She is an innate leader/athlete*~~. Say: *She is a natural leader/athlete.*

Innate is usually used with words like "ability," "quality," or "need": *The coach seems to have an innate ability to motivate his players.*

ADVERBS

You can make the adjectives that mean "an ability or quality that you are born with" into adverbs by using an **-ly** ending: *She is naturally good at sports.* | *New parents instinctively talk to their babies in high-pitched voices, which babies seem to prefer.*

nature /ˈneɪtʃɚ/ *noun*

- nature
- the environment
- wilderness
- the wild

nature
everything in the world that is not made by people, such as wild plants and animals, lakes, oceans, and mountains, or the weather: *We lived on a ranch, surrounded by the beauty of nature.* | *The fish grow bigger in an aquarium than they do in nature.*

the environment
the air, water, and land in which people, animals, and plants live: *Car engines produce pollution, which is bad for the environment.*

→ GRAMMAR: When used with this meaning, **environment** is a singular noun. Don't say: ~~*We need to protect our environments*~~. Say: *We need to protect our environment.*

wilderness
a large area of land that is natural, where people do not live and there are no buildings: *Bears, elk, and many other animals live in the Alaskan wilderness.*

→ GRAMMAR: **Wilderness** is a singular noun. Don't say: ~~*It is easy to get lost in wildernesses*~~. Say: *It is easy to get lost in the wilderness.*

the wild
the natural conditions in which animals and plants live, where they are not taken care of by people: *Pandas are now rare* ***in the wild****, and most pandas live in zoos.*

→ see **country (2)**, **landscape**

→ see **character** for **nature** meaning "the character you are born with"

near *preposition* → see Function Word **close²**

nearby *adverb, adjective* → see Function Word **close²**

nearly *adverb* → see Function Word **almost**

neat /nit/ *adjective*

- ► neat
- ► tidy
- ► organized
- ► immaculate
- ► orderly

ANTONYMS → see **messy**

neat
carefully arranged so that everything is in the place where it belongs: *Their house was so neat and clean I was always afraid of making a mess.* | *The logs were stacked in neat piles along one wall.*
→ If a person is **neat**, that person likes to have things in the right place. You can also use **neat** about the way people are dressed, or about their hair, to mean that they look very clean and everything is in the right place: *He was dressed in a neat gray suit.*

tidy
tidy means the same as **neat** but seems a little old-fashioned. You use **tidy** about places but not about people: *My sister's bedroom is always tidy, but mine is usually a complete mess.*

organized
planned or arranged carefully so that everything is in the right place or happens in the right order: *The event was well organized and nothing went wrong.*
→ If a person is **organized**, that person plans things carefully and always has things in the right order: *She is the most organized person I know – she never forgets to do anything!*

immaculate
very clean and neat, with everything in exactly the right place: *They must have cleaned the whole house because it was immaculate.*

orderly
arranged in a neat way and in a particular order: *The cans and jars were arranged in orderly rows that made it easy to find the one you wanted.*

ADVERBS

You can make the adjectives **neat**, **tidy**, and **immaculate** into adverbs by using an **-ly** ending: *Her hair was neatly tied back in a ponytail.* | *She was tall, slim, and immaculately dressed.* **Orderly** looks like an adverb, but it is an adjective.

necessary /ˈnesəˌseri/ *adjective*

1 necessary and important
- ► necessary
- ► essential
- ► vital
- ► crucial
- ► critical
- ► imperative (*formal*)

ANTONYMS → see **unnecessary**

2 necessary because a rule or law says you must
- ► required
- ► compulsory
- ► mandatory
- ► obligatory (*formal*)

ANTONYMS → see **optional**

1 necessary and important

necessary
if something is necessary, you need to have it or do it: *My doctor thinks **it is necessary for** me **to** have an operation.* | *Some fat is necessary in your diet to provide heat and energy.* | *Make sure you have all the necessary documents for your trip, like your passport and ticket.*

essential
if something is essential, you need it in order to do something or for something to happen: *Oxygen is **essential for** plants and animals to live.*

vital
if something is vital, it is extremely important and you will have serious problems if you do not have it or do it: ***It is vital that** you turn off the electricity before touching the wires.*

crucial (AWL)
important and necessary, because other things depend on it: *Learning through play is **crucial for** the development of young children.*

critical
critical means the same as **crucial**: *Having a positive attitude is **critical to** achieving your goals.*

imperative (*formal*)
very important and needing to be done or dealt with immediately: ***It is imperative that** the report is ready by tomorrow.*
→ see **important**

N

ADVERBS

You can make the adjectives **necessary**, **vital**, **crucial**, **critical**, and **imperative** into adverbs by using an **-ly** ending: *The company's future will necessarily depend on whether it can satisfy its customers.* | *Are these weapons vitally needed for national defense?* | *The attention a baby gets from its parent is crucially important to its development.*

The adjective **essential** can be made into an adverb, but it has a different meaning.

N

2 necessary because a rule or law says you must

required
something that is required is necessary in order to do or achieve something, and someone in authority says you must do it: *The book is required reading for the class.* | *To be elected, a candidate must receive the required number of votes.*

compulsory
something that is compulsory must be done because a rule or law says that you must: *English classes are compulsory for all students.*

mandatory
something that is mandatory must be done because of a law: *Wearing a helmet when riding a motorcycle is mandatory.*

obligatory (*formal*)
something that is obligatory must be done because of a rule or law: *In Israel, military service is obligatory for boys and girls.*

necessity *noun* → see **need²**

need¹ /nid/ *verb*

- ► need
- ► require (*formal*)
- ► demand

need
if you need something, you must have it, especially in order to do something: *I need a new cell phone because this one is broken.* | *You will need three eggs to make this cake.* | *I was thirsty and needed a drink.*

require (AWL) (*formal*)
to need something: *If his leg is broken, it will require surgery.* | *Most house plants require regular watering.*

demand
if something demands your time, skill, attention, etc. it needs a lot of your time, etc. to do it correctly: *I started my own business, which demanded a lot of time and effort.*

need² /nid/ *noun*

- ► need
- ► requirement
- ► necessity
- ► essentials

need
your need for something is the fact that you need it in order to be healthy or happy, or in order to achieve something: *She felt trapped by the baby's* ***need for*** *constant care.* | *There is a real* ***need for*** *good teachers.* | *The medical needs of old people are different from the needs of children.*

requirement (AWL)
a need or request: *To meet the requirements of wheelchair users, they put a ramp up to the door.*

necessity
something you need to have in order to live or do something: *Water is the most basic necessity of life.* | *A truck or car is a necessity in this area of the country, because there are no buses or trains.*

essentials
the most important and basic things that people need in order to live: *The group supplied food, water, and other essentials to the refugees at the camp.*

negative *adjective* → see **bad**, **pessimistic**

negotiate *verb* → see **discuss**

neighborhood *noun* → see **area**

nervous /ˈnɚvəs/ *adjective*

- ► nervous
- ► anxious
- ► tense
- ► uneasy
- ► on edge (*informal*)
- ► flustered

ANTONYMS → see **relaxed**

nervous
worried and a little bit frightened about something: *I felt so* ***nervous about*** *flying that I could not sleep.* | *It is natural to be nervous before a job interview.*

anxious
very nervous about something so that you think about it a lot. **Anxious** is more formal than **nervous**: *I was very* ***anxious about*** *taking the exam because I can't go to college unless I pass it.*

tense AWL
nervous and not able to relax so that you become angry or upset easily: *Everyone was feeling tense as we waited for news from the hospital about Dad.*

uneasy
nervous because you think something bad might happen: *I felt **uneasy about** being alone in the house with him.*

on edge (*informal*)
feeling nervous and worried, usually because you are expecting something bad to happen very soon: *The soldiers were on edge as they moved through the jungle, because they expected to be attacked at any time.*

flustered
if you are flustered, you feel confused and nervous: *When I stood in front of the class, I got flustered and forgot what I was going to say.*
→ see **worried**, Topic **Describing People's Emotions**

ADVERBS

You can make the adjectives **nervous**, **anxious**, **tense**, and **uneasy** into adverbs by using an **-ly** ending: *He walked nervously up and down the room, waiting for news.* | *Paula looked anxiously at her daughter, who was very pale.* | *The street was dark, and she looked around uneasily.*

nervousness /ˈnɚvəsnəs/ *noun*

- nervousness
- tension
- anxiety

nervousness
the feeling of being worried and a little frightened about something: *As she spoke, Maria's nervousness showed in her voice.* | *The bad economy is causing nervousness on Wall Street.*

tension AWL
a feeling of being nervous and not able to relax so that you become angry or upset easily: *The tension was almost unbearable as we waited to hear whether Ramon was all right.*

anxiety
the feeling of being very nervous and worried about something so that you think about it all the time: *I had just lost my job and was filled with **anxiety about** the future.*
→ see **worry² (1)**

never /ˈnevɚ/ *adverb*

- never
- not once
- at no time

ANTONYMS → see **always (2)**

never
not at any time, or not on any occasion: *It never gets really cold in Los Angeles, even in the winter.* | *I'll never make that mistake again.*
→ GRAMMAR: **Never** is not used at the end of a sentence. Don't say: ~~*They visit me never*~~. Say: *They never visit me.*

not once
never. Use **not once** when you are surprised or annoyed that someone did not do something he or she should have done: *Not once has he apologized for what he did.*

at no time
never. **At no time** is used to emphasize that something did not happen: *Although the situation was serious, at no time was the public in any danger.*

GRAMMAR CHECK: never

If you use **never**, **not once**, or **at no time** at the beginning of a sentence, you must change the normal word order. Don't say: ~~*Never I have been so excited*~~. Say: *Never have I been so excited.*

nevertheless *adverb* → see Function Word **but**

new /nu/ *adjective*

1 made or done only a short time ago
- new
- brand-new
- recent
- latest

ANTONYMS → see **old (2)**

2 new and different from other things
- novel
- fresh
- original
- innovative
- revolutionary

1 made or done only a short time ago

new
if something is new, it was made, produced, or bought only a short time ago: *We decided to sell our old car and buy a new one.* | *The band will*

release their new album on Monday. | *I like your coat – is it new?*

brand-new
new and never used before. You use **brand-new** to emphasize that something is new: *Inside the box was a brand-new laptop.*

recent
made or done a short time ago: *He met her on a recent visit to New York.* | *She showed me a recent photograph of Laura, which had been taken last Saturday.*

latest
the most recent thing or action, when other similar things were done or made before it: *I think that her latest novel is her best yet.*

ADVERBS
You can make the adjectives **new** and **recent** into adverbs by using an **-ly** ending: *The dog dug up the newly planted bushes.* | *Lenny recently got a raise at work.*

2 new and different from other things

novel
new and unusual: *Chili ice cream sounds like a novel idea, but I don't think I would like it.*

fresh
fresh ideas or ways of doing something are new, different, and interesting: *The new coach has lots of fresh ideas about how to improve the team.*

original
new and different from what other people do or think: *The artist's paintings were completely original – until then no one had painted like that.*

innovative (AWL)
new and better than in the past: *The students came up with some innovative ideas for recycling household waste.*

revolutionary (AWL)
completely new and different, and usually much better than before: *A revolutionary new treatment for cancer could save thousands of lives.*

news /nuz/ *noun*

- ▶ news
- ▶ developments
- ▶ the latest (*informal*)

news
reports about things that are happening in the world. People get **news** from newspapers, television, the radio, and the Internet: *I usually listen to **the news** on the radio while I drive to work.* | *Environmental issues have been **in the news** a lot recently.*
→ **GRAMMAR: News** is followed by a singular verb: *Not all the economic news is bad.*

News is often used before another noun to talk about stories and programs about things happening in the world: *I saw an interview with the president on a TV news program.*

developments
the most recent changes in an important situation: *The president said today that he was watching developments in Asia with great interest.*

the latest (*informal*)
the most recent news: *What is **the latest on** the election?*
→ see **media**, **report**

newspaper *noun* → see **media**

next[1] /nekst/ *adjective*

- ▶ next
- ▶ the following
- ▶ this coming
- ▶ a later
- ▶ future
- ▶ subsequent (*formal*)
- ▶ succeeding (*formal*)
- ▶ forthcoming (*formal*)

ANTONYMS → see **last[1] (2)**

next
the next person or thing is the one after this one: *The next flight to Chicago leaves in 45 minutes.* | *The doctor wanted Juan to come back the next day to see if he was doing any better.* | *You should call me next time you are in town.*
→ **GRAMMAR:** Don't say: ~~*The wedding will take place on next Sunday/in next June*~~. Say: *The wedding will take place next Sunday/next June.*

the following
used when you are talking about a time in the past that came immediately after another time: *He was sick in the evening, but the following day he felt better.*
→ You can also use **the following** to introduce the next thing in a piece of writing: *Please look at the following example and correct any mistakes.* | *You can write to me at the following address: 52 Main Street, Anytown, IL.*

this coming
used about a time that is happening soon. You use **this coming** before the name of a day or a month to show that you mean the next one that happens: *This coming Sunday is the first day of spring.* | *They're getting married this coming June.*

a later
coming in the future, or after something else. You use **a later** especially before words like "date" and "time": *It was raining, so the game was postponed to a later date.*

future
happening or existing at a time after the present, especially at a time that is far ahead: *We are a small company today, but we are planning for future growth.* | *Alberto is my future brother-in-law* (=he will be my brother-in-law in the future).

subsequent (AWL) (*formal*)
happening after something else: *The matter was discussed again in subsequent meetings.* | *In the months **subsequent to** his accident, he had three surgeries.*

succeeding (*formal*)
happening after something else. You use **succeeding** especially before words that mean a period of time, such as "days," "months," or "decades": *In the succeeding weeks, he gradually grew stronger.*

forthcoming (AWL) (*formal*)
happening soon: *The president was convinced that he could win the forthcoming election.*

GRAMMAR CHECK: next

All the words meaning **next** must be used before a noun, except for **subsequent**. Don't say: ~~*the week that was following/next/coming etc.*~~ Say: *the following/next/coming etc. week.*

next² *adverb* → see Function Word **after**

next to *preposition* → see Function Words

nice /naɪs/ *adjective*

1 used about a person
- nice
- kind
- friendly
- likeable
- pleasant
- charming
- sweet (*informal*)

ANTONYMS → see **mean²**

2 used about a nice experience or place
- nice
- enjoyable
- fun
- pleasant
- delightful (*formal*)
- charming

3 used about a nice object, story, or picture
- nice
- enjoyable
- delightful
- charming
- appealing

1 used about a person

nice
behaving toward other people in a way that shows that you like them, want to help them, and care about them: *Maddie is really nice.* | *He is one of the nicest people I know.* | *Be **nice to** your little brother.* | *It was **nice of** them **to** offer to help.*
→ **GRAMMAR:** Don't say: ~~*They were nice with me*~~. Say: *They were **nice to** me.*

kind
if you are kind, you show that you care about people and want to help them: *The nurses were all very kind.* | *It is really **kind of** you **to** let us use your swimming pool.*
→ **GRAMMAR:** Don't say: ~~*They were kind with me*~~. Say: *They were **kind to** me.*

friendly
behaving toward other people in a way that shows that you like them and are ready to talk to them or help them: *Most people in the class seemed friendly.* | *The local people are generally **friendly toward** tourists.*

likeable
easy to like, and seeming nice and friendly: *Paula is very likeable, and she has always had a lot of friends.*

pleasant
friendly, polite, and easy to talk to. **Pleasant** sounds more formal than **nice** and is used especially about someone you do not know very well: *I only met her once or twice, but she seemed pleasant.*

charming
behaving in a polite and friendly way that makes people like you and want to do things for you: *He was charming, good-looking, and in his early forties.*
→ Sometimes someone who is **charming** behaves this way in order to get an advantage: *She can be very charming when she wants something.*

sweet (*informal*)
someone who is sweet is kind and gentle, and tries to make other people happy: *He is a sweet guy who likes to bring his wife flowers.*
→ see **friendly**, **kind²**

2 used about a nice experience or place

nice
if something is nice, you like it or enjoy it: *Did*

you have a nice day? | ***It was nice to** be back home again.*

enjoyable
an enjoyable experience gives you pleasure because it is interesting, exciting, or amusing: *Games can make learning more enjoyable.*

fun
enjoyable, and making you feel happy, excited, and interested. **Fun** sounds more informal than **enjoyable**: *The party was so much fun! Everyone had a great time.* | *Try snowboarding - it's fun!*

pleasant
a pleasant place, occasion, or activity is one that you like, especially because it is calm, peaceful, easy, or relaxing. **Pleasant** sounds more formal than **nice**: *We sat on the porch together and had a pleasant conversation.*

delightful (*formal*)
very nice and making you feel pleased: *We ate at a delightful little Italian restaurant.*

charming
pretty and making you feel pleased: *We found a charming picnic spot near the river.*
→ see **beautiful**, **good**, **sunny**, Topic **The Weather**

3 used about a nice object, story, or picture

nice
if something is nice, you like it because it is good to look at, or because it has parts that are useful or attractive: *He got a really nice bike for his birthday.* | *The flowers in the park are nice this year - a lot of them are blooming now.*

enjoyable
a story, movie, or picture that is enjoyable is good and gives you pleasure: *The book was enjoyable, even though it wasn't very well written.*

delightful
if something is delightful, you like it a lot because it is good to look at, touch, smell, taste, or hear: *Bread and cheese make a simple but delightful meal.*

charming
making you feel pleased, because something is pretty or enjoyable. You usually use **charming** about small things or about stories that do not deal with serious or sad subjects: *The book shows how to make charming little gifts using your sewing machine.* | *It is a charming movie about friendship.*

appealing
something that is appealing has interesting or unusual qualities that make you like it: *The desserts are displayed in an appealing way.* | *Samoyeds are appealing dogs, because they are fluffy and friendly.*

ADVERBS
You can make the adjectives **nice**, **kind**, **pleasant**, **charming**, **sweet**, **enjoyable**, and **delightful** into adverbs by using an **-ly** ending: *"Here, let me help you," she said kindly.* | *The smell of bread baking rose pleasantly into the air.* | *The book is delightfully funny.*

nicely *adverb* → see **well**

nickname *verb* → see **name²**

night /naɪt/ *noun*

- ► night
- ► nighttime
- ► midnight
- ► the middle of the night
- ► the early hours of the morning

ANTONYMS → see **day**

night
the time when it is dark and the sun cannot be seen: *It was a cold night and I could hear the wind outside.* | *I stayed up all night to finish writing the paper.* | *She reads in bed **at night** before going to sleep.*
→ When you are mentioning a time before midnight, use **night**: *It was ten o'clock **at night**.* When you are mentioning a time after midnight, use **morning**: *The phone rang at three **in the morning**.*

Use **tonight**, not "this night," to mean the night that will come after the time when you are speaking. Don't say: *~~I'll call you this night~~*. Say: *I'll call you tonight.*

nighttime
the time during the night when the sky is dark: *It was nighttime and the streets were dark and empty.*
→ **GRAMMAR: Nighttime** can be used before other nouns to talk about things that happen during the night: *The troops were preparing for a possible nighttime battle.*

midnight
twelve o'clock at night: *It was **after midnight** when we finally got home.*

the middle of the night
the time during the night when most people are asleep: *I woke up when I heard a strange noise **in the middle of the night**.*

the early hours of the morning
so late at night that it is almost the time when

the sun comes up: *The baby wakes up **in the early hours of the morning** because she is hungry.*
→ see **evening**

no /noʊ/ *adverb*

- ► **no**
- ► **nope** (*informal*)

ANTONYMS → see **yes**

no
used to answer a question when something is not true or when you do not want something: *"Are you Italian?" "No, I'm Spanish." | "Do you want any more coffee?" "No, thanks." | When I asked him, he said "no."*

nope (*informal*)
no: *"Are you hungry?" "Nope, I just ate."*
→ see **refuse** for words that mean "to say no"

noise /nɔɪz/ *noun*

- ► **noise**
- ► **sound**
- ► **racket** (*informal*)
- ► **din** (*formal*)
- ► **clamor** (*formal*)

ANTONYMS → see **silence**

noise
something that you hear that is loud or annoying: *Don't make too much noise – Dad's trying to work. | Traffic noise is a real problem in our neighborhood. | The **noise of** the machines made it hard to talk.*

sound
something that you hear: *The only sound in the room was the ticking of the clock. | We could hear the **sound of** rain falling on the roof of the house.*

racket (*informal*)
a loud unpleasant noise: *I wish those kids would stop making such a racket in the street.*

din (*formal*)
a loud unpleasant noise that continues for a long time, especially a noise made by a large number of people talking loudly or doing something: *We had to speak loudly to hear each other in the **din of** the school cafeteria.*

clamor (*formal*)
a loud noise, especially the noise made by an excited or confused crowd. **Clamor** is used especially in literature: *He shouted over the rising **clamor of** voices.*
→ see **sound¹**, Topic **To Make a Sound**

SYNONYM CHECK
Noise or sound?

Sound is anything you hear. A **noise** is a sound that is loud or annoying. Don't say: ~~*Stop making so much sound.*~~ Say: *Stop making so much noise.*

noisy *adjective* → see **loud**

none *pronoun* → see Function Words

nonfiction /ˌnɑnˈfɪkʃən/ *noun*

- ► **nonfiction**
- ► **textbook**
- ► **reference book**
- ► **biography**
- ► **autobiography**

ANTONYMS → see **story (1)**

nonfiction
books about real events, people, or places: *Do you like fiction or nonfiction? | I like to read nonfiction, especially books about history.*
→ **GRAMMAR:** You can also use **nonfiction** before a noun: *She is the author of several nonfiction books.*

textbook
a book about a subject which students use: *The teacher gave us each a math textbook.*

reference book
a book such as a dictionary that you look at to find information: *Reference books, such as encyclopedias, are at the back of the library.*

biography
a book about a real person's life, written by another person: *I just finished reading the new **biography of** Albert Einstein.*

autobiography
a book in which someone writes about his or her own life: ***In her autobiography**, the movie star writes about her difficult childhood.*
→ see **book¹**, Topic **Books and Literature**

nonsense /ˈnɑnsens/ *noun*

- ► **nonsense**
- ► **foolishness**
- ► **gibberish**
- ► **garbage** (*informal*)

nonsense
statements, ideas, or opinions that are not true or that seem very stupid: *"Nobody cares about me." "That's nonsense, Kayla." | Some of these*

"organic foods" are not healthy at all – it is a lot of nonsense.

foolishness
things that someone says or does that shows he or she is not thinking sensibly: *That's enough of this foolishness. You guys are fighting over nothing.*

gibberish
words someone says that have no meaning or are difficult to understand: *Did you understand what the lawyer just said? It sounded like gibberish to me.*

garbage (*informal*)
statements or ideas that are silly or wrong: *Don't believe all the garbage that advertisers tell you.*

N

normal /ˈnɔrməl/ *adjective*

- ► normal
- ► ordinary
- ► usual
- ► regular
- ► typical
- ► conventional

ANTONYMS → see **strange**, **special**

normal (AWL)
happening or existing in the way that people expect, because it is what happens most often. You use **normal** especially about situations, ways of doing things, and feelings, as well as about amounts and levels: *It is **normal to** feel nervous when you start a new job.* | *Rainfall has been higher than normal this month.*

ordinary
not special in any way and not very different from other people or things of the same type: *The book is about ordinary people – not anyone famous or important.* | *It looks like an ordinary pen, but it actually has a tiny camera in it.*

usual
happening, done, or existing in the same way as always. You use **usual** especially about situations and ways of doing things: *Is it **usual** for Tom to be so late?*
→ You can also use **usual** about objects that you always use or people who always do something: *Tomás sat at his usual table in the cafeteria.* | *We will be meeting with the usual people from the head office.*

regular
usual or normal, and not special or different: *Call any time during regular business hours between 9 a.m. and 5 p.m.*

typical
having the usual qualities of a particular person, group, or thing: *How much do you spend on food in a typical week?*

conventional (AWL)
belonging to the type that is usually used or has been used for a long time: *Hybrid cars get better gas mileage than conventional cars.*
→ see **common**, **ordinary**, **usual**

normally *adverb* → see **usually**

note *noun* → see **letter**, **message**, **record**, **remark²**

notice¹ /ˈnoʊtɪs/ *verb*

- ► notice
- ► observe
- ► note (*formal*)
- ► spot
- ► detect

notice
to see, feel, or hear someone or something and pay attention to it: ***I noticed that** his hands were shaking.* | *Did you **notice how** quiet Olivia was at dinner?*

observe
to notice something because you are watching or studying it closely. **Observe** is more formal than **notice**: *Researchers **observed that** the mice fought with each other more when they were put in smaller cages.*

note (*formal*)
to notice or pay careful attention to something: *She **noted that** the man was wearing a wedding ring.* | *The coach noted which players were able to listen to his advice and improve their game.*

spot
to see something that is difficult to notice, or something that no one else notices. **Spot** sounds a little more informal than **notice**: *I'm glad you spotted that mistake before it was too late.*

detect (AWL)
to notice something that is difficult to see, feel, or hear because it is very small or unclear. **Detect** sounds more formal than **notice**: *He thought he detected a slight sadness in her eyes.*

notice² *noun* → see **sign**, **warning**

novel *noun* → see Topic **Books and Literature**

now /naʊ/ *adverb*

- ► now
- ► currently (*formal*)
- ► presently (*formal*)
- ► at the moment
- ► at present (*formal*)

now
at this time: *Where are you living now? | The population is much larger now than it used to be.*

currently (*formal*)
currently means the same as **now** but sounds more formal. You usually use **currently** about a situation: *The company currently employs 113 people.*

presently (*formal*)
presently means the same as **now** but sounds more formal. You often use **presently** when the situation is likely to change: *He is presently working on a new novel.*

at the moment
if something is true at the moment, it is true now but you do not expect it to be permanent. You use **at the moment** especially in spoken or informal English: *I am working in a restaurant at the moment, but I hope to go to college next year.*

at present *also* **at the present time** (*formal*)
at present means the same as **at the moment**. **At present** is used in written and formal spoken English: *Many roads are closed at present due to heavy snow. | There is no good treatment for the disease at the present time.*
→ see **present² (2)**

nude *adjective* → see **naked**

nudge *noun* → see **push²**

nuisance *noun* → see **annoyance**

number /ˈnʌmbɚ/ *noun*

- ► number
- ► digit
- ► numeral
- ► integer

number
a word or sign that represents an amount or quantity: *Pick any number between one and ten. | Some people think that the number 13 is unlucky.*

digit
any of the numbers between 0 and 9, for example 1, 5, or 8: *The number 839 has three digits. | The children are learning how to add double-digit numbers* (=numbers that are between 10 and 99).

numeral
a written sign that represents a number in a particular number system: *The clock has Roman numerals – XII means 12.*

integer
a whole number, not a fraction or a decimal. **Integer** is used when talking about math: *6 is an integer, but 6.4 is not.*
→ see **amount**, **count**

nutritious *adjective* → see **healthy**, Topic **Describing Food**

N

Oo

obedient /əˈbidiənt/ *adjective*

- ► **obedient**
- ► **dutiful** (*formal*)
- ► **law-abiding**

ANTONYMS → see **rebellious**

obedient
always doing what parents, teachers, or other people in authority tell you to do: *Lily is a quiet and obedient child, and her work is always done on time.* | *We can show you how to train your dog to be obedient.*

dutiful (*formal*)
doing what you are expected to do and behaving in a loyal and obedient way: *He is a dutiful son who always helps his mother.*

law-abiding
a law-abiding person respects and obeys the law: *She is an honest law-abiding citizen – she doesn't even drive faster than the speed limit.*

ADVERBS
You can make the adjectives **obedient** and **dutiful** into adverbs by using an **-ly** ending: *The dog laid down in his basket obediently.* | *I wrote dutifully to my parents every week.*

obese *adjective* → see **fat**, Topic **Describing People's Looks**

obey /əˈbeɪ/ *verb*

- ► **obey**
- ► **do what someone says**
- ► **follow**
- ► **respect** (*formal*)
- ► **comply** (*formal*)

ANTONYMS → see **disobey**, **rebel[2]**

obey
to do what someone in authority tells you to do: *Soldiers must obey the orders that they are given.* | *I told my dog to sit, but he won't obey.*
→ You also use **obey** to talk about doing what a law says you must do: *If all drivers obeyed the law, the roads would be much safer.*

do what someone says
do what someone says means the same as **obey** but is more common in everyday English: *I expect you to do what your father and I say without complaining!*

follow
to do what someone says you should do, for example when someone gives orders, advice, or instructions: *You must follow your doctor's orders.* | *He followed her advice and began saving money regularly.* | *Follow the instructions on the back of the box to build the toy car.*

respect (*formal*)
to obey the law or customs of a place, especially because you believe it is important to obey them: *I respect my Chinese friend's customs, so I take my shoes off before going inside her house.*

comply (*formal*)
to do what a law, rule, or agreement says: *Companies must **comply with** employment laws.*

object[1] *noun* → see **thing**, **purpose**

object[2] *verb* → see **oppose**, **complain**, **protest[2]**

objection /əbˈdʒekʃən/ *noun*

- ► **objection**
- ► **disagreement**
- ► **dissent**

objection
the reason someone gives for not approving of an idea or plan: *My main **objection to** the marriage is that Mateo and his girlfriend are too young.* | *The school wants to increase class sizes, but the teachers have many objections.*

disagreement
a situation in which people have different opinions about something and sometimes argue: *There is some **disagreement** among medical experts **about** the best treatment for back pain.*

dissent
an opinion that is different from an official decision or different from most people's opinion: *In some countries, **dissent against** the government is not allowed.*
→ see **complaint**, **protest[1]**

objective[1] /əbˈdʒektɪv/ *adjective*

- ► **objective**
- ► **impartial**
- ► **neutral**
- ► **unbiased**

objective (AWL)
thinking only about facts, and not influenced by your own feelings, beliefs, or ideas: *Students must try to be objective when doing an*

experiment. | *It is hard to be* ***objective about*** *the people you love.*

impartial
not giving special attention or support to any one person or group: *A jury is supposed to be impartial and make a decision based on the facts.*

neutral (AWL)
not supporting either side in an argument, competition, or war: *I always try to stay neutral when my parents start arguing.*

unbiased (AWL)
fair and not influenced by your own or someone else's personal opinions: *The best news reporters try to give the public unbiased information about what is happening in the world.*
→ see **fair**[1]

ADVERBS

You can make the adjectives **objective**, **impartial**, and **neutral** into adverbs by using an **-ly** ending: *It is difficult to think objectively about the people you love.* | *The jury must try to listen to the case impartially.*

objective[2] *noun* → see **goal**

observant /əbˈzɚvənt/ *adjective*

- ► observant
- ► perceptive

observant
good at noticing the things that happen around you: *Brittany is very observant – she noticed my new haircut right away.* | *Doctors have to be observant to do their job well.*

perceptive
good at noticing and understanding situations or people's feelings: *Children can be very perceptive about how their parents are feeling.*

ADVERBS

You can make the adjectives **observant** and **perceptive** into adverbs by using an **-ly** ending: *The novel observantly follows the lives of an ordinary family.* | *He spoke perceptively about how children deal with difficult situations.*

observation *noun* → see **comment**[1]

observe *verb* → see **comment**[2], **notice**[1], **remark**[2], **say**, **watch**

obsessed *adjective* → see **interested**

obstacle /ˈɑbstɪkəl/ *noun*

1 something that blocks a road or passage so that people or things cannot go through
- ► obstacle
- ► barrier
- ► obstruction

2 something that makes it difficult for someone to do or achieve something
- ► obstacle
- ► stumbling block
- ► barrier
- ► obstruction

1 something that blocks a road or passage so that people or things cannot go through

obstacle
something that blocks a road or path so that you must go around it, over it, under it, etc.: *The soldiers have to climb over or go under all the obstacles as they run around the course.*

barrier
a fence or wall that stops people from entering a place: *A barrier was put up to stop cars from entering the street.*

obstruction
something that blocks something such as a road or passage completely so that nothing can go past or through: *Doctors had to operate to remove the obstruction in his bowel.* | *A tree fell, causing an obstruction in the road.*
→ see **wall**

2 something that makes it difficult for someone to do or achieve something

obstacle
something that makes it difficult for someone to do or achieve something, but that does not make it impossible to achieve it: *There are many* ***obstacles to*** *peace in the region.* | *The team had to deal with many obstacles this season, but they still went to the finals.*

stumbling block
stumbling block means the same as **obstacle** but sounds more informal: *The biggest stumbling block for students is usually finding enough money to go to college.*

barrier
a situation or problem that stops someone from doing something: *The law says that being disabled cannot be a* ***barrier to*** *getting a job.*

obstruction
the act of preventing or delaying a legal or political process. **Obstruction** is used especially

in the phrase **obstruction of justice**, when someone does something to make it hard for the police or other officials to find out about a crime: *He destroyed the documents about the crime, and was later accused of **obstruction of justice** in court.*

obstacle

A fallen tree has caused an **obstruction** in the road.

The soldiers climbed over the **obstacles**.

A **barrier** stops car from entering the street.

obtain *verb* → see **get**

obvious /ˈɑbviəs/ *adjective*

- ► obvious
- ► clear
- ► plain
- ► noticeable
- ► blatant
- ► conspicuous

obvious (AWL)
very easy to notice or understand. You use **obvious** to emphasize that something is so easy to notice or understand that it is surprising if someone does not notice or understand it: *She tried not to show it, but her disappointment was obvious.* | *It is **obvious that** he is in love with you.* | *There were obvious signs that someone had been in the house – for one thing, the cupboard doors were open.*

clear
easy to notice or understand, and impossible to doubt or make a mistake about: *It was **clear to me that** he was lying.* | *There are clear signs of an economic recovery.*

plain
very clear and easy to understand or recognize: *It was **plain that** she was unhappy.*

noticeable
easy to see, hear, smell, or feel: *After she had taken the medicine for two days, there was a noticeable improvement in her health.*

blatant
very obvious and offensive. You use **blatant** when someone does something bad, but does not seem to be ashamed of it: *Mark said he did not hit Antonio, but it was a blatant lie – we saw him do it, and he knows that.*

conspicuous
very easy to notice, especially because someone or something looks very different from everyone or everything else: *Everyone was wearing black or gray, and I felt conspicuous in my red coat.*

obviously /ˈɑbviəsli/ *adverb*

- ► obviously
- ► clearly
- ► noticeably
- ► plainly
- ► blatantly

obviously (AWL)
used to emphasize that something is easy to notice or understand, and it is surprising if someone does not notice or understand: *We are obviously going to need more help – three people aren't enough.* | *Obviously, we are disappointed that we lost.*

clearly
used to say that something is easy to notice or understand and difficult to make a mistake about: *Clearly, the situation is more complicated than we first thought.* | *Everyone was clearly confused, so I explained the rules of the game again.*

noticeably
in a way that is easy to see, hear, smell, or feel: *The birds were similar, but one of them was noticeably darker.*

plainly
in a way that is clear and easy to recognize: *Tom was plainly nervous as he began his speech.*

blatantly
in a way that is very obvious and offensive. You use **blatantly** when someone does something bad, but does not seem to be embarrassed about it: *The referee's decision seemed blatantly unfair, because we could all see that the ball was out of bounds.*

occasion *noun* → see **event**, **time**

occasionally *adverb* → see **sometimes**

occupation *noun* → see **job**, Topic **Jobs and Work**

occupied *adjective* → see **busy**

occupy *verb* → see **live**

occur *verb* → see **exist**, **happen**

occur to *phrasal verb* → see **think**

ocean /ˈoʊʃən/ *noun*

- ► ocean
- ► sea
- ► bay
- ► gulf

ocean
one of the very large areas of salt water on Earth: *I like to swim* ***in the ocean*** *in the summer.* | *We crossed the Atlantic Ocean when we flew from New York to France.*

sea
an area of salt water that is part of an ocean and that is partly surrounded by land: *Fishing boats go out into the Bering Sea from the coast of Alaska.*
→ A **sea** is also a large area of salt water, or sometimes fresh water, enclosed by land: *The Caspian Sea is so big that five countries are on its borders.*

bay
a place where the coast curves around the ocean: *The explorers left their ships and rowed in smaller boats across the shallow waters of the bay.*

gulf
a large area of ocean that is surrounded by land on three sides: *The beaches along the Gulf of Mexico have white sand and calm waters.*

odd *adjective* → see **strange**

odor *noun* → see **smell**[1]

off *adjective* → see **bad**, **rotten**, Topic **Describing Food**

offend /əˈfend/ *verb*

- ► offend
- ► insult
- ► cause offense

offend
to make someone angry and upset by doing or saying something rude or unkind: *His jokes about old people offended me.* | *I was careful about what I said, because I did not want to offend anyone.*

insult
to make someone very angry and upset by showing a lack of respect or saying something unkind: *In some cultures, you insult your host if you do not accept their offer of food.* | *He tried to pick a fight by insulting my mother.*

cause offense *also* **give offense**
cause offense and **give offense** mean the same as **offend** but sound more formal: *A joke that seems funny to people in one culture can* ***cause offense to*** *people from another culture.* | *If you do not shake hands, you may* ***give offense.***
→ see **hurt (3)**

offense *noun* → see **crime**

offensive /əˈfensɪv/ *adjective*

1 likely to upset someone

- ► offensive
- ► insulting
- ► abusive
- ► tasteless

2 offensive and often about sex

- ► offensive
- ► dirty (*informal*)
- ► foul
- ► obscene
- ► crude
- ► indecent
- ► vulgar

1 likely to upset someone

offensive
likely to upset or offend someone: *I think that the advertisement is* ***offensive to*** *women, because it seems to say that women are only good for cleaning houses.* | *The teacher sent the student to the principal because he was using offensive language.*

insulting
very offensive and mean, or showing a complete lack of respect: *It is* ***insulting to*** *Eva to suggest that she got the job only because she is a woman.* | *She made an insulting remark about his weight.*

abusive
criticizing someone in an unfair and very offensive way that can cause harm: *He had to leave his job because he was abusive toward another employee.*

tasteless
tasteless jokes and remarks are a little shocking, because they seem unkind and not appropriate: *The comedian was making tasteless jokes about people with no arms.*

2 offensive and often about sex

offensive
likely to upset and offend someone, especially because of being about sex: *One of the men made an offensive remark about Joel's wife.*

dirty *(informal)*
relating to sex in a way that people think is bad: *He got in trouble for saying a dirty word.* | *One of the men told a dirty joke.*

foul
foul language is very rude and offensive, and uses swear words: *My dad didn't want us to see the movie, because it was full of foul language.*

obscene
showing or talking about sex in a way that is offensive or shocking: *The movie was banned because it was obscene.* | *He got in trouble for using obscene language on a radio show.*

crude
talking about sex or about people in an offensive and impolite way: *One of the men made a crude joke about her body.*

indecent
shocking and offensive, and involving sex: *The man was found guilty of possessing indecent photographs.*

vulgar
vulgar jokes or remarks are about things that it is not polite to talk about, for example sex or body waste: *He was telling vulgar jokes that embarrassed all the women.*
→ see **rude**

ADVERBS
You can make the adjectives **offensive**, **abusive**, **tasteless**, **obscene**, **crude**, **indecent**, and **vulgar** into adverbs by using an **-ly** ending: *He made offensively rude remarks about her weight.* | *The player was sent off the court for verbally and vulgarly abusing a referee.*

offer /ˈɔfɚ/ *verb*

- ► offer
- ► volunteer
- ► come forward

offer
to say that you will do something in order to help someone: ***I offered to** give her a ride into town.* | *She is a great teacher who is always ready to offer help and encouragement.*

volunteer (AWL)
to offer to do something, especially something difficult or unpleasant: *Will anyone **volunteer to** help me clean up this mess?*

come forward
to offer to give help, information, or money, especially after someone has publicly asked for something: *The teacher is asking parents to **come forward to** help with the school party.*

office /ˈɔfɪs/ *noun*

- ► office
- ► workplace

office
a room, set of rooms, or building where people work at desks: *Is Mr. Kim **in his office**?* | *I am not going to the office today – I'll be working from home.*

workplace
the office, factory, or other building where people work. You use **workplace** when you are talking in a general way about the places or situations in which people work: *It is important to have good relationships with your co-workers **in the workplace**.*
→ **GRAMMAR: Office** and **workplace** are also used before other nouns: *The new law is designed to improve workplace safety.* | *They sell office equipment.*

officer *noun* → see **police officer**, **soldier**

official /əˈfɪʃəl/ *adjective*

- ► official
- ► formal

ANTONYMS → see **informal (2)**

official
done by someone who has an important position in the government or in an organization, or approved of by someone in authority: *The secretary of state is on an official trip to India.* | *The official statement to the press said that he resigned because of health problems.*

formal
done or produced in a way that has been officially agreed: *The two countries have now signed a formal agreement limiting the number of nuclear weapons they have.*

ADVERBS
You can make the adjectives **official** and **formal** into adverbs by using an **-ly** ending: *One in four residents of the city officially live in poverty.* | *The senator has not yet formally announced that he will run for president.*

often /ˈɔfən/ *adverb*

- ► often
- ► frequently
- ► a lot
- ► regularly
- ► repeatedly
- ► constantly

ANTONYMS → see **rarely**

often
many times: *If you wash your hair too often, it can get very dry.* | *My aunt lives nearby, so we go to her house fairly often.*

frequently
very often. **Frequently** is more formal than **often**: *Some of the patients frequently forget to take their medicine.*

a lot
a lot means the same as **often** but sounds more informal: *He runs a lot because he is on the track team.*

regularly
often, especially with the same amount of time between each event: *Buses go to the airport regularly every 15 minutes.*

repeatedly
many times, one after the other: *I've called Kevin repeatedly, but he is not answering the phone.*

constantly (AWL)
very often over a long period of time in a way that is annoying: *Susan is constantly complaining. She finds something wrong with everything.*

oily /ˈɔɪli/ *adjective*

- ► oily
- ► greasy

oily
covered with oil, or containing a lot of oil: *There were oily stains on his clothes from working on the car.* | *My skin is really oily, so I have to wash my face a lot.*

greasy
If something is greasy, it has too much oil on it, in an unpleasant way: *His hair was really greasy, like he hadn't washed it in a week.*
→ You often use **greasy** about food that has been fried and has a lot of fat in it: *The French fries were soft and greasy.*

old /oʊld/ *adjective*

1 having lived a long time – used about people
- ► old
- ► elderly
- ► aging
- ► aged

ANTONYMS → see **young**[1]

2 having existed a long time – used about things
- ► old
- ► ancient
- ► antique
- ► vintage

ANTONYMS → see **new**

1 having lived a long time – used about people

old
having lived for a long time: *Mr. Johnson is very old – I think he is about 90.* | *Grandma is too old to go skiing.*

elderly
elderly means the same as **old** but sounds more polite or formal: *Andy helped the elderly woman with a cane cross the street.*

aging
becoming old: *The aging actress had surgery on her face to try to look younger.*

aged
very old. **Aged** sounds formal or literary and is

old

an **ancient** temple

an **old** van

an **antique** dresser

a **vintage** car

O

used mostly in writing: *Cecilia's aged father was near death in the hospital.*
→ see Topic **Describing People's Looks**

2 having existed a long time – used about things

old
having existed for a long time: *The old house was built in the 1850s.* | *The car was so old that it was not safe to drive anymore.*

ancient
thousands of years old: *The ancient city walls were built by the Romans.*

antique
antique objects are old and valuable: *Be careful! That antique vase is worth a lot of money.*

vintage
old, and valuable or interesting. Use **vintage** about wine, cars, or clothes: *Dan collects and repairs vintage cars from the 1950s.*
→ see **last**[1] for **old** meaning "the one you had before now"

old-fashioned /ˌoʊld ˈfæʃənd/ *adjective*

- ► old-fashioned
- ► outdated
- ► out-of-date
- ► dated
- ► obsolete

ANTONYMS → see **modern**

old-fashioned
no longer modern or popular. You use **old-fashioned** about styles, words, or ideas: *That dress is too old-fashioned. It looks like something my mom would wear.* | *My grandpa has some really old-fashioned ideas about how only women should do the cooking and cleaning.*

outdated
old and no longer useful, because newer things are better. You use **outdated** about machines, equipment, or methods: *The computer I bought in college is completely outdated now – new computers are a lot faster.*

out-of-date
old and no longer containing the most recent information. You use **out-of-date** about written information, especially when it contains numbers, prices, dates, or times: *That bus schedule is out-of-date. Here's the new one with the current times.*

dated
no longer fashionable or modern. You use **dated** about styles that were popular until fairly recently but now seem old-fashioned: *I liked the food, but the inside of the restaurant is very dated. It looks like it was done in the 1990s.*

obsolete
old and no longer used or needed, because something newer and better has been made. You use **obsolete** especially about equipment and machines: *Within two years, my cell phone was almost obsolete and I had to buy a new one.*

old person /ˈoʊld ˌpɚsən/ *noun*

- ► old person
- ► senior citizen
- ► the elderly

ANTONYMS → see **child (1)**, **teenager**

old person *also* **old man, old woman, old lady**
someone who has been alive for a long time. **Old man**, **old woman**, etc. does not always sound very polite: *The bus tours are a good way for old people to travel because everything is taken care of for them.* | *A little old lady with gray hair sat on the park bench feeding the pigeons.*
→ If you want to sound more polite, you can use **elderly person/man/woman** or **older person/man/woman**. **Older person** is more informal: *He was an elderly man – probably in his eighties.* | *The older woman with Elsa is her grandmother.*

senior citizen *also* **senior**
an old person. **Senior citizen** or **senior** is more formal than **old person**, and you use it especially when you are talking about old people as a group. People also use it to avoid saying the word "old," because some people get upset about being called old: *Seniors get a discount at the movie theater.* | *She works with senior citizens at a nursing home.*

the elderly
people who are old. **The elderly** sounds more polite and formal than **old people**: *The government spends a lot of money on health care for the elderly.*

omit *verb* → see **leave out**

on *preposition* → see Function Words

online *adjective, adverb* → see Topic **Computers and the Internet**

only[1] *adverb* → see Function Words

only² /ˈoʊnli/ *adjective*

- ► only
- ► single
- ► sole
- ► lone
- ► solitary (*formal*)
- ► unique

only
used for saying that there is not more than one person or thing of a particular kind: *There were seven girls at the party, and I was the only boy.* | *This is the only way to get to the beach. The other trails don't go there.*
→ **GRAMMAR:** Don't say: ~~*He was an only person who believed me*~~. Say: *He was the only person who believed me.* Don't say: ~~*There is an only way to solve this problem*~~. Say: *There is only one way to solve this problem.* "An" is not used before **only** except when you say that someone does not have a brother or sister: *He is an only child.*

single
used to emphasize that you mean one, and only one: *Dad fired a single shot from his rifle and hit the bird.*

sole (AWL)
sole means the same as **only** but sounds more formal or literary: *Anna was the sole survivor of the plane crash.* | *His sole responsibility was to protect the children.*

lone
used to emphasize that someone or something is the only one doing an activity or existing in a place. **Lone** is used especially in literary writing: *A lone figure* (=person) *in a heavy coat walked down the dark snowy street.*

solitary (*formal*)
a solitary object is the only one you can see in a place, and it may seem a little lonely or sad: *A solitary light shone in the window.*

unique (AWL)
a unique thing is the only one of its kind: *Each person's fingerprints are unique.*

ADVERBS

You can make the adjectives **sole** and **unique** into adverbs by using an **-ly** ending: *The reporter was held solely responsible for the mistakes in the article.* | *The story gives the reader a sense of place and character that is uniquely American.*

on time /ɔn ˈtaɪm/ *adverb, adjective*

- ► on time
- ► prompt
- ► punctual (*formal*)

ANTONYMS → see **late**

on time
arriving or happening at the right time, and not early or late: *I'm always **on time for** the meetings, but everyone else is always late.* | *If you want to keep your job, you have to be on time.* | *The program started on time, but it finished late.*

prompt
someone who is prompt arrives or does something at the right time and is not late: *She is always **prompt with** her replies to my emails.* | *The meeting will start at nine. Please be prompt.*

punctual (*formal*)
someone who is punctual arrives at exactly the right time: *Students are expected to be punctual and tardiness is not tolerated.*
→ see **early**

ADVERBS

You can make the adjectives **prompt** and **punctual** into adverbs by using an **-ly** ending: *Feeney came into my office promptly at ten.* | *The students arrived punctually.*

open¹ /ˈoʊpən/ *adjective*

- ► open
- ► ajar
- ► unlocked

ANTONYMS → see **closed**

open
not closed so that things, people, air, or light can get in or out: *I am leaving the door open, so the cat can get back inside.* | *He fell asleep in the chair with his mouth wide open.*
→ If a store is **open**, it is allowing customers to go in: *Is the bank still open?*

ajar
a door or window that is ajar is open a little bit: *The door was ajar, so she looked into the room.*

unlocked
if a door, window, or container is unlocked, the lock is not fastened so that it can be opened easily: *I'll leave the front door unlocked, so you won't need a key.*

open² /ˈoʊpən/ *verb*

- open
- unlock
- unwrap
- unfasten

ANTONYMS → see **close¹**

open
to move a door or window so that things, people, air, or light can go in or out: *Open the window and let some air in – it's too hot in here.*
→ **Open** also means to remove the cover from something: *Gayle opened the letter and read it nervously.*
→ You also use **open** about your mouth and eyes: *He opened his eyes and looked at her.*
→ If a store **opens**, it starts letting customers in: *The store opens at 9 a.m.*

unlock
to open a door, window, or container with a key: *Unlock the car, so we can get in.*

unwrap
to remove the paper, plastic, or other material that is around something: *The children sat around the Christmas tree unwrapping their presents.*

unfasten
to open something that is fastened or tied: *It was hot, so Ricky unfastened the top button of his shirt.*

openly *adverb* → see **publicly**

operate /ˈɑpəˌreɪt/ *verb*

1 to use a machine
- operate (*formal*)
- run
- control
- work (*informal*)

2 to cut into someone's body to repair it
- operate
- do surgery

1 to use a machine

operate (*formal*)
to use and control a machine or piece of equipment. **Operate** is used especially in written English, for example in warnings or instructions: *Do not operate the chainsaw without safety glasses.* | *You should not drive or operate heavy machinery when taking the medicine.*

run
to make a machine or engine do what it is supposed to do: *We only run the air conditioner when it's really hot outside.*

control
to make a machine or vehicle do what you want it to do: *You can use the radio device to control the toy car.*

work (*informal*)
to make a complicated machine or piece of equipment do what it is supposed to do. You use **work** especially in spoken English: *Does anyone here know how to work this microwave?*
→ see **work¹**

2 to cut into someone's body to repair it

operate
if a doctor operates, he or she cuts into someone's body in order to repair or remove a part that is damaged: *They had to **operate on** my arm because it was broken in two places.*

do surgery
do surgery means the same as **operate** but is less formal: *The doctors had to do emergency surgery to stop the bleeding.*
→ see Topic **Medical Treatment**

operation /ˌɑpəˈreɪʃən/ *noun*

- operation
- surgery
- procedure (*formal*)

operation
a medical treatment in which a doctor cuts into someone's body to fix or remove a damaged part: *He had an **operation on** his right eye to try to get his sight back.* | *How long will the operation last?*

surgery
medical treatment in which a doctor cuts into someone's body to fix or remove a damaged part: *Her doctor says she'll need surgery to remove the tumor.*

procedure (AWL) (*formal*)
a medical treatment or operation. **Procedure** is less specific than **operation** or **surgery** and can mean any medical treatment that needs several steps: *Greta was in the hospital for a medical procedure, but she didn't say what it was.*
→ see **treatment**, Topic **Medical Treatment**

SYNONYM CHECK

Operation or surgery?

When you talk about having medical treatment involving cutting, you can use either **have surgery** or **have an operation**. Don't say: ~~*He had a surgery on his knee*~~. Say: *He had surgery on his knee* or *He had an operation on his knee.*

opinion /əˈpɪnyən/ *noun*

- opinion
- point of view
- view
- attitude
- feeling
- sentiment (*formal*)

opinion
your ideas about someone or something, for example whether you think he, she, or it is good or right: ***In my opinion****, the movie was terrible, but you might like it.* | *Everyone had a different* ***opinion about*** *how to solve the problem, so we could not decide what to do.*

point of view
your opinion about something, especially when this is influenced by the situation you are in: *If you had been there, you might have a different* ***point of view about*** *what happened.*

view
your opinion about something, especially about a serious or important subject: ***I don't agree with the view that*** *longer prison sentences stop people from committing crime.*

attitude AWL
the way you think or feel about someone or something, especially when you show this in the way you behave: *As Carlo made more friends, his* ***attitude toward*** *school improved a lot.* | *She comes in to work with a good attitude.*

feeling
your opinion about someone or something, especially an opinion that is based on emotions: *Kids'* ***feelings about*** *exercise are influenced a lot by their parents.* | *I have a feeling that this was the wrong thing to do.*

sentiment (*formal*)
an opinion or feeling that you have about something: *Many people share the* ***sentiment that*** *the war should end.*
→ see **idea**

opponent /əˈpoʊnənt/ *noun*

- opponent
- competitor
- opposition
- rival
- adversary (*formal*)

opponent
someone who tries to defeat someone else in a competition, game, or election: *The Tigers are strong opponents, but we think we can beat them.* | *Who will be the mayor's opponent in the next election?*

competitor
a person, team, or company that is competing with another one: *The company's phone is selling much better than the phone produced by its competitors.*

opposition
the team you are competing against: *We lost the game because the opposition played better than we expected.*

rival
if two people, companies, or teams are rivals, they are always trying hard to do better than the other one in business or a sport: *When I played football in high school, Medford High School was our biggest rival* (=the team it was most important to beat).

adversary (*formal*)
someone you are fighting or competing against, especially in politics or sports. **Adversary** sounds formal or literary and is often used in writing: *The president's political adversaries are trying to make voters feel that he cannot be trusted.*

opportunity *noun* → see **chance**

oppose /əˈpoʊz/ *verb*

- oppose
- be against
- object

ANTONYMS → see **approve**

oppose *also* **be opposed to**
to disagree with an idea or action: *Many people oppose the plan to build a new airport because it will be very noisy.* | *He was opposed to the idea and said that it was not practical.*

be against
to not agree with an idea or plan and not want it to happen. **Be against** is less formal than **oppose**: *She wants to marry him, but her parents are against it.* | *Many people were against the war.*

O

object
to say that you do not approve of something. **Object** is more formal than **be against**: *She **objected to** the changes that he wanted to make.*

opposite[1] *preposition* → see Function Words

opposite[2] /ˈɑpəzɪt/ *noun*

1 someone or something that is completely different
- the opposite
- the reverse (*formal*)
- the contrary (*formal*)
- the converse (*formal*)

2 a word or meaning that is completely different
- the opposite
- antonym

1 someone or something that is completely different

the opposite
someone or something that is as different as possible from someone or something else: *Anna is quiet and shy, but her sister is just the opposite: she is very friendly.* | *Russ asked for my opinion of what he should do, and then did the opposite. I wonder why he even asked!*

the reverse (*formal*)
the opposite of a situation that you have just mentioned: *In most of the world, populations are growing, but in Europe, the reverse is true: the number of births is going down.*

the contrary (AWL) (*formal*)
the opposite of what has just been said or suggested. Use this in the expressions **on the contrary**, **to the contrary**, or **quite the contrary** to emphasize that the opposite of what has been asked or suggested is in fact true: *No, Amanda is not jealous about her boyfriend. On the contrary, she seems happy when he makes new friends.*

the converse (*formal*)
the exact opposite of a fact or statement: *We know that building more roads leads to more cars and more traffic. **The converse of** this is also true: fewer or smaller roads will reduce traffic.*

2 a word or meaning that is completely different

the opposite
a word or meaning that is as different as possible from another word or meaning: *"Light" **is the opposite of** both "dark" and "heavy."* | *I forgot to write "not," so the sentence says **the opposite of** what I meant.*

antonym
a word that means the opposite of another word: *"Old" is an **antonym of** "young."*

opposition /ˌɑpəˈzɪʃən/ *noun*

- opposition
- resistance
- hostility
- antagonism (*formal*)

opposition
if there is opposition to something, people disagree with it or protest against it: *There has been **opposition to** the war since it started.* | *The plan to raise taxes has met strong opposition.*

resistance
if there is resistance to something, people do not accept it and they try to stop it: *There is **resistance to** the new school uniforms from both parents and students.*

hostility
angry statements or behavior that show that someone opposes someone or something strongly: *The local people showed a lot of **hostility toward** the soldiers and sometimes threw rocks at them.*

antagonism (*formal*)
a feeling that you strongly oppose or hate someone or something: *Ron's **antagonism toward** people in authority has gotten him in trouble many times.*

→ see **opponent**

oppress /əˈpres/ *verb*

- oppress (*formal*)
- persecute
- keep down

oppress (*formal*)
if people with power oppress other people, they treat them badly or do not let them do what they want. **Oppress** sounds fairly formal or literary: *The plantation owners oppressed their slaves, often separating families or treating them cruelly.*

persecute
to treat someone cruelly and unfairly because of his or her ideas: *People of all religions have come to the U.S. because they were persecuted in their own countries.*

keep down
keep down means the same as **oppress** but sounds more informal: *The land owners kept slaves down by refusing to give them an education.*

oppressed /ə'prest/ *adjective*

- ► oppressed
- ► persecuted
- ► downtrodden (*formal*)

oppressed
treated badly and not allowed to do what you want: *For centuries in this country, minorities were oppressed and the white majority had all the power.*

persecuted
treated cruelly and unfairly because of your beliefs: *The persecuted writer had spent years in prison because of his political beliefs.*

downtrodden (*formal*)
treated badly by people who have power over you. **Downtrodden** sounds literary or formal: *The organization helps downtrodden workers and poor families.*

optimism *noun* → see **hope²**

optimistic *adjective* → see **hopeful**, Topic **Describing People's Character**

option *noun* → see **choice**

optional /'ɑpʃənəl/ *adjective*

- ► optional
- ► voluntary

ANTONYMS → see **necessary (2)**

optional (AWL)
if something is optional, you do not have to do it or have it: *Name tags are optional at the meeting, but we recommend that you use them.* | *The car has optional features, like leather seats, that you can pay extra for.*

voluntary (AWL)
done because you want to and not because you must: *Donations are completely voluntary. You don't have to pay anything if you don't want to.*

ADVERBS

You can make the adjectives **optional** and **voluntary** into adverbs by using an **-ly** ending: *Add some pepper and, optionally, a clove of garlic.* | *He was not forced to resign; he resigned voluntarily.*

ordeal /ɔr'dil/ *noun* (*formal*)

- ► ordeal
- ► trauma
- ► horror

ordeal
a very bad or difficult experience: *The trip home in the snowstorm was a real ordeal.* | *They were kidnapped, which was a terrible ordeal.*

trauma
an extremely upsetting experience that affects you for a long time: *Children often find it hard to deal with traumas such as the death or divorce of a parent.*

horror
a terrible experience that is extremely shocking or frightening. You often use **horror** in its plural form in the phrase **the horrors of something**: *The people of Afghanistan know* ***the horrors of*** *war very well.*

order¹ /'ɔrdɚ/ *noun*

1 the way a number of things are arranged or happen
- ► order
- ► arrangement
- ► sequence
- ► pattern

2 something that someone tells you to do
- ► order
- ► command

1 the way a number of things are arranged or happen

order
the way that you arrange things or put them on a list, or the way events follow each other: *We lined up* ***in*** *alphabetical* ***order****, so the people with names starting with "A" were at the front.* | *We had to put the paragraphs* ***in order*** *to make a story.* | *The program listed the order in which the singers would perform.*

arrangement
the way you put all the things in a group into a particular position: *The arrangement of desks in rows is not good for a class discussion.*

sequence (AWL)
the order in which a series of related things happens or exists: *Give the directions* ***in a sequence*** *so that they're easy to follow.*

pattern
the order in which things happen, which stays the same even in different situations or times:

O

Women's lives used to follow a pattern: first school, then marriage, and then motherhood.
→ A **pattern** is also a regular arrangement of repeated shapes, lines, and colors: *The pattern of diamonds on the curtains is like our curtains at home.*

2 something that someone tells you to do

order
something that someone in authority tells you to do: *The captain gave the soldier the* ***order to*** *shoot.* | *She asked the judge for a court order to stop him from coming to her house.*
→ An **order** is also something you ask for from a business or restaurant: *I gave the waitress my order and asked for some water.* | ***Orders for*** *new cars have gone down in the past three years.*

command
an official order from an important person, especially someone like a king, queen, or military leader: *When the sergeant gave the command, the soldiers ran up the hill.*
→ see **request**

order[2] /ˈɔrdɚ/ *verb*

- ► order
- ► tell
- ► give orders
- ► command
- ► give instructions
- ► instruct (*formal*)
- ► direct (*formal*)

order
to say to someone that he or she must do something, using your official power or authority: *Police* ***ordered*** *the man* ***to*** *put down the gun.* | *"Stop right there," he ordered.*

tell
to say to someone that he or she must do something: *My older sister is always* ***telling*** *me what to do.* | *Mom* ***told*** *me* ***to*** *wait for her by the fountain.*

give orders
to tell someone exactly what he or she must do, using your official power or authority: *The commander* ***gave orders to*** *burn the fort.*

command
if a king, queen, or military leader commands a less important person to do something, he or she officially tells that person to do something: *The general* ***commanded*** *the troops* ***to*** *retreat.*

give instructions
to tell someone exactly what he or she must do and how to do it: *Mrs. Gonzalez* ***gave instructions about*** *how to give the cat its medicine.*

instruct (AWL) (*formal*)
instruct means the same as **give instructions**: *She takes three pills a day, as her doctor* ***instructed*** *her* ***to*** *do.*

direct (*formal*)
to give someone an official or legal order to do something: *The judge* ***directed*** *the jury* ***to*** *think about all the evidence when making their decision.*
→ see **ask**, **organize**

ordinary /ˈɔrdnˌeri/ *adjective*

- ► ordinary
- ► usual
- ► normal
- ► regular
- ► typical
- ► average
- ► everyday
- ► conventional

ANTONYMS → see **strange**, **special**

ordinary
not special in any way, and not very different from other people or things of the same type: *The book is about ordinary people – not anyone famous or important.* | *It looks like an ordinary pen, but it actually has a tiny camera in it.*

usual
happening, done, or existing in the same way as always. You use **usual** especially about situations and ways of doing things: *Is it* ***usual for*** *Tom* ***to*** *be so late?*
→ You can also use **usual** about objects that you always use or people who always do something: *Tomás sat at his usual table in the cafeteria.* | *We will be meeting with the usual people from the head office.*

normal (AWL)
happening or existing in the usual way that people expect. You use **normal** especially about situations, ways of doing things, and feelings, as well as about amounts and levels: *It is* ***normal to*** *feel nervous when you start a new job.* | *Rainfall has been higher than normal this month.*

regular
usual or normal, and not special or different: *Call any time during regular business hours between 9 a.m. and 5 p.m.*

typical
having the usual qualities of a particular person, group, or thing: *How much do you spend on food in a typical week?*

average
typical or ordinary, not particularly big or small, or high or low: *The average American family will spend about $3,000 on food and a place to stay during their vacation this summer.*

everyday
ordinary, usual, or happening every day: *The movie gives you an idea of what everyday life was like in Mexico in the 1950s.*

conventional (AWL)
belonging to the type that is usually used or has been used for a long time: *Hybrid cars get better gas mileage than conventional cars.*
→ see **common**

ADVERBS

You can make the adjectives **usual**, **normal**, **typical**, and **conventional** into adverbs by using an **-ly** ending: *Tom is usually late.* | *It normally rains in April.* | *Typically, I spend about $100 a week on food.*

organic *adjective* → see **natural**, Topic **Describing Food**, **The Environment**

organization /ˌɔrgənəˈzeɪʃən/ *noun*

- organization
- institution
- association
- society
- club

organization
a group that has formed for a particular purpose: *Matt works for an organization that provides food and housing for poor people.* | *A terrorist organization took responsibility for the bombing.*

institution (AWL)
a large important organization, such as a bank, hospital, or university: *The changes in the law will affect banks, insurance companies, and other financial institutions.*

association
an organization for people who do the same type of job or activity. **Association** is used especially in the names of these types of organizations: *Doctors are going to the American Medical Association's annual meeting in Chicago.*

society
an organization for people with the same interests or ideas. **Society** is used especially in the names of these organizations: *The local historical society is collecting antiques for the town's museum.*

club
a group of people who meet regularly to do something that they are all interested in, for example an activity or hobby: *His mother started the local gardening club.*

SYNONYM CHECK
Society or club?

Both **society** and **club** are used for groups of people who share an interest in something.

A **society** is often for people interested in a subject, for example history or music: *The Tucson Jazz Society is hosting the concert.*

A **club** is often for people who are interested in a particular activity or hobby: *She is the captain of the chess club.*

organize /ˈɔrgəˌnaɪz/ *verb*

1 to put things into an order or system
- organize
- arrange
- structure
- order

2 to do everything necessary for an event to happen successfully
- organize
- make arrangements
- plan
- coordinate (*formal*)

1 to put things into an order or system

organize
to put people or things into a particular order or system: *The software helps you organize all your digital photos, so they're easy to find.* | *The clothes in the store are **organized by** style and size.*

arrange
to put a group of things in particular positions: *Mom wants us to help her arrange the living room furniture.*

structure (AWL)
to organize information or a schedule carefully, so the parts of it are in a particular order and they connect together in a sensible way: *Structure your essay so that each paragraph talks about a different point.*

order
to arrange things in a particular order: *The list of names is ordered alphabetically.*

O

2 to do everything necessary for an event to happen successfully

organize
to do all the things that are necessary to prepare for an event so that it can happen successfully: *I'm organizing a party for Juan's 21st birthday.* | *The unemployed people organized a protest on Wall Street.*

make arrangements
to do all the things that are necessary for something that is planned to happen, for example by calling people and making reservations: *The couple* ***made*** *all the* ***arrangements for*** *the wedding and invited over 100 guests.*

plan
to think carefully about how you will do something that you want to do: *We spent months planning our trip.* | *The robbery had obviously been carefully planned, and the thieves were all dressed as security guards.*

coordinate (AWL) *(formal)*
to organize an activity so that people involved in it work well together and achieve a good result: *The government is coordinating efforts to rescue people trapped by the flooding.*

organized /ˈɔrgəˌnaɪzd/ *adjective*

- ► organized
- ► systematic
- ► methodical
- ► orderly
- ► efficient

ANTONYMS → see **messy**

organized
planned or arranged carefully, sensibly, or neatly: *There has been an organized effort by the neighborhood to clean up the park.* | *The exhibit is well organized, so it is easy to see how the artist's work developed over time.*
→ You can also say that a person is **organized** when he or she plans things carefully: *He is very organized; everything always goes well when he is in charge.*

systematic
using an organized and thorough plan in a careful way in order to do everything that you should. You can use **systematic** about the method you use or about the person who uses it: *We need a systematic way to grade students' work so that we treat everyone the same.* | *Nurses who work in an operating room need to be very systematic about organizing the instruments.*

methodical (AWL)
done in a careful and organized way so that you do not miss anything: *The researchers check every detail in a methodical way.*
→ You can also use **methodical** about a person who does something in a careful and organized way: *The researchers are very methodical when they check the details.*

orderly
arranged or organized in a sensible neat way. You use **orderly** especially about the way objects or people are organized: *The tools were arranged in orderly rows.* | *There was smoke coming from the top floor, but people were leaving the building in an orderly way.*

efficient
someone or something that is efficient works well, is organized, and does what needs to be done without wasting time, money, or energy: *Email is an efficient way of contacting a large number of people because it's very quick.*
→ see **neat**, **thorough**, **careful**, Topic **Describing People's Character**

ADVERBS

You can make the adjectives **systematic**, **methodical**, and **efficient** into adverbs by using an **-ly** ending: *We had to go through the paperwork systematically, checking that everything was done correctly.* | *The police methodically searched the room.* | *Good students learn to manage their time efficiently.*

origin *noun* → see **beginning**, **source**

original *adjective* → see **first**, **new**

origins *noun* → see **cause**[1]

ornament *noun* → see **decoration**

ought to *verb* → see **should**

out *adverb* → see Function Words

outdoor *adjective* → see **outside**[1]

outdoors *adverb* → see Function Word **out**

outer *adjective* → see **outside**[1]

outgoing /ˈaʊtˌgoʊɪŋ/ *adjective*

- ► outgoing
- ► extroverted
- ► sociable
- ► gregarious

ANTONYMS → see **shy**

outgoing
someone who is outgoing is lively and confident,

and enjoys meeting and talking to people: *Whitney is outgoing and loves talking to people, but I'm too shy.* | *Mañuel has become more outgoing as he has gotten to know people at his new school.*

extroverted
extroverted means the same as **outgoing** but sounds more formal and scientific: *Extroverted people often make good salespeople, because they like talking to others.*

sociable
someone who is sociable is friendly and enjoys being with other people: *Alex is very sociable and is always doing things with his friends.*

gregarious
someone who is gregarious is friendly and likes to talk to people: *Cicely is a gregarious, fun-loving young woman who has plenty of friends.*

outside[1] /ˌaʊtˈsaɪd/ *adjective*

1 on the outside part of something
- ► **outside**
- ► **exterior** (*formal*)
- ► **outer**
- ► **external** (*formal*)

ANTONYMS → see **inside[2]**

2 happening or used outside
- ► **outside**
- ► **outdoor**
- ► **open-air**

1 on the outside part of something

outside
on the part of something that is outdoors, especially on the part of a building that is outdoors: *Check the outside door – is it locked?* | *You get to the apartment by an outside staircase at the back of the building.*

exterior (*formal*)
exterior means the same as **outside**: *The exterior walls of the museum are covered in polished metal.*

outer
on or near the outside of something, especially when there are different layers or similar parts inside: *Boil the beans for ten minutes and remove the tough outer skin.*

external (AWL) (*formal*)
relating to the outer part of something, or to the skin of a person's body: *The external walls of the castle are beginning to crumble.* | *There were no external signs of injury, but doctors found internal* (=inside the body) *bleeding.*

ADVERBS

The adverb for **outside** is also **outside**: *We went outside.*

You can make the adjective **external** into an adverb by using an **-ly** ending: *The medicine is applied externally to the infected area.*

2 happening or used outside

outside
existing or done outside a building, not inside: *The outside faucet is dripping.* | *You should wear sunscreen for outside activities.*

outdoor
happening or used outside: *The restaurant has indoor and outdoor seating.* | *Outdoor pools have to be cleaned every few days.*

open-air
happening or existing outside. You use **open-air** especially about things that usually happen or exist under a roof, for example a theater or a restaurant: *The town has an open-air fruit and vegetable market on the weekends.*

GRAMMAR CHECK: outside

When **outside**, **outdoor**, and **open-air** are adjectives, they are only used before a noun. Don't say: ~~*The swimming pool is outdoor.*~~ Say: *The swimming pool is an outdoor one.*

However, **outside** can also be used as an adverb, and the adverb for **outdoor** is **outdoors**. These words do not need to be used before a noun: *The swimming pool is outside/outdoors.*

outside[2] /ˌaʊtˈsaɪd/ *noun*

- ► **the outside**
- ► **exterior** (*formal*)
- ► **surface**

ANTONYMS → see **inside[1]**

the outside
the outer part of something, that is farthest from the center of it: *The outside of the house was painted white.* | *Fry the sausage until it is brown* ***on the outside.***

exterior (*formal*)
exterior means the same as **the outside**, but is used especially in writing about technical subjects: *Raisa checked the exterior of the car for scratches and dents.*

surface
the outside or top layer of something: *The surface of the planet is very rocky.*

outside³ *adverb* → see Function Word **out**

oval¹ *noun* → see **circle¹**

oval² *adjective* → see **round¹**

oven /ˈʌvən/ *noun*

- ► oven
- ► kiln
- ► furnace

oven
a piece of equipment that you cook food inside, shaped like a metal box with a door on it. An **oven** is usually part of a stove: *Heat the oven before you put the pizza in.* | *The chicken is **in the oven**. It should be ready in a half hour.*

kiln
a special oven for baking pots, bricks, and other things made of clay: *The artist uses a special tool to remove the pots from the kiln.*

furnace
a large container with a very hot fire inside it, used to melt metal: *The large furnaces are used to produce steel.*
→ A **furnace** is also a piece of equipment that produces heat to make a building warm: *We have a gas furnace in the basement.*

oven

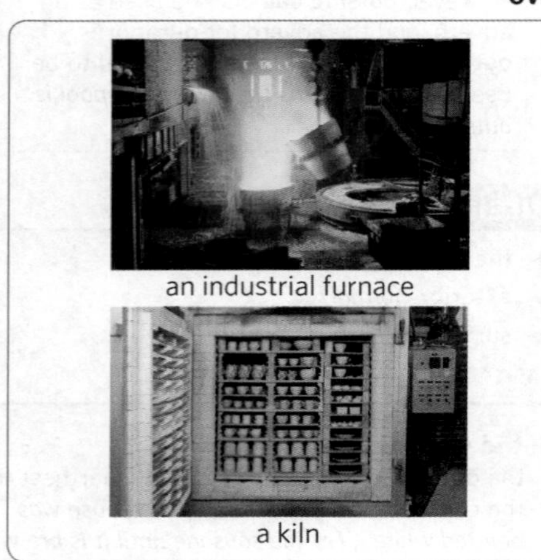
an industrial furnace

a kiln

over *preposition, adverb* → see Function Word **above**, **across**, **again**, **during**

overseas *adverb* → see **abroad**

overweight *adjective* → see **fat**, Topic **Describing People's Looks**

owe /oʊ/ *verb*

- ► owe
- ► be in debt
- ► be overdrawn

owe
to have to give money back to someone because you borrowed it from him or her: *How much do I owe you for the movie ticket?* | *Janet **owes** a lot of money **to** her credit card company.*

be in debt
to owe a lot of money, and often to have difficulty paying it back: *Sean was $50,000 in debt when he graduated from college.*

be overdrawn
to owe money to your bank because you have spent more than you had in your bank account: *I paid some bills before I got my paycheck, and now I'm overdrawn.*

own¹ /oʊn/ *verb*

- ► own
- ► have
- ► possess (*formal*)
- ► belong to

own
if you own something, it is legally your property. You use **own** especially about large things such as houses or cars: *Does your family own your house, or do you rent it?* | *You have to ask the farmer who owns the land if you want to hunt there.*

have
if you have something, you own it and it is available for you to use. You use **have** especially about smaller things that most people own: *What kind of bike do you have?* | *I have some extra pens if anyone needs one.*

possess (*formal*)
to own or have something. **Possess** is often used in legal language to talk about having or owning illegal things, or to talk about someone who does not own something that most people own: *The country is believed to possess nuclear weapons.* | *They never watch TV – they don't even possess one!*

belong to
if something belongs to you, it is yours and not someone else's: *Do you know who this jacket belongs to? I found it after the party.*
→ see **possession** for words meaning "something that you own"

own² *adjective* → see **personal**

owner /ˈoʊnɚ/ *noun*

- ► **owner**
- ► **homeowner**
- ► **landlord**
- ► **landlady**
- ► **proprietor** (*formal*)

owner
someone who owns something: ***The owner of the house wants to paint it white. | Small business owners say the new tax will hurt profits.***

homeowner
someone who owns his or her house. **Homeowner** sounds a little formal and is used especially in reports and contracts: ***When you are a homeowner, you are responsible for all the repairs on your house.***

→ In everyday English you are more likely to talk about a person who **owns** his or her home: ***Do you own your home, or do you rent?***

landlord
someone who owns a house or apartment that someone else rents: ***I have to give the landlord the rent check by the first day of the month.***

landlady
a woman who owns a house or apartment that someone else rents: ***Whenever there's a problem with the apartment, we call the landlady and she takes care of it.***

proprietor (*formal*)
an owner of a business: ***Because he is the proprietor of the only grocery store in town, Mr. Harris knows everyone.***

oxygen *noun* → see **air**

Pp

pack /pæk/ *verb*

- pack
- load
- fill
- jam
- cram

pack *also* **pack up**
to put things into boxes or bags so that you can take them somewhere: *We're going on vacation tomorrow, so I need to pack tonight.* | *Help me pack up these dishes. I'm going to take them to Linda's garage sale.*

load *also* **load up**
to put a lot of something inside a vehicle or container, especially so that you can do something with it or take it somewhere: *Help me load the dishwasher.* | *The car was* ***loaded up with*** *our camping equipment.*

fill *also* **fill up**
to put something in a container or space so that it becomes full: *We* ***filled*** *the baskets* ***with*** *cookies, nuts, and candy.* | *It is going to be a long trip, so fill up the gas tank.*

jam
to push things into a small space using a lot of force so that they do not move: *She* ***jammed*** *the suitcases* ***into*** *the trunk of the car.*

cram
to force a lot of things into a small space: *She* ***crammed*** *the boxes* ***in*** *the closet and closed the door.*
→ see **group**, **package**

package /'pækɪdʒ/ *noun*

- package
- pack
- packet

package
a box or bag that holds food or other things so that they can be sold: *He took out a package of chicken breasts from the freezer.* | *The package held 250 paper napkins.*
→ A **package** can also be something that you have wrapped in paper, or put in a box or bag so that you can mail it: *You got a package in the mail today. What did you order?*

pack
a small box or paper bag that you buy a set of things in: *He pulled a* ***pack of*** *gum out of his pocket and offered me a piece.*

packet
a small paper or plastic container like an envelope, used for holding liquid or small things: *Ask for a* ***packet of*** *ketchup with the fries.*
→ see **box**[1]

packed *adjective* → see **full**

paddle /'pædl/ *noun*

- paddle
- oar

paddle
a short pole with a wide flat end, that you use to move a small boat across water. **Paddles** are used especially with canoes, kayaks, or rubber boats: *We pushed the canoe away from the dock using the paddles.*

oar
a long pole with a wide flat end, used for rowing a boat and usually used in pairs: *Use both oars with the same force, or the boat will go in circles.*

page *noun* → see **sheet**

pain /peɪn/ *noun*

- pain
- ache
- soreness
- tenderness
- discomfort (*formal*)
- suffering
- agony

pain
the feeling you have when part of your body hurts: *She felt a sharp pain in her leg and was afraid she had broken it.* | *After the surgery, I was* ***in*** *a lot of* ***pain*** *for a few days.*

ache
pain that continues without stopping, especially one that is not very bad. **Ache** is usually used in words such as **headache**, **toothache**, **backache**, and **stomachache**: *Josh had a dull ache in his back from moving boxes all day.*

soreness
pain in a part of your body that you have used too much or that is infected: *Jordan was complaining about soreness in his knees after the race.*

tenderness
pain that you feel in a part of your body when it

is touched, because it is injured or infected: *The tenderness will go away as the wound heals.*

discomfort (*formal*)
slight painful or unpleasant feelings in your body: *Women who are seven or eight months pregnant often suffer discomfort that prevents them from sleeping.*

suffering
a long period of mental or physical pain that does not go away: *When an animal is so sick that it cannot get better, it is best to let it die and end its suffering.*

agony
extremely bad pain: *She screamed out* ***in agony*** *as the knife cut into her skin.*
→ see **suffer**

painful /ˈpeɪnfəl/ *adjective*

1 feeling pain
- ► **painful**
- ► **sore**
- ► **tender**
- ► **stiff**

2 causing pain
- ► **painful**
- ► **agonizing**
- ► **excruciating** (*formal*)

1 feeling pain

painful
if a part of your body is painful, it hurts: *I'd love to come on the hike, but my leg is still painful.* | *The doctor gave her exercises for her painful joints.*

sore
if a part of your body is sore, it is painful because you have used it too much or because it is infected: *My throat is really sore. I think I'm catching a cold.* | *My muscles were sore after working out yesterday.*

tender
if a part of your body is tender, it is painful when you touch it, because it is injured or infected: *Your arm may be tender for a few days after the injection.*

stiff
if a part of your body is stiff, your muscles or joints hurt and it is difficult to move: *I've got a stiff neck from trying to sleep on the bus.*

2 causing pain

painful
making part of your body hurt: *She was worried that getting her tooth pulled would be painful.* | *Grandpa finds it painful to sit up, so he lies down most of the time.*

agonizing
extremely painful and making you suffer: *Burns can cause agonizing pain, so strong pain medicine is used.*

excruciating (*formal*)
so painful that you can barely think or do anything: *He nearly passed out from the excruciating pain in his kidneys.*
→ see **upsetting** for **painful** meaning "making someone very sad"

ADVERBS

You can make the adjectives **painful**, **agonizing**, and **excruciating** into adverbs by using an **-ly** ending: *His leg ached painfully.* | *I kept running, even though I was gasping agonizingly for breath.*

P

painting *noun* → see **art**, **picture[1]**

pair /per/ *noun*

1 two things
- ► **pair**
- ► **a couple**

2 two people
- ► **pair**
- ► **couple**
- ► **twins**
- ► **duo**

1 two things

pair
two things of the same type that are used together: *I need to buy a new* ***pair of*** *shoes for the wedding.* | *Do you have a* ***pair of*** *gloves I could borrow?*
→ A **pair** of things can also be something made of two similar parts that are joined together: *Could you hand me that pair of scissors?* | *a pair of pants*

a couple
two things or people of the same type: *Do you have any stamps? I just need a couple.*
→ People sometimes use **a couple** to mean a small number, but more than two. It can sometimes be difficult to be sure whether someone means two or more than two: *There were only a couple of other people there.*
→ see **group** (**2**), Function Word **few**

2 two people

pair
two people who do something together or who are often seen together: *The students often work*

in pairs or groups of three. | *They are an unusual pair: she is very tall, and he is very short.*

couple (AWL)
two people who are married or who have a romantic relationship: *It was mostly married couples at the party, but there were a few single people.*

twins
two children who were born on the same day to the same mother: *George and Gerald are identical twins – they look exactly alike.*

duo
two people who do something together: *Deven and Juan perform together as a comedy duo.*
→ see **group (1)**

pair

The students are working **in pairs**.

palace *noun* → see **castle**

pale *adjective* → see **light²**

pan /pæn/ *noun*

- ► pan
- ► pot
- ► dish

pan
a round metal container with low sides and a handle, that you cook food in: *Mom made scrambled eggs in the frying pan.* | *You can heat the sauce in a small pan.*
→ A **pan** can also be a flat metal container with low sides for baking: *Pour the cake batter in a pan and place it in the oven.*

pot
a round metal container with high sides that you cook things in: *There was a big* ***pot of*** *soup on the stove.*

dish
a special container used for cooking food in an oven: *Arrange the chicken in the bottom of a baking dish before adding the potatoes and sauce.*
→ A **dish** is also something you eat your food from: *Put the dishes on the table, and get some knives, spoons, and forks for everyone.*
→ see **plate**

pan

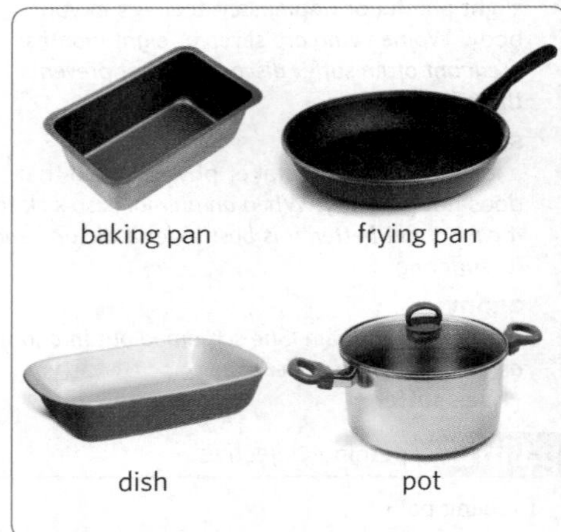

panic¹ *noun* → see **fear¹**

panic² *verb* → see **worry¹**

pants /pænts/ *noun*

- ► pants
- ► slacks
- ► jeans
- ► shorts

pants
a piece of clothing that covers you from your waist to your feet, and that has a separate part for each leg: *Are you planning to wear pants or a skirt to the concert?* | *I gained some weight and now my pants are too tight.*

slacks
pants made out of good material, which are not part of a suit: *Gregor was wearing a clean white shirt and a pair of gray slacks.*

jeans
pants made from a thick rough cloth called denim: *On the weekends, I usually just wear a T-shirt and a pair of jeans.*

shorts
pants that cover only the top part of your legs: *It was so hot that most people were wearing shorts.*

paper *noun* → see **document**, **essay**, Topic **Education**

P

parade /pəˈreɪd/ *noun*

- ► parade
- ► march
- ► procession

parade
a celebration in which musical bands, decorated trucks, and groups of people move in a long line along a street: *This Friday kids will march in the town's Halloween parade, wearing their costumes.* | *We waited on Main Street to watch the parade go by.*

march
an event in which many people walk together in order to protest against or support something: *The annual* ***march for*** *breast cancer raises money for research.*

procession
a line of people or cars moving slowly in the street as part of a ceremony: *The city streets were closed for the president's funeral procession.*

paragraph *noun* → see **part**

pardon *noun* → see **forgiveness**

park /pɑrk/ *noun*

- ► park
- ► playground
- ► field

park
a large area with grass and trees in a town, where people can walk, play games, have a picnic, or relax: *I like to go to the park after school to walk the dog.* | *Let's have a picnic in the park.*

playground
an outdoor area where children can play, often with equipment to play on: *My elementary school had a playground with swings and places to play games.*

field
an area of ground where sports are played: *The fans ran out on the football field when their team won the game.*

part *noun* → *go to pages 458-459*

participate *verb* → see **take part**

particular /pəˈtɪkyələ/ *adjective*

- ► particular
- ► specific
- ► certain

particular
a particular person or thing is the one you are talking about and not any other: *In this particular case, no one was hurt, but the situation is still dangerous.* | *Is there a particular type of food you would like to eat tonight?*

specific (AWL)
one particular person or thing, not people or things in general: *Do you need to travel on a specific day, or can you go any time?*

certain
used to talk about a particular person or thing, without saying exactly which one: *There are certain things I don't want to talk to my mother about.*
→ see **special**

particularly *adverb* → see **especially**

partner /ˈpɑrtnə/ *noun*

- ► partner
- ► coworker
- ► colleague
- ► associate
- ► accomplice

partner (AWL)
someone with whom you own a business: *I can't make any decisions about the store without talking to my business partner.* | *Donna is a partner in a successful law firm, so she makes a lot of money.*

coworker
someone who works with you in the same office or organization: *Some of my coworkers and I are going out for dinner after work on Wednesday.*

colleague (AWL)
colleague means the same as **coworker** but sounds more formal. You use **colleague** especially about people you work with in a profession, for example teachers or doctors: *She found out that her male colleagues were earning more money for the same job.*

associate
someone with whom you work or have a business relationship. **Associate** is more formal than **coworker**: *Goodman and his associates worked closely together to produce the report.*

accomplice
someone who works with a criminal to help do something wrong: *Police believe the murderer must have had an accomplice – he could not have done it on his own.*
→ see **husband**, **wife**, Topic **Relationships and Marriage**

part-time *adjective, adverb* → see Topic **Jobs and Work**

P

part /pɑrt/ *noun*

1 a part of a thing or area
- ► part
- ► piece
- ► section
- ► component
- ► portion (*formal*)
- ► segment (*formal*)

2 a part of a piece of writing, story, movie, or piece of music
- ► part
- ► section
- ► chapter
- ► paragraph
- ► scene
- ► episode
- ► excerpt
- ► passage
- ► clip

3 a part of a process
- ► part
- ► step
- ► stage
- ► phase

4 part of a total amount or number
- ► part
- ► portion (*formal*)
- ► fraction
- ► percentage
- ► proportion

5 a part of a situation, activity, or experience
- ► part
- ► aspect (*formal*)
- ► factor (*formal*)
- ► element (*formal*)
- ► component (*formal*)

1 a part of a thing or area

part
an area of something, but not the whole thing: *Only the top part of the submarine was sticking out of the water.* | *In parts of Canada, French is the main language.*
→ A **part** is also one of the pieces that a machine is made of: *They had to order a part in order to fix the car's engine.*

piece
a part of an object that can be separated from or joined with other parts: *One of the pieces of the puzzle was missing.* | *Do you want a piece of pie?*

section (AWL)
a part of something that is clearly different and separate from other parts: *Restaurants used to have smoking sections, but now people have to go outside to smoke.*

component (AWL)
a part of a machine: *The company's electronic components are used in computers.*

portion (AWL) (*formal*)
a part of something larger, especially a part that is different from the other parts: *She did not do very well on the written portion of the exam.*

segment (*formal*)
one part of something that is divided into clearly separate parts: *An ant's body is divided into three distinct segments.*

2 a part of a piece of writing, story, movie, or piece of music

part
some of a piece of writing, a story, a movie, or a piece of music, but not the whole thing: *You should add more detail to this part of your essay.* | *The first part of the movie was boring, but the rest was great!*

section (AWL)
one of the main separate parts of a piece of writing or speech: *The history test has two sections: true/false questions and multiple choice.*

chapter (AWL)
one of many separate parts that a book is divided into: *There are ten chapters in the book, and I'm reading chapter five now.*

paragraph (AWL)
a part of a piece of writing that contains several sentences, starts on a new line, and deals with one idea: *The last paragraph of an essay is usually a summary of your main points.*

scene
a short part of a play or movie, during which the events happen in the same place: *The car chase is the best scene in the movie.*

episode
a television show that is one of a series of shows that tell a story, usually shown over a period of weeks or months: *What happened on last night's episode of the show?*

excerpt
a short part that you take from a longer piece of writing, often used as an example of something: *The following excerpt is from one of my students' essays.*

passage
a short piece of writing or music, that is taken from a longer piece, and is often used as an example of something. You usually use **passage**

about parts from famous works of literature or music: *The book includes passages from the Bible, the Koran, and other holy books.*

clip
a short part of a movie or other recording that is used in another movie or television program: *During the interview, they showed several clips from Harrison Ford's old movies.*
→ see **quotation**

3 a part of a process

part
one of the periods of time in a process, activity, or event: *She spent the early part of her life in Alaska.* | *Planning the trip was the easy part. Getting my parents to agree was much harder.*

step
one of the parts of a process that you must do in a particular order: *The first step is to make a list of everything you need.* | *Step one: Boil the water in a large pot. Step two: Add the pasta to the water. Step three: Boil the pasta for eight minutes. Step four: Drain the water from the pasta.*

stage
one of several steps of a long process, which happen one after the other: *At this stage, Aaron should be reading better than he is.*

phase AWL
one of the clearly different stages in the development or growth of something. You use **phase** especially about scientific processes, or about processes that have been very carefully planned: *There are three phases in the life cycle of a butterfly.*

4 part of a total amount or number

part
some of a total amount, but not all of it: *Part of the money will be used to repair the school, and the rest will be used to hire new teachers.* | *The official unemployment rate is only part of the total number of people looking for work.*
→ GRAMMAR: When used with this meaning, **part** does not usually come after "a." Don't say: ~~*A part of the money will be used to repair the school.*~~

portion AWL *(formal)*
portion means the same as **part**: *Sam's portion of the rent is smaller than his roommate's because his room is smaller.*

fraction
a very small part of a total amount: *Luckily, the disease affects only a small fraction of the population.*

percentage AWL
a part of an amount or number, that you express as part of 100: *The percentage of students who passed the test went up this year, but it is still only 75%.*

proportion AWL
an amount or quantity that is part of a whole, used when you are talking about the size of that part compared to the total amount: *Poorer families spend a higher proportion of their income on food than richer families do.*

5 a part of a situation, activity, or experience

part
something that, when it is together with other things, forms a whole activity, situation, or experience: *Part of the problem is that we don't have enough time.* | *The trip was great. The best part was visiting the Grand Canyon.*

aspect AWL *(formal)*
one of the most important parts of something such as a situation, problem, or activity: *His illness affects every **aspect of** his life – his work, his family life, and his leisure time.* | *Several **aspects of** our language program will have to change because of the budget cuts.*

factor AWL *(formal)*
one of many things that affect a situation. A **factor** can be important or not very important: *The weather could be an important **factor in** tomorrow's game – if it snows, our team will have the advantage.*

element AWL *(formal)*
a basic or important part of a situation, activity, or experience: *Love is an important **element in** the mother-child relationship, but so is power.*
→ In phrases such as "an element of surprise/truth/risk/doubt," **element** means a small but important part: *When you watch the movie the second time, the element of surprise at the end is gone.*

component AWL *(formal)*
one of the several parts that make up a whole situation, system, activity, or experience: *Exercise is an important component of a healthy lifestyle.*
→ see **take part**

Online Thesaurus

Go to **www.longmandictionariesusa.com**
→ ***Longman Thesaurus of American English*** – with pronunciation of all the words
→ **Study Center** – interactive practice to help you learn synonyms, Academic Words, and Topic Vocabulary

party /ˈpɑrti/ *noun*

- ► party
- ► celebration
- ► bash (*informal*)
- ► reunion
- ► shower
- ► reception
- ► get-together (*informal*)
- ► gathering

party
an occasion when people enjoy themselves by eating, drinking, playing games, or dancing together, for example when it is someone's birthday: *Can you come to my birthday party on Sunday? | There were lots of interesting people at the party, and the music was great.*

celebration
a party, meal, or event that you have for a special occasion: *The fireworks are part of the town's 4th of July celebration.*

bash (*informal*)
a big party: *The kids are having a big bash to celebrate the end of the school year.*

reunion
a party for people who have not met for a long time, often with food, dancing, and other activities. Schools and families usually have **reunions**: *She is going to her high school reunion in Dallas this weekend.*

shower
a party at which you give presents to a woman who is going to get married or have a baby: *We're having a shower for Sue a week from Saturday. She is having her baby next month.*

reception
a large formal party to celebrate something or to welcome someone. **Receptions** usually follow an event such as a wedding or speech: *The reception will immediately follow the wedding ceremony.*

get-together (*informal*)
a small party, usually without decorations, dancing, or other party activities: *There's a neighborhood get-together at the Martins' house tomorrow night at eight.*

gathering
an occasion when a group of people meet together to have fun, especially a group of family or friends: *Every summer we have a family gathering at the lake.*
→ see **group** for **party** meaning "a group of people who do something together"

pass[1] /pæs/ *verb*

1 to become a later time
- ► pass
- ► go by
- ► progress (*formal*)
- ► elapse (*formal*)

2 to move past someone
- ► pass
- ► go past
- ► go by

3 to succeed at school
- ► pass
- ► graduate

ANTONYMS → see **fail** (**2**)

4 to officially accept a law or proposal
- ► pass
- ► approve
- ► ratify (*formal*)

1 to become a later time

pass
if time passes, the minutes, hours, etc. happen and it becomes a later time: *The days passed slowly as he waited for her letter. | As the years passed, Hayley became more self-confident.*

go by
go by means the same as **pass** but sounds a little less formal: *This year went by so quickly. I can't believe it's December already.*

progress (*formal*)
if time or an event progresses, time passes, or the event happens over a period of time: *As the football season progressed, the team began to win a few games.*

elapse (*formal*)
elapse means the same as **pass** but sounds formal or literary: *Three days had elapsed before anyone noticed the young man was missing.*

2 to move past someone

pass
to move past someone or something: *Mark always says hello when he passes me in the hall. | After you pass the park, our house is the second one on the right.*

go past *also* **run/walk/drive past**
go/run/walk etc. past mean the same as **pass** but are slightly less formal. You can also use them to be more specific about how someone is moving: *If you're going past the library on your way home, could you give me a ride? | Lisa ran past me so fast I thought someone must be chasing her.*

go by *also* **run/walk/drive by**
go by means the same as **go past**: *I walk by Elena's house every day on my way to school.* | *We lay on our backs and watched the clouds float by.*

3 to succeed at school

pass
to succeed in a test or class: *You need to get at least 60% of the answers right to pass the test.* | *I didn't pass algebra, so I have to take it again next semester.*

graduate
to succeed in completing your studies at a school, college, or university so that you get a diploma or degree: *Are you going to go to college after you graduate from high school?*

4 to officially accept a law or proposal

pass
to officially accept a law or idea, especially by voting: *The House of Representatives passed the bill.*

approve
to officially accept a plan or proposal. **Approve** is very similar in meaning to **pass**, but is a more general word. It can be used for a situation that may or may not involve voting: *Congress voted to approve the President's plans for cutting the arms budget.*

ratify (*formal*)
to make a written agreement official by signing it: *The treaty was ratified by the Senate last year.*

→ see **give** for **pass** meaning "to give someone something by putting it in his or her hand," **spend** for **pass** meaning "to spend time doing something," **throw**[1] for **pass** meaning "to throw a ball in a sport"
→ see **pass around** at **give**
→ see **pass away** at **die**
→ see **pass up** at **miss**
→ see **pass out** at **faint**

pass[2] *noun* → see **license**, **throw**[2], **ticket**

passage *noun* → see **hall**, **part**, **tunnel**

passenger /ˈpæsəndʒɚ/ *noun*

- passenger
- commuter
- traveler

passenger
someone who is traveling in a car, bus, airplane, or boat, but is not driving it: *My car holds me and three passengers.* | *Neither the bus driver nor the passengers were hurt in the accident.*

commuter
someone who travels to work regularly, either driving or as a passenger in a bus, train, etc.: *Every day thousands of commuters come into the city from the suburbs for work.*

traveler
someone who is on a trip from one place to another, especially someone using planes, trains, buses, or cars: *Two days after the storm, the airport was still full of tired travelers.*

passing *noun* → see **death**

passive /ˈpæsɪv/ *adjective*

- passive
- apathetic
- docile

passive AWL
a passive person lets things happen to him or her without getting involved or trying to change things: *You're being too passive. You should just tell her you don't want to go.* | *Students are expected to take an active part in discussions, not just be passive listeners.*

apathetic
not caring about something, and not willing to try to change or improve things: *Many citizens have become apathetic and don't even vote in elections.*

docile
quiet and easy to control: *She was extremely docile and did everything her husband said without complaining.*

ADVERBS
You can make the adjectives that mean **passive** into adverbs by using an **-ly** ending: *They did not passively accept his decision; they argued and tried to persuade him to change it.* | *The children followed docilely behind their mother.*

past[1] /pæst/ *noun*

- the past
- the old days (*informal*)
- history

ANTONYMS → see **future (1)**

the past
the time that existed before the present: *The events of the past influence what happens in the future.*

the old days (*informal*)
a long time ago when things were different from

how they are now: *In the old days, we listened to the radio because there wasn't any TV.*

history
all the things that happened in the past in a place: *This book is about the history of India.*
→ see **history**

past² /pæst/ *adjective*

- ► past
- ► last
- ► previous
- ► preceding (*formal*)

ANTONYMS → see **next¹**

past
the past week, year, few days, etc. is the period of time up until now: *The past few months have been very difficult for our family.*
→ GRAMMAR: Don't say: ~~*Past week has been tiring*~~. Say: *The past week has been tiring.*
→ Don't use **past** when talking about the period of time before the present one. Don't say: ~~*I saw him the past week*~~. Say: *I saw him last week.*

last
relating to the most recent time before the present time: *Last night we went to the movies.* | *The last time I saw you, you were only eight years old.*
→ GRAMMAR: Don't say: ~~*It happened in last week/month/year*~~. Say: *It happened last week/month/year.*

previous (AWL)
the previous time, event, or thing is the one before the one you are talking about now. **Previous** sounds more formal than **last**: *The dog's previous owner did not take good care of it.* | *The economic problems we are having now are worse than the previous troubles we had.*

preceding (AWL) (*formal*)
coming before the time you have just mentioned, or coming before the part of the piece of writing that you are reading now: *After you have read the last paragraph, read through the preceding paragraphs again.*
→ Don't use **preceding** about activities or relationships. Don't say: ~~*She had two children from her preceding marriage*~~. Say: *She had two children from her previous marriage.*
→ see **last¹**

paste *verb* → see **stick¹**

pastime *noun* → see **hobby**

pastor *noun* → see **minister**

pat *verb* → see **touch**

path /pæθ/ *noun*

- ► path
- ► sidewalk
- ► trail

path
a long narrow area on the ground that is made for people to walk along: *A path took us down to the river.* | *I walked along a path through the garden.*

sidewalk
a hard path built along the side of a street for people to walk on: *Walk **on the sidewalk**, not in the street, so you don't get hit by a car.*

trail
a path that you walk on through a forest or in the mountains: *The trail leads up to the top of the mountain.*

patience /ˈpeɪʃəns/ *noun*

- ► patience
- ► self-control
- ► tolerance

patience
the ability to deal with a problem or wait for something without becoming angry or upset: *Teachers need a lot of patience, because dealing with children is not always easy.* | *I finally lost my patience and told Ken to shut up.*

self-control
the ability to control your behavior even when you are angry, excited, or upset: *Young children often have problems with self-control, and cannot stop talking with their friends in the classroom.*

tolerance
willingness to let people do, say, or believe what they want without criticizing or punishing them, even when you do not agree with them: *For society to work, we all need to show **tolerance for** different religions and lifestyles.*
→ see **tolerance**

patient¹ /ˈpeɪʃənt/ *adjective*

- ► patient
- ► calm
- ► tolerant

patient
able to deal with a problem or wait for something without getting angry or upset: *I'm almost finished – just be patient.* | *Good teachers are very patient.*

calm
relaxed and quiet, not angry or upset: *How can you be so calm when everyone else is yelling?*

tolerant
willing to let other people do, say, or believe what they want without getting angry and criticizing or punishing them, even when you do not agree with them: *You should be more **tolerant** of other people's mistakes – nobody is perfect, you know.*
→ see **tolerant**, Topic **Describing People's Character**

ADVERBS
You can make the adjectives that mean **patient** into adverbs by using an **-ly** ending: *We waited patiently for her to finish.* | *I breathed deeply and began to think more calmly.*

patient² /ˈpeɪʃənt/ *noun*

- ► patient
- ► sufferer
- ► case
- ► invalid

patient
someone who is getting medical treatment from a doctor or hospital: *The doctor is with a patient right now. Can he call you back?* | *Dr. Lan mainly treats patients with cancer.*

sufferer
someone who has a particular disease or medical condition: *The drugs have been successful with AIDS sufferers.*

case
an example of a disease, or a person who has this disease: *The hospital has treated 13 cases of measles this year.*

invalid
someone who is sick, injured, or old and needs other people to do things for him or her: *Lucy's grandfather is an invalid and has a nurse who lives with him.*

patriot *noun* → see **citizen**

patriotic /ˌpeɪtriˈɑtɪk/ *adjective*

- ► patriotic
- ► nationalistic

patriotic
having or showing a lot of love for your country: *Kurt has always been very patriotic. I'm not surprised he joined the army.* | *The band played patriotic songs at the 4th of July celebrations.*

nationalistic
believing that your country is very good, or that it is better than any other country. **Nationalistic** usually sounds bad, because nationalistic people often do not show respect for people from other countries: *The congressman gave a nationalistic speech against immigrants.*

ADVERBS
You can make the adjectives that mean **patriotic** into adverbs by using an **-ly** ending: *He was willing to patriotically serve his country.*

patronizing /ˈpeɪtrəˌnaɪzɪŋ/ *adjective*

- ► patronizing
- ► condescending
- ► superior
- ► snobbish

patronizing
a patronizing person treats you as though you are less important or less intelligent than he or she is: *"You did a great job boiling the water." "Stop being so patronizing."* | *My boss has a patronizing attitude. He doesn't explain his decisions because he thinks we cannot understand the situation.*

condescending
condescending means the same as **patronizing** but sounds more formal. You usually use **condescending** about people in important positions who treat other people as less important: *The director was so **condescending to** the musicians that some of them quit the band.*

superior
superior means the same as **patronizing**, but you use it when you want to emphasize that someone is behaving as though he or she is better than other people: *"It is simple, really," she said in a superior tone of voice.*

snobbish *also* **snobby**
showing that you think you are better than other people because you are richer or know more: *Megan is very snobbish and always makes fun of the other girls' clothes.* | *The health club was full of snobby rich kids.*
→ see **proud** (**2**) for words meaning "thinking you are better than other people," **talk¹** (**2**) for the verb **patronize**

P

ADVERBS

You can make the adjectives **patronizing**, **condescending**, and **snobbish** into adverbs by using an **-ly** ending: *"You did that very well," she said patronizingly, as though she were much older than I.* | *He went on to say condescendingly that her work was surprisingly good for a woman.*

pattern /ˈpætə-n/ *noun*

- ► pattern
- ► design
- ► markings
- ► motif (*formal*)

P

pattern
an arrangement of shapes, lines, and colors on the surface of something: *Mom chose a flower pattern for the bathroom wallpaper.* | *Each zebra is covered with a unique pattern of black and white stripes.*

design (AWL)
a pattern used for decorating something, especially cloth or paper: *The dress has a floral design on the skirt.*

markings
the natural patterns on the skin, fur, or feathers of animals or birds: *The bird can be recognized by its red and yellow markings.*

motif (*formal*)
a single shape that is repeated to form a pattern: *Islamic art frequently uses the star motif.*
→ see **order**[1]

pause[1] /pɔz/ *verb*

- ► pause
- ► stop
- ► break off
- ► hesitate

pause
to wait for a short time before you continue speaking or doing something. **Pause** is used especially in writing. In everyday English, people usually say **stop**: *She* ***paused for*** *breath and then continued to speak.* | *Larry paused halfway up the stairs to see if Ann was behind him.*

stop
to pause while you are doing something or going somewhere in order to do something else: *Let's stop at the next restaurant and get something to eat.*

break off
to suddenly stop talking: *Ed broke off in the middle of his story to greet the guest who had just arrived.*

hesitate
to wait for a moment before you do or say something, because you are thinking about what to do or say: *Ping hesitated for a moment before he knocked on the door.*
→ see **delay**[2], **stop**[1]

pause[2] /pɔz/ *noun*

- ► pause
- ► break
- ► intermission
- ► interruption
- ► lull
- ► lapse (*formal*)

pause
a short time when someone or something stops doing something and then starts again: *There was a pause, after which he asked me if I wanted to get something to eat.* | *We had a bad phone connection and there were long* ***pauses in*** *the conversation.*

break
a period of time when something stops happening, or you stop doing something before you start again. **Break** is more informal than **pause**: *There was a little* ***break in*** *the rain, so the kids went outside.* | *We took a* ***break from*** *studying and went out for coffee.*

intermission
a break in the middle of a play or concert, when the performance stops before starting again a short time later: *There will be a 15-minute intermission between the first and second act.*

interruption
a time when someone makes someone else stop what they are saying or doing for a short time. An **interruption** is something that you do not want to happen: *I can't concentrate on my homework with all the noise and interruptions at home.*

lull
a short period when there is less activity or noise than usual: *There was a* ***lull in*** *the fighting for about an hour, but the soldiers have started firing again.*

lapse (*formal*)
the period of time when you do not do something, between two times when you do it: *There was a* ***lapse of*** *ten years before they met again.*
→ see **delay**[1]

pay[1] /peɪ/ *verb*

- ► pay
- ► spend
- ► repay
- ► refund
- ► tip
- ► settle
- ► reimburse (*formal*)
- ► compensate (*formal*)
- ► finance

pay
to give money to someone when you buy something or when the person has done work for you: *How much does Mrs. Lee* ***pay*** *you* ***to*** *mow her yard?* | *I got the jeans on sale and only* ***paid*** *$20* ***for*** *them.*

spend
to use your money to buy or pay for something: *You* ***spend*** *too much money* ***on*** *fast food.*

repay *also* **pay back**
to give money back to someone you have borrowed it from. **Repay** sounds more formal than **pay back**: *Hong promised to repay me the money as soon as she got her paycheck.* | *Mom gave me some money for clothes, but she says I have to pay her back.*

refund
if a business refunds a customer's money, the business gives back the money the customer paid for something, especially because the customer is not satisfied with it: *I took the phone back because it wouldn't work, and the store refunded my money.*

tip
to give an additional amount of money to someone who has done a job for you, as a way of thanking him or her: *I usually tip waiters and waitresses 15% of the bill or more.*

settle
if you settle a bill, account, or debt, you pay all the money that you owe: *Luis settled the bill at the front desk of the hotel before he left.*

reimburse (*formal*)
to give someone the amount of money he or she paid to someone else. You often use **reimburse** when an employer gives an employee money for something that the employee has bought while he or she is working: *Will the company* ***reimburse*** *you* ***for*** *the cost of meals on your business trip?*

compensate (AWL) (*formal*)
to pay someone money because he or she has been injured or lost something important, or because his or her property has been damaged: *The state will compensate teachers who are hurt while doing their job.*

finance (AWL)
to provide the money needed to pay for something important or expensive. You use **finance** especially when you are talking or writing about business or economics: *The government uses money from taxes to finance education.*

pay[2] /peɪ/ *noun*

- ► pay
- ► wage
- ► salary
- ► income
- ► earnings (*formal*)
- ► compensation (*formal*)
- ► pension
- ► payment
- ► tip

pay
money that someone gives you for work you have done: *Taxes are taken out of your pay every week.* | *If they want us to work without pay, I'm not going to do it.*

wage *also* **wages**
the money that you get each day, week, or month for doing a job, based on the number of hours that you work. **Wage** is used especially in official documents and in news reports about business: *The minimum wage in California is $8 per hour, but that's not enough to support a family on.* | *Martin sends some of his wages to his family in Guatemala every week.*

salary
money that you get regularly as payment for the job you do. You usually talk about someone's **salary** by saying how much he or she earns each year, but part of the salary is paid each month: *The average salary for a school teacher in this district is around $42,000.*

income
all of the money that you get in a particular period of time, for example the pay you get for working or the profit from investments: *People with higher incomes generally pay more taxes.*

earnings (*formal*)
all the money that you earn by working. **Earnings** is used in official documents and news reports about business: *Many working mothers spend a large part of their earnings on childcare.*

compensation (AWL) (*formal*)
the money that someone is paid for doing his or her job. **Compensation** is used especially in

official and legal language: *The total compensation for the new job, including health insurance, is a little more than he was making at his last job.*

→ You also use **compensation** to talk about the money someone is paid when something bad has happened to him or her, for example an injury: *Should criminals have to pay compensation to their victims?*

pension
the money that a company pays regularly to someone who used to work for the company: *She gets a pension because she worked for the city for 40 years before she retired.*

payment
an amount of money that someone pays for something. Some **payments** are made only once, but others may be made in smaller amounts until they are completely paid: *Marie received a **payment of** $150 when her story was printed in the magazine.* | *I made a $300 car payment every month for three years.*

tip
an additional amount of money that you give to someone who has done a job for you, as a way of thanking him or her: *I left a tip for the waitress on the table.*

→ see Topic **Jobs and Work**

SYNONYM CHECK

Salary or wages?

You talk about a **salary** by saying how much a person earns each year: *His salary is $65,000 per year.* If you are on a **salary**, the amount you are paid each month does not depend on how many hours you have worked.

Your **wage** is the amount you earn for each hour you work. You usually talk about someone's **wages** by saying how much a person earns each hour, week, or month: *Hourly wages have risen by 2%.*

pay attention /ˌpeɪ əˈtenʃən/ *verb phrase*

- ► pay attention
- ► concentrate
- ► focus
- ► keep your mind on something (*informal*)
- ► be absorbed in
- ► be engrossed in

pay attention
to listen to or watch something or someone carefully so that you know what to do, what is happening, or what someone is saying: *Kayla always pays attention in class – that's why she is doing so well.* | *The TV was on, but no one was really **paying attention to** it.*

concentrate (AWL)
to pay attention and think carefully about something without stopping for a period of time, without noticing or thinking about other things: *To do the job well, you must be able to concentrate for long periods of time.* | *I was tired, but I tried to **concentrate on** the road ahead.*

focus (AWL)
to pay careful attention to one thing, and not to other things: *You need to **focus on** getting better grades, and not play so many sports.*

keep your mind on something (*informal*)
to continue paying attention to something, even if you want to think about something else: *It is hard to keep your mind on school when summer vacation is about to start.*

be absorbed in
to be so interested in something that you pay attention only to it and not to other things: *The book has a really good story and I was completely absorbed in it.*

be engrossed in
be engrossed in means the same thing as **be absorbed in** but it is a little more formal: *He was so engrossed in watching the game on TV that he did not hear me go out.*

→ see **listen**

payment /ˈpeɪmənt/ *noun*

- ► payment
- ► deposit
- ► down payment
- ► installment
- ► subscription

payment
an amount of money that you pay for something, often one that you pay each month until a final amount is reached: *When is your next credit card payment due?* | *My sister had to sell her car because she couldn't afford the monthly car payment anymore.*

deposit
a small first payment for something you want to rent or use. The **deposit** is either used as part of the whole amount or it is given back to you if the thing you are renting is not damaged: *The hotel asks for a $50 deposit to reserve a room.*

down payment
the first payment for something you want to own that costs a lot, for example a house or car. You pay a **down payment** when you are going to pay the rest of the money later: *We've been saving to make a **down payment** on a new house.*

installment
one of a series of payments that you make regularly until you have paid all the money you owe: *Ron is paying back the loan in monthly installments of $250.*

subscription
an amount of money you pay, usually once a year, to get a magazine, newspaper, or service: *How much is a **subscription to** the "New York Times"?*

→ see **pay²**

PC *noun* → see Topic **Computers and the Internet**

peace /pis/ *noun*

1 when there is no fighting or violence
- peace
- ceasefire
- truce
- order
- calm
- harmony

ANTONYMS → see **war**

2 a time in which everything feels quiet, relaxed, and simple
- peace
- quiet
- calm
- tranquility (*formal*)

1 when there is no fighting or violence

peace
a time when there is no war or fighting: *There has been peace in the region since the war ended six years ago. | People of different religions have lived here together **in peace*** (=without fighting) *for centuries.*

ceasefire *also* **cease-fire**
a time during a war when the enemies agree to stop fighting for a time, especially so that they can discuss making peace: *Military leaders agreed to a temporary ceasefire before the peace talks.*

truce
truce means the same as **ceasefire**, but you can also use it about the time when people agree to stop arguing: *The truce has put an end to three months of fighting between the two armies, at least for now.*

order
a situation in which people obey rules and do not behave violently: *It took the police several days to restore order after the riots began.*

calm
a situation in which there is no violence, fighting, or protest: *The bombing on Sunday ended the brief period of calm in the city.*

harmony
a situation in which people do not fight or argue with each other. You usually use **harmony** about situations that involve arguing or disagreement, but not war or violence: *In the end my father agreed with my mother to keep harmony in the family.*

2 a time in which everything feels quiet, relaxed, and simple

peace
a situation that is calm and quiet, with no interruptions, worry, or excitement: *We go to the cabin on weekends for some peace and quiet. | I'll go now and let you study **in peace.***

quiet
a time or situation in which there is little or no noise: *Damien loved the quiet of the forest.*

calm
a relaxed time when there is no trouble, worry, or excitement. You use **calm** especially to compare a calm situation with a more noisy, difficult, or exciting situation: *A loud scream suddenly broke the late afternoon calm.*

tranquility (*formal*)
the quality of being pleasantly calm, quiet, and peaceful. **Tranquility** is often used in literature or more formal writing: *I feel a deep tranquility when I am walking in the mountains.*

peaceful /ˈpisfəl/ *adjective*

- peaceful
- quiet
- calm
- restful
- tranquil (*formal*)

peaceful
quiet and without any worry or excitement: *Life is more peaceful in the country. | It is very peaceful around the house now that the kids have gone back to school.*

quiet
without a lot of noise: *It was quiet by the lake, with only the sound of the birds to disturb us.*

calm
relaxed and with no worry, excitement, or trouble. You use **calm** especially to compare a calm situation with a more noisy, difficult, or exciting situation: *The city is calm again after three nights of rioting.*

P

restful
peaceful and making you feel relaxed: *I'm looking forward to a restful vacation, just lying on the beach and reading a book.*

tranquil (*formal*)
pleasantly calm, quiet, and peaceful. **Tranquil** is often used in literature or more formal writing: *The hotel is in a tranquil little village in the mountains.*
→ see **calm**[1] **(2)**, **quiet**[1] **(2)**

ADVERBS

You can make the adjectives that mean **peaceful** into adverbs by using an **-ly** ending: *I floated peacefully in the warm ocean water.* | *He sat quietly by himself, reading.*

P

peak *noun* → see **mountain**, **top**[1]

peculiar *adjective* → see **strange**

peel /pil/ *noun*

- peel
- skin
- rind
- zest

peel
the thick outer covering of a fruit such as a banana, orange, or apple. You usually use **peel** when you are talking about taking the covering off the fruit: *She threw the banana peel in the garbage.*

skin
the outer covering of some fruits and vegetables, especially when this covering is thin. For example, you use **skin** about the covering on onions and potatoes: *The skin of the baked potato was nice and crispy.*

rind
the hard outer covering of fruits such as oranges, lemons, or melons, or of vegetables such as squash: *Cut off the rind and slice the melon into cubes.*

zest
the outer layer of the peel of an orange, lemon, or lime, used in cooking: *Add a little lemon zest for flavor.*
→ see **cut**[1]

penalty *noun* → see **punishment**

pension *noun* → see **pay**[2]

people /ˈpipəl/ *noun*

- people
- folks (*informal*)
- the public
- population
- society
- the human race
- humankind
- humanity (*formal*)

people
men, women, and children, thought of as a group: *Most people really liked the movie.* | *People are the same everywhere – they just want a better life for themselves and their families.*
→ **GRAMMAR: People** is a plural noun. Don't say: ~~*Peoples are mean sometimes*~~ or ~~*People is mean sometimes*~~. Say: *People are mean sometimes.*

folks (*informal*)
folks means the same as **people**. **Folks** is not usually used in formal writing, but is sometimes used to show that you are talking about ordinary working people: *Folks in Iowa are proud to be the first to vote in the presidential primary elections.*

the public
all the ordinary people in a place, not people who belong to the government or a particular organization: *The information is available to the public on the website.*

population
all the people who live in a particular area such as a city, state, or country: *In this county, most of the population live on farms.*

society
all the people who live in a country. You use **society** to talk about people as an organized group with a system of laws and ways of behaving: *Society's views on marriage have changed a great deal in the past 50 years.*

the human race
all the people in the world, thought of together as one type of living thing: *Pollution is a threat to the future of the whole human race.*

humankind *also* **mankind**
people in general. You use **humankind** or **mankind** especially when talking about human history or how something affects the way people will develop: *Traveling into space was a great achievement for mankind.*
→ Some people think that the word **mankind** makes women seem unimportant, and choose to use **humankind** instead.

humanity (*formal*)
all people in general. You use **humanity**

especially when you are talking about people's rights and living conditions: *Thirty percent of humanity live in conditions of terrible poverty.*
→ see **person**, **race**[1]

perfect /ˈpɚfɪkt/ *adjective*

1 with no mistakes or problems
- ► perfect
- ► flawless
- ► impeccable (*formal*)

ANTONYMS → see **imperfect**

2 exactly right for something
- ► perfect
- ► ideal

ANTONYMS → see **imperfect**

1 with no mistakes or problems

perfect
if something is perfect, it is so good that it could not be better: *Manuel got a perfect score on the test – he didn't miss a single question.* | *She wore braces and now her teeth are perfect.*

flawless
perfect, with no mistakes or unattractive marks. You use **flawless** about the way someone does something, or about the way an object or someone's skin looks: *Nasrin's English is flawless. How long has she lived in the U.S.?*

impeccable (*formal*)
so good that you cannot find anything wrong. You use **impeccable** about someone's behavior or someone's ability to choose good things: *The food at the restaurant was delicious and the service was impeccable.* | *She has impeccable taste in clothes.*
→ see **clean**[1], Topic **Describing the Condition of Something**

2 exactly right for something

perfect
exactly right or exactly what is needed for something: *This is a* ***perfect*** *tree* ***to*** *build a tree house in.* | *"I'll pick you up around seven." "That's perfect."*

ideal
the best or most appropriate that is possible: *I still need to lose five pounds to reach my ideal weight.* | *Plastic glasses are* ***ideal for*** *an outdoor party, because they won't break.*

GRAMMAR CHECK: perfect

Don't use "very" with **perfect**, **flawless**, **impeccable**, or **ideal**. Don't say: ~~*It was very perfect*~~. Say: *It was absolutely perfect* or *It was just perfect.*

ADVERBS

You can make the adjectives that mean **perfect** into adverbs by using an **-ly** ending: *"I understand perfectly," she said.* | *The skirt fit her perfectly.* | *She played the song flawlessly.* | *Ideally, both parents should help take care of the baby.*

perfectly /ˈpɚfɪktli/ *adverb*

- ► perfectly
- ► flawlessly
- ► impeccably (*formal*)

perfectly
extremely well, without any mistakes or problems: *Nothing went wrong – the plan worked perfectly.* | *The steaks were perfectly cooked: not too red and not too tough.*

flawlessly
without any mistakes at all: *He could still repeat the poem flawlessly from memory, 40 years later.*

impeccably (*formal*)
in a way that you cannot find anything wrong about. You use **impeccably** especially about the way someone is dressed or how he or she looks: *Montgomery was impeccably dressed in a dark blue suit.*

perform /pɚˈfɔrm/ *verb*

1 to do something to entertain people
- ► perform
- ► appear
- ► be in

2 to give or organize a performance of something
- ► perform
- ► put on
- ► stage
- ► present (*formal*)

1 to do something to entertain people

perform
to act in a play, play music, sing, dance, do tricks, tell jokes, or do anything else to entertain people: *Several local bands will perform at the town festival.* | *I always get nervous when I have to perform on stage.*

appear
to perform in a concert, movie, television show, play, or other performance: *Anderson had* ***appeared in*** *a number of movies before becoming famous.*

P

be in
be in means the same as **appear in** and is what most people say in everyday English: *Isn't he the actor who was in the horror movie we saw last week?*
→ see **act¹ (1)**

2 to give or organize a performance of something

perform
to act in a play, play music, sing a song, do a dance, do tricks, or do other similar things to entertain people: *The kids perform two plays each school year.* | *She performed all of my favorite songs at the concert.*

put on
to arrange for a play or concert to happen, or to perform in it: *As kids, we were always putting on plays for our friends in the backyard.*

stage
to arrange for a play or concert to happen: *The play has been staged only twice before.*

present (*formal*)
to arrange for a play, movie, television program, or concert to take place. **Present** is used especially in advertising to show who is organizing a performance: *The Rose Theater Company will present six performances of "A Christmas Carol."*

performance *noun* → see **play²**, **show²**

performer /pə-ˈfɔrmə-/ *noun*

- ► performer
- ► entertainer
- ► artist
- ► actor
- ► singer
- ► musician
- ► star
- ► comedian

performer
someone who acts, plays music, dances, does tricks, or does other similar things to entertain people: *Most performers feel nervous before they go on stage.* | *Magicians and circus performers entertained the crowd.*

entertainer
a performer who does something such as tell jokes or sing for people, for example on stage or on television: *He was one of the most famous entertainers of the 1960s, and had regular shows in New York City and Las Vegas.*

artist
a professional performer, especially a singer, dancer, or actor who is very good or important: *Nashville is home to many country music recording artists.*

actor
someone who performs in plays, movies, or television shows. A female actor can also be called an **actress** but many female actors now prefer **actor**: *I really like the actor who played Gandalf in "The Lord of the Rings."* | *Natalie Portman won the Oscar for Best Actress in 2011.*

singer
a performer who sings: *The singer has just released a new album.*

musician
a performer who plays or sings music: *The group is made up of three musicians who have been performing together for 20 years.*

star
a famous actor or musician: *Lady Gaga is one of today's biggest pop stars.*

comedian *also* **comic**
a performer whose job is to tell jokes and make people laugh: *Robin Williams started out as a comedian and later became an actor.*
→ see **musician**

perfume /ˈpə-fyum/ *noun*

- ► perfume
- ► cologne
- ► fragrance (*formal*)
- ► aftershave

perfume
a liquid with a pleasant smell that women put on their skin: *The perfume she was wearing smelled really good.*

cologne
a liquid with a pleasant smell that men or women put on their skin: *Miguel put a little cologne on his neck before he went out for the evening.*

fragrance *also* **scent** (*formal*)
a perfume or cologne. **Fragrance** and **scent** are used especially in stores and advertisements: *David Beckham has produced a new fragrance for men.*

aftershave *also* **aftershave lotion**
a liquid with a pleasant smell that a man puts on his face after he shaves: *The aftershave stung his freshly shaved face.*
→ see **smell¹**

perhaps *adverb* → see **maybe**

period *noun* → see **class**, **time**, Topic **Education**

permanent /ˈpɚmənənt/ *adjective*

- ► permanent
- ► perpetual (*formal*)
- ► eternal
- ► everlasting
- ► lasting

ANTONYMS → see **temporary**

permanent
continuing for a long time, forever, or for the rest of your life: *The deep cut left a permanent scar on her forehead.* | *Joel had a temporary job, but the company just offered him a permanent position.*

perpetual (*formal*)
continuing forever or for a long time without changing or stopping: *He was searching for a fountain that would give perpetual youth to anyone who drank the water.*

eternal
continuing forever: *Do you believe in eternal life, or do you think we stop existing when we die?*

everlasting
everlasting means the same as **eternal**: *They believe that sinners will suffer everlasting punishment.*

lasting
having an effect for a very long time: *The story my grandmother told me as a child left a lasting impression on me.*
→ see **constant**, **lasting**

ADVERBS

You can make the adjectives that mean **permanent** into adverbs by using an **-ly** ending: *The accident left her permanently scarred.* | *In the winter, the sky is perpetually gloomy.* | *Juan had helped him at a difficult time, and he would be eternally grateful.*

permanently *adverb* → see **always**

permission /pɚˈmɪʃən/ *noun*

- ► permission
- ► consent
- ► authorization
- ► clearance
- ► approval
- ► assent (*formal*)

permission
if you are given permission to do something, someone allows you to do it: *We have to get our parents' **permission to** go on the field trip.* | *Don't come in my room **without** my **permission**, Rachel.*

consent (AWL)
formal permission to do something important, especially something that could affect your rights or safety: *Vera was only 16, but her parents gave their **consent for** her **to** get married.*

authorization
formal permission to do something from someone in authority: *The president needs **authorization from** Congress to declare war.*

clearance
official permission from someone in authority who has checked to make sure something is safe, legal, or likely to be successful: *The plane was given **clearance to** land.* | *His security clearance allows him to read secret documents.*

approval
if someone gives something his or her approval, he or she accepts an idea or plan and gives permission to do it: *I have to get my teacher's **approval of** my topic before I start working on my research paper.*

assent (*formal*)
assent means the same as **approval** but sounds very formal: *All decisions require the assent of all the board members.*
→ see **allow**

permit¹ *noun* → see **license**

permit² *verb* → see **allow**

permitted *adjective* → see **legal**

person /ˈpɚsən/ *noun*

- ► person
- ► individual
- ► human
- ► character
- ► citizen
- ► figure

person
a man, woman, or child: *I was the only person who could speak Spanish.* | *Her son is the most important person in her life.*

individual (AWL)
a person. You use **individual** when you are thinking about each person separately from the group: *Each student in the class needs to be treated as an individual.* | *The coach took a group of talented individuals and built a great team.*

human *also* **human being**
a person, not an animal or machine: *The disease cannot be passed from animals to humans.* | *Computers can do some tasks much quicker than human beings.*

P

character
a person in a book, play, or movie: *In the story, the main character is a 15-year-old girl.*

citizen
someone who lives in a particular town, state, or country and has legal rights there, such as the right to vote and live there permanently: *Noriko is a U.S. citizen, but her parents are originally from Japan.*

figure
someone who is important or famous in some way: *Muhammad Ali was one of the great sports figures of the 20th century.*
→ see **people**

P

personal /ˈpɚsənəl/ *adjective*

1 belonging to you
- personal
- own
- subjective

2 done or experienced yourself
- personal
- direct
- first-hand

1 belonging to you

personal
personal things or opinions belong to you and not other people: *Please make sure you take all your personal belongings with you when you leave the plane.* | *My personal opinion is that we need to reduce the amount of pollution from cars.*

own
belonging to you: *You can use your own tennis racket, or you can rent one for $5.* | *I have my own opinion about what should be done.*
→ **GRAMMAR: Own** is always used after a word such as "my" or "your." Say: *I have my own room.* You can also use the phrase **of my/your/his etc. own**: *I wanted a room of my own.*

subjective
relating to your feelings or opinions, and not based on facts: *Art is very subjective – some people will like a painting, but other people will hate it.*

2 done or experienced yourself

personal
done or experienced yourself, instead of asking someone else to do it or hearing about it: *I know from personal experience that being bullied can affect your whole life.* | *The president made a personal visit to the army hospital.*

direct
done without involving other people: *The manager has direct control over five salespeople.*

first-hand
relating to knowledge that you get or learn yourself, not from other people: *He wrote a first-hand account of what happened during the battle.*
→ see **private (1)** for **personal** meaning "relating to your own life and things you do not want other people to know about"

ADVERBS
You can make the adjectives **personal**, **subjective**, and **direct** into adverbs by using an **-ly** ending: *It is often better to get advice from someone who is not personally involved in the situation.* | *Personally, I think our project is more important.* | *I was not directly involved in the argument, but I saw what happened.*

personality *noun* → see **character**

personally /ˈpɚsənəli/ *adverb*

- personally
- in person
- face to face

personally
if you do something personally, you do it yourself rather than asking someone else to do it: *The managing director wrote personally to thank me.*

in person
if you do something in person, you do it by going to a place, not by writing, using the phone, or asking someone else to do it: *I think it is better that you tell him in person, rather than sending an email.*

face to face
in the same place and very close to someone so that you can talk or see each other very clearly: *I have heard a lot about her, but we have never met face to face.* | *I was standing* ***face to face with*** *a big brown bear.*

personnel *noun* → see **worker**

perspiration *noun* → see **sweat**[2]

perspire *verb* → see **sweat**[1]

persuade /pəˈsweɪd/ *verb*

- ► persuade
- ► talk someone into something (*informal*)
- ► convince
- ► encourage
- ► discourage
- ► coax
- ► cajole
- ► sway

persuade
to make someone decide to do something by giving him or her good reasons: *My friends* ***persuaded*** *me* ***to*** *go and see the movie.* | *See if you can* ***persuade*** *him* ***to*** *change his mind.*

talk someone into something (*informal*)
to persuade someone to do something, especially something he or she does not really want to do: *I managed to talk my parents into lending me the money.*

convince (AWL)
to persuade someone that he or she should do something, especially because it is the best thing to do: *Each candidate tries to* ***convince*** *voters* ***that*** *he or she is the best person for the job.*

encourage
to try to persuade someone to do something, especially because you think it will be good for him or her: *People should be* ***encouraged to*** *eat healthy foods.*

discourage
to persuade someone not to do something, especially by making it seem difficult or bad: *We do everything we can to* ***discourage*** *kids* ***from*** *smoking.*

coax
to persuade someone to do something, by talking gently and kindly to him or her: *I tried to coax my brother into the pool by saying that it was nice and warm.*

cajole
to persuade someone to do something, by praising him or her, or by promising things: *She* ***cajoled*** *the kids* ***into*** *going to church by telling them they could have an ice cream afterward.*

sway
to persuade someone who is not sure about something to make the decision that you want: *The governor said he would cut taxes in an effort to sway voters.*

persuasion /pəˈsweɪʒən/ *noun*

- ► persuasion
- ► encouragement
- ► pressure
- ► propaganda

persuasion
things that you say or do to persuade someone to do something: *It took a lot of persuasion, but she finally agreed to help.* | *The president will need to use all of his powers of persuasion to make Congress accept his plan.*

encouragement
things that you say in order to make someone want to do something: *With some encouragement from her teacher, Brooke wrote a story about a princess.*

pressure
things that people say or do in order to make someone feel that he or she must do something: *Her parents are putting pressure on her to get married.*

propaganda
false information used by a government or organization to make people believe things that are not true: *The ads about the senator are just propaganda, but it's amazing how many people believe them.*

persuasive /pəˈsweɪsɪv/ *adjective*

1 making you think that something is true or right
- ► persuasive
- ► convincing
- ► compelling

2 good at persuading people to accept your ideas
- ► persuasive
- ► eloquent

1 making you think that something is true or right

persuasive
making people think that something is probably true or right. You use **persuasive** about arguments or evidence: *There is some persuasive evidence that changes in diet can help reduce heart disease.* | *He made a persuasive case for changing the law.*

convincing (AWL)
making you feel sure that something is true or right. You use **convincing** about arguments,

evidence, or explanations: *Her lawyer says there is clear and convincing evidence that shows that she is innocent.*

compelling
making you feel that something must be true or that you must do something. You use **compelling** about evidence, reasons, or arguments: *There are several compelling reasons for believing her story.*

2 good at persuading people to accept your ideas

persuasive
good at persuading other people to accept your ideas: *She is very persuasive. It is hard to say no when she wants you to do something.* | *Like many politicians, he is a very persuasive speaker, but you need to think about his arguments carefully.*

eloquent
good at using words to talk about your ideas, especially in speeches: *The president is very eloquent; he knows how to get his point across to his audience.* | *He made an eloquent speech about the need to help the people in the war zone.*

ADVERBS

You can make the adjectives that mean **persuasive** into adverbs by using an **-ly** ending: *He spoke persuasively about the need to change the law.* | *Newton was able to demonstrate convincingly that his ideas were correct.* | *She writes eloquently about the need to spend time in the wilderness.*

P

pessimism /ˈpesəˌmɪzəm/ *noun*

- ► **pessimism**
- ► **negativity**

ANTONYMS → see **hope²**

pessimism
the feeling that bad things will happen, not good things: *A feeling of pessimism has followed the team's latest defeat.* | ***Pessimism about** the country's economy has grown stronger.*

negativity
the attitude of someone who only sees the bad parts of a situation, without thinking about the good parts. You use **negativity** when someone is behaving in an unreasonable way: *His constant negativity is having a bad effect on the people he works with.*

pessimistic /ˌpesəˈmɪstɪk/ *adjective*

- ► **pessimistic**
- ► **gloomy**
- ► **negative**
- ► **cynical**

ANTONYMS → see **hopeful**

pessimistic
someone who is pessimistic thinks that bad things will happen, not good things: *He is **pessimistic about** his chances of getting the job because he doesn't think he has enough experience.*

gloomy
not having much hope for the future: *Some experts are **gloomy about** the future of the U.S. economy.*

negative (AWL)
thinking only about the bad parts of a situation, not the good parts. You use **negative** when you think someone is behaving in a way that is unreasonable: *She has been very **negative about** school, and I'm wondering if something is wrong.*

cynical
a cynical person never believes that people have good or honest reasons for doing something: *People are **cynical about** politicians and they find it hard to trust them.*
→ see Topic **Describing People's Character**

ADVERBS

You can make the adjectives that mean **pessimistic** into adverbs by using an **-ly** ending: *"I don't think I'll get the job," he said pessimistically.* | *"So, what does he get from helping us?" asked Roy cynically.*

pest /pest/ *noun*

1 an annoying person
- ► **pest** (*informal*)
- ► **nuisance**
- ► **pain** (*informal*)

2 an annoying insect or animal that causes problems
- ► **pest**
- ► **vermin** (*formal*)

1 an annoying person

pest (*informal*)
a very annoying person who keeps bothering you, especially a child: *Stop being such a pest, and leave me alone!*

nuisance
an annoying person who causes problems, especially someone who keeps asking for things: *I don't want to be a nuisance, but could you help me fix my computer?*

pain (*informal*)
an annoying person: *I know he is a pain, but he is your brother.*

GRAMMAR CHECK: pest
These words are not often used in the plural.

2 an annoying insect or animal that causes problems

pest
an annoying insect or animal that damages things and causes problems for people: *Pests such as moths can make holes in your clothes.*

vermin (*formal*)
animals and insects that damage things, spread disease, and cause other problems for people: *Leaving food on the floor for your cats may attract mice and other vermin.*
→ see **annoyance** for words meaning "an annoying thing or situation"

pet¹ *noun* → see **animal**

pet² *verb* → see **rub**, **touch**

phone *verb* → see **call**

phony *adjective* → see **fake²**

photo *noun* → see **photograph¹**

photocopy¹ *noun* → see **copy¹**

photocopy² *verb* → see **copy²**

photograph¹ /ˈfoʊtəˌgræf/ *noun*

- ► photograph
- ► photo (*informal*)
- ► picture
- ► snapshot
- ► shot (*informal*)
- ► print

photograph
a picture you make using a camera: *Visitors are not allowed to take photographs inside the museum. | Ansel Adams was famous for his beautiful photographs of Yosemite National Park.*

photo (*informal*)
a photograph: *I found some old photos of my grandparents.*

picture
a painting, drawing, or photograph: *There was a picture of her in her wedding dress. | Did you take many pictures on your vacation?*

snapshot
a photograph that you take quickly and without thinking carefully about how it will look, for example when you are on vacation: *She showed me some snapshots of her friends.*

shot (*informal*)
a photograph. You use **shot** when you want to talk about the way that the photograph was taken: *I got some great shots of the Grand Canyon.*

print
a photograph that has been printed on special paper: *When you have a digital camera, you don't always get prints of all your pictures.*

photograph² /ˈfoʊtəˌgræf/ *verb*

- ► photograph (*formal*)
- ► take a picture
- ► shoot
- ► snap (*informal*)

photograph (*formal*)
to make a picture of someone or something using a camera: *Kate agreed to let me photograph her. | The astronauts photographed the surface of the Moon.*

take a picture *also* **take a photograph**
to photograph someone or something. **Take a picture/photograph** sounds less formal than **photograph**: *We stopped the car to take a picture of the view.*

shoot
to take photographs or make a movie of something: *I shot hundreds of pictures before I got the one I wanted. | They shot the movie in Arizona.*

snap (*informal*)
to quickly photograph someone or something: *The actor was snapped coming out of a nightclub.*

photography *noun* → see **art**

phrase /freɪz/ *noun*

- ► phrase
- ► expression
- ► idiom
- ► cliché
- ► saying
- ► proverb
- ► slogan

phrase
a group of two or more words that have a particular meaning: *He uses the phrase "let me be clear" when he wants to explain what he means.* |

In English, the phrase "something to eat" is often used instead of the word "food" when you are asking if someone is hungry: "Do you want something to eat?"

expression
expression means the same as **phrase**. You often use **expression** about a phrase that is commonly used in a language: *"See you later" is an expression which people use when saying goodbye.*

idiom
a group of words that have a special meaning that is different from the usual meaning of each word: *"Under the weather" is an idiom which means "sick."*

cliché
a phrase that has been used so often that it is boring: *It may be a sports cliché, but players really must only think about "one game at a time."*

saying
a phrase that many people know that gives advice or information about life: *Do you know the saying "A problem shared is a problem halved"? It means that if you tell someone about your problem, he or she can help you.*

proverb
an old saying: *There is an old Chinese proverb which states "A journey of a thousand miles starts with a single step."*

slogan
a short phrase that is easy to remember, especially one that is used in advertising or politics: *In his 2008 election campaign, Barack Obama used the slogan "Yes we can."*

physical /ˈfɪzɪkəl/ *adjective*

- ► physical
- ► bodily (*formal*)

ANTONYMS → see **mental**

physical (AWL)
relating to your body, not your mind or emotions: *The doctor said that I was in good physical health.* | *She was suffering severe physical pain.*

bodily (*formal*)
relating to the human body. **Bodily** is used especially in scientific, medical, or legal writing: *The disease is spread from one person to another through bodily fluids such as blood.* | *He threatened the reporter with bodily harm* (=he threatened to hurt the reporter).

ADVERBS

You can make the adjective **physical** into an adverb by using an **-ly** ending: *For some jobs, it is necessary to be physically strong.*

Bodily looks like an adverb, but it is an adjective.

physician *noun* → see **doctor**

physics *noun* → see Topic **Science and Technology**

pick /pɪk/ *verb*

1 to remove a flower or fruit from a plant
- ► pick
- ► pluck
- ► harvest

2 to decide which thing or person you want
- ► pick
- ► choose
- ► decide on
- ► select (*formal*)
- ► opt for

1 to remove a flower or fruit from a plant

pick
to remove a flower, fruit, or nut from a plant or tree: *Amy picked a small bunch of flowers.* | *We picked lemons and made fresh lemonade.*

pluck
to pull something quickly in order to remove it: *Reaching up, she plucked an apple off the tree.*

harvest
to cut and collect crops when they are ready: *The corn is harvested at this time of year.*

2 to decide which thing or person you want

pick
to decide which one of a group of things or people you want. You often use **pick** in situations where the choice you are making is easy or quick: *Pick a number from one to five.* | *In P.E., I was always picked last for any team games.*

choose
choose means the same as **pick** but sounds slightly more formal: *I can't decide which dessert to get. You choose for me.* | *She was only 16 when the director **chose** her **to** be in the movie.*

decide on
to choose one thing from many possible choices, after thinking carefully about the choice: *Have you decided on a date for the wedding?*

select (AWL) *(formal)*
select means the same as **decide on** but sounds formal: *It is important for parents to select the right school for a child with special needs. | From the menu, select "copy" and then paste the picture into the correct place.*
→ **Select** is also used in official or formal documents to mean the same as **choose**: *Select "privacy" from the pull-down menu if you would like to change your computer's settings.*

opt for
to choose to have one thing instead of another: *I think I would* ***opt for*** *the blue dress rather than the red one.*
→ see **decide (1)** for **choose** meaning "to choose to do something"
→ see **choice**

pick on /ˈpɪk ɔn/ *phrasal verb*

- pick on
- bully
- tease
- persecute *(formal)*
- victimize

pick on
to treat one person in a group in an unfair and unkind way: *At school some of the boys used to pick on him. They called him names and sometimes even pushed or hit him.*

bully
to be cruel to someone who is weaker or less powerful than you: *The manager* ***bullies*** *his staff* ***into*** *working for more hours than they should.*

tease
to make jokes about someone in order to embarrass or annoy him or her. You can **tease** someone in either a friendly way or an unkind way: *Sam's sisters used to tease him because he was overweight.*

persecute *(formal)*
to be cruel to a group of people, especially because of their religious beliefs or their race: *Many people came to America because they were being* ***persecuted*** *in Europe* ***for*** *their religious beliefs.*

victimize
to treat one person in a very unfair way, which is different from how other people are treated: *None of the other students who missed class were punished, so Elena feels that she is being victimized.*

pick up /ˌpɪk ˈʌp/ *phrasal verb*

- pick up *(informal)*
- get
- fetch

pick up *(informal)*
to go to a place in order to bring someone or something back with you: *What time do you need to pick up the kids at school? | I'll pick up a pizza on the way home from work.*

get
to bring someone or something back from somewhere: *I can go and get Katie if her parents can't drive her over here.*

fetch
if a dog fetches something, it runs to it and brings it back to you: *The dog fetched the chewed-up tennis ball.*

picture[1] /ˈpɪktʃɚ/ *noun*

- picture
- painting
- drawing
- illustration
- portrait
- artwork
- image
- graphics

picture
a drawing, painting, or photograph: *There was a picture of his wife and children on his desk. | Georgia O'Keeffe was famous for painting pictures of flowers.*

painting
a picture that is made using paint: *The painting now hangs in the Museum of Modern Art.*

drawing
a picture that is made using a pencil or pen: *The teachers asked the students to do a drawing of a tree.*

illustration (AWL)
a picture in a book: *The book has over 100 illustrations, most of them in color.*

portrait
a painting, drawing, or photograph of a person: *The artist painted a portrait of his mother.*

artwork
paintings, drawings, or other pieces of art: *The school displays the children's artwork in the hall.*
→ **Artwork** can also mean the pictures and photographs that are used in a magazine or book.

P

image (AWL)
a picture that you can see on a television, on a computer screen, in a mirror, or in a photograph. You use **image** especially when talking about what the picture is like, or the effect it has on you: *Some of the images in this news report are very disturbing.*

graphics
pictures or images, especially those produced on a computer: *The graphics in some of today's computer games are really amazing.*
→ see **art**, **drawing**, **photograph**[1]

picture[2] *verb* → see **imagine**

piece *noun* → *go to pages 480-481*

pier /pɪr/ *noun*

- pier
- dock
- wharf

pier
a long structure that goes from the land into the ocean. People can walk along a **pier**, or boats can stop next to it: *We went for a walk along the pier.* | *Some boys were fishing from the pier.*

dock
an area of water where a ship or boat stops so that people can get on or off, or so that goods can be put on or taken off. **Docks** can be in the ocean or in rivers or lakes, and they can be big or small: *The ship slowly came into the dock and the passengers waited to get off.*
→ Many people use **dock** to mean the structure next to the water where the ship or boat stops, but some people think this use is wrong: *He stood on the dock, waiting for the boat to pull up beside it.*

wharf
a long structure that is built out into the water, so that boats can stop next to it. **Wharves** are usually in harbors: *We watched the fishing boats arriving at the wharf.*

pierce /pɪrs/ *verb*

- pierce
- prick
- poke a hole
- punch
- puncture
- drill
- penetrate

pierce
to make a hole in something with a sharp object: *The arrow pierced his leg, and he fell down onto the ground.*
→ **Pierce** is often used about making a hole in your ear so that you can wear an earring: *I had my ears pierced when I was 14.*

prick
to make a small hole in something using something sharp: *Prick holes in the skin of the potatoes before you cook them in the microwave, or they may explode.*

poke a hole
to make a hole in something by pushing something pointed into it: *Use your finger to poke a hole in the dough.*

punch
to make a hole using a special tool, especially in paper: *In the old days, the train conductor used to punch everybody's tickets.*

puncture
to make a small hole in something so that air or liquid comes out: *Luckily, the knife had not punctured his skin and he wasn't bleeding.*

drill
to make a hole with a special tool: *We'll have to drill some holes in the wall to put up the shelves.*

penetrate
to pass into or through something that is deep or thick, and usually make a hole in it: *The bullet penetrated the door and went through the other side.*

pig /pɪg/ *noun*

- pig
- hog
- sow
- boar
- piglet

pig
a fat farm animal with short legs, a flat nose, and a short curved tail. **Pigs** are kept for their meat, which includes pork, bacon, and ham: *We used to keep pigs on the farm.*

hog
a large pig. **Hog** is used especially by farmers who keep pigs and sell them for their meat: *He has a hog farm in central Minnesota.*

sow
a fully grown female pig: *Each sow produces around 20 piglets every year.*

boar
a male pig: *The boars can weigh over 200 pounds.*
→ A **wild boar** is a type of pig that lives in forests and in the country.

piglet
a young pig: *Last night the sow gave birth to ten piglets.*

pile¹ /paɪl/ *noun*

- pile
- heap
- stack
- mound
- mountain

pile
a lot of things on top of each other: *The books were arranged* ***in neat piles*** *on the table. | There is a big pile of towels that need to be washed.*

heap
a large messy pile of things: *A heap of clothes lay on the floor.*

stack
a group of things that have been neatly placed on top of each other: *There was a stack of magazines on the table.*

mound
a pile of something with a round shape: *She had a huge mound of rice on her plate.*

mountain
a very large pile of something. **Mountain** sounds informal: *His desk is always covered in a mountain of papers.*

pile

a **heap** of clothes

a **mound** of soil

a **stack** of magazines

a **pile** of books

pile² /paɪl/ *verb*

- pile
- heap
- stack

pile
to put a lot of things on top of each other: *Dirty dishes were left piled in the sink. | Books were piled up on the desk.*

heap
to put a lot of things on top of each other in a messy way: *Jim heaped some more logs on the fire. | Magazines were heaped on the table.*

stack
to put things into a neat pile: *We stacked the boxes neatly in one corner of the room.*

pinch *verb* → see **press¹**

pioneer /ˌpaɪəˈnɪr/ *noun*

- pioneer
- settler

pioneer
one of the first people to travel to a new place and begin living there: *In the 1880s, thousands of pioneers traveled across the United States until they reached California or Oregon.*

settler
someone who goes to live in a new place, where there were few people before: *Many of the early settlers died from hunger or disease.*
→ see **explorer**

pipe /paɪp/ *noun*

- pipe
- hose
- tube
- pipeline
- duct

pipe
a long round hollow object with hard sides, especially one that carries water or gas: *A water pipe broke in the bathroom and flooded the floor.*

hose
a long soft pipe that water or air can flow through: *The firefighters held the hose and sprayed water on the burning building.*

tube
a long pipe that can be soft or hard, and that often carries liquid or gas: *While he was in the hospital, he was fed through a tube to his stomach.*

pipeline
a system of pipes that carry oil or gas over long distances: *The pipeline transports oil 800 miles across Alaska.*

duct
a pipe in a building, especially for carrying air or electric wires: *Air is heated and then carried through large ducts to all parts of the building.*

piece /pis/ *noun*

1 a piece
► piece
► fragment
► bit (*informal*)
► scrap
► crumb
► chip
► splinter
► sliver
► flake
► shard

2 an extremely small piece
► particle
► speck

3 a flat piece
► piece
► sheet
► slice
► strip
► slip
► slab

4 a piece that has a particular shape
► block
► cube
► bar
► wedge

5 a piece that does not have a regular shape
► chunk
► lump
► hunk

1 a piece

piece
a part of something that has been separated from the rest: *The plate broke into two pieces.* | *The floor is made of* ***pieces of*** *polished wood.*

fragment
a small piece from something that was broken: *I dropped the bowl and it shattered into a thousand tiny fragments.*

bit (*informal*)
a very small piece: *There were* ***bits of*** *glass all over the road after the accident.*

scrap
a small piece of paper or cloth that is no longer needed: *Do you have a* ***scrap of*** *paper that I can write my address on?*

crumb
a very small piece of food such as bread or cake: *After he had finished eating, he wiped the crumbs from his mouth with his napkin.*

chip
a small piece of wood or stone, especially one that comes off a larger piece after someone has been cutting it: *The floor of the workshop is covered in wood chips.*

splinter
a small sharp thin piece of wood, glass, or metal, especially one that goes into someone's skin: *I have a splinter in my finger from the wooden fence – it really hurts!*

sliver
a very small thin piece of something: *She cut her foot on a* ***sliver of*** *glass.* | *I don't want a big piece of pie – just a sliver is fine.*

flake
a very thin flat piece of something such as snow or stone, which breaks easily: *The first* ***flakes of*** *snow were beginning to fall.*

shard
a sharp piece of broken glass, metal, or pottery: *They found shards of ancient pots buried in the ground.*

2 an extremely small piece

particle
an extremely small piece of something: *The air was full of tiny particles of dust.*
→ **Particle** is often used in science when talking about atoms and other very small things: *Matter consists of tiny particles called atoms.*

speck
an extremely small piece of dirt or dust: *He brushed a* ***speck of*** *dust from his jacket.*

3 a flat piece

piece
a part of something that is flat and that has been separated from the rest: *Could I have another* ***piece of*** *cake?* | *The teacher gave each child a big* ***piece of*** *paper to paint on.*

sheet
a thin flat piece of paper, glass, metal, or another material. A **sheet** usually has four straight sides: *Write each answer on a separate* ***sheet of*** *paper.*

slice
a piece of food that has been cut from a bigger piece, and that is usually flat and thin: *Could you put a* ***slice of*** *bread in the toaster for me?* | *My lemonade had* ***a slice of*** *lemon floating in it.* | *I had a slice of apple pie for dessert.*

strip
a thin narrow flat piece of something such as cloth or paper: ***He used a strip of cloth as a bandage.***

slip
a small narrow piece of paper, especially one that you use for writing on: ***She wrote her telephone number on a slip of paper.***

slab
a thick flat heavy piece of something such as stone: ***The graves are covered with slabs of marble.***

4 a piece that has a particular shape

block
a large solid piece of wood, stone, or ice that has straight sides, especially one that is square or rectangular: ***I put a big block of wood behind the back wheel of the car so it wouldn't roll down the hill.***

cube
an object with six square sides: ***She dropped another sugar cube into her coffee.***

bar
a thick rectangular piece of chocolate, soap, or metal: ***The boy was eating a big bar of chocolate.***

wedge
a piece with sides shaped like a triangle, which has a thin end and a thick end: ***The fish was served with a wedge of lemon on the side.***

→ When **wedge** is used about pie or cake, it means a very large slice.

5 a piece that does not have a regular shape

chunk
a piece of something that does not have a regular shape: ***Cut the pineapple into chunks.***

lump
a solid piece of something that does not have a regular shape. A **lump** is usually smoother and more round than a **chunk**: ***There were lumps of ice mixed in with the snow.***

hunk
a large piece of something that has been cut or torn from a bigger piece, especially a big piece of bread, cheese, or meat: ***He tore off a hunk from the loaf of bread and put it on his plate.***

piece

fragments

a **scrap** of paper

wood **chips**

lumps of charcoal

a **slice** of lemon

a lemon **wedge**

pineapple **chunks**

a **shard** of glass

a **bar** of chocolate

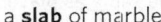

a **slab** of marble

Online Thesaurus

Go to **www.longmandictionariesusa.com**

→ ***Longman Thesaurus of American English*** – with pronunciation of all the words

→ **Study Center** – interactive practice to help you learn synonyms, Academic Words, and Topic Vocabulary

pitch *verb* → see **build[1]**, **throw[1]**

pity[1] *noun* → see **sympathy**

pity[2] *verb* → see **sorry (3)**

place[1] /pleɪs/ *noun*

1 the place where something is
- ► place
- ► location
- ► position
- ► spot (*informal*)

2 the place where something happened
- ► place
- ► spot (*informal*)
- ► site
- ► scene
- ► setting

1 the place where something is

place
an area, building, city, or country: *Florida is a great place for a vacation.* | *I put the money in a secret place.*

location (AWL)
the place where someone or something is. **Location** is more formal than **place**: *The company plans to move its offices to a new location.* | *The map shows the location of all the hotels in the area.*

position
the exact place where someone or something is, in relation to other people or things: *The length of your shadow depends on the position of the sun in the sky.*

spot (*informal*)
a place, especially the place where people do something: *The area is a favorite* ***spot for*** *windsurfers.*

2 the place where something happened

place
an area, city, country, etc. where something happened: *The place where the battle happened is now a national park.*

spot (*informal*)
spot means the same as **place**: *This is the spot where the Pilgrims landed in their ship, the "Mayflower."*

site (AWL)
a place that will be used for a particular purpose, or where something important happened: *There are plans to develop the site for housing.* | *Vicksburg was the site of a famous battle in the Civil War.*

scene
the place where something bad, such as an accident or crime, happened: *The ambulance arrived at the scene of the accident within minutes.*

setting
the place where something is and the area around it: *The hotel is in a beautiful setting next to a lake.*
→ You often use **setting** about the place where a book, movie, or event happens: *The* ***setting for*** *the book is New York in the 1920s.*
→ see **area**, **safe place**, **take place** at **happen**

place[2] *verb* → see **put**

plain /pleɪn/ *adjective*
- ► plain
- ► simple
- ► bare

plain
something that is plain does not have any decorations, patterns, or extra things added: *The girl was wearing a plain white blouse.* | *The room is very plain, with no pictures on the walls.*

simple
not complicated and without a lot of things added: *The restaurant serves simple but delicious food.* | *The kitchen had a simple wooden table at one end.*

bare
with no covering or decoration: *There was no carpet or anything, just bare wooden floorboards.*
→ You say that a room is **bare** when there is no furniture or anything else in it: *The room was bare, except for a bed in the corner.*
→ see **simple**, Topic **Describing People's Looks**

ADVERBS

You can make the adjectives **plain** and **simple** into adverbs by using an **-ly** ending: *The room is plainly decorated.* | *The food is simply cooked, but tastes fantastic.* The adverb **barely** is not used in this meaning.

plan[1] /plæn/ *noun*
- ► plan
- ► strategy
- ► policy
- ► program
- ► schedule
- ► plot
- ► conspiracy
- ► scheme

plan
something that you have decided to do: *The plan is to finish the work by the end of the year. | Two of the guests can't come on Saturday, so we may have to change our plans.*

strategy (AWL)
a plan or method that you use to achieve what you want: *Their strategy was to attack the enemy with as much force as possible.*

policy (AWL)
a plan of how a government or organization will deal with a particular subject or problem: *He advises the president on economic policy. | The college has a policy of welcoming students from all minority groups.*

program
a series of activities that have been officially planned by a government or organization in order to achieve something: *The president announced a program that will create thousands of new jobs.*

schedule (AWL)
a plan of what someone is going to do: *Lisa has a busy schedule tomorrow – she is in meetings all day.*

plot
a secret plan to do something very bad: *The men were involved in a plot to blow up a plane.*

conspiracy
a secret and usually complicated plan by two or more people to do something illegal together. **Conspiracy** is more formal than **plot**: *The idea that there was a conspiracy by the CIA to kill President Kennedy is just stupid.*
→ **Conspiracy** also means the crime of secretly planning to do something illegal: *The authorities have charged 11 people with conspiracy to murder.*

scheme (AWL)
a plan to do something, especially something bad or illegal: *They participated in a scheme to cheat people out of their money.*

plan² /plæn/ *verb*

- plan
- organize
- make arrangements
- plot
- scheme

plan
to think carefully about how you will do something that you want to do: *We spent months planning our trip. | The robbery had obviously been carefully planned, and the thieves were all dressed as security guards.*

organize
to do all the things that are necessary to prepare for an event so that it can happen successfully: *I'm organizing a party for Juan's 21st birthday. | The unemployed people organized a protest on Wall Street.*

make arrangements
to do all the things that are necessary for something that is planned to happen, for example by calling people and making reservations: *The couple **made** all the **arrangements for** the wedding and invited over 100 guests.*

plot
to make secret plans to do something bad or illegal: *The terrorists were **plotting to** kill thousands of people.*

scheme (AWL)
to make secret plans to do something using dishonest methods: *The king's brother **schemes against** him until he is able to take the throne from the king.*

planet *noun* → see **world**

plant¹ /plænt/ *noun*

- plant
- weed
- crop
- undergrowth
- vegetation (*formal*)
- flora (*formal*)

plant
a living thing that has leaves and roots and grows in soil: *I like plants that have pretty flowers. | Plants need water and sunlight in order to grow.*

weed
a wild plant that grows where you do not want it to grow: *The farmers use chemicals to control the weeds.*

crop
a plant such as corn, wheat, or potatoes that farmers grow for food: *Farmers plant their crops in spring.*

undergrowth
small bushes and other plants that cover the ground, especially between the trees in a forest: *They made their way through the undergrowth and reached the edge of the jungle.*

vegetation (*formal*)
plants and trees: *The fire destroyed a lot of the vegetation on the island.*

flora (*formal*)
the plants that grow somewhere. **Flora** is used in

scientific writing, often in the phrase **flora and fauna** (=plants and animals): *Tourism is having a bad effect on the flora and fauna of the region, as natural habitats are destroyed for hotels.*
→ see **flower**, **tree**

plant² /plænt/ *verb*

- ► plant
- ► sow

plant
to put plants, seeds, or trees in the soil to grow: *We planted some beautiful flowers.*

sow
to put seeds in the soil so that they will grow into plants: *Sow the seeds in early spring.*

P

plan to /ˈplæn tu/ *verb*

- ► plan to
- ► intend to
- ► be going to
- ► propose to (*formal*)
- ► aim to
- ► mean to

plan to
if you plan to do something, you have decided that you will do it in the future: *We're planning to visit my brother when we're in New York.* | *Are you planning to go to college?*

intend to
to plan to do something at some time in the future. **Intend to** sounds more formal than **plan to**: *I don't know who did this, but I intend to find out.*

be going to
to be planning to do something. You use **be going to** especially when you have already made arrangements to do something: *We're going to stay at the Hyatt Hotel for three nights.*

propose to (*formal*)
to say that you will probably do something: *The company is proposing to build a theme park.*

aim to
to hope to achieve something, although you do not know if you will succeed: *We're aiming to finish the work by Friday.*

mean to
to plan to do something. You use **mean to** especially in negative sentences to show that someone did not do something deliberately: *I didn't mean to upset you.*

plate /pleɪt/ *noun*

- ► plate
- ► dish
- ► bowl
- ► platter

plate
a flat round object that you put food on to eat: *He ate everything on his plate.*

dish
a container with low sides that you serve food on or cook food in: *The pasta was served in a big dish.*
→ If you **wash the dishes**, you wash all the plates, bowls, and cups that have been used in a meal: *Mom asked me to wash the dishes.*

bowl
a round container with high sides, used for eating or serving food: *We ordered two bowls of soup.*

platter
a large plate used for serving food: *Place the meat on a warm serving platter.*

play¹ /pleɪ/ *verb*

1 to take part in a game or sport
- ► play
- ► compete
- ► enter

2 to do things that you enjoy
- ► play
- ► have fun
- ► enjoy yourself

1 to take part in a game or sport

play
to take part in a game or sport: *Two old men were playing chess.* | *I play tennis once a week.*

compete
to take part in a race or competition: *Over 1,000 cyclists will **compete in** the race.*

enter
to arrange to take part in a race or competition: *If you want to enter the competition, all you have to do is call this number.*
→ see Topic **Sports and Exercise**

2 to do things that you enjoy

play
to do things that you enjoy. You use **play** about what children and pets do: *After school I usually go out and play with my friends.* | *Cats love to play with balls of string.*

have fun
to get pleasure from doing something: *It was a good party and everyone was laughing and having fun.*

enjoy yourself
enjoy yourself means the same as **have fun** but is more formal: *Her son seems to be enjoying himself at college.*

play² /pleɪ/ *noun*

- ► play
- ► musical
- ► drama
- ► show
- ► performance
- ► production

play
a story that actors perform in a theater: *"Romeo and Juliet" is a famous play by William Shakespeare.*

musical
a play in which the characters sing songs and dance to tell the story: *She performed in the musical "Wicked."*

drama (AWL)
a play, television program, or movie that tells a serious story about people's lives: *The show is a new TV drama which is set in a hospital.*
→ You also use **drama** about the study of plays in general: *She is planning to go to drama school.*

show
something people watch on stage or television, or listen to on the radio. **Show** sounds fairly informal and you do not usually use it about a performance of classical music, an opera, or a ballet: *Parents and friends came to watch the young musicians and dancers perform in the show.* | *He was in the TV show "Friends."*

performance
an occasion when people perform a play or show on stage: *This evening's performance of the play will begin at 8 p.m.*

production
a play, opera, or ballet. You use **production** when you are talking about how the play will be performed by a particular group of actors: *There is a new production of Arthur Miller's famous play "Death of a Salesman."*
→ see **fun¹** for **play** meaning "things you do for fun"
→ see **theater**, Topic **Books and Literature**

player /ˈpleɪɚ/ *noun*

- ► player
- ► athlete

player
someone who plays a game or sport: *He is one of the college's best tennis players.* | *The players were disappointed that they didn't win.*

athlete
someone who is good at sports, especially someone who takes part in competitions: *The country's best athletes will be going to the Olympic Games.*
→ see Topic **Sports and Exercise**

playground *noun* → see **park**

pleasant *adjective* → see **comfortable**, **nice**

please /pliz/ *verb*

- ► please
- ► satisfy

please
to make someone feel happy, especially by doing or saying something that he or she likes: *Young children often try hard to please their parents.* | *Mr. McClellan was* ***pleased with*** *my work.*

satisfy
to make someone feel happy by providing everything that he or she wants: *Companies have to satisfy their customers.*
→ see **happy** for **pleased** meaning "happy that something good has happened"

pleased *adjective* → see **happy**, **proud**

pleasure /ˈpleʒɚ/ *noun*

- ► pleasure
- ► enjoyment
- ► satisfaction
- ► delight

pleasure
a happy feeling because you like something very much: *Their music has brought pleasure to millions of people.* | *She ate her meal* ***with obvious pleasure.***

enjoyment
the feeling that you get when you enjoy doing something: *I get a lot of enjoyment out of playing the piano.*

satisfaction
the feeling that you have done something good or useful, or have gotten what you wanted: *As a*

P

teacher he got great satisfaction from helping people to learn.

delight
a strong feeling of happiness and excitement, because something good has happened: *She screamed **with delight** when she found out that she had passed her driving test.*
→ see **enjoyment**, **happiness**

plentiful /ˈplentɪfəl/ *adjective*

- plentiful
- abundant (*formal*)
- ample
- copious (*formal*)

ANTONYMS → see **scarce**

plentiful
existing in large amounts so that there is as much or more than is needed: *During the summer, tomatoes are plentiful and cheap.* | *The river provides a plentiful supply of clean water to the village.*

abundant (*formal*)
existing in large amounts so that there is more than is necessary. **Abundant** sounds fairly literary: *In summer, there is an abundant supply of fresh vegetables, and we are able to store some for the winter.*

ample
as much or more than is needed. You use **ample** especially about a supply of something, the space or time you need for something, or opportunities to do something: *You should have ample time to finish the test, so don't rush.* | *There is ample scientific evidence that global warming is happening.*

copious (*formal*)
existing or produced in very large amounts: *The writer took copious notes on his travels so that he could later write a book.*
→ see Function Word **enough**

ADVERBS

You can make the adjectives that mean **plentiful** into adverbs by using an **-ly** ending: *At this time of year, fresh vegetables are abundantly available.* | *You will be amply rewarded for your work.*

plenty *pronoun* → see Function Word **enough**, **a lot**

plot¹ *noun* → see **plan¹**, **story**, Topic **Books and Literature**, **Entertainment**

plot² *verb* → see **plan²**

plump *adjective* → see **fat**

poem /ˈpoʊɪm/ *noun*

- poem
- poetry
- verse
- rhyme

poem
a piece of writing with short lines, which often end with words with the same sound: *There is a famous poem by Robert Frost that has the lines "The woods are lovely, dark and deep. But I have promises to keep, And miles to go before I sleep."*

poetry
poems in general: *I like reading poetry by Emily Dickinson and other American poets.*

verse
words that are arranged in the same way as poetry: *The play is written in verse.*

rhyme *also* **nursery rhyme**
a short poem or song for children: *"Humpty Dumpty sat on the wall. Humpty Dumpty had a great fall" is a line from a well-known children's rhyme.*
→ see Topic **Books and Literature**

poet *noun* → see **writer**, Topic **Books and Literature**

poetry *noun* → see **poem**, Topic **Books and Literature**

point¹ /pɔɪnt/ *noun*

- the point
- the essence
- the core

the point
the most important fact or idea, especially of something that you want to talk about: *The point is that he gets paid more than I do, even though we both do the same work.* | *Now she has gotten to the point. Nothing else she has said really matters.*

the essence
the most basic and important part of something, which makes it how it is: *Freedom of speech is the essence of any democracy.*

the core
the most important part of something, especially when this is the cause of other things: *The core of the problem is that there are not enough jobs.*
→ see Topic **Sports and Exercise**

point² /pɔɪnt/ *verb*

1 to show which person or thing you mean
- ► **point**
- ► **indicate**

2 to hold something so that it is aimed at a person or thing
- ► **point**
- ► **aim**

3 to look in or show a direction
- ► **point**
- ► **face**

1 to show which person or thing you mean

point
to show the person or thing you mean, by holding your finger out toward him, her, or it: *"Look!" she said, and **pointed at** a small boat on the lake. | "Sit down," he said, **pointing to** a chair. | As we drove by, Jenna **pointed out** the house she used to live in.*

indicate (AWL)
to show which person or thing you mean, by moving your hand or your head slightly or looking toward him, her, or it: *"I'd like you to meet Todd," he said, indicating a tall man standing next to him.*

2 to hold something so that it is aimed at a person or thing

point
to hold something so that the end of it is toward a person or thing: *He **pointed** his **gun at** the prisoner. | The cameras were **pointed at** the stage.*

aim
to choose the person or place that you want to hit and point your gun or weapon at him, her, or it carefully: *Which part of the target were you **aiming at**?*

3 to look in or show a direction

point
if something long and thin points somewhere, the end of it shows that direction: *The arrow on a compass always points north. | The big hand **pointed to** the number five on the clock.*

face
to be looking at or pointing toward someone or something. You usually use **face** about people or about buildings: *The front of the school faces south. | John turned to face me, looking angry.*

point

indicate

point

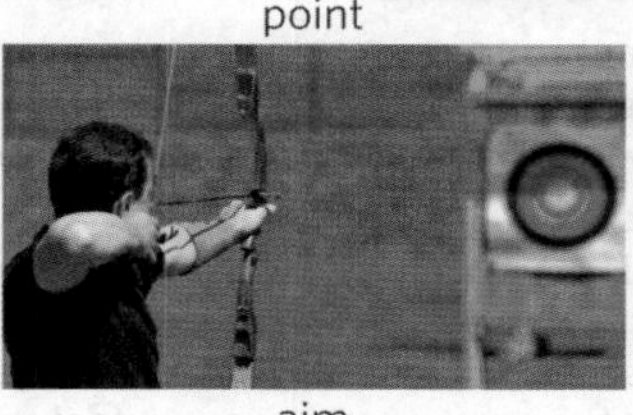
aim

point of view /ˌpɔɪnt əv ˈvyu/ *noun phrase*
- ► **point of view**
- ► **perspective**

point of view *also* **viewpoint**
the way you think about something, when this is influenced by your situation or the kind of person you are: *As an adult, I knew we didn't walk far, but **from** the child's **point of view** it was a long way. | **From** our **point of view**, this was the right thing to do, but I can understand that you disagree.*

perspective (AWL)
a way of thinking about a subject: ***From** a business **perspective**, selling the factory is good for the company.*
→ see **opinion** for **point of view** meaning "your opinion about something"

poison /ˈpɔɪzən/ *noun*
- ► **poison**
- ► **venom**
- ► **toxin**

poison
a substance that can kill or harm you: *Someone tried to kill him by putting poison in his food.*

venom
poison from a snake or spider. **Venom** is a

technical word: *The venom from this snake can kill you.*

toxin
a dangerous substance that causes disease, especially one that is produced by bacteria. **Toxin** is a technical word: *High levels of toxins were found in the town's drinking water.*

poisonous /ˈpɔɪzənəs/ *adjective*

- ► poisonous
- ► venomous
- ► toxic

poisonous
containing a substance that can kill or harm you: *Some wild mushrooms are very poisonous, so you need to be careful when you are picking them.*

venomous
a venomous animal produces poison: *A venomous snake bit him on the ankle, and he died.*

toxic
toxic chemicals are dangerous because they are harmful to people and the environment. **Toxic** is a technical word: *The fish died because a factory had been putting toxic waste into the river.*

poke *noun* → see **push²**

police officer /pəˈlis ˌɔfəsɚ/ *noun*

- ► police officer
- ► officer
- ► cop (*informal*)
- ► policeman/policewoman
- ► detective

police officer
a member of the police: *Police officers arrested the men and took them away for questioning.*

officer
a police officer. You use **officer** when it is clear from the situation that you mean a police officer, and not another kind of officer: *We need more officers on the streets to protect the public.*

cop (*informal*)
a police officer: *The old lady saw someone breaking a window and immediately called the cops.*

policeman/policewoman
a police officer. You use **policeman** or **policewoman** when you want to show whether the officer was a man or woman: *The policeman told the driver to get out of the car.*

detective (AWL)
a police officer whose job is to find out who has committed a crime: *Detectives think they know who the killer is, but they do not have enough evidence to arrest him.*

polish /ˈpɑlɪʃ/ *verb*

- ► polish
- ► shine

polish
to make something clean and shiny, by rubbing it with a cloth or brush: *She dusted and polished the wooden furniture.*

shine
to polish shoes: *These shoes need shining.*

polite /pəˈlaɪt/ *adjective*

- ► polite
- ► respectful
- ► courteous (*formal*)

ANTONYMS → see **rude**

polite
following the usual rules of good behavior when you are with other people, for example by saying "please" and "thank you" and offering to help: *The man was very polite and offered to carry our bags for us.* | *Remember to be **polite to** your grandmother. Don't forget to say "please."*

respectful
showing respect to a person, religion, or organization and not doing anything that might cause offense: *It is important to be **respectful toward** people of other religions.*

courteous (*formal*)
polite and thinking about what other people need, especially in a formal situation with people you do not know well: *We received a courteous welcome when we arrived at the hotel.*

ADVERBS

You can make the adjectives that mean **polite** into adverbs by using an **-ly** ending: *"Thank you," she said politely.* | *The woman at the reception desk greeted us courteously.*

politeness *noun* → see **manners**

politician *noun* → see Topic **Government and Politics**

pollute /pəˈlut/ *verb*

- ► pollute
- ► contaminate

pollute
to make air, water, or a place dangerous for

people and other living things, by putting harmful chemicals into it: *Cars pollute the air.* | *The factory polluted the river with chemical waste.*

contaminate
to make food, water, or land dirty or unsafe to use, by adding harmful chemicals or bacteria: *Two people became sick after eating meat that was **contaminated with** bacteria.*

→ **GRAMMAR: Polluted** and **contaminated** are often used before a noun: *We could hardly breathe the polluted air of the city.* | *They drank contaminated water.*

polluted *adjective* → see **dirty**

pollution /pəˈluʃən/ *noun*

- ► pollution
- ► smog
- ► greenhouse gases
- ► acid rain
- ► contamination

pollution
substances that make air, water, or soil dirty and dangerous to people and other living things. **Pollution** is usually caused by chemicals from vehicles, factories, and things people do: *Cars burn gas, which causes air pollution.* | *The pollution in the river comes from chemicals that farmers put on their fields.*

smog
dirty air in cities, caused especially by smoke from cars and trucks: *The roads are full of traffic and the city is covered in smog.*

greenhouse gases
gases that surround the Earth and stop heat from escaping. These gases are not natural, and come from factories, cars, etc. The gases make the air around the Earth gradually become warmer, and this is known as the "greenhouse effect": *The U.S. produces 25% of the world's greenhouse gases.*

acid rain
rain that has harmful acid in it which damages the environment, caused especially by smoke from cars and factories: *The trees were dying because of acid rain.*

contamination
the fact of being dirty and unsafe to use, because harmful chemicals or other substances are there: *The contamination was caused by waste from factories getting into the river.*

→ see Topic **The Environment**

pond *noun* → see **lake**

pool *noun* → see **lake**, Topic **Sports and Exercise**, **Travel and Vacations**

poor /pʊr/ *adjective*

- ► poor
- ► needy
- ► disadvantaged (*formal*)
- ► underprivileged (*formal*)
- ► poverty-stricken (*formal*)
- ► developing
- ► penniless

ANTONYMS → see **rich (1)**

poor
not having enough money: *Her family was very poor, and it didn't have enough money to buy her new clothes.* | *People in poor countries often cannot get safe drinking water.*

needy
needy people are very poor and need help: *They provide free medical care for needy children.*

disadvantaged (*formal*)
disadvantaged people have a smaller chance of being successful than richer people, because they are poor: *The school wants to give disadvantaged children a good education that will help them go to college or get jobs.*

underprivileged (*formal*)
underprivileged people are very poor and do not have the same education, health care, and other things that most other people in society have: *The program changed the lives of thousands of underprivileged people in Pittsburgh, by helping them get jobs and a better education.*

poverty-stricken (*formal*)
very poor, especially because something very bad has happened: *After their father died, the family was left poverty-stricken.*

developing
a developing country is poor and does not have many businesses or factories: *The disease is found mainly in developing countries.*

penniless
having no money. **Penniless** is old-fashioned and is used especially in written descriptions of people's lives: *He lost all his money by gambling and he died penniless.*

→ see **bad** for **poor** meaning "not good quality," **poverty** for words meaning "a situation in which people are poor"

poorly *adverb* → see **badly**

popular /ˈpɑpyələ˞/ *adjective*

- ► popular
- ► well-liked

popular
liked by a lot of people: *Their music is very*

popular with young people. | She was a popular student who had many friends.

well-liked
liked by the people that you know and work with: *He is respected and well liked by his co-workers. | Bill Cosby is a familiar and well-liked TV actor.*
→ see **fashionable**

population /ˌpɑpyəˈleɪʃən/ *noun*

- population
- inhabitant
- resident
- citizen

population
the number of people who live in a place: *The city has a population of over a million people. | California has a large Chinese population.*

inhabitant
someone who lives in a place: *The island's inhabitants are very poor. | The town has over 15,000 inhabitants.*

resident (AWL)
someone who lives in a particular street, building, or area of a town: *Parking spaces are for residents only.*

citizen
someone who has the legal right to live in a country or state: *U.S. citizens are able to vote in the election.*

port /pɔrt/ *noun*

- port
- harbor
- marina

port
a place where ships can stop so that goods or people can go on or come off: *The ship left the port of Miami and set off to Mexico.*

harbor
an area of calm water next to the land, where ships can stay safely: *The harbor was full of fishing boats.*

marina
an area of water where people keep boats used for pleasure: *He keeps a sailboat at the marina.*

portrait *noun* → see **picture**[1]

pose /poʊz/ *verb*

- pose
- sit for
- model

pose (AWL)
to sit or stand in a particular position so that someone can take a photograph or paint a picture of you: *The couple **posed for** a photograph in front of the Capitol building.*

sit for
to sit somewhere, usually for a long time, so that an artist can paint a picture or take a photograph of you: *The artist asked her to sit for him when he was painting his famous picture of the "Weeping Woman."*

model
to wear new clothes so that people can photograph them for fashion magazines or look at them in fashion shows: *Elizabeth is really pretty – she **models for** fashion magazines.*

position /pəˈzɪʃən/ *noun*

- position
- pose
- posture

position
the way someone is standing, sitting, or lying: *Make sure that the injured person is lying in a comfortable position. | I pushed myself up into a sitting position.*

pose (AWL)
the way you stand or sit, especially when someone paints a picture or takes a photograph of you: *The artist asked her to keep the same pose while he painted her face.*

posture
the way you stand or sit, and whether your back is straight or not. You use **posture** especially when saying how your posture affects your health: *Bad posture can result in back problems.*
→ see **job**, **place**[1], **rank**, **situation**

positive *adjective* → see **hopeful**, **sure**

possess *verb* → see **own**[1]

possession /pəˈzeʃən/ *noun*

- possession (*formal*)
- things (*informal*)
- belongings
- property
- assets

possession (*formal*)
something that someone owns: *They lost all their*

possessions in the fire. | *The old teddy bear is her most treasured possession.*

things (*informal*)
objects and clothes that you own: *Brian had left some of his things at his father's house.*

belongings
the things that you own, especially clothes and other things that you take with you when you are going somewhere: *I quickly packed a few belongings in a suitcase.*

property
the things that someone owns, especially valuable things or land: *The police asked her to make a list of any property that was stolen.*

assets
all the things that a company owns, including money, land, or equipment: *The company has $6 million in assets.*

SYNONYM CHECK

Possessions, belongings, or property?

Your **possessions** are everything you own, including large things such as furniture, and small things such as clothes or jewelry.

Things and **belongings** are used about smaller possessions, especially ones that you can easily carry with you.

Property is a more formal word, and it is used about small or large objects and land.

possibility *noun* → see **chance**

possible /ˈpɑsəbəl/ *adjective*

1 able to be done
- ► possible
- ► feasible
- ► workable
- ► realistic
- ► doable (*informal*)

ANTONYMS → see **impossible**

2 able to happen or be true
- ► possible
- ► likely
- ► probable

3 used about a person or thing who might do something in the future
- ► possible
- ► potential
- ► prospective (*formal*)

1 able to be done

possible
if something is possible, it can be done or achieved: ***Is it possible to** get tickets for the game?* | *Please call me as soon as possible.*

feasible
if an idea or plan is feasible, it is possible and you can find a practical way of doing it: ***It is not feasible to** have security cameras in every part of the building.*

workable
a workable plan, system, or solution is one that you can use: *I hope we can find a workable solution to the problem.*

realistic
possible and based on what someone can really achieve: *Do you think the team has a realistic chance of winning?*

doable (*informal*)
if something is doable, you have enough time, money, or skill available to do it: *We have two hours to get to the airport, which should be doable.*

2 able to happen or be true

possible
if something is possible, it could happen or be true: *Do you think **it is possible that** there could be life on other planets?* | *There are three possible answers for each question, and you must choose the right one.*

likely
if something is likely, you expect that it will happen or be true: *Young drivers are more **likely to** have accidents than older drivers.* | *Snow is likely later tonight.*

probable
probable means the same as **likely**, but is more formal and is used especially in writing or in scientific language: ***It is probable that** global warming will cause higher sea levels.*

3 used about a person or thing who might do something in the future

possible
if someone is a possible candidate, suspect, partner, etc., that person might become a candidate, etc. in the future: *Rubio is a possible candidate for the Senate.*

potential (AWL)
used for describing something that might happen or develop in the future: *Advertisers want to reach as many potential customers as they can.* | *Can you think of any other potential problems?*
→ **GRAMMAR: Potential** is only used before a noun. Don't say: ~~*a problem that is potential*~~. Say: *a potential problem.*

prospective (AWL) (*formal*)
used for describing someone who might become something in the future: *The salesman wants to*

P

get prospective customers to buy the cars he is selling. | *He sent his résumé to prospective employers.*
→ **GRAMMAR: Prospective** is only used before a noun. Don't say: ~~*a customer who is prospective*~~. Say: *a prospective customer.*

possibly *adverb* → see **maybe**

post *noun* → see **job**

poster *noun* → see **advertisement**, **sign**

postpone *verb* → see **delay²**

pot *noun* → see **pan**

P

pour /pɔr/ *verb*

- ► pour
- ► spill
- ► drizzle
- ► run

pour
to make a liquid or another substance come out of a container: *She poured another cup of coffee.* | *He poured some milk into the pan.*

spill
to accidentally make a liquid or another substance come out of a container: *I spilled orange juice all over my new shirt.*

drizzle
to pour a small amount of liquid slowly onto some food. **Drizzle** is often used in cooking instructions: *Drizzle the salad dressing onto the lettuce.*

run
to make water come out of a faucet into a container: *He ran water into the tub for a bath.*
→ see **flow** for words meaning "to flow somewhere,"
→ see **it pours** at **rain²**, Topic **The Weather**

pour

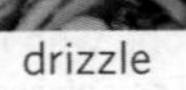
drizzle

pour

poverty /ˈpɑvə·ti/ *noun*

- ► poverty
- ► hard times

poverty
a situation in which people have very little money: *Half of the world is living* ***in poverty****, with not even enough money for food.* | *People in the area suffer from high rates of poverty and unemployment.*

hard times
a time when life is difficult because you do not have much money: *After the hurricane, a lot of people went through hard times, because they had lost their houses and their jobs.*
→ see **poor**

power /ˈpaʊə·/ *noun*

1 the ability to influence what people do
- ► power
- ► authority
- ► influence
- ► strength
- ► might

2 physical force or strength
- ► power
- ► force
- ► strength

1 the ability to influence what people do

power
the ability to control people or have an effect on what they do: *The military government has a lot of power and people have very little freedom.* | *Parents have* ***the power to*** *decide what is best for their children.*

authority (AWL)
the power you have because of your official position: *The President has* ***the authority to*** *declare war.*

influence
the power to affect what people do: *The Internet has a big* ***influence on*** *our lives.*

strength
the power of a country or leader: *The country's economic and military strength means that it has a lot of influence in the region.*

might
power, especially a country's military or economic power. **Might** is a formal or literary word: *The military might of the U.S. has not been able to win the war in Afghanistan.*

2 physical force or strength

power
the strong physical energy that something has: *The power of the explosion smashed windows across the street. | We use the power of the wind to generate electricity.*

force
the physical power with which something moves or hits another thing: *The force of the waves nearly knocked her over.*

strength
the physical power that something has, especially something natural: *The strength of the earthquake broke windows and knocked down walls.*

powerful *adjective* → see **important**, **strong**, Topic **Describing People's Emotions**

practical *adjective* → see **realistic**, **sensible**

practice¹ /ˈpræktɪs/ *noun*

1 the activity of doing something many times in order to become better at it
- ► practice
- ► training
- ► drill

2 an occasion when you practice doing something
- ► practice
- ► rehearsal

3 something that people usually do
- ► practice
- ► custom
- ► habit
- ► procedure

1 the activity of doing something many times in order to become better at it

practice
the activity of doing something many times so that you become better at doing it: *It takes a lot of practice to become a good golfer. | **With practice**, the piece of music will become easier.*

training
activities that help you learn how to do something: *All new employees receive **training in** how to use the computer system.*

drill
a way of teaching in which you make students do the same thing many times so that they learn it: *We do drills to learn the multiplication tables.*

2 an occasion when you practice doing something

practice
an occasion when you play a sport so that you become better at it: *Baseball practice is every Thursday after school. | Did you go to practice today?*

rehearsal
an occasion when people practice for a play, concert, or show: *We're having our first rehearsal of the play this evening.*

3 something that people usually do

practice
something that people usually do in a situation. **Practice** sounds a little formal: *Different religions have different beliefs and practices.*
→ You can also say that something is often done by saying **it is common practice**: ***It is common practice for** fathers **to** take time off work when their new baby is born.*

custom
something that people in a society usually do, because it is a tradition (=activity that has existed for a long time): ***It is the custom for** the bride's father **to** pay for the wedding.*

habit
something that you often or regularly do, especially without thinking about it: *The doctor said that she needed to change her eating habits by eating more healthy food. | I got into the habit of waking up early.*

procedure AWL
the correct or normal way of doing something, especially a way that has been officially agreed: *If you want to complain, please follow the company's complaints procedure.*
→ see **tradition**

practice² /ˈpræktɪs/ *verb*

- ► practice
- ► rehearse
- ► train
- ► work on
- ► drill

practice
to do something a lot, in order to become better at doing it: *He practices the guitar for two hours every day. | I wanted to practice my Spanish before we went to Mexico.*

rehearse
to practice for a play, concert, or show before people come to see it: *The actors are rehearsing for the first performance of the play.*

train
to learn the skills that you need to do a job or activity: *She is training to be a pilot.*

work on
to try to improve the way you do something, especially a particular skill: *His written English is good, but he needs to work on his spoken English.*

drill
to teach people something by making them do the same thing many times: *The teacher was **drilling** the class **in** irregular verbs.*

P

praise[1] /preɪz/ verb

- ► praise
- ► congratulate
- ► compliment
- ► flatter
- ► applaud (*formal*)
- ► commend (*formal*)

ANTONYMS → see **criticize**

praise
to say that someone has done something well, or that something is good: *His teacher **praised** him **for** all his hard work. | The movie was praised by the critics, but audiences hated it.*

congratulate
to tell someone that you are pleased about his or her success, or about something good that has happened to him or her: *Smith called to **congratulate** her **on** winning the election.*

compliment
to tell someone that he or she looks nice, or has done something well: *We all **complimented** her **on** the cheesecake, which was delicious.*

flatter
to say nice things about someone in a way you do not really mean, especially in order to make the person like you, or to get something that you want: *He seemed to be trying to flatter me, and I didn't trust him.*

applaud (*formal*)
to publicly praise a decision, action, or idea: *Business leaders applauded the government's decision to lower taxes.*

commend (*formal*)
to praise someone publicly and officially for his or her actions: *The police officer was **commended for** his bravery and given a special medal.*

praise[2] /preɪz/ noun

- ► praise
- ► compliment
- ► flattery
- ► approval
- ► credit
- ► recognition

praise
the things you say when you think someone has done something well: *The teacher gives the students plenty of praise and encouragement when they work hard. | Tom deserves **praise for** all the help he has given us.*

compliment
something nice that someone says to you about the way you look, or about the things you can do: *I got a lot of **compliments on** my new shoes.*

flattery
nice things that you say about someone when you do not really mean them, usually because you want to get something from him or her, or because you want him or her to like you: *I don't think you'll be able to use flattery to persuade him. You'll need better reasons than that.*

approval
words or behavior that show that you like someone or something, or think someone is doing the right thing: *By that age, children are often trying to win the approval of their friends.*

credit (AWL)
praise given to someone because he or she made something good happen: *The coach deserves the **credit for** the team's success – they couldn't have won without him.*

recognition
respect and praise from society for someone's work, especially after a long time: *It was many years before Van Gogh received **recognition for** his achievements as an artist.*

pray /preɪ/ verb

- ► pray
- ► worship
- ► praise

pray
to talk to God, for example to ask for help or give thanks: *We **pray for** the sick and their families. | She prays every day.*

worship
to show respect for God by praying, singing, and taking part in religious ceremonies: *The ancient Egyptians worshipped many gods.*

praise
to give thanks to God, especially by singing and praying in a church: *Every Sunday they come to the church to praise God.*

prayer /prer/ *noun*

- prayer
- worship
- praise

prayer
words that you say to God, or the activity of talking to God: *The children said their prayers and got into bed.* | *In Islam, prayer is very important, and a Muslim prays five times each day.*

worship
things that you do to show respect to God, such as praying, singing, or taking part in a religious ceremony: *The temple has been used as a place of worship for over 100 years.*

praise
thanks to God: *They sang songs of praise in the church.*

preacher *noun* → see **minister**

precious *adjective* → see **valuable**

precise *adjective* → see **exact**

precisely *adverb* → see **exactly**

precision /prɪˈsɪʒən/ *noun (formal)*

- precision
- accuracy

precision (AWL)
if a machine, method, or weapon does something with precision, it does something in a very careful and exact way and does not make any mistakes: *The weapon's precision is impressive – it can hit a target from hundreds of miles away.* | *The laser allows the surgeon to operate **with precision**.*

accuracy (AWL)
if a person or weapon throws or hits something with accuracy, it exactly reaches the target it is aiming at: *He throws the passes **with a high degree of accuracy**.*

predict /prɪˈdɪkt/ *verb*

- predict
- forecast
- foresee *(formal)*
- prophesy
- foretell
- anticipate *(formal)*
- project

predict (AWL)
to say what is going to happen before it happens: *The newspapers **predicted that** the president would be re-elected.* | *It is not possible to predict exactly when an earthquake will happen.*

forecast
to say what is likely to happen in the future, especially to say what the weather will be like or what will happen in the economic or political situation: *They are forecasting another very cold winter.*

foresee *(formal)*
to know that something is going to happen before it happens, especially a problem or something bad: *More people lost their jobs, just as the economists had foreseen.*

prophesy
to predict that an important event will happen, using special religious or magical powers: *Many years ago, a man called Nostradamus **prophesied that** the world would end in 2012.*

foretell
foretell means the same as **prophesy** but seems more old-fashioned or literary. **Foretell** is often used in the phrase **foretell the future**: *He was a poor but lucky boy, and it was **foretold that** he would marry the king's daughter.*

anticipate (AWL) *(formal)*
to expect that something will happen and be ready for it: *Luckily we had **anticipated that** it might rain, and there was a big tent for the wedding guests.*

project (AWL)
to calculate what the amount or cost of something will be in the future, using the information that you have now: *Energy prices are **projected to** rise by over 50% in the next ten years.*

prediction /prɪˈdɪkʃən/ *noun*

- prediction
- forecast
- prophecy

prediction (AWL)
a statement saying what you think will happen

P

in the future: *It is too early to make any **predictions about** who will win the election.* | *The students made predictions about which plants would grow best – the plants in the dark cupboard or the ones on the windowsill.*

forecast
a prediction about what the weather will be like, or about what will happen in the economic or political situation: *According to the weather forecast, it's going to stay hot this week.*

prophecy
a prediction made by someone with special religious or magical powers, especially about an important event: *This verse in the Bible is seen as a prophecy about the birth of Jesus.*

P

prefer /prɪˈfɚ/ *verb*

- ► prefer
- ► like something better
- ► would rather
- ► favor

prefer
to like something more than something else. **Prefer** sounds fairly formal: *"Which one do you like?" "I prefer the red one."* | *I **prefer** baseball **to** football.*

like something better
like better means the same as **prefer**, but sounds more informal and is what most people use in everyday English: *I'm good at math, which is probably why I **like it better than** English.*

would rather
to prefer to do or have one thing more than another: *I feel too tired to go out – I would rather stay home.* | *I **would rather** have less money and do a job that I love **than** have more money and hate my work.*

favor
to like one person or idea better than other things, and show this in the way you behave: *A good teacher never **favors** one student **over** the others.* | *The president faces opposition from politicians who favor cutting taxes.*
→ see **favorite[1]**, **favorite[2]**

preference *noun* → see **favorite[2]**

preferred *adjective* → see **favorite[1]**

pregnant /ˈpregnənt/ *adjective*

- ► pregnant
- ► be going to have a baby
- ► be expecting a baby

pregnant
if a woman is pregnant, she has a baby growing in her body: *She found out last week that she is pregnant.* | *I got up and gave the pregnant woman my seat.*

be going to have a baby
be going to have a baby means the same as **be pregnant**, but sounds more informal and is what most people use in everyday English: *Marco was so happy when his wife told him that she was going to have a baby.*

be expecting a baby *also* **be expecting a child**
if a woman is, or a couple are, expecting a baby, the woman is pregnant. You use this especially to talk about when the baby will be born: *Kimberly and Peter are expecting their first child in April.* | *He called his parents to tell them that he and his wife are expecting a baby.*
→ see **baby**

prejudice /ˈpredʒədɪs/ *noun*

- ► prejudice
- ► racism
- ► discrimination
- ► sexism
- ► bigotry
- ► intolerance
- ► bias

ANTONYMS → see **tolerance**

prejudice
an unfair belief that someone who is of a different sex, race, or religion is not as good as you are: *Even now, black people still have to deal with prejudice.* | *There is **prejudice against** disabled people, which makes it difficult for them to find a job.*

racism
bad and unfair treatment of people who belong to a different race: *Because of racism, black people didn't have the same rights as white people.*

discrimination
different and unfair treatment of people because of their sex, race, religion, or the way they look: *There are laws to prevent **discrimination against** women.* | *Racial discrimination is no longer acceptable in American society.*

sexism AWL
the unfair treatment of one sex, usually women, because of the belief that one sex is weaker, less intelligent, or less important than the other: *I accused him of sexism when he said that men were better drivers than women.*

bigotry
the actions or beliefs of someone who does not like people who belong to a different race,

religion, or country: *His speech was full of bigotry and religious hatred against Jewish people.*

intolerance
an unwillingness to accept a way of behaving or a belief that is different from your own: *Religious intolerance forced many people to leave Germany and come to America.*

bias (AWL)
an unfair opinion about someone, that makes you treat that person differently: *He accused the umpire of showing **bias toward** the home team.*
→ see **unfair**

prejudiced /ˈpredʒədɪst/ *adjective*

- ► prejudiced
- ► racist
- ► sexist
- ► biased
- ► discriminatory (*formal*)
- ► bigoted
- ► narrow-minded

ANTONYMS → see **tolerant**

prejudiced
believing unfairly that someone who is of a different race, sex, or religion is not as good as you are: *Some men are **prejudiced against** women and don't like having a female boss.*

racist
treating people of other races badly because you think your race is better than theirs: *There have been several racist attacks against Jewish businesses.*

sexist
believing that one sex is weaker, less intelligent, and less important than the other. You usually use **sexist** when men believe this about women: *He is always making sexist comments, like saying girls are no good at sports.*

biased (AWL)
thinking that one person or group is better than another, and treating them differently and unfairly: *He accused the witness of being **biased against** his clients because they are rich.*

discriminatory (*formal*)
discriminatory actions, rules, or laws unfairly treat one person or group of people differently from others: *The lawyers argued that a law that stops a gay couple from getting married is discriminatory.*

bigoted
someone who is bigoted dislikes people who belong to a different race, religion, or country: *He is just a bigoted old man who hates all foreigners.*

narrow-minded
narrow-minded people are unwilling to accept ideas or customs that are new or different: *My mother is one of those narrow-minded people who does not believe that popular music can be an art form.*

premier *adjective* → see **top[2]**

prepare *verb* → see **cook[1]**, **ready (2)**

prepared *adjective* → see **ready**

prescribe *verb* → see **treat**, Topic **Medical Treatment**

prescription *noun* → see **medicine**, Topic **Medical Treatment**

presence /ˈprezəns/ *noun*

- ► presence
- ► existence
- ► attendance

ANTONYMS → see **lack[1]**

presence
the state of being in a particular place at a particular time: *Our tests showed the presence of dangerous chemicals in the water. | He lay there asleep, completely unaware of my presence.*

existence
the fact that something exists somewhere: *The scientists thought they had discovered the existence of water on one of Saturn's moons.*

attendance
the act of being at an event or in a place, such as a meeting or school, especially when you go there regularly: *Her attendance at school this year has been very good, with just one absence last month.*

present[1] /ˈprezənt/ *adjective*

1 in a particular place or at a particular event
- ► present
- ► in attendance

ANTONYMS → see **absent**

2 happening or existing now
- ► present
- ► current
- ► existing

1 in a particular place or at a particular event

present
in a particular place or at a particular event: *Oxygen and hydrogen are both **present in** the*

Earth's atmosphere. | *Business leaders from around the globe were* ***present at*** *the meeting.*
→ GRAMMAR: You cannot use **present** with this meaning before a noun. Don't say: ~~*All the present people heard him say it.*~~ Say: *All the people present heard him say it* or *All the people who were present heard him say it.*

in attendance
if you are in attendance at an important event, you are there: *They had a private funeral with only a few close friends and family* ***in attendance.***

2 happening or existing now

present
happening or existing now: *The present economic situation is difficult, but it will improve.* | *There are no new updates to the software at the present time.*

current
happening or existing at this time. **Current** is used especially about something that is not expected to stay the same: *Read about current events in a newspaper.* | *He wore his jeans down low on his hips, in the current fashion.*

existing
an existing thing is one that exists now or that you have now. **Existing** is used especially about something that may change: *The new classrooms will be added to the existing building.*
→ GRAMMAR: When **present**, **current**, and **existing** are used with this meaning, they are always used before a noun. Don't say: ~~*We will make our decision based on the situation that is present/current/existing*~~. Say: *We will make our decision based on the present/current/existing situation.*
→ see **modern**

ADVERBS
You can make the adjectives **current** and **present** into adverbs by using an **-ly** ending: *The company currently employs 113 people.* | *The writer is presently working on a new novel.*

present² /ˈprezənt/ *noun*

1 something that you give someone
- present
- gift
- donation
- reward

2 the time that is happening now
- the present
- the present day
- today
- modern times

1 something that you give someone

present
something that you give someone on a special occasion: *I need to get a birthday* ***present for*** *my dad.* | *The watch was a* ***present from*** *my folks.*

gift
gift means the same as **present** but sounds slightly more formal: *These earrings were a* ***gift from*** *my boyfriend for my birthday.*

donation
money that you give to help a group of people or an organization: *People gave* ***donations of*** *food and money to help the victims of the flood.*

reward
something that you give to someone for doing something good: *The man who lost his wallet is offering a $100 reward to the person who brings it back.*

2 the time that is happening now

the present
the time that is happening now: *In school, we studied the history of the United States from 1776 to the present.* | *Try to stop worrying about the past and think about the present.*

the present day
the period of history in which we are now living. You often use **the present day** when you are comparing something to a time in history: *This traditional way of making rugs is still used in* ***the present day.***
→ GRAMMAR: **The present day** is always singular. Don't say: ~~*It is still used in the present days*~~. Say: *It is still used in the present day.*

today
today means the same as **the present day** but is less formal: *The young people of today face an uncertain future.* | *Today's cell phones are much smaller than the early models.*

modern times
modern times means the same as **the present day**, and is often used to compare technology and ways of living to earlier times in history: *In modern times, we travel long distances much more quickly than ever before.*
→ see **future (1)**, **now**, **past¹**

presentation *noun* → see **speech**

preserve *verb* → see **protect**

president *noun* → see **chairman**, **leader**, Topic **Government and Politics**

press¹ /pres/ *verb*

- ► press
- ► crush
- ► squeeze
- ► compress
- ► squash
- ► pinch
- ► mash

press
to firmly push something hard against something else: *The point of the pencil snapped as he pressed it against the paper.* | *Press down on the dough and flatten it into a circle.*
→ You also use **press** to mean "to touch a button or switch with your finger in order to make a piece of equipment start or stop working": *Press the right-hand button to stop the machine.*

crush
to push down hard on something and break or damage it: *Be careful not to crush the strawberries when you pack them into the boxes.*

squeeze
to press something firmly together with your fingers or hands: *If you squeeze the toy, it makes a funny noise.* | *I squeezed some ketchup onto my fries.*

compress
to press something, or make it smaller, so that it takes up less space. **Compress** is more formal than **press**: *The machine **compresses** the pieces of cardboard **into** a small solid block.*

squash
to press something so that it becomes flatter, often damaging it: *I squashed my hat when I sat on it.*

pinch
to press someone's skin between your finger and thumb: *Ouch! Stop pinching me!*

mash
to crush food until it is soft: *Mash the potatoes with milk and butter until they are really smooth.*
→ see **push¹**

press² *noun* → see **media**

pressure /ˈpreʃɚ/ *noun*

1 the force of one thing pressing on something else
- ► pressure
- ► strain
- ► stress

2 the state or feeling of having too many problems
- ► pressure
- ► demands
- ► stress
- ► strain

3 an attempt to persuade or force someone to do something
- ► pressure
- ► coercion (*formal*)
- ► duress (*formal*)

1 the force of one thing pressing on something else

pressure
the force of one thing pressing on or against something else: *The nurse put **pressure on** the wound to stop it bleeding.* | *The pressure of the water behind the dam became too great, and the dam burst* (=broke).

strain
a force that pulls, stretches, or pushes something: *The **strain on** the cables supporting the bridge is enormous.*

stress (AWL)
a force that affects or damages something, especially by pressing or pulling: *Running puts **stress on** the joints in your legs, so it is important to wear good shoes.*

2 the state or feeling of having too many problems

pressure
the state or feeling of having too many problems or difficult things to do, which makes people worry: *We have to take a lot of tests, and dealing with the pressure can be tough.* | *The deadline for the work was two days away, and we were feeling the pressure.*

demands
the difficult things that you need to do, that take up your time: *With every year, the **demands of** the job seem to increase, and I spend more and more time at work.*
→ **GRAMMAR:** You always use **demands** in its plural form. Don't say: ~~*A demand of the job is dealing with customers*~~. Say: *One of the demands of the job is dealing with customers.*

stress (AWL)
a continuous feeling of worry about work or your personal life, which prevents you from relaxing: *Your headaches are probably caused by stress from all the work you have been doing this month.* | *Mark has been **under** a lot of **stress** lately because he can't find a job.*

strain
a feeling of worry that is caused by having to work too hard or deal with too many problems: *I found the **strain of** working 12 hours a day too much to handle.*

3 an attempt to persuade or force someone to do something

pressure
an attempt to persuade or force someone to do something, usually by using influence, arguments, or threats: *The salesman kept putting **pressure on** me to buy the most expensive model.* | *We're **under pressure** at work **to** get the project done quickly.*

coercion (*formal*)
the use of threats or physical force to make someone do something he or she does not want to do: *Torture is an illegal form of coercion.*

duress (*formal*)
illegal or unfair threats that are used to make someone do something he or she does not want to do. **Duress** is almost always used in the phrase **under duress** and is used especially in legal language: *If the police put the man **under duress** to get the confession, the judge could dismiss the case.*

→ see **persuasion**

presume *verb* → see **think**

pretend /prɪˈtend/ *verb*

- ► pretend
- ► make believe (*informal*)
- ► imagine
- ► suppose

pretend
to behave as if something is true or real, when it is not: *She closed her eyes and **pretended to** be asleep.* | *Daddy, let's **pretend that** we are going to the Moon.*

make believe (*informal*)
to pretend that something is true, especially as a game. **Make believe** is used especially by children or when talking to children: *Make believe you are animals in a jungle.*

imagine
to use your mind to think what something could be like or must have been like: *I want you all to **imagine that** you are pirates looking for buried treasure.* | *Can you **imagine what** it would be like to have no food for days?*

suppose
to imagine what might happen if a particular situation existed. **Suppose** is usually used at the beginning of a question: *Suppose you lost your job tomorrow. What would you do?*

→ see **act**[1]

pretty[1] *adverb* → see **fairly**

pretty[2] *adjective* → see **beautiful**, Topic **Describing People's Looks**

prevent /prɪˈvent/ *verb*

- ► prevent
- ► stop
- ► avoid
- ► deter (*formal*)

prevent
to do something now so that something will not happen or is not done in the future: *To prevent arguments, Mom made us share the candy equally.* | *We wrapped the vase carefully to **prevent** it **from** breaking.*

stop
to end something that is happening or being done now, or to prevent something: *We want to **stop** teenagers **from** smoking so that they can become healthy adults.* | *How can we **stop** this **from** happening again?*

→ **GRAMMAR: Prevent** and **stop** are never followed by "to do something". Don't say: *~~We want to prevent/stop kids to smoke~~*. Say: *We want to **prevent/stop** kids **from** smoking.*

avoid
to do something in order to prevent something bad from happening to you: *I jumped out of the way to avoid being hit by the falling rocks.*

deter (*formal*)
to stop someone from doing something by making it difficult or unpleasant: *The store uses closed-circuit TV cameras to **deter** people **from** stealing.*

→ see **block**[1] for words meaning "to prevent someone or something from moving or making progress"

preventable /prɪˈventəbəl/ *adjective*

- ► preventable
- ► avoidable

preventable
if something bad is preventable, someone could stop it before it happens. You use **preventable** about things that are very serious, like accidents, diseases, and deaths: *The accident was easily preventable – it never should have happened.* | *Deaths from the disease are preventable if patients take the right medicine.*

avoidable
avoidable means the same as **preventable**, but is not used to talk about diseases. You use **avoidable** about more situations than preventable: *The mistakes that led to this disaster were all easily avoidable.*

prevention /prɪˈvenʃən/ *noun*

- ► prevention
- ► deterrence (*formal*)
- ► prohibition (*formal*)

prevention
the things you do in order to stop something bad from happening: *We started to focus on the* ***prevention of*** *the disease, rather than just treating it.* | *One basic rule of fire prevention is to make sure that electrical cords are in good condition.*

deterrence (*formal*)
the use of a punishment or a threat to make people less likely to do something, because they understand that it will have bad results: *The threat of going to jail is supposed to act as a* ***deterrence against*** *crime.*

prohibition (AWL) (*formal*)
the act of not allowing people to do something, especially by making it illegal: *To keep the sand clean, there is a* ***prohibition of*** *dogs and other pets on the beach.*

previous *adjective* → see **last¹**

previously *adverb* → see Function Word **before**

price /praɪs/ *noun*

- ► price
- ► cost
- ► value
- ► charge
- ► fee
- ► rate

price
the amount of money that you must pay in order to buy something that is being sold: *Airline ticket prices have gone up again.* | *For* ***the price of*** *a cup of coffee, you can help a child in Africa get the vaccines he or she needs.*

cost
the amount of money you have to pay for something: *The stadium was built* ***at a cost of*** *over $300 million.* | *Does this include the cost of delivery?*

value
the amount of money that something is worth: *A new kitchen can increase the value of your home.*

charge
the amount of money you have to pay to do or use something: *There's a small charge for Internet access at the hotel.*

fee (AWL)
an amount of money that you pay to do something, especially to enter a place, join a group, or get advice from a lawyer or doctor: *The gym membership fee is $100 a year.*

rate
a charge that is different at different times, for different people, or for other reasons: *Some hotels offer special rates for senior citizens.* | *You may be able to get a lower rate in the winter.*

pride /praɪd/ *noun*

1 a feeling of satisfaction and pleasure because of something you have done
- ► pride
- ► self-esteem
- ► self-respect
- ► dignity

2 a belief that you are better than other people
- ► pride
- ► arrogance
- ► conceit
- ► vanity
- ► self-righteousness

ANTONYMS → see **modesty**

1 a feeling of satisfaction and pleasure because of something you have done

pride
a feeling of satisfaction and pleasure that you have because you have done something well or have something good: *I love my job and take great* ***pride in*** *my work.* | *Margo's parents watched* ***with pride*** *as she collected the award.*

self-esteem
the feeling that you are a good person and that people should like you: *Losing his job was a real blow to his self-esteem.*

self-respect
the feeling that you are a good person and that people should respect you: *Now, with a new job and her own apartment, Juanita finally has her self-respect back.*

dignity
calm and controlled behavior that makes other people respect you: *She walked with great dignity through the screaming crowd.*

P

2 a belief that you are better than other people

pride
a belief that you are better than other people and do not need their help or support: *He had too much pride to ask for help.* | *One day, your pride will get you in trouble.*

arrogance
a rude and unfriendly attitude that shows that someone thinks he or she is better or more important than other people: *He always assumes he is right, and his arrogance makes him unpopular with the other students.*

conceit
an attitude that shows that you are too proud of what you can do, how you look, or how important you are: *She talked about her very impressive achievements without showing any conceit.*

vanity
too much pride in yourself so that you are always thinking about yourself and your appearance: *Losing my hair was a blow to my vanity.* | *Teresa was beautiful, but she was also modest and totally lacking in vanity.*

self-righteousness
the feeling of being very sure that your beliefs, opinions, and actions are the only ones that are right: *The self-righteousness of people who say that mothers should stay home with their children annoys me. I should be able to make my own choices!*
→ see **proud**

priest *noun* → see **minister**

principle *noun* → see **conscience**, **morality**, **rule[1]**

print[1] *verb* → see **publish**, **write**

print[2] *noun* → see **photograph[1]**

printer *noun* → see Topic **Computers and the Internet**

prior to *preposition* → see Function Word **before**

prison /ˈprɪzən/ *noun*

1 a building or room where criminals are kept (nouns)
- prison
- jail
- penitentiary (*formal*)
- cell
- dungeon
- custody

2 to make someone be kept in a prison (verbs)
- put someone in prison/jail
- lock up (*informal*)
- jail
- imprison (*formal*)
- incarcerate (*formal*)

ANTONYMS → see **free[2]**

1 a building or room where criminals are kept (nouns)

prison
a large building where criminals are sent to stay as punishment for a crime: *She was sent to prison for five years because of the robbery.* | *He spent 26 years* ***in prison*** *for killing a policeman.*

jail
a prison, or a place where people who have been charged with a crime are kept before they are judged in a court of law. **Jail** sounds more informal than **prison**: *He is being held in the LA County Jail until his trial.* | *Curtis has been* ***in jail*** *for nearly nine years.*

penitentiary (*formal*)
a prison, especially a large one: *The judge sent her to the state penitentiary for five years.*

cell
a small room where a prisoner is kept: *Some prisoners were locked up in their cells for 24 hours a day.*

dungeon
a dark prison that is under a building such as a castle. **Dungeons** were used in the past: *He was captured by the king and thrown in the dungeon.*

custody
if someone is in custody, that person is in prison before a trial, or while the police find facts about a crime: *Your son will be held* ***in custody*** *until the trial date.* | *When the plane landed, the men were taken* ***into custody*** *by the FBI.*

2 to make someone be kept in a prison (verbs)

put someone in prison/jail *also* **send someone to prison/jail**
to officially order someone to be taken to a prison or jail and kept there: *Police put the young man in jail overnight for drunk driving.* | *If Rogers is found guilty of murder, he could be sent to prison for life.*

lock up (*informal*)
to put and keep someone in prison. Use **lock up** especially when you think someone deserves to be in prison: *I think rapists should be locked up for the rest of their lives.*

jail
to put and keep someone in prison as a punishment, or to keep someone in prison before he or she goes to court to be judged for a crime. **Jail** is used especially in newspaper reports: *Most of the local drug dealers have now been jailed.*

imprison (*formal*)
to put and keep someone in prison. Use **imprison** especially when you think the punishment is wrong or unfair: *Government forces imprisoned and beat many of the protesters.*

incarcerate (*formal*)
incarcerate means the same as **put in prison**: *Williams has been **incarcerated for** the murder since 1996.*

prisoner /ˈprɪzənɚ/ *noun*

- ► **prisoner**
- ► **convict**
- ► **inmate**
- ► **captive** (*formal*)
- ► **hostage**
- ► **prisoner of war**

prisoner
someone who must stay in a prison as a punishment for a crime: *The prisoner will not be released until she has served her sentence.* | *There are two prisoners in each cell.*
→ You can also use **prisoner** to talk about a person who is being kept in a place when he or she does not want to be there: *The wicked witch kept the princess as her prisoner for 20 years.*

convict
someone who has been proven to be guilty of a crime and sent to prison: *State police are still looking for a convict who escaped from prison last night.*

inmate
someone who is kept in a prison or mental hospital: *Many of the inmates work in the prison kitchen or laundry room.*

captive (*formal*)
someone who is kept as a prisoner, especially in a war: *The captives spent the rest of the war in a prison camp.*

hostage
someone who is kept as a prisoner by a person or group, until they get the things they want: *The group took four hostages and demanded that one of their members be released from prison by the government.*

prisoner of war *also* **POW**
a member of the military who is caught by the enemy during a war and kept as a prisoner: *Senator John McCain was a prisoner of war during the Vietnam War.*
→ see **criminal**

privacy /ˈpraɪvəsi/ *noun*

- ► **privacy**
- ► **solitude**
- ► **seclusion**

privacy
the state of being alone or separated from other people so that they do not see or hear you: ***With seven brothers and sisters all living at home, you don't get much privacy!*** | ***The yard was surrounded by trees, giving us complete privacy.***

solitude
the state of being alone, especially when you enjoy it: *I had a few wonderful hours of solitude before the rest of the family got home.*

seclusion
the state of being away from other people, especially because you do not want people near you: *After their son's death, the family remained **in seclusion** for months.*

private /ˈpraɪvət/ *adjective*

1 secret and not for other people to know about
- ► **private**
- ► **secret**
- ► **personal**
- ► **confidential** (*formal*)
- ► **innermost**
- ► **intimate**
- ► **classified**

2 relating to a quiet place without other people
- ► **private**
- ► **secluded**

1 secret and not for other people to know about

private
if something is private, it is secret or is about things that you do not want other people to know: *Please don't read that letter – it's private.* | *Go away! We're having a private conversation!*

secret
if something is secret, only a few people know about it, and it is kept hidden from others: *I keep my jewelry in a secret place that my sister will never find.* | *They kept their relationship secret from their parents.*

personal
if something is personal, it relates to your own

P

life, especially to things that you do not want other people to know about: *The movie star refused to answer questions about his girlfriend or his personal life.*

confidential (*formal*)
if information is confidential, you must not show it or talk about it to other people. You use **confidential** especially in official or legal language: *Doctors must keep information about their patients confidential.*

innermost
your innermost feelings or thoughts are your most personal and private ones: *She was able to express her innermost feelings through poetry.*

intimate
relating to very private or personal subjects, especially things about love or sex: *I told my sister my most intimate secrets.*

classified
if information is classified, the government has ordered it to be kept secret: *He is accused of giving classified information to the press.*

ADVERBS

You can make the adjectives **private**, **secret**, **confidential**, and **intimate** into adverbs by using an **-ly** ending: *Can I talk to you privately?* | *They met secretly, without their parents knowing about it.* | *Doctors talk to their patients confidentially.*

2 relating to a quiet place without other people

private
if a place is private, there are not a lot of other people there: *Let's go somewhere more private where we can talk without being overheard.*

secluded
a secluded building or area outdoors is very private and quiet: *The beach can only be reached by boat, so it is quiet and secluded.*
→ see **secret**

privately /'praɪvətli/ *adverb*

- privately
- in private
- secretly
- in secret
- in confidence

ANTONYMS → see **publicly**

privately
if you say something privately, you say it to someone when you are away from other people so that nobody else can hear you: *Can we talk about this privately? I don't want to discuss our problems in front of our friends.* | *A few parents have complained privately to the principal about the coach's behavior.*

in private
an action that happens in private happens in a place where other people cannot see or hear it: *We believe that the government has no right to say what we can do in private.*

secretly
if you do something secretly, you try to do it so that other people do not know it is happening: *Mom had been secretly planning the trip for months, and we were all completely surprised.*

in secret
in a place or way that other people do not know about: *The couple got married in secret because they knew their families would not approve.* | *The police had been listening in secret to their phone conversations.*

in confidence
if you tell someone something in confidence, you do not want him or her to tell anyone else: *I'm telling you this in confidence, so don't repeat it to anyone.*

privilege *noun* → see **advantage**

privileged *adjective* → see **rich**

prize /praɪz/ *noun*

- prize
- award
- medal
- trophy
- reward
- honor

prize
something that someone gets for winning or doing something very well, especially in a competition or game: *I was so proud of Jorge when he won first prize in the poetry competition.* | *She won the Nobel Peace Prize in 2011.*

award
a prize given to a person, group, or organization for making or doing something well or better than others: *The show won an **award for** the best television drama.* | *Who received the best player award?*

medal
a round flat piece of metal that someone gets as a prize, or for doing something brave: *He won four gold medals at the Olympics.*

trophy
a metal cup or a similar object that someone

gets for winning a game or race: *She won several **trophies for** swimming when she was at UCLA.*

reward
something that you are given for doing something good: *My parents bought me the game as a **reward for** getting good grades.* | *The man offered a $150 **reward for** the return of his phone.*

honor
something that people give to someone to show that they respect and admire what he or she has done: *The firefighters received their country's highest **honor for** bravery.*

probable *adjective* → see **likely**

probably *adverb* → see **maybe**

problem /ˈprɑbləm/ *noun*

- ► problem
- ► difficulty
- ► trouble
- ► complication
- ► setback
- ► pitfall
- ► dilemma

ANTONYMS → see **answer[2] (2)**

problem
a bad situation or event that is hard to deal with, that is causing harm, or that is stopping you from doing something: *She began to have problems at school after she got sick and missed a lot of classes.* | *Unemployment is a serious problem, and it is getting worse.* | *The computers aren't working, which is causing a lot of problems.*

difficulty
a problem that makes it hard to do something, or a situation in which you have problems: *The project ran into difficulties when the government cut its funding.* | *Some of the children have difficulty understanding English.*
→ **GRAMMAR:** Don't say: ~~*I had a difficulty learning English*~~. Say: *I had difficulty learning English* or *I had difficulties learning English.*

trouble
trouble means the same as **difficulty** but sounds more informal: *I have trouble sleeping when it's this hot.* | *Our troubles began when I lost my job.*
→ **GRAMMAR:** Don't use "a" before **trouble**. Don't say: ~~*I've been having a trouble with my car*~~. Say: *I've been having trouble with my car*.

complication
another problem that makes something even more difficult to do or deal with: *When we were planning the wedding dinner, one complication was that some of the guests didn't eat meat.*

setback
a problem that prevents progress or makes a situation worse than it was: *The Colts suffered a major setback when their star quarterback got injured.*

pitfall
a problem that is likely to happen in a particular job or activity: *The book helps you avoid some of **the pitfalls of** buying a used car.*

dilemma
a situation in which you have to make a difficult choice between two things: *I am **in a dilemma** about taking the job because it means moving to New York, which I don't want to do.*
→ see **puzzle** for "a math problem"

process *noun* → see **system**

produce[1] /prəˈdus/ *verb*

1 to produce food, oil, or other things as part of a natural process

- ► produce
- ► yield (*formal*)
- ► bear (*formal*)

2 to produce results or an effect

- ► produce
- ► yield (*formal*)
- ► generate (*formal*)

1 to produce food, oil, or other things as part of a natural process

produce
to grow something or make it as part of a natural process. You use **produce** about areas of land or about farmers: *The area produces grapes that are used in wine.* | *The U.S. does not produce as much oil as it uses.* | *Our bodies produce carbon dioxide as we breathe.*

yield (*formal*)
to produce something such as oil or food, especially through a natural process. You use **yield** especially when you are talking about how much something produces: *Each cow yields about six gallons of milk a day.* | *The bread dough did not rise correctly and yielded a small heavy loaf.*

bear (*formal*)
if a tree bears fruit or nuts, it produces them: *The old apple tree no longer bears fruit.*

2 to produce results or an effect

produce
to make something happen or have a particular effect: *Higher temperatures will produce a rise in sea levels.* | *New drugs are producing very good results in treating cancer.*

yield (*formal*)
to produce results or profit: *Our research has yielded some important evidence that global warming exists.*

generate (AWL) (*formal*)
if a company generates revenue (=money), jobs, sales, etc., it does something that makes money, creates jobs, sells things, etc.: *This year the company generated $1.2 million in revenue.*
→ see **make** for **produce** meaning "to make something in a factory to sell"
→ see **cause²**

produce² *noun* → see **product**

producer *noun* → see **maker**, Topic **Entertainment**

product /ˈprɑdʌkt/ *noun*

- ► **product**
- ► **goods**
- ► **merchandise**
- ► **produce**
- ► **export**
- ► **import**

product
something that people grow or make in order to sell: *All the products we sell are organic.* | *Most people go to the drugstore to buy beauty products.*

goods
things that are produced in order to be sold: *The store sells sporting goods such as golf clubs and tennis rackets.* | *The goods are transported across the country on trains.*

merchandise
the goods that are being sold in a particular store: *You can buy a range of baseball merchandise from the team's website.*
→ **GRAMMAR: Merchandise** cannot be used in the plural. Don't say: ~~*They looked at the merchandises*~~.

produce
food, especially fruit and vegetables, that people grow to sell: *All the produce at the farmers' market is so fresh – the tomatoes I bought tasted fantastic.*

export (AWL)
a product that one country sells to another country: *Fruit is one of Chile's main* ***exports to*** *the U.S.*

import
a product that is brought into a country to be sold: *Imports such as toys and clothing often come from Asia.*
→ see **result¹** for **product** meaning "the result of a situation or someone's actions"

production /prəˈdʌkʃən/ *noun*

- ► **production**
- ► **output**
- ► **manufacturing**
- ► **the making of something** (*informal*)

production
the process of making or growing things in order to sell them: *This land will be used for the* ***production of*** *food.* | *The new model of the car is now* ***in production.***
→ **Production** is also the amount of something that is made: *The company increased production to meet the demand for its products.*

output (AWL)
the amount of goods or work that a company, machine, or country produces: *The newer faster machines allowed the factory to increase its output by 10%.*

manufacturing
the activity of making goods in factories: *In the recession, thousands of jobs were lost in manufacturing in the south.*

the making of something (*informal*)
the process or business of producing something: *The cast and crew lived on the island for five months during the making of the movie.*
→ see **play²**, **show²**

productive /prəˈdʌktɪv/ *adjective*

- ► **productive**
- ► **fruitful**
- ► **prolific**
- ► **fertile**

productive
producing or achieving a lot: *At work, I am more productive in the morning.* | *The mine gradually became less productive as the coal began to run out.*

fruitful
a fruitful activity or period of time produces results that are good or useful: *We had a fruitful meeting and made a lot of progress.*

prolific
a prolific artist, musician, or writer produces a lot of art, music, or literature: *She is a prolific author who has written 22 novels and several books of poetry.*

fertile
fertile land or soil is able to produce good crops: *Crops are grown all year round on the fertile land near the river.*
→ see **hard-working**, **successful**, **useful**

ADVERBS

You can make the adjectives **productive**, **fruitful**, and **prolific** into adverbs by using an **-ly** ending: *The new software helps us work more productively.* | *The countries are working together closely and more fruitfully than in the past.*

profession *noun* → see **job**, Topic **Jobs and Work**

professor *noun* → see **teacher**, Topic **Education**

profit /ˈprɑfɪt/ *noun*

- profit
- earnings
- interest
- dividend

profit
money that you make by selling something for a higher price than the amount that it cost you to produce or buy it: *The oil companies made huge profits following the rise in oil prices.* | *The cost of making each doll is $2 and we sell them for $3.50, so there is a **profit of** $1.50 on every doll.*

earnings
the profit a company or country makes: *Earnings from tourism in the first six months of this year reached $2.53 billion.*

interest
money that a bank pays you regularly on the amount you have saved: *The bank is offering to pay 3% interest on this type of savings account.*
→ **Interest** also means the extra money that you must pay back on money you have borrowed: *If the interest is 5%, you will pay back $105 if you borrow $100.*

dividend
a part of a company's profit that the company pays back to people who have shares in the company: *The company paid shareholders a dividend of 70 cents a share.*

program *noun* → see **plan[1]**, **show[2]**, Topic **Computers and the Internet**, **Entertainment**

progress[1] /ˈprɑgrəs/ *noun*

- progress
- development
- advance
- breakthrough

progress
the process of getting better at doing something or closer to achieving something: *The tests help to show the students' **progress in** each subject.* | *The **progress of** the peace talks has been slow at times.*

development
the process of gradually getting bigger, stronger, or more advanced: *The disease affects Bobby's physical development so that he is smaller than other children of his age.*
→ You can also use **development** to talk about the process of making something that is more advanced, for example a product or idea: *The company is working on the **development of** a new drug.*

advance
a change that brings progress: ***Advances in** technology have led to computers that are smaller and much more powerful.*

breakthrough
an important new discovery in something you have been studying, that comes after a lot of hard work and brings progress: *Detectives believe they have made an important **breakthrough in** solving the case.*
→ see **success**

progress[2] *verb* → see **improve**, **move**, **pass[1]**

prohibit *verb* → see **forbid**

prohibited *adjective* → see **forbidden**, **illegal**

project /ˈprɑdʒekt/ *noun*

- project
- mission
- undertaking

project (AWL)
an important piece of work that you plan carefully, and that often takes a long time: *Work on the new freeway project will begin next month.* | *Each student will do a research project in science this semester.*

mission
an important job or task that someone has been given to do: *Our mission is to make sure that every child receives good health care.*

undertaking (AWL)
an important or difficult job that takes a lot of time, effort, and money: *Building the Hoover Dam was a massive undertaking.*
→ see **work[2]** (**3**) for **project** meaning "a piece of work that you do for school"

prom *noun* → see **dance**

promise¹ /ˈprɑmɪs/ *verb*

- ► promise
- ► swear
- ► vow
- ► guarantee
- ► give someone your word
- ► take an oath
- ► pledge
- ► assure

promise
to tell someone that you will definitely do something: *Maria has **promised to** take me to the zoo on Saturday.* | *I **promised** my parents **that** I would clean my room.*

swear
to make a very serious promise to do something: *He **swore to** tell the truth in court.* | *I **swore that** I would find her wherever she was.*

vow
vow means the same as **swear** but is used especially in literature: *When she left home, she **vowed that** she would never go back.*

guarantee (AWL)
to make a strong promise to do something, or to promise that something will happen. If you **guarantee** something, you are emphasizing that it will definitely happen: *Can you **guarantee that** this won't happen again?* | *The company **guarantees to** replace the product if it doesn't work.*

give someone your word
to make a sincere promise to someone that you do not intend to break. You use **give someone your word** when you want someone to know that he or she can trust you to do what you say: ***I give you my word that** I won't tell anyone else about this.*

take an oath *also* **swear an oath**
to make a formal or official promise to do something, especially to do a job or to support someone or something: *Doctors have to **take an oath to** do everything they can to save lives.* | *New citizens are asked to **swear an oath** of loyalty **to** the United States.*

pledge
to make a formal promise to do something. A **pledge** is usually something official that you sign your name to or say in public: *The mayor **pledged to** reduce crime.* | *"I pledge allegiance to the flag of the United States of America" means that you promise to be loyal to our country.*

assure (AWL)
to tell or promise someone that something will happen so that he or she feels less worried: *I want to **assure** fans **that** we will do all we can to make the team successful.*

promise² /ˈprɑmɪs/ *noun*

- ► promise
- ► vow
- ► oath
- ► pledge
- ► assurance
- ► guarantee
- ► warranty

promise
if you make a promise, you say that you will definitely do something: *Juan made a **promise to** quit smoking.* | *He broke his **promise to** me* (=he didn't do what he promised), *and I can't forgive him.*

vow
a very serious promise that you make to yourself or someone else. **Vow** sounds formal or literary: *He made a public **vow to** continue the fight against organized crime.* | *Millions of viewers watched the royal couple exchange wedding vows.*

oath
a formal or official promise, especially to do a job or to support someone: *The governor raised his hand to take **the oath of** office* (=the promise to do his job well and honestly).

pledge
a public or written promise to do something: *The president made a **pledge to** spend more on education.*

assurance (AWL)
a promise that something is definitely true, or will definitely happen, so that someone will feel less worried: *Despite **assurances that** everything is fine, many of us are still worried that we might lose our jobs.*

guarantee (AWL)
a promise by a company to repair or replace a product if it breaks or stops working: *All the store's products come with a money-back guarantee.*

warranty
a guarantee to fix or replace a product within a particular time period: *The laptop has a three-year warranty.*

prompt *verb* → see **remind**

pronounce /prəˈnaʊns/ *verb*

- ► pronounce
- ► say (*informal*)

pronounce
to make the sound of a word or letter: *When*

I first started learning English, I pronounced the "d" in Wednesday. | *I know how to spell his name, but I don't know how to pronounce it.*

say (*informal*)
say means the same as **pronounce** but is informal: *I know how to spell his name, but I don't know how to say it.*
→ see **say**

proof /pruf/ *noun*

- ► **proof**
- ► **evidence**
- ► **documentation**
- ► **confirmation**

proof
facts that prove something is true: *The police don't have any* ***proof that*** *he stole the money.* | *Do you have any* ***proof of*** *your identity, such as a driver's license or a passport?*

evidence (AWL)
things that you see, hear, or learn that make you believe that something exists or is true: *Scientists are looking for* ***evidence of*** *life on Mars.* | *There is no* ***evidence that*** *vitamin C actually prevents colds.*
→ **Evidence** also means the facts and information that are used to prove that someone is guilty or not guilty of a crime: *The police collected a lot of evidence showing that Morris committed the robbery.*
→ **GRAMMAR: Evidence** cannot be used in the plural. Don't say: ~~*We can show you evidences that this is true*~~. Say: *We can show you evidence that this is true.*

documentation (AWL)
official documents or written reports that prove that something is true or correct: *You must provide documentation when opening a bank account, for example some form of ID and a bill with your address on it.*

confirmation (AWL)
proof, for example facts or evidence, that makes you sure that something is true or correct: *We have a report of a fire in the downtown area, but we are still waiting for official* ***confirmation of*** *this.*

properly *adverb* → see **well**

property /ˈprɑpɚti/ *noun*

- ► **property**
- ► **land**
- ► **real estate**

property
an area of ground or a building, or both together. You use **property** when you are talking about who owns it: *He owns several properties, including a large house near the beach.* | *The sign on the gate said: "Private Property. Keep Out."*

land
an area of ground. You use **land** when you are talking about an area of ground that someone wants to buy, sell, or use in a particular way: *He bought a small piece of land and built a house on it.* | *Most of the land around here belongs to the university.*

real estate
property. You use **real estate** when you are talking about the business of buying and selling property: *He made a lot of money buying and selling real estate.*
→ see **building**, **possession**

proposal *noun* → see **suggestion**

propose *verb* → see **plan to**, **suggest**

prosecute /ˈprɑsəˌkyut/ *verb*

- ► **prosecute**
- ► **charge**
- ► **indict** (*formal*)
- ► **impeach** (*formal*)
- ► **put someone on trial**
- ► **take someone to court**

prosecute
to say officially that a court of law should judge whether someone is guilty of a crime, and give the court the facts about the crime: *Police believe she is guilty and will prosecute her.* | *Simpson was* ***prosecuted for*** *murder.*

charge
if the police charge someone, they officially say he or she may be guilty of a crime: *Police* ***charged*** *him* ***with*** *theft.*

indict (*formal*)
to say officially that someone may be guilty of a crime, and take him or her to a court of law. **Indict** is used in formal legal situations: *Wu was* ***indicted for*** *the killing.* | *Fernandez was* ***indicted on*** *charges of fraud.*

impeach (*formal*)
to say officially that a president, mayor, etc. may be guilty of a serious crime: *The President was* ***impeached for*** *breaking an election law.*

put someone on trial
to send someone to a court of law to decide whether he or she is guilty of a crime: *He was arrested and* ***put on trial for*** *murder.*

take someone to court
to start the legal process in which someone is

P

judged in a court of law: *His ex-wife will take him to court if he does not send money to help support their children.*

→ see **accuse**, **punish**

protect /prəˈtekt/ *verb*

- ► protect
- ► defend
- ► guard
- ► shield
- ► shelter
- ► preserve
- ► safeguard

protect
to prevent someone or something from being harmed or damaged: *To protect the environment, use your car less often.* | *Exercise can help **protect** you **against** heart disease.* | *It is a parent's job to **protect** children **from** harm.*

defend
to do things in order to protect someone or something from attack: *If someone tries to hit you, you're allowed to defend yourself.* | *The soldiers defended the city.*

guard
to stand near a person or place and watch carefully for danger so that you can protect them: *Soldiers guarded the government buildings.*

shield
to put something in front of something else, in order to protect it from harm or damage: *I held up a hand to **shield** my eyes **from** the sun.*
→ You also use **shield** to talk about protecting someone such as a child from something that might upset him or her: *Many parents try to **shield** children **from** unpleasant things such as death.*

shelter
to protect a person or animal from bad weather or danger, especially by providing a safe place to stay: *The tree **sheltered** us **from** the rain a little.*

preserve
to prevent something from being changed a lot or destroyed: *The Navajo Indians want to preserve their traditions.* | *The group is working to preserve old buildings.*

safeguard
to do something that protects someone or something from harm or bad things that could happen, for example by making a law: *In order to safeguard children, some websites are blocked from the school computers.* | *The Constitution helps to safeguard the rights of all citizens.*

protection /prəˈtekʃən/ *noun*

1 the state of being protected, or the act of protecting something
- ► protection
- ► safeguard
- ► preservation
- ► conservation

2 something that gives you protection
- ► shield
- ► guard

1 the state of being protected, or the act of protecting something

protection
the state of being protected from harm or damage: *A hat gives some **protection from** the sun.* | *The shot will provide **protection against** diseases such as measles.*

safeguard
something that protects someone or something against bad things that could happen: *Congress included safeguards for the environment in the new law.* | *The crop insurance acts as a safeguard in case the harvest fails.*

preservation
the act of preventing something from being changed a lot or destroyed: *The preservation of these old buildings is important to keep our history alive.*

conservation
the protection of natural things such as plants, animals, and forests, for example by not allowing building on the areas where they live or by not allowing them to be destroyed or hunted: *The group will spend four months carrying out conservation work in the rain forest.*

2 something that gives you protection

shield
something that you put in front of something else in order to protect it: *He used a newspaper as a **shield against** the wind and rain.* | *The police carried shields and wore helmets.*

guard
something you wear to protect yourself when playing sports: *Hockey players often wear face guards.*
→ A **guard** is also a person who helps protect a place or person: *Guards stood at the door of the store.*
→ see **safety**

protest[1] /ˈproʊtest/ *noun*

1 things that groups do to show publicly that they think something is unfair
- ► **protest**
- ► **demonstration**
- ► **march**
- ► **boycott**

2 something you say to show you disagree with something
- ► **protest**
- ► **objection**
- ► **outcry**
- ► **uproar**

1 things that groups do to show publicly that they think something is unfair

protest
the things that a group of people do to show that they think something is wrong or unfair: ***Protests over** the war took place in several cities this week.* | *The students joined in a peaceful **protest against** the new dress code.*

demonstration (AWL)
an event when a lot of people meet somewhere or walk together to protest against something: *About 12,000 people held a **demonstration against** the changes to the law.*

march
an event when a lot of people walk together to protest against something: *Six thousand people joined the march through the city to protest the plans.*

boycott
a type of protest in which people refuse to buy, use, or do something as a way of protesting: *The **boycott of** South African goods put pressure on the government to change the way black people were treated.*

2 something you say to show you disagree with something

protest
something that you say to show you disagree with something or think it is unfair: *She ignored the children's protests and turned off the TV.*

objection
a statement in which someone says that he or she opposes an idea or plan: *The mayor wants to close some schools, but there have been strong objections from the community.*

outcry
a situation in which a lot of people complain about something because they feel so angry: *There was a public **outcry over** the oil spill in the Gulf of Mexico.*

uproar
a situation in which a lot of people express angry feelings, shock, or disappointment at something they think is very wrong or unfair: *There was an uproar when the company announced that it would be cutting workers' pay.*

→ see **complaint**

protest[2] /prəˈtest/ *verb*

1 to show publicly that you think something is wrong or unfair
- ► **protest**
- ► **demonstrate**
- ► **march**
- ► **boycott**

2 to disagree or disapprove of something
- ► **protest**
- ► **object**

1 to show publicly that you think something is wrong or unfair

protest
if a group of people protest, they show that they think something is wrong or unfair, for example by having a public meeting: *A million people gathered to **protest against** the war.* | *Local people protested the plan to close the school.*

demonstrate (AWL)
to protest about something by having a large outdoor meeting or by walking from one place to another with other people: *Thousands of workers **demonstrated against** changes to their pay.*

march
to walk with a lot of people from one place to another to show that you think something is wrong or unfair: *Hundreds of protesters marched past the White House to protest against the law.*

boycott
to protest against something by refusing to buy, use, or do something: *People are boycotting companies that use child labor to make their products.*

2 to disagree or disapprove of something

protest
to say that you disagree with something and think it is wrong or unfair: *"It wasn't my fault! Juana did it!" Helena protested.* | *I **protested that** there was not enough time to finish the test.*

object
to say that you do not like or approve of

something: *She wanted to go to New York by herself, but her parents* ***objected to*** *the idea because they thought she was too young.*

→ see **oppose** for words meaning "to oppose an idea or plan"

→ see **complain**

protester /prəˈtestɚ/ *noun*

- ► protester
- ► demonstrator
- ► marcher

protester *also* **protestor**
someone who is protesting about something with other people: *Protesters marched in front of the White House to protest against the war.*

demonstrator (AWL)
someone who is protesting about something by being at an outdoor meeting or by walking somewhere with other people: *Demonstrators were carrying signs saying "Save our jobs."*

marcher
someone who is walking somewhere with a large group of people in order to protest about something: *Marchers walked toward the city's main square.*

proud /praʊd/ *adjective*

1 happy because you, your family, etc. have done something good
- ► proud
- ► pleased

2 too proud in a way that other people do not like
- ► proud
- ► stuck up (*informal*)
- ► conceited
- ► vain
- ► arrogant
- ► smug
- ► self-righteous
- ► snobbish

ANTONYMS → see **modest**

1 happy because you, your family, etc. have done something good

proud
very happy about what you, your family, your country, etc. have done, or happy about something you have because it is special: *Marco's parents were very* ***proud of*** *him when he won the race.* | *Shula was very* ***proud of*** *her Indian heritage.*

pleased
happy about something good that you, your family, etc. have done: *Maria was very* ***pleased*** *with her daughter's report card.*

ADVERBS

The adjective **proud** can be made into an adverb by using an **-ly** ending: *"My son just graduated from college," he said proudly.* | *She proudly held up the trophy for everyone to see.*

2 too proud in a way that other people do not like

proud
very pleased with yourself so that you think that you are better or more important than other people: *Eduardo was a proud man who would never admit that he had made a mistake.*

stuck up (*informal*)
unfriendly because you think you are better than other people: *She was too stuck up to talk to people who didn't wear the right clothes.*

conceited
too proud of what you can do or of the way you look: *He is so conceited! He thinks every girl likes him.*

vain
too proud of the way you look: *Eva was too vain to wear glasses.*

arrogant
behaving in a rude way because you think you are more important or intelligent than other people: *He is a smart boy, but he can be very arrogant about it.*

smug
too happy about how smart, lucky, or good you are, in a way that annoys other people: *"I've already done my homework," she said with a smug smile.*

self-righteous
very sure that your beliefs and actions are right, in a way that annoys other people: *She criticizes other people in a self-righteous way, and forgets that everyone makes mistakes.*

snobbish
thinking that you are better than other people because you are from a higher social class or because you know more: *Her snobbish parents didn't like her boyfriend because he hadn't been to college.*

→ see **pride**

ADVERBS

You can make the adjectives **proud**, **arrogant**, **smug**, **self-righteous**, and **snobbish** into adverbs by using an **-ly** ending: *He proudly refused any help.* | *"The test was easy for me," she said arrogantly.* | *"I've already finished reading the book," said Paul smugly.*

prove /pruv/ *verb*

- ► prove
- ► confirm
- ► verify (*formal*)
- ► support
- ► back up (*informal*)

prove
to show that something is true: *He thinks Anna took some money from him, but he can't prove it.* | *Tests* ***proved that*** *Perez was the girl's father.*

confirm (AWL)
to show that something is definitely true, when you thought before that it was probably true: *The blood test* ***confirmed that*** *he had diabetes.*

verify (*formal*)
to prove that something is true by getting or giving more information: *He said he was home alone, but the police have not been able to verify his claim.*

support
to help to show that an idea or belief is probably true: *There is evidence to support the belief that climate change is affecting plants and animals.*

back up (*informal*)
to give more information that helps to show that a belief is true, or that what someone says is true: *Research does not back up his claim that the pills will help you lose weight.*
→ see **show**[1]

proverb *noun* → see **phrase**

provide *verb* → see **give**

provide for /prəˈvaɪd fɔr/ *phrasal verb*

- ► provide for someone
- ► support

provide for someone
to give someone the things he or she needs to live, such as food, money, and clothes: *She needed to earn money to provide for her children.*

support
to give someone the money he or she needs to live: *He had a wife and three kids to support.* | *How will you support yourself and your family if you don't have a job?*

psychiatrist *noun* → see **doctor**

public[1] *adjective* → see **social**

public[2] *noun* → see **people**

publication *noun* → see **book**[1]

publicly /ˈpʌblɪkli/ *adverb*

- ► publicly
- ► in public
- ► openly

ANTONYMS → see **privately**

publicly
if you do or say something publicly, you do or say it so that everyone knows about it: *He publicly accused the President of telling lies.* | *Douglas has never spoken publicly about his illness.*

in public
in a place where anyone can see or hear: *She was embarrassed about kissing him in public.*

openly
if you do something openly, you do it in a public place without feeling embarrassed or trying to keep anything secret: *It can be difficult to speak openly about having diseases such as AIDS.*

publish /ˈpʌblɪʃ/ *verb*

- ► publish
- ► print
- ► issue

publish (AWL)
to print and sell a book, magazine, or newspaper: *The dictionary was published in 2009.*
→ You can also use **publish** when you make an official document or report available for people to read: *Scientists published a report on the effects of global warming.*

print
to use a machine that puts ink on paper to produce a lot of books, newspapers, etc.: *More than 20,000 copies of the book were printed.*

issue (AWL)
to produce an official document and make it available for people to read: *The company issued a financial report.*

puddle *noun* → see **lake**

P

pull¹ /pʊl/ *verb*

1 to use your hands to move something toward you
- ► pull
- ► tug
- ► drag
- ► haul
- ► draw (*formal*)
- ► yank (*informal*)

ANTONYMS → see **push¹ (1)**

2 to make something move behind you
- ► pull
- ► tow

3 to remove something from its place by using force
- ► pull
- ► tear
- ► pry
- ► pluck
- ► extract

1 to use your hands to move something toward you

pull
to use your hands to move something toward you: *When I count to three, start pulling the rope.* | *She pulled the door open and hurried inside.*

tug
to pull something suddenly with a quick movement, often to get someone's attention: *"I'm hungry," the little boy said,* ***tugging at*** *his mother's skirt.*

drag
to pull something along the ground, often because it is too heavy to carry: *The mattress was too heavy, so we had to drag it into the room.*

haul
to pull something big and heavy using a lot of effort, especially using a rope: *They were hauling their boats farther up the beach.*

draw (*formal*)
to pull something or someone gently in a particular direction: *He put his arm around her and drew her closer.*

yank (*informal*)
to pull something with a sudden strong movement: *She yanked on the cord and the parachute opened.*

2 to make something move behind you

pull
to make something move behind you in the direction you are moving. **Pull** is often used when animals or heavy vehicles make something move in this way: *The car was pulling a camper behind it.* | *The queen's carriage was pulled by two white horses.*

tow
to pull a vehicle along using a rope or chain: *He parked the car by a fire hydrant, and the police* ***towed*** *it* ***away****.*

3 to remove something from its place by using force

pull
to remove something from its place, especially using your hands and using force: *Vicky had* ***pulled*** *the arm* ***off*** *her doll.* | *Daniela* ***pulled*** *the phone* ***out of*** *her brother's hands and walked away with it.*

tear
to pull something violently from a person or place: *He* ***tore*** *the letter* ***from*** *my hand.* | *The storm almost* ***tore*** *the roof* ***off*** *the house.*

pry
to pull something that is stuck tightly in or on another thing: *The child would not let go of the toy – his mother had to* ***pry*** *it* ***out of*** *his hands.*
→ You also use **pry** to talk about forcing something open, such as a door, by using an

pull

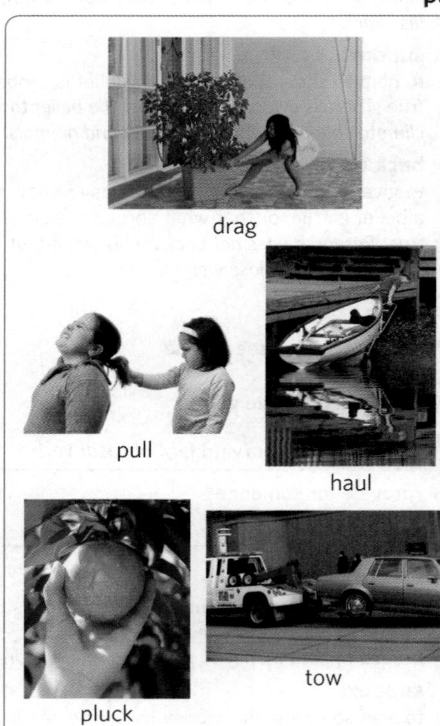
drag
pull
haul
pluck
tow

object to help you: *The police used a long iron bar to pry open the door.*

pluck
to pull something small from something that is larger: *She reached up and* ***plucked*** *an apple* ***off*** *the tree.*

extract (AWL)
to remove something from a place where it grows or from a place that it is part of. You use **extract** about things like teeth or things that you get from under the ground, such as oil or minerals: *The dentist is going to extract my wisdom teeth.* | *Next month, the company will begin extracting oil and gas from under the farmland south of the city.*
→ see **pull out** at **remove**

pull² /pʊl/ *noun*

- ► pull
- ► tug
- ► yank (*informal*)

ANTONYMS → see **push²**

pull
the act of using force to move something toward you or in the same direction as you are going: *I gave the door a pull, but it did not open.* | *One more strong pull will get the sofa through the door.*

tug
a quick pull, often to get someone's attention: *I felt a* ***tug on*** *my skirt and turned to see what the little boy wanted.*

yank (*informal*)
a quick strong pull: *When you tie the cord, give it a yank to make sure it is tight.*

pun *noun* → see **joke¹**

punch¹ *verb* → see **hit¹**, **pierce**

punch² *noun* → see **hit²**

punctual *adjective* → see **on time**

puncture *noun* → see **hole**

punish /ˈpʌnɪʃ/ *verb*

- ► punish
- ► penalize
- ► discipline
- ► sentence

punish
to make someone suffer because he or she has done something bad: *We will catch the people responsible for this crime, and we will punish them.* | *I don't spank my kids to* ***punish*** *them* ***for*** *doing bad things; I usually send them to their rooms.*

penalize
to officially punish someone for breaking a rule or law: *The company will be* ***penalized for*** *polluting the river – it will have to pay a $10,000 fine.*
→ **Penalize** can also be used in games where someone loses points or has a disadvantage for not following the rules. Don't say: ~~*The team was punished for wasting time.*~~ Say: *The team was* ***penalized for*** *wasting time.*

discipline
to punish someone for behaving in the wrong way, especially in order to keep control of a person or situation: *Young teachers are sometimes unsure about how to discipline their students.*

sentence
if a judge sentences someone who is guilty of a crime, he or she gives the person an official punishment: *The thief was* ***sentenced to*** *three years in prison.*
→ see **prosecute**

punishment /ˈpʌnɪʃmənt/ *noun*

- ► punishment
- ► penalty
- ► sentence
- ► sanction

punishment
something that is done to punish someone: *The* ***punishment for*** *her crime was a year in prison.* | *Emillio was sent to bed early* ***as a punishment*** *for his bad behavior.*
→ **GRAMMAR:** Don't say: ~~*He received a big/heavy/strict punishment*~~. Say: *He received a* ***harsh/severe punishment.***

penalty
an official punishment for someone who breaks a rule or law: *What is the* ***penalty for*** *driving without a license?* | *Texas and Florida have the* ***death penalty*** (=a law that says someone can be killed as a punishment).

sentence
a punishment that a judge gives to someone who is guilty of a crime: *He was given a two-year prison* ***sentence for*** *robbing a grocery store.*

sanction
a punishment that can be used if someone disobeys a rule or law: *One sanction that the school uses for bad behavior is to send a child into a different class.*

pupil *noun* → see **student**

P

purchase *verb* → see **buy**

pure /pyʊr/ *adjective*

► pure
► solid

pure
a pure substance or material is not mixed with anything else: *I felt the scarf and knew that it was pure silk.* | *The restaurant says that their hamburgers are made from pure beef.*
→ **Pure** can also be used about water or air that is very clean and does not contain any harmful substances or chemicals: *The water in the stream was pure and cold.*

solid
solid wood or metal has not been mixed with any other substance: *She was wearing a solid gold bracelet.* | *The dining room table is made of solid oak.*
→ see **clean[1]** and **natural** for **pure** meaning "very clean and containing no harmful substances"

purely *adverb* → see Function Word **only**

purify /ˈpyʊrəˌfaɪ/ *verb*

► purify
► refine

purify
to remove the dirty parts from something such as water or air: *Houseplants can help purify the air in your home.* | *We boiled and filtered the water to purify it.*

refine (AWL)
to remove things from a substance to make it more pure, for example a substance such as oil or sugar: *The factory refines oil into gasoline.*

purpose /ˈpɚpəs/ *noun*

► purpose
► object (*formal*)
► point
► function

purpose
the reason you do something, and the thing you want to achieve when you do it: ***The purpose of** the exercise is to strengthen your stomach muscles.* | *My **purpose in** writing this book was to bring attention to global warming.*

object (*formal*)
the specific purpose of an activity, or the result you hope to get by doing the activity: *The **object** of the game is to get as many points as possible.*

point
the purpose of doing something and the reason why it is important or necessary: *The **point of** this experiment is to show how this chemical reacts with water.* | *There is no **point in** trying to explain – they won't understand.*

function (AWL)
the purpose that something has, for example a machine, tool, or piece of equipment: ***The main function of** the bars is to protect the driver's legs.*
→ see **reason**, **goal**, **on purpose** at **deliberately**

purse *noun* → see **bag**

push[1] /pʊʃ/ *verb*

1 to move something or someone away from you

► push
► shove
► poke
► nudge
► thrust
► press
► stuff
► tackle

ANTONYMS → see **pull[1] (1)**

2 to push someone so that you can get somewhere or do something

► push
► shove
► jostle

1 to move something or someone away from you

push
to move something away from you by pressing it with your hand or finger: *He pushed the door open and went into the room.* | *The little boy wanted to push the grocery cart around the supermarket.* | *If you push the red button, the power will turn off.*

shove
to push someone or something with your hand or arm, using force: *Mary shoved the box back under the bed.*

poke
to push your finger or something pointed into something or someone: *He poked the snake with a stick but it was dead.*

nudge
to push someone gently with your elbow to get his or her attention: *Carla nudged me and said "Look over there!"*

thrust
to push something somewhere suddenly or using force: *She thrust a letter into my hand.*

press
to push something with your finger: *Press the switch to turn the light on.*

stuff
to push something quickly into a small space: *Martha stuffed the money into her pocket.*

tackle
to push a player to the ground to stop that player from running or throwing, in the game of football: *Two guys tackled the quarterback before he could pass the ball.*

2 to push someone so that you can get somewhere or do something

push
to push people so that you can go to a place near you: *Amy pushed past me to get to the front of the line. | Tom had to push his way through the crowd of people.*

shove
to push people in a rough way so that you can go to a place near you: *The subway was busy and people were pushing and shoving to get onto the train.*

jostle
to push roughly against other people in a crowd, usually so that you can get somewhere or do something before them: *Photographers* ***jostled for*** *the best position to photograph the movie star.*

push

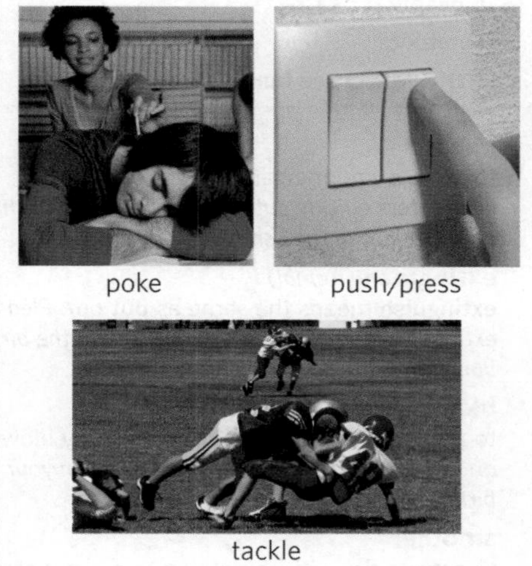
poke push/press
tackle

push² /pʊʃ/ *noun*

- ► push
- ► shove
- ► poke
- ► nudge
- ► tackle

ANTONYMS → see **pull²**

push
the action of moving someone or something away from you using your hand: *Mom, can you give me a push on the swing? | With a push, she managed to open the window.*

shove
a hard rough push with your hand or shoulder: *Lee gave the boy a shove which sent him flying onto the floor.*

poke
a quick push with your finger or with something pointed such as a stick: *She gave Josh a playful poke in the stomach.*

nudge
a gentle push with your elbow, especially to get someone's attention: *Taylor fell asleep in class so I gave him a nudge.*

tackle
the action of pushing a player to the ground to stop that player from running, in the game of football: *Hovan had 85 tackles last season.*

put /pʊt/ *verb*

1 to move something to a place
- ► put
- ► place
- ► set
- ► position
- ► stand
- ► lay
- ► dump
- ► leave

2 to put something into a place
- ► put
- ► shove
- ► stick
- ► insert
- ► slip
- ► slide
- ► thrust
- ► tuck

P

1 to move something to a place

put
to move something to a place: *Dino put the books on his desk.* | *"Where did you put my cell phone?" "It is on the table."*

place
to put something somewhere carefully. **Place** is more formal than **put** and is used especially in written descriptions: *She placed the vase back on the shelf.*

set
to put a person or a large or heavy object somewhere carefully. **Set** is more formal than **put** and is used especially in written descriptions: *Talia carried the boy into the house and set him down in the hall.*

position
to put someone or something carefully into the right place so that he, she, or it is ready: *Position the golf ball carefully on the tee, and prepare to hit it.*

stand
to put something somewhere in an upright position: *Sean stood the bottle next to the glass.*

lay
to put something down carefully in a flat position: *She laid the clothes on the bed before she got dressed.*

dump
to drop or put something somewhere in a careless way: *The kids came home from school and dumped their backpacks in the kitchen.*

leave
to put something in a place and not take it with you when you go: *Do you want me to leave your keys on the table?*
→ see **pile²**

2 to put something into a place

put
to move something into a place: *I put the letter in the envelope.* | *Kevin put the tissue in his pocket.*

shove
to push something somewhere quickly and roughly: *She shoved some clothes into a suitcase and got in her car.*

stick
to put something somewhere quickly, often without thinking carefully: *I stuck the photos in a box and forgot about them.*

insert (AWL)
to put something inside or into something else. **Insert** is more formal than **put**: ***Insert** the coins **into** the machine and select the type of candy you want.*

slip
to put something somewhere quietly and smoothly: *Rachel slipped the book into her bag and hoped no one had noticed.*

slide
to put something smoothly into a small narrow space: *To get money out, first slide your card into the machine.*

thrust
to put something somewhere suddenly, often with a lot of force: *He thrust the letter into her hand and said "Read this!"*

tuck
to put the edge of a piece of cloth or clothing into or under something else: *Tuck the sheets under the mattress.*
→ see **put off** at **delay²**
→ see **put up** at **build¹**

put on /ˌpʊt ˈɔn/ *phrasal verb*

- put on
- apply (*formal*)

put on
to put something such as makeup or lotion on your skin: *I don't usually wear much makeup, but I do put on mascara.* | *Don't forget to put on some sunscreen!*

apply (*formal*)
apply means the same as **put on**: *The instructions say to apply the medicine to the burn three times a day.*
→ see **dress²**, **perform**

put out /ˌpʊt ˈaʊt/ *phrasal verb*

- put out
- extinguish (*formal*)
- blow out
- smother

ANTONYMS → see **burn (3)**

put out
to make a fire or cigarette stop burning: *Firefighters quickly put out the fire.* | *She put her cigarette out in the ashtray.*

extinguish (*formal*)
extinguish means the same as **put out**: *Please extinguish all cigarettes before entering the airport building.*

blow out
to make a flame or fire stop burning by blowing on it: *Did you blow out all the candles on your birthday cake?*

smother
to cover a fire with something to make it stop

burning: *The pan was on fire and I tried to smother the flames with a wet towel.*

put up with /ˌpʊt ˈʌp wɪθ/ *phrasal verb*

- ► put up with
- ► tolerate
- ► stand
- ► bear
- ► endure (*formal*)

put up with
to accept a bad situation without complaining or trying to change it: *I couldn't put up with the noise any longer and I told him to turn it down.* | *I don't know how she puts up with those kids. They never help in the house.*

tolerate
to accept a bad situation without complaining or trying to change it. **Tolerate** is more formal than **put up with** and is often used when you are annoyed with someone's behavior: *Teachers will not tolerate violent behavior from students.*

stand
to accept a bad situation or pain: *I don't know if I can stand another day in this job – it's so boring.*
→ **Stand** is usually used in the phrase **can/can't stand**.

bear
to accept a very bad situation or pain. **Bear** is more formal than **stand** and is often used about situations that make you very upset or angry: *When someone dies, the sadness you feel does not go away, but it becomes easier to bear.* | *The pain was hard to bear.*

endure (*formal*)
to suffer great pain or deal with a difficult situation for a very long time: *Jennifer endured months of pain after breaking her leg.*

puzzle /ˈpʌzl/ *noun*

- ► puzzle
- ► riddle
- ► problem

puzzle
a game in which you have to think hard to solve a problem: *I like doing Sudoku and other number puzzles.*

riddle
a question that seems silly or confusing but has a funny or smart answer: *Here's a riddle: What belongs to you, but is used more by your friend than you? The answer is "your name."*

problem
a question in which you have to use math or think very carefully to find the answer: *The teacher gave us some math problems to solve.*
→ see **confuse**

puzzled *adjective* → see **confused**

puzzling *adjective* → see **confusing**

P

Qq

qualify *verb* → see **allow**

quality /'kwɑləti/ *noun*

1 a quality that a person has
- ► quality
- ► characteristic
- ► good point/bad point
- ► trait (*formal*)

2 a quality that something has
- ► quality
- ► characteristic
- ► feature
- ► property
- ► good point/bad point

3 how good or bad something is
- ► quality
- ► level
- ► standard
- ► grade

1 a quality that a person has

quality
a part of someone's character, especially a good part such as kindness or intelligence: *Good teachers have qualities such as patience and confidence.* | *What qualities do you want in a girlfriend or boyfriend?*

characteristic
a quality that is typical of someone: *You are very determined, and that is a characteristic that will help you in life.*

good point/bad point
a particular good or bad quality that someone has. **Point** is more informal than **quality**: *One of her good points is that she is a good listener. She'll always listen to you when you have a problem.*

trait (*formal*)
a particular quality in someone's character, especially a basic quality that someone is born with and that does not change easily: *Do we get personality traits such as kindness or aggression from our parents?*

2 a quality that something has

quality
something that is typical or important about a thing, especially something good that makes that thing different from other things: *The island has a magical quality that makes it a popular vacation spot.* | *They are a pop band, but some of their music has a country quality.*

characteristic
a quality that is typical of something: *Speech is a human characteristic. No other animals can talk.*

feature (AWL)
an important, interesting, or typical part of something: *The phone has some new features, such as faster Internet access.*

property
a quality that a substance or object has. **Property** is used especially in science: *One of the properties of water is that it freezes at 0°C.*

good point/bad point
a particular good or bad quality that something has. **Point** is more informal than **quality**: *Being the eldest child has its good and bad points. For example, I get to do things first, but often my parents expect more of me.*

3 how good or bad something is

quality
how good or bad something is: *The quality of the food at this restaurant is very good.* | *Parents complained about the poor quality of children's TV shows.*

level
how good someone or something is compared to other people or other things of the same type: *At the beginner's level, people start with how to hold a tennis racket and learning how to hit the ball.* | *I've reached the fifth level of the computer game.*

standard
a level that people think is the correct or acceptable level: *The school expects a high standard of behavior from all students.*

grade (AWL)
a level of quality that a product, material, etc. has: *The best grades of meat are expensive.*

quantity *noun* → see **amount**

quarter *noun* → see Topic **Education**

question[1] /'kwestʃən/ *noun*
- ► question
- ► query
- ► inquiry (*formal*)
- ► riddle

ANTONYMS → see **answer**[2]

question
something you say or write to ask something:

Can I ask you a question? Where do you live? | Martina answered the question honestly.

query
a question asking for more information or to check whether something is correct or you have understood it: *If you have any queries about what you have to do, ask your teacher.*

inquiry (*formal*)
a question you ask because you want to get information or details: *I'll make some inquiries and see if I can find a good hotel.*
→ If a group of people officially try to find out what happened in a situation or the cause of a problem, this process is also called an **inquiry**: *The company is facing an* ***inquiry into*** *its financial dealings.*

riddle
a question that seems silly or confusing but has a funny or smart answer: *Here's a riddle: What belongs to you, but is used more by your friend than you? The answer is "your name."*
→ see **subject** for **question** meaning "a problem that needs to be dealt with"

question² /ˈkwestʃən/ *verb*

- ► question (*formal*)
- ► interrogate
- ► interview
- ► cross-examine

question (*formal*)
to ask someone questions so that you can get information about something: *The police are* ***questioning*** *two men* ***about*** *the theft. | Louie continued to question her: "Why did you come here?"*

interrogate
if the police interrogate someone, they ask him or her a lot of questions for a long time in order to get information: *The men were interrogated for five hours because police believed they were involved in the bombing.*

interview
to ask a famous person questions on a television program or for a newspaper: *The singer was interviewed on television.*
→ You also use **interview** about asking someone questions when he or she wants a job or has applied for a college: *Mr. Nuñez interviewed me for a job at the store.*

cross-examine
to ask someone questions in a court of law after another lawyer has already asked that person questions: *The defense lawyer cross-examined the first witness.*
→ see **ask**

questionnaire *noun* → see **survey**

quick /kwɪk/ *adjective*

1 done without any delay
- ► quick
- ► prompt

2 moving with a lot of speed
- ► quick
- ► rapid
- ► brisk

3 doing things in a very short time
- ► quick
- ► fast
- ► rapid
- ► swift (*formal*)
- ► speedy

ANTONYMS → see **slow**

1 done without any delay

quick
done or happening very soon, without any delay: *Doctors have to make quick decisions to save people's lives. | It is quicker to drive to school, but I like to walk.*

prompt
done immediately at the correct time: *Prompt action is needed to stop the problem getting worse.*

2 moving with a lot of speed

quick
moving with a lot of speed: *He took a quick step backward.*

rapid
rapid means the same as **quick** but sounds more formal: *During this period of sleep, people make rapid eye movements.*

brisk
moving fast and with a lot of energy: *We went for a brisk walk in the fresh air.*
→ see **fast¹ (1)**

3 doing things in a very short time

quick
doing something in a short time: *I'll just have a quick shower before we go out. | You've finished already? That was quick!*

fast
doing something in a very short time: *She is a very fast reader – she finished that book in just two days. | The fast growth of the population has caused economic problems.*

rapid
happening very quickly, or doing something very quickly. You use **rapid** especially about changes,

Q

increases, and improvements: *There has been a rapid increase in the number of people who have the disease.*

swift (*formal*)
doing something very quickly: *She gave him a swift hug goodbye.* | *My letter got a swift response.*

speedy
happening quickly in the way that you want: *She sent him a letter wishing him a speedy recovery from his illness.*
→ see **short** for **quick** meaning "continuing for only a short time," **smart** for **quick** meaning "quick at learning new things"

quickly /ˈkwɪkli/ *adverb*

1 without taking much time
► quickly
► shortly
► promptly
► swiftly (*formal*)
► speedily
ANTONYMS → see **slowly**
2 with a lot of speed
► quickly
► fast
► rapidly
► swiftly (*formal*)
► briskly
► at high speed
ANTONYMS → see **slowly**

1 without taking much time

quickly
without taking much time: *The show quickly became very popular.* | *John quickly realized that she was lying.*

shortly
within a very short time: *The plane crashed shortly after take-off.* | *Details of the event will be announced shortly.*

promptly
without any delay: *The company responds promptly to complaints from customers.*

swiftly (*formal*)
very quickly and without any delay: *Luckily, the pilot reacted swiftly and they avoided hitting the other plane.*

speedily
quickly, especially in the way that you want: *I hope that the problem can be solved speedily.*
→ see **immediately**

2 with a lot of speed

quickly
if you move or do something quickly, you move or do it with a lot of speed: *He ate his lunch quickly.* | *Joanna walked quickly through the hall to her classroom.*

fast
fast means the same as **quickly** but sounds even quicker: *You're driving too fast – slow down!* | *She can run much faster than I can.*

rapidly *also* **at a rapid rate**
moving, happening, or done very quickly. You use **rapidly** especially about changes, increases, and improvements: *The population is growing rapidly.* | *Her heart was beating rapidly and she was short of breath.*

swiftly (*formal*)
moving or doing something very quickly: *The river was flowing swiftly after the heavy rain.* | *The president swiftly took action.*

briskly
quickly and with a lot of energy. You use **briskly** especially to say how someone walks: *He walked briskly back along the path.*

at high speed
if something moves at high speed, it moves very fast. You use **at high speed** about vehicles: *The car was traveling at high speed.*
→ see **go faster**

quiet[1] /ˈkwaɪət/ *adjective*

1 a quiet voice or sound
► quiet
► low
► soft
► faint
► silent
► hushed
► inaudible (*formal*)
ANTONYMS → see **loud**
2 a quiet place
► quiet
► silent
ANTONYMS → see **loud**

1 a quiet voice or sound

quiet
not making a lot of sound: *"What about me?" Ahmed asked in a quiet voice.* | *Listening to quiet music can help you fall asleep.*

low
quiet in a way that does not annoy or interrupt

people: *"Don't wake him up," said Ben in a low voice.* | *I turned the volume of the TV down low.*

soft
quiet and pleasant. You use **soft** especially about voices, music, and similar sounds: *Ellie's voice was soft and calming.* | *It was a romantic dinner, with soft music and candlelight.*

faint
a faint sound is quiet and difficult to hear, especially because it comes from a long way away: *We heard the faint sound of a train in the distance.*

silent
not talking or not making any sound: *Anja was silent for a moment, wondering what to say next.* | *She said a silent prayer.*

hushed
if people talk in hushed voices or hushed tones, they talk quietly so that other people cannot hear: *Everyone in the library was speaking in hushed voices.*

inaudible (*formal*)
too quiet to hear: *I could see that he was saying something, but his comments were inaudible through the glass of the window.*

ADVERBS

You can make the adjectives **quiet**, **soft**, **faint**, **silent**, and **inaudible** into adverbs by using an **-ly** ending: *Music played quietly on the radio.* | *"Everything's all right," she said softly.* | *He turned away and looked silently out the window.*

2 a quiet place

quiet
not having much noise: *The house is very quiet when the kids are out.* | *The hotel is in a quiet street with hardly any traffic.*

silent
having no noise at all: *Everyone was asleep and the house was silent.*
→ see **peaceful** for "describing places that are quiet and calm"
→ see Topic **Describing Sounds and Voices**

quiet² /ˈkwaɪət/ *verb*

- quiet
- become quiet
- fall silent
- fade
- die down
- lower your voice

quiet *also* **quiet down** (*formal*)
to become calmer and less noisy: *When the crowd had quieted, he started to speak.* | *Quiet down, everyone, or you won't be able to hear what I'm saying.*

become quiet
to stop speaking or making any noise: *The class became quiet when the teacher began reading the story aloud.*

fall silent
to suddenly stop talking and become quiet. **Fall silent** is used mainly in books: *Everyone fell silent as she walked into the room.*

fade *also* **fade away**
if a sound fades or fades away, it slowly becomes quieter until you cannot hear it: *At the end of the song, the music fades away.*

die down
if shouting, music, laughter, etc. dies down, it becomes quieter after being very loud: *The talking and laughter died down, and Mendez was able to speak.*

lower your voice
to start speaking more quietly because you do not want other people to hear: *Peter lowered his voice and leaned toward Linda.*

quit /kwɪt/ *verb*

- quit
- resign
- leave
- drop out (*informal*)

quit
to stop doing your job and not go back. **Quit** sounds informal, and you should not use it in official letters or more formal writing: *Bianca quit her job and started her own business.* | *I really want to quit – this job is driving me crazy!*
→ You can also use **quit** to say that someone stops going to school and does not come back: *My grandfather quit school at the age of 16 and always regretted it.*

resign
to officially say you will stop doing your job and not come back. **Resign** sounds more formal than **quit** and is the best word to use in official letters and other writing: *She is going to resign from the company and take a job in another state.*

leave
to stop doing a job and not return to it. **Leave** is a more general word that is less formal than **resign** and more formal than **quit**, so you can use it in both spoken and written language: *I am going to leave as soon as I find another job.*

drop out (*informal*)
to stop going to school or college before you

have finished it: ***Many students drop out of college because of financial problems.***

→ see **stop[1]** for **quit** meaning "to stop doing something"

quite *adverb* → see **fairly**, **very**

quiz *noun* → see **test[1]**

quotation /kwoʊˈteɪʃən/ *noun*

- quotation
- quote
- reference
- citation (*formal*)

quotation (AWL)
a sentence or phrase from a book or speech that you repeat in your own speech or writing. You use a **quotation** because it is interesting or funny, or because it supports what you are saying: ***She began her speech with a quotation** from Abraham Lincoln.* | *If you use quotations in your essay, choose them carefully and make sure they support what you are saying.*

quote (AWL)
quote means the same as **quotation** but sounds more informal: *This quote comes from a poem by Pablo Neruda.*

reference
something that you say or write that mentions someone or something else: *Her writing is full of references to Chicago.*
→ **References** are also the books and articles you use when you are writing a book, article, or research paper. You usually show **references** in a list at the end of what you are writing: *Be sure to read over your list of references to check for punctuation mistakes.*

citation (AWL) (*formal*)
a quotation or reference to another person's sentence or phrase in writing. A **citation** usually includes information about where the quotation comes from, so someone can find more information if he or she is interested: *There are a lot of citations in her essay, so she must have done a lot of research.*

SYNONYM CHECK
Quotation or quote?

You can use both **quotation** and **quote** about words that you take from writing or speeches, but **quote** sounds more informal than **quotation**: *I started the essay with a short* ***quotation/quote*** *from Shakespeare.*

When you are repeating a sentence or phrase from informal speech or an interview, you should use **quote**. Don't say: ~~*The newspaper article included quotations from the candidates.*~~ Say: *The newspaper article included* ***quotes*** *from the candidates.*

quote /kwoʊt/ *verb*

- quote
- cite (*formal*)
- repeat

quote (AWL)
to say or write exactly what someone else has said or written: *"Imagination is more important than knowledge," he said, quoting Albert Einstein.* | *A newspaper article **quoted** the football player as saying that he will retire at the end of this year.*

cite (AWL) (*formal*)
to give the exact words of something that has been written, especially in order to support an opinion or prove an idea. When you **cite** something, you give detailed information about where it came from: *The judge cited parts of the U.S. Constitution as he read his decision in court.*

repeat
to say or write something again: *I promise that I will not **repeat** anything you say **to** anyone else.*
→ see **quotation**

Q

Rr

race¹ /reɪs/ noun

- ► race
- ► people
- ► tribe
- ► ethnic group
- ► ethnicity (*formal*)
- ► minority

race
one of the groups that humans can be divided into because of the color of their skin and the way they look: *Students of many different races and religions attend our school.* | *People should be treated equally, regardless of their race.*

people
a race or group of people who live in a particular country. The plural of this meaning of **people** is **peoples**: *Every four years, the American people choose their president.* | *The sun is an important symbol for many native peoples of Mexico.*

tribe
a group of people of the same race who have the same beliefs, customs, and language. A **tribe** usually lives in one particular area ruled by its leader: *In school we are learning about Native American tribes of the southwest.*

ethnic group
a group of people of the same race, nation, or tribe. **Ethnic group** is used especially when the group lives in a place where there are other races or nationalities: *There are hundreds of different ethnic groups living in San Francisco.*

ethnicity (*formal*)
the race or nationality that someone belongs to: *It is illegal for an employer to ask you about your ethnicity or religion.*

minority (AWL)
a group of people with a different race, religion, etc. from most other people in a country: *The company tries to hire minorities or women if they are the best people for the job.*

race² *verb* → see **run¹**, Topic **Sports and Exercise**

racial /ˈreɪʃəl/ adjective

- ► racial
- ► ethnic
- ► cultural

racial
relating to people of the same race, or to the relationships between different races: *Racial discrimination is still a problem in the United States.* | *In his famous speech, Martin Luther King talked about his dream of racial equality.*

ethnic (AWL)
relating to a group of people who have the same culture or religion, or who come from the same country: *Can you guess my ethnic background? I am Hispanic – Peruvian, to be exact.*

cultural (AWL)
relating to a society and its way of life: *There are many cultural differences between Chinese and American families.*

GRAMMAR CHECK: racial

Racial is always used before a noun, and **ethnic** and **cultural** are usually used before nouns: *The city has many racial/ethnic/cultural groups.*

ADVERBS

You can make the adjectives that mean **racial** into adverbs by using an **-ly** ending: *The city is still racially divided.* | *The U.S. has a culturally diverse population* (=it has people from many different cultures).

racism *noun* → see **prejudice**

racist *adjective* → see **prejudiced**

rage *noun* → see **anger¹**

rain¹ /reɪn/ noun

- ► rain
- ► drizzle
- ► shower
- ► downpour
- ► sleet
- ► raindrop
- ► rainfall

rain
water that falls in small drops from clouds in the sky: *Why do you want to go out in the rain?* | *The rain began to fall in the afternoon and continued all night.*
→ A **light rain** is when the rain falls gently in

small amounts. A **heavy rain** is when the rain falls in large amounts.
→ **GRAMMAR:** Don't say: ~~*I've been standing under the rain for an hour*~~. Say: *I've been standing **in the rain** for an hour.*

drizzle
rain that has very small drops of water and that does not come down in large amounts: *A light drizzle was falling as I left the house.* | *In the winter the weather is a constant drizzle.*

shower
a short period of rain: *The weather forecast said that showers are possible over the weekend.*

downpour
a lot of rain that falls in a short time: *I walked back to my apartment **in the downpour** and got soaking wet.*

sleet
a mixture of rain and snow: *The rain had turned to sleet and the roads were becoming icy.*

raindrop
a single drop of rain: *As we sat down on the beach, I felt a few raindrops fall on my face.*

rainfall
the amount of rain that falls somewhere: *It rains a lot in Seattle – the average rainfall is about 36 inches a year.*
→ see **snow¹**, Topic **The Weather**

rain² /reɪn/ *verb*

- ► it rains
- ► it pours
- ► it drizzles
- ► it sprinkles
- ► it sleets
- ► rain falls
- ► rain comes down

it rains
if it rains, drops of water fall from clouds in the sky: *It is raining – you should take an umbrella.* | *It started to rain in the afternoon and rained hard all night.*
→ If **it rains hard** or it **rains heavily**, a lot of rain comes down in a short period of time.

it pours
if it pours, it rains a lot without stopping: *It was a horrible camping trip – it poured the whole time and we could hardly leave the tent.*

it drizzles
if it drizzles, it rains in small amounts, usually when this continues for a fairly long time: *It is only drizzling – let's go for a walk anyway.*

it sprinkles
if it sprinkles, a little rain falls from the sky, but it does not last long: *It is sprinkling now, but the sky is sunny over there.*

it sleets
if it sleets, it rains and snows at the same time: *I hate it when it sleets and the roads freeze, because driving is so dangerous.*

rain falls
if rain falls, it comes down from the sky: *As the rain began to fall, we ran to stand under a tree.*

rain comes down
rain comes down means the same as **rain falls** but sounds more informal: *We were still outside playing basketball with friends when the rain started coming down.*
→ see **snow²**, Topic **The Weather**

GRAMMAR CHECK: rain

When you are talking about rain that is falling right now, don't say: ~~*It rains/pours/drizzles/sleets*~~. Say: *It is raining/pouring/drizzling/sleeting.*

rainy /ˈreɪni/ *adjective*

- ► rainy
- ► wet
- ► damp
- ► gray

ANTONYMS → see **dry (2)**

rainy
if it is rainy, there is rain: *It was a cold rainy day.* | *For most of our vacation, it was windy and rainy.*

wet
wet means the same as **rainy** but sounds a little more formal: *We had two weeks of cold wet weather.* | *It was a wet Sunday afternoon.*

damp
a little rainy, or having just rained: *It was cloudy and damp outside.* | *The day felt damp and gloomy.*

gray
if it is gray or a gray day, there are a lot of clouds and sometimes rain: *It was a gray day in early March.*
→ see **humid** for words meaning "when the air feels wet but it is not raining"

raise /reɪz/ *verb*

1 to collect money to help people
- raise
- collect

2 to take care of animals
- raise
- keep
- rear
- breed

1 to collect money to help people

raise
to do things to make money, which you use to help people or an organization: *The students are washing cars to **raise** money **for** a school trip.* | *We had a yard sale and **raised** $500 **to** help victims of the earthquake.*

collect
to ask people to give you money or things to help an organization or other people: *The fifth graders at school are **collecting** food **for** homeless people.*
→ see **give** for words meaning "to give money or things to an organization or group"

2 to take care of animals

raise
to take care of animals, especially smaller farm animals, so that you can sell them or sell their products such as milk, meat, or eggs: *We raised chickens and sold the eggs at the market.* | *The farmers raise sheep for their wool.*

keep
to own and raise farm animals in order to use or sell their products. You usually use **keep** when you only have a few animals: *Mrs. Koto keeps a few chickens in her backyard.*

rear
to do the work of caring for and feeding animals. You use **rear** especially when you are talking about methods used to raise and feed a particular kind of animal: *Hilly land is a good place to rear sheep.*

breed
to bring male and female animals together to create baby animals, especially when you do this to sell the baby animals: *She breeds Dalmatian dogs and sells the puppies for very high prices.*
→ see **grow** for raising crops, **lift** for raising your hand, **improve** for raising standards, **increase**[1] for raising prices, **mention** for raising a subject in conversation

ranch *noun* → see **farm**

random /ˈrændəm/ *adjective*
- random
- arbitrary
- haphazard
- chance

random (AWL)
happening or chosen without any plan, reason, or pattern: *The police will be doing random searches of cars coming across the border.* | *The people in the groups were chosen **at random** – our teacher picked names out of a hat.*

arbitrary (AWL)
decided or arranged without any reason or plan, often in a way that seems unfair: *It seems arbitrary that bikes are allowed, but not skateboards.*

haphazard
happening or done in a way that is not planned or organized well. You use **haphazard** when you do not approve of the way something is done: *She had packed in a haphazard way, and left many of the things she needed at home.*

chance
not planned or expected: *Their relationship started with a chance meeting on a train.*
→ **GRAMMAR: Chance** is only used before a noun. Don't say: ~~*Their meeting was chance*~~. Say: *It was a chance meeting* or *They met by chance.*

ADVERBS

You can make the adjectives **random**, **arbitrary**, and **haphazard** into adverbs by using an **-ly** ending: *Cars will be randomly searched at the border.* | *The park seems to be acting arbitrarily by banning skateboards but allowing bikes.*

range /reɪndʒ/ *noun*
- range
- scope
- spectrum
- breadth

range (AWL)
a group of things that are different, but belong to the same general type: *The classroom has a wide **range of** books, so everyone can find something to read.* | *In his speech, the president discussed a **range of** topics, including education, health care, and unemployment.*

scope (AWL)
the range of ideas or subjects that something

R

includes: *Algebra is beyond **the scope of** this math textbook, which covers only the basics.*

spectrum
a complete range of different types of things or people: *She is a popular singer and her music appeals to a broad **spectrum of** people.*

breadth
the quality of including a wide range or variety of things, especially experiences or ideas: *Mr. Lee has been a teacher for 25 years and has a great **breadth of** experience.*
→ see **variety**

rank /ræŋk/ *noun*

- ► rank
- ► position
- ► level
- ► status
- ► standing
- ► seniority

rank
someone's rank in an organization is how important he or she is and whether he or she is in charge of other people. **Rank** is used especially about the military, the police force, or similar organizations: *The fire chief is the officer with the highest rank in the fire department.* | *He holds **the rank of** lieutenant in the U.S. army.*

position
someone's job in an organization, company, or profession. **Position** is used for talking about how important someone is and how much responsibility he or she has: *She has a very important position in the company – she is responsible for major financial decisions.*
→ Don't say: ~~*He holds the rank of assistant manager at the company*~~. Say: *He holds the position of assistant manager at the company.*

level
all the jobs in an organization that are similar in importance and for which people earn similar amounts of money: *The company provides training for staff **at all levels**.* | *I am working hard so that my career will advance to the next level.*

status (AWL)
someone's position in a group or society, that shows how important he or she is to the group: *The status of women has improved, but women still earn less money than men.*
→ You use **high status** or **low status** to show how much status someone has: *Doctors usually have high social status.*

standing
someone's position within a group or society, based on how much respect and admiration other people have for him or her: *He has been making a lot of mistakes recently, and this has hurt his standing at work.*

seniority
the state of having a higher rank or position than other people, usually because you have worked for an organization for a longer time: *Although I disagreed with him, he has seniority, so he made the final decision.*

rapid *adjective* → see **fast[1]**

rapidly *adverb* → see **fast[2]**

rare /rer/ *adjective*

- ► rare
- ► not common
- ► infrequent
- ► scarce

ANTONYMS → see **common (1)**

rare
not seen or found very often, or not happening very often: *Snow is very rare in Florida.* | *It is **rare for** Ava to miss school – I hope everything is okay.* | *These rare plants grow only in South Africa.*

not common *also* **uncommon**
rare or unusual. **Uncommon** is more formal than **not common**: *Tigers still exist, but they are not common.* | *In my country, **it is uncommon for** men to cook.*
→ **Uncommon** is often used in the phrase **not uncommon** to say that something happens or is done often: ***It is not uncommon for** students to have loans to pay back after their college education.*

infrequent
not happening or coming often: *She moved away, and as time passed her letters became more and more infrequent.*

scarce
if something is scarce, there is not much of it and it is difficult to get. **Scarce** is used especially about things people need to live, such as food and water: *After the war, food and clothing were scarce.*

> **ADVERBS**
> You can make the adjectives **rare**, **uncommon**, and **infrequent** into adverbs by using an **-ly** ending: *Snow is rarely seen in Florida.* | *His letters began coming more infrequently.*

R

rarely /ˈrerli/ *adverb*

- ► rarely
- ► seldom
- ► hardly ever

ANTONYMS → see **often**

rarely
not often: *He is really intelligent, but he rarely speaks in class.* | *The tablecloth still looks new because it is rarely used.*

seldom
seldom means the same as **rarely**, but sounds more formal and is used especially in written English: *She seldom talks about her personal life.*

hardly ever
almost never. **Hardly ever** is more common in spoken English than **rarely** or **seldom**: *We hardly ever see Amanda now that she has a boyfriend.*

GRAMMAR CHECK: rarely

You use **rarely**, **seldom**, and **hardly ever** before the main verb, unless the main verb is "be": *He is rarely/seldom/hardly ever at home.*

Don't say: ~~*I see him rarely/seldom/hardly ever.*~~
Say: *I rarely/seldom/hardly ever see him.*

rate /reɪt/ *verb*

- ► rate
- ► rank
- ► grade
- ► place

rate
to decide how good, bad, or important something is when compared to others: *I would **rate** Babe Ruth **as** the best baseball player of all time.* | *The traffic in Los Angeles was rated the worst in the nation.*

rank
to have a particular position in a list that shows how good someone or something is: *Our soccer team has won every game this year – we are ranked number one in the league.*

grade (AWL)
to arrange things into groups that show their quality or rank: *The most expensive beef is graded "Prime" by the U.S. Department of Agriculture.*

place
to say how good or important you think someone or something is in relation to other people or things. You often talk about "placing something above/below" another thing or "placing something high/low" on a list: *Some schools seem to **place** high test scores **above** real learning.*

→ see **cost**[1], **level**, **speed**

rather *adverb* → see **fairly**

ratio /ˈreɪʃiˌoʊ/ *noun*

- ► ratio
- ► proportion
- ► scale

ratio (AWL)
a relationship between two amounts that shows how much bigger one amount is than another. For example, "20:1" and "5:1" are **ratios**, and when you say these **ratios**, you say "twenty to one" and "five to one": *There are six men and six women in class, so the **ratio of** males **to** females is exactly 1:1.* | *The **ratio of** nurses **to** doctors at the hospital is 2:1* (=two nurses for each doctor).

proportion (AWL)
the general relationship between a number or group and the larger number or group that it is part of: *The **proportion of** young people **to** old people in the country is changing because fewer babies are being born.*

scale
the relationship between the size of a map, drawing, or model and the actual size of the place or thing that it represents: *The map is drawn **to scale** – every 1 centimeter shown on the map is 25 kilometers in reality.*

rattle /ˈrætl/ *verb*

- ► rattle
- ► clatter
- ► clink
- ► clank
- ► knock

rattle
if a hard object rattles, it moves or shakes and makes short sounds as it hits against things. **Rattle** is used especially when part of something is loose and is hitting against something hard: *There's something rattling inside the washing machine.* | *The wind was rattling the windows so hard I thought they might break.*

clatter
if a hard object clatters, it makes several loud short sounds as it hits another hard object or surface, especially because it has fallen: *The pot fell out of my hand and **clattered onto** the stone floor.*

clink
if glass or metal objects clink, they make a short

R

ringing sound when they touch: *Spoons* ***clinked against*** *cups as the women stirred their tea.*

clank
if a heavy metal object clanks, it makes a short loud sound as it hits another metal object: *The gate clanked shut behind him.*

knock
to hit a hard surface with a short quick action and a short sound, either once or many times: *The branches were* ***knocking against*** *the windows in the wind.*

raw /rɔ/ *adjective*

- ► raw
- ► uncooked
- ► fresh

raw
not cooked: *You should wash the counter carefully after cutting raw meat.* | *Carrots can be eaten raw or cooked.*

uncooked
uncooked food has not yet been cooked, but should be cooked before it is eaten: *Add half a cup of uncooked rice to the soup and cook it for 15 more minutes.*

fresh
fresh food has recently been picked or prepared, and is not frozen or preserved: *The tomatoes are fresh from the garden.*
→ see Topic **Describing Food**, **Describing People's Emotions**

ADVERBS

You can make the adjective **fresh** into an adverb by using an **-ly** ending: *The tomatoes are freshly picked.*

ray *noun* → see **light¹**

reach /ritʃ/ *verb*

- ► reach
- ► stretch

reach
to move your hand or arm to touch or pick up something: *Can you get that book on the top shelf for me? I can't reach it.* | *He* ***reached*** *across the table* ***for*** *the salt.*

stretch *also* **stretch out**
to reach out your arms, legs, or body as far as possible: *I got up and stretched.* | *Jimmy stretched out his hand to take the candy.*
→ see **reach an agreement** at **agree (2)**, **reach a place** at **come (1)**, **reach someone by telephone** at **communicate**

react /ri'ækt/ *verb*

- ► react
- ► respond
- ► overreact

react (AWL)
to do or say something because of what someone has done or said to you: *"How did she* ***react to*** *the news that you are quitting your job?" "She was really surprised."* | *The audience* ***reacted by*** *cheering and shouting.*

respond (AWL)
to react to something, especially by giving an answer in words or doing something: *When I asked for help, she* ***responded that*** *I could do it myself.* | *The soldiers* ***responded to*** *the attack* ***by*** *shooting at the rebels.*

overreact
to react too strongly to something, especially by becoming extremely angry, worried, or afraid: *I get jealous when my boyfriend talks to other girls – do you think I am overreacting?*

reaction /ri'ækʃən/ *noun*

- ► reaction
- ► response

reaction (AWL)
the way you feel or the things you do when something happens: *My first* ***reaction to*** *the news was shock.* | *When someone attacks you, your natural reaction is to try to defend yourself.*

response (AWL)
something you say or do when another person says or does something to you: *I asked him if he wanted to come with us, but there was no response.*

read /rid/ *verb*

- ► read
- ► skim
- ► scan
- ► browse
- ► flip through
- ► look through
- ► study

read
to look at words and understand them: *Most children can read by the age of seven.* | *Steve was reading a book about airplanes.*

skim
to read something very quickly so that you get a general idea of what it is about: *She **skimmed through** the article on the elections.*

scan
to read something quickly to find the specific information you want: *He scanned the list, looking to see if his name was on it.*

browse
to look at pages of a magazine or book, stopping to read parts that interest you: *There was time to **browse through** some magazines at the library.*

flip through
to quickly turn the pages of a magazine or book without reading much: *I flipped through the magazine, hoping to find something interesting to read.*

look through
to turn the pages of something and look at them without reading everything: *The teacher looked through my report and said she thought it was fine.*

study
to read something very carefully to find out information: *Lisa studied the menu in the restaurant, hoping to find something that was not too fattening.*

readers *noun* → see **audience**

ready /ˈredi/ *adjective*

1 having done everything you need in order to deal with something
- ready
- prepared
- set (*informal*)

2 to become ready (verbs)
- get ready
- prepare
- make preparations
- ready (*formal*)

1 having done everything you need in order to deal with something

ready
if you are ready, you have done everything you need to do in order to deal with something: *Is everyone ready yet? It is almost time to go.* | *Maria was getting **ready for** school and putting her books in her backpack.*

prepared
ready to deal with something, because you know what is going to happen: *The city is **prepared for** the thousands of sports fans who are coming to watch the Olympics.* | *I wasn't **prepared for** his next question.*

set (*informal*)
if you are set, you are completely ready to do something: *Are you all **set for** your trip?*
→ see **ready to** at **willing**

GRAMMAR CHECK: ready

You cannot use **ready**, **prepared**, or **set** before a noun. Don't say: ~~a ready/prepared/set person~~. Say: *She was ready/prepared/set.*

2 to become ready (verbs)

get ready
to make plans or do things that need to be done for something that will happen in the future: *I have to go **get ready for** work.* | *The army was **getting ready to** attack.*

prepare
prepare means the same as **get ready** but sounds more formal: *He only had a few hours to **prepare for** the interview.* | *The company is **preparing to** move to Texas.*

make preparations
to prepare for an event that needs a lot of planning: *The couple are **making preparations for** their wedding next year.*

ready (*formal*)
to do all the things that need to be done before you can do an activity or process. **Ready** sounds formal or literary: *The fisherman readied his nets.*

real /rɪəl/ *adjective*

- real
- genuine
- authentic
- true
- actual
- sincere
- literal

ANTONYMS → see **artificial**, **fake²**, **imaginary**

real
not false or artificial: *These white flowers aren't real – they're made of plastic.* | *We call him "Biff" but his real name is Bernard.*
→ **Real** is also used about things that exist or happen and are not imaginary: *The book was based on real events.* | *She was in real pain.*

R

genuine
a genuine feeling, thing, or person really is what they seem to be: *He showed a genuine interest in what I was doing.* | *We thought the painting was by Picasso, and an expert confirmed that it was genuine.*

authentic
done in the correct or traditional way, and not an imitation: *The restaurant serves authentic Japanese food.*
→ You can also say that a painting, document, etc. is **authentic** when it has been proved to be the original work and not a copy: *The photographs were authentic and had not been changed in any way.*

true
having all the qualities that you think a particular kind of person or feeling should have: *When you are in trouble, you soon find out who your true friends are.* | *She says that she has finally found true happiness.*
→ **GRAMMAR:** With this meaning, **true** is always used before a noun. Don't say: ~~*This happiness is true*~~. Say: *This is true happiness.*

actual
real, but different from what people think or expect: *The news reports said that around 2,000 people died in the earthquake, but the actual number may never be known.* | *The actual cost of the building work was much higher than the planned cost.*
→ **GRAMMAR: Actual** is always used before a noun. Don't say: ~~*The movie is based on events that are actual*~~. Say: *The movie is based on actual events.*

sincere
really feeling or believing something, and not pretending: *Eduardo listened with sincere interest.*

literal
the literal meaning of a word or expression is its basic or original meaning: *A trade war is not a war in a literal sense. It just means that there is very strong competition between countries.*

realistic /rɪəˈlɪstɪk/ *adjective*

1 sensible and understanding what is possible or not possible
- ► realistic
- ► practical
- ► pragmatic
- ► rational

2 seeming real
- ► realistic
- ► lifelike
- ► true to life

1 sensible and understanding what is possible or not possible

realistic
sensible and understanding what is possible or not possible: *She is **realistic about** her chances of winning the race.* | *We need to be realistic. How much can we really get done in just two weeks?*
→ You can also use **realistic** about something that it is possible to achieve: *He has a realistic chance of being elected.*

practical
using methods that are likely to help you deal with common situations and problems: *Tom's very practical and I'm sure he can think of a solution to our problems.*
→ You can also use **practical** about things that are likely to work well in a particular situation: *This car is a good practical choice for people with young children.*

pragmatic
willing to change your ideas or what you are doing so that you can find methods that work in a situation: *We need to be **pragmatic about** reducing crime and not just think about putting people in prison.*

rational (AWL)
able to think in a calm and sensible way without letting emotions affect your decision or opinion: *When you are scared of losing your job, it is difficult to make a rational decision about what to do next.*

ADVERBS

You can make the adjectives **realistic**, **pragmatic**, and **rational** into adverbs by using an **-ly** ending: *Realistically, we are not likely to finish in just two weeks.* | *You must approach the problem rationally, and not let your feelings influence your decision.*

The adverb **practically** is not used in this meaning.

2 seeming real

realistic
if something is realistic, it seems real: *The picture is very realistic and you can almost imagine that the woman is sitting in front of you.* | *The movie gives a realistic picture of what life was like for the soldiers.*

lifelike
a lifelike model or image looks a lot like a real person or thing: *The dinosaurs in the museum are very lifelike and they can be scary for kids.*

true to life
a book, story, or movie that is true to life is similar to what really happens in people's lives: *His stories are very true to life and are based on real events.*

reality /riˈæləti/ *noun*

- reality
- the real world

reality
the real situation: *Some people think it is easy to get a job, but the reality is very different.* | *If you spend all your life playing computer games, there is a danger that you will lose touch with reality.*

the real world
life as it really is, with all its problems: *We try to prepare students for the real world outside school.* | ***In the real world**, doctors often have to make decisions very quickly.*

realize /ˈrɪəˌlaɪz/ *verb*

- realize
- become aware
- it dawns on me/him/her etc.
- understand

realize
to know that something is happening or is true: *I could smell burning, and I suddenly **realized that** the house was on fire.* | *Her parents knew college was expensive, but they didn't **realize how** much it would really cost.*

become aware
to start to realize something: *We first **became aware that** our son had reading problems last year.*

it dawns on me/him/her etc.
used when saying that someone realizes something for the first time: ***It dawned on** me **that** she had been lying to me and was only interested in my money.*

understand
to know why or how something happens, or the effect that it has: *I still don't **understand why** she hates me so much.* | *People need to understand the importance of healthy eating.*

really /ˈrɪəli/ *adverb*

- really
- actually
- in fact
- in reality
- in practice
- in effect
- truly
- genuinely
- sincerely
- literally

really
used when saying that something is true, especially when the situation seems different: *Is she really 70? She looks younger than that.* | *David seems confident but he is a shy person really.*

actually
really. You use **actually** especially when the situation is different from what you expect, in a way that seems surprising. **Actually** is used especially in spoken English: *Dan lost his job, but he is actually happy about it.* | *Did you actually meet the president when you went to the White House?*

in fact
used when the situation is different from what people think: *Making bread sounds difficult, but in fact it is very simple.*

in reality
used when the situation is different from what you have just said: *She was young, beautiful, and seemed to have everything she wanted, but in reality she was deeply unhappy.*

in practice
used when something is different from what is supposed to happen: *Marco was supposed to finish work at 5:30, but in practice this rarely happened.*

in effect
used when saying what the real or true situation is, when it is not clear: *The college has given a new name to what is, in effect, the same class.*

truly
used when emphasizing that you really mean what you are saying: *I'm truly sorry for what I've done.*

genuinely
used when a person, feeling, or thing is really what he, she, or it seems to be: *He seemed genuinely interested in what I was doing.*

sincerely
used when emphasizing that someone really

R

feels or believes something, and is not pretending: *She made a mistake, and sincerely apologized.*

literally
used to emphasize that something, especially a large number, is actually true even though it is difficult to believe: *The Olympic Games were watched by literally billions of people.*
→ see **very** for **really** meaning "very much"

reason /ˈrizən/ *noun*

1 a fact that explains something
- ► reason
- ► explanation
- ► motive
- ► excuse
- ► pretext
- ► justification
- ► grounds
- ► rationale (*formal*)

2 the ability to make sensible decisions or behave sensibly
- ► reason
- ► logic
- ► judgment
- ► sense

1 a fact that explains something

reason
a fact that explains why something happens or why someone does something: *Marta gave no* ***reason for*** *her decision.* | *There are many* ***reasons why*** *some young people fail in school.*
→ **GRAMMAR:** Don't say: ~~*the reason of something*~~. Say: *the reason for something.*

explanation
a reason that helps you to understand why something happens. **Explanation** is often used when something is difficult to understand: *Climate change is one possible* ***explanation for*** *the increase in the number of these insects.*

motive (AWL)
the reason why someone decides to do something. You use **motive** especially about why someone commits a crime: *Police believe the* ***motive for*** *the murder was money.*

excuse
a reason that someone gives for doing something wrong, especially one that you do not believe is true: *When I asked him why he was late, he made some excuse about his alarm clock not working.*

pretext
a false reason that you give for doing something, because you want to hide the real reason: *The man said he needed to check the water pipes, but it was just a pretext so that he could get into the old lady's house.*

justification (AWL)
a good reason that explains why someone has done something bad: *The* ***justification for*** *the war was the fear that the enemy had nuclear weapons.*

grounds
an official reason that makes it legally right or fair to do something: *If your husband or wife has an affair, that is usually* ***grounds for*** *a divorce.*

rationale (*formal*)
the reasons that you use to make a decision: *The chairman explained the* ***rationale for*** *the company's decision to close the factory.*

2 the ability to make sensible decisions or behave sensibly

reason
the ability to make sensible decisions, or a way of behaving that seems sensible: *He loved her, which had nothing to do with reason and everything to do with emotion.* | *At about age seven, children reach the "age of reason," when they can understand the difference between right and wrong and act responsibly.*
→ If someone **sees reason** or **listens to reason**, he or she starts to behave in a sensible way or is persuaded to behave in a sensible way: *We've tried to make him change his mind but he won't listen to reason.*

logic
the way in which someone connects facts and reasons together in order to explain something: *I can see the logic in his argument - you can't spend money that you don't have.*

judgment
the ability to make sensible decisions about what to do in a situation: *If you are feeling tired and hungry, it can affect your judgment.*

sense
the ability to make good decisions and not do stupid things: *I was very sick, but luckily Jim had the sense to call a doctor.*
→ see **cause**[1]

reasonable *adjective* → see **cheap**, **fair**[1], **sensible**

reasonably *adverb* → see **fairly**

rebel[1] /ˈrebəl/ *noun*

- ► rebel
- ► revolutionary
- ► guerrilla
- ► freedom fighter
- ► terrorist

rebel
someone who fights against the leader or government of his or her own country: *Rebels have taken control of government buildings.*
→ A **rebel** is also someone, especially a young person, who refuses to do what people in authority want him or her to do: *I was kind of a rebel in high school – I even almost dropped out.*

revolutionary (AWL)
someone who wants to get rid of the old government, especially by using force: *In the 1800s, revolutionaries in Uruguay wanted to be free of Spanish rule.*

guerrilla
a member of a group of fighters who are not part of an official army and are fighting for political reasons: *The guerrillas attacked an army patrol and killed four U.S. soldiers.*

freedom fighter
someone who fights to get rid of the government so that the people in a country can be free. You usually use **freedom fighters** when you support what they are doing: *Some people thought they were freedom fighters. Other people said they were terrorists.*

terrorist
someone who uses violent actions for political reasons: *Terrorists blew up the ship in the harbor.*

rebel[2] /rɪˈbel/ *verb*

- ► rebel
- ► revolt
- ► disobey
- ► defy

ANTONYMS → see **obey**

rebel
to refuse to do what your parents, teachers, or people in authority tell you to do: *Teenagers often **rebel against** their parents and argue with them.* | *Voters are openly **rebelling against** the government.*

revolt
to refuse to obey the government, and use violence to try to change it: *In Egypt, the people **revolted against** the government and held big demonstrations in the main square in Cairo.*
→ You can also use **revolt** when a group of people refuse to accept a decision or law: *Shareholders revolted against the plan to increase the Chief Executive's pay.*

disobey
to not do what someone or something tells you to do: *He disobeyed his commanding officer and refused to shoot.* | *If you disobey the law, you can expect to be punished.*

defy
to deliberately disobey a person, government, or law, in a way that shows you do not care if you make someone angry or get punished: *The workers defied federal law and went on strike.* | *She defied her parents and married him against their wishes.*

rebellious /rɪˈbelyəs/ *adjective*

- ► rebellious
- ► disobedient
- ► defiant

ANTONYMS → see **obedient**

rebellious
a rebellious young person often behaves badly and refuses to do what parents, teachers, and people in authority tell him or her to do: *James Dean plays the role of a rebellious teenager who is always fighting with his parents.*

disobedient
a disobedient child or animal refuses to do what someone says: *Our dog is very disobedient, and he never comes back when you tell him to.*

defiant
refusing to do what someone tells you to do, in a way that shows you do not care if you get punished or make the person angry: *There is a famous picture of a defiant student protester who stands in front of a line of government tanks.*

ADVERBS
You can make the adjectives that mean **rebellious** into adverbs by using an **-ly** ending: *"I won't go!" she shouted rebelliously.* | *The students defiantly stood in front of a line of government tanks.*

receive /rɪˈsiv/ *verb*

- ► receive (*formal*)
- ► get
- ► inherit

ANTONYMS → see **give**, **send** (**1**)

receive (*formal*)
to be given something or be sent something:

R

Cecilia never received an invitation to the party. | *She walked up to the stage to receive her award.*

get
get means the same as **receive** but is less formal: *I get about 50 emails every day.* | *Ben* ***got*** *a new computer* ***from*** *his parents* ***for*** *Christmas.*

inherit
to get something from someone after he or she has died: *Jim* ***inherited*** *a lot of money* ***from*** *his mother when she died.*

recent /ˈrisənt/ *adjective*

- ► recent
- ► latest

recent
happening or done a short time ago: *In recent years, the city has become a much safer place to live.* | *A recent survey showed that most people wanted lower taxes.*

latest
most recent: *Have you seen his latest movie?*

ADVERBS

You can make the adjective **recent** into an adverb by using an **-ly** ending: *The city has recently become a much safer place to live.* | *Have you seen Lisa recently?*

recession /rɪˈseʃən/ *noun*

- ► recession
- ► depression
- ► crash
- ► downturn

recession
a time when a country's economy stops growing and there is much less business activity and fewer jobs: *The U.S. economy went into recession and many companies were forced to close down.* | *The bank failed during the recession.*

depression (AWL)
a long period of time when there is very little business activity and many people are poor because they do not have jobs. A **depression** is much more serious than a **recession**: *My grandfather remembers the Great Depression of the 1930s, when millions of people lost their jobs.*

crash
a sudden fall in the value of companies, with the result that many companies close and people lose jobs: *The 1929 stock market crash caused investors to lose a lot of money, and was the starting point of the Great Depression.*

downturn
a time when there is less business activity than before, and economic conditions are less good. A **downturn** in the economy is less serious than a **recession**: *A big rise in gas prices could lead to a downturn in the economy.*

recipe *noun* → see **instructions**

recognize /ˈrekəgˌnaɪz/ *verb*

- ► recognize
- ► identify
- ► can tell
- ► distinguish
- ► differentiate (*formal*)

recognize
to know who someone is or what something is, because you have seen or heard him, her, or it before: *I hadn't seen him in a while, and because of his haircut I didn't recognize him at first.* | *Ramón* ***recognized*** *the girl* ***as*** *the one he had seen at the party.*

identify (AWL)
to say who someone is or what something is: *There were three different types of butterflies, and I was able to identify them all.*

can tell
to be able to recognize someone or something: *Marcia looks different in the photograph but* ***you can tell it is*** *her because of her red hair.*

distinguish
to recognize the difference between things or people: *It is often difficult to* ***distinguish*** *a real diamond* ***from*** *a fake one.*

differentiate (AWL) (*formal*)
differentiate means the same as **distinguish** but is used more in science writing: *Some children were unable to* ***differentiate between*** *the sounds /th/ and /f/.*

recommend *verb* → see **advise**, **suggest**, Topic **Eating in a Restaurant**

recommendation *noun* → see **advice**, **suggestion**

record /ˈrekəd/ *noun*

- ► record
- ► diary
- ► journal
- ► blog
- ► log
- ► minutes
- ► transcript
- ► note

record
information about something that you keep by writing it down or storing it on a computer: *The doctor asked me to keep a **record** of what I eat.* | *The school's records are kept in computer files.*

diary
a book in which you write about the things that happen to you each day and about your thoughts: *On February 7, 1907, Margaret wrote in her diary: "Jane has asked me to be her bridesmaid. I am thrilled!"*

journal (AWL)
journal means the same as **diary**, but seems more serious and is more commonly used by adults: *He wrote in his journal that he felt "alone in the world."*

blog
a record in which you talk about the things you have done or your opinions, which you write regularly on the Internet: *He wrote in his blog that he was planning to take a trip to Mexico.*

log
an official record of the things that have happened on a ship or plane: *The ship's captain recorded this information in the log.*

minutes
a written record of the things that were said or decided at a meeting: *I can't go to the meeting, but could you send me a copy of the minutes?*

transcript
a written record of the exact words that someone said: *In court, we were given a transcript of the interview between Phillips and the police.*

note
something that you write down quickly, to help you remember something: *I'll just make a note of your address.*

recover *verb* → see **better (2)**, **get back**

recovery *noun* → see **improvement**

recycle /ri'saɪkəl/ *verb*

- ► recycle
- ► reuse

recycle
to make paper, glass, plastic, or metal able to be used again, by collecting it and putting it through a special process: *We collect and recycle empty bottles and cans.* | *The chairs are made from recycled plastic.*

reuse
to use something again, instead of throwing it away: *Try to reuse plastic bags.*
→ see Topic **The Environment**

reduce /rɪ'dus/ *verb*

1 to make something less in amount or level
- ► reduce
- ► decrease (*formal*)
- ► lower
- ► bring down
- ► cut
- ► cut down
- ► slash
- ► minimize
- ► lessen

ANTONYMS → see **increase[1] (3)**

2 to make pain, worry, etc. less
- ► reduce
- ► relieve
- ► ease
- ► lessen
- ► soothe

1 to make something less in amount or level

reduce
to make something such as an amount or level become less than it was before: *The shirt was **reduced from $30 to $15**.* | *Better public transportation will reduce the number of cars on the road.*

decrease (*formal*)
to reduce the amount or level of something: *The law has decreased the number of guns on the street.*

lower
to reduce a level, amount, or limit. **Lower** is often used in writing about business, technical, or health subjects: *Stores lower their prices in the after-Christmas sales.* | *The drug is used to lower your blood pressure.*

bring down
to reduce something such as prices or costs, or reduce the level of something. **Bring down** is less formal than **lower**: *More competition between companies should bring prices down.* | *The government wants to bring down unemployment by creating new jobs.*

cut
to reduce something such as prices, costs, jobs, or time: *The company is looking at ways to cut its costs.*

cut down
to reduce the amount you eat or drink, or to reduce the number of times you do something: *Doctors want kids to cut down on the amount of soda they drink.*

R

slash
to reduce an amount or price by a lot. **Slash** is usually used in newspapers or advertisements: *Stores have slashed prices to attract more customers.*

minimize (AWL)
to reduce something bad or dangerous to the smallest possible amount: *Keep your car locked to minimize the risk of theft.*

lessen
to make a chance or risk become less, or to make the importance or effect of something less: *If you eat healthily, you lessen your chances of having a heart attack.* | *The campground is being made smaller to lessen the impact on the environment.*
→ see **decrease²** for "to become less"

2 to make pain, worry, etc. less

reduce
to make pain, worry, or an unpleasant feeling less than it was before: *Doctors gave him a drug to reduce the pain.* | *The aim of the treatment is to reduce anxiety and help you relax.*

relieve
to make pain or an unpleasant feeling easier to deal with: *Doctors had to relieve the pressure on his brain caused by the injury.* | *Mohammed read a book to relieve the boredom of waiting.*

ease
to reduce pain or an unpleasant feeling and make someone feel more comfortable: *He took a warm bath to ease the pain in his legs.*

lessen
to reduce pain or an unpleasant feeling by a small amount: *Time can help lessen the pain when someone you love dies.*

soothe
to reduce pain, or reduce someone's worry, fear, etc.: *The cream will soothe the pain of sunburn.* | *She soothed his fears with some calming words.*

reduction *noun* → see **decrease¹**

referee /ˌrefəˈri/ *noun*

- ► referee
- ► umpire
- ► judge

referee
the person who makes sure that the players obey the rules in sports such as soccer, football, hockey, basketball, volleyball, and boxing: *The referee called a foul on Johnson.*

umpire
the person who makes sure that the players obey the rules in sports such as baseball or tennis: *The umpire said the pitch was a strike.*

judge
the person in some sports who helps the referees: *The line judge said that the ball was out.*
→ see Topic **Sports and Exercise**

refer to *phrasal verb* → see **mention**

reflect *verb* → see **think**

refreshments *noun* → see **food**

refusal /rɪˈfyuzəl/ *noun*

- ► refusal
- ► rejection
- ► veto
- ► denial

ANTONYMS → see **agreement (3)**

refusal
an act of saying that you will not do something or will not allow something: *I wondered if Jane's **refusal to** talk to me meant she was angry with me.* | *His **refusal to** eat worried his parents.*

rejection (AWL)
the act of saying or showing that you do not want something or someone: *He was disappointed by the **rejection of** his plans to build a new golf course.*

veto
the act of officially refusing to allow something, especially a new law: *There was a presidential **veto of** the bill to change the tax laws.*

denial (AWL)
a refusal to allow someone to have or do something that he or she has a right to expect: *Refusing to allow prisoners to talk is a **denial of** basic human rights.*

refuse /rɪˈfyuz/ *verb*

1 to say you will not do something

- ► refuse
- ► say no (*spoken*)
- ► veto
- ► decline (*formal*)

ANTONYMS → see **agree**

2 to say no to an offer or suggestion

- ► refuse
- ► say no (*spoken*)
- ► reject (*formal*)
- ► turn down
- ► decline (*formal*)

ANTONYMS → see **accept**

3 to not give or allow someone something that he or she wants or should have
- ► refuse
- ► deny
- ► turn down
- ► take away
- ► deprive

ANTONYMS → see **let**

1 to say you will not do something

refuse
to say that you will not do something: *I asked Diego to help us but he refused.* | *If they* ***refuse to*** *leave, call the police.*

say no (*spoken*)
to say that you will not do something when someone asks you: *Remember, you can say no. No one has the right to pressure you to take drugs.*

veto
if someone in a powerful position vetoes something such as a new law, he or she refuses to agree to it: *The president vetoed the bill that had been passed by Congress.*

decline (AWL) (*formal*)
to politely refuse to do something: *The governor* ***declined to*** *comment on the rumors.*

2 to say no to an offer or suggestion

refuse
to say that you do not want something that someone offers you: *I refused his offer of a meal because I had just had lunch.*

say no (*spoken*)
to say that you do not want something that someone offers you: *I asked him if he wanted to come with us, but he said no.*

reject (AWL) (*formal*)
to refuse to accept an idea, plan, suggestion, or offer. **Reject** can seem more rude or angry than **refuse**: *Teachers rejected the pay offer because it was too low.*

turn down
to not accept an offer or invitation. **Turn down** is often used when the offer is good and it seems surprising that someone has refused it: *Anna was offered a place at Harvard University, but she turned it down so she could stay closer to home.*

decline (AWL) (*formal*)
to politely refuse to accept an invitation or offer: *He was invited to go to their wedding but he declined.*

3 to not give or allow someone something that he or she wants or should have

refuse
to not give or allow someone something that he or she wants: *Mom* ***refused to*** *let me go to the movie. She said I was too young.* | *The government refused him a visa, so he had to leave the country.*

deny (AWL)
to not allow someone to have something that he or she wants or needs: *He was denied the opportunity to appeal the court's decision.*

turn down
to not allow someone to do something that he or she has officially asked to do: *His application to build a new house on the land was turned down.*

take away
to not allow someone to have something that he or she had before: *The law took away their right to vote.*

deprive
to stop someone from having something that he or she needs or should have: *The court said that they had been* ***deprived of*** *their rights as citizens.*

regard *verb* → see **think**

region *noun* → see **area**

regret[1] *verb* → see **sorry (2)**

regret[2] *noun* → see **sadness**

regular /ˈregyələ/ *adjective*

- ► regular
- ► routine
- ► daily/weekly/monthly
- ► yearly

regular
happening or repeated at the same time every hour, day, year, etc.: *It is important to get regular check-ups at your dentist.* | *The camp was so popular that it became a regular event each summer.*

routine
happening regularly as part of the normal system and not because of any special problem: *A problem with the airplane was found during a routine check.*

daily/weekly/monthly
happening every day, week, or month: *The airline has a daily flight from San Francisco to Honolulu.*

yearly *also* **annual**
happening every year: *The conference is an*

R

annual event. | *In their yearly report, the police said that crime had fallen two percent.*
→ see **usual** for **regular** meaning "not different from usual"
→ see **frequent**, **ordinary**

regularly *adverb* → see **often**, **usually**

regulation *noun* → see **law**, **rule**[1]

rehearsal *noun* → see **practice**[1]

rehearse *verb* → see **learn**, **practice**[2]

reject *verb* → see **refuse**

rejection *noun* → see **refusal**

related *adjective* → see **connected**

relate to *phrasal verb* → see **connect**

relation *noun* → see **family**

relationship /rɪˈleɪʃənˌʃɪp/ *noun*

1 the situation when people spend time together and love each other
- relationship
- romance
- affair

2 the way that people or groups feel about each other, and the way they behave toward each other
- relationship
- friendship
- bond
- partnership
- relations
- association

1 the situation when people spend time together and love each other

relationship
a situation in which two people are together because they love each other: *"Are you in a relationship right now?" "Yes, I'm seeing a guy called Dan."* | *I had just left my husband and wasn't ready to start another relationship.*

romance
an exciting relationship between two people who love each other: *Their romance began on a date their friends had arranged for them.*

affair
a secret sexual relationship between two people, when one or both of them are married to someone else: *His wife found out that he was having an affair, and she asked for a divorce.*

2 the way that people or groups feel about each other, and the way they behave toward each other

relationship
the way that people or groups feel about each other and behave toward each other: *It is important for teachers to have a good **relationship with** their students.* | *The **relationship between** the two countries has always been difficult.*

friendship
the way that friends feel about each other and behave toward each other: *The two women formed a close friendship in college.*

bond (AWL)
a strong and special relationship between two people that makes them love each other or want to help each other: *The **bond between** a mother and her child is very strong.*

partnership (AWL)
a relationship between business partners, or between organizations that work together: *The school and local companies have formed a partnership to provide work experience for students.*

relations
the way people, groups, or countries behave toward each other, especially when this affects how well they work together: *The U.S. has good **relations with** Britain.*

association
a relationship with a person or organization, especially a business relationship: *His **association with** the company dates back to 1990 when he began work in the marketing department.*
→ see **connection**, **marriage**

relative *noun* → see **family**

relax /rɪˈlæks/ *verb*

- relax
- rest
- unwind
- take it easy (*informal*)

relax (AWL)
to not do very much and not think about things you need to do: *A long hot bath helps me to relax.* | *The pilot told us to relax and enjoy the flight.*

rest
to spend time relaxing or sleeping: *After the trip I was tired and needed to rest.*

unwind
to relax, especially after you have been working hard: *Exercise helps me to unwind after a long day at work.*

take it easy (*informal*)
to relax and not do very much, sometimes because you do not feel very strong: *The doctor told him to take it easy for a while after the operation.*

relaxed /rɪˈlækst/ *adjective*

- relaxed
- comfortable
- at ease

ANTONYMS → see **nervous**

relaxed
calm and not worried: *Dana looked relaxed and happy as she talked with her friends.* | *Marc was feeling relaxed after his vacation.*

comfortable
relaxed because you are in a situation you know, or because you are with people you like and trust: *I have known Ricardo for a long time, and I feel very comfortable with him.*

at ease
feeling relaxed in a situation that often makes people feel nervous: *It is part of a nurse's job to make patients feel at ease.*
→ see **calm**[1], **comfortable**, **informal**

ADVERBS
You can make the adjective **comfortable** into an adverb by using an **-ly** ending: *We chatted comfortably, as though we had known each other for years.*

relaxing /rɪˈlæksɪŋ/ *adjective*

- relaxing
- restful

relaxing
making you feel calm, or making your body feel less stiff: *We spent a relaxing weekend at the beach.* | *A relaxing massage can help the pain of sore muscles.*

restful
peaceful, quiet, and making you feel relaxed: *It is so quiet and restful here at the lake.*
→ see **comfortable**

release *verb* → see **drop**[1], **free**[2]

reliable *adjective* → see **responsible**

relief /rɪˈlif/ *noun*

- relief
- reassurance
- consolation

relief
happiness because something bad did not happen or has finished: *I don't like going to the dentist, and it was a relief when it was over.* | *The woman sighed **with relief** when she found her wallet.*

reassurance
something that helps you feel calmer and less worried about something: *The doctor gave the patient reassurance that everything would be fine.*

consolation
something that makes you feel less sad or disappointed, when what you wanted did not happen: *He lost the game but took some consolation in knowing he had done his best.*
→ see **help**[2]

religion /rɪˈlɪdʒən/ *noun*

1 belief in a god or gods
- belief
- religion
- faith

2 a system of beliefs about a god or gods
- religion
- faith
- denomination
- church
- sect
- cult

1 belief in a god or gods

belief
a feeling that a god or gods exist: *Many people who never go to any kind of church still say that religious belief is important to them.*

religion
a belief in one or more gods: *Religion is very important to us, and we pray and go to the mosque regularly.* | *We don't usually talk about religion in our family, because my uncle doesn't believe in God.*

faith
a strong belief in a particular god or religion: *My faith really helped me when my mom died.*

2 a system of beliefs about a god or gods

religion
a particular system of beliefs in one or more gods. Each **religion** has different rules and ceremonies: *Islam, Judaism, and Christianity are three of the main religions in the world.*

faith
a religion, especially one of the main religions of

the world: *Jacob was brought up in the Jewish faith and went to the synagogue every Saturday.* | *People of many different faiths came to live in America.*

denomination
a religious group that has slightly different beliefs from other groups who belong to the same religion: *The Armenian Orthodox Church is one of the world's oldest Christian denominations.*

church
a religious group that is part of the Christian religion: *The Catholic Church does not allow women to be priests.*

sect
a religious group that has separated from a larger group: *The sect split from the Catholic Church and believes that Jesus was an African man.*

cult
a small religious group with strange or extreme ideas and a strong leader who controls the group: *Members of the cult are not allowed to see their families.*

→ see **church**, **minister**

R

religious /rɪ'lɪdʒəs/ *adjective*

1 relating to a god or religion
- ► **religious**
- ► **spiritual**
- ► **holy**
- ► **sacred**
- ► **divine**

2 believing in a god or gods
- ► **religious**
- ► **devout**
- ► **faithful**
- ► **pious**

1 relating to a god or religion

religious
relating to religion: *Jewish people don't eat pork for religious reasons.* | *Buddhists and Christians have different religious beliefs.*

spiritual
relating to religion and the soul, and not relating to physical things: *She believes that spiritual life is more important than possessions.*

holy
relating to a god or religion, and believed to be special in some way: *Mecca is a holy city for Muslims.*

sacred
sacred means the same as **holy**: *Ayers Rock is the most sacred site of the Aborigines in Australia.*

divine
relating to or coming from a god: *At that time, people believed the floods were a divine punishment for their sins.*

SYNONYM CHECK

Holy or sacred?

Holy and **sacred** mean the same thing. They are used with many of the same words: *a holy/sacred book* | *a holy/sacred place.* However, you cannot use **sacred** about a person. Don't say: ~~*a sacred man/woman*~~. Say: *a holy man/woman.*

2 believing in a god or gods

religious
having a strong belief in a god or gods: *Maria is very religious and goes to church every week.*

devout
very religious, and careful to follow all the rules of your religion: *Ahmed is a devout Muslim who prays several times a day.*

faithful
continuing to believe in a particular religion, and following its rules: *It was Easter Sunday, and many faithful Catholics had gathered to hear the Pope.*

pious
having strong religious beliefs and showing this in the way you behave: *On Yom Kippur, pious Jews do not eat or drink, and they ask God to forgive them for the bad things they have done.*

ADVERBS

You can make the adjectives **spiritual**, **divine**, **devout**, **faithful**, and **pious** into adverbs by using an **-ly** ending: *I felt that my choice was divinely guided.* | *Walking in the mountains makes me feel better both spiritually and mentally.* | *He was a devoutly religious man.*

rely on *phrasal verb* → see **trust**[1]

remain *verb* → see **stay**

remark[1] /rɪ'mɑrk/ *noun*

- ► **remark**
- ► **comment**
- ► **observation**
- ► **point**
- ► **statement**

remark
something that you say, for example about your opinion or something you have noticed: *He made*

*a rude **remark about** my clothes. | Her **remarks on** the banking crisis were very interesting.*

comment (AWL)
something you say that shows your opinion about someone or something: *Jill made some interesting **comments about** the movie. | OK, does anyone have any comments or questions?*

observation
a comment on what you have noticed about something. **Observation** is more formal than **comment**: *Someone made the **observation that** Jenny has missed a lot of work lately.*

point
an idea or opinion that someone says in an argument or discussion: *Mrs. Woodall made a good **point about** the way bullying is dealt with at the school.*

statement
something that you say or write publicly and officially: *The president is expected to make a **statement about** the situation in the Middle East later today.*

remark² /rɪˈmɑrk/ *verb*

- ► **remark**
- ► **comment**
- ► **observe**
- ► **note** (*formal*)
- ► **point out**

remark
to say something, especially about something you have noticed: *"You look tired," he remarked. | Barbara **remarked that** she thought the movie was very good. | Her father **remarked on** how hard she had worked.*

comment (AWL)
to say what you have noticed: *"The two boys seem very alike," she commented. | He **commented that** Ryan had grown a lot since he last saw him.*

observe
to say or write what you have noticed about something. **Observe** is slightly more formal than **remark** or **comment**: *"Tom and Rick argue a lot," she observed. | The doctor **observed that** some patients do not take their medications.*

note (*formal*)
to say or write that you have noticed that something is true, important, or interesting: *"Girls do just as well in math as boys," he noted. | The judge **noted that** Miller had never been arrested before.*

point out
to tell people about a fact that you think is important, especially something that other people do not already know or have not yet noticed: *"Let's go to the park." "But it has started to rain," Bill pointed out. | The teacher pointed out several spelling mistakes. | Researchers have **pointed out that** children whose parents read aloud to them often learn to read more quickly at school.*

SYNONYM CHECK

Remark or comment?

Remark and **comment** can often be used in place of each other. However, you cannot use **remark** when you are asking for someone's opinion or saying that he or she will not give an opinion. Don't say: ~~*The president refused to remark on the progress of the talks.*~~ Say: *The president refused to comment on the progress of the talks.*

remarkably *adverb* → see **extremely**

remember /rɪˈmembɚ/ *verb*

- ► **remember**
- ► **recall**
- ► **recollect** (*formal*)

ANTONYMS → see **forget (1)**

remember
to have an idea or picture in your mind about something you did in the past, a place you went to, etc.: *I still remember my first day at school. | Do you remember when we went camping in the mountains?*

recall
to remember something from the past, especially so that you can tell someone about it: *Lewinsky **recalled that** he had seen a young man standing outside the house on the day of the robbery.*

recollect (*formal*)
recollect means the same as **recall**: *Johnson was able to recollect every detail of his first baseball game.*

→ see **remind** for words meaning "to make someone remember something"

→ see **memory**

remind /rɪˈmaɪnd/ *verb*

1 to make someone remember something they must do or say

- ► **remind**
- ► **prompt**

2 to make someone remember something that happened in the past

- ► **remind**
- ► **bring back memories**

R

1 to make someone remember something they must do or say

remind
to make someone remember something that he or she must do: *The teacher **reminded** us **that** our projects are due on Friday.* | *Please will you **remind** me **to** call Giorgio later?*

prompt
to tell an actor the words that he or she has forgotten so that he or she remembers the rest of the words: *If you forget your words, someone will prompt you.*

2 to make someone remember something that happened in the past

remind
to make you remember someone or something from the past: *That song **reminds** me **of** our first date.*

bring back memories
to make you remember something that happened in the past: *For some soldiers, the sound of fireworks can bring back terrible memories of the war.*
→ see **suggest (3)**, **look¹ (3)** for **remind you of** someone

SYNONYM CHECK
Remind or bring back memories?

You can use either **remind** or **bring back memories** about an event that makes you think of another event in the past: *Seeing the circus again reminded me of the time I saw it with my parents.* | *Seeing the circus again brought back memories of the time I saw it with my parents.*

You can use **remind** about a person who makes you think of someone else because they are similar in some way: *You remind me of my mom.* Don't say: ~~*You bring back memories of my mom.*~~

R

removal /rɪ'muvəl/ *noun*

- ► removal
- ► extraction
- ► withdrawal

removal (AWL)
the act of taking something away: *Snow removal costs about $57 million every winter.* | *You can use a drop of olive oil in your ear to help with the removal of ear wax.*

extraction (AWL)
the process of removing a natural substance from the ground or from a plant: *The extraction of oil from under the ocean is a difficult process.*
→ You also use **extraction** about removing a tooth from someone's mouth.

withdrawal
the act of taking soldiers away from the area where they were fighting: *The President wants a complete withdrawal of all U.S. troops from the country.*
→ **Withdrawal** can also be used to talk about taking away something such as support or an offer: *The withdrawal of financial support meant that the work had to stop.* It can also be used about taking money from a bank account: *He made a large cash withdrawal from a bank in Los Angeles.*

remove /rɪ'muv/ *verb*

1 to take something away from a place
- ► remove
- ► take out
- ► cut out
- ► pull out
- ► detach (*formal*)
- ► withdraw (*formal*)

2 to take something away permanently
- ► remove
- ► delete
- ► erase
- ► extract (*formal*)

1 to take something away from a place

remove (AWL)
to take something away from a place: *Eva used a razor to **remove** the hair **from** her legs.*

take out
to remove something from inside a container or place: *She opened her bag and took out a letter.*

cut out
to remove something from a place by cutting it: *The magazine article was interesting, so I cut it out and sent it to my friend.*

pull out
to remove something from a place such as a bag or pocket: *He pulled out a tissue and wiped his nose.*

detach (*formal*)
to remove something from the thing that it is attached to: *You can detach the legs of the pants to make them into shorts.*

withdraw (*formal*)
to take soldiers away from the place where they are fighting: *The government plans to **withdraw** troops **from** the area.*

→ **Withdraw** can also be used about taking money out of a bank account: *I want to withdraw $100 from my account.* It can also be used about taking away something such as support or an offer: *The company withdrew the job offer when they realized he had lied about his experience.*

2 to take something away permanently

remove (AWL)
to take something away from a place permanently: *Two trees had to be removed because they were dangerous.*

delete
to remove part of something you are writing on a computer. You can also **delete** all of a computer document: *The program lets you delete or move sentences as you are writing.*

erase
to remove writing or drawing with an eraser: *I used a pencil, so I could erase any mistakes.*

extract (AWL) *(formal)*
to remove a natural substance from the ground or from a plant: *The oil is* ***extracted from*** *the plant and used for making soap.*
→ **Extract** can also be used to say that a dentist removes a tooth from someone's mouth: *The dentist extracted his wisdom teeth.*
→ see **get rid of**

rent /rent/ *verb*

1 to pay money to use something that someone else owns
- ► rent
- ► lease

2 to let someone pay money to use something you own
- ► rent
- ► lease

1 to pay money to use something that someone else owns

rent
to pay money to live in a place or use something that someone else owns: *I* ***rent*** *the apartment* ***from*** *my aunt.* | *We rented a car when we were on vacation.*

lease
to pay money to a company to use a building, a car, or some equipment for a long time, especially for your business: *The company's airplanes are leased to several airlines under long-term contracts.*

2 to let someone pay money to use something you own

rent *also* **rent out**
to let someone pay to live in a place you own, or pay to use something for a short time: *We* ***rented*** *the house* ***to*** *a young couple.* | *There's a place on the lake that rents out boats.*

lease
to let a company or organization pay to use buildings, land, or equipment for a particular period of time: *We* ***lease*** *the building* ***to*** *a dance company.*
→ see **cost**[1]

repair /rɪˈper/ *noun*

- ► repair
- ► maintenance
- ► service

repair
something that you do to fix something that is damaged or not working: *The railroad track had been closed for repairs.* | *The building is very old and in need of repair.*

maintenance (AWL)
work that is done regularly to keep something in good condition and working correctly: *An older house usually needs more maintenance.*

service
a regular check of a car or machine, to make sure that it is working correctly: *The car needs a service every 20,000 miles.*
→ see **fix**

repeat[1] /rɪˈpit/ *verb*

- ► repeat
- ► say/do something again
- ► redo
- ► rerun
- ► echo

repeat
to say or do something again: *I didn't hear you. Can you repeat the question?* | *"What?" said Lou. "It is time to go," Amy repeated.* | *Repeat the exercise as many times as you can.*

say/do something again
say/do something again means the same as **repeat** but it is less formal: *I lost my homework on my computer and had to do it all again.*

redo
to do a piece of work again, especially because you did not do it well enough, or it needs changing: *We painted the kitchen but we had to redo it because it was the wrong color.*

rerun
to show a television program again: *The TV show "I Love Lucy" has been rerun many times.*

R

echo
if a sound echoes, you hear it again because it comes back off a wall or other surface: *His voice echoed around the empty hall.*
→ **Echo** can also mean "to repeat what another person has just said, because you agree with him or her": *Joel thanked her, and Lisa echoed, "Yes, thanks for all your help."*
→ see **quote**

repeat² /rɪˈpit/ *noun*

1 a television program that is shown again
► repeat
► rerun
2 something that happens again in the same way
► repeat
► repetition
► echo

1 a television program that is shown again

repeat
one show in a television series that is shown again: *I'm sure this is a repeat – I've seen it before.*

rerun
a television show or series that is shown again: *Reruns of "The X-Files" are on Channel 13.*

2 something that happens again in the same way

repeat
something that happens again in the same way: *The team is trying to avoid a* ***repeat of*** *last year's game when they lost 45–5.*

repetition
repetition means the same as **repeat**: *We don't want a repetition of the problems we had before.*
→ **Repetition** also means "saying or doing the same thing many times": *Repetition of words can help when you are learning a language.*

echo
a sound that you hear again, because it comes back off a wall or other surface: *He could hear the echo of the gunshots around the valley.*

repeated *adjective* → see **frequent**

repeatedly *adverb* → see **often**, Function Word **again**

repetition *noun* → see **repeat²**

replace /rɪˈpleɪs/ *verb*

1 to be used instead of something else
► replace
► take the place of
2 to do something instead of someone
► replace
► take someone's place
► stand in for
► substitute for

1 to be used instead of something else

replace
to be used instead of another thing: *Computers have replaced typewriters.* | *Do you think we should* ***replace*** *inches, feet, and miles* ***with*** *metric system measurements?*

take the place of
take the place of means the same as **replace**: *In Los Angeles, cars quickly took the place of the old bus and trolley system.*

2 to do something instead of someone

replace
to do something instead of another person, especially when this is a permanent change: *Maria will replace Joseph, who is leaving for a new job in Ohio.*

take someone's place
to do something instead of another person: *If you can't get to the meeting, I'll take your place.*

stand in for
to do someone's job for a short time or on a particular occasion, because he or she cannot be there: *The Vice President stood in for the President at the dinner.*

substitute for (AWL)
to ask someone to do someone else's job for a short time until he or she is able to do it again. **Substitute for** is used especially in sports: *The coach substituted Ruiz for Jordan, who wasn't playing well.*

replacement /rɪˈpleɪsmənt/ *noun*

1 something that you use or do instead of another thing
► replacement
► alternative
► substitute
► spare
2 someone who does a job instead of another person
► replacement
► substitute
► successor

1 something that you use or do instead of another thing

replacement
a new thing that you use instead of the one you had before, especially because there was something wrong with the old one: *If you have a problem with your phone, the store will give you a **replacement** free of charge.* | *My grandmother had a hip replacement last year.*

alternative (AWL)
something you can use or do instead of something else: *Low-fat yogurt is a healthy **alternative to** cream if you are trying to lose weight.*

substitute (AWL)
something that you can use if the usual thing is not available: *You can use frozen strawberries as a substitute, if you can't find fresh strawberries.*

spare
an extra key, tire, etc. that you keep so that you can use it if you need to: *I had to change a flat tire, so I got the spare out of the trunk.*

2 someone who does a job instead of another person

replacement
a new person who does the job that another person did before: *The director is leaving her job, and we are looking for a replacement.*

substitute (AWL)
someone or something that does what another person or thing usually does, especially a teacher or sports player: *There was a substitute in math today, because Mrs. Norris was sick.*

successor (AWL)
the person who does a job after someone else: *Kate is leaving the job next week, and her successor will be Ricardo Mendez.*

reply[1] *verb* → see **answer[1]**

reply[2] *noun* → see **answer[2]**

report /rɪ'pɔrt/ *noun*

- ► report
- ► article
- ► story
- ► account
- ► study
- ► review

report
a piece of writing or a statement that gives the facts about a situation or event: *The report said that over 500 people had been injured.* | *The teacher asked students to write a **report on** their visit to the museum.*

article
a piece of writing about someone or something in a newspaper or magazine: *There is an interesting **article about** climate change in today's "New York Times."*

story
a report in a newspaper or magazine or on the television news. **Story** is more informal than **report**: *Did you see the story in the paper about the fire?*

account
a written or spoken description of something that happened, especially based on your experience of it: *She wrote an **account of** her childhood in China.*

study
a piece of work that scientists or other people do to find out more about a subject or problem: *The study showed that women are much less likely to have car accidents than men.*

review
a piece of writing in a newspaper or magazine that says what is good and bad about a new movie, play, book, etc.: *Her latest movie got good reviews and I'd really like to see it.*
→ see **essay**, **tell**, **work[2] (3)**

reporter /rɪ'pɔrtɚ/ *noun*

- ► reporter
- ► journalist
- ► correspondent
- ► columnist

reporter
someone who writes reports for newspapers, magazines, television, or radio: *She is a **reporter for** "The Boston Globe."* | *Reporters waited outside the courtroom for the news.*

journalist
a reporter, or someone who writes articles for a newspaper. **Journalist** is more formal than **reporter**: *The journalist interviewed several farm workers for his story.*

correspondent
someone who reports news about one particular subject or place for a newspaper or news program. **Correspondent** is more formal than **reporter**: *He is the war **correspondent for** "The New York Times."*

columnist
someone who regularly writes an article for a newspaper or magazine: *Smith was a political **columnist for** "Time" magazine.*
→ see **writer**

R

represent *verb* → see **mean**[1]

representative *noun* → see **spokesperson**

reproduce /ˌriprəˈdus/ *verb*

- reproduce (*formal*)
- breed
- bear young (*formal*)

reproduce (*formal*)
if animals, plants, or cells reproduce, they make more animals, plants, or cells. You use **reproduce** especially in science writing: *Many plants and animals reproduce in the spring.* | *DNA controls the way cells reproduce in your body.*

breed
if animals breed, they have sex and produce baby animals: *Rabbits breed very quickly.*

bear young (*formal*)
if an animal bears young, it produces baby animals: *The cows will soon be old enough to bear young.*

R

reputation /ˌrepyəˈteɪʃən/ *noun*

- reputation
- image
- standing
- prestige
- good/bad name

reputation
the opinion that people have of someone or something and how good he, she, or it is: *The scandal could damage the reputation of the company.* | *The senator has a reputation as a hard-working politician.*

image (AWL)
the idea that people have about what someone or something is like, especially from the news or advertisements: *When you meet the president, he is very different from the image that most people have of him.*

standing
someone or something's position, and how important he, she, or it is compared to other people or things: *In recent years, China's standing in the world has changed and it is now an economic superpower.*

prestige
a good reputation that makes people admire and respect you for your achievements: *The Nobel Prize for Literature is an award that carries great prestige.*

good/bad name
the good or bad reputation that someone or something has compared to other people or things: *Dishonest car dealers give other dealers a bad name.* | *He said that the story in the newspaper had ruined his good name.*

request /rɪˈkwest/ *noun*

- request
- demand
- appeal
- plea
- application
- order
- petition

request
the action of asking for something, especially officially or politely: *The college has had a lot of* ***requests for*** *information about the class.* | *The singer granted the request for an interview* (=said yes to the request).

demand
a request in which you say very strongly and firmly that you want something: *The workers say they will go on strike if the company does not agree to their* ***demands for*** *better working conditions.*

appeal
an urgent request for help, money, or information from the public: *The police made an* ***appeal for*** *information to help them find the missing boy.*

plea
an urgent request for help because you are in a very bad situation: *Someone heard the man's* ***pleas for*** *help and pulled him out of the river.*

application
an official written request for something such as a job, entry into a college, or permission to do something: *The company received more than 100* ***applications for*** *the job.* | *You have to fill out a visa application if you want to travel to Argentina.*

order
something that you ask for in a restaurant or from a business: *The waiter got our order wrong and brought orange juice instead of lemonade.* | *The company received an* ***order for*** *50 trucks.*

petition
a document that a lot of people sign, in order to ask for something or complain about something: *Thousands of people signed a* ***petition against*** *plans to close the school.*
→ see **ask**

require *verb* → see **expect**, **need**[1]

requirement *noun* → see **need**[2]

rescue *verb* → see **save**

research¹ /ˈrisɚtʃ/ *noun*

- research
- study
- experiment
- investigation
- analysis
- work

research (AWL)
the activity of trying to find out more information about a subject, especially done by scientists or people who are studying the subject: *Scientists have been doing* ***research into*** *the causes of the disease. | Her* ***research is on*** *Native American culture before the Pilgrims arrived.*

study
a piece of work that is done to find out more about a particular subject or problem: *Recent studies have shown that women still get paid less than men.*

experiment
a scientific test that you do to find out something, or show that something is true: *In class, we did an experiment to find out which metals conduct electricity.*

investigation (AWL)
a process to find out the reasons why something bad happened, or to find the person who was responsible for a crime: *Police are carrying out an* ***investigation into*** *the accident.*

analysis (AWL)
a careful examination of something in order to understand it or to find out what it contains: *The blood samples were sent off to the laboratory for analysis. | Researchers carried out a detailed* ***analysis of*** *the data.*

work
the things that you do when you are studying something: *Edison is known for his* ***work on*** *light bulbs, but he also invented a lot of other things.*
→ see Topic **Science and Technology**

research² /rɪˈsɚtʃ/ *verb*

- research
- do research
- study
- investigate
- analyze

research (AWL)
to study a subject so you can find out more about it, especially for scientific or academic work: *She spent many years researching the history of the island before she wrote her book.*

do research *also* **carry out research**
do research or **carry out research** means the same as **research**, but it is more common in writing and speech, and it is less formal: *The company is* ***doing research into*** *the use of banana leaves to make paper. | The research was carried out by a team of scientists at the National Institutes of Health.*

study
to try to find out more about a subject: *They studied the way in which different students learn languages.*

investigate (AWL)
to try to find out the reasons why something happened, especially an accident or crime: *Police officers are investigating a robbery in which thieves stole over $10 million.*

analyze (AWL)
to examine something carefully, in order to understand it or to find out what it contains: *The researchers analyzed data from over 1,000 patients to see if the drug had any side effects. | Scientists analyzed the water and discovered that it contained dangerous levels of pollution.*
→ see Topic **Science and Technology**

researcher *noun* → see Topic **Science and Technology**

resemble *verb* → see **look¹ (3)**

reserve *verb* → see **save**, **supply**, Topic **Eating in a Restaurant**

reserved *adjective* → see **shy**

residence *noun* → see **house**

resident /ˈrezədənt/ *noun*

- resident
- inhabitant (*formal*)
- occupant (*formal*)
- tenant

resident (AWL)
one of the people who live in a city or town, or in a part of a city or town: *The beach is popular with local residents as well as tourists. | Residents of San Francisco were shaken awake by an earthquake.*

inhabitant (*formal*)
one of the people who live in a city, town, or part of a country. You use **inhabitant** especially when saying how many people live in a place: *Los Angeles is a city with over three million inhabitants. | The village has no electricity and the inhabitants live in mud huts.*

R

occupant (AWL) *(formal)*
someone who is in a particular house, apartment, or room, especially someone who lives there: *The occupants were all asleep when the fire started. | George W. Bush is a former occupant of the White House.*

tenant
someone who pays the owner of a house, apartment, or office building money to live or work there: *The tenants pay $1,500 a month to live in the apartment.*
→ see **population**

resign *verb* → see **quit**

resources *noun* → see **supply**

respect /rɪˈspekt/ *noun*

1 the feeling that someone or something should be treated politely and well
► respect
► honor
► self-esteem

2 the feeling when you think that someone is good
► respect
► regard *(formal)*
► admiration
► esteem *(formal)*

1 the feeling that someone or something should be treated politely and well

respect
the feeling that you should treat someone politely and well: *Kids should show respect toward their parents and not shout at them. | She is a cruel and selfish woman and I have no* ***respect for*** *her.*
→ You can also use **respect** about treating something in a way that shows you think it is important: *The gangs have no respect for the law. | We should show respect for other people's religious beliefs.*

honor
the respect that you, your family, or country get from other people, which makes you feel proud: *For the Mexican fans, tomorrow's game is a matter of national honor.*

self-esteem
the feeling that you are a good person and that you deserve to be liked and respected: *Students who have been bullied often have low self-esteem.*

2 the feeling when you think that someone is good

respect
the feeling that you think someone is good at what he or she does: *Venus is a great player and I have a lot of* ***respect for*** *her.*

regard *(formal)*
regard means the same as **respect**. You use it especially in the phrase **have a high regard for** (=to respect someone or something a lot): *I have a high* ***regard for*** *the teachers. I think they have a very difficult job.*

admiration
the feeling that you think someone or something is very good, especially so that you want to be like that person: *He felt great* ***admiration for*** *the work of writers such as Hemingway and F. Scott Fitzgerald. | The other students all looked at her* ***in admiration.***

esteem *(formal)*
if you hold someone in high esteem, you have a lot of respect for him or her: *Carter was clearly held in high esteem by his colleagues.*
→ see **admire**, **obey**

respectable *adjective* → see **good**

respond *verb* → see **answer[1]**, **react**

response *noun* → see **answer[2]**, **reaction**

responsibility /rɪˌspɑnsəˈbɪləti/ *noun*
► responsibility
► job *(informal)*
► duty
► obligation

responsibility
something that you must do because it is part of your job and you are in charge of doing it: *My boss has given me more responsibility at work. | Parents have many responsibilities, from making sure their children are clean and fed to making sure they go to school.*

job (AWL) *(informal)*
something you do because someone in authority has asked you to do it: *Your job is to help your classmates with any math problems that they do not understand.*
→ **Job** is usually used in the phrases **it's my/your/his job to do something** or **my/your/his job is to do something**.

duty
something that you have to do because it is right or it is part of your job: *One of your duties is keeping records of what happens at every*

meeting. | *As a police officer I have a* ***duty to*** *uphold the law.*

obligation
something that you must do because it is the law or your duty: *If you are in a car accident, you have a legal* ***obligation to*** *stay at the place where the accident happened until the police come.*

responsible /rɪˈspɑnsəbəl/ *adjective*

- ► **responsible**
- ► **reliable**
- ► **dependable**
- ► **conscientious**
- ► **trustworthy**

responsible
always behaving in a sensible way. You use **responsible** when someone can be trusted to do something without another person checking: *Young children should always be left in the care of a responsible adult.* | *He is not responsible enough to have his own key to the house.*

reliable (AWL)
always doing what you say you will do, or always doing what you are supposed to do: *Marco is very reliable and he always comes to the class on time.*

dependable
always doing what someone needs or wants: *He is a very dependable player who is able to score consistently.* | *The mail is usually dependable and letters normally arrive within a day or two.*

conscientious
always careful to do things as well as you can: *She is a conscientious student who sometimes spends four hours a day on her homework.*

trustworthy
honest and able to be trusted to do what you say: *Voters want politicians who are trustworthy.*
→ see **fault** for **responsible** meaning "responsible for something bad that happened"
→ see **guilty** (**2**), **sensible**

ADVERBS

You can make the adjectives **responsible**, **reliable**, **dependable**, and **conscientious** into adverbs by using an **-ly** ending: *I know that I can trust my son to act responsibly.* | *Most customers pay their bills reliably.* | *She does her homework conscientiously every night.*

rest[1] /rest/ *noun*

1 the part that is left after other parts have gone
- ► **the rest**
- ► **the remainder** (*formal*)
- ► **the balance**
- ► **the remains**

2 a time when you can relax or sleep
- ► **rest**
- ► **relaxation**
- ► **break**

1 the part that is left after other parts have gone

the rest
the part of a thing or group that is still there after all the other parts have gone: *He spent half the money and put the rest in the bank.* | *Cheryl is in New York, but* ***the rest of*** *the family will be here for Thanksgiving.*

the remainder (*formal*)
the remainder means the same as **the rest**: *The school will be closed for* ***the remainder of*** *the week because of problems with the heating system.*

the balance
the amount of something that is left after some has been spent or used. You use **the balance** about money or time: ***The balance of*** *the money must be paid back before the end of the year.* | *Profits are expected to increase during* ***the balance of*** *the year.*

the remains
the parts of something that are left after the rest has been destroyed: *You could see* ***the remains of*** *buildings that had been destroyed by the earthquake.*

2 a time when you can relax or sleep

rest
a time when you can relax or sleep: *I was taking care of five children, and I just needed a rest.* | *Why don't you go lie down and get some rest?*

relaxation (AWL)
things you do to help you rest and stop thinking about work or studying: *"What do you do for relaxation?" "I play computer games or watch TV."*

break
a short time when you stop working so that you can rest or eat: *He had worked all day without a break, so he was really tired.*

R

rest² /rest/ verb

- ► rest
- ► relax
- ► lie down
- ► take a break

rest
to spend time sleeping or not doing very much: *After the trip I was tired and needed to rest. | Don't disturb Dad! He is resting.*

relax (AWL)
to not do very much and not think about things you need to do: *A long hot bath helps me to relax.*

lie down
to lie on a bed so that you can rest: *Ellie went to lie down because she was tired.*

take a break
to stop what you are doing for a short time so that you can rest: *We've been working hard this morning. Let's take a break.*

R

restaurant /ˈresˌtrɑnt/ noun

- ► restaurant
- ► café
- ► coffee shop
- ► cafeteria
- ► diner

restaurant
a place where you can buy and eat a meal: *We ate at a Mexican restaurant on 23rd Street. | The restaurant serves Vietnamese food.*

café
a small restaurant where you can buy drinks and simple meals: *We stopped at a café for a sandwich.*

coffee shop
a small restaurant that serves cheap meals or coffee and snacks: *A group of men were sitting in the coffee shop eating pie and drinking coffee.*

cafeteria
a restaurant in a school, office, or factory where people take food from a counter and then sit down: *I always eat lunch in the school cafeteria.*

diner
a small restaurant that serves cheap meals: *We went to the diner for breakfast.*
→ see Topic **Eating in a Restaurant**

restroom *noun* → see **bathroom**

result¹ /rɪˈzʌlt/ noun

- ► result
- ► effect
- ► consequences
- ► implications (*formal*)
- ► outcome
- ► product (*formal*)

result
something that happens or exists because of something else happening first: *The store's closure was the* ***result of*** *poor sales. | They didn't play well and* ***as a result*** *they lost the game.*

effect
a change that is caused by an action or event: *Watching too much television has a bad* ***effect on*** *a child's development.*

consequences
the things that happen because of a decision or action, especially things that are bad or serious: *If you don't wear a seat belt in a car, this could have serious consequences if you get in an accident.*
→ **Consequences** is often plural, but you can also say something happens **as a consequence** or that something is **a consequence of** something else. **Consequence** is formal: *They broke the rules. As a consequence, they were sent home. | Mood swings may be a consequence of poor sleep.*

implications (*formal*)
the things that might happen because of something: *The company needs to consider the financial* ***implications of*** *any business decision.*

outcome (AWL)
the final result of something: *This decision changed* ***the outcome of*** *the war.*

product (*formal*)
the result of a situation or of someone's actions: *The report was* ***the product of*** *four years' hard work.*
→ see **grade¹**, **score¹**

result² *verb* → see **cause²**

return *verb* → see **give back**, **go back**

revenge /rɪˈvendʒ/ noun

- ► revenge
- ► vengeance (*formal*)
- ► retaliation (*formal*)
- ► reprisal

revenge
something you do in order to punish someone

who has done something bad to you, and who you hate because of this: *Maria had hurt him and he wanted revenge.* | *To get* ***revenge on*** *her ex-husband, she burned all his clothes.*

vengeance (*formal*)
something violent that you do to someone because he or she has done something bad to you, and who you hate because of this: *The movie is about a mother's desire for vengeance when her daughter is killed.*

retaliation (*formal*)
something bad that you do to someone because he or she has done something bad to you: *The shooting was* ***in retaliation for*** *the killing of another gang member.*

reprisal
something that you do to punish an enemy, after he or she has done something bad to you: *People in the community would not talk to the police because they were afraid of reprisals from the criminals.*

reverse *verb* → see **change**[1], **undo**

review[1] *noun* → see **report**

review[2] *verb* → see **judge**[2], **study**[1]

revolution /ˌrevəˈluʃən/ *noun*

- ► revolution
- ► rebellion
- ► revolt
- ► uprising
- ► coup

revolution (AWL)
a time when people change a government or political leader by using violence: *The American Revolution took place in the late 1700s, and America broke free from the British Empire.* | *Many people left Cuba and stayed in the U.S. after the revolution in Cuba in 1958.*

rebellion
an attempt to remove a government or political leader by using violence. You use **rebellion** especially when this is not successful: *The colonel was arrested after the* ***rebellion against*** *the government failed.*

revolt
an attempt to get rid of a government or leader, especially by using violence. A **revolt** is usually not successful and is shorter than a **rebellion**: *In 1712, there was a revolt by slaves in New York against their masters, but it was quickly stopped.*

uprising
an attempt to get rid of the government that is done by many of the ordinary people of a country: *In Egypt, the uprising against the government involved thousands of people and led to a revolution.*

coup *also* **coup d'état**
a situation in which a powerful group of people, who are usually in the army, take control of a country by force: *A military coup ended the president's rule.*
→ see **rebel**[1], **rebel**[2]

reward /rɪˈwɔrd/ *noun*

- ► reward
- ► incentive

reward
something that you get because you have done something good: *The new job was a* ***reward for*** *all her hard work.* | *There is a $50,000 reward for information that leads to the arrest of the robbers.*

incentive (AWL)
something that you offer someone, in order to persuade him or her to do something: *Companies are being offered tax incentives to reduce pollution.*
→ see **prize**

rewrite /ˌriˈraɪt/ *verb*

- ► rewrite
- ► revise
- ► edit

rewrite
to write something again so that you improve it or make it correct: *I rewrote the first part of my paper because it wasn't very good.* | *He needed to rewrite some paragraphs and cut others out altogether.*

revise (AWL)
to change a piece of writing by adding new information, removing mistakes, or making improvements: *The book needed to be revised because the law had changed.*

edit
to make a book, newspaper, magazine, or movie ready for people to read or see, by removing mistakes and deciding what to include: *The newspaper edits letters before printing them.*

rhyme *noun* → see **poem**

rhythm /ˈrɪðəm/ *noun*

- ► rhythm
- ► beat
- ► tempo

rhythm
a regular repeated pattern of sounds or

R

movements: *She started moving to the rhythm of the music. | The rhythm of his heart seemed to have changed.*

beat
the main regular pattern of sounds in a piece of music: *The song has a good beat that you can dance to.*

tempo
the speed at which a person or band plays a piece of music: *This piece should be played at a slow tempo.*

rich /rɪtʃ/ *adjective*

1 having a lot of money
- ► rich
- ► wealthy
- ► affluent
- ► well off
- ► prosperous (*formal*)
- ► well-to-do
- ► privileged

ANTONYMS → see **poor**

2 used about food that makes you feel full
- ► rich
- ► heavy

1 having a lot of money

rich
having a lot of money: *He is very rich, and has houses in Santa Barbara, Los Angeles, and France. | Rich countries need to do more to help poor countries.*

wealthy
a person or place that is wealthy has a lot of money over a long period of time: *Margaret was born into a very wealthy family and she always had everything she wanted. | Switzerland is one of the wealthiest countries in the world.*

affluent
having a lot of money to spend. You use **affluent** about places and groups of people: *Lisa is from an affluent suburb of Boston. | In today's affluent society, people don't seem to care how much food gets wasted.*

well off
having enough money to have a good life, with all the things you want: *His family are well off, and they can afford to pay for him to go to college.*

prosperous (*formal*)
rich and successful because of your business. You use **prosperous** about places and people: *The city became prosperous through trade with Europe. | She became a prosperous businesswoman who owned several successful stores.*

well-to-do
rich and having a high position in society. **Well-to-do** is usually used in writing: *He was born into a well-to-do Jewish family in the 1920s.*

privileged
having more advantages than other people because your family is rich: *Most of the students at this expensive school come from privileged backgrounds.*

2 used about food that makes you feel full

rich
rich food contains a lot of butter, cream, or eggs that make you feel full very quickly: *The dessert was covered in cream, and was too rich for me.*

heavy
heavy food makes your stomach feel full and uncomfortable: *A heavy meal makes you want to sleep.*

→ see **dark[1]** for **rich** meaning "having a strong color"

ride /raɪd/ *verb*

- ► ride
- ► pedal

ride
to sit on a bicycle, motorcycle, or horse and make it move forward: *I learned to ride a bicycle when I was five. | Have you ever ridden a horse?*

pedal
to ride a bicycle by pushing the pedals with your feet: *He pedaled the bike slowly up the hill.*

ridiculous *adjective* → see **silly**

right[1] /raɪt/ *adjective*

1 true and correct
- ► right
- ► correct
- ► accurate

ANTONYMS → see **wrong**

2 best for a situation or purpose
- ► right
- ► appropriate
- ► suitable
- ► acceptable

ANTONYMS → see **unacceptable (1)**

3 morally right
- ► right
- ► fair
- ► moral
- ► ethical
- ► justified

ANTONYMS → see **evil**[1]

1 true and correct

right
based on true facts, not having any mistakes, and not wrong: *Put up your hand if you think you know the right answer.* | *I'm not sure if this is the right address.*
→ You can also use **right** about people who have said or done something that is true and without mistakes: *I think you're right. We should have gone the other way.*

correct
right or without any mistakes. **Correct** sounds more formal than **right**: *The information you have is correct.* | *Make sure that your seat is in the correct position.*
→ You can also use **correct** about people who are right: *If the scientists are correct, there could be a big increase in average world temperatures.*

accurate (AWL)
exactly right in every detail, without any mistakes: *Make sure that your measurements of the room are accurate.* | *He was able to give the police an accurate description of his attacker.*

ADVERBS
You can make the adjectives that mean **right** into adverbs using an **-ly** ending: *He guessed, rightly, that the answer was "Peru."* | *The student needs to weigh the substances accurately.*

2 best for a situation or purpose

right
the right person, thing, method, etc. is the one that is best for a situation or purpose: *I think you have made the right decision.* | *Anna is the right person for the job because she has a lot of experience.*
→ **GRAMMAR:** In this meaning, you always use "the" before **right**. Don't say: ~~*He made a right decision*~~. Say: *He made the right decision.*

appropriate (AWL)
good for a person or situation: *The apartment is on the ground floor and is* ***appropriate for*** *young children.* | *It seemed an appropriate time to thank him for all his hard work.*

suitable
suitable means the same as **appropriate**: *T-shirts and shorts are* ***suitable for*** *days when the weather is hot.*

acceptable
good enough for a particular situation: *The students must be able to produce work of an acceptable standard before they can move to the next level.*

ADVERBS
You can make the adjectives **appropriate**, **suitable**, and **acceptable** into adverbs by using an **-ly** ending: *He was appropriately dressed for the wedding.* | *The motel room was acceptably clean.*

3 morally right

right
if something is right, people should do it because it is good or treats people equally: *Obviously, telling the truth is the right thing to do.* | *It is* ***right to*** *give disabled people the same opportunities as other people.*

fair
treating people in an equal way: *It is not fair if you give Marcus $5 and me only $3.* | *Everyone should have a fair chance at getting an education.*

moral
a moral duty is based on what you think is right, not on a law or rule: *Many people feel they have a moral duty to care for their elderly parents.*

ethical (AWL)
right according to principles about how people should behave: *It is not* ***ethical for*** *a doctor to start a romantic relationship with a patient.*

justified (AWL)
if something is justified, there is a good reason for doing it: *Violence against children is never justified, in any situation.*

ADVERBS
You can make the adjectives **fair**, **moral**, and **ethical** into adverbs by using an **-ly** ending: *The law makes sure that people are treated fairly.* | *Ethically, a doctor cannot start a romantic relationship with a patient.*

right[2] *adverb* → see **well**

right away *adverb* → see **immediately**

rim *noun* → see **edge**

R

ring¹ /rɪŋ/ verb

- ► ring
- ► strike
- ► chime
- ► toll
- ► clang
- ► jingle
- ► buzz

ring
if a bell or telephone rings, it makes a sound: *The church bells were ringing.*
→ You also use **ring** when someone makes a bell produce a sound: *I rang the doorbell and waited outside the front door.*

strike
if a clock strikes three, four, etc., it makes a noise like a bell to tell you that it is three o'clock, four o'clock, etc.: *I heard the clock strike twelve, so I knew it was midnight.*

chime
if a clock or bell chimes, it makes a ringing sound: *A clock chimed in the next room. It was two o'clock.*

toll
if a church bell tolls, it rings slowly because someone has died: *The church bell tolled as we went into the church for the funeral.*

clang
if a piece of metal clangs, it makes a loud sound when it hits something: *The gates clanged shut again.*

jingle
if small metal things jingle, they make a high sound when they hit each other. You use **jingle** especially about keys or coins: *The keys jingled in his pocket.*

buzz
if a phone, doorbell, or alarm buzzes, it makes an electronic sound instead of ringing: *The doorbell buzzed and she went downstairs to answer it.*
→ You also use **buzz** when someone presses a button that makes an electronic sound: *He buzzed for the elevator and went down to the basement.*
→ see Topic **To Make a Sound**

ring² *noun* → see **circle¹**

rinse *verb* → see **wash**

rip¹ *verb* → see **tear¹**

rip² *noun* → see **tear²**

rise¹ *verb* → see **go up**, **increase¹**, **stand**

rise² *noun* → see **increase²**

risk¹ /rɪsk/ noun

- ► risk
- ► gamble
- ► chance

risk
a possibility that something bad might happen: *Car racing is a dangerous sport and there is always the risk of an accident.*
→ You often use **risk** in the phrase **take a risk** (=to do something that could make something bad happen): *You're taking a risk if you lend him money. He might not pay you back.*

gamble
an action that you hope will be successful, but it may not be: *It was a gamble using a player who had been injured, but luckily he played well.*

chance
a possibility that something might happen: *There is a* ***chance that*** *it might rain tomorrow. I think we should have the picnic on a different day.*
→ see **danger** for **risk** meaning "a possibility that something bad might happen"

risk² /rɪsk/ verb

- ► risk
- ► take a risk
- ► be at risk
- ► endanger (*formal*)
- ► jeopardize (*formal*)

risk
to make it possible that something bad could happen to someone or something: *She risked her own life by jumping into the water to save the child.* | *If you lend him the money, you risk losing it.*

take a risk
to do something even though there is a possibility that something bad will happen: *He took a risk and gave up his job so that he could start his own restaurant.*

be at risk
if something important is at risk, it could be harmed or lost: *The jobs of over 2,000 workers are at risk if the factory closes.*
→ If you **put something at risk**, you start a situation in which something could be harmed or lost: *Smoking puts your health at risk.*

endanger (*formal*)
to put someone or something in a dangerous or harmful situation: *People who drive too fast are endangering the lives of all road users.*

jeopardize (*formal*)
to make it possible that someone will not be able to do something or have something: *The injury may jeopardize Whitman's basketball career.*

risky *adjective* → see **dangerous**

river /ˈrɪvɚ/ *noun*

- ► river
- ► stream
- ► creek
- ► brook
- ► canal
- ► delta
- ► tributary

river
a long line of water that flows into the ocean or a lake: *The Mississippi River flows into the Gulf of Mexico near the city of New Orleans.* | *The Nile is the longest river in the world.*

stream
a long narrow line of water that flows into a lake or into a river. A **stream** is usually too small to use a boat on: *They drank water from mountain streams.*

creek
a small river. A **creek** can be small and narrow and dry in the summer, or it can be wide enough to use a boat such as a canoe on it and have water all year: *We were fishing in a little creek.*

brook
brook means the same as **stream** and is usually used in written descriptions: *A little frog hopped into the brook.*

river

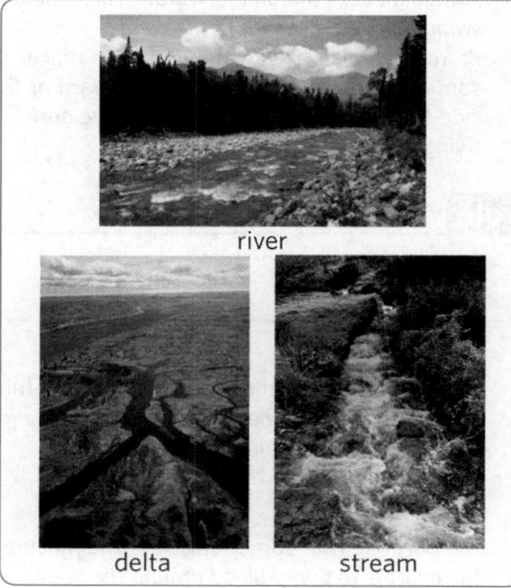
river
delta
stream

canal
a river that people have made so that boats or water can go from one place to another: *The Panama Canal joins the Atlantic Ocean with the Pacific Ocean.*

delta
a place where a large river spreads out and often divides into smaller rivers, before the water flows into the ocean: *The Mississippi Delta is home to many kinds of wild birds and animals.*

tributary
a river or stream that flows into a larger river: *The Yellowstone River is a major tributary of the Missouri River.*

road /roʊd/ *noun*

- ► road
- ► street
- ► avenue
- ► freeway
- ► highway
- ► alley
- ► lane

road
a hard surface for vehicles to travel on, which goes from one place to another: *They drove down the road until they came to the next town.* | *We live on Canyon Road.*

street
a road in a town or city with houses, stores, or offices along it: *The city streets are always full of cars.* | *The theater is on Fifth Street.*

avenue *also* **boulevard**
a wide road in a town or city: *The hotel is located on Santa Monica Boulevard.* | *Do you know who lives at 1,600 Pennsylvania Avenue, Washington D.C.?*

freeway *also* **expressway**
a wide fast road: *She was driving along the freeway at 55 miles an hour.* | *They are building a new six-lane expressway to the airport.*

highway
a wide fast road between cities: *The highway between Vancouver and Whistler was closed following an accident.*

alley
a narrow street or passage between buildings: *The alley was lined with garbage cans.*

lane
one of the parts that a wide road is divided into so that people can drive along next to each other: *The freeway had three lanes in each direction.*

roast *verb* → see **cook**[1]

rob *verb* → see **steal**

robber *noun* → see **thief**

robbery *noun* → see **theft**

robot *noun* → see **machine**

rock[1] /rɑk/ *noun*

- ► rock
- ► stone
- ► boulder
- ► pebble
- ► fossil

rock
a piece of a hard natural substance on or in the ground. A **rock** can be big or small: *Finn sat on a rock at the bottom of the trail.* | *The waves washed over the rocks at the bottom of the cliff.* | *She picked up a rock and threw it into the water.*
→ **Rock** also means the hard substance that forms part of the Earth's surface: *You can see the different layers of rock in the Grand Canyon.*

stone
a small rock: *Protesters threw stones at the police.*
→ **Stone** also means rock that has been shaped to use for building things: *The houses are made of stone.*

boulder
a large rock: *A huge boulder rolled down the mountain.*

pebble
a small smooth stone: *I got a pebble in my shoe as I was walking down the trail.*

rock

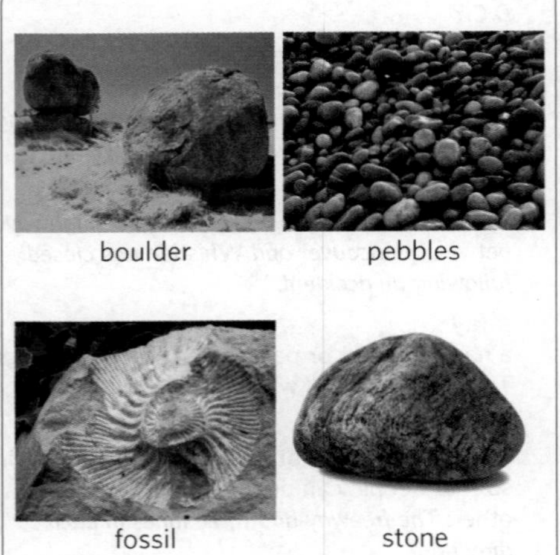

boulder pebbles fossil stone

fossil
a rock that shows part of an animal or plant that lived thousands or millions of years ago: *Scientists found dinosaur fossils that were over 130 million years old.*

rock[2] /rɑk/ *verb*

- ► rock
- ► sway
- ► wobble
- ► swing

rock
to move from side to side or backward and forward in a gentle way: *The boat rocked with the movement of the waves.* | *He sat in the chair, rocking backward and forward.*
→ You can also use **rock** when you make something move from side to side or backward and forward: *She was rocking the baby in her arms.*

sway
to move slowly from side to side. People, buildings, and trees **sway**: *Office buildings started to sway as the earthquake hit.* | *Her body swayed with the music.*

wobble
to move from side to side in an unsteady way: *The ladder wobbled and I was worried that it was going to fall over.*

swing
to move backward and forward or from side to side with long movements. You use **swing** when talking about the movement of things that hang from something or are attached to something at one side: *Jack tried to grab the rope which was swinging backward and forward.* | *The door kept swinging open and shut in the wind.*
→ You can also use **swing** when you make something move backward and forward or from side to side: *The girl was sitting on the desk, swinging her legs.*

role /roʊl/ *noun*

- ► role
- ► function

role (AWL)
the job or purpose that someone or something has in a situation: *The nurse's role is to care for the patients.* | *The United Nations plays a peacekeeping role in the world.*

function (AWL)
the purpose that something has: *The function of the heart is to pump blood around the body.*

roll¹ /roʊl/ *verb*

► roll
► wheel

roll
to move by turning over and over, or to make something move in this way: *The ball rolled under a car.* | *If you roll your clothes rather than fold them, they get fewer wrinkles in the suitcase.*

wheel
to move something that has wheels: *He wheeled the shopping cart out of the store.*
→ see **roll over** at **turn¹**

roll² /roʊl/ *noun*

► roll
► bundle
► wad

roll
a long piece of paper, tape, etc. that has been wound around itself many times so that it is in the shape of a tube: *There was a roll of paper towels for mopping up spills in the kitchen.* | *Before digital cameras, you had to put a roll of film into a camera.*

bundle
a group of things that have been tied together, for example papers, clothes, or sticks: *The delivery man was carrying bundles of newspapers into the store.*

wad
a thick pile of money or paper that is folded over or crushed together: *He took a wad of $20 bills out of his pocket.*

roll

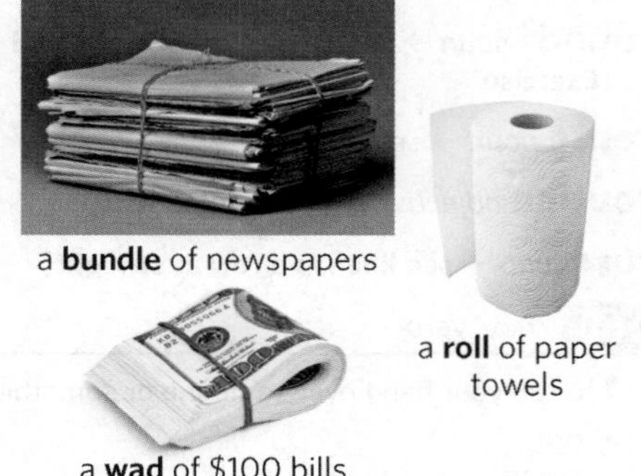

a **bundle** of newspapers

a **roll** of paper towels

a **wad** of $100 bills

romance *noun* → see **marriage**, **relationship**, Topic **Books and Literature**, **Relationships and Marriage**

romantic *adjective* → see **loving**, Topic **Describing People's Character**

room *noun* → see **space**

root *noun* → see **cause¹**

rope /roʊp/ *noun*

► rope
► cable
► line

rope
strong thick string: *The boat was tied to a post with a piece of rope.*

cable
a thick strong metal rope: *Some bridges are supported by cables.*

line
string that is used for a particular purpose, for example hanging things or catching things: *Maisie hung the wet clothes on the clothesline.* | *There was a fish hanging from the end of the fishing line.*
→ see **string**, **wire**

rotate *verb* → see **turn¹**

rotten /ˈrɑtn/ *adjective*

1 in bad condition
► rotten
► decayed
2 bad to eat and having a bad smell
► rotten
► spoiled
► moldy
► stale
► sour
► rancid
► bad
► off

1 in bad condition

rotten
in bad condition and starting to become soft or disappear, because of natural chemical changes: *The wood around the window was completely rotten and we had to replace it.*

decayed
in bad condition, and beginning to break apart. You use **decayed** especially about someone's teeth, but it can also be used about natural things such as leaves: *Several of his teeth are decayed and he needs to go to the dentist.*

2 bad to eat and having a bad smell

rotten
rotten food is old and starting to become soft because of natural chemical changes, and usually has a bad smell: *The apples were soft and rotten.* | *Rotten eggs have a terrible smell.*

spoiled
if food is spoiled, it is no longer fresh or it is damaged, and it is not suitable to eat: *Some of the strawberries were spoiled.* | *Several people became seriously ill after eating some spoiled food.*

moldy
covered in a soft green, gray, or black substance that grows on food which has been kept too long: *The only thing in the fridge was a piece of moldy cheese.*

stale
stale bread or cake is no longer fresh or good to eat, and is often too hard: *The cookies were hard and stale.*

sour
sour milk has a bad taste because it is no longer fresh: *The milk is sour. We'll have to throw it out.*

rancid
rancid butter, milk, or meat has a strong bad smell, because it is no longer fresh: *There was a horrible smell of rancid meat in the kitchen.*

bad
if food goes bad, it becomes rotten: *The meat has gone bad – don't eat it.*

off
if food is off, it is no longer fresh and it has a bad smell or taste: *The milk is off – it has a funny smell.*
→ **GRAMMAR:** Do not use **off** before a noun. Don't say: *~~off meat~~*. Say: *The meat is off.*

rough /rʌf/ *adjective*

► rough
► uneven
► bumpy
► coarse
► rugged

ANTONYMS → see **smooth**

rough
not smooth or flat. You use **rough** about the surface of the ground or about the surface of something you touch: *The truck had thick tires for driving over rough ground.* | *His big rough hands were covered in dirt.*

uneven
not flat, or not all at the same level: *The sidewalk was uneven and had cracks in it.* | *His teeth were yellow and uneven.*

bumpy
not smooth and having a lot of raised parts and holes. You use **bumpy** especially about roads: *The truck went down the bumpy road to the farm.*

coarse
having a rough surface that feels slightly hard. **Coarse** is used about cloth, skin, hair, and things such as sand or rock: *He covered himself with a coarse woolen blanket.*

rugged
a rugged place is not flat and has a lot of rocks and mountains: *The road passes through the rugged landscape of southern Utah.*
→ see Topic **Describing Texture**

roughly *adverb* → see Function Word **about**

round[1] /raʊnd/ *adjective*

► round
► circular
► spherical (*formal*)
► oval

round
shaped like a circle or ball: *She drew a round yellow sun in the center of the picture.* | *His eyes were big and round.*

circular
shaped like a circle. **Circular** is more formal than **round**: *We sat around a circular table to have lunch.*

spherical (AWL) (*formal*)
shaped like a ball: *The planet Saturn is not completely spherical.*

oval
shaped like a circle, but longer than it is wide: *She has an oval face.* | *Football players use an oval-shaped ball.*
→ see **circle[1]**

round[2] *noun* → see **game**, Topic **Sports and Exercise**

route *noun* → see **direction**

routine *adjective* → see **regular**, **usual**

row *noun* → see **line[1]**, **in a row** at **straight[2]**

rub /rʌb/ *verb*

1 to rub your hand over someone or something
► rub
► stroke
► pet
► caress
► massage
► scratch

2 to rub something against another thing, especially in a way that damages it

- ► rub
- ► scrape
- ► scratch

1 to rub your hand over someone or something

rub
to move your hand, or something you are holding, backward and forward over a surface. You can **rub** a part of someone's body to make it feel better, or you can **rub** an object, for example to make it clean: *The boy rubbed his bruised arm.* | *He rubbed the oil into his baseball mitt to soften it.*

stroke
to move your hand gently over something, especially to make someone feel calm: *Michelle stroked her daughter's hair and sang to her.*

pet
to move your hand over an animal's fur to show that you like it: *Can I pet your dog?*

caress
to gently touch someone in a way that shows love. **Caress** is used especially in literature and stories: *She bent over and caressed the baby's cheek.*

massage
to press and rub someone's body with your hands to help him or her feel relaxed or to reduce the pain in his or her muscles: *Can you massage my neck for me?*

scratch
to rub the skin on part of your body with your fingernails, because it feels uncomfortable: *If you have an insect bite, you shouldn't scratch it.*

2 to rub something against another thing, especially in a way that damages it

rub
to move something backward and forward against another thing many times: *We tried to make a fire by* ***rubbing*** *two pieces of wood* ***together.*** | *Her new shoes rubbed her heels and she got a blister.*

scrape
to accidentally rub something against a rough surface in a way that damages it: *I scraped my knee when I fell down.* | *He accidentally scraped the side of the car against the wall when he was backing into the garage.*

scratch
to accidentally rub something against a sharp surface, in a way that causes lines or cuts: *I scratched my arm when I was going through the bushes.*

rub

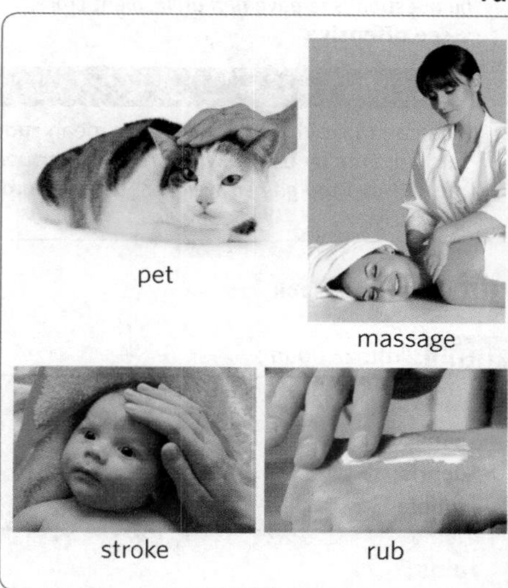

pet massage stroke rub

rude /rud/ *adjective*

- ► rude
- ► impolite (*formal*)
- ► tactless
- ► disrespectful
- ► obnoxious
- ► insolent (*formal*)

ANTONYMS → see **polite**

rude
speaking or behaving in a way that is not polite and upsets or offends people: ***It is rude to*** *stare at people.* | *Why were you so* ***rude to*** *her?*

impolite (*formal*)
not polite: ***It is impolite to*** *ask a woman her age.*

tactless
carelessly saying things that are likely to upset or embarrass someone, without intending to: ***It was tactless of*** *you* ***to*** *ask if she had gained weight.*

disrespectful
rude to someone who you should respect, especially your parents, your teachers, or other people in authority: *Shouting and swearing at teachers is disrespectful and is never allowed.*

obnoxious
behaving very badly and very rudely, especially in a way that is annoying: *One drunk and obnoxious customer was making rude comments about the waitresses.*

R

insolent *(formal)*
deliberately behaving in a way that is very rude to someone in authority. You use **insolent** especially about children: *Instead of answering the question, she gave him an insolent stare.*
→ see **offensive**

ADVERBS
You can make the adjectives that mean **rude** into adverbs by using **-ly**: *He rudely interrupted me.* | *"Have you gained weight?" asked Sharon tactlessly.*

ruin *verb* → see **spoil**

ruins /ˈruɪnz/ *noun*

- ruins
- wreckage
- debris
- rubble

ruins
the parts of a building that remain, when most of the rest has been destroyed: *We visited the **ruins of** an ancient temple.*

wreckage
the broken parts of a vehicle or building that was destroyed in an accident: *The driver was pulled from the **wreckage of** his car after the accident.*

debris
the broken pieces of something that remain after an accident or explosion: *Debris was scattered everywhere after the explosion.*

rubble
broken stones or bricks from a building or wall that was destroyed: *The building was reduced to a pile of rubble by the earthquake.*

R

rule[1] /rul/ *noun*

- rule
- regulation
- restriction
- guidelines
- principles
- code
- protocol *(formal)*

rule
something that says what people can or cannot do: *Can you explain the rules of the game to me?* | *Students are not allowed to eat in class – it is **against** the rules.*

regulation (AWL)
an official rule that is part of a set of rules about how people should do something: *The men ignored safety regulations and worked without protective clothing and helmets.*

restriction (AWL)
a rule that limits what you are allowed to do: *There are **restrictions on** what you can take on planes – for example, you are not allowed to take knives or scissors.*

guidelines (AWL)
official instructions or advice about how to do something: *Most public libraries provide **guidelines about** which books are appropriate for children of different ages.*

principles
basic moral rules or beliefs about what is right or wrong, which affect your behavior: *He doesn't eat meat – it's **against his principles**, because he thinks killing animals is wrong.*

code
a set of rules that a group of people agrees to obey: *The school dress code says that students should not wear very short skirts.*

protocol (AWL) *(formal)*
a system of rules about the correct way to behave on an official occasion: *Strict protocol must be followed when meeting the President.*
→ see **law**

rule[2] *verb* → see **govern**, Topic **Government and Politics**

rumor /ˈrumɚ/ *noun*

- rumor
- gossip
- speculation

rumor
information that someone hears and tells other people, which may not be true: *There is a **rumor that** they are going to get married – do you know if they are?* | *Most of the kids had heard the **rumors about** Roy and Linda getting suspended, but no one knew the truth.*

gossip
things that people say about what has happened in other people's private lives, especially things that are not kind or not true: *The magazine is full of **gossip about** famous people – who is getting a divorce, or who has gained weight.*

speculation
things that people say when they are trying to guess what has happened or what might happen: *There was some **speculation** in the newspapers **that** the vice president was planning to resign.*

run¹ /rʌn/ verb

- run
- sprint
- jog
- dash
- race
- tear
- dart
- scamper
- scurry
- gallop
- trot

run
to move very quickly using your legs: *Run as fast as you can to the tree and back.* | *The children came running out of the house.*

sprint
to run quickly for a short distance: *The runners sprinted toward the finishing line.*

jog
to run at a slow steady speed for exercise: *I jog a mile every morning.*

dash
to go somewhere quickly, especially by running or walking very fast: *He dashed into the store just as it was closing.*

race
to go somewhere very quickly. **Race** is even quicker than **dash**: *She could smell something burning and raced into the kitchen to see what it was.*

tear
to run somewhere very quickly, especially in a dangerous or careless way: *A masked man came tearing out of the bank and jumped into a waiting car.*

dart
to run suddenly and quickly in a particular direction: *A rabbit darted across the trail in front of us.*

scamper
to run quickly with quick short steps. You use **scamper** about children or animals: *The bears scampered back into the woods.*

scurry
to run quickly with small steps, especially because you are nervous or afraid. You use **scurry** about people, small animals, and insects: *The mice scurried back into their hole.* | *News reporters were scurrying around, trying to find out what was happening.*

gallop
if a horse gallops, it runs very fast: *The horse started galloping down the hill.*

trot
to run fairly slowly, taking short steps. You use **trot** especially about horses and dogs: *A little dog was trotting behind her.*

→ see **flow**, **govern**, **manage**, **operate**
→ see **run after** at **follow**
→ see **run into** at **hit¹**, **meet**
→ see **run out** at **end²**, **use¹**

run² /rʌn/ noun

- run
- jog
- sprint
- dash
- gallop
- trot

run
an occasion when you run, for example for exercise or in a race: *He usually goes for a run before breakfast.* | *She came second in the six-mile run.*

jog
a slow run, which you do for exercise: *I went for a jog in the park.*

sprint
a very fast run for a short distance: *Bolt won the 100-meter sprint in a time of just under 9.7 seconds.*

dash
a short fast run, because you need to go somewhere quickly: *It started to rain, so we made **a dash for** the car.*

gallop
the running of a horse at its fastest speed: *A man on a horse approached them **at a gallop**.*

trot
the movement of a horse or dog when it is running fairly slowly and taking small steps: *A little dog was running behind her **at a trot**.*

run-down *adjective* → see **condition** (**3**), Topic **Describing the Condition of Something**, **Describing Places**

rush¹ /rʌʃ/ verb

- rush
- hurry
- dash
- hustle (*informal*)
- speed up

R

rush
to go somewhere or do something very quickly: *Everyone rushed out into the street to see what was happening.* | *When you are taking a test, it's best not to rush. Read the questions carefully.*

hurry
to go somewhere or do something quickly, especially because you do not have much time: *You need to hurry, or you're going to be late for school!*

dash
to go somewhere quickly, especially by running or walking quickly: *He dashed into the store just as it was closing.*

hustle (*informal*)
to go somewhere or do something quickly, because there is not much time: *You'll have to hustle or you'll miss the bus.*

speed up
to move or do something faster: *Come on, speed it up! You can walk faster than that.* | *We are looking for ways to speed up the children's progress in reading.*

→ see **fast**[1], **fast**[2]

R

rush[2] /rʌʃ/ *noun*

- ► **rush**
- ► **hurry**
- ► **haste** (*formal*)

rush
a situation in which you have to do things very quickly, because you do not have much time: *There was a rush to get everything ready for the party.* | *He did his homework **in a rush** just before school.*

hurry
hurry means the same as **rush**, but **hurry** is usually used in the phrase **in a hurry**: *I'm **in a hurry** – can we talk about this later?* | *They left **in a hurry** because they were afraid of missing their train.*

haste (*formal*)
a lot of speed in doing something, especially so that you make mistakes: ***In his haste** to leave, he forgot his briefcase.*

Ss

sack *noun* → see **bag**

sacred *adjective* → see **religious**

sad /sæd/ *adjective*

1 sad
- ► **sad**
- ► **unhappy**
- ► **upset**
- ► **homesick**
- ► **gloomy**
- ► **down** (*informal*)

2 very sad
- ► **miserable**
- ► **depressed**
- ► **heartbroken**

3 making you feel sad
- ► **depressing**
- ► **tragic**
- ► **pitiful** (*formal*)
- ► **somber**
- ► **bleak**
- ► **dreary**

ANTONYMS → see **happy**

1 sad

sad
not happy, especially because a happy time has ended: *He felt **sad about** leaving home.* | *You look sad. What is the matter?*

unhappy
not happy, especially for a long time, because you are in a situation, job, or relationship that you do not enjoy at all, and it seems likely to continue: *I was unhappy at school because I didn't have any friends.* | *She feels trapped in an unhappy marriage.*

upset
sad and worried because something bad or disappointing has happened, especially so that you feel shocked or want to cry: *She is still very **upset about** her uncle's death.*

homesick
sad because you are away from your home, your family, and your friends, and you wish you were back there: *You might be very homesick when you first go away to college, but you will soon make new friends.*

gloomy
sad, especially because you think something bad will continue: *"No job yet, Frank?" asked Joe. Frank shook his head, looking gloomy.*

down (*informal*)
unhappy about the things that are happening in your life: *She has been feeling down since she lost her job.*

SYNONYM CHECK

Sad or unhappy?

You use **sad** when something has happened that you did not want: *I'm sad that the summer vacation is over.* **Sad** is used about short periods of time: *a sad moment/occasion/day.*

You use **unhappy** about a feeling that continues for a long time: *He is unhappy with his job.* **Unhappy** is used about long periods of time: *an unhappy childhood/marriage.*

2 very sad

miserable
very sad: *He has been miserable ever since his wife left him.*

depressed
very sad and without hope for a long time, because things are wrong in your life or because of a medical condition: *After he lost his job, he became depressed and stopped going out.*

heartbroken
very sad because of something that has happened to something or someone that you care about a lot: *Holly was heartbroken when her dog died.*

ADVERBS

You can make the adjectives **sad**, **unhappy**, **gloomy**, and **miserable** into adverbs by using an **-ly** ending: *She looked at me sadly as I left.* | *My aunt was unhappily married for years.* | *Frank shook his head gloomily.*

3 making you feel sad

depressing
making you feel very sad: *The news is always so depressing – it is all about wars, accidents, and murders.*

tragic
a tragic event makes you feel very sad, because something very bad happens to someone: *Both sisters died in a tragic car accident.*

pitiful (*formal*)
looking or sounding very sad, in a way that makes you feel sorry for someone: *The starving children were a pitiful sight.*

somber
sad, quiet, and serious: *The funeral was a somber occasion.*

bleak
without anything to make you feel cheerful or hopeful about the future: *The future of the company looks bleak and people are worried about their jobs.* | *We looked out on the bleak winter landscape.*

dreary
not at all interesting or enjoyable, and making you feel sad or bored: *They lived in a dreary apartment building that smelled of sweat and old meals.*

→ see **grieve** for words meaning "to feel sad because someone has died"

→ see **disappointed**, Topic **Describing People's Emotions**

ADVERBS

You can make the adjectives that mean "making you feel sad" into adverbs by using an **-ly** ending: *The weather was depressingly cold and gray.* | *He died tragically at the age of 24.* | *The child looked pitifully thin.* | *She thought bleakly about her future without her family.*

S

sadden /ˈsædn/ *verb*

- sadden (*formal*)
- make someone sad/unhappy
- depress
- upset

ANTONYMS → see **cheer up**

sadden (*formal*)
to make someone feel sad: *We were deeply saddened by the news of his death.*
→ GRAMMAR: **Sadden** is usually used in the passive.

make someone sad/unhappy
to cause someone to feel sad: *It made her sad to remember all the friends she had left behind.*

depress (AWL)
to make someone feel very sad and not have much hope: *It depresses me when I think how long it will take to pay back all the money.*

upset
to make someone feel sad and want to cry, especially because another person has been unkind or something bad has happened: *He was careful not to say anything that would upset her.*

sadly *adverb* → see **unfortunately**

sadness /ˈsædnəs/ *noun*

1 sadness
- sadness
- unhappiness
- regret
- melancholy (*formal*)

2 a lot of sadness
- despair
- grief
- sorrow
- misery
- depression
- heartbreak
- anguish

ANTONYMS → see **happiness**

1 sadness

sadness
a sad feeling: *I could see the sadness in her eyes when we said goodbye.* | *The song filled her with sadness.*

unhappiness
sadness, especially because you are in a bad situation that lasts for a long time: *After years of unhappiness, she finally decided to leave her husband.*

regret
sadness because you wish that you had not done something, or that something had not happened: *The country's leaders expressed regret for the deaths of innocent people in the attack.*

melancholy (*formal*)
a feeling of sadness, especially one that lasts for a long time and that affects your attitude: *"I knew I would not go home again," he said, with a touch of melancholy.*

2 a lot of sadness

despair
deep sadness because the situation is very bad and you have no hope that anything will change: *They watched **in despair** as the ship slowly began to sink.*

grief
deep sadness because someone you know well has died: *He was overcome with grief when his wife died.*

sorrow
a lot of sadness because something terrible has

happened: *There was great sorrow when the news of President Kennedy's death was announced.*

misery
great sadness and suffering, especially because you have to live or work in very bad conditions: *It is hard for us to imagine the misery of slavery.*

depression (AWL)
a lot of sadness that lasts for a long time and makes you think there is no hope, often caused by mental illness: *People who suffer from depression feel hopeless and stop enjoying their usual activities.*

heartbreak
deep sadness because someone you love leaves you or dies: *She suffered the heartbreak of losing two of her sons in the war.*

anguish
the feeling when you are very upset and worried about something: *She told us about the anguish of waiting to hear if her daughter was still alive.*

safe /seɪf/ *adjective*

1 not in danger of being harmed or stolen (adjectives)
- ► **safe**
- ► **secure**
- ► **unharmed**

2 not likely to cause any harm (adjectives)
- ► **safe**
- ► **harmless**
- ► **non-toxic**

ANTONYMS → see **dangerous**

3 a safe place (nouns)
- ► **shelter**
- ► **refuge** *(formal)*
- ► **sanctuary**
- ► **reserve**

1 not in danger of being harmed or stolen (adjectives)

safe
not in danger of being harmed or stolen: *She doesn't feel safe when she's alone in the house. | Your money will be safe in the bank.*
→ You also use **safe** about a place where someone or something is not likely to be harmed or stolen: *Keep your passport in a safe place.*

secure (AWL)
if something is secure, it is safe from thieves and criminals: *How do I know that my card number and address are secure if I buy something over the Internet?*
→ You also use **secure** about a place where something is safe: *The jewels are kept in a very secure place.*

unharmed
not hurt or harmed after something happens: *The girl escaped unharmed from the burning building.*
→ **GRAMMAR:** Do not use **unharmed** before a noun. Don't say: ~~the unharmed girl~~. Say: *The girl was unharmed.*

2 not likely to cause any harm (adjectives)

safe
not likely to cause any injury or harm: *Is it safe to swim here? | Flying is one of the safest forms of travel.*

harmless
completely safe. You use harmless when something seems dangerous but is not: *The snake is harmless – it will not bite you.*

non-toxic
non-toxic substances are not harmful to your health: *Make sure that you use non-toxic paint.*

ADVERBS

You can make the adjectives **safe**, **secure**, and **harmless** into adverbs by using an **-ly** ending: *His passport was stored safely in a locked drawer. | You can send files securely using this software. | The rocks fell harmlessly into the lake.*

3 a safe place (nouns)

shelter
a place where you are protected from bad weather or danger: *The trees provided **shelter from** the wind. | The shelter gives homeless people a place to stay for a time.*

refuge *(formal)*
a place where people or animals are protected from danger: *The United States became a refuge for people escaping from wars and poverty in other parts of the world. | The Arctic National Wildlife Refuge is home to bears and other animals.*
→ **Refuge** is often used in the phrase "take refuge somewhere" (=go there because it is safe): *The men took refuge in a cave.*

sanctuary
a safe area for animals, where people cannot hunt them: *The park is the largest wildlife sanctuary in the U.S.*

reserve *also* **preserve**
an area of land where animals and plants are protected: *You can see many rare birds at the wildlife reserve.*

safety /ˈseɪfti/ noun

► safety
► security
► protection
ANTONYMS → see **danger**

safety
a situation in which someone or something is safe from danger or harm: *New plans have been announced to improve safety at the factory.* | *The firefighters carried the children to safety.*

security (AWL)
safety from being attacked or stolen: ***For the security** of passengers, all luggage is checked before you get on the plane.*

protection
something that is done to protect someone or something: ***For your own protection,** you should always wear a helmet when you are riding a bicycle on the road.*
→ see **safe**

salary *noun* → see **pay²**, Topic **Jobs and Work**

sale /seɪl/ noun

► sale
► discount
► special

sale
a time when a store sells things at lower prices than usual: *The store is having a sale, so I'm hoping to get some shoes at a good price.*
→ You can also say that a product is **on sale** when it is being sold for less than the usual price: *I got a beautiful coat on sale!*

discount
an amount that is taken off the price of something, usually for a special reason: *The airline is offering a 25% discount to students on all plane tickets.*

special
a lower price for a product that is available for a short period of time: *The store has a special this week on their own brand of ice cream.*
→ see **sell**

salty *adjective* → see Topic **Describing Food**

same /seɪm/ adjective, pronoun

► the same
► identical
► equal
► indistinguishable (*formal*)
► uniform (*formal*)
► constant
► consistent (*formal*)
ANTONYMS → see **different (1)**

the same
not different: *The students in this class are all the same age.* | *The two photographs look exactly the same.* | *His car is **the same as** mine.*
→ **GRAMMAR:** You always say **the same**. Don't say: ~~*We are same height*~~. Say: *We are the same height.*

identical (AWL)
exactly the same in every way: *The picture is **identical to** the one in the Museum of Modern Art in New York.* | *The two sisters were **identical in** appearance.*

equal
the same in size, number, or amount: *Draw two lines of equal length.* | *The two girls are about **equal in** their reading ability.*

indistinguishable (*formal*)
so similar that it is impossible to see any differences: *The copy of the painting was **indistinguishable from** the real one.*

uniform (AWL) (*formal*)
always the same in all parts or in all cases: *The fruit in supermarkets is always very **uniform in** size and shape.* | *It is important to have a uniform system of tests so that students are all graded in the same way.*

constant (AWL)
always at the same level: *The room is kept at a constant temperature of 68 degrees.*

consistent (AWL) (*formal*)
always doing something well or in the same way: *She is one of the most consistent players in the team.*

ADVERBS
You can make the adjectives **identical**, **equal**, **indistinguishable**, **uniform**, and **consistent** into adverbs by using an **-ly** ending: *The two sisters were identically dressed.* | *The bird's feathers blended indistinguishably with the bark of the tree.* | *She has played consistently well all season.*

same time /ˌseɪm ˈtaɪm/ *noun phrase*

- at the same time
- at once
- simultaneously (*formal*)

at the same time
doing something or happening together: ***We both got home at the same time.** | **Can you pat your head and rub your stomach at the same time?***

at once
at the same time. You use **at once** when several things happen at the same time, especially in a way that is surprising or difficult to deal with: ***Don't all talk at once!***

simultaneously (*formal*)
at exactly the same time: ***At the end of the show, ten huge fireworks went up into the air and exploded simultaneously.***

sample /ˈsæmpəl/ *noun*

- sample
- specimen
- example

sample
a small amount of something that shows you what the rest is like: ***The doctor took a sample of his blood to see what was wrong with him.** | **They asked me to bring some samples of my work to the interview.***

specimen
a small amount or piece of something that is taken to be tested or examined, so it can show you what the rest is like: ***Scientists are examining specimens of** rock from the area.*

example
something that is typical of a group of things, that tells you what other things in the group are probably like: *The church is a good **example of** Spanish mission architecture.*

sandy *adjective* → see Topic **Describing Places**

sarcasm /ˈsɑrˌkæzəm/ *noun*

- sarcasm
- irony

sarcasm
the use of words that have the opposite meaning to what you are saying, especially in order to criticize someone or something: ***"Well, that is just great. What a good job you've done," he said with sarcasm.***

irony
a type of humor in which you say the opposite of what you really mean: ***"She is just very talented," Simmons said with heavy irony.***

satisfaction /ˌsætɪsˈfækʃən/ *noun*

- satisfaction
- pride
- contentment (*formal*)

satisfaction
the happy feeling that you get when you are pleased with what you have done: ***I get a lot of satisfaction from helping other people.** | **"I got an A!" she said with satisfaction.***

pride
a feeling of pleasure and respect that you have when you have done something well, or when someone you know has done something well: ***He talked with great pride about his son's work.***

contentment (*formal*)
satisfaction with your life, because you feel you have everything you want and you do not want to change anything: ***She had a feeling of peace and contentment as she watched her family playing on the beach.***
→ see **pleasure**

satisfactory /ˌsætɪsˈfæktəri/ *adjective*

- satisfactory
- good enough
- acceptable
- adequate
- decent

satisfactory
reaching a fairly good standard, but not a high standard: ***Her grades are satisfactory, but with a little more work she could do better.***

good enough
having a high enough standard to do something or be used for something: ***The coach says that he is good enough to play college basketball.***

acceptable
if something is acceptable to you, you think it is good enough and you are willing to take it or agree to it: ***We need to find a solution that is acceptable to** both sides.*

adequate AWL
good enough for doing something. **Adequate** sounds a little formal and is often used in official documents or statements: ***Companies have to provide adequate heating for employees.***

decent
having a good enough standard and quality: ***Where can I get a decent cup of coffee?***

S

ADVERBS

You can make the adjectives **satisfactory**, **acceptable**, **adequate**, and **decent** into adverbs by using an **-ly** ending: *The students performed satisfactorily on the tests.* | *Seventy-five percent of the restaurants were rated "acceptably clean."* | *He played decently in the tournament.*

satisfied /ˈsætɪsˌfaɪd/ *adjective*

- ► satisfied
- ► content
- ► fulfilled

satisfied
feeling that something is as good as it should be, or that something has happened in the way that you want: *The teacher is* ***satisfied with*** *his progress.* | *Our goal is to have satisfied customers, because they'll come back again.*

content *also* **contented**
feeling that you have all the things you want or need so that you are happy. You often use **content** when someone could have more things but is satisfied with what he or she has: *She has a good job and good friends, and is* ***content with*** *her life.*

fulfilled
feeling that you have achieved enough in your life, and that you do not need other things to make you feel happy: *I love being a mother, but I feel more fulfilled when I work.*
→ see **happy**, Topic **Describing People's Emotions**

ADVERBS

You can make the adjective **contented** into an adverb by using an **-ly** ending: *They lived together contentedly in their little house.*

satisfy /ˈsætɪsˌfaɪ/ *verb*

1 to make someone feel happy about his or her achievements
- ► satisfy
- ► fulfill

2 to be good enough for what people need or want
- ► satisfy
- ► meet
- ► fulfill (*formal*)

1 to make someone feel happy about his or her achievements

satisfy
to make someone feel happy and pleased about what he or she is doing or has achieved: *I tried a few different jobs before I became a teacher, but none of them really satisfied me.*

fulfill
if you fulfill your wish, dream, or hopes, you achieve something that you have always wanted and you feel completely satisfied: *She finally fulfilled her dream of becoming an Olympic athlete.*

2 to be good enough for what people need or want

satisfy
to be good enough for what people need or want. You use **satisfy** about needs or requirements (=things people ask for or want): *Students must take a science class, and General Science satisfies this requirement.* | *It wasn't a great meal, but it satisfied my hunger.*

meet
meet means the same as **satisfy**, but you use it about requirements, standards, and criteria (=standards used when making a decision or judgment): *The hotel met all our requirements – it was comfortable, clean, and near the beach.*

fulfill (*formal*)
fulfill means the same as **satisfy** but is more formal. You use **fulfill** about requirements, criteria, and conditions: *New power plants must fulfill security requirements.*
→ see **please** for **satisfy** meaning "to make someone feel happy by providing what he or she wants or needs"

satisfying /ˈsætɪsˌfaɪ-ɪŋ/ *adjective*

- ► satisfying
- ► rewarding
- ► fulfilling
- ► gratifying (*formal*)

satisfying
making you feel happy by giving you what you want or need: *It is particularly satisfying when people say that they have enjoyed the show.* | *We prepared a satisfying meal of eggs and bacon.*

rewarding
satisfying because you feel that you are doing something interesting or useful: *Working with Neil was a really rewarding experience. I learned a lot from him.*

fulfilling
making you feel happy and satisfied with your

life because you are using your abilities in a useful way: *Teaching young students can be very fulfilling.*

gratifying (*formal*)
making you feel pleased and satisfied because people like what you have done, or because you feel that you were right about something: *It is always gratifying to get praise for your work.*

ADVERBS

You can make the adjectives **satisfying**, **rewarding**, and **gratifying** into adverbs by using an **-ly** ending: *I felt satisfyingly full after breakfast.* | *The novel is rewardingly complex.*

save /seɪv/ *verb*

1 to gradually collect money
- ► save
- ► save up
- ► set aside

ANTONYMS → see **spend (1)**

2 to use less of something
- ► save
- ► economize
- ► conserve

ANTONYMS → see **waste**

3 to save someone or something from being harmed or destroyed
- ► save
- ► rescue
- ► salvage

4 to keep something for someone to use later
- ► save
- ► reserve
- ► book

1 to gradually collect money

save
to put money in the bank or in a safe place so that you can keep it or use it later: *He doesn't earn much, but he still manages to save a few dollars each week.* | *She is* ***saving for*** *a new bike.*

save up
to save money in order to buy something: *I'm saving up to buy a new car.*

set aside
to regularly save part of the money you earn, especially over a long period of time: *Each month she sets aside a little money for her retirement.*

2 to use less of something

save
to use less of something such as time, money, or energy, so that you do not waste any: *We'll save time if we go by car.* | *You can save energy by washing clothes in warm water instead of really hot water.*

economize
to spend less money on something, for example by buying cheaper things or by buying less of something: *We're trying to* ***economize on*** *food by buying the cheaper brands.*

conserve
to use something carefully and use less of it so that there is enough for the future. You use **conserve** especially about natural things such as water and energy: *There has been very little rain, and people are being asked to conserve water.*

3 to save someone or something from being harmed or destroyed

save
to make someone or something safe from danger: *His friend* ***saved*** *him* ***from*** *drowning by dragging him back to the shore.* | *Wearing a seat belt can help save your life.* | *We want to save the forest and protect it for future generations to enjoy.*

rescue
to save someone by removing him or her from a dangerous situation: *Firefighters rescued two people who were trapped in a burning building.*

salvage
to save something when other things have been damaged or destroyed in an accident or other situation: *After the tornado had passed, they went to see if they could* ***salvage*** *anything* ***from*** *the wreckage of their house.*

→ see **protect**

4 to keep something for someone to use later

save
to keep something for someone to use later: *I'll save you some of my birthday cake.* | *Will you save me a seat? I'll be back in a minute.*

reserve
to ask for something to be kept for you to use in the future, for example a table in a restaurant, a room at a hotel, or a seat on a plane: *I would like to reserve a table for two people at seven o'clock.*

book
book means the same as **reserve**. You use **book** about reserving tickets for concerts, shows, planes, or trains: *To get tickets for the show, you have to book in advance.*

say *verb* → *go to pages 572-573*

saying *noun* → see **phrase**

scale *noun* → see **level**, **ratio**

S

say /seɪ/ *verb*

1 to say something
► say
► mention
► add
► specify
► utter (*formal*)
► pronounce
► recite
► dictate
► declare

2 to say something in an official or public way
► announce
► state
► testify

3 to tell people about something that you have noticed
► remark
► observe

4 to say something suddenly
► exclaim
► blurt out

5 to say something in an angry way
► snap
► snarl
► growl

6 to use words to show your feelings, opinions, or ideas
► express
► comment
► put

7 to say that something is definitely true or not true
► insist
► claim
► argue
► swear
► confirm
► deny (*formal*)
► protest

1 to say something

say
to use particular words to tell someone something: *"It is time for dinner," she said.* | *Tom* ***said that*** *he got a new bike.* | *Did she* ***say what*** *time she would be home?*

→ You use **say** about the words someone uses when speaking. You can also use it about the words someone writes: *He said in his email that he was enjoying his vacation.*

→ **GRAMMAR:** Don't say: ~~*She said me that she was a doctor*~~. Say: *She said that she was a doctor.*

mention
to say someone or something's name, or say that something has happened, without giving a lot of information: *She* ***mentioned that*** *he has a new girlfriend, but didn't tell me her name.* | *I didn't know he won! He never even mentioned it!*

add
to say another thing about something that you have just been talking about: *"It was a long drive," Paul said. Jane added, "We're really tired."* | *She* ***added that*** *the weather had been very bad.*

specify (AWL)
to say something in an exact and detailed way: *The rules* ***specify that*** *the ball must land inside the court.* | *He did not specify how much I would get paid.*

utter (*formal*)
to say something, usually one word or a few words: *No one uttered a word.*

pronounce
to make the sounds of a word or letter: *You don't pronounce the "b" in "lamb."*

recite
to say the words of a poem or story that you have learned, without reading it: *He recited the speech that President Lincoln gave at Gettysburg.*

dictate
to say something to someone so that he or she can write the exact words that you are saying: *She dictated the letter to her secretary.*

declare
to say something very firmly. **Declare** is mainly used in writing: *"I won't go!" she declared.* | *He* ***declared that*** *he would not help her anymore.*

2 to say something in an official or public way

announce
to tell people officially that something will happen or has happened: *"I will retire in June," he announced.* | *The publishing company* ***announced that*** *the book would be in stores by July.* | *The president announced an agreement to reduce the number of nuclear missiles.*

state
to say something publicly or officially, in a clear way: *"He no longer works for this company," Smith stated.* | *The police officer* ***stated that*** *the driver*

testify
to tell a court what you know about something: *Williams **testified that** Hayes had stolen the money.*

3 to tell people about something that you have noticed

remark
to say what you have noticed about something: *"You look tired," he remarked.* | *Her father **remarked on** how hard she had worked.*

observe
observe means the same as **remark**: *"Tom and Rick argue a lot," she observed.* | *The doctor **observed that** some patients do not take their medications.*

4 to say something suddenly

exclaim
to say something loudly and suddenly because you are surprised, excited, or angry: *"You've grown so much!" exclaimed Jake's aunt.* | *He looked at his watch and **exclaimed that** he was late for work.*

blurt out
to say something suddenly and without thinking, especially because you are nervous, surprised, or excited: *"Mark! I never expected to see you here," she blurted out.* | *Peter blurted out the news before we could stop him.*

5 to say something in an angry way

snap
to say something suddenly in an angry way: *"Oh, never mind!" Josie snapped.* | *The singer **snapped at** reporters who were shouting questions at him.*

snarl
to say something in a mean angry way: *"You can wait!" he snarled.* | *She angrily snarled an answer.*

growl
to say something in a low angry voice: *"Get out of my way," he growled.* | *A man with a beard **growled at** her in Spanish.*
→ **Snarl** and **growl** are like the noises animals such as dogs make when they are angry.

6 to use words to show your feelings, opinions, or ideas

express
to use words to tell people your feelings or ideas: *The teacher expressed concern about Lucy's lack of progress.* | *At two years old, she cannot express her ideas because she doesn't have the words to do so.*

comment (AWL)
to give your opinion about something: *The judge refused to **comment on** the case because the trial was still going on.* | *He **commented that** the decision had been unfair.*

put
to use particular words to talk about something: *The machine is difficult to use. As one parent put it, "calculus is easier."*
→ You often use **put** in the phrase "put sth into words": *It is hard to **put into words** what I feel right now.*

7 to say that something is definitely true or not true

insist
to say and repeat firmly that something is true, even when other people think you may not be telling the truth: *"This diet is easy and it works," Cowan insists.* | *Adamson's lawyer insisted that he was innocent.*

claim
to say that something is true, even though it has not been proved to be true or when many people do not believe that it is true: *The doctor claimed to have discovered a cure for cancer.* | *Martin **claims that** he was with friends at the time of the murder.*
→ **Claim** is not often used to say exactly what someone said, but it can also be used that way: *"It was my idea," claimed Robinson.*

argue
to say that you think something is true and give reasons for this: *Some people **argue that** there is a link between poverty and crime.* | *The Senator **argued against** taking any military action and said that he thought it was too risky.*

swear
to say firmly that what you are saying is true. You use **swear** when you want to show how serious you are about telling the truth: *I swear I never meant to hurt him!* | *She **swore that** she had seen Milton leaving the house that night.*

confirm (AWL)
to say that something that other people have said is true: *The police have **confirmed that** the two men are being held on terrorism charges.* | *No one has been able to confirm reports of troops crossing the border.*

deny (AWL) (*formal*)
to say that something is definitely not true, especially when other people have accused you of doing something bad: *Smith denied any involvement in the robbery.* | *Hale **denied that** he had ever asked Moran for a loan.*

protest
to say that something is not true, when someone else says that it is true: *"I'm not a baby!" Corinna protested.* | *They **protested that** the new program would not create jobs, as government officials had said.*
→ see these entries for other words you can use instead of "say": **answer**[1], **mumble**, **repeat**[1], **shout**[1], **suggest**, **whisper**

scarce /skers/ *adjective*

- scarce
- in short supply
- rare
- sparse

scarce
if something is scarce, there is not much of it and it is difficult to get. **Scarce** is used especially about things people need to live, such as food and water: *Because of the bad harvest, food was scarce.*

in short supply
if something is in short supply, there is not much of it available: *Clean water is in short supply in areas affected by the floods.*

rare
if something is rare, not many of that thing exist: *He had to pay a lot of money for the book because it was so rare.*

sparse
if things or people are sparse, there are not many of them and they are not close together: *This large island has a sparse population – only 3,000 people.*

ADVERBS
You can make the adjective **sparse** into an adverb by using an **-ly** ending: *The island was sparsely populated.*

scare /sker/ *verb*

- scare
- frighten
- terrify
- alarm
- startle
- intimidate
- terrorize

scare
to make someone feel afraid and that something bad will happen to him or her: *There is no ghost – you're just trying to scare me!* | *Fireworks can scare dogs and other pets.*

frighten
frighten means the same as **scare** but is a little more formal: *The crazy look in his eyes frightened her.*

terrify
to make someone feel very afraid: *The thought of making a speech to hundreds of people terrified her.*

alarm
to make someone feel worried or afraid: *I was alarmed by the strange noise the elevator was making.*

startle
to make someone feel a little afraid, because something happens very suddenly: *The doorbell suddenly rang, startling him.*

intimidate
to deliberately make someone feel afraid of you, especially to make him or her do what you want: *The criminals intimidated witnesses so that they would not give evidence in court.*

terrorize
to make people feel extremely afraid of you by attacking them and threatening to hurt them: *The gang had terrorized the neighborhood for years, and everyone was afraid of them.*

scared /skerd/ *adjective*

- scared
- afraid
- frightened
- terrified
- petrified
- alarmed
- fearful
- intimidated

scared
unhappy or worried because you think something bad might happen. **Scared** is used in more informal or spoken language: *When he was little, he was **scared of** clowns.* | *We could hear the guns, and we were so scared.*

afraid
afraid means the same as **scared** but sounds slightly more formal: *My sister is **afraid of** flying.* | *Don't be afraid – it is just the wind making that noise.*

frightened
frightened means the same as **scared** but sounds more formal or literary: *The dog, **frightened by** the thunder, was found hiding in the barn.*

terrified
extremely afraid: *The little girl was terrified because she couldn't find her mother.*

petrified
petrified means the same as **terrified**, but is used to emphasize that someone is completely terrified: *She stood still, **petrified that** the snake would bite her if she moved.*

alarmed
suddenly very worried and frightened because

you realize there is a problem or danger: *Her parents were alarmed when she didn't get home on time, but luckily everything was fine.*

fearful
afraid of something that could happen in the future. **Fearful** sounds slightly formal or literary: *Many people are **fearful of** losing their jobs in this bad economy.*

intimidated
feeling worried or afraid because you do not have enough confidence to deal with a situation: *Don't feel **intimidated by** the other team just because they're bigger.*
→ see **fear²**, Topic **Describing People's Emotions**

GRAMMAR CHECK: scared

Scared, **afraid**, and **frightened** mean the same thing, but there are some differences in the ways you can use them.

You can say: *a scared/frightened child*, but don't say: ~~*an afraid child*~~. You can say: *She was **frightened/scared by** the loud noise*, but don't say: ~~*She was afraid by the loud noise*~~.

You can use all three adjectives before "of," "that," and "to": *He's **scared of** the dark.* | *I was **frightened that** no one would help me.* | *Women are **afraid to** walk alone at night.*

ADVERBS

You can make the adjective **fearful** into an adverb by using an **-ly** ending: *The boys looked at each other fearfully as the storm came closer.*

scary /ˈskeri/ *adjective*

- ► scary
- ► frightening
- ► terrifying
- ► alarming
- ► intimidating
- ► eerie
- ► spooky
- ► creepy

scary
making you feel frightened: *I didn't want to watch the movie before I went to bed, because it was too scary.*

frightening
frightening means the same as **scary** but sounds more formal or literary: *It was frightening to realize that we were completely alone.*

terrifying
making someone extremely frightened: *Seeing the tornado coming closer was the most terrifying thing that has happened to me.*

alarming
making you feel suddenly frightened and worried because you realize there is a problem or danger: *Bees are dying at an alarming rate, which is worrying for farmers.*

intimidating
making you feel worried or afraid because you feel you do not have enough confidence to deal with a situation: *He finds long books intimidating.*

eerie
strange and scary. You use **eerie** especially about sounds and things you see: *There was an eerie howling sound coming from the backyard.* | *The fire made an eerie glow on the man's face.*

spooky
scary because something reminds you of ghosts or similar things. You use **spooky** especially about places, and sometimes about people: *The empty rooms upstairs were spooky in the dark.*

creepy
making you feel frightened and slightly sick or uncomfortable to think about. You use **creepy** especially about people and places: *The way the old woman looked at me was really creepy.*

ADVERBS

You can make the adjectives that mean **scary** into adverbs by using an **-ly** ending: *The building was scarily dark and quiet.* | *The number of people dying from the disease is alarmingly high.* | *An owl called out eerily in the dark forest.* | *The empty room was spookily quiet.*

scene *noun* → see **part**, **place¹**, **sight**, **view**, Topic **Entertainment**

scenery *noun* → see **landscape**

scenic *adjective* → see **beautiful**

scent *noun* → see **smell¹**

schedule *noun* → see **list¹**, **plan¹**

school *noun* → see **group**, Topic **Education**

scientific /ˌsaɪənˈtɪfɪk/ *adjective*

- ► scientific
- ► technical
- ► technological

scientific
relating to science: *There is no scientific evidence that the herb can prevent colds.* | *Scientific*

S

knowledge continues to grow as we learn more about the universe.

technical (AWL)
relating to the practical use of science to do things, especially using machines and systems: *We are having technical difficulties and are unable to play the recording at this time.* | *His explanation of how genes work was too technical for me to understand.*

technological (AWL)
relating to new and advanced machines: *We are living in a time of rapid technological change.*
→ see Topic **Science and Technology**

ADVERBS

You can make the adjectives that mean **scientific** into adverbs by using an **-ly** ending: *The theory has been scientifically proven.* | *We are a technologically advanced society.*

scientist *noun* → see Topic **Science and Technology**

scold /skoʊld/ *verb*

- ► scold
- ► tell off
- ► reprimand (*formal*)
- ► rebuke (*formal*)
- ► reproach (*formal*)

scold
to tell someone in an angry way that he or she has done something wrong: *Mom* ***scolded*** *me* ***for*** *being mean to my sister.*

tell off
tell off means the same as **scold** but sounds more informal: *We were making a lot of noise and the neighbor came over to tell us off.*

reprimand (*formal*)
to tell someone officially that he or she has done something wrong: *He was* ***reprimanded*** *by his boss* ***for*** *arriving late three times in a week.*

rebuke (*formal*)
to criticize someone in a serious way because he or she has done something wrong: *He* ***rebuked*** *journalists* ***for*** *not checking their facts.*

reproach (*formal*)
to criticize someone in a way that shows your disappointment and makes that person feel sorry for what he or she has done: *She* ***reproached*** *me* ***for*** *not letting her know I was safe.*
→ see **criticize**

score[1] /skɔr/ *noun*

- ► score
- ► point
- ► result
- ► tally

score
the number of points that you get in a game or on a test: *The final score was 62–56.* | *The school is working on improving students' test scores.*

point
a unit used for showing the score in a game or sport: *After 20 minutes, our team had 12 points.*

result
the final number of points at the end of a competition or votes after an election: *Everyone is waiting for the election results to be announced.*

tally
a record you keep when you are counting something, for example points or votes: *He added another goal to his tally this season.*
→ see **grade[1]**

score[2] /skɔr/ *verb*

- ► score
- ► get
- ► make

score
to earn points in a game or on a test: *Deng scored 28 points for the Bulls.* | *He scored well on the math and reading tests.*

get
to score a point, or receive a grade on a test: *I got a B in biology.*

make
to score points by doing something in a game: *Which member of the basketball team made the winning basket?* | *He ran 30 yards to make his second touchdown.*

scorn /skɔrn/ *noun*

- ► scorn
- ► contempt
- ► disrespect

scorn
a strong lack of respect for someone or something because you think that person or thing is not important or good: *Tyson was full of* ***scorn for*** *his opponent and said he could beat him easily.*

contempt
a strong lack of respect that makes you dislike

someone or something, because you think that person or thing is very bad, weak, or stupid: *He seems to feel a deep contempt for anyone who disagrees with him.*

disrespect
a lack of respect for someone or something: *I don't like to see the American flag treated with disrespect.*

scrap *noun* → see **piece**

scrape *verb* → see **rub**

scratch *verb* → see **cut**[1], **damage**[2], **rub**, **touch**

scream[1] *verb* → see **shout**[1]

scream[2] *noun* → see **shout**[2]

screen *noun* → see **wall**, Topic **Computers and the Internet**

sculpture /ˈskʌlptʃɚ/ *noun*

- sculpture
- statue
- carving

sculpture
an object that someone has made from stone, wood, or metal as a piece of art: *The sculpture consists of a curved metal shape with a hole in it.*
→ You also use **sculpture** about the activity of making objects from stone, wood, or metal as art: *She studied sculpture at art school.*

statue
a large stone or metal model of a person or animal: *There was a big statue of a man on a horse.*

sculpture

carving

statue

sculpture

carving
an object or decoration made by cutting parts off a piece of wood or stone: *The wooden door is decorated with carvings of leaves and flowers.*

sea *noun* → see **ocean**

seal *verb* → see **close**[1]

search[1] /sɚtʃ/ *noun*

- search
- hunt
- raid
- quest

search
an attempt to find someone or something by looking very carefully: *Everyone joined in the **search for** the family's missing dog. | A search of the Internet turned up several web pages.*

hunt
an attempt to find someone or something, especially so that you can catch him, her, or it: *The **hunt for** the bombers is continuing.*

raid
an occasion when the police suddenly go into a place in order to try to find illegal things or catch a criminal: *Police officers carried out a **raid on** his home and found drugs there.*

quest
a long and difficult search for something, especially something that exists but cannot be seen, such as love or the truth: *She said she would not give up her **quest for** the truth about what happened to her son.*

search[2] /sɚtʃ/ *verb*

- search
- look for
- seek
- hunt
- frisk
- raid

search
to try to find someone or something by looking very carefully: *She began **searching through** the trash in case the letter had been thrown away. | Rescue workers are **searching** the buildings **for** survivors after the earthquake.*

look for
to try to find someone or something: *Could you help me look for my keys? I can't remember where I put them.*

S

seek (AWL)
to try to find or get something, especially help, advice, or information: *She was worried about her son and decided to seek help.*

hunt
to look for something or someone in many places. You do not usually use **hunt** about people unless they have done something wrong: *The police are **hunting for** more clues.*
→ **Hunt** also means "to look for and kill wild animals": *He uses the gun for hunting rabbits.*

frisk
to search someone by feeling his or her body with your hands, especially when looking for hidden weapons: *The security guard frisked us before letting us inside the building.*

raid
if the police raid a place, they go there suddenly to look for something illegal or to catch a criminal: *The police raided his house and found a large amount of stolen jewelry.*
→ see **find**

season *noun* → see **time**

seat *noun* → see **chair**

S

secret /ˈsikrət/ *adjective*

- ► secret
- ► covert
- ► clandestine
- ► undercover
- ► private
- ► confidential

secret
if something is secret, only you or only a few people know about it: *He hid the money in a secret place. | You should keep your computer password secret.*

covert
covert activities are done secretly, especially by a government or other organization: *The soldiers were sent on a covert mission in enemy territory.*

clandestine
clandestine activities are done secretly, because you do not want other people to find out about them: *The couple had clandestine meetings in the park. | They said the country has a clandestine program to develop a nuclear weapon.*

undercover
working or done secretly, in order to catch criminals or find out information: *An undercover police officer became a member of the gang to find out about their activities.*

private
if something is private, it is about your personal life and you do not want many other people to know about it: *My family problems are a private matter and I do not wish to discuss them.*

confidential
if information is confidential, you must not let other people know about it: *A doctor should not discuss confidential information about patients with other people.*

ADVERBS

You can make the adjectives **secret**, **covert**, **clandestine**, **private**, and **confidential** into adverbs by using an **-ly** ending: *The men met secretly to discuss their plan. | The country's leaders clandestinely developed a nuclear weapon. | Everything you tell your doctor will be treated confidentially.*

secretly *adverb* → see **privately**

section *noun* → see **part**

secure *adjective* → see **confident**, **safe**, **stable**

securely *adverb* → see **tightly**

security *noun* → see **safety**, Topic **Travel and Vacations**

see /si/ *verb*

- ► see
- ► look at
- ► notice
- ► spot
- ► observe
- ► catch sight of
- ► catch a glimpse of
- ► make out
- ► perceive (*formal*)
- ► witness

see
to know that someone or something is there, using your eyes: *I saw two kids sitting on the grass. | He looked out of the window and **saw that** it was raining.*

look at
to pay attention to something using your eyes, or to move your eyes so that you see something: *She was looking at the big painting on the wall. | Look at this dress – isn't it beautiful?*

notice
to see something interesting, or see that something is happening: *Emma noticed a van*

parked outside the house. | ***I noticed that** his hands were shaking.*

spot
to see something that is difficult to notice, or something that no one else notices. **Spot** sounds more informal than **notice**: *I'm glad you spotted that mistake before it was too late.*

observe
to look at someone or something carefully so that you notice anything unusual: *We sat and observed the ants as they carried food to their underground home.*

catch sight of
to suddenly see someone or something: *As she passed a store window, she caught sight of her reflection.*

catch a glimpse of *also* **glimpse**
to see someone or something, but only for a very short time: *The crowd had waited for ages to catch a glimpse of the singer as he arrived.* | *We glimpsed the ocean ahead of us, before the fog came down again.*

make out
to see something that is difficult to see clearly: *I could just make out the words on the old gravestone.*

perceive (AWL) *(formal)*
to see something, especially because you are physically able to see: *Rattlesnakes can perceive infrared light, but people cannot.*
→ You can also use **perceive** when you understand something from what you see: *He **perceived that** she was tired and asked if she wanted to sit down and rest.*

witness
to see an accident or crime happen: *If you witnessed the accident, please contact the police.*
→ see **find out**, **look[1]**, **watch**
→ see **understand** for **see** meaning "understand something"

seem /sim/ *verb*

- ► seem
- ► appear
- ► look
- ► sound
- ► feel
- ► come across as
- ► give the impression of
- ► strike me/her/them etc. as

seem
used to say what quality you think someone or something has, because of what you can see, hear, touch, or notice: *She seems happy at her new school.* | *The man didn't answer me and **seemed to** be asleep.* | *It seems possible that ice on the wings of the plane caused the crash.*

appear
appear means the same as **seem** but is more formal: *A quick end to the war appears unlikely.* | *The building **appeared to** be empty.*

look
to seem when you look at or think about someone or something: *Sit down – you look tired.* | *The situation looked hopeless.* | ***It looks like** things are going to be OK.*

sound
to seem from what you hear or read, or from what someone has told you: *When Martin called me yesterday, he sounded worried.* | *Mexico **sounds like** a great place for a vacation.*

feel
to seem when you touch something, or based on your feelings about something: *The rugs and cushions make the room feel cozy.*

come across as
to seem because of someone's behavior or what someone says: *In interviews, she comes across as being very intelligent.*

give the impression of
to seem. You use **give the impression of** especially when what seems true is not true: *Because he spoke quickly, he gave the impression of being nervous, but he was just excited.*

strike me/her/them etc. as
to seem. You use **strike me/her/them etc. as** when you give your opinion about someone or something: *Their reaction to the news struck me as odd.*

segregated *adjective* → see **separate[1]**

segregation *noun* → see **separation**

seize *verb* → see **catch**, **take**

seldom *adverb* → see **rarely**

select *verb* → see **choose**

selection *noun* → see **choice**, **variety**

selfish /ˈselfɪʃ/ *adjective*

- ► selfish
- ► self-centered

selfish
caring only about yourself and not about other

S

people: *Don't be so selfish! Share the candy with your brother.* | *Her selfish son never comes to visit or help her.*

→ You can also use **selfish** about someone's actions: *Leaving your friends to do all the work was a very selfish thing to do.*

self-centered

believing that what you want or need is most important, and not noticing what is happening to other people: *Very young children are naturally self-centered, but they gradually learn to sympathize with other people.*

→ see Topic **Describing People's Character**

ADVERBS

You can make the adjective **selfish** into an adverb by using an **-ly** ending: *She selfishly decided not to share the candy.*

sell /sel/ *verb*

- sell
- export
- auction
- trade
- peddle

ANTONYMS → see **buy**

sell

to give something to someone in exchange for money: *The drugstore sells everything from medicines to makeup.* | *We* ***sold*** *the house* ***for*** *$300,000.*

export AWL

to sell things to another country: *India now* ***exports*** *software* ***to*** *many countries, including the U.S.*

auction

to sell something at an event where things are sold to the person who offers the most money: *The painting, by a Mexican artist, will be auctioned next week.*

trade

to buy and sell things as your job or business: *She ran a small company that* ***traded with*** *China.*

peddle

to sell cheap things in the street. **Peddle** can also be used when people sell illegal or harmful things: *A man with a cart was* ***peddling*** *ice cream* ***to*** *the families in the park.*

→ see **sale**

seller /'selə/ *noun*

- seller
- dealer
- retailer
- trader
- merchant

seller

a person or company that sells something: *Toy sellers are busy during the holiday season.* | *The seller accepted the offer we made on the house, so we will sign the contract soon.*

dealer

a person or company that buys and sells a particular type of thing: *They are buying a small car from a local dealer.* | *The painting was bought by an art dealer.*

retailer

a person or company that sells things to people in a store. **Retailer** is usually used in business English: *The clothing retailer reported a 13% increase in sales in the past three months.*

trader

someone who buys and sells stocks on a financial market: *He is one of the best bond traders on Wall Street.*

→ **Trader** also means someone who sells things in a market or on the street rather than in a store: *The city of Montreal was founded by French fur traders in the 17th century.*

merchant

someone who buys and sells large amounts of something as a business. **Merchant** sounds slightly formal or old-fashioned, and you use it especially about someone who sells a particular type of goods: *He is a successful wine merchant.*

semester *noun* → see Topic **Education**

seminar *noun* → see **class**, Topic **Education**

senate *noun* → see Topic **Government and Politics**

senator *noun* → see Topic **Government and Politics**

send /send/ *verb*

1 to arrange for something to go to another place

- send
- mail
- ship
- forward
- circulate
- dispatch (*formal*)

ANTONYMS → see **get (1)**

2 to tell someone to go to a place
- ► send
- ► put
- ► station

1 to arrange for something to go to another place

send
to arrange for something to go or be taken to another place, for example by mail, email, or fax: *I will **send** a copy of the report **to** you.* | *We sent Mom flowers for Mother's Day.* | *I sent her an email about tomorrow's meeting.*
→ **GRAMMAR:** Don't say: ~~*I sent to him some money*~~. Say: *I sent him some money.* You can also say: *I **sent** some money **to** him.*

mail
to send a letter or package to someone, usually by putting it in a mailbox or taking it to the post office: *Your new driver's license will be **mailed to** you.* | *I have to go to the post office to mail some letters.*
→ **GRAMMAR:** Don't say: ~~*She mailed to me the photographs*~~. Say: *She mailed me the photographs.* You can also say: *She **mailed** the photographs **to** me.*

ship
to send or deliver goods to customers: *The book that you ordered online will ship within 24 hours.* | *All our packages are shipped by air.*

forward
to send a letter or email that has been sent to you: *When we moved, we asked our landlord to **forward** the mail **to** us.* | *If you email me your résumé, I will **forward** it **to** the manager.*

circulate
to send information to a group of people: *Information about the graduation ceremony was **circulated to** all the students in the school.*

dispatch (*formal*)
to send something somewhere for a particular purpose. You use **dispatch** to talk about the government or military sending something: *Water and relief supplies were **dispatched to** the island after the earthquake.*

2 to tell someone to go to a place

send
to ask or tell someone to go to a place: *He **sent** the others **out** of the room so that we could speak in private.* | *The teacher **sent** the boys **to** the principal's office because they were fighting in class.*

put
to arrange for someone to go to a place, especially when it will be for a long time. You often use **put** when someone is sent to a place where he or she does not want to go, for example a prison or hospital: *It was too difficult to take care of our grandmother, so we had to **put** her **in** a nursing home.*

station
to send someone to work in a place for a period of time as a military duty: *He joined the army and **was stationed in** Japan for three years.*

sensation *noun* → see **feeling**

sensational *adjective* → see **exciting**

sense *noun* → see **intelligence**, **meaning**, **reason**

sensible /ˈsensəbəl/ *adjective*

- ► sensible
- ► reasonable
- ► rational
- ► logical
- ► practical
- ► responsible
- ► mature
- ► pragmatic

ANTONYMS → see **silly**, **illogical**

sensible
showing good judgment and an ability to make practical decisions: *It is sensible to allow plenty of time to get to the airport.* | *He is a sensible man. I'm sure he will think about everything before making a decision.*

reasonable
showing that you make sensible decisions that are fair to other people: *We need to discuss this in a reasonable way, and not let our emotions cloud our thinking.*

rational AWL
based on facts or sensible reasons, not on your feelings: *It can be difficult to make a rational decision when you're under pressure.*

logical AWL
based on good thinking in which facts and ideas are connected in a sensible way: *She has always been interested in the environment, so studying environmental law is a logical thing to do.*

practical
sensible and based on a good understanding of what is possible and what is not possible: *Martin made some very practical suggestions about how to change the system without wasting too much time.*

responsible
sensible and able to be trusted: *Young children should always be left in the care of a responsible adult.*

mature (AWL)
behaving in a sensible and responsible way, like an adult: *Katherine is only 14, but she is very mature and I trust her to babysit.*

pragmatic
dealing with something in a sensible and practical way, without being afraid to change your ideas as a situation changes: *Both sides need to have a pragmatic attitude if the peace talks are going to be successful.*
→ see **realistic (1)** for words meaning "sensible and understanding what is possible"
→ see Topic **Describing People's Character**

ADVERBS
You can make the adjectives that mean **sensible** into adverbs by using an **-ly** ending: *Think sensibly about everything before making a decision.* | *Logically, we know we should spend less when we have less money.* | *She behaves very maturely for a 14-year-old.* | *We have to think pragmatically if we want to succeed.*

S

sensitive /ˈsensətɪv/ *adjective*

- ► sensitive
- ► emotional
- ► sentimental

sensitive
able to understand other people's feelings and problems: *She is a sensitive child who always knows when her mother is unhappy.* | *The work made me more sensitive to the needs of disabled people.*

emotional
showing strong feelings to other people, especially by crying: *I try not to get too emotional when I talk about him, but I miss him so much.*

sentimental
a person who is sentimental is affected by emotions such as love, pity, and sadness, sometimes in a way that seems silly or not sincere: *As I get older, I have become more sentimental about the people and places in my past.*
→ A **sentimental** movie, song, or book deals with emotions, often in a silly or insincere way: *She was singing a sentimental love song.*
→ see **sympathetic**, **tactful**, **thoughtful**

ADVERBS
You can make the adjectives that mean **sensitive** into adverbs by using an **-ly** ending: *You dealt with a difficult issue very sensitively.* | *He spoke emotionally about his father's death.*

sentence /ˈsentəns/ *noun*

- ► sentence
- ► clause
- ► phrase

sentence
a group of words with a subject and a verb, that makes a statement or asks a question. In written English, a **sentence** begins with a capital letter and ends with a period, question mark, or exclamation point: *"We are going to Vancouver next week" is a sentence.* | *In the sentence "The children go to school on the bus," "the children" is the subject of the sentence.*

clause (AWL)
a group of words that contains a subject and a verb. A simple sentence may have one **clause**, and a more complicated sentence may have several **clauses**: *The sentence "We'll have a picnic if the weather is good" contains two clauses: "We'll have a picnic" and "if the weather is good."*

phrase
a group of words that is not a complete sentence: *"After a while" and "during the day" are phrases.*

sentimental *adjective* → see **sensitive**

separate[1] /ˈseprɪt/ *adjective*

- ► separate
- ► apart
- ► segregated

separate
put or kept in different places or groups: *Keep raw meat **separate from** cooked meat.* | *They divided the students into three groups and put them in separate rooms.*

apart
not together or not next to each other: *She hated being **apart from** her boyfriend, even for a day.* | *Plant the seeds two inches apart.*
→ **GRAMMAR: Apart** is an adverb and is never used before a noun. Don't say: ~~*They are apart towns*~~. Say: *The towns are far apart.*

segregated
if a place is segregated, people of different races, religions, or sexes are not allowed to be

there together: *In the 1940s, black and white children went to segregated schools.*

ADVERBS

You can make the adjective **separate** into an adverb by using an **-ly** ending: *The raw meat is stored separately from the cooked meat.*

separate[2] /ˈsepəˌreɪt/ *verb*

- ► separate
- ► divide
- ► split
- ► segregate
- ► isolate
- ► part

ANTONYMS → see **join (2)**

separate
to put people or things that were together into different places or groups: *We **separated** the cans **from** the bottles for recycling.* | *The teacher separated Alex and me because we were talking in class.*

divide *also* **divide up**
to separate something into smaller parts or groups: *The coach **divided** the kids **into** two teams.* | *We will **divide up** the money **between** us.*

split *also* **split up**
to separate something into two or more parts. **Split** is used especially when the parts are equal, and sounds less formal than **divide**: *The boys **split** the rest of the candy **between** them.* | *The teacher asked us to **split up into** three groups.*

segregate
to separate one group of people from others, because they belong to a different race, sex, or religion: *In the past, mentally disabled people were **segregated from** the rest of society in special hospitals.*

isolate (AWL)
to keep one person or thing alone and separate from others: *The hospital isolates patients who have infectious diseases.*

part
to separate two things or parts that are together and make a space in the middle: *She pushed through the thick bushes, parting the branches with her hands.*

separated *adjective* → see **married**, Topic **Relationships and Marriage**

separation /ˌsepəˈreɪʃən/ *noun*

- ► separation
- ► division
- ► segregation
- ► split

separation
the act of separating people or things that were together, or the fact of being separated: *Most people in Quebec said they did not want a formal **separation from** Canada.* | *For the families of men and women in the military, the **separation from** their loved ones is always difficult.*

division
the act of separating something into two or more different parts: *The **division of** Korea took place after the war, and North Korea and South Korea were formed.*
→ **Division** also means the way that something is divided or shared: *Some women felt that the **division of** housework was unfair, and that they did far more than their husbands.*

segregation
the act of separating groups of people because they are of a different race, sex, or religion: *Racial segregation is now illegal in U.S. schools.*

split
a clear separation between two things. **Split** sounds fairly informal: *The **split between** the richer and poorer parts of town is very noticeable.*

series /ˈsɪriz/ *noun*

- ► series
- ► sequence
- ► string
- ► stream
- ► chain of events

series (AWL)
several events, actions, or things of the same kind that happen one after the other: *The police are investigating a **series of** robberies in the area.* | *The doctors are giving her a **series of** tests to try to find out what is wrong.*

sequence (AWL)
a series of related things that happen in a particular order: *The **sequence of** movements for this dance is very difficult to learn.* | *Put the pictures **in** the correct **sequence**, so they tell a story.*

string
a series of similar events that happen very close together. You often use **string** to talk about a series of bad events: *The team has had a **string of** losses – they have not won a game in three weeks.*

S

stream
a long and almost continuous series of events, people, or things: ***A steady stream of people were coming into the concert hall.***

chain of events
a connected series of events or actions that lead to a final result: ***The history teacher described the chain of events that led to the First World War.***
→ see Topic **Entertainment**

serious /ˈsɪriəs/ *adjective*

1 very bad
- ► serious
- ► severe
- ► big (*informal*)
- ► desperate
- ► grave (*formal*)
- ► acute (*formal*)

2 not laughing or joking
- ► serious
- ► solemn
- ► earnest

1 very bad

serious
very bad. You use **serious** about problems, accidents, illnesses, or crimes: ***Unemployment is a serious problem across the country.*** | ***Scientists say that the consequences of the oil spill could be serious.***

severe
very bad. You use **severe** especially to describe serious medical conditions and bad weather: ***He suffered severe injuries in a car crash.*** | ***The flight was canceled because of the severe weather conditions.***

big (*informal*)
very bad. You use **big** especially about problems or mistakes: ***AIDS remains a big problem in many parts of the world.*** | ***Buying that car was a big mistake – there is always something wrong with it.***
→ **GRAMMAR: Big** is only used before a noun. Don't say: ~~The mistake was big~~. Say: ***It was a big mistake.***

desperate
a desperate situation or problem is very serious or dangerous, especially because people need something in order to live or be safe: ***The situation is becoming desperate – many people in the country have no food.***

grave (*formal*)
a grave situation is very serious and makes you worry because it is dangerous or seems likely to get worse: ***The country is at war and foreign tourists there may be in grave danger.***

acute (*formal*)
an acute illness, problem, or situation is one that has become very serious or dangerous and needs to be dealt with quickly: ***The ambulance took him directly to the hospital because he was having acute chest pains.***

ADVERBS
You can make the adjectives **serious**, **severe**, **desperate**, **grave**, and **acute** into adverbs by using an **-ly** ending: ***The oil spill seriously affected wildlife in the Gulf of Mexico.*** | ***The people desperately need food.*** | ***She was gravely ill.*** | ***The wounds were acutely painful.***

2 not laughing or joking

serious
someone who is serious thinks and behaves carefully and sensibly, without laughing or joking about something: ***Be serious for a minute – this is really important.*** | ***Laura is very serious about her schoolwork.***
→ You can also use **serious** about writing, events, etc. that are not funny and that are about important things: ***The magazine mostly has stories about celebrities, but there is a serious article about breast cancer.***

solemn
someone who is solemn is very serious because of an important or sad occasion: ***The judge read the verdict in a solemn voice.***
→ You can also use **solemn** about something important that is done in a very serious way: ***A funeral is a very solemn occasion.*** | ***He made a solemn promise to help us.***

earnest
an earnest person is serious and sincere, and tries very hard to behave in the right way. **Earnest** is often used about someone who is young and not very experienced: ***She is an earnest young teacher who believes that education can change people's lives.***

ADVERBS
You can make the adjectives that mean "not laughing or joking" into adverbs by using an **-ly** ending: ***Laura is talking seriously about moving to the city.*** | ***He solemnly promised to help us.*** | ***She spoke earnestly about how education changes lives.***

seriously *adverb* → see **very**

serve *verb* → see **give**, Topic **Eating in a Restaurant**

service *noun* → see **ceremony**, **repair**, **work[2]**

set[1] *verb* → see **go down**, **harden**, **put**

set[2] *noun* → see **game**, **group**

set[3] *adjective* → see **ready**

set fire *verb phrase* → see **burn**

set free *verb phrase* → see **free**[2]

set off *phrasal verb* → see **leave**

set up *phrasal verb* → see **start**[1]

several *adjective, pronoun* → see Function Word **some**

severe *adjective* → see **extreme**, **serious**

severely *adverb* → see **very**

sew /soʊ/ *verb*

- ► sew
- ► stitch
- ► hem

sew
to use a needle and thread to make or repair clothes or other things from cloth: *My mother is teaching me how to sew.* | *Can you sew a patch on my jeans?*

stitch
to sew two pieces of cloth together, or to sew something onto a piece of cloth: *I **stitched** two pockets **onto** the skirt.*
→ You also use **stitch** when a doctor sews a cut or wound in someone's skin: *The doctor stitched the cut together neatly.*

hem
to fold and sew the edge of a piece of clothing: *The jeans were too long for me, so I cut an inch off the bottom and hemmed them.*

sex /seks/ *noun*

1 the fact of being male or female
- ► sex
- ► gender

2 the activity that produces babies
- ► sex
- ► reproduction (*formal*)

1 the fact of being male or female

sex (AWL)
the fact of being male or female: *Put your name and sex at the top of the form.* | *I don't care what sex the baby is – we will be happy either way.*
→ **Sex** is also used to describe all men or all women, thought of as groups, in phrases like these: *He is nervous around people of **the opposite sex** (=women).* | *Some people think that **single-sex** (=with only boys or only girls) schools are a good idea.*

gender (AWL)
gender means the same as **sex**, but you use it especially when you are talking about how men and women behave in society: *Are there really gender differences in the ways that little boys and girls play?* | *The change in the number of women who work has had an effect on gender roles, as men are expected to do more child care.*

2 the activity that produces babies

sex (AWL)
the physical activity that two people do together in order to produce babies, or for pleasure: *They believe it is wrong to have sex before they are married.* | *There is too much sex and violence on TV.*

reproduction (*formal*)
the act of producing babies, young animals, or plants. **Reproduction** is used when you are reading or talking about science: *We learned about human reproduction in science class in the seventh grade.*

sexism *noun* → see **prejudice**

sexist *adjective* → see **prejudiced**

shabby *adjective* → see **condition** (**3**), Topic **Describing the Condition of Something**, **Describing Places**

shade *noun* → see **color**[1], **shadow**

shadow /ˈʃædoʊ/ *noun*

- ► shadow
- ► shade
- ► silhouette

shadow
a dark shape on a surface, made when someone or something blocks the light: *A shadow fell across the table and I looked up to see who was there.* | *It was late in the afternoon, and the **shadows of** the trees had become long.*

shade
an area that is cooler and darker because the light of the sun does not reach it: *We sat outside **in the shade**, under a tree.*

silhouette
a dark shape that you see against a light background. When you see the **silhouette** of something, you see a dark shape without any

S

details or features: *I saw the **silhouette of** a bird in the pale sky.*

shadow

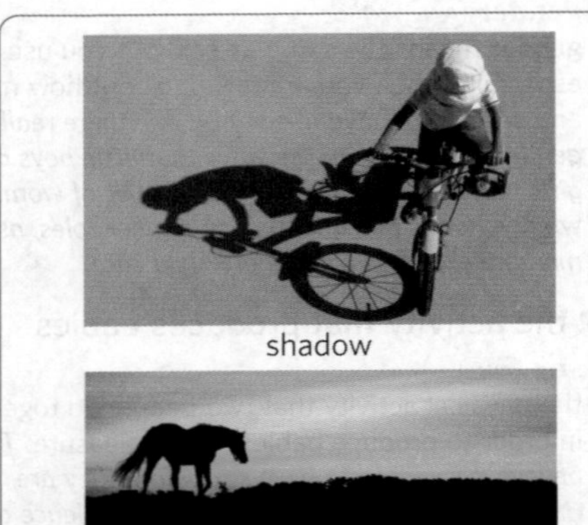
shadow

silhouette

shady *adjective* → see **dishonest**, **dark[1]**, Topic **Describing Places**

shake /ʃeɪk/ *verb*

1 to shake – used about people
- shake
- shiver
- tremble
- shudder
- quiver

2 to shake – used about things
- shake
- vibrate
- rattle
- tremble
- quiver
- shudder

1 to shake – used about people

shake
to move up and down or from side to side with quick movements: *I was nervous and my hands were shaking. | She shook the blanket to get rid of all the dust.*

shiver
to shake because you are very cold: *You're shivering! Do you want to go inside?*

tremble
to shake very slightly because you are frightened or upset. You use **tremble** especially in writing: *Jane's lip began to tremble and I thought she was going to cry.*

shudder
to shake for a short moment, especially because something is very unpleasant or upsetting: *I saw a mouse run across the kitchen floor and shuddered.*

quiver
to shake so slightly that it is difficult for other people to notice, especially because you are nervous, scared, angry, or excited. You use **quiver** about people or animals, and especially in writing: *The children stood there **quivering with** excitement as we opened the package.*

GRAMMAR CHECK: shake

When you want to say that someone shakes something, you can only use the word **shake**: *She shook the present to try to guess what was inside.* You cannot use the words **shiver**, **tremble**, etc. for saying that someone **shakes** something.

2 to shake – used about things

shake
to move suddenly from side to side or up and down, usually with a lot of force: *The branches of the tree were shaking in the wind. | The floor shook from the force of the explosion.*

vibrate
to shake continuously with small fast movements: *The music was so loud that the whole car vibrated.*

rattle
to shake and make a noise: *The windows rattled in the wind.*

tremble
to shake slightly. You usually use **tremble** when the earth moves a little and makes things shake: *The whole house trembles as the huge trucks go by.*

quiver
to shake very slightly: *The flowers quivered in the breeze.*

shudder
if a machine or vehicle shudders, it shakes strongly for a short time. **Shudder** is used mainly in literary writing: *Cyrus braked, and the old truck shuddered to a stop.*
→ see **rock[2]** for words meaning "to move from side to side or backward and forward"

shallow *adjective* → see Topic **Describing Size**

shame /ʃeɪm/ *noun*

- ► shame
- ► humiliation
- ► dishonor (*formal*)
- ► disgrace
- ► stigma (*formal*)

ANTONYMS → see **pride (1)**

shame
the feeling that you have when you know that you have behaved badly and lost the respect of other people: *He felt a deep sense of shame because he could not help his poor mother.* | *She lowered her head* ***in shame*** *when the teacher caught her cheating.*

humiliation
a feeling of shame and embarrassment because you look weak or stupid in front of other people: *The* ***humiliation of*** *losing the game so badly stayed with the team for weeks.*

dishonor (*formal*)
the loss of other people's respect for someone's profession, country, or family, which happens because of his or her bad actions: *The soldiers who hurt their prisoners brought dishonor on their country.*

disgrace
the loss of other people's respect because you have done something very bad and shocking: *He faced public disgrace when his affair with another woman was reported in the papers.*
→ If someone is a **disgrace to** something, he or she has done something bad or unacceptable, and has made people feel ashamed of him or her: *After he was arrested and put in jail, his father told him that he was a* ***disgrace to*** *the family.*

stigma (*formal*)
a strong feeling of shame and a feeling that other people disapprove of you. **Stigma** is used especially when this seems unfair and unreasonable: *Even when someone has been found innocent of a crime, the* ***stigma of*** *being accused of the crime often remains.*
→ see **embarrassment**, **guilt**

shape /ʃeɪp/ *noun*

- ► shape
- ► form
- ► outline
- ► figure

shape
the fact of an object being square, round, triangular, rectangular, etc.: *"What shape is your kitchen table?" "It is square."* | *You can get pasta in many different shapes.* | *She baked a cake* ***in the shape of*** *a heart.*
→ You can also use **shape** to talk about things such as squares, circles, and triangles: *She is two years old, and she is learning all her shapes and colors.*

form
the shape or outline of someone's body: *He could see her slender form walking toward him in the dim light.*

outline
a line around the edge of something that shows its shape, but not any other details: *In the distance, we could see the* ***outline of*** *the Statue of Liberty.*

figure
the shape of a person, especially when he or she is far away or difficult to see: *There was a dark figure running across the yard.*
→ see **in shape** at **healthy**, Topic **Sports and Exercise**

share[1] /ʃer/ *verb*

- ► share
- ► take turns
- ► divide
- ► split

share
to separate something into parts and give one part to each person in a group. You usually separate something you **share** into equal parts, so that everyone gets the same amount: *I* ***shared*** *some of the candy* ***with*** *my friends.*
→ You can also use **share** to say that more than one person uses something, such as a room or a book: *Mrs. Garcia* ***shares*** *an office* ***with*** *another teacher.*

take turns
if a group of people take turns doing something, one person does it, then another person does it, so that everyone gets a chance: *There was only one swing, so the children took turns.*

divide *also* **divide up**
to separate something into smaller parts or groups: *The coach* ***divided*** *the kids* ***into*** *two teams.* | *We* ***divided up*** *the rest of the pie* ***between*** *us.*

split *also* **split up**
to divide something. **Split** is less formal than **divide**, and you use it especially when the parts are equal: *The boys* ***split*** *the candy* ***between*** *them.* | *The teacher asked us to* ***split up into*** *three groups.*

S

share² /ʃer/ *noun*

- ► share
- ► portion (*formal*)

share
the part of something that you own, deserve, or are responsible for: ***When Grandpa died, we each got a share of his money. | Everyone should do a fair share of the work on the group project.***

portion (AWL) (*formal*)
a part of something larger: ***He sends a large portion of his salary home to El Salvador.***
→ see **part**

shared *adjective* → see **common**

sharp /ʃarp/ *adjective*

- ► sharp
- ► spiky
- ► jagged

ANTONYMS → see **blunt**

sharp
with a very thin edge or point that can cut things easily: ***Be careful with that knife – it is very sharp. | The dog's teeth were very sharp.***

spiky
with a lot of points: ***There were spiky cactus plants along the path. | He had a leather jacket and short spiky hair.***

jagged
having a rough uneven edge with a lot of sharp points: ***After the window broke, the floor was covered with jagged pieces of glass.***
→ see **clear (3)** for **sharp** meaning "easy to see," **smart (1)** for **sharp** meaning "understanding things quickly"

sharp

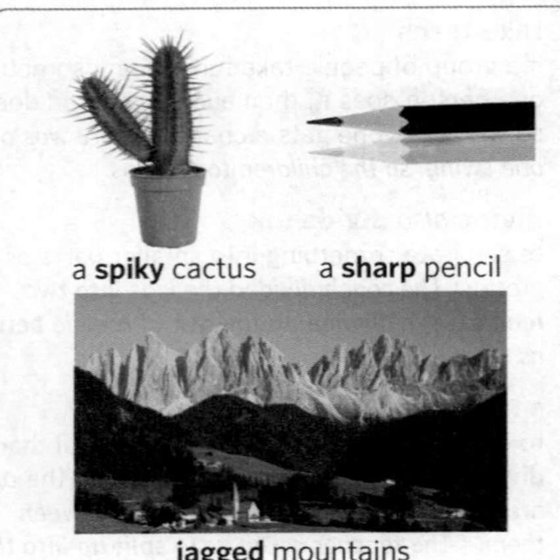

a **spiky** cactus a **sharp** pencil

jagged mountains

shave *verb* → see **cut¹**

sheep /ʃip/ *noun*

- ► sheep
- ► lamb
- ► ram
- ► ewe

sheep
a farm animal that is kept for its wool and its meat: ***Sheep were grazing on the hills. | The farm sells wool and cheese from its large flock of sheep.***

lamb
a young sheep, or the meat of a young sheep: ***New lambs are born in early spring.***

ram
a male sheep: ***A huge ram with curving horns was staring at us.***

ewe
a female sheep: ***The flock is made up of 100 ewes and 4 rams.***

sheet /ʃit/ *noun*

1 a thin flat piece of paper
- ► sheet
- ► page
- ► piece
- ► slip
- ► side

2 a thin flat piece of glass
- ► sheet
- ► pane

1 a thin flat piece of paper

sheet
a thin flat piece of paper for writing, drawing, or printing on: ***I wrote my name at the top of a blank sheet of paper. | The package has 500 sheets of 8.5 by 11 inch white paper.***

page
a sheet of paper in a book, magazine, or newspaper: ***One of the pages in the book was missing.***
→ A **page** can be one or both sides of a piece of paper. When **page** is used with a number, it usually means one side of a sheet of paper in a book, magazine, or newspaper: ***Turn to page 150 in your textbook.***

piece
a sheet of paper, especially one that is taken or cut off from a larger set of similar sheets. You usually use **piece** in the phrase **piece of paper**, especially when you are mentioning it for the

first time: ***I'll get you a piece of paper, so you can write the number down.***

slip
a small piece of paper: ***He wrote his address on a slip of paper.***

side
one of the two surfaces of a sheet of paper: ***The teacher told us to write on only one side of the paper.***

2 a thin flat piece of glass

sheet
a thin flat piece of glass: ***The construction workers were carrying a huge sheet of glass toward the building.***

pane
a piece of glass in a window or door: ***One of the panes in the window is broken and needs to be replaced.***
→ see **layer**

shelter *noun* → see **house**, **safe (3)**

shield *noun* → see **protection**

shine /ʃaɪn/ *verb*

1 to produce light
- ► shine
- ► glow
- ► flash
- ► blaze
- ► glisten
- ► gleam

2 to produce light that changes or moves
- ► sparkle
- ► glitter
- ► flicker
- ► twinkle
- ► shimmer

1 to produce light

shine
if something such as the sun or a lamp shines, it produces light: ***The sun was shining, so we decided to go to the beach. | From the plane window, she could see the lights shining from cities below.***
→ A surface can also **shine** when it reflects light from the sun or a lamp: ***The car was so clean that it shone in the sunlight.***

glow
to shine with a soft steady light. You use **glow** especially in writing: ***One candle was glowing in the dark room.***

flash
to shine brightly for a very short time: ***I saw lightning flash across the sky.***

blaze
to shine very brightly with a lot of heat. You use **blaze** especially in writing about fires or lights that feel hot in the way a fire does: ***It was noon and the hot sun blazed in their faces.***

glisten
if something glistens, it shines because it is wet or oily and is reflecting light. **Glisten** is used especially when saying that someone's eyes are full of tears, or someone's skin is covered with sweat: ***As they were leaving, her eyes glistened with tears.***

gleam
if something gleams, it shines because it is very clean. You usually use **gleam** about smooth surfaces: ***She polished the old dining table until it gleamed.***

2 to produce light that changes or moves

sparkle
if something sparkles, it shines with many small bright points of light. Things like water and glass **sparkle**: ***The lake sparkled in the sunlight.***

glitter
glitter means the same as **sparkle** but you usually use it about hard shiny things: ***Jewels glittered around her neck.***

flicker
to produce a light that is not steady. You use **flicker** about a weak flame or a light that almost stops shining: ***The candles flickered in the wind.***

twinkle
if a star or small light twinkles, it shines with a light that keeps changing from bright to less bright: ***The stars twinkled in the black sky.***

shimmer
to shine with a soft light that seems to shake slightly. You use **shimmer** especially about things that shine in an attractive way: ***Her golden dress shimmered in the light from the candles.***

shiny /ˈʃaɪni/ *adjective*

- ► shiny
- ► glossy

shiny
something that is shiny has a smooth bright surface that reflects light: ***The little girl's shoes were black and shiny. | A shiny silver car was parked in front of the building.***

glossy
very shiny and smooth. **Glossy** hair or fur looks

S

shiny and healthy, and **glossy** magazines and books use expensive shiny paper: *She brushed her long glossy black hair.* | *There was a stack of glossy magazines on the table.*

ship *noun* → see **boat**

shirt /ʃɚt/ *noun*

- ► shirt
- ► blouse
- ► top

shirt
a piece of clothing that covers the top half of your body: *I like cotton shirts.* | *He put on a clean shirt after working in the yard.*
→ There are many different kinds of **shirts**. A **shirt** that a man wears that has a collar, long sleeves, and buttons down the front can be called a **shirt**, a **button-down shirt**, or a **dress shirt**: *He put on a white shirt and a tie.* A **T-shirt** is soft, and has short sleeves and no collar: *The boy was wearing jeans and a T-shirt.* A **polo shirt** is soft and has short sleeves, a collar, and a few buttons near the neck: *The students wear polo shirts as part of their school uniform.*

blouse
a shirt for a woman or girl. A **blouse** often has buttons, but not always, and it does not always have sleeves or a collar. A blouse is usually worn on more formal occasions, such as for work or a special party: *She put on a silk blouse and a long skirt.*
→ A woman's **blouse** that looks more like a man's **dress shirt** can also be called a **shirt**.

top
a piece of clothing that covers the upper part of your body. A **top** can be any kind of shirt, and does not usually look as formal as a **blouse**: *The girl was wearing shorts and a pink top.*
→ You usually use **top** about a piece of clothing that a woman or girl wears.

shiver *verb* → see **shake**

shock[1] /ʃɑk/ *noun*

- ► shock
- ► horror
- ► dismay (*formal*)

shock
the feeling of surprise you have when something very bad happens that you did not expect: *I lost my job this morning – I'm still **in shock**.* | *Mom has never really gotten over the **shock of** Dad's death.*

horror
shock and fear: *She watched **in horror** as the firefighters pulled her sister from the car.*

dismay (*formal*)
a feeling of surprise and worry: *As I looked at the test questions, I realized **with dismay** that I did not know any of the answers.*
→ see **fright**, **surprise[1]**

shock[2] /ʃɑk/ *verb*

- ► shock
- ► stun
- ► horrify

shock
to make someone feel very surprised and upset: *Their apartment was filthy, which really shocked me.* | ***It shocked** us **to** see how ill she looked.*

stun
to surprise or shock someone so much that he or she cannot react immediately: *Mr. Kim stunned us all by suddenly resigning.*

horrify
to make someone feel very shocked and upset or afraid: *The gang fights in the park have horrified people in the neighborhood.*
→ see **surprise[2]**

GRAMMAR CHECK: shock

Don't say: ~~*The news about the explosion was shocking/stunning/horrifying us.*~~ Say: *The news about the explosion shocked/stunned/horrified us.*

shocked /ʃɑkt/ *adjective*

- ► shocked
- ► stunned
- ► horrified
- ► shaken
- ► appalled

shocked
feeling surprised and upset by something very unexpected and unpleasant: *I **was shocked by** how much weight my aunt had gained.* | *We were **shocked to** hear about Brian's heart attack – he is so young.*

stunned
so shocked that you are not able to do or say anything immediately: *She looked stunned when I told her that I had quit my job.*

horrified
very shocked by something very unpleasant or

S

frightening that has happened: *We were **horrified** to hear that he had been hurt in the accident.*

shaken
shocked and feeling weak and nervous, because something very unpleasant or frightening has happened: *Victims of crime are usually badly **shaken by** the experience.*

appalled
very shocked by behavior or a situation that is very bad or unpleasant: *I was **appalled by** how rude the children were to their mother.*

shocking *adjective* → see **surprising**

shoot /ʃut/ *verb*

- ► shoot
- ► fire
- ► launch

shoot
to make a bullet come out of a gun: *Gang members started **shooting at** each other. | Don't shoot! I'm coming out with my hands up.*
→ **Shoot** also means "to injure or kill someone using a gun": *The guards shot the man as he was trying to escape.*

fire
to shoot bullets from a gun, or to shoot an explosive from a larger weapon: *The police **fired** two shots **at** the men before they stopped running.*

launch
to send a weapon such as a rocket into the sky or through water: *The missile was launched from a submarine and aimed at an enemy ship.*
→ see **photograph**[2] for **shoot** meaning "make a movie"
→ see **shot**

shop *noun* → see **store**

shore *noun* → see **coast**

short /ʃɔrt/ *adjective*

1 not tall
- ► short
- ► small
- ► petite
- ► little
- ► low

ANTONYMS → see **tall**

2 continuing for only a little time
- ► short
- ► brief
- ► quick
- ► momentary
- ► short-lived
- ► temporary

ANTONYMS → see **long**[1]

3 using only a few words
- ► short
- ► brief
- ► concise (*formal*)

1 not tall

short
not as tall as most people: *Michael is a short man – only five foot four inches tall. | I am a little bit shorter than my sister. | The gymnast was short and strong.*

small
short and usually thin: *A small woman with straight dark hair was sitting in front of me. | The girl was small for her age* (=smaller than other girls of the same age).

petite
a woman who is petite is short and thin. You use **petite** to show approval: *She was a petite woman with blonde hair.*

little
short and small. **Little** is used especially to describe children or old people: *We saw a little old lady with a walking stick. | The little girl was sitting on her mother's lap.*

low
not high, or not far above the ground: *The kids built a low wall around the sandcastle. | I picked an apple that was hanging from a low branch.*
→ see Topic **Describing People's Looks**, **Describing Size**

SYNONYM CHECK
Short or low?
You use **low** about things such as mountains and walls, and **short** about people. Don't say: *~~There was a short wall around the yard~~*. Say: *There was a low wall around the yard.*

2 continuing for only a little time

short
continuing for only a little time, or for less time than usual: *I lived in Tokyo for a short time. | Our group is going to have a short meeting after lunch.*

brief (AWL)
brief means the same as **short** but sounds a

little more formal: *We stopped at Alice's house for a brief visit.*

quick
a quick action or activity takes a very short time: *He had a quick shower and then went out.*

momentary
lasting a very short time. You use **momentary** about feelings or pauses: *After a momentary silence, he spoke again.*

short-lived
continuing only a short time. You use **short-lived** about something good that does not last long, for example a feeling or relationship: *Their happiness was short-lived, as their marriage soon developed problems.*

temporary (AWL)
not permanent. Something **temporary** is usually planned to last only a short time: *She took a temporary job working in a store at Christmastime.*

ADVERBS

You can make the adjectives **brief**, **quick**, **momentary**, and **temporary** into adverbs by using an **-ly** ending: *We visited Alice's house briefly.* | *He quickly took a shower and went out.* | *He stopped speaking momentarily.* | *She worked temporarily in a store at Christmastime.*

3 using only a few words

short
a short piece of writing or a speech does not have many pages or words: *I wrote a short note to explain.* | *She was reading a book of short stories by Chekhov.*

brief (AWL)
using only a few words and not describing things in detail. Use **brief** especially to describe something someone says: *I'll try to be brief – I know it is late.* | *The President made a brief statement to reporters.*

concise (*formal*)
short and giving only the information that is necessary and important: *Your letter should be concise and polite.*

ADVERBS

You can make the adjectives **brief** and **concise** into adverbs by using an **-ly** ending: *We listened to the President's briefly worded statement.* | *She spoke concisely about her plan.*

shortage *noun* → see **lack**[1]

shorten /ˈʃɔrtn/ *verb*

- ► shorten
- ► cut
- ► condense
- ► abridge (*formal*)

ANTONYMS → see **lengthen**

shorten
to make something shorter. You can use **shorten** to talk about making something physically shorter, or shorter in the amount of time something uses: *She wants to shorten the skirt by one inch.* | *The new high-speed train will shorten travel time between Beijing and Shanghai.*

cut
to make something shorter. You can use **cut** to talk about making a movie or piece of writing shorter, or about making hair or grass shorter: *The original version of the movie was 120 minutes long, but the director later **cut** it **to** 100 minutes.* | *The hairdresser was cutting my hair.*
→ You can also use **cut** to talk about making something shorter in time: *The new road will cut travel time between the two cities.*

condense
to make a piece of writing or something you say shorter by not giving as many details or by not using as many words: *The information could be **condensed into** one book rather than two books.*

abridge (*formal*)
to make a book or play shorter without changing the basic story: *The book has been abridged to make it easier for children to read.*

shortly *adverb* → see **quickly**, **soon**

shorts *noun* → see **pants**

shot /ʃɑt/ *noun*

- ► shot
- ► gunfire
- ► shooting

shot
if you fire a shot, you make a bullet come out of a gun: *He fired several shots from his gun.* | *We called police after we heard shots.*

gunfire
a lot of shots fired from guns – used especially about the sound of shots being fired: *The gunfire went on throughout the night as soldiers continued fighting.*

shooting
a situation in which someone is killed or injured by shots fired from a gun: *Thirty people were*

killed in the shooting.
→ see **photograph**[1] for **shot** meaning "a photograph"

should /ʃəd, strong ʃʊd/ *verb*

- ► should
- ► ought to
- ► had better
- ► be supposed to

should
used when you say or ask what is the right or sensible thing to do: ***You should leave a note for your mom to tell her where you will be.*** | ***What should I do with the money?***
→ **GRAMMAR:** Don't say: ~~*I should to do it now*~~. Say: ***I should do it now.***

ought to
used for saying that someone should do something because it is right or the best thing to do. **Ought to** sounds slightly more formal than **should** and is not used in questions: ***You look tired. You ought to go to bed.***

had better
used for giving advice or for saying what is the best thing to do. **Had better** is usually used in spoken English and is not used in questions: ***It is late – I had better go home now.***
→ **GRAMMAR:** Don't say: ~~*You had better to leave*~~. Say: ***You had better leave.***

be supposed to
used for saying what a rule or someone in authority has told you to do: ***We're supposed to check out of the hotel by 11 a.m.*** | ***Are we supposed to hand in our math homework today?***

shout[1] /ʃaʊt/ *verb*

- ► shout
- ► yell
- ► scream
- ► call
- ► raise your voice
- ► cry
- ► cheer
- ► roar
- ► shriek
- ► screech

ANTONYMS → see **whisper**

shout
to say something in a very loud voice: ***"Wait for me!" he shouted.*** | ***The captain shouted at him to hurry up.*** | ***I could hear someone shouting for help.***

yell
yell means the same as **shout** but is more informal: ***"Nate!" she yelled. "We're over here!"*** | ***Sarah yelled at her mother to stop.***

scream
to shout in a very loud high voice because you are frightened, angry, or excited: ***Everyone screamed as the roller coaster started downward.*** | ***At the airport, a woman was screaming at the ticket clerk because her luggage had not arrived.***

call *also* **call out**
to shout or speak loudly to make sure that someone can hear you: ***"Can you give me a hand?" Tina called from the kitchen.*** | ***I could hear someone calling for help.***

raise your voice
to say something more loudly than normal, often because you are angry about something. **Raising your voice** is not as loud as **shouting**: ***The teacher had to raise her voice to get the kids to pay attention.***

cry *also* **cry out**
to shout something suddenly and loudly, especially because you are hurt, frightened, or excited: ***"There it is!" cried Stephen.*** | ***People in the water cried out for help.***

cheer
to shout as a way of showing that you like or approve of someone or something: ***The crowd cheered when the band came on stage.***

roar
to shout something in a loud deep voice: ***"Let me out of here!" Collins roared.***
→ If people in a crowd **roar**, they make a very loud sound together, usually to show approval for something: ***The fans roared as the football players ran onto the field.***

shriek
to shout loudly in a high voice that hurts people's ears, because you are frightened, angry, or excited: ***"Watch out!" she shrieked.*** | ***She shrieked at him to leave and not come back.***

screech
screech means the same as **shriek**, but people usually screech only when they are angry: ***She screeched at me to take off my muddy boots.***
→ You can use **screech** about other high loud sounds, for example the sound of some large birds: ***The seagulls screeched as they flew over the beach.*** You can also use it about the sound that tires on a vehicle make when it stops quickly: ***We heard a car screech to a stop outside.***

GRAMMAR CHECK: shout

If you say that someone **shouts**, **yells**, or **screams at** someone, you usually mean that he or she is shouting in an angry way: *I shouted at Jim to go away.*

If someone **shouts to** someone, he or she uses a loud voice but is not angry: *I shouted to Jim, "I'm over here!"*

shout² /ʃaʊt/ *noun*

- ► shout
- ► yell
- ► scream
- ► cry
- ► cheer
- ► shriek
- ► screech

shout
the loud sound that someone makes when he or she says something in a very loud voice: *As we got near the stadium, we could hear the shouts of the crowd.* | *I heard a shout from the street and looked out the window to see what was happening.*

yell
yell means the same as **shout** but is more informal: *Mom gave a yell to tell us it was time for dinner.*

scream
a loud high sound that you make when you are frightened or angry: *Did no one notice the screams coming from the apartment next door?*

cry
a short loud shout that you make suddenly, especially because you are hurt, frightened, or excited: *We heard a child's* ***cries for*** *help coming from the river.*

cheer
a shout to show that you like or approve of someone or something: *There were loud* ***cheers from*** *the crowd when Tanya scored a goal.*

shriek
a scream that hurts your ears because it is so loud and high: *With a* ***shriek of*** *delight, she jumped into the swimming pool.*

screech
a very loud high scream that is unpleasant to listen to: *I could hear the screech of children yelling in the playground.*
→ A **screech** can also be the high loud sound that some large birds make: *We heard the screech of an owl outside in the darkness.* You can also use it about the sound that tires on a vehicle make when it stops quickly: *The car stopped suddenly with a screech of tires.*

shove *verb* → see **push¹**, **put**

show¹ /ʃoʊ/ *verb*

1 to let someone see something
- ► show
- ► display
- ► reveal
- ► expose
- ► exhibit

ANTONYMS → see hide

2 to teach someone how to do something by doing it yourself
- ► show
- ► demonstrate

3 to show an emotion
- ► show
- ► display
- ► exhibit (*formal*)

4 to prove that something exists or is true
- ► show
- ► indicate
- ► demonstrate (*formal*)
- ► prove
- ► illustrate

1 to let someone see something

show
to let someone see something: *Pedro showed me his drawings.* | *You have to* ***show*** *your passport* ***to*** *the border guards.*

display (AWL)
to show something to people, or put it in a place where people can see it easily: *Your parking permit must be displayed in your car window.* | *The museum displays Serra's huge artworks in a large well-lighted room.*

reveal (AWL)
to show something that could not be seen before. **Reveal** is usually used in writing: *Marcus lifted the lid of the box to reveal a snake.*

expose (AWL)
to show something that is usually covered or hidden. **Expose** is usually used in writing: *He undid the buttons of his shirt, exposing his hairy chest.*

exhibit (AWL)
to show something such as art in a public place: *Picasso's paintings have been exhibited around the world.*

2 to teach someone how to do something by doing it yourself

show
to teach someone how to do something by

doing it yourself so that he or she can copy you: *Can you* ***show*** *me* ***how*** *to draw a flower? | I'll* ***show*** *you* ***where*** *to put the paper for recycling.*

demonstrate (AWL)
to show someone how to use or do something. **Demonstrate** sounds more formal than **show**, and is used especially when you show a group of people how to do something: *At the event, Alice Carter will* ***demonstrate how*** *to decorate a wedding cake.*
→ see **explain**

3 to show an emotion

show
to let people clearly see your feelings, attitudes, or qualities: *Men do not always find it easy to show their emotions. | The soldiers showed great courage when they went to help their wounded friend.*

display (AWL)
to clearly show a feeling or attitude by what you do or say: *He displayed little interest in his own children.*

exhibit (AWL) *(formal)*
exhibit means the same as **show** but is formal: *She was exhibiting signs of depression.*

4 to prove that something exists or is true

show
to give facts that prove something exists or is true: *Studies* ***show that*** *exercise helps prevent heart disease. | The economy is showing signs that it may be improving.*

indicate (AWL)
to show that something is likely to be true. **Indicate** sounds more formal than **show** and is usually used in writing: *The evidence* ***indicates that*** *the killer was working alone.*

demonstrate (AWL) *(formal)*
demonstrate means the same as **show** and is usually used in official or scientific writing: *Harrison's research clearly* ***demonstrates that*** *the disease can be controlled.*

prove
to show that something is certainly true: *Is there evidence to* ***prove that*** *he carried out the attack?*

illustrate (AWL)
to give an example that shows that something is true or that a situation exists: *I'm telling this story to illustrate how dangerous the drug can be.*
→ You can also say that a fact or situation **illustrates** something: *The increase in test scores illustrates how successful this program has been.*
→ see **express** for **show** meaning "let someone know what you are feeling or thinking," **lead**[1] for **show** meaning "go with someone to help him or her find a place"
→ see **show off** at **brag**
→ see **show up** at **come**

show[2] /ʃoʊ/ *noun*

1 a play, television program, etc.
► **show**
► **performance**
► **production**
► **program**

2 an event for people to go to
► **show**
► **display**
► **exhibition**

1 a play, television program, etc.

show
something people watch on stage or TV, or listen to on the radio. **Show** sounds fairly informal, and you do not usually use it about a performance of classical music, an opera, or a ballet: *Parents and friends came to watch the young musicians and dancers perform in the show. | Danson starred in the TV show "Cheers."*

performance
an occasion when people perform a play or show on stage: *This evening's* ***performance of*** *the play will begin at 8 p.m.*

production
a play, opera, or ballet. You use **production** when you are talking about a play, opera, or ballet being performed by a particular group: *Have you seen the new* ***production of*** *"Romeo and Juliet" at the Arts Center?*

program
a show on television or radio. **Program** sounds more formal than **show**: *"The Simpsons" is still a very popular TV program.*
→ see **play**[2], Topic **Entertainment**

2 an event for people to go to

show
an event where people can see and learn about a special group of things: *The fashion shows are a great place to see all the new styles. | Ellis is attending a computer trade show in Japan.*

display (AWL)
an arrangement of things for people to come and see or learn about: *The library has a display of travel books in the front hall.*
→ You can also use **display** to mean a show of fireworks or lights: *The city has a fireworks display on New Year's Eve.*

exhibition *also* **exhibit** (AWL)
a public show of art or other things, that is in a

S

museum or place where people can go to see it: *There's a new exhibition at the Museum of Science, starting next week.* | *An* ***exhibit of*** *his paintings runs from September 21 at the San Diego Museum of Art.*

shower *noun* → see **party**, **rain**[1], Topic **The Weather**

shriek *noun* → see **shout**[2]

shut[1] *verb* → see **close**[1]

shut[2] *adjective* → see **closed**

shut down *phrasal verb* → see Topic **Computers and the Internet**

shy /ʃaɪ/ *adjective*

- ► shy
- ► bashful
- ► timid
- ► reserved
- ► quiet
- ► introverted (*formal*)
- ► self-conscious

ANTONYMS → see **outgoing**

shy
nervous about meeting people and talking to them: *Amy is a shy child who finds it difficult to make friends.* | *I was* ***shy about*** *meeting him for the first time.*

bashful
shy and easily embarrassed in social situations: *Don't be bashful! Just ask her for a date.*

timid
very shy and not having much courage or confidence: *He was too timid to stand up and say what he was feeling.*

reserved
not willing to show or talk about your feelings: *He is a very reserved man, who thinks that showing emotion is embarrassing.*

quiet
someone who is quiet does not usually say very much: *Anna is very friendly and chatty but her husband is very quiet.*

introverted (*formal*)
an introverted person is quiet and shy, and does not enjoy being with other people: *Parties can be difficult experiences for introverted people.*

self-conscious
worried about what other people think about the way you look or behave: *Dean is very* ***self-conscious about*** *the pimples on his face.*
→ see Topic **Describing People's Character**

ADVERBS
You can make the adjectives **shy**, **bashful**, **timid**, **reserved**, **quiet**, and **self-conscious** into adverbs by using an **-ly** ending: *Amy greeted us shyly.* | *He bashfully asked her to go out with him.* | *She looked self-consciously in the mirror.*

sick /sɪk/ *adjective*

1 having an illness
- ► sick
- ► ill
- ► not feel good
- ► unhealthy

ANTONYMS → see **healthy (1)**

2 feeling that you will vomit
- ► sick
- ► queasy
- ► nauseated (*formal*)

1 having an illness

sick
having a disease or illness: *I got sick and had to stay home.* | *People sometimes need time off work to care for a sick child.*

ill
someone who is ill is sick, especially with something that is fairly serious or dangerous: *The woman is seriously ill and is being treated in the hospital.* | *Several people became ill after eating food in the hotel.*
→ **GRAMMAR:** You do not usually use **ill** before a noun unless it is used with an adverb such as "mentally," "seriously," or "terminally": *Many terminally ill patients want to be cared for at home.*

not feel good *also* **not feel well**
to feel slightly sick. Both **not feel good** and **not feel well** are used in spoken English, but **not feel well** is more formal and can also be used in written English: *I don't feel good. I'm going to go home.* | *Your son wasn't feeling well, so the teacher sent him to the nurse.*

unhealthy
not physically healthy, and often sick: *If you don't exercise or eat well, you become unhealthy.*

2 feeling that you will vomit

sick *also* **sick to your stomach**
feeling that you are going to vomit: *Suddenly she felt sick and dizzy and had to sit down.* | *I feel sick to my stomach. I think I'm going to throw up.*

queasy
having a sick feeling in your stomach and head,

as if you are going to vomit: *Eating that much fried food made me queasy.*

nauseated (*formal*)
feeling that you are going to vomit. **Nauseated** is often used in medical language: *The treatments may leave patients feeling nauseated.*

sickness /ˈsɪknəs/ *noun*

- sickness
- illness
- disease
- condition
- infection

sickness
the state or feeling of being sick: *Cara had to take a day off work due to sickness.*

illness
something wrong with you that makes you feel sick: *The patients in this part of the hospital are suffering from serious illnesses.*
→ **Illness** also means the state of being sick: *Ahmed has missed a lot of school because of illness.*

disease
a serious illness: *More drugs are being developed to fight diseases such as cancer.*

condition
a health problem that affects you for a long time: *Please tell the school if your child has any medical conditions such as asthma.*

infection
an illness that affects a part of your body, usually making it red and sore or swollen. An **infection** is caused by bacteria or a virus: *Kids often get ear and throat infections.*
→ see **medicine**

side /saɪd/ *noun*

- side
- face
- surface

side
a part of something that is not the front, back, top, or bottom: *Your ears are on the side of your head.* | *One of the windows on the side of the house is broken.*
→ **Side** can also mean one of the flat parts on the outside of something, even if the flat part is the front or back of the object: *Sean wrote "Do not drop" on the side of the box.*

face
a side of a mountain, cliff, or tall building: *They climbed up the north face of the mountain.*

surface
one of the sides of an object that has many sides, including the top, bottom, back, and front: *"How many surfaces does a cube have?" "Six."*
→ see **edge**

side

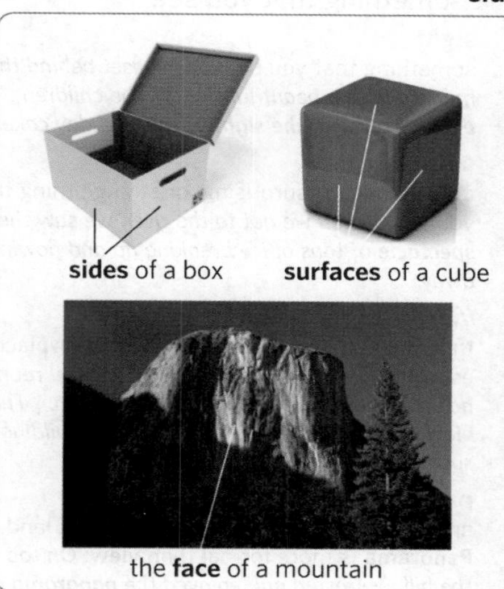

sigh¹ *verb* → see **breathe**

sigh² *noun* → see **breath**

sight /saɪt/ *noun*

1 the ability to see
- sight
- eyesight
- vision (*formal*)

2 something that you see
- sight
- spectacle
- view
- panorama
- scene

1 the ability to see

sight
the ability to see things: *There are five senses: sight, smell, hearing, taste, and touch.* | *He lost his sight when he was very young.*

eyesight
eyesight means the same as **sight**, but you use it mainly with adjectives like "good" and "poor" to describe how well someone can see: *My grandfather does not drive anymore because of his poor eyesight.*

vision (AWL) *(formal)*
vision means the same as **sight** but is used especially in medical language: *She has poor vision.* | *The disease can affect your vision and make it hard to see things clearly.*

2 something that you see

sight
something that you see: *The sunset behind the mountains is a beautiful sight.* | *The children became quiet at **the sight of** the birthday cake.*

spectacle
a very unusual, surprising, or strange thing that you see: *When we got to the river, we saw the **spectacle of** tons of ice breaking up and flowing away.*

view
the area you can see from a window or place, especially when it is beautiful: *The hotel room had a beautiful **view of** the Pacific Ocean.* | *The **view from** the top of the Empire State Building was spectacular.*

panorama
an impressive view over a wide area of land. **Panorama** is more formal than **view**: *On top of the hill, we rested and enjoyed the **panorama of** the mountains stretched out before us.*

scene
the things and people you see in a place, especially when you see people moving around and doing things: *The photograph shows a street scene in New York, about 70 years ago.*
→ see **look**[1], **look**[2], **see**

sightsee *verb* → see Topic **Travel and Vacations**

sightseeing *noun* → see **travel**[2]

sign /saɪn/ *noun*

1 something that gives people information or instructions
- ► sign
- ► notice
- ► poster

2 an event or fact that shows something is true or will happen
- ► sign
- ► indication *(formal)*
- ► symptom
- ► trace

3 a picture or shape that has a particular meaning
- ► sign
- ► symbol
- ► emblem
- ► logo

1 something that gives people information or instructions

sign
a piece of paper, metal, or wood with words or a picture that gives people information, warnings, or instructions: *The sign on the door of the restaurant said "Open."* | *In some parts of Canada, the road signs are in both French and English.*

notice
a piece of paper with information, that someone has put on a wall or door in a public place: *I'll put up a **notice about** the book sale on the bulletin board of the coffee shop.*

poster
a large printed piece of paper that is put on a wall in a public place, and that gives information about something that is going to happen, for example a movie or concert: *At the theater there are old movie posters hanging on the walls.*

2 an event or fact that shows something is true or will happen

sign
an event or fact that shows that something is true or that something will happen: *A score of 80 or more on the physical test is a **sign that** you are very healthy.* | *Clara is only four years old but already shows **signs of** great talent in art.*

indication (AWL) *(formal)*
indication means the same as **sign**: *There are **indications that** we can easily win the election.* | *There was no **indication of** forced entry to the building.*

symptom
a sign that someone has an illness or that a serious problem exists: *Common **symptoms of** diabetes are weight loss and fatigue.* | *Rising crime rates are another **symptom of** a society in trouble.*

trace (AWL)
a very small sign that a particular situation exists or is true: *He tried to look serious, but there was a **trace of** a smile on his face.*

3 a picture or shape that has a particular meaning

sign
a picture or shape that has a particular meaning: *The sign "%" is the percentage sign.* | *Remember to put the dollar sign before the total amount.*

symbol (AWL)
a picture, shape, or design that has a particular meaning or represents an idea: *For many people, a red rose is a **symbol of** love.*

emblem
a picture, shape, or object that represents something such as a country or organization: *The bald eagle is the official **emblem of** the United States.*

logo
a sign that has been designed to represent an organization, company, or product: *His baseball cap has the Yankees baseball team logo on it.*

→ see **signal¹**, **signal²**, **write**

sign

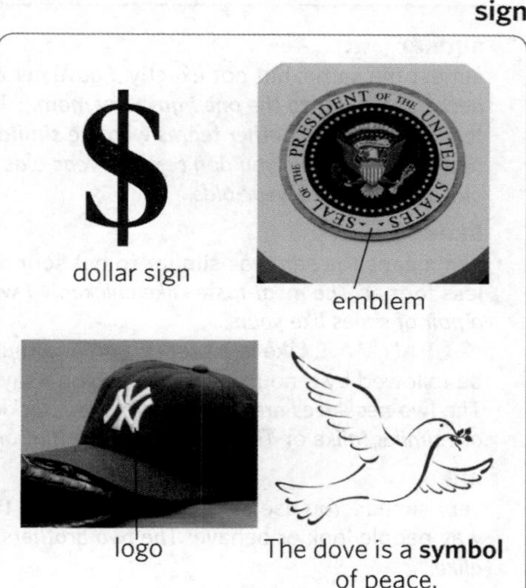

signal¹ /'sɪgnəl/ *noun*

- ► signal
- ► sign
- ► cue

signal
a sound or action that tells someone to do something: *The runners were waiting for the **signal to** start the race. | When I wave my arm, that's the **signal for** you **to** follow me.*

sign
a movement that you make to tell someone something: *I made a sign to say that we were OK.*

cue
an action or event that tells someone it is time to do something. You often use **cue** when people are acting and need to know when to go on stage or do something: *When the customer's water glass is almost empty, that is your **cue to** go to the table and fill the glass. | Andy missed his cue and didn't go on stage at the right time!*

signal² /'sɪgnəl/ *verb*

- ► signal
- ► sign
- ► gesture
- ► indicate
- ► motion

signal
to make a movement or sound that tells someone to do something: *We finished our meal and I **signaled for** the check. | Eduardo **signaled to** the men with a quick whistle, and they all got on their horses.*

sign
to make a movement to tell someone something or ask him or her to do something: *He **signed to** them **to** stay back.*

gesture
to move your hand or head to show or tell someone something: *She **gestured toward** a chair where he could sit. | I **gestured for** him **to** come closer.*

indicate (AWL)
to move your hand to show someone what to do or which direction to look: *The police officer stopped my car and **indicated that** I should lower the window. | "That's her!" he said, indicating a woman on the other side of the room.*

motion
to move your head or hand to show someone what to do, where to go, or what to look at: *She **motioned to** him to be quiet. | "Over here!" he shouted, **motioning toward** the door.*

signature /'sɪgnətʃə/ *noun*

- ► signature
- ► autograph
- ► initials

signature
your name written by you, for example at the end of a letter or on a check: *We need your signature on the contract. | Byron's signature was difficult to read.*

autograph
a famous person's name that he or she writes on something for someone to keep: *Fans surrounded the actor and asked him for his autograph.*

initials
the first letters of each of your names: *If your name is John Patrick Mullen, your initials are J.P.M.*

significance *noun* → see **importance**, **meaning**

S

significant *adjective* → see **important**

silence /ˈsaɪləns/ *noun*

- silence
- quiet
- stillness

ANTONYMS → see **noise**

silence
a situation when there is no sound: *A loud scream broke the silence.* | *She sat in the silence of the small church and prayed.*

quiet
a situation when there is not much noise: *If you're looking for peace and quiet, you'll find it on this island.*

stillness
a situation when nothing is moving or making a sound. **Stillness** is usually used in stories and poems: *Somewhere in the stillness of the night, an owl hooted.*

silent *adjective* → see **quiet**[1]

silly /ˈsɪli/ *adjective*

- silly
- ridiculous
- absurd
- funny

ANTONYMS → see **sensible**

silly
stupid or not sensible: *You're being silly – you can't wear shoes with high heels in the snow.* | *He annoyed me by asking lots of silly questions.*

ridiculous
very silly: *Marc looked ridiculous with his hair sticking up like that.*

absurd
absurd means the same as **ridiculous** but sounds more formal or literary: *It seems absurd to spend so much money on something that is not effective.*

funny
silly in a way that makes people laugh: *He looked funny with a big pink hat on.*
→ see **stupid**

ADVERBS

You can make **ridiculous** and **absurd** into adverbs by using an **-ly** ending: *Marc's hair was sticking up ridiculously.* | *The amounts of money they spent were absurdly large.*

similar /ˈsɪmələ/ *adjective*

- similar
- like
- alike
- close
- equivalent
- comparable
- corresponding
- matching

similar (AWL)
almost the same, but not exactly: *I gave her a necklace **similar to** the one I gave my mom.* | *The teams play against other teams who are **similar in** age, so for example you don't get 10-year-olds playing against 15-year-olds.*

like
like means the same as **similar to** but sounds less formal: *The meat tastes like chicken.* | *I want a pair of shoes like yours.*
→ **GRAMMAR: Like** is a preposition and must be followed by a noun or pronoun. Don't say: ~~*The two necklaces are like*~~. Say: *The two necklaces are similar/alike* or *This necklace is like that one.*

alike
very similar. You use **alike** especially about the way people look or behave: *The two brothers look alike.*
→ **GRAMMAR:** You cannot use **alike** before a noun. Don't say: ~~*We wear alike clothes*~~. Say: *We dress alike.*

close
very similar: *We want to make the movie as **close to** the original as possible.*
→ **GRAMMAR: Close** is not usually used before a noun with this meaning, but you can say that something **is the closest thing to** something: *My mother died when I was little, so my Aunt Ruth was the closest thing to a mother I had.*

equivalent (AWL)
the same in value, level, size, or importance as something of a different type: *The visa costs $25 or the equivalent amount in pesos.* | *People say that one year in the life of a dog is **equivalent to** seven human years.*

comparable
similar to something else in size, number, or quality so that you can easily compare the two things: *An apartment of comparable size costs much less in the suburbs than it costs in the city.*

corresponding (AWL)
relating to or similar to something else that existed in a different time or situation: *Sales in May were 10% higher than in the corresponding period last year.*

matching
similar to something else in color, style, pattern, or material: *She was wearing silver earrings and a matching silver bracelet.*
→ see **same**, **equal**

ADVERBS

You can make the adjectives **similar**, **close**, **equivalent**, **comparable**, and **corresponding** into adverbs by using an **-ly** ending: *The kids were dressed similarly.* | *The plot of the movie follows the book closely.* | *A comparably sized apartment in the suburbs would cost much less.*

similar

The sisters look **alike**.

matching hat and scarf

The two bags are **similar**.

similarity /ˌsɪməˈlærəti/ *noun*

- ► similarity
- ► resemblance
- ► parallel (*formal*)

ANTONYMS → see **difference**

similarity (AWL)
something that is the same about two people or things: ***There are some similarities between the two football players. They are both from Chicago, and they are both very fast.*** | *This part of Oregon has some **similarities to** the French region of Burgundy.*

resemblance
if there is a resemblance between two people or

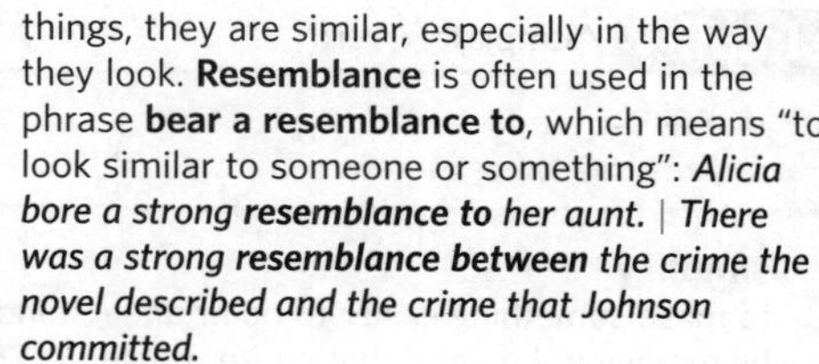

things, they are similar, especially in the way they look. **Resemblance** is often used in the phrase **bear a resemblance to**, which means "to look similar to someone or something": *Alicia bore a strong **resemblance to** her aunt.* | *There was a strong **resemblance between** the crime the novel described and the crime that Johnson committed.*

parallel (AWL) (*formal*)
a similarity between things that happen or exist in different places or times: *There are many interesting **parallels between** the political situation now and the one in the 1970s.*

simile *noun* → see Topic **Books and Literature**

simple /ˈsɪmpəl/ *adjective*

- ► simple
- ► uncomplicated
- ► basic
- ► crude

ANTONYMS → see **complicated**

simple
only having one or a few parts, and not made in a complicated way: *They used hammers, saws, and other simple tools.* | *You can make a simple shelter using a large sheet of plastic and some rope.*

uncomplicated
simple and without a lot of parts or features that could cause problems: *Older cars were uncomplicated and easier to repair than modern cars.*

basic
only having the necessary parts or features, and not able to do anything unusual or complicated: *The farm equipment was old and fairly basic.*

crude
made or done in a simple way that is not very good: *Computers in the 1980s were crude by modern standards.*
→ see **easy** for **simple** meaning "easy to do," **plain** for **simple** meaning "not decorated"

ADVERBS

The adjectives **simple** and **crude** can be made into adverbs by using an **-ly** ending: *The room was simply decorated.* | *They put up a crudely built shelter.*

S

simplify /ˈsɪmpləˌfaɪ/ *verb*

- ► simplify
- ► make something easier

simplify
to make something easier to do or understand, by removing the parts that cause problems: *The company has simplified its payment system.* | *The story has been simplified so that younger children can understand it.*

make something easier
to make something become less difficult or complicated: *Computers have made my job much easier.*

simply *adverb* → see Function Word **only**

sin *noun* → see **evil²**

since *preposition, conjunction* → see Function Word **because**, **for**

sincere *adjective* → see **honest**, **real**

sing /sɪŋ/ *verb*

- ► sing
- ► hum
- ► whistle

sing
to make musical sounds with your voice: *Mike was singing a song he heard on the radio.* | *Birds were singing in the trees.*

hum
to sing a tune with your mouth closed: *Maria hummed as she worked.* | *He hummed a tune to himself.*

whistle
to make musical sounds by blowing air through your lips: *Someone was whistling the song "America the Beautiful."* | *Jack was whistling as he came down the stairs.*
→ see **song**

singer /ˈsɪŋɚ/ *noun*

- ► singer
- ► vocalist
- ► soloist

singer
someone who sings, especially as his or her job: *The singer will perform in several concerts this summer.* | *José Carreras is an opera singer.*

vocalist
someone who sings with a band: *He was one of the vocalists in the group the Grateful Dead.*

soloist
a singer or musician who performs alone: *The director chose a soloist from the members of the choir.*
→ see **musician**, **performer**

single *adjective* → see **only**, Topic **Relationships and Marriage**

sink /sɪŋk/ *verb*

- ► sink
- ► dive
- ► submerge

ANTONYMS → see **float**

sink
if a ship, boat, or other object sinks, it goes down below the surface of water: *If you drop a rock into water, it will sink.* | *The "Titanic" was a ship that hit an iceberg and sank.*

dive
to jump into water with your head and arms going in first: *Martha **dived into** the pool.*

submerge
to make something go under the surface of water: *Floodwater submerged roads and cars.*
→ see **get wet**, **go down**

sister /ˈsɪstɚ/ *noun*

- ► sister
- ► sibling (*formal*)

ANTONYMS → see **brother**

sister
a girl or woman who has the same parents as you: *John has one sister and two brothers.* | *I'm 15, and my little sister is 10.*

sibling (*formal*)
a brother or sister: *Older siblings sometimes take care of their younger brothers and sisters.*

sit /sɪt/ *verb*

- ► sit
- ► sit down
- ► take a seat
- ► sit up
- ► lounge
- ► perch
- ► slump
- ► slouch

ANTONYMS → see **stand**

sit
to have your bottom on something such as a

chair or the ground, with your body upright: *I sit next to Tom in class.* | *Grandpa was sitting in a chair by the fire.*

sit down
to move so that you are sitting on something, after you have been standing up: *I was tired of standing, so I sat down.*

take a seat
to move in order to sit on a chair: *Karen took a seat at the kitchen table.*
→ You can also use **take a seat** as a polite way of telling someone to sit down: *Please take a seat. The doctor will see you in a minute.*

sit up
to move so that you are sitting, after you have been lying down: *Mary sat up in bed and turned on the light.*
→ **Sit up** also means "to sit with your back straight": *Try to sit up straight, and keep your shoulders back.*

lounge
to sit or lie in a place in a very relaxed way without doing much: *He found her out on the porch lounging in a chair.*

perch
to sit on something high up, or on the edge of something: *Mohammed perched on a stool by the sink.*

slump
to sit with the top part of your body leaning forward or sideways: *He was slumped in the chair, fast asleep.*

slouch
to sit or stand with your shoulders bent forward: *Sit up straight – don't slouch!*

site *noun* → see **place¹**

situation /ˌsɪtʃuˈeɪʃən/ *noun*

- situation
- circumstances
- case
- position
- conditions
- scenario

situation
all the things that are happening at a particular time, or the things that are happening in someone's life: *The country's economic situation is very bad.* | *We're **in a difficult situation**, and we're not sure what to do next.*

circumstances
the situation at a particular time, which influences what people do or what can happen: *In some circumstances we will hire people who do not have a college degree.*
→ **Circumstances** can also be used in official language to talk about someone's personal situation, such as whether he or she is married and how much money he or she has: *Please notify us if your circumstances change.*

case
a particular situation. You use **case** to talk about what happens or what someone does in a particular situation: *The flu affects people in different ways. **In** Suzanna's **case**, she got a very bad cough and fever.* | *"I don't need the book anymore." "**In that case**, can I keep it?"*

position
the situation that someone is in, especially when it affects what he or she does: *What would you do if you were in my position?*

conditions
the situation in which someone works or lives, or in which something happens: *The working conditions in some factories are terrible. The buildings are hot, and workers get paid very little.*

scenario (AWL)
a situation that could possibly happen: *If a player breaks the rules, the most likely scenario is that he will have to pay a big fine, but he could be banned from the game.*

sit up *phrasal verb* → see **sit**

size /saɪz/ *noun*

1 how big or small something is physically
- size
- measurements
- dimensions
- area
- volume
- capacity

2 the fact of being very big physically
- size
- extent
- bulk
- magnitude (*formal*)

3 how big or important something is
- size
- scale
- extent
- magnitude (*formal*)

1 how big or small something is physically

size
how big or small something is: *"What size is that*

shirt?" "Large." | Your desk is exactly the same size as mine. | The price will depend on the ***size of*** *the carpet.*

measurements
the exact length, width, or height of something, or of someone's body: *I need to check the* ***measurements of*** *the stove to make sure it will fit in the kitchen.*

dimensions (AWL)
dimensions means the same as **measurements** but sounds more formal. You do not use **dimensions** to talk about someone's body: *What are the* ***dimensions of*** *the table?*

area (AWL)
the amount of space that a flat surface such as a floor or wall covers: *Calculate the* ***area of*** *the walls and ceiling before you buy the paint.*

volume (AWL)
the amount of space that a substance such as a liquid or gas fills: *This instrument measures the* ***volume of*** *air in your lungs.*
→ You can also use **volume** to talk about the amount of a substance that a container will hold: *Help me figure out* ***the volume of*** *this fish tank.*

capacity (AWL)
the amount that a container, vehicle, or structure will hold: *The tank has a* ***capacity of*** *around 500 gallons. | All the flights to Dallas are filled* ***to capacity*** (=as full as possible).
→ see **measure**

2 the fact of being very big physically

size
the fact of being very big: *You should see* ***the size of*** *their house! | The* ***size of*** *the classes makes learning difficult for students.*

extent
the length or size of an area: *The fire covered an area four acres* ***in extent****. | The rope was stretched out* ***to its full extent****.*

bulk (AWL)
the very large size of something, especially something heavy that takes up a lot of space: *The sheer* ***bulk of*** *the statue made it very difficult to move.*

magnitude (*formal*)
the large size of something: *The* ***magnitude of*** *the universe is difficult to imagine.*
→ In scientific writing, **magnitude** is used to describe the size of an earthquake: *The earthquake was a magnitude 5.6 on the Richter scale.*

3 how big or important something is

size
how big or important something is: *I'm not sure he understands* ***the size of*** *the problem. | Economists measure* ***the size of*** *the economy by adding up the value of all the goods and services we produce.*

scale
how big or important something such as a problem or change is, when other similar problems or changes are different sizes: *Scientists are just beginning to understand* ***the scale of*** *the problem.*

extent
how large, important, or serious something is, especially something such as a problem or injury: *Doctors did several tests to determine* ***the extent of*** *his injury.*

magnitude (*formal*)
the large size and importance of something: *We need more people to work on the project, because of* ***the magnitude of*** *the job.*
→ see **amount (1)**, **level**

sketch[1] *noun* → see **drawing**

sketch[2] *verb* → see **draw**

skill /skɪl/ *noun*

- skill
- expertise
- competence
- proficiency

skill
an ability to do something very well because you have learned and practiced it: *He plays the piano* ***with great skill****. | Reagan's* ***skill at*** *talking to the American people made him a popular president.*
→ You can also use **skill** to talk about something you learn to do for a job or activity: *You need computer skills for most office jobs.*

expertise (AWL)
special skills or knowledge that you get from experience: *The doctor has* ***expertise in*** *treating knee injuries.*

competence
the ability and skill to do something, especially a job, in a way that people think is acceptable or good: *The test measures the students'* ***competence in*** *math. | The doctor has made mistakes in surgery, and people are questioning his professional competence.*

proficiency
the ability and skill to do something well because of training and practice: *As you gain* ***proficiency in*** *English, you will be able to speak and write about more difficult subjects.*
→ see **ability**

skilled /skɪld/ *adjective*

- ► skilled
- ► skillful
- ► good
- ► expert
- ► experienced
- ► accomplished
- ► proficient
- ► competent
- ► advanced

skilled
having a lot of training and experience and able to do a job well: *A highly skilled chef can earn a lot of money. | The school counselor is very* ***skilled at*** *working with teenagers.*

skillful
good at doing something, especially something that needs special ability or training: *It took her several years of practice to become a skillful photographer. | He's one of the most skillful players in professional tennis.*

good
able to do something well: *Susie is really* ***good at*** *playing the piano, because she practices every day. | Fortunately he was a good swimmer and managed to swim to shore.*

expert (AWL)
very skillful at doing something because you have a lot of knowledge or experience: *This ski run is very difficult – it is only for expert skiers.*

experienced
good at doing something because you have been doing it for a long time: *Ms. Jiménez is one of our most experienced teachers.*

accomplished
very skillful because you have had a lot of experience doing something. **Accomplished** is used especially about artists or musicians: *His mother is an accomplished painter.*

proficient
able to do something well because of training and practice: *There is only one way to become* ***proficient at*** *math – practice!*

competent
able to do a job in a way that people think is acceptable or good: *Mr. Johnson was a competent lawyer, but not a brilliant one.*

advanced
someone who is advanced has reached a high level in a subject that he or she is studying: *The college offers English classes for elementary, intermediate, and advanced learners.*
→ see Topic **Jobs and Work**

ADVERBS

The adjectives **skillful**, **expert**, **proficient**, and **competent** can be made into adverbs by using an **-ly** ending: *The dancers moved skillfully across the floor. | She skied expertly through the trees.* The adverb for **good** is **well**: *Susie plays the piano very well.*

skillful *adjective*

→ see **talented**, **skilled**

skillfully *adverb*

→ see **well**

skin /skɪn/ *noun*

1 the skin of a person or animal
- ► skin
- ► hide
- ► pelt

2 the skin of a fruit or vegetable
- ► skin
- ► peel
- ► rind
- ► zest

1 the skin of a person or animal

skin
the outer covering of a person's or animal's body: *The skin on his hands was dry and rough. | Snakes grow new skin and shed their old skin one or two times each year.*

hide
the skin of an animal, especially when it is removed to be used for leather: *Native Americans used buffalo hides for their clothing and shelter.*

pelt
the skin of a dead animal with the fur on it: *The hats were made from the pelts of rabbits.*

2 the skin of a fruit or vegetable

skin
the outer covering of some fruits and vegetables, especially when this covering is thin. For example, you use **skin** about the covering on onions and potatoes: *The skin of the baked potato was nice and crispy.*

peel
the thick outer covering on a fruit such as a banana, orange, or apple. You usually use **peel** when you are talking about taking the covering off the fruit: *She threw the banana peel in the garbage.*

rind
the hard outer covering of fruits such as oranges, lemons, or melons, or of vegetables

S

such as squash: *Cut off the rind and slice the melon into cubes.*

zest
the outer layer of the peel of fruits such as oranges, lemons, or limes, used in cooking: *Add a little lemon zest for flavor.*

skinny *adjective* → see **thin**, Topic **Describing People's Looks, Describing Clothes**

skip *verb* → see **jump[1]**, **leave out**, **miss**

sky /skaɪ/ *noun*

- ► sky
- ► air
- ► atmosphere
- ► space

sky
the area above the Earth where you see the sun, clouds, and stars: *It was a summer afternoon and the sky was blue.* | *In the mountains, you can see a lot of stars in the* ***sky*** *at night.*

air
the space that is above the ground or around things: *I kicked the ball up* ***into the air****.* | *The plane flies* ***through the air*** *very fast.*

atmosphere
the mixture of gases that surrounds the earth: *The Earth's atmosphere is made up mostly of nitrogen and oxygen.*

space
the area beyond the earth where the stars and planets are. **Space** is beyond the Earth's atmosphere: *The photograph shows what the Earth looks like* ***from space****.*

slang *noun* → see **language**, **word**

slant /slænt/ *noun*

- ► slant
- ► angle
- ► slope

slant
the fact of something being higher at one end than it is at the other: *The ceiling follows the slant of the roof, so it is higher in the middle of the room.*
→ If something is **at a slant**, it is higher at one end than the other: *The bed is* ***at a slant****, allowing the patient to sit up easily.*

angle
the shape that is formed when two straight lines meet each other. **Angles** are measured by degrees: *Each corner of the triangle has* ***an angle of*** *60 degrees.*
→ If something is **at an angle**, one side or end is higher than the other: *The plane comes down at an angle, with its nose lower than its tail.*

slope
the angle of something that is higher at one end than it is at the other: *The roof of the house has a 20 degree slope.*
→ You can also use **slope** about something that has one end higher than the other: *The skiers raced down the slope.* | *The children rolled cars down the slope to see which car reached the bottom first.*

slanted /ˈslæntɪd/ *adjective*

- ► slanted
- ► sloping
- ► tilted
- ► angled

ANTONYMS → see **flat**, **vertical**

slanted
higher at one end than at the other end: *The room on the top floor of the house has a slanted ceiling.* | *It was an old-fashioned desk with a slanted top.*

sloping
sloping land or surfaces have a slight slant: *The sloping path led down to the river.*

tilted
leaning to one side, not pointing straight up or across: *She was asleep in the chair with her head* ***tilted to*** *one side.*

slanted

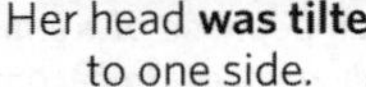
Her head **was tilted** to one side.

a **sloping** field

an **angled** lamp

a **slanted** roof

angled
higher at one end than the other, or forming an angle: *An angled ramp led up to the door.*

SYNONYM CHECK
Slanted or sloping?
Slanted and **sloping** have similar meanings.
Slanted is used especially about things like roofs that have a fairly steep angle.
You can also use **sloping** about roofs, but it is most often used about things such as paths and fields that go downhill at a gentle angle.

slap *verb* → see **hit¹**

sleep¹ /slip/ *verb*

- sleep
- be asleep
- fall asleep
- nap
- doze
- snooze (*informal*)
- oversleep
- hibernate

ANTONYMS → see **wake (1)**

sleep
to rest your mind and body with your eyes closed: *Most people sleep for about eight hours.* | *She looked as if she had slept well.*
→ When saying that someone starts to sleep, use **fall asleep** or **go to sleep**. Don't say: ~~*I usually sleep at 10:00*~~. Say: *I usually go to sleep at 10:00.*

be asleep
to be sleeping now: *The baby is asleep – don't wake her up.*
→ **GRAMMAR:** You cannot use **asleep** before a noun. Don't say: ~~*an asleep boy*~~. Say: *The boy is asleep.*

fall asleep *also* **go to sleep**
to start to sleep: *I was so tired that I fell asleep watching TV.* | *He lay down and went to sleep.*
→ If you want someone to start to sleep, don't say: ~~*Fall asleep*~~! Say: *Go to sleep!*

nap *also* **take a nap**
to sleep for a short time during the day: *I closed my eyes and napped for a few minutes on the airplane.* | *If you are tired, why don't you go upstairs and take a nap?*

doze
to sleep lightly for a short time, often waking up and going back to sleep again, especially when you are not in your bed: *Grandpa was dozing by the fire.*
→ You use **doze off** to say that someone starts to doze: *I dozed off in my chair while we were watching TV.*

snooze (*informal*)
snooze means the same as **nap** but sounds much more informal: *Maria was snoozing on the couch when the doorbell rang.*

oversleep
to sleep for longer than you intended so that you wake up late in the morning: *He overslept and missed his first class.*

hibernate
if an animal hibernates, it sleeps for the whole winter: *Bears must eat a lot of food before they hibernate in their caves.*

sleep² /slip/ *noun*

- sleep
- nap
- doze
- snooze (*informal*)
- slumber (*formal*)
- hibernation

sleep
the state of resting your mind and body with your eyes closed, usually at night: *A noise in the street woke her from a deep sleep.* | *Grandpa died peacefully in his sleep.* | *It's late – why don't you go home and get some sleep?*
→ A **deep sleep** is when you sleep very well and do not wake up easily. A **light sleep** is when you wake easily.

nap
a short sleep during the day: *You will feel much better after you take a nap.* | *I put the baby in his crib for a nap.*

doze
a sleep that lasts for a short time, during which you wake up easily. You use **doze** especially when you are not in your bed: *It was hot in the classroom, and I kept slipping into a doze.*

snooze (*informal*)
snooze means the same as **nap** but sounds much more informal: *Maya is having a little snooze in the back of the car.*

slumber (*formal*)
slumber means the same as **sleep** but is a literary or formal word: *The princess was lying deep in slumber on the bed.*

hibernation
a long sleep for the whole winter, that some animals do in order to stay alive: *During hibernation, an animal's body temperature drops and breathing slows down.*

sleepiness /ˈslipinəs/ *noun*

- ► sleepiness
- ► drowsiness

sleepiness
the feeling of being very tired and wanting to sleep: *Sleepiness is common after eating a big meal.* | *I put the baby down for a nap when he showed signs of sleepiness.*

drowsiness
the feeling of wanting to sleep, often in a situation when it is not appropriate or safe to sleep: *The medication can cause drowsiness, so do not drive while you are taking it.*

sleepy /ˈslipi/ *adjective*

- ► sleepy
- ► drowsy

sleepy
wanting to sleep because you are very tired: *I was too sleepy to study.* | *He carried the sleepy child upstairs to bed.*

drowsy
wanting to sleep, often in a situation when it is not appropriate or safe to sleep: *Mai was feeling hot and drowsy in the back of the car.*

ADVERBS

You can make the adjectives meaning **sleepy** into adverbs by using an **-ly** ending: *The child looked at him sleepily.* | *Andrew waited drowsily in the back of the car.*

slender *adjective* → see **thin**

slice¹ *noun* → see **piece**

slice² *verb* → see **cut¹**

slide /slaɪd/ *verb*

- ► slide
- ► slip
- ► skid
- ► glide
- ► slither

slide
to move smoothly across a surface: *The children were having fun **sliding** around **on** the ice.* | *Several glasses slid off the tray and crashed to the floor.*

slip
to accidentally slide while walking on a smooth surface and fall down or almost fall down: ***I slipped on** the stairs and landed on my back.* | *Running is not allowed by the pool because you might slip and fall.*

skid
if a vehicle skids, it suddenly slides, and it is difficult for the driver to control it: *The car **skidded on** the ice and went off the road.*

glide
to move smoothly and quietly across a surface in a graceful way: *The skaters were **gliding across** the frozen pond.*

slither
to slide close to the ground in a smooth way, twisting or moving from side to side: *A snake **slithered through** the grass.*

slide

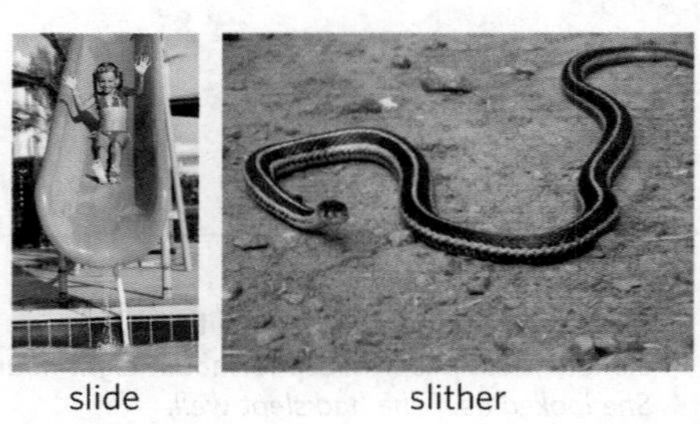
slide slither

slight *adjective* → see **small**

slim *adjective* → see **narrow**, **thin**, Topic **Describing People's Looks**

slip¹ *verb* → see **fall¹**, **put**, **slide**, **trip²**

slip² *noun* → see **mistake¹**, **piece**, **sheet**

slippery /ˈslɪpəri/ *adjective*

- ► slippery
- ► slick

slippery
a slippery surface is so smooth or wet that it is difficult to stand or move safely on it without falling: *Be careful – the floor is very slippery.* | *Drive at slower speeds on slippery roads.*

slick
very slippery. **Slick** is sometimes used when a surface is covered with something slippery like oil or water: *We walked carefully over the slick surface of the rocks.* | *Dario felt very nervous, and his hands were **slick with** moisture.*

slogan *noun* → see **phrase**

slope[1] *noun* → see **slant**

slope[2] *verb* → see **lean**

sloping *adjective* → see **slanted**

sloppy *adjective* → see **messy**

slow /sloʊ/ *adjective*

- slow
- gradual
- unhurried
- sluggish
- leisurely

ANTONYMS → see **fast[1], quick**

slow
not moving quickly or not doing something quickly: *My computer is really slow compared to the ones at school. | I was always one of the slowest runners in my class. | Service at the restaurant was slow – we had to wait 30 minutes for our food.*

gradual
happening slowly over a long period of time. You use **gradual** about changes, increases, and improvements: *Her teacher has noticed a gradual improvement in her writing. | Over the past 100 years, there has been a gradual increase in temperatures on the earth.*

unhurried
moving or doing something in a slow and calm way, without rushing at all. **Unhurried** is used especially in writing: *The island is peaceful, with an unhurried pace of life.*

sluggish
moving or reacting more slowly than usual, especially because someone or something does not have enough power or energy: *The car felt sluggish as we drove up the hill. | The morning after the party I felt sluggish and tired.*

leisurely
moving or doing something slowly, especially because you are enjoying what you are doing and do not have to hurry. **Leisurely** is used especially in writing: *We had a leisurely lunch in the garden.*

ADVERBS

You can make the adjectives **slow, gradual, unhurried**, and **sluggish** into adverbs by using an **-ly** ending: *She ran slowly across the finish line. | Gradually, there was an improvement in her writing. | I got out of bed sluggishly.*

slow down /ˌsloʊ ˈdaʊn/ *phrasal verb*

- slow down
- brake
- reduce speed (*formal*)

ANTONYMS → see **fast[1] (3)**

slow down
to move or do something more slowly: *Drivers should slow down when they are near schools. | We should have been here hours ago, but the rain slowed us down. | At the end of the song, she slowed down and sang more quietly.*

brake
to make a bicycle, car, or other vehicle go more slowly or stop by using its brakes: *The car in front of me suddenly stopped, and I braked hard.*

reduce speed (*formal*)
to drive more slowly than before. **Reduce speed** is used especially in road signs or in official instructions: *Reduce your speed as you go through the construction area.*

slowly /ˈsloʊli/ *adverb*

- slowly
- gradually
- at low speed

ANTONYMS → see **quickly**

slowly
at a slow speed: *She was walking slowly and carefully up the stairs. | Doctors slowly removed the bandages from Kendra's arm.*

gradually
slowly, over a long period of time. You use **gradually** about changes, increases, and improvements: *I practiced the piano every day, and I gradually got better. | Many of our forests are gradually disappearing.*

at low speed
more slowly than usual. You use **at low speed** about the movement of a vehicle or machine: *A car was coming in our direction at low speed.*

small /smɔl/ *adjective*

1 not large in size (adjectives)
- ► small
- ► little
- ► tiny
- ► low
- ► miniature
- ► compact
- ► minute
- ► microscopic
- ► minuscule

ANTONYMS → see **big** (**1**), **big** (**2**)

2 not large in amount or number (adjectives)
- ► small
- ► low
- ► tiny
- ► minuscule
- ► minute
- ► meager

ANTONYMS → see **big** (**3**)

3 not important or not having a large effect (adjectives)
- ► small
- ► slight
- ► little
- ► minor
- ► superficial

ANTONYMS → see **big** (**4**), **important** (**1**)

4 to become smaller (verbs)
- ► get smaller
- ► shrink
- ► shrivel
- ► contract

ANTONYMS → see **increase**[1] (**1**), **grow** (**1**)

1 not large in size (adjectives)

small
not large in size: *It is easier to drive a small car in the city.* | *These shoes are too small for me.* | *A small woman with straight dark hair was in the kitchen.*

little
small in size: *The little boy was walking home from school.* | *The cake was decorated with little flowers.*
→ **Little** is often used with other adjectives to describe someone or something small, and shows that you like the person or thing: *What a cute little kitten!* | *They bought a nice little house near the beach.*

tiny
very small: *Have you seen her apartment? It is tiny.* | *He touched the tiny fingers of the baby.*

low
not high, or not far above the ground. You use **low** about things such as mountains or walls: *The kids built a low wall around the sandcastle.*

miniature
much smaller than the usual size. You use **miniature** especially about things that are made to look just like something larger: *The children made miniature houses out of cardboard.*

compact
small, but comfortable, convenient, or easy to carry: *The kitchen in the apartment was perfect – compact but with everything we needed.* | *I want a compact camera that will fit easily in my pocket.*

minute
very small and difficult to see: *Many larger fish eat these minute shrimp.*

microscopic
extremely small and impossible to see without a scientific tool called a microscope: *Your body contains trillions of microscopic cells, for example skin cells or blood cells.*

minuscule
extremely small, especially in a way that seems surprising: *Compared to its adult size, a newborn kangaroo is minuscule.*
→ see Topic **Describing Size**, **Describing Places**

2 not large in amount or number (adjectives)

small
not large in amount or number: *Only a small number of people came to the meeting.* | *The water contained small quantities of dangerous chemicals.*

low
small in amount, or less than the usual amount. **Low** is used especially about prices, rents, and levels: *People on low incomes are finding it difficult to pay for gas.* | *It is a safe neighborhood, and the crime rate is low.*

tiny
a tiny amount or number is very small: *Millions of people buy lottery tickets, but only a tiny number of them ever win anything.*

minuscule
extremely small, especially in a way that seems surprising: *The risks of flying are minuscule compared to the risks of driving.*

minute
a minute amount is extremely small, and often so small that it makes very little difference to something: *The amount of blood on her shoe was*

minute, but scientists were still able to say that it belonged to the murdered man.

meager
very small in amount and much less than you need. You use **meager** to talk about food or things relating to money: *Her meager earnings as a cleaner are barely enough to feed her family.*

3 not important or not having a large effect (adjectives)

small
not important or not having a large effect: *We may have to make a few small changes. | There is only a small difference between the two prices.*

slight
small and not very important or noticeable: *The doctor says there has been a slight improvement in her condition. | There was a slight smile on his face.*

little
little means the same as **slight** but sounds more informal: *Nick gave a little nod of his head. | The program has had little effect on poverty in the area.*

minor (AWL)
not important enough or serious enough to worry about: *We have made some minor changes to the schedule.*

superficial
not serious or important and not having much effect on the way something works: *Fortunately her injuries were not serious – they were just superficial cuts and bruises.*

> **ADVERBS**
> You can make the adjectives **slight** and **superficial** into adverbs by using an **-ly** ending: *The doctor says her condition has improved slightly. | The building was only superficially damaged in the earthquake.*

4 to become smaller (verbs)

get smaller
to become less large in size or amount: *Computers are getting smaller, faster, and more powerful all the time. | My family drove away, and I watched as their car got smaller and smaller.*

shrink
to get smaller. Use **shrink** especially about clothes that become smaller when you wash them in hot water or dry them in a hot dryer: *Do you think this sweater will shrink if I wash it?*
→ You can also use **shrink** to talk about numbers or amounts that get smaller, especially when you do not want them to. This meaning is used especially in journalism: *States will have to cut many programs as their budgets continue to shrink.*

shrivel *also* **shrivel up**
if something shrivels, it becomes smaller because it is dry or old. Use **shrivel** especially about something such as a plant or a fruit: *Eventually the grapes will shrivel and become raisins. | The plants were beginning to shrivel up in the heat.*

contract (AWL)
contract means the same as **get smaller**, but sounds more formal and is used especially in science or business: *Metal contracts as it cools. | The economy has contracted by 3% since last year.*
→ see **decrease²**

smart /smɑrt/ *adjective*

1 smart – used about a person
- ► smart
- ► intelligent
- ► bright
- ► brilliant
- ► gifted
- ► wise
- ► quick
- ► sharp
- ► clever
- ► shrewd
- ► intellectual

ANTONYMS → see **stupid**

2 smart – used about ideas, actions, or things
- ► smart
- ► intelligent
- ► brilliant
- ► ingenious
- ► wise
- ► shrewd
- ► intellectual

1 smart – used about a person

smart
able to learn and understand things quickly: *Diego is so smart. He'll probably become either a doctor or a lawyer. | She is a smart girl, and she works hard at school.*

intelligent (AWL)
intelligent means the same as **smart** but is more formal: *Dolphins are very intelligent animals that can be easily trained to do tricks.*

bright
able to learn and understand things quickly. Use **bright** especially about children and young

S

people: *Spencer is a bright kid – I'm sure he'll do well in kindergarten.*

brilliant
extremely smart and good at the work that you do: *The case was won by a brilliant young lawyer from Memphis.*

gifted
having a higher level of intelligence than most people, and likely to do well in school: *Some of the high school's gifted students also attend classes at the community college nearby.*

wise
able to make good decisions and give sensible advice, especially because you have a lot of experience: *As I became older and wiser, I realized that I had made many mistakes.*

quick
able to learn new things and react quickly: *Jen is so quick – she has a funny answer for everything!*

sharp
smart and able to notice and understand things quickly so that you are not easily tricked or confused: *A sharp salesman knows how to get you to buy the car at the right price.*

clever
smart and good at thinking of new ideas or ways of doing things. You often use **clever** about people who are good at thinking of new ways to do bad things: *The thief was clever enough to avoid being caught by the police for six years.*

S

shrewd
good at understanding situations or people and at making decisions to get what you want: *Sachs was a shrewd judge of character and chose his staff well.*

intellectual
smart and interested in thinking and talking about serious ideas: *Mark is very intellectual and prefers reading literature to watching TV.*

2 smart – used about ideas, actions, or things

smart
a smart idea or action is good or sensible and shows that someone used his or her intelligence: *It was **smart to** call first to see if the store was open before driving all the way there.* | *She is a young businesswoman with a lot of smart ideas.*

intelligent (AWL)
an intelligent idea, question, decision, etc. is done by someone who has thought about the subject carefully and understands it well: *After the lecture, Amanda asked some intelligent questions.*

brilliant
brilliant ideas are very good and show a lot of intelligence and imagination: *Sandra came up with a brilliant plan to raise money for the school.*

ingenious
an ingenious thing or method works very well or solves a problem that nothing else solves, and is usually designed in an intelligent way: *This ingenious gadget chops onions without making your eyes water.*

wise
a wise idea or action is sensible and shows that someone has learned from his or her experiences: *It was **wise to** leave when you did, because you avoided a fight.*

shrewd
a shrewd decision or choice is likely to be right because the person who makes it is good at understanding situations or people: *Charles made some shrewd investments when he was young, and now he has so much money that he doesn't have to work.*

intellectual
relating to serious ideas or subjects that interest intelligent people: *There aren't many TV shows on intellectual subjects, but this news and opinion show often makes me think more deeply about things.*

ADVERBS

You can make the adjectives **intelligent**, **brilliant**, **wise**, **ingenious**, **clever**, and **shrewd** into adverbs by using an **-ly** ending: *The young lawyer argued the case brilliantly.* | *It is an ingeniously designed machine.* | *Charles has invested his money shrewdly.*

smart person /ˌsmɑrt ˈpɚsən/ *noun phrase*

► **genius**
► **intellectual**
► **brain** (*informal*)

genius
someone who has much more intelligence, ability, or skill than is usual: *Albert Einstein was a genius whose scientific work has had a huge influence.*

intellectual
an intelligent person who is interested in serious subjects or complicated ideas: *Keynes was a British intellectual who came up with his economic ideas during the Great Depression.*

brain (*informal*)
someone who is very smart, especially someone who does very well in school: *Susan always gets A's – she is a real brain.* | *We need the country's best brains to go into the field of medicine.*

smash *verb* → see **break**[1]

smell[1] /smel/ *noun*

1 something you recognize with your nose
- ► smell
- ► whiff

2 a good smell
- ► scent
- ► aroma
- ► fragrance
- ► perfume (*formal*)

3 a bad smell
- ► smell
- ► odor
- ► stench
- ► stink

1 something you recognize with your nose

smell
the quality that you recognize by using your nose: *What is that smell? Is something burning?* | *I love the smell of roses.*

whiff
a smell of something that you notice for only a short time: *There was a whiff of lavender in the air from the gardens nearby.*

2 a good smell

scent
a pleasant smell: *The candles give off a scent like flowers.* | *We walked through the forest, breathing in the scent of the pines.*

aroma
a strong pleasant smell, especially from food or drinks: *The aroma of fresh bread filled the kitchen.*

fragrance
a very pleasant smell. You use **fragrance** about the smell of sweet things such as flowers or fruit: *The fragrance of the flowering trees drifted in the window.*

perfume (*formal*)
a pleasant sweet smell: *In the garden, the perfume of the jasmine flowers was strong.*
→ see **perfume**

3 a bad smell

smell
an unpleasant smell: *The smell is coming from the refrigerator.* | *I cleaned the whole garage, but the smell is still there.*

odor
a strong unpleasant smell that is easy to recognize: *The spray is supposed to get rid of household odors, such as the smell of dogs or old cooking smells.*

stench
a very strong unpleasant smell: *The meat was decaying, and the stench made him feel sick to his stomach.*

stink
stink means the same as **stench** but is a little more informal: *The stink of rotting fish near the harbor was horrible.*

smell[2] /smel/ *verb*

1 to have a smell
- ► smell
- ► stink
- ► give off

2 to use your nose to recognize a smell
- ► smell
- ► sniff
- ► catch a whiff of (*informal*)

1 to have a smell

smell
to have a smell: *That fried chicken smells good!* | *The room **smells like** flowers.* | *Her breath **smelled of** peppermint.*
→ You can use **smell** without anything after it to say that something smells bad: *The milk spoiled and now the whole kitchen smells.*

stink
to have a very strong bad smell: *How can you eat that cheese? It stinks!*

give off
to produce a particular smell: *The old books gave off a slightly moldy smell.*

2 to use your nose to recognize a smell

smell
to notice the smell of something, especially by putting your nose near it: *I could smell her perfume from across the room.* | *Smell this spice, and tell me what you think it is.*

sniff
to breathe quickly in through your nose in order to smell something: *He sniffed his shirt and decided to put it in the wash.*

catch a whiff of *also* **get a whiff of** (*informal*)
to notice a smell, just for a short time: *Marta caught a whiff of apple pie coming from the kitchen.*

S

smelly /ˈsmeli/ *adjective*

- ► smelly
- ► stinky (*informal*)
- ► stinking
- ► stale
- ► musty
- ► pungent (*formal*)

smelly
having a bad smell: *Don't leave your smelly sneakers in the living room.* | *The inside of the car was dirty and smelly.*

stinky (*informal*)
having a strong bad smell: *Put your stinky running clothes in the washing machine!*

stinking
having a very strong bad smell. **Stinking** is used more in writing than **smelly** or **stinky**: *Flies buzzed around the stinking garbage cans.*

stale
having an unpleasant smell that is no longer fresh: *The curtains held a stale smell of cigarette smoke and sweat.*

musty
having an unpleasant wet smell: *The basement apartment was dark and musty.*

pungent (*formal*)
having a strong sharp smell: *The pungent smell of sulfur told her that the eggs were rotten.*

ADVERBS

You can change the adjective **pungent** into an adverb by using an **-ly** ending: *The shop smelled pungently of unusual spices.*

smile[1] /smaɪl/ *verb*

- ► smile
- ► grin
- ► beam
- ► smirk

ANTONYMS → see **frown**

smile
to raise the corners of your mouth because you are happy or being friendly: *A cute girl smiled at me, but I was too shy to say hello.* | *Let's take another picture, and smile this time!*

grin
to give a big smile, especially because you are very happy: *Ted was grinning all day after he heard the good news.*

beam
to smile in a very happy way for a long time because you are very pleased or proud: *Alex's parents beamed when he accepted the award.*

smirk
to smile in a way that is not nice, for example because you are pleased by someone else's bad luck: *The other girls looked at her old clothes and smirked.*

smile[2] /smaɪl/ *noun*

- ► smile
- ► grin
- ► smirk

ANTONYMS → see **frown**

smile
a happy expression on your face in which the corners of your mouth curve up: *Ina has a perfect teeth and a beautiful smile.* | *Mr. Ko welcomed his guests with a warm smile.*

grin
a big smile: *We knew by Dan's grin that he had passed the test.*

smirk
a smile that is not nice, for example when you are pleased by someone else's bad luck: *He had an arrogant smirk on his face as he walked to the front of the line.*

smoke[1] /smoʊk/ *noun*

- ► smoke
- ► smog
- ► fumes
- ► exhaust

smoke
the white, gray, or black gas that comes from something when it burns: *People could see the smoke from the fire from a mile away.* | *The cigarette smoke burned Joe's eyes and made him cough.*

smog
dirty air caused by smoke from cars and factories in cities: *Most days, there is a layer of brown smog hanging over Los Angeles.*

fumes
strong-smelling gas or smoke that is unpleasant or dangerous to breathe in: *The air in the city was filled with diesel fumes from the buses and cars.*

exhaust
the gas that is produced when a machine such as a car is working: *Car exhaust is damaging to the environment.*

→ see **fire[1]**

S

smoke² /smoʊk/ *verb*

1 to breathe in smoke
► smoke
► inhale
2 to produce smoke
► smoke
► smolder

1 to breathe in smoke

smoke
to light a cigarette or pipe and breathe in the smoke: *If you're going to smoke, at least open a window.* | *Several men stood outside the building, smoking cigarettes.*

inhale
to breathe in once when you are smoking a cigarette: *Vivien lit another cigarette and inhaled deeply.*
→ see **breathe**

2 to produce smoke

smoke
to produce smoke: *The fire was out but parts of the building were smoking.* | *The car's engine was smoking.*

smolder
to burn slowly with smoke but no flames: *The green plants smoldered but did not catch fire.*
→ see **burn (1)**

smooth /smuð/ *adjective*

► smooth
► sleek
► silky
ANTONYMS → see **rough**

smooth
having a surface that is nice to touch, with no rough parts, raised parts, or holes: *The pond was covered with a smooth sheet of ice.* | *Grandpa is bald, and the top of his head is completely smooth.*

sleek
having a smooth, attractive, and often shiny surface. You use **sleek** especially about hair, fur, material, or metal: *She was dressed in a sleek black dress and expensive shoes.*

silky
soft and smooth, and often shiny like silk cloth. You use **silky** about hair, fur, skin, or material: *Lisa stroked the cat's silky fur.*
→ see **flat**, Topic **Describing Texture**

ADVERBS
You can make the adjectives **smooth** and **sleek** into adverbs by using an **-ly** ending: *Apply the paint smoothly to the surface.* | *Her hair was combed back sleekly in a bun.*

snack *noun* → see **food**, **meal**

snooze¹ *verb* → see **sleep¹**

snooze² *noun* → see **sleep²**

snore *verb* → see **breathe**

snow¹ /snoʊ/ *noun*

1 frozen water that comes from the sky
► snow
► snowflake
► slush
► sleet
► hail
► frost
2 when snow falls from the sky
► snow
► snowfall
► flurry
► snowstorm
► blizzard
► frost

1 frozen water that comes from the sky

snow
soft white pieces of frozen water that fall from the sky when it is very cold: *Outside snow was falling silently.* | *It was easy to follow the footprints in the snow.*

snowflake
one soft white piece of frozen water that falls from the sky when it is very cold: *A snowflake landed on the tip of her nose and melted.*

slush
snow on the ground that has started to melt: *Temperatures rose and the streets were filled with slush.*

sleet
a mixture of snow and rain that falls from the sky: *The sleet on the highway is making driving very dangerous.*

hail
hard round pieces of ice that fall from the sky: *Hail bounced off the roof onto the lawn.*

frost
a white powder of ice that covers things that are outside when it is very cold: *The grass and trees*

in the park were white with frost.
→ see **rain¹**

2 when snow falls from the sky

snow
a time when snow falls from the sky: *The first snow of the season often takes drivers by surprise. | There will be snow tonight in northern parts of the state.*

snowfall
snowfall means the same as **snow** but sounds more formal. **Snowfall** is used especially in reports about the weather: *We are expecting heavy snowfall, so drive carefully. | The mountain gets an average annual snowfall of 210 inches.*

flurry *also* **snow flurry**
a time when a small amount of snow falls and blows around: *There were snow flurries last night, but there was no snow on the ground this morning.*

snowstorm
a storm with wind and a lot of snow: *Flights were canceled because of the snowstorm.*

blizzard
a very bad snowstorm with very strong wind and a lot of snow: *Suddenly we were driving in a blizzard and couldn't see anything in front of the car.*

frost
the weather conditions when it is cold enough for water to freeze outside, especially at night when the temperature is lowest: *Even in May we can sometimes get a late frost.*
→ see **rain¹**, **storm**, Topic **The Weather**

snow² /snoʊ/ *verb*

- ► it snows
- ► it sleets
- ► it hails
- ► fall
- ► come down

it snows
if it snows, soft white pieces of frozen water fall from the sky when it is very cold: *If it snows a lot, maybe school will be canceled. | It is so cold that it feels like it might snow.*

it sleets
if it sleets, rain and snow fall from the sky at the same time: *It was sleeting hard, and we could barely see the road ahead of us.*

it hails
if it hails, hard round pieces of ice fall from the sky: *It started hailing, and a lot of crops were damaged.*

fall
if snow falls, it comes from the sky onto the ground: *The snow began to fall; it was so beautiful.*

come down
come down means the same as **fall** but sounds more informal: *The snow was coming down hard, so we decided to go home.*
→ see **rain²**

GRAMMAR CHECK: snow

When you are talking about **snow**, **sleet**, or **hail** that is falling right now, don't say: ~~*It snows/sleets/hails.*~~ Say: *It is snowing/sleeting/hailing.*

so *conjunction* → see Function Words

soak *verb* → see **wash**, **wet (2)**

sob *verb* → see **cry¹**

social /ˈsoʊʃəl/ *adjective*

- ► social
- ► public
- ► popular
- ► civic

social
relating to the people in a society and the way they live: *High unemployment often leads to more social problems. | Social changes in the 1960s and 1970s gave women more freedom.*

public
relating to all the people in an area or country: *Public opinion about nuclear energy has changed since the accident* (=the way people think about nuclear energy has changed).

popular
involving many or most of the people in a society or group: *The new president has a lot of popular support.*

civic
relating to being a citizen of a country or state: *It is your civic duty to vote.*
→ You can also use **civic** to talk about things that are related to a city, the people who live in it, or its government: *Last night there was a meeting of civic and religious leaders at City Hall.*

GRAMMAR CHECK: social

Social is usually used before a noun, and **public**, **popular**, and **civic** are always used before a noun. Don't say: ~~*the opinion is public.*~~ Say: *public opinion.*

ADVERBS

You can make the adjectives **social**, **popular**, and **civic** into adverbs by using an **-ly** ending: *This is a socially conservative town.* | *The singer is popularly known as Shanta.* The adverb **publicly** is not used in this meaning.

society /səˈsaɪəti/ *noun*

- society
- community
- civilization
- culture

society
all the people who live in a country, and the way they live: *Education is important for the success of a democratic society.* | *As a society, we no longer approve of smoking.*

community
all the people who live in the same town or area: *The new recreation center will be open to the whole community.*

civilization
a society that is well organized and developed: *The ideas from the ancient Greek and Roman civilizations still affect the way we live today.*

culture (AWL)
the way people in a society live and the ideas they have: *In American culture, it is rude to ask people how much money they earn.*
→ see **organization**, **people**

soft /sɔft/ *adjective*

1 not hard and nice to touch
- soft
- fluffy
- silky
- velvety

2 not hard or firm
- soft
- limp
- floppy
- squishy
- tender

ANTONYMS → see **hard**

1 not hard and nice to touch

soft
not hard, sharp, or rough, and nice to touch: *Use a soft cloth to polish the silver spoons and forks.* | *Your hair is so soft. Do you wash it every day?*

fluffy
covered in soft light threads, fur, or feathers: *She held the fluffy little chick in her hands.*

silky
soft and smooth, and often shiny, like silk cloth. You use **silky** about hair, fur, skin, or material: *Ronald was stroking the cat's silky fur.*

velvety *also* **like velvet**
with a thick soft smooth surface, like velvet cloth. **Velvety** and **like velvet** are used especially in literature and stories: *The rocks by the river are covered with velvety moss.* | *The baby's skin was like velvet.*
→ see **smooth**

2 not hard or firm

soft
a soft substance is not hard or firm, but is easy to press or make a mark on: *The clay is soft and easy to work with.* | *The foam mattress made the bed really soft.*

limp
if something is limp, it is not as stiff or firm as it should be: *Carolyn passed out and her whole body went limp.* | *The lettuce was limp and not crisp.*

floppy
soft and hanging loosely down: *The woman's large floppy sun hat flapped in the breeze.*

squishy
very soft, wet, and easy to press: *I could feel the squishy mud on the bottom of the lake between my toes.*

tender
tender food is soft and easy to cut or eat: *Boil the potatoes until they are tender.*
→ see Topic **Describing Texture**

ADVERBS

You can make the adjectives **limp** and **floppy** into adverbs by using an **-ly** ending: *Carolyn fell limply to the floor.* | *The dog's ear hung floppily over its eye.*

soften /ˈsɔfən/ *verb*

- soften
- get soft

ANTONYMS → see **harden**

soften
to become less hard, firm, or rough: *The cream will help to soften your skin.* | *The leather in the shoes will soften as you wear them.*

get soft
get soft means the same as **soften** but is less formal: *Boil the beans until they get soft.*

S

software *noun* → see Topic **Computers and the Internet**

soil *noun* → see **dirt**

soldier /ˈsoʊldʒɚ/ *noun*

- ► soldier
- ► troops
- ► service member
- ► officer
- ► warrior

soldier
someone in the army, especially someone who is not an **officer**: *Three soldiers were injured in the bomb attack.* | *Soldiers with guns guarded the entrance to the embassy.*

troops
people in the military: *American troops started coming home soon after the war ended.*
→ **Troop** is not usually used in the singular form, unless you are a member of the military.

service member *also* **serviceman** *or* **servicewoman**
a person in the military. **Service member** sounds formal and is often used in official speeches or reports: *The number of service members killed or missing in the war continues to rise.* | *The monument honors all the servicemen and women who fought in the war.*

officer
someone who has an important position in the army, navy, air force, or marines, and who is in charge of a group of service members: *The officer told the soldiers to wait for his command to fire their weapons.*

warrior
a person who fights bravely in a war. **Warrior** is a literary word: *The mighty warriors protected the kingdom from the invaders.*
→ see **army**, **military**

SYNONYM CHECK
Soldier, troops, or service member?

To people who are in the military, **soldier** means only "a person who is in the army."

Service member can be used about someone in the army, navy, air force, or marines.

Troops can also be used for people in all the different armed forces, but it is not usually used to mean one person.

sole *adjective* → see **only**

solid *adjective* → see **hard**, **pure**

solution *noun* → see **answer²**, **liquid**, **mixture**

solve /sɑlv/ *verb*

1 to think of the correct answer or explanation
- ► solve
- ► find an answer
- ► figure out

2 to successfully deal with a problem
- ► solve
- ► find a solution
- ► resolve (*formal*)
- ► work something out

1 to think of the correct answer or explanation

solve
to think of the correct answer or explanation for something that is difficult to understand: *Police are asking for help in solving the murder case.* | *You need to use math to solve the puzzle.*

find an answer *also* **find an explanation**
to think about a problem or question and use the information you have to find the correct reason to explain it: *Nobody understands why young people are getting the disease, but scientists are trying to find the answer.* | *They haven't* ***found an explanation for*** *why the birds suddenly died.*

figure out
figure out means the same as **find an answer**, but sounds more informal and is used more in spoken English: *I could not figure out why he would do that - it was so weird.* | *The math problem was hard, but I finally figured it out.*

2 to successfully deal with a problem

solve
to successfully deal with a problem so that the problem goes away: *The pipes were leaking under the sink, so Dad tightened them and that seemed to solve it.* | *Congress needs to try some new ideas to solve the unemployment problem.*

find a solution *also* **come up with a solution**
to think of a way to solve a large complicated problem: *Until both sides agree to discuss the issue, they will never find a solution.* | *The neighbors worked together to* ***come up with a solution to*** *the graffiti problem.*

resolve (AWL) (*formal*)
to do something that ends a problem or disagreement: *The leaders hope to resolve the conflict by discussion rather than war.*

work something out
if two people or groups work something out, they end a disagreement by finding a solution that satisfies everyone: *If the kids are fighting, sometimes it is best to let them work it out themselves.*

some *adjective, pronoun* → see Function Words

sometimes /ˈsʌmtaɪmz/ *adverb*

- ► sometimes
- ► at times
- ► occasionally
- ► on occasion (*formal*)
- ► once in a while
- ► now and then
- ► from time to time
- ► every so often

sometimes
on some occasions, but not always: *Sometimes I walk to school, and sometimes I ride my bike.* | *Carla sometimes doesn't understand what the teacher says.*

at times
at times means the same as **sometimes** but sounds more formal: *At times, we worried that we could not finish the project on time.*

occasionally
sometimes, but not often: *Occasionally we go to a restaurant, but mostly we eat at home.*

on occasion (*formal*)
on occasion means the same as **occasionally** but sounds formal or literary: *The bone she had broken in her leg years ago still hurt on occasion.*

once in a while
sometimes, but not regularly or often: *I only play video games once in a while. I would rather play sports.*

now and then *also* **now and again**
now and then and **now and again** mean the same as **once in a while**: *It is fun to go hiking now and then.* | *Dad still smokes now and again, but he is trying to quit.*

from time to time
from time to time means the same as **once in a while**: *Even experienced doctors make mistakes from time to time.*

every so often *also* **every once in a while** *or* **every now and then**
sometimes, at fairly regular periods, but not very often: *The dog barked every so often, breaking the silence.* | *Every once in a while we stay in and watch a movie.* | *The coach yells at the kids every now and then, but he is generally very nice.*

song /sɔŋ/ *noun*

1 a piece of music with words
- ► song
- ► lullaby
- ► national anthem
- ► hymn
- ► carol

2 part of a song
- ► verse
- ► chorus

1 a piece of music with words

song
a short piece of music with words that you sing: *What song are you singing? It is really pretty.* | *I love that song, but I can never remember the words.*

lullaby
a quiet slow song that you sing to small children to make them go to sleep: *Tina hummed a lullaby as she rocked the baby.*

national anthem
a song used to represent a particular country, especially one with words that praise the country: *The fans stand up to sing the national anthem before the game.*

hymn
a song that people sing in Christian churches: *The pastor asked everyone to stand to sing the hymn.*

carol
a song that people sing at Christmas: *We stood around the piano singing Christmas carols.*

2 part of a song

verse
one of the parts of a song that is repeated with the same tune but different words each time: *The song has three verses, but we only sang the first two.* | *The first verse starts with the words, "Oh beautiful, for spacious skies ..."*

chorus
the part of a song that is repeated between each verse. The **chorus** has the same words every time you sing it: *Everybody started singing when we got to the chorus.*
→ see **music**

S

soon /sun/ adverb

- ► soon
- ► shortly
- ► before long
- ► in a minute
- ► in the near future

soon
after a short time: *It will be dark soon.* | *The guests arrived sooner than I expected.*

shortly
shortly means the same as **soon** but sounds more formal: *Her last novel was published shortly after her death.*

before long
fairly soon, and not a very long time later: *Don't worry – I'm sure he will be back before long.* | *Before long, the company had increased its sales by 70%.*

in a minute *also* **in a moment**
very soon, and within a few minutes from now: *The coffee will be ready in a minute.*

in the near future
in a few years or months from now, although you do not know exactly when: *Scientists may find a cure for the disease in the near future.*

S

sophisticated /səˈfɪstəˌkeɪtɪd/ adjective

- ► sophisticated
- ► worldly
- ► experienced

ANTONYMS → see **naive**

sophisticated
knowing a lot about things such as art, culture, and fashion: *Her friends all seemed very sophisticated as they talked about the latest novels they had read.* | *Jazz and classical music appeal to a sophisticated audience.*

worldly
having a lot of experience about life and dealing with people. A **worldly** person is not easily shocked when other people behave badly: *The other students were much older and more worldly than I was.*

experienced
knowing a lot about a situation because you have done it or dealt with it for a long time: *The more experienced players on the team handle the pressure much better than new players.*
→ see **advanced** for **sophisticated** meaning "using modern technology and methods"

ADVERBS
You can make the adjective **sophisticated** into an adverb by using an **-ly** ending: *Her friends talked sophisticatedly about art and literature.*

sore *adjective* → see **painful**

sorrow *noun* → see **sadness**

sorry /ˈsɑri/ adjective

1 feeling unhappy about something you have done (adjectives)
- ► sorry
- ► apologetic
- ► ashamed

2 to feel unhappy because you have done something (verbs)
- ► be sorry
- ► regret

3 to feel sad for someone (verbs)
- ► feel sorry for
- ► pity
- ► sympathize

1 feeling unhappy about something you have done (adjectives)

sorry
feeling unhappy because you know that you should not have done something: *I'm sorry if I upset you.* | *Afterward, he felt **sorry for** some of the things he had said.*
→ **GRAMMAR:** Don't say: ~~*He is a sorry person.*~~ Say: *He is sorry* or *He feels sorry.*

apologetic
saying or showing you are sorry about something you have done: *The waiter was very **apologetic about** our food taking so long to come.*

ashamed
feeling very sorry, because you know you have done something bad and you are worried about what other people think of you: *Karen felt **ashamed that** she had lied to her parents.*
→ see **guilty (1)**

ADVERBS
You can make the adjectives **apologetic** and **ashamed** into adverbs by using an **-ly** ending: *She smiled at me apologetically.* | *Karen admitted ashamedly that she had lied to her parents.*

2 to feel unhappy because you have done something (verbs)

be sorry *also* **feel sorry**, **seem sorry**
if you are sorry, you feel unhappy because

something has happened or because you have done something, especially something you should not have done: *I'm sorry I'm late.* | *She seemed genuinely **sorry for** her behavior.*

regret
to wish that you had not done something: *It was a stupid thing to say, and I immediately regretted it.*

3 to feel sad for someone (verbs)

feel sorry for
to feel sad for someone because something bad has happened to him or her: *Dave felt sorry for Tina – she seemed so lonely.*

pity
to feel very sorry for someone who is in a much worse situation than you: *The man had a violent temper and I pitied his poor wife.*

sympathize
to feel sorry for someone because you understand how he or she feels: *She could **sympathize with** anyone whose parents were going through a divorce.*

sort /sɔrt/ verb

► sort
► group
► categorize
► classify

sort
to put things into groups or into a particular order: *He sorted the letters into two piles – bills and junk mail.* | *Next, you sort the list of names into alphabetical order.*

group
to divide people or things into groups: *The book has 15 chapters, which are grouped into three sections.* | *The teacher grouped the students into teams of five.*

categorize
to put people or things into groups with other people or things that belong to the same type: *Her novels are categorized as romances.*

classify
to categorize something using an official or scientific system: *Tomatoes are officially classified as a fruit, even though people think of them as a salad vegetable.*

soul /soʊl/ noun

► soul
► spirit

soul
the part of you that has your character and makes you different from other people. Your **soul** is what goes to heaven or hell when you die, according to many religions: *We pray for the souls of the dead.*

spirit
spirit means the same as **soul**, but you do not talk about spirits going to heaven or hell: *The school run by the church wants to educate the mind, body, and spirit.*

sound¹ /saʊnd/ noun

► sound
► noise
► tone

sound
something that you hear: *I could hear the sound of a child crying.* | *There were strange sounds coming from the next room.*

noise
a sound, especially one that is loud or annoying: *Don't make too much noise – Dad's trying to work.* | *I couldn't sleep because of the noise of the traffic.*

tone
a sound made by a piece of equipment, for example the sounds made by a telephone when you press the buttons: *When I picked up the phone, there was no dial tone.*
→ **Tone** can also mean "the sound of someone's voice," especially whether it is low or high: *They were talking together in low tones.*
→ see **noise, rhythm**

sound² verb → see **seem**

sour /saʊə/ adjective

► sour
► tart
► tangy
► acidic (*formal*)
► bitter
► sharp

ANTONYMS → see **sweet**

sour
having a strong taste, like the taste of a lemon or a fruit that is not ready to eat: *The strawberries are a little sour but they taste good with honey on them.*
→ You also use **sour** about milk that tastes bad because it is no longer fresh.

tart
sour, but usually in a pleasant way. You use **tart**

S

especially about apples and other fruit: *Use a tart apple to make the pie.*

tangy
having a nice strong sour taste. You use **tangy** about foods that have sour fruits, wine, or vinegar in them: *The lemon cake is delicious and tangy.*

acidic (*formal*)
very sour, like lemon juice or vinegar: *If the tomato sauce is too acidic, you can always add some sugar.*

bitter
having a strong sour taste that is not sweet at all and not pleasant. You use **bitter** especially about coffee, chocolate, or medicine: *The medicine tasted bitter and I didn't want to drink it.*

sharp
having a strong sour taste that is not sweet. You use **sharp** especially about cheese or wine: *The cheese has a sharp taste.*

source /sɔrs/ *noun*

- ► source
- ► origin
- ► roots
- ► birthplace
- ► cradle (*formal*)

source (AWL)
the place or thing where something comes from or where you get something from: *Most Americans rely on television as their main* ***source of*** *news.* | *Oil and coal are running out and we need to find other* ***sources of*** *energy.* | *Vegetarians don't eat meat, so they have to get their protein from other sources.*

origin
the place or situation where something starts to exist: *The word "restaurant" is French in origin.* | *Scientists are studying the* ***origin of*** *the universe.*

roots
the original things that something is based on, and from which it developed: *Reggae has its* ***roots in*** *a range of different musical styles.*

birthplace
the place where something first started to happen or exist: *New Orleans is* ***the birthplace of*** *jazz.*

cradle (*formal*)
the place where something very important began, for example civilization, democracy, or a religion: *Ancient Greece is often regarded as* ***the cradle of*** *democracy.*

→ see **cause**[1]

space /speɪs/ *noun*

1 the area outside the Earth's atmosphere
- ► space
- ► outer space
- ► universe
- ► galaxy
- ► solar system

2 an area that can be used
- ► space
- ► room
- ► capacity

1 the area outside the Earth's atmosphere

space
the area beyond the sky, where the Moon and stars are: *The rocket set off into space on a three-year mission to Mars.*

outer space
the part of space that is a long way from the Earth: *In the movie, the Earth is invaded by strange creatures from outer space.*

universe
space and everything in it, including the Earth and all the planets and stars: *Are there any other planets with life on them in the universe?*

galaxy
a very large group of stars: *A spaceship moving at the speed of light would take more than 100,000 years to cross our galaxy.*

solar system
a star and the planets that go around it. You use **solar system** especially about the Sun and the Earth, and other planets that move around the Sun: *As far as we know, the Earth is the only planet in our solar system that contains life.*

2 an area that can be used

space
an empty area that can be used for putting things or people in: *It is a big apartment with a lot of space.* | *There is enough space for one more person in the car.*

room
enough space to put things in, or to use for a particular purpose: *There is room in the trunk of the car for all our suitcases.* | *The roof of the cave was so low that there was not enough room to stand up straight.*

capacity (AWL)
the amount of liquid, things, or people that something can contain: *The fuel tank has a*

S

capacity of 15 gallons. | *The hall has a seating capacity of 1,500 people.*
→ see **hole (1)** for words meaning "a space between two things"

spacious *adjective* → see **big**

span *verb* → see **cross**, **go across**

spank *verb* → see **hit¹**

spare¹ *adjective* → see **another**

spare² *noun* → see **extra²**, **replacement**

sparse /spɑrs/ *adjective*

- ► sparse
- ► scarce

sparse
if something is sparse, there are only a few in a large area: *Montana is a large state with a sparse population.*

scarce
if something is scarce, there is not enough available for people: *Hotel rooms are scarce in the summer.*

ADVERBS

You can make the adjective **sparse** into an adverb by using an **-ly** ending: *Montana is a sparsely populated state.*
In this meaning, the adverb **scarcely** is only used in the phrase **scarcely any**, meaning "almost no" or "almost none": *There has been scarcely any improvement in quality.*

speak /spik/ *verb*

- ► speak
- ► be fluent in
- ► know

speak
to be able to talk in a language: *Do you speak English?* | *The ambassador can speak several languages, including English, Spanish, and Portuguese.*

be fluent in
to be able to speak a language very well, without making mistakes or stopping to think of the right word: *Kelly went to high school in Japan and she is fluent in Japanese.*

know
to be able to speak or understand some words in a language: *I only know a few words of Spanish.*
→ see **speech (2)**, **talk¹**, **whisper**, **mumble** for words meaning "to speak in an unclear way"

special /ˈspeʃəl/ *adjective*

- ► special
- ► unusual
- ► unique
- ► distinctive
- ► particular

ANTONYMS → see **ordinary**

special
something that is special is different from other things, for example because it is better, more important, or is for a particular purpose: *Today is a very special day for them. It was 50 years ago today when they first met.* | *Did you do anything special on the weekend?*

unusual
different from what is usual or normal: *We had snow in May, which is very unusual.* | *Did you notice anything unusual about the man's behavior?*

unique (AWL)
if something is unique, it is very special or unusual and the only one of its kind: *The islands are famous for their unique wildlife.*
→ Don't use "very" with **unique**. Just say **unique**: *Each handmade bowl is unique.*

distinctive (AWL)
having a special feature or appearance that makes something different from other things, and makes it easy to recognize: *The male birds have distinctive blue and yellow feathers.*

particular
different from or more important than other things: *Pineapple has a very particular taste and not everyone likes it.* | *Is there a particular reason why you want to go to Florida and not California?*

ADVERBS

You can make the adjectives **unusual**, **unique**, **distinctive**, and **particular** into adverbs by using an **-ly** ending: *Unusually, we had snow in May.* | *He paints in a style that is uniquely his own.* | *The male birds are distinctively colored.*

specific *adjective* → see **particular**

specifically /spəˈsɪfɪkli/ *adverb*

- ► specifically
- ► namely

specifically (AWL)
used when adding more exact information so that people know exactly what you are talking

S

about: *In her books she writes about her fears, specifically the fear of being alone.*

namely
used when saying which people or things you are talking about: *Three students were mentioned, namely Maria, Lisa, and Carole.*
→ see **especially** for words meaning "more than other times, or more than other people or things"

spectacular *adjective* → see **good**

spectators *noun* → see **audience**, Topic **Sports and Exercise**

speech /spitʃ/ *noun*

1 an occasion when someone talks about a subject to a group of people (nouns)
- ► speech
- ► talk
- ► lecture
- ► sermon
- ► presentation
- ► address

2 to talk about a subject for a group of people (verbs)
- ► give a speech
- ► speak
- ► address
- ► lecture
- ► preach

1 an occasion when someone talks about a subject to a group of people (nouns)

speech
an occasion when someone talks about a subject in a formal way to a group of people, for example at an official meeting: *The bride's father usually gives a speech at a wedding.* | *President Kennedy made a famous speech in which he said: "Ask not what your country can do for you – ask what you can do for your country."*

talk
a short speech about one subject. A **talk** is done in a less formal way than a **speech**: *The students have to give a talk to the rest of the class about a book they have read.*

lecture
a talk about a subject, especially to students at a university: *The lecture was about Mark Twain's novel "Adventures of Huckleberry Finn."*

sermon
a talk about a religious subject, given by a priest or minister in church: *The sermon in church this week was about the need for forgiveness.*

presentation
a talk in which you explain or describe something to a group of people, for example a new idea or product for your company: *At the end of his presentation, the chairman asked if there were any questions.*

address
a formal speech to a group of people, especially one by a leader on an important occasion: *In his **address to** Congress, the President talked about the need to create more jobs.*

2 to talk about a subject for a group of people (verbs)

give a speech *also* **make a speech**
to talk about a subject in a formal way to a group of people: *When the senator visited the university, he **gave a speech to** all the students.*

speak
to give a speech at an event such as a meeting or funeral: *Professor Altman will be speaking at the conference.*

address
to give a speech to a large group of people: *She stepped up to the microphone and addressed the crowd.*

lecture (AWL) *also* **give a lecture**
to give a formal talk about a subject to a group of people, especially to teach them about it: *He has written and **lectured on** the subject of early jazz.*
→ You can also use **lecture** to mean "to talk to someone in a serious way about how he or she should behave": *His dad **lectured** him **about** the dangers of drugs.*

preach
to give a speech on a religious subject in church: *The minister preached a sermon about love.*

speed /spid/ *noun*

- ► speed
- ► rate
- ► pace
- ► velocity (*formal*)
- ► tempo

speed
how fast something moves or travels: *The car has a top speed of 132 mph.* | *The train was traveling **at high speed**.*

rate
how fast things happen, change, or develop: *The population is growing **at a rate of** 12% a year.*

pace
the speed at which someone does something, for example walks, runs, or works, or the speed at which something happens: *The soldiers were marching **at a steady pace**. | The pace of change in computer technology is amazing.*

velocity (*formal*)
the speed at which something moves in a particular direction. **Velocity** is a technical word used in scientific writing: *The instrument is used for measuring wind velocity.*

tempo
the speed at which a person or band plays a piece of music: *It is important to play the music at the right tempo.*

speed up *phrasal verb* → see **fast[1] (3)**, **rush[1]**

spell /spel/ *noun*

- ► spell
- ► curse

spell
words or actions that are intended to make something magic happen. **Spell** is used in children's stories: *The witch put a magic spell on the prince and changed him into a frog.*

curse
words or actions that bring people bad luck. **Curse** is used in children's stories: *Things kept going wrong and it seemed like someone had put a curse on the house.*

spend /spend/ *verb*

1 to use money to pay for things
- ► spend
- ► invest
- ► squander
- ► economize

ANTONYMS → see **save (1)**

2 to use time doing something
- ► spend
- ► devote
- ► pass the time

1 to use money to pay for things

spend
to use money to pay for something: *We spend about $200 a week **on** food. | The state **spends** millions of dollars a year **on** education.*

invest AWL
to spend a large amount of money in order to improve something or help something succeed: *The city has **invested** a lot of money **in** the subway system.*

squander
to waste money on things you do not need, instead of saving it or using it carefully: *He used to be rich, but he **squandered** all his money **on** fast cars.*

economize
to use your money carefully so that you spend less: *We economize by cooking our own meals, instead of eating out in restaurants.*
→ see **pay[1]**

2 to use time doing something

spend
to use time doing something, or do something for a period of time: *I want to spend more time with my family. | Her childhood was spent in Brazil.*

devote AWL
to use a lot of your time to do something: *He has devoted his life to helping people.*

pass the time
to spend time doing something so that you do not feel bored: *It was a long trip and we passed the time by playing computer games.*

spending /ˈspendɪŋ/ *noun*

- ► spending
- ► expenditure (*formal*)

spending
the amount of money that a person or organization spends: *People are reducing their spending, because they are worried about the future. | There has been a big increase in government spending on education.*

expenditure (*formal*)
the total amount of money that a government or organization spends: *Military expenditure has been growing in recent years.*

spicy /ˈspaɪsi/ *adjective*

- ► spicy
- ► hot
- ► peppery

spicy
hot food has a taste that burns your mouth: *The chicken dish is very spicy, but the pork is milder.*

hot
hot means the same as **spicy**: *The salsa was hot. | The ghost pepper is supposed to be the hottest chili pepper in the world.*
→ It can be clearer to use **spicy** instead of **hot** when you are talking about food. If you use **hot**, people may not know if you are talking about the temperature of the food or the spice in the food.

S

peppery
having a spicy taste like pepper. You can use **peppery** to describe food that has pepper in it, or to describe food that tastes like pepper: *The cheese had a peppery taste that made it interesting.* | *The sausages were too peppery for me.*
→ see Topic **Describing Food**

spill /spɪl/ *verb*

- ► spill
- ► splash
- ► overflow

spill
to accidentally pour liquid onto a surface: *She accidentally **spilled** some coffee **on** the carpet.* | *I passed him the glass of milk carefully, so it wouldn't spill.*

splash
to make drops of a liquid fall onto someone or something: *Be careful you don't **splash** any paint **on** your clothes.* | *Water from the bucket **splashed** onto the carpet.*

overflow
if something overflows, it becomes so full of liquid that the liquid comes out over the top: *She left the water running when she answered the phone, and the sink overflowed.*

spirit *noun* → see **ghost**, **soul**

spiritual *adjective* → see **religious**

splash¹ /splæʃ/ *verb*

- ► splash
- ► spray
- ► sprinkle
- ► squirt

splash
to make someone or something wet with a lot of small drops of water or other liquid: *He **splashed** water **on** his face.* | *The kids were splashing each other in the pool.*

spray
to make a liquid come out of something in very small drops: *The farmers **spray** chemicals **on** the plants to protect them from insects.*

sprinkle
to scatter small pieces of something or drops of liquid onto another thing: ***Sprinkle** some salt **onto** the vegetables.* | *If you **sprinkle** water **on** the clothes, they are easier to iron.*

squirt
to force liquid to come out of a narrow hole in a thin fast stream: *I squirted some oil in the lock, to make the key turn more easily.*

splash

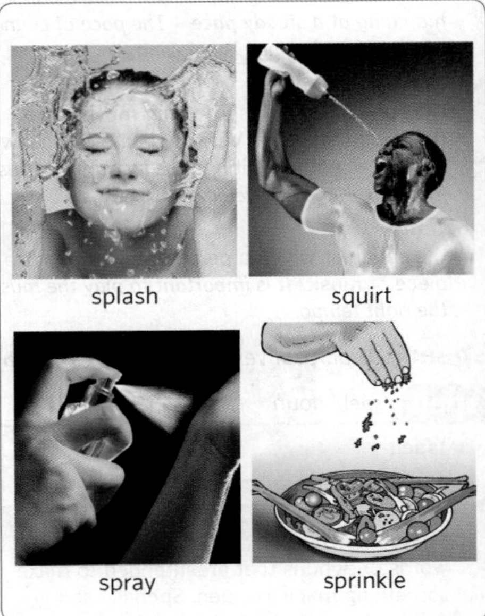

splash² /splæʃ/ *noun*

- ► splash
- ► spray
- ► squirt

splash
a large drop of liquid: *Add a splash of lemon juice to your cola.* | *There were a few splashes of paint on the floor.*
→ You also use **splash** about the sound or movement that is made when liquid hits something, or when something hits liquid: *There was a big splash when he jumped in the pool.*

spray
a lot of very small drops of liquid that come out of a container: *Farmers use sprays to protect their crops from insects.*

squirt
a short fast thin stream of liquid: *He put a squirt of ketchup on his French fries.*

split¹ *verb* → see **separate²**, **tear¹**

split² *noun* → see **break²**, **separation**

split up *phrasal verb* → see **divorce**, Topic **Relationships and Marriage**

S

spoil /spɔɪl/ *verb*

1 to have a bad effect on something
- ► spoil
- ► ruin

2 to treat someone too kindly
- ► spoil
- ► pamper
- ► indulge

1 to have a bad effect on something

spoil
to make something less good, attractive, or enjoyable: *The bad weather spoiled our vacation.* | *It is an ugly building, and it spoils the view.*

ruin
to spoil something completely: *The scandal ruined his career as a politician.* | *I spilled milk on the book and ruined it.*

2 to treat someone too kindly

spoil
to give a child everything he or she wants, because you are trying to be very kind. If you **spoil** someone, he or she often behaves badly: *His grandparents spoiled him, buying him little presents and treats.*

pamper
to spend a lot of time trying to make a person or animal happy and comfortable. Sometimes you can **pamper** in a way that is not good for someone's health or character: *Lisa really pampers her dog – she feeds it steak!*

indulge
to let someone have or do the things that he or she wants, even if it is not good for his or her health or character: *Her mother tries to set limits, but her father indulges her.*
→ You can also **indulge** yourself by buying something expensive or letting yourself eat something you know is not good for you: *I decided to indulge myself and bought a new pair of nice boots.*

spoiled *adjective* → see **bad**, **rotten**, Topic **Describing Food**

spoken /ˈspoʊkən/ *adjective*

- ► spoken
- ► oral
- ► verbal

ANTONYMS → see **written**

spoken
relating to saying words, rather than writing or reading words: *At the beginning, the lessons focus on spoken English rather than reading or writing the language.*

oral
spoken, not written. You use **oral** when something that is usually written, such as a report, history, test, etc., is spoken instead: *The students each gave an oral report on a book that they had read.*

verbal
spoken and not written down. You use **verbal** about official things, such as agreements or contracts, that are usually done by writing a formal document: *If an employee is regularly late, he or she will first receive a verbal warning; a written warning will be given if no improvement is made.*
→ You can also use **verbal** to mean "relating to words or using words, especially while speaking": *The students' verbal communication has improved greatly.*

ADVERBS

You can make the adjectives **oral** and **verbal** into adverbs by using an **-ly** ending: *The students are tested orally and in written form.* | *The employee was warned verbally and then in writing.*

spokesperson /ˈspoʊksˌpɚsən/ *noun*

- ► spokesperson
- ► representative
- ► delegate

spokesperson *also* **spokesman** *or* **spokeswoman**
a man or woman who speaks officially for an organization: *A **spokesperson for** the company answered questions from reporters.*

representative
someone who people have chosen to speak, vote, or make decisions for them: *The class chose him as their representative for the school's student government.*

delegate
someone who represents a country, organization, or group, especially at an important meeting: *Delegates from more than 30 countries will meet to discuss the world economic situation.*

S

sponsor /ˈspɑnsɚ/ *noun*

- ► sponsor
- ► donor
- ► contributor
- ► patron

sponsor
a company or person that gives money to help pay for an event, show, team, etc., especially as a way to advertise their products: *A well-known sportswear company will be the sponsor of the competition.*

donor
someone who gives something, especially money, to help an organization: *The museum was built with $5 million from private donors.*

contributor (AWL)
someone who gives money or help to a party or organization: *Westbrook was a major contributor to the Democratic Party.*

patron
someone who gives money to help artists, musicians, etc. do their work: *Sam was a great patron of the arts. He often bought work by young artists.*

sport /spɔrt/ *noun*

- ► sport
- ► game
- ► recreation

sport
a physical activity in which players or teams compete against each other, for example by running or throwing a ball: *My favorite sports are basketball and tennis.* | *Which sports do you play at school?*

game
an activity that you do for enjoyment, which has rules and which you play to win: *Chess is such a difficult game.* | *She likes playing computer games.*

recreation
activities people do for fun, which can include sports and games. **Recreation** is often used in formal or official language: *What do the local people do for recreation in the winter?*
→ **GRAMMAR: Recreation** is often used before another noun: *The state has decided to make the lake and the park around it a recreation area, with boating and horse riding.*
→ see **exercise¹**, **game**, Topic **Sports and Exercise**

spot¹ *noun* → see **mark¹**, **place¹**

spot² *verb* → see **notice¹**

spouse *noun* → see **husband**, **wife**, Topic **Relationships and Marriage**

spray¹ *verb* → see **splash¹**

spray² *noun* → see **splash²**

spread /spred/ *verb*

1 to move something over a wide area
- ► spread
- ► scatter

2 to open something and arrange it on a surface
- ► spread
- ► lay out
- ► unfold

1 to move something over a wide area

spread
to move something over a big area: *Spread the paint all over the wall with a big brush.* | *The seeds are spread by the wind.*
→ You can also use **spread** when something affects a bigger area or more people: *Fire spread quickly through the building.*

scatter
to throw or drop things over a wide area in an irregular way: *He scattered his father's ashes in the mountains where he loved to hike.*

2 to open something and arrange it on a surface

spread *also* **spread out**
to open something such as a sheet, map, or newspaper, and arrange it so that it lies flat on a surface: *Spread the map out and let's take a look.*

lay out
to spread something carefully on a surface: *I laid the blanket out on the ground.*

unfold
to open something that was folded: *He unfolded the sheet of paper and began to read it.*
→ see **infect** for **spread** meaning "give someone a disease"

spy *verb* → see **watch**

squeak /skwik/ *verb*

- ► squeak
- ► creak
- ► screech
- ► squeal

squeak
to make a short high sound that is not loud: *The*

mouse squeaked and ran into the bushes. | I used some oil to make the gate stop squeaking.

creak
if something creaks, it makes a long high sound when someone stands on it or moves it: *The floorboards creaked as she walked across the room. | The door creaks when you open it.*

screech
to make a loud high unpleasant sound or cry for a long time. You use **screech** especially about someone's voice or about brakes or tires: *The plane's tires screeched as they touched the ground. | "Don't do that!" she screeched.*

squeal
to make a long loud high sound or cry: *The train squealed to a stop. | She tickled the baby's feet until he squealed.*

squirt *noun* → see **splash²**

stable /'steɪbəl/ *adjective*

- stable
- steady
- secure

ANTONYMS → see **unstable**

stable (AWL)
staying in the same position and not moving: *The ladder doesn't look very stable – do you want me to hold it for you?*

steady
firmly held in a particular position and not moving or shaking: *It is important to keep the camera steady when you take a picture.*

secure (AWL)
firmly fastened or tied, and not likely to fall down: *Make sure all the ropes are secure when you put up your tent.*
→ see **constant** for **stable** meaning "not changing"

ADVERBS
You can make the adjectives **steady** and **secure** into adverbs by using an **-ly** ending: *Hold the camera steadily. | Make sure your seat belt is securely fastened.*

stadium *noun* → see Topic **Sports and Exercise**

staff *noun* → see **worker**, Topic **Jobs and Work**

stage *noun* → see **part**

stain¹ *noun* → see **mark¹**

stain² *verb* → see **dirty (2)**

stale *adjective* → see **bad**, **hard**, **rotten**, **smelly**, Topic **Describing Food**

stand /stænd/ *verb*

- stand
- stand up
- get up
- get to your feet
- rise (*formal*)
- be on your feet

ANTONYMS → see **sit**

stand
to be on your feet, in an upright position: *There were no seats, so we had to stand. | They were standing at the bus stop.*

stand up
to move so that you are on your feet, after you have been sitting or lying down: *She stood up and went over to the window.*

get up
get up means the same as **stand up** but is a little more informal: *I heard someone knock on the door and I got up to see who it was.*

get to your feet
to stand up, especially slowly or with difficulty: *I helped the old man get to his feet.*

rise (*formal*)
to stand up: *The audience rose to their feet and started clapping and cheering.*

be on your feet
to be standing for a long time, so you feel tired: *I've been on my feet all day and I need a rest.*
→ see **lean** and **put** for **stand** meaning "put something against a wall or other surface," **put up with** for **stand** meaning "accept a bad situation"
→ see **stand by** at **wait**
→ see **stand for** at **mean¹**
→ see **stand in for** at **replace**
→ see **stand up for** at **defend**, **support**
→ see **stand up to** at **disobey**
→ see **cannot stand** at **hate**

standard /'stændɚd/ *noun*

- standard
- criteria
- yardstick (*informal*)

standard
a level used when measuring how good something is: *All her work is of a very high standard. | The restaurant failed to meet food safety standards and it was closed down.*

S

criteria
standards and other things that you think about when you are making a decision or judgment about something: *The **criteria** for the job are that you must have at least three years' work experience and a college degree.*
→ **GRAMMAR: Criteria** is a plural noun. The singular form **criterion** is more formal and less common: *When choosing which food to buy, the price is often the main criterion.*

yardstick (*informal*)
something that you use to compare another thing with, in order to decide how good or successful it is: *If we take last year's performance **as a yardstick**, this year has been a very good year for the team.*
→ see **level** (**2**), **usual**

standards *noun* → see **conscience**

star /stɑr/ *noun*

- ► **star**
- ► **celebrity**
- ► **legend**

star
a famous and successful actor, musician, or sports player: *He has become one of basketball's biggest stars.* | *Many Hollywood movie stars live in Beverly Hills.*

celebrity
someone who often appears in newspapers, on television, etc. and is well known to the public: *The magazine is full of stories about the private lives of celebrities.*

legend
someone who has been very famous for a long time, who people admire a lot: *Michael Jackson was a pop legend who recorded a lot of good songs.*
→ see Topic **Entertainment**

S

stare¹ *verb* → see **look¹**

stare² *noun* → see **look²**

start¹ /stɑrt/ *verb*

1 to start doing something
- ► **start**
- ► **begin**
- ► **launch**
- ► **take up**
- ► **initiate** (*formal*)

ANTONYMS → see **stop¹**, **finish**

2 to start happening
- ► **start**
- ► **begin**
- ► **commence** (*formal*)
- ► **break out**

ANTONYMS → see **end²** (**1**)

3 to start doing something again
- ► **start over**
- ► **resume**

4 to make something start to exist
- ► **start**
- ► **establish**
- ► **found**
- ► **set up**

1 to start doing something

start
if you start doing something, you were not doing it before but you are doing it now: *The clown fell down and the kids all started laughing.* | *When do you start your new job?* | *She tried to start a conversation with him.*

begin
begin means the same as **start** but is more formal: *They slowly began to climb up the mountain.* | *The company plans to begin work on the bridge next year.* | *She began reading.*

launch
to start something new or important, such as an effort to do something or an attack: *The town launched a campaign to attract more tourists.*

take up
to become interested in a sport or activity, and start doing it regularly: *When did Bryan take up golf?*

initiate (AWL) (*formal*)
to start something, especially something important such as a new process, discussion, or plan: *Both sides have agreed to initiate peace talks in an effort to end the war.*

SYNONYM CHECK

Start or begin?

Start and **begin** both mean the same, but **begin** is a little more formal. With some words, you can only use **start**. You say: *start an argument/war/fire*. You do not use **begin** with these words.

2 to start happening

start
if something starts happening, it was not happening before but is happening now: *What time does the movie start? | The rain started again.*

begin
begin means the same as **start** but is more formal: *The meeting begins at 10:30 a.m. | It began to snow.*

commence (AWL) *(formal)*
to start. **Commence** is more formal than **start** and **begin**: *Work on the new building will commence immediately.*

break out
to start happening. You use **break out** about unpleasant things such as wars, fires, or diseases: *The fire broke out on the top floor of the hotel.*

3 to start doing something again

start over
to start doing something again from the beginning, especially because you want to do it better: *If you make a mistake, just erase it and start over.*

resume
to start something again after stopping it or being interrupted: *The court does not work on the weekend and the trial will resume on Monday morning.*

4 to make something start to exist

start
if someone starts a business or organization, it did not exist before but it exists now: *She started her own company five years ago.*

establish (AWL)
to start a company or organization, especially a big or important one that lasts for a long time: *The company was established in 1938.*

found (AWL)
to start a company or an organization such as a school or hospital, especially by providing money for it: *Stanford University was founded by Leland and Jane Stanford in 1885.*

set up
to start a business, organization, or system, and make the arrangements for it: *The leaders of the different groups in this African country will meet to set up a new government.*

→ see **turn on/off**

start[2] /stɑrt/ *noun*

- ► start
- ► beginning
- ► introduction
- ► origin
- ► birth
- ► outbreak
- ► outset

ANTONYMS → see **end[1] (1)**

start
the time or moment when something begins: ***At the start of** the second half of the basketball game, the score was 32 to 28. | She was in charge of the project **from start to** finish.*

beginning
the first part of an event, period of time, story, etc., when something begins: ***At the beginning of** the movie, the two main characters hate each other. | We hope this is the beginning of a time of peace in our country. | The show lasts **from the beginning** until the end of August.*

introduction
the part at the beginning of a book, report, or speech, that explains what it is about: *In the **introduction to** her book, Julia writes about how she first became interested in cooking.*

origin *also* **origins**
the beginning of something that started a long time ago: *Scientists still have many questions about **the origins of** language in humans.*

birth
the time when something starts to exist, especially something important that has a big effect on people's lives: *The website is about the singers and bands of the 1950s and **the birth of** rock 'n' roll.*

outbreak
a time when fighting or a disease starts: ***At the outbreak of** the war, he was living in Boston. | There was an **outbreak of** food poisoning at the hotel.*

outset
the time when you start doing something or something starts happening: *We knew **from the outset** that it was not going to be an easy task.*
→ **Outset** is only used in the phrases **from the outset** and **at the outset**.

S

SYNONYM CHECK

Beginning or start?

Beginning and **start** mean the same thing. However, if you use **beginning**, the amount of time seems longer than the **start** of something: *Did you see the beginning of the game?* means the moment it started and a period of time after that. *Did you see the start of the game?* means only the moment it started.

You usually use **beginning** about stories or movies, or about long periods of time such as months.

You usually use **start** about events, such as meetings or races.

state[1] *noun* → see **condition**, **country**

state[2] *verb* → see **say**

statement /ˈsteɪtmənt/ *noun*

- ► statement
- ► announcement
- ► declaration
- ► testimony

statement
something that someone says or writes publicly and officially: *The president made a statement saying that the government would help the victims of the earthquake.* | *In a written statement, the head of the company promised to deal with the problem.*

announcement
a public statement that tells people some important news: *The company made a surprise* ***announcement that*** *it plans to close the factory in Dallas.*

declaration
an official announcement that says you will do something: *The president issued a* ***declaration of*** *war.*

testimony
the things you say in a law court about what you know about a crime: *The man who is accused of her murder will give testimony tomorrow.*
→ see **say** (**2**)

station[1] /ˈsteɪʃən/ *noun*

- ► station
- ► channel
- ► network

station
a company that broadcasts television or radio programs: *Radio stations began playing her music.* | *Reporters from CNN and a local TV station wanted to interview him.*

channel (AWL)
the number on a television set that you turn to in order to find a particular station: *The game will be shown on Channel 36.*

network (AWL)
a company that broadcasts the same programs in different parts of a country. A **network** is made up of many smaller **stations**: *The comedy show was broadcast on the Fox network.*

station[2] *verb* → see **send**, Topic **Travel and Vacations**

stationary *adjective* → see **still**[1]

statue *noun* → see **sculpture**

stay /steɪ/ *verb*

1 to continue to be in the same place
- ► stay
- ► remain (*formal*)
- ► linger

ANTONYMS → see **go** (**1**)

2 to continue being something
- ► stay
- ► keep
- ► remain (*formal*)

1 to continue to be in the same place

stay
to continue to be in the same place and not leave: *He was sick, so he stayed at home.* | *I'm coming with you. I'm not staying here by myself.*

remain (*formal*)
to stay in the same place: *The mayor reminded everyone to remain indoors during the storm.*

linger
to stay in a place for a little longer because you do not want to leave: *On the weekends, he lingered in bed with a book.*
→ You can also use **linger** to say that smells, memories, or effects stay for a long time: *The effects of the flu can linger for weeks.*

2 to continue being something

stay
to continue being something: *Doing exercise can help you to stay healthy.* | *I don't know how they stayed alive in such cold conditions.*

keep
keep means the same as **stay** but sounds a little more informal: *He lit a fire to keep warm.*

remain (*formal*)
remain means the same as **stay** but is formal: *Twenty-five schools remain closed because of damage caused by the hurricane.*
→ see **live (2)** for **stay** meaning "to live in a place for a short time"

GRAMMAR CHECK: stay

Stay and **remain** can be followed by an adjective or a noun, but **stay** is usually followed by an adjective: *I tried to stay/remain calm.* | *He has remained my friend ever since.* **Keep** can only be followed by an adjective: *He told us to keep calm.*

steady *adjective* → see **constant**, **stable**

steal /stil/ *verb*

- steal
- take
- rob
- burglarize
- mug
- shoplift
- hijack

steal
to remove and keep something that belongs to someone else, in a dishonest way: *He was accused of stealing a car.* | *She had **stolen** money and jewelry **from** the family she worked for.*

take
to steal something. You use **take** when it is clear from what you have said that someone has taken something dishonestly. **Take** is more informal than **steal**: *The robber took money from the cash register and ran away.*

rob
to steal something from a person or place: *Bennett was in prison after robbing a bank and stealing $200,000.* | *He was beaten and robbed by two men.*

burglarize
to go into a building and steal things. **Burglarize** is used especially in news reports: *Woodward burglarized apartments to get money to buy drugs.*

mug
to attack and rob someone: *I was mugged outside the hotel. They forced me to give them my wallet and cell phone.*

shoplift
to take something from a store and not pay for it: *Some of the kids shoplifted candy from the supermarket.*

hijack
to take control of an airplane by using force: *Terrorists hijacked the plane.*
→ see **theft** for words meaning "the crime of stealing something," **thief** for words meaning "someone who steals something"

SYNONYM CHECK

Steal or rob?

You say that someone **steals** a thing, but **robs** a person or a place such as a bank. Don't say: ~~*He robbed my watch*~~. Say: *He stole my watch.* Don't say: ~~*He stole me*~~ or ~~*He stole me my watch*~~. Say: *He robbed me* or *He **robbed** me **of** my watch.*

steam /stim/ *noun*

- steam
- vapor
- condensation
- moisture

steam
the gas or mist that hot water produces: *Steam was rising from the pan of boiling water.* | *Old trains and ships were powered by steam.*

vapor
a gas that comes from a liquid or solid substance that has been heated: *A huge cloud of gas vapor was rising into the air after the explosion.*

condensation
small drops of water that form on a cold surface when warm air touches it: *After I took a shower, there was a lot of condensation on the bathroom window.*

moisture
small amounts of water that make something a little wet: *Plants need plenty of sunlight and moisture.*

steer *verb* → see **drive**

stem /stem/ *noun*

- stem
- stalk
- trunk

stem
the long narrow part of a plant, that leaves or flowers grow on. You use **stem** especially to talk about the longest or main part that grows up from the ground: *He gave her a dozen red roses on long stems.* | *The flower was bending over because the stem had broken.*

stalk
the narrow part of a plant, that grows from the stem or branch and that leaves, flowers, or fruit grow on: *When you pick an apple off a tree, the stalk sometimes stays on the apple.*

trunk
the thick wooden stem of a tree: *Teresa sat under the tree and leaned against the trunk.*

stem

step¹ /step/ noun

- step
- footstep
- stride
- pace

step
the movement of lifting one foot and putting it down in front of the other foot: *Manuel nervously took a step toward the dog.* | *Babies take their first steps when they are about a year old.*

footstep
the sound of each step when someone is walking: *Juanita could hear footsteps outside the door.*

stride
a long step that you make when you walk: *The little girl found it difficult to keep up with her father's long strides.*

pace
a step that you make when you walk. You usually use **pace** when you are counting the steps someone takes: *He walked three or four paces past Jody and then turned.*
→ see **action** for **step** meaning "one of several things you do in order to achieve something," **part** (**3**) for **step** meaning "a part of a process"
→ see **step back** at **back²**
→ see **step up** at **increase¹**

step² /step/ verb

- step
- step on
- stamp
- trample

step
to move one foot forward and put it down in front of the other foot, in order to walk: *Jemma stepped into the hallway.* | *When your name is called, please step forward.*

step on
to put your foot on something: *I stepped on her foot by accident.*

stamp
to put your foot down very hard onto something or when you are walking: *Marco* ***stamped on*** *the fire to try to put it out.* | *Dickinson stamped angrily out of the room.*

trample
to step on something and damage it: *There was a low fence to stop people from trampling on the flowers.*
→ You can also use **trample** when a person or animal hurts or kills someone by stepping on them: *He was trampled by a horse.*

stick¹ /stɪk/ verb

- stick
- glue
- paste

stick
to join one thing to another thing using something such as glue or tape (=a narrow length of sticky material): *He stuck pictures all over his bedroom wall.* | *Ella was sticking stamps on the envelopes.*

glue
to stick things together using glue: *I glued the broken handle back onto the cup.*

paste
to stick something using thick wet glue: *Maria is pasting some pictures in her scrapbook.*
→ see **stick to** at **continue**
→ see **stick up** at **stick out**
→ see **stick up for** at **defend**

stick² /stɪk/ noun

1 a piece of wood from a tree
- stick
- branch
- twig
- log

2 a piece of wood or other material, that you use to support you when you walk
- ► stick
- ► cane
- ► crutch
- ► pole

1 a piece of wood from a tree

stick
a long thin piece of wood from a tree: *The dog had a stick in its mouth.* | *We collected some dry sticks for the fire.*

branch
a part of a tree that grows out from the main part: *A bird was sitting on a branch of the tree.*

twig
a very thin branch that grows on a larger branch of a tree: *Twigs and leaves were blown to the ground during the storm.*

log
a thick piece of wood that has fallen off or been cut off a tree: *There was a big pile of logs by the fire.*

2 a piece of wood or other material, that you use to support you when you walk

stick *also* **walking stick**
a long strong stick you use to help you walk in difficult places: *He found a branch to use as a walking stick as they climbed higher into the hills.* | *The shepherd leaned on his stick as he watched the sheep come in.*

cane
a smooth piece of wood or metal, often with a curved end that you hold, which you use to help you walk: *The old lady walked slowly with a cane.*

crutch
a special stick that you put under your arm to help you walk: *He broke his leg and had to use crutches for six weeks.*

pole
a long stick used for skiing or walking, that is usually made of metal: *Using two poles as you walk takes the pressure off your knees.*

stick out /ˌstɪk ˈaʊt/ *phrasal verb*

- ► stick out
- ► stick up
- ► protrude (*formal*)
- ► project (*formal*)

stick out
if something sticks out, it comes out further than the edge or surface of something: *If your teeth stick out, you will need to wear braces.* | *There was an umbrella* ***sticking out of*** *her bag.*

stick up
if something sticks up, the top of it shows above a surface and the rest is hidden beneath the surface: *A bottle was* ***sticking up out of*** *the sand.*

protrude (*formal*)
protrude means the same as **stick out**. You often use **protrude** when something sticks out in a way that is not wanted or is not attractive: *Her bony ankles* ***protruded from*** *beneath her long dress.*

project (AWL) (*formal*)
project means the same as **stick out**. You usually use **project** about something long and thin that sticks out from something larger: *The insect's sting* ***projects from*** *its body like a tail.*

sticky *adjective* → see **humid**, Topic **The Weather**

stiff *adjective* → see **hard**, **painful**, Topic **Describing Texture**

still[1] /stɪl/ *adjective*

- ► still
- ► motionless
- ► stationary
- ► at a standstill
- ► calm

still
not moving, or moving very little: *Keep still while I cut your hair.* | *The deer was standing very still with only its ears moving slightly.*

motionless
completely still. **Motionless** is used especially in writing: *Adam stood motionless, waiting to see what the other man was going to do.*

stationary
not moving. **Stationary** is usually used about vehicles: *He was riding his bike and hit a stationary car.*

at a standstill
if traffic is at a standstill, it is not moving: *The streets are full of cars, and traffic is at a standstill.*

calm
water or wind that is calm is not moving very much: *The ocean was very calm, so nobody on the boat got sick.*

still[2] *adverb* → see Function Word **but**

sting *verb* → see **bite**, **hurt**

stink[1] *verb* → see **smell[2]**

stink[2] *noun* → see **smell[1]**

S

stir /stɚ/ *verb*

- stir
- beat
- blend
- whisk

stir
to mix a liquid or food by moving a spoon around in it: *Stir the sauce until it boils.* | *Beth **stirred** some sugar into her coffee.*

beat
to mix a liquid or food quickly using a fork or kitchen tool: *Break the eggs into a bowl and beat them.* | *Beat the butter and sugar together.*

blend
to mix things together thoroughly, so they become smooth: *Blend the cream cheese and sugar.*

whisk
to mix liquids or soft foods together very quickly using a kitchen tool. The tool is called a **whisk** and has a handle with long curved pieces of wire attached: *Whisk the egg whites until they are stiff.*

stomach /ˈstʌmək/ *noun*

- stomach
- abdomen

S

stomach
the front part of your body between your chest and your legs: *He was lying on his stomach.*
→ Your **stomach** is also the part inside your body that digests food after you have eaten it: *After dinner, I started having pains in my stomach.*

abdomen
abdomen means the same as **stomach** but is used by doctors and in medical books: *She had a pain in her lower abdomen.*

stone *noun* → see **rock[1]**

stool *noun* → see **chair**

stop[1] /stɑp/ *verb*

1 to stop doing something
- stop
- quit
- give up
- abandon
- cease (*formal*)

ANTONYMS → see **start[1] (1)**

2 to stop moving
- stop
- come to a halt

3 to stop doing something for a short time
- stop
- take a break (*informal*)
- pause
- break for lunch/coffee

ANTONYMS → see **start[1] (3)**

4 to make someone or something stop
- stop
- end
- put an end to something
- discontinue (*formal*)
- halt
- block
- suspend (*formal*)
- terminate (*formal*)

1 to stop doing something

stop
to not continue doing something: *I stopped playing tennis because I injured my arm.* | *Stop treating me as if I'm a child.*
→ You also use **stop** to say that something stops happening: *We waited for the rain to stop.*

quit
quit means the same as **stop** but sounds more informal: *He quit smoking cigarettes last year.* | *Quit fighting, you two!*

give up
to stop doing something because it is harmful or not healthy: *I decided to give up eating chocolate.*

abandon (AWL)
to stop doing something because there are too many problems: *The country has abandoned its nuclear weapons program.*

cease (AWL) (*formal*)
to stop doing something. **Cease** is used in very formal writing or literature: *The company lost a lot of money and ceased trading in 2010.*
→ see **end[2]** for "to stop happening," **quit** for "to stop working or going to school"
→ see **finish**

2 to stop moving

stop
to not continue moving: *The bus stopped and three men got out.* | *She stopped and turned to look behind her.*
→ You can also use **stop** when someone makes something stop moving: *He stopped the car and looked at the map.*

come to a halt
to get slower and then stop. **Come to a halt** is usually used in writing and is often used to say where something stops: *The bus slammed on its*

brakes and came to a halt a few inches from the car.

3 to stop doing something for a short time

stop
to stop doing something for a short time before starting again: *Let's* ***stop for*** *lunch.* | *They* ***stopped to*** *look at the view.*

take a break (*informal*)
to stop working for a short time so that you can rest, have a drink, or eat something. **Take a break** is usually used in informal or spoken English: *I'm getting tired. Let's take a break.*

pause
to stop speaking or doing something for a short time. **Pause** is usually used in writing: *Paolo was talking, but he paused when Eduardo walked into the room.*

break for lunch/coffee
if you break for lunch or coffee, you stop working to eat lunch or drink a cup of coffee. **Break for lunch/coffee** is usually used in informal or spoken English: *Let's break for lunch and come back at 1:30.*

4 to make someone or something stop

stop
to make someone or something stop: *We need to stop the destruction of the rain forests.* | *I tried to stop him from running away.*

end
to make a situation or something that is happening stop: *She told him she wanted to end their relationship.*

put an end to something
to stop something, especially so that it never starts again: *The injury could put an end to her dancing career.*

discontinue (*formal*)
to stop doing something that has been done or has been happening regularly for a while: *Doctors decided to discontinue his treatment because it did not seem to be working.*
→ **Discontinue** is also used when a company stops making something and you cannot buy it anymore: *This model of phone has been discontinued. The company stopped making it last year.*

halt
to make something stop changing, developing, or making progress. **Halt** is used especially in writing, for example in news reports: *Doctors say that if people have better information, we could halt the spread of the disease.*

block
to stop something from happening because you believe it is wrong or bad. You use **block** especially when you are talking or writing about legal or political situations: *The government filed lawsuits to block the company's plans to drill for oil in the wildlife refuge.*

suspend (AWL) (*formal*)
to officially stop something from continuing for a period of time. You use **suspend** when you plan to start it again later: *Coal production was suspended until safety checks had been carried out.*
→ If someone is **suspended** from school, a team, or work, he or she is not allowed to take part for a period of time, as a punishment for something he or she has done: *She was* ***suspended from*** *school because she was rude to a teacher.*

terminate (AWL) (*formal*)
to end a legal agreement: *The management cannot terminate an employee's contract without talking to the union.*
→ see **prevent**

stop² /stɑp/ *noun*

- ► **stop**
- ► **halt**
- ► **suspension** (*formal*)

stop
the act of not continuing to move or happen. **Stop** is most often used in the phrase **come to a stop**: *The car came to a stop outside the house.* | *Work has come to a stop because there is no money left.*

halt
a stop. **Halt** sounds more formal than **stop**: *Heavy snow brought traffic to a halt.* | *The president called for a* ***halt to*** *the fighting.*

suspension (AWL) (*formal*)
the act of officially stopping something for a period of time before starting it again: *The government announced a month-long* ***suspension of*** *oil exports.*
→ see **end¹**

store /stɔr/ *noun*

- ► **store**
- ► **shop**
- ► **supermarket**
- ► **mall**

store
a building where people go to buy things: *He bought some milk at the grocery store.* | *We tried a couple of stores on Main Street, but nobody sells radios.*

S

→ The phrase **go to the store** is a common phrase that usually means that someone is going to a store that sells food: *I'm going to the store – do we need anything for dinner?*

shop
a small store that sells only a particular type of thing: *Juan works in a gift shop.*

supermarket
a large store that sells food and things that people need at home: *Could you buy some bread and potatoes for me if you're going to the supermarket?*

mall
a very large building with a lot of stores in it. **Malls** have a large variety of stores and restaurants: *Mia met her friends **at the mall** to get some pizza and see a movie.*

storm /stɔrm/ *noun*

- ► storm
- ► snowstorm
- ► blizzard
- ► thunderstorm
- ► tornado
- ► hurricane
- ► typhoon
- ► cyclone

storm
if there is a storm, there is a lot of wind and rain or snow: *The tree had blown down in the storm.* | *A violent storm sent waves onto the deck of the boat.*

snowstorm
a storm with strong winds and a lot of snow: *A snowstorm struck the New York area.*

blizzard
a very bad storm with a lot of snow and wind: *This week's blizzard closed many airports on the East Coast.*

thunderstorm
a storm with thunder and lightning: *The plane waited for the thunderstorm to clear before taking off.*

tornado
a violent storm on land with strong winds that move quickly in a circle: *A tornado flipped cars and ripped mobile homes to pieces.*

hurricane
a storm with very strong fast winds and heavy rain, that forms over the ocean, moves in a large circle, and can cause a lot of damage: *The hurricane destroyed more than 30 homes near the beach.*
→ The word **hurricane** is used to describe this kind of storm when it happens in the Atlantic Ocean or the Northeast Pacific Ocean.

typhoon
a **typhoon** is the word for a **hurricane** in countries around the Northwest Pacific Ocean: *A powerful typhoon caused widespread damage to the city.*

cyclone
a **cyclone** is the word for a **hurricane** in countries around the South Pacific and Indian Oceans: *The South Pacific cyclone season is from November through April.*
→ see Topic **The Weather**

stormy *adjective* → see Topic **The Weather**

story /ˈstɔri/ *noun*

1 a description of events to entertain people
- ► story
- ► tale
- ► myth
- ► legend
- ► fable
- ► fiction

2 the events in a book, movie, or play
- ► story
- ► plot
- ► narrative (*formal*)

1 a description of events to entertain people

story
a description of real or imaginary events that is intended to entertain people: *Dad told us a **story about** the time when he went to Mexico.* | *This is the **story of** a young woman who finds true love in a very unusual place.*

tale
a story, usually about events that are not real: *The movie is a **tale of** friendship between two women in different parts of the world.* | *The book is a collection of folk tales from around the world.*

myth
an old story about gods, brave people, or strange creatures: *In Greek myths, Zeus is the god of the sky and thunder.*

legend
an old well-known story, especially one about people who lived long ago, that is usually not true: *According to the legend, drinking the water from the spring brings good luck.*

fable
a story, especially one with animals, that teaches us something: *The **fable of** the boy and*

the wolf teaches us that it is important not to tell lies.

fiction
books and stories about people and events that are not real: *J.K. Rowling is a children's fiction writer.*

2 the events in a book, movie, or play

story *also* **storyline**
the things that happen in a book, movie, or play: *The acting in the movie was good, but the storyline was boring. | I haven't read "The Three Musketeers," but I know the story.*
→ **Storyline** and **plot** are used more commonly than **story** in this meaning.

plot
the story that is told in a book, movie, or play: *The plot was very complicated, and I didn't understand what was happening.*

narrative (*formal*)
a story or the way that events are described in a story. **Narrative** is often used in writing about literature: *The writer based the narrative on his time in Japan.*
→ see Topic **Books and Literature**

straight¹ /streɪt/ *adverb*

1 without doing anything else first
- straight
- directly
- right

2 in a direction that is not curved, and usually with nothing in between
- straight
- right
- directly

1 without doing anything else first

straight
immediately, without doing anything else first: *I was tired, so I went straight to bed when I got home. | He went straight home after school.*

directly
without doing anything else first. **Directly** sounds more formal than **straight**: *He had gone directly from high school to university.*

right
immediately, and without any delay: *Come home right after school. Don't go to Dan's house today. | I need you here **right away**!*

2 in a direction that is not curved, and usually with nothing in between

straight
in a line or direction that is not curved or bent, especially when there is nothing in between one person or thing and another: *She looked straight at me. | The book was on the table straight in front of you - how could you miss it?*

right
exactly in a position or place, with nothing in between: *My uncle's house is right next to ours.*

directly
directly means the same as **right** but sounds more formal: *The girl was sitting directly opposite him.*

straight² /streɪt/ *adjective*

1 not bent or at an angle
- straight
- level
- upright

2 happening one after another
- straight
- consecutive
- in a row

1 not bent or at an angle

straight
not bent or curved, and not at an angle: *Use a ruler to draw a straight line. | None of the pictures on the walls were straight.*

level
flat and having no part higher than any other part: *Make sure the shelves are level before you put the screws in the wall.*

upright
straight up, and not lying flat or leaning: *Stand the books upright on the shelves, in alphabetical order.*

2 happening one after another

straight
happening one after the other: *The team has had five straight wins. | We had ten straight days of rain.*

consecutive
consecutive means the same as **straight** but sounds more formal: *Crops have been badly affected by three consecutive years of very little rain.*

in a row
one after the other: *I've eaten at restaurants for three nights in a row, so I'm going to stay home tonight.*
→ **GRAMMAR:** You put **in a row** after the noun.

ADVERBS

You can make the adjective **consecutive** into an adverb by using an **-ly** ending: *Crops have been badly affected for three years consecutively.*

strange /streɪndʒ/ *adjective*

1 different from what is usual

- strange
- weird
- funny
- odd
- peculiar (*formal*)
- bizarre
- eccentric
- unusual
- abnormal
- atypical (*formal*)

ANTONYMS → see **normal**, **ordinary**, **usual**

2 not known

- strange
- unfamiliar
- unknown

S

1 different from what is usual

strange
different from what is usual or normal, often in a way that is difficult to understand or explain: *She was wearing strange clothes – a red cowboy hat and a pink dress.* | *He is a little strange. Sometimes I see him talking to himself as he walks along the sidewalk.*

weird
strange in a way that you do not like or in a way that frightens you: *I had a weird feeling in my stomach as I walked up the stairs to meet her.*
→ When you use **weird** or **strange** to describe other people, it shows that you do not approve of them, and it can be insulting: *Marcus is so weird sometimes!* | *She said some strange things in class.*

funny
funny means the same as **strange** but is more informal: *The car is making a funny noise.*

odd (AWL)
strange, especially in a way that does not seem right or normal: *The police stopped him and checked his car because of his odd behavior.*

peculiar (*formal*)
peculiar means the same as **odd** but sounds formal: *Her grandfather looked at her in a peculiar way, as if he had never seen her before.*

bizarre
very unusual and strange: *He has some very bizarre ideas about using insects to cure cancer.*

eccentric
behaving in a way that is unusual and different from most people. You use **eccentric** when you want to say that someone is a little strange or different but you do not want to sound disapproving or insulting: *Their neighbor was an eccentric man who had over 30 cats.*

unusual
different from what is usual or normal: *It is a very unusual knife. I've never seen one like it before.*

abnormal (AWL)
different from what is normal, especially in a way that seems worrying or dangerous: *Doctors were concerned because she had abnormal levels of sugar in her blood.*

atypical (*formal*)
not having the features that something usually has. **Atypical** is used especially in scientific language: *The steep roof on the house is atypical because most houses in the area have flat roofs.*

ADVERBS

You can make the adjectives that mean "different from what is usual" into adverbs by using an **-ly** ending: *Angela was dressed strangely.* | *The police picked him up because he was behaving oddly.* | *The levels of sugar in her blood were abnormally high.*

2 not known

strange
a strange place, person, or thing is one that you do not know, so that you feel a little frightened or worried: *I was on my own in a strange town and was feeling lonely.* | *When a strange man approached me in the dark, I got scared and ran.*

unfamiliar
if something is unfamiliar, you have never seen it or heard about it before: *The handwriting on the envelope was unfamiliar, and Jo wondered who the letter was from.*

unknown
unknown means the same as **unfamiliar**, but sounds more formal and is used especially in writing: *The first explorers were visiting unknown territory.* | *The man seemed to be suffering from a disease that was **unknown to** doctors.*

stream *verb* → see **flow**, **move**, **river**, **series**

street *noun* → see **road**

strength /streŋkθ/ *noun*

- ► strength
- ► power
- ► force
- ► energy
- ► stamina
- ► endurance
- ► might

strength
the physical ability to lift, move, or do things: ***Regular exercise will improve both your health and strength.*** | ***I didn't have enough strength to climb any farther.*** | ***It took all my strength to lift the heavy box.***
→ You can also use **strength** to mean "the mental ability to be brave or determined in difficult situations": ***It took all my strength to say "no" to him. I could not leave my family.***

power
a lot of physical strength in a particular part of your body. **Power** sounds more formal than **strength**: ***The power of the tiger's legs allows it to leap 30 feet in the air.***

force
physical strength that is needed to be able to push, pull, or lift something: ***I had to use force to get the window open.***

energy (AWL)
the physical and mental strength that makes you able to move and do things: ***Anna is usually full of energy, but she seems tired recently.***

stamina
physical strength that lets you continue doing something for a long time without getting tired: ***Basketball players need to have both speed and stamina on the court.***

endurance
the physical and mental strength you need to continue doing something difficult or painful for a long time: ***You need to increase your strength and endurance before you try to run a marathon.***

might
great strength and power. **Might** is used especially in literature: ***He swung the axe with all his might and cut down the tree.***

strengthen /ˈstreŋkθən/ *verb*

- ► strengthen
- ► reinforce
- ► toughen

ANTONYMS → see **weaken**

strengthen
to become stronger or to make something stronger. You use **strengthen** to talk about making your body, a building, or structure stronger: ***He was doing some exercises to strengthen his leg muscles.*** | ***The walls were strengthened with steel rods.***
→ You can also use **strengthen** about feelings, beliefs, or relationships: ***Our friendship has steadily strengthened over the years.*** | ***As he became older, his belief in God strengthened.***

reinforce (AWL)
to make something stronger by adding something to it. You use **reinforce** about materials and buildings or structures: ***The wall is being reinforced with tons of cement.***
→ You can also use **reinforce** about beliefs, opinions, or behavior: ***Being robbed reinforced his view that the city is a dangerous place.***

toughen
to make a rule or law stronger: ***The governor plans to toughen the laws on air pollution in the state.***

stress *verb* → see **emphasize**, **pressure**

stretch *verb* → see **expand**, **lengthen**, **reach**, **tighten**, Topic **Sports and Exercise**

strict /strɪkt/ *adjective*

- ► strict
- ► firm
- ► tough
- ► stern
- ► demanding
- ► rigid
- ► harsh
- ► authoritarian

strict
someone who is strict expects people to obey rules or do what he or she says. You use **strict** about people in authority such as teachers, parents, or schools: ***Her parents are strict, and she will get in trouble if she comes home late.*** | ***The school is very strict about the way students dress.***
→ You can also use **strict** to describe rules or laws that have strong punishments if they are not obeyed: ***The laws against drunkdriving are very strict in this state.***

firm
if you are firm, you show that you are in control of the situation and will not change your opinion: ***It is important to be firm with young children.*** | ***Emily's answer was polite but firm. "No, I do not want to go on a date with you," she said.***

tough
someone who is tough is very strict, and is

S

determined that his or her orders will be obeyed. **Tough** sounds more informal than **strict**, and you use it especially when you think that someone is strict in a good way: *We need a government that is **tough on** crime.*

→ **Tough** is also used about rules or actions that are strict: *Tough measures are needed to prevent terrorism.*

stern
a stern person is strict in a serious, disapproving, and unfriendly way: *Her grandfather was a stern man who rarely smiled.*

demanding
a demanding person expects other people to work very hard and do things exactly the way he or she wants: *My piano teacher is very demanding, but I don't mind working hard to get things right for her.*

rigid (AWL)
systems or rules that are rigid are strict and difficult to change. Use **rigid** especially when these rules do not change even when the situation is different: *Some teenagers fight with their parents because they think the rules at home are too rigid.*

harsh
too strict, severe, or unkind. You use **harsh** especially about words, criticism, or punishment that seem too extreme and unfair: *The punishment was very harsh – he was sent to prison for stealing a loaf of bread.*

authoritarian
an authoritarian government or person forces people to obey strict rules or laws, and punishes them severely if they do not. You use **authoritarian** especially about governments that are too severe and do not respect the rights of people: *The population has lived under an authoritarian government for more than 40 years.*

ADVERBS

You can make the adjectives **strict**, **firm**, **stern**, **demanding**, **rigid**, and **harsh** into adverbs by using an **-ly** ending: *The laws are strictly enforced.* | *He told her sternly to go home.* | *The man was punished harshly for stealing the bread.*

strictly /ˈstrɪktli/ *adverb*

- ► strictly
- ► firmly
- ► sternly
- ► rigidly
- ► harshly

strictly
in a clear and definite way that you must obey: *My sister and I were **strictly forbidden** to enter the room.* | *They brought their children up very strictly.*

firmly
in a way that shows you are in control of the situation and will not change your opinion: *"No," she said firmly, "you can't go."*

sternly
in a serious and strict way: *The librarian sternly told the group of teenagers to be quiet.*

rigidly
in a way that is very strict and must be obeyed exactly, and will not change for any reason: *You will have one hour for the exam, and the time limit will be rigidly enforced.*

harshly
in a way that is strict, severe, or unkind: *The prisoners were harshly treated and often received no food.*

strike¹ *verb* → see **hit¹**, **ring¹**

strike² *noun* → see **attack¹**

string /strɪŋ/ *noun*

- ► string
- ► thread
- ► twine
- ► rope

string
a long thin material that is used for tying things: *I need a piece of string to tie this package.* | *Her key hung on a string around her neck.*

thread
a long very thin string that you use for sewing

string

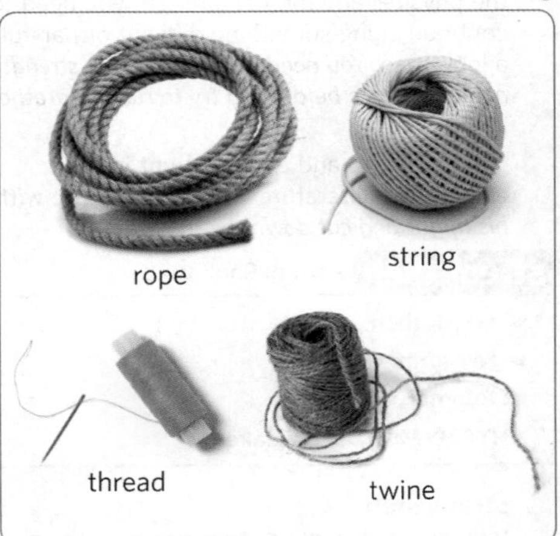

cloth: *She took a needle and thread, and sewed the two pieces of material together.*

twine
a strong rough string made by twisting together two or more strings: *I tied up the stack of newspapers with twine.*

rope
a very strong thick string, made by twisting together many threads or strings: *The climbers used a rope to keep them safe while they climbed.*

strip *noun* → see **piece**

stripe /straɪp/ *noun*

- ► stripe
- ► band
- ► streak

stripe
a long narrow line of color, usually part of a pattern where the line is repeated many times: *The American flag has red and white stripes. | She was wearing a shirt with pink and brown stripes.*

band
a thick colored line that is different from the areas around it: *The bird has a white head with a black band across it.*

streak
a colored line, especially one that is not straight or that has been made without any plan or pattern: *At sunset, the clouds made beautiful long pink streaks across the sky.*
→ see **line¹ (2)**

stripe

strong /strɔŋ/ *adjective*

1 able to lift or carry heavy things and do a lot of physical work
- ► strong
- ► powerful
- ► muscular
- ► well-built
- ► tough

ANTONYMS → see **weak (1)**

2 determined and confident
- ► strong
- ► forceful
- ► tough

3 not easily broken or damaged
- ► strong
- ► sturdy
- ► heavy-duty
- ► durable
- ► tough (*informal*)
- ► robust (*formal*)

ANTONYMS → see **weak (2)**

4 clear and definite, and having an effect on you
- ► strong
- ► deep
- ► powerful
- ► profound (*formal*)
- ► intense
- ► overwhelming
- ► irresistible
- ► acute

1 able to lift or carry heavy things and do a lot of physical work

strong
having a lot of physical power, so you can lift heavy things or do hard physical work: *It took four strong men to lift the piano. | Can you open this jar? You're stronger than I am.*

powerful
very strong. **Powerful** is used especially in writing, and you use it about muscles or a part of someone's body: *He has very powerful arms and shoulders because he swims so much.*

muscular
having big strong muscles and looking strong: *If you want a more muscular body, you should try lifting weights.*

well-built
a well-built man is strong and tall in an attractive way. **Well-built** is used especially in

S

writing: *A well-built young man in a military uniform entered the room.*

tough
physically strong and able to deal with difficult situations or pain: *I worried when my grandma got sick, but she is tough and got better quickly.*

ADVERBS
You can make the adjective **powerful** into an adverb by using an **-ly** ending: *His arms were powerfully strong from lifting weights.*

2 determined and confident

strong
determined, confident, and able to deal with difficult situations: *Mom had to be very strong when our father left us.* | *The country needs a strong leader at this difficult time.*

forceful
strong and confident, and expressing opinions firmly or clearly in a way that makes other people agree with you: *He gave a forceful reply to the criticisms.*

tough
strong and confident, and able to deal with difficult situations without changing your mind. **Tough** seems more informal than **strong**: *As a lawyer, she is known for being tough and getting her clients what they want.*

ADVERBS
You can make the adjectives **strong**, **forceful**, and **tough** into adverbs by using an **-ly** ending: *We strongly appeal to the committee to reconsider.* | *He replied forcefully to the criticisms.* | *She wrote a toughly worded letter to the school.*

3 not easily broken or damaged

strong
not easily broken or damaged: *The bags are made of strong black plastic.* | *You'll need a strong piece of rope for towing the car.*

sturdy
strong and often thick, and not likely to fall over or get broken. You use **sturdy** about things that people make, such as buildings or furniture: *The furniture is simple but sturdy.* | *The fence was made with sturdy wooden posts.*

heavy-duty
extremely strong. You use **heavy-duty** about things like materials, tools, or machines that have to be stronger than usual because they will be used a lot or used in difficult conditions: *I wear heavy-duty rubber gloves when I clean the bathrooms.*

durable
substances or products that are durable are strong and will last a long time, even if they are used a lot. **Durable** is especially used to describe products, for example in advertising: *Aluminum is stronger and more durable than plastic.*

tough (*informal*)
tough means the same as **durable** but sounds informal: *The rubber on the tires is tough enough to last for two years of constant use.*

robust (*formal*)
strongly made. You use **robust** especially about the structure of something, for example a vehicle or machine: *It is a light but robust bike, probably the best you can get for that price.*

ADVERBS
You can make the adjectives **sturdy** and **durable** into adverbs by using an **-ly** ending: *The furniture is simple but sturdily built.* | *Their products are durably made.*

4 clear and definite, and having an effect on you

strong
a strong feeling or belief is one that you feel or believe a lot: *Many people have strong feelings about the issue.* | *She became a teacher because of a strong desire to help children.*

deep
a deep feeling is one that you feel very strongly. **Deep** is used especially about a feeling of love, disappointment, or sympathy: *The news came as a deep disappointment to us all.* | *He never found a way to express his deep love for her.*

powerful
having a strong effect on your thoughts and feelings: *Jealousy is a very powerful emotion.*

profound (*formal*)
having a very strong effect on you: *If the mother is depressed, this will have a profound effect on the young child.*

intense (AWL)
a feeling that is intense is extremely strong: *As we waited for the winner to be announced, the excitement was intense.*

overwhelming *also* **overpowering**
an overwhelming feeling is so strong that you cannot think or behave normally: *Sasha had the overwhelming desire to get up and leave.* | *His sadness after her death was overpowering, and he became very depressed.*

irresistible
too strong or powerful to be stopped. You use **irresistible** about a need or a feeling that you

want to do something: *I was overcome by an irresistible urge to cry.* | *The temptation to take a chocolate was irresistible.*

acute
an acute feeling is very strong. **Acute** is used especially about a feeling of pain, embarrassment, or anxiety: *As he stood on stage, he felt acute embarrassment when he realized that his zipper was open.*
→ see Topic **Describing People's Emotions**

ADVERBS
You can make the adjectives that mean "clear and definite, and having an effect on you" into adverbs by using an **-ly** ending: *She believed strongly that she could help the children.* | *It was an intensely exciting moment.* | *He stood on stage, feeling acutely embarrassed.*

strongly /ˈstrɔŋli/ *adverb*

- ► strongly
- ► powerfully
- ► forcefully

strongly
in a way that is meant to persuade someone, or that shows how sure or serious you are: *The senator strongly opposed the changes in the law.* | *We strongly believe that she is innocent.*

powerfully
in a way that is strong or has a very strong effect: *His research powerfully demonstrates how effective the new medicine is.*

forcefully
in a way that is clear and shows strong reasons: *She spoke forcefully against the war.*

structure[1] *noun* → see **building**, **system**

structure[2] *verb* → see **organize**

struggle[1] *verb* → see **campaign[2]**, **fight[1]**, **try[1]**

struggle[2] *noun* → see **campaign[1]**, **fight[2]**

stubborn /ˈstʌbɚn/ *adjective*

- ► stubborn
- ► determined
- ► obstinate
- ► willful

stubborn
refusing to change your opinions or behavior because you believe you are right: *I told him it was a bad idea, but Dave is so stubborn that he did it anyway.* | *The city wants to build a shopping center here, but a stubborn old man has refused to sell his land to them.*

determined
if you are determined to do something, you have decided that you are definitely going to do it, and you will not let anything stop you: *I was* ***determined to*** *be a professional dancer and practiced every day.* | *She was* ***determined that*** *her children should have the best possible education.*

obstinate
very stubborn in a way that is annoying and unreasonable: *You know I'm right. You are just being obstinate.*

willful
deliberately continuing to do what you want, even after you have been told to stop. You use **willful** especially about a child or young person who is behaving badly, or about someone who knows that what they are doing breaks the law: *It was a mistake, not a willful violation of the law* (=a deliberate act of breaking the law).

SYNONYM CHECK
Stubborn or determined?
Stubborn, **obstinate**, and **willful** are usually used when you disapprove of someone's behavior. You use **determined** when you think that the behavior is good.

ADVERBS
You can make the adjectives that mean **stubborn** into adverbs by using an **-ly** ending: *He stubbornly refused to sell his land.* | *You obstinately do the opposite of what I tell you!* | *Did the boys willfully break the law?*

stubbornness /ˈstʌbɚn-nəs/ *noun*

- ► stubbornness
- ► determination
- ► obstinacy

stubbornness
the quality of refusing to change your opinions or behavior because you believe you are right: *She wouldn't change her mind, and her stubbornness was annoying.* | *He refused any help, just out of stubbornness and a desire to do it himself.*

determination
the quality of deciding to do something so that you keep trying, even when a situation is difficult: *Success requires hard work and determination.*

obstinacy
the quality of being stubborn in a way that is

S

annoying and not reasonable: *His obstinacy caused the deal to fall through.*

stuck /stʌk/ *adjective*

- stuck
- jammed

stuck
someone or something that is stuck is in a particular position or place, and cannot move: *I tried to open the window, but it was stuck.* | *The boat was* ***stuck in*** *the mud.* | *We got* ***stuck in*** *a traffic jam.*

jammed
something that is jammed cannot move because it is trapped between two surfaces or parts of something: *The paper got* ***jammed in*** *the printer.*
→ see **trapped**

stuck up *adjective* → see **proud**

student /ˈstudnt/ *noun*

- student
- pupil (*formal*)
- learner
- scholar

ANTONYMS → see **teacher**

student
someone who is studying at a school, college, or university: *How many students are there in your class?* | *Johanna is a student at Cornell University.* | *High school students are required to take at least two years of mathematics.*

pupil (*formal*)
someone who is being taught at a school, especially a child: *The school has around 500 pupils between 11 and 18.*

learner
someone who is learning a particular subject or skill: ***Learners of*** *English often have problems with pronunciation.* | *He missed a few weeks of school, but he is a quick learner and soon caught up with everyone.*

scholar
someone who studies a subject and knows a lot about it: *Some scholars argue that the building was used for storage, not for housing.*
→ see Topic **Education**

study[1] /ˈstʌdi/ *verb*

- study
- work
- review

study
to spend time reading, writing, or learning about a subject for school or college, when you are not in the classroom: *I have to stay home and study tonight.* | *She spent the morning at the library,* ***studying for*** *her final exams.*

work
to spend time and effort in order to study and do assignments (=work a teacher has told you to do for your classes at school): *You'll have to work hard to pass the exams.* | *Mandy has been* ***working on*** *a school project about the solar system all weekend.*

review
to look at something you have already studied, such as books, notes, and assignments, usually so that you can prepare for a test: *I'll just review my notes and go to bed.* | *The instructor said that we'll spend next week* ***reviewing for*** *the final exam.*
→ see **examine**, **learn**, **read**, **research[2]**

study[2] *noun* → see **experiment**, **report**, **research[1]**, Topic **Education**, **Science and Technology**

stuff[1] *noun* → see **substance**, **thing**

stuff[2] *verb* → see **fill**, **push[1]**

stupid /ˈstupɪd/ *adjective*

- stupid
- dumb (*informal*)
- foolish
- unwise (*formal*)
- idiotic

ANTONYMS → see **smart**

stupid
not intelligent, or not showing good judgment: *That was a stupid thing to say.* | ***It was stupid of*** *me* ***to*** *leave my keys in the car.* | *It is a stupid idea, and it will never work.*

dumb (*informal*)
dumb means the same as **stupid**: *She is always asking such dumb questions.* | *He told me a lot of lies, and I was dumb enough to believe him.*

foolish
stupid and not thinking about the possible results of what you do. **Foolish** sounds more formal than **stupid** and is used especially in writing: ***It was foolish of*** *her* ***to*** *spend all the money and not save anything.* | *I was afraid of looking foolish in front of the whole class.*

unwise (*formal*)
actions or decisions that are unwise are not based on good judgment: ***It is unwise to*** *keep medicine in a place that children can reach.*

idiotic
very stupid: *Never dive into water when you can't see the bottom – it is idiotic.*
→ see **silly**

SYNONYM CHECK
Stupid, dumb, and idiotic
It is rude to say that someone else is **stupid** or **dumb**. People usually only say these words when they are very annoyed with someone. Saying that someone is **dumb** is not as rude as saying he or she is **stupid**, but it is still very impolite. **Idiotic** is also rude and shows that you are strongly criticizing someone.

ADVERBS
You can make the adjectives that mean **stupid** into adverbs by using an **-ly** ending: *I stupidly locked my keys in the car.* | *The child's parents unwisely left the medicine where he could find it.* | *The kids idiotically dived into very shallow water.*

style /staɪl/ *noun*

- ► style
- ► elegance
- ► sophistication
- ► glamour

style (AWL)
a confident and attractive quality that makes people admire you or admire the way something looks. **Style** can be used to talk about the way someone behaves as well as the way someone dresses or decorates the place where he or she lives or works: *The actress is an old woman now, but she still has a lot of style.* | *The hotel has been decorated* ***with style****, and it was a pleasure to stay there.*

elegance
an attractive and graceful quality. You often use **elegance** when something looks as though it is expensive: *Their townhouse in Manhattan has a simple elegance.* | *The best ice skaters possess both strength and elegance.*

sophistication
a quality that shows someone knows a lot about art, fashion, and modern life: *She is from a small town, but she has gained a new sophistication after living in the city for a few years.*

glamour
a quality that makes someone or something seem very exciting, attractive, or fashionable: *I love the glamour of Hollywood actresses from the 1950s.*
→ see Topic **Books and Literature**

stylish /ˈstaɪlɪʃ/ *adjective*

- ► stylish
- ► in fashion
- ► fashionable
- ► trendy (*informal*)
- ► elegant
- ► sophisticated
- ► chic
- ► glamorous

stylish (AWL)
attractive in a way that people admire, and popular now: *Monica was wearing a stylish black dress.* | *The furniture looked very stylish and modern.*

in fashion *also* **in style**
if something is in fashion or in style, it is popular at a particular time. You use **in fashion** or **in style** especially about clothing or hair: *In the 1960s, long hair was in fashion for men.* | *Tight jackets are back in style.*

fashionable
if something is fashionable, it is popular at a particular time: *She likes wearing fashionable clothes.* | *Bright colors are very fashionable this year.*

trendy (*informal*)
very popular and fashionable now. You use **trendy** about something that is not likely to remain popular for very long: *They went to a trendy new restaurant in Manhattan for dinner.*

elegant
stylish, attractive, and graceful, in a way that looks expensive: *She is a tall elegant woman in her 40s.* | *We stayed in one of Boston's most elegant hotels.*

sophisticated
stylish and confident. You use **sophisticated** about someone who knows a lot about art, fashion, and modern life: *I always admired my cousin who lived in New York City – she seemed so glamorous and sophisticated to me.*

chic
very stylish and showing good judgment about what is attractive and fashionable: *She looks very chic with her hair cut short.*

glamorous
attractive and exciting. You use **glamorous** about people who are rich, successful, or famous, and about the things they do or use: *The actress wore a glamorous black evening gown to the awards ceremony.*
→ see **fashionable**

ADVERBS

You can make the adjectives that mean **stylish** into adverbs using an **-ly** ending, except for **in fashion**: *Monica was stylishly dressed.* | *They sell bags in fashionably bright colors.* | *The restaurant was trendily decorated.*

subject /ˈsʌbdʒɪkt/ *noun*

1 the thing you are talking or writing about
- subject
- topic
- issue
- matter (*formal*)
- question
- theme

2 something you study at a school or university
- subject
- class
- major
- field

1 the thing you are talking or writing about

subject
the thing you are talking or writing about: *I like to read books about astronomy – it is a very interesting subject.* | *I could see John was embarrassed, so I changed the subject.* | *While we are* ***on the subject of*** *money, do you have the $10 you owe me?*
→ In everyday English, people often use **about** to say what the subject of a book or movie is. *The movie is about war* sounds less formal than *The subject of the movie is war.*

topic (AWL)
a subject that people often talk or write about, for example in books, newspapers, or at school: *The teacher gave us a list of topics to choose from – I chose The Environment.* | *Their main topic of conversation seems to be football.*

issue
an important subject that people discuss and argue about: *The cost of health care is an issue that affects everyone.*

matter (*formal*)
an important idea or problem that you have to think about, discuss, or deal with: *There are important things we need to discuss, especially the* ***matter of*** *how to pay for the trip.*

question
a difficult subject or problem that has often been discussed but still needs to be solved: *What is the best way to help less developed countries? That is the really important question.*

theme (AWL)
an important idea that appears several times in something such as a book, movie, or poem: *One of the central themes of the book is the relationship between people and nature.*

2 something you study at a school or university

subject
one of the things that you study at a school or university, such as English, history, or mathematics: *English was my favorite subject in school.* | *What subjects are you studying this semester?*

class
a series of lessons in one subject, often with an examination at the end: *The statistics class is really hard.*
→ Don't say: ~~*I'm making a class in art history*~~. Say: *I'm taking a class in art history.*

major
the main subject that someone studies in college: *"What is your major?" "Biology."* | *She's a business major.*

field
a subject that people study at a very high level, or that people are involved in as part of their work: *Dr. Kim is famous for his work* ***in the field of*** *heart surgery.*
→ see Topic **Education**

substance /ˈsʌbstəns/ *noun*

- substance (*formal*)
- material
- stuff (*informal*)
- matter (*formal*)

substance (*formal*)
any type of solid, liquid, or gas such as a chemical or mineral: *A substance called chlorophyll makes the leaf green.* | *All the poisonous substances are clearly labeled.*

material
any solid substance that can be used for making things: *Steel is a stronger material than iron.* | *The company supplies building materials such as bricks and cement.*

stuff (*informal*)
stuff means the same as **substance** but sounds much more informal. You use **stuff** especially when you do not know exactly what something is called, or it is not important to say exactly what it is: *I've got some sticky stuff on my shoe.* |

Do you have any of that clear plastic stuff to cover food with?

matter (*formal*)
any physical substance. **Matter** is used especially in science: *Matter is made up of particles called atoms and molecules.*

subtle /'sʌtl/ *adjective*

- ► subtle
- ► inconspicuous
- ► faint

ANTONYMS → see **clear (3)**

subtle
not easy to notice unless you pay careful attention: *The patterns look very similar, but there are subtle differences between them.* | *The warning signs of the disease are so subtle that they are often ignored.*

inconspicuous
an inconspicuous person or thing is difficult to notice, especially because they look the same as the people or things around them: *The laboratory was in an inconspicuous low gray building downtown.*

faint
a faint sound, smell, or light is difficult to hear, smell, or see because it is not strong or clear: *I heard a faint sound downstairs.*

ADVERBS

You can make the adjectives that mean **subtle** into adverbs by using an **-ly** ending: *The man's appearance had subtly changed.* | *We tried to leave the theater inconspicuously.* | *"It was my fault," she said faintly.*

subtract /səb'trækt/ *verb*

- ► subtract
- ► take away (*informal*)
- ► minus
- ► deduct

ANTONYMS → see **add**

subtract
to take one number from another and calculate the answer: *Most of the children in the class know how to add and subtract.* | *If you* ***subtract*** *6* ***from*** *10, you get 4.*

take away (*informal*)
take away means the same as **subtract** but is informal: *If you* ***take away*** *6* ***from*** *10, you get 4.*

minus
used in mathematics to show that you subtract one number from another: *Nine minus five equals four and is written as 9 – 5 = 4.*

deduct
to subtract an amount from a total. You use **deduct** especially about money or points that are subtracted when following official rules or an official system: *Points will be deducted for spelling mistakes.* | *Your employer will* ***deduct*** *income tax from your salary.*

succeed /sək'sid/ *verb*

- ► succeed
- ► be successful
- ► achieve
- ► accomplish
- ► manage
- ► attain (*formal*)
- ► prosper (*formal*)
- ► thrive (*formal*)
- ► flourish (*formal*)

ANTONYMS → see **fail (1)**

succeed
to do something you tried or wanted to do: *She wanted to climb to the top of the mountain, and she succeeded.* | *You need to work hard to* ***succeed in*** *work or college.*
→ **GRAMMAR:** Don't say: ~~*She succeeded to climb the mountain*~~. Say: *She* ***succeeded in*** *climbing the mountain.*

be successful
be successful means the same as **succeed**: *Researchers have* ***been successful in*** *developing drugs to treat many illnesses.*
→ If a person or business **is successful**, he, she, or it makes money: *She opened two restaurants and both were very successful.*

achieve AWL
to succeed in doing something important, especially something that other people will admire you for: *She has achieved many things in the short time she has been with the company.* | *After long years of fighting, the country finally achieved independence.*

accomplish
to succeed in doing or finishing something good that you planned to do, after trying hard for a long time. You use **accomplish** especially with words like "goal," "objective," and "task": *After many years of hard work, she finally accomplished her goal and graduated from medical school.*

manage
to succeed in doing something difficult after trying very hard or almost failing: *I finally* ***managed to*** *get the bed down the stairs.*

attain (AWL) *(formal)*
to succeed in achieving a position or level of quality after trying hard: *More women are attaining positions of power.*

prosper *(formal)*
to be successful or become rich. **Prosper** sounds formal or literary and you use it about people or businesses: *Most parents want their children to get a good education and prosper.*

thrive *(formal)*
to become very successful. You use **thrive** especially about a company or industry that is very successful: *The coffee shop on the corner is thriving – it is always full of customers.*
→ You can also use **thrive** about a person, plant, or animal that is healthy and growing or developing in a successful way: *Their two sons are both thriving in their new school.*

flourish *(formal)*
flourish is very similar in meaning to **thrive** but you often use it about an organization or activity that had problems or seemed small before succeeding: *Once people began to understand the Internet, online shopping flourished.*

success /sək'ses/ *noun*

1 something that has the result you wanted
- ► success
- ► achievement
- ► accomplishment
- ► progress

ANTONYMS → see **failure (1)**

2 the state of achieving what you want to achieve
- ► success
- ► effectiveness

1 something that has the result you wanted

success
something that is a success has the result that you wanted or planned for: *The party was a big success – the whole class came and had a great time.* | *Critics have called the play a success, but audiences do not seem to like it as much.*

achievement (AWL)
something important or difficult that you do and that other people admire: *Winning three gold medals is a remarkable achievement.*

accomplishment
accomplishment means the same as **achievement**: *My biggest accomplishment was losing 50 pounds through diet and exercise.*

progress
the process of getting better at doing something and gradually getting closer to the result that you want to achieve: *We are very pleased with your son's* ***progress in*** *school.*
→ see **win²**

2 the state of achieving what you want to achieve

success
the state of having achieved what you wanted or planned: *He has finally achieved* ***success in*** *his career.* | *All of the players are important to the* ***success of*** *the team.*

effectiveness
the state of achieving the result you want in the best way possible. You use **effectiveness** about methods of doing something, medical treatments, or medicines: *The group has been looking at the* ***effectiveness of*** *the new reading program, to see if more children are reading at the right level.*

successful /sək'sesfəl/ *adjective*

1 achieving the result that you wanted
- ► successful
- ► effective
- ► productive
- ► fruitful

ANTONYMS → see **unsuccessful**

2 earning a lot of money from your business
- ► successful
- ► booming
- ► thriving
- ► prosperous
- ► profitable

3 a successful book, movie, game, etc. is very popular, so that many people watch it or buy it
- ► successful
- ► hit
- ► bestselling

1 achieving the result that you wanted

successful
achieving the result that you wanted: *The surgery was successful and the patient was soon able to walk again.* | *The firefighters were* ***successful in*** *preventing the fire from spreading.* | *I tried to change his mind, but I wasn't successful.*

effective
achieving the result that you want in the best way possible. You use **effective** about methods of doing something, medical treatments, or medicines: *What is the most effective way of teaching children to read?*

→ You can also use **effective** about a person who does his or her work in the best way and successfully: *She is a very effective teacher.*

productive
producing good results and achieving a lot of things: *We had a very productive meeting and made a lot of decisions.* | *How can we make the workers more productive?*

fruitful
fruitful means the same as **productive**, and is used especially about a relationship or discussion: *The two men had a fruitful partnership and wrote many songs together.*

ADVERBS
You can make the adjectives that mean "achieving the result that you wanted" into adverbs by using an **-ly** ending: *The surgeons successfully performed the operation.* | *We are teaching children effectively using this method.* | *The two men worked together fruitfully for years.*

2 earning a lot of money from your business

successful
a successful person, company, or product earns a lot of money: *Barbara is a successful businesswoman who owns several local restaurants.* | *Apple became one of the most successful companies in the U.S.*

booming
a booming economy or industry is very successful, and is producing more or making more money quickly: *In China, the economy is booming and people are becoming much wealthier.* | *Venezuela has a booming oil industry.*
→ You can also say that **business is booming** (=business is very good and companies are making a lot of money from selling things).

thriving
a thriving company or place is successful: *He started repairing computers in his dad's garage and built up a thriving business.* | *Los Angeles is the second largest city in the United States and is a busy thriving city.*

prosperous
a prosperous place or person is rich and successful: *The town became prosperous because of the fishing industry.* | *He was the son of a prosperous farmer and landowner.*

profitable
if a business is profitable, you can earn money from it: *It was no longer profitable to make the clothes in the U.S. and the company decided to close the factory.*

ADVERBS
You can make the adjectives **successful**, **prosperous** and **profitable** into adverbs by using an **-ly** ending: *Today the country is developing prosperously.* | *The business operated profitably for two decades.*

3 a successful book, movie, game, etc. is very popular, so that many people watch it or buy it

successful
if a book, movie, game, etc. is successful, it is very popular and many people watch it or buy it: *"Avatar" was one of the most successful movies of all time – it was seen by millions of people around the world.*

hit
a hit record, song, movie, or play is one that many people buy or pay to see: *"Just Dance" was Lady Gaga's first hit song.*

bestselling
a bestselling book or product is bought by a lot of people: *The movie is based on Stephenie Meyer's bestselling book "Twilight."*

suck *verb* → see **lick**

sudden /ˈsʌdn/ *adjective*

- ► sudden
- ► abrupt
- ► dramatic
- ► sharp

sudden
happening quickly or when you did not expect something to happen: *A sudden wind blew the leaves off the tree.* | *He complained of a sudden pain in his ear, that stopped as quickly as it started.*

abrupt
very sudden and unexpected. You use **abrupt** especially when you did not want something to happen, or it seems a little strange: *His career came to an abrupt end when he was injured.* | *No one could explain her abrupt departure.*

dramatic (AWL)
a dramatic change is sudden and very big: *There has been a dramatic improvement in his behavior this semester – he is much more polite and hard-working.*

sharp
a sharp increase or decrease is sudden and very big: *There has been a sharp fall in profits, from over $20 million to $1.8 million.*

S

ADVERBS

You can make the adjectives that mean **sudden** into adverbs by using an **-ly** ending: *Suddenly he felt a pain in his ear.* | *His behavior has dramatically improved.* | *Profits fell sharply last year.*

suddenly /'sʌdnli/ *adverb*

- ► suddenly
- ► all of a sudden
- ► abruptly
- ► without warning

suddenly
if something happens suddenly, it happens quickly or when you are not expecting it: *Suddenly, a rabbit ran across in front of them.* | *I suddenly realized I had forgotten to bring my flashlight.*

all of a sudden
all of a sudden means the same as **suddenly**, and is used at the beginning or end of a sentence: *All of a sudden, we heard a loud bang.*

abruptly
in a sudden, unexpected, and usually strange way: *When I asked him what his name was, he turned abruptly and walked away.*

without warning
if something bad happens without warning, it happens suddenly and there are no signs that it is going to happen: *The disease struck without warning – one day he was fine, the next day he was unable to move.*

suffer /'sʌfɚ/ *verb*

- ► suffer
- ► be in pain
- ► go through
- ► endure

suffer
to feel a lot of pain or unhappiness: *The people are suffering because they do not have enough food to eat.* | *The animals are kept in small cages and are clearly suffering a lot of discomfort.*
→ You can also say that someone **suffers from** an illness or medical problem: *My father suffers from heart disease.*

be in pain
to be feeling pain: *The boy was crying because he was in so much pain.*

go through
to have a very upsetting or difficult experience: *I was very stressed because I was going through a divorce.*

endure
to experience something bad for a long time: *The country's people have endured four years of civil war.* | *As a football player, he learned to endure pain.*
→ see **experience²** for **suffer** meaning "to experience an injury, illness, or damage"

suggest /səg'dʒest/ *verb*

1 to tell someone what he or she should or could do
- ► suggest
- ► recommend
- ► advise
- ► propose (*formal*)

2 to say something in an indirect way
- ► suggest
- ► imply
- ► hint
- ► indicate
- ► mean

3 to make someone imagine or remember something
- ► suggest
- ► evoke
- ► remind

1 to tell someone what he or she should or could do

suggest
to tell someone what he or she should or could do: *I* ***suggested that*** *we should go for a picnic.* | *The teacher suggested a few changes to his essay.* | *"Maybe," I suggested, "you could ask your mother to help."*
→ **GRAMMAR:** Don't say: ~~*She suggested him to take an English class.*~~ Say: *She suggested that he take an English class* or *She suggested taking an English class.*

recommend
to suggest something, because you have special knowledge about it or because you know it is good: *Can you recommend any good hotels in the area?* | *Dentists* ***recommend that*** *you brush your teeth twice a day.*

advise
to tell someone what you think he or she should do, especially when you know a lot about the subject: *His doctor* ***advised*** *him* ***to*** *rest.*

propose (*formal*)
to suggest a plan or idea: *They have proposed*

changes that will cut the budget by 20%.
→ see **advise**

2 to say something in an indirect way

suggest
to say something that makes your real meaning clear without saying it directly, especially when you say something bad about someone: *They seemed to be **suggesting that** I had done something wrong.*

imply (AWL)
to say one thing which seems to show that another thing is true, but without saying the true meaning directly: *He **implied that** Lynne agreed with him, but she has never talked to him about it!*

hint
to say something so that someone else can guess what you mean, even though you have not said it directly: *When Joe said it was getting late, I thought he was **hinting that** he wanted to leave.*

indicate (AWL)
to say what you think or what you intend to do in an indirect way. **Indicate** is more formal than **suggest**: *She has **indicated that** she wants to run for governor.*

mean
to intend something you say to have a particular meaning: *When people say they are not sure if they want to do something, they usually mean "no."*

3 to make someone imagine or remember something

suggest
to make someone think of or imagine something: *The stage was bare, but the lighting suggested it was meant to be a prison.*

evoke
to make someone think of a memory or feeling: *The Vietnam Memorial, with its list of names on black stone, is meant to evoke feelings of sadness and loss.*

remind
to make someone think of something that is similar: *The landscape reminded me of the desert mountains of California.*

suggestion /səg'dʒestʃən/ *noun*

- suggestion
- proposal
- recommendation

suggestion
an idea given to someone about what he or she should or could do: *Does anyone have any **suggestions about** what to do tomorrow? | The booklet gave some **suggestions for** games to play that would help your child in math.*

proposal
an idea or plan that someone suggests officially: *Republicans in the House have objected to a **proposal to** raise taxes.*

recommendation
a piece of official advice from a person or group who has studied a situation carefully: *After the crash, the Safety Board made several safety recommendations to the airlines.*
→ see **hint¹ (1)** for words meaning "a useful piece of advice"
→ see **advice**

suitable *adjective* → see **appropriate**, **right¹**

sum *noun* → see **amount**, **total**

summarize /'sʌməˌraɪz/ *verb*

- summarize
- sum up

summarize (AWL)
to make or write a short statement that gives the main information about something, but not all the details or everything that was said: *The president's speech was summarized on the front page of the newspaper. | Summarize Chapter 7 for homework.*

sum up
to summarize what someone has said in a few words, especially at the end of a speech, report, or essay: *At the end of your essay, write a paragraph summing up the arguments.*
→ You can also use **sum up** to mean "describe something using only a few words": *The coach summed up the season in two words: "A disaster."*

summary /'sʌməri/ *noun*

- summary
- overview
- outline
- synopsis (*formal*)

summary (AWL)
a short statement that gives the main information in or about something, but not all the details: *There was a short summary of the interview on the singer's website. | Write a summary of Chapter 7 for homework.*

overview
a summary of a large or complicated subject, situation, or series of events: *The book gives a useful overview of the history of Latin America.*

S

outline
a summary of the main ideas or facts, especially in a piece of writing: *He presented an **outline of** the research he was planning.*

synopsis (*formal*)
a short summary of the main things that happen in a movie, book, or story: *I read the **synopsis of** the book on the back cover to see if the story sounded interesting.*

sun /sʌn/ *noun*

- ► sun
- ► sunlight
- ► sunshine
- ► daylight

sun
the star in the sky that we see during the day, and the heat and light that come from it: *The sun was shining.* | *Our cat likes lying **in the sun**.*
→ When you are writing about the **Sun** in relation to space, planets, or other stars, use a capital S: *The Earth revolves around the Sun.*

sunlight
light from the sun: *Plants need sunlight and water to grow.*

sunshine
light and heat from the sun, when it is not covered by clouds: *The lake sparkled **in the sunshine**.* | *The city of Phoenix has over 200 days of sunshine every year.*

daylight
the light that comes from the sun during the day, or the hours when there is light from the sun: *I hadn't seen the house **in daylight** before, only at night.*

sunny /ˈsʌni/ *adjective*

- ► sunny
- ► fine
- ► nice
- ► bright
- ► clear

sunny
if it is sunny, the sun is shining and the sky is not covered by clouds: *What a beautiful sunny day!* | *The weather was warm and sunny.*

fine
if it is fine, it is sunny and the weather is good: *It was a fine day, so he decided to go for a walk.*

nice
if it is nice, it is sunny and warm, and the weather is good. **Nice** is more informal than **fine**: *We had nice weather and spent most of the day on the beach.*

bright
with a lot of sunlight: *It was a bright spring morning and the flowers were starting to bloom.*
→ **Bright** is also used to describe strong sunlight: *You should wear sunglasses in bright sunlight.*

clear
if it is clear, there are no clouds or mist: *On a clear day you can see the mountains from here.*
→ see Topic **The Weather**

ADVERBS
You can make the adjective **bright** into an adverb by using an **-ly** ending: *The sun was shining brightly that day.* The adverbs **finely**, **nicely**, and **clearly** are not used in this meaning.

sunrise /ˈsʌnraɪz/ *noun*

- ► sunrise
- ► dawn
- ► daybreak
- ► sun-up
- ► first light

ANTONYMS → see **sunset**

sunrise
the sky when the sun first appears, or the time when this happens: *I got up early to see the sunrise.* | *She awoke **at sunrise**.*

dawn
the time of day when light first appears as the sun comes up: *The general had planned to attack **at dawn** the next day.*

daybreak
daybreak means the same as **dawn** and is used especially in writing: *His father left the house before daybreak.*

sun-up
sun-up means the same as **dawn** but is more informal: *I've been working since sun-up.*

first light
the time when light first appears in the sky in the morning. **First light** sounds more poetic than **sunrise**: *We camped at the foot of the mountain for the night, and started up the trail **at first light**.*

sunset /ˈsʌnset/ *noun*

- ► sunset
- ► sundown
- ► dusk
- ► twilight
- ► nightfall

ANTONYMS → see **sunrise**

sunset
the sky when the sun goes down each evening, or the time when this happens: *There was a photograph of a beautiful pink and orange sunset on the wall.* | *The bats leave the caves* ***at sunset*** *each day.*

sundown
the time when the sun goes down at the end of the day: *We worked until sundown.* | *The two girls agreed to meet each other* ***at sundown*** *by the lake.*

dusk
the time when it starts to become dark in the early evening: *The streetlights come on* ***at dusk****.*

twilight
the time when it starts to become dark in the early evening, or the pale light at this time. **Twilight** sounds slightly literary: *They watched for the first stars to appear* ***at twilight****.*

nightfall
the time when it becomes dark in the evening and night begins. **Nightfall** sounds fairly literary: *We hurried to get back to camp before nightfall.*

superb *adjective* → see **good**

superior *adjective* → see **better**, **patronizing**

supervise /ˈsupəˌvaɪz/ *verb*

- ► supervise
- ► oversee

supervise
to make sure that someone is doing something correctly or behaving correctly: *Children should be supervised when they are doing chemistry experiments.* | *The investigation is being supervised by a senior police officer.*

oversee
to make sure that a group of workers do a piece of work correctly: *He oversaw the construction of the bridge.*
→ see **manage**

supper *noun* → see **meal**

supplement *noun* → see **extra²**

supply /səˈplaɪ/ *noun*

- ► supply
- ► stock
- ► stockpile
- ► hoard
- ► reserve
- ► resources

supply
an amount of something that you can use when you need it: *I only have a week's* ***supply of*** *my heart medicine left.* | *Supplies of food and water are being sent to the flood victims.*

stock
a supply of something that is kept by an organization to be sold or used later: *The hospital keeps large stocks of blood for emergencies.*

stockpile
a large supply of something that you collect in order to use in the future: *They have a big stockpile of firewood for the winter.*

hoard
a large amount of something that someone has hidden to keep it safe: *They found a hoard of gold that someone had buried under the ground.*

reserve
a supply. You use **reserve** about large quantities of materials such as oil, gas, or coal: *The country has huge gas reserves.*

resources (AWL)
all the money, materials, equipment, or people that you have available to use: *The school doesn't have the resources to buy new textbooks.* | *Russia is very rich in natural resources, including gas and oil.*

support /səˈpɔrt/ *verb*

1 to agree with a person, group, or idea
- ► support
- ► back
- ► endorse
- ► stand up for
- ► uphold (*formal*)

2 to be under something so that it does not fall
- ► support
- ► hold up
- ► prop up
- ► hold
- ► bear

1 to agree with a person, group, or idea

support
to agree with a person, group, or idea and want

him, her, or it to be successful: *Which political party do you support? | She supports the idea of lower taxes for companies that develop solar or wind power.*

back
to support someone or something, and usually to do something to help that person or idea be successful: *The peace plan is backed by the UN.*

endorse
to say officially that you support or approve of someone or something: *The president endorsed the proposal and said that it would improve air safety.*

stand up for
to support someone or something by defending him, her, or it from being attacked or criticized: *When other people said you were wrong, I stood up for you. | He was not afraid to stand up for his rights.*

uphold (*formal*)
to support a law or decision officially: *The court agreed with the lower court and upheld its decision.*

2 to be under something so that it does not fall

support
to be under something so that it does not fall: *The tin roof was supported by wooden posts. | I'm not strong enough to support your weight.*

hold up
hold up means the same as **support** but is more informal: *One of the poles that was holding up the tent broke.*

prop up
to stop something from falling or keep it in a high position by putting something under it: *The fence was leaning over, so I propped it up with a piece of wood. | He was sitting in bed, propped up by pillows.*

hold
to be able to support the weight of someone or something and not break: *The wooden ladder was old, and I didn't think it would hold me.*

bear
bear means the same as **hold** but is a little more formal: *Is the ice thick enough to bear our weight?*
→ see **encouragement**, **help²**, **provide for**

supporter /sə'pɔrtə-/ *noun*

- ► supporter
- ► sponsor
- ► follower

supporter
someone who supports a person, group, or plan: *The mayor's supporters are working to help him be re-elected. | The senator is a supporter of the proposal to change the fundraising rules.*

sponsor
a person or company that supports someone or something by providing money, for example to help pay for a television show, sports team, sports event, etc.: *The team's main sponsor is a software company.*

follower
someone who believes in someone's religious or political ideas or supports a leader: *What did Jesus teach his followers?*

suppose *verb* → see **pretend**, **think**

supposedly /sə'poʊzɪdli/ *adverb*

- ► supposedly
- ► apparently
- ► seemingly

supposedly
used when saying what other people say about someone or something, when you do not think they are right: *His bike was expensive and supposedly better than the others, but there really didn't seem to be any difference between them.*

apparently
used when saying something that other people say is true, although you do not know whether it is really true: *I didn't see it, but apparently the movie was very good.*

seemingly
used to say that something seems to be true but is not really true or correct: *We spent seemingly endless hours just playing outside.*

supposed to /sə'poʊzd tu/ *adjective*

1 used when saying that someone should do something (verbs)
- ► be supposed to
- ► be expected to
- ► have to

2 used when saying what someone wants or expects to happen (verbs)
- ► be supposed to
- ► be meant to
- ► be intended to
- ► be designed to

1 used when saying that someone should do something (verbs)

be supposed to
if you are supposed to do something, you should do it, for example because a rule or someone in

authority says you should: *You're supposed to write your full name at the top of the test.* | *People are not supposed to park on the red lines.*

be expected to
if someone is expected to do something, it is his or her duty to do it: *Students are expected to do their own research.* | *Women were expected to stay home and raise children.*

have to *also* **have got to**
if you have to do something, you must do it: *I have to be home before six o'clock.* | *Nurses have to buy their own uniforms.*
→ see **have to**, **should**

2 used when saying what someone wants or expects to happen (verbs)

be supposed to
used when saying what someone wants or expects to happen, especially when it does not happen: *The fence is supposed to keep animals out of the vegetable garden, but some rabbits got in anyway.*

be meant to
be meant to means the same as **be supposed to**: *This was meant to be a private meeting – what are all these people doing here?*

be intended to
used when saying the result that someone wants something to have: *The changes are intended to make the company more efficient.*

be designed to
to be made or planned for a particular purpose: *The equipment was designed to be easy to use.* | *This exercise is designed to strengthen your legs.*

sure /ʃʊr/ *adjective*

1 having no doubts about something (adjectives)
- **sure**
- **certain**
- **positive**
- **convinced**
- **confident**

2 to do what is necessary so that something definitely happens (verbs)
- **make sure**
- **make certain**
- **ensure** (*formal*)
- **guarantee**

3 to find out if something is true or has happened (verbs)
- **make sure**
- **make certain**
- **check**
- **verify** (*formal*)

1 having no doubts about something (adjectives)

sure
if you are sure that something is true, you have no doubts about it: *I'm **sure that** she lives on this street, but I don't know which is her house.* | *"He wouldn't lie to me." "Really? Are you **sure about** that?"*

certain
completely sure. **Certain** is more formal than **sure** and sounds more definite: *Do not eat wild berries unless you are **certain that** they are safe to eat.*

positive (AWL)
very sure that something is true. You use **positive** especially when other people say that it might not be true: *"Mina is getting married." "Are you sure?" "I'm positive."*

convinced (AWL)
feeling sure that something is true, especially when it is hard to know if something is really true: *She was **convinced that** the man was lying, but she didn't have any proof.*

confident
sure that what you want will happen, or that you can do something: *We have a lot of good players and we are **confident that** we can win tonight's game.* | *He was feeling **confident of** success in the test.*

ADVERBS

You can make the adjectives **certain**, **positive**, and **confident** into adverbs by using an **-ly** ending: *You are certainly too sick to leave the hospital.* | *I was positively convinced that he was lying.* | *The player commented confidently that her team could win.*

2 to do what is necessary so that something definitely happens (verbs)

make sure
to do what is necessary so that something definitely happens, because this is important: *Make sure you get to the airport on time – we don't want to miss our plane.* | *You must **make sure that** you put your name at the top of the test paper.*

make certain
to make completely sure that something will

happen. **Make certain** sounds a little more formal and a little more definite than **make sure**: *She bought a large turkey, just to* ***make certain that*** *there would be enough for everyone.*

ensure (AWL) (*formal*)
to make sure that something happens. You use **ensure** especially in official situations: *Please* ***ensure that*** *you have your passport with you.*

guarantee (AWL)
to make it completely sure that something will happen or exist: *The team needs to win this game in order to guarantee that they will stay in the competition.* | *The constitution guarantees the right to freedom of speech.*

3 to find out if something is true or has happened (verbs)

make sure
to find out if what you want is true or has happened: *He called to* ***make sure that*** *we got home okay.* | *Can you* ***make sure that*** *I turned the oven off?*

make certain
to make completely sure that something is true or has happened. **Make certain** sounds a little more formal and a little more definite than **make sure**: *Before buying a sofa,* ***make certain that*** *it will fit in your living room.*

check
to find out if something is true or has happened: ***Check that*** *you have entered your password correctly.* | *I wanted to* ***check if*** *the company had received my order.*

verify (*formal*)
to make sure officially that something is true: *They will need to* ***verify that*** *the letter was written by Abraham Lincoln – if it is, it could be worth a lot of money.*

surely *adverb* → see **certainly**

surface[1] *noun* → see **outside[2]**

surface[2] *verb* → see **appear**

surge *noun* → see **increase[2]**

surplus /ˈsɚpləs/ *noun*

- ► surplus
- ► excess
- ► glut

ANTONYMS → see **lack[1]**

surplus
an amount that is more than people need or can use: *Farmers are finding it easy to get workers because there is a* ***surplus of*** *labor.* | *The city will have a small budget surplus at the end of the year* (=it will have a little bit of money left).

excess
an amount that is more than you need or should have. You use **excess** especially when this has a bad effect: ***It is not healthy to have an excess of salt in your body.***

glut
an amount that is more than people need, because too many have been produced at one time: *Bananas are cheap right now because there is a* ***glut of*** *them.*
→ see **extra[2]**

surprise[1] /sɚˈpraɪz/ *noun*

1 something that you did not expect to happen
- ► surprise
- ► shock
- ► revelation

2 the feeling you have when something happens that you did not expect
- ► surprise
- ► shock
- ► amazement
- ► astonishment
- ► wonder

1 something that you did not expect to happen

surprise
something that you did not expect to happen: *I'm not going to tell you what I got for your birthday – I want it to be a surprise.* | *The news that she was getting married came as a surprise.*

shock
something that you did not expect that makes you feel very surprised and upset: *We didn't know he was sick, so it was a* ***shock to*** *us when we were told he had died.*

revelation (AWL)
something that is very surprising. You use **revelation** about surprising information that was hidden or private before, especially when it is in a news report: *There were more* ***revelations about*** *the senator's private life on the news.*

2 the feeling you have when something happens that you did not expect

surprise
the feeling you have when something happens that you did not expect: ***To my surprise,*** *the company offered me the job.* | *His friends looked at him* ***in surprise*** *when they saw his new haircut.*

shock
the feeling of surprise you have when something very bad happens that you did not expect: *I lost my job this morning – I'm still **in shock**.*

amazement
a feeling of very strong surprise, and a feeling that something cannot really be true, even though it is: *He stared **in amazement** at his watch. He had slept for over 16 hours.*

astonishment
a feeling of very strong surprise. You use **astonishment** to show that something is difficult to believe, even though it is true. **Astonishment** is a stronger word than **amazement**: ***To my astonishment**, a huge fish suddenly jumped out of the water in front of me.*

wonder
a feeling of strong surprise and admiration, because something does not seem real or true, even though it is. **Wonder** is used mainly in literature: *People stared **in wonder** at the first steam trains.*
→ see **shock[1]**

surprise[2] /sə'praɪz/ *verb*

- surprise
- take someone by surprise
- amaze
- astonish
- startle
- stun
- shock

surprise
if something surprises you, you do not expect it to happen: *His reaction surprised me – I thought he would be pleased, but he was angry.* | *Shh, be quiet! I want to surprise him.*

take someone by surprise *also* **catch someone by surprise**
if something takes you by surprise, it happens suddenly when you are not ready to deal with it: *The heavy snowfall took us by surprise and we didn't have any chains for the car tires.*

amaze
to surprise someone very much, especially because something is unusual: *Her ability to learn languages amazed her teachers.* | *It amazes me how easy it is to fool some people.*

astonish
to surprise someone very very much. If you use **astonish**, something seems even more surprising and hard to believe than when you use **amaze**: *He astonished theater audiences by making an elephant disappear.*

startle
to surprise someone by appearing suddenly or making a sudden noise: *The sound of the gun startled the birds and they all flew away.*

stun
to surprise or shock people very much, especially so that they are not sure how to react: *The young player's unexpected victory stunned the tennis world.*

shock
to make someone feel very surprised and upset: *It shocked us to see how sick she looked.*
→ see **shock[2]** for more words meaning "to surprise and upset someone"

surprised /sə'praɪzd/ *adjective*

- surprised
- amazed
- astonished
- stunned
- startled
- taken aback
- shocked

surprised
if you are surprised by something, you did not expect it to happen: *I was **surprised that** she invited me to her party because I thought she didn't like me.* | *"I didn't realize you were coming," he said in a surprised voice.*

amazed
very surprised, especially because something is very unusual: *The meal was really cheap and I was **amazed at** how good it tasted.*

astonished
extremely surprised, and finding something difficult to believe: *Scientists were **astonished to** find that the tree was over 3,000 years old.*

stunned
very surprised and shocked so that you do not know what to say or do: *When he asked for a divorce, she was stunned, because she had thought everything was okay.*

startled
surprised because you suddenly hear or see someone or something: *She was **startled by** a sudden knock at the door.*

taken aback
surprised and not sure what to say or do: *They were taken aback when the manager of the restaurant asked them to leave, even though they had done nothing wrong.*

S

shocked
surprised and upset because of something bad that has happened: *I was **shocked by** the sudden change in his appearance – he looked awful.*
→ see **shocked** for more words meaning "surprised and upset"

surprising /sə'praɪzɪŋ/ *adjective*

- ► surprising
- ► amazing
- ► astonishing
- ► startling
- ► unexpected
- ► shocking
- ► unforeseen

surprising
if something is surprising, you do not expect it to happen or be true: *It was an easy question and **it was surprising that** no one knew the answer.* | *A surprising number of people have never read a single book.*

amazing
very surprising. You use **amazing** especially about good or impressive things: *He hit two home runs in one game, which is pretty amazing.*

astonishing
extremely surprising and difficult to believe: *The students improved at an astonishing rate using the new program.*

startling
very surprising. You use **startling** when you suddenly find out about a piece of information: *NASA scientists made the startling discovery that life may have existed on Mars more than three billion years ago.*

unexpected
if something is unexpected, it is surprising because you did not think it would happen: *Her victory was unexpected – everyone thought her opponent would win.*

shocking
very surprising and upsetting: *The conditions in the refugee camps were shocking – there was very little food or water.*

unforeseen
an unforeseen situation is one that you did not expect to happen and causes problems: *The bridge took a long time to build because of a series of unforeseen problems.*
→ see **strange**

ADVERBS

You can make the adjectives **surprising**, **amazing**, **astonishing**, **startling**, **unexpected**, and **shocking** into adverbs by using an **-ly** ending: *Surprisingly, no one knew the answer.* | *His offer was startlingly generous.* | *The conditions were shockingly poor.*

surrender /sə'rendə/ *verb*

- ► surrender
- ► give in
- ► yield
- ► submit (*formal*)

surrender
to say officially that you want to stop fighting, because you know that you cannot win: *When the soldiers realized they would be defeated, they put down their guns and surrendered.*

give in
to finally agree to do something that you do not really want to do: *She kept asking her parents for a laptop computer until they gave in and bought her one.*

yield
yield means the same as **give in** but is more formal: *We will not **yield to** the terrorists' demands.*

submit (AWL) (*formal*)
to agree to obey someone who is stronger or has authority over you: *Your dog must learn to **submit to** you, but that does not mean that you can be cruel to make him obey.*

surround /sə'raʊnd/ *verb*

- ► surround
- ► be enclosed by
- ► be ringed by

surround
to be all around something or go all around something: *An island is a piece of land surrounded by water.* | *Police officers surrounded the building so that the robbers could not escape.*

be enclosed by
to be surrounded by something, especially a fence or wall: *The backyard is enclosed by a high brick wall.*

be ringed by
to be completely surrounded by people or things that are in the shape of a circle. **Be ringed by** sounds literary: *The town is ringed by mountains on every side, which makes it hard to get to.*

S

survey /ˈsɚveɪ/ *noun*

- ► survey
- ► poll
- ► questionnaire

survey (AWL)
a set of questions that an organization asks a lot of people in order to find out what they think about something, what they do, what they buy, etc.: *The survey found that only 10% of Americans really enjoyed their work.*

poll
a set of questions that an organization asks a lot of people in order to find out what they think, especially about politics: *According to a recent opinion poll, 65% of voters support the president.*

questionnaire
a written set of questions that someone gives to people in order to collect information: *The students filled out a* ***questionnaire about*** *their health.*

survive *verb* → see **live**

survivor *noun* → see **living**[3]

suspect *verb* → see **disbelieve**, **think**

suspense /səˈspens/ *noun*

- ► suspense
- ► tension
- ► uncertainty

suspense
a situation that makes you feel excited or worried, because you do not know what will happen next: *There's no suspense – it's obvious how the movie will end.* | *Don't keep us in suspense! Who won?*

tension (AWL)
a nervous feeling that you have because something is very exciting or frightening, or because something important is going to happen: *You could feel the tension in the audience when the host came onto the stage to announce the winner.*

uncertainty
a worrying feeling because you are not sure what will happen in the future: *There is a lot of uncertainty right now because people are worried about losing their jobs.*

suspicion *noun* → see **belief (2)**, **distrust**[2]

swamp /swɑmp/ *noun*

- ► swamp
- ► marsh
- ► bog
- ► wetlands

swamp
land that is usually partly covered with shallow water, and often has trees growing in it. **Swamps** are usually in hot places: *The swamp is full of alligators.*

marsh
an area of soft very wet ground, often with grasses growing in it: *This plant is found in marshes and shallow water.*

bog
an area of soft wet muddy ground: *My foot sank in the bog and when I tried to pull it out I lost my shoe.*

wetlands
land that is partly covered with water, and has grasses and other plants growing in it. **Wetlands** are often important places for birds or animals to live in: *We must protect these wetlands and not let them be turned into farmland.*

swamp

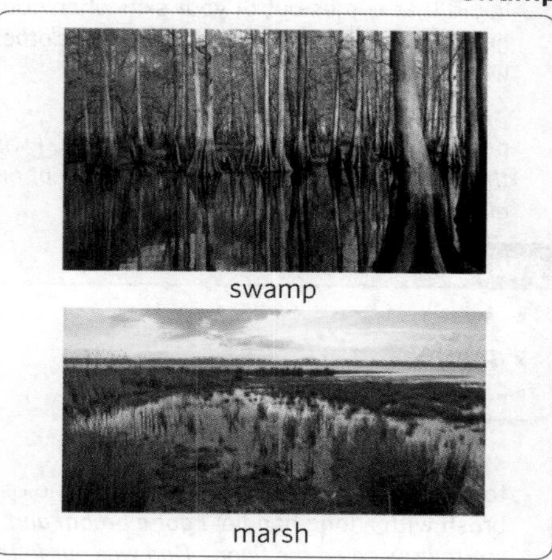
swamp
marsh

swear /swer/ *verb*

- ► swear
- ► curse

swear
to say very bad words: *If you swear, the kids will copy you and use bad words too.*

curse
to say bad words that show you are angry: *His dad tripped over a toy truck on the floor and*

cursed. | *Men cursed at their bad luck.*

→ see **promise¹** for **swear** meaning "to make a serious promise to do something"

sweat¹ /swet/ *verb*

- ► **sweat**
- ► **perspire** (*formal*)
- ► **break into a sweat**

sweat
if you sweat, liquid comes out of your skin, for example because you are hot or nervous: *He was sweating because he had been out running.*

perspire (*formal*)
perspire means the same as **sweat**: *The woman was perspiring and kept wiping her forehead.*

break into a sweat
to begin to sweat, especially because you are nervous or sick: *He broke into a sweat and then asked if he could lie down.*

sweat² /swet/ *noun*

- ► **sweat**
- ► **perspiration** (*formal*)

sweat
liquid that comes out of your skin when you are hot or nervous: *It was so hot that their clothes were soaked with sweat.*

perspiration (*formal*)
perspiration means the same as **sweat**: *I wiped the perspiration from my forehead and kept on digging.*

sweep /swip/ *verb*

- ► **sweep**
- ► **brush**
- ► **scrub**

sweep
to clean dirt from the floor or the ground using a brush with a long handle: *I got a broom and started sweeping the floor.* | *Dad was out in the yard, sweeping leaves off the patio.*

brush
to clean your teeth or make your hair look neat using a brush: *Do you brush your teeth after every meal?* | *She was brushing her hair in front of the mirror.*

scrub
to clean something by rubbing it very hard with a brush or cloth, using water and soap: *Tom was on his knees, scrubbing the floor to try and remove the stain.*

→ see **clean²**

sweet /swit/ *adjective*

- ► **sweet**
- ► **sugary**

ANTONYMS → see **sour**

sweet
tasting like sugar or containing sugar: *I love sweet things like chocolate and ice cream.* | *The strawberries were sweet and so good.*

sugary
containing a lot of sugar. You use **sugary** especially when you do not like something because it contains too much sugar: *Sugary foods and drinks are bad for your teeth.*

switch on/off *phrasal verb* → see **turn on/off**

symbol *noun* → see **sign**, Topic **Books and Literature**

sympathetic /ˌsɪmpəˈθetɪk/ *adjective*

- ► **sympathetic**
- ► **understanding**
- ► **compassionate**
- ► **caring**
- ► **sensitive**
- ► **empathetic** (*formal*)

sympathetic
kind when someone has a problem and showing that you feel sorry for him or her: *When I lost my job, my friends were very sympathetic and tried to help when they could.*

understanding
kind and not getting angry when someone has a problem, because you understand it. You use **understanding** about someone who is in charge of you, such as an employer, a teacher, or parents: *My boss was very understanding and she said I should go home and rest.*

compassionate
feeling sorry for people who are in a bad situation, and wanting to help them: *As a teacher, she is compassionate but firm with the children.*

caring
kind to other people and trying to make sure that they are all right: *She was a good caring mother who always did her best for her children.*

sensitive
able to understand other people's feelings and careful not to upset them: *If you were more sensitive, you would realize that she doesn't want to talk about her accident.*

empathetic (*formal*)
able to understand other people's feelings and problems, especially because you have been through a similar experience yourself: *In the classes, prisoners learn to have a more* ***empathetic*** *attitude* ***toward*** *other people.*
→ see **kind²**

ADVERBS

You can make the adjectives that mean **sympathetic** into adverbs by using an **-ly** ending: *Laura smiled sympathetically and hugged him.* | *Many people have compassionately given their time to help us.* | *The counselors are trained to listen empathetically.*

sympathize /ˈsɪmpəˌθaɪz/ *verb*

- ► sympathize
- ► understand
- ► empathize
- ► appreciate

sympathize
to realize that someone is having problems and feel sorry about that: ***I sympathize with*** *the families who have had to wait so long for help.* | *The president* ***sympathized with*** *people who had lost their jobs.*

understand
to know how someone feels: *My parents just don't understand me.* | *She understands what it is like to be a teenager.*

empathize
to understand someone else's feelings and problems, because you can imagine being in his or her situation: *She had a difficult childhood, which helps her to empathize with the suffering of other children.*

appreciate (AWL)
to realize that a situation is true or that someone has a particular feeling. You use **appreciate** especially when you think something else is more important: *We* ***appreciate that*** *many families will not like the tax increases, but we have no choice.*
→ see **sorry (3)**

sympathy /ˈsɪmpəθi/ *noun*

- ► sympathy
- ► understanding
- ► empathy
- ► pity
- ► compassion

sympathy
the feeling that you have when you are sorry for someone who is having problems: *When his wife died, people sent cards to express their sympathy.* | *I felt some* ***sympathy for*** *the other team, because they were unlucky to lose the game.*

understanding
an attitude that shows that you know how someone feels and why he or she behaves in that way: *Troubled teenagers need to be treated with understanding.*

empathy
sympathy for someone, because you can imagine what it is like to be in his or her situation: *You feel a lot of* ***empathy for*** *the characters in the book – they seem very real.*

pity
a strong feeling of sympathy, especially for someone who is in a very bad situation: *She felt* ***pity for*** *the lonely little girl and tried to help her.*

compassion
sympathy for people who are in a bad situation, especially so that you want to help them, not punish them or treat them unkindly: *The judge showed compassion and did not jail the woman, because she was very sick.*
→ see **kindness**

system /ˈsɪstəm/ *noun*

1 an organized way of doing something
- ► system
- ► process
- ► procedure

2 a group of things or parts that work together
- ► system
- ► network
- ► structure
- ► framework

1 an organized way of doing something

system
an organized way of doing something, in which people have to follow certain rules: *The United States has a democratic system of government.* | *Some people want to change the tax system so that rich people pay more tax.*

process (AWL)
a series of things that you do in order to achieve something: *He has just begun the* ***process of*** *rewriting his movie script.* | *Getting permission to stay in the U.S. is often a long process for new immigrants.*

procedure (AWL)
the correct or usual way of doing something, in which you have to do a series of things based on

S

official rules: *The company has changed its procedure for dealing with complaints from customers.*

→ see **way**

2 a group of things or parts that work together

system
a group of things or parts that work together for a particular purpose: *Your stomach is part of your digestive system.* | *They want to improve the city's transportation system.*

network (AWL)
a group of things, places, or people that are connected to each other: *All the company's offices are linked by a computer network.* | *It is important to have a good network of friends and family whom you can ask for help.*

structure (AWL)
the way that the parts of something are arranged and connect with each other: *A new management structure has been introduced in the company, so that there are fewer levels between workers and managers.*

framework (AWL)
the basic parts of a system, which the other parts depend on: *The U.S. constitution is the framework on which our political system is based.* | *Einstein used the work of other scientists as a framework for his ideas.*

S

Tt

table *noun* → see **list**[1]

tackle *noun* → see **push**[2]

tact /tækt/ *noun*

- ► tact
- ► sensitivity
- ► discretion

tact
the ability to say things in a kind and polite way so that you do not upset someone. You use **tact** especially when you are talking about criticizing someone or giving your opinion in a way that does not hurt his or her feelings: *When you criticize someone else's work, use tact. Be polite and make helpful comments.* | *If you don't like her dress, tell her so – but do it* ***with tact****. Tell her she looks great in a different one!*

sensitivity
the ability to understand other people's feelings and problems, so you deal with a situation in a way that does not upset them: *The movie director handled the subject of mental illness* ***with sensitivity****.*

discretion (AWL)
the ability to be careful about what you say to people so that you do not tell them other people's secrets or embarrass anyone: *All the information in your school records is treated* ***with discretion****, so we will only give information about you to people who really need to know.*

tactful /ˈtæktfəl/ *adjective*

- ► tactful
- ► sensitive
- ► discreet
- ► diplomatic

ANTONYMS → see **tactless**

tactful
careful to say something in a way that will not upset someone, especially when you are criticizing him or her, or giving your opinion: *I wish you would be more tactful – you shouldn't have said she looks heavier than before.* | *I knew he had failed the test, but I was tactful enough not to mention it.*

sensitive
able to understand other people's feelings and problems, so you deal with situations in a way that does not upset them: *The police should be* ***sensitive to*** *the needs of crime victims.*

discreet
careful not to let too many people know something that might embarrass someone: *Please be discreet – I don't want people to know I lost my job.*

diplomatic
careful to deal with people politely in a difficult situation, so you do not upset them: *Barkley was diplomatic, saying that the other team had played a great game.*
→ see **polite**, **thoughtful**

ADVERBS

You can make the adjectives that mean **tactful** into adverbs by using an **-ly** ending: *I tactfully didn't mention the test, because I knew he had failed.* | *A good friend knows how to listen sensitively.* | *Barkley diplomatically praised the other team.*

tactless /ˈtæktləs/ *adjective*

- ► tactless
- ► thoughtless
- ► insensitive
- ► indiscreet

ANTONYMS → see **tactful**

tactless
saying things that can upset someone because you have not thought carefully enough about how he or she will feel: *I thought* ***it*** *would be* ***tactless to*** *ask her about her divorce.* | ***It was tactless of*** *Larry* ***to*** *criticize the meal that Lori had spent all day preparing.*

thoughtless
not thinking about someone else's feelings: *"What's wrong with your hair?" he said, not realizing that his thoughtless comment would hurt her feelings.*

insensitive
not noticing or caring when you say something that upsets someone, because you do not understand other people's feelings or problems: *The article described the plane crash in detail, which was* ***insensitive to*** *the victims' families.*

indiscreet
talking about things that should be kept secret because they will embarrass someone: *He should not have mentioned the money; it was very*

indiscreet.

→ see **thoughtless** for "doing things that may hurt someone else's feelings"

→ see **rude**

ADVERBS

You can make the adjectives that mean **tactless** into adverbs by using an **-ly** ending: *She tactlessly asked me about my divorce.* | *The article insensitively described the details of their deaths.* | *Charlie indiscreetly mentioned the huge sum of money they were paying him.*

take /teɪk/ *verb*

1 to take something with you from one place to another
- ► take
- ► bring
- ► carry
- ► deliver
- ► transport (*formal*)

2 to take something away from someone
- ► take
- ► grab
- ► seize
- ► snatch
- ► confiscate (*formal*)

ANTONYMS → see **give (1)**

1 to take something with you from one place to another

take
to move someone or something from one place to another: *I'm going to **take** my lunch **to** school tomorrow.* | *Would you mind taking Olivia home? We're not ready to leave yet.* | *I took Spencer one of the cookies.*

bring
to take someone or something with you to a place or person: *Can you bring me a pen?* | *Don't forget to bring your bike if you want to go riding with us.* | *I didn't expect Curtis to **bring** so many friends **to** the party.*

carry
to have something in your hands or arms, or in your pockets or handbag as you go somewhere: *Ann carried the baby upstairs.* | *Could you help me **carry** these suitcases **to** the car?*

→ You can also say that a vehicle, pipe, or wire **carries** people or things when it takes them from one place to another: *The new plane can carry up to 600 passengers.* | *These wires carry electricity to the house.*

deliver
to take things such as letters, packages, and goods to a place or person: *Unfortunately, the package was **delivered to** the wrong address.*

transport (AWL) (*formal*)
to move things or people from one place to another in a vehicle: *The plane is used to transport military equipment.*

SYNONYM CHECK

Take or bring?

You use **take** when you are moving things away from a place: *Don't forget to take your umbrella* (=you should take your umbrella with you when you leave).

You use **bring** when you are moving things with you toward a place: *Don't forget to bring your umbrella* (=you should bring your umbrella with you when you come to where I am).

2 to take something away from someone

take
to take something from someone: *Let me take your bags – they look heavy.* | *He **took** our coats **from** us and hung them up.*

→ You also often use **take** when saying that someone steals something: *I turned around for a minute and someone took my phone.*

grab
to take something from someone suddenly, in a rough or violent way: *When I wasn't looking, she grabbed the ball out of my hands.*

seize
to take something from someone quickly and in a forceful way. **Seize** sounds more formal than **grab**: *Jen **seized** the letter **from** her and ripped it up.*

→ You can also say that an official organization such as the police **seizes** illegal goods when it takes them from someone: *Police seized 53 weapons and made 42 arrests.*

snatch
to take something from someone very quickly, especially when it is something that you should not be taking: *The thief snatched her purse and ran off down the street.*

confiscate (*formal*)
if the police or people in authority confiscate something, they take it away from someone, either as a punishment or because that person is not allowed to have it: *The teacher confiscated all the students' candy, because eating is not*

allowed in classrooms.
→ see **take away** at **refuse**, **subtract**
→ see **take off** at **leave**, **undress**
→ see **take out** at **remove**

take advantage of *verb phrase*

- ► take advantage of
- ► use
- ► exploit
- ► abuse

take advantage of
to treat someone in a way that is not fair in order to get what you want: *Don't let him take advantage of you. You are his roommate, not his cook, so you shouldn't have to make meals for him.* | *I worry that people might take advantage of him because he trusts everyone.*

use
to treat someone in a nice way, in order to get something that you want. If you **use** someone, you treat someone nicely but do not really have the kind feelings you show to the other person. **Use** is more informal than **take advantage of**: *He doesn't love you. He is just using you to get a free place to live.*

exploit (AWL)
to treat someone or something in an unfair way, in order to gain an advantage for yourself. **Exploit** sounds more formal than **take advantage of**: *Some businesses exploited their workers, making them work long hours in poor conditions.* | *The company exploits people's fear of crime to sell them products they do not need.*

abuse
to use your power or position in a wrong or harmful way, in order to gain an advantage for yourself: *Officials abused their power by giving jobs to their friends.*
→ see **use**[1] for **take advantage of** meaning "to use a situation in a good way to do something you need or want to do"

take care of *verb phrase*

- ► take care of
- ► look after
- ► babysit
- ► care for

take care of
to make sure a person or animal is safe and has the things he or she needs: *Taking care of three small children all day is hard work.* | *When the old woman got sick, there was no one to take care of her.* | *You can have a dog if you are willing to take care of it.*

→ You can also **take care of** plants or objects by doing things to make sure they stay in good condition: *Who is taking care of the house while you're away?*

look after
to take care of a person or animal for a short time, especially a child: *Can you look after the kids for me this afternoon?* | *I usually look after my little brother after school before Mom gets home.*

babysit
to take care of a child while his or her parents are not at home, especially when you are paid to do this: *Amanda* ***babysits for*** *the neighbors to earn extra money.*

care for
to make sure that someone who is old or sick has the things he or she needs. **Care for** sounds a little more formal than **take care of** or **look after**: *Louise has spent the last three years caring for her sick father.*
→ see **take care of sth** at **deal with**

take part *verb phrase*

- ► take part
- ► participate (*formal*)
- ► join in
- ► contribute

take part
to do an activity with other people: *More than 10,000 people* ***took part in*** *the celebrations.* | *The school runs a sports program, and lots of the students take part.*

participate (AWL) (*formal*)
to do an activity with other people: *Researchers are looking for people to* ***participate in*** *a study on the effects of sleep.*

join in
to start to do something that other people are already doing: *Chris, would you join in the discussion? What do you think?* | *We're playing a game. Why don't you join in?*

contribute (AWL)
to take part by giving or saying something: *When we're having a class discussion, the teacher likes it when we all contribute.* | *We all* ***contributed to*** *the picnic. I brought sandwiches, Martina brought fruit, and Juan brought the drinks.*

GRAMMAR CHECK: take part
You say **take part in** something, **participate in** something, **join in** something, but **contribute to** something.

take turns *verb phrase* → see **share**[1]

T

tale *noun* → see **story**

talent /ˈtælənt/ *noun*

- ► talent
- ► ability
- ► gift
- ► flair
- ► knack

talent
an ability to do something well, especially one that you are born with: *Evan's parents noticed his **talent for** drawing very early.*

ability
if you have an ability to do something, you can do it well: *The coach is looking for kids with good athletic ability.*

gift
an unusual or very strong talent: *Clara has a real **gift for** languages and speaks Spanish, Russian, and Japanese.*

flair
a talent for doing something well, especially something artistic: *You can see from her artwork that she has a real **flair for** design.*

knack
an ability to do something easily, especially something that other people think is difficult: *Everyone likes Bob – he just has a **knack for** making people feel comfortable and relaxed.*
→ see **skill**

talented /ˈtæləntɪd/ *adjective*

- ► talented
- ► good
- ► skillful
- ► gifted
- ► promising

talented
having a natural ability to do something well: *He is a very talented writer and has had several short stories published. | These drawings are amazing – I didn't know you were so talented!*

good
able to do something well: *I am **good at** sports and win a lot of competitions. | A good actor makes you believe in the character he is playing.*

skillful
good at doing something that you have learned and practiced: *Ms. Davis is a skillful teacher who gets the students excited about chemistry.*

gifted
having a natural ability to do something extremely well: *She is a gifted child who can do very difficult math problems. | He is a gifted poet.*

promising
likely to be good or successful: *Williams is a promising young player who hopes to win a basketball scholarship.*
→ see **skilled** for "able to do sth well because you have been doing it for a long time"

ADVERBS

You can make the adjectives **skillful** and **promising** into adverbs by using an **-ly** ending: *The teacher skillfully takes his students through the difficult math problems. | The team looks promisingly strong this season.*

talk[1] /tɔk/ *verb*

1 to say things to someone
- ► talk
- ► speak
- ► have a conversation
- ► converse (*formal*)
- ► chat
- ► gossip
- ► chatter

2 to talk to someone in a way that shows you think they are less important than you
- ► talk down to
- ► patronize
- ► condescend (*formal*)

1 to say things to someone

talk
to say things to someone, especially as part of a conversation: *I could hear Sarah and Andy talking in the next room. | I don't want to **talk about** the test – I'm just glad it's over. | Ed is over there **talking to** the woman in the red dress.*

speak
to talk to someone about something, especially for a particular reason. **Speak** sounds a little more formal than **talk**: *Hello, may I **speak to** Darren Taylor, please? | The mayor refused to **speak with** reporters.*

have a conversation
to talk to someone for a period of time about everyday things: *One customer was **having a long conversation with** the waitress about the weather. | We **had a good conversation about** what should happen next.*

converse (*formal*)
converse means the same as to **have a**

conversation but is more formal: *I was glad to have the chance to* ***converse with*** *someone who spoke Spanish.*

chat
to talk with someone in a friendly way about things that are not important: *It was nice* ***chatting with*** *you, but we really should get back to work.*

gossip
to talk about other people's behavior, often saying things that are not kind or not true: *Everyone at school was* ***gossiping about*** *Tania and her new boyfriend.*

chatter
to talk a lot without stopping about things that are not important: *She* ***chattered*** *happily* ***about*** *the party until she noticed I wasn't listening.*
→ see **speak** for "talk in another language"

2 to talk to someone in a way that shows you think they are less important than you

talk down to
to talk to someone in a way that shows you think that he or she is less intelligent or important than you: *The professor never talks down to his students. Instead, he assumes that they can understand his complicated explanations.*

patronize
patronize means the same as **talk down to** but is more formal: *Just because you're older than me, it doesn't give you the right to patronize me.*

condescend (*formal*)
condescend means the same as **talk down to**. You usually use **condescend** about people in important positions who behave as though they are much better than other people: *A lawyer should never* ***condescend to*** *a jury, because they will stop listening to his case fairly.*
→ see **talk into** at **persuade**
→ see **talk over** at **discuss**

talk² *noun* → see **conversation**, **speech**

talks *noun* → see **discussion**

tall /tɔl/ *adjective*

- tall
- high
- high-rise
- towering

ANTONYMS → see **short (1)**

tall
bigger in height than most other people or things. **Tall** is used especially about people or things that are high and narrow, such as trees and buildings: *Who is taller – Russ or me? | The Empire State Building used to be the tallest building in the world, but now there are many buildings that are taller. | Redwood trees are very tall.*

high
tall. **High** is used about things such as mountains and walls: *Mount Kilimanjaro is the highest mountain in Africa. | The prison was surrounded by a high fence.*

high-rise
a high-rise building is tall: *High-rise apartment buildings surround the park.*

towering
very tall, in a way that seems impressive but also often a little frightening. **Towering** is used in books: *The storm sent towering waves over the deck of the ship.*
→ see **grow**, Topic **Describing People's Looks**, **Describing Size**

tame /teɪm/ *adjective*

- tame
- domesticated

ANTONYMS → see **wild (1)**

tame
a tame animal is one that was wild but is not afraid of people anymore, because it has become used to them: *The elephants were really tame – you could go right up and touch them. | He has a tame squirrel as a pet.*

domesticated AWL
domesticated animals are the types of animals that live with people as pets or on a farm: *Cows have been domesticated for thousands of years. | Dogs and wolves are related species, but dogs are domesticated and wolves are wild.*

tantrum /ˈtæntrəm/ *noun*

- tantrum
- outburst
- fit (*informal*)

tantrum *also* **temper tantrum**
a time when a young child suddenly becomes angry and starts shouting and crying: *She throws a tantrum when she can't have the toy she wants. | Owen had a temper tantrum in the middle of the store, and I couldn't get him to stop screaming.*

outburst
a time when someone suddenly becomes angry and starts shouting or complaining: *After he calmed down, he apologized for his outburst.*

fit (*informal*)
a time when someone suddenly becomes very

T

angry, because he or she finds out about something. You use **fit** in the phrase "someone will have a fit": *If Gina finds out you went to the movie without her, she'll have a fit.*

tap[1] *noun* → see **hit[1]**

tap[2] *verb* → see **hit[1]**, Topic **To Make a Sound**

tape *verb* → see **attach**

tardy *adjective* → see **late**

target *noun* → see **goal**, **victim**

task *noun* → see **challenge**, **job**

taste[1] /teɪst/ *noun*

- ► taste
- ► flavor

taste
the feeling that something produces in your mouth when you eat or drink it: *The barbecue sauce has a slightly sour taste.* | *I have never liked the taste of onions.*

flavor
the particular taste that food or drink has. A **flavor** is the special taste that makes one type of food or drink different from another: *What's your favorite flavor of yogurt? I like cherry.* | *The ice cream comes in over 30 different flavors.*
→ You often use **flavor** when a food has been specially designed to taste like another food. Don't say: ~~*strawberry taste ice cream*~~. Say: *strawberry flavor ice cream.*
→ see Topic **Describing Food**

taste[2] /teɪst/ *verb*

1 to have a particular taste
- ► taste

2 to eat a small amount of something to find out what it is like
- ► taste
- ► try
- ► sample
- ► have a taste

1 to have a particular taste

taste
to produce a particular feeling on your tongue when you eat or drink something: *The chocolate cookies taste really good.* | *The berries tasted a little sour and I decided to add some sugar.*

2 to eat a small amount of something to find out what it is like

taste
to eat or drink a small amount of something to find out what it is like: *Taste the soup and see if it is too salty.* | *I'm not sure what flavor it is – you taste it.*
→ **Taste** also means to be able to recognize the taste of a food or drink: *You can really taste the garlic in the spaghetti sauce.* | *Can you taste the difference between these two colas?*

try
to taste a new food or drink to find out what it is like: *Try one of these cookies and tell me what you think.* | *Each time I go to the restaurant, I like to try something new.*

sample
to taste a little bit of a food or drink in order to decide if you want to have more of it: *We sampled six different kinds of cheese, but we decided not to buy any.*

have a taste
have a taste means the same as **taste** something: *Can I have a taste of your milkshake?*

tasteless /ˈteɪstləs/ *adjective*

- ► tasteless
- ► bland
- ► mild
- ► flavorless

tasteless
tasteless food or drink is unpleasant because it has no particular taste: *Why is airplane food always so tasteless?* | *The tasteless, overcooked vegetables were hard to eat.*

bland
bland food has very little taste and is not interesting to eat or drink. **Bland** food is often given to sick people: *If the sauce is bland, add some salt and spices.*

mild
mild food has a taste that is not strong or hot: *Do you want mild or spicy salsa with your burrito?*

flavorless
flavorless food and drink has no taste: *The flavorless liquid vitamins can be easily mixed with other drinks.*
→ see **offensive** (**2**)

T

ADVERBS

You can make the adjective **mild** into an adverb by using an **-ly** ending: *The dish is made with mildly seasoned pork.* The adverbs **tastelessly** and **blandly** are rarely used in this meaning.

tasty *adjective* → see **delicious**, Topic **Describing Food**

tax /tæks/ *noun*

- ► tax
- ► duty
- ► tariff

tax
money that you have to pay the government, based on how much you earn, what you buy, etc.: *How much income tax did you have to pay last year? | The state is planning to raise the **tax on** cigarettes.*

duty
a tax you pay on something you buy when you bring it into another country: *If you spend more than $400 on things you buy abroad, you will have to pay a customs duty on them when you bring them home.*

tariff
a tax on goods that enter or leave a country. A country often uses **tariffs** to protect its industry from cheap goods from other countries: *The government put new **tariffs on** chicken products imported from the U.S.*

teach /titʃ/ *verb*

- ► teach
- ► instruct (*formal*)
- ► train
- ► coach
- ► tutor
- ► educate (*formal*)

ANTONYMS → see **learn**

teach
to help someone learn something by giving lessons: *I **teach** English **to** new immigrants. | She has been teaching for 12 years at a middle school. | My dad **taught** me **how to** ride.*

instruct (AWL) (*formal*)
to teach someone about something by explaining it or showing what to do. You use **instruct** especially about a practical subject or skill: *The flight attendants always **instruct** passengers **on** what to do if the plane has to make an emergency landing.*

train
to teach someone the skills needed to do something: *He **trained** the dog **to** sit when he told it to. | New employees are **trained in** how to deal with customers.*

coach
to help a sports team improve their skills or help someone do an activity better, by making them practice: *Who's coaching the football team this year? | The people who worked on the project were **coached in** problem-solving skills by their managers.*

tutor
to teach a subject to one student or only a few students. You usually **tutor** students to help them with a difficult subject that they are studying at school: *Adam is **tutoring** me **in** math after school.*

educate (*formal*)
to teach someone. You use **educate** especially when talking about where someone went to school or college, or about teaching someone about an important subject: *Ms. Langford was educated at Northwestern University. | The program aims to educate visitors about how they can help save the environment.*
→ see Topic **Education**

teacher /ˈtitʃɚ/ *noun*

- ► teacher
- ► professor
- ► instructor
- ► coach
- ► tutor
- ► educator (*formal*)
- ► faculty

ANTONYMS → see **student**

teacher
someone whose job is to teach, especially in a school: *Rob is an elementary school teacher. | Amanda decided to become a teacher.*

professor
a teacher at a university: *She is a professor of history at Arizona State University. | Professor Rosen teaches biology.*

instructor (AWL)
someone who teaches a sport, such as dancing or skiing, or a skill, such as driving: *My driving instructor got mad when I made a turn without signaling first.*

coach
someone who helps a person or team get better

T

at a sport by practicing particular skills: *The basketball coach makes the team practice hard, and their playing has really improved.*

tutor
someone who gives lessons to one student or a small group of students. A **tutor** usually helps students with a difficult subject that they are studying at school: *My parents hired a Spanish tutor for me when I was having trouble in Spanish class.*

educator (*formal*)
a teacher at a school, college, or university. You use **educator** about someone who knows a lot about education and methods of teaching and learning: *Most educators agree that class sizes should be smaller.*

faculty
all the teachers in a school, college, or university: *Both the college's faculty and students oppose the new rules.*
→ see Topic **Education**

teaching *noun* → see **education**

team /tim/ *noun*

- ► team
- ► squad
- ► lineup

team (AWL)
a group of people who play together in a sport or game: *Which teams are in the Superbowl this year?* | *Sarah plays **on the** high school volleyball **team**.*

squad
a sports team. A **squad** can also mean a larger group of players from which the playing team is chosen: *There are currently 22 players on the national soccer squad.*

lineup
the players on a sports team who play in a particular game: *The starting lineup is usually made up of the best players on a team.*
→ see Topic **Sports and Exercise**

tear[1] /ter/ *verb*

- ► tear
- ► rip
- ► tear up
- ► shred
- ► split
- ► fray

tear
to make a hole in paper or cloth by pulling it apart or pulling it on something sharp: *I tore a hole in my jacket when I climbed over the fence.* | *She unwrapped the present carefully, trying not to tear the paper.*

rip
to tear paper or cloth quickly or violently: *Arnie **ripped open** the package excitedly.*

tear up
to tear paper or cloth into many small pieces: *He ripped up the letter and threw it in the trash.*

shred
to tear or cut something into thin pieces, with your hands or using a special machine: *We shredded some old newspapers to make a bed for our pet mice.* | *You should shred your bank statements, so no one can get your personal information.*

split
to tear a hole in your clothes when they fit too tightly. The hole is usually where pieces of cloth are sewn together: *When he bent over, he split his pants along the seam in the back.*

fray
if a piece of cloth or rope frays, its threads become loose at the edge because it is old or torn: *She was wearing an old pair of jeans that were fraying at the bottom.*

tear[2] /ter/ *noun*

- ► tear
- ► hole
- ► rip

tear
a hole in a piece of paper or cloth, where it has been torn: *I got a **tear in** my jacket when it caught on a nail.* | *There's a small tear near the corner of the painting.*

hole
an empty space in something: *The pin left a **hole in** her blouse.* | *The sweater was old and full of holes.*

rip
a long straight tear in cloth or paper: *There was a **rip in** her jeans where they had caught on a nail.*

tear[3] /tɪr/ *noun*

- ► tear
- ► teardrop

tear
a drop of salty liquid that comes out of your eye when you are crying: *As she walked away, a tear*

ran down Dan's cheek. | *Rianne tried to smile, but I could see there were tears in her eyes.*

→ **Tears** is also used in phrases such as "be in tears" (=be crying), "burst into tears" (=start crying), and "be close to tears" (=be almost crying): *The children were so frightened that they were all* ***in tears.*** | *Bridget suddenly* ***burst into tears*** *and ran out of the room.* | *Anna looked* ***close to tears*** *after hearing the news.*

teardrop

one tear. **Teardrop** sounds literary, and is used especially in stories and songs: *A large teardrop fell from her eye and onto the letter she was writing.*

→ see **cry[1]**

tease *verb* → see **joke[2]**, **pick on**, **laugh at**

technical /ˈteknɪkəl/ *adjective*

- technical
- technological
- scientific
- mechanical

technical (AWL)

relating to the practical use of science to do things, especially using machines and systems: *The job requires specialized technical knowledge about computers.* | *We are having technical difficulties and are unable to play the recording at this time.*

→ You sometimes use **technical** when saying that something is difficult for an ordinary person to understand: *His explanation of how genes work was too technical for me to understand.*

technological (AWL)

relating to new and advanced machines and systems: *We are living in a time of rapid technological change.*

scientific

relating to science: *There is no scientific evidence that the herb can prevent colds.* | *Scientific knowledge continues to grow as we learn more about the universe.*

mechanical

relating to machines, or a knowledge of how they work: *The flight was delayed because of mechanical problems.* | *I don't have much mechanical ability, so I would never try to fix my own car.*

→ see Topic **Science and Technology**

ADVERBS

You can make the adjectives that mean **technical** into adverbs by using an **-ly** ending: *The students are technically very well trained.* | *We live in a technologically advanced society.* | *The herb has not been scientifically tested yet.*

technological *adjective* → see **scientific**, Topic **Science and Technology**

technology *noun* → see Topic **Science and Technology**

teen *noun* → see **teenager**

teenage *adjective* → see **young[1]**

teenager /ˈtineɪdʒɚ/ *noun*

- teenager
- teen (*informal*)
- adolescent (*formal*)
- young adult
- young person
- the young (*formal*)
- juvenile (*formal*)
- youth (*formal*)

teenager

someone who is between 13 and 19 years old: *To teenagers, friends are often more important than parents.* | *Teenagers from local high schools took part in the competition.*

teen (*informal*)

a teenager: *Online video games are popular with teens.*

adolescent (*formal*)

a young person between 12 and 18 years old, when his or her body is changing to become more like an adult's: *Adolescents need almost as much sleep as young children, because their brains and bodies are changing.*

young adult *also* **young man** *or* **young woman**

someone who is between about 15 and 22: *The vampire novel is intended for young adults.* | *Sarah is a bright young woman who is beginning college.*

young person

a teenager or young adult: *More young people are going to college than ever before.*

the young (*formal*)

children, teenagers, or young adults in general: *The young are often better at using computers than their parents.*

juvenile (*formal*)

a young person who is not yet an adult,

especially if he or she has committed a crime. **Juvenile** is often used when talking about the law: *He was sent to a special prison for violent juveniles.*

youth (*formal*)
a teenage boy or girl. **Youth** is sometimes used especially in newspapers about an older teenage boy who is violent or involved in crime: *He was attacked by a gang of youths.*
→ You can also use **youth** to mean young people as a group: *Are the youth of America getting the education and skills they need?*
→ see **child**

telephone *verb* → see **call**

tell /tel/ *verb*

1 to give someone information by talking
- ▸ tell
- ▸ let someone know (*informal*)
- ▸ inform (*formal*)
- ▸ announce
- ▸ report
- ▸ notify (*formal*)
- ▸ recount (*formal*)
- ▸ narrate

2 to tell someone secret information
- ▸ reveal
- ▸ disclose (*formal*)
- ▸ divulge (*formal*)
- ▸ confide (*formal*)

1 to give someone information by talking

tell
to give someone information by talking or writing to him or her: *No one told me the meeting was canceled.* | ***Tell*** *me more* ***about*** *your summer plans.*
→ **GRAMMAR:** Don't say: ~~*He told that he was an engineer*~~. Say: *He told me that he was an engineer.*

let someone know (*informal*)
to tell someone something, especially about something that is happening or that has recently happened: ***Let me know how*** *your job interview goes.* | *Could you* ***let*** *Bob* ***know if*** *you're going to be late?*

inform (*formal*)
to tell someone important information in an official way: *We will* ***inform*** *you* ***if*** *there are any changes to the schedule.*
→ **GRAMMAR:** Don't say: ~~*He informed that my stolen car had been found*~~. Say: *He informed me that my stolen car had been found.*

announce
to tell people publicly and officially about an important plan or decision: *The president of the company announced his resignation on Friday.*

report
to tell people in a formal way about something that has happened or is happening: *The newspaper* ***reported that*** *the peace talks are not going well.*
→ **Report** can also mean to tell the police about a crime or accident that has happened: *She called the police to report the theft.*

notify (*formal*)
to tell someone officially about something that has happened or that will happen: *The police are notifying the families of the accident victims.*

recount (*formal*)
to tell what happened in a series of events: *Alan recounted the story of how he and Joyce met.*

narrate
to say what is happening in a movie, a television program, or a story: *The actor has agreed to narrate a documentary about hunger in Africa.*
→ see **advise**, **order²**

2 to tell someone secret information

reveal (AWL)
to let someone know about something that is secret or has not been known until now: *He* ***revealed that*** *he had been in prison twice before.*

disclose (*formal*)
to publicly reveal something that has been kept secret, such as a fact or a name: *The company did not disclose details of the agreement.*

divulge (*formal*)
to reveal important or personal information that people did not know before: *Company officials would not divulge the name of the person who had offered to buy the company.*

confide (*formal*)
to tell someone you trust about something very private or secret, especially a personal problem: *I was having trouble at school, and the only person I felt I could* ***confide in*** *was my mother.*
→ see **tell of** at **scold**

temple *noun* → see **church**

temporarily *adverb* → see **briefly**

T

temporary /ˈtempəˌreri/ *adjective*

- ► temporary
- ► brief
- ► short-lived
- ► short-term
- ► passing

ANTONYMS → see **lasting**, **permanent**

temporary (AWL)
existing or happening for a short time only. Something **temporary** is usually planned to continue for only a short time: *John is living with his grandmother now, but it's only temporary.* | *She took a temporary job working in a store at Christmastime.*

brief (AWL)
brief is similar to **temporary** but is used about something that may or may not be planned: *We stopped at Alice's house for a brief visit.*

short-lived
continuing only a short time. Use **short-lived** about something good that does not last long, for example a feeling or relationship: *Their happiness was short-lived, as their marriage soon developed problems.*

short-term
continuing for only a short time into the future. Use **short-term** especially about the way something is done in business or politics: *The company was more interested in short-term profits than in planning for the future.* | *Your short-term goals should be steps on the way to achieving a long-term aim.*
→ **Short-term** is often used to show disapproval, because the people who plan something **short-term** are not thinking about the future enough.

passing
continuing only a short time. You use **passing** about an interest, thought, or feeling that is short and not very serious: *It was an exciting game, even for people who only had a passing interest in the sport.* | *The toy was a passing fad, but while they were popular they sold in huge numbers.*

ADVERBS

You can make the adjectives **temporary** and **brief** into adverbs by using an **-ly** ending: *John is temporarily living with his grandmother.* | *She briefly worked at a store during Christmas vacation.*

tender *adjective* → see **loving**, **painful**, **soft**

tenderness *noun* → see **pain**

tense *adjective* → see **nervous**, Topic **Describing People's Emotions**

tension *noun* → see **nervousness**, **suspense**

term *noun* → see **name¹**, **time**, **word**

terminal¹ *noun* → see Topic **Travel and Vacations**

terminal² *adjective* → see **incurable**

terrible *adjective* → see **bad**

terribly *adverb* → see **badly**

terrific *adjective* → see **good**

terrified *adjective* → see **scared**, Topic **Describing People's Emotions**

terrify *verb* → see **scare**

terrifying *adjective* → see **scary**

terror *noun* → see **fear¹**

terrorize *verb* → see **scare**

test¹ /test/ *noun*

1 a set of questions used to find out how much you know

- ► test
- ► exam
- ► quiz
- ► final
- ► midterm

2 something you do to find out information about something or find out whether it works

- ► test
- ► trial
- ► examination
- ► experiment

1 a set of questions used to find out how much you know

test
a set of questions or activities that are used to find out how much you know about a subject or how well you do something: *I have a biology test tomorrow.* | *You can take a test to get your driver's license when you are 16.*

exam
an important test, especially one that you take at the end of a semester in school or

T

college. **Exam** is short for **examination**, which is more formal: *At the end of the semester, the students take exams in every subject.* | *She finished law school and passed the bar exam soon afterward.*

quiz
a short test, especially one that you take without having a lot of time to prepare: *Read Chapter 11 for homework; there will be a **quiz on** it tomorrow.*

final (AWL) *also* **final exam**
an important test that students take at the end of a semester in high school or college. A final exam usually tests students on everything they have learned in a class: *I'm studying for my history final.* | *Final exams are given during the last week of school.*

midterm
a test that students take in the middle of a semester, especially in college: *For most English classes, you will have to write two papers and take a midterm and final exam.*

2 something you do to find out information about something or find out whether it works

test
something you do to find out information about something, for example whether something works correctly or whether someone has an illness: *The blood test shows that she has diabetes.* | *The company carries out safety tests on all its products.*

trial
a test in which a small group of people use something new to find out whether it is safe or works well. Use **trial** about new medicines, methods, or machines: *The trial showed that the drug worked well for breast cancer patients.*

examination *also* **exam**
a test in which a doctor examines someone's body to find out if there is anything wrong with him or her: *Every soldier is given a thorough medical examination.* | *You should have an eye exam every year.*

experiment
a scientific test to find out what the effects of doing something are: *The students carried out an experiment to see whether heating the liquid made the chemical reaction faster.*
→ see Topic **Medical Treatment**, **Science and Technology**

T

test² /test/ *verb*

1 to measure someone's knowledge or skill by asking questions
- ► test
- ► quiz
- ► assess (*formal*)

2 to use something to find out whether it works
- ► test
- ► try something out
- ► experiment

1 to measure someone's knowledge or skill by asking questions

test
to measure someone's knowledge or skill by asking questions or making him or her do things: *Each year we test the children's reading and math skills.* | *You will be **tested on** everything we have learned this semester.*

quiz
to measure someone's knowledge by asking a small number of questions: *The teacher **quizzed** them **on** the state capitals.*

assess (AWL) (*formal*)
to judge how good or bad someone's work is: *The teacher had assessed her writing as being at sixth-grade level.*

2 to use something to find out whether it works

test
to use something to find out whether it works: *The games have to be tested before they are sold, to make sure that everything works correctly.* | *The new medicine was **tested on** a group of cancer patients.*

try something out
to use something in order to find out if it works or is good. Use **try out** about a new method, new product, or something you have learned. **Try out** is more informal than **test**: *I tried out several different cameras, and this one was the best.*

experiment
to try using different things in order to find out what the results are: *The children had to build a model bridge, and they **experimented with** different designs and materials to see what would work best.* | *I like to experiment when I'm cooking, so I try different spices or foods.*

text *noun* → see **book**[1], **message**, **writing**

texture /ˈtekstʃɚ/ *noun*

- ► texture
- ► feel
- ► consistency
- ► to the touch

texture
the kind of surface that something has and whether it is rough, smooth, hard, or soft: *The clay has a smooth, soft texture that is pleasant to work with.* | *The toy has different textures for your baby to feel: soft cloth, hard metal, and squishy rubber.*

feel
the way that something feels when you touch it, especially something soft or smooth that feels good: *Velvet is a type of cloth that has a nice soft feel.* | *I love the feel of a baby's skin; it is so soft and warm.*

consistency (AWL)
how thick or smooth a liquid or soft substance is: *Stir the paint until it is the consistency of thick cream.* | *The pudding should have a smooth consistency, with no lumps.*

to the touch
if something is warm, soft, etc. to the touch, it feels warm, soft, etc. when you touch it: *In a fire, if the door is warm to the touch, do not open it.*

thank /θæŋk/ *verb*

- ► thank
- ► express your thanks/gratitude (*formal*)
- ► show your appreciation (*formal*)

thank
to tell someone that you are pleased about something that he or she has done for you or given you: *He helped me a lot and I wanted to thank him.* | *I* ***thanked*** *her* ***for*** *the present.* | *Mr. Barnes shook his hand and* ***thanked*** *him* ***for*** *coming.*

express your thanks/gratitude (*formal*)
to thank someone for something that he or she has done. Use this especially in speeches or letters: *I would like to express my thanks to the ambulance and hospital workers who helped me.* | *In her speech, Mrs. Robinson expressed her gratitude to all her coworkers.*

show your appreciation (*formal*)
to thank someone by giving him or her something, or by doing something special: *We invite our volunteers to a special dinner as a way of showing our appreciation for all their hard work.*

thankful /ˈθæŋkfəl/ *adjective*

- ► thankful
- ► grateful
- ► appreciative (*formal*)

thankful
feeling glad about something, especially that something bad did not happen or is over: *We have so much to be* ***thankful for*** *– a house to live in, enough money, and our health.* | *I am so* ***thankful that*** *no one was hurt.*

grateful
wanting to thank someone who has been kind or helpful: *I am very* ***grateful for*** *all the help I have been given.* | *She was* ***grateful to*** *her parents for their support.* | *The doctor received a thank-you letter from a grateful patient.*

appreciative (*formal*)
showing that you are pleased and feel grateful for something that someone has done: *The teacher gives them a lot of help, and the students are very appreciative.*

SYNONYM CHECK

Thankful or grateful?

You use **grateful** to say that you want to thank someone, and you use **thankful** when you are pleased or relieved about something that has happened: *I am grateful to all the doctors who helped me.* | *I am thankful that the doctors were able to help me.*

ADVERBS

You can make the adjectives that mean **thankful** into adverbs by using an **-ly** ending: *Thankfully, I have a house, enough money, and my health.* | *She thanked us gratefully for all our help.* | *The students applauded appreciatively for their teachers.*

thanks /θæŋks/ *noun*

- ► thanks
- ► gratitude
- ► appreciation (*formal*)

thanks
the things that you say or do to thank someone:

They prayed and gave thanks to God. | *He waved his thanks to the lady at the desk who let him in.*

gratitude
the feeling of being grateful and wanting to thank someone because he or she has been kind or helpful to you: *They accepted our help **with gratitude**.* | *Her eyes filled with tears of gratitude for their kindness to her.*

appreciation (AWL) (*formal*)
the feeling of knowing that someone has done something for you and being grateful for it: *I look back on my school days with **appreciation for** my teachers.* | *They gave her the award **in appreciation of** all her volunteer work.*

theater /ˈθiətɚ/ *noun*

- theater
- auditorium
- concert hall

theater
a building where actors perform plays and shows: *He has performed in musicals in several Broadway theaters.* | *The theater is small and every member of the audience can see the stage clearly.*

auditorium
a large building or room that usually has a stage and is used for concerts, plays, or public meetings: *The Congresswoman addressed 400 people who crowded into the auditorium.* | *Parents filled the school auditorium to watch the play.*

concert hall
a building where musicians and singers perform: *His magnificent voice filled the concert hall.*
→ see **actor**, **play²**

theft /θeft/ *noun*

- theft
- robbery
- burglary
- shoplifting
- larceny (*formal*)
- fraud
- embezzlement

theft
the crime of stealing something: *He was arrested for the theft of three laptop computers.* | *The men are suspected of crimes including car theft and drug selling.*

robbery
a crime in which someone steals something from a place or person, especially using threats or violence: *About $300 in cash was stolen during the robbery.* | *The man was arrested as a suspect in two grocery store robberies.*

burglary
the crime of going into someone else's home or a building and stealing things: *There have been several burglaries in our neighborhood recently.* | *Cash and jewelry were taken in the burglary of the woman's home.*

shoplifting
the crime of taking things from a store without paying for them: *Dina was arrested for shoplifting when she walked out of the store with a dress she hadn't paid for.*

larceny (*formal*)
the crime of stealing something, used by lawyers and judges when talking about theft: *He was charged with larceny for breaking into houses in the Beverly Hills area.*

fraud
the crime of deceiving people in order to get money, goods, or something else you want: *The couple lost all their savings in this fraud, which worked by paying the first investors the money paid in by later ones.*

embezzlement
the crime of stealing money from an organization that you work for: *Police are investigating the embezzlement of $25,000 from the business by one of the partners.*
→ see **steal**

theme *noun* → see **subject**, Topic **Books and Literature**

then /ðen/ *adverb*

- then
- at that time
- at that point
- at that stage

then
at a time in the past, or at a time in the future: *My grandparents were living on the farm then, not in town.* | *She sat down for dinner and just then the phone rang.* | *I'll be back on Tuesday, so I'll call you then.*

at that time *also* **at the time**
used when saying what the situation was at a particular time in the past, when it is different now: *At that time the area was farmland, but the city grew and now there are houses there.* | *I was just five years old at the time.*

at that point
at that exact time during an event or period of time: *He got up to speak, and at that point several people walked out.* | *It was at that point that I began to think she was wrong.*

at that stage
at a particular time during a series of events: ***At that stage of*** *the game they were behind by three runs.* | *The disease can be difficult for a doctor to recognize at that stage.*

theory /ˈθiəri/ *noun*

- theory
- hypothesis
- idea
- concept

theory (AWL)
an idea or set of ideas that tries to explain why something happens. In science, a **theory** is a set of ideas that are accepted as true by most scientists, even though some parts of the theory are not proven: *Darwin's* ***theory of*** *evolution explains how species change over time.* | *Jean Piaget developed a theory which says that children go through four stages as they learn and grow.*

hypothesis (AWL)
an idea that tries to explain something and that is based on facts. In science, a **hypothesis** is an idea that can be tested by carefully studying something or doing scientific tests: *There is evidence that supports the* ***hypothesis that*** *all the continents once formed one large land mass.*

idea
a thought that someone has about something: *Freud's* ***ideas about*** *the mind are still important in psychology today.*

concept (AWL)
a general idea of what something is like, especially an idea about something that is not physical and cannot be touched: *Young children understand the* ***concept of*** *fairness and are often upset when something is not fair.*
→ see **idea**, Topic **Science and Technology**

therefore *adverb* → see Function Word **so**

thick /θɪk/ *adjective*

1 having a large distance between one side and the other
- thick
- heavy

ANTONYMS → see **narrow**, **thin**, **wide**

2 having a lot of things close together
- thick
- dense

3 difficult to see through
- thick
- dense

1 having a large distance between one side and the other

thick
if something is thick, there is a large distance between one side and the other: *The walls of the old farmhouse were thick.* | *The cake was cut into thick slices.* | *The carpet was thick and soft.* | *She carried a thick notebook stuffed with papers.*

heavy
thick. You use **heavy** about cloth or clothes that are thick and warm, or thick and strong: *He was wearing a heavy sweater.* | *The beds had heavy wool blankets on them.*

2 having a lot of things close together

thick
thick hair grows close together. A thick forest contains a lot of trees growing close together: *His hair is black and thick.* | *The trail leads through a thick pine forest that blocks out the sun.*

dense
a dense forest or jungle has a lot of trees or plants growing close together. A dense crowd has a lot of people standing close together: *The crowd was so dense that I couldn't push my way through.*
→ In science, **dense** is used when you are describing the mass of an object: *If an object is less dense than water, it will float on the water* (=the molecules of the object have more space between them than the molecules of water, so the object floats).

3 difficult to see through

thick
thick cloud or smoke is difficult to see through: *You could hardly see the firefighters through the thick smoke.*

dense
very thick: *The dense fog made driving dangerous.*
→ see Topic **Describing Size**

T

ADVERBS

You can make the adjectives **thick** and **dense** into adverbs by using an **-ly** ending: *The room was thickly carpeted.* | *The area is thickly forested.* | *I live in a densely populated area.* | *The mountains were densely covered in fog.*

thickness /ˈθɪknəs/ *noun*

- thickness
- depth

thickness
the distance from one side of something to the other: *Cook the steaks about 3 minutes on each side, depending on their thickness.* | *The wire is only about the thickness of a hair.*

depth
the distance from the top to the bottom of something, such as a river or hole: *The diving pool has a depth of 5 meters.*
→ **Depth** is also used to describe the distance from the front to the back of an object: *The depth of the shelves is 8 inches.*
→ see **length**, **width**

thief /θif/ *noun*

- thief
- robber
- burglar
- shoplifter
- pickpocket
- mugger

thief
someone who steals things: *A car thief took the car from their driveway!* | *Police are still looking for the thieves who stole the painting.*

robber
someone who steals money or valuable things from a bank or store: *Armed robbers entered the store and demanded that the cashier give them all the money.*

burglar
someone who goes into a house or other building to steal things, especially when no one is in it: *The burglars entered the house while the owners were away on vacation.*

shoplifter
someone who secretly takes things from a store and leaves without paying for them: *The security cameras caught the shoplifter putting jewelry into her pocket.*

pickpocket
someone who steals things from someone's pocket when he or she is not paying attention: *Pickpockets often work on crowded subways.*

mugger
someone who attacks someone in a public place and steals from him or her: *A mugger beat up Andy and took his watch and wallet.*
→ see **steal**, **theft**

thin /θɪn/ *adjective*

1 not fat
- thin
- slim
- slender
- lean
- skinny
- anorexic

ANTONYMS → see **fat**

2 not thick
- thin
- paper-thin
- fine

ANTONYMS → see **thick (1)**

1 not fat

thin
not having much fat on your body: *He is tall and thin – about 6 feet and 160 pounds.* | *The child held up her thin arms, asking to be picked up.*

slim
thin in a way that looks good: *She stays slim through diet and exercise.* | *He has broad shoulders and a slim waist.*

slender
thin in a way that looks good or seems graceful. Use **slender** especially about women: *She is a tall slender woman with a short haircut.* | *Her short skirt showed off her long slender legs.*

lean
thin in a healthy way: *He has the lean muscular body of an athlete.*

skinny
very thin, in a way that is not attractive. Use **skinny** to show that someone is thinner than he or she should be: *Eat something – you're too skinny!*

anorexic
someone who is anorexic is extremely thin because he or she has a mental illness that makes him or her stop eating: *She was so thin she looked almost anorexic.*
→ see Topic **Describing People's Looks**

2 not thick

thin
having a small distance between one side and the other: *The blankets were thin and did not keep us warm.* | *The road was covered with a thin layer of ice.*

paper-thin
extremely thin, like paper: *The beef was cut into paper-thin strips that cooked very quickly.*
→ You can use **paper-thin** to describe walls that are so thin that sound goes through them: *The walls of the motel were paper-thin, and I could hear the people next door arguing.*

fine
very thin or delicate. **Fine** is used about things that are long, or flat and thin, for example hair, thread, cloth, or layers: *She wore a fine silver chain around her neck.*
→ see **narrow**, Topic **Describing Size**

> **ADVERBS**
> You can make the adjectives **thin** and **fine** into adverbs by using an **-ly** ending, when they mean "not thick": *The road was thinly covered in ice.* | *Chop the onion finely.*

thing /θɪŋ/ noun

- ► thing
- ► object
- ► item (*formal*)
- ► article (*formal*)
- ► artifact
- ► stuff (*informal*)

thing
an object. Use **thing** instead of the name of something, when you do not know or cannot remember the name: *Do you see that thing over by the car – what is it?* | *I'm bringing them a few little things as gifts.*

object
a solid thing that you can touch or hold. **Object** sounds more formal than **thing**: *There were several small square objects sitting on the shelf.* | *His art is made from objects he finds on beaches.*

item (AWL) (*formal*)
a single thing on a list or in a group: *A few of the items have been sold already.* | *The first item on the list is milk.*

article (*formal*)
one of several things of the same type: *The police found some **articles of clothing** in the bushes, including a pair of shoes.*

artifact
an object such as a tool or weapon that was made a long time ago and is historically important: *They found several iron artifacts in the grave.*

stuff (*informal*)
things of different types: *How are we going to get all this stuff into the car?*
→ see **possession**

think verb → *go to pages 682-683*

thirst /θɚst/ noun

- ► thirst
- ► dehydration

thirst
the feeling of wanting a drink: *Thousands of people are suffering from hunger and thirst.* | *He took a long drink, trying to quench his thirst* (=make him not feel thirsty).

dehydration
a weak condition because there is not enough water in your body: *Many of the runners were suffering from dehydration because of the heat.*

thirsty /ˈθɚsti/ adjective

- ► thirsty
- ► dehydrated (*formal*)
- ► need a drink

thirsty
feeling that you want to drink something: *Are you thirsty? Do you want some water?* | *On a hot day, animals can become very thirsty.*

dehydrated (*formal*)
if you are dehydrated, you do not have enough water in your body so that you may feel weak or sick: *Some of the runners had not drunk enough and were becoming dehydrated.*

need a drink
to feel thirsty. **Need a drink** is used especially in spoken language: *It is hot out here. I need a drink.*

> **ADVERBS**
> You can make **thirsty** into an adverb by using an **-ly** ending: *She drank thirstily from the bottle.*

think /θɪŋk/ *verb*

1 to think of an idea
- think
- come up with (*informal*)
- think up (*informal*)
- occur to
- conceive
- brainstorm

2 to think about something carefully
- think
- consider
- think something over
- reason (*formal*)
- contemplate (*formal*)
- reflect
- dwell on
- weigh

3 to think that something is probably true
- think
- believe
- feel
- be under the impression
- assume
- presume (*formal*)
- suspect
- suppose (*formal*)
- infer (*formal*)
- conclude
- deduce (*formal*)

4 to have a particular opinion
- think
- consider
- regard
- view

1 to think of an idea

think
to use your mind to produce an idea or solve a problem: *You'll have to* ***think of*** *a different way to do it.* | *"What should we do?" "Wait a minute – I'm thinking."*

come up with (*informal*)
to think of an idea or a way to solve a problem **Come up with** sounds more informal than **think**: *We'll have to come up with a new plan.* | *Scientists have not come up with any solutions to the problem.*

think up (*informal*)
to think of a new idea. **Think up** sounds more informal than **come up with**: *I was trying hard to think up a good excuse to give the teacher.*

occur to (AWL)
if a new thought or idea occurs to you, you suddenly think it: *It occurred to me that I could use my travel diaries as the start of a book.*

conceive (AWL)
to imagine or understand something that is new or difficult. **Conceive** sounds more formal than **think**: *Einstein was the first person to* ***conceive of*** *the idea of relativity.*

brainstorm
to try to think of a lot of different ideas, even if they are not good ideas: *Employees regularly get together and brainstorm ideas.*

→ see **imagine**

2 to think about something carefully

think
to spend time trying to understand a situation or make a decision: *I was* ***thinking about*** *what you said.* | *Think carefully before you answer the question.*

consider
to spend time thinking about something, especially before making a decision. **Consider** sounds more formal than **think**: *The Senator was considering running for president.* | *We're* ***considering whether*** *to buy him a new phone.*

think something over
to think carefully about a situation, problem, or decision before giving an answer or making a decision. **Think over** is more informal than **consider**: *Think it over, and we can talk about it again tomorrow.* | *I've been thinking over what you said last night.*

reason (*formal*)
to decide that something is true after thinking carefully about all the facts: *The ancient Greeks* ***reasoned that*** *the Earth must be the center of the universe, but scientists later proved that this was not true.*

contemplate (*formal*)
to think seriously and for a long time about something: *He is contemplating a change in his career, from being a lawyer to becoming a professor.*

reflect
to think about something that happened in the past, especially when you are thinking about your own experiences or behavior: *Take some time to stop and* ***reflect on*** *what happened. You might choose to do things differently next time.*

dwell on
to spend too much time thinking about something, so that it makes you feel unhappy or upset: *Try not to dwell on what you did wrong – just think about the positive things.*

weigh
to compare two things that you might do in order to decide which one is best: *When you are choosing a college, you have to weigh your options and decide what feels right to you.*

3 to think that something is probably true

think
to have an opinion that information or facts are true or correct: *My teacher **thinks that** it's time for me to move up to the next level.*
→ You can also use **think** to show that you are not completely sure that something is true, for example because someone else told you: *I think his sister's name is Tammy, but I'm not sure.*

believe
believe means the same as **think** but sounds more formal. You often use **believe** to show you have a strong opinion about something: *I **believe that** improving our schools is very important for our economy. | My family believes hard work and a good attitude are the keys to success.*
→ You can also use **believe** to show that you are not completely sure that something is true, for example because someone else told you: *I believe the movie starts at 7:00, but I'm not sure.*

feel
feel means the same as **think** but sounds more formal. You sometimes use **feel** when what you think is based more on your feelings than on facts: *The principal **feels that** students need to have more time at recess. | I feel that he has been treated very unfairly.*

be under the impression
to think something is true because of information you have received from someone or something: *I **was under the impression that** Danny was bringing the drinks.*

assume (AWL)
to think that something is true, although you do not have definite proof. You often use **assume** in situations when you think something is true and then find out that it is not true: *The light in her room was on, so I **assumed that** she was still awake.*

presume (AWL) (*formal*)
to be fairly sure that something is true, especially because you have a good reason to think so, although you have no proof: *"Are his parents still alive?" "I presume so." | Many scientists presumed the damage to the forests to be the result of pollution.*

suspect
to think that something is likely to be true because you have a little information: *Sophia **suspected that** he was lying to her.*

suppose (*formal*)
to think that something is true when you have some information but cannot be sure that it is correct. **Suppose** sounds very formal and is mostly used in written language. It is not usually used to show what someone else thinks: *We have no reason to **suppose that** the girl is dead.*

infer (AWL) (*formal*)
to decide that something is probably true because of information which you already know: *It is easy to **infer from** his comments that the marriage was not a very happy one.*

conclude (AWL)
to decide that something is true or to make a judgment about it after carefully thinking about all the facts: *The jury listened carefully to the evidence and **concluded that** the man was guilty.*

deduce (AWL) (*formal*)
deduce means the same as **conclude**, but is more formal and is used especially to talk about scientific or technical judgments: *The police were able to deduce the probable time of death from the temperature of the body.*

4 to have a particular opinion

think
to have a particular opinion about something: *I didn't think the movie was very exciting. | Do you think I should go to Dan's party?*
→ You can use **think** to talk about what you like and do not like: *I think her dress is beautiful.*

consider
to have an opinion about someone or something after carefully thinking about it: *Liz is **considered to** be an excellent teacher who works very hard.*

regard
to think about someone or something in a particular way, or as being a particular type of person or thing: *Picasso is **regarded as** one of the most important artists of the 20th century.*

view
view means the same as **regard**: *Laws can be **viewed as** a way of controlling how people in a society behave.*
→ see **imagine**

Online Thesaurus
Go to www.longmandictionariesusa.com
→ ***Longman Thesaurus of American English*** – with pronunciation of all the words
→ **Study Center** – interactive practice to help you learn synonyms, Academic Words, and Topic Vocabulary

thorough /ˈθɚoʊ/ *adjective*

- ► thorough
- ► detailed
- ► comprehensive
- ► in-depth
- ► close

thorough
very careful, and checking or including everything: *Congress is demanding a thorough investigation into the causes of the problem.* | *Students will develop a thorough understanding of the biology of plants.*

detailed
including or showing a lot of details: *You can find more detailed information on our website.* | *The book contains detailed maps of the area.*

comprehensive AWL
including everything because it is important that nothing be left out: *The governor asked for a comprehensive report on the situation.*

in-depth
an in-depth study, discussion, or report is thorough and complete, and considers all details: *"Sports Night" gives you the most in-depth coverage of Major League Baseball anywhere.*

close
paying special attention to every detail. You use **close** with words like "look," "examination," and "inspection": *Pay close attention to the instructions.* | *A closer examination of the case showed that the police officer's actions were completely legal.*
→ see **careful**

ADVERBS

You can make **thorough**, **comprehensive**, and **close** into adverbs by using an **-ly** ending: *The problem is being thoroughly investigated by Congress.* | *The issue is comprehensively discussed in Parker's book.* | *Listen closely to the directions for the test.*

though *conjunction* → see Function Word **although**

thought /θɔt/ *noun*

- ► thought
- ► consideration
- ► contemplation (*formal*)
- ► deliberation (*formal*)

thought
the act of thinking: *I like the idea. I'll give it some thought.* | *This is a difficult subject that needs careful thought.*

consideration
careful thought about something. **Consideration** sounds more formal than **thought**: *I hope you will give this opportunity serious consideration.* | *After careful consideration, the judge made her decision.*

contemplation (*formal*)
the act of thinking about serious or important ideas, for example in religion or literature: *We will take a few minutes for silent contemplation before we begin the service.*

deliberation (*formal*)
the act of thinking carefully about something before making a decision, especially when you think about all the possibilities: *After months of deliberation, I announced my decision.*
→ see **idea** for **thought** meaning "something that you think"

thoughtful /ˈθɔtfəl/ *adjective*

1 thinking about something
- ► thoughtful
- ► preoccupied

2 kind and thinking about what other people need or want
- ► thoughtful
- ► considerate
- ► tactful
- ► sensitive

ANTONYMS → see **thoughtless**

1 thinking about something

thoughtful
serious and quiet because you are thinking about something: *He stopped talking and became thoughtful for a moment.* | *"She was upset?" Roger asked, looking thoughtful. "I hadn't realized."*

preoccupied
thinking about something a lot so that you do not pay attention to other things. You use **preoccupied** especially when someone is worrying about something: *He was too **preoccupied with** his own problems to think about anything else.*

2 kind and thinking about what other people need or want

thoughtful
kind and thinking about what other people need or want, especially by doing things that will please them: *He is a thoughtful boy who is always willing to help.* | *Jenny called to see if I was feeling better – that was really **thoughtful of** her.*

considerate
thinking about other people's feelings and what they want, and careful not to worry or cause problems for them: ***It was considerate of** Sheila **to** call and tell us that she would be late.* | *The neighbors had a party, but they were considerate and turned the music down at eleven o'clock.*

tactful
careful to say or do something in a way that will not upset someone, especially when you are criticizing him or her, or giving your opinion: *Is there a tactful way to tell Sophie that I don't like her boyfriend?*

sensitive
able to understand other people's feelings and problems, and trying to deal with situations in a way that does not upset them: *A good teacher is **sensitive to** learners' needs.*
→ see **kind²**

ADVERBS
You can make the adjectives **thoughtful**, **considerate**, **tactful**, and **sensitive** into adverbs by using an **-ly** ending: *"Wait a minute," he said thoughtfully.* | *Sheila considerately remembered to call and tell us she would be late.* | *I tried to tell Sophie tactfully that I didn't like her boyfriend.*

thoughtless /ˈθɔtləs/ *adjective*

- ► thoughtless
- ► inconsiderate
- ► tactless
- ► insensitive

ANTONYMS → see **thoughtful (2)**

thoughtless
not thinking about how something will affect another person's feelings – used especially when you forgot to do or say something: *He forgot his mother's birthday – how could he be so thoughtless?*

inconsiderate
very thoughtless. **Inconsiderate** sounds stronger than **thoughtless** and is used when you disapprove of someone's behavior: ***It is really inconsiderate of** you not **to** call when you are going to be late.* | *An inconsiderate driver turned without signaling first, making the other car stop suddenly.*

tactless
saying or doing things that offend other people or hurt their feelings, without intending to: ***It was tactless of** you **to** ask Joanne if she has gained weight.*

insensitive
not thinking about other people's feelings, and not realizing that something you say or do will upset them: *Reporters want to get a story, and sometimes they are **insensitive to** the feelings of crime victims.*

ADVERBS
You can make the adjectives that mean **thoughtless** into adverbs by using an **-ly** ending: *He thoughtlessly forgot his mother's birthday.* | *You tactlessly asked Joanne if she had gained weight.* | *The reporter's questions were insensitively worded.*

thread *noun* → see **string**

threat /θret/ *noun*

- ► threat
- ► warning
- ► ultimatum

threat
a statement in which you say you will hurt someone or cause problems for someone, if he or she does not do what you want: *Some parents use **threats of** punishment to get their children to behave.* | *Security officers at the airport say they received a bomb threat today.*

warning
a statement saying that something bad might happen: *The mayor's office issued a **warning of** more snow and icy roads.* | *The teacher gave Eric several **warnings about** his bad behavior before she sent him to the principal's office.*

ultimatum
a final warning that if someone does not do what you want, something bad will happen. **Ultimatum** sounds more formal than **warning**: *The coach gave him an ultimatum: if he misses another practice, he won't play in Saturday's game.*
→ see **danger** for **threat** meaning "the danger that something might happen"

threaten /ˈθretn/ *verb*

- ► threaten
- ► make threats
- ► bully
- ► intimidate
- ► blackmail

threaten
to say that you will do something bad to someone if he or she does not do what you want: *Suzy's mother **threatened to** throw away all*

T

of her things if she doesn't pick up her room. | *He robbed them and* ***threatened*** *them* ***with*** *violence.*

make threats
to say repeatedly that you will do something bad to someone if he or she does not do what you want: *Threats have been made against the witness, but he is still going to testify in court.*

bully
to frighten or hurt someone, especially someone who is smaller or weaker: *Matthew was being bullied by a boy at school who kept punching him.*

intimidate
to deliberately make someone feel frightened of you so that he or she does what you want: *Some voters say they were* ***intimidated into*** *voting for the ruling party.*

blackmail
to threaten to tell someone's secrets if he or she does not give you money or do what you want: *The man's secretary found out about his affair and began to blackmail him.*

threatening /ˈθretnɪŋ/ *adjective*

- ► threatening
- ► menacing
- ► intimidating
- ► ominous
- ► sinister

threatening
making you think that someone intends to harm you: *"If you tell anyone, you'll be sorry," he said in a threatening way.* | *The lawyer has received threatening phone calls from members of the gang.*
→ You can also use **threatening** to describe the sky or clouds when bad weather is coming: *The sky suddenly looked dark and threatening, like it was about to rain.*

menacing
frightening and making you think that someone is going to hurt you: *Two policemen were walking beside a menacing criminal in handcuffs.*
→ You can also use **menacing** when clouds are very dark and it looks like it may rain very soon: *The sky was filled with menacing black clouds.*

intimidating
making you feel frightened and nervous and lacking in confidence: *Big schools can seem intimidating to small children.* | *He was tall and intimidating.*

ominous
making you feel worried that something bad is going to happen: *There were ominous signs that the country was working on making nuclear weapons.*
→ You can also use **ominous** to describe the sky or clouds when bad weather is coming: *Ominous dark clouds covered the sky.*

sinister
strange and frightening, and making you feel that something bad will happen to you: *A sinister-looking man in dark glasses seemed to be watching me.*

ADVERBS

You can make the adjectives that mean **threatening** into adverbs by using an **-ly** ending: *"You'll be sorry!" he said threateningly.* | *The dog looked menacingly at me from behind the wall.* | *Dark clouds were gathering ominously in the western sky.*

thrifty /ˈθrɪfti/ *adjective*

- ► thrifty
- ► careful with money
- ► frugal

ANTONYMS → see **extravagant**

thrifty
good at using money carefully and wisely without wasting any, and saving money when possible: *Mrs. Jones was a thrifty woman who never wasted anything.* | *By being thrifty and shopping wisely, you can feed an entire family on $100 a week.*

careful with money
careful to spend as little money as possible: *Sandra is careful with money and always saves most of her allowance.*

frugal
spending very little money and careful to only buy what is necessary: *He is a frugal man who lives in a clean but small apartment and drives an old car.*
→ see **cheap**

ADVERBS

You can make **thrifty** and **frugal** into adverbs by using an **-ly** ending: *The company has thriftily cut its budget by 20%.* | *He lived frugally in a small clean apartment.*

thrill *verb* → see **excite**

thrilled *adjective* → see **excited**, **happy**, Topic **Describing People's Emotions**

thrilling *adjective* → see **exciting**

through *preposition, adverb* → see Function Word **across**, **because**

throughout *preposition, adverb* → see Function Word **during**

throw[1] /θroʊ/ *verb*

1 to make something go through the air
- ► throw
- ► toss
- ► fling
- ► hurl

2 to throw a ball in a game
- ► throw
- ► pass
- ► pitch
- ► shoot

1 to make something go through the air

throw
to make something go through the air, by moving your arm and letting it go out of your hand: *John stood on the beach, **throwing** stones **into** the water. | Kids were **throwing** snowballs **at** each other.*
→ **GRAMMAR:** You "throw something at someone or something" when you want it to hit that person or thing. You "throw something to someone" when you want him or her to catch it.

toss
to throw something, especially in a careless or relaxed way: *She **tossed** the map **onto** the back seat of the car.*

fling
to throw a light object quickly with a lot of force, often in a careless way: *The child started screaming and **flinging** toys **against** the wall.*

hurl
to throw an object using a lot of force, especially because you are angry: *He picked up his chair and **hurled** it **across** the room.*

2 to throw a ball in a game

throw
to throw a ball in a game: *Luis caught the ball and **threw** it back **to** the pitcher. | I **threw** the basketball straight **into** the net and scored.*

pass
to throw the ball to another member of your team, especially in football or basketball: *Murray **passed** the ball **to** Barry, who dunked it for two points.*

pitch
to throw the ball for a player to hit in baseball: *Do you know who is pitching in tonight's baseball game?*

shoot
to throw a ball toward the basket or goal in a sport such as basketball: *She dribbled up to the basket, shot, and scored!*

throw[2] /θroʊ/ *noun*

- ► throw
- ► pass
- ► pitch

throw
an action of throwing something such as a ball: *The throw was high, and I had to jump to catch it.*

pass
a throw of the ball to another member of your team, especially in football or basketball: *Johnson threw a pass to Muller, who scored.*

pitch
a throw of the ball for a player to hit in baseball: *The first pitch looked good, and the batter swung.*

throw away /ˌθroʊ əˈweɪ/ *phrasal verb*

- ► throw away
- ► throw out
- ► get rid of
- ► discard (*formal*)
- ► dispose of (*formal*)
- ► scrap

throw away
to get rid of something that you do not want or need, usually by putting it in the garbage: *I threw away the empty box. | The cake tasted bad, so I threw it away.*

throw out
to get rid of something that you do not want or need in your house, usually by putting it in the garbage: *The orange was moldy, so I threw it out. | We threw out a lot of stuff when we moved.*

get rid of
to remove something that you no longer want or need, for example by giving it to someone or throwing it away: *It is time to get rid of all these toys – you don't play with them anymore.*

discard (*formal*)
throw or leave something carelessly somewhere: *Empty bottles had been discarded on the beach.*

dispose of (*formal*)
to get rid of something by putting it somewhere. You use **dispose of** especially about things that you must be careful with: *Dispose of cooking oil in the trash. Do not pour it down the drain. | The problem with nuclear energy is how to dispose of dangerous nuclear waste.*

T

scrap
to get rid of an old machine or vehicle so that the metal in it can be used for other things: *The old ship is being scrapped this year.*
→ see **get rid of**, **waste**

throw up /ˌθroʊ ˈʌp/ *phrasal verb*

- ► throw up
- ► vomit (*formal*)
- ► feel sick to your stomach
- ► feel nauseated (*formal*)
- ► gag

throw up
if you throw up, food comes up from your stomach and out through your mouth: *He often throws up in the car – even on short journeys.*

vomit (*formal*)
vomit means the same as **throw up**: *Mrs. Smith called the doctor because her son had a fever and he had been vomiting.*

feel sick to your stomach
to feel that you might throw up: *The ride made me feel dizzy and sick to my stomach.*

feel nauseated (*formal*)
feel nauseated means the same thing as **feel sick to your stomach**: *The smell of the garbage made me feel nauseated.*

gag
if you gag, your throat moves as though you are going to **throw up**, for example because you have tasted or smelled something very unpleasant: *The awful smell from the trash can made her gag.*

thunderstorm *noun* → see **storm**, Topic **The Weather**

ticket /ˈtɪkɪt/ *noun*

- ► ticket
- ► pass
- ► voucher

ticket
a small piece of paper that shows that you have paid to see a movie, travel on a bus, etc.: *I have two **tickets for** the concert.* | *The plane ticket to Calgary was really expensive.*

pass
an official piece of paper that allows you to enter a building, travel on a bus, etc. You can usually use a **pass** more than once: *If you buy a bus pass, it is cheaper than paying every time you travel.* | *We didn't have to stand in line at the museum because we had a pass.*

voucher
a piece of paper that you can use instead of money to pay for something: *Poorer families can receive food stamps and rent vouchers.*

tidy *adjective* → see **neat**

tie /taɪ/ *verb*

- ► tie
- ► tie up
- ► bind
- ► knot

tie
to fasten something by making a knot in rope, string, etc.: *I kept all his letters tied together with a ribbon.* | *She **tied** the scarf **around** her neck.*

tie up
to tie someone's arms and legs with rope so that he or she cannot move: *The gang tied up the man and his wife, and stole money and jewelry from their home.*
→ If you **tie up** a boat or dog, you fasten it to something with a length of rope so that it cannot move away.

bind
to tie someone or something tightly with rope or string: *Bind the newspapers together with string in a stack about 6 inches high.* | *The workers in the bank had been bound, and all of the money had been taken.*

knot
to tie something in a knot: *He was wearing a dark suit, and his red tie was perfectly knotted.*
→ see **fasten**

tied /taɪd/ *adjective*

- ► tied
- ► one to one, 18 to 18, etc.
- ► one-all, three-all, etc.

tied
if two players or teams are tied in a game, each player or team has an equal number of points. You can also talk about the game being **tied**: *The teams were tied 13-13 at half time.* | *The score is **tied at** 36.*

one to one, 18 to 18, etc.
used when giving the score of a game in which both players or teams have the same number of points: *At the end of the first half, the score was 28 to 28.*

T

one-all, three-all, etc.
used when giving the score of a game in which both players or teams have the same number of points: *The game ended one-all.*
→ see Topic **Sports and Exercise**

tight /taɪt/ *adjective*

1 fitting very closely to your body
► tight
2 pulled or stretched as far as possible
► tight
► taut
3 holding something so that it cannot move
► tight
► firm
ANTONYMS → see **loose**

1 fitting very closely to your body

tight
tight clothes fit very closely to your body and are difficult to put on or take off: *These jeans are very tight. I can hardly button them at the waist.* | *She wore a tight black dress that showed off her figure.*
→ see Topic **Describing Clothes**

2 pulled or stretched as far as possible

tight
if a rope or strap is tight, it is pulled or stretched as far as possible: *If the straps aren't tight enough around the horse, the saddle can slip.*

taut
stretched very tight. Use **taut** especially about rope, wire, muscles, or skin: *It is important to keep the safety rope taut so that the climber cannot fall very far.*

3 holding something so that it cannot move

tight
unable to move, or holding something so that it cannot move: *His mother kept a tight hold on his hand as they crossed the street.*
→ You also use **tight** when something is in a fixed position where it cannot move: *Turn the screw to the right until it is tight.*

firm
holding something so that it cannot move, especially by squeezing your hand: *A firm handshake shows confidence.* | *Keep a firm hold on the bat.*

ADVERBS
You can make the adjectives that mean **tight** into adverbs by using an **-ly** ending: *The strap was not fastened tightly enough.* | *His muscles flexed tautly under his T-shirt.* | *She shook hands firmly with me.*

tight

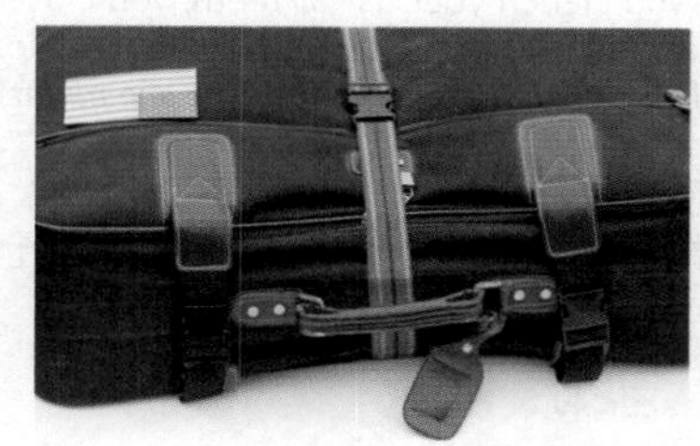

The strap around the suitcase is **tight**.

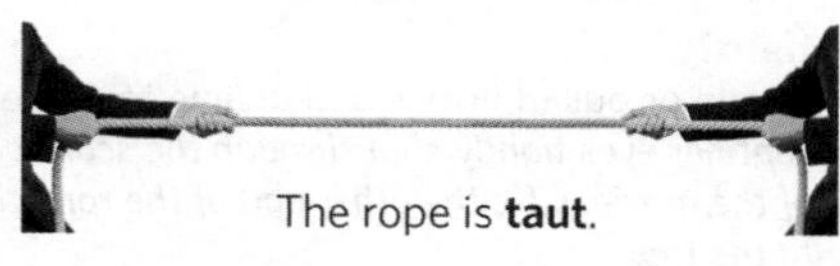

The rope is **taut**.

tighten /ˈtaɪtn/ *verb*

1 make something tight
► tighten
► pull something tight
► stretch
2 make your muscles tight
► tighten
► stiffen
► clench

1 make something tight

tighten
make a rope, wire, etc. tight, or become tight: *He pulled on the loose ends of the string to tighten the knot.* | *The horse felt the rope tighten around its neck.*

pull something tight
to pull something so that it becomes tight: *She pulled her jacket collar tight to keep her neck warm.*

stretch
to make something longer or wider by pulling it: *We stretched a rope between two trees to hold up the top of the tent.* | *His T-shirt was stretched tight across his back.*

2 make your muscles tight

tighten
to make a part of your body stiff or straight by

using your muscles: *Brenda tightened her grip on the cup.* | *He tightened his mouth into a thin angry line.*

stiffen
to tighten your muscles so that your body becomes stiff or straight: *He touched her on the shoulder and she stiffened.*

clench
if you clench your fist or teeth, you close your hand or mouth tightly using your muscles: *She clenched her fist and looked like she might punch something.*

tightly /ˈtaɪtli/ *adverb*

- ► tightly
- ► firmly
- ► securely
- ► closely

tightly
closed or pulled firmly, and unable to move: *She kept her eyes tightly shut through the scary parts of the movie.* | *Tie the other end of the rope tightly to the tree.*

firmly
in a way that does not allow something to move: *There was a small window, but it was firmly closed and he could not open it.* | *To start the exercise, stand with both feet firmly on the floor.*

securely (AWL)
in a way that will not allow something to open or move. You use **securely** about the way you fasten something: *Bethany keeps the door securely locked when she is home.*

closely
in a way that is so close to other people or things that there is not enough space to move very much: *Crowds of people were standing closely together trying to see the president.*

time /taɪm/ *noun*

1 when something happens
- ► time
- ► occasion
- ► moment
- ► point
- ► the instant

2 a length of time
- ► time
- ► period
- ► a while
- ► season
- ► term
- ► spell
- ► interval (*formal*)

3 a period of time in history
- ► time
- ► period
- ► century
- ► decade
- ► age
- ► era

1 when something happens

time
a time when something happens or when you do something: *The last time I saw her she was just a baby.* | *Remember that time we got lost on our way to the lake?* | ***By the time** I got to the phone, it had stopped ringing.*

occasion
Occasion means the same as **time** but is more formal: *The actress and the mayor have been seen together **on** several **occasions**.*

moment
a particular point in time when something happens, especially when it happens very quickly: *He jumped on the bus, and the next moment he was gone.* | ***At that moment** the phone rang, and it was Joan!*

point
a particular time during a longer period of time: ***At** one **point** during the flight, I thought I was going to throw up.*

the instant *also* **the minute**
the exact time when something happens. Use **the instant** or **the minute** when you are saying that one thing happens immediately after something else: *He was so tired he fell asleep the instant he closed his eyes.* | *Let me know the minute she gets here – I have something important to tell her.*

2 a length of time

time
a group of minutes, hours, days, or years, during which something happens or someone does something: *It takes a long time to learn to speak another language well.* | *The two women talked for a short time before entering the store.* | *That summer was a really happy time for me.*

period (AWL) *also* **period of time**
a length of time with a beginning and an end. **Period** sounds more formal and exact than **time**: *The medicine was tested over a five-week period.* | *His violin playing has improved in a very short period of time.*

a while
a period of time. You use **a while** when you are not being specific about how long the period is: *Ricky played with the ball **for a while** until he got*

bored. | *I'll be back **in a little while*** (=not a very long time).

→ If you use **while** in the phrase **take a while**, you mean something takes a fairly long time to happen: *It took her a while to recover from the operation.*

season
a time of the year which has its own type of weather. The seasons are winter, spring, summer, and fall: *As the season changes from fall into winter, the leaves drop off the trees.*

→ **Season** also means a period of weeks or months, when people do a type of sport or activity. A season happens at the same time every year: *The baseball season usually starts in April and finishes at the end of October.*

term
a period of time during which someone does a job, especially a government job: *The governor has served two terms in office.*

→ **Term** also means a period of time that a school year is divided into: *The paper is due at the end of the term.* You can also use **term** to talk about the period of time someone spends in prison: *Smith is serving a 19-year prison term.*

spell
a short period during which someone does something or there is a type of weather: *The dry spell lasted several months, but it finally began to rain in June.* | *After a brief spell in the army, he went to college.*

interval (AWL) (*formal*)
a period of time between two events or activities: *He left the room, returning after a short interval with a message.*

3 a period of time in history

time
a length of time in history, especially one in which particular events happened: *The 1960s were an important time in U.S. history.* | *People had to work hard during pioneer times.* | *Women were not allowed to vote until modern times.*

period (AWL)
a time in history. You often use **period** about a time in history that has a particular name: *By the end of the colonial period, 30,000 people lived in Philadelphia.* | *During that period many people moved from farms in the South to cities in the North.*

century
a period of 100 years: *The U.S. became a world leader during the 20th century.*

decade (AWL)
a period of ten years: *In the first decade of the 2000s, cell phones became very common.*

age
a long period of time in history, especially a time when the use of new tools or technology began: *Communication has changed greatly in the age of the Internet.* | *In the modern age, life is much faster and more stressful.* | *People began to use stone tools during the Stone Age.*

era
a long period of time in history during which things changed a lot, making the era different from other times: *Rock 'n' roll music first became popular in the post-World War II era.*

→ see **same time** for **at the same time**

timid *adjective* → see **shy**

tiny *adjective* → see **small**, Topic **Describing Size**

tip[1] *noun* → see **advice**, **end**[1], **hint**[1], **pay**[2], **top**[1]

tip[2] *verb* → see **pay**[1]

tired /taɪə-d/ *adjective*

1 feeling you want to sleep
- ► **tired**
- ► **exhausted**
- ► **worn out**
- ► **fatigued** (*formal*)
- ► **weary**

2 to start feeling tired (adjectives)
- ► **get tired**
- ► **tire** (*formal*)
- ► **exhaust** (*formal*)
- ► **tire out**

1 feeling you want to sleep

tired
feeling that you want to sleep or rest: *I stayed up late last night, so I'm really tired today.* | *Everybody looks tired. Let's take a break and finish cleaning later.*

→ A part of your body is **tired** when the muscles are sore because you have used them a lot: *My arms were tired from carrying boxes.*

exhausted
extremely tired and not having any energy left, especially because you have been working very hard or have not slept: *We were exhausted after the long trip home.* | *The exhausted firefighters had worked through the night to put out the fire.*

worn out
very tired because you have been working or playing hard: *The children were worn out after a day at the water park.*

fatigued (*formal*)
very tired, especially because you have used

T

your body or mind a lot: *They were too fatigued to continue with the climb.*

weary
very tired because you have been doing something for a long time and do not have any energy left. **Weary** is used mostly in written descriptions: *When the weary travelers finally arrived, they were cold and hungry.*
→ see **sleepy**

ADVERBS
You can make **tired**, **exhausted**, and **weary** into adverbs by using an **-ly** ending: *The team walked tiredly off the field.* | *She sat down wearily on the couch.*

2 to start feeling tired (adjectives)

get tired
to begin to feel that you want to sleep or rest: *It was a long walk, and I got very tired.*
→ **Get tired** is used much more often than **tire**.

tire (*formal*)
to become tired, or to make someone feel tired: *The runners were beginning to tire.* | *Only one visitor was allowed at a time, so as not to tire the patients.*

exhaust (*formal*)
to make someone feel very tired and without energy: *She had been sick, and the effort of standing up exhausted her.*

tire out
to make someone feel very tired, especially because he or she has done something active: *A day at the beach usually tires out the kids.*
→ see **bored** for **tired of**

tiredness /ˈtaɪɚdnəs/ *noun*

- tiredness
- exhaustion
- fatigue
- jet lag
- weariness

tiredness
the feeling that you want to sleep or rest: *If you work too late, you will start making mistakes because of tiredness.*

exhaustion
the feeling of being extremely tired and not having any energy left, especially because you have been working very hard or have not slept: *The soldiers were suffering from exhaustion after three days of marching.*

fatigue
the feeling of being very tired and weak. **Fatigue** is used especially about illnesses: *The signs of the disease are fever, fatigue, and not wanting to eat.*

jet lag
the feeling of being very tired after traveling a long distance in an airplane to a part of the world where the time is different: *I had jet lag after I got back from India, and I kept falling asleep in the afternoon.*

weariness
the feeling of being very tired because you have been doing something for a long time, and do not have any energy left: *He knew from the weariness in her face that she had been up all night worrying.*
→ see **sleepiness**

tiring /ˈtaɪərɪŋ/ *adjective*

- tiring
- exhausting
- hard
- grueling
- strenuous

tiring
making you feel that you want to rest, because you have to use a lot of effort: *Painting a house is very tiring.* | *My father has a tiring job working in a factory.*

exhausting
making you feel extremely tired and that you have no energy to do anything: *I had to drive nine hours without a break – it was exhausting.* | *He works in a coal mine, and it's a difficult and exhausting job.*

hard
difficult and tiring, and needing a lot of effort: *After a hard day at work, I just want to watch TV.* | *Cleaning the garage was hard work.*

grueling
something that is grueling makes you feel very tired, because it is difficult and unpleasant and because you have to keep doing it for a long time: *We finally arrived after a grueling five-hour bus ride on bumpy mountain roads.*

strenuous
needing a lot of effort and strength: *His doctor said that he must not do any strenuous exercise until his back was completely better.*

T

ADVERBS

You can make **exhausting** and **strenuous** into adverbs by using an **-ly** ending: *The two-year-old was exhaustingly full of energy.* | *If you exercise too strenuously, you will hurt your back again.*

title *noun* → see **name**[1]

today *noun* → see **present**[2]

tolerance /ˈtɑlərəns/ *noun*

- ► tolerance (*formal*)
- ► open-mindedness
- ► acceptance

ANTONYMS → see **prejudice**

tolerance (*formal*)
an attitude in which you let people do, say, or believe what they want, even if you do not agree with them: *The school has no **tolerance for** bullying, so bullies will be punished.* | *Religious tolerance is important – no one should lose a job because of their religious beliefs.*

open-mindedness
a willingness to think about and accept new ideas, opinions, or ways of doing things: *The group showed open-mindedness by listening to everyone's ideas, even if they were strange.*

acceptance
an attitude in which you allow something to happen without trying to prevent it, and without getting angry or upset: *His **acceptance of** his daughter's decision to not go to college surprised everyone.*
→ see **patience**

tolerant /ˈtɑlərənt/ *adjective*

- ► tolerant
- ► open-minded
- ► liberal

ANTONYMS → see **prejudiced**

tolerant
letting other people do, say, or believe what they want, even if you do not agree with them: *In this job you deal with many different kinds of people, so you have to be tolerant.* | *My parents don't like the music I listen to, but they are **tolerant of** it.*

open-minded
willing to accept new ideas, opinions, or ways of doing things: *Living in Brazil for a year has made Margo more open-minded about the way different cultures do things.*

liberal (AWL)
willing to respect other people's ideas and behavior even if they are different from your own: *I went to school with lots of different types of people, and that made me more liberal.*
→ see **patient**[1]

ADVERBS

You can make **tolerant** into an adverb by using an **-ly** ending: *My mom listened tolerantly to my complaining.*

tolerate *verb* → see **put up with**

too *adverb* → see Function Word **also**

tool /tul/ *noun*

- ► tool
- ► instrument
- ► gadget
- ► device
- ► utensil
- ► implement (*formal*)

tool
something that you hold in your hand and use for doing a particular job: *The tool set includes a hammer, screwdriver, drill, and wrenches.* | *Painting tools such as brushes and rollers are kept in the garage.*

instrument
a piece of scientific equipment or a medical tool: *Microscopes are useful scientific instruments.* | *The dentist's instruments were spread out on a tray.*

gadget
a small tool or machine, especially one that is new or interesting. People sometimes use **gadget** when they think that something is useful but not really necessary: *This handy kitchen gadget grates cheese or slices onions in no time.*

device (AWL)
a machine or small tool that is used to do a particular thing: *A corkscrew is a **device for** opening wine bottles.*

utensil
something that you use for preparing and eating food: *Knives, pots, and other kitchen utensils lay on the counter.*

implement (AWL) (*formal*)
a tool, especially one used for outdoor work: *The*

T

barn contained old farm implements, such as plows that could be pulled by horses.
→ see **equipment**

tool

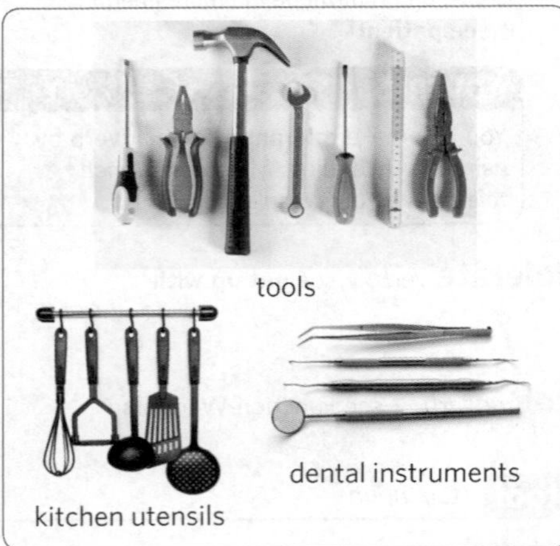
tools
kitchen utensils
dental instruments

tooth /tuθ/ *noun*

- ► tooth
- ► tusk
- ► fang

tooth
one of the hard white things in your mouth that you use for biting food: *Brush your teeth twice a day.* | *One of his front teeth was loose.*

tusk
one of the two very long teeth that stick out of the mouth of some animals, such as elephants, walruses, and wild boar: *Mammoths had curved tusks that were 14 feet long.*

fang
one of the long sharp teeth that a snake, dog, tiger, etc. has: *A rattlesnake injects poison into its prey through its fangs.*
→ Vampires also have **fangs**.

top[1] /tɑp/ *noun*

1 the highest part of something
- ► top
- ► summit
- ► peak
- ► crest
- ► tip

ANTONYMS → see **bottom (1)**

2 something you put on a container to close it
- ► top
- ► lid
- ► cap

1 the highest part of something

top
the highest part of something: *Beth was shorter, and Marcia could see over the top of her head.* | *The page number was* ***at the top of*** *the page.*

summit
the top of a high mountain: *It took the climbers four hours to reach the summit of the mountain.*

peak
the pointed top of a mountain: *On a clear day, the snow-covered peaks of the mountains can be seen from miles away.*

crest
the top of a hill or a wave: *When we reached the crest of the hill, we stopped to enjoy the view.*

tip
the pointed end of something, often the top end: *The tip of the iceberg was visible above the water.*

2 something you put on a container to close it

top
the cover for any container or a pen: *Who left the top off the toothpaste again?*

lid
a cover for a pot, box, or other container: *Put the lid on the pot, so the water will boil faster.*

cap
a cover that closes a bottle or tube, or goes on the end of a pen: *She was having trouble getting the cap off the pill bottle.*
→ see **shirt** for **top** meaning "clothes such as a T-shirt or a sweater"

top

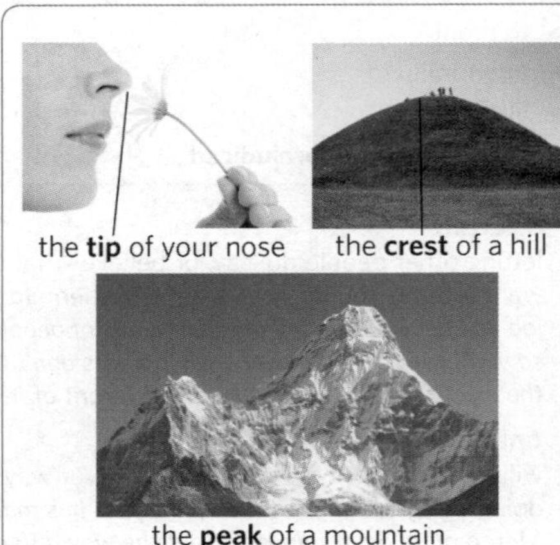
the **tip** of your nose
the **crest** of a hill
the **peak** of a mountain

top² /tɑp/ *adjective*

1 highest
- ► **top**
- ► **highest**
- ► **upper**
- ► **uppermost** (*formal*)

2 best or most important
- ► **top**
- ► **leading**
- ► **chief**
- ► **premier**
- ► **foremost**

1 highest

top
farthest from the bottom: *He undid the top button of his shirt because his collar was too tight.* | *Some of the top layer of paint had come off, but there were still more layers underneath.*

highest
farthest from the ground or from the bottom of something: *The cookies were on the highest shelf, so the kids couldn't reach them.*

upper
in a higher position than another part of something: *Several of her upper teeth were missing.* | *The stairs led to the upper floors of the building.*

uppermost (*formal*)
at the top of something, above all of its other parts: *She climbed the stairs and sat on the uppermost step.*

2 best or most important

top
best, most important, or most successful: *As the world's top tennis player, he is expected to win easily.* | *Money problems are among the top ten reasons for divorce.*

leading
best, most important, or most successful: *The nation's leading politicians attended the meeting.*

chief
most important: *Safety is our chief concern.*

premier
best in quality or most important: *The president stayed at the city's premier hotel.*

foremost
the best, most skilled, or most important: *One of the country's foremost surgeons will perform the surgery.*
→ see **best**

GRAMMAR CHECK: top

The words for **top** that mean "best" or "most important" are always used before a noun: *The secretary of state will meet with top Chinese officials.* | *The company is a leading provider of Internet services.*

topic *noun* → see **subject**

total /ˈtoʊtl/ *noun*
- ► **total**
- ► **subtotal**
- ► **sum**

total
the number that you get when you add or count everything together: *You had 29 points plus 33 more points, so the total is 62.* | *The three defendants were jailed for ten years each, **a total of** thirty years.*

subtotal
the amount you get when you add some but not all of a set of numbers: *The subtotal for parts was $43 and labor costs were $48.55, so the total bill came to $91.55.*

sum (AWL)
the total of numbers that are being added. You use **sum** only when you are doing a math problem that involves addition: ***The sum of** 14 and 20 is 34.* | *Add up both columns to find the sum.*
→ see **amount**

totally *adverb* → see **completely**

touch /tʌtʃ/ *verb*

1 to put your hand on someone or something
- ► **touch**
- ► **feel**
- ► **rub**
- ► **scratch**
- ► **tickle**

2 to touch someone in a gentle, loving, or approving way
- ► **stroke**
- ► **caress**
- ► **pat**
- ► **pet**

3 to touch someone or something accidentally
- ► **brush**

1 to put your hand on someone or something

touch
to put your finger, hand, etc. on something or

T

someone for a short time: *Don't touch the iron, it's hot! | Anna touched him on the arm and said, "Don't worry."*

feel
to use your fingers or hands to find out what something is like or where something is: *David's mother felt his head to see if he had a fever. | Dobbs **felt in** his pocket for any loose change.*

rub
to move your hand, or something you are holding, backward and forward over a surface. You can **rub** a part of someone's body to make it feel better, or you can **rub** an object, for example to make it clean: *Let me rub your back. | He used a rag to **rub** his fingerprints **off** the door handles.*

scratch
to rub your skin with your fingernails: *She tried to scratch her back where the sunburn was itching.*

tickle
to move your fingers lightly on parts of someone's body to try and make him or her laugh: *Dad tickled us under our arms until we screamed with laughter.*

2 to touch someone in a gentle, loving, or approving way

stroke
to move your hand gently over something, especially to make someone feel calm: *Michelle stroked her sister's hair and sang to her. | He sat, thinking and stroking his beard.*

caress
to gently touch someone in a way that shows love. **Caress** is used especially in literature and stories: *She bent over and caressed the baby's cheek.*

pat
to touch something lightly several times, with your hand flat, especially to show approval or love: *The politicians were shaking hands and **patting** each other **on** the shoulder.*

pet
to move your hand over an animal's fur to show that you like it: *Can I pet your dog?*

3 to touch someone or something accidentally

brush
to touch someone or something lightly with a part of your body, usually accidentally: *He sat back in the chair, and his leg accidentally **brushed against** hers.*

tough *adjective* → see **determined**, **difficult**, **strict**, **strong**

tour¹ *noun* → see **trip¹**, Topic **Travel and Vacations**

tour² *verb* → see **travel¹**

tourism *noun* → see **travel²**

tourist /ˈtʊrɪst/ *noun*

- ► tourist
- ► visitor
- ► sightseer

tourist
someone who goes to a place for a vacation: *We live in a beach town, so there are lots of tourists in the summer.*
→ **GRAMMAR: Tourist** is often used before other nouns to talk about places and things that tourists visit or use: *She wants to see the Statue of Liberty and some of the other tourist attractions before she leaves.*

visitor
someone who comes to see or stay in a place: ***Visitors to** the theme park come from all over the world.*

sightseer
someone who goes to famous or interesting places while he or she is visiting a city or country: *The bus was full of sightseers looking at the Eiffel Tower.*
→ see **traveler**, Topic **Travel and Vacations**

tournament *noun* → see **competition**, Topic **Sports and Exercise**

toward *preposition* → see Function Words

town /taʊn/ *noun*

- ► town
- ► city
- ► metropolis
- ► suburb
- ► village
- ► capital
- ► settlement

town
a place with many buildings and streets, that is smaller than a city: *I was born in a small town in Illinois. | The sculpture is in the Black Hills near **the town of** Custer, South Dakota.*

city
a very large town: *New York is the biggest city in the U.S. | He works for the city government.*

metropolis
a very large city, especially an important city: *New York quickly grew into a busy and crowded metropolis.*

suburb
a town that has houses and businesses, and which is near a city so that people can easily travel to the city to work: *Malden is **a suburb of** Boston that is north of the city. | After years of living **in the suburbs**, the family moved to a farm.*

village
a very small town, usually far from cities. **Village** is usually used about places outside of the U.S.: *His parents come from a village in Thailand.*

capital
a large city where a country's or state's main government is: *Many people do not realize that Albany is **the capital of** New York State.*

settlement
a group of houses and buildings where people live, especially in a place where few people have lived before: *The pioneers lived in a small settlement on the edge of the desert.*

toxic *adjective* → see **poisonous**

toy /tɔɪ/ *noun*

- ► **toy**
- ► **plaything** (*formal*)

toy
a thing for children to play with: *We watched the kids playing with their toys in the yard.*
→ **GRAMMAR: Toy** is often used before another noun to show that something is a toy: *I asked for a toy truck for Christmas that year.*

plaything (*formal*)
a toy. **Plaything** is usually used in writing: *Many parents worry about whether their children's playthings are safe to use.*

trace *noun* → see **sign**

tracks *noun* → see **line**[1]

trade[1] /treɪd/ *noun*

- ► **trade**
- ► **exchange** (*formal*)
- ► **swap** (*informal*)

trade
the act of giving someone something in order to get something from him or her: *You want my old video game for your soccer ball? Sounds like a good trade.*

exchange (*formal*)
the act of trading one thing for another. **Exchange** means the same as **trade** but is more formal: *In the marriage ceremony there is usually **an exchange of** rings. | You can get a free download **in exchange for** tweeting about the website.*

swap (*informal*)
swap means the same as **trade** but is more informal: *We did a swap – two cookies for a bag of chips.*
→ see **business** for **trade** meaning "the activity of buying and selling things"
→ see Topic **Jobs and Work**

trade[2] /treɪd/ *verb*

- ► **trade**
- ► **exchange**
- ► **swap** (*informal*)
- ► **barter**

trade
to give someone something and get something else from him or her. The things that each person **trades** may be very different: ***I'll trade** you these earrings **for** that necklace. | Neither of us liked our present, so we decided to trade.*

exchange
to give someone something and get something else from him or her. The things you **exchange** are usually similar: *At Christmas we exchange gifts. | The boys exchanged cell numbers and agreed to call each other later.*
→ You use **exchange** when you go to a store and give back what you bought in order to get something that costs a similar amount: *I'd like to **exchange** this sweater **for** a larger size.*

swap (*informal*)
swap means the same as **trade** but is more informal: *I liked her shoes, and she liked mine. So we swapped. | Jon and Felipe swapped pens.*

barter
to pay for something by giving another thing or doing work, rather than using money: *During the war her grandmother had to **barter** pieces of jewelry **for** bread and milk.*
→ see **sell** for **trade** meaning "buy and sell things in order to make money"

tradition /trəˈdɪʃən/ *noun*

- ► **tradition**
- ► **custom**
- ► **practice**
- ► **norms** (*formal*)

tradition
a belief or activity that has existed for a long time in a culture or country: *In Germany, the **tradition of** exchanging gifts on Christmas Eve is still common. | In the U.S., it is a **tradition** that the bride wears a long white dress.*

T

custom
a traditional activity or way of behaving that most people in a society do: *In my country **it is the custom to** eat at 9:00 or 9:30 in the evening.*

practice
a method of doing something that is used by most people in an organization, profession, or society: *In France, **it is a common practice to** have cheese at the end of a meal instead of dessert.*

norms (*formal*)
ways of behaving that are acceptable in a group or society, and that are normal: *Because of social networking sites, the **norms of** privacy are changing. People post many things they would not say in public.*

SYNONYM CHECK

Tradition or custom?

Tradition and **custom** have similar meanings.
You use **tradition** when you are talking about beliefs or activities that people pass on to their children: *At Thanksgiving, it is a tradition that families get together and eat a turkey dinner.*
You use **custom** to talk about activities or ways of behaving that people in a society think are normal or polite: *It is the custom in Japan to take your shoes off when you go into the house.*

traditional /trəˈdɪʃənəl/ *adjective*

- traditional
- conservative
- customary (*formal*)

traditional (AWL)
based on ideas and ways of doing things that people in a place have used for a long time: *They sang traditional African songs.* | *In the U.S. **it is traditional to** dress up in costumes on Halloween.*

conservative
typical of someone who likes attitudes, styles, and ways of doing things to remain the same and does not like new ones: *Grant's ideas about women are very conservative.* | *She was dressed in a conservative blue suit and pumps.*
→ You can also use **conservative** about people who like things to remain the same: *My parents were very conservative and did not like me going to parties with boys.*

customary (*formal*)
if something is customary, it is the usual thing that people do in that situation: ***It is customary for** the man **to** ask the woman to marry him.* | *The man at the hotel welcomed us with the customary greeting.*

ADVERBS

You can make the adjectives that mean **traditional** into adverbs by using an **-ly** ending: *Traditionally, we sing the national anthem before every game.* | *Mara was dressed conservatively in a blue suit.* | *Customarily, the man asks the woman to marry him.*

traffic /ˈtræfɪk/ *noun*

- traffic
- traffic jam
- congestion (*formal*)

traffic
the vehicles moving along a road at a particular time: *There is so much traffic in the city that driving is stressful.* | *The traffic is heavy on the freeway at rush hour, because everyone leaves work at the same time.*

traffic jam
a long line of vehicles on the road that are moving very slowly or not moving at all: *An earlier accident caused a traffic jam on the highway.* | *I'm sorry we're late – we got stuck in a traffic jam.*

congestion (*formal*)
a situation in which there is too much traffic in a particular area: *There is congestion downtown because everyone drives to work.*
→ see **transportation**

train *verb* → see **exercise²**, **practice²**, **teach**

training *noun* → see **exercise¹**, **practice¹**

translate /trænzˈleɪt/ *verb*

- translate
- interpret

translate
to change something that someone has spoken or written into a different language: *The book was written in French, and he **translated** it **into** English.* | *Shakespeare's plays have been **translated into** over 80 different languages.*

interpret (AWL)
to change what someone is saying in one language into another language, as he or she is speaking: *The witness speaks only Spanish, so she needs someone to **interpret for** her in court.*

transparent *adjective* → see **clear**

transportation /ˌtrænspəˈteɪʃən/ *noun*

1 a way that people use to travel from one place to another
- ► **transportation**
- ► **transit** (*formal*)

2 the process of moving people or things from one place to another
- ► **transportation**
- ► **transit** (*formal*)
- ► **traffic**

1 a way that people use to travel from one place to another

transportation (AWL)
a way that people use to travel from one place to another: *Many people in China rely on bicycles **for transportation**. | Cars are the most common form of transportation in the U.S.*

transit (AWL) (*formal*)
a system of buses or trains that people use to travel around a city or area: *You can use public transit to get to the airport.*
→ **Public transit**, **mass transit**, and **public transportation** can all be used to talk about the system of buses and trains in a city: *New York City's mass transit system is one of the biggest in the world. | There is good public transportation, so you don't need a car to get downtown.*

2 the process of moving people or things from one place to another

transportation (AWL)
the process of moving people or things from one place to another: *The **transportation of** products across the United States is faster today than ever before.*

transit (AWL) (*formal*)
the process of moving people or things from one place to another: *When our airplane landed in Dallas, we found out that our suitcases had been lost **in transit**.*

traffic
the number of airplanes, ships, or trains that are moving from one place to another: *Because of the increase in air traffic, the city needs to build a bigger airport.*

trap /træp/ *noun*

- ► **trap**
- ► **snare**

trap
a piece of equipment for catching animals: *I need to set some traps because we have mice in the house.*

snare
a trap for catching an animal. A **snare** has a wire or rope that pulls tightly around the animal: *He used snares to catch rabbits.*
→ see **trick[1]** for **trap** meaning "something that is intended to trick someone"
→ see **catch**

trapped /træpt/ *adjective*

- ► **trapped**
- ► **stuck**
- ► **imprisoned** (*formal*)

trapped
unable to escape from a dangerous place or a bad situation: *The miners have been trapped underground for three days. | He feels trapped in a job that he doesn't enjoy anymore.*

stuck
unable to move or to get out of an unpleasant or boring situation. **Stuck** sounds more informal than **trapped**: *My boot got stuck in the mud, and I couldn't get out. | Our flight was delayed, and we were stuck at the airport for hours.*

imprisoned (*formal*)
unable to escape from a place because you are locked in, or feeling as though you are locked in a place: *The story is about a princess who is imprisoned in a tower. | The violence in the neighborhood makes many residents feel imprisoned in their own homes.*

trash /træʃ/ *noun*

- ► **trash**
- ► **garbage**
- ► **litter**
- ► **refuse** (*formal*)
- ► **waste** (*formal*)
- ► **junk**

trash
things that you throw away: *There was a pile of trash by the side of the road. | I cleaned up the backyard and took out three bags of trash.*

garbage
things that you throw away. **Garbage** is used especially about food and containers for food: *We used paper plates for the party, so there was a lot of garbage afterward. | This garbage smells bad – let me take it out for you.*
→ If you throw things **in the trash** or **in the garbage**, you put things in a bag or a can used for trash.

litter
pieces of paper, food containers, or other trash that people leave on the ground in public places: *I picked up the wrapper I dropped, so I wouldn't leave any litter on the street.*

refuse (*formal*)
trash. You use **refuse** especially to talk about a lot of trash: *Each truck collects nine tons of refuse every day.*

waste (*formal*)
things that are left after you have used something. **Waste** is often used about the things that are left after an industrial process, for example making something in a factory: *Recycling is an important way to reduce waste.* | *Nuclear waste is stored deep underground for safety reasons.*

junk
old or unwanted things that have no use or value: *There was an old car without wheels, some broken garden tools, and lots of other junk in the backyard.*

travel¹ /ˈtrævəl/ *verb*

- ► travel
- ► go
- ► explore
- ► visit
- ► tour
- ► commute
- ► journey (*formal*)

travel
to go from one place to another: *He travels a lot on business.* | *The president will **travel to** Mexico later this month.* | *After I graduate from college, I want to travel around Europe.*

go
to go somewhere. **Go** is often used instead of **travel**: *We're **going to** Hawaii for our vacation this year.* | *If it's too expensive to fly, you can always **go by** bus.*

explore
to travel around an area in order to find out what it is like: *We explored some of the different neighborhoods in Miami.*

visit
to go somewhere to see a place: *You must visit the Colosseum while you are in Rome.*

tour
to travel around an area and visit different places, especially as part of a vacation: *We toured northern California and went to see the redwood trees.*

commute
to travel to work regularly in a car, train, or bus: *He **commutes to** work **on the train**.*

journey (*formal*)
to travel, especially a long distance. **Journey** is used especially in books: *In 1804, Lewis and Clark journeyed up the Missouri River.*
→ see **go**, Topic **Travel and Vacations**

travel² /ˈtrævəl/ *noun*

- ► travel
- ► traveling
- ► sightseeing
- ► tourism

travel
the activity of traveling: *Her interests are politics, music, and travel.* | *One hundred years ago, travel between the two countries was extremely difficult.*
→ **Travel** can also be used to describe a particular kind of traveling: *Air travel is generally very safe, but some people are still scared of flying.*

traveling
the activity of traveling. **Traveling** is used especially to talk about the trips that a particular person makes: *My father did a lot of traveling around Europe when he was younger.* | *I wish I had more time for traveling – I would love to go to India.*

sightseeing
the activity of traveling and visiting famous or interesting places: *We will be doing some sightseeing while we are in Greece.*

tourism
the business of providing hotels, flights, etc. for people who are traveling to a place for a vacation: *The new aquarium has been good for tourism – there were thousands more visitors to the city last year.*
→ see **trip¹**, Topic **Travel and Vacations**

traveler /ˈtrævələ˞/ *noun*

- ► traveler
- ► tourist
- ► visitor
- ► sightseer
- ► commuter

traveler
someone who goes on a trip somewhere: *Business travelers will enjoy the train's new larger seats.*

tourist
someone who goes to a place for a vacation: *We*

T

live in a beach town, so there are lots of tourists in the summer.

→ **GRAMMAR: Tourist** is often used before other nouns to talk about places and things that tourists visit or use: ***She wants to see the Statue of Liberty and some of the other tourist attractions before she leaves.***

visitor
someone who comes to see or stay in a place: ***Visitors to** the theme park come from all over the world.*

sightseer
someone who goes to famous or interesting places while he or she is visiting a city or country: *The bus was full of sightseers looking at the Eiffel Tower.*

commuter
someone who travels to work regularly, in a car, bus, train, etc.: *The subway was full of commuters.*

→ see **passenger**, Topic **Travel and Vacations**

traveling *noun* → see **travel[2]**

travels *noun* → see **trip[1]**

treasure /ˈtreʒɚ/ *noun*

- ► treasure
- ► valuables

treasure
a group of valuable things, such as gold, silver, or jewels: *A pirate had stolen the treasure and then buried it on the island.*

valuables
things you own that are valuable, such as jewelry, cameras, or important documents: *Guests should leave their valuables in the hotel safe.*

treat /trit/ *verb*

1 to deal with people or situations in a particular way
- ► treat
- ► deal with
- ► handle
- ► behave toward

2 to do something to make a sick or injured person better
- ► treat
- ► cure
- ► heal
- ► nurse
- ► operate
- ► prescribe

1 to deal with people or situations in a particular way

treat
to behave toward someone or deal with something in a particular way: *Please treat this information as a secret.* | *The school treated their concerns about bullying very seriously.*

deal with
to do something to make a situation better, for example to solve a problem: *We need to deal with problems like pollution and climate change.*

→ You can also use **deal with** about the way you behave and the things you do when you are with someone: *He dealt with the angry customer very well.*

handle
to deal with people or situations, especially in an effective or confident way: *Most customers were happy with the way their complaints had been handled.*

behave toward
to do things in a particular way when you are dealing with someone: *He began to behave differently toward me when he found out I was rich.*

2 to do something to make a sick or injured person better

treat
to do something to make a sick or injured person better, or to make an illness or injury go away: *In some countries, it is difficult to treat patients because there is not enough medicine.* | *Nowadays, malaria can be **treated with** drugs.*

cure
to make an injury or illness go away completely so that someone is well again: *When the disease is found early, it can be easily treated and cured.*

heal
to make someone's body get better after an injury: *Vitamin C helps your body to heal wounds.*

nurse
to take care of people who are sick or injured: *The boy was very sick, but his mother nursed him back to health.*

operate
if a doctor operates, he or she cuts into someone's body in order to repair or remove a part that is damaged: *They had to **operate on** my arm because it was broken in two places.*

prescribe
if a doctor prescribes medicine, he or she says what medicine or treatment a sick person should have: *Dr. Gordon said that the baby had an ear infection and prescribed an antibiotic.*

treatment /'tritmənt/ *noun*

- treatment
- cure
- operation
- surgery
- therapy

treatment
a way of making an illness or a sick person better: *Doctors are testing the drug as a* ***treatment for*** *depression.* | *Injured passengers were rushed to the hospital* ***for treatment.***

cure
a medicine or type of medical treatment that makes a disease go away completely: *Scientists are still working hard to find a* ***cure for*** *AIDS.*

operation
a medical treatment in which a doctor cuts into someone's body to fix or remove a damaged part: *He had* ***an operation on*** *his right eye to try to get his sight back.*

surgery
medical treatment in which a doctor cuts into someone's body to fix or remove a damaged part: *If the drugs don't work, her doctor says she'll need surgery to remove the tumor.*

therapy
treatment of an illness or injury over a long period of time: *After the accident, Don had months of physical therapy to help him walk again.*
→ see **behavior** for **treatment** meaning "the way people behave toward someone"
→ see Topic **Medical Treatment**

SYNONYM CHECK
Operation or surgery?
You can often use either **surgery** or **operation**. However, you use **operation** with "an": *He had an operation on his knee.* You use **surgery** without "a": *He had surgery on his knee.*

tree /tri/ *noun*

- tree
- sapling
- conifer

tree
a tall plant that has a wooden trunk, branches, and leaves: *Mom and Dad planted that maple tree when I was born.* | *It was fall and the trees were losing their leaves.*

sapling
a young tree: *Saplings were growing where the fire had destroyed older trees.*

conifer
a tree that has leaves that look like needles. **Conifers** do not lose their leaves in winter, and produce cones containing their seeds: *There is a layer of dry pine needles on the forest floor from all the conifers.*
→ see **forest**

trend /trend/ *noun*

- trend
- transition
- shift
- movement

trend
a gradual change so that something happens differently or people do things differently: *The trend is for gas prices to go even higher.* | *There is a general trend toward part-time work.*

transition (AWL)
the process of changing from one situation or state to another: *The* ***transition from*** *communism* ***to*** *democracy was difficult in many Eastern European countries.*

shift (AWL)
a clear change in the way most people think about something, or in the way something is done: *There's been a huge* ***shift in*** *attitudes toward divorce since the 1960s, and it is much more common now.*

movement
a slow change in a situation or in the way people think about something: *There has been some* ***movement toward*** *more freedom in the country, but the changes will be slow.*
→ see **fashion** for **trend** meaning "something that is becoming popular"

trial /'traɪəl/ *noun*

- trial
- case
- lawsuit
- hearing

trial
the process by which a court of law decides whether someone is guilty of a crime: *The murder trial is expected to take several months.* | *Bolin will go* ***on trial for*** *robbery next Tuesday.*

case
a particular crime or legal problem that is judged in a court of law: *A jury is being selected*

to hear the case against Simons, who is accused of stealing.

lawsuit *also* **suit**
a formal complaint that someone takes to a court of law so that a judge can decide who is right and who is wrong: *She filed a **lawsuit against** her employer, saying the company had fired her unfairly.*

hearing
a meeting of a court to find out the facts about a case: *During the court hearing, the judge decided that there was enough evidence to go ahead with the trial.*

trick[1] /trɪk/ *noun*

- ► trick
- ► trap
- ► scam
- ► hoax
- ► deception (*formal*)
- ► bluff

trick
something that you do to make someone believe something that is not true, in order to get something or to have fun: *Don't give her any money – it might be a trick.* | *When Abby opened the empty bag, she realized the man had played a trick on her.*

trap
a trick for catching or harming someone: *I didn't follow him into the bar because I thought it might be a trap.*

scam
a dishonest plan to get money by tricking people: *The scam involved saying that someone had won a free vacation and then charging them for plane tickets that never arrived.*

hoax
a trick to make a lot of people believe that something bad will happen, or that something is true when it is not: *Police could not find a bomb and now believe the bomb threat was a hoax.*

deception (*formal*)
lies or behavior that is intended to make someone believe something that is not true: *Her husband had lied to her, and she only found out about his deception by accident.*

bluff
a situation in which you pretend something, in order to make something happen the way you want it to: *It was all a bluff: she was never really going to run away – she just wanted attention.*

trick[2] /trɪk/ *verb*

- ► trick
- ► deceive (*formal*)
- ► fool
- ► bluff

trick
to make someone believe something that is not true in order to make him or her do something: *She **tricked** me **into** coming to the party by telling me that Stuart would be there.* | *A man pretending to be an insurance agent **tricked** her **out of** thousands of dollars.*

deceive (*formal*)
to make someone believe something that is not true: *The senator deceived the public by saying that he had not taken money from the organization.*

fool
to make someone believe something that is not true, especially in a way that makes him or her look stupid: *The fake painting was so good it even fooled art experts.*

bluff
to pretend that something is true, especially in order to get an advantage: *She says she is going to tell on us if we don't let her come along, but I think she is bluffing – she won't really tell.*

trip[1] /trɪp/ *noun*

1 a trip
- ► trip
- ► visit
- ► commute
- ► drive
- ► flight

2 a trip for fun
- ► tour
- ► excursion
- ► cruise

3 a long trip
- ► journey
- ► voyage
- ► expedition
- ► travels

1 a trip

trip
an occasion when you travel from one place to another: *I will be taking a **trip to** Seattle.* | *We had a lot of fun **on** our **trip**, but it's good to be home.* | *The museum is just a short **trip from** here.*

T

visit
an occasion when someone goes to a place to spend time: *On Ed's first* ***visit to*** *New York, he went to the top of the Empire State Building.* | *Why don't you come* ***for a visit*** *next summer?*

commute
the trip that someone makes regularly to get to work: *He is tired of the long commute, so he is looking for a job closer to home.*

drive
a trip in a car: *They went for a drive in the mountains.*

flight
a trip in a plane: *It is a three-hour flight from here to Los Angeles.*

2 a trip for fun

tour
a trip to several different places in a country, city, or area: *We went* ***on*** *a bike* ***tour of*** *the city and stopped at all the major tourist sights.*

excursion
a short trip made for pleasure, often as part of a longer trip: *The trip to Las Vegas includes a one-day* ***excursion to*** *the Grand Canyon.*

cruise
a trip for pleasure on a ship that travels to different places: *We went* ***on*** *a Caribbean* ***cruise*** *and visited some of the islands there.*

3 a long trip

journey
a trip from one place to another, especially over a long distance: *Their* ***journey across*** *America took six months.*

voyage
a long trip on a ship: *Columbus made his first* ***voyage to*** *North America in 1492.*

expedition
a long trip to a place that is dangerous or not well known: *The scientists are planning an* ***expedition to*** *the rainforest to study the plants and animals there.*

travels
trips to places that are far away: *She has written books about her* ***travels through*** *Asia.*
→ see **travel²**, Topic **Travel and Vacations**

T

trip² /trɪp/ *verb*

- ► trip
- ► stumble
- ► slip

trip
to hit your foot against something so that you fall or almost fall: *She tripped and fell.* | *Pick up your toys – someone might* ***trip on*** *them.* | *He* ***tripped over*** *the cat and broke his arm.*

stumble
to almost fall down while you are walking, especially because your foot hits something: *We kept* ***stumbling over*** *rocks in the dark cave.*

slip
to accidentally slide on a smooth surface and fall down or almost fall down: *He walked carefully to avoid* ***slipping on*** *the ice.*

troops *noun* → see **army**, **military**, **soldier**

trouble /ˈtrʌbəl/ *noun*

- ► trouble
- ► unrest
- ► disturbance
- ► mischief
- ► prank

trouble
a situation in which people fight or behave in a violent or frightening way: *Just let me go – I don't want any trouble.* | *If those kids start any trouble, I'm going to call the police.*

unrest
a situation in which people protest or behave violently: *High unemployment is causing unrest in the country, where thousands of people have joined in the protests.*

disturbance
a situation in which people fight or make a lot of noise in public: *Witnesses said the man was yelling and causing a disturbance.*

mischief
bad behavior, especially by children, that causes trouble or damage but no serious harm: *That boy is always getting into mischief – he has tied everyone's shoelaces together.*

prank
a joke in which you play a trick on someone in order to make him or her look silly: *As a prank, they emptied the wastebasket onto her desk after she had left for the day.*
→ see **problem** for **trouble** meaning "problem"

true /tru/ *adjective*

- ► true
- ► right
- ► correct
- ► accurate
- ► factual

ANTONYMS → see **false**

true
based on facts, and not imagined or invented:

Do you think the rumors are true? Are they really breaking up? | The movie is based on a true story. | I never know if what he says is true or made up.

right
based on true facts and not wrong. You can say that information is **right**, or you can say that a person is **right** when he or she says something that is correct: *What is the right answer to question number 3? | I think you're right. We should have gone the other way.*

correct
right or without any mistakes. **Correct** sounds more formal than **right**: *The information you have is correct.*

accurate (AWL)
exactly correct without any mistakes. Use **accurate** about descriptions, information, and numbers: *I was there and I can assure you that the story is accurate.*

factual
true and based on facts: *The court makes its decision based on factual evidence that can be proved.*

→ see **real**

ADVERBS

You can make **correct**, **accurate**, and **factual** into adverbs by using an **-ly** ending: *You answered the question correctly. | I have accurately described the situation to you. | The news broadcast reported the story as factually correct, but they have no evidence.*

truly *adverb* → see **really**, **very**

trust¹ /trʌst/ *verb*

- ► trust
- ► believe in
- ► have faith in
- ► depend on
- ► rely on
- ► be reliant on
- ► count on

trust
to feel sure that someone will do what he or she says or what is right: *David is one of my oldest friends – I trust him completely. | I wouldn't trust Tina to babysit – she is too immature.*
→ **Trust** can also mean to feel sure that something is correct or will work correctly: *She needs a car she can trust.*

believe in
to trust that someone or something is good or will be successful: *My mother believed in me even when others weren't sure I would succeed. | She believes in the power of education to improve lives.*

have faith in
to trust that someone or something is good or will do the right thing: *Antonio will be here to help – I have faith in him.*

depend on
to trust that someone or something will do something that you need or that you expect him or her to do: *You can depend on Jane – she always keeps her promises.*

rely on (AWL)
to trust that someone or something will do something that you need: *The city relies on the police to keep people safe.*
→ **Depend on** and **rely on** have very similar meanings and you can usually use either expression in a sentence: *I knew I could depend on you for help. | I knew I could rely on you for help.*

be reliant on
to rely on someone or something completely to do or provide something: *When she got older and could not drive, she **was reliant on** her family **to** take her to the supermarket, to church, and anywhere else she needed to go.*

count on
to trust that someone or something will do something that you want. **Count on** is a little more informal than **depend on** or **rely on**: *I knew I could count on my older brother for protection.*
→ You can also use **count on** to say that you expect someone to do something, even if it is not a good thing: *You can always count on Jack to say the wrong thing.*

trust² /trʌst/ *noun*

- ► trust
- ► confidence
- ► faith

ANTONYMS → see **distrust²**

trust
the belief that someone is honest or that you can depend on someone or something: *The doctor-patient relationship is based on trust. | Children need to have **trust in** the adults around them.*

confidence
a strong belief that someone or something is good or will be successful: *Voters have lost **confidence in** the president and no longer believe he will do what he promised.*

faith
a strong belief that someone or something is good or will do the right thing: *I always had **faith***

in the legal system and was sure that my husband would be proven innocent.

truth /truθ/ *noun*

- ► truth
- ► fact
- ► accuracy

truth
the true facts about something: *The truth is that he didn't borrow the money, he stole it.* | *Joe is telling the* ***truth about*** *what happened – I was there, and I saw it.*

fact
a piece of information that is true: *The police are trying to find out the* ***facts about*** *what happened.*

accuracy (AWL)
the quality of being correct or true: *Has anyone checked the accuracy of his statement? Is there any proof that what he says is true?*
→ see **reality**

truthful *adjective* → see **honest**

try[1] /traɪ/ *verb*

1 to attempt to do something
- ► try
- ► attempt
- ► make an effort
- ► struggle
- ► fight
- ► strive (*formal*)
- ► endeavor (*formal*)

2 to examine the evidence and decide whether someone is guilty of a crime
- ► try
- ► put someone on trial
- ► judge

1 to attempt to do something

try
to make an effort to do something, especially when you are not sure if you can do it: *I* ***tried to*** *explain why I was upset.* | *Can you* ***try to*** *open the window? I think it's stuck.* | *He tries hard in class, but his test scores are still low.*

attempt
to try to do something, especially something difficult. **Attempt** sounds a little more formal than **try**: *He was* ***attempting to*** *climb one of the world's highest mountains.*

make an effort
to try hard to do something, especially when you do not want to do it: *She* ***made a big effort to*** *be nice to him even though she didn't like him.*

struggle
to try very hard for a long time to do something difficult, especially when you are not completely successful: *Many poor families* ***struggle to*** *buy food and pay their bills.*

fight
to try hard to do or get something, when this is difficult: *Women are still* ***fighting for*** *equal rights in some countries.*

strive (*formal*)
to try very hard to achieve a goal: *Our team always* ***strives to*** *do the best we can.*

endeavor (*formal*)
to try hard to do something new or important: *The people* ***endeavored to*** *protect the town from the flood.*

2 to examine the evidence and decide whether someone is guilty of a crime

try
to examine the evidence and decide whether that person is guilty of a crime, in a court of law: *Lowden will be tried for murder.* | *The lawyer agreed to try the case.*

put someone on trial
to bring someone to a court of law to be judged: *He was arrested last year and put on trial for robbery.*

judge
to decide whether someone is guilty of a crime in a court of law: *The court judged her guilty and sentenced her to two years in prison.*
→ see **taste**[2] for **try** meaning "eat a little of something to find out if you like it"
→ see **try on** at **dress**[2]
→ see **try out** at **test**[2]

try[2] /traɪ/ *noun*

- ► try
- ► attempt
- ► effort
- ► endeavor (*formal*)

try
the act of trying to do something: *She didn't break the school record, but it was a good try.* | *Only half the students passed the test on the first try.*

attempt
the act of trying to do something. **Attempt** is a little more formal than **try**: *She made several* ***attempts to*** *escape, but she was always caught.*

effort
an attempt to do something, especially something that you find difficult: *Tom's **efforts to** stop smoking have not been very successful.*

endeavor (*formal*)
an attempt to do something new or important: *They are doing tests **in an endeavor to** understand what caused the accident.*
→ see **campaign¹** for words meaning "try to persuade people to change something"

tube /tub/ *noun*

- ► tube
- ► pipe
- ► hose
- ► cylinder

tube
a hollow object with circular ends and long sides, especially one for a liquid or gas to flow through: *While he was in the hospital, he was fed through a tube to his stomach.* | *The toilet paper is wrapped around a cardboard tube.*

pipe
a hard tube for water, gas, oil, etc. to flow through: *A water pipe burst in the bathroom and flooded the floor.*

hose
a long soft tube that water or air can flow through: *The firefighters held the hose and sprayed water on the burning building.*

cylinder
a container with circular ends and hard straight sides: *The cylinder contained three tennis balls that were stacked one on top of the other.*

tug *noun* → see **pull²**

tune *noun* → see **music**

tunnel /ˈtʌnl/ *noun*

- ► tunnel
- ► passage
- ► shaft

tunnel
a passage through a mountain or under the ground: *You have to go through a tunnel to get to the other side of the mountain.* | *My cell phone stopped working when the train went through the tunnel.*

passage *also* **passageway**
a long narrow area with walls on either side, that connects one room or place with another: *There was an underground passage that connected the two buildings.*

shaft
a narrow passage that goes down into the ground or from the top to the bottom of a building: *It is too dangerous to go down that old mine shaft.* | *The elevator went down through the elevator shaft.*

turn¹ /tɚn/ *verb*

1 to turn in a circle
- ► turn
- ► spin
- ► rotate
- ► revolve (*formal*)
- ► go around (*informal*)
- ► whirl
- ► twirl

2 to turn your body around
- ► turn
- ► turn around
- ► turn away
- ► turn over
- ► roll over
- ► twist
- ► spin
- ► twirl

3 to change direction
- ► turn
- ► turn around
- ► turn back
- ► change direction
- ► swerve

1 to turn in a circle

turn
to move around, or make something move around: *The wheels began to turn and the wagon rolled away.* | *I turned the door handle and pushed the door open.* | *Turn the key to start the engine.*

spin
to turn something around many times, very quickly: *He can spin a basketball on the end of his finger.*

rotate
to turn around a central point. You use **rotate** about things that have the shape of a circle or that form a circle: *The helicopter blades rotate at very high speeds.* | *Rotate the knob under the chair to change the height of the seat.*

revolve (*formal*)
to make a circular movement around a central point. **Revolve** is a scientific word: *All the planets **revolve around** the Sun.*

T

go around (*informal*)
to make a circular movement around a central point. **Go around** means the same as **revolve** but it is more informal: *Mars takes almost 687 days to go around the sun once.* | *Out in the ocean, you can see the wind turbines going around and around.*

whirl
to spin with a lot of energy. **Whirl** is very similar in meaning to **spin**, but you use it to make your words more interesting, for example in a story: *White clouds of snow were whirled around by the strong winds.*

twirl
to turn something long and thin, such as a stick, around many times in a circular movement: *The marchers at the front of the parade twirled their batons in time to the music.*

2 to turn your body around

turn
to change the direction that your body is facing: *Michael turned and walked away.* | *She turned to face him, looking excited.*

turn around
to turn your body so that you are facing the opposite direction: *Anna turned around so that her back was to me.*

turn away
to turn your body so that you are not looking at someone, especially when you are upset or angry: *I turned away so that she wouldn't see the tears in my eyes.*

turn over
to turn your body to face a different direction when you are lying down: *Ryan **turned over** onto his stomach.*

roll over
to turn your body to face a different direction when you are lying down. **Roll over** and **turn over** mean the same thing: *She rolled over and stared at the ceiling.*

twist
to turn part of your body while the rest of it points forward: *He **twisted around** in his seat to see what the other kids were doing.*

spin
to turn your body around many times, very quickly: *The skater was spinning faster and faster.*

twirl
to spin around in a graceful way. **Twirl** is similar in meaning to **spin**, but you use it to talk about things or people that seem pretty: *Katy twirled in front of the mirror, admiring the dress.*

3 to change direction

turn
to change direction, or make something face in a different direction: *The truck turned left at the traffic lights.* | *I turned the picture to face the wall.*

turn around
to turn so that you are facing the opposite direction: *We turned around and drove home.* | *Tim stopped, turned around, and went back into the house.*

turn back
to stop going in one direction and start going in the opposite direction, especially because something is stopping you from going forward: *The traffic was so bad that we had to turn back.* | *We walked for about a mile and then turned back toward the parking lot.*

change direction
to move in a different direction: *The plane changed direction and flew west.* | *The wind*

turn

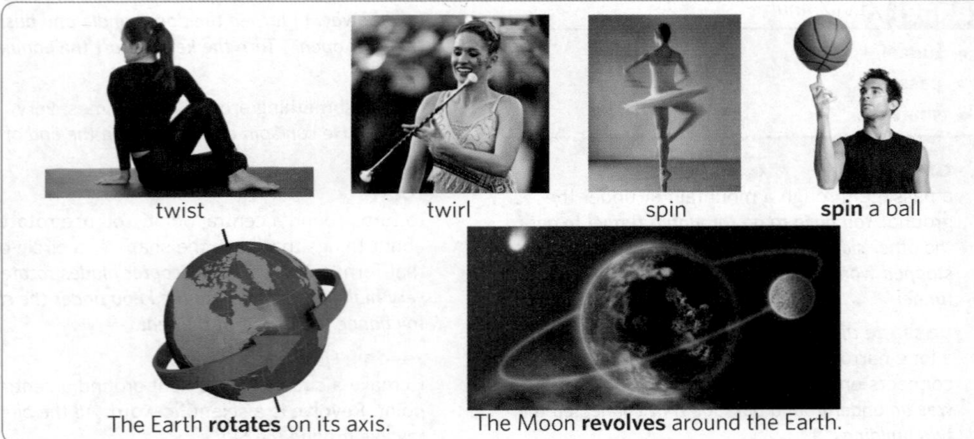
twist
twirl
spin
spin a ball
The Earth **rotates** on its axis.
The Moon **revolves** around the Earth.

changed direction and started blowing from the north.

swerve
to move suddenly to the left or right, especially so that you do not hit something. You usually **swerve** when you are driving or riding a bike: *She swerved to the right, almost hitting another car.*
→ see **turn down** at **refuse**
→ see **turn into** at **become**

turn² /tɚn/ *noun*

- turn
- spin
- twist
- rotation
- revolution (*formal*)

turn
the action of moving something around in a circle: *With every **turn of** the wheels, we came closer to home. | To open the lock on your locker, make one **turn to** the right, then a turn to the left, and then right again, stopping at the correct numbers.*

spin
a movement in which something turns around quickly, especially several times: *The plane suddenly dropped downward and went into a spin. | The boy gave the top a spin.*

twist
a movement in which you turn something in a circle: *She gave the light bulb a twist, and it broke off in her hand.*

rotation
movement around a central point, like the movement of a wheel. You use **rotation** about the movement a planet makes around its own central point: *The **rotation of** Earth on its axis takes 24 hours. | With each rotation of the bike pedals, he became more and more tired.*

revolution (AWL) (*formal*)
one complete 360 degree turn of something around a central point, used when talking about scientific subjects. You use **revolution** to talk about the way parts of a machine move, or about the movement of a planet in its path around a star: *The Earth makes one **revolution around** the Sun each year. | The drill turns at 150 revolutions per minute on its lowest speed.*
→ see **bend²** for words meaning "a place where a road or river changes direction"
→ see **take turns** at **share¹**

turn on/off /ˌtɚn ˈɔn, ˈɔf/ *phrasal verb*

- turn on/off
- switch on/off
- start
- come on
- go on/off
- go out

turn on/off
to make something that uses electricity, gas, or water start or stop working, especially by pushing a button or moving a switch: *Turn on the oven and set it to 350 degrees. | Save water by turning off the faucet when you are brushing your teeth.*

switch on/off
to turn on or off something that uses electricity: *Can you switch on the bedside lamp? | Liam switched off the engine and got out of the car.*

start
to make the engine on a vehicle begin working: *I'm going out to start the car. | The engine wouldn't start in the cold.*

come on
if something that uses gas, water, or electricity comes on, it starts working, especially because you have set a time for this to happen: *What time did you set the water heater to come on? | We were sitting in the dark with one candle when the lights and the radio came back on.*

go on/off
if something that uses gas, water, or electricity goes on or off, it starts or stops working, especially because you have set a time for this to happen. **Go on** means the same as **come on** but it is more informal: *The heat goes off at 11:00 at night.*
→ You can also use **go off** to say that something that makes a loud warning sound turns on suddenly: *We had to leave the building because the fire alarm was going off.*

go out
if a light goes out, it stops working unexpectedly or accidentally: *As they entered the cave the flashlight went out.*

turn over /ˌtɚn ˈoʊvɚ/ *phrasal verb*

- turn something over
- turn something upside down
- flip
- overturn
- capsize

turn something over
to turn something so that the top side is facing

T

down, especially so that you can look at it: *Please turn over your test papers now.*

turn something upside down
to turn something over, especially in a way that causes problems: *The baby turned his bowl upside down and watched the milk run onto the floor.*

flip *also* **flip over**
to turn something over with a single quick movement: *Flip the pancake over when it is brown on the bottom.*

overturn
if a vehicle overturns, it goes onto its side by accident: *The truck overturned and completely blocked the highway.*

capsize
if a boat capsizes or you capsize it, it turns over in the water: *The ship capsized because too many people were on board.* | *A huge wave capsized the boat.*
→ see **turn**[1]

twins *noun* → see **pair**

twist *verb* → see **bend**[1], **change**[1], **hurt**, **turn**[1]

twisted *adjective* → see **bent**

type /taɪp/ *verb*

- type
- enter

type
to write something using keys on a computer: *Please type your answers to these homework questions, instead of writing them with a pen.*

enter
to put numbers or information into a computer by pressing the keys on the keyboard: *Her job was to **enter** the information **into** the database.*
→ see **kind**[1]

typical /ˈtɪpɪkəl/ *adjective*

- typical
- characteristic
- classic

typical
like most people or things of the same type: *It was a typical week at school, without any real problems or excitement.*
→ You also use **typical** when someone behaves in the way he or she usually behaves: *It is **typical of** Sara to be so thoughtful.*

characteristic
typical and showing you what something is like: *This pasta dish is **characteristic of** the region.*

classic (AWL)
very typical. You use **classic** when something is a very good example of something: *This is a classic example of some of her best poetry.*

ADVERBS

You can make the adjectives that mean **typical** into adverbs by using an **-ly** ending: *The pasta dish is typically made with spinach.* | *The birds characteristically fish early in the morning.* | *He was a classically good-looking man.*

typically *adverb* → see **usually**

T

Uu

ugly /ˈʌgli/ *adjective*

- ugly
- unattractive
- plain
- homely
- hideous
- grotesque

ANTONYMS → see **beautiful**

ugly
extremely unpleasant to look at. You can use **ugly** about people, places, or things: *The witch was an ugly old woman with a long bent nose.* | *It is one of the ugliest buildings I have ever seen.*

unattractive
unattractive means the same as **ugly** but sounds more formal and more polite: *At 16, I felt skinny and unattractive.* | *The neighborhood was gray and unattractive.*

plain
a plain woman or girl is not beautiful or attractive: *She was a plain girl, but her eyes were nice.*

homely
a homely person is not attractive. **Homely** is less attractive than **plain**. **Homely** is usually used about men, but it can also be used about women: *He showed me a photo of his brother, a homely boy with teeth that stuck out and hair in all the wrong places.*
→ **Plain** and **homely** are more polite ways of saying that someone is **unattractive**.

hideous
extremely ugly. You use **hideous** especially about things or places, and if you use it about people it sounds very rude: *He was wearing a brown suit with a hideous green and orange tie.*

grotesque
ugly in a way that is very strange and frightening: *In my dream, I was being chased by a grotesque monster with two heads and a long tail.*
→ see Topic **Describing People's Looks**

ADVERBS

You can make the adjectives **unattractive**, **hideous**, and **grotesque** into adverbs by using an **-ly** ending: *The house is unattractively decorated.* | *The monsters in the movie are hideously ugly.* | *The man's body had been grotesquely injured.*

Ugly and **homely** look like adverbs, but they are adjectives.

umpire *noun* → see **referee**, Topic **Sports and Exercise**

unacceptable /ˌʌnəkˈseptəbəl/ *adjective*

1 bad and not right for a situation
- unacceptable
- inappropriate
- unsuitable
- unsatisfactory

ANTONYMS → see **right**[1] **(2)**

2 so bad that you cannot stand it
- intolerable
- unbearable

ANTONYMS → see **acceptable**

1 bad and not right for a situation

unacceptable
something that is unacceptable is wrong or bad and should not be allowed to happen: *Shouting or running around is unacceptable behavior in class.* | *The store thinks **it is unacceptable to** try to sell damaged fruit.*

inappropriate (AWL)
not right for a particular situation or person: *Yelling is inappropriate in a restaurant.* | *The movie is very violent, so it is **inappropriate for** children.*

unsuitable
unsuitable means the same as **inappropriate**: *Several parents thought the language in the book was **unsuitable for** young teenagers.*

unsatisfactory
not good enough. **Unsatisfactory** is usually used in official language, for example at work or school: *Your report is unsatisfactory, and you need to rewrite it.*

SYNONYM CHECK

Inappropriate or unsuitable?

Inappropriate and **unsuitable** can often be used in the same sentences.

Inappropriate is used more often about things that are not right because society does not approve of them: *He made an inappropriate comment about how she looked.*

Unsuitable is also used that way, but it is often used about things that are not right because they do not work well in a situation: *The land is unsuitable for farming.*

2 so bad that you cannot stand it

intolerable
more difficult, bad, or painful than you can deal with: *The pain in his leg became intolerable and he eventually had to go to the hospital.*

unbearable
unbearable means the same as **intolerable**: *The heat from the midday sun was becoming unbearable, so they found some shade under a tree.*

ADVERBS

You can make the adjectives that mean **unacceptable** into adverbs by using an **-ly** ending: *The noise level was intolerably loud.* | *The wound on her leg was unbearably painful.* | *The girls were behaving inappropriately.* | *The workers took an unsatisfactorily long time to finish the project.*

U

unaware /ˌʌnəˈwer/ *adjective*

- unaware (*formal*)
- oblivious
- unsuspecting

ANTONYMS → see **aware**

unaware (AWL) (*formal*)
not knowing something, or not seeing what is happening: *She was **unaware that** he was watching her.* | *Many people are **unaware of** their rights.*

oblivious
not knowing about something, or not noticing that something is happening. You usually use **oblivious** when you should notice something but do not: *She continued talking, **oblivious to** the fact that Fernandez wasn't listening to her.* | *Young children are **oblivious to** the danger of water.*

unsuspecting
not knowing that something bad is going to happen: *The product is dangerous, yet it is still being sold to unsuspecting customers.*

→ see **ignorant** for words meaning "not knowing something"

ADVERBS

You can make the adjectives **oblivious** and **unsuspecting** into adverbs by using an **-ly** ending: *Obliviously, she kept on talking while he ignored her.* | *Farmers unsuspectingly sprayed the dangerous chemical on their lands.*

unbelievable /ˌʌnbəˈlivəbəl/ *adjective*

- unbelievable
- hard/difficult to believe
- incredible
- implausible (*formal*)

unbelievable
something that is unbelievable is impossible to believe, and seems untrue or very different from what really happens: *The story in the movie was fun, but it was completely unbelievable in some places.*

hard/difficult to believe
if something is hard or difficult to believe, it does not seem possible that it is true, even when it is true: *It is hard to believe she is 19 – she looks like she is 11!*

incredible
something that is incredible is very difficult to believe because it is surprising or strange, even though it may be true: *The cars were traveling very fast, and it is incredible that anyone survived the accident.*

implausible (*formal*)
something that is implausible seems unlikely and difficult to believe: *She said she was late because she forgot she had a class, but her explanation sounded **implausible to** me.*

→ see **unlikely**

ADVERBS

You can make the adjectives **unbelievable**, **incredible**, and **implausible** into adverbs by using an **-ly** ending: *Unbelievably, I got a call saying I had won the competition.* | *The cars were traveling incredibly fast.* | *Her writing was implausibly good for a ten-year-old.*

unbutton *verb* → see **undo**

uncertain *adjective* → see **unclear**, **unsure**

uncertainty *noun* → see **doubt**, **suspense**

unclear /ˌʌnˈklɪr/ *adjective*

- ► unclear
- ► vague
- ► uncertain (*formal*)
- ► in doubt
- ► ambiguous

ANTONYMS → see **clear (2)**

unclear
not easy to understand or feel sure about: *The meaning of the first sentence is unclear.* | ***It was unclear whether** she would be well enough to come with us on the trip.*

vague
not clear in your mind because of not having enough details: *Kieran had only a vague idea about how car engines worked.*

uncertain (*formal*)
not definite, decided, or clear: *The cause of the accident is still uncertain.*

in doubt
in doubt means the same as **uncertain** but is slightly less formal: *The financial future of the company is in doubt because of its huge debt.*

ambiguous (AWL)
an ambiguous idea or statement is not clear because it can be understood in more than one way: *The jury couldn't make a decision because the law was ambiguous.*
→ see **blurred** for "not easy to see clearly"

ADVERBS
You can make the adjectives **unclear**, **vague**, and **ambiguous** into adverbs by using an **-ly** ending: *The first sentence was unclearly written.* | *Kieran only vaguely understood how car engines worked.* | *The law was ambiguously written.*

uncomfortable *adjective* → see **embarrassed**

unconscious /ʌnˈkɑnʃəs/ *adjective*

- ► unconscious
- ► stunned
- ► dazed

unconscious
unable to see, move, feel, or hear in the normal way for a period of time because you have been hit very hard on the head or are sick: *The man was struck by lightning and was unconscious for several minutes.*

stunned
unable to say or do anything for a short period of time, especially because of a shock or because you have been hit on the head: *The accident left him feeling stunned and unsure about what had happened.*

dazed
unable to think clearly, especially because of a shock or because you have been hit on the head: *After the car accident, he looked dazed and was bleeding from a cut on his forehead.*
→ see **faint**

ADVERBS
You can make the adjective **dazed** into an adverb by using an **-ly** ending: *After the accident, he got out of the car and looked dazedly around.*

uncooked *adjective* → see **raw**

under *preposition, adverb* → see Function Words

undergo *verb* → see **experience²**

underline *verb* → see **emphasize**

underneath *preposition, adverb* → see Function Word **under**

understand /ˌʌndəˈstænd/ *verb*

- ► understand
- ► get (*informal*)
- ► comprehend (*formal*)
- ► grasp
- ► appreciate (*formal*)
- ► see (*informal*)
- ► follow
- ► make sense of

understand
to know the meaning of an idea, a situation, or what someone is saying: *He was having trouble understanding the first math problem.* | *At first I didn't **understand that** we were experiencing an earthquake.*

get (*informal*)
get means the same as **understand**: *I don't get it. Why is the answer 43 and not 44?* | *Carrie finally got the joke after we explained it to her.*

comprehend (*formal*)
to understand something, especially something that is very difficult or complicated: *For many people, it is difficult to comprehend how global warming can cause freezing weather in some places.*

grasp
grasp means the same as **comprehend** but

sounds less formal: *It is almost impossible for humans to grasp how large the universe is.*

appreciate (AWL) (*formal*)
to understand that something is important because it affects what will happen: *I began to **appreciate that** it takes a lot of time and money to sell a house.*

see (*informal*)
to understand a situation or the reason for something. **See** is very common in spoken language, but it is better not to use it in writing: *Now I see what Randy was trying to do – he was trying to change the settings on the camera.* | *"I told you the car was a mess." "Yeah, I see what you mean."*

follow
to understand a story, explanation, or talk that continues for a long time: *The movie's plot was hard to follow.* | *I know a little Spanish, but long conversations are hard for me to follow.*

make sense of
to understand something that is not clear or easy to understand. Often you spend a lot of time trying to **make sense of** something: *The information was confusing and it took me some time to make sense of it all.*
→ see **misunderstand** for words meaning "to understand something wrongly," **realize** for words meaning "to understand something you did not know before," **sympathize** for words meaning "to understand how someone feels"

understanding *noun* → see **sympathy**

underwater /ˌʌndəˈwɔtə/ *adjective, adverb*

- underwater
- submerged
- sunken
- flooded

underwater
below the surface of the water: *The old dock was now underwater.* | *She can swim underwater for 20 yards.*

submerged
completely covered by water: *The entrance to the cave is submerged at high tide.*

sunken
a sunken ship or building is now under the water in a lake, river, or ocean: *Workers began to remove the pieces of the sunken ship from the harbor.*

flooded
a building or area of land that is flooded is covered or filled with water because of storms or an accident: *No cars could get through because the road was flooded.*

undo /ʌnˈdu/ *verb*

1 to open something that is fastened
- undo
- unfasten
- untie
- unscrew
- unzip
- unbutton

2 to change something back to how it was before
- undo
- reverse

1 to open something that is fastened

undo
to open something that is fastened, tied, or wrapped: *I was trying to undo the knot in the string.* | *He took off his tie and undid the top button of his shirt.*

unfasten
to open something that is fastened or tied: *Lewis unfastened his seat belt and got out of the car.*

untie
to undo string, rope, etc. that someone has tied in a knot: *I untied the rope and got into the boat.*

unscrew
to remove something by twisting it or taking screws out: *Turn off the light before unscrewing the bulb.*

unzip
to unfasten clothing, a bag, etc. by opening the zipper on it: *Lucy unzipped her jacket because she was hot.*

unbutton
to unfasten a piece of clothing that is closed with buttons: *He unbuttoned his shirt and took it off.*

2 to change something back to how it was before

undo
to change something back to how it was before: *One careless mistake could undo all our good work and spoil everything.* | *It is going to be difficult to undo the effects of years of discrimination.*

reverse (AWL)
to change something so that it goes back to what it was before, or so that it is the opposite: *It will take years to reverse the damage done by*

pollution. | *The Supreme Court reversed the lower court's decision.*

undo

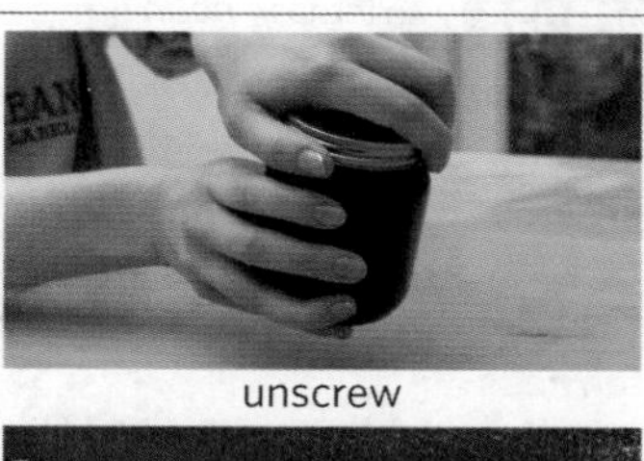

unscrew

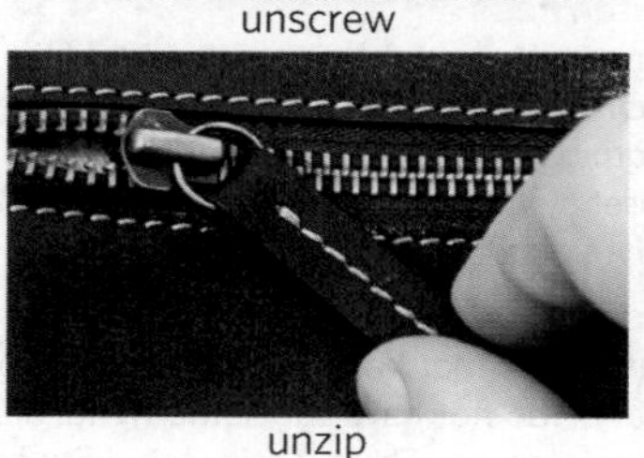

unzip

undone *adjective* → see **unfinished**

undress /ʌn'dres/ *verb*

- ► undress
- ► get undressed
- ► take off
- ► change
- ► strip

ANTONYMS → see **dress²**

undress
to remove the clothes you are wearing. **Undress** sounds more formal than **get undressed**: *Matt undressed and stepped into the shower.* | *Ann didn't want to undress in front of the other girls.*

get undressed
to remove your clothes: *Get undressed and put this robe on. The doctor will be in to see you in a moment.*

→ **Get undressed** and **take your clothes off** are the usual phrases to use in everyday English.

take off
to remove something you are wearing: *She took off her clothes and put on her pajamas.* | *If you are too warm, take your sweater off.*

change *also* **get changed**
to take off your clothes and put on different clothes: *I'll be ready in a second – I just have to get changed.* | *Ed* ***changed out of*** *his suit and* ***into*** *a T-shirt and pair of jeans.*

strip
to take off your clothes quickly, especially all of your clothes: *The boys stripped and jumped in the lake.*

→ You cannot use **strip** before pieces of clothing. Don't say: ~~*He stripped his sweater*~~. However, you can use **strip off**: *He stripped off his sweater.*

undressed *adjective* → see **naked**

uneducated *adjective* → see **ignorant**

unemployed /ˌʌnɪm'plɔɪd/ *adjective*

- ► unemployed
- ► out of work
- ► jobless

unemployed
without a job: *Lou has been unemployed since he lost his job in March.* | *There are few jobs in the area, and 50% of the men are unemployed.*

out of work
unemployed, especially for a long time. You use **out of work** when someone had a job before: *My dad's been out of work for two years.*

jobless
without a job. **Jobless** is used especially in news reports about all the people who do not have jobs: *The jobless rate rose to 8.6%* (=8.6 percent of people do not have jobs).

→ see Topic **Jobs and Work**

uneven *adjective* → see **rough**

unexpected *adjective* → see **surprising**

unfair /ˌʌn'fer/ *adjective*

1 not treating people in a way that is fair (adjectives)

- ► unfair
- ► unreasonable
- ► unequal
- ► biased
- ► unjust (*formal*)
- ► arbitrary (*formal*)

ANTONYMS → see **fair¹**

2 ways of treating people that are unfair (nouns)

- ► persecution
- ► oppression
- ► discrimination

1 not treating people in a way that is fair (adjectives)

unfair
not right or fair, especially because some people are treated better than others: *His father was one of the judges of the essay competition, so he had an unfair advantage.*

unreasonable
not fair, or asking someone to do too much: *It is **unreasonable of** your boss **to** expect you to do all the work by yourself.*

unequal
unfair because people are treated in different ways when they should be treated the same, or because some people have more advantages than others when they should be treated the same: *In some countries, girls receive unequal treatment in schools, because boys are seen as more important.*

biased (AWL)
treating one person or group unfairly because you think one is better than the other: *He said that some radio talk shows are **biased against** the Democrats.*

unjust (*formal*)
a law, system, or action that is unjust is not fair because it is not morally right: *The laws were unjust because they did not allow blacks to go to the same schools as white people.*

arbitrary (AWL) (*formal*)
arbitrary rules or decisions seem unfair because there are no good reasons for them: *The coach's decisions about who would go on the team seemed arbitrary – one of the best players didn't make it!*

ADVERBS

You can make the adjectives that mean **unfair** into adverbs by using an **-ly** ending, except for **biased**: *When I am treated unfairly, I am not afraid to complain.* | *Boys and girls were treated unequally.* | *The coach seems to make his decisions arbitrarily.*

U

2 ways of treating people that are unfair (nouns)

persecution
bad or unfair treatment of a person because of his or her beliefs: *He left the country because of religious persecution.* | *In some countries, the **persecution of** people who disagree with the government is common.*

oppression
unfair treatment of people by a powerful person or government. **Oppression** is used when people are not free to do what they want: *People suffered years of oppression under this government.*

discrimination
unfair treatment of someone because of something such as his or her race, sex, age, or religion: *The law says that it is sexual discrimination when a man is paid more than a woman for doing exactly the same job.*
→ see **prejudice**

unfairness /ʌnˈfernəs/ *noun*

- unfairness
- inequality
- injustice

ANTONYMS → see **fairness**

unfairness
the quality of not being equal and fair: *I remember the feeling of unfairness when my brother got a new bike and I didn't.* | *Maria was upset by **the unfairness of** the decision. Why was John not punished too?*

inequality
unfairness that happens when two people or groups do not have the same rights and opportunities: *There is still **inequality between** men and women in many countries.*

injustice
unfairness, especially because someone does not have the rights that he or she should have: *She fought against **the injustice of** the slave trade.*

unfamiliar *adjective* → see **strange**

unfashionable /ʌnˈfæʃənəbəl/ *adjective*

- unfashionable
- out of fashion
- dated

ANTONYMS → see **fashionable**

unfashionable
not popular or fashionable at the present time: *She was wearing a pair of unfashionable lace-up shoes.*

out of fashion
no longer popular or fashionable: *I used to love this jacket, but it's really out of fashion now.*

dated
if something is dated, it is no longer fashionable or modern because it comes from an earlier time: *The hotel was built in the 1960s, and the design is somewhat dated now.*

SYNONYM CHECK

Unfashionable and out of fashion

Unfashionable and **out of fashion** are mostly used about clothes, but you can use them about other things too: *Slang words quickly go out of fashion.* | *Sometimes it seems like being polite has become unfashionable.*

ADVERBS

You can make the adjective **unfashionable** into an adverb by using an **-ly** ending: *I didn't want to go into the party, because I knew I was unfashionably dressed.*

unfasten *verb* → see **open²**, **undo**

unfinished /ʌnˈfɪnɪʃt/ *adjective*

- unfinished
- not over yet
- incomplete
- undone

ANTONYMS → see **done**

unfinished
if something is unfinished, you have not done all of it: *On her desk was an unfinished letter to her mother.*

not over yet
if a bad situation is not over yet, it is not finished and still needs to be dealt with: *The situation at work has been awful, and it's not over yet.*

incomplete
not having all of the work done, or not having all of the parts that are needed: *The building is still incomplete, but it will be finished next September.* | *The form you sent was incomplete – it was missing the last two pages.*

undone
not completed. Use **undone** about something that should be finished but is not: *He left much of the work undone, and Angie had to finish it for him.*

ADVERBS

You can make the adjective **incomplete** into an adverb by using an **-ly** ending: *The effects of the economic problems are still incompletely understood.*

unforgettable *adjective* → see **memorable**

unfortunate *adjective* → see **unlucky**

unfortunately /ʌnˈfɔrtʃənətli/ *adverb*

- unfortunately
- sadly

ANTONYMS → see **luckily**

unfortunately
used when you wish something were not true or had not happened: *Unfortunately, I didn't get your text message until after I had left.* | *I took some great pictures but, unfortunately, I lost my camera.*

sadly
used when you wish that events or situations that are very serious or sad had not happened or were not true: *Sadly, the old theater was destroyed by a fire in 2005.*

unfriendly /ʌnˈfrendli/ *adjective*

- unfriendly
- not nice
- cold
- hostile

ANTONYMS → see **friendly**

unfriendly *also* **not friendly**
not behaving in a kind or pleasant way toward other people: *The hotel staff was unfriendly and unhelpful.* | *It is no surprise Bryan doesn't have many friends – he is not very friendly.*

not nice
not friendly, kind, or polite. **Not nice** is used especially in spoken English: *He wasn't very **nice to** me when I asked for help. In fact, he just laughed at me.*

cold
very unfriendly and not seeming to care at all about other people: *Mark was really **cold to** me at the party, but I don't know what I did to offend him.* | *She gave him a cold stare.*

hostile
very unfriendly and ready to argue or fight: *The audience was hostile and disagreed with almost everything she said.*

ADVERBS

You can make the adjective **cold** and **hostile** into adverbs by using an **-ly** ending: *She looked at him coldly.* | *The audience reacted hostilely to almost everything he said.*

unhappiness *noun* → see **sadness**

unhappy *adjective* → see **sad**, Topic **Describing People's Emotions**

unharmed *adjective* → see **safe**

unhealthy *adjective* → see **sick**

uniform¹ *noun* → see **clothes**

uniform² *adjective* → see **same**

U

unimportant /ˌʌnɪmˈpɔrtnt/ *adjective*

- ► unimportant
- ► of no importance (*formal*)
- ► minor
- ► trivial
- ► irrelevant
- ► insignificant (*formal*)
- ► secondary

ANTONYMS → see **important**

unimportant
not important: *The education of girls used to be seen as unimportant.*

of no importance *also* **of little importance** (*formal*)
not important: *Price is of no importance – I'm ready to pay whatever it costs.* | *It is of little importance who said it; what matters is whether it's true.*

minor (AWL)
small and not likely to have an important effect. Use **minor** about changes, problems, injuries, damage, or differences: *I've made a few minor changes, but overall the essay is really good.*

trivial
not at all important and not worth spending time on: *She wastes a lot of time on trivial things like what color nail polish to wear.*

irrelevant (AWL)
something that is irrelevant is not important because it does not relate to the situation that you are talking about: *Lawson's behavior as a teenager is* ***irrelevant to*** *the criminal charges against him now.*

insignificant (AWL) (*formal*)
very small and not very important: *Losing 5 pounds seems insignificant when I still need to lose over 100 pounds.*

secondary
not as important as something else: *For many women, a career is* ***secondary to*** *being mother.*

ADVERBS

You can make the adjectives **trivial**, **irrelevant**, **insignificant**, and **secondary** into adverbs by using an **-ly** ending: *The number of people who will be affected by the change is trivially small.* | *We were talking about school, when, irrelevantly, Helen said she would like to go to San Francisco.*

unintentional *adjective* → see **accidental**

unintentionally *adverb* → see **accidentally**

uninterested /ʌnˈɪntrəstɪd/ *adjective*

- ► uninterested
- ► indifferent
- ► apathetic

ANTONYMS → see **interested**

uninterested
not wanting to know about something. **Uninterested** is more formal than **not interested**: *When I tried to tell her about my vacation, she seemed completely uninterested.*

indifferent
not at all interested in something and not caring about what is happening, especially not caring about other people's problems or feelings: *He seems* ***indifferent to*** *her problems and has done nothing to help her.*

apathetic
not interested in something and not caring what happens, because you do not think it is important and do not want to be involved in it: *A lot of people have become* ***apathetic about*** *politics and don't even bother to vote anymore.*

ADVERBS

You can make the adjectives **indifferent** and **apathetic** into adverbs by using an **-ly** ending: *"Do whatever you want," he said indifferently.* | *At first she listened apathetically, but gradually she became more interested in what he said.*

uninteresting *adjective* → see **boring**

unique *adjective* → see **only**, **special**

unit *noun* → see **machine**

unite /yuˈnaɪt/ *verb*

- ► unite
- ► unify
- ► integrate
- ► merge

unite
to cause people or groups to join together and feel a connection to each other, especially in order to do something important: *We need a strong leader who can unite the Republican Party.* | *He believes that the different Christian churches in his country need to unite in order to survive.*

unify (AWL)
to bring the different parts of a country or organization together so that they become one: *In 1990, West and East Germany unified to become one country instead of two.*

integrate (AWL)
to join systems or ways of working together in an effective way to do a job: *The company has announced that it will* ***integrate*** *some of its operations* ***with*** *another German engineering company.*

merge
to make two companies or organizations join together to make one company or organization: *They made a deal that will merge the two companies to form one large company.* | *In 2007, the school* ***merged with*** *another nearby high school and became Parklands High School.*
→ see **cooperate**

unkind *adjective* → see **mean²**

unknown *adjective* → see **strange**

unless *conjunction* → see Function Word **if**

unlike *adjective* → see **different**

unlikely /ʌnˈlaɪkli/ *adjective*

- unlikely
- improbable (*formal*)
- doubtful

ANTONYMS → see **likely**

unlikely
if something is unlikely, it will probably not happen or it is probably not true: *A small amount of the medicine is* ***unlikely to*** *have any harmful effects.*

improbable (*formal*)
improbable means the same as **unlikely**: *It seemed highly* ***improbable that*** *the small army could win the battle.*

doubtful
very unlikely to happen, or very unlikely to be true: *There's so much work to do –* ***it's doubtful that*** *we'll finish tonight.*

GRAMMAR CHECK: unlikely

You can use **unlikely** with "to": *The medicine is unlikely to have any harmful effects.*

You cannot use **improbable** or **doubtful** with "to." Instead you say: ***It is improbable/doubtful that*** *the medicine will have any harmful effects.*

ADVERBS

You can make the adjective **improbable** into an adverb by using an **-ly** ending: *The movie seems to be getting improbably large audiences, considering how bad it is.*

unload *verb* → see **empty²**

unlock *verb* → see **open²**

unlocked *adjective* → see **open¹**

unlucky /ʌnˈlʌki/ *adjective*

- unlucky
- unfortunate
- jinxed

ANTONYMS → see **lucky**

unlucky
having bad luck, or causing bad luck: *We were really* ***unlucky with*** *the weather – it rained every day.* | *A lot of people think* ***it's unlucky to*** *break a mirror.*

unfortunate
having bad luck, or happening because of bad luck. **Unfortunate** sounds more formal than **unlucky** and is used mainly in writing: *He was* ***unfortunate to*** *lose his job just after his wife had a baby.* | ***It was unfortunate that*** *the old woman was in the store when the robbers came in.*

jinxed
having or causing a lot of bad luck: *That house is jinxed – everyone who has lived there has died within a few years.*
→ **Jinxed** is often used as a joke when it seems like you have bad luck because someone else has put a spell on you: *I think we're jinxed. We've lost every game!*

ADVERBS

You can make the adjectives **unlucky** and **unfortunate** into adverbs by using an **-ly** ending: *A jellyfish will sting you if you unluckily brush against it in the water.* | *Unfortunately, he lost his job.*

U

unmarried *adjective* → see Topic **Relationships and Marriage**

unnecessary /ʌnˈnesəˌseri/ *adjective*

- unnecessary
- needless (*formal*)
- gratuitous
- superfluous

ANTONYMS → see **necessary**, **important (2)**

unnecessary
not necessary: *Her parents felt that a new TV was an unnecessary expense, since the old one still worked.*

needless (*formal*)
not necessary. Use **needless** to describe bad

things that could have been avoided: *The new safety rules will prevent needless injuries.*

gratuitous
unnecessary and likely to upset people: *My mother hated the movie because it had so much gratuitous violence.*

superfluous
more than is needed or wanted: *The story was filled with superfluous details, so it was a lot longer than it needed to be.*

ADVERBS

You can make the adjectives that mean **unnecessary** into adverbs by using an **-ly** ending: *I don't want to spend money unnecessarily; the old TV still works.* | *Children should not be suffering needlessly from diseases that we can prevent.*

unpack *verb* → see **empty²**

unpleasant *adjective* → see **bad**

unqualified /ʌnˈkwɑləˌfaɪd/ *adjective*

- ► unqualified
- ► inexperienced
- ► unskilled
- ► incompetent

ANTONYMS → see **skilled**

unqualified
not having the education or experience to do a job: *An unqualified pilot was flying the plane when it crashed.* | *I don't want to give the job to someone who is unqualified.*

inexperienced
not having much experience of doing a job: *As an inexperienced salesman, he did not make many sales in the first year.*

unskilled
an unskilled worker has not had any training in any kind of work: *Wages for unskilled workers are usually very low.*

incompetent
not having the ability needed to do your job well, although you should have this ability: *Her lawyer was incompetent and she deserves a new trial.*

ADVERBS

You can make the adjective **incompetent** into an adverb by using an **-ly** ending: *The judge decided that she had been incompetently represented by her lawyer.*

unreasonable *adjective* → see **illogical**, **unfair**

unsafe *adjective* → see **dangerous**

unsatisfactory *adjective* → see **inadequate**, **unacceptable**

unselfish *adjective* → see **kind²**

unstable /ʌnˈsteɪbəl/ *adjective*

- ► unstable (*formal*)
- ► unsteady
- ► shaky (*informal*)
- ► precarious
- ► wobbly (*informal*)

ANTONYMS → see **stable**

unstable (AWL) (*formal*)
likely to fall or move. You use **unstable** about things that will no longer provide support for something if they fall or move: *The building is very old and the walls have become unstable.* | *Some of the houses had been built on unstable soil on the west side of the mountain.*

unsteady
unable to balance well: *I felt very unsteady when I stood up for the first time after six weeks in bed.* | *The boat became more and more unsteady as the wind and waves hit it.*

shaky (*informal*)
weak and unsteady. If a person is **shaky**, it is because of illness, old age, or shock. If a thing is **shaky**, it is because it is not in good condition or not made well: *It is normal to feel a little shaky when you have the flu.* | *The ladder was a little shaky.*

precarious
not safe, and likely to fall or make someone fall. **Precarious** sounds slightly formal or literary, and is usually used about something that is in a high place: *He was sitting in a precarious spot in the highest branches of the tree.*

wobbly (*informal*)
moving from side to side in an unsteady way: *The table was a little wobbly, so I tried not to lean on it.*

→ see **changeable** for **unstable** meaning "likely to change suddenly and become worse"

ADVERBS

You can make the adjectives **unsteady**, **shaky**, and **precarious** into adverbs by using an **-ly** ending: *She walked unsteadily down the hall to her bedroom.* | *The lamp was balanced precariously on a pile of boxes.*

unsteady *adjective* → see **unstable**

U

unsuccessful /ˌʌnsəkˈsesfəl/ *adjective*

- ► unsuccessful
- ► ineffective
- ► useless

ANTONYMS → see **successful**

unsuccessful
not succeeding in doing something. You use **unsuccessful** especially about attempts to do something which have failed: *The prisoners made an unsuccessful attempt to escape from the jail.* | *We tried to find out where the noise was coming from, but were unsuccessful.*

ineffective
something that is ineffective does not do what you want. You use **ineffective** about drugs and methods that do not work: *The medicine proved to be **ineffective against** the disease.*

useless
not helpful or useful at all. **Useless** sounds much stronger and more informal than **ineffective**: *The instructions they gave me were useless. I couldn't understand them at all.* | *It is useless telling him he is wrong. He never listens to anyone.*

ADVERBS
You can make the adjectives that mean **unsuccessful** into adverbs by using an **-ly** ending: *We tried unsuccessfully to find out where the noise was coming from.* | *My broken arm hung uselessly at my side.*

unsuitable *adjective* → see **unacceptable**

unsure /ʌnˈʃʊr/ *adjective*

- ► unsure
- ► uncertain
- ► unconvinced
- ► undecided
- ► doubtful
- ► dubious
- ► skeptical

ANTONYMS → see **sure**

unsure
not sure about something: *If you're **unsure about** what you're supposed to do, just ask.*

uncertain
uncertain means the same as **unsure** but is more formal: *David is **uncertain about** which classes he will take next fall.*

unconvinced
not sure that you believe something, especially when someone has tried to persuade you that it is true: *Mrs. Jones was **unconvinced that** we could paint the house all by ourselves.*

undecided
not sure because you have not made a decision about something yet: *I'm still **undecided about** whether or not to get a part-time job.*

doubtful
not sure whether something is true or good: *Everyone says that the trip will be fun, but I'm still doubtful.*

dubious
dubious means the same as **doubtful** but is more formal: *Reggie was **dubious about** the diet, but he was willing to try anything to lose some weight.*

skeptical
not sure, but believing that something is probably not true or right: *Voters are **skeptical that** the mayor will actually do what he promised to do.*

ADVERBS
You can make the adjectives **unsure**, **uncertain**, **doubtful**, **dubious**, and **skeptical** into adverbs by using an **-ly** ending: *We stood there uncertainly, waiting for someone to tell us what to do.* | *"I'm not sure the trip will be much fun," he said doubtfully.* | *After he answered the question, the police officer looked at him skeptically.*

untrue *adjective* → see **false**, **wrong**

untruthful *adjective* → see **dishonest**

unusual *adjective* → see **special**, **strange**

unwilling /ʌnˈwɪlɪŋ/ *adjective*

- ► unwilling
- ► reluctant
- ► not prepared to

ANTONYMS → see **willing**

unwilling
if you are unwilling to do something, you do not want to do it: *She was **unwilling to** admit that she had made a mistake.* | *Should you force an unwilling child to do chores?*

reluctant (AWL)
not wanting to do something that you should do or that someone wants you to do: *I was **reluctant to** get up because the bed was warm and comfortable, and I was still sleepy.*

not prepared to *also* **not ready to**
if you are not prepared to do something, you

U

refuse to do it. **Not ready to** means the same as **not prepared to** but sounds less formal: *I offered to buy the house, but he wasn't prepared to sell it.* | *He was not ready to accept that she wanted a divorce.*

ADVERBS

You can make the adjectives **unwilling** and **reluctant** into adverbs by using an **-ly** ending: *The boy unwillingly followed his mother into the dentist's office.* | *Reluctantly, she got out of the warm bed.*

unwrap *verb* → see **open²**

unzip *verb* → see **undo**

up *preposition, adverb* → see Function Words

upper *adjective* → see **top²**

upright *adjective* → see **vertical**

upset¹ /ʌp'set/ *adjective*

- ► upset
- ► hurt
- ► disturbed
- ► troubled
- ► distressed
- ► dismayed
- ► devastated

upset
sad, worried, or angry because something bad has happened: *She is **upset that** she didn't get the job.* | *John was so **upset about** what she had done that he didn't talk to her for a month.*

hurt
sad because someone has been mean to you, especially someone that you trusted to be kind: *I was really **hurt that** she didn't invite me to her party – I thought we were friends.*

disturbed
nervous and unhappy about something: *Julie was **disturbed to** learn that her son had started smoking.*

troubled
worried about a problem so that you think about it a lot: *Ben looked troubled, so she knew something was wrong.*

distressed
very worried or unhappy about something: *His parents are distressed because he has dropped out of school.*

dismayed
worried and unhappy about something that is an unpleasant surprise: *The team was **dismayed by** the coach's decision to quit in the middle of the year.*

devastated
very sad or shocked about something that has happened: *The whole family was **devastated by** Alan's sudden death.*
→ see **sad**

upset² /ʌp'set/ *verb*

- ► upset
- ► hurt
- ► bother
- ► disturb
- ► trouble
- ► distress (*formal*)
- ► shake

upset
to make someone feel sad, worried, or angry: *It still upsets me to think about the way he lied to me.* | *Why are you crying? Did I say something that upset you?*

hurt
to make someone feel sad by being mean to him or her, especially when that person trusts you to be kind: *He really hurt her when he said he didn't love her anymore.* | *I wanted to tell her what I really thought, but I didn't want to hurt her feelings.*

bother
to make someone feel slightly upset, worried, or annoyed: *Does it bother you that he forgot your birthday again?*

disturb
to make someone feel nervous or unhappy: *The movie was scary, and it disturbed her so much that she couldn't get to sleep.*

trouble
to make someone feel worried or unhappy. Use **trouble** especially to talk about problems that upset someone: *How can I help you if you won't tell me what's troubling you?*

distress (*formal*)
to make someone feel very worried or unhappy: *It distressed us to know that Ron might be in danger.*

shake
to make someone feel very upset or shocked. You use **shake** when something very unpleasant suddenly affects you: *Luckily Mica wasn't injured in the accident, but she was badly shaken.*
→ see **sadden**

U

upsetting /ʌpˈsetɪŋ/ *adjective*

- ► upsetting
- ► painful
- ► disturbing
- ► troubling
- ► worrisome (*formal*)
- ► distressing
- ► traumatic

upsetting
making someone feel upset: *The night he spent in jail was a very upsetting experience.* | *His nasty comments were really* ***upsetting to*** *me.*

painful
making someone feel very sad: *Talking about her ex-husband brought up painful memories and she began to cry.*

disturbing
making someone feel nervous or unhappy: *There has been a disturbing increase in crime in the past year.*

troubling
making someone feel worried and unhappy. You use **troubling** about problems and worrying situations: *It is troubling that no one tried to stop the bullying.*

worrisome (*formal*)
worrisome means the same as **troubling**: *The recent rise in drug use among teenagers is a worrisome trend.*

distressing
making someone feel very worried or unhappy: *Being in a strange city with no money was extremely distressing.*

traumatic
extremely shocking and upsetting, and affecting someone for a long time: *The time I almost drowned was the most traumatic experience of my life.*

up-to-date *adjective* → see **modern**

upward *adverb* → see Function Word **up**

urban /ˈɚbən/ *adjective*

- ► urban
- ► metropolitan
- ► municipal
- ► civic

urban
relating to towns or cities: *Air pollution is particularly bad in urban areas.* | *Young people were moving from farms to urban centers to look for work.*

metropolitan
relating to a big city: *The population of the Houston metropolitan area is about six million.*

municipal
relating to the government of a town or city: *The mayor and other municipal officials will meet tomorrow.*

civic
relating to the government or to public activities of a town or city: *The courthouse is in the civic center.* | *It is your civic duty to vote.*

urge[1] /ɚdʒ/ *noun*

- ► urge
- ► impulse
- ► whim

urge
a strong feeling that you want to do something very much: *I felt the* ***urge to*** *go back home, so I decided to buy a plane ticket.* | *Runners have to resist the* ***urge to*** *quit when the run gets hard.*

impulse
a sudden feeling that you want to do something: *I felt a sudden* ***impulse to*** *laugh, but I managed to control myself.* | *She bought the book* ***on impulse*** *when she was in the bookstore.*

whim
a sudden feeling that you want to do something, when there is no reason to do it: *We didn't plan to go to the restaurant. We just stopped off there* ***on a whim*** *on our way home.*
→ see **wish**

urge[2] *verb* → see **advise**

usage *noun* → see **use[2]**

use[1] /yuz/ *verb*

1 to use something for a particular purpose
- ► use
- ► make use of
- ► employ (*formal*)
- ► utilize (*formal*)
- ► consume (*formal*)
- ► exploit
- ► take advantage of

2 to use all of something, so there is none left
- ► use up
- ► exhaust (*formal*)
- ► run out

1 to use something for a particular purpose

use
if you use something, you do something with it for a particular purpose: *Can I **use** your phone **to** call my mother? | Let's **use** these old rags **to** wash the car.*
→ **Use** is often used when talking about how much of something you use: *We use about a gallon of milk each week. | The new light bulbs use less energy and last longer.*

make use of
to use something that is available in order to achieve something: *Make use of the library to research your report.*

employ (*formal*)
to use a particular method or skill in order to achieve something: *The methods that teachers employ in the classroom are very different today from how teachers taught 50 years ago.*

utilize (AWL) (*formal*)
to use something for a particular purpose. **Utilize** sounds a little bit technical, and people usually choose **use** in everyday English: *The company has developed a new way to utilize solar energy.*

consume (AWL) (*formal*)
to use oil, energy, water, and other natural resources. **Consume** is used especially to talk about the amount of natural resources that people as a group use: *The U.S. imports 45% of the oil that it consumes.*

exploit (AWL)
to use something as completely and effectively as possible: *The business will exploit the Internet to advertise and sell its products.*
→ **Exploit** can also mean "to use someone or something in an unfair way": *The farm workers were exploited by landowners, who forced them to work long hours for little pay.*

take advantage of
to use an opportunity in order to do what you want or need to do: *You should take advantage of the warm weather by taking your lunch to the park.*

2 to use all of something, so there is none left

use up
to use all of something so that there is none left: *She took a shower and used up all the hot water.*

exhaust (*formal*)
to use up all of something, especially a supply of something when it will be difficult to get more of it: *What will happen when we have exhausted the world's oil supply?*

run out
if something runs out, or you run out of something, there is none left because you have used it all: *I have some money you can borrow if you run out. | We have **run out of** milk again. I'll buy some more when we go to the supermarket.*
→ see **take advantage of** for **use** meaning "to use a person in an unfair way"

use² /yus/ *noun*

- ► use
- ► usage
- ► utilization (*formal*)
- ► consumption (*formal*)

use
the act of using something, or the way in which it is used: *The use of smart phones has increased rapidly. | The drug has been approved **for use in** treating cancer.*

usage
the amount of something that is used, or the act of using something: *The meter measures water usage. | The usage of computers in businesses increased rapidly in the 1990s.*
→ **Usage** can also be used to talk about the way people use words in a language: *Can you explain the correct usage of "whom"?*

utilization (*formal*)
the act of using something for a particular purpose: *We want to encourage the utilization of wind and solar power.*

consumption (AWL) (*formal*)
the amount of oil, energy, water, or other natural resources that people use, or the act of using oil, gas, water, etc.: *The company managed to cut its energy consumption by 20%. | The amount of oil that is imported for domestic consumption has increased* (=the oil imported for use in a country has increased).

used to /ˈyustə, ˈyustu/ *adjective*

- ► used to
- ► familiar with
- ► accustomed to (*formal*)
- ► at home with

used to
having experienced something many times, so it does not seem strange or difficult: *I grew up on a farm, so I'm used to working hard. | It took a few years, but Miguel finally got used to the cold winters here.*

familiar with
knowing something well and feeling comfortable

U

with it: *She is familiar with Paris because she spent a year there in college.*

accustomed to (*formal*)
having experienced something many times, so it does not seem strange or difficult. **Accustomed to** means the same as **used to** but is more formal: *They were accustomed to waiting, so no one complained.*

at home with
so used to something that you feel comfortable and happy doing it. **At home with** is more informal than **used to**: *Teenagers often feel more at home with computers than their parents do.*

useful /ˈyusfəl/ *adjective*

- ► useful
- ► handy
- ► helpful
- ► valuable
- ► invaluable
- ► worthwhile
- ► productive
- ► beneficial
- ► of use

ANTONYMS → see **useless**

useful
if something is useful, it is good because you can use it to do something: *The basket would be* ***useful for*** *picnics.* | *You can find a lot of useful information on the Internet.*

handy
useful and easy to use. **Handy** is more informal than **useful**, and you use it about things that are useful: *It is a handy little camera, and not too expensive.*

helpful
useful and helping you to do something: *She made some helpful suggestions, and I was able to really improve my essay.* | ***It might be helpful to*** *practice your speech in front of your parents.*

valuable
if something is valuable, it is very useful because it helps you to do something. Use **valuable** especially about advice, information, or help: *The information will be very* ***valuable to*** *the police.* | *She gave me valuable advice to help me prepare for the job interview.*

invaluable
extremely useful and helping you to do something, and difficult to do without. **Invaluable** is even stronger than **valuable**: *The drug could be* ***invaluable for*** *treating cancer patients.*

worthwhile
if something you do is worthwhile, it is useful for you and you gain something from doing it: *The training was certainly worthwhile – we learned how to use a new computer program.*

productive
useful because a lot is produced or achieved: *The meeting was very productive. Some important decisions were made and lots of ideas were discussed.*

beneficial (AWL)
useful because of having a good effect: *Bike riding is* ***beneficial*** *both* ***to*** *your health and* ***to*** *the environment.*

of use
if something is of use, it is useful in some way: *She kept the pieces of material, thinking they might be of use one day.*

SYNONYM CHECK
Useful, handy, helpful, etc.

You use **useful**, **handy**, **invaluable**, and **of use** about things that help you to do something: *The device is a useful tool.*

You use **useful**, **helpful**, **valuable**, **invaluable**, and **of use** about information, ideas, advice, etc. that help you: *Her advice was invaluable.*

You use **worthwhile**, **productive**, and **beneficial** about activities that are useful and help you to do something: *The study group was really worthwhile – I learned a lot.*

useless /ˈyusləs/ *adjective*

- ► useless
- ► futile (*formal*)
- ► pointless

ANTONYMS → see **useful**

useless
not useful, or not worth doing. You use **useless** when something is annoying because it does not work or has no effect: *The scissors are totally useless – I can't cut anything with them.* | ***It is useless to*** *say anything – he won't listen to you.*

futile (*formal*)
futile actions have no chance of being successful and do not have any effect: *She looked everywhere, but her efforts to find the lost ring were futile.*

pointless
useless and having no purpose, and so not worth doing: ***It is pointless to*** *argue with him – he will never change his mind.*

U

usual /ˈyuʒuəl/ *adjective*

- ► usual
- ► normal
- ► regular
- ► routine
- ► standard

ANTONYMS → see **strange (1)**

usual
the usual thing is the thing that happens most often: *She greeted me in the usual way, with a kiss on the cheek.* | *I'm tired because I went to bed later than usual last night.*

normal (AWL)
usual and what happens most often so that this is what you expect to happen: *Temperatures have been higher than normal.* | ***It is normal to** feel nervous when you start a new job.*

regular
usual, and not special or different from normal: *He is in a regular classroom but gets extra help after school.*

routine
happening regularly as part of the usual system and not because of any special problem: *A problem with the airplane was found during a routine check.*

standard
happening as part of the usual system, or of the most usual type: *It is standard practice to X-ray all luggage at the airport.* | *The standard size is six feet by four feet.*
→ see **ordinary**

usually /ˈyuʒuəli/ *adverb*

- ► usually
- ► generally
- ► normally
- ► typically
- ► routinely
- ► as a rule
- ► regularly

usually
used when saying what happens most of the time: *I usually get up at 6:30.* | *The museum is usually really crowded on weekends.*

generally
usually. **Generally** is more formal than **usually**: *She generally works late on Fridays.* | *Insects are generally small in size.*

normally (AWL)
usually. You use **normally** when something is what you expect to happen: *Normally, it takes me 20 minutes to get to work.*
→ You often use **normally** to show what usually happens in a situation, before saying that something different from usual has happened: *I normally eat cereal for breakfast, but there was none left, so I had toast.*

typically
in the way that something usually happens: *I typically get around 30 emails a day.*

routinely
done as a normal part of a process or job: *The cars are routinely tested for safety before leaving the factory.*

as a rule *also* **as a general rule**
usually or most of the time. **As a rule** is sometimes used to give advice about what usually works best: *As a rule, roses grow best in full sunlight and shouldn't be planted in the shade.*

regularly
at the same time each day, week, month, etc.: *The teachers meet regularly, every Friday at 3:00.*

utter *verb* → see **say**

U

Vv

vacant *adjective* → see **empty¹**

vacation /veɪˈkeɪʃən/ *noun*

- **vacation**
- **holiday**
- **break**
- **leave**
- **time off** (*informal*)

vacation
a time when you do not go to work or school, when you can relax: *Mr. Wilson is **on vacation** this week – he will be back in the office next week.* | *Let's take a vacation and go camping for a week.*

holiday
a day when officially no one has to go to work or to school: *School was closed for the Columbus Day holiday.*

break
a short vacation from your work or school: *The students get a short break in February.*

leave
time that you are allowed to spend away from work, for example because you have had a baby or are sick: *Anna took three months of maternity leave after the birth of her child.*

time off (*informal*)
time when you are officially allowed not to be at your place of work or studying: *She'll **take** some **time off** when she has her baby.*
→ When you want to be more specific, you can say how many days, weeks, or months someone will have **off**. So, for example, you can say: *She'll take four months off when she has her baby.*
→ see Topic **Travel and Vacations**

vague /veɪg/ *adjective*

- **vague**
- **inexact** (*formal*)
- **imprecise** (*formal*)

ANTONYMS → see **exact**

vague
not clear because of not having enough details. You use **vague** to talk about ideas, memories, and things people say: *I have a vague memory of meeting him when I was a young child, but all I really remember is that he was tall.* | *Carla made some vague promises about coming back to see us, but I didn't really believe her.*

inexact (*formal*)
not exact or not completely clear. You use **inexact** about things such as ideas, descriptions, and knowledge: *His directions to the restaurant were frustratingly inexact, and we got lost.*

imprecise (AWL) (*formal*)
not exact. You use **imprecise** especially about things like numbers, calculations, and measurements, but you can also use it about words: *In the past, measurements were often imprecise because people did not have good equipment for weighing things.*
→ see **unclear**

ADVERBS

You can make the adjectives that mean **vague** into adverbs by using an **-ly** ending: *I remembered him vaguely, but not well enough to remember his name.* | *In law, you cannot use terms like "legacy" imprecisely. It has a specific meaning in legal situations.*

vain *adjective* → see **proud**, Topic **Describing People's Character**

valley /ˈvæli/ *noun*

- **valley**
- **canyon**
- **gorge**
- **ravine**

valley
a low area of land between hills or mountains. A **valley** often has a river flowing through it: *The village is in a valley, surrounded on all sides by mountains.*

canyon
a deep narrow valley with very steep sides of rock, that usually has a river running through it. **Canyon** is used mostly about places in the U.S. or places in Spanish-speaking countries: *We hiked to the bottom of the Grand Canyon until we reached the Colorado River.*

gorge
a deep narrow valley with very steep sides of rock, that usually has a river running through it. **Gorge** means the same as **canyon**, but a small gorge may be part of a canyon: *In the spring, the river is full and rushes along the bottom of the gorge.*

ravine
a deep narrow valley with steep sides, that usually has a small river running through it. A

ravine is smaller and narrower than a **canyon** or **gorge**: *The trail through the ravine goes along beside the creek.*

valuable /ˈvælyəbəl/ *adjective*

- ► valuable
- ► priceless
- ► precious
- ► worth a lot (*informal*)

valuable
worth a lot of money: *It is my grandmother's ring and it's very valuable.* | *Their home is full of valuable antiques.*

priceless
very valuable: *The painting by Van Gogh is priceless.*

precious
precious metals or stones are very rare and expensive: *In the past, coins contained precious metals like gold and silver.*

worth a lot *also* **worth a fortune** (*informal*)
worth a very large amount of money: *Some rare baseball cards are worth a fortune.*
→ see **useful** for **valuable** meaning "very useful"

value¹ /ˈvælyu/ *verb*

- ► value
- ► prize
- ► treasure
- ► cherish (*formal*)

value
to think that something or someone is very important: *I value the relationship I have with him.* | *Stefan valued life, and would never hurt a person or animal.*

prize
to value something very highly. You use **prize** especially about people and objects: *Japan is a culture which prizes its young children.* | *These shoes are highly prized by fashionable young people.*

treasure
to keep and care for something because it is very special or important to you. You usually use **treasure** about memories or objects that relate to the past: *My aunt treasured this photo of her grandfather.*

cherish (*formal*)
to love and value something very much so that you do not forget how important it is: *He cherishes the time he spends with his children.*

GRAMMAR CHECK: value

You can use **valued**, **prized**, **treasured**, and **cherished** before a noun: *We are only making this offer to our valued customers.* | *Her grandmother's ring is her most prized possession.*

value² *noun* → see **cost¹**, **importance**, **morality**

vanish *verb* → see **disappear**

variable *adjective* → see **changeable**, **flexible**

variation *noun* → see **difference**

varied *adjective* → see **different**

variety /vəˈraɪəti/ *noun*

1 a lot of different types of something
- ► variety
- ► range
- ► selection

2 a situation in which there are a lot of different people or things
- ► variety
- ► variation
- ► diversity (*formal*)

1 a lot of different types of something

variety
a lot of different types of a particular thing: *You can cook the meat in **a variety of** ways – frying, broiling, roasting, and barbecuing.* | *People become homeless for **a** wide **variety of** reasons.* | *The store has **a** huge **variety of** Christmas decorations.*

range (AWL)
a lot of different types of a particular thing: *Lake Tahoe offers **a range of** accommodations from top-class hotels to youth hostels.* | *Smoking can cause **a** wide **range of** serious illnesses.*

selection (AWL)
a lot of different types of a particular thing from which you can choose: *The café offers **a selection of** hot and cold snacks.*

V

SYNONYM CHECK

Variety or range?

Variety and **range** can often be used in the same situations, but **range** is more often used when you want to emphasize the number of different things, and **variety** is more often used when you want to emphasize the difference between the things: *The store carries a good range of sports equipment from all the major sporting goods manufacturers.* | *The store carries a large variety of sports equipment, from swimming gear to baseball gloves.*

2 a situation in which there are a lot of different people or things

variety
a situation in which there are a lot of different people or things, especially when this is interesting or enjoyable: *The city has a lot of variety to offer visitors – theme parks and beaches, museums and the theater.*

variation (AWL)
a situation in which things are different in amount or level: *There is a lot of* ***variation in*** *temperature – it can be very hot in the daytime, and very cold at night.*

diversity (AWL) (*formal*)
a situation in which there are a lot of very different people or things in a place, or very different opinions about a subject: *The United States is a country with enormous diversity – there are people from many countries and ethnic backgrounds.* | *We found a huge* ***diversity of*** *views about the war.*
→ see **kind**[1] for **variety** meaning "a type of something"

vary /ˈveri/ *verb*

- ► **vary**
- ► **differ** (*formal*)

vary (AWL)
if several things of the same type vary, they are all different from each other: *The eggs* ***vary in*** *size.* | *Prices vary considerably between stores.*

differ (*formal*)
if two or more things differ, they are different: *The tax rules in the U.S.* ***differ from*** *the rules in Canada.* | *Medical treatments differ according to the age of the patient.*

verse *noun* → see **poem**, **song**, Topic **Books and Literature**

vertical /ˈvɚtɪkəl/ *adjective*

- ► **vertical**
- ► **upright**
- ► **perpendicular**
- ► **erect**

vertical
pointing straight up: *To write the letter "I" you need to draw a vertical line.* | *The shirt has pink and white vertical stripes.*

upright
in a vertical position: *The ceiling was so low that he couldn't stand upright.*

perpendicular
exactly vertical and not leaning to one side or the other: *I was holding the bat up so that it was almost* ***perpendicular to*** *the ground.*
→ **Perpendicular** is used in math to mean that two straight lines form an angle of 90 degrees where they cross: *In the graph, the y-axis is* ***perpendicular to*** *the x-axis.*

erect
in a vertical position that is straight and stiff: *The soldier stood erect, staring straight ahead.*
→ see **flat** to describe surfaces or objects that are flat and go straight across, **slanted** to describe surfaces or objects that are at an angle

ADVERBS

You can make the adjectives **vertical**, **perpendicular**, and **erect** into adverbs by using an **-ly** ending: *The words were printed vertically on the page, rather than the usual left to right way of printing.* | *Huge rocks rose perpendicularly above the flat desert.*

very /ˈveri/ *adverb*

- ► **very**
- ► **really** (*informal*)
- ► **highly**
- ► **deeply**
- ► **truly**
- ► **extremely**
- ► **quite**
- ► **seriously**
- ► **severely**
- ► **acutely** (*formal*)

very
used to emphasize that something has a lot of a particular quality: *That is a very good idea.* | *They*

were running very quickly. | It was a very upsetting experience.

→ GRAMMAR: **Very** is not used before adjectives that have a strong or extreme meaning. Don't say: ~~It was very excellent~~ or ~~It was very terrible~~.

Very is not used before comparative forms such as "better," "bigger," and "faster." Don't say: ~~*His house is very bigger than mine*~~. Say: *His house is much bigger than mine.*

really (*informal*)
very or very much. You use **really** mainly in informal spoken English: *It was really cold last night.* | *What he said really upset me.*

highly
very or very much. **Highly** is more formal than **very**. You use **highly** especially with words like **successful**, **popular**, **intelligent**, or **unusual**: *He is a highly successful businessman.*

deeply
very or very much. You use **deeply** when your emotions are strongly affected by something: *We were all deeply saddened by Bill's sudden death.*

truly
used when emphasizing that something is true about someone or something: *Brady has become a truly international star.*

extremely
used when you want an even stronger word than **very**: *She was extremely angry.*

quite
very, but not extremely: *Our new house is quite big, but not huge.*

seriously
very much or to a great degree. You use **seriously** especially with words like **ill**, **hurt**, and **injured**, and before adjectives that show an emotion: *Was she seriously hurt in the accident?* | *I'm seriously worried about Ben. He has been behaving very strangely today.*

severely
very badly or to a great degree. You use **severely** especially with words like **damaged** and **wounded**, **injured**, or **disabled**: *The town was severely damaged during the war.*

acutely (*formal*)
feeling or noticing something very strongly: *He was acutely aware that everyone was looking at him.*
→ see **extremely**

veto *noun* → see **refusal**

victim /ˈvɪktɪm/ *noun*

1 someone who has been attacked
- ► victim
- ► casualty
- ► target

2 someone who suffers because of a bad event or illness
- ► victim
- ► sufferer

1 someone who has been attacked

victim
someone who has been attacked: *The victim was tied up and robbed.* | *Men are more likely than women to be the **victims of** violent crime.*

casualty
someone who is hurt or killed in an attack or war: *The battle was fierce and there were **heavy casualties*** (=many casualties) *on both sides.*

target (AWL)
if someone is a target, he or she has been chosen to be attacked: *Her purse was open, so she was an easy **target for** thieves.*

2 someone who suffers because of a bad event or illness

victim
someone who is affected when something bad happens, or someone who has a serious illness: ***Victims of** the earthquake need food and shelter.* | *The charity supports breast cancer victims.*

sufferer
someone who has a disease or medical condition: *The spring is a difficult time of year for many allergy sufferers.*

SYNONYM CHECK

Victim or sufferer?

Both **victim** and **sufferer** are used about people who have illnesses.

Victim is used when an illness is very serious and someone will die from it: *The hospice is for AIDS victims.*

Sufferer is used when an illness lasts for a long time: *The pollution in the air is a problem for asthma sufferers.*

victory *noun* → see **win²**

view /vyu/ *noun*

- ► view
- ► sight
- ► scene
- ► panorama

view
the area you can see from a window or place, especially when it is beautiful: *The hotel room had a **view of** the Pacific Ocean. | The **view from** the top of the Empire State Building was spectacular. | We had a good **view of** the fireworks.*

sight
something that you see: *The sunrise over the mountains is a magnificent sight. | The children became quiet at the **sight of** the birthday cake.*

scene
what you see happening in a place. Use **scene** especially when you see people moving around and doing things, or when a place has a particular feeling: *The photograph shows a street scene in New York, about 70 years ago. | It was a strange scene, unlike anything I had seen before.*

panorama
an impressive view over a wide area of land. **Panorama** is more formal than **view**: *On top of the hill, we rested and enjoyed the **panorama of** the mountains stretched out before us.*
→ see **opinion** for **view** meaning "your opinion about something"

SYNONYM CHECK
View or scene?
When you are talking about what you are able to see from a window, use **view**: *There is a nice view from my window.*
Use **scene** when you are talking about the activities you see, or when you are talking about what you see in a picture of a place: *The kids were having a snowball fight, and I watched the whole scene from my window.*

village *noun* → see **town**

violence /ˈvaɪələns/ *noun*

- ► violence
- ► aggression
- ► force
- ► brutality
- ► ferocity (*formal*)
- ► savagery (*formal*)

violence
behavior in which people use physical force to attack and hurt other people: *There was so much violence in the movie. People were always fighting or shooting each other. | **Violence against** women is a serious problem in many parts of the world.*

aggression
angry feelings or behavior that often result in fighting: *Do you think video games that show fighting or wars encourage aggression in kids?*

force
the use of violent actions in order to do something: *The police used force when arresting the man – they pushed him to the ground and handcuffed him.*

brutality
deliberately cruel and violent behavior: *The brutality of the murders shocked the nation.*

ferocity (*formal*)
extreme violence in fighting or in attacking someone: *The knife had snapped in two from the ferocity of the attack.*

savagery (*formal*)
extreme and uncontrolled violence in which people are attacked and killed: *Local people were shocked by the savagery of the attack.*

violent /ˈvaɪələnt/ *adjective*

- ► violent
- ► aggressive
- ► rough
- ► vicious
- ► savage
- ► brutal
- ► fierce
- ► ferocious

violent
using physical force to hurt people, for example by hitting or attacking someone: *Hitting, kicking, or other violent behavior is not acceptable at school. | There were a lot of angry people in the room, but the situation never became violent.*

aggressive
behaving in an angry way that shows you want to fight or argue with someone: *She suddenly became more aggressive and pushed him.*

rough
using force or violence but not causing serious injury: *The boys get rough with each other when they're playing, but they don't hurt each other.*

vicious
extremely violent and cruel, and intended to hurt someone. You use **vicious** about a person or about actions: *The vicious attack on a brave young policewoman shocked the city.*

savage
extremely violent. You use **savage** about people's actions that seem as though they were done by animals: *The man nearly died in the savage attack.*

brutal
very violent and cruel, in a way that shows no human feelings for other people: *The police are investigating a series of brutal murders.*

fierce
a fierce animal or person looks frightening and ready to attack: *The dog looked fierce at first, but then she began to lick Joe's hand.*

ferocious
a ferocious animal or action is violent, frightening, and powerful, and can cause a lot of harm: *A ferocious growl came from the lion.* | *The woman was the victim of a ferocious attack.*

ADVERBS

You can make the adjectives that mean **violent** into adverbs by using an **-ly** ending: *He reacted violently when she criticized him.* | *The boys were playing roughly, and Tom got hurt.* | *The dog began to bark ferociously.*

visit /ˈvɪzɪt/ *verb*

1 to go and spend time with someone
- visit
- pay someone a visit (*formal*)
- come over/by (*informal*)
- drop in/by (*informal*)
- look someone up
- go to see (*informal*)
- go to

2 to go and spend time in a place
- visit
- go to (*informal*)
- spend time in
- go sightseeing

1 to go and spend time with someone

visit
to go and spend time with someone, especially in his or her own home: *We're going to visit Vicky this weekend.* | *Paul visited her every day when she was in the hospital.*

pay someone a visit (*formal*)
to visit someone, especially for a particular reason. **Pay a visit** sounds more formal than **visit**: *Melissa decided to pay a visit to her old teacher.*

come over/by (*informal*)
to visit someone in his or her home, especially for a short time: *Can you come by on Tuesday to pick up the keys?*

drop in/by (*informal*)
to visit someone for a short time, especially when he or she is not expecting you: *I was in the neighborhood, so I decided to drop in – I hope you don't mind.*

look someone up
to visit someone you know, especially when you go to the place where he or she lives for another reason: *I looked up an old friend while I was in Boston for a conference.*

go to see (*informal*)
to visit someone, either for enjoyment or in order to get advice or help: *He goes to see his mother once a week.* | *I think you should go to see a doctor.*

go to
to visit a doctor or dentist. **Go to** is more informal than **visit**: *I went to the doctor because I had a bad cough.*

2 to go and spend time in a place

visit
to go somewhere: *The Secretary of State visited Thailand in 2010.* | *We want to visit Navy Pier while we are in Chicago.*

go to (*informal*)
to visit a place. In everyday English, **go to** is often used instead of **visit**: *They went to the museum.*

spend time in
to visit a place and stay there for a period of time: *I've spent time in many different countries because my father is in the military and we move around a lot.* | *We spent a week in Florida.*

go sightseeing
to visit famous and interesting places: *Let's go sightseeing tomorrow. I would like to see the Empire State Building and Central Park.*
→ see **travel**[1], **trip**[1]

visitor *noun* → see **foreigner**, **guest**, **traveler**

vital *adjective* → see **important**, **necessary**

vocabulary *noun* → see **language**, **word**

voice /vɔɪs/ *noun*

- voice
- tone

voice
the sound you make when you speak or sing: *Michael recognized his daughter's voice instantly.* | *"Go to sleep," she said **in a quiet voice**.*

V

tone
the way someone speaks, especially when this shows the way he or she feels: *It was obvious from her tone of voice that she didn't like me.* | *"There is something I need to tell you," she said **in a serious tone**.*

volume *noun* → see **amount**, Topic **Describing Size**

vomit *verb* → see **throw up**

vote[1] /voʊt/ *verb*

- vote
- cast your vote (*formal*)
- go to the polls
- take a vote

vote
to show which person or plan you choose by marking a piece of paper, pressing a button, or raising your hand. When you **vote for** someone or something you are saying that you choose him, her, or it. When you **vote against** someone or something you are saying that you do not want to choose him, her, or it: *You can call in and **vote for** your favorite singer.* | *Citizens have to be 18 to be able to vote.*

cast your vote (*formal*)
to vote in an election: *You have until 8:00 p.m. to cast your vote.*

go to the polls
if the people of a country or area go to the polls, they vote in an election. **Go to the polls** is used in news reports: *The people of Houston will go to the polls next week to elect a new mayor.*

take a vote *also* **have a vote**
if a group of people have or take a vote, they choose something by voting. People **take** or **have a vote** as a formal way of deciding what to do: *The class **took a vote on** which book they wanted the teacher to read aloud.*
→ see **election**, Topic **Government and Politics**

vote[2] /voʊt/ *noun*

- vote
- election
- ballot
- referendum
- show of hands
- polls

vote
an occasion when a group of people vote to choose or decide something: *The results of the vote were surprising – we have a new mayor who has little experience in politics.*

election
an event in which people vote to choose someone for an official position: *Don't forget to vote in the student government election!* | *John F. Kennedy won the presidential election of 1960.*

ballot
the system of voting in secret, or an occasion when people vote this way: *The union members chose a leader by secret ballot.*
→ A **ballot** is also the piece of paper that you mark to vote for someone or something: *I wrote a name on the ballot and dropped it in the box.*

referendum
an occasion when people in a state or country vote in order to make a decision about a subject: *The city held a **referendum on** whether a new stadium should be built or not.*

show of hands
an occasion when a group of people vote informally by raising their hands: *Let's have a show of hands – who wants the next meeting to be on a Friday?*

polls
the place where people vote in an election: *The polls will close at 8:00 p.m.*
→ If someone wins or loses **at the polls**, he or she wins or loses an election because of people's votes: *Richards won a huge victory at the polls.*
→ see **election**, Topic **Government and Politics**

voter *noun* → see **citizen**

vow *noun* → see **promise[1]**

voyage *noun* → see **trip[1]**

V

Ww

wage *noun* → see **pay²**, Topic **Jobs and Work**

wait /weɪt/ *verb*

- ► wait
- ► hold on (*informal*)
- ► stand in line
- ► await (*formal*)
- ► stand by

wait
to stay somewhere or not do something until something else happens: *Hurry up! Everyone's waiting.* | *He said he was **waiting for** a friend.*

hold on *also* **hang on** (*informal*)
to wait for a short time: *Hold on – I'm almost ready.* | *Hang on a minute while I find her phone number.*

stand in line
to stand in a line of people who are all waiting for the same thing: *There were about 50 people **standing in line for** tickets outside the theater.*

await (*formal*)
to wait for something. **Await** is used about something that you know will happen or arrive: *Two men have been charged with robbery and are now in prison awaiting trial.*

stand by *also* **be on standby**
to wait and be ready to do something if needed. **Stand by** and **be on standby** are used especially about soldiers, police, medical teams, etc.: *An ambulance was standing by in case any of the firefighters got injured.*

wake /weɪk/ *verb*

1 to stop sleeping
- ► wake
- ► wake up
- ► awake (*formal*)
- ► get up
- ► get out of bed
- ► stir (*formal*)

ANTONYMS → see **sleep¹**

2 to make someone stop sleeping
- ► wake
- ► wake up
- ► disturb
- ► get someone up
- ► get someone out of bed

1 to stop sleeping

wake
to stop sleeping. **Wake** is more formal than **wake up** and is usually used in writing: *Margaret woke from her long sleep and opened her eyes.*

wake up
to stop sleeping. **Wake up** means the same thing as **wake**, but it is more common and less formal: *I woke up at 6:00 this morning.*

awake (*formal*)
to wake. **Awake** means the same thing as **wake**, but it is formal and is used more in literature or poetry: *She awoke to the sound of birds outside the window.*

get up
to get out of bed after you have been sleeping, especially so that you can get ready for the day: *What time do you need to get up tomorrow?*

get out of bed
to stand up and move out of your bed after you have been sleeping. **Get out of bed** means the same thing as **get up**: *Don't stay up too late or you won't be able to get out of bed in the morning.*

stir (*formal*)
to wake for a short time and move slightly, and then go back to sleep again: *As I entered the room, she stirred slightly and then went back to sleep.*

2 to make someone stop sleeping

wake
to make someone stop sleeping: *Try not to wake the baby.*

wake up
to make someone stop sleeping: *The alarm clock woke me up at 8:00.*

disturb
to accidentally wake someone who is sleeping, by making a noise or movement. Use **disturb** especially when you think you might annoy someone by doing this: *I hope my snoring won't disturb you too much.*

get someone up
to wake someone up and make him or her get out of bed, especially so that he or she can get ready for the day: *Go and get your brother up or he'll be late for work.*

get someone out of bed
to wake someone up and make him or her leave the bed: *I'm sorry for calling so early – I hope I didn't get you out of bed.*

walk[1] *verb* → *go to pages 738-739*

walk[2] /wɔk/ *noun*

- walk
- stroll
- hike

walk
a time when you walk somewhere, especially for pleasure: *Let's go for a walk on the beach.* | *We took a walk after dinner.*

stroll
a slow relaxed walk: *They went for a stroll in the park.*

hike
a long walk in the mountains or countryside: *The hike to the waterfalls takes about three hours.*

wall /wɔl/ *noun*

- wall
- fence
- barrier
- partition
- screen

wall
a structure made of brick, stones, wood, or other material, that divides one area from another area or supports part of a building: *The walls in the dining room are painted blue.* | *Some old cities have a wall around them.*

fence
a structure made of wood or metal that surrounds a piece of land and keeps people or animals in or out: *Burglars climbed over the fence to get into the yard.*

barrier
a fence or wall that stops people or cars from entering a place: *A barrier was put up to stop cars from using the street.*

partition
a thin wall that divides one part of a room from another: *She could hear someone talking behind the partition.*

screen
a piece of material on a frame that you use to keep one part of a room private: *Patients at the hospital undress behind a screen.*

wallet *noun* → see **bag**

wander *verb* → see **walk[1]**

want /wʌnt/ *verb*

- want
- would like
- wish
- would love
- desire (*formal*)
- crave
- long
- yearn

want
to feel that you will be happy if you have or do something: *My son wants a puppy for his birthday.* | ***I want to** be a famous actress.*

would like
would like means the same as **want**. It is used especially in spoken English, and can be used to offer or ask for something politely: *She **would like to** visit Africa some day.* | *I would like some coffee, please.*

wish
to want something to happen even though it is unlikely or impossible: *I wish I could run as fast as a cheetah.*
→ **Wish** is also used in formal English to say that someone wants to do something: ***I wish to** apologize.*

would love
if you would love something, you want it very much. **Would love** is used especially in spoken English: *She said she **would love to** come to my party.* | *I would love another slice of this cake.*

desire (*formal*)
to want something very much: *Why is she unhappy? She has everything she could possibly desire.*
→ **Desire** is very formal and it is unusual to say that you **desire** something.

W

crave
to want something very much and be very eager to get it, in a way that is difficult to control. You often use **crave** about food or substances that may be harmful, or about emotional needs such as love or attention: *I was tired and craved chocolate.* | *Do you think people go on TV because they crave fame?*

long
to want very much to have something or do something, especially when you are unlikely to get it or do it soon: *I used to* ***long for*** *a room of my own.* | *She was* ***longing to*** *see her family again after being away from them for so long.*

yearn
to long for something, and feel slightly sad because you do not have it. **Yearn** is used mostly in literature: *She* ***yearned to*** *be slim and pretty like her friends.* | *The prisoners* ***yearned for*** *freedom.*
→ see **wish**

war /wɔr/ *noun*

- war
- fighting
- combat
- battle
- conflict
- rebellion
- warfare

ANTONYMS → see **peace (1)**

war
a time when countries fight each other: *My father fought in the first Gulf War.* | *The government decided to go to war for the second time in three years.* | *When World War II ended in 1945, Europe was in chaos.*

fighting
a situation in which people or groups attack each other and try to hurt each other: *Fighting continued today in the streets of the capital.* | *About 200 people were injured in* ***fighting*** *between the protesters and troops.*

combat
fighting by soldiers during a war: *He was injured* ***in combat.***

battle
an occasion when armies fight each other in a war: *Six hundred men were killed in the first battle.*
→ **Battle** can also mean the same as **combat** but is used more in stories: *In the movie, he asks her to marry him before going into battle.*

conflict AWL
a time when countries or groups fight each other. **Conflict** is used especially in news reports: *There is some good news to report from the conflict in Afghanistan.*

rebellion
an attempt to remove a government or political leader by using violence: *The* ***rebellion against*** *the president was led by the military.*

warfare
the way of fighting or attacking enemies in a war, using particular weapons or methods: *The special suits protect soldiers from nuclear, biological, or chemical warfare.*

warm *adjective* → see **friendly**, **hot**

warmth *noun* → see **heat**[1]

warn /wɔrn/ *verb*

- warn
- give a warning
- alert
- beware
- forewarn (*formal*)

warn
to tell someone that something bad or dangerous may happen so that he or she can avoid it: *The teacher* ***warned*** *us* ***that*** *if she sees us doing it again, we will go to the principal's office.* | *The sign* ***warns*** *people* ***of*** *the dangers of not cooking meat thoroughly.*

give a warning
to warn someone: *The fire alarm gave the family enough warning to get out of the house.*
→ You can also use **give a warning** in official situations to say that someone only has one chance to stop doing something: *I'm giving you a warning this time, but if you do it again you'll lose your job.*

alert
to warn someone of a problem or of danger. **Alert** sounds more formal than **warn** and is used especially in official language: *Please alert the police if you see anything unusual.*

beware
used to warn someone to be careful about something. **Beware** is mainly used on signs: *The sign said "Beware! Falling Rocks."*

forewarn (*formal*)
to warn someone about something dangerous or unpleasant that may happen. **Forewarn** is mainly used in literature or formal writing: *The rebels were forewarned, giving them time to prepare to fight.*

W

warning /ˈwɔrnɪŋ/ *noun*

- ► warning
- ► alarm
- ► notice
- ► alert

warning
something that tells you that something bad or dangerous might happen so that you can avoid it: *There are **warnings about** the dangers of smoking on every pack of cigarettes.* | *The enemy attacked **without warning**.*

alarm
a piece of equipment that makes a noise to warn people of danger: *The fire alarm went off in the kitchen and woke us all up.* | *The movement in the yard set off the alarm.*

notice
an official or legal warning that something will end soon: *He received a notice that said he would have to move out of his apartment.*

alert
an official warning to be ready for possible danger, especially one on the TV or radio, or printed in a newspaper: *There is a severe weather alert starting at 9 p.m. this evening.*
→ see **alarm** for words meaning "a piece of equipment that warns you about something"
→ see **threat**

wash /wɑʃ/ *verb*

1 to wash something using water
- ► wash
- ► clean
- ► mop
- ► scrub
- ► soak
- ► rinse
- ► wash the dishes
- ► do laundry

2 to wash yourself or someone else
- ► wash
- ► take a bath
- ► take a shower
- ► shower
- ► bathe

1 to wash something using water

wash
to use water and usually soap to get the dirt off something: *He was outside washing his car.* | *I **washed** the clothes **in** hot water.*

clean
to wash something using a cloth or brush, and usually soap or a special product: *What can I use to clean the floor?* | *She was **cleaning** the windows **with** paper towels.*

mop
to clean the floor with a mop (=tool with a long handle and a soft part that you put into water): *The janitor was mopping the floor in the bathroom.*

scrub
to wash something by rubbing it hard with soap and water, especially using a brush or cloth: *She was on her knees scrubbing the kitchen floor.*

soak
to clean something by leaving it in water or another liquid for a long time: ***Soak** the stain **in** water mixed with a little bleach.*

rinse
to pass water through or over something to remove soap or other substances: ***Rinse** the sweater **in** cold water.*

wash the dishes *also* **do the dishes**
to make dishes clean by washing them with water and soap in the sink: *I'll do the dishes if you clean up the rest of the kitchen.*

do laundry
to wash clothes and sheets, usually in a washing machine: *She did a load of laundry before she went to school.*

2 to wash yourself or someone else

wash
to clean yourself with soap and water: *Make sure you wash your hands thoroughly.*
→ You can also say **wash up** when you mean "to wash your hands and sometimes your face": *Go wash up before dinner.*

take a bath
to wash yourself by sitting in a bathtub: *My little sister takes a bath after dinner.*

take a shower
to wash yourself by standing under a shower: *I like to take a shower in the morning, because it helps me wake up.*

shower
to wash yourself by standing under a shower. **Shower** sounds more formal than **take a shower**: *He showered, dressed, and ate breakfast.*

bathe
to wash yourself or someone else in a bathtub. **Bathe** means the same as **take a bath** but sounds more formal: *One of the nurses' jobs is to bathe the patients.*
→ see **clean²**

walk /wɔk/ *verb*

1 to walk
- walk
- go on foot
- hike
- pace
- march
- wade
- waddle
- roam

2 to walk slowly
- wander
- stroll
- amble
- trudge
- shuffle
- crawl

3 to walk proudly or confidently
- stride
- strut
- parade

4 to walk quietly
- tiptoe
- sneak
- creep

5 to walk with difficulty
- limp
- stagger

1 to walk

walk
to move forward by putting one foot in front of the other: *"How did you get here?" "We walked."* | *We walked twenty miles that day.*

go on foot
to walk rather than use a vehicle such as a car: *It takes 30 minutes to get there if you go on foot, and 5 minutes by car.*
→ **GRAMMAR:** Don't say: ~~go by foot~~.

hike
to walk a long way in the country or the mountains: *We hiked to a lake.* | *Every year a few people hike the length of the Appalachian Trail.*

pace
to walk first in one direction and then in another, when you are waiting or worried about something: *Coach Stafford started pacing along the side of the court.*

march
to walk with firm regular steps. You often use **march** about people who walk at the same time, such as soldiers, or about someone who is angry: *The band will march in the New Year's Day parade.* | *She marched into the room and started shouting.*

wade
to walk through deep water: *There was no bridge, so we had to wade across the river.*

waddle
to walk with short steps, with your body moving from one side to another. You use **waddle** about birds or people with fat bodies: *Half a dozen ducks waddled along the riverbank.*

roam
to walk around an area without intending to go to any particular place, usually for a long time: *Tourists roamed around the old city.*

2 to walk slowly

wander
to walk slowly around a place without having a clear idea of where you want to go: *My sister and I spent the afternoon wandering around in the mall.*

stroll
to walk in a slow and relaxed way, especially for pleasure: *They strolled along the riverbank, enjoying the evening sun.*

amble
to walk in a slow and relaxed way, especially when you are going a short distance, or when you are not going to a particular place: *A few people were ambling around the botanical gardens.*

trudge
to walk with slow heavy steps because you are tired, it is difficult to walk, or you do not want to go somewhere: *She trudged back up the hill, loaded down with heavy bags of groceries.*

shuffle
to walk slowly and in a noisy way, without lifting your feet off the ground: *The old man shuffled toward the door.*

crawl
to move along on your hands and knees, with your body close to the ground: *He watched the baby crawl across the floor.*

3 to walk proudly or confidently

stride
to walk with long steps in a determined, confident, or angry way: *She strode to the front of the stage and began speaking to the audience.*

strut
to walk in a proud and confident way, with your head up and your chest pushed forward. You use **strut** to show that someone thinks he or she is important or impressive, when you do not think this: *The hotel was full of rich people strutting around in expensive clothes.*

parade
to walk proudly around a place, in a way that shows you want people to notice and admire you: *Three girls in bikinis were parading up and down the beach.*

4 to walk quietly

tiptoe
to walk quietly and carefully on your toes because you do not want to make a noise: *I tiptoed out of the room, trying not to wake the baby.*

sneak
to walk quietly so that no one notices you, especially when you are doing something you should not be doing: *I sneaked out of the house after my parents were asleep.*

creep
to walk quietly and slowly because you do not want anyone to see or hear you: *Nobody noticed that the little boy had crept into the room and was sitting there, listening.*

5 to walk with difficulty

limp
to walk with difficulty because your leg hurts so that you put most of your weight on the other leg: *His knee hurt, and he was limping.*

stagger
to walk in an unsteady way and almost fall over: *John pushed him and he staggered backward.*

hike wade waddle
tiptoe march crawl

Online Thesaurus

Go to **www.longmandictionariesusa.com**
→ ***Longman Thesaurus of American English*** – with pronunciation of all the words
→ **Study Center** – interactive practice to help you learn synonyms, Academic Words, and Topic Vocabulary

waste /weɪst/ verb

- waste
- let something go to waste
- squander
- throw away

ANTONYMS → see **save (2)**

waste
to use more of something than you need, or not use something in a useful way: *Turn off the faucet – you're wasting water.* | *I wish he would stop wasting my time with stupid questions.*
→ You also use **waste** when you do not use a chance or opportunity that you should use: *You shouldn't waste the chance to go on the trip if you can afford it.*

let something go to waste
to throw something away when it could have been used: *Please eat! We can't let all this good food go to waste.*

squander
to carelessly waste money, time, or an opportunity: *The company has* ***squandered*** *money on programs that do not work.*

throw away
to spend more money than you need to, or not use an opportunity that could help you: *I don't want to throw away good money on something that will break right away.* | *The team threw away its best chance at a goal in the second half.*
→ see **trash**

wasteful /ˈweɪstfəl/ adjective

- wasteful
- inefficient
- excessive (*formal*)

wasteful
using more of something than you need, or using it badly, so that it is wasted: *The politicians always argue about how to cut wasteful spending.*

inefficient
working or done in a way that wastes time, money, or energy. **Inefficient** is used especially about systems, organizations, and machines that do not work well: *The company became too large and inefficient, so they closed several factories.*

excessive (*formal*)
an amount or level that is excessive is a lot more than you need or want: *Do not use an excessive amount of shampoo when you wash your hair.*
→ see **extravagant**

W

ADVERBS

You can make the adjectives that mean **wasteful** into adverbs by using an **-ly** ending: *He accused the mayor's office of spending the money wastefully on programs that were not needed.* | *We do not want our employees to be working inefficiently.* | *The costs of the program seemed excessively high.*

watch /wɑtʃ/ verb

- watch
- observe (*formal*)
- see
- monitor
- keep an eye on (*informal*)
- spy on

watch
to look at something that is happening or moving and give it your attention: *She watched the birds fly away over the trees.* | *We were watching some boys playing baseball.*

observe (*formal*)
to watch something carefully, especially for a long time, in order to find out more about it: *Scientists observed the monkeys in the wild in order to find out about their behavior.*

see
to watch a movie, television show, or sports game: *Did you see the basketball game last night?*
→ Don't say: ~~*I saw television last night*~~. Say: *I saw a good show on television last night* or *I watched television last night.*

monitor (AWL)
to carefully watch a situation over a period of time to see how it changes or develops: *The nurses monitor the patients after surgery.*

keep an eye on (*informal*)
to watch someone or something to make sure nothing bad happens: *Can you keep an eye on our house while we're on vacation?*

spy on
to watch someone or something secretly in order to get information about him or her: *The company was spying on foreign businesses.* | *My little brother spies on me and tells my parents what I'm doing.*
→ see **see**

wave /weɪv/ verb

- wave
- flap
- flutter
- wag

wave
to move from side to side: *The flag was waving in the breeze.* | *Protesters waved signs as they marched through the streets.*
→ You also use **wave** when you move your hand from side to side as a way of saying hello or goodbye, or as a way of making someone notice you: *The princess **waved at** the children in the front row.*

flap
to move quickly from side to side or up and down, and make a noise: *The sheets hanging on the line were flapping in the wind.*

flutter
to make small gentle movements from side to side in the air: *A Mexican flag fluttered in the breeze.*

wag
if a dog wags its tail, it shakes it from one side to another. You can say that "a dog wags its tail" or that "the dog's tail wags": *The dog was happy to see us and was wagging his tail.* | *My friend's dog came to us with her tail wagging.*

way /weɪ/ *noun*

1 a way of doing something
- ► **way**
- ► **method**
- ► **technique**
- ► **approach**
- ► **strategy**
- ► **means**

2 a way of behaving or happening
- ► **way**
- ► **manner** (*formal*)

1 a way of doing something

way
how you do something in order to achieve something: *I am always looking for new **ways to** cook chicken.* | *The best **way of** traveling down the coast is by train.*

method (AWL)
a way of doing something, especially one that is well known and often used. **Method** sounds more formal than **way**: *Scientists use this method to find out how old something is.* | *The best **method of** removing fruit stains is to pour boiling water through them.*

technique (AWL)
a special way of doing something, especially one that involves skill or training: *My dad helped me improve my skiing technique.*

approach (AWL)
a way of doing something that is carefully planned: *The company is trying a new approach to deal with the problem.*

strategy (AWL)
a set of carefully planned methods for doing something over a long time: *The school has a new **strategy for** helping students who are struggling with reading.*

means
a method or thing that you use to do something: *I had no cell phone and no other means of communication.*
→ see **direction**, **system**, Function Word **how**

2 a way of behaving or happening

way
how someone does something or how it happens: *"Hello," she said, in a friendly way.* | *Don't talk to me that way! You need to be more polite!* | *He was handsome in an old-fashioned way.*

manner (*formal*)
the way in which something is done or happens. **Manner** is used especially about someone's behavior: *The managers always treat their employees **in a** professional **manner**.*

weak /wik/ *adjective*

1 weak people are not strong
- ► **weak**
- ► **frail**
- ► **feeble**
- ► **shaky**
- ► **vulnerable**
- ► **defenseless**

ANTONYMS → see **strong (1)**

2 weak things are not strong and break easily
- ► **weak**
- ► **fragile**
- ► **flimsy**
- ► **delicate**
- ► **brittle**

ANTONYMS → see **strong (3)**

3 not able to persuade or influence people
- ► **weak**
- ► **ineffective**
- ► **feeble**
- ► **powerless**

ANTONYMS → see **strong (2)**

1 weak people are not strong

weak
not physically strong: *My grandmother had been*

W

sick, and she looked weak and tired. | *Do these exercises to strengthen weak stomach muscles.*

frail
someone who is frail is thin and weak, especially because of being old or ill: *My uncle had seemed so big and strong when I was little, but now he looked old and frail.*

feeble
extremely weak, especially because of being old, young, or sick: *The old man was very feeble and needed someone to take care of him.*

shaky
weak and unsteady because of illness, old age, or shock: *I am still feeling shaky after falling off my bike.*

vulnerable
easy to harm, hurt, or attack: *I felt vulnerable and afraid as I sat waiting in the dark.*

defenseless
unable to protect yourself from violence: *The soldiers apparently attacked defenseless civilians.*

ADVERBS

You can make the adjectives **weak**, **feeble**, and **shaky** into adverbs by using an **-ly** ending: *He raised his arm weakly and let it fall back onto the bed.* | *She stood up shakily.* | *She feebly waved her bandaged hand as he left.*

2 weak things are not strong and break easily

weak
not able to support much weight, and likely to break: *The sign said "Weak bridge – no trucks."* | *The metal structure of the building was weak.*

fragile
made of a thin material, such as glass, that is easy to break or damage. **Fragile** is often written on boxes containing fragile things to warn people that they are easily broken: *The old doll was fragile, so we weren't allowed to touch it.* | *The mirror was packed inside a box marked "Fragile. Do Not Drop."*

flimsy
not strong or well made, and easy to break or damage. You use **flimsy** about things such as furniture, houses, or fences: *The poorest people live in flimsy wooden shacks on the hillside.*

delicate
easy to damage. **Delicate** is often used about soft things such as cloth, skin, or flowers: *Silk is a delicate fabric, and it needs special care.*

brittle
hard or stiff, but easily broken: *As we get older our bones grow more brittle and can break easily.* | *The old newspaper was stiff and brittle with age.*

ADVERBS

You can make the adjective **flimsy** into an adverb by using an **-ly** ending: *The book was flimsily bound, and several pages fell out when I opened it.* The adverb **delicately** is not used in this meaning.

3 not able to persuade or influence people

weak
not likely to be able to persuade or influence people to do something: *The evidence against him is weak, so the case will not go to trial.* | *Thirty-eight percent of people said they thought the president was a weak leader.*

ineffective
not achieving what people want to be achieved: *The police operation was ineffective, and crime continued to rise in the area.* | *The country has a largely ineffective government, and its military leaders are much stronger.*

feeble
weak and not achieving what you want: *His mother ignored his feeble protest that he wasn't tired and sent him to bed.*

powerless
not able to stop or control people or events, because you do not have the ability, strength, or legal right to stop them: *The government seems* ***powerless to*** *stop the fighting in the region.*

ADVERBS

You can make the adjectives **weak**, **ineffective**, and **feeble** into adverbs by using an **-ly** ending: *"I'm not sure we should do this," Gary protested weakly.* | *The country is governed ineffectively, and the military is much more organized.*

weaken /ˈwikən/ *verb*

- ► **weaken**
- ► **undermine**
- ► **impair** (*formal*)

ANTONYMS → see **strengthen**

weaken
to make someone or something less strong, powerful, or important: *A long illness had weakened him.* | *A series of bad decisions weakened the government.* | *There are signs that the economy is weakening, so more people are worried about their jobs.*

W

undermine
to make someone or something less strong or effective over a period of time: *Constant criticism will undermine a child's confidence.*

impair (*formal*)
to make something less good or useful, especially something such as an ability: *Being very tired can impair your judgment, so you make bad decisions.*

weakness *noun* → see **flaw**

wealth *noun* → see **money**

wealthy *adjective* → see **rich**

weapon /ˈwepən/ *noun*

- ► **weapon**
- ► **arms**
- ► **firearm** (*formal*)
- ► **ammunition**

weapon
a thing used for fighting or attacking people, for example a knife, gun, or bomb: *The police found guns and other weapons in the man's house.*

arms
weapons such as guns and bombs, especially used to fight wars: *The group had been supplying arms to the rebels.*

firearm (*formal*)
any gun that you can carry: *In many states, it is illegal to carry a hidden firearm.*

ammunition
things such as bullets that are fired from guns: *He tried to buy ammunition and other supplies in the store.*

wear /wer/ *verb*

- ► **wear**
- ► **have on** (*informal*)
- ► **be dressed in**

wear
if you are wearing a particular piece of clothing or jewelry, it is on your body: *Angela was wearing a dark blue sweater and jeans.* | *He always wore trainers.*

have on (*informal*)
to be wearing something: *Mr. Fielding has a jacket and tie on.* | *She had on an old sweatshirt.*

be dressed in
to be wearing particular clothes. **Be dressed in** is more formal than **wear**: *She was dressed in a black suit.*
→ see **clothes**

wear away /ˌwer əˈweɪ/ *phrasal verb*

- ► **wear away**
- ► **erode**
- ► **crumble**
- ► **disintegrate**

wear away
if something wears away, it starts to disappear or become thinner because something else has rubbed or touched it a lot: *The painted lines on the road had worn away.* | *The soles of his shoes are starting to wear away.* | *The stairs are made of stone, and long years of using them have worn the rock away in places.*

erode (AWL)
if land, rock, or soil erodes, the wind, rain, or water gradually destroys it: *The cliffs along the coast are eroding, and houses built on the cliffs may fall into the ocean.* | *Wind and water had eroded the soil.*

crumble
if things made of stone or rock crumble, small pieces begin to fall off, especially because they are old, and wind, rain, and snow are gradually breaking them: *The stone walls of the old church are crumbling.*

disintegrate
to break up into very small pieces: *The paper was very old and just disintegrated in my hands.*

weather /ˈweðɚ/ *noun*

- ► **weather**
- ► **conditions**
- ► **climate**

weather
the weather in a place is how warm or cold it is and whether it is raining, sunny, windy, etc.: *The weather on the island is always warm and usually sunny.* | *"What is the weather going to be like tomorrow?" "It will be hot."*

conditions
the weather at a particular time or in a particular place. **Conditions** is used especially in reports about the weather: *Icy conditions on the highway have caused several accidents.*

climate
the type of weather that a place usually has: *The plant will not grow in a cold climate.*

Web *noun* → see Topic **Computers and the Internet**

website *noun* → see Topic **Computers and the Internet**

wedding /ˈwedɪŋ/ *noun*

- wedding
- marriage (*formal*)
- reception
- honeymoon
- engagement

wedding
a ceremony in which two people get married: *Their wedding will be in the church on Main Street.* | *There were over a hundred people at the wedding.* | *The couple received lots of wedding presents.*

marriage (*formal*)
a wedding. **Marriage** is more formal than **wedding**, and is used to talk about the wedding as an event that happens at a particular time in a particular place: *The marriage will take place in October.*

reception *also* **wedding reception**
a large party to celebrate after a wedding: *There was dancing at the reception.*

honeymoon
a vacation that people take after they get married: *Two days after the wedding, they went to Greece on their honeymoon.*

engagement
an agreement to get married: *The couple announced their engagement in March.*
→ see **marriage**, Topic **Relationships and Marriage**

weed *noun* → see **plant¹**

weigh *verb* → see **measure**, **think**

weird *adjective* → see **strange**

welcome /ˈwelkəm/ *verb*

- welcome
- greet

welcome
to say friendly things or behave in a friendly way to someone who has just arrived: *My job is to welcome guests when they arrive at the hotel.* | *He stood at the door welcoming his friends to the party.*

greet
to say something such as "hello" to someone when you see him or her. **Greet** is used more in writing than in speech: *A man stood at the door of the church greeting visitors.*

well /wel/ *adverb*

- well
- nicely
- skillfully
- competently
- properly (*formal*)
- right (*informal*)
- adequately

ANTONYMS → see **badly**

well
in a good or very good way: *You played well today, and you even hit a home run!*

nicely
in a pleasant, attractive, or satisfactory way: *She behaved very nicely at the party.* | *The food was nicely cooked and looked beautiful.*

skillfully
in a way that shows a lot of skill or ability, especially physical skill: *She landed the plane skillfully in the bad weather.*

competently
in a way that shows you have knowledge or skill: *He does his job competently.* | *She drives very competently.*

properly (*formal*)
in the best, most correct, or most complete way: *They did not fix the car properly, so we will be taking it back to the garage.*

right (*informal*)
in the best, most correct, or most complete way: *Make sure you finish it tonight, and get it done right.*

adequately
in a way that is good enough for a particular purpose, but not very good: *The family did not have enough money to adequately heat their home.*
→ see **healthy**, **better** (**2**) for "to get well"

SYNONYM CHECK
Skillfully or competently?

You use **skillfully** about things that need physical skill: *He juggled the three balls skillfully.*

Competently can also be used about physical skills, but you usually use it about things that need mental ability: *The lawyer presented the case competently in court.*

well-behaved *adjective* → see **good**

well-dressed *adjective* → see Topic **Describing People's Looks**

well-known *adjective* → see **famous**

well-off *adjective* → see **rich**

wet /wet/ adjective

1 covered in liquid
- wet
- soaked
- drenched
- soggy
- saturated (*formal*)
- waterlogged

ANTONYMS → see **dry (1)**

2 to become wet (verbs)
- get wet
- wet (*formal*)
- soak
- dampen
- moisten
- sprinkle
- saturate (*formal*)
- immerse (*formal*)

1 covered in liquid

wet
covered in or containing liquid: *Be careful. I just cleaned the floor and it is still wet.* | *My hair was wet because I had just taken a shower.*

soaked *also* **soaking**
very wet all the way through: *I fell in the stream, and my clothes were soaked.* | *You're soaking! Come in out of the rain.*

drenched
completely wet, because a lot of rain or water has poured onto someone or something: *A huge wave hit the boat and we all got drenched.*

soggy
too wet and soft, because of taking in too much liquid, and looking or feeling unpleasant: *The eggs were dry, and the toast was soggy.*

saturated (*formal*)
so wet that no more water can be contained. **Saturated** is used especially in scientific writing: *The soil is completely **saturated with** water.*

waterlogged
completely wet and holding a lot of liquid. Use **waterlogged** about the ground or natural materials: *They found the waterlogged wood from an old ship at the bottom of the river.*
→ see **damp**, **rainy**, Topic **The Weather**

2 to become wet (verbs)

get wet
to make something wet: *I stepped in a puddle and got my feet wet.* | *When wood gets wet, it must dry completely or it will begin to rot.*

wet (*formal*)
to make something wet. **Wet** is less common than **get wet**: *She wet the cloth and then squeezed it out over the sink.*

soak
to leave something in water or another liquid for a period of time: ***Soak** the bread **in** the egg and milk mixture.*

dampen
to make something a little wet, especially with water: ***Dampen** a cloth **with** soap and water and gently rub the mark.*

moisten
to make something a little wet, especially to stop it from getting dry: *Moisten the soil in the pot regularly, but do not put too much water on the plant.*

sprinkle
to put small drops of liquid onto the surface of something, especially food: ***Sprinkle** the fish **with** lemon juice and melted butter.*

saturate (*formal*)
to make something become wet all the way through so that no more liquid can be taken in: *Heavy rains saturated the ground and caused flooding.*

immerse (*formal*)
to cover something with water or another liquid: ***Immerse** the beans **in** water for 24 hours.*

when *conjunction, adverb* → see Function Words

whenever *conjunction, adverb* → see Function Word **when**

while *conjunction* → see Function Words

whine *verb* → see **complain**, Topic **To Make a Sound**

whisper /ˈwɪspɚ/ verb

- whisper
- murmur
- mumble
- mutter

ANTONYMS → see **shout[1]**

whisper
to speak very quietly, using your breath to make words and not your voice: *"The baby has just gone to sleep," she whispered. "Don't wake him up."* | *Two girls were **whispering to** each other at the back of the class.*

murmur
to say something in a quiet gentle voice: *"It is all right," she murmured.* | *He held her hand and murmured her name.*

W

mumble
to say something quietly, in a way that is not clear: *"Who were you with?" his mother asked. "Nobody," Rob mumbled.* | *He looked down at his feet and mumbled an apology.*

mutter
to say something quietly because you are annoyed or do not want people to hear: *"I don't like you," Sofia muttered.* | *Neil angrily muttered something about Sam being late.*

whistle *verb* → see **sing**

whole /hoʊl/ *adjective*

- ► whole
- ► entire
- ► complete

whole
all of something: *The whole family came to celebrate his 100th birthday.* | *We spent the whole day just talking and having fun.*
→ GRAMMAR: **Whole** is always used before a noun: *I read the whole book in two days.*

entire
all of something. You often use **entire** to show that you are surprised or annoyed: *Anna sat down and ate the entire cake!*
→ GRAMMAR: **Entire** is always used before a noun: *He lived his entire life in the same town.*

complete
including everything or everyone. You use **complete** to emphasize that nothing is missing: *The prize included a complete set of expensive dishes.* | *I think the list is complete. We haven't forgotten anyone.*

wholly *adverb* → see **completely**

wide /waɪd/ *adjective*

1 measuring a large distance from one side to the other
- ► wide
- ► broad

ANTONYMS → see **narrow (1)**

2 including many different things or people
- ► wide
- ► broad

1 measuring a large distance from one side to the other

wide
measuring a large distance from one side to the other: *The pants have wide legs.* | *The highway is wide and straight.*

broad
broad means the same as **wide** but sounds more formal: *The Hudson River is very broad in some places.* | *The jacket fit perfectly on his broad shoulders.*
→ see Topic **Describing Size**

SYNONYM CHECK

Wide or broad?

Wide is the more usual word to use. You can say: *a wide river/road/area*. You can also say that someone has *a wide mouth/face/smile*.

Broad sounds more formal and is often used to make a road, river, or area seem attractive: *He drove down the broad tree-lined streets of the town.*

You can describe a person's chest, back, or shoulders as **broad**, but you do not usually use it about any other parts of the body. You can, however, say that someone has *a broad smile/grin*.

2 including many different things or people

wide
including many different things or people: *The show reaches a wide audience, so men and women of all ages enjoy it.*

broad
broad means the same as **wide** but sounds more formal: *The piano students have a broad range of skill, from beginners to the more advanced.*

SYNONYM CHECK

Wide or broad?

You can often use **wide** or **broad** with the same words: *a wide/broad range* | *a wide/broad selection* | *He has wide/broad experience of teaching.*

With some words, you can only use **broad**: *a broad category* | *a broad generalization*.

With other words, you can only use **wide**: *a wide variety* | *a wide choice*. Both **wide** and **broad** are usually used before a noun.

ADVERBS

When the adjectives **wide** and **broad** mean "including many different things or people," you can make them into adverbs by using an **-ly** ending: *She is very widely read* (=she has read many different types of books). | *The movie has been broadly popular with the public.* For other meanings, see **generally**.

widely *adverb* → see **generally**

width /wɪdθ/ *noun*

- width
- breadth (*formal*)
- depth
- diameter

width
the distance from one side of something to the other: *The width of the river is about 25 feet.* | *The pool is fifty feet in length and twenty feet* ***in width.***

breadth (*formal*)
breadth means the same as **width** but is more formal or literary: *He traveled the length and breadth of the country.*

depth
the distance from the front of an object to the back. You use **depth** especially when you are talking about a piece of furniture: *The closet is seven feet high, ten feet wide, and has a depth of three feet.*
→ **Depth** is also used to describe the distance from the top to the bottom of something such as a hole, river, ocean, etc: *The diving pool has a depth of five meters.*

diameter
the distance from one side of a circle to the other, through the center: *The tree trunk is about six inches in diameter.*
→ see **height**, **length**, Topic **Describing Size**

width

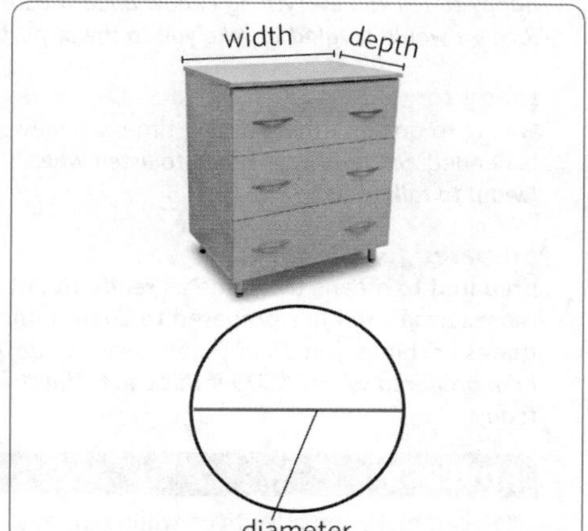

wife /waɪf/ *noun*

- wife
- bride
- fiancée
- spouse (*formal*)
- widow
- partner

ANTONYMS → see **husband**

wife
the woman that a man is married to: *Jonathan's wife is a doctor.*

bride
a woman who is getting married at a wedding ceremony: *The bride was standing at the back of the church.*

fiancée
the woman that a man has promised to marry: *I'm going to Mexico to meet my fiancée's family before the wedding.*

spouse (*formal*)
someone's husband or wife. **Spouse** is used mostly on official forms: *The application asks for the name of your spouse.*

widow
a woman whose husband is dead: *She became a widow at age 27 when her husband died in a car accident.*

partner (AWL)
someone's husband, wife, girlfriend, or boyfriend. You often use **partner** when someone is in a relationship and living with someone else but is not married to that person: *He and his partner are going to New York for a week.*
→ see Topic **Relationships and Marriage**

wild[1] /waɪld/ *adjective*

1 in a natural state
- wild
- natural
- untamed
- unspoiled
- virgin

ANTONYMS → see **tame**

2 behaving in a very excited, noisy, or uncontrolled way
- wild
- disruptive
- unruly
- rowdy

W

1 in a natural state

wild
wild plants, animals, and areas of land are in their natural state, and have not been changed or controlled by people: *The wild flowers in the desert begin blooming in April. | The animals that live in the national parks are wild.*

natural
something that is natural was not made or caused by people: *The river had worn away the rock to form a natural bridge. | Natural disasters such as earthquakes can cause enormous amounts of damage.*

untamed
untamed areas of land have never been changed or used by people: *The trail goes through the untamed wilderness of the Sierra Nevada mountains.*

unspoiled
unspoiled places have not been changed or polluted (=made dirty) by people: *The island has few visitors, and the beaches are white and unspoiled.*

virgin
virgin forests or wilderness have no roads or buildings in them, and trees have not been cut down: *The law will protect virgin rain forests.*
→ see **natural**

ADVERBS
You can make the adjective **natural** into an adverb by using an **-ly** ending: *The bridge is formed naturally as water wears away the rock.*

2 behaving in a very excited, noisy, or uncontrolled way

wild
behaving in a very excited way and not controlling your behavior: *The crowd went wild when the team scored another touchdown.*

disruptive
behaving in a way that causes problems or interrupts something, for example a class or meeting: *Disruptive behavior in the classroom, such as talking or fighting, makes it hard for the teacher to teach.*

unruly
behaving in a way that is difficult to control. You use **unruly** especially about children, young people, and crowds that someone is in charge of: *The book gives advice on dealing with an unruly child who will not do anything you ask.*

rowdy
a rowdy group of people make a lot of noise, especially in a way that disturbs other people: *They held a rowdy party that kept everyone in the neighborhood awake.*

ADVERBS
You can make the adjectives **wild**, **disruptive**, and **rowdy** into adverbs by using an **-ly** ending: *The crowd cheered wildly as their team scored. | The students rushed rowdily down the hall.*

wild² *noun* → see **nature**

wilderness *noun* → see **nature**

willing /ˈwɪlɪŋ/ *adjective*

- willing
- happy to
- ready to
- prepared to (*formal*)

ANTONYMS → see **unwilling**

willing
doing something because you want to do it, not because you have to: *I am always **willing to** help if you ask me. | Was Thompson a willing partner in the crime, or was he forced to take part?*

happy to *also* **glad to**
willing and pleased to do something: *I would be **happy to** tell you everything I know about Costa Rica. | I would be **glad to** take you to the airport.*

ready to
willing to do something at any time, whenever it is needed: *She is always **ready to** listen when I want to talk to her.*

prepared to (*formal*)
prepared to means the same as **ready to** but is more formal. You use **prepared to** about difficult things or things you do not really want to do: *I am **prepared to** pay $500 if this can be finished today.*

ADVERBS
You can make the adjectives **willing**, **happy**, and **ready** into adverbs by using an **-ly** ending: *The boys don't always join in willingly when there are chores to be done. | She readily agreed to help.*

W

willingly /ˈwɪlɪŋli/ *adverb*

- willingly
- gladly
- voluntarily
- of your own free will

willingly
in a way that shows you want to do something, not that you are being forced to do it: *The man went with the police officer to the station willingly because he wanted to tell the police what he saw.*

gladly
in a way that shows that you are pleased to do something and want to do it: *I'll gladly answer all of your questions at the end of class.*

voluntarily (AWL)
because you choose to do something, not because you are forced to do it: *The police didn't arrest him – he gave himself up voluntarily.*

of your own free will
of your own free will means the same as **voluntarily** but is more formal: *He left his country of his own free will, and he may return at any time.*

win[1] /wɪn/ *verb*

- win
- come in first
- be leading

ANTONYMS → see **lose (2)**

win
to be the best or be first in a game, competition, or election: *We're winning, and there are only two minutes left in the game!* | *Sharon won the math competition last year.*

come in first *also* **get first place**
to win a race or competition in which more than two people or teams compete. **Get first place** sounds a little more informal than **come in first**: *Laura came in first, and Janet got second place.* | *The swimmer who got first place was from Canada.*

be leading *also* **be in the lead**
to be in the first position in a race, competition, or election while it is still happening: *Our favorite horse is in the lead!* | *The congresswoman is still leading in the polls.*
→ see **beat**

win[2] /wɪn/ *noun*

- win
- victory
- triumph
- conquest
- success

ANTONYMS → see **loss**

win
an occasion when you win a game, competition, or election: *The basketball team was celebrating its **win against** Lakeland High School.*

victory
a win in a game, competition, war, or election. You use **victory** especially in writing about sports, politics, and war: *The team's **victory over** the Dodgers means that they will be in the World Series.*

triumph
a great win or success: *The navy's triumph in the Battle of Midway was the first step in defeating Japan in World War II.*

conquest
an occasion when a country defeats a group of people in a war and takes control of their land: *The book is about the history of the Spanish **conquest of** Mexico.*

success
an occasion when someone wins or achieves something that he or she has been competing for: *The party's recent success in the election brings a lot of excitement.*

wind[1] /wɪnd/ *noun*

- wind
- breeze
- gust
- gale
- draft

wind
a moving current of air: *It was a big storm with strong winds and rain.* | ***The wind** was blowing old newspapers up and down the street.*
→ If the **wind** or a **breeze** blows, this means that the air is moving: *A damp cold wind was blowing.*

breeze
a light gentle wind: *A breeze was coming in off the ocean.*

gust
a sudden strong wind that is faster then the rest of the wind that is blowing: *There were gusts of*

wind up to 60 miles per hour. | *The wind wasn't bad, but there were some stronger gusts near the coast.*

gale
a very strong wind that blows for a long period, for example during a storm: *The rain started to fall, followed by a gale from the south.*

draft (AWL)
cold air blowing into a room, especially through the space around a window or door: *There is a draft coming in under the door.*
→ see **storm**, Topic **The Weather**

wind² *verb* → see **bend¹**

windy /ˈwɪndi/ *adjective*

- ► windy
- ► breezy
- ► blustery

windy
if it is windy, there is a lot of wind: *It was a windy day, and leaves were being blown off the trees.*

breezy
with the wind blowing gently: *A breezy day is good for flying kites.*

blustery
very windy and having many strong sudden winds: *The weather was damp, gray, and blustery, and I wanted to stay inside.*
→ see Topic **The Weather**

winner /ˈwɪnɚ/ *noun*

- ► winner
- ► champion
- ► medalist
- ► prize winner
- ► frontrunner

ANTONYMS → see **loser**

winner
someone who wins a competition, race, game, or election: *The* ***winner of*** *the 200-meter race is Sandra Hernandez.* | *The Republican was declared the winner by only 200 votes.*

champion
a person or team that has won a series of sports competitions: *She is a world champion swimmer.*

medalist
someone who wins a medal for coming first, second, or third in a sports competition such as the Olympics: *Johnson was the gold medalist two years in a row.*

prize winner
someone who wins a prize, especially the person who wins the most important prize: *The Nobel Peace prize winner in 2007 was Al Gore.*

frontrunner
the person who is most likely to win an election: *She is the* ***frontrunner for*** *the senate seat in the coming election.*
→ Do not use **frontrunner** about sports competitions.

wipe *verb* → see **clean²**

wire /waɪɚ/ *noun*

- ► wire
- ► cord
- ► cable

wire
a long thin piece of metal that carries electricity or electrical signals: *You shouldn't touch electrical wires.* | *The two wires touched, making a spark.*

cord
a piece of wire covered with plastic, used for connecting electrical or electronic equipment: *I made sure the computer cord was plugged in correctly.*

cable
a thick cord containing several wires. A **cable** carries electricity, telephone signals, or television signals: *Workers accidentally cut through a power cable and thousands of homes were left without electricity.*

wise *adjective* → see **smart**

wish /wɪʃ/ *noun*

- ► wish
- ► desire (*formal*)
- ► want
- ► craving
- ► longing
- ► yearning
- ► inclination (*formal*)

wish
a feeling that you want something to happen: *I could understand her* ***wish to*** *go back to her home country.* | *His* ***wish that*** *his son become a doctor did not come true.*

desire (*formal*)
a strong feeling of wanting something: *Reese had a strong* ***desire to*** *help people in the community.*

want
a feeling of wanting something that you do not have. **Wants** are wishes for things that would

make you happy, but that are not necessary: *Thinking about your needs and wants can help you to set goals for yourself.*

craving
a very strong feeling that you want a particular type of food or drink, a drug, or something like fame or attention: *Sometimes pregnant women have **cravings for** unusual foods.*

longing
a strong feeling of wanting someone or something very much, especially when it is difficult or impossible to have it: *She was filled with **longing for** her family, whom she hadn't seen in five years.*

yearning
yearning means the same as **longing** but is used mostly in literature and poetry: *His **yearning for** home was very strong, but he did not have the money to travel.*

inclination (AWL) (*formal*)
a feeling that makes you want to do something: *He asked if he could borrow my car, and my natural inclination was to say no.*
→ see **hope[1]**, **need[2]**, **urge[1]**, **want**

witch *noun* → see **magician**

witness /ˈwɪtnəs/ *noun*

- ► witness
- ► bystander
- ► observer

witness
someone who saw a crime or accident happen, especially someone who makes a formal statement in court saying what happened: *Nina was the only **witness to** the crime.* | *In court, the defense lawyer called their second witness to testify.*

bystander
someone who is in a place when something happens but who did not plan to take part: *Bystanders described the scene to the reporters.* | *Two innocent bystanders were hurt during the fight.*

observer
someone who watches someone or something, especially someone who does this carefully over a long period to see how something develops or happens: *Observers say that the election was not carried out legally.*

wizard *noun* → see **magician**

woman /ˈwʊmən/ *noun*

- ► woman
- ► lady
- ► girl
- ► female
- ► Mrs.
- ► Ms.
- ► Miss

ANTONYMS → see **man**

woman
an adult female person: *Do you know that woman in the blue dress?* | *Most of the teachers at this school are women.*

lady
a polite word for a woman, used when you do not know her name, or when you are speaking to a group of people: *I said thank you to the lady who had given me the pen.* | *Ladies and gentlemen, I would like to welcome you to our show.*

girl
a female child: *The little girl waved at us.*
→ You can also use **girl** to talk about a person's female child: *Marianne's girls are in high school now.*

female
a person or animal that belongs to the sex that can have babies or produce eggs. You use **female** in scientific language, but you do not use it to talk about a particular person: *The monkeys all look similar, but the females are smaller than the males.*
→ **GRAMMAR:** Don't say: ~~*Do you see that female standing by the door*~~? Say: *Do you see that woman standing by the door?*

Mrs.
used before the family name of a married woman: *My homeroom teacher's name is Mrs. Longwood.*

Ms.
used before the family name of a woman. **Ms.** does not show if the woman is married or not: *Ms. Ginelli asked me to call her about the job.*

Miss
used before the family name of a girl or a woman who is not married: *Miss Gretsky is 17 years old.*
→ see **female[1]**

wonderful *adjective* → see **good**

wood /wʊd/ *noun*

- ► wood
- ► log
- ► lumber
- ► timber

wood
the hard material that trees are made of. **Wood** is used for making things such as furniture and houses or for burning in a fire: *The table is made of wood.* | *Perez was chopping wood for the fire.*
→ **GRAMMAR:** When you want to say that something is made from wood, you can use the adjective **wooden**: *He kept the papers in a wooden box.*

log
a thick piece of wood that has fallen off or been cut off a tree. A **log** is usually from the trunk (=main part) or a thick branch: *There was a pile of logs by the fire.* | *He lived in a log cabin in the mountains.*

lumber
wood that is cut and prepared to be used for building things: *The lumber is for building a new room on the house.*

timber
timber means the same as **lumber**, but it is used more about cut wood that is very thick, or when you are talking about using trees to produce **lumber**: *Spruce trees are valuable for their timber because they are strong.*

woods *noun* → see **forest**

word /wɚd/ *noun*

- ► word
- ► vocabulary
- ► term
- ► slang
- ► jargon

word
a group of sounds or letters that have a particular meaning: *"Casa" is the Spanish* ***word for*** *"house."* | *There was a word I didn't know, so I looked it up in a dictionary.*

vocabulary
all the words that you know and use: *Reading is a good way to increase your vocabulary.*
→ You can say **vocabulary words** when you are talking about a set of words that someone is learning: *I need to study a list of vocabulary words for tomorrow's test.*

term
a word or phrase that has a special meaning and is used by people in a particular job or people who know a lot about a subject: *Business people use the term "bull market" when stock prices are rising.*

slang
very informal spoken words, especially words used by a particular group of people, such as young people: *"Sick" is* ***slang for*** *"good" or "cool."*
→ You use **slang word**, **slang term**, or **slang expression** when talking about a particular word or phrase: *New slang expressions come into the language all the time.*

jargon
words and phrases that are used only by people who are doing the same type of work or who are interested in a particular subject. **Jargon** can be difficult for other people to understand: *The document was full of legal jargon, and I had to ask a lawyer to explain it to me.*
→ see **phrase** for "a group of words with a particular meaning"
→ see **language**

work[1] /wɚk/ *verb*

1 to do a job in order to earn money
- ► work
- ► be employed (*formal*)
- ► practice

2 to use time and effort to achieve something
- ► work
- ► labor (*formal*)
- ► toil (*formal*)

3 to make a machine do what it is supposed to do
- ► work
- ► operate
- ► function

1 to do a job in order to earn money

work
to do a job to earn money: *"Where do you work?" "I* ***work at*** *a museum downtown."* | *My father* ***works for*** *the electric company.*
→ Use **work for** to talk about the company or organization where someone works: *She works for a software company.*

Use **work in** with words like "school," "bank," or "hospital" to talk about the kind of place where someone works: *He works in a restaurant.*

Use **work at** for the specific place where someone works: *She works at the bookstore on Court Street.*

be employed (*formal*)
to work for a company or organization,

especially when you have a permanent job there: *Mr. Hardy has been employed as the school's music teacher since 1995.*

practice
to work as a doctor or lawyer. **Practice** sounds more formal than **work**: *My sister has been practicing law for 16 years.* | *Dr. Cho is applying for a license to practice medicine in California.*
→ see **cooperate** for words meaning "to work with someone else"

2 to use time and effort to achieve something

work
to use time and effort trying to achieve something: *Mom had been working hard in the kitchen all morning.* | *We have been* ***working to*** *get the house ready to sell.*

labor (AWL) (*formal*)
to use a lot of effort doing work that is difficult. **Labor** is especially used about physical work: *Farmers labored all day in the fields.*

toil (*formal*)
to use a lot of effort for a long time to do work that is difficult and tiring. **Toil** is especially used about physical work: *Workers spent long days toiling in the coal mines.*

3 to make a machine do what it is supposed to do

work
to make a machine or piece of equipment do what it is supposed to do: *Does anyone here know how to work this microwave?* | *The delete key on my computer doesn't work.*

operate
operate means the same as **work** but is more formal: *Clive was experienced in operating the computers.* | *Make sure the equipment is operating safely.*

function (AWL)
to work in the correct or intended way – used about a machine or system: *The alarm system was not functioning when the paintings were stolen.*
→ see **work out** at **practice**[2]
→ see **work out** at **exercise**[2]

work[2] /wɚk/ *noun*

1 activity that is done in order to achieve something
- ► work
- ► effort
- ► labor

2 work that you do for your job
- ► work
- ► housework
- ► duties (*formal*)
- ► workload
- ► service

3 work that you do for school
- ► work
- ► homework
- ► classwork
- ► assignment
- ► project
- ► report
- ► essay
- ► paper

1 activity that is done in order to achieve something

work
activity that involves using physical or mental energy in order to achieve something: *Organizing the party was a lot of work.* | *It was hard work climbing up the mountain!*

effort
the physical or mental energy that you use to do something: *She put a lot of effort into the project and we were all really impressed.*

labor (AWL)
hard work that you do using your body and hands: *They spent long hours in the fields doing hard physical labor.*
→ see **effort**

2 work that you do for your job

work
the things that you do or produce at home or in your job: *She has a busy job and she often takes work home with her.* | *The house needs a lot of work before it is ready to move into.*

housework
the work that you do to keep a house clean, such as cleaning, washing clothes, etc.: *I hate housework, especially dusting.*
→ **GRAMMAR: Housework** cannot be used in the plural. Don't say: *~~I don't like doing houseworks~~*.

duties (*formal*)
the things that you have to do as part of your job: *The police officer's duties include patrolling and investigating crime.*

W

workload
the amount of work that you must do: *Teachers have a heavy workload, because they teach during the day and prepare and grade papers in the evenings.*

service
a particular type of help or work that is provided by a business to customers, but not one that involves producing goods: *The company provides a delivery service to over 160 countries.*
→ see **duty**, **job**, Topic **Jobs and Work**

3 work that you do for school

work
the things that you do or produce for school: *The teacher wrote some comments on his work.*

homework
work for school that students do at home: *I have a lot of homework tonight – math problems, an essay for English, and some Spanish.*
→ GRAMMAR: **Homework** cannot be used in the plural. Don't say: ~~*I don't like doing homeworks*~~.

classwork
the work that students do during classes: *The teacher corrected tests while the students did their classwork.*

assignment (AWL)
a piece of work that a teacher has told you to do: *Please hand in your history assignment before Wednesday.*

project (AWL)
a piece of work for a class in school that involves careful study and gathering of information on a particular subject over a period of time: *Our class is doing a **project on** the effects of pollution.* | *I'm going to Katia's house to work on our science project.*

report
a piece of writing telling about something you have learned: *We each had to read a different book and write a book report for class.*

essay
a piece of writing about a particular subject, that involves writing about people or events that are real: *The teacher told us to write a two-page **essay on** our favorite musician.*

paper
a long piece of writing about something you have studied: *I have to write two research papers this semester.*
→ see **research**[1], Topic **Education**

worker /ˈwɚkɚ/ *noun*

- ► worker
- ► employee
- ► colleague
- ► co-worker
- ► staff
- ► staff member
- ► workforce
- ► personnel
- ► laborer

ANTONYMS → see **boss**

worker
someone who does a job, but who is not a manager: *Factory workers at the auto manufacturer get paid around $25 an hour.* | *We need better communication between the management and the workers.*

employee
someone who is paid to work at a job with a person, company, or organization. **Employee** is more formal than **worker**: *Marcia has been an **employee at** the bank for ten years.* | *Government employees usually receive good wages and benefits.*

colleague (AWL)
someone who works with you in the same office or organization. **Colleague** is used especially by people who work in jobs that need special training, such as teachers, doctors, or lawyers: *The research was carried out by Dr. Francis and her colleagues at Johns Hopkins University in Baltimore.*

co-worker
someone who works with you. You use **co-worker** especially when someone works closely with you and does a similar job: *I went out to dinner with two of my co-workers from the office.*

staff
all the people who work for an organization. You usually use **staff** about people who work in offices, not about people who do physical work: *Our library staff will be able to help you find the book you want.* | *The school has a **staff of** around 20 people.*
→ GRAMMAR: **Staff** can be followed by a singular verb or a plural verb: *The staff is/are helpful.*

Staff can be used before other nouns to talk about activities for people who work for an organization: *We have a staff meeting every Friday morning.*

staff member
one of the people who work for a company or

organization. You use **staff member** especially about someone who works in offices, not about people who do physical work: *Two of the congressman's staff members went to the meeting.*

workforce
all the people who work in a country, industry, or large organization: *Women make up about 40% of the workforce in this country.*

personnel
the people who work in a company, organization, or military force. **Personnel** is used especially in official documents or statements: *All personnel must attend the meeting.*

laborer
someone whose work needs physical strength: *His father was working as a farm laborer, picking fruit.*
→ see Topic **Jobs and Work**

workplace *noun* → see **office**

world /wɚld/ *noun*

- ► the world
- ► earth
- ► the planet
- ► the globe

the world
the planet that we live on, and its countries, people, mountains, oceans, etc.: *Athletes from **all over the world** compete in the Olympics. | What is the tallest building **in the world**?*

earth *also* **Earth, the Earth**
the name of the planet that we live on: *The Earth revolves around the Sun. | In the story, Hercules is the strongest man **on earth**.*
→ **GRAMMAR:** You write **Earth** when you are thinking about it as a planet in space. You write **earth** when you are thinking about it as the planet that we live on.

the planet
the large round object in space that we live on. You use **the planet** when you are talking about problems that affect the environment: *Global warming affects **the whole planet**.*
→ A **planet** is a large round object that moves around a star. The Earth is one of eight planets that go around the Sun.

the globe (AWL)
the planet that we live on. You use **the globe** when you are thinking about how big the world is, the fact that it is round, and how far apart things are on it: *Water covers over half of **the globe**. | People **around the globe** watched the Olympic Games.*

SYNONYM CHECK
World or Earth?

Use **world** when you are thinking of the world as a place where there are people and countries: *In some parts of the world, people do not have enough food.*

Use **Earth** when you are thinking about the Earth as compared to things in space or to other planets: *The space shuttle returned to Earth safely.* You also use **Earth** when you are talking about scientific subjects such as geology: *Earthquakes happen when parts of the Earth's surface move.*

GRAMMAR CHECK: world

You say the biggest, smallest, best, etc. **in the world**, but you say the biggest, smallest, best, etc. **on earth**: *It is the highest mountain **in the world**. | It is the highest mountain **on earth**.*

worn *adjective* → see **condition** (**3**), Topic **Describing the Condition of Something**

worried /ˈwɚid/ *adjective*

- ► worried
- ► anxious
- ► concerned
- ► preoccupied
- ► frantic

worried
unhappy or frightened because you think something bad might happen: *Her parents are **worried about** how she is doing in school. | "Are you feeling sick?" she said, giving him a worried look.*

anxious
very worried that something bad might happen **Anxious** is more formal than **worried**: *A lot of workers are **anxious about** their jobs.*

concerned
worried, usually about a problem that affects other people. **Concerned** is more formal than **worried** and you often use it in writing: *Police say they are **concerned for** the safety of the missing girl.*

preoccupied
worrying so much about a particular problem that you cannot think about anything else: *Alan seems preoccupied – do you know what is bothering him?*

frantic
extremely worried and frightened about a situation and unable to think or behave calmly:

There is still no news of the missing child, and her parents are becoming frantic.
→ see **nervous**, Topic **Describing People's Emotions**

ADVERBS

You can make the adjectives **anxious** and **frantic** into adverbs by using an **-ly** ending: *The workers waited anxiously for news.* | *The child's parents frantically searched the park for her.*

worry¹ /ˈwɚi/ *verb*

1 to feel worried about something
► worry
► fret
► panic
2 to make someone feel worried
► worry
► trouble
► bother

1 to feel worried about something

worry
to keep thinking about a problem or about something bad that might happen so that you cannot relax or feel happy: *He began to* ***worry that*** *he might lose his job.* | *My parents were always* ***worrying about*** *money.*

fret
to worry about something a lot. You use **fret** especially when you think someone is worrying about something that is not very important: *Don't* ***fret about*** *the kids – they will be fine with the babysitter.*

panic
to feel very worried or frightened about a situation so that you are not able to think clearly or behave sensibly. People often run or shout when they **panic**: *Ben started to panic when he realized the test was in an hour and he hadn't studied.* | *Some people panicked when the earthquake hit.*

2 to make someone feel worried

worry
to make someone feel worried: *It worries me that she gets out of breath just walking up the stairs.* | *I didn't tell my parents about the accident because I didn't want to worry them.*

trouble
if a problem troubles you, it makes you feel worried because you do not know what to do about it. **Trouble** is a little more formal than **worry**: *Find out if anything is troubling him. For example, has something happened at school?*

bother
if something bothers you, it worries you a little bit. **Bother** is used especially about problems that do not seem serious: *It bothers me when my boyfriend talks to other girls.*

worry² /ˈwɚi/ *noun*

1 the feeling of being worried
► worry
► anxiety (*formal*)
► stress
► strain
► concern
2 something that makes you feel worried
► worry
► concern
► care

1 the feeling of being worried

worry
the feeling of being upset and frightened about something because you think something bad might happen: *When he didn't come home that night, we were sick with worry.* | *He lost his job, so there was constant* ***worry about*** *money.*

anxiety (*formal*)
the feeling of being very worried because you think something bad might happen: *Some children suffer from anxiety before they start at a new school.*

stress (AWL)
the feeling of being worried all the time, usually caused by problems at work or personal problems: *The huge amount of homework has been causing Andrea a lot of stress.* | *Felipe has been* ***under*** *a lot of* ***stress*** *lately because he can't find a job.*

strain
stress that continues for a long time, often causing mental or physical problems: ***The strain of*** *working seven days a week finally caused Ricky to get very sick.*

concern
a feeling of worry about something. You use **concern** especially when many people are worried about a problem that affects everyone. **Concern** sounds more formal than **worry** and is often used in writing: *There is some* ***concern about*** *the safety of the old bridge.*

2 something that makes you feel worried

worry
something that makes you feel worried: *Her*

W

biggest worry is that the children will get hurt. | *Money is a **worry for** most people.*

concern
something that makes you feel worried, especially a problem that affects a lot of people. **Concern** sounds more formal than **worry** and is often used in writing: *The destruction of the rainforest is a **concern to** us all.*

care
something that causes problems and makes you worried or sad. **Care** is more literary than **worry**: *They went on vacation and left their cares behind* (=did not think about their worries).
→ **GRAMMAR: Care** is usually used in the plural. You only use **a care** in the phrase **not have a care in the world**.
→ see **pressure (2)**, **problem**

worse /wɚs/ *adjective*

1 not as good as before, or of a lower standard, quality, or level than something else (adjectives)
- ► **worse**
- ► **not as good**
- ► **worst**
- ► **inferior** (*formal*)

ANTONYMS → see **better**

2 to become more unpleasant, bad, or severe (verbs)
- ► **get worse**
- ► **worsen**
- ► **deteriorate** (*formal*)
- ► **decline** (*formal*)

ANTONYMS → see **improve (1)**

3 to become more sick (verbs)
- ► **get worse**
- ► **worsen**
- ► **deteriorate** (*formal*)
- ► **relapse**
- ► **aggravate** (*formal*)

ANTONYMS → see **better (2)** for "to get better"

1 not as good as before, or of a lower standard, quality, or level than something else (adjectives)

worse
more unpleasant or severe: *The traffic is much worse after five o'clock.* | *Conditions in the prison were **worse than** anything I had seen before.*
→ **Worse** is used when you are comparing two things that are both bad: *The food was awful, and the service was even worse.*

not as good
of a lower standard, quality, or level than something else: *I like this town better than Harrisburg, but the schools aren't as good.* | *The food at the restaurant is **not as good as** it used to be.*

worst
worse than all the others, or worse than at any other time: *That's **the worst** movie I've ever seen.*

inferior (*formal*)
not as good as something else: *His later novels are **inferior to** his earlier books.*

2 to become more unpleasant, bad, or severe (verbs)

get worse *also* **become worse**
become more unpleasant, bad, or severe: *The roads became worse as the snow continued to fall.* | *The problems got worse and worse because we had no money to fix them.*

worsen
worsen means the same as **get worse** but sounds more formal: *The fires in the mountains worsened yesterday morning, and more firefighters came to help.*

deteriorate (*formal*)
to gradually become worse. **Deteriorate** is used especially about the condition of something: *The building has deteriorated to the point where it is just not safe anymore.*

decline (AWL) (*formal*)
to gradually become worse. **Decline** is used especially about the quality or standard of something: *Do you think standards of education are declining?*

3 to become more sick (verbs)

get worse *also* **become worse**
if someone's health gets worse, he or she becomes more sick than before. You can use **get worse** to talk about a person or about the condition or illness the person has: *The doctors told us his infection was getting worse.* | *The flu became worse and worse, and finally I had to go to the hospital.* | *Claudia says she is better, but she looks like she is getting worse to me.*

worsen
worsen means the same as **get worse** but is more formal: *As my grandmother's condition worsened, we all gathered at the house to sit with her.*

deteriorate (*formal*)
to gradually become worse: *George's health was deteriorating, so we moved him to a nursing home.*

relapse
to become sick again with the same illness after being healthy. You only use **relapse** to talk about

a person, not his or her illness: *Only two of the women relapsed and died after having surgery.*

aggravate (*formal*)
to make an illness, pain, or injury worse: *Is the pain aggravated by coughing or laughing?*

worsen *verb* → see **worse (3)**

worship¹ *verb* → see **pray**

worship² *noun* → see **prayer**

worst *adjective* → see **worse**

wound¹ *noun* → see **cut²**, **injury**

wound² *verb* → see **hurt**

wrap *verb* → see **cover¹**

wrinkle *noun* → see **fold²**, **line¹**

write /raɪt/ *verb*

1 to put letters or words on paper
- write
- print
- write down
- make a note of
- take down
- fill out
- fill in
- sign
- scribble
- put something in writing

2 to write someone a letter, email, or message
- write
- contact
- email
- correspond (*formal*)
- get in touch (*informal*)
- keep in touch

3 to write a story, essay, list, etc.
- write
- draft
- compose (*formal*)

1 to put letters or words on paper

write
to put letters or words on paper, using a pen or pencil: *Write your name and address on the top of the paper.* | *You learn to read and write during your first years at school.*

print
to write words without joining the letters together: *Please print your name in capital letters in the first box on the form.*

write down *also* **jot down**
to write information on a piece of paper so that you have a record of it and can use it later. **Jot down** is more informal than **write down**, and seems quicker: *Here, I've written the address down for you.* | *I jotted down a few ideas for my story while I was on the bus.*

make a note of
to write a few words or a piece of information down in order to remember it or use it later: *Let me **make a note of** those prices, and I'll call you back.*

take down *also* **get down**
to write information down at the same time as you hear or see it. **Get down** is more informal than **take down**: *I took down the license plate number as the car drove away.*

fill out
to write all the information that is needed in the spaces on an official document: *Please fill out the application form using a pen.*

fill in
to put information in the spaces on an official document or test: *Fill in the blanks with the correct answer.*

sign
to write your name on an official document or letter to show that you wrote it or approve it: *Don't forget to sign and date the check.* | *She signed the letter, "Love, Marcia."*

scribble
to write something quickly in a messy way: *Carla scribbled a few words on a piece of paper and passed it to me.*

put something in writing
to make something legal or official by writing it down and usually signing it: *Make sure the company puts its promises in writing.*

2 to write someone a letter, email, or message

write
to write a letter, email, or message: *I'm sorry I haven't written in so long.* | *Wendy is **writing** a letter **to** the company to complain.*

contact (AWL)
to write a letter or email to someone, or to call someone on the telephone: *We have been trying to contact Mr. Wright by email.*

email
to send a message to someone's computer using email: *I emailed Mrs. Compton to say thank you.*

correspond (AWL) (*formal*)
if two people correspond, they write letters or emails to each other: *The two scientists*

W

corresponded for several years after meeting in London.

get in touch (*informal*)
to call or write after a period of time when you have not talked or written to someone: *My best friend from high school* ***got in touch with*** *me again after ten years.*

keep in touch *also* **stay in touch**
to continue to write to or call someone regularly, especially a friend: *The men have stayed in touch, even after leaving college.*

3 to write a story, essay, list, etc.

write
to write a story, essay, list, report, etc.: *For homework, I want you to write a report on volcanoes or earthquakes.*
→ You can also use **write** about songs and music: *The song was written by Bob Dylan.*

draft (AWL)
to write something that you plan to make changes to later, until it is the way you want it: *He drafted an article for the newspaper about traveling in Spain.*

compose (*formal*)
to write something and choose the words you use carefully, especially when writing a speech or letter: *It took him hours to compose the letter to his father.*
→ You can also use **compose** about songs and music: *He composed five symphonies.*
→ see **describe**, **rewrite**

writer /ˈraɪtɚ/ *noun*

- writer
- author
- novelist
- playwright
- poet
- reporter
- journalist

writer
someone whose job is to write books, stories, or articles: *When I was young, I wanted to be a writer or a poet.* | *The class is reading the works of some young short story writers.*

author (AWL)
someone who writes books or short stories. You use **author** especially about someone whose books are well respected and are considered to be literature, or someone who wrote a particular book: *The* ***author of*** *the book was signing copies in the bookstore.*

novelist
someone who writes novels (=books that tell stories rather than give facts): *She is a successful novelist whose latest book won a children's fiction prize.*

playwright
someone who writes plays: *The playwright came onto the stage after the performance.*

poet
someone who writes poems: *Emily Dickinson is one of the most famous American poets.*

reporter
someone who writes reports for newspapers, magazines, television, or radio: *She is a* ***reporter for*** *the "Daily News."*

journalist
journalist means the same as **reporter** but sounds more formal: *The journalist interviewed several farm workers for his story.*
→ see Topic **Books and Literature**

writing /ˈraɪtɪŋ/ *noun*

- writing
- handwriting
- text
- inscription

writing
words or letters that are written by hand or printed: *His writing was too messy to read.* | *The writing at the bottom of the label was very small.*

handwriting
the way someone writes with a pen or pencil: *His handwriting is very neat and easy to read.*

text (AWL)
the written part of a book, newspaper, magazine, or document, not including pictures: *In a children's book, the print is large so that the text is easy to read.*

inscription
words that are cut into stone, metal, or wood: *The inscription on the gravestone read "Rest In Peace."*

W

written /ˈrɪtn/ *adjective*

- written
- in writing
- on paper
- handwritten

written
if something is written, someone has put the words on paper, on a computer, etc.: *The company's president gave out a written statement explaining the reasons for her decision.* | *Before the 1820s the Cherokee Indians did not have a written*

language, but Chief Sequoyah created a way for the Cherokees to write down their words.

in writing
a promise or agreement that is in writing has been written down in a way that is legal or official: *I know they told you the price, but make sure you get it in writing.*

on paper
if you put ideas or information on paper, you write them down so that there is a record of them: *The secretary takes notes so that everything that happens at the meeting is on paper.*

handwritten
written with a pen or pencil, not printed or written on a computer: *Maria sent me a handwritten note to thank me.*

→ see **spoken**

wrong /rɔŋ/ *adjective*

- wrong
- incorrect (*formal*)
- inaccurate
- untrue
- mistaken
- misleading

ANTONYMS → see **right[1] (1)**

wrong
not correct: *I think he is from Morocco, but I may be wrong.* | *She got the wrong answer on question 2 on the test.*

incorrect (*formal*)
incorrect means the same as **wrong** but is more formal: *There were several incorrect spellings in the paper.*

inaccurate (AWL)
inaccurate information, numbers, or statements are not exactly right: *The information in the article was inaccurate. The company is twenty-five years old, not five, and does not have financial problems.*

untrue
not true. **Untrue** is more formal than **wrong**: *The rumors about the school closing were later shown to be untrue.*

mistaken
someone who is mistaken has made a mistake and said something that is wrong. People often say that someone is **mistaken** as a polite way of saying that he or she is wrong: *She says it happened last May, but I think she is mistaken. I'm sure it was June.*

misleading
a misleading statement or piece of information is likely to make someone believe something that is not true: *The advertisements are misleading because they make you think the drink is healthy when it's not.*

→ see **bad**, **evil[1]**

ADVERBS

You can make the adjectives **wrong**, **incorrect**, **inaccurate**, and **mistaken** into adverbs by using an **-ly** ending: *He wrongly believed that Salim was from Morocco; Salim is from Egypt.* | *A lot of the words were spelled incorrectly.* | *She mistakenly thought the wedding was in May, when it was in June.*

W

Yy

yard /yɑrd/ *noun*

- yard
- courtyard
- grounds

yard *also* **backyard**
the land around a house, which is usually covered with grass: *The dog was **in the yard**. | The kids are playing in the backyard.*

courtyard
an open area with walls around it, either within a building or surrounded by buildings: *The apartment building has a courtyard in the center with a pool.*

grounds
the land or gardens that surround a large building: *There is a concert today **on the grounds of** the library. | Students are not allowed to leave the school grounds during lunch.*

yeah *adverb* → see **yes**

yearly /ˈyɪrli/ *adjective, adverb*

- yearly
- annual

yearly
happening every year: *Sara is going to the doctor for her yearly flu shot. | About 195 million barrels of beer are produced yearly in the U.S.*

annual (AWL)
happening once a year, especially at about the same time each year: *The school is having its annual Fourth of July picnic this weekend.*
→ see **regular**

ADVERBS

You can make the adjective **annual** into an adverb by using an **-ly** ending: *The picnic happens annually, each July.* **Yearly** looks like an adverb, but it is an adjective.

yell[1] *verb* → see **shout[1]**

yell[2] *noun* → see **shout[2]**

yes /yes/ *adverb*

- yes
- yeah (*informal*)

ANTONYMS → see **no**

yes
used to answer a question when something is true, or when you want something or agree to something: *"Are you from Costa Rica?" "Yes, I am." | "Do you want some lemonade?" "Yes, please." | Yes, you can go to the party.*

yeah (*informal*)
yes: *"Are you hungry?" "Yeah, I'm starving!"*

young[1] /yʌŋ/ *adjective*

- young
- little
- teenage
- adolescent
- youthful
- juvenile

ANTONYMS → see **old** (**1**)

young
a young person or animal has only lived for a short time: *When she was young, she lived in Costa Rica. | The young bears played together by the river.*

little
a little girl or boy is very young, but older than a baby: *She babysits for a little boy who is three years old. | When I was little, I was very shy.*

teenage
between the ages of 13 and 19: *The band is a big hit with teenage boys.*
→ **GRAMMAR: Teenage** is always used before a noun. Don't say: ~~*He is teenage*~~. Say: *He is a teenager* or *He is in his teens.*

adolescent
relating to or typical of a young person between 12 and 18, when his or her body is changing to become more adult. You use **adolescent** especially when you are talking about a young person's body or behavior: *Adolescent girls are often shy about the changes taking place in their bodies.*

youthful
looking or behaving in a way that is typical of a much younger person: *At 50, he still has plenty of youthful energy.*

juvenile
relating to children who are not old enough to be legally considered adults. **Juvenile** is used

especially in legal language about crime: *The program is supposed to reduce juvenile crime.*
→ You can also use **juvenile** in scientific writing to describe young animals: *The juvenile monkeys hold onto their mothers' backs.*
→ see Topic **Describing People's Looks**

ADVERBS
You can make the adjective **youthful** into an adverb by using an **-ly** ending: *He was 38 years old, with a youthfully attractive face and dark hair.*

young² *noun* → see **child**, **young person** at **teenager**

youth *noun* → see **childhood**, **man**, **teenager**

zip *verb* → see **fasten**

Z

Topic Vocabulary

Function Words

BOOKS AND LITERATURE

1 Fiction

fiction *noun*
books and stories about people and events that are not real: *I mostly read fiction.* | *She writes historical fiction for adults and children.*

literature *noun*
books, plays, and poems, especially famous ones that people think are important: *She studied Latin American literature in college.*

novel *noun*
a book about people and events that are not real: *The novel "The Bluest Eye" was written by Toni Morrison.*

story *noun*
a description of an event that is intended to entertain people: *I'm reading a* ***story about*** *a man who loses his memory.* | *The children like their mother to tell them a story before bed.*

short story *noun*
a short piece of writing in which the writer tells a story: *The writer Flannery O'Connor is famous for her short stories.*

classic (AWL) *noun*
a book or play that is considered to be very good and has been admired for a long time: *"Anna Karenina" is a classic of Russian literature.*

tale *noun*
a story about exciting events or people that are not real: *The* ***tales of*** *Poe are really scary.* | *The novel is a* ***tale of*** *mystery and romance.*

science fiction *noun*
stories about things that happen in the future or in other parts of the universe: *The novel is science fiction and set on another planet, but its themes of love and loss are universal.*

mystery *noun*
a story in which someone tries to find who is responsible for a crime, especially a murder: *Connelly writes mysteries about a police detective.*

fantasy *noun*
stories that are based on imagination, and not on things that can really happen: *If you like fantasy, I think you will enjoy the Harry Potter books about a boy who finds out he is a wizard.*

romance *noun*
a story about people who fall in love: *"Twilight" is a romance novel about a girl and a vampire who fall in love.*

fable *noun*
a story, especially one about animals, that teaches us a lesson about life: *In the fable, the tortoise wins the race because he keeps going and doesn't give up.*

myth *noun*
an old story about gods, brave men, strange creatures, or events at the beginning of the world: *The myth tells us how the gods sent fire to the earth in flashes of lightning.*

fairy tale *noun*
a traditional children's story in which magical things happen: *When I was a little girl, my favorite fairy tale was "Snow White."*

folktale *noun*
a traditional story from a particular area or country: *The teacher was reading from a collection of Chinese folktales.*

tall tale *noun*
a folktale in which someone is described as better or bigger or stronger than he or she really was: *In the tall tales about Paul Bunyan, he is as big as his father by the time he is a year old.*

prose *noun*
written language in its usual form, not as poetry: *He is the author of several books of prose and poetry.*

2 Nonfiction

nonfiction *noun*
books about real events, people, or places: *The books in the library are divided into fiction and nonfiction.*

biography *noun*
a book about a real person's life, written by another person: *She has written a very interesting* ***biography of*** *Martin Luther King.*

autobiography *noun*
a book in which someone writes about his or her own life: ***In her autobiography, the movie star writes that she was shy as a child.***

textbook *noun*
a book about a subject which students use: ***The homework assignment is to read Chapter 3 in the science textbook.***

reference book *noun*
a book that you read in order to get information, especially a dictionary or encyclopedia: ***Carlos was looking for photos and facts about elephants in the reference books.***

dictionary *noun*
a book that shows words in alphabetical order and explains what they mean: ***I looked up the word "mansion" in my dictionary and found out it means "a large house."***

encyclopedia *noun*
a book, or set of books, that has a lot of facts about many different subjects, usually arranged in alphabetical order: ***I looked up "opera" in the "Encyclopedia of Music."***

atlas *noun*
a book of maps: ***We looked at a road atlas and planned our route from New York to Georgia.***

3 Poetry

poem *noun*
a piece of writing that usually has short lines, often using words that end with the same sound: ***The students had to write a poem about rain.***

poetry *noun*
poems in general: ***The book has a selection of Latin American poetry by different writers.***

verse *noun*
words arranged in the form of poetry. **Verse** does not usually deal with important ideas or emotions, like **poetry** does: ***The verse written by Ogden Nash was often funny.***

4 Plays

play *noun*
a story that actors perform in a theater: ***Arthur Miller's play "Death of a Salesman" was first performed in 1949.***

drama (AWL) *noun*
plays in general: ***Japanese drama traditionally includes music, dance, and acting.***

5 The People Who Write Books, Plays, and Poems

writer *noun*
someone whose job is to write books, stories, or articles: ***The class will cover works by American writers.***

author (AWL) *noun*
someone who writes books: ***Maurice Sendak is the author of several books for children.***

novelist *noun*
someone who writes novels: ***The novelist is from Baltimore, and most of her stories take place there.***

poet *noun*
someone who writes poems: ***What does the poet mean when he says, "I took the road less traveled by?"***

playwright *noun*
someone who writes plays: ***Ben Jonson was a 17th-century playwright.***

6 What Happens in a Story

story *noun*
the things that happen in a novel, play, etc.: ***Her novels always seem to have the same story – boy meets girl, they argue, make up, and get married.***

plot *noun*
the events that happen in a novel, short story, etc., and the way in which these events are connected: ***The plot was very complicated, and I kept getting confused about what had happened.***

action *noun (informal)*
the events that happen and the things the characters do in a story or play: ***Most of the action in the play takes place on a ship.***

narrative *noun (formal)*
the description of the series of events that happen in a novel, play, etc.: ***The narrative moves back and forth between the past and present.***

conflict (AWL) *noun*
an issue or problem in a novel, play, etc., which the story is about: ***The conflict of the story focuses on the family's struggle to survive a flood.***

climax *noun*
the most exciting or important part of a story, which usually comes near the end: ***The climax occurs when the hero discovers the buried treasure.***

ending *noun*
the things that happen at the end of a book: ***Does the book have a happy ending?***

resolution (AWL) *noun (formal)*
the part of a story after the climax, when the conflict is solved: ***In the novel's resolution, the prisoners escape to freedom.***

7 The People in a Book

character *noun*
a person in a novel, play, etc.: ***The main character***

***of** the book is a 16-year-old girl.* | *Each chapter of the book is narrated by a different character.*

hero *noun*
the man or boy who is the most important character in a story. A **hero** usually has good qualities that you admire: ***The hero of the story is strong and brave, and he defeats the enemy.***

heroine *noun*
the woman or girl who is the main character in a story. A **heroine** usually has good qualities that you admire: *The author has based the **heroine of** the novel on herself.*

narrator *noun*
the person in a novel, play, etc. who explains what happens during the story: *The **narrator of** the novel is also the main character, so you see the story from her point of view.*

protagonist *noun (formal)*
the most important character in a novel, play, etc.: *Jay Gatsby is the **protagonist of** Fitzgerald's novel "The Great Gatsby."*

antagonist *noun (formal)*
the opponent of the main character in a novel, play, etc.: *The main character is a 12-year-old boy, and his antagonist is a bully.*

8 What People Say in a Book or Play

dialogue *also* **dialog** *noun*
conversation in a movie, television program, novel, or play: *The author uses dialogue to show us what the relationship between the characters is really like.*

monologue *noun*
a long speech by one person in a play: *Shakespeare's plays have many famous monologues.*

9 Where a Book or Play Takes Place

setting *noun*
the place or time where the events in a novel, play, etc. happen: *A castle in Romania is the **setting for** part of the novel "Dracula."*

be set in *verb phrase*
if a book is set in a place or period of time, the story happens in that place or during that time: *Most of her short stories are set in small towns in Canada.*

10 The Ideas or Subject of a Book

be about *verb phrase*
if a book is about someone or something, that person or thing is the main subject of the book: *What do you think the poem is about?* | *The novel is about the importance of love and family.*

be based on *verb phrase*
if a book or story is based on an event, the things that happen in the book are very similar to the things that really happened in the event: *The novel is based on a true story.*

theme (AWL) *noun*
one of the main ideas that an author writes about in a book: *The **theme of** jealousy appears in many of his stories.*

11 The Parts of a Book

contents *noun*
the list at the beginning of a book that tells you the name of each part of the book: *The table of contents helps a reader know how a book is organized.*

chapter (AWL) *noun*
one of many separate parts that a book is divided into: *I have only read the first chapter, but I already know that I am going to like the novel.*

index (AWL) *noun*
a list of names and subjects at the back of a book, with the numbers of the pages where they can be found. In an **index**, the names and subjects are in alphabetical order: *Look under "F" in the index to see which page the map of Florida is on.*

foreword *also* **introduction** *noun*
a short piece of writing at the beginning of a book that introduces the book or its writer: *An English literature professor wrote the **foreword to** the new edition of the novel.* | ***In the introduction**, the author explains what her purpose was in writing the book.*

bibliography *noun*
a list of all the books and articles that a writer used when he or she wrote something: *The bibliography should show all the books that a writer used for research.*

12 The Parts of a Poem

verse *noun*
a set of lines that forms one part of a poem or song, and that usually has a pattern that is repeated in other parts: *The poem actually has four verses, but I only know the first two.*

stanza *noun*
stanza means the same as **verse**: *Each stanza in the poem has three lines, and the first and the third lines rhyme.*

couplet *noun*
two lines of poetry that follow each other and are the same length, and that usually rhyme: *He recited a couplet from a poem his father had taught him.*

13 The Parts of a Play

act *noun*
one of the main parts that a long play is divided into. An **act** is usually divided into several scenes: *In Act 1, Macbeth decides to kill the king.*

scene *noun*
a short part of a play in which the events all happen in one place: *The main character of the play first appears in Act 1, Scene 2.*

14 Words Used for Writing about Poetry or Literature

genre *noun*
a type of literature: *Within the category of "fiction" there are many different genres, such as mystery and fantasy.*

style (AWL) *noun*
a way in which a writer uses words in order to express ideas or tell a story: *The writer has her own very distinctive style.*

characterization *noun*
the way in which a writer makes a person in a novel, play, etc. seem like a real person: *His books have humor, good characterization, and lively dialogue.*

first/second/third person *adjective phrase*
writing that is in the **first person** uses "I," "me," and "we." Writing that is in the **second person** uses "you." Writing in the **third person** uses "he," "she," "it," and "they": *She writes her poems in the first person and describes her own feelings in a very direct way.*

symbol (AWL) *noun*
someone or something that represents a particular quality or idea: *In the story, the snake is a symbol of evil.*

imagery (AWL) *noun*
the use of words to describe things in a way that makes you see pictures in your mind when you read or listen to the words: *Water imagery is used throughout the poem.*

metaphor *noun*
a way of describing someone or something by comparing it to something else, which suggests that the two things are similar in some way. **Metaphors** do not use the words "like" or "as": *The writer uses winter metaphors to describe the character, saying that "her heart is ice."*

simile *noun*
an expression that describes something by comparing it with something else, using the words "as" or "like": *When he says "time is like a river," he is using a simile.*

figurative *noun*
a figurative word or phrase is used in a different way from its usual meaning, to give you a particular idea or picture in your mind: *In the phrase "a mountain of papers," "mountain" is used in a figurative way and means "a large amount."*

personification *noun*
a way of describing something so that it seems like a person or has qualities that people have: *The poet uses personification when he writes that "the flowers sing."*

rhyme *noun*
the use of words or lines of poetry that end with the same sound: *Rhyme is an important part of many traditional forms of poetry.*
→ You can also use **rhyme** as a verb: *The words "house" and "mouse" rhyme.*

meter *noun*
the way that the words of a poem are arranged into a pattern of weak and strong beats: *To read the poem properly, you need to know the meter and which syllables should be stressed.*

alliteration *noun*
the use of several words together that all begin with the same sound, especially in poetry: *The poet uses alliteration in the line "wet and windy weather."*

assonance *noun*
similarity in the vowel sounds of words that are close together in a poem: *There is assonance at the ends of lines in the poem, as in the words "warm" and "born."*

onomatopoeia *noun*
the use of words that sound like the thing that they are describing: *The poem uses onomatopoeia like "Crash, bang!" to show that doors are being closed angrily.*

oxymoron *noun*
a combination of two words that seem to mean the opposite of each other: *The phrase "deafening silence" is an oxymoron.*

irony *noun*
the use of words that are the opposite of what you really mean, in order to be amusing or show that you are annoyed: *There is irony in the name of the ship, "Rose Bud," because the ship smells of dead fish.*

hyperbole *noun*
a way of describing something by saying that it is much bigger, smaller, worse, etc. than it really is: *It is hyperbole to say that the bag weights a ton – it is heavy, but it does not weigh a ton.*

cliché *noun*
an idea or phrase that has been used so much that it is not effective, or does not have any meaning any longer: *The teacher told us to avoid using clichés like "no pain, no gain" in our writing.*

COMPUTERS AND THE INTERNET

1 Types of Computer

computer (AWL) *noun*
an electronic machine that stores information and uses programs to help you find, organize, or change the information: *He was playing a game on the computer.*

PC *noun*
a computer that is used by one person at home or at work, with a separate screen and keyboard: *Her PC is old, and it is really slow.*
→ **PC** stands for "personal computer."

laptop *noun*
a small computer that you can carry, with a screen and a keyboard that are not separate: *Some of the students bring laptops to class.*

notebook *noun*
a small **laptop**: *The notebook is really light and easy to take anywhere.*

tablet *noun*
a small computer that you can carry. A **tablet** has a screen that you write on with a special pen or that you touch with your finger in order to tell the computer what to do: *I use my tablet to look up information on the web.*

2 Computer Equipment

hardware *noun*
computers and all the machinery and equipment connected with them: *Hardware includes all the physical parts of the computer, like the keyboard and the monitor.*

flash drive *also* **memory stick, USB drive** *noun*
a small piece of electronic equipment that stores information and can be fitted into a computer: *You can save your presentation on a flash drive and bring it to class.*

mouse *noun*
a small object which you move with your hand to give instructions to the computer: *Click on the right mouse button.*

keyboard *noun*
a piece of equipment with buttons that have letters or numbers on them, which you press to put information into a computer: *I sat looking at the keyboard, thinking about what I should write.*

screen *also* **monitor** *noun*
the part of a computer where the picture or information appears: *It is a good idea to correct your work* ***on screen*** *before you print it.* | *She was staring at her computer monitor.*

hard drive *noun*
the part of a computer where information and programs are stored: *The hard drive is where the operating system is stored on your computer.*

router *noun*
a piece of electronic equipment that makes sending messages between different computers, or between different networks, easier and faster: *Routers keep data flowing between networks.*

modem *noun*
a piece of electronic equipment that allows information to be sent along telephone wires from one computer to another computer: *A modem plugs the computer in to a phone or cable line.*

printer *noun*
a machine that puts the words or pictures from a computer onto paper: *Make sure the printer is connected to your computer.*

scanner *noun*
a piece of equipment that copies a picture or piece of writing onto a computer: *I used a scanner to transfer drawings into my computer.*

CD-ROM *noun*
a flat round object on which large amounts of information can be stored and used on a computer: *The textbook comes with a CD-ROM, so you can do practice tests on your computer at home.*

DVD *noun*
a flat round object similar to a CD-ROM, but which can store much more information, sound, pictures, and video: *He saved his video project to a DVD.*

memory *noun*
the amount of space that a computer has for keeping information: *How can I find out how much memory is available on my computer?*

3 Software and Programs

software *noun*
a set of programs that tells a computer to do

something: *The children in school were using special software to practice math.*

program *noun*
a set of instructions for a computer that makes it do something: *After I wrote the paragraph, I used a program to check my grammar.*

application *also* **app** *noun*
a piece of computer software that you use online or on a cell phone, tablet, computer, etc.: *I downloaded an app for the game on my phone.*

operating system *noun*
a system in a computer that helps all the programs in it work together: *The operating system usually comes with the computer when you buy it.*

database *noun*
a very large collection of information that is kept on a computer: *Libraries use databases to keep a record of the books that people borrow.*

spreadsheet *noun*
a computer program that lets you organize information into rows and columns, and make calculations: *The business keeps a detailed spreadsheet of all the money that it earns and spends.*

firewall *noun*
a system that protects a computer network from being used or looked at by people who do not have permission to do so: *A firewall can help prevent a virus from infecting your computer.*

4 What Is on the Screen

icon *noun*
a small picture on a computer screen that represents a program that you can use or a job that a program will do: *Click on the icon to start the program.*

window *noun*
one of the separate areas on a computer screen where different programs are operating: *I had one window open with the Internet and another window with the essay I was writing.*

cursor *noun*
a mark that you can move around the computer screen to show where you are working: *You can use the arrow keys to move the cursor up or down.*

document (AWL) *noun*
a piece of written work that is stored on a computer: *Don't forget to save the changes you make to your document.*

file (AWL) *noun*
information on a computer that you store under a particular name: *I closed the file by clicking on the X.*

5 Using a Computer

start up *also* **boot up** *phrasal verb*
if you start up or boot up a computer, you turn it on and it starts working: *I waited while she started up her computer.* | *The computer is old and it needs a little time to boot up.*

password *noun*
a word or group of letters and numbers that you need to use some computer systems or software: *To look at your email account, type in your user name and password.*

log on *phrasal verb*
to do the things that will allow you to start using a computer, such as putting in your name or password: *I **logged on to** the university website and looked up my grades for the semester.*

open *verb*
to make a document or computer program ready to use: *Select your file from the list and open it.*

enter *verb*
to put information into a computer by pressing the keys: *Enter your credit card information on the payment page.*

access (AWL) *verb*
if you access information on a computer, you use the computer to find and show the information: *The new website makes it easier for students to access financial aid information.*

download *verb*
to copy a file from the Internet onto your own computer: *You can **download** music **from** the Internet.*

upload *verb*
to copy something from your computer onto the Internet: *I **uploaded** the video of my dance performance **to** my personal website.*

click *verb*
to press a button on a mouse in order to choose something on the screen and make the computer do something: *Click here for more information.* | ***Click on** the picture if you want to make it larger.*

save *verb*
to make a computer keep the work that you have done in its memory or on a disk: *I saved the document and then printed it.*

cut and paste *verb phrase*
to remove information from one place in a computer program or document and put it in another place: *If you want to move parts of your essay around, you can cut and paste.*

close *verb*
to do the things you need to do when you want to stop using a document or a computer

program: *Close all applications before shutting down your computer.*

log out *also* **log off** *phrasal verb*
to do the things that you need to do when you finish using a computer system: *You should always log out after you have done online banking. | I'll log off, and then you can use this computer.*

shut down *phrasal verb*
if you shut a computer down, you turn it off: *I shut down my computer and went home.*

6 Problems with Computers

crash *verb*
if a computer crashes, it suddenly stops working: *The computer crashed, and I lost a whole afternoon's work.*

freeze *verb*
if a computer screen freezes, the computer will not do anything because of a fault, and everything stays in the same position: *The computer screen froze, so I had to restart the computer.*

virus *noun*
a set of instructions that have been secretly put on a computer, and that can change or destroy the information that is stored there. **Viruses** spread easily from one computer, or computer program, to another: *Be careful opening email attachments – they may have viruses.*

bug *noun*
a small fault with a computer program that stops it from working correctly: *The software has some kind of bug in it, so I can't get it to do what I want.*

worm *noun*
a type of computer virus that can make copies of itself and destroy information on computers that are connected to each other: *Computer worms cause even more problems than normal viruses.*

hack *verb*
to use a computer in order to secretly and illegally enter someone else's computer system: *Somebody* ***hacked into*** *the company's central database.*
→ Someone who hacks into computers is called a **hacker**.

7 The Internet

Internet, the *noun*
a system that allows computer users around the world to send messages and information to each other: *You can find all kinds of information* ***on the Internet***.

Web, the *also* **the web** *noun*
the system on the Internet that allows you to find and use information that is held on computers all over the world: *When you need to do research, the Web is a great resource. | I usually read the news* ***on the web***.

online *adjective, adverb*
connected to other computers through the Internet, or available through the Internet: *I'll just* ***go online*** *and look up her address.*

broadband *noun*
a system of connecting computers to the Internet and moving information, such as messages, at a very high speed: *Most Americans in cities can get broadband, but some people in farming areas cannot.*

search engine *noun*
a computer program that helps you find information on the Internet: *A search engine works by matching the words you type into the search to websites containing those words.*

browser *noun*
software that allows your computer to find and show web pages: *Which browser do you use?*

website *also* **site** *noun (informal)*
a place on the Internet that gives you information about a particular company, organization, or person: *For more information, visit our website. | The company's new site is really cool.*

web page *also* **page** *noun (informal)*
one of the areas that you can go to on a website: *The company website has web pages for each department.*

homepage *noun*
the first place you go to on a website: *You can reach all the other pages on a website from its homepage.*

social networking site *noun*
a website where people can put pictures of themselves, send messages to their friends, etc.: *Teenagers and young people can spend a lot of time on social networking sites.*

blog *noun*
a web page that has information about someone's activities and opinions: *She writes a blog about her life as a small town farmer.*

link *noun*
a word or picture on a website or computer document that will take you to another page or document if you click on it: *Click on a link to explore other related websites.*

8 Using the Internet

browse *verb*
to search for information on the Internet: *I found*

an interesting article while I was browsing the web.

post *verb*
to put a message or piece of writing on a website or blog: ***She has posted the recipe on her blog.***

bookmark *verb*
to put a website in your list of favorite websites so that you can find it again easily: ***I found the math website really helpful, so I bookmarked it.***

9 Email

email *noun*
a written message that is sent from one computer to another: ***I sent him an email two weeks ago, but I haven't heard anything back.***

email *verb*
to send a message to someone's computer using email: ***I'll email you directions to the party.***

bounce *verb*
if an email bounces, it comes back to you because there is a problem with the system and it cannot be delivered to the person you sent it to: ***I tried to email her several times, but the message always bounced.***

spam *noun*
email messages and advertisements that you receive but do not want to read: ***I was getting so much spam that I changed my email address.***

attachment (AWL) *noun*
a computer file that you put with an email in order to send them together: ***I sent her a picture as an attachment.***

send *verb*
to make an email go to someone else's computer: ***Danilo sent everyone an email about the meeting.***

receive *also* **get** (*informal*) *verb*
to get an email from someone else: ***She receives up to a hundred emails a day.***

10 Studying Computers

computer science *noun*
the study of computers and what they can do: ***I have a Masters degree in Computer Science.***

tablet

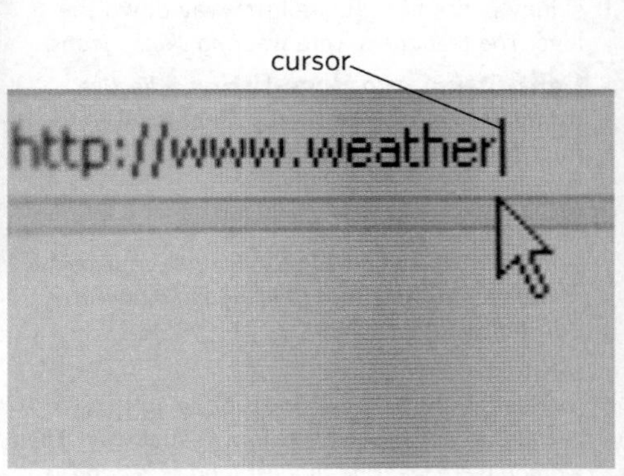

DESCRIBING CLOTHES

1 How Does It Fit?

baggy *adjective*
baggy clothes are big and loose: *She was relaxing on the couch in comfortable baggy pajamas.*

loose *adjective*
loose clothes do not fit your body tightly, so you feel comfortable when you wear them: *In hot weather, loose clothing is more comfortable.*

oversized *adjective*
bigger than usual or too big: *The girl was wearing an oversized shirt with a pair of leggings.*

tailored *adjective*
clothing that is tailored is made to fit very well: *A woman in a tailored suit walked into the office.*

tight *adjective*
tight clothes fit your body very closely: *He was wearing tight jeans.* | *These shoes feel too tight.*

skinny *adjective*
skinny pants fit tightly all the way down the legs: *The teenagers were wearing skinny jeans.*

tight-fitting *also* **close-fitting** *adjective*
fitting very closely or tightly: *She was wearing a tight-fitting skirt.* | *She had on a close-fitting sweater.*

skin-tight *adjective*
skin-tight clothes fit tightly against your body: *The singer walked onto the stage in a pair of skin-tight leather pants.*

modest *adjective*
modest clothing covers your body so that people do not look at you in a sexual way: *The women were wearing modest long skirts and blouses.*

revealing *adjective*
revealing clothes show parts of your body that you usually keep covered: *I think her swimsuit is a little too revealing.*

2 Are the Clothes Formal, Informal, or Stylish?

formal *adjective*
formal clothes are worn at events such as weddings or dances, where men are asked to wear tuxedos (=special suits) and women wear very nice dresses: *I need a formal dress that I can wear to the wedding.*

dressy *adjective*
dressy clothes are suitable for special occasions, such as parties or a dinner at a nice restaurant, when you want to look very nice: *Everyone was wearing dressy clothes at the party.*

best *adjective*
your best clothing is the clothing that you wear for special occasions: *The children put on their best clothes for the party.*

casual *also* **informal** *adjective*
casual or informal clothes are not formal, and you usually wear them when you are not working: *Most people were wearing casual clothes like jeans or chinos.* | *The invitation for the party says "informal dress," so don't wear a suit.*

stylish *also* **fashionable** *adjective*
looking good in a fashionable way: *A stylish scarf was wrapped around her neck.*

sensible *adjective*
sensible clothing or shoes are practical rather than fashionable: *We'll be walking a lot, so wear sensible shoes – no high heels!*

unfashionable *adjective*
not stylish any more, so not looking good: *She wore a pair of unfashionable lace-up brown shoes.*

old-fashioned *adjective*
not looking stylish or popular now, but worn in the past: *The pictures, taken in the late 1800s, were of women in old-fashioned long dresses.*

3 How Long or Warm Are the Clothes?

light *also* **thin** *adjective*
light clothes are thin and not very warm: *It gets cool in the evening, so you might want to take a light jacket.*
→ You usually use **light** when you do not want clothing that is very warm.

thin
thin means the same as light, but you use it when you are describing clothes that are not warm enough: *She pulled her thin sweater tighter around her body and shivered.*

heavy *also* **thick** *adjective*
heavy clothes are thick and warm: *You need a heavy winter coat for the winters in Chicago.* | *He wore a thick wool sweater.*

long *adjective*
covering all of your arms or legs: *Her long skirt*

almost touched the ground. | *He was wearing a long-sleeved shirt.*

short *adjective*
covering only a small part of your arms or legs: *He was wearing a short-sleeved shirt.* | *Alice had on a short skirt and a white top.*

full-length *adjective*
a full-length dress or skirt reaches the ground: *The actress was wearing a full-length blue gown.*

knee-length *adjective*
long enough to reach your knees: *Knee-length skirts are popular this fall.*

4 Describing a Feature of Clothes

low-cut *adjective*
a low-cut dress or blouse is shaped so that it shows a woman's neck and the top of her chest: *She was wearing a low-cut dress.*

open-necked *adjective*
an open-necked shirt has buttons down the front that you wear without fastening the top button: *He was wearing an open-necked shirt under his jacket.*

sleeveless *adjective*
a sleeveless jacket, dress, etc. has no sleeves: *She looked elegant in a simple sleeveless black dress.*

formal clothes

a **tailored** suit

casual clothes

dressy

DESCRIBING EMOTIONS

1 To Feel an Emotion

feel happy/sad etc *verb phrase*
to experience a particular feeling or emotion: *I feel so happy to be back home.* | *She felt a little nervous about the test.*

be happy/sad etc. *verb phrase*
to experience a particular feeling or emotion. **Be** means the same as **feel**: *The little boy was scared of the dog.* | *Dad will be angry when he finds out you lost his camera.*

2 Happy

happy *adjective*
feeling good and satisfied with your life: *They returned from their vacation feeling happy and relaxed.* | *Congratulations! I'm so **happy for** you.*

thrilled *adjective*
very happy, pleased, or excited: *His parents are **thrilled with** his progress in school this year.*

delighted *adjective*
very happy because something good has happened. **Delighted** sounds more formal than **happy** or **thrilled**: *We were **delighted that** she invited us to the wedding.*

ecstatic *adjective*
feeling extremely happy and excited: *When he heard he had gotten the job, he was ecstatic.*

content *adjective*
feeling happy and satisfied so that you do not want anything else: *She is **content with** her quiet country life.*

3 Sad

sad *adjective*
not happy, especially because a happy time has ended: *She felt sad as she waved goodbye.* | *Why does Sandra look so sad?*

unhappy *adjective*
not happy, especially for a long time, because you are in a situation, job, or relationship that you do not enjoy at all and it seems likely to continue: *Neil was very unhappy at school.* | *Divorce can leave children feeling confused and unhappy.*

upset *adjective*
sad and worried because something bad or disappointing has happened, especially so that you feel shocked or want to cry: *Margo was very upset when her husband forgot her birthday.*

disappointed *adjective*
sad because something does not happen or is not as good as you expected it to be: *She was **disappointed that** she could not get a ticket for the concert.*

miserable *adjective*
very sad because of the situation you are in, especially because you are lonely, hungry, cold, etc.: *We had been waiting outside in the rain for hours, and were cold and miserable.*

depressed *adjective*
very sad because of a difficult or bad situation, and feeling that your life will never get better. If someone is **depressed** for a long time, it can be a serious mental illness: *Her husband has been very depressed since he lost his job.*

4 Angry

angry *adjective*
feeling strong emotions because you think someone has behaved badly, or because a situation seems bad: *My parents were really angry when I got a D on the math test.* | *She was **angry with** him because he had lied to her.*

annoyed *adjective*
a little angry: *Meg was **annoyed with** me because I was a little late.*

upset *adjective*
angry and disappointed: *The teacher was upset when she realized that no one had done their homework.*

furious *adjective*
very angry: *When Dad finds out you wrecked his car, he will be furious.*

5 Scared

scared *also* **frightened** *adjective*
unhappy or worried because you think something bad might happen. **Scared** is used in more informal or spoken language: *The first time*

*I went on a motorcycle, I was really scared. | Are you **frightened of** spiders?*

afraid *adjective*
afraid means the same as **scared** but sounds slightly more formal: *Children are often **afraid of** the dark. | He was **afraid that** he would get in trouble if he told the truth.*

alarmed *adjective*
suddenly very worried and frightened because you realize there is a problem or danger: *I am becoming **alarmed at** how thin she looks.*

terrified *adjective*
extremely afraid: *The child ran into the busy street, and we were all **terrified that** she would be hit by a car.*

petrified *adjective*
petrified means the same as **terrified** but is used to emphasize that someone is completely terrified: *I realized that someone was following me and I felt absolutely petrified.*

6 Worried

worried *adjective*
not feeling happy or relaxed, because you keep thinking about a problem or about something bad that might happen: *The economy is bad, and a lot of people are **worried about** losing their jobs. | I got worried when you were late and didn't call.*

nervous *adjective*
worried and a little bit frightened about something: *I'm always nervous before tests.*

anxious *adjective*
very nervous about something so that you think about it a lot. **Anxious** is more formal than **nervous**: *She knew it was a simple operation, but she still felt anxious.*

tense (AWL) *adjective*
nervous and not able to relax so that you become angry or upset easily: *You seem a little tense lately – is anything wrong?*

7 Jealous

jealous *adjective*
feeling unhappy or angry because someone else has something that you want and cannot have: *She was **jealous of** me because I got better grades.*

envious *adjective*
wishing that you had something nice or special that someone else has: *My friends will be really envious when I tell them I won a trip to Hawaii.*
→ **Jealous** and **envious** can be used to mean the same thing, especially in spoken English. However, if you are **jealous**, you feel angry and unhappy that someone has something and you do not. If you are **envious**, you wish you had something that someone else has, but you do not feel angry about it.

8 Guilty

guilty *adjective*
feeling unhappy and sorry because you have done something that you know is wrong: *Ed felt **guilty about** leaving work so early. | I felt really guilty after spending all that money.*

embarrassed *adjective*
feeling nervous and uncomfortable, especially in front of other people: *I was **embarrassed about** how messy my house was.*

ashamed *adjective*
feeling guilty and very embarrassed about something bad you have done: *He felt **ashamed of** the cruel things he had said to his mother.*

9 Adjectives that Describe How Strong an Emotion Is

strong *adjective*
a strong feeling is one that you feel a lot and are very serious about: *The students have a strong desire to succeed and they work very hard.*

deep *adjective*
a deep feeling is one that you feel very strongly. **Deep** is used especially about a feeling of love, disappointment, or sympathy: *The letters show her deep affection for him.*

powerful *adjective*
having a great effect on your thoughts and feelings: *Anger is a powerful emotion that can be difficult for children to control.*

profound *adjective*
a profound feeling is very strong. **Profound** is very similar to **deep**: *I was alone in the city for the holidays and I felt a profound sense of loneliness.*

intense (AWL) *adjective*
a feeling that is intense is extremely strong: *The game was tied and the crowd was filled with intense excitement.*

overwhelming *adjective*
an overwhelming feeling is very strong, often so strong that you cannot think or behave normally: *After stealing the money, she felt an overwhelming sense of guilt.*

fierce *adjective*
with very strong feelings and a lot of energy. Use **fierce** especially when people are fighting or competing with each other in an angry or determined way: *There was a fierce debate between the two candidates.*

bitter *adjective*
a bitter argument, battle, etc. is one in which people oppose or criticize each other with strong feelings of hate and anger: *They have always been bitter enemies.*

acute *adjective*
an acute feeling is very strong. **Acute** is used especially about a feeling of pain, embarrassment, or anxiety: *I felt acute embarrassment when I realized my mistake.*

heartfelt *adjective*
very strongly felt and sincere: *She wrote a letter to the doctors, in which she expressed her heartfelt thanks.*

raw *adjective*
raw feelings are strong and natural, but not fully controlled: *Her performance was filled with raw emotion.*

burning *adjective*
a burning feeling is one that you feel very strongly. Use **burning** about desires, needs, or ambitions: *He has a burning desire to win the competition.*

DESCRIBING PEOPLE'S LOOKS

1 Height
2 Body Size
3 Age
4 Appearance
5 Clothes
6 Hair
7 Face and Skin

1 Height

tall *adjective*
bigger in height than most other people: *There was a tall man standing in front of her, so she couldn't see the stage.*

short *adjective*
not as tall as most people: *He was so short he couldn't reach the top shelf.*

average height *also* **medium height** *adjective phrase*
neither tall nor short. It is more formal to say that someone is **of average/medium height**: *He told the police that the man was of average height and had dark hair.*

be five feet/six feet etc. tall *verb phrase*
used to say exactly how tall someone is: *He was six feet five inches tall.*

2 Body Size

fat *adjective*
having too much fat on your body: *The driver was a short fat man with glasses.* | *You'll get fat if you eat too many cookies.*
→ It is rude to say that someone is **fat**. It is better to say that someone is **overweight**. If you are talking to someone who is **fat**, it is better not to say anything about it at all.

chubby *adjective*
a little fat in an attractive way. **Chubby** is used especially about babies and children: *She was holding a chubby little baby boy.*

overweight *adjective*
weighing more than you should: *His doctor told him that he was overweight and that he needed to do more exercise.* | *I'm a couple of pounds overweight.*

obese *adjective*
extremely fat in a way that is very unhealthy: *People who are obese often suffer from heart problems.*

big *adjective*
tall and having a large body: *He was big and strong, and I knew he would beat me in a fight.*

thin *adjective*
not having much fat on your body: *He is tall and thin – about 6 feet and 160 pounds.*

slim *adjective*
thin in a way that looks good: *She stays slim through diet and exercise.*

skinny *adjective*
very thin, in a way that is not attractive. You use **skinny** when you think that someone is thinner than he or she should be: *He was skinny and looked like he didn't eat enough.*

weigh 115/182/205 etc. pounds *verb phrase*
used to say how heavy someone is: *He weighs 250 pounds and wants to lose weight.*

slight/athletic/medium etc. build *adjective phrase*
used to describe the size and shape of someone's body. Someone with a **slight build** is thin and looks like he or she has small bones. Someone with an **athletic build** looks like he or she exercises a lot. Someone with a **medium build** is neither big nor small. **Build** is used in writing: *He had the lean build of an athlete.* | *She was of slight build.*

3 Age

young *adjective*
having lived for a short time: *When she was young, she wanted to be an actress.*

teenage *adjective*
between 13 and 19 years old: *She allowed her teenage son to use her car.*

middle-aged *adjective*
between about 40 and 65 years old: *A middle-aged woman and her two teenage sons were standing in the line.*

old *adjective*
having lived for a long time: *Mr. Johnson is very old – I think he is about 90.*

elderly *adjective*
elderly means the same as **old** but sounds more polite: *Many elderly people live alone but need help taking care of themselves.*

be 10/25/48 etc. years old *verb phrase*
used to say exactly how old someone is: *His parents got divorced when he was ten years old.*

be in your teens/20s/30s etc. *verb phrase*
to be between 13 and 19, 20 and 29, 30 and 39,

etc.: *He looked young – I guessed he was in his early 20s.*

4 Appearance

beautiful *adjective*
very nice to look at. **Beautiful** is used especially about women, girls, or babies: *She looked beautiful in her wedding dress.*

pretty *adjective*
nice to look at. **Pretty** is not as strong as **beautiful** and is used about women and girls: *His mother was a pretty woman with red hair.*

handsome *adjective*
nice to look at. **Handsome** is stronger than **attractive** or **good-looking** and is used about men and boys: *Jill's new boyfriend is very handsome.*

attractive *adjective*
nice to look at. **Attractive** sounds slightly more formal than **pretty** and is used about adult men and women: *He is an attractive guy, but I don't think he is very interesting.*

good-looking *also* **nice-looking** *adjective*
nice to look at. **Good-looking** is not as strong as **beautiful** or **handsome**, and is used slightly more often about men than women: *He is a good-looking man in his early 30s.*

cute *adjective*
nice to look at. **Cute** is used about babies and small children: *Your little sister is so cute!*
→ You can also use **cute** as an informal way to describe a young woman or man: *She hoped the cute guy in the coffee shop would ask her out.*

ugly *adjective*
extremely unpleasant to look at: *The witch was an ugly old woman with a long bent nose.*

homely *adjective*
not at all attractive: *He thought he was homely, and that no one would ever want to be his girlfriend.*

plain *adjective*
not attractive. **Plain** is used about women and girls: *A plain girl can make herself prettier using makeup.*

5 Clothes

be wearing *verb phrase*
if you are wearing a particular piece of clothing, it is on your body: *Angela was wearing a dark blue sweater and jeans.*

be dressed in *verb phrase*
be dressed in means the same as **be wearing** but sounds more formal: *She was dressed in a black suit.*

have on *phrasal verb*
have on means the same as **be wearing** but sounds more informal: *Mr. Fielding has a jacket and tie on today.* | *She had on an old sweatshirt.*

in *preposition*
wearing a particular color or piece of clothing: *Who's the woman in the green dress?*

well-dressed *adjective*
wearing clothes that are of good quality, attractive, and usually formal: *A well-dressed businessman was getting into a cab.*

casually dressed *adverb phrase*
wearing clothes that are not formal, like the ones you wear at home or with friends: *He was casually dressed in jeans and a blue plaid shirt.*

stylish *adjective*
wearing attractive fashionable clothes: *The perfume was advertised by a beautiful and stylish actress.*

6 Hair

long/short/medium-length hair *adjective phrase*
used to say how long someone's hair is: *He has very short hair.* | *Her hair was medium-length, and fell just below her shoulders.*

dark/fair/brown/blonde/red/gray hair *adjective phrase*
used to say what color someone's hair is: *The girl with blonde hair smiled at him.* | *His hair was beginning to go gray.*
→ You can say that someone with dark hair is **dark-haired**, someone with red hair is **red-haired**, etc.

straight/curly hair *adjective phrase*
used to say what someone's hair is like: *The little girl had curly brown hair.*

bald *adjective*
having no hair on your head: *By age 40 he was completely bald.* | *Dan has a bald spot on top of his head.*

beard *noun*
hair that grows on a man's chin: *Santa Claus is shown as an old man with a white beard.*

mustache *noun*
hair that grows above a man's mouth: *My brother thought he would look older if he had a mustache.*

clean-shaven *adjective*
a man who is clean-shaven has no hair on his face: *One of the men had a beard and the other was clean-shaven.*

7 Face and Skin

strong/regular/small features *adjective phrase*
used to describe the size or shape of the parts of someone's face. **Strong features** are big but usually attractive, for example a big nose and mouth. **Regular features** do not have any unusual shapes. **Small features** are small: *He was good-looking, with regular features and neat dark hair.*
→ You can also describe the parts of someone's face separately: *He had blue eyes and a thin mouth.*

have blue/brown/green etc. eyes
to have eyes that are blue, brown etc.: *He has dark hair and brown eyes.*

pale/fair/dark/olive/black skin *adjective phrase*
used to describe the color of someone's skin. **Pale** and **fair skin** are light in color. **Dark skin** is brown. **Olive skin** is light brown. **Black skin** is dark brown: *He has pale skin and gets sunburned easily.*
→ You can say that someone with olive skin is **olive-skinned**, someone with fair skin is **fair-skinned**, etc.

tan *also* **tanned, suntanned** *adjective*
having darker skin after spending time in the sun: *By the end of the summer she was very tan.*

freckles *noun*
small light brown spots on someone's skin, especially on the face: *The little girl had red hair and freckles.*
→ You can say that someone who has freckles is **freckled**.

mole *noun*
a small dark brown mark on your skin that is often slightly higher than the skin around it: *She has a small mole above her eyebrow.*

wrinkles *noun*
lines on your face that you get when you are old: *She wasn't looking forward to having gray hair and wrinkles.*
→ You can say that someone who has wrinkles is **wrinkled**.

scar *noun*
a permanent mark on your skin, caused by a cut or by something that burns you: *He has a bad scar on his ear where a dog once bit him.*

tattoo *noun*
a permanent picture or word on your skin, done using a needle and ink: *The man had a tattoo of an eagle on his right arm.*

freckles

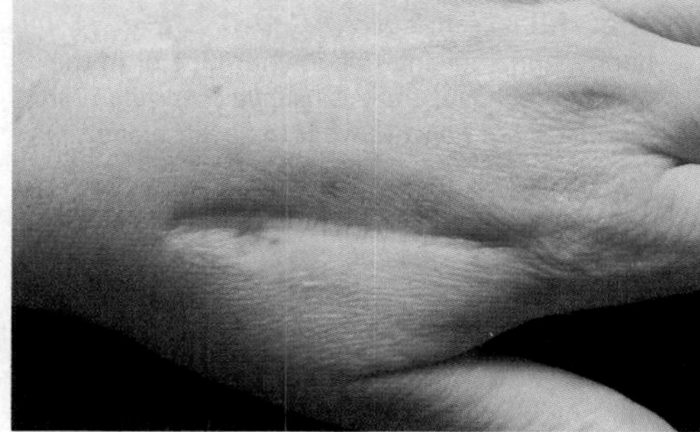
scar

wrinkles

mole

DESCRIBING PEOPLE'S CHARACTER

1 Good Qualities
2 Bad Qualities

1 Good Qualities

adventurous *adjective*
liking to do new and exciting things: *She is an adventurous traveler who likes going to new places where there are not many tourists.*

ambitious *adjective*
wanting very much to be successful in your job: *She is an ambitious politician who may someday be president.*

artistic *adjective*
good at painting, drawing, or making beautiful things: *John's very artistic – in fact, he painted that picture on the wall.*

brave *adjective*
not afraid to do things that other people find dangerous or difficult: *You have to be very brave to be a firefighter.*

calm *adjective*
not angry, upset, or excited, even in a difficult situation: *Jennifer looked surprisingly calm as she went up onto the stage to give her speech.*

cheerful *adjective*
happy, and showing this in your face or in the way you behave: *Emily is usually cheerful in the mornings, but I always want to be left alone.*

confident *adjective*
believing that you can do something well and not feeling nervous about it: *You will feel more **confident about** riding when you have been on a horse a few times.*

considerate *adjective*
thinking about other people's feelings and what they want, and careful not to cause problems for them: ***It was considerate of** Sheila to call and tell us that she would be late.*

creative *adjective*
good at thinking of new ideas or making new things: *The art class gives you the chance to be creative.*

decisive *adjective*
good at making decisions quickly: *We want a leader who is decisive at important moments.*

energetic *adjective*
very active and doing things with a lot of energy: *My aunt is an energetic woman who always has several projects going at the same time.*

enthusiastic *adjective*
showing a lot of interest and excitement about something: *Adam is **enthusiastic about** helping the younger kids improve their soccer skills.*

friendly *adjective*
wanting to talk to and be nice to people you do not know: *When I first came to the school, Michaela was friendly and helpful.*

funny *adjective*
someone who is funny makes you laugh: *Josh is so funny – he tells great jokes.*

generous *adjective*
liking to give people things or do things for them: *Mr. Marianelli has been **generous with** his time and money.*

hard-working *adjective*
using a lot of effort and spending a lot of time on the work you do: *She is a very hard-working student who gets good grades.*

helpful *adjective*
always willing to help people: *A helpful woman at the tourist office gave me some suggestions about places to visit.*

honest *adjective*
someone who is honest is good and does not lie or steal: *Maria is very honest. She would never cheat on a test.*

kind *adjective*
nice to other people: *The children liked their teacher because she was always **kind to** them.*

loyal *adjective*
someone who is loyal always supports a person, group, or country: *She has a group of loyal friends who helped her when her mother was so sick.*

mature *adjective*
behaving in a sensible and responsible way, like an adult: *They should stop fighting and start behaving like mature adults.*

optimistic *adjective*
believing that good things will happen in the future: *After talking to my teacher, I felt more **optimistic about** the class, and I thought I could do well.*

organized *adjective*
liking to plan things carefully so that everything gets done: *Nilza is the most organized person I know – she never forgets to do anything!*

patient *adjective*
able to deal with a problem or wait for something without getting angry or upset: *If you are patient and practice the notes slowly, you will learn how to play the song.*

quiet *adjective*
someone who is quiet does not usually say very

much: *Anna is very friendly and likes to talk, but her husband is very quiet.*

romantic *adjective*
liking to do things that show strong feelings of love for someone you are attracted to: *I want a romantic boyfriend who surprises me with love notes and flowers.*

sensible *adjective*
showing good judgment and an ability to make practical decisions: *He is a sensible man. I'm sure he won't spend the money on something of bad quality.*

shy *adjective*
nervous about meeting people and talking to them: *Amy is a shy child who finds it difficult to make friends.*

sociable *adjective*
friendly and liking to spend time with other people: *The teacher said that he was a sociable child who got along well with everyone.*

sympathetic *adjective*
someone who is sympathetic when you have a problem is kind to you and shows that he or she feels sorry for you: *When I lost my job, my friends were very sympathetic and said it wasn't my fault.*

2 Bad Qualities

aggressive *adjective*
behaving in an angry way that makes it seem like you want to fight or argue with someone: *Some of the children were aggressive, pushing and hitting to get what they wanted.*

conceited *adjective*
too proud of what you can do or of the way you look: *He is so conceited! He thinks every girl likes him.*

cruel *adjective*
very unkind and often deliberately hurting people or animals: *It is cruel to leave the dog chained up in the snow all day.*

dishonest *adjective*
a dishonest person tells lies, cheats, or steals things: *You wouldn't go into business with him if you knew he was dishonest – that would be stupid.*

immature *adjective*
behaving in a way that seems more like a younger person than people your own age. Someone who is **immature** does not always make responsible decisions or cannot control his or her emotions as well as other people of the same age: *He is 18, but he is still very immature. I wouldn't lend him your car.*

impatient *adjective*
quickly becoming angry if you have to wait or if someone else does something too slowly or badly: *I'll come and help you in a minute – don't be so impatient!*

indecisive *adjective*
not good at making decisions quickly, or often changing your mind: *A president cannot be indecisive, because the issues are so important.*

lazy *adjective*
not wanting to work, or not wanting to make any effort: *Stop being so lazy! Get off the couch and help me.*

materialistic *adjective*
caring more about getting money and buying things than about anything else: *Some lawyers want to help people, but others are more materialistic and just want to earn a lot of money.*

mean *adjective*
treating people in a way that is not nice and makes them unhappy: *He is always calling his little brother "stupid" and being* ***mean to*** *him.*

moody *adjective*
often becoming annoyed or unhappy suddenly, especially when there seems to be no good reason: *Teenagers can be moody – happy one minute and miserable the next.*

negative *adjective*
thinking only about what is bad or wrong with a situation or person, not what is good or right: *Don't be so negative – it might be fun!*

pessimistic *adjective*
thinking that bad things will happen, not good things: *He is* ***pessimistic about*** *his chances of getting the job because he doesn't think he has enough experience.*

picky *adjective*
difficult to please because there are a lot of things you do not like: *My sister is a very picky eater, but my parents make her try the foods she doesn't like.*

reckless *adjective*
behaving in a dangerous way and not thinking about your safety or the safety of other people: *The police arrested him for reckless driving after he drove through several red lights at 60 miles per hour.*

selfish *adjective*
caring only about yourself and not about other people: *He is a selfish person who refuses to help his parents.*

stubborn *adjective*
refusing to change your opinions or behavior because you believe you are right: *I told him it was a bad idea, but Dave is so stubborn he did it anyway.*

vain *adjective*
too proud of the way you look: *Eva was too vain to wear glasses.*

DESCRIBING PLACES

1 A City or Town

big *adjective*
covering a lot of land. **Big** is used to describe cities, but is not often used to describe towns: *In the past, people lived on farms and in small towns, but now most people live in big cities.*

large *adjective*
large means the same as **big**: *There are not many large towns in Alaska.*

small *adjective*
not covering much land: *I grew up in a small Midwestern town.*

modern *adjective*
built recently and using the latest designs: *Modern skyscrapers fill the downtown area.*

ancient *adjective*
very old: *London, England, is an ancient city that was founded by the Romans.*

historic *adjective*
old and often important in history: *When we went to England, we visited the historic town of Stratford-upon-Avon, where Shakespeare was born.*

quaint *adjective*
pretty, in an old-fashioned way that you like: *The main street is quaint and charming, with small shops and nice places to eat.*

picturesque *adjective*
pretty and interesting to look at, especially in an old-fashioned way: *I took some photographs of the city's picturesque main square.*

busy *adjective*
full of people, vehicles, and activity: *The normally busy downtown streets were deserted.*

bustling *adjective*
very busy because a lot of people are there: *The little village grew into a bustling tourist resort.*

congested *adjective*
too full of vehicles so that it is hard to move along: *They are trying to reduce the amount of traffic in congested areas.*

rundown *adjective*
in very bad condition. You use **rundown** about buildings and areas: *He rented a cheap apartment in a rundown area.*

shabby *adjective*
looking old and in fairly bad condition. You use **shabby** about buildings and rooms: *The company is based in a shabby little office on 4th Street.*

crumbling *adjective*
crumbling buildings are in such bad condition that they are nearly falling down: *The 1960s buildings are already crumbling.*

clean *adjective*
without dirt or garbage: *Boulder, Colorado, seems like a clean safe city where people care about their surroundings.*

dirty *adjective*
covered in dirt: *I wanted to get out of the hot dirty city and into the mountains.*

2 A Beach

sandy *adjective*
made of sand: *They took off their shoes and walked along the sandy beach.*

rocky *adjective*
made of rocks: *The waves crashed onto the rocky beach.*

golden *adjective*
with yellow sand: *This area has miles of golden beaches which are popular with families.*

white *also* **white sand** *adjective*
with white sand: *Except on weekends, the long white beach was empty.*

crowded *adjective*
with a lot of people: *The beach was so crowded it was hard to find somewhere to sit.*

deserted *adjective*
with no people: *If you want a quiet day, there are plenty of deserted beaches.*

3 Mountains, Hills, or Rocky Areas

rugged *adjective*
not flat and having a lot of rocks and mountains: *The scenery varies from rugged mountains to gentle valleys.*

rough *adjective*
ground that is rough is not smooth or flat: *The truck had thick tires for driving over rough ground.*

rocky *adjective*
with a lot of rocks, or made of bare rock: *They landed on a small rocky island.*

jagged *adjective*
rough and having a lot of sharp uneven points: *The Sawtooth Mountains in Idaho got their name because the jagged mountaintops look like the teeth of a saw.*

craggy *adjective*
a craggy mountain or canyon is steep and covered in rough rocks: *The mountain goat leaped down the craggy slope.*

snow-capped *adjective*
a snow-capped mountain has snow on the top: *The snow-capped mountains stood out against the bright blue sky.*

majestic *adjective*
very big, beautiful, and impressive: *From our hotel window we had a breathtaking view of the majestic mountains.*

4 A Forest or Jungle

dense *adjective*
with a lot of trees or other plants growing close together: *The dense jungles of Central America are home to animals such as monkeys.*

lush *adjective*
with a lot of plants growing very well: *Many strange plants and animals can be found in the lush rain forest.*

wooded *adjective*
covered with trees. **Wooded** is used mainly in writing: *The plane crashed in a wooded area, and it took rescuers some time to reach it.*

dark *adjective*
without much light, because there are so many trees: *She was afraid to go into the deep dark forest.*

shady *adjective*
protected from the light of the sun by trees: *I found a shady place to sit, under an old oak tree.*

towering *adjective*
towering trees are very tall and impressive. **Towering** is used in writing: *The tops of the towering trees swayed in the wind.*

5 A Desert

hot *adjective*
having a lot of heat: *The sun beat down as they crossed the baking hot desert.*

dry *adjective*
a dry area has no water or rain: *The soil was dry and cracked.* | *The driest place on earth is the Atacama Desert in Chile.*

arid *adjective*
an area that is arid gets very little rain and is very dry: *The cactus grows in the arid regions of the Southwest.*

parched *adjective*
soil that is parched is extremely dry. **Parched** is used especially in literature and news reports: *Each night they prayed for rain to come and soak the parched earth.*

6 A Beautiful Landscape

beautiful *adjective*
very nice to look at: *We walked around the city looking at the beautiful old buildings.*

pretty *adjective*
nice to look at. **Pretty** is not as strong as **beautiful**: *We stopped in a pretty little town in the mountains to have dinner.*

lovely *adjective*
very pretty, in a way that pleases you: *Graz, in Austria, is a lovely 900-year-old city.*

magnificent *adjective*
very beautiful, and very impressive or large: *The mountains looked magnificent in the sunshine.*

breathtaking *adjective*
beautiful in a way that excites or surprises you. You use **breathtaking** especially about a large area of land or water that you can see: *The views of the ocean from the cliffs were breathtaking.*

stunning *adjective*
very beautiful in an exciting way: *The room has a stunning view of the city.*

scenic *adjective*
surrounded by views of beautiful countryside: *We traveled to the coast by a very scenic route.*

7 An Unpleasant Landscape

desolate *adjective*
empty and making you feel sad and lonely: *The road is beside a desolate stretch of land without trees, grass, or buildings.*

dreary *adjective*
not at all interesting or attractive, and making you feel sad or bored: *He gazed out of the train window at the flat dreary landscape.*

harsh *adjective*
unpleasant to live in, especially because the weather is either very cold or very hot: *Not many animals can survive in the harsh environment of northern Canada.*

windswept *adjective*
windy and usually without many trees: *Tumbleweeds roll across the windswept plain.*

barren *adjective*
if land is barren, plants cannot grow there: *As the world gets warmer, some farmland will become a barren desert.*

DESCRIBING SIZE

1 Size

size *noun*
how big or small something is: *What size is that shirt? | Your desk is exactly the same size as mine. | The price will depend on the* ***size of*** *the carpet.*

dimensions (AWL) *noun*
the measurement or size of something. The **dimensions** of something usually include the exact height, width, and length: *What are the* ***dimensions of*** *the table?*

area (AWL) *noun*
the amount of space on a flat surface, which is usually measured by multiplying the length by the width of the surface: *Calculate the* ***area of*** *the walls and ceiling before you buy the paint.*

volume (AWL) *noun*
the amount of space that a substance fills, or that an object contains: *Help me figure out the* ***volume of*** *this fish tank. | This instrument measures the* ***volume of*** *air in your lungs.*

2 Big or Small

big *adjective*
more than usual in size: *They live in a big house in New York. | Canada is a big country.*

large *adjective*
large means the same as **big**, but is slightly more formal and used more in written English: *She ordered a large pizza.*

huge *adjective*
very big: *Her house is huge – it has ten bedrooms.*

enormous (AWL) *adjective*
enormous means the same as **huge**: *The office is in an enormous 75-story building.*

small *adjective*
not big in size: *It is easier to drive a small car in the city. | These shoes are too small for me. | A small woman with straight dark hair was in the kitchen.*

little *adjective*
little means the same as **small** but sounds slightly less formal: *The little boy was walking home from school. | The cake was decorated with little flowers.*

tiny *adjective*
very small: *Have you seen her apartment? It is tiny. | He touched the tiny fingers of the baby.*

3 Tall or Short

height *noun*
the distance from the top to the bottom of something: *Some of the redwood trees reach a* ***height of*** *more than 360 feet.*

tall *adjective*
bigger in height than most other people or things. **Tall** is used especially about people and things that are high and narrow, such as trees and buildings: *Who is taller – Russ or me? | The Empire State Building used to be the tallest building in the world, but now there are many buildings that are taller. | Carly is five feet tall.*

high *adjective*
bigger in height than most things. **High** is used about things such as mountains and walls: *Mount Kilimanjaro is the highest mountain in Africa. | The fence around the prison is 15 feet high.*
→ Do not use **high** to talk about a person's height.

short *adjective*
not as tall as most people: *Who is the short man with gray hair standing over there? | I am a little bit shorter than my sister.*
→ Do not use **short** to talk about the height of things.

low *adjective*
not high, or not far above the ground: *The wall was low and broken in places. | I picked an apple that was hanging from a low branch.*
→ Do not use **low** to talk about a person's height.

4 Long or Short

length *noun*
the distance from one end of something to the other end: *The wall was about 60 feet* ***in length*** *and 8 feet high.*

long *adjective*
measuring a large distance from one end to the other: *Dan can run really fast because he has long legs. | The movie theater is a long way from here – we should probably drive.*
→ You use **long** to talk about the measurement

of something: *Each piece of string should be three inches long.*

short *adjective*
measuring a small distance from one end to the other: *Kris cut her hair really short.* | *The shortest way to get to the store is through the park.*

5 Wide or Narrow

width *noun*
the distance from one side of something to the other: *The width of the river is about 25 feet.*

breadth *noun (formal)*
breadth means the same as **width**: *The boat measured 15 feet in length and 4 feet in breadth.*

wide *adjective*
measuring a large distance from one side to the other: *The pants have wide legs, so they're easy to put on.* | *The highway is wide and straight.*
→ You use **wide** to talk about the measurement of something: *The door is 3 feet wide.*

broad *adjective*
broad means the same as **wide** but sounds more formal: *The Hudson River is very broad in some places.* | *The jacket fit perfectly on his broad shoulders.*
→ You can say that someone's back, chest, or shoulders are **broad**, but do not use **broad** about other parts of the body.

narrow *adjective*
measuring only a small distance from one side to the other: *The city's narrow roads were jammed with traffic.* | *The space between the rocks was very narrow, and we could barely squeeze through it.*

6 Thick or Thin

thickness *noun*
the distance through one side of an object or material to the other side: *The thickness of the glass was about 5 inches.*

thick *adjective*
a thick object or material has a large distance from one side through to the other side: *The walls of the old farmhouse were thick.* | *The cake was cut into thick slices.* | *The carpet was thick and soft.*
→ You use **thick** to talk about the measurement of something: *The walls are only about an inch thick.*

thin *adjective*
having only a small distance from one side of an object or material through to the other side: *The ice was covered by a thin layer of snow, making it even more dangerous.*

7 Deep or Shallow

depth *noun*
the distance from the top to the bottom of something, such as a river or hole: *The diving pool has a depth of 5 meters.*
→ **Depth** is also used to describe the distance from the front to the back of an object: *The depth of the shelves is 8 inches.*

deep *adjective*
going a long way down from the top to the bottom of something like a river, hole, or soft substance: *You can't walk across the river – it is too deep.* | *In the morning, the snow was so deep it blocked the front door.*
→ You use **deep** to talk about the measurement of something: *Dig a hole around 12 inches deep.*

shallow *adjective*
measuring only a short distance from the top to the bottom of something such as a river, hole, or soft substance: *The little kids all played in the shallow end of the pool.*

a **wide** street

a **narrow** trail

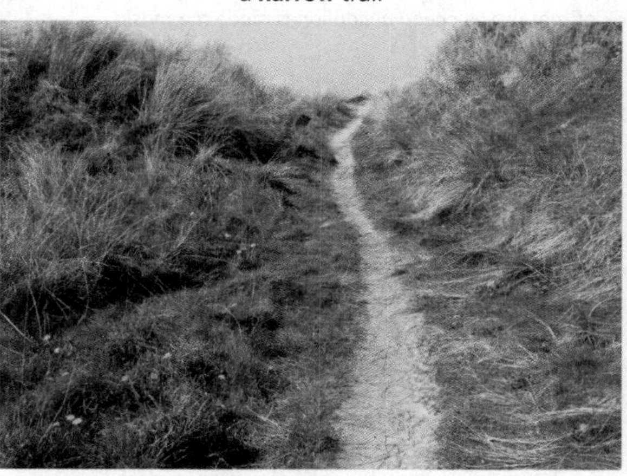

DESCRIBING SOUNDS AND VOICES

1 A High Voice or Sound

high *adjective*
near the top of the range of sounds that humans can hear. You use **high** especially about voices and musical notes: *He still has the high voice of a little boy.* | *Dogs can hear sounds that are too high for humans to hear.*

high-pitched *adjective*
a high-pitched sound or voice is high and sometimes unpleasant: *The lock made a high-pitched squeak as I turned the key.* | *People often use high-pitched voices when they talk to babies.*

piercing *adjective*
a piercing sound or scream is very high and loud in a way that sounds unpleasant and almost painful to your ears: *A piercing whistle got everyone's attention.* | *She gave a piercing scream as she fell.*

shrill *adjective*
a shrill voice or sound is very high and loud in a way that sounds unpleasant: *Her aunt's shrill voice could be heard from downstairs.*

squeaky *adjective*
making short high sounds: *Put some oil on that squeaky door!*

tinny *adjective*
a tinny sound is high, weak, and unpleasant, and sounds like it is coming out of something made of metal: *The cheap headphones made the music sound tinny.*

2 A Low Voice or Sound

low *adjective*
a low voice or sound is near the bottom of the sounds that human ears can hear: *Boys' voices usually become much lower as they get older.* | *Suddenly we heard the long, low blast of a ship's horn.*

deep *adjective*
a deep voice or sound is very low, strong, and pleasant: *He's a big man with a very deep voice.*

rich *adjective*
a rich voice is low, strong, and pleasant to listen to: *The songs, sung in his rich voice, are wonderful.*

husky *adjective*
a husky voice is deep, quiet, and rough-sounding, especially in a way that is attractive: *His voice dropped to a husky whisper.*

bass *adjective*
if a man has a bass voice, he has a very low voice: *He spoke in a deep bass voice.*

3 A Quiet Voice or Sound

quiet *adjective*
not making a lot of sound: *"What about me?" Ahmed asked in a quiet voice.* | *Listening to quiet music can help you fall asleep.*

soft *adjective*
a soft voice or sound is quiet and pleasant: *Ellie's voice was soft and calming.* | *It was a romantic dinner, with soft music and candlelight.*

low *adjective*
a low voice or sound is quiet so that you do not wake or annoy other people: *"Don't wake him up," said Ben in a low voice.* | *I turned the volume of the TV down low.*

gentle *adjective*
a gentle voice is quiet, pleasant, and caring: *"Come sit by me," Grandma said in a gentle voice.*

faint *adjective*
a faint sound or voice is quiet and difficult to hear, especially because it comes from a long way away: *We heard the faint sound of a train in the distance.* | *She had been very sick, and her voice was faint.*

hushed *adjective*
if people talk in hushed voices or hushed tones, they talk quietly so that other people cannot hear: *Everyone in the library was speaking in hushed voices.*

4 A Loud Voice or Sound

loud *adjective*
making a lot of sound: *The music is too loud – can you turn it down?* | *In the restaurant, a group of friends were talking in loud voices and laughing.*

noisy *adjective*
making a lot of annoying sound: *They have noisy neighbors.* | *The room was so noisy I couldn't hear her.*

booming *adjective*
a booming voice or laugh is loud and low: *The P.E. teacher's booming voice filled the gym.*

deafening *adjective*
a noise that is deafening is so loud you cannot

hear anything else: ***As the band walked on stage, the screams and yells of the fans were deafening.***

ear-splitting *adjective*
an ear-splitting noise or scream is very loud and unpleasant, and hurts your ears: ***There was an ear-splitting roar as the jets took off.***

5 A Rough Voice or Sound

rough *adjective*
not sounding soft or gentle, especially because the person speaking is angry or rude: ***"What are you doing in here?" the man demanded in a rough voice.***

grating *adjective*
a grating voice or sound is rough, unpleasant, and annoying, and sounds like rough things rubbing together: ***The elevator began to rise, making a grating noise that was a little frightening.*** | ***His voice was grating and hard to listen to.***

harsh *adjective*
a harsh voice or sound is rough and unpleasant, and often sounds angry: ***"You'll do what I tell you," he said, his voice harsh in her ear.*** | ***The sound from the speakers was harsh rather than pleasant.***

husky *adjective*
a husky voice is slightly rough, as though you have a sore throat, but also attractive and deep: ***The singer James Brown had a scratchy husky voice that fans loved.***

gravelly *adjective*
a gravelly voice is very low and rough-sounding: ***She had a gravelly voice from years of smoking.***

gruff *adjective*
a gruff voice is low and rough, especially when the speaker is feeling annoyed or is being rude, and does not want to talk much: ***The old man rarely talked except to say "hello" in a gruff voice.***

hoarse *adjective*
a hoarse voice is rough and not very clear, especially because your throat is sore as a result of illness or too much shouting or singing: ***You sound hoarse. Do you have a cold?***

throaty *adjective*
a throaty voice is deep and rough, as if the sounds are produced deep down in your throat: ***Julie had a throaty voice that made her sound older than she was.***

DESCRIBING TEXTURE

1 The Texture of Something

texture *noun*
the way that something feels when you touch it, for example whether it is rough or smooth, hard or soft: *The clay has a smooth soft texture that is pleasant to work with.* | *The toy has different textures for your baby to feel: soft cloth, hard metal, and squishy rubber.*

feel *noun*
the way that something feels when you touch it, especially something soft or smooth that feels good: *Velvet is a type of cloth that has a nice soft feel.* | *I love the feel of warm sand under my feet at the beach.*

consistency (AWL) *noun*
how thick or smooth a liquid or soft substance is: *Stir the paint until it is the consistency of thick cream.* | *The pudding should have a smooth consistency, with no lumps.*

2 Feeling Rough

rough *adjective*
having a surface that is not smooth or flat, and that is unpleasant to touch: *His big rough hands were covered in dirt.* | *Sandpaper has a very rough surface.*

coarse *adjective*
having a rough surface that is slightly hard. **Coarse** is used about cloth, skin, hair, and things such as sand or rock: *He covered himself with a coarse woolen blanket that scratched his face.*

bumpy *adjective*
having a surface with a lot of small raised parts on it: *Rashes can cause skin to change color, itch, and become bumpy.*

lumpy *adjective*
a bed or chair that is lumpy has small hard parts under the surface so that it is uncomfortable to sit or lie on: *The couch was lumpy and uncomfortable to sit on.*

sticky *adjective*
made of or covered with a slightly wet substance that sticks to surfaces: *I spilled some juice and now the floor is sticky.*

3 Feeling Smooth

smooth *adjective*
flat and without any raised or rough areas: *The pond was covered with a smooth sheet of ice.* | *He stroked her smooth soft hair.*

sleek *adjective*
having a smooth, curved, attractive shape. **Sleek** things are often a little bit shiny. You use **sleek** especially about hair, fur, cars, or people's bodies and the clothes they wear: *Several women at the party were wearing sleek black dresses and expensive shoes.*

silky *adjective*
soft and smooth like silk cloth. You use **silky** about hair, fur, skin, or cloth: *The little dog had silky brown hair.*

4 Feeling Soft

soft *adjective*
not hard, sharp, or rough, and nice to touch: *Use a soft cloth to polish the silver.* | *Your hair is so soft. What conditioner do you use?*

fluffy *adjective*
covered in soft light threads, fur, or feathers: *She held the fluffy little chick in her hands.*

velvety *also* **like velvet** *adjective*
with a thick, soft, smooth surface that is nice to touch: *The rocks by the river were covered with velvety moss.* | *The baby had skin like velvet.*

silky *adjective*
soft and smooth like silk cloth. You use **silky** about hair, fur, skin, or cloth: *Ronald was stroking the cat's silky fur.*

squishy *adjective*
very soft, wet, and easy to press: *I could feel the squishy mud on the bottom of the lake between my toes.*

soggy *adjective*
too wet and soft, and looking or feeling unpleasant: *The eggs were dry, and the toast was soggy.*

5 Feeling Hard

hard *adjective*
not soft, and difficult to bend, break, or cut: *The workers wear hard hats to protect their heads.* | *I wish this chair wasn't so hard and uncomfortable.*

firm *adjective*
not bending easily when pressed, but not completely hard either. You use **firm** to show

that this is good: ***It is best to buy pears when they are still firm.** | **A bed with a firm mattress is good for your back.***

stiff *adjective*
something that is stiff keeps its shape and is not easy to bend. You use **stiff** when something is harder than usual or harder than you expect: ***His collar felt stiff and rubbed against his neck.***

crisp *adjective*
slightly hard and making a pleasant noise when it breaks. You use **crisp** about food, dry leaves, and snow: ***The cookies were crisp at the edges and chewy in the middle.***

6 Describing Liquids

thick *adjective*
a thick liquid flows slowly because it is almost solid: ***To make the sauce thicker, add flour.***

creamy *adjective*
thick and smooth like cream: ***The tomato soup was creamy and delicious.***

smooth *adjective*
a liquid that is smooth has no big pieces in it: ***Beat the eggs and flour until they are smooth.***

lumpy *adjective*
a liquid that is lumpy contains small solid pieces, so it is not as smooth as it should be: ***This gravy is lumpy – did you stir it?***

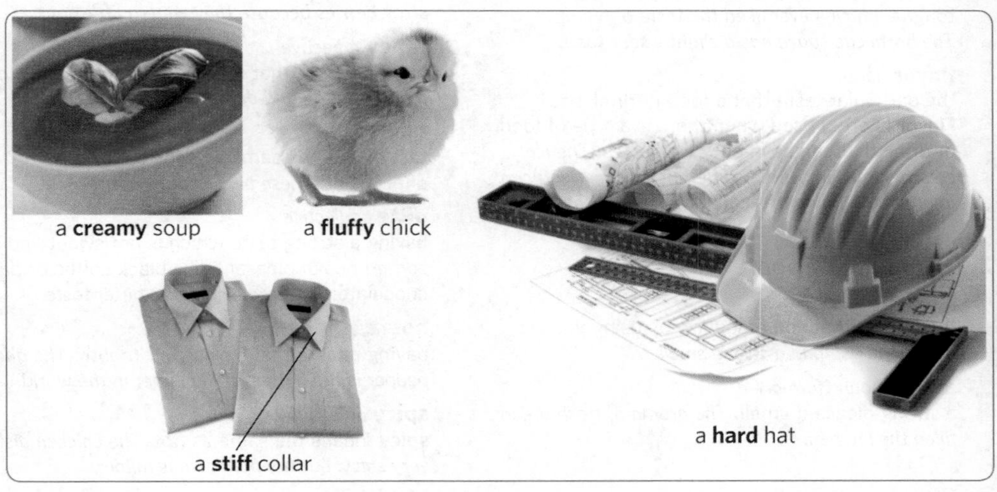

a **creamy** soup

a **fluffy** chick

a **stiff** collar

a **hard** hat

DESCRIBING FOOD

1 The Taste of Food

taste *noun*
the quality that you recognize by using your tongue: *I have never liked the taste of onions.* | *The barbecue sauce has a slightly sour taste.*

flavor *noun*
the particular taste that a food or drink has. **Flavor** is often used when there is a type of food or drink that can have different tastes: *The ice cream comes in over 30 different flavors.* | *You can improve the flavor of soups by adding herbs.*

2 The Smell of Food

smell *noun*
the quality that you recognize by using your nose: *The fish had a strong smell.*

aroma *noun (formal)*
a strong pleasant smell: *The aroma of fresh bread filled the kitchen.*

3 A Good or Bad Taste

delicious *adjective*
tasting very good: *The soup is delicious! You'll have to give me the recipe.* | *He served a delicious chocolate dessert.*

appetizing *adjective (formal)*
looking or smelling good, and making you feel that you want to eat it: *The appetizing smell of baked apples filled the house.*

tasty *adjective (informal)*
having a good strong taste. **Tasty** is not used about sweet things: *She makes a really tasty chicken and rice dish.*

disgusting *adjective*
tasting or smelling very bad so that it makes you feel sick: *The meat was so disgusting that he spat it out.*

awful *adjective*
tasting or smelling very bad: *The stew tasted awful, but she ate it because she was hungry.*

horrible *adjective*
tasting or smelling very bad: *I couldn't eat the horrible food they gave us.*

4 What Food Tastes Like

sweet *adjective*
tasting like sugar or containing sugar: *I love sweet things like chocolate and ice cream.*

salty *adjective*
containing a lot of salt: *The ham was very salty.*

sour *adjective*
having a strong taste like the taste of a lemon or a fruit that is not ready to be eaten. **Sour** tastes are usually unpleasant: *I put some sugar on the strawberries because they were a little sour.*

tangy *adjective*
having a taste that is pleasantly sour: *The lemon pie was tangy and delicious.*

tart
tart means the same as **sour** but is less unpleasant: *These berries have a tart taste.*

bitter *adjective*
having a strong taste which is not sweet and is sometimes unpleasant, like black coffee or dark chocolate: *The medicine had a bitter taste.*

hot *adjective*
having a taste that burns your mouth: *The ghost pepper is the hottest chili pepper in the world.*

spicy *adjective*
spicy means the same as **hot**: *The chicken dish is very spicy, but the pork dish is milder.*

bland *adjective*
having very little taste, and not interesting to eat or drink. **Bland** food is often given to sick people: *If the sauce is bland, add some salt and spices.*

5 What Food Is Like to Eat

crunchy *adjective*
food that is crunchy is firm and makes a noise when you bite it: *She ate a bite of crunchy cereal.*

crisp *adjective*
pleasantly hard or firm: *She bit into the crisp apple.*

crispy *adjective*
pleasantly hard after being cooked or dried: *Fry the bacon until it is crispy.*

chewy *adjective*
food that is chewy has to be chewed a lot before it is soft enough to eat: *Do not overcook steaks or they will be chewy.*

juicy *adjective*
containing a lot of juice: *The oranges were ripe and juicy.*

greasy *adjective*
covered or cooked in too much fat or oil: *The French fries were too soft and greasy.*

rich *adjective*
containing a lot of butter, cream, or eggs, and making you feel full very quickly: *The chocolate cake was very rich, so I only had a small slice.*

heavy *adjective*
solid and making your stomach feel full and uncomfortable: *Avoid eating a heavy meal before sleeping.*

6 Food That Is Good for You

healthy *adjective*
good for your body and making you strong: *She eats plenty of healthy food, especially fruit and vegetables.*

nutritious *adjective*
full of the natural substances that your body needs to stay healthy and grow well: *Eggs are a nutritious food, with lots of protein to help build strong muscles.*

organic *adjective*
grown or produced without using chemicals: *She only buys organic food, because she thinks the chemicals used in farming harm the environment.*

7 Food That Is Not Cooked or Frozen

raw *adjective*
not cooked: *You should wash the counter carefully after cutting raw meat.* | *Carrots can be eaten raw or cooked.*

fresh *adjective*
fresh food has recently been picked or prepared, and is not frozen or preserved: *The tomatoes are fresh from the garden.*

8 Food That Is Not Fresh

stale *adjective*
stale bread or cake is no longer fresh or good to eat, and is often too hard: *The bread was stale and dry.*

rancid *adjective*
rancid butter, milk, or meat has a strong bad smell because it is no longer fresh: *There was a horrible smell of rancid meat in the kitchen.*

sour *adjective*
if milk is sour, it is no longer fresh and has a bad smell and taste: *The milk wasn't in the fridge, and it had gone sour.*

spoiled *adjective*
if food is spoiled, it is no longer fresh or it is damaged, and it is not suitable to eat: *Several children were sick after eating hamburgers made of spoiled meat.*

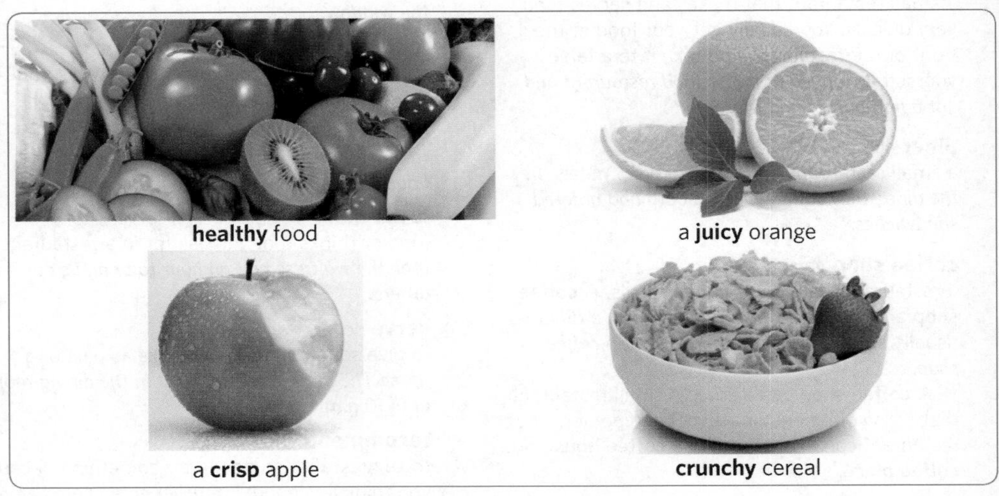

healthy food

a **juicy** orange

a **crisp** apple

crunchy cereal

EATING IN A RESTAURANT

1 A Restaurant

restaurant *noun*
a place where you can buy and eat a meal: *We ate at a Mexican restaurant on 23rd Street.* | *Marc works as a waiter in a restaurant.*

café *noun*
a restaurant where you can buy drinks and simple meals: *We stopped at a café for a sandwich.*

cafeteria *noun*
a restaurant in a school, office, or factory where people take food from a counter and then sit down to eat it: *I always eat lunch in the school cafeteria.*

fast-food restaurant *also* **fast-food place** (*informal*) *noun*
a small restaurant that makes and serves food very quickly. You usually get your food at the front of the restaurant and take it to a table yourself: *I stopped at a fast-food restaurant and got a hamburger and fries.*

diner *noun*
a small restaurant that serves cheap meals: *In the diner, they sat down in a booth and ordered sandwiches.*

coffee shop *noun*
a restaurant that serves cheap meals. A **coffee shop** and a **diner** are very similar, but a diner is usually smaller: *We had breakfast at a coffee shop.*
→ A **coffee shop** can also be a small restaurant that sells coffee and snacks. This type of restaurant can also be called a **coffee house** or a **coffee place**.

deli *also* **delicatessen** *noun*
a small restaurant that sells sandwiches and small meals, and that usually has a shop where you can also buy cooked meats, cheese, or salads: *I got a turkey sandwich and some coleslaw at the deli.*

2 To Go to a Restaurant to Eat

eat out *phrasal verb*
to have a meal in a restaurant, not at home: *We often eat out on Fridays so that I don't have to cook.*

go out to dinner/lunch/breakfast *also* **go out for a meal** *phrase*
to go to a restaurant and have a meal: *We went out for dinner to celebrate Kate's birthday.* | *Do you want to go out for a meal on Saturday?*

reserve *verb*
to arrange for a table at a restaurant to be kept for you to use: *The restaurant is busy on Fridays – you should call and reserve a table.*

reservation *noun*
an arrangement for a table at a restaurant to be kept for you to use: *Our reservations are at 7:30, so we should leave here at 7:15.*

3 Being Served at a Restaurant

waiter, waitress, server *noun*
the person who brings food to tables in a restaurant. **Server** is used for both men and women; a **waiter** is a man; a **waitress** is a woman: *Ask the waiter to bring us more bread.* | *Hi, I'm Brad, and I'll be your server tonight.*

host *or* **hostess** *noun*
the person who takes you to your table in some restaurants: *The hostess seated us at a table by the window.*

menu *noun*
a list of food that you can eat in a restaurant: *Are there any fish dishes* ***on the menu****?*

order *verb*
to ask for food or drinks in a restaurant: *I decided to order pasta with meatballs.*

order *noun*
food or drinks that you ask for in a restaurant: *It took the waitress half an hour to bring us our orders.*

serve *noun*
to give someone food or drinks as part of a meal: *The inn serves breakfast in the dining room until 10 a.m.*

recommend *noun*
to suggest that someone try something because you think it is good: *I've never eaten here before – what do you recommend?*

4 Paying for Your Meal

bill *also* **check** *noun*
a piece of paper that you get in a restaurant that

shows how much you must pay: *The waiter put the bill down next to Mr. Forrester. | Could I have the check, please?*

tip *noun*
money that you give to the waiter or waitress, in addition to the money you pay for your meal. You leave a **tip** on the table to show your thanks: *They left a $10 tip.*

service *noun*
the charge for serving your food, in addition to the cost of the food. Many restaurants do not put a **service** charge on the bill, but some do: *There was a note on the bill that said, "Service not included in the total."*

5 The Person Who Makes the Food

cook *noun*
someone who makes food in a restaurant for people to eat: *One of the cooks at the diner accidentally started a fire in the kitchen.*

chef *noun*
someone who has had special training to cook and works in a restaurant: *The chef has decided to put lamb on the menu tonight.*

6 The Food or Meals at a Restaurant

meal *noun*
the food that you eat at a particular time: *The restaurant serves big meals at reasonable prices.*

dish *noun*
food that is prepared or cooked in a particular way: *You should try the coconut chicken - it's my favorite dish.*

ingredient *noun*
one of the things that you use to make a particular dish: *All of our food is made using fresh ingredients.*

cooking *noun*
food made in a particular way or by a particular person: *Herbs are used a lot in French cooking.*

cuisine *noun (formal)*
the particular type of food served in a restaurant or hotel: *Enjoy the delicious Asian cuisine created by our award-winning chef.*

specialty *noun*
a type of food that is always very good in a particular restaurant: *The restaurant is famous for its seafood specialties.*

takeout *noun*
food that you buy at a restaurant to eat at home: *We get takeout from the Mexican restaurant almost every Friday night.*

buffet *noun*
a meal in which food is put on a table and you go and take what you want: *The lunch buffet at the Indian restaurant is delicious and it's only $10.*

banquet *noun*
a formal meal for many people on an important occasion: *A huge banquet was served to the winning team and its owners.*

7 The Parts of a Meal

appetizer *noun*
a small dish that you eat at the beginning of a meal: *I'm really hungry, so let's order some appetizers to get started.*

main course *also* **entrée** *noun*
the main dish of a meal served in a restaurant: *I'll start with a salad, and for the main course, I'd like the steak. | The restaurant has several delicious vegetarian entrées to choose from.*

side order *also* **side** *noun*
a small amount of a particular food you order in a restaurant to eat with the main dish: *I'd like a side order of French fries, please. | The chicken comes with any two sides.*

dessert *noun*
sweet food that you eat after the main part of a meal: *Let's order ice cream for dessert.*

8 The Amount of Food You Get

serving *noun*
an amount of food that is enough for one person: *The servings are so big here that you and I could probably share a meal.*

portion *noun (formal)*
an amount of food for one person: *To lose weight, you need to eat smaller portions.*

helping *noun*
an amount of food that you put on your plate: *He went back to the buffet to get another helping of potatoes.*

DESCRIBING THE CONDITION OF SOMETHING

1 Bad Condition

in bad/poor/terrible condition *also* **in bad/poor/terrible shape** *(informal) phrase*
broken or damaged because of being used a lot or because of being old: *The house is in bad shape, and it will need a lot of work before we can live in it.* | *After being left out in the rain, the old chair was in worse condition than it was before.*

broken *adjective*
damaged or in pieces because of being hit, dropped, etc.: *Some of the chairs were broken and couldn't be used.*

broken-down *adjective*
in very bad condition and not working. **Broken-down** is used especially about vehicles, furniture, and houses: *There was a broken-down old truck rusting in the front yard.*

crumbling *adjective*
a crumbling building or wall is breaking into pieces because it is very old and damaged by the weather: *The castle walls were crumbling.*

rickety *adjective*
in very bad condition and likely to break. **Rickety** is used about structures or furniture: *I wasn't sure the rickety old ladder could hold my weight.*

ramshackle *adjective*
a ramshackle building is in bad condition and looks as though it is likely to fall down: *No one had lived in the ramshackle farmhouse for years.*

dilapidated *adjective (formal)*
a building that is dilapidated is in very bad condition and has broken things that need to be repaired: *We stayed in an old dilapidated hotel with a leaky roof.*

decrepit *adjective (formal)*
decrepit buildings or objects are old and in very bad condition. If something is **decrepit**, it is very weak and likely to break: *The decrepit wooden bridge looks like it could collapse at any moment.*

derelict *adjective (formal)*
a derelict building or piece of land is in very bad condition because no one has used it in a long time: *The warehouses by the dock are derelict and will probably be demolished.*

2 Having Been Used a Lot

be falling apart *verb phrase*
if something is falling apart, it is in very bad condition and is breaking into pieces because it has been used a lot: *The old bicycle was rusty and falling apart.*

rundown *adjective*
a building or area that is rundown is in very bad condition, especially because it has been used a lot, but no one has repaired it: *All we could afford was a small room in a rundown motel.*

shabby *adjective*
shabby clothes, places, or objects are in bad condition because they are old and have been used a lot: *Paul was wearing a shabby old suit.* | *The apartment was dark and shabby.*

battered *adjective*
something that is battered is in bad condition and looks old because it has been used a lot. You usually use **battered** about objects: *He arrived with a battered old suitcase in his hand.*

worn *adjective*
old and a little bit damaged from use. **Worn** is usually used about cloth that is thinner or weaker in some places: *There was some old furniture and a worn rug in the living room.*

tattered *adjective*
tattered clothes or books are old and torn: *He kept his tattered baby blanket in a drawer.*

threadbare *adjective*
clothes, carpets, or other things made of cloth that are threadbare are very thin and almost have holes because they have been used so much: *His coat was old and threadbare, but he wore it because he could not afford another one.*

3 Good Condition

in good/excellent/great condition *also* **in good/excellent/great shape** *(informal) phrase*
if something is in good shape or in good condition, it is the way it should be with little or no damage: *I'll only buy used clothes if they're in really good condition.* | *Dad takes good care of his car, and it's still in great shape.*

like new *also* **as good as new** *phrase*
if something is like new, or as good as new, it is in very good condition even though someone has used it: *Your watch just needs cleaning and it'll be as good as new.*

perfect *adjective*
in the best possible condition: *She wore braces for a couple of years, and now her teeth are perfect.*

EDUCATION

1 Education

education *noun*
the process of teaching and learning: *The education of children is very important if we want our nation to be successful.*
→ Your **education** is also the knowledge and skills that you have learned: *She has a good education so she should be able to get a good job.*

learning *noun*
the process of studying or practicing a subject or activity so that you know about it or know how to do it: *Our teacher uses games and stories to make learning fun.*

academic (AWL) *adjective*
relating to education, especially to studying and learning in schools and colleges about subjects such as math, English, history, and science: *The school has worked hard to raise the academic achievement of its students.*

educational *adjective*
relating to teaching people about a subject: *The national parks have educational programs to teach children about nature.*

2 Types of Schools

school *noun*
a place where children go to learn: *What did you learn **at school** today? | We live a long way from the school, so I take the bus to get there.*

elementary school *also* **grade school** *noun*
a school in the U.S. for the first five or seven years of a child's education, usually between the ages of about five and ten or eleven: *I went to the same elementary school from kindergarten through sixth grade. | In grade school you learn to read and write and do basic math.*

middle school *noun*
a school in the U.S. for students in fifth or sixth grade through eighth grade, between the ages of about 11 and 14 years old: *Kids meet new friends when they start middle school.*

junior high school *also* **junior high** *noun*
a school in the U.S. for students in seventh grade through eighth or ninth grade, between the ages of about 12 and 14 or 15 years old: *Helen started studying Spanish in the last year of junior high school.*

high school *noun*
a school in the U.S. for students in ninth or tenth grade through twelfth grade, between the ages of about 14 or 15 and 18 years old: *Dan started studying harder in high school so he could get into a good college.*

community college *also* **junior college** *noun*
a college that people can go to, usually for two years, in order to learn a skill or to prepare to go to another college or university: *My brother went to a community college for two years before he transferred to Idaho State University. | Why don't you take some computer classes at the junior college to see if you like it?*

college *also* **university** *noun*
a large school where you can study after high school to get a degree: *It costs a lot to go to college, but having a degree will help you find a good job. | Cara is studying biology at the University of Texas.*

3 A Period of Time at School

school year *also* **academic year** *noun*
the period of time during a year when there are classes at a school, college, or university: *The school year runs from September through the middle of June.*

grade (AWL) *noun*
one of the 12 years that students are in school in the U.S.: *My sister is **in eighth grade** now, so she'll be in high school next year.*

period *noun*
one of the equal times that divide the school day, in which you have a class: *Which period do you have chemistry class?*

semester *noun*
one of two equal periods of time into which a school year is divided in most schools and some colleges: *I'm taking Spanish I during the fall semester, and Spanish II in the spring semester.*

quarter *noun*
one of four equal periods of time into which the

school year at some colleges is divided: *How many classes are you taking this quarter?*

4 A Class or Lesson

class *noun*
a period of time during which students are taught, or a series of these classes: ***In class** we were learning about how to write newspaper reports.* | *I want to take an art class next semester.*

course *noun*
a series of classes on a particular subject, especially at a college or university: *The college is offering three basic computer courses this year.*

lesson *noun*
an occasion when a teacher teaches a particular skill or subject, especially to only one person or to a small group: *How much do guitar lessons cost?* | *A good teacher plans lessons with the students' individual needs in mind.*

lecture *noun*
a long talk on a subject that someone gives to a group of people, especially students at a university: *Dr. Hernandez gave a lecture on Spanish literature.*

seminar *noun*
a class at a college or university in which a small group of students learn about a particular subject: *Students must take a writing seminar in their freshman year.*

5 What You Are Studying

subject *noun*
something you study at school: *"What's your favorite subject this year?" "History."*

major *noun*
the main subject that you study at college or university: *Jeff changed his major from economics to engineering.*

major in *phrasal verb*
to study something as your main subject at college or university: *I like to write, so I'm planning to major in English.*

minor *noun*
the second main subject that you study for your college or university degree: *Mañuel has a major in math with a minor in business.*

6 Learning and Teaching

learn *verb*
to study a subject or activity so that you know about it: *It is important to learn another language.* | *We **learned about** the Revolutionary War this week.*

study *verb*
to spend time going to classes and reading to learn about a subject: *José can't come – he's studying for his math test tomorrow.* | *What do you plan to study at college?*

teach *verb*
to give lessons in a school or college to help people learn about something: *I **teach** English **to** new immigrants.* | *Mrs. Sherwood has been teaching at the school for 15 years.*

test *verb*
to measure someone's knowledge or skill by asking questions or making him or her do things: *Each year we test the children's reading and math skills.* | *You will be **tested on** everything we have learned this semester.*

7 The Work You Do for School

schoolwork *noun*
the work that students do for school or during classes, such as reading or writing: *Rick spends too much time on sports and not enough on his schoolwork.*

homework *noun*
the work that students do for school while they are at home: *I have a lot of homework to do tonight – math problems and an essay for English.*

classwork *noun*
the work that students do during classes: *The students had some classwork to do.*

coursework *noun*
the work that students do for classes at a college or university: *Lou did some college coursework, but he never graduated.*

assignment (AWL) *noun*
a piece of work that a teacher has told you to do for school: *The social studies assignment was to write a report on how the Civil War started.*

report *noun*
a piece of writing telling about something you have learned: *We each had to read a different book and write a book report for class.*

essay *noun*
a piece of writing about a particular subject: *The teacher told us to write a two-page **essay on** our favorite musician.*

paper *noun*
a long piece of writing about something you have studied: *I have to write two research papers.*

8 Tests

test *noun*
a set of questions you are given at school to find out how much you know about something: *I didn't study for the test, so I got a bad grade.*

quiz *noun*
a short test: *The teacher gave us a quiz at the beginning of class to see if we had read the chapter.*

exam *also* **examination** *(formal) noun*
an important test at the end of a class in school or college: *Logan is studying hard for his final exams.*

9 Students

student *noun*
someone who is studying at a school, college, or university: *Johanna is a student at Cornell University. | High school students are required to take at least two years of mathematics.*

class *noun*
a group of students who are taught together: *My class is going on a field trip to a TV station next week.*

freshman, sophomore, junior, senior *noun*
a student in his or her first, second, third, or fourth year of high school or college: *Maddie is a senior in high school and will graduate in June.*

undergraduate *noun*
a student in college who is working for his or her college degree: *I studied English, but I also took psychology classes while I was an undergraduate.*

graduate student *noun*
a student at university who is studying for another degree after completing his or her first degree: *The course is for graduate students.*

10 Teachers

teacher *noun*
someone whose job is to teach, especially in a school: *Rob is an elementary school teacher.*

professor *noun*
a teacher at a college or university: *She is a professor of history at Arizona State University. | Professor Rosen teaches biology.*

11 To Go to School

go to *phrasal verb*
to regularly study at a particular school: *I go to Milton Middle School.*

attend *verb (formal)*
attend means the same as **go to**: *I am the first person in my family to attend college.*

be in school/college/second grade/your freshman year etc. *verb phrase*
to be studying at a particular level of school or college: *Rosa is in tenth grade.*

be at elementary school/college/UCLA etc. *verb phrase*
to be studying at a particular school or college regularly: *Lars is at Indiana State University this year.*

apply *verb*
to formally ask to be allowed to study at a particular college or university, by filling out a form: *I* ***applied to*** *five colleges, but I only got accepted at two.*

12 Finishing School

graduate *verb*
to finish your studies at a school or college successfully, and get a diploma or a degree: *80% of Americans* ***graduate from*** *high school.*

diploma *noun*
an official document that you get when you have successfully completed your studies at a high school, college, or university: *Each graduating student received a diploma during the ceremony.*

degree *noun*
an official statement that you have successfully completed all your studies at a college or university: *Applicants for the job must have a bachelor's* ***degree in*** *computer science.*

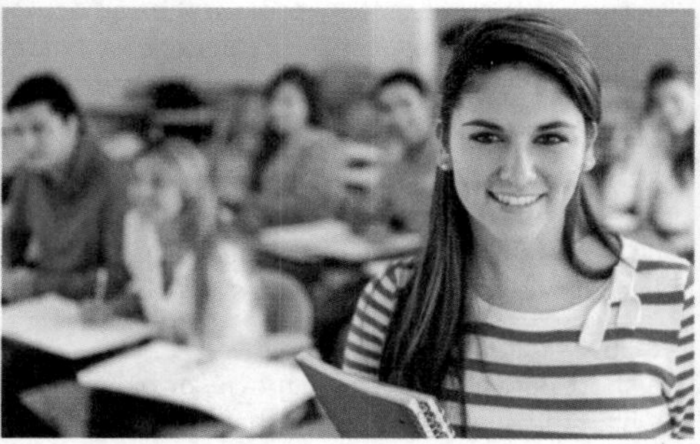

ENTERTAINMENT

1 TV, Movies, and Plays

television *also* **TV** *noun*
the programs that you can watch on a television set: *Is there anything good* ***on TV*** *tonight? | When she's bored, Ashley just lies on the couch and watches television.*

movie *also* **film** (*formal*) *noun*
a story that is told using moving pictures and sound, which is usually about 1½ or 2 hours long. A **movie** is shown at a theater or on television: *We went to see a movie last night.*

play *noun*
a story that actors perform in a theater: *I'm going to be the king in our school play.*

show *noun*
a play, performance, or program on television: *There's a new show on TV tonight that I want to watch. | The show starts at 7:30, but we should get there early to get good seats.*

program *noun*
a play, news report, or performance that you watch on television. **Program** is more formal than **show**: *They always argue about which television program to watch.*

episode *noun*
a television program that is one in a series of programs that tell a story or have the same characters: *I missed last week's episode, so I didn't understand what was happening on tonight's show.*

series *noun*
a set of television programs with the same characters or on the same subject: *The series has been on TV for five years and it's still popular.*

scene *noun*
a short part of a TV show, movie, or play, during which the events happen in the same place: *The car chase is the best scene in the movie.*

act *noun*
one of the main parts of a play, which is made up of one or more scenes: *I got to the theater late and missed the first act.*

2 Watching TV, a Movie, or a Play

watch TV/a show *verb phrase*
to look at and listen to television or a particular program on television: *Do you want to come over and watch TV tonight? | I used to watch that show, but it got boring.*
➔ You can also **watch** a movie if it is on the television, but you **see** a movie at a theater.

be on *verb phrase*
if something is on TV, it is being broadcast by a television station: *The show is on at 8:00.*

be showing *also* **be playing** *verb phrase*
if a movie or play is showing or playing at a theater, people can go to the theater and see it: *The movie is now showing at theaters.*

go to a movie/the movies/a play *verb phrase*
to go to a theater to see a movie or a play: *There's nothing on TV – let's go to the movies.*

3 Types of TV Shows

sitcom *noun*
a funny television program that has the same people in different situations each week: *A few of the new sitcoms are really funny.*

drama (AWL) *noun*
a television program that tells a serious story about people's lives: *Courtroom dramas are very popular, but most lawyers' lives aren't so interesting.*

reality show *noun*
a television program that shows real people doing real things, or real people who have been put in different situations and filmed over a long period: *The reality show follows the lives of eight young people who live together.*

soap *also* **soap opera** *noun*
a story on television about the lives of a group of people: *Aunt Gina watches her favorite soap opera every afternoon.*

documentary *noun*
a television program that gives facts and information on something: *We watched a TV documentary on the Iraq War.*

game show *noun*
a television program in which people play a game in order to win prizes: *On the game show people guess the correct prices of things to win.*

talk show *noun*
a television program in which famous people answer questions about themselves: *Matt Damon was on a talk show last night talking about his new movie.*

cartoon *noun*
a television program with characters that are drawn and not real: *The kids always get up early Saturday morning to watch cartoons.*

4 Types of Movies

comedy *noun*
a funny movie: *It's a comedy about two policemen who always get everything wrong.*

drama (AWL) *noun*
a movie that tells a serious story: *The drama tells the story of a young mother who is dying of cancer.*

romantic comedy *noun*
a funny movie about two people who meet and have a romantic relationship: *All romantic comedies end the same way: the two people always end up together.*

thriller *noun*
a movie that tells an exciting story about murder or other crime: *"Psycho" is a classic thriller about a woman who stops at a motel and disappears.*

action movie *noun*
a movie with a lot of exciting events in it, for example people fighting or chasing each other in cars: *Will Smith has been in a lot of action movies with car chases and gunfights.*

horror movie *noun*
a movie that makes you feel frightened, because dangerous or frightening things happen to the characters: *The horror movie scared me so badly I couldn't get to sleep.*

war movie *noun*
a movie about people fighting a war: *There have already been several war movies about Iraq.*

science fiction movie *also* **sci-fi movie** (*informal*) *noun*
a movie about imaginary events in the future or in outer space: *We saw a science fiction movie that takes place in a world with flying cars.*

animated movie *noun*
a movie made using drawings or photographs of clay models that are put together to look as if they are moving: *Most animated movies, like "Toy Story," are for children.*

western *noun*
a movie about cowboys and life in the late 1800s in the western U.S.: *Jeff Bridges plays a U.S. marshal in the western "True Grit."*

buddy movie *noun*
a movie about two friends and the things that happen to them: *Buddy movies are usually about two men who become close friends even though they have different personalities.*

road movie *noun*
a movie about people who take a long trip in a car and the things that happen to them: *The characters in a road movie develop a lot as they travel around.*

documentary *noun*
a movie that gives facts and information on something: *I learned a lot from the documentary on penguins.*

sequel *noun*
a movie that continues the story of an earlier one: *"Spider-Man 2" was a really great sequel.*

trailer *also* **preview** *noun*
an advertisement that shows small pieces of a new movie: *Have you seen the trailer for the new James Bond movie? It looks really good.*

5 Types of Plays

drama (AWL) *noun*
a play that tells a serious story: *There are a couple of funny moments in the play, but it's really a drama about growing up.*

comedy *noun*
a funny play: *There's a comedy at the Orpheum Theater that's supposed to be very funny.*

tragedy *noun*
a serious play with a very sad ending, especially the death of a main character: *"Romeo and Juliet" is a tragedy in which the young lovers die.*

musical *noun*
a play that includes singing and dancing: *You have to be a great singer or dancer to be in a Broadway musical.*

6 The Story of a TV Show, Movie, or Play

plot *also* **storyline** *noun*
the story that is told in a television show, movie, or play: *The plot was very complicated and I didn't understand what was happening.*

script *noun*
the written words of a television show, movie, or play: *As soon as she read the script, Angela knew the part she wanted in the play.*

7 People Who Work in TV, Movies, and Plays

actor *noun*
someone who performs in television shows, movies, or plays: *He has wanted to be a professional actor since he was in 6th grade.*

actress *noun*
a woman who performs in television shows, movies, or plays. Some women prefer to be called **actors**: *Laura went to New York to become an actress.*

star *noun*
a famous actor: *Many movie stars live in Los Angeles, because a lot of movies are made there.*
→ **The star** of a television show, movie, or play is the person who plays the most important role: *Daniel Radcliffe is* ***the star of*** *the "Harry Potter" movies.*

costar *noun*
one of two or more famous actors who appear together in a television show, movie, or play: *Brad Pitt and Michael Fassbender are costars in the new movie.*

cast *noun*
all the actors in a television show, movie, or play: *Two new actors joined the cast of the popular TV show this fall.*

director *noun*
the person who tells actors what to do when they are making a television show, movie, or play: *Ron Howard started as a child actor, but as an adult, he has been the director of many successful films.*

producer *noun*
someone whose job is to control how a television show, movie, or play is prepared: *Hollywood producers earn a lot of money if their movies are successful.*

8 Music and Musicians

concert *noun*
a performance given by a musician or musicians: *Are you going to the Beyoncé concert?*

musician *noun*
someone who plays music well, especially as a job to entertain people: *Greg is a talented musician who can play three instruments.*

guitar/saxophone/piano etc. player *noun*
someone who performs music using a guitar, saxophone, piano, etc.: *The singer wasn't that great, but her piano player was amazing.*

singer *noun*
someone who sings as a job: *The lead singer of the band is a girl.*

rock/pop/country etc. star *noun*
a singer or musician who is very famous for performing rock, pop, etc. music: *My sister has pictures of pop stars all over her bedroom wall.*

band *noun*
a group of musicians that plays popular music: *We're still looking for a band to play at next month's dance.*

orchestra *noun*
a large group of musicians that plays classical music: *Julia plays violin in the school orchestra.*

conductor *noun*
someone who stands in front of an orchestra and directs the playing of the musicians: *The conductor was waving his arms around while the orchestra played.*

9 Types of Music

pop *also* **pop music** *noun*
a type of modern music that is popular with young people, and usually has simple tunes and a strong beat: *Katy Perry's pop music is fun to dance to.*

rock *also* **rock music** *noun*
a type of popular music with a strong loud beat, made using drums and electric guitars: *I could hear the drumbeat of the rock music he was listening to coming out of his headphones.*

rap *also* **rap music** *noun*
a type of popular music in which someone speaks words instead of singing them: *I like rap because it's like poetry with a beat.*

hip hop *also* **hip-hop music** *noun*
a type of popular music that can include rapping, scratching records, using small pieces of other songs, and using your voice to make drumbeats and other musical sounds: *My brother breakdances to hip-hop music.*

R & B *noun*
a type of popular music developed by African Americans that has strong rhythms and smooth singing: *Alicia Keys is an amazing R & B singer.*

dance music *also* **club music** *noun*
a type of popular music made using electronic equipment, with a very fast strong beat that young people dance to: *The dance music at the club was so loud I couldn't talk to my friends.*

country *also* **country music, country and western** *noun*
a type of popular music from the southern and western U.S.: *A couple of guys in cowboy hats were listening to country music on the radio.*

jazz *noun*
a type of music in which the musicians often change the music or add notes as they play: *My friend Al plays trumpet in a jazz band.*

classical *also* **classical music** *noun*
a type of music that is considered to be serious and has been popular for a very long time, for example the music of Beethoven or Mozart: *Orchestras usually play classical music.*

THE ENVIRONMENT

1 The Environment

the environment *noun*
the natural world, including water, air, land, plants, and sometimes animals, that can be harmed by the way humans live: *Chemicals from the factory are dangerous to the environment.* | *What effect will the dam have on the environment?*

ecology *noun*
the relationship between the environment and all the plants, animals, and people living there: *The oil spill could affect* ***the ecology of*** *the seashore.*

ecosystem *noun*
all the plants and animals in a place, that are all connected with each other and affect each other: *The decrease in the number of birds is affecting the island's ecosystem.*

habitat *noun*
the place in which a plant or animal lives: *The jungle is the tiger's natural habitat.*

biome *noun*
a type of environment that has a particular type of weather and particular types of plants: *The snake is found only in desert biomes.*

biodiversity *noun*
all the different types of plants and animals in a particular place: *Cutting down forests and planting single crops like corn have greatly reduced biodiversity.*

food chain *noun*
a system of plants and animals in an area, in which a plant is eaten by an insect or other animal, which is then eaten by a larger animal, and so on: *If one part of the food chain is harmed, it affects every other part of the chain.*

food web *noun*
all the food chains in an area that are connected with each other: *The living things in the ocean form a food web.*

2 Damage to the Environment

global warming *noun*
an increase in world temperatures, caused by an increase of carbon dioxide, and other gases, around the Earth: *Because of global warming, sea levels will rise as the ice caps melt.*

climate change *noun*
changes in the weather across large areas of the Earth as the Earth gets warmer: *Farmers may eventually have to plant different crops as a result of climate change.*

greenhouse effect *noun*
the process by which the air around the Earth is slowly getting warmer because gases like carbon dioxide stop the heat from escaping: *Burning coal and oil over the past 200 years has greatly increased the greenhouse effect.*

ozone layer *noun*
the layer of gases around the Earth that stops a type of heat from the sun from harming the Earth. Chemicals that people use cause the **ozone layer** to become thinner so that more harmful heat from the sun reaches the Earth: *If the ozone layer keeps getting thinner, more people will probably get skin cancer.*

ice cap *also* **polar ice cap** *noun*
an area of thick ice that permanently covers the North and South Poles. As the Earth becomes warmer, the **ice caps** will melt and raise the levels of the oceans: *Melting ice caps could mean that some island countries would be completely flooded.*

deforestation *noun*
the process of cutting down too many trees in an area so that the environment is badly damaged: *Deforestation in the rain forest has destroyed the homes of many animal species.*

erosion (AWL) *noun*
the gradual destruction of land by the weather or by water: *Erosion on the hills is worse where too many trees have been cut down.*

endangered species *noun phrase*
a type of animal or plant that soon might not exist anymore because there are very few left: *If the wetlands are destroyed, the endangered species that live there will disappear forever.*

extinct *adjective*
a plant or animal that is extinct no longer exists: *The tigers could become extinct if the forests they live in are not protected.*

3 Things That Damage the Environment

pollution *noun*
substances that make air, water, or soil dirty and dangerous to people or other living things: *They tested the level of water pollution in local rivers.*

→ You can use **pollute** as a verb: *The factory pollutes the air and water.* **Polluted** is the adjective: *The river is polluted and lots of fish have died.*

smog *noun*
dirty air caused by smoke from cars and factories in cities: *The city is covered in smog for much of the year.*

greenhouse gas *noun*
a type of gas that traps heat above the Earth and causes the air around the Earth to gradually warm up. **Greenhouse gases** cause the greenhouse effect: *Greenhouse gases are produced by factories and vehicles.*

fossil fuel *noun*
a substance such as coal, gas, or oil that can be burned for energy. **Fossil fuels** are formed from plants and animals that died millions of years ago. Burning these fuels can pollute the air and produce carbon dioxide, which is a greenhouse gas: *We should reduce our use of fossil fuels and find cleaner sources of energy.*

carbon emissions *noun*
carbon dioxide that is put in the air when fossil fuels are burned: *As the number of cars and factories have increased, so have carbon emissions.*

carbon footprint *noun*
the amount of carbon dioxide that a person or organization produces by the things they do. Someone's **carbon footprint** is a measurement of the harm he or she does to the environment: *You can reduce your carbon footprint by driving your car less.*

acid rain *noun*
rain that contains harmful chemicals that can damage the environment. **Acid rain** is caused by chemicals in the air, for example from cars and factories: *The reason the trees were dying was acid rain.*

toxic waste *also* **hazardous waste** *noun*
waste products such as chemicals that are harmful to people, animals, or the environment: *Toxic waste from the factory ended up in the river and killed the fish.*

4 Things That Are Good for the Environment

conservation *noun*
the activity of protecting wild plants and animals: *Forest conservation protects the habitat of the brown bear and many other species.*

environmentally friendly *adjective*
not harmful to the environment: *Is there such a thing as an environmentally friendly car?*

green *adjective*
green methods and products are intended not to cause damage to the environment: *Green cleaning products often work as well as harmful chemicals.*

clean *adjective*
clean fuels or forms of energy do not put harmful substances in the air: *We should use more clean energy sources like solar power.*

organic *adjective*
organic food is grown or produced naturally, without using chemicals: *The restaurant uses only organic meat and vegetables.*

sustainable (AWL) *adjective*
a sustainable method of doing something can continue for a long time, because it does not cause damage to the environment or use up all of the resources: *Sustainable farming methods keep the soil healthy.*

recycle *verb*
to put used newspapers, bottles, cans, etc. through a process so that they can be used again for making new things: *We collect and recycle empty bottles and cans.*
→ **Recycling** is the noun: *The city has increased the amount of recycling it does.*

5 Clean Power or Energy

solar/wind/wave power *also* **solar/wind/wave energy** *noun*
energy that is taken from the sun, wind, or ocean and turned into electricity: *If we use more wind power, we could use less oil that comes from foreign countries.*

wind turbine *noun*
a very large structure with parts that turn around in the wind, used for producing electricity: *The wind turbines in the desert turn the high winds into electricity.*

wind farm *noun*
a place where a lot of wind turbines have been built in order to produce electricity: *We can expect to see more wind farms in windy areas across the plains.*

solar panel *noun*
a piece of equipment, usually put on a roof, that collects and uses the sun's energy to heat water or make electricity: *The solar panels on the roof provide all the electricity the family needs.*

biofuel *noun*
a substance made from plants or animal waste that can be used to produce heat or power: *Corn*

is being used to make biofuels, but biofuels still take energy to produce, and release carbon when they are burned.

alternative (AWL) *adjective*
alternative forms of energy are ones that are used instead of fossil fuels, because they do less damage to the environment: ***Wind and solar power are two common types of alternative energy.***

renewable *adjective*
renewable energy comes from things like the wind or the sun, and you will always be able to get more of it because it continues to be produced all the time: ***The building is heated using renewable energy from the sun.***

6 People Who Protect the Environment

environmentalist (AWL) *noun*
someone who is concerned about protecting the environment: ***As an environmentalist, Maria has worked hard to clean up the parks in her area.***

environmental group *noun*
an organization that works to protect the environment: ***Environmental groups are asking the government for stricter rules on pollution.***

conservationist *noun*
someone who works to protect and manage natural resources such as water, forests, and land: ***Conservationists believe the dam would harm local wildlife.***

solar panels

wind farm

GOVERNMENT AND POLITICS

1 Government

government *noun*
the organization that controls a country, state, or city, and that makes all the decisions and laws: *People like to blame the government when the economy is bad, but how much control does it really have?*

administration (AWL) *noun*
the U.S. president and the people who work for him or her: *The new administration aims to reduce unemployment in America.*

the authorities *noun*
an organization or government department that controls something: *If you have any information about the crime, please report it to the authorities.*

federal (AWL) *adjective*
relating to the government of the U.S. as a whole: *Federal officials ordered that the new security equipment had to be used in all airports.*

2 Parts of the U.S. Government

a branch of government *noun phrase*
a part of the government that does a particular thing: *In the U.S. system, there are three branches of government – the executive, the legislative, and the judiciary.*

the executive *noun*
the part of the government that includes the president and the people who work for him or her: *The executive can introduce a bill, but it must be approved by Congress before it will become a law.*

the legislature (AWL) *noun*
the part of the government that makes laws. In the U.S., **the legislature** is called Congress and it includes the House of Representatives and the Senate: *Both houses in the legislature must pass a bill before it can be signed by the president and become law.*

the judiciary *noun*
the part of the government that includes the courts. **The judiciary** makes decisions about whether a law has been broken and how laws should be understood and used in different situations: *The judiciary must be fair and not involved in politics, so that peoples' rights are protected.*
→ The highest court in the U.S. **judiciary** is **the Supreme Court**.

Congress *noun*
the two parts of the U.S. **legislature** as a whole: *Congress is not allowed to make any law that limits people's freedom of speech.*

the House of Representatives *also* **the House** *(informal) noun*
one of the two parts of the U.S. **legislature**. **The House of Representatives** is made up of people who have been elected from each state. Representatives are elected every two years: *Because California is such a large state, it has 53 representatives in the House of Representatives.*

the Senate *noun*
one of the two parts of the U.S. **legislature**. **The Senate** is made up of 100 people called senators, two from each state. Senators are elected every six years: *The Senate has passed the bill, and now it will be discussed in the House.*

the Cabinet *noun*
the group of people who give advice to the president and who are chosen by him or her. **The Cabinet** is made up of the vice president and the heads of the 15 departments of government: *She was appointed to the Cabinet as Secretary of State in 2009.*

3 Politicians in the U.S.

politician *noun*
someone who is elected as a member of the government, or who wants to be elected: *Politicians should be working together to solve our country's problems.*

representative *also* **congressman** *or* **congresswoman** *noun*
an elected member of the U.S. **House of Representatives**: *Congressman Capuano will make a statement later today.* | *Ms. Pingree is the representative from the 1st District in Maine.*

senator *noun*
an elected member of the U.S. **Senate**: *The senators from North Carolina were both at the meeting.*
→ States also have legislatures. Some state legislatures are also called the **House of Representatives** and the **Senate**, but other states call the legislature the **Assembly** and the **Senate**. A politician who is elected to these is

called a **representative**, **senator**, **assemblyman**, or **assemblywoman**.

4 Government Leaders

leader *noun*
the person who is in charge of a country or group of people: *Several important community leaders attended the meeting, including the imam from the local mosque.*

president *noun*
the leader of some countries, for example the U.S.: ***The president of** the U.S. can be elected for two four-year terms.* | *President Obama was the first African-American president of this country.*

head of state *noun phrase*
the official leader of a country, for example a king or a president. The **head of state** is not always the same person as the political leader of the country's government: *The queen acts as the head of state in England, and the prime minister is the leader of the government.*

secretary *noun*
one of the members of the U.S. president's **Cabinet**. Each **secretary** is in charge of a different department of the government: *The **Secretary of State** is in charge of relations with foreign countries.* | *Secretary Vasquez will visit several Asian countries next week.*

governor *noun*
the leader of a U.S. state: *Governor Dayton visited the Minnesota State Fair today.* | *She was elected **governor of** New Mexico in 2010.*

mayor *noun*
the leader of a city: *He ran for **mayor of** Chicago last year.*

5 The Government in Other Countries

parliament *noun*
the part of government, in some countries, that makes laws and is made up of elected officials: *The English parliament will discuss the issue today.*

member of parliament *also* **MP** *noun*
one of the people who has been elected to be in a parliament: *She is a member of parliament from North Wales.* | *Several MPs disagree with the treaty.*

prime minister *noun*
the political leader of a country with a parliament. The **prime minister** is usually the most important leader in the political party that has power: *The Canadian prime minister is visiting Washington today.*

minister *noun*
a person chosen by a leader to be in charge of a government department: *He was appointed **Minister of** Education in 2012.*

premier *noun*
the leader of a state or province in some countries: *He was the premier of Ontario during some very difficult economic times.*
→ In some countries **premier** is used to mean the same as **prime minister**.

king *also* **queen** *noun*
the male or female ruler of a country who has the position because he or she comes from a royal family: *In 1016 he became the **king of** Norway.*

dictator *noun*
a leader of a country who has complete power over that country: *Josef Stalin was a dictator in the Soviet Union who sent many people to their deaths.*

6 To Govern or Rule a Country

govern *verb*
to legally control a country, state, or city, and make all the decisions and laws: *Both political parties must work together to govern the country.*

rule *verb*
to govern a country. You use **rule** about a king, queen, military leader, or foreign government that has power over a country and the people in it: *India was ruled by the British until it became independent in 1947.*

run *verb (informal)*
run means the same as **govern** but sounds informal: *If you don't like the way the president is running the country, then vote for someone else.*

be in power *verb phrase*
to be the political leader or group that controls a country at a particular time: *Republicans plan to cut taxes when they are in power again.*

hold office *verb phrase*
to have an important position in government, especially one that you are elected to do: *Senators hold office for six years between elections.*

7 Choosing a Leader or Government

vote *verb*
to show which person or plan you choose by marking a piece of paper, pressing a button, or raising your hand: *People over age 18 are able to vote in elections.* | *Who will you **vote for** in the next presidential election?* | *Fourteen representatives **voted against** the bill.*

elect *verb*
to choose someone for an official position by

voting: *She was **elected to** the state House of Representatives in 2010.*

nominate *verb (formal)*
if a group of people nominates someone, they choose that person to be considered for a particular job. There are usually several people who are **nominated**, and then there is a vote to officially choose one of them: *Elena, Chris, and Josh were nominated for class representative, and then we voted to choose one of them.*
→ The person who is nominated is called a **nominee**.

candidate *noun*
someone who is trying to win an election, for example to become a senator or president: *The candidates are taking part in a debate on Thursday.*

election *noun*
an occasion when people choose a government official or leader by voting: *In a fair election, every vote is counted.* | *Ronald Reagan **won the** U.S. presidential **election** in 1980.*

primary *noun*
a vote in U.S. politics in which people decide who will be their political party's candidate in an election: *Mitt Romney won the Republican primary in New Hampshire in 2012.*

the White House

the Capitol
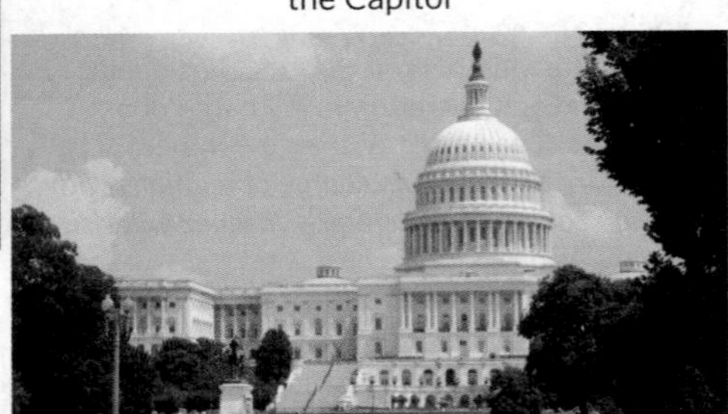

JOBS AND WORK

1 Jobs and Work

work *noun*
activities that you are paid for doing: *What time do you start work? | Why were you late for work this morning?*

job (AWL) *noun*
work that you do regularly for a particular person or company, in order to earn money: *She got a job at a bank.*

profession *noun*
a job that needs special education and training, such as being a lawyer or a doctor: *There are now many women in the legal profession.*

occupation (AWL) *noun (formal)*
the type of job that someone does. **Occupation** is often used on official documents: *Please give your name, age, and occupation.*

career *noun*
the work you do or plan to do for most of your life: *During his **career as** a journalist he interviewed many famous people.*

trade *noun*
a job that involves using your hands, and for which you need special training: *Most of the men had worked in skilled trades such as carpentry and printing.*

self-employed *adjective*
working for yourself or having your own company, rather than working for a company that someone else owns: *When you are self-employed, you have to carefully manage your own financial accounts.*

freelance *adjective*
doing work for several companies, rather than being an employee of only one company: *She is a freelance journalist who writes about travel.*
→ **Freelance** can also be used about the work that someone does: *Eleni has been doing freelance work from home and taking care of her two children.*

manual labor *also* **manual work** *noun*
difficult physical work that is done with your hands or body, especially when you do not need special skills to do the work: *After years of manual labor in the fields, he developed serious problems with his back.*

skilled *adjective*
a skilled worker has a lot of training and experience, and is able to do a job well: *A highly skilled chef can earn a lot of money.*

white-collar *adjective*
white-collar workers have jobs in offices rather than doing physical work, and they usually need a college degree. You can also use **white-collar** to describe jobs: *Many white-collar jobs in banking were lost during the most recent recession.*

blue-collar *adjective*
blue-collar workers have jobs in which they do physical work, and they do not need a college degree. You can also use **blue-collar** to describe jobs: *There are fewer jobs in factories for blue-collar workers than there were in the 1950s.*

2 To Work

work *verb*
to do a job to earn money: *Corinne **works at** a bookstore. | My uncle **works for** the fire department.*

be employed *verb phrase (formal)*
to work for a company or organization, especially when you have a permanent job there: *Mr. Hardy has **been employed as** the school's music teacher since 1995.*

3 People Who Work

worker *noun*
someone who does a job, but who is not a manager: *Factory workers at the auto manufacturer get paid around $25 an hour.*

employee *noun*
someone who has a job with a person, company, or organization. **Employee** is more formal than **worker**: *Marcia has been an **employee at** the bank for ten years.*

staff *noun*
all the people who work for an organization. You usually use **staff** about people who work in offices, not about people who do physical work: *The library staff will be able to help you find the book you want.*

colleague (AWL) *noun*
someone who works with you in the same office

or organization. **Colleague** is used especially by people who work in jobs that need special training, such as teachers, doctors, or lawyers: *The research was carried out by Dr. Francis and her colleagues at Johns Hopkins University in Baltimore.*

coworker *noun*
someone who works with you in the same office or organization: *Some of my coworkers and I are going out for dinner after work on Wednesday.*

temporary worker *also* **temp** *noun*
someone who is hired by a company to do a job for a short period of time: *We hire temps to answer the phones when we are very busy.*

4 To Give Someone a Job or Lose a Job

hire *verb*
to give someone a job: *It's still a small company, but they want to hire 20 new employees before June.*

employ *verb*
to have someone working for you and being paid: *The factory employs over 200 people.*

lay off *phrasal verb*
if a company lays off workers, it stops employing them because it does not have enough work for them: *Peter was laid off when his employer cut jobs to save money.*

fire *verb*
to make someone leave his or her job, especially because he or she has not been doing it well or has done something wrong: *He was fired from his job because he was caught stealing.*

lose your job *verb phrase*
to be forced to leave your job: *I lost my job when my company was bought by one of our competitors.*

unemployed *adjective*
without a job: *There are few jobs in the area, and 50% of the men are unemployed.*

be out of work *verb phrase*
to be unemployed, especially for a long time. You use **out of work** when someone had a job before: *My dad has been out of work for two years.*

5 Money You Get for Working

earn *verb*
to get money for the work you do: *Kevin is looking for a job on the weekends to earn some extra money.*

pay *verb*
to give money to someone because he or she has done work for you: *The company pays their employees at the end of every month.*

wages *noun*
money that you get each day, week, or month for doing a job, based on the number of hours you work: *The farm workers waited in line for their wages at the end of the week.*

salary *noun*
money that you get regularly as payment for the job you do. You usually talk about someone's **salary** by saying how much he or she earns each year, but part of the salary is paid each month: *The average salary for a school teacher in this district is around $42,000.*

benefits *noun*
health insurance, vacation time, and other advantages that you get from an employer in addition to the money you earn: *The salary at his new job is good, and the benefits include three weeks of vacation.*

6 The Person You Work For

employer *noun*
a person, company, or organization that pays people to work for them: *She was a good employer and always treated me fairly.* | *The shoe factory is the largest employer in the area.*

boss *noun (informal)*
someone who is in charge of a group of people at work and tells them what to do: *I asked my boss if I could have a day off next week.*

manager *noun*
someone who is in charge of a store or part of an organization: *He is a manager in the sales department, with ten people who work for him.*

supervisor *noun*
the person who is in charge of a group of workers, and who makes sure that they do the right things while they work: *Every year, I have a meeting with my supervisor to discuss my job performance.*

7 Finding a Job

look for a job *verb phrase*
to spend time trying to get a job, for example by looking online or in newspapers, sending letters to companies, and going to interviews: *Katia's been looking for a job for six months, and she finally found one at a department store.*

apply *verb*
to try to get a job by writing a letter and sending information about yourself and your skills to a company that has a job available: *I'm* ***applying*** *for a job at the new restaurant on Water Street.*

fill out *phrasal verb*
to write information in the spaces on a form, for

example a job application: *Fill out the online form, and send it to us with your cover letter.*

résumé *also* **resume** *noun*
a document that shows the jobs you have had, your skills, and your education, which you send to a company that you want to work for: *Please send your résumé and a cover letter to the email address above.*

cover letter *noun*
a letter you send with your **résumé** that you use to explain briefly why you think you would be good at a particular job: *Keep your cover letter short, with only the most important points in it.*

application *noun*
a form on which you write information about yourself and your skills when you apply for a job: *The company received more than 100* ***applications for*** *the job.*

interview *noun*
an occasion when someone at a company asks you questions so that they can decide whether they want to hire you: *I have an* ***interview for*** *a job at a law firm next week.*
→ You can also use **interview** as a verb: *This week the director was* ***interviewing*** *people* ***for*** *the marketing job.*

8 Time That You Spend Working

shift *noun*
one of the periods during each day and night when workers in a factory, hospital, etc. are at work: *I told my boss I could do some extra shifts if he needed more help. | Cara is a nurse who works* ***the night shift*** *at the hospital.*

part-time *adjective, adverb*
if you work part-time, you work for only part of each day or week: *I got a part-time job washing dishes at a restaurant. | He works part-time as a librarian.*

full-time *adjective, adverb*
if you work full-time, you work 35 or more hours each week: *When she got out of college, she could not find a full-time job, so she took two part-time jobs. | He works full-time as a chef.*

overtime *noun*
extra hours that someone works at a job, in addition to the normal number of hours he or she works in a week: *I* ***worked*** *15 hours of* ***overtime*** *last month, because they needed help with the Christmas displays.*

plant **workers**

office **staff**

TO MAKE A SOUND

1 To Make a Sound or Noise

make a sound *also* **make a noise** *verb phrase*
to produce something that can be heard. You usually use **make a noise** for a sound that is loud or annoying: *Ed left without making a sound, so we didn't even know he was gone.* | *Dry soil makes a noise when you walk on it.*
→ You can also use words to describe the particular type of **sound** or **noise** that is made: *The automatic door made a sucking sound as it closed behind me.*

go bang/pop/beep etc. *verb phrase (informal)*
to make a banging, popping, beeping, etc. noise: *The answering machine goes beep beep beep when there's a message on it.*

with a bang/crash/thud etc. *phrase*
used to describe the sound that is made when something else happens: *The book fell to the floor with a thud.*

go off *phrasal verb*
if an alarm, timer, or something similar goes off, it makes a loud noise: *Everyone left the building when the fire alarm went off.*

sound *verb (formal)*
to produce something you can hear: *The bell sounded for everyone to go to class.*
→ You can also use **sound** to describe how something seems when you hear it: *He sounded angry.* | *The washing machine sounds funny – is it working all right?*

2 To Make a High Sound

squeak *verb*
to make a short high sound that is not loud: *A rat squeaked and ran into the bushes.* | *This chair squeaks every time I move.*

creak *verb*
if something creaks, it makes a long high noise when it is moved or pressed. You use **creak** especially about something wooden such as a door, bed, or stairs: *The floorboards creaked as she walked across the room.*

screech *verb*
to make a loud long high noise that is unpleasant. **Screech** is used especially about someone's voice, or about brakes or tires: *The plane's tires screeched as it landed.* | *She screeched at me to take off my muddy boots.*

squeal *verb*
to make a long high sound or cry: *The tires squealed as they drove off.* | *The children squealed with excitement.*

scream *verb*
to make a loud high noise with your voice because you are frightened, hurt, excited, etc.: *Charlie's sister screamed when he bit her finger.*

shriek *verb*
to make a loud unpleasantly high noise with your voice because you are frightened, excited, or angry: *"Watch out!" she shrieked.*

cheep *verb*
if a young bird cheeps, it makes a weak high noise: *The chicks were cheeping in the nest.*

3 To Make a Sound When Hitting or Falling onto Something

bang *verb*
to make a loud noise by hitting something hard, especially something metal: *The kids were banging pots with wooden spoons.* | *The gate keeps banging in the wind.*

crash *verb*
to make a sudden loud sound by hitting hard against something big: *The big waves crashed against the shore.*

thud *verb*
if something heavy thuds, it makes a low sound when it hits the ground: *The tree branch thudded to the ground.*

crack *verb*
to make a quick loud sound like the sound of something breaking: *The dry branches cracked under his feet.* | *Rob rubbed his hands together and cracked his knuckles.*

clatter *verb*
if a hard object clatters, it makes several loud short sounds as it hits another hard object or surface, especially because it has fallen: *The pot fell out of my hand and* ***clattered onto*** *the floor.*

thump *verb*
to hit something in a way that makes a low noise: *His feet thumped loudly down the hallway.*

4 To Make a Sound by Repeatedly Hitting Something

knock *verb*
to hit a door with your knuckles to make a noise and get someone's attention: *Someone's* ***knocking at*** *the door – go see who it is.*

tap *verb*
to gently hit your fingers or knuckles against a door or window to get someone's attention: *I heard someone* ***tapping on*** *my door.*

rap *verb*
to knock on something with force and a loud sound: *The officer* ***rapped on*** *the door and shouted "Police!"*

rattle *verb*
if a hard object rattles, it moves or shakes and makes short knocking sounds. **Rattle** is used especially when part of something is loose and is hitting against something repeatedly: *There's something rattling inside the washing machine.* | *The wind was rattling the windows so hard I thought they might break.*

patter *verb*
if water patters, it makes quiet sounds as it keeps hitting a surface lightly and quickly: *Rain* ***pattered against*** *the tin roof of the shed.*
→ You can also use **patter** to describe the sound that small children make when they walk: *Eddie pattered up the stairs in his bare feet.*

5 To Make the Sound that Glass or Metal Makes When It Hits Something

clink *verb*
if glass or metal objects clink, they make a short ringing sound when they touch: *Spoons* ***clinked against*** *cups as the women stirred their tea.*

clank *verb*
if a heavy metal object clanks, it makes a short loud sound as it hits another hard or metal object: *The car's snow chains clanked on the ice.*

clang *verb*
if a piece of metal clangs, it makes a loud ringing sound when it hits something: *The gates clanged shut again.*

jingle *verb*
to shake small metal objects together so that they produce a noise: *Cody jingled the car keys in his pocket.*

tinkle *verb*
to make a high soft repeated sound, like a small bell: *Ice tinkled in their glasses as they drank.*

6 To Make the Sound of a Storm, Gun, or Bomb

boom *verb*
to make a deep loud sound, like the sound of guns or drums: *Cannons boomed in the distance.*

roar *verb*
if a storm or strong wind roars, it makes a continuous loud noise: *Outside the wind roared and shook the house.*

rumble *verb*
to make a series of long low sounds: *The sky clouded over, thunder rumbled, and lightning flashed.* | *The sound of the big guns rumbled in the night.*

crack *verb*
to make a loud fast sound, like something breaking: *Thunder cracked overhead, and then it began to rain hard.* | *His rifle cracked as he took a shot.*

7 To Make the Sound of Something Burning or Cooking

crackle *verb*
to make repeated short sounds, like something burning in a fire: *In the living room, a log crackled on the fire.*

sizzle *verb*
to make the sound of food cooking in hot oil: *Bacon was sizzling in the frying pan.*

8 To Make a Quiet Gentle Sound

murmur *verb*
to make a soft low sound: *A small stream murmured near the campsite.* | *She murmured something in her sleep.*

rustle *verb*
if something such as leaves or papers rustle, they make a soft noise as they rub against each other: *Her long silk skirt rustled as she walked.* | *The breeze rustled the leaves in the trees.*

rumble *verb*
if your stomach rumbles, it makes a series of

long low sounds: *He was hungry, and his stomach rumbled.*

swish *verb*
to move quickly through the air with a quiet sound: *The curtains swished open.* | *An arrow swished through the air.*

9 To Make the Sound of Gas or Air Escaping

pop *verb*
if a bubble or balloon pops, it breaks with a short loud sound: *She stuck a pin in the balloon and it popped.*

hiss *verb*
if something such as a tire or ball hisses, it makes a continuous quiet high sound as air leaves it: *Air hissed out of the punctured tire.*

fizz *verb*
to make the continuous quiet high sound that is made by some kinds of drinks with bubbles: *The cola fizzed in the glass.*

10 To Make the Sound of a Machine, Engine, or Car

buzz *verb*
to make a continuous noise like the sound of a bee: *Police helicopters buzzed overhead.*

hum *verb*
to make a low steady sound like "mmm": *The computer was still on and humming.*

whirr *verb*
to make a fairly quiet, regular sound, like something turning very quickly and beating against the air: *It was quiet in the room except for a fan that was whirring in the window.*

whine *verb*
if a machine whines, it makes an unpleasant continuous high sound: *The scooter strained and whined as it went up the hill.*

tick *verb*
if a clock or other machine ticks, it makes a quiet regular repeated sound: *I don't even hear the clock tick anymore – I'm so used to it.*

beep *verb*
if a machine beeps, it makes a short high sound: *The microwave beeps three times when it's done cooking.*

roar *verb*
if an engine roars, it makes a very loud noise when it is working hard: *The Ferrari roared and shot off down the road.*

rumble *verb*
if traffic, vehicles, or engines rumble, they make a series of long low sounds: *Big trucks rumbled over the bridge.*

11 To Make the Sound of a Bell or Horn

ring *verb*
if a bell or telephone rings, it makes a sound: *The church bells were ringing.* | *I rang the doorbell, but no one came.*

toll *verb*
if a large bell tolls, it keeps ringing slowly: *The big bell in the clock tower tolled precisely at noon.*

chime *verb*
if a clock or bell chimes, it makes a ringing sound: *It was one o'clock, and the clock chimed.*

tinkle *verb*
to make a high soft ringing sound: *She tinkled a little brass bell to get the servant's attention.*

honk *verb*
if a car horn honks, it makes a clear loud sound: *The cab driver honked his horn when the light turned green.*

12 To Make the Sound of Liquid or Wet Things

splash *verb*
if a liquid splashes, it falls or hits against something and makes a noise: *The waves splashed against the dock.*

squish *verb*
to make a soft sucking sound by moving in or through something soft and wet: *His tennis shoes were wet, and they squished when he walked.*

gurgle *verb*
if water gurgles, it makes a low irregular sound, like water flowing through a pipe: *The pipes in the attic gurgle in the night and keep me awake.*

bubble *verb*
to make the continuous repeated sound that water makes when it boils: *He took the lid off the pan when he heard the water bubbling.*

plop *verb*
to make a sound like something solid falling into water: *Noah threw the rock, and it plopped in the river.*

→ All of these verbs can also be used as nouns: *I heard the rumble of traffic on the freeway.* | *Please leave a message after the beep.* | *There was a murmur of voices coming from the kitchen.* | *We listened to the crash of the waves.*

MEDICAL TREATMENT

1 Health and Medicine

medicine *noun*
the treatment and study of illnesses and injuries: *Dr. Thompson has practiced medicine for 30 years.* | *Modern medicine can cure many more illnesses than in the past.*

medical (AWL) *adjective*
relating to medicine and the treatment of illnesses and injuries: *The injury required immediate medical attention.*

health care *noun*
medical treatment and care: *Amanda is considering nursing school and a career in health care.*

health insurance *noun*
an arrangement by which you pay a company an amount of money regularly, and they pay for your medical treatment if you need it: *We don't have very good health insurance, so we don't go to the doctor very often.*

2 People Who Work in Medicine

doctor *noun*
someone whose job is treating people who are sick or hurt: *Josh went to the doctor because his stomach hurt.*

surgeon *noun*
a doctor who cuts open someone's body to fix or replace something inside: *The surgeon operated on the patient's knee.*

pediatrician *noun*
a doctor who treats children who are sick or hurt: *When Bobby started throwing up, his dad called the pediatrician.*

gynecologist *noun*
a doctor who treats medical conditions and illnesses that affect only women: *If you think you may be pregnant, you should see a gynecologist.*

dentist *noun*
a doctor whose job is to work on people's teeth: *The dentist said I didn't have any cavities.*

nurse *noun*
someone whose job is to take care of people who are sick or hurt: *The school nurse sent Chris home because he had a fever.*

paramedic *noun*
someone who works in an ambulance and whose job is to help sick or hurt people until they get to a hospital: *Paramedics carried the man out of the house and put him into the ambulance.*

3 Where You Go for Medical Treatment

hospital *noun*
a building where doctors and nurses help people who are sick or hurt: *Grandma's in the hospital because she broke her hip.*

clinic *noun*
a place where people can get medical treatment or advice: *They're giving free flu shots at the clinic.*

doctor's office *noun*
the place where a doctor works, and sees and treats patients: *Try to get to the doctor's office 15 minutes before your appointment.*

emergency room *noun*
the part of a hospital that treats people who have been hurt or are very sick, and need immediate treatment: *The emergency room was full of people injured in the bus accident.*

4 Illnesses and Being Sick

illness *noun*
something wrong with you that makes you feel sick: *He is in the hospital suffering from a serious illness.*
→ **Illness** also means the state of being sick: *Ahmed had missed a lot of school because of illness.*

sickness *noun*
the state or feeling of being sick: *She had to take a day off work due to sickness.*

disease *noun*
an illness that has a particular cause. You usually use **disease** about a serious illness: *More drugs are being developed to fight diseases such as cancer.*

cold *noun*
a common illness that blocks your nose, makes your throat painful, makes you cough, etc.: *My nose is running and my throat is scratchy, so I think I'm getting a cold.*

virus *noun*
a very small living thing that causes infectious illnesses, or the illness caused by this: *Rick*

caught a virus at school and was sick for a week with a fever and sore throat.

the flu *noun*
a disease that makes it hard for you to breathe, gives you a fever, and makes your muscles hurt: *I was so sick with the flu, I couldn't get out of bed.*

be sick *verb phrase*
to have a disease or illness: *If you're sick, stay home from school.*

be ill *verb phrase*
be ill means the same as **be sick** but is more formal: *I'm sorry I couldn't come to the meeting, but I was ill.*

5 At the Doctor's Office

check-up *noun*
a medical check that happens regularly to make sure you are healthy: *It's good to go to the dentist for a check-up every six months.* | *The children have an annual check-up with the pediatrician.*

exam *also* **examination** (*formal*) *noun*
a medical check of all or part of your body: *The examination of her chest showed that the infection was gone.* | *New pilots should have a medical exam before being allowed to fly.*

physical *also* **physical examination** *noun*
a medical check of your body to make sure that you are healthy, especially one that you have before you start a new job or new activity: *All team members have to have a complete physical before playing.*

examine *verb*
if a doctor examines you, he or she looks at your body to see if you are healthy: *The doctor examined my leg to see if it was broken.*

test *noun*
a short medical examination of part of your body: *We had hearing tests at school.*

prescribe *verb*
if a doctor prescribes medicine, he or she says what medicine or treatment a sick person should have: *Dr. Gordon said that the baby had an ear infection and prescribed an antibiotic.*

6 Medical Treatment

treatment *noun*
a medical method for making a sick or injured person better: *Doctors are testing the drug as a* ***treatment for*** *depression.* | *Injured passengers were rushed to the hospital* ***for treatment.***

treat *verb*
to do something to make a sick or injured person better, or to make an illness or injury go away: *In some countries, it is difficult to treat patients because there is not enough medicine.* | *Malaria can be* ***treated with*** *drugs.*

heal *verb*
to make a wound or sick person get better: *Vitamin C helps your body to heal wounds.*

cure *noun*
a medicine or medical treatment that makes a disease go away completely: *Scientists are still working hard to find a* ***cure for*** *AIDS.*

cure *verb*
to make an injury or illness go away so that someone is well again: *When the disease is found early, it can be easily treated and cured.*

surgery *noun*
medical treatment in which a doctor cuts into someone's body to fix or remove a damaged part: *If the drugs don't work, her doctor says she'll need surgery to remove the tumor.*

operation *noun*
a medical treatment in which a doctor cuts into someone's body to fix or remove a damaged part: *He had* ***an operation on*** *his right eye to try to get his sight back.*
→ **GRAMMAR:** **Surgery** and **operation** mean the same thing. However, you use **operation** with "an," and **surgery** without "a": *She had an operation.* | *She had surgery.*

physical therapy *also* **PT** *noun*
the treatment of injuries and muscle problems with exercises, rubbing, or heat: *After her shoulder operation, she had ten sessions of physical therapy.*

operate *verb*
if a doctor operates, he or she cuts into someone's body in order to repair or remove a part that is damaged: *They had to* ***operate on*** *my arm because it was broken in two places.*

cast *noun*
a hard cover that doctors put around a broken bone until it gets better: *Her leg was* ***in a cast*** *for six weeks.*

scan *verb*
an examination of part of the inside of your body using a machine that can see inside your body: *The scan of his brain showed that there was a small tumor.*

X-ray *noun*
a special photograph of the inside of your body, used to check whether your body is healthy: *You could see the break in the bone on the X-ray.*

7 Medicine for an Illness

medicine *noun*
a substance used for treating illness: *You have to take the medicine twice a day.*

medication *noun*
medicine that a person takes over a period of time for a particular illness: *My grandmother is **on medication** for high blood pressure.*

drug *noun*
a medicine, or a substance for making medicines: *There are many different drugs that are used in the treatment of cancer.*

prescription *noun*
a particular medicine ordered by a doctor for a sick person: *I need to pick up my prescription at the drug store.*

painkiller *noun*
a medicine that stops you from feeling too much pain: *My mom took painkillers for a week after her surgery.*

antibiotics *noun*
medicine that kills bacteria and cures infections: *Antibiotics should clear up the infection in a few days.*

8 Shots

shot *also* **injection** (*formal*) *noun*
the act of putting medicine into your body using a needle: *I get a flu shot every year.* | *The nurse gave me a tetanus injection.*

inject *verb*
to put a drug into someone's body using a special needle: *Brad has to inject himself with insulin.*

vaccine *noun*
a medicine that stops you from getting a disease. A **vaccine** is made with a weak or dead form of the thing that causes the disease so that your body will develop protection against the disease naturally: *The smallpox vaccine eventually got rid of the disease completely.*

vaccinate *verb*
to give someone a vaccine: *All children should be vaccinated against measles.*
→ The noun is **vaccination**: *Children must have some vaccinations before they can attend school.*

inoculate *verb*
to protect someone against getting a serious form of a disease by putting the disease into his or her body so that the body can develop protection naturally: *The children were inoculated with a version of the polio virus.*
→ The noun is **inoculation**: *Your baby may have a slight fever after the inoculations.*

immunize *verb*
to give someone vaccinations and inoculations in order to prevent them from getting diseases: *Children can be immunized against diseases such as measles and mumps.*
→ The noun is **immunization**: *Has your baby had her immunizations?*

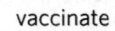

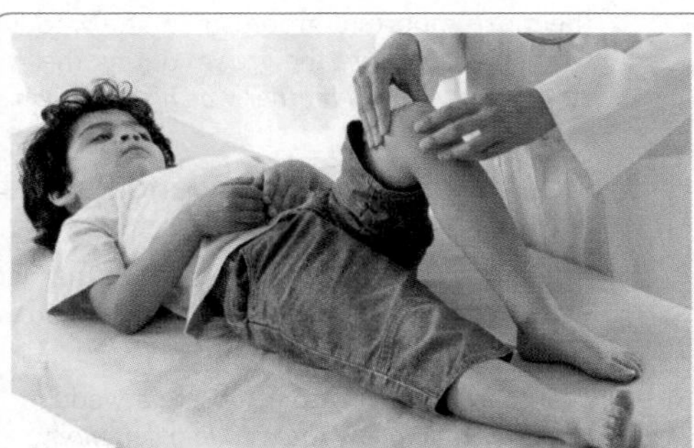

examine

vaccinate

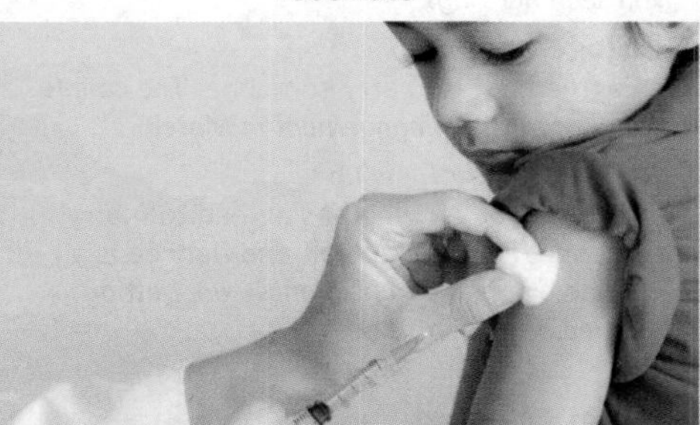

RELATIONSHIPS AND MARRIAGE

1 Dating Someone

date *verb*
to go to places and do things with someone you like, especially with someone you have a romantic relationship with: *Miguel and Carla started dating in high school.*

go out *phrasal verb*
go out means the same as **date**: *How long have you and Tom been going out?*

date *noun*
an arrangement to meet someone, especially a boyfriend or girlfriend, and do something together such as see a movie or go to a restaurant: *On their first date they went out for lunch together.*

2 When People Are Going to Get Married

engaged *adjective*
if someone is engaged, he or she has agreed to marry someone: *Sharon just got engaged – have you seen her ring?*

engagement *noun*
an agreement to marry someone: *The couple announced their engagement in March.*

fiancé *or* **fiancée** *noun*
a man or woman who has agreed to marry someone. **Fiancé** is a man and **fiancée** is a woman: *Hernan and his fiancée are getting married next month.*

3 To Get Married

get married *verb phrase*
to become someone's husband or wife: *My parents got married in 1986.* | *Alicia was 30 years old when she* ***got married to*** *Bryan.*

marry *verb*
marry means the same as **get married** but is more formal: *Will you marry me?* | *Alicia was 30 years old when she married Bryan.*

remarry *verb*
to get married again: *He remarried three years after his wife died.*

4 The People at a Wedding

bride *noun*
a woman who is getting married at a wedding ceremony: *The bride was wearing a white dress and standing at the back of the church.*

groom *noun*
a man who is getting married at a wedding ceremony: *The groom stood at the front of the church waiting for his bride.*

bridesmaid *noun*
a girl or woman who helps a bride at her wedding and stands with her during the ceremony: *The three bridesmaids were wearing matching dresses.*

maid of honor *or* **matron of honor** *noun*
a single or married woman who is the most important bridesmaid at a wedding and stands next to the bride during the ceremony: *The maid of honor held the bride's flowers.*

groomsman *noun*
a friend of the groom who stands with him during the wedding: *The groomsmen were three of the groom's friends from college.*

best man *noun*
the most important groomsman at a wedding, who stands next to the groom during the ceremony: *Adam's brother was his best man.*

5 The Wedding Ceremony and Parties

wedding *noun*
a ceremony at which two people get married: *Their wedding will be in the church on Main Street.*

reception *noun*
a large formal party to celebrate a wedding: *The reception will follow the wedding ceremony.*

honeymoon *noun*
a vacation that people take after they get married: *Two days after the wedding, they went to Greece* ***on their honeymoon****.*

shower *noun*
a party at which you give presents to a woman who is going to get married soon: *We're having a shower for Lara a week from Saturday.*

bachelor party *also* **stag party** (*informal*) *noun*
a party for a man and his male friends just before he gets married: *His bachelor party was the night before the wedding.*

6 People Who Are Married

wife *noun*
the woman that a man is married to: *Jonathan and his wife have been married for five years.*

husband *noun*
the man that a woman is married to: *Stella and her husband are both very tall.*

partner *noun*
the person that someone lives with and has a romantic relationship with, but is not married to: *Pedro and his partner are going to New York.*

spouse *noun (formal)*
someone's husband or wife. **Spouse** is used mostly on official forms: *The application asks for the name of your spouse.*

couple *noun*
two people who are married or have a romantic relationship: *It was mostly married couples at the party.*

7 People Who Are Not Married

single *adjective*
someone who is single is not married: *When I was single, I went out with my friends a lot.*

unmarried *adjective*
unmarried means the same as **single** but is a little more formal: *Mrs. Ling's two unmarried adult sons still live at home.*

girlfriend *noun*
a girl or woman someone has a romantic relationship with: *Have you met his girlfriend?*

boyfriend *noun*
a boy or man someone has a romantic relationship with: *Marissa's boyfriend is nice.*

lover *noun*
someone's lover is a person he or she is having a sexual relationship with but is not married to: *The two were secret lovers for years.*

8 When Someone Stops Being in a Relationship or Married

break up *phrasal verb*
to end a relationship with a boyfriend or girlfriend: *Sara* ***broke up with*** *her boyfriend because he was cheating on her.*

split up *phrasal verb*
to end a marriage or other romantic relationship: *When did your parents split up?*

breakup *noun*
the act of ending a romantic relationship: *I just went through a bad breakup, and I'm not ready to date again yet.*

get divorced *also* **divorce** *(formal) verb phrase*
to legally end a marriage: *They got divorced only three years after they got married. | David's parents divorced when he was six.*

divorce *noun*
the legal ending of a marriage: *Why doesn't she get a divorce if she's so unhappy?*

divorced *adjective*
no longer married because you have legally ended your marriage: *It has become common for children to grow up with divorced parents.*

ex-husband *or* **ex-wife** *noun*
the man or woman that someone used to be married to: *Jorge has two boys with his ex-wife and a daughter with his current wife.*

leave *verb*
to stop living with your husband or wife because you want to end your marriage: *He left his wife after ten years of marriage.*

separate *verb*
if a married couple separates, the two people start living apart because they are having problems in their marriage: *Mara's parents separated for a while.*

separated *adjective*
if a husband and wife are separated, they are living apart because they are having problems in their marriage: *She is separated from her husband.*

separation *noun*
a situation in which a husband and wife agree to live apart even though they are still married: *They hoped that the separation would help them fix their marriage.*

9 A Type of Relationship

relationship *noun*
a situation in which two people spend time together or live together because they have romantic feelings for each other: *Are you* ***in a relationship*** *right now, or are you single?*

romance *noun*
an exciting relationship between two people who love each other: *Their romance began on a date their friends had arranged for them.*

marriage *noun*
the relationship between two people who are married, or the time that they are married: *My grandparents had a long and happy marriage.*

affair *noun*
a secret sexual relationship between two people, when one or both people are married to someone else: *His wife found out that he was having an affair, and she asked for a divorce.*

SCIENCE AND TECHNOLOGY

1 Science and Technology

science *noun*
the study of animals, plants, and the physical world, and the knowledge and facts about them that are based on testing and proving ideas: *Science has led to the cure of many diseases.*

technology (AWL) *noun*
scientific knowledge and the way people use it to make machines, or the machines themselves: *The producers of the CD used modern technology to get rid of some of the flaws in the old recordings from the 1930s.*

engineering *noun*
the job or activity of designing and building machines, equipment, roads, bridges, etc.: *The Golden Gate Bridge is an impressive example of good engineering.*

scientific *adjective*
relating to science: *There is no scientific evidence that the herb can prevent colds. | Scientific knowledge continues to grow as we learn more about the universe.*

technological (AWL) *adjective*
relating to new and advanced machines and systems: *We are living in a time of rapid technological change, with one example being computers that have gotten smaller and smaller.*

technical (AWL) *adjective*
relating to the practical use of science to do things, such as build or use machines: *The radio station had technical difficulties and was unable to play the recording.*

2 New Developments in Science and Technology

discovery *noun*
a fact or thing that someone finds out about, when no one else knew about it before: *The large telescope has helped astronomers to make new discoveries about the universe.*

discover *verb*
if someone discovers a new fact or thing, they are the first person to find it or know that it exists: *Scientists believe they have discovered the gene that causes the disease.*

invention *noun*
a new type of thing that has been made or designed: *The dishwasher is a wonderful invention.*

invent *verb*
to make, design, or think of something that is completely new and different: *Alexander Graham Bell invented the telephone in 1876.*

innovation (AWL) *noun*
a new idea, invention, or way of doing something: *The company's innovations in cell phones have kept their products popular.*

breakthrough *noun*
an important new discovery in something you have been studying, that comes after a lot of hard work: *Researchers have made a major **breakthrough** in the treatment of cancer.*

advance *noun*
a change that brings progress: ***Advances** in technology have led to computers that are smaller and much more powerful.*

cutting-edge *adjective*
relating to the newest and most exciting development in science or technology: *Many people are willing to pay more for cutting-edge technology, just to have the newest thing.*

high-tech *also* **hi-tech** *adjective*
using very advanced technology: *Melanie bought a high-tech digital camera with all the latest features.*

3 People Who Work in Science and Technology

scientist *noun*
someone who does scientific work: *Scientists are studying the virus, but they still do not completely understand it.*

inventor *noun*
someone who thinks of or makes something completely new and different: *Thomas Edison was the inventor of a long-lasting electric light bulb.*

researcher *noun*
someone who studies a subject to find out new facts about it: *Medical researchers reported the results of a new study on cancer today.*

engineer *noun*
someone whose job is to design, build, and repair machines, equipment, roads, bridges, etc.: *Structural engineers are checking the building for earthquake damage.*

technician *noun*
someone whose job involves using special machines or scientific equipment: *Sylvia is studying to become an X-ray technician.*

4 Learning about Science

laboratory *also* **lab** *(informal) noun*
a room or building where scientists work and do experiments: *The laboratory has a lot of very advanced equipment. | We haven't gotten the test results back from the lab yet.*

experiment *noun*
a scientific test to find out what the effects of doing something are: *The students carried out an experiment to see whether heating the liquid made the chemical reaction faster.*

experiment *verb*
to do a scientific test in order to find out or show something: *The scientists* ***experimented on*** *mice to see what the effects of the drug might be.*

test *noun*
something you do to find out information about something, for example whether something works correctly or whether someone has an illness: *The blood test shows that she has diabetes. | The company carries out safety tests on its products.*

test *verb*
to use something to find out whether it works: *The new medicine was tested on cancer patients.*

study *noun*
a piece of work that is done to find out more about a particular subject or problem: *Recent studies have shown that the best way to treat back pain is by exercise, such as swimming.*

study *verb*
to examine something carefully to find out more about it: *Doctors have studied the effects of the drug on children.*

research (AWL) *noun*
a study of a subject in order to find out new information: *Scientists have been doing* ***research into*** *the causes of breast cancer. | New research shows that women have less free time than men.*

research (AWL) *verb*
to study a subject and do experiments or tests so you can find out more about it: *Scientists are researching the effects of global warming.*

hypothesis (AWL) *noun*
an idea that tries to explain something, which can be tested by carefully studying something or doing experiments: *There is evidence that supports the hypothesis that all the continents once formed one large area of land.*

theory (AWL) *noun*
a set of ideas that explain something, which most scientists accept as true even though some parts of the theory are not proven: *Darwin's theory of evolution explains how species change over time. | Jean Piaget developed a theory which says that children go through four stages as they learn and grow.*

5 Science Subjects

biology *noun*
the scientific study of living things: *Doctors need a good understanding of biology.*

physics *noun*
the scientific study of natural forces, such as heat, light, and movement: *The story says that Isaac Newton understood one of the laws of physics - gravity - when an apple fell on his head.*

chemistry *noun*
the scientific study of substances and the way they change or combine with each other: *People who study chemistry often end up working for medical companies.*

astronomy *noun*
the scientific study of stars, planets, space, etc.: *Dad likes astronomy - ask him which star that is.*

geology *noun*
the scientific study of rocks and soil: *In geology class, we learned how rocks are formed.*

meteorology *noun*
the scientific study of weather: *I took a meteorology class, but I still can't predict the weather!*

botany *noun*
the scientific study of plants: *My botany teacher showed us some really unusual plants.*

zoology *noun*
the scientific study of animals: *If you want to be a veterinarian, you should study zoology.*

life science *noun*
a scientific subject in which scientists study humans, plants, or animals. **Biology**, **botany**, and **zoology** are **life sciences**: *I like life sciences more than physical sciences because living things are more interesting to me.*

physical science *noun*
the scientific study of natural forces or things that are not living. **Physics**, **chemistry**, **geology**, and **astronomy** are **physical sciences**: *If you are planning to study a physical science, it is useful to also study mathematics.*

earth science *noun*
the scientific study of anything related to the planet Earth and the air around it. **Geology** and **meteorology** are **earth sciences**: *I'm interested in earth sciences and want to work to protect the environment.*

SPORTS AND EXERCISE

1 Sports and Exercise

sport *noun*
a physical activity in which people compete against each other: *My favorite sports are swimming and tennis.* | *Which sports do you play at school?*

game *noun*
a sport or enjoyable activity in which you try to win or score points: *Kickball is a really fun game.*

exercise *noun*
a physical activity that you do in order to stay strong and healthy: *I needed more exercise, so I started walking three miles every day.* | *The coach made us do stretching exercises before we started running.*

workout *noun*
a set of exercises that you do, especially in a gym or exercise class: *Dan does a workout at the gym every morning.*

warm-up *noun*
a set of gentle exercises or practices that you do to get your muscles ready before playing a sport: *The team does a half-hour warm-up before the game.*

2 Being Healthy and Strong from Sports or Exercise

fit *also* **physically fit** *adjective*
having a body that is healthy and strong, especially because you exercise regularly: *She keeps fit by biking to work.* | *Being physically fit is good for your heart.*

in shape *phrase*
in shape means the same as **fit** but is more informal: *Jogging keeps me in shape.*

athletic *adjective*
physically strong and good at playing sports: *Raj is an athletic young man who plays basketball and swims.*

3 A Competition

competition *noun*
an organized event in which people or teams try to be the best at doing something: *We were watching the swimming competition on TV.*

game *noun*
an occasion when two people or teams compete against each other in a sport or other activity: *We won our first football game last night.* | *Let's play a game of volleyball.*

match *noun*
a game or competition between two people or teams, in boxing, soccer, tennis, and some other sports: *The boxing match was really exciting!*

race *noun*
a competition to find out who can move or do something fastest, for example, running, driving, or swimming: *There were six runners in the race.*

tournament *noun*
a competition in which many players or teams compete against each other until there is one winner: *Our team is playing in the state basketball tournament in March.*

championship *noun*
a competition to find the best player or team in a sport: *Shannon Miller has won more world championships than any other American gymnast.*

round *noun*
one of the parts of a competition that you must win to get to the next part: *The second round of the NCAA championships starts tomorrow.*

semifinal *noun*
one of the two sports games that are played in a competition before the final game. Teams have to win one or more **rounds** of a competition to play in a **semifinal**. The winners of the two **semifinals** then play each other in the **final** to decide the winner of the competition: *All four teams in the semifinals have a chance to win the tournament.*

final *noun*
the last and most important game or race in a competition: *We have to play the Tigers in the final, and they're a very good team.*

4 To Play a Sport or to Exercise

play *verb*
to take part in a game or sport: *Liz started playing basketball when she was eight.* | *The coach says I can't play in the game this week because I hurt my knee.*

compete *verb*
to take part in a race or competition: *Over 1,000 cyclists will **compete in** the race.*

do *verb*
to perform an activity: *How many push-ups can you do? | The doctor said I should do more exercise.*

exercise *verb*
to do physical activity so that you stay strong and healthy: *I've been exercising a lot, and I've lost five pounds.*

stretch *verb*
to spread or reach out your arms or legs as far as possible in order to keep your muscles loose: *Always stretch before exercising.*

warm up *phrasal verb*
to prepare for an activity or sport by doing gentle exercises or practicing just before the activity or game starts: *Make sure you warm up and stretch before you start playing.*

work out *phrasal verb*
to exercise in a way that uses all the important muscles in your body, especially in a gym or exercise class: *I went running, and then I went to the gym to work out.*

5 People Who Play Sports

player *noun*
someone who plays a game or sport: *She is one of the college's best tennis players.*

athlete *noun*
someone who is good at playing sports, especially someone who takes part in sports competitions in running, jumping, and throwing: *Some of the country's finest athletes will be taking part in the competition.*

sportsman, sportswoman, sportsperson *noun*
a man, woman, or person who plays sports well. **Sportsman**, **sportswoman**, and **sportsperson** are used mainly in journalism: *Pérez is a former Olympic athlete and Ecuador's most famous sportsperson.*

competitor *noun*
a person or team that is competing with another one: *Two of the competitors didn't show up for the race.*

team *noun*
a group of people who play together in a sport or game: *Which teams are in the Superbowl this year? | Sarah is **on the** high school volleyball **team**.*

league *noun*
a group of teams in a particular sport that play against each other to see who is best: *How many teams are there in your bowling league?*

6 Referees in Sports

referee *noun*
the person who makes sure that players obey the rules in sports such as soccer, football, hockey, basketball, volleyball, and boxing: *The referee called a foul on Johnson.*

umpire *noun*
the person who makes sure that the players obey the rules in sports such as baseball or tennis: *The umpire said the pitch was a strike.*

judge *noun*
the person who decides how well an athlete has done something in gymnastics, ice skating, diving, and some other sports: *Three of the judges gave her a 7.5 for her balance beam performance.*
→ In some sports, such as volleyball or tennis, a judge helps the referee: *The line judge said that the ball was out.*

7 People Who Watch Sports

spectator *noun*
someone who is watching a game or sports event: *There were thousands of spectators at the basketball game.*

fan *noun*
someone who likes a sport or sports team very much: *Are you a baseball fan? | My brother is a Denver Broncos fan and watches all their games on TV.*

8 Places to Play a Sport or to Exercise

field *noun*
an area of ground where sports are played: *The fans ran out on the football field when their team won the game.*

court *noun*
an area with a hard surface made for playing a sport such as tennis or basketball: *Some kids were on the court playing basketball.*

track *noun*
a course with a special surface on which people, cars, horses, etc. race: *To run a mile, you have to go around the track four times.*

diamond *noun*
a field for playing baseball, especially the area inside the four bases: *The pitcher stands in the middle of the diamond.*

ballpark *noun*
a field for playing baseball, with seats for people to sit and watch the game: *The New York Yankees started playing at their new ballpark in 2009.*

stadium *noun*
a building used for sports games that consists of a field surrounded by rows of seats: ***The race was held in the Olympic stadium.***

pool *also* **swimming pool** *noun*
a structure that is filled with water for people to swim in: ***We go swimming at the public pool during the summer.***

gym *noun*
a building or a room that has equipment for doing physical exercise: ***I usually lift weights at the gym.***
→ You can also use **gym** to mean a **health club** or a **fitness center**.

gymnasium (*formal*) *also* **gym** *noun*
a large room in a school where students can exercise and play sports such as basketball and volleyball: ***The third graders were running around the gymnasium.*** | ***The basketball game was in the gym.***

health club *also* **fitness club** *noun*
a place where people who have paid to become members can go to do physical exercise: ***I should really join a health club and get in shape.***

fitness center *noun*
a room or building that has equipment for doing exercise, especially at a hotel, at a company's office, in a college etc.: ***My mom's office has a fitness center, and she usually exercises there at lunch time.***

9 Scoring Points in a Sport or Game

point *noun*
a unit used for showing who has made a goal, run, touchdown, basket, etc. in a game or sport: ***After 20 minutes, our team had 12 points.***

score *noun*
the number of points that you get in a game: ***The final score was 23-11.*** | ***Helen Schmidt won the women's competition with a score of 46.2.***

score *verb*
to get points in a game: ***Deng scored 28 points for the Bulls.***

tied *adjective*
if teams, players, or the score is tied in a game, each team or player has the same number of points: ***The teams were tied 13–13 at halftime.*** | ***The score is tied at 36.***

spectators

work out

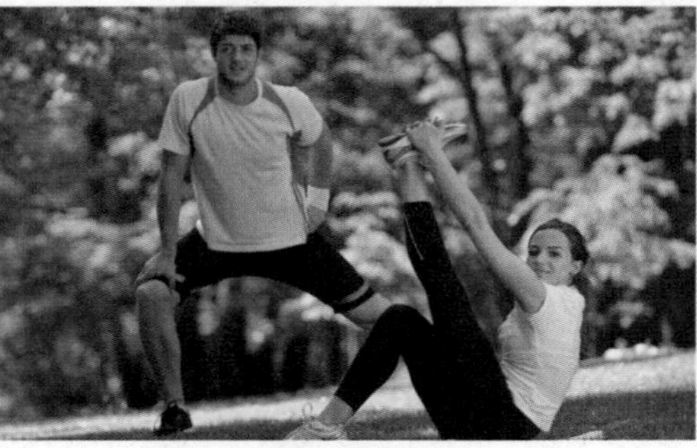
stretch

TRAVEL AND VACATIONS

1 Trips and Traveling

travel *noun*
to go from one place to another, especially when you go long distances: *The president will* ***travel to*** *Mexico later this month.* | *After I graduate from college, I want to* ***travel around*** *Europe.*

vacation *noun*
a time when you do not go to work or school, especially when you travel away from home: *"What did you do during your summer vacation?" "We went camping in the mountains."* | *The family was* ***on vacation*** *in Florida when their car broke down.*

go on vacation *also* **take a vacation** *verb phrase*
to travel away from home, especially for more than a few days: *We're* ***going on vacation to*** *New Mexico next week, and we won't be back until the 23rd.* | *Javier's family* ***took a vacation*** *in the mountains.*

trip *noun*
a visit to a place, especially a place where you do not usually go and that you travel to get to: *We went to three national parks* ***on our trip*** *this summer.* | *The whole senior class is going* ***on a*** *ski* ***trip*** *in February.*

tour *noun*
a trip to several different places in a country, city, or area so that you can see important or beautiful places: *We went* ***on a*** *bike* ***tour*** *of the city and stopped at all the major tourist sights.*

cruise *noun*
a trip for pleasure on a large ship that travels to different places. You take a **cruise** on a very large ship called a cruise ship, which is like a hotel on water: *Cruises are becoming more popular with families as ships offer activities for children.*

2 Someone Who Is Traveling

tourist *noun*
someone who travels to a place for pleasure: *We live in a beach town, so there are lots of tourists in the summer.*

traveler *noun*
someone who goes on a trip. You use **traveler** when you are writing about travel to places that are far away and about people who travel on trains, buses, and other transportation: *Business travelers will enjoy the train's new larger seats.*

sightseer *noun*
someone who goes to famous or interesting places while he or she is visiting a city or country: *The bus was full of sightseers looking at the Eiffel Tower.*

3 What You Do on Vacation

go sightseeing *verb phrase*
the activity of looking at the most famous or interesting places in a city or area that you are visiting: *We went sightseeing while we were in New York, and saw the Statue of Liberty and the Empire State Building.*

tourist attraction *noun*
a famous or interesting place that many tourists visit: *She wants to see the Statue of Liberty and some of the other tourist attractions before she leaves.*

tour *verb*
to travel and visit different places: *We toured northern California and went to see the giant redwood trees.*

road trip *noun*
a trip in which you drive to different places: *My friends and I went on a road trip along the coast when we finished high school.*

go on a cruise *also* **take a cruise** *verb phrase*
to travel on a large ship for fun: *We are going on a cruise along the coast of Alaska.* | *They took a Caribbean cruise for their anniversary.*

backpack *verb*
to travel, usually with just one bag that you wear on your back, staying in very cheap places: *When they finished college, they backpacked across Europe.*
→ The bag you carry on your back when you are backpacking is called a **backpack**: *You can leave your backpack in the lockers at the train station.*

go camping *verb phrase*
to take a vacation in which you camp, either in a tent or in a special vehicle called a **recreational vehicle** or **RV**: *His family went camping in the Rockies this summer.*

campground *noun*
a place where people can go and stay in a tent

or a special vehicle when they are camping: *The campground was right next to a lake where we could fish.*

hike *verb*
to walk a long way in the country or the mountains: *We **hiked to** a lake and had a picnic.*
→ The walk that you take when you hike is called a **hike**: *We went **on a hike** to the bottom of the canyon and back up.*

go backpacking *verb phrase*
to hike in the country or mountains and carry your food, a tent, etc. in a special bag on your back: *We went backpacking for a week in the Sierras.*

swim *verb*
to move yourself through the water: *The kids were jumping off the rocks and swimming in the river.*

sunbathe *verb*
to sit in the sun in order to make your skin become darker: *A crowd of teenagers was sunbathing on the beach.*

pool *also* **swimming pool** *noun*
a large container that is filled with water for people to swim in: *There were only a few people swimming in the outdoor pool.*

beach *noun*
an area of sand or small stones at the edge of an ocean or a lake: *The beaches in Mexico were so beautiful.*

4 Where You Stay on Vacation

hotel *noun*
a building where you pay to stay when you are traveling or on vacation: *We stayed at a hotel right by the beach in Hawaii.*

motel *noun*
a hotel you stay in when you are traveling by car, with a place for your car near your room: *I walked over to the motel office to get the key.*

resort *noun*
a large hotel, or group of hotels, which usually has swimming pools, tennis courts, golf courses, and other activities. **Resorts** are often by the ocean or in the mountains near a ski area: *It was a huge resort with its own golf course and a private beach.*

B & B *noun*
a place where you can pay to stay in a room and have breakfast in the morning. **B & B** stands for "bed and breakfast." A **B & B** is often a house where the owner lets people stay in the extra rooms: *We stayed in a B & B near the ski area in Vermont.*

5 Using a Plane, Bus, or Train

get on a plane/bus/rain *or* **get off a plane/bus/train** *verb phrase*
to go onto or out of a plane, bus, or train on which you are traveling: *We got on the plane at 7:00, but we didn't leave the ground until 8:30!* | *You'll need to get off the train in San Diego.*

board *verb*
board means the same as **get on**, but sounds more formal and is used especially in announcements or in writing: *We will begin boarding the plane about 30 minutes before the flight.*

catch *verb*
to get on a bus, train, or airplane at the right time and not miss it: *Were you on time to catch the train to Washington?*

change *verb*
to go from one bus, plane, or train to another during a trip from one place to another: *When I was flying to Denver, I had to change planes in Chicago.*

by car/bus/plane/train *phrase*
traveling in a car, bus, plane, or train: *I like traveling by train better than by bus.*

take *verb*
if you take a bus, train, or plane, you travel in a bus, train, or plane: *We took the train to Seattle.*

6 Tickets for Traveling

ticket *noun*
a printed piece of paper that shows you have paid to travel on a bus, train, plane, etc.: *Keep your plane tickets in a safe place.*

fare *noun*
the amount of money you pay to travel by bus, train, or plane: *I didn't have enough money for bus fare to get home!*

one-way *adjective*
a one-way ticket or fare is what you use or pay to go from one place to another, but not back again: *I went to the bus station and got a one-way ticket to Los Angeles.*

round-trip *adjective*
a round-trip ticket or fare is what you use or pay to go from one place to another, and then back again: *You usually save money if you buy a round-trip ticket.*

7 Traveling by Plane

flight *noun*
a trip from one place to another on a particular plane. Each flight has a different number: ***Flight 442 to** Vancouver is now boarding.* | *How was your flight?*

terminal (AWL) *noun*
one of the large buildings in an airport that planes leave from. **Terminals** usually have numbers or letters to help you to know where to go: *All international flights leave from Terminal 2.*

gate *noun*
the area in a terminal where a plane waits for passengers to get on. **Gates** usually have numbers to help you to know where to go: *The flight for Miami is now boarding* ***at Gate 27.***

take off *phrasal verb*
if an airplane takes off, it leaves the ground: *The plane took off about 45 minutes after we boarded.*

land *also* **touch down** *verb*
if an airplane lands, it comes down onto the ground when it has finished flying: *The plane landed at 7:05.* | *It was raining when we touched down in Atlanta.*

check in *phrasal verb*
to show your ticket and identification to the people who work for an airline so that you can get on a plane. You can also usually **check in** online, for example by giving passport information : *Please check in at least one hour before your flight leaves.*

check-in counter *noun*
the desk where you check in at an airport: *There was nobody* ***at the check-in counter****, so I had to wait.*

security (AWL) *noun*
the area where you and the things you are carrying onto a plane are checked to make sure you do not have weapons or other dangerous materials: *It took more than 30 minutes to* ***go through security.***

boarding pass *noun*
the piece of paper you show in order to be allowed to get on a plane: *Please have your boarding passes and passports ready to show the security officer.*

baggage claim *noun*
the area where you go to get your luggage after traveling on a plane: *We waited in the baggage claim area for our suitcases to come off the plane.*

immigration (AWL) *noun*
the place in an airport, or at the border of a country, where you show your passport to be allowed into the country: *The man was stopped* ***at immigration*** *and taken away by the FBI.*

customs *noun*
the place in an airport, or at the border of a country, where you tell officials about any money or other goods you are bringing into the country: *They opened my bags and searched them* ***in customs.***

8 Traveling by Train or Subway

station *noun*
a building where trains or subways stop so that people can get on and off: *Many people stood waiting as the train came into the station.*

stop *noun*
one of the places where a train or subway stops so that people can get on and off: *Get off* ***at the first stop*** *after the Medical Center.*

car *noun*
one of the parts of a train or subway train: *The first two cars of the train are for first-class passengers.*

buffet car *also* **dining car** *noun*
the car on a train where you can buy food and drinks: *He sat in the dining car, eating a hot dog.*

sleeper car *also* **Pullman car** *noun*
a car on a train with beds for people to sleep in if they travel overnight: *Sandra bought a ticket for the sleeper car on a train going to Italy.*

hike

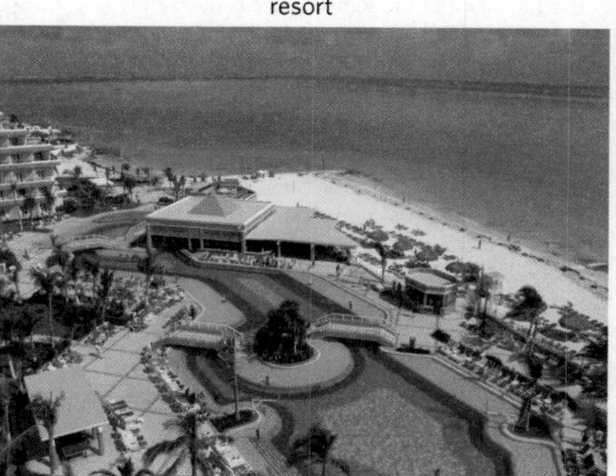
resort

THE WEATHER

1 The Weather

weather *noun*
the weather in a place is how warm or cold it is, and whether it is raining, sunny, windy, etc.: *The weather on the island is always warm and usually sunny.* | *"What is the weather going to be like tomorrow?" "It will be hot."*

climate *noun*
the type of weather that a place usually has: *The plant will not grow in a cold climate.*

2 Talking about How Warm or Cold the Air Is

temperature *noun*
how hot or cold the air is: *The temperature got as high as 98°F in the middle of the day.*

it's hot *phrase*
used to say that the temperature is high: *It's so hot - let's go swimming!*

it's warm *phrase*
used to say that the temperature is pleasantly hot: *It's nice and warm - you don't need a jacket.*

it's cool *phrase*
used to say that the temperature is not warm but not very cold either: *It's fairly cool today, and it looks like it might rain.*

it's cold *phrase*
used to say that the temperature is low: *Wear a coat - it's cold outside!*

it's freezing *phrase*
used to say that the temperature is extremely cold: *It was freezing all winter long!*
→ You can also say that the weather is **hot**, **warm**, **cool**, **cold**, or **freezing**, or that a day is **hot**, **warm**, **cool**, **cold**, or **freezing**: *It was a nice warm day in early summer.* | *The winter weather can be extremely cold.* | *I hate going outside on freezing mornings.*

above/below freezing *phrase*
higher or lower in temperature than 32°F or 0°C, at which water freezes: *If it stays above freezing, the ice on the lake will melt.* | *The temperature here fell below freezing only four times last winter.*

below zero *phrase*
lower in temperature than 0°C or 32°F: *It was freezing - at least five degrees below zero!*

in the 30s/60s/90s, etc. *phrase*
having a temperature between 30 and 40 degrees Fahrenheit, 60 and 70 degrees Fahrenheit, etc.: *It was a beautiful spring day with temperatures in the 60s.*

3 Describing Good Weather

sunny *adjective*
if it is sunny, the sun is not covered by clouds: *What a beautiful sunny day!*

good *adjective*
good weather is pleasant, and usually sunny and warm: *If we have good weather tomorrow, let's go for a hike.*

nice *adjective*
if it is nice, it is sunny and warm: *We had nice weather and spent most of the day on the beach.*

fine *adjective*
if it is fine, it is not raining and is not very cloudy: *It was a fine day, so he decided to go for a walk.*

beautiful *adjective*
very pleasant and sunny: *We had beautiful weather the whole trip - no rain at all.*

bright *adjective*
with a lot of sunlight: *It was a bright spring morning and I felt full of hope.*
→ **Bright** is also used to describe strong sunlight: *You should wear dark glasses in bright sunlight.*

clear *adjective*
with no clouds or mist: *On a clear day you can see the mountains from here.*

4 Describing Bad Weather

bad *adjective*
bad weather is unpleasant, and usually rainy or stormy: *The plane was delayed by bad weather.*

awful *also* **terrible** *adjective*
awful weather is very unpleasant ,and rainy or stormy: *The weather was awful - it didn't stop raining all week.* | *What terrible weather! Let's just stay home.*

5 Rain

rain *noun*
water that falls in small drops from clouds in the sky: *Why do you want to go out* ***in the rain****? | The rain began to fall in the afternoon.*

rain *verb*
if it rains, drops of water fall from clouds in the sky: ***It is raining*** *– you should take an umbrella. |* ***It rained*** *hard all night.*

drizzle *noun*
light rain with very small drops of water: *A light drizzle was falling as I left the house.*
→ **Drizzle** can also be used as a verb: ***It is only drizzling*** *– let's go for a walk anyway.*

sprinkle *verb*
if it sprinkles, a little rain falls from the sky, especially for a short time: ***It is sprinkling*** *now, but the sky is sunny over there.*

pour *verb*
if it pours, it rains heavily without stopping: *If* ***it pours*** *tomorrow, we will have to cancel the game.*

fall *also* **come down** *verb*
if rain falls or comes down, it comes down from the sky. **Come down** is less formal than **fall**: *As the rain began to fall, we ran to stand under a tree. | We were still outside in the fields when the rain started coming down.*

rain drop *noun*
a single drop of rain: *As we sat down on the beach, I felt a few rain drops fall on my face.*

shower *noun*
a short period of rain: *The weather forecast said that showers are possible over the weekend.*

downpour *noun*
a lot of rain that falls in a short time: *I walked back to my apartment* ***in the downpour****.*

rainy *adjective*
if it is rainy, there is rain: *It was rainy last night, but the sun is out now. | For most of our vacation, it was windy and rainy.*

wet *adjective*
wet weather or a wet time is one in which there is a lot of rain: *We had two weeks of cold wet weather. | It was a wet Sunday afternoon.*

damp *adjective*
a little rainy, or having just rained: *It was cloudy and damp outside.*

6 Snow

snow *noun*
soft white pieces of frozen water that fall from the sky when it is very cold: *Outside, snow was falling silently. | It was easy to follow the footprints in the snow.*

snow *verb*
if it snows, soft white pieces of frozen water fall from the sky when it is very cold: *If* ***it snows*** *a lot, maybe school will be canceled.*

sleet *noun*
a mixture of snow and rain: *The sleet on the highway makes driving very dangerous.*
→ **Sleet** can also be used as a verb: ***It was sleeting*** *so hard we could only see a few yards in front of us.*

hail *noun*
small hard pieces of frozen rain that fall from the sky: *Hail bounced off the roof onto the lawn.*
→ **Hail** can also be used as a verb: *The roof of our car got damaged when* ***it started hailing****.*

snowflake *noun*
a soft white piece of frozen water that falls from the sky when it is very cold: *A snowflake landed on the tip of her nose and melted.*

frost *noun*
a white powder of ice that covers things that are outside when it is very cold: *The grass and trees were white with frost.*

slush *noun*
snow on the ground that has started to melt: *Temperatures rose and the streets were filled with slush.*

snowy *adjective*
if it is snowy, there is a lot of snow on the ground or snow is falling: *It was snowy and school was canceled. | We could see the snowy mountaintops from the valley.*

icy *adjective*
very cold, or covered with ice: *Even her thick coat couldn't keep out the icy wind. | Several accidents were caused by the icy roads.*

frosty *adjective*
very cold, or covered with frost: *It is hard to get out of a warm bed on frosty mornings.*

slushy *adjective*
covered with slush: *My shoes got wet on the slushy sidewalks.*

7 Wind

wind *noun*
air outside that moves quickly along: *It was a big storm with strong winds and rain. |* ***The wind was blowing*** *old newspapers up and down the street.*
→ If the **wind** or a **breeze** blows, this means that the air is moving: *A damp cold wind was blowing.*

breeze *noun*
a light gentle wind: *A breeze was coming in off the ocean.*

gust *noun*
a sudden strong wind that happens when the

wind is blowing: *There were gusts of wind up to 60 miles per hour.*

gale *noun*
a very strong wind that blows for a long period, for example during a storm: *The rain started to fall, followed by a gale from the south.*

windy *adjective*
if it is windy, there is a lot of wind: *It is windy, so hang on to your hat!* | *Leaves get blown all over the yard on windy days.*

breezy *adjective*
with the wind blowing gently: *A breezy day is good for flying kites.*

blustery *adjective*
very windy and having many strong sudden winds: *The weather was damp, gray, and blustery.*

8 Rain, Snow, and Wind Storms

storm *noun*
if there is a storm, there is a lot of wind and rain, or snow: *The tree had blown down in the storm.* | *A large storm on New Year's Day knocked out power and left many people without heat.*

stormy *adjective*
if the weather is stormy, there are strong winds, heavy rain, and dark clouds: *We went inside when the sky started to look stormy.*

thunderstorm *noun*
a storm with thunder, lightning, and rain: *The plane waited for the thunderstorm to clear before taking off.*

rainstorm *noun*
a storm with a lot of rain: *A heavy rainstorm flooded the town.*

snowstorm *noun*
a storm with strong winds and a lot of snow: *There was a big snowstorm and we couldn't leave the house.*

blizzard *noun*
a very bad storm with a lot of snow and wind: *This week's blizzard closed airports on the Eastern Coast of the U.S.*

hurricane *noun*
a storm with very strong fast winds that comes from the ocean: *The hurricane destroyed several homes.*

tornado *noun*
a short violent storm with strong winds that go around and around: *A tornado flipped cars and ripped mobile homes to pieces.*

cyclone *noun*
a very strong wind that moves fast in a circle. **Cyclone** is a general word for any storm in which winds go around in a circle, but it can also be used to mean a very large storm that lasts a few days. You usually use **cyclone** about storms in the Indian Ocean and South Pacific: *The South Pacific cyclone season usually runs from November through April.*

typhoon *noun*
a cyclone in the western part of the Pacific Ocean: *A powerful typhoon caused widespread damage to the city.*

9 Cloud

cloud *noun*
a white or gray thing in the sky, that rain sometimes falls from. **Clouds** are made of many small drops of water: *There was a bright blue sky with a few white clouds.*

fog *noun*
clouds that are near the ground and that are difficult to see through: *Traffic was moving slowly because of the thick fog.*

mist *noun*
cloudy air near the ground that is not as thick as fog: *A gray mist was hanging over the water.*

cloudy *adjective*
if it is cloudy, there are a lot of clouds in the sky: *It was cloudy and cold, and looked like it might rain.* | *We left San Francisco on a cloudy afternoon.*

overcast *adjective*
if the sky is overcast, it is completely covered with clouds and makes the day seem dark, and it is likely to rain soon: *The day was overcast and it soon began to drizzle.*

gray *adjective*
cloudy, so there is no blue sky and no sun showing: *The weather was cold and gray.*

foggy *adjective*
if it is foggy, there is a lot of thick low cloud near the ground that is difficult to see through: *It was really foggy, and we could barely see the road.* | *The accident took place on a foggy highway.*

misty *adjective*
if it is misty, there is a lot of thin low cloud that is difficult to see through, but that is not as thick as fog: *It was a cool misty morning by the lake.*

10 Weather that Is Warm and Feels Wet

humid *adjective*
if the weather is humid, the air feels warm and wet: *It was hot and so humid that we were sweating just sitting there.*

sticky *also* **muggy** *adjective (informal)*
sticky weather is very hot, and the air feels wet: *In the summer, it's hot and sticky in Florida.* | *It was muggy, and we didn't feel like moving.*

Function Words

about /əˈbaʊt/ *adverb, preposition*

1 used to say that a number or amount is not exact
- ► about
- ► approximately
- ► roughly
- ► just over
- ► just under

2 used to say what the subject of something is
- ► about
- ► on
- ► relating to
- ► concerning (*formal*)
- ► with regard to (*formal*)
- ► as to (*formal*)

1 used to say that a number or amount is not exact

about *also* **around** *adverb, preposition*
a little more or less than a particular number, amount, distance, size, or time. Use **about** or **around** to show that you are guessing or not being exact: *The beach is about a mile away.* | *The jeans only cost about $30.* | *We should leave around 8:30 if we want to get there by 9:00.*

approximately *adverb*
approximately means the same as **about** but is more formal. **Approximately** is used especially in technical or scientific situations: *The disease affects approximately 10% of the population.*

roughly *adverb*
a little more or less than a number, size, or amount. Use **roughly** when you know a number is not exact: *The tree is roughly 15 feet tall.* | *Roughly 25% of the players on the team are from other countries.*

just over *adverb*
slightly more than a number or amount: *The new building cost just over $1 million to build.*

just under *adverb*
slightly less than a number or amount: *Kevin is just under 6 feet tall.*

2 used to say what the subject of something is

about *adverb, preposition*
used when you say what the subject of something is: *In her novels she writes about her childhood in Mississippi.* | *Do you have any questions about tomorrow's test?* | *Why didn't you tell me about your accident?*

on *preposition*
about a particular subject. You use **on** when giving the subject of a book, article, or speech that gives information, or when giving the subject of someone's opinions or ideas: *I have to write a report on Abraham Lincoln for school.* | *Researchers studied young people's views on marriage.*

relating to *also* **related to** *preposition*
used to say what information, records, laws, documents, etc. are about: *She asked several questions related to the rental agreement.* | *The city has laws relating to acceptable noise levels.*

concerning *also* **regarding** *preposition (formal)*
used to say what questions, information, decisions, documents, laws, and suggestions are about: *Police asked him several questions concerning the robbery.* | *Thank you for your letter regarding next month's music festival.*

with regard to *also* **in regard to** *preposition (formal)*
about one particular subject and not a different one: *Wilson has not spoken to reporters with regard to his work at the company.*
→ **With regard to** or **in regard to** can also be used to introduce the subject that you are going to talk or write about: *I am writing to you with regard to the bill you sent me on June 8.*

as to *conjunction (formal)*
used to say what a question, explanation, decision, reason, or doubt is about: *The senator never gave a clear explanation as to why he decided to quit.* | *There were no clues as to where he had gone.*
→ **GRAMMAR: As to** is often followed by "why," "when," "how," "who," "what," "where," or "whether."

SYNONYM CHECK
About

Only **about** can be used to give the subject of a story, or of a movie that tells a story: *She wrote a story about a boy who finds out he is a wizard.*

On is used to give the subject of a book or movie that gives information: *She wrote a book on wild animals.*

Do not use **relating to, concerning, with regard to**, or **as to** to give the subject of a book or movie.

above /əˈbʌv/ preposition, adverb

1 higher than
- ► above
- ► over
- ► overhead
- ► up
- ► overlooking

ANTONYMS → see Function Word **under**

2 more than
- ► above
- ► over
- ► beyond
- ► exceeding (*formal*)

ANTONYMS → see Function Word **under**, **less**

1 higher than

above *preposition, adverb*
in a higher position than something: *Scott had a red mark above his left eye.* | *I could hear voices coming from the apartment above.*
→ **Above** is also used in a piece of writing when referring to something that comes before: *The graph above shows the increase in pollution levels.*

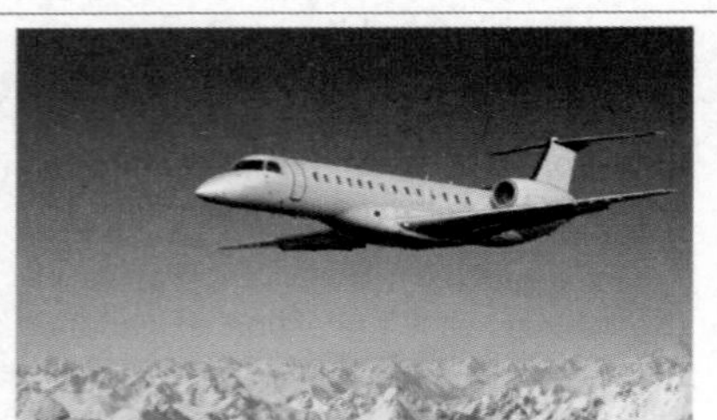
The plane is flying **above** the mountains.

over *preposition, adverb*
above something without touching it: *A small lamp hung over the desk.* | *Everyone looked up when the helicopter flew over.*

overhead *adverb*
above your head: *The big birds were flying in circles overhead.*

up *adverb*
in a higher position than where you are: *The cat is up on the roof again.*
→ **GRAMMAR:** Don't say: *~~The cat is up~~*. Say: *The cat is up on the wall* or *The cat is up there.* **Up** must be followed by an adverb or phrase showing position, such as "on the roof."

overlooking *preposition*
with a view of something from a higher position: *We asked for a room overlooking the ocean.*

2 more than

above *preposition, adverb*
more than a number, amount, or level: *The temperature was two degrees above zero last night.* | *To pass the test, you need a score of 60 or above.* | *Our high school scored above average on the test.*

over *preposition, adverb*
more than a number, amount, or age. Use **over** especially when it is not important to say exactly how much more: *Our office receives over 2,000 applications a year.* | *The class is only for children aged 13 and over.*

beyond *preposition*
more than a particular number or amount. Use **beyond** especially when the other amount is a particular level or limit: *The price was beyond what we could afford to pay.*

exceeding *preposition* (*formal*)
exceeding means the same as **above** but is only used before a number: *Income exceeding $82,250 is taxed at a higher level.*

across /əˈkrɔs/ preposition, adverb

- ► across
- ► over
- ► through

across *preposition, adverb*
from one side of something wide or large to the other side: *He ran across the street.* | *When you look across the lake, you can see the mountains.* | *The river is deep, so you can't go across without a good boat.*

The girls are running **across** the street.

over *preposition, adverb*
from one side of something that is high or deep

to the other side: *We flew over the mountains into Italy.* | *Katie ran up to the wall and climbed over.*

There is a bridge **over** the river.

through *preposition, adverb*
from one side or end of a hole, crowd, forest, town, or country to the other side or end: *I pushed my way through the crowd.* | *We drove through Baltimore on our way to Washington.* | *We found a gap in the fence and climbed through.*
→ You also use **through** when talking about someone seeing something on the other side of a window: *Through the window I could see Mike in the kitchen.*

The train has gone **through** the tunnel.

after /ˈæftɚ/ *preposition, conjunction, adverb*

- ► after
- ► following (*formal*)
- ► then
- ► afterward
- ► next
- ► in

ANTONYMS → see Function Word **before**

after *preposition, conjunction, adverb*
at a later time than something else: *I go swimming every day after school.* | *What did you do after she left?* | *After that, he went home.*
→ **GRAMMAR: After** is usually only used as an adverb after a word such as "soon" or a phrase such as "two days": *They moved here in 2009, and their first child was born* ***soon after.***

following *preposition (formal)*
after an event or as a result of an event. **Following** sounds fairly formal or literary: *Following the war, many people left the country.*

then *adverb*
after an event that has already been mentioned: *We could have lunch and then go shopping.*

afterward *adverb*
after an event that has already been mentioned. You can use words such as "soon" and "shortly" before **afterward**: *The class ended at 4:00 p.m. and I went home shortly afterward.*

next *adverb*
after an action that has already been mentioned. Use **next** especially when talking about a series of actions: *Fry the onions. Next add the bell peppers. Finally add the mushrooms.*

in *preposition*
after a particular amount of time has passed: *He is out, but he'll be back in ten minutes.*
→ see **later**

again /əˈgen/ *adverb*

- ► again
- ► over
- ► again and again
- ► repeatedly
- ► over and over (*informal*)

again *adverb*
one more time: *I liked the movie so much that I decided to watch it again.* | *He played tennis on Monday, and again on Thursday.*

over *adverb*
if you start over or do something over, you do something again, especially because you did not do it right the first time: *If you make a mistake when you're writing, you can do it over.* | *I didn't like the drawing, so I started over.*

again and again *adverb*
many times: *During the trial, she was accused again and again of being a liar.*

repeatedly *adverb*
many times. **Repeatedly** is slightly more formal than **again and again**: *She repeatedly warned him not to be late.*

over and over *adverb (informal)*
many times. You use **over and over** when something happens many times in a boring or tiring way: *He read the poem over and over until he knew it perfectly.*
→ see **often**

almost /ˈɔlmoʊst/ *adverb*

- ► **almost**
- ► **nearly**
- ► **virtually**
- ► **practically**
- ► **more or less**
- ► **just about** (*informal*)
- ► **pretty much** (*informal*)
- ► **hardly**
- ► **barely**

almost *adverb*
a little less than a number or amount, or not completely happening or true: *He goes swimming almost every day.* | *I have almost finished my math homework. I just have one more problem to do.* | *It is almost midnight.*

nearly *adverb*
nearly means the same as **almost**: *It will take nearly two hours to get there.* | *She is nearly 12 years old. Her birthday is next week.*

virtually (AWL) *adverb*
nearly but not completely. **Virtually** sounds more formal than **almost**. It is not used before numbers: *Virtually all the children go to school by bus.*

practically *adverb*
practically means the same as **virtually** but is used more often in spoken English. It is not used before numbers: *These shoes are practically new – I bought them a month ago.*

more or less *adverb*
almost – used especially when the difference between a description and the exact truth is small and not important: *All his friends gave him more or less the same advice.*

just about *adverb* (*informal*)
almost: *I play tennis just about every day.*

pretty much *adverb* (*informal*)
almost: *The day was pretty much a disaster – nearly everything went wrong.*

hardly *adverb*
almost none, or almost not at all: *He doesn't have many friends and hardly anyone visits him.* | *I hardly ever go to that store because it is very expensive.*

barely *adverb*
almost not: *He was speaking so quietly that I could barely hear him.*

SYNONYM CHECK
Almost or nearly?

In most sentences, you can use either **almost** or **nearly**. However, you use **almost**, not **nearly**, before "no," "nobody," and "nothing": *Almost nobody liked my idea.*

also /ˈɔlsoʊ/ *adverb*

- ► **also**
- ► **too**
- ► **as well**
- ► **either**
- ► **in addition**
- ► **besides**
- ► **moreover** (*formal*)
- ► **furthermore** (*formal*)

also *adverb*
used when saying that something else is true about someone or something, or that the same thing is true about another person or thing: *She sings and also plays the piano.* | *Information about the club is also available on our website.*
→ **GRAMMAR:** **Also** usually comes after the verb "be" or before other main verbs: *He is also a guitar player.* | *He also plays the guitar.*

too *adverb*
too means the same as **also**: *Aunt Linda laughed, and Grandpa laughed too.* | *It is a more efficient system, and it is cheaper too.* | *Can I come too?* | *"I'm really hot." "Me too."*
→ **GRAMMAR:** **Too** is usually used at the end of a sentence.

as well *adverb*
as well means the same as **too** but sounds more formal: *The chickens are producing more eggs and the egg size is bigger as well.* | *Mark has been to Malaysia* **as well as** *Thailand.*
→ **GRAMMAR:** **As well** is usually used at the end of a sentence.

either *adverb*
used in sentences with "not" to mean **too**: *Angie wasn't in class today and Ron wasn't either.* | *"I can't swim." "I can't either."*
→ **GRAMMAR:** In this meaning, **either** is used at the end of a sentence.

in addition *adverb*
used to add another piece of information: *On election day, 36 states will be voting for their governor. In addition, all states will be voting for their representatives in Congress.* | ***In addition to*** *teaching all day, teachers have a lot of grading to do.*

besides *adverb*
used to add another reason or more information. **Besides** sounds more informal than **in addition**: *I babysit because I need the money. Besides, I enjoy it.* | *Besides running three times a week, he lifts weights in the gym.*

moreover *adverb (formal)*
used when giving more information that adds to or supports what you have already said: *The students' science grades improved. Moreover, more of them went on to study science in college.*

furthermore (AWL) *adverb (formal)*
used when adding another piece of information, especially when you want to persuade someone to agree with you: *The drug has dangerous side effects. Furthermore, it is addictive.*

although /ɔlˈðoʊ/ *conjunction*

- ► although
- ► though (*informal*)
- ► even though (*informal*)
- ► despite
- ► in spite of
- ► even so
- ► while
- ► whereas (*formal*)

although *conjunction*
used when mentioning a fact that makes the other part of your sentence seem surprising or less definite: *I like playing basketball, although I'm not very good at it.* | *Although she said she would visit us while she was here, she never even called.*

though *conjunction (informal)*
Though means the same as **although** but sounds a little more informal: *I really like Ben, though I don't see him very often.* | *Though my mother doesn't always agree with my decisions, she still supports me completely.*
→ GRAMMAR: **Though** is not used at the beginning of a sentence as often as **although**.

even though *conjunction (informal)*
even though means the same as **although**, but it is used to emphasize that a situation is very surprising: *He can still remember that day, even though it was more than 20 years ago.*

despite (AWL) *preposition*
used to say that although something bad happens or exists, something good or surprising still happens or exists: *Despite our worries, I'm sure the show will go well.* | *Cats will drink from puddles outside, despite the fact that they have a clean bowl of water in the kitchen.*
→ GRAMMAR: Don't say: ~~*despite of our worries*~~ or ~~*despite we are worried*~~. Say: *despite our worries.*

in spite of *preposition*
in spite of means the same as **despite** but is less common: *Watching the game was fun, in spite of the rain.*
→ GRAMMAR: Don't say: ~~*in spite of raining*~~ or ~~*in spite that it was raining*~~. Say: *in spite of the rain.*

even so *adverb*
despite what you have just mentioned: *She knew she was well prepared for the test. Even so, she felt nervous.*

while *conjunction*
used to say that although something is true of one person, thing, or situation, it is not true of another: *Some plants need lots of sunlight, while others grow better in the shade.* | *While some of the children speak English well, others are still learning the language.*
→ You can also use **while** to start a sentence by saying something that makes the rest of the sentence seem surprising or the opposite of what you said before: *While I like Ryan, I don't like what he's doing.*

whereas (AWL) *conjunction (formal)*
whereas means the same as **while**: *In most societies women travel to live with their husbands, whereas men tend to remain close to their relatives.*

away /əˈweɪ/ *adverb*

- ► away
- ► from
- ► off

ANTONYMS → see Function Word **toward**

away *adverb*
in a direction that takes you farther from someone or something: *He turned his back on me and walked away.* | *Why did you run **away from** me?*

from *preposition*
used to mention the place that someone or something leaves: *You can fly from St. Louis to San Francisco.* | *He broke his leg when he jumped from an upstairs window.*

off *adverb, preposition*
away from a place, or down from something: *Travis got into his car and drove off.* | *He was carried off the field after being injured.* | *I accidentally knocked a book off the shelf.*

back /bæk/ *adverb*

- ► back
- ► backward

ANTONYMS → see Function Word **forward**

back *adverb*
toward a place behind you: *He looked back over his shoulder.* | *I stepped back to let them pass.*

He looked **back** over his shoulder.

backward *also* **backwards** *adverb*
toward a place behind you, but while facing forward: *She slipped and fell backward into the snow.* | *Can you skate backwards?*

because /bɪˈkɔz/ *conjunction*

- ► because
- ► since
- ► as (*formal*)
- ► as a result of
- ► due to (*formal*)
- ► through
- ► thanks to
- ► out of

because *conjunction*
used when you are giving the reason that something happens or is done: *I can't come to the party, because I have to play in a baseball game.* | *Because the college is losing money, they cannot hire new teachers.*
→ You can also use **because of** like a preposition: *The hotel is popular because of its location near the beach.*

since *conjunction*
used to give the reason why someone decides to do something: *Since it was a sunny day, I decided to walk to the store.*

as *conjunction* (*formal*)
used to give the reason why someone decides to do something: *James decided not to go out as he was still really tired.*

as a result of *preposition*
as a result of means the same as **because of** but is more formal: *Hundreds of people lost their homes as a result of the war.*

due to *preposition* (*formal*)
due to means the same as **because of** but is used in more formal or official situations: *Due to problems with the engine, the flight will be canceled.*

through *preposition*
used to say why something good or bad happens: *Your father got that job through hard work.* | *The business finally failed through lack of good management.*

thanks to *preposition*
used to say that something happened or is possible because of someone's actions or a particular situation. **Thanks to** is used especially in public speeches and news reporting: *The trip now only takes an hour, thanks to new high-speed trains.* | *Our college is now rated Number 1 in the state, thanks to our great teachers.*

out of *preposition*
used to mention the feeling that causes someone to do something: *I asked her how long she had been playing the guitar, just out of interest.*

before /bɪˈfɔr/ *preposition, conjunction, adverb*

1 earlier than something
- ► before
- ► prior to (*formal*)
- ► beforehand
- ► ahead of time
- ► in advance
- ► by
- ► by the time

ANTONYMS → see Function Word **after**

2 at a time in the past
- ► before
- ► earlier
- ► previously (*formal*)
- ► formerly (*formal*)

1 earlier than something

before *preposition, conjunction, adverb*
earlier than a time or event: *A decision is expected before the end of the month.* | *Before I met you, I was miserable.* | *You should brush your teeth before going to bed.*
→ **GRAMMAR:** In this meaning, **before** is used as an adverb after words such as "day" and "week": *She arrived too late – he had left **the day before**.*

prior to (AWL) *preposition (formal)*
prior to means the same as **before**: *He served two years in the state Senate prior to his election as governor in 1986.*

beforehand *adverb*
before something happens or before you go somewhere, especially in order to be ready: *I will remind you three days beforehand, so you don't forget.*

ahead of time *adverb*
ahead of time means the same as **beforehand**: *Can you tell him ahead of time what he'll need to bring?*

in advance *adverb*
in advance means the same as **beforehand** but sounds more formal: *I made the dinner in advance so that I would not have to cook when my friends came.*

by *preposition*
at some time before a particular time or date, and definitely not after it: *I promise I'll be home by 6:00.* | *They're coming at 5:00, so I want everything to be ready by then.* | *The company grew, and by 1973 it had a staff of 1,400.*

by the time *conjunction*
at some time before something happens: *By the time we arrived, the game had already started.*

2 at a time in the past

before *adverb*
at a time in the past: *I remember meeting you before at Jon's party.* | *There are more cars parked here than before.*

earlier *adverb*
at a time before now, especially a time during the same day or period of time: *I saw Julia earlier, but she is not here now.* | *Earlier today, we recorded an interview with the President.*

previously (AWL) *adverb (formal)*
previously means the same as **before** but sounds more formal: *I had met her previously at church.* | *Previously, he was a teacher at a community college.*

formerly *adverb (formal)*
before, but no longer: *He formerly worked for ABC, but he is now a reporter for CNN.*

behind /bɪˈhaɪnd/ *preposition, adverb*

- behind
- in back of
- at the rear of (*formal*)

ANTONYMS → see Function Word **in front of**

behind *preposition, adverb*
near the back of someone or something: *There is a big yard behind the house.* | *I heard someone coming up behind us.* | *A bear appeared, with its two cubs following close behind.*

The bear appeared, with its cubs following **behind**.

in back of *preposition*
in the area behind something: *The car is parked in back of the building.*

at the rear of *preposition (formal)*
at the rear of means the same as **in back of** but sounds more formal: *There were huge piles of garbage at the rear of the restaurant.*

between /bɪˈtwin/ *preposition*

- between
- among
- in the middle
- surrounded by

between *preposition*
with a person or thing on each side: *He is sitting between Steve and Jane.*

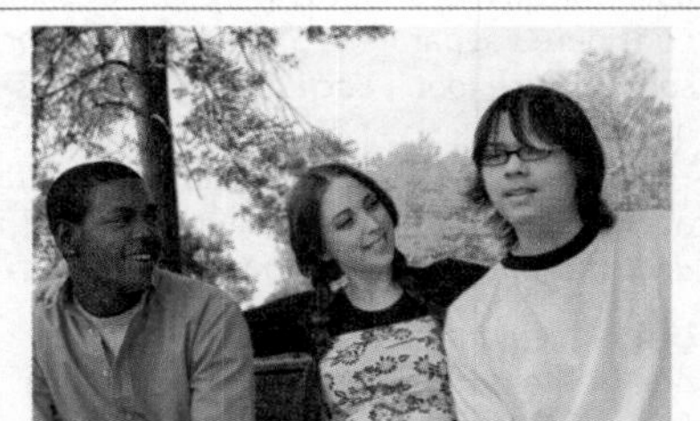

She is sitting **between** Steve and John.

→ **Between** is also used in the phrase **in between**: *There were two armchairs with a small table in between.*

among *preposition*
with people or things all around someone or something: *I saw him standing among a group of students.*

in the middle *adverb*
in the center, with one or more people or things on each side: *In the photo, Bill is on the left, Sam is on the right, and Jim is in the middle.*

surrounded by *preposition*
with a group or line of people or things all around someone or something: *The field was surrounded by trees.*

The house is **surrounded** by a fence.

both /boʊθ/ *adjective, pronoun*

- both
- each
- either
- neither

both *adjective, pronoun*
used to emphasize that you mean the two people or things you mention, and not just one of them: *Paul and I are both on the swim team.* | ***Both of*** *my sisters have black hair.* | *Hold the bowl with both hands, so you won't drop it.*

each *pronoun, adverb, determiner*
used for talking about two people or things, considered separately: *She had a different colored sock on each foot.* | ***Each of*** *the two rooms has its own shower.*
→ **Each** can also be used when you are talking about more than two people or things: *The dentist examined **each of** my teeth.*

either *determiner, pronoun*
one or the other of two people or things: *Do you know **either of** these two women?* | *There's chocolate or vanilla ice cream – you can have either.* | *Either spelling can be used.*

neither *determiner, pronoun*
not one and not the other of two people or things: *"Do you want milk or lemon in your tea?" "Neither, thanks."* | *Fortunately, **neither of** the passengers was hurt in the car accident.* | *Neither team played well.*

but /bət, strong bʌt/ *conjunction*

- but
- however (*formal*)
- still
- nevertheless (*formal*)
- then again (*informal*)
- on the other hand

but *conjunction*
used to join two words or parts of a sentence, when you say something that is different or surprising compared with what you just said: *Rob is a very nice guy, but I don't want to go out with him.* | *It was sunny but cold outside.*
→ **GRAMMAR:** In formal writing you should not start a sentence with **but**.

however *adverb (formal)*
used when mentioning something that is different or surprising compared with what you just said: *The vegetables tasted good. The meat loaf, however, was terrible.* | *The senator felt better after a few minutes. However, the doctor said he should go to the hospital anyway.*
→ **GRAMMAR: However** is sometimes used at the beginning of a sentence, but is most often used in the middle of a sentence.

still *adverb*
in spite of what has just been mentioned: *He wasn't always very nice to me. Still, I miss him.*
→ **GRAMMAR: Still** is used at the beginning of a sentence.

nevertheless (AWL) *also* **nonetheless** *adverb (formal)*
in spite of what has just been mentioned: *It was a terrible accident. Nevertheless, traveling by air is still safer than traveling by car.* | *They haven't won a single game, but the team is nonetheless showing great improvement.*
→ **GRAMMAR: Nevertheless** and **nonetheless** are often used at the beginning of a sentence.

then again *adverb (informal)*
used when mentioning something different that is also true: *He might lend us the money. Then again, he might not.*
→ **GRAMMAR: Then again** is used at the beginning of a sentence or after "but": *I was nervous, but then again, I was excited too.*

on the other hand *adverb*
used when mentioning a very different fact or idea: *This change may be significant. On the other hand, it could just be a coincidence.*
→ **GRAMMAR: On the other hand** is often used at the beginning of a sentence.

close /kloʊs/ *adverb, adjective*

- ► close
- ► near
- ► nearby

ANTONYMS → see Function Word **far**

close *adverb, adjective*
not far away from someone or something: *She was sitting* ***close to*** *the window. | The closest town is about ten miles away from the farm.*

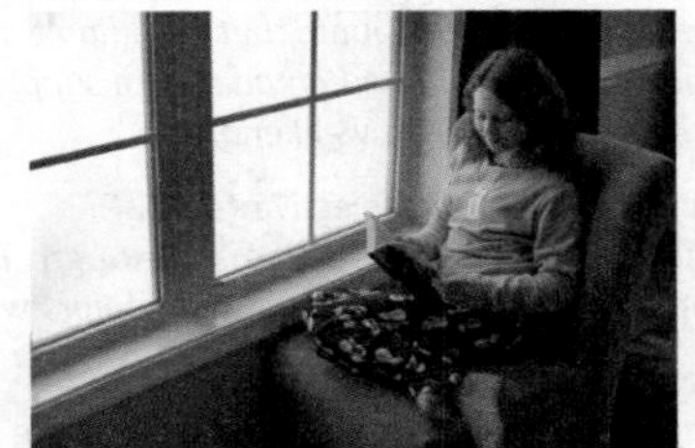
She is sitting **close to** the window.

near *preposition*
near means the same as **close**: *He lives near here. | They moved to be nearer the school.*

nearby *adverb, adjective*
close to here or close to a particular place: *We stopped at a nearby gas station. | Is there a post office nearby?*
→ see **similar, thorough**

GRAMMAR CHECK: close

Close and **near** are both used to talk about short distance between things.

Don't say: ~~*The hotel is close the beach.*~~ Say: *The hotel is* ***close to*** *the beach.* **Close** must be followed by the preposition "to" and then a noun: *They live* ***close to*** *the park.*

Near is usually followed directly by a noun: *The hotel is* ***near*** *the beach.*

People do not often say that someone or something "is close" or "is near," although you can say that someone or something **is closer** or **nearer**, or **gets** or **comes closer**: *Which school is closer? | The dog came closer.*

down /daʊn/ *adverb, preposition*

- ► down
- ► downward
- ► downhill
- ► downstairs

ANTONYMS → see **up**

down *adverb, preposition*
toward or to a lower place: *He tripped and fell down. | If you are scared of heights, don't look down! | The ball bounced down the stairs.*

downward *adverb*
toward a lower place: *She was standing on the bridge, staring downward into the water.*
→ If you want to say that something or someone comes onto the ground or floor from a higher position, use **down**, not **downward**: *Come down from that tree!*

downhill *adverb*
down a hill or sloping piece of ground to a lower level: *The car began to roll downhill.*

They rode **downhill**.

downstairs *adverb*
toward or to the bottom of the stairs: *She went downstairs to look for the book.*

during /ˈdʊrɪŋ/ *preposition*

1 for the whole of a period of time

- ► during
- ► in
- ► over
- ► in the course of (*formal*)
- ► throughout
- ► all through
- ► all day/week/year etc.

2 at some point in a period of time

- ► during
- ► in
- ► on
- ► within

1 for the whole of a period of time

during *preposition*
for the whole of a period of time or an event: *There wasn't much to eat during the winter.* | *He was silent during breakfast.*

in *preposition*
used to say what generally happens for the whole of a part of the day or a season, or what change happened during a period of time: *The house is cool in the summer and warm in the winter.* | *In 2011, profits rose by 5%.*

over *preposition*
during a particular period of time, such as the summer or a weekend: *She and her friends are going to Miami over Spring Break.*

in the course of *also* **during/over the course of** *preposition (formal)*
in the course of means the same as **over** but is more often used in writing: *There will be some important changes happening at the school in the course of the next two years.*

throughout *preposition, adverb*
used to emphasize that something happens or stays the same from the beginning to the end of a long period of time: *He loved to hike, and throughout his life he made time to go to the mountains and walk.* | *The speaker was booed throughout by the crowd.*

all through *preposition*
all through means the same as **throughout** but sounds more informal: *It snowed all day yesterday, and all through the night.*

all day/week/year etc. *adverb*
throughout the day, week, year, etc.: *I've had a headache all day.* | *Why have you avoided me all week?*

2 at some point in a period of time

during *preposition*
at some point in a period of time or an event: *A car alarm went off during the night.* | *During the voyage, his wife died.*

in *preposition*
during a part of the day, a month, a season, a year, or a century. **In** is also used when talking about some events, for example wars: *He left early in the morning.* | *She was born in 1933.* | *His father was killed in World War II.*

on *preposition*
during a day: *We're going out to dinner on Friday.* | *They were married on 7 August 1967.*

within *preposition*
before a period of time ends: *Within 20 minutes he was back from the store.*

enough /ɪˈnʌf/ *adjective, pronoun, adverb*

- ► enough
- ► adequate
- ► sufficient *(formal)*
- ► plenty
- ► ample

enough *adjective, pronoun, adverb*
as much or as many as you need or want: *Are there enough chairs for everyone?* | *Is that enough, or would you like some more rice?*
→ **GRAMMAR: Enough** can also be used after an adjective: *I wasn't tall enough to reach the shelf.*

adequate (AWL) *adjective*
enough or good enough for a particular purpose. **Adequate** is more formal than **enough**: *How can we make the right decision if we do not have adequate information?* | *The service at the restaurant was adequate, but I wouldn't go there again.* | *The cabin had an adequate supply of drinking water for a weekend.*

sufficient (AWL) *adjective (formal)*
sufficient means the same as **enough**: *There was sufficient evidence to prove that Majors was guilty.*

plenty *pronoun*
enough or more than enough: *There are **plenty of** restaurants near here, so we'll have no trouble finding something to eat.* | *It is a big tent, with **plenty of** room for two people.* | *There is **plenty to** do and see on the island.*
→ **GRAMMAR:** Use **plenty of**, not **plenty**, before a noun: *We have plenty of time.*

ample *adjective*
ample means the same as **plenty of** but sounds more formal: *Don't worry – you'll have ample time to ask questions later.*
→ **GRAMMAR: Ample** is not used before plural nouns. Don't say: ~~*There were ample hamburgers for everyone*~~. Say: *There were plenty of hamburgers for everyone.* You can say: *There was ample food for everyone.*

every /ˈevri/ *adjective*

- ► every
- ► each
- ► all
- ► everything

ANTONYMS → see Function Word **none**

every *adjective*
used to refer to all the people or things in a group, considered separately: *We picked up every*

piece of garbage in the park. | *Every child received a gift, so no one was unhappy.*

each *adjective, pronoun*
every one of two or more people or things: *Each member of the team has a different job to do.* | *The dentist examined* ***each of*** *my teeth.* | *Tickets cost $20 each, so I'll need $80 if you want four.*

all *adjective, pronoun*
used for talking about the whole of a group of people or things: *I want all the girls to come here and all the boys to stand over there.* | ***All of*** *the cookies are gone – who ate them?* | *I used to have a lot of comic books, but I gave them all away.*

everything *pronoun*
all the things: *Don't believe everything he says.*
→ see **everyone**

GRAMMAR CHECK: every

Every, **each**, and **everything** are followed by a singular verb: *Every child is different.*

except /ɪk'sept/ *preposition*

- except
- other than
- but
- apart from
- not including
- with the exception of *(formal)*

except *preposition*
used when saying something that shows why your statement is not completely true or exact. You also use **except** to show which person or thing is not included in your statement: *Everyone except me knew why he had quit.* | *The weather was sunny,* ***except for*** *one day when it rained hard.* | *Her sister looks just like her,* ***except that*** *she is taller.*
→ **GRAMMAR:** At the beginning of a sentence, always use **except for**, not just **except**: *Except for the ticking of the clock, the room was quiet.*

other than *preposition*
other than means the same as **except**: *I did nothing all day, other than play video games.*
→ **GRAMMAR: Other than** is used in sentences with words such as "no," "nothing," "no one," and "not any": *There was no one else there, other than me and Elise.* | *I don't speak any Spanish, other than "por favor" and "gracias."*

but *preposition*
but means the same as **except**: *He eats nothing but vegetables.*
→ **GRAMMAR: But** is used after words such as "any," "nothing," "all," "anyone," and "everyone."

apart from *preposition*
apart from means the same as **except** but sounds more formal or literary: *There was no light in the room, apart from the glow of a candle.*

not including *preposition*
used when you want to show which things or people in a group are not included in a statement. You often use **not including** when you are talking about things that are not included in a price: *I pay $14.95 per month for 1,000 minutes of long distance calls, not including any local charges.*

with the exception of *phrase (formal)*
used when you want to show that one person or thing, or a small group, is different from a larger group: *All the passengers have arrived, with the exception of Mrs. Laura Ferrara.*

far /fɑr/ *adverb*

- far
- a long way
- distant *(formal)*
- faraway *(formal)*
- remote
- in the distance
- nowhere near

ANTONYMS → see Function Word **close²**

far *adverb*
a long distance. You use **far** in questions, in sentences with "not," or with "too" or "so": ***How far*** *is it to the store?* | *My house is* ***not very far*** *away.* | *It is* ***too far*** *to walk.* | *Maybe they feel sad because they are* ***so far from*** *home.*

a long way *noun*
a long distance: *Her house was* ***a long way from*** *the office where she worked.* | *It is a long way to the next town.*

distant *adjective (formal)*
a long distance from a place, and difficult to see or hear: *I could hear the distant sound of thunder.*

faraway *adjective (formal)*
a very long distance from a place. **Faraway** is used especially in stories: *One day a stranger arrived from a faraway land.*
→ **GRAMMAR: Faraway** is always used before a noun: *She told us stories about faraway places.*

remote *adjective*
a very long distance from the nearest town or city. **Remote** is used about places that are difficult to get to. It sounds fairly formal: *He comes from a remote village in the mountains.*

in the distance *adverb*
a long distance from where you are. You use **in the distance** when you can only just see or hear something: *You can see the mountains in the distance.*

You can see the mountains **in the distance**.

nowhere near *preposition*
a very long distance from a place. You use **nowhere near** when saying very strongly that two places are not near each other: *Our house is nowhere near the school – it is on the other side of town.*

few /fyu/ *adjective, pronoun*

1 not many
- ► few (*formal*)
- ► not many
- ► hardly any
- ► almost no

2 a very low number
- ► a few
- ► a small number
- ► a handful
- ► a minority (*formal*)

ANTONYMS → see Function Word **many**

1 not many

few *adjective, pronoun (formal)*
not a lot of people or things: *Very few types of birds are unable to fly. | The city has changed a great deal and* ***few of*** *the original buildings remain.*

not many *adjective, pronoun*
a smaller number of people or things than you expected or wanted: *Not many people know about this place, so there's usually no one here. |* ***Not many of*** *my old friends are still around – most of them have moved away.*

hardly any *adjective, pronoun*
only a very small number: *There are hardly any T-shirts left, so order yours today.*

almost no *adjective*
so small a number that it is almost none: *We saw almost no other cars all day.*

2 a very low number

a few *adjective, pronoun*
a number of people or things that is very low: *There are only a few cookies left. | A few people complained about having to wait, but most people were patient. | The firefighters managed to save* ***a few of*** *the people in the building.*

a small number *pronoun*
a few people or things – used especially when they are part of a much larger group: ***A small number of*** *students asked for some extra help.*

a handful *pronoun*
a very small number of people or things – used especially when the number is disappointing or surprising: ***A handful of*** *people stayed after the party to help clean up.*

a minority *pronoun (formal)*
a small group of people or things that is less than half of a larger group: *Most of the people in the country are Buddhist, but a small minority are Christian.*

GRAMMAR CHECK: few

A few and **few** are both used before plural nouns.

A few means "a low number": *A few people laughed.*

Few means "not many." It emphasizes how small the number is, and sounds formal: *Few people knew that he was sick.*

for /fɚ, strong fɔr/ *preposition*

- ► for
- ► since
- ► ago

for *preposition*
used to say how long something has been happening or lasts: *The meeting continued for five hours. | I have known Jim for 20 years.*

since *preposition, conjunction*
used to say that something has happened from a particular time in the past until now: *He has been competing in quizzes since 2005. | Sally and I have been best friends since we were children.*

ago *adverb*
used to say how much time has passed since something happened: *Jeff left for work 10 minutes ago. | I met her once, but it was a long time ago and I don't remember her very well.*

GRAMMAR CHECK: for

For, **since**, and **ago** are all used in order to talk about time.

You use **for** before an amount of time: *She has been living in the U.S. for ten years.*

You use **since** before a day, date, or time: *I've been waiting here since ten o'clock.*

You use **ago** after an amount of time: *Nora graduated from high school two years ago.*

forward /ˈfɔrwɚd/ *adverb*

- ► forward
- ► ahead
- ► straight ahead
- ► along
- ► onward

ANTONYMS → see Function Word **back**

forward *also* **forwards** *adverb*
toward a place or point in front of you – used when talking about movement or position: *One of the guards stepped forward and put his hand out to stop us.* | *She leaned forward to speak to the driver.* | *Sit facing forward with your legs stretched out.*

He is leaning **forward**.

ahead *adverb*
toward what is in front of you – used when talking about looking: *It was impossible to see ahead through the fog.*

straight ahead *adverb*
directly forward, not to the left or right – used when talking about movement or looking: *At the intersection, go straight ahead.* | *He was staring straight ahead toward the gates at the end of the road.*

along *adverb, preposition*
forward, especially on a road or path – used when talking about movement: *I was driving along, listening to the radio.* | *We walked along the path by the river.*

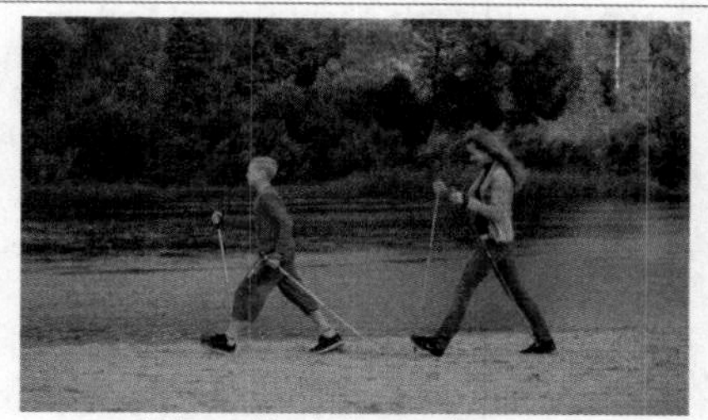
We walked **along** the river.

onward *also* **onwards** *adverb*
forward – used when talking about someone or something that is continuing to move, usually on a long journey: *The army marched onward.*

how /haʊ/ *adverb, conjunction*

1 used to ask or talk about the way something is done

- ► how
- ► the way
- ► the manner (*formal*)

2 used to ask or talk about the amount of something

- ► how
- ► to what extent (*formal*)
- ► the extent to which (*formal*)

1 used to ask or talk about the way something is done

how *adverb, conjunction*
used to ask or talk about a method of doing something, or what makes something possible: *How did you make the earrings?* | *I don't know how he can afford to pay for that car.*

the way *noun*
used to talk about or ask about how to do something, or how someone behaves or talks: *Let me show you the way I do it.* | *What's the fastest way to get there?* | *I don't like the way that he treats you.*

the manner *noun* (*formal*)
the manner means the same as **the way**: *The scientists explained the manner in which they found the answer.*
→ Don't say: ~~*The scientists explained the manner that they found the answer*~~.

2 used to ask or talk about the amount of something

how *adverb*
used to ask or talk about the amount of something, or about the age or size of someone or something: *How many pets do you have?* | *How much does it cost?* | *Happy Birthday! How old are you today?*

to what extent *adverb* (*formal*)
used in questions to ask how much something happens or is true: *To what extent should the government support poor families?*

the extent to which *adverb* (*formal*)
used in statements to talk about how much something happens or is true: *They were researching the extent to which preschool improves children's education later.*

if /ɪf/ *conjunction*

- ► **if**
- ► **unless**
- ► **even if**
- ► **as long as**
- ► **provided (that)**
- ► **in case**
- ► **or**
- ► **otherwise**

if *conjunction*
used when talking about something that might happen or that might have happened: *If the snow doesn't stop, I won't be able to get to work.* | *If you had been here yesterday, you could have met my sister Michelle.*

unless *conjunction*
if something does not happen or is not true: *Unless you work harder, you'll fail the test.*

even if *conjunction*
used when mentioning an action or situation that will not stop something happening or being true: *Even if we leave now, we'll still be late.*

as long as *also* **so long as** *conjunction*
only if something happens or is true: *You can have a party as long as it is over by eleven.*

provided (that) *also* **providing (that)** *conjunction*
provided (that) means the same as **as long as** but is more formal: *Any student can go to any public school in the city, provided that there is space available.*

in case *conjunction*
used when mentioning something that might happen, which someone wants to be prepared for: *Take an umbrella in case it rains.*

or *conjunction*
used when mentioning a bad thing that will happen if something is not done: *Stop that or I'll tell Mom!*

otherwise *adverb*
otherwise means the same as **or** but is more formal: *I'd better go now; otherwise my husband will wonder where I am.*
→ **GRAMMAR:** You must use a period or a semicolon before **otherwise**.

GRAMMAR CHECK: if

Use the present tense, not "will," after **if**, **unless**, **even if**, **as long as**, **provided (that)**, and **in case** when talking about the future. Don't say: ~~*He will be disappointed if he will lose*~~. Say: *He will be disappointed if he loses.*

in /ɪn/ *preposition, adverb*

1 used to mention the place or container where something is
- ► **in**
- ► **at**
- ► **on**
- ► **inside**
- ► **indoors**

2 to the inside of something
- ► **in**
- ► **into**
- ► **inside**
- ► **indoors**

ANTONYMS → see Function Word **out**

1 used to mention the place or container where something is

in *preposition*
used to mention the place where someone or something is, or the container where something is: *My sister lives in Pittsburgh.* | *Jim's watching TV in his room.* | *There's some juice in the refrigerator.*

at *preposition*
used to say exactly where someone or something is: *I was waiting at the bus stop.* | *Let's meet at Bill's house.*

He is waiting **at** the bus stop.

on *preposition*
used to mention a particular place where someone or something is: *Napoleon spent the rest of his life on the island of St. Helena.* | *Los Angeles is on the west coast.* | *His office is on the fifth floor.*

inside *preposition, adverb*
in a container or building: *What is inside the box?* | *It was dark inside the church.* | *He shook the box, trying to guess what was inside.*

indoors *adverb*
in a building: *Our dog gets bored if he is left indoors all day.*

2 to the inside of something

in *preposition, adverb*
to the inside of a room, vehicle, or container, especially to the place where you are or that you have just mentioned: *When I knocked at the door, the principal said "Come in!"* | *Put the scissors back in the drawer.*
→ After the verbs "put," "throw," drop," and "look" it is more natural to use **in** rather than **into**: *I dropped my book in the mud.*

The flowers are **in** the vase.

into *preposition*
to the inside of a room, vehicle, or container: *She went into the living room.* | *Pour the milk into a pan.*

inside *preposition, adverb*
into a building or container: *It started to rain, so we went inside.* | *I looked inside the closet for my shoes.*

indoors *adverb*
into a building: *You should bring the plant indoors for the winter.*

in front of /ɪn ˈfrʌnt ʌv/ *preposition*

- ► in front of
- ► in front
- ► out front
- ► ahead

ANTONYMS → see Function Word **behind**

in front of *preposition*
if something is in front of you, you are facing it. If something is in front of a building or vehicle, the front of the building or vehicle is facing it: *There was a tall man standing in front of me, so I couldn't see what was happening.* | *She parked her car right in front of the main entrance.*
→ Don't confuse **in front of** (=directly next to the front of a building) and **opposite** (=on the other side of the street).

in front *adverb*
further forward, and usually near or without anyone or anything else in between: *The car in front suddenly slowed down and we nearly ran into it.*

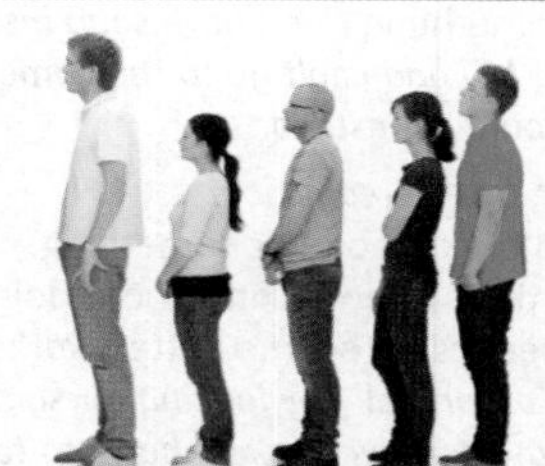
There was a tall man **in front of** me.

out front *adverb*
in the area near the entrance to a building: *I looked out of the window and saw there was a police car parked out front.*

ahead *adverb*
further forward than you, when you are moving: *I shouted at him to stop, but he was too far ahead and didn't hear me.* | *We could still see their car*

ahead of us. | *The road ahead was closed because of an accident.*

in order to /ɪn ˈɔrdɚ tu/ *conjunction*

- ► in order to
- ► to
- ► so

in order to *conjunction*
used when saying what someone's purpose is. **In order to** sounds more formal than **to**: *I practice the piano every day in order to improve.*
→ **In order that** is also used, but is very formal: *He hid the letter in order that his wife might not read it.*

to *used before a verb in the infinitive*
to means the same as **in order to** but is less formal: *I went upstairs to change.*

so *also* **so that** *conjunction*
used to say what result someone wants his or her action to have: *I'm saving up so I can go to the concert.* | *He turned the doorknob slowly so that it would make no noise.*

instead /ɪnˈsted/ *adverb*

- ► instead
- ► rather than
- ► in place of
- ► in someone's place
- ► in favor of

instead *adverb*
used when talking about using or doing a different thing from the usual or expected one. You also use **instead** when a different person does something: *Can I have soup* ***instead of*** *salad?* | *My dad can't go to the game, but he said that I could go instead.*

rather than *preposition*
instead of someone or something. You often use **rather than** when talking about doing a different thing because it seems better: *Rather than driving around all day looking for somewhere to park, why don't you take a bus into town?*

in place of *preposition*
instead of the thing or person that is usually used or that was used before. **In place of** sounds more formal than **instead of**: *For this recipe you can always use olive oil in place of butter.* | *The coach put in Rogers to start in place of Murray, who was injured.*

in someone's place *adverb*
instead of the person who was going to do something: *If Maria can't go, you can go in her place.*

in favor of *preposition*
used before the thing that someone chooses instead, because it seems better: *They rejected the original plan in favor of a new one.*

just /dʒʌst/ *adverb*

- ► just
- ► hardly
- ► barely
- ► narrowly

just *adverb*
used when saying that something happens, but it almost did not happen: *I just got to the airport on time – a few minutes later and I would have missed the plane.* | *The bullet* ***only just*** *missed his head.*

hardly *adverb*
if you can hardly do something, you can do it, but it is very difficult and only just possible: *The music is so loud that I can* ***hardly*** *hear what you are saying.*

barely *adverb*
barely means the same as **hardly**: *Because of the thick fog we could barely see the road in front of us.*
→ You often use **can** or **could** with **barely** and **hardly**.

narrowly *adverb*
used when someone almost does not avoid, escape, or miss something: *He narrowly escaped death when his car went over a cliff.*
→ You also use **narrowly** when someone wins or loses by a very small number of points or votes: *She narrowly won the election, with just 57 more votes than the other candidate.*

least /list/ *adjective, pronoun*

- ► least
- ► the fewest
- ► minimum

ANTONYMS → see Function Word **most (2)**

least *adjective, pronoun*
the smallest amount of something: *You should do what causes the least harm to the environment.* | *Let's buy the one that costs the least.*

the fewest *adjective, pronoun*
the smallest number of things or people: *The men who had the best family relationships had the fewest health problems.*

minimum (AWL) *adjective, noun*
the smallest number or amount that is possible or allowed: *You should exercise for* ***a minimum of***

20 minutes every day. | *What is the minimum age for marriage?*

less /les/ *adjective, pronoun*

- ► less
- ► not as much
- ► fewer
- ► not as many
- ► lower
- ► under
- ► below

ANTONYMS → see Function Word **more**

less *adjective, pronoun*
a smaller amount of something: *There was* ***less*** *water in the bucket* ***than*** *before.* | *She earns* ***less than*** *I do.*

not as much *adjective, pronoun*
not as much means the same as **less** but sounds less formal: *There was* ***not as much*** *water in the bucket* ***as*** *before.* | *She doesn't earn* ***as much as*** *I do.*

fewer *adjective, pronoun*
a smaller number of people or things: *There were* ***fewer*** *people at the meeting* ***than*** *I expected.*

not as many *adjective, pronoun*
not as many means the same as **fewer** but sounds less formal: *There* ***weren't as many*** *people at the meeting* ***as*** *I expected.*

lower *adjective*
less than another amount, level, or price: *Their prices are* ***lower than*** *ours, so more people shop there.* | *The pollution levels in the air around the city are lower today.*

under *preposition, adverb*
less than a particular number, amount, or age: *Do you have any shoes for under $50?* | *Tickets are free for children aged 12 and under.*

below *preposition*
below means the same as **under**: *There were hundreds of people there, but the total number was below 1,000.*
→ **GRAMMAR: Below** can also be used as an adverb to mean "less than zero" when talking about a temperature: *Temperatures drop to 40 below at night.*

like /laɪk/ *conjunction*

- ► like
- ► as if
- ► as

like *conjunction*
in a way that makes it seem that something is true: *He looked at me like I was crazy.* | *I feel like I belong here.*
→ **Like** can also mean "in the same way": *I was doing my homework at the table, like I always do.*

as if *also* **as though** *conjunction*
in a way that makes it seem that something is true. **As if** sounds a little more formal than **like** and is more often used in writing: *Graciela looked as if she was about to start crying.* | *She moved her legs slowly, as though she were in pain.*

as *conjunction*
in the same way or state: *Make sure you leave this room as you found it.*

little /ˈlɪtl/ *adjective, pronoun*

1 not much
- ► little (*formal*)
- ► not much
- ► hardly any
- ► almost no

2 a small amount
- ► a little
- ► a small amount
- ► a little bit of

ANTONYMS → see Function Word **a lot**

1 not much

little *adjective, pronoun (formal)*
not a lot of something, especially when this is less than what you want or expect: *We have very little time to finish the project.* | *There is little chance that the dog will be found.* | *Leslie could understand* ***little of*** *what they were saying.*
→ **GRAMMAR: Little** is not used before plural nouns. Don't say: ~~*There are little hours left*~~. Say: *There is little time left* or *There are few hours left.*

not much *adjective, pronoun*
a smaller amount of something than you wanted, expected, or needed: *It is very cold, but there's not much snow on the ground.* | *You can use my shampoo, but there's not* ***much of*** *it left.*
→ **GRAMMAR: Not much** is not used before plural nouns.

hardly any *adjective, pronoun*
only a very small amount: *There's hardly any milk left. Should I buy some more?*

almost no *adjective*
so small an amount that there is almost none: *By the end of the trip, we had almost no money.*
→ see Function Word **few** (**1**)

2 a small amount

a little *adjective, pronoun*
an amount that is not large: *"Is there any coffee*

left?" "Only a little." | Just use a little glue, not too much. | He was a little upset, but he's okay now.

a small amount *pronoun*
an amount that is not large, especially when the amount is measured: *Pour **a small amount of** oil in the pan.*

a little bit of *adjective*
a little bit of means the same as **a little** but is more informal: *I just want to have a little bit of fun.*
→ see **short**, **small**

a lot /ə ˈlɑt/ *pronoun, adverb*

1 a large amount or number
- ► a lot
- ► much
- ► a great deal (*formal*)
- ► quite a bit
- ► plenty

ANTONYMS → see Function Word **little**

2 to a large degree
- ► a lot
- ► much
- ► a great deal (*formal*)
- ► quite a bit

1 a large amount or number

a lot *also* **lots** *pronoun (informal)*
a large amount of something, or a large number of people or things: *I ate a lot for lunch, and I'm still full. | Will has **a lot of** friends, so he's always busy on the weekends. | There's still **lots to** do if you want to help.*

much *pronoun, adjective*
a large amount of something: *He didn't say much about his trip, so I don't know if he had fun or not. | Can you pay? I don't have much money with me. | There was too much work for one person.*
→ **GRAMMAR: Much** is used mainly in questions, in sentences with "not," or after "too" or "so." In other types of sentences, use **a lot of**. Don't say: ~~*Terry has much money*~~. Say: *Terry has a lot of money.*

a great deal *also* **a good deal** *pronoun (formal)*
a large amount of something: *It took **a great deal of** time and effort to paint the mural. | She earns a **good deal of** money from her business.*

quite a bit *pronoun*
a fairly large amount. **Quite a bit** is fairly informal: *Don has gained **quite a bit of** weight, because he isn't exercising.*

plenty *pronoun*
enough or more than enough: *Make sure the plants get **plenty of** water. | There's **plenty to** do in New York – you won't be bored.*

GRAMMAR CHECK: a lot

A lot of, **much of**, **a great deal of**, etc. are also used to talk about a large part of a group, amount, or thing: ***A lot of** my friends have kids now. | **Much of** the town was destroyed in the war.*

2 to a large degree

a lot *adverb*
to a large degree: *Ken likes Sarah a lot, and he's going to ask her out to dinner. | The test was a lot harder than the others. I wish I had studied more.*

much *adverb*
much is similar in meaning to **a lot** but you use it in different ways in a sentence: *Thank you very much. | Olivia is much taller than her sister, so she seems more grown up.*
→ **GRAMMAR: Much** is used mainly before comparative words such as "more" or "bigger," or after "too," "very," or "so": *Their house is much bigger than mine. | I ate too much. | It was so much fun!* In other types of sentences, use **a lot**. Don't say: ~~*I like it much*~~. Say: *I like it very much* or *I like it a lot.*

a great deal *also* **a good deal** *adverb (formal)*
a great deal means the same as **a lot**: *The problem is a great deal more complicated than anyone expected. | His spelling used to be very bad but it has improved a good deal.*

quite a bit *adverb*
to a fairly large degree: *In the past five years the town has changed quite a bit, with hundreds of new houses being built.*
→ see **often**

many /ˈmeni/ *adjective, pronoun*

- ► many
- ► hundreds/thousands/millions
- ► numerous (*formal*)
- ► countless

ANTONYMS → see Function Word **few**

many *adjective, pronoun*
used about a large number of people or things: *Andrea is from Brazil, but she has lived in Chicago for many years. | Many people voted against the proposal.*
→ **GRAMMAR: Many of** is used to talk about a large part of a group: ***Many of** her books are set in Egypt, where she grew up.*

Many sometimes sounds formal, and **a lot of** is often used instead in everyday English: *They have a lot of problems.*

You use **many** after "how," "too," and "so": *How many people are in your class? | You ask too many questions. | I've made so many mistakes.*

hundreds/thousands/millions *pronoun*
used about a large number that is more than a few hundred, thousand, or million: ***Hundreds of** people came to see our concert. | The ships carry **millions of** tons of cargo every year.*

numerous *adjective (formal)*
a number of people or things that is large but can still be counted: *He has received numerous awards for his work in the community.*

countless *adjective*
an extremely large number of people or things, that is too high to be counted or imagined: *Some kids spend countless hours playing video games.*

more /mɔr/ *adjective, pronoun*

1 an additional amount
- ► **more**
- ► **another**
- ► **further** *(formal)*
- ► **additional** *(formal)*
- ► **extra**

2 a larger number or amount
- ► **more**
- ► **higher**
- ► **greater**
- ► **above**
- ► **over**
- ► **beyond**
- ► **exceeding** *(formal)*

ANTONYMS → see Function Word **less**

1 an additional amount

more *adjective, pronoun*
an amount of something that comes or is given after an amount of the same thing: *She offered her guest some more coffee. | There will be more rain tomorrow. | Could I have a little more? I'm still hungry.*
→ **More** is used when talking about amounts or groups, but you can also talk about **one more** person or thing: *I would like to ask you one more question.*

another *adjective, pronoun*
one more person, thing, or amount of the same kind: *They decided to have another child. | Let's wait another ten minutes – I'm sure he'll be here soon. | He scored a goal, and then quickly scored another.*

further *adjective (formal)*
more, or another thing or amount: *If you need further information, just ask. | They made a further attempt to restart the peace talks.*

additional *adjective (formal)*
more, or another person, thing, or amount: *No additional details about the arrest were provided. | The Democrats need to gain an additional 20 seats to win control of the House.*

extra *adjective*
more than the usual amount or price: *Can I have extra fries with my burger? | If you want air conditioning, you have to pay extra.*

2 a larger number or amount

more *adjective, pronoun*
a larger number or amount, or a larger part of a group or amount: *You should spend more time checking your spelling. | He earns **more** money **than** I do. | We want **more of** our students to go to college.*

higher *adjective*
more than another amount, level, or price: *Housing prices there are **higher than** in other areas of the city. | The workers are demanding higher wages.*

greater *adjective*
a larger amount of a quality, feeling, action, etc. **Greater** is fairly formal: *Nothing is of greater importance to us than our children.*

above *preposition, adverb*
more than a number, amount, or level: *The temperature was two degrees above zero last night. | To pass the test, you need a score of 60 or above. | Our high school scored above average on the test.*

over *preposition, adverb*
more than a number, amount, or age. Use **over** especially when it is not important to say exactly how much more: *Our office receives over 2,000 applications a year. | The class is only for children aged 13 and over.*

beyond *preposition*
more than a particular number or amount. Use **beyond** especially when the other amount is a particular level or limit: *The price was beyond what we could afford to pay.*

exceeding *preposition (formal)*
more than a number, amount, or level. **Exceeding** is only used before a number: *Income exceeding $82,250 is taxed at a higher level.*

most /moʊst/ *adjective, pronoun*

1 almost all
- ► most
- ► the majority
- ► the bulk

2 the largest number or amount
- ► most
- ► maximum

ANTONYMS → see Function Word **least**

1 almost all

most *adjective, pronoun*
almost all, or a lot more than half: *Most people like ice cream.* | ***Most of** the children had finished the test but a few were still writing.* | *We've already eaten **most of** the cake, but there's still a little bit left.*

the majority *noun*
the majority means the same as **most** but sounds more formal: *I believe that **the majority of** people are honest.*
→ **A majority** means "more than half," but it may not be a lot more than half: ***A majority of** the people who voted (54% of them) supported the plan.*

the bulk *noun*
most of a large amount, group, or thing: ***The bulk of** the money they spend on research comes from the federal government.* | ***The bulk of** the work has been completed and they expect the building to be finished soon.*

2 the largest number or amount

most *adjective, pronoun*
the largest number or amount of something: *The team that scores the most points wins.* | *Who should we ask? Who knows the most about cars?*

maximum (AWL) *adjective, noun*
the largest number or amount that is possible or allowed: *The road was designed for **a maximum of** 35,000 vehicles a day.* | *The train was traveling at its maximum speed.*

next to /ˈnekst tu/ *preposition*

- ► next to
- ► beside
- ► by
- ► at the side of
- ► next door
- ► along
- ► alongside
- ► side by side
- ► adjacent to (*formal*)
- ► neighboring
- ► adjoining (*formal*)

next to *preposition*
close to the side of a person or thing, with no other person or thing in between – sometimes used when there are several people, rooms, buildings, etc. in a line: *She asked the person standing next to her what was going on.* | *His office is next to mine.*
→ **The next room** can be used to describe a room that is next to another one: *I could hear people talking in the next room.*

beside *preposition*
next to a person or thing. **Beside** sounds more formal than **next to**, and is not usually used about rooms and buildings: *He sat down beside her and started talking to her.*

by *preposition*
next to or close to something: *Ask for a table by the window.* | *We had a picnic by the lake.*

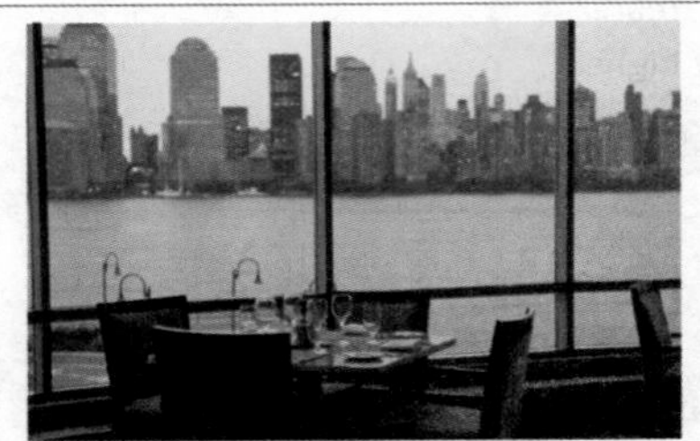
Ask for a table **by** the window.

at the side of *preposition*
next to something, especially a road or building: *Richard left his motorcycle at the side of the road and started to walk.*
→ You can say that someone is **at someone's side**: *He spoke to reporters with his wife at his side.*

next door *adverb*
next to another building, or living in the house

next to someone: *There's a bookstore **next door to** the bank.* | *Mrs. Cottrell lived **next door to** my parents.* | *The house next door has been sold.*
→ The person who lives next door to someone is their **next-door neighbor**.

along *preposition*
close to the side of a river, coast, border, etc. - used about movement or position: *Walk along the river as far as the bridge.* | *They are planning to build a fence along the border.*

alongside *preposition*
next to something: *A boat came alongside the ship to take the sick passenger off.* | *There were people running alongside the car, taking the star's picture.*

side by side *adverb*
if two people are walking, sitting, or lying side by side, they are next to each other: *We walked along slowly, side by side.*

We walked **side by side**.

adjacent to (AWL) *preposition (formal)*
used when saying that a building or area is next to a building or area, or that one room is next to another: *The hotel is adjacent to the park.*
→ **Adjacent** can be used as an adjective to describe a room, building, or area that is next to another one: *The fire spread to two adjacent houses.*

neighboring *adjective*
next to another country, state, or town: *People affected by the fighting have fled to neighboring countries.*
→ **GRAMMAR: Neighboring** is always used before a noun: *a neighboring town/country.*

adjoining *(formal)*
next to another room, building, or area: *They were called into an adjoining room for their interviews.*
→ **GRAMMAR: Adjoining** is always used before a noun: *an adjoining room/building/apartment.*

none /nʌn/ *pronoun*

► none
► no
► not any
► nothing
► no one

ANTONYMS → see Function Word **every**

none *pronoun*
not even one person or thing in a group, or not even one part of something: ***None of** my friends are here this weekend.* | *I was going to offer you some cake, but there is none left.*

no *adjective*
used to talk about nobody or nothing of a particular kind: *The house has no air conditioning.* | *There is no excuse for rudeness.*

not any *adjective, pronoun*
no or none: *He didn't have any money.* | *She was looking for potato chips, but there weren't any.*

nothing *pronoun*
not anything: *There was nothing in the box – it was completely empty.*

no one also **nobody** *pronoun*
not anyone: *The truck was badly damaged in the accident, but no one was hurt.* | *Nobody told me about the party for Farid.*

on /ɔn/ *preposition*

► on
► on top
► onto

on *preposition*
used to mention the surface where something is resting or where it is put: *You'll have to sleep on the floor.* | *Put those magazines on the table.* | *There were pictures on the walls.*

on top *adverb*
on the highest surface of something: *There was a pile of papers **on top of** the filing cabinet.* | *When the cake has cooled, you can put frosting on top.*

onto *preposition*
to a position on the surface of something: *The dog leaped onto the couch.*

only /ˈoʊnli/ *adverb*

1 not more than a small amount or number
► only
► just
► no more than

2 nothing or no one else
- ► only
- ► just
- ► nothing but

3 not anything more important or serious
- ► only
- ► just
- ► merely (*formal*)

4 for no other reason
- ► only
- ► just
- ► simply
- ► merely (*formal*)
- ► purely

1 not more than a small amount or number

only *adverb*
not more than a small amount or number, especially when this is surprising: *Naomi was only 18 when she got married.* | *There were only eight people in the restaurant, so it was very quiet.*

just *adverb*
just means the same as **only**, but sounds a little more informal and is used more in spoken English: *"How many pins do you need?" "Just one."*

no more than *adverb*
no more than means the same as **only** but sounds more formal: *These insects are no more than an inch long, but they can destroy a forest.*

2 nothing or no one else

only *adverb*
nothing or no one except for a particular person, thing, or group: *We use only the best ingredients.* | *Only the students with the highest grades are accepted to the college.*
→ **GRAMMAR:** In signs and instructions, you can use **only** after a noun: *The parking lot is for staff only.*

just *adverb*
just means the same as **only**, but sounds a little more informal and is used more in spoken English: *"Can all the students leave school for lunch?" "No, just the seniors."*

nothing but *adverb*
only a particular thing, and no other things: *He eats nothing but vegetables.*

3 not anything more important or serious

only *adverb*
used for saying that something or someone is not very important or serious: *Firefighters told the crowd that it was only smoke, and that there was no reason to worry.* | *She was only the manager's assistant and could not help me.*

just *adverb*
just means the same as **only** but sounds more informal and is used more in spoken English: *"What's for dinner?" "Just pasta – nothing exciting."* | *I just said hello to her – I didn't even get her name.*

merely *adverb (formal)*
merely means the same as **only**: *Jackson is merely one player on the team – the game does not depend entirely on him.*

4 for no other reason

only *adverb*
for one reason or purpose, and not for any others. You use **only** to explain why someone does something: *Everyone thinks Daria only married him for his money.* | *The man said he took the food only because his family was very hungry.*

just *adverb*
just means the same as **only**, but sounds a little more informal and is used more in spoken English: *I didn't mean to bother you – I was just trying to help.*

simply *adverb*
for one reason or purpose that is easy to understand, and not for any others. **Simply** is more formal than **only** or **just**: *Maybe I am sleeping so much simply because I have so much free time.*

merely *adverb (formal)*
used to emphasize that something is done only for the reason you say, and not for a more serious or more important reason: *I was not trying to blame you; I was merely asking what happened.*

purely *adverb*
only for the reason or purpose you say, or only of the type you say: *The colorful plants are purely for decoration – they cannot be eaten.*

opposite /ˈɑpəzɪt/ *preposition*

- ► opposite
- ► across from
- ► across
- ► facing

opposite *preposition*
directly in front of a thing or person and on the other side of a road, path, area, or table. **Opposite** is used mostly in writing, and it is more common to say **across from**: *The bathroom*

is opposite my bedroom upstairs. | *The museum is opposite the library.*

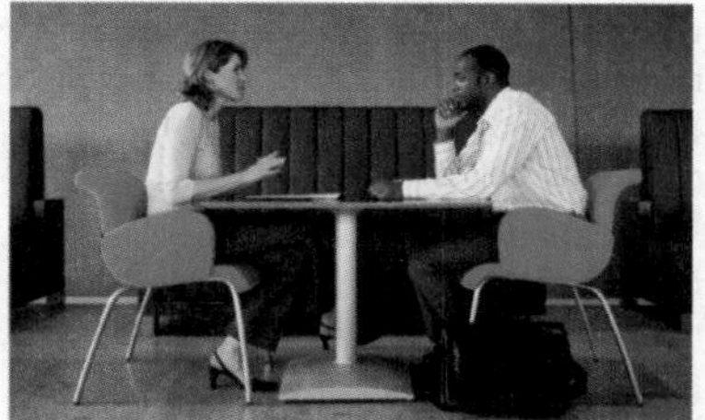

They are sitting **opposite** each other.

across from *preposition*
across from means the same as **opposite**: *I was sitting across from her at the table, so I heard everything she said.*

across *preposition*
on the other side of a road, river, border, or area: *Barbara lives here, and my house is across the street.*

facing *verb*
in a position in which the front parts of two people or things are toward each other: *We asked for a hotel room facing the ocean.*
→ **GRAMMAR: Facing** is used like a preposition, but it is a form of the verb **face**, which means "to be looking or pointing toward someone or something": *The back windows face west, so you can watch the sun set.*

SYNONYM CHECK
Across or across from?

If you are mentioning the road, river, etc. between things, you use **across**: *We took a picture of the waterfall across the lake.*

If you are mentioning the person or thing that is on the other side, you use **across from**: *The library is across from the auditorium.*

out /aʊt/ *adverb*

1 from the inside of something
- ► out
- ► outside

2 not in a building or room
- ► out
- ► out of
- ► outside
- ► outdoors

ANTONYMS → see Function Word **in**

1 from the inside of something

out *adverb*
from the inside of a building, room, vehicle, or container: *Gary had gone out to buy a newspaper.* | *She opened her bag and took out her passport.* | *People came rushing* ***out of*** *their houses to see what had happened.*
→ **GRAMMAR: Out** can also be used as a preposition, without **of** after it: *She looked out the window.*

outside *adverb*
out of a building or room: *I went outside to get some fresh air.*

2 not in a building or room

out *adverb*
not in a building or room: *Why are you standing out here in the corridor?*
→ If you say that someone is **out**, you mean that he or she is not at home or not at work: *I'm sorry, Mr. Robbins is out. Can I take a message?*

out of *preposition*
no longer in a place, or not in a place at that time: *He was glad to be out of jail.* | *I'm going to be out of town for two weeks.*

outside *adverb, preposition*
not inside a building or room, but near it: *She asked me to wait outside her office for a minute.* | *I like sitting outside in the sunshine.*
→ You can also use **outside** or **outside of** before a noun to mean "not in a city, but near it" or "not in a country": *He had a farm just outside of Kinston.* | *Toyota has many factories outside Japan.*

I like sitting **outside** in the sunshine.

outdoors *also* **out of doors** *adverb*
not in a building: *He has a lot of energy and likes spending time outdoors.*

so /soʊ/ *conjunction*

- ► so
- ► therefore (*formal*)
- ► as a result
- ► thus (*formal*)
- ► consequently (*formal*)
- ► for this reason
- ► thereby (*formal*)

so *conjunction*
for the reason that you have mentioned: *It was a lovely day, so they went to the beach.*
→ **And so** is also used, but it is more informal and is used more in speech: *I was tired and so I said, "Can we go home, please?"*

therefore *adverb (formal)*
for the reason that you have mentioned: *This house is smaller, and therefore cheaper.*

as a result *adverb*
used when you are giving the result of something: *Her husband was having to work longer hours. As a result, they spent less time together.* | *They were given new information and changed their minds as a result.*
→ **GRAMMAR: As a result** can be used at the beginning or end of a sentence.

thus *adverb (formal)*
as a result of what you have just mentioned: *The problem was more serious than they had thought, and thus took longer to solve.*

consequently (AWL) *adverb (formal)*
as a result of what you have just mentioned: *He did no work and consequently failed the exam.*

for this reason *adverb*
because of what you have just mentioned: *It is important that your résumé contains no errors. For this reason, you should check it carefully.*

thereby (AWL) *adverb (formal)*
with the result that something happens: *The equipment was left in a dangerous state, thereby creating a risk of injury to workers.*

some /səm, strong sʌm/ *adjective, pronoun*

- ► some
- ► any
- ► several
- ► a number of
- ► a few
- ► a little
- ► a bit
- ► a couple

some *adjective, pronoun*
an amount of something, or a number of people or things: *Do you want some ice cream?* | *I needed batteries, so I went out to buy some.*

any *adjective, pronoun*
some – used mainly in questions, in sentences with "not," "never," etc., and in sentences beginning with "if": *Did you see any dolphins?* | *We didn't have any money.* | *If you have any questions, call us.*

several *adjective, pronoun*
three or more people, things, or events, etc., but not a lot: *I've spoken to him several times.*

a number of *adjective*
a number of means the same as **several** but is slightly more formal: *A number of people were forced to leave their homes.*

a few *adjective, pronoun*
a small number of people or things: *There are only a few cookies left.* | *A few people complained about having to wait, but most people were patient.*

a little *adjective, pronoun*
a small amount of something: *If the sauce is too thick, add a little milk.* | *"Is there any coffee left?" "Only a little."*

a bit *pronoun*
a fairly small amount: *He had gained **a bit of** weight, and his jeans were now too tight.*

a couple *pronoun*
about two, or a small number: *I haven't seen Ryan for **a couple of** years.* | *They were handing out free pens, so I took a couple.*
→ **GRAMMAR:** In informal English, **a couple** is sometimes used before a noun instead of **a couple of**: *It is going to take a couple days.*

GRAMMAR CHECK: some

You use **some of**, **any of**, **several of**, **a few of**, and **a little of** when you are talking about part of a group or amount: ***Several of** his friends had become teachers.* | *I spent **some of** the money on a computer.*

toward /tɔrd/ *preposition*

- ► toward
- ► to
- ► in the direction of
- ► up

ANTONYMS → see Function Word **away**

toward *preposition*
used to say that someone or something is moving closer to someone or something: *Wright noticed two policemen walking toward him.*
→ **Toward** is also used to say what someone or

something faces or points at: *All the windows face toward the sea.*

They walked **toward** the library.

to *preposition*
used to say where someone goes. You use **to** to mention the place where someone will be after he or she has finished moving: *He has gone to Australia.* | *She stood up and walked to the door.*
→ Don't say: ~~*We're going to home*~~. Say: *We're going home.*

in the direction of *also* **in someone's direction** *preposition*
toward the area where a place or person is. **In the direction of** is used, for example, when it is not clear if someone intends to get to the place or not: *"Where's Rick?" "I saw him walking in the direction of Harry's house."* | *I tried to get the waitress's attention but she wasn't looking in my direction.*

up *adverb*
if you go up to a person or building, you go nearer and then stop when you are near him, her, or it: *An old man came* ***up to*** *me in the street and asked for money.* | *He saw a police car drive up and park outside his house.*

under /ˈʌndɚ/ *preposition, adverb*

1 in a lower position
- ► under
- ► below
- ► underneath
- ► beneath (*formal*)

ANTONYMS → see Function Word **above**

2 less than
- ► under
- ► below

ANTONYMS → see Function Word **above**, **more**

1 in a lower position

under *preposition, adverb*
in a lower position than something or covered by it: *The dog sat under the table by her feet.* | *Is my bag under your coat on the couch?*
→ **GRAMMAR:** Don't use **under** as an adverb unless you are talking about being under the surface of water: *The sperm whale can dive a mile and stay under for two hours.*

below *preposition, adverb*
in a lower place or position than someone or something: *I looked out of the window of the airplane at the islands far below us.* | *They skied down the mountain to the valley below.*
→ **Below** is also used in a piece of writing when referring to something that comes afterward: *Discuss the topics listed below.*

underneath *preposition, adverb*
underneath means the same as **under**. You use **underneath** especially when something is hidden or covered by something else: *She found the letter underneath a pile of papers.* | *The birds were moving the fallen leaves to get at the insects underneath.*

beneath *preposition, adverb (formal)*
beneath means the same as **under** but is used mainly in stories and descriptions: *The ship sank beneath the sea.* | *Because the trees cast so much shade, the ground beneath is bare.*

2 less than

under *preposition*
less than a particular number, amount, or age: *Do you have any shoes for under $50?* | *Tickets are free for children aged 12 and under.*

under

The dog is sitting **under** the chair.

below *preposition*
below means the same as **under**: *There were hundreds of people there, but the total number was below 1,000.*
→ **GRAMMAR: Below** is usually used as a preposition, but can be used as an adverb to mean "less than zero" when talking about a temperature: *Temperatures drop to 40 below at night.*

up /ʌp/ *adverb, preposition*

► up
► upward
► uphill
► upstairs

ANTONYMS → see Function Word **down**

up *adverb, preposition*
toward or to a higher place: *Don't let the cat jump up onto the table.* | *He lay on his bed staring up at the ceiling.* | *He had climbed up a tree to get a better view.*

upward *adverb*
toward a higher place: *The balloon floated upward into the sky.*

uphill *adverb*
up a hill or sloping piece of ground to a higher level: *It is hard work riding a bicycle uphill.*

upstairs *adverb*
toward or to the top of the stairs: *They carried her upstairs to the bedroom.*

when /wen/ *conjunction, adverb*

► when
► whenever
► as soon as
► the minute

when *conjunction, adverb*
at, around, or during the time that something happens: *When I got up, Mom had already gone to work.* | *I used to play chess when I was younger.*
→ **When** is also used to ask questions about the time of something, or to talk about the time that something will happen: *When did you meet your boyfriend?* | *She didn't tell us when she would be arriving.*

whenever *conjunction, adverb*
every time something happens: *Whenever we are alone together, he stops talking to me.*

as soon as *conjunction*
immediately after something has happened: *I'll call you as soon as I get any news from the hospital.*

the minute *also* **the moment** *conjunction*
the minute/the moment means the same as **as soon as** but sounds slightly more informal: *The minute I walked in the room, I knew something was wrong.*

while /waɪl/ *conjunction*

► while
► meanwhile

while *conjunction*
during the time that something is happening: *The parents talk to each other while their kids play together.* | *While he was sleeping, I wrapped his present.*

meanwhile *adverb*
while something else is happening: *I did my homework. Meanwhile, my brother practiced the guitar.*

Academic Writing Guide

by Lynn Bonesteel, Teacher and ESL Writer

1 Overview of Basic Organizational Structure

Many texts in English follow a predictable pattern of organization. The length and style differ depending on the purpose of the text, but the basic organizational structure remains the same.

Basic Organizational Structure

❶ Title

- Indicates the topic of the text
- Sometimes stated in a clever or unusual way in order to attract the attention of the reader

❷ Introduction

- Introduces the topic of the text in a way that makes the reader want to continue reading

Hook

Introductions often begin with a hook. The hook could be an anecdote (a very short story), a series of questions, a quotation, a vivid description, or a surprising statement or question. The hook is sometimes just one or two sentences, or it can be a whole paragraph.

Topic and Background Information

After the hook, either in the same paragraph or in a new one, the writer introduces the general topic of the text and gives some background information.

Central Idea

Usually at the end of the introduction (but sometimes at the beginning or in the middle) the writer gives the *central idea*. The central idea includes the topic of the text as well as the *controlling idea*, that is, the writer's purpose, point of view, opinion, or attitude concerning the topic. It is this central idea that will be supported in the rest of the text.

❸ Body

- Supports the central idea in body paragraphs. Some topics are developed in one paragraph. Other topics require two or more paragraphs.

Transition

The opening sentence(s) of each body paragraph refers to information from the previous paragraph, and introduces the new topic. This is called a *transition*. The transition might be one or more sentences, depending on how complex the topics are. The sentence or part of the sentence that introduces the new topic is often called the *topic sentence* of the paragraph.

Development and Support

Details such as facts, examples, descriptions, anecdotes, reasons, steps in a process, or references to authoritative sources develop and support the topics in the body paragraphs.

❹ Conclusion

- Summarizes all the information in the preceding paragraphs
- Provides the reader with a satisfactory ending
- Closely relates to the central idea and purpose of the essay. It doesn't include any new ideas.

Restatement of the Central Idea

The central idea is usually restated in the conclusion, either at the beginning or end, by using synonyms to rephrase it and by changing the sentence structure.

A Satisfactory Ending

A satisfactory ending depends on the central idea and purpose. For example, the conclusion might end with a call for future action (what the writer wants the reader to do), an unanswered question that the writer wants the reader to think about, or a prediction for the future.

Unity

A piece of writing is unified when all of the sentences in the text are related to the central idea.

Cohesion

Cohesion happens when the relationship among ideas is clear, and the sentences in the text flow logically. Cohesion is accomplished through the use of grammatical patterns and vocabulary. There are several good ways to achieve cohesion.

1. Repeating key terms

Repeating the most important words in your essay makes the reader pay attention to your main idea. It also helps link different parts of your essay together:

> *In the* ***United States****, the* ***average*** *family* ***size*** *continues to decrease. At the same time, the* ***average home size*** *has grown. According to the U.S. Census, the* ***average home size*** *in the* ***United States*** *was 2,479* ***square feet*** *in 2007, up from 983* ***square feet*** *in 1950.*

2. Repeating grammatical patterns

Using a similar sentence structure and word choice in your essay, especially at the beginning of a body paragraph, helps link different parts of your essay together so that it is more cohesive:

> *Commensalism* ***refers to an association*** *in which one or more species benefit.*
>
> *Mutualism* ***refers to an association*** *that is beneficial to both species.*
>
> *Parasitism* ***refers to an association*** *in which one species, the parasite, lives on or in a second species, the host, for a significant period of its life.*

3. Substituting a pronoun for a full noun or phrase

The second time you mention a noun in a sentence, it is better to use a pronoun to replace it. This avoids repetition, which can make your writing sound boring and stiff:

> *The simple design of the* ***houses*** *means that* ***they*** *can be built in just three weeks ...*

4. Using linking words

Linking words and expressions help you to join ideas, sentences, and paragraphs together in a clear way. You can use them to show what order something happens in, for giving reasons, for adding information, etc.:

> *Owning a small house is not just about saving money. It is* ***also*** *about saving the environment.*

5. Using synonyms

Using a synonym adds variety and interest to your writing. It also helps to link sentences or ideas together by saying the same thing in a different way:

> *One way of understanding symbiosis is to consider the benefit or harm to each species in the* ***relationship****. However, it is important to note that many* ***associations*** *between species do not fit neatly into one category.*
>
> *For their owners, these* ***vast homes*** *represent a piece of the American dream. However, a growing number of people ... have started to question the need for such* ***large domestic spaces****.*

Model Text 1: Informative Report (Social Studies)

❶

The Small House Movement

❷ Ⓐ In the United States, the average family size continues to decrease. **At the same time**, the average home size has grown. Ⓑ **According to** the U.S. Census, the average home size in the United States was 2,479 square feet in 2007, up from 983 square feet in 1950. In communities across the United States, it is possible to see homes that are larger than 10,000 square feet. For their owners, these **vast homes** represent a piece of the American dream[1]. **However**, a growing number of people, including artists, architects[2], city planners, and environmentalists[3], have started to question the need for such large **domestic**[4] **spaces.** Ⓒ They point out that small homes offer a number of benefits, **not just** to their owners, **but** to the world.

❸ "I have been living in houses smaller than some people's closets," says California architect Jay Shafer. Ⓓ Shafer **currently** lives with his wife in a 70-square-foot home that he built himself outside San Francisco. The narrow[5] wooden home has a small working fireplace, a kitchen, and a table that lifts up to **reveal** a computer. Beyond the main room is a bathroom with a shower; upstairs is a **tiny** loft[6] with a bed and storage[7] for clothing. ❸

Ⓓ Shafer is one of the original members of the "Small House Movement,"[8] a group of artists and architects that **promote** small living spaces. The group's goal is to help people create a balanced and enjoyable life by living simply. The group has become more popular **as more and more** people have discovered the benefits of small living spaces. ❸

Ⓓ One obvious reason to live in smaller homes is their low price. **Whereas prices** in downtown New York City easily reach $1,200 per square foot or more, **costs** of construction company Jot House's small homes are as little as $100 per square foot, depending on location. Jot House founder Bryant Yeh says he wanted to create low-cost homes with modern designs. The Los Angeles company's one-story[9] homes have a simple **layout**[10], with a kitchen and bath. The simple **design** of the houses means that they can be built in just three weeks, ❸

❶ Title and topic
❷ Introduction
❸ Body paragraph
❹ Conclusion
Ⓐ Hook
Ⓑ Background information
Ⓒ Central idea

1 **the American dream** the belief that everyone in the U.S. has the opportunity to become successful and rich if they work hard
2 **an architect** someone whose job is to design buildings
3 **an environmentalist** someone who believes in protecting the natural world from the negative effects of the way that humans live
4 **domestic** relating to life at home
5 **narrow** measuring only a small distance from side to side; the opposite of wide
6 **a loft** an area with a floor that is above a room
7 **storage** a place where you can keep things when they are not being used
8 **a movement** a group of people who share the same ideas or beliefs, and work together on a particular goal

3 **compared to** the typical year-long building process for many homes.

3 (D) The low price of smaller homes makes them **especially** useful in difficult times. After Hurricane Katrina flooded much of the city of New Orleans in 2005, thousands of people were left homeless. Among them were Julie Martin and her family. "**Prior to** Katrina we specialized in **restoring** beautiful historic homes," she says. **Since then**, Martin has worked with Shafer to create the Martin House Company, which sells small homes. Many hurricane victims[11] like Martin have been able to rebuild their lives by moving to small homes. The U.S. government has spent millions to **assist** in their construction. The low price of the houses makes them a better **option** than keeping hurricane victims in hotels or government buildings.

3 (D) For Small House Movement founding member[12] Susan Susanka, owning a small house is **not just** about saving money. It is **also** about saving the environment. In her book *The Not So Big House*, the North-Carolina-based architect points out that half of the energy use in the United States is for buildings. **Reducing**[13] the size of homes is an easy way to **limit** energy use and pollution. By focusing on detail and making **maximum** use of available space, Susanka says residents[14] can have a better **living experience**, without wasting natural resources[15]. 3

(D) Perhaps the greatest advantage of small houses is the flexibility[16] they offer the people who live in them. The small size and weight of many small homes means they can be moved by truck. This allows people to live in a variety of places without having to pack and move their possessions[17]. The small homes are also easy to take care of. This gives their owners more time to do the things they **truly** love. "The reason I've [lived in small homes] is mostly because I don't like … taking care of a lot of **stuff** that I'm not really using," says Shafer. 3

(E) **In many ways**, the Small House Movement represents a return to the past and a time of simplicity. People who choose a small house point to a past when people had fewer possessions and children played outside. (F) For these homeowners, bigger is not better after all. 4

(D) Transition from old to new information
(E) Satisfactory ending
(F) Restatement of central idea

○ Unity and cohesion: Using linking words
○ Unity and cohesion: Using synonyms

9 **a story** a floor or level of a building
10 **a layout** the way in which a room or building is arranged
11 **a victim** someone who suffers because of a bad situation
12 **founding member** someone who begins a movement
13 **to reduce** to make smaller
14 **a resident** someone who lives in a particular place
15 **a natural resource** something such as land, minerals, or natural energy that exists in a country and can be used to increase its wealth
16 **flexibilty** the quality of being able to change easily
17 **a possession** something that you own

Model Text 2: Informative Report (Science)

Notice how in a scientific report, consistent section headings and subheadings often serve the purpose of signaling the sections of the report which correspond to the introduction, body, transitions between topics in the body, and conclusion. Charts, tables, and diagrams contain supporting information that is also explained in the text.

Symbiosis ❶

Ⓐ **Definition** Symbiosis is an important concept[1] in biology. Biologists define symbiosis as the close, interactive association (living together) of members of two or more species[2] over a period of time. ❷

Ⓑ **Classification of Symbiotic Relationship** Symbiosis may have a good, bad, or neutral effect on one or more of the species. One way of understanding symbiosis is to consider the benefit (positive effect) or harm (negative effect) to each species in the relationship, as shown in Figure 1. However, it is important to note that many associations between species do not fit neatly into one category. (See *One Final Note on Classification Systems* below.)

Ⓒ

SPECIES A	SPECIES B	TERMINOLOGY USED TO DESCRIBE SYMBIOTIC RELATIONSHIPS
+	0	Commensalism
+	+	Mutualism
+	–	Parasitism

0 = no effect (neutral)
+ = beneficial effect
– = harmful effect

Figure 1

Ⓓ **Commensalism (+, 0)** Commensalism **refers to an association** in which one or more species benefits. The other species is not affected. **One example of** commensalism **is the association between** the marine sponge[3] and a variety of small marine organisms[4], including shrimp and certain species of worms[5]. The marine sponge serves as a "living hotel" for these marine organisms. There are many benefits to the organisms living in the sponge. These include shelter[6], protection from predators[7], and easy access[8] to food that is washed into the sponge by the ocean. The sponge does not appear to be affected by the association. ❸

❶ Title and topic
❷ Introduction
❸ Body paragraph
❹ Conclusion
Ⓐ Background information
Ⓑ Central idea
Ⓒ Development and support

1 **a concept** an idea of how something is, or how something should be done
2 **a species** a group of animals or plants which are all similar and can breed together to produce young animals or plants of the same kind as them
3 **a marine sponge** a simple sea creature that is full of small holes
4 **an organism** a living thing, especially a very small one
5 **a worm** a long thin creature with a soft body and no legs
6 **shelter** protection from danger or the weather
7 **a predator** an animal that kills and eats other animals
8 **access** the ability to have or use something

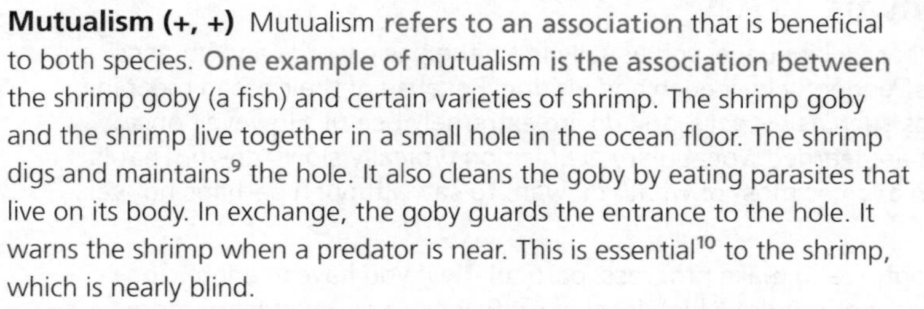

❸ **Mutualism (+, +)** Mutualism refers to an association that is beneficial to both species. One example of mutualism is the association between the shrimp goby (a fish) and certain varieties of shrimp. Ⓓ The shrimp goby and the shrimp live together in a small hole in the ocean floor. The shrimp digs and maintains[9] the hole. It also cleans the goby by eating parasites that live on its body. In exchange, the goby guards the entrance to the hole. It warns the shrimp when a predator is near. This is essential[10] to the shrimp, which is nearly blind.

❸ When the shrimp emerges[11] from the hole, it always keeps one of its antennae[12] on the goby. Ⓒ If the goby goes back into the hole, the shrimp feels the movement and quickly follows. If the shrimp is inside the hole and the goby is outside, the shrimp reaches out with one of its antennae and touches the fish's tail. If it is safe for the shrimp to emerge, the goby will move its tail from side to side. Otherwise the shrimp will remain inside, protected from potential predators by its constant companion.

❸ **Parasitism (+, –)** Parasitism refers to an association in which one species, the parasite, lives on or in a second species, the host, for a significant period of its life. Ⓓ It uses the host for food, shelter, and/or protection. In the process, it harms the host in some way. A parasite does not usually kill its host. However, the harmful effects of the parasite's actions can lead to the death of the host.

❸ One example of parasitism is the association between a tape worm and a dog. Ⓒ The tape worm lives and reproduces[13] inside the intestine[14] of the dog. It has no mouth, so it feeds by absorbing[15] the contents of the dog's intestines through its skin. If the tape worm is not removed, the dog's health will be harmed.

❹ **One Final Note on Classification Systems** Clearly, manmade classification systems with distinct[16] categories help us understand the natural world. However, in nature such distinct categories do not exist. Ⓔ Rather, you might think of relationships among species as existing on a continuum[17]. For example, symbiotic relationships exist on a continuum from beneficial (+) to harmful (-). Very few relationships fit neatly into just one category. Ⓕ

Ⓓ Transition from old to new information
Ⓔ Satisfactory ending
Ⓕ Restatement of central idea

○ Unity and cohesion: Repeating grammatical patterns

[9] **to maintain** to take care of
[10] **essential** important and necessary
[11] **to emerge** to come out of a place
[12] **antennae** two long things on an animal's head that it uses to feel things
[13] **to reproduce** if a person or animal reproduces, it has babies
[14] **intestines** the long tube in an animal's body that food passes through after it leaves the stomach and before it leaves the body
[15] **to absorb** to take into the body and hold it in
[16] **distinct** clearly different or separate
[17] **a continuum** something that changes or develops very gradually so that each part is very similar to previous and following parts

LANGUAGE BANK

Using Synonyms

When you first learn a language, you usually learn the basic words and phrases that occur most frequently in speech and writing. Because of their broad meaning and usage, words such as *be*, *have*, and *do* are extremely useful. However, once these key words are learned, vocabulary acquisition typically slows down. That is because you can express most of what you want to say, although perhaps not very precisely.

If you want to continue to make progress, particularly if you have academic or professional goals that require a high level of proficiency, you must learn more formal and precise ways of expressing your ideas. That is when a thesaurus can be very helpful. Before using a word or expression from the *Longman Thesaurus*, however, you should check not only its meaning, but also its usage. It will almost certainly have a more limited usage than the simpler word you are replacing.

When reading, get into the habit of noticing words that express simple ideas in a more formal, precise manner. Here are some examples taken from the model text *The Small House Movement*.

Simple verb or verb phrase	More formal, precise synonym	Example
get smaller	*decrease*	*In the United States, the average family size **has decreased**.*
be/stand for	*represent*	*For their owners, these vast homes **represent** the American dream.*
ask about	*question*	*A growing number of people have started to **question** the need for such large domestic spaces.*
have/give	*offer*	*They point out that small homes **offer** a number of benefits.* *Perhaps the greatest advantage is the flexibility they **offer** to their residents.*
do	*achieve*	*This can be **achieved** by living simply and practically.*
help with	*assist in*	*The U.S. government has spent millions to **assist in** their construction.*

Using Linking Words

Linking words help you to join ideas, sentences, and paragraphs together in a clear way. You can use them to show what order something happens in (time/sequence linking words), for giving reasons, for adding information, etc. The *Longman Thesaurus* will help you select the right linking word for your writing. Here are some examples of linking words taken from the model text *The Small House Movement*.

Time/Sequence	*after, as, at the same time, before, currently, for a period, in the process, now, over a period of time, prior to, since then, when, while*
Emphasis	*especially, in fact, clearly*

LANGUAGE BANK *continued*

Restatement	*... means that ...*
Addition or simple listing	*not just ... but, also, one way*
Compare/Contrast	*however, whereas, or, as little as, compared to, rather*
Reason	*because, the reason that ... is because, so*
Concession	*despite, while, in many ways*
Condition	*if, otherwise*

PRACTICE

Using the Thesaurus

A Read the model text *The Small House Movement* again and pay attention to the words in boldface. In the exercise below, look at the key words from the *Longman Thesaurus* and write the boldfaced word that you think is a synonym for the key word next to it.

	KEY WORD IN THESAURUS	BOLDFACED WORD FROM TEXT
1	small	
2	encourage	
3	large	
4	show (*verb*)	
5	most	
6	before	
7	really	
8	choice	
9	thing	
10	fix	
11	help (*verb*)	

B Now check your answers to Exercise A by looking up the key words in the *Longman Thesaurus*. If you have matched the words correctly, you should find the boldfaced word from the text under the key word entry. Look carefully at the definition of the word from the text. Circle the parts of the definition that make the meaning more specific than the definition of the key word.

Linking Words

C Find and circle the linking words that are used in the model texts. Pay attention to how they are used.

2 Informative Essays

The purpose of an informative essay is to inform the reader. Regardless of the subject, the essay needs to present factual information on a topic that is likely to be unfamiliar to the reader. In other words, an informative essay should teach the reader something new.

Basic Structure of Informative Essays

❶ Introduction

- Introduction of the central idea or topic
- The controlling idea
- A hook (sometimes) to get the reader's attention
- Background information about the topic

❷ Body

- Details about the topic
- Transitions from old information to new information (usually at the beginning of a new body paragraph)
- Words that let the reader know when the writer is certain and when he or she is hedging
- Use of specific tenses (simple present, present perfect, simple past, and past perfect)

❸ Conclusion

- Restatement of the central idea or topic
- Satisfactory ending

GRAMMAR BANK

VerbTenses

In informative essays, it is important to let the reader know when details are facts. One way to do this is to use specific verb tenses like the simple present, present perfect, simple past, and past perfect.

Simple present – use to describe facts that are true now and in the future, and were true in the past:

*Humans **have** only two legs.*

Present perfect – use to describe a situation or trend that develops over time, from past to present:

*Running **has played** a significant role in human life and culture.*

Simple past and past perfect – use to report on past events:

*Europeans travelling in Turkey **admired** the beautiful flowers.*

*Merchants in Holland **had become** very rich.*

LANGUAGE BANK

Expressing Certainty

Writers can also let their readers know when they are certain about something by using expressions that indicate their certainty.

Words or phrases that indicate certainty	*undeniably, certainly, of course, without a doubt, definitely, always*
Modal verbs	*must, will, cannot, have to*
Quantity words	*all, no, whole, everyone, everything*

Hedging

In academic writing, it is important not to overstate a point or make an absolute claim that you cannot support. Thus, it is important to be able to express degrees of uncertainty as well as certainty. When writers are not certain about some information, they hedge. Writers hedge to qualify what they are writing, to avoid making statements that are overly broad or making assertions that have not been fully proven or cannot be verified. There are many ways to hedge in English.

Words that express probability or possibility	*probably, perhaps, few, most, not often, not much, many*
Reporting verbs	*say, report*
Modal verbs	*might*
Verbs that express probability or possibility	*seem, tend*

Model Text 1: Informative Essay (History)

Tulip Fever

❶ It **might** come as **a bit** of a surprise, but Ⓐ tulips, the vividly colored yet rather ordinary flowers, Ⓑ have an extraordinary history. Today the country most commonly **associated** with tulips is Holland. However, that was **not always** true. Ⓒ **No one is sure** where the first tulips came from, but we do know that it was not Holland. The first wild tulips **probably** grew thousands of years ago **somewhere** in the **region** between Northern China and Southern Europe.

❷ Ⓔ Turkish rulers, called sultans, were **fascinated** by Ⓓ the tulip. From the late 15th to early 18th centuries, tulips were associated with wealth and high social position in Turkey. There were special festivals to celebrate the tulip. On the night of the full moon, crystal[1] vases filled with the most **exceptional** tulip **varieties** were placed around the sultan's gardens. Crystal lanterns[2] lit up the **charming** flowers. Songbirds in cages entertained the guests, who dressed in a wide range of colors to match the beautiful flowers. Access[3] to the distinctive flowers was controlled by law. It was illegal for **most** ordinary Turks to grow, buy, or sell them. ❷

Ⓔ Europeans traveling in Turkey admired the beautiful flowers, and brought back descriptions of the extraordinary Turkish tulips. **As far as we know**, the first tulip bulbs[4] from Turkey Ⓔ were sent to the famous botanist[5] Carolus Clusius (1526–1609) at the Royal Medicinal Gardens in Prague in the late 1500s. The bulbs arrived in Holland **some years later**, when Clusius moved to Leiden taking the Turkish bulbs with him. There he planted them in the Leiden Botanical Gardens. ❷

Ⓓ At that time, merchants[6] in Holland had become very rich from trading with other countries. These Dutch merchants built large, luxurious houses to show off their wealth. Ⓓ And like the Turkish sultans, they ❷

❶ Introduction
❷ Body paragraph
❸ Conclusion
Ⓐ Topic
Ⓑ Controlling idea
Ⓒ Background information
Ⓓ Old information/topic

[1] **crystal** high quality glass
[2] **a lantern** a type of lamp you can carry, that has a metal frame and glass sides
[3] **access** the ability to have or use something
[4] **a bulb** a root shaped like a ball, that grows into a plant
[5] **a botanist** a scientist who studies plants
[6] **a merchant** someone who buys and sells large quantities of goods

2 Ⓔ wanted the most dramatic varieties of tulips for their gardens. But there was a problem. Clusius did not want to share his tulips. To get them, people **had to** sneak[7] into the botanical garden and steal the bulbs.

2 Ⓓ Because tulips were so difficult to get and so **many wealthy** people wanted them, Ⓔ the flowers became very expensive. At first, only wealthy merchants could afford them. Ⓔ But in 1630 a new profession emerged[8]: tulip trading. Traders bought tulip bulbs and then resold them at a much higher price. It **seemed** an easy way to make money fast.

2 Ⓓ Soon the obsession[9] with tulips Ⓔ had become widespread. **Everyone** was borrowing money to buy tulip bulbs. Ordinary farmers and workers risked their livelihoods to buy them. In 1633, one man traded his farmhouse for three bulbs. In 1636, one bulb sold for an astonishing 5,200 guilders[10]. That was as much money as a rich merchant made in a year! The **whole** country was wild for tulips. Soon **everyone** had tulip fever. 2

Ⓓ Today, we can see that the Dutch were not thinking clearly. They believed that tulip prices would rise forever. But, **of course**, that was an illusion. The traders came to their senses[11] first. From one day to the next, they stopped buying tulip bulbs. The demand for tulip bulbs evaporated, and Ⓔ the tulip markets crashed. Bulbs worth 5,000 guilders one day, were worth nothing the next. The lives of ordinary people were destroyed. They lost **everything**: their homes, their land, their farms, and their life savings. 2

Ⓕ Tulip fever was a disaster for ordinary people in Holland, but the financial markets survived. Today, the tulip is a flower for everyone, not just the rich. Ⓖ That is good news for the Dutch, who make hundreds of millions of dollars a year from tulip sales to ordinary people **all over the world**. 3

Ⓔ New topic
Ⓕ Restatement of central idea
Ⓖ Satisfactory ending
○ Hedging
○ Expressing certainty

[7] **to sneak** to go somewhere quietly because you do not want people to see or hear you
[8] **to emerge** to appear
[9] **an obsession** something that you think about too much, in a way that is not normal
[10] **a guilder** the money used in the past in Holland
[11] **to come to one's senses** to realize what is sensible

Model Text 2: Informative Essay (Social Studies)

Running Around the World

❶ (A) If a cheetah[1], a wolf, and a well-trained human all entered a marathon[2], who would win? The cheetah would **definitely** take an early lead. The wolf would **probably** pass the cheetah after **a few** miles. But at the end of the 26 miles, the human would be the first to cross the finish line.

❷ (B) Humans have only two legs, but an incredible capacity[3] for running. Our powerful lungs[4] give us the stamina[5] needed to run great distances. And because we can sweat[6], we can control our body temperature while we run. Why are we so good at running? Running was necessary for early human survival. **Of course**, we **don't often** need to run for survival these days. All the same, (C) running continues to play (D) an important role in human cultures all over the world.

❷ (F) Marathon running is perhaps the best-known example of (E) human running culture. That is because it is big business. Millions of people worldwide watch as elite[7] runners compete for millions of dollars on television. And **of course** businesses promote products such as athletic shoes during the competition.

❷ (F) How does someone become (E) an elite marathoner? The legendary[8] runners of Kenya **seem** to have found the answer. Iten is a small farming town in Kenya's western highlands. It is also home to seven of the world's top ten marathon winners. **Most** of them are members of the Kalenjin tribe. The Kalenjini **tend** to have ideal bodies for running. Their slim bodies, long legs, and short waists[9] concentrate power where a runner needs it most—the legs. And because Iten is 8,000 feet above sea level, the Kalenjini develop an enormous lung capacity. They need it to get oxygen out of the thin air. This gives the Kalenjini an important advantage when they compete in races at lower altitudes.

❷ Thousands of miles away from (E) Iten, (F) in the mountains in western Mexico, live the Tarahumara. They call themselves the running people. The Tarahumara do **not** have **much** contact

❶ Introduction
❷ Body paragraph
❸ Conclusion
(A) Hook
(B) Background information
(C) Topic
(D) Controlling idea

[1] **a cheetah** a member of the cat family that can run very fast

[2] **a marathon** a race in which competitors run 26 miles and 385 yards

[3] **capacity** the ability to do or produce something

[4] **a lung** one of the two parts inside your body that you use for breathing

[5] **stamina** physical or mental strength that lets you do something for a long time

[6] **to sweat** to have salty liquid coming through the skin when you are hot, ill, scared, or exercising

[7] **elite** an elite group has the best people or things, and therefore is highly respected

❷ with the outside world. However, their amazing capacity for long-distance running has caught the attention of researchers. Unlike elite marathon runners, the Tarahumara do not compete for prize money. Instead, they run when playing traditional games and when competing in two- to three-day-long races over mountains. There is **no** million-dollar prize waiting for them. For the Tarahumara, running **seems** to be its own reward.

❷ Ⓕ A group of monks high in the mountains near Kyoto, Japan, run for a different reason. They run to reach enlightenment[10]. The 1,000-day challenge of the monks of Hiei involves intense periods of running, as well as a period of extreme physical deprivation[11]. The challenge takes seven years to complete. Only 46 monks have ever finished it.

❷ A monk begins the challenge by running 40 kilometers every day for 100 days. The distance is similar to that of a marathon. The monk completes three of these 100-day cycles. There are periods of rest between the cycles. Next, the monk **must** run 40 kilometers a day for 200 days without a single day of rest. Then comes a different type of challenge. For nine days, the monk **cannot** eat, drink, or sleep. At the end of the nine days, he is often near death. ❷

If the monk survives, he **will** go on to complete the final year of the challenge. There are two 100-day cycles in the final year. During each cycle, the monk runs 84 kilometers every day. He **must** complete the run within 18 hours. Then he **must** repeat it again the next day. That means that in each 100-day cycle, he is running two marathons a day. ❷

The **few** monks who have completed the rigorous[23] 1,000-day challenge **say** that they now see the world in a new way. They **report** that they experience things more intensely; they can see, hear, taste, and smell much better than before. They also **say** that they have a much greater appreciation[12] for life. ❷

It is **undeniable** that the running cultures of the Kalenjini, the Tarahumara, and the monks of Hiei are very different. However, they all remind us that Ⓖ running has **always** played a significant role in human life and culture. Ⓗ The tradition continues today as people all over the world continue to run for money, sport, exercise, enlightenment, or just plain fun. ❸

Ⓔ Old information/topic
Ⓕ New topic
Ⓖ Restatement of central idea
Ⓗ Satisfactory ending
○ Hedging
○ Expressing certainty

[8] **legendary** famous and admired
[9] **a waist** the part in the middle of your body just above your hips
[10] **enlightenment** the state in the Hindu and Buddhist religions of not having any more human desires
[11] **deprivation** the state of not having the things that you need for a comfortable or happy life
[12] **rigorous** involving a lot of work or effort
[13] **appreciation** the feeling of being grateful for something

PRACTICE

Using the Thesaurus

A Read the model text *Tulip Fever* again and pay attention to the words in boldface. In the exercise below, look at the key words from the *Longman Thesaurus* and write the boldfaced word that you think is a synonym for the key word next to it.

	KEY WORD IN THESAURUS	BOLDFACED WORD FROM TEXT
1	rich	
2	interested	
3	area	
4	connected	
5	good	
6	nice	

B Now check your answers to Exercise A by looking up the key words in the *Longman Thesaurus*. If you have matched the words correctly, you should find the boldfaced word from the text under the key word entry. Look carefully at the definition of the word from the text. Circle the parts of the definition that make the meaning more specific than the definition of the key word.

Linking Words

C Find and circle the linking words that are used in the model texts. Pay attention to how they are used.

Persuasive Writing: The Book Review

A review is a particular type of persuasive writing. A review is a report on a book, short story, poem, movie, play, piece of music or art, or exhibition. The purpose of a review is to introduce the reader to the piece, express the reviewer's opinion about it, and finally persuade the reader that the piece is (or is not) worth reading, seeing, or hearing.

Book reviews are one type of persuasive writing. They usually contain a brief overview of the content of the book, followed by a commentary on its strengths and weaknesses. The reviewer concludes with a recommendation as to whether someone should read the book or not. The recommendation can be stated directly or implied. Book reviews can be of fiction or non-fiction books.

Reviews of fiction books, such as a novel, usually have an overview that contains some basic information about the plot (basic story), the setting (physical environment, period of time), and the characters (people, animals), without revealing information that tells the end of the story and spoils the reader's enjoyment. The reviewer then points out strengths and/or weaknesses in the plot, setting, characters, and writing style.

Reviews of non-fiction books, such as a popular science book, have an overview that usually contains an outline of the basic theories, concepts, or arguments presented in the book. The reviewer then comments on the strengths and/or weaknesses in the content and writing style.

In both fiction and non-fiction reviews, the reviewer often uses descriptive language and provides short excerpts, quotations, and/or examples from the book. The language and examples support the reviewer's opinion of the book, and give the reader an idea about the content of the book.

Basic Structure of a Book Review

❶ Introduction

- Author's full name
- Title of the book
- Basic information about author, genre, audience, themes, characters, and/or plot
- Indication of reviewer's opinion

❷ Body

- Overview of content, plot, and/or themes
- Presentation of central argument (non-fiction)
- Character description (fiction)
- Strengths and/or weaknesses
- Quotations, excerpts, and/or specific examples from text to illustrate reviewer's main points

❸ Conclusion

- Reviewer's recommendation (directly stated or implied)

Model Text 1 : Book Review (Fiction)

Girl with a Pearl Earring

❶ Ⓐ GIRL WITH A PEARL EARRING by Tracy Chevalier is a Ⓑ thoroughly engaging Ⓒ historical novel that follows the life-changing experiences of Ⓓ a quiet housemaid named Griet over the two years she serves the Delft painter, Johannes Vermeer (1632–1675). Ⓑ It is hard not to like this good and obedient protagonist[1], Ⓔ for she struggles with universal yearnings[2] such as love and an escape from poverty[3]. Her life is a fairly **solitary** one as she finds herself growing apart from her family while living as an outsider in another's home.

❷ Ⓓ The Vermeer family, with the exception of the painter himself, is not fond[4] of the strange [...] girl; and as Maria Thins, the grandmother, says, Ⓖ "Never so much trouble with a maid before." The real trouble comes, however, when the artist takes a liking to the young girl and allows her to assist him in his work.

❷ Ⓕ Griet is granted the **privilege** that no other family member has—helping Vermeer in his studio. Not even his wife Catharina is allowed to enter the studio, so this arrangement causes a great deal of tension within the household. Griet begins her work by cleaning the various still life objects[5] that Vermeer will paint later that day. She is also given the responsibility of grinding[6]

❶ Introduction
❷ Body paragraph
❸ Conclusion

Ⓐ Book title and author
Ⓑ Reviewer's opinion of the book

Ⓒ Genre
Ⓓ Introduction of main characters

[1] **a protagonist** the main character in a play, movie, or story

[2] **yearning** a strong desire for something or someone, especially someone or something that is difficult to get

[3] **poverty** the state of being poor

[4] **to be fond of someone or something** to like someone or something

[5] **still life objects** objects such as fruit or flowers that a painter arranges and then paints

[6] **to grind** to crush something into small pieces

the paints and even **purchasing** the colors from the apothecary[7]. As if these "privileges" were not causing enough disquietude[8] within the family, matters only get worse when Vermeer agrees, at a friend's request, to paint Greit. ❷

The moments in which Vermeer paints Griet are the Ⓗ most spellbinding[9] of the book. The reader feels Griet's nervous emotions as she sits as still as possible under the close eye of the awe-inspiring[10] man she has grown to love. Ⓕ Her inner struggle is **intensified** by jealous Pieter, the butcher's son, who has made no secret of his intention to marry Griet. The young maid, however, seems **devoted** only to her master and obeys his every wish. When he tells her to wear his wife's pearl earrings for the painting, Griet agrees even though she knows it could lead to her downfall[11]. ❷

This book is Ⓘ written with the same extreme care that Griet takes when cleaning her master's studio. While Griet is quiet and obedient, the reader can see how full her heart is, as the emotions are **conveyed** magnificently across the page. The reader also has a very clear image of what Vermeer himself may have been like, and his Ⓙ remarkable character draws the reader in as much as Chevalier's **charming** history of a most **intriguing** painting. ❸

Ⓔ Introduction of book's themes
Ⓕ Plot
Ⓖ Supporting quotation
Ⓗ Book's strengths
Ⓘ Comment on style
Ⓙ Reviewer's recommendation

[7] **an apothecary** a person who mixed and sold medicines and other chemicals in the past

[8] **disquietude** feelings of being anxious or not satisfied about something

[9] **spellbinding** extremely interesting and holding your attention completely

[10] **awe-inspiring** someone or something that is awe-inspiring causes you to feel great admiration and respect for that person or thing

[11] **downfall** a sudden loss of money, power, social position, etc.

Model Text 2: Book Review (Non-Fiction)

The First Home-Cooked Meal

❶ Have you ever wondered when early humans first began cooking their food? Harvard professor Ⓐ Richard Wrangham has some ideas. His latest book, *Catching Fire: How Cooking Made Us Human*, explores the role of cooking in human evolution. In this Ⓑ fascinating and very readable book, Wrangham challenges us to look at one of the most common of human activities in a completely new way.

❷ Scientists have found evidence of campfires from 800,000 years ago. Archaeologists[1] believe that humans first learned how to control fire around that time. And because fire is needed to cook, archaeologists believe that the first home-cooked meal could not have been served any earlier than 800,000 years ago. Ⓒ But biological anthropologist[2] Wrangham does not agree with those dates. He argues that early humans started cooking long before that. In fact, Wrangham believes that cooking played an essential[3] role in the evolution of our ancestor, Homo erectus, 1.8 million years ago. In other words, modern humans did not invent cooking—cooking invented modern humans. ❷

Wrangham does not deny that the archaeological evidence of cooking goes back only 800,000 years. Ⓒ However, he uses the evolutionary record, not the archaeological one, to support his theory. In evolutionary biology, it is widely accepted that modern humans' early ancestor, Homo erectus, first appeared about 1.8 million years ago, when it evolved from an earlier species, Homo habilis. ❷

Homo habilis had larger stomachs, teeth, and jaws[4] than Homo erectus, but much smaller brains. Why were their bodies like that? Ⓒ Wrangham thinks it was because they ate raw food. Those early human ancestors needed big teeth and jawsto chew all that raw food. They also needed large stomachs and intestines[5] to digest[6] it. And eating and digestion used up so much energy that there wasn't enough energy left to feed a large brain. ❷

❶ Introduction
❷ Body paragraph
❸ Conclusion
Ⓐ Book title and author
Ⓑ Reviewer's opinion of the book

[1] **an archaeologist** a person who studies ancient societies by examining what remains of their buildings, tools, etc.

[2] **an anthropologist** a person who studies people, their societies, and cultures

[3] **essential** important and necessary

[4] **a jaw** the bottom part of your face that contains the two bones that your teeth are in

[5] **intestines** the long tube, consisting of two parts, that takes digested food from your stomach out of your body

[6] **to digest** when you digest food, it changes in your stomach into a form your body can use

[7] **a shift** a change in the way most people think about something, or in the way something is done

2 (C) Wrangham argues that the shift[7] from eating raw to cooked food enabled the evolution of the larger-brained Homo erectus. How? Cooking makes more energy from food available for the body to use. Cooked food is also softer than raw food, so the body uses less energy digesting what it takes in. Thus, cooking is extremely important to supporting a large brain, which consumes[8] a quarter of the body's energy. (D) "It's hard to imagine the leap[9] to Homo erectus without cooking's nutritional[10] benefits," writes Wrangham. "It's the development that underpins[11] many other changes that have made humans so distinct from other species."

2 Cooking also makes eating faster and easier. Most of our primate[12] relatives spent half the day chewing tough[13] raw food, such as the stems[14] and roots of plants. (C) Wrangham argues that because cooking freed early humans from all of that chewing, they could then spend time on more productive activities, such as the development of tools[15] for agriculture, and social networks. 2

Many other scientists believe that eating meat, rather than cooking food, led to the evolution of Homo erectus. (C) That might explain Homo erectus's large brains, but not their small jaws and teeth, argues Wrangham. Wrangham does not deny the importance of meat-eating to human evolution. However, he believes that meat-eating played a role in an earlier stage of evolution, from Australopithecines to Homo habilis—a species about the size of a chimpanzee, but with a larger brain. 2

Wrangham's book leaves at least one important question unanswered. Why isn't there any archaeological evidence of cooking until 800,000 years ago, at the earliest? (E) Many scientists see this gap[16] in the archaeological record as evidence against Wrangham's theory. They have a very good point. Nevertheless, (F) *Catching Fire: How Cooking Made Us Human* provides the reader with some very rich food for thought. 3

(C) Central argument
(D) Supporting quotation
(E) Book's weaknesses
(F) Reviewer's recommendation

8 **to consume** to use energy, time, etc.
9 **a leap** a sudden big change
10 **nutritional** relating to the substances in food that help you to stay healthy and grow well
11 **to underpin** to support
12 **a primate** a member of the group of animals that includes monkeys and humans
13 **tough** hard and difficult to cut or chew
14 **a stem** a long thin part of a plant, from which leaves or flowers grow
15 **a tool** any object that you hold in your hand and use for doing a particular job
16 **a gap** something that is missing so that something else is not good or complete

LANGUAGE BANK

Reporting the Author's Words and Ideas

The first time the author's name is mentioned, the reviewer uses his/her full name. After that, only the last name is used. When reporting what an author has written, reviewer use a variety of reporting verbs and expressions. Several are used in the review of *The First Home-Cooked Meal*.

1. Common reporting verbs followed by a noun clause

Many reporting verbs are followed by a noun clause (= group of words with a subject and a verb) that usually begins with *that*:

say	*write*	*argue*	*believe*	*think*

*Wrangham **argues that** early humans started cooking long before that.*
*Wrangham **thinks** (**that**) it was because they ate raw food.*

2. Common reporting verbs not followed by a noun clause

Other reporting verbs are followed by different grammatical patterns:

challenge (someone to do something)
explore (something)
provide (someone with something)

*Wrangham **challenges** us **to look** at one of the most common of human activities in a completely new way.*
*His latest book **explores the role** of cooking in human evolution.*
*The book **provides** the reader **with** some very rich food for thought.*

Using Specific Descriptive Language and Examples As Support

Reviewers use specific, descriptive language and examples that will give the reader an idea of what they can expect from the book, rather than just saying that they liked or disliked a book:

It is hard not to like this good and obedient protagonist, for she struggles with universal yearnings such as love and an escape from poverty.

The reader can expect to like the main character, who is good and obedient. The reader can also expect the book to discuss universal themes such as love and escape from poverty:

In this fascinating and very readable book, Wrangham challenges us to look at one of the most common of human activities in a completely new way.

The reader can expect the book to be fascinating and easy to read, but at the same time challenging because it has completely new ideas.

GRAMMAR BANK

Verb Tenses

For reviews of fiction, the narrative simple present and present progressive are used to write about the action taking place in the book as you read it:

*Her life **is** a fairly solitary one as she **finds** herself growing apart from her family while living as an outsider in another's home.*

For reviews of non-fiction, the reviewer uses the same tenses that the author has used in presenting the information:

*In evolutionary biology, it **is** widely accepted that modern humans' early ancestor, Homo erectus, first **appeared** about 1.8 million years ago, when it **evolved** from an earlier species, Homo habilis.*

In both fiction and non-fiction writing, the reviewer's comments, opinions, and recommendations are typically written in the simple present, as are the reviewer's summary of the author's arguments:

*The reader **feels** Griet's nervous emotions as she **sits** as still as possible under the close eye of the awe-inspiring man she has grown to love.*

*Wrangham **does** not deny that the archaeological evidence of cooking **goes** back only 800,000 years.*

*Wrangham's book **leaves** at least one important question unanswered.*

PRACTICE

Using the Thesaurus

A Read the model text *Girl with a Pearl Earring* again and pay attention to the words in boldface. In the exercise below, look at the key words from the *Longman Thesaurus* and write the boldfaced word that you think is a synonym for the key word next to it.

KEY WORD IN THESAURUS		BOLDFACED WORD FROM TEXT
1	increase (*verb*)	
2	lonely	
3	express	
4	interesting	
5	buy (*verb*)	
6	advantage	
7	nice	
8	loving	

B Now check your answers to Exercise A by looking up the key words in the *Longman Thesaurus*. If you have matched the words correctly, you should find the boldfaced word from the text under the key word entry. Circle the parts of the definition that make the meaning more specific than the definition of the key word.

4 Narrative Writing: Historical Narrative

A narrative is a story about events that have happened. It is usually told in chronological order, that is, in the order in which the events occurred. Writers often use narratives when they write about historical events or people. True stories about people's lives—biographies, autobiographies, and memoirs—are historical narratives.

Basic Structure of a Historical Narrative

❶ Introduction

- Introduction of the characters, setting, and any background information or interesting details that the reader needs to follow the story
- Information about why this event is significant or this person is important
- Description of the significant problem or conflict

❷ Body

- The story, describing what happened and answering the questions who, what, when, where, why, and how
- Paragraphs or sections organized by time periods and including interesting details
- Many time words and expressions
- Chronological order, or a pattern that clearly signals any shifts in time, so readers can tell the story is moving forward or backward from the "now"
- Details and descriptive language to bring the story alive

❸ Conclusion

- Description of the end of the story that solves the problem or conflict in a satisfactory way
- Comment on the significance or importance of the subject

LANGUAGE BANK

Adverbs of Manner

Adverbs of manner describe how an action is done and they can help to make a story come alive. Most adverbs of manner end in **-ly**:

deliberately, quickly, successfully, nervously, formally, frequently, closely, highly

*Jenner, and other scientists and doctors, waited **nervously** for the results.*

Prepositions of Time

Prepositions of time show when something happens:

in, at, on, by, during, for, after, before, until, from

***In** 1694, **at** the age of 49, a remarkable poet died.*

Transitions: Adverbs

Transitions help your writing move from one idea, sentence, or paragraph to the next in a clear way. Adverbs used as transitions help show when something happened, so that the reader understands the sequence of events in chronological order.

Use adverbs at the beginning of a sentence, in front of the main verb, or after the verb *be*:

finally, then, soon, today, eventually, now, while, fortunately

*The little boy was **then** locked in a barn with other children.*
***Eventually**, Jenner's contributions to science were formally recognized.*
***Soon**, Matsuo had his own school and students.*

GRAMMAR BANK

Verb Tenses

Different verb forms are used to show whether actions are completed or still happening at a particular time.

Simple past – use to describe single, completed actions or events in the past:

*They **stayed** there until they either **died** or **recovered**.*
*Matsuo's life **began** in 1644 in Ueno, a small town in Iga Province.*

Past progressive – use to indicate that a particular action or event was in progress at a particular point in the past:

*By 1770, he **was studying** anatomy and surgery at St. George's Hospital in London.*

Would – use to indicate that a completed action or event happened *after* another action or event in the past (the past of the future):

*Edward Jenner **would never forget** his terrible days in the barn.*
*Now 40 years old, Basho knew the trip **would be** difficult and dangerous.*

Model Text 1: Historical Account

The Father of Vaccination[1]

❶ ⒶIn a small town in England, in the middle of the eighteenth century, a doctor infected[2] an eight-year-old boy named Edward Jenner with a **deadly** disease. The little boy was **then** locked in a barn[3] with other children who had been infected in the same way. They stayed there until they either died or **recovered**. Ⓑ**Fortunately** for humanity[4], Jenner survived.

❷ ⒷChild abuse[5]? No—variolation. Variolation was a common medical practice in the eighteenth century. It involved **deliberately** infecting a healthy person with smallpox, a **highly** contagious[6] disease that killed one in three infants and young children. ⒸAt the time, doctors believed that healthy people infected with the pus[7] of patients sick with **mild** cases of smallpox would develop only a mild form of the disease. They would then be protected from smallpox for the rest of their lives. Although variolation was the only way of fighting smallpox at that time, it was quite dangerous. About 10 percent of variolated patients became sick with a **severe** case of smallpox, and many of them died.

Edward Jenner would never forget his terrible days in the barn. Perhaps that was why he decided to become a doctor. ⒹIn 1761, at just 13, Jenner began his medical studies. By 1770, he was studying anatomy[8] and surgery[9] at St. George's Hospital in London. ❷

ⒹAfter two years in London, Jenner returned to his hometown. He was a popular doctor, due to his gentle personality and surgical skill. Jenner's patients **frequently** requested variolation. He **performed** the procedure many times; however, he never locked children in a barn, as had been done to him! Jenner **observed** that some of his variolated patients never developed even a mild case of smallpox. Jenner wanted to understand why. He discovered that they had all had cowpox before. Cowpox was a mild illness which affected **mostly** people who worked **closely** with cows. Jenner observed that cowpox, while much less severe than smallpox, was very similar to it. He also knew of a traditional belief that people who had had cowpox never got smallpox. Based on his observations, Jenner developed a theory[10]. He believed that cowpox ❷

❶ Introduction
❷ Body paragraph
❸ Conclusion

Ⓐ Character and setting
Ⓑ Problem and significance of story
Ⓒ Background information

1 **vaccination** the act of putting a medicine into a person to stop that person from getting a disease
2 **to infect** to give someone a disease
3 **a barn** a large farm building in which animals are kept
4 **humanity** all the people in the world
5 **abuse** cruel or violent treatment of someone
6 **contagious** a contagious disease can pass from one person to another
7 **pus** a thick, yellowish liquid produced in an infected part of the body

2 could be **deliberately** passed from one person to another. The infected person would **then** get cowpox, but the cowpox would protect them from the much more serious disease of smallpox.

2 Ⓓ In May 1796, Jenner was **finally** able to test his theory. He learned that a young woman from a local farm, Sarah Nelmes, had cowpox. Jenner asked the parents of an eight-year-old boy named James Phipps for permission to perform a **risky** experiment on their son. Jenner chose James because he had never had cowpox or smallpox. Jenner removed pus from Sarah's hand and spread it on scratches[11] he had made on the boy's arms. As he had expected, the boy developed a mild case of cowpox, but **quickly** recovered. Jenner was now ready for the second part of his experiment. On July 1, 1796, Jenner variolated Phipps with pus from a smallpox patient. Jenner, and other scientists and doctors, waited **nervously** for the results.

2 In fact, James Phipps never developed smallpox. This was clear support for Jenner's theory. However, more data[12] were needed. Jenner experimented **successfully** on 13 more patients, Ⓓ and at the end of 1796 wrote a report describing his work for the Royal Society. However, the Society refused to publish it. Jenner's theory was just too different from the medical beliefs of the time. 2

Jenner ignored[13] the criticism and continued experimenting. Ⓓ In 1798, he published his own book. It was based on 23 cases in which vaccination (named for the vaccinnia virus of cowpox) resulted in protection against smallpox. Although many people continued to criticize Jenner, some well-known London physicians were starting to vaccinate their patients. Ⓔ By the beginning of the nineteenth century, the practice of vaccination had spread throughout the world. 2

Eventually, Jenner's contributions to science were **formally** recognized. However, he never tried to get rich through his discovery. Instead, he spent much of his time working, without pay, to spread the good news about vaccination. In 1977, the final person with smallpox recovered. Ⓕ No new cases appeared, and in 1980 the World Health Assembly announced that "the world and its peoples" were free of smallpox. 3

Ⓓ Time periods and chronological order
Ⓔ Shift forward in time
Ⓕ Problem solved/significance of subject
○ Adverbs of manner
○ Transition: Adverbs

8 **anatomy** the scientific study of the structure of human or animal bodies
9 **surgery** medical treatment in which a doctor cuts open someone's body to fix or replace something inside
10 **a theory** a scientific idea that tries to explain why something happens
11 **a scratch** a thin, not very deep cut on someone's skin
12 **data** information or facts
13 **to ignore** to not pay any attention to someone or something

Model Text 2: Biography

The Haiku Master

❶ Ⓐ**In** 1694, **at** the age of 49, a remarkable[1] Japanese poet died. **Before** his death, Matsuo Kinsaku, better known as "Basho," wrote this final poem:

Fallen sick on a journey[2]
my dream goes wandering[3]
over a field of dried grass

Ⓑ Basho's last poem, like much of his work, was a *haiku*—a traditional Japanese poetic form. Most haiku share certain characteristics. First, they are short: only three lines. Second, they describe a remarkable moment in a few simple words. Third, they mention nature in some way—usually the seasons. Ⓒ Matsuo was one of the greatest masters of haiku; he wrote over 1,000 of these small, surprising poems. His haiku reflect his life experiences.

❷ ⒶⒺ Matsuo's life began **in** 1644 in Ueno, a small town in Iga Province. **After** the death of his father **in** 1656, Matsuo left home and became a servant[4]. His master was Todo Yoshitada, a wealthy young man. Todo and Matsuo quickly discovered they had something in common: they both loved writing poetry. Ⓓ One of their favorite poetic subjects was an old cherry tree in Todo's garden. Matsuo wrote many haiku about it, such as this one **from** 1664:

The old-lady cherry
is blossoming[5]*—in her old age*
an event to remember

❷ Ⓔ **Until** 1666, Matsuo enjoyed a simple life of working and writing poetry. **Then** Todo suddenly died. Matsuo lost his job and best friend. Filled with sadness, he traveled to the capital of Edo (modern-day Tokyo) to start a new life. There, he studied and wrote poetry. His poetry began to attract fans[6]. **Soon**, Matsuo had his own school and many students. His life was comfortable again.

❶ Introduction
❷ Body paragraph
❸ Conclusion
Ⓐ Character and setting
Ⓑ Background information
Ⓒ Significance of person and story

[1] **remarkable** unusual or surprising, usually in a good way
[2] **a journey** a trip from one place to another, especially over a long distance
[3] **to wander** to walk slowly, without having a clear direction or purpose
[4] **a servant** someone who is paid to work in someone else's house
[5] **to blossom** to produce flowers
[6] **a fan** someone who likes a particular famous person very much

ⒶⒹ Inside, however, Matsuo felt empty. Although his friends liked the many shops and crowded streets of Edo, Basho felt out of place in the city. He wanted a change. Looking for inspiration[7], Ⓔ he moved to a small hut[8] outside of Edo **in** the winter **of** 1680. Ⓓ In front of this simple house, he planted a banana tree, called a *basho* in Japanese. It became the subject of many haiku: ❷

The banana plant in the autumn[9] storm
rain dripping in the tub[10]
listening that night

Ⓓ Because he loved his banana tree so much, Matsuo's friends began calling him Basho. The poet enjoyed this and began signing his poems *Basho*. Ⓔ **Then**, one cold winter day, a fire burned down his hut. **For** the third time in his life, Matsuo was without a home. ❷

Ⓐ Feeling lost and without purpose, Basho traveled the countryside of Japan. He planned to visit the twelve provinces between Edo and Kyoto, Japan's second largest city. Ⓔ **Now** forty years old, Basho knew the trip would be difficult and dangerous. He expected to die from illness or be killed by robbers. But he traveled safely. Basho began to enjoy his long journey. He met many people and made new friends. As he traveled, the topics of his haiku began to change. He focused less on his feelings and more on nature. **While** on the road, Basho wrote some of his best haiku: ❷

How admirable[11]!
to see lightning and not think
life is fleeting[12]

Ⓔ **For** the rest of his life, Matsuo traveled the Japanese countryside. His travels took him east to the Pacific coast. He climbed the mountains of Honshu in the north. He traveled west to the inland sea. His final journey was south to the city of Osaka, where he wrote his final poem. Ⓒ **Today**, his haiku inspire writers and readers from countries all over the world. His poems encourage people to see their lives and the things around them in a new way. ❸

Ⓓ Interesting details
Ⓔ Time periods and chronological order
○ Prepositions of time
○ Transition: Adverbs

7 **inspiration** someone or something that makes you want to achieve something, or that gives you new ideas
8 **a hut** a small simple house or building
9 **autumn** the season before winter, when the leaves fall off the trees
10 **a tub** a large round container
11 **admirable** having many good qualities that you respect
12 **fleeting** lasting for only a short time

5 Persuasive Writing: Opinions

Unit 3 talked about persuasive writing and book reviews. A book review is one type of persuasive writing that persuades the reader to read (or not read) a book. In general, the purpose of persuasive writing is to convince the reader to agree with the writer's opinion on an issue. Effective persuasive writing contains vivid, persuasive language. There are many types of persuasive writing.

Types of Persuasive Writing

Editorials are written by the editor of a newspaper or magazine and express his or her opinion about a particular subject.

Op-ed pieces are written for newspapers and magazines by experts on an issue. These experts are not employed by the newspaper or magazine. In op-ed pieces, they express their expert opinion on the issue.

Letters to the editor are letters written by readers of a newspaper or magazine and sometimes published in that particular newspaper or magazine. These letters express the reader's opinion on an article or on a particular issue.

Book reviews are written by critics and express an opinion on a particular book.

Persuasive essays are written following a logical structure to convince the reader to agree with the writer's position on an issue.

Persuasive speeches are speeches that are written to convince a particular audience to believe or do something, such as speeches by politicians who want people to vote for them.

Basic Structure of Persuasive Writing

❶ Introduction

- A clear description of the issue and why it is important
- A thesis statement that clearly states the writer's opinion on the issue

❷ Body

- Factual evidence to support the writer's opinion, particularly data such as percentages, statistics, and clear comparisons
- References to opinions from experts on the issue
- Arguments that support the writer's opinion
- A presentation of the arguments of the opposing side (Sometimes these are presented before the writer's arguments.)
- Counter-arguments that respond to the opposing side's arguments

❸ Conclusion

- A forceful restatement of the writer's opinion
- An appeal to action, requesting that the reader do something, for example write a letter to an elected official of the government, or vote in a particular way

LANGUAGE BANK

Counter-arguments and Concessions

In good persuasive writing, the writer must not only present his or her own strongest arguments. He or she must also try to imagine all arguments on the opposing side, present them, and then demonstrate that they are wrong. Often the writer's argument will seem more persuasive if he or she **makes a concession** before demonstrating why he or she disagrees with the opposing side. When making a concession, the writer agrees that some part of the opposing argument is correct, while still arguing that the opposing argument is mostly wrong.

Language to start counter-arguments and concessions
Some people claim that ... *They argue that ...* *Despite ...* *While I do not disagree with this argument ...* *However ...*

> ***While I do not disagree with this argument**, at the moment the only pathway to success ... is a college diploma.*
>
> ***Despite** the large amount of research, some people still insist that prevention programs are too costly.*

Referring to Authoritative Sources of Data

To persuade the reader, the writer must support his or her point of view with factual information, examples, and details. When doing so, it is important to refer to the source of the information.

According to ... [respected authority] *[Respected Authority] reports that ...*

> ***The New York Times reports that** for every dollar spent on early childhood programs ...*

Model Text 1: Op-Ed Article

The Economic Impact of High School Dropouts[1]

❶ Ⓐ In a recent speech, President Obama discussed the **startling** rise in students dropping out of high school in the United States. Although in 1970 the United States was at the top of the world in both college and high school graduation rates, our position has dropped **dramatically** since then. Ⓑ According to the Organization for Economic Cooperation and Development, Ⓒ the United States is currently 21st in the world for high school graduation, and 15th for university graduation. Ⓓ Such a **sharp drop** in graduation rates has **damaged** our economy and is costing the American people billions of dollars. This is an **unacceptable** situation that **deserves our immediate attention**.

❷ Ⓔ President Obama has suggested a possible solution: making high school attendance **mandatory** until a student graduates or turns 18. Currently only 21 states require this. Ⓕ While a good idea, Ⓖ this proposal is an example of **too little, too late**. Ⓒ Scores[2] of research studies have shown that **addressing** this issue cannot wait until high school. The best prevention programs start in pre-school, when the children are just 3 or 4 years old. These programs usually include small group instruction, **nutritious** meals, home visits by teachers, regular parent/teacher meetings, and higher salaries for teachers.

❶ Introduction
❷ Body paragraph
❸ Conclusion

Ⓐ Clear description of the issue
Ⓑ Reference to authority

Ⓒ Factual supporting evidence
Ⓓ Thesis statement

[1] **a dropout** someone who leaves school or college without finishing it

[2] **scores** a large number

F It can certainly be argued that such programs are **costly**. However, G not paying now will be even more costly over the long term. B According to the *New York Times*, C cutting the current number of dropouts in half would result in 700,000 more high school graduates every year. Since many studies have shown that the average high school graduate earns 50 to 100% more during his or her lifetime than the student who quits, more high school graduates would result in much higher tax revenues[3]. ❷

What does this mean in dollars and cents? B The *New York Times* reports that C for every dollar spent on early childhood programs to prevent students from quitting, there is a return of $1.45 to $3.55. In other words, effective programs save the public $127,000 per graduate in tax dollars per year. With 700,000 fewer dropouts per year, this totals an **astonishing** $1 trillion dollars in savings in just 11 years! ❷

Despite the large amount of research, E some people still insist that prevention programs are just too costly. G However, we now have **sufficient** evidence that better educated high school graduates help the economy. H It has become clear that we cannot afford *not* to invest in prevention programs. In fact, our economic future depends on it. ❸

E Counter-argument
F Concession
G Argument
H Appeal to action
O Persuasive language

[3] **tax revenues** money that government receives from taxes

Letter to the Editor

A letter to the editor is a specific type of persuasive writing in direct response to a newspaper op-ed or editorial. The writer gives his or her own opinion or perspective on the issue addressed in the op-ed or editorial, agreeing or disagreeing with it. Letters to the editor are usually short and direct. The introduction is generally a simple statement of agreement or disagreement, along with a reference to the original article and its writer in parentheses. This is the letter writer's "thesis statement."

The body of the letter is also brief, usually just one or two paragraphs. In the body of the letter, the writer presents the reasons for his or her opinion. These can be based on the writer's personal experience. They can also be based on factual evidence.

In the conclusion to the letter, the writer often includes a request that the reader take action, for example write a letter to an elected official of the government or vote in a particular way. This request is the writer's "call to action." It either contradicts or supports the original writer's call to action.

Model Text 2: Letter to the Editor

1 Introduction
2 Body paragraph
3 Conclusion

A Reference to personal experience
B Statement of agreement (the writer's thesis)
C Reference to op-ed
D Counter-argument
E Concession
F Argument
G Appeal to action

O Persuasive language

❶ Ⓐ As a high school dropout with **first-hand** knowledge of the negative economic **impact** that the lack of a high school diploma can have, Ⓑ I **fully** agree with the recent commentary on the high school dropout **crisis** Ⓒ ("The Economic Impact of High School Dropouts").

❷ Ⓐ At 16, I made a **foolish** decision to leave school and get a job. At the time, it seemed obvious to me that earning a salary as a cashier made a lot more sense than sitting in a classroom, **bored out of my mind**. I have regretted that decision for the past 24 years. I have **struggled** to support myself at jobs that pay little more than minimum wage[1]. When I compare myself to my friends who graduated, I am always reminded of how **foolish** my decision to quit was. Those who graduated and went on to college, **easily earn twice what I do**. Perhaps even more importantly, they enjoy the approval of a society that values professionals more than those who work with their hands.

❷ Ⓓ Some people claim that college is not for everyone. They argue that there should be other pathways to success for kids who are not academically-oriented. Ⓔ While I do not disagree with this argument, Ⓕ at the moment the only pathway to success for most young people is a college diploma. And to **obtain** that diploma, a high school degree is a necessity.

❸ Ⓐ I wish the programs that are proposed in the op-ed piece had been there when I was a teen—perhaps I would have made a different choice. Ⓖ I **urge** everyone who cares about the economic future of our country to support all efforts to decrease the high school dropout rate.

[1] **minimum wage** the lowest amount of money that can be paid per hour to a worker

PRACTICE

Using the Thesaurus

A Read the model text *The Economic Impact of High School Dropouts* again and pay attention to the words in boldface. In the exercise below, look at the key words from the *Longman Thesaurus* and write the boldfaced word that you think is a synonym for the key word next to it.

KEY WORD IN THESAURUS		BOLDFACED WORD FROM TEXT
1	enough	
2	expensive	
3	healthy	
4	decrease *(verb)*	
5	necessary	
6	surprising	
7	deal with	

B Now check your answers to Exercise A by looking up the key words in the *Longman Thesaurus*. If you have matched the words correctly, you should find the boldfaced word from the text under the key word entry. Look carefully at the definition of the word from the text. Circle the parts of the definition that make the meaning more specific than the definition of the key word.

C Read the model text *Letter to the Editor* again and pay attention to the words in boldface. In the exercise below, look at the key words from the *Longman Thesaurus* and write the boldfaced word that you think is a synonym for the key word next to it.

KEY WORD IN THESAURUS		BOLDFACED WORD FROM TEXT
1	effect	
2	completely	
3	advise	
4	stupid	
5	personal	
6	get	

D Now check your answers to Exercise C by looking up the key words in the *Longman Thesaurus*. If you have matched the words correctly, you should find the boldfaced word from the text under the key word entry. Circle the parts of the definition that make the meaning more specific than the definition of the key word.

Expository Essays: Compare and Contrast

An expository essay is an essay in which the writer shares information with the reader. The writer supports the main points with factual information. The writer's personal experience or point of view is not usually included in an expository essay, except perhaps as a hook to get the reader interested in the essay.

Different Types of Expository Essays

There are several types of expository essays, including cause and effect, compare and contrast, classification, and problem and solution. Sometimes, the writer of an expository essay will use more than one pattern of organization in the essay, such as cause and effect and compare and contrast. The choice of organizational pattern depends on the writer's topic and audience.

Expository Essay: Compare and Contrast

A compare and contrast essay is a type of expository writing. The purpose is to point out the similarities and/or differences between two things, such as historical periods, people, or phenomena. In some compare and contrast essays, there is a focus on similarities; in others, the focus is more on the differences. In others, the similarities and differences are discussed evenly.

The compare and contrast organizational pattern is used in many disciplines or areas of study:

Science – to describe and differentiate natural phenomena or living creatures

Literature – to examine the work of two authors or compare two fictional characters

Social Studies – to discuss cultural differences and similarities

History – to compare two historical periods, events, or characters

It is important that the writer's main points are easy to follow. Thus, the use of clear signal words indicating whether the writer is addressing a similarity or a difference is an important feature of compare and contrast essays. It is also important that the supporting evidence be well-researched, relevant, and clearly presented. When writing a compare and contrast essay, the writer cannot simply state that two things are similar or different; he or she must support those statements with details, facts, observations, and examples.

Basic Structure of Compare and Contrast Essays

❶ Introduction

- Announcement of the topic
- A thesis statement that clearly states what the writer will compare and/or contrast

❷ Body

The precise organization of a compare and contrast essay depends on the writer's purpose. For example:

- Similarities and/or differences
- Transitional sentences between paragraphs
- Supporting evidence: details, facts, observations, and examples
- Signal words to indicate similarities and/or differences

❸ Conclusion

- Restatement of central idea
- Satisfactory ending

Model Text 1: Compare and Contrast (Social Studies)

Minding Our Manners[1]

❶ Ⓐ Many people think that the rules for polite behavior are the same everywhere. They may not realize that Ⓑ how you define *politeness* depends upon the culture that you grow up in.

❷ For example, countries have **different** customs for offering and receiving food and drinks. Ⓒ In Latin America, offering food or drink to all visitors is very important. If a visitor does not accept the food, it is considered rude, unless there is a health reason. Ⓒ In the United States, **on the other hand**, it is appropriate for a guest to say "no" if he or she doesn't want anything. Many hosts accept this refusal and are not offended[2] by it.

❷ Ⓓ Politeness is **also** expressed by the way people speak to each other. Some cultures are more open and friendly; others are more reserved[3]. Ⓒ For example, in the United States, it is common for strangers to strike up[4] a conversation. They may start talking on the bus, at

❶ Introduction
❷ Body paragraph
❸ Conclusion

Ⓐ Topic
Ⓑ Thesis statement
Ⓒ Supporting evidence

[1] **to mind one's manners** to behave or speak in a polite way
[2] **offended** angry or upset because of something that someone else has done
[3] **reserved** not liking to show or talk about your thoughts and feelings
[4] **to strike up a conversation** to start a conversation

a subway station, or in a supermarket. **C** **On the other hand**, in the United Kingdom, it is less common for strangers to talk. Many British people are more reserved than Americans, so talking to strangers is not always considered polite. **2**

D **Different** customs can **also** be seen at restaurants. **C** In the United States, for example, people say "Excuse me" to call to a waiter or waitress. They do not snap their fingers[5] because they think it is rude. **C** In some cultures, **in contrast**, people gesture[6] with their hands or snap their fingers. **Unlike** in the United States, it is appropriate in those countries, and the server will not be offended. **2**

Politeness is based on a desire to treat other people well, **but** **E** countries show politeness in **different** ways. **E** Each culture has its own customs and expectations. **F** If we understand this, we are less likely to be offended by customs that are **different** from our own. **3**

D Transitional sentences: old to new topic
E Restatement of central idea
F Satisfactory ending

○ Expressing differences
○ Expressing similarities

[5] **to snap one's fingers** to move one of your fingers against your thumb to make a noise

[6] **to gesture** to move your hand, arms, or head, in order to tell someone something

Model Text 2: Compare and Contrast (Social Studies)

Fashionable Men

❶ Researchers have made an interesting discovery about Ⓐ modern-day men: they spend a lot of time and money on their appearance. Ⓒ Today, global sales of male grooming[1] products are billions of dollars a year, and the industry is not expected to slow down. Is this a sign that the modern man is becoming **more** concerned about his appearance? Ⓑ Some people might think that fashion-conscious[2] men are a new phenomenon[3], **but** a look through history reveals that men have **actually** been concerned about their **looks** for thousands of years.

❷ Ⓒ The first documented[4] cases of fashionable men occurred around 10,000 BCE in ancient Egypt. The Egyptians stressed the importance of good hygiene[5] and health. Men **applied** oils and creams to their skin to protect themselves from the hot sun and dry winds of the desert. **In addition** to the perfumes they wore, men **also** had their own colored makeup, which they applied to their eyes, lips, cheeks, and nails. All of this was done not to impress others, **but rather** to keep their ancient gods happy.

❷ Ⓓ The ancient Greeks **also** valued male health and beauty, **but in contrast to** the Egyptians, the Greeks' use of cosmetics was for purely[6] aesthetic[7] reasons. Ⓒ Greek men applied flower-based oils to their skin, and quickly adopted Egyptian oils after the Greek king Alexander the Great took over Egypt in 332 BCE. Alexander was the man responsible for making the use of oils common practice in daily Greek life. During his conquests[8], he would take plant cuttings and send them to Athens, where they were grown and made into perfumes and various skin oils for men to use before and after bathing.

❷ Ⓓ Around 100 AD, the Romans took men's grooming products to a whole new level. Ⓒ **Like** the Greeks, Roman men used skin oils before and after bathing, **but** they were also passionate

❶ Introduction
❷ Body paragraph
❸ Conclusion

Ⓐ Topic
Ⓑ Thesis statement
Ⓒ Supporting evidence

[1] **grooming** the act of taking care of your appearance by keeping your hair and clothes clean and neat
[2] **fashion-conscious** very concerned about and interested in fashion
[3] **a phenomenon** something that happens or exists in society, science, or nature that is unusual or difficult to understand
[4] **documented** written down
[5] **hygiene** things you do to keep people and things clean in order to prevent diseases
[6] **purely** completely and only
[7] **aesthetic** relating to beauty
[8] **a conquest** the act of defeating an army or taking land by fighting
[9] **blush** cream or powder used for making your cheeks slightly red or pink

2 about the beauty of their face and hair. They used nail polish and frequently dyed their hair blond to make themselves look younger. They had their own versions of eye shadow, blush[9] for the cheeks, and powder for whitening the face. Vanity did not have a negative **connotation**, **but instead** was viewed as a natural **consequence** of health and beauty.

2 (D) In 16th century England, the emphasis on male beauty was directly tied to financial **status**. Rich English men would use face-whitening powder because they believed a **pale** face was a sign of wealth. Keeping their skin healthy was an **elaborate** procedure that consisted of bathing in wine, applying oils to the skin, and using an egg and honey mask on the face to hide wrinkles[10]. On formal occasions, men further **enhanced** their appearance by using lipstick, bleaching[11] their hair, and wearing wigs[12].

2 (D) Men today, and especially young men, are **equally** concerned about their appearance and body image[13], and this **trend**[14] is not necessarily culture-specific. (C) In 2006, American men spent $4.8 millions on male grooming products; in parts of Asia, the male cosmetic[15] industry is **just as** strong, if not stronger. [These] men are **rejecting** the modern-day "**masculine**" stereotype[16] which says that men aren't supposed to care about their appearance. In today's world, that assumption is simply not true. Modern-day society is becoming **more** liberal[17], and **no longer** expects all men to fit one definition of "masculinity."

3 (F) It is often said that history repeats itself—trends come and go as people's beliefs and values change over time and cultures interact with one another. (E) Modern man's interest in grooming and cosmetic products is not a new phenomenon. The eye creams, facial masks, and moisturizers that men are buying today are simply **different** versions of the **same** idea, one that began 12,000 years ago.

(D) Transitional sentence: old to new information
(E) Restatement of central idea
(F) Satisfactory ending

○ Expressing differences
○ Expressing similarities

10 **a wrinkle** a line on your face that you get when you are old
11 **to bleach** to make something whiter or lighter in color
12 **a wig** something that has been made for someone to wear as hair
13 **body image** the way that you see or think about your body
14 **a trend** the way that a change in society is developing
15 **cosmetic** a substance that people use to make their faces more attractive
16 **a stereotype** a common idea of what a particular type of person is like, which is often not correct
17 **liberal** willing to accept or respect other people's ideas and behavior even if it is different from your own

LANGUAGE BANK

Expressing Similarities and Differences

The following words are used to introduce similarities and differences. These words help give your essay a clear structure and are often used as a transition (= change) from one idea to another.

Differences
less, more ... than, some ... others, different, on the other hand, but, unlike, but instead, but rather, but actually, in contrast, in contrast to

Similarities
also, the same, equally, just as, like, in addition

1. At the beginning of a paragraph

Use these words at the beginning of a paragraph to transition from the topic of the previous paragraph to a similar or contrasting topic of the new paragraph:

[Topic of previous paragraph: *One way of expressing politeness ...*]

*Politeness is **also** expressed by the way people speak to each other.*

2. In the middle of a paragraph

Use these words in the middle of a paragraph to show a similarity or contrast with the point made in the preceding sentence:

[Point of preceding sentence: *... in the United States, it is common for strangers to strike up a conversation.*]

***On the other hand**, in the United Kingdom, it is less common for strangers to talk.*

PRACTICE

Using the Thesaurus

A Read the model text *Fashionable Men* again and pay attention to the words in boldface. In the exercise below, look at the key words from the *Longman Thesaurus* and write the boldfaced word that you think is a synonym for the key word next to it.

	KEY WORD IN THESAURUS	BOLDFACED WORD FROM TEXT
1	put on	
2	male (*adj*)	
3	fashion	
4	improve	
5	refuse	
6	light (*adj*)	
7	rank	
8	result (*noun*)	
9	meaning	
10	complicated	
11	appearance	

B Now check your answers to Exercise A by looking up the key words in the *Longman Thesaurus*. If you have matched the words correctly, you should find the boldfaced word from the text under the key word entry. Look carefully at the definition of the word from the text. Circle the parts of the definition that make the meaning more specific than the definition of the key word.

7 Expository Essays: Cause and Effect

An expository essay is an essay in which the writer shares information with the reader. The writer supports the main points with factual information. The writer's personal experience or point of view is not usually included in an expository essay, except perhaps as a hook to get the reader interested in the essay.

Different Types of Expository Essays

There are several types of expository essays, including cause and effect, compare and contrast, classification, and problem and solution. Sometimes, the writer of an expository essay will use more than one pattern of organization in the essay, such as cause and effect and compare and contrast. The choice of organizational pattern depends on the writer's topic and audience.

Expository Essay: Cause and Effect

A cause and effect essay is a type of expository essay that explains the causes or reasons for an event or natural phenomenon. Writers must be careful to write only facts and make sure that there is a clear relationship between causes and effects or reasons and results. If the relationships between events or phenomena are not absolutely certain, it is important to use appropriate hedging language.

Ways of Expressing Cause and Effect

There are many ways of expressing cause and effect relationships. Some state the cause and effect relationship directly. For example, the words *because* and *so* clearly mark the cause and effect in a sentence. Other ways of expressing cause and effect are less direct, and the cause and effect relationship is merely implied, rather than stated directly. For example, the time word *when* is sometimes used to suggest that one thing leads to another. Writers might use less direct ways of expressing cause and effect if the facts suggest, but do not prove, a clear cause and effect relationship.

Basic Structure of an Expository Essay

Because the purpose of an expository essay is to share information, it is important that the writer's main points are easy to understand and that the supporting details are well-researched, relevant, and clearly explained.

❶ Introduction

- A clear thesis statement that states the central idea of the essay

❷ Body

- A topic sentence for each body paragraph
- Development of each topic with relevant factual support
- Clear transitions from one body paragraph to the next

❸ Conclusion

- Restatement of central idea
- A satisfactory ending

LANGUAGE BANK

Showing Cause and Effect

Some statements of cause and effect are very clear: one thing happens because of another thing. Other statements are less direct, and the cause and effect is implied. For example, *when* is often used to imply that one action leads to another action.

There are several ways to express cause and effect.

1. Verb phrases – many different verbs can suggest that one thing caused another:

*That is why college students **play** such an influential **role in the success or failure of low-budget films**.*

2. Infinitives of purpose – by using an infinitive, you can show why something happens or what the purpose of an action is:

*Other ants follow the trail **to find** the food.*

3. Coordinating conjunctions – the coordinating conjunctions are: *and, but, for, nor, or, so, yet*. These join two parts of a sentence (=independent clauses), and are useful for showing why something happens, why someone does something, and for comparing one action with another. The coordinating conjunctions *for* and *so* are used to express cause and effect relationship:

*He needed an inexpensive way to promote the film, **so** he went on the Internet and visited science fiction chat rooms.*

4. Subordinating conjunctions – subordinating conjunctions join a subordinate (= dependent) clause to an independent clause. They can show why something happens. Common subordinating conjunctions are: *because, after, though, unless, when, while*

*And **because** the pheromones don't wear off for several hours, male moths have enough time to find the females and breed.*

5. Prepositional phrases – phrases that begin with a preposition can also give the reasons why something happens, either directly or indirectly:

*Pheromones are chemicals that animals, including insects, produce **for a variety of reasons**.*

6. Other expressions – expressions such as *that is why, the more ... the more* are ways of directly showing a cause and effect relationship:

***The more** serious the threat, **the more** alarm pheromones the ant produces.*

Verb Tenses

Simple present – the simple present tense is used for a general statement of fact. When the cause and effect relationship is one that involves a scientific fact or phenomenon, use the simple present tense.

Simple past – when the cause and effect relationship is one that involves the causes or reasons for a past event, use the past tense.

Reference to Authority

The following pattern is often used when referring to authority:

[authority] +	[verb] +	[noun clause stating fact]
Studies	*show*	*that flowers use pheromones to attract bees.*

Model Text 1: Cause and Effect (Science)

The Language of Insects

❶ Pheromones are chemicals that animals, including insects, produce **for many reasons**. Plants also produce pheromones. **Studies show that flowers use pheromones to attract[1] bees.** Ⓐ For many creatures, life would not be possible without pheromones.

❷ Ⓑ Moths[2] are one insect that could not survive without pheromones. Ⓒ Moths have poor eyesight, and most species[3] cannot use sound to communicate. Instead, they communicate through pheromones. Female moths, for example, release[4] pheromones from their legs and wings. A male moth can identify female moth pheromones from as many as five miles away. **And because the pheromones don't wear off for several hours, male moths have enough time to find the females and breed.**

❷ Ⓑ **Ants have different pheromones for different purposes.** Ⓒ **Like moths, ants use pheromones to find each other. They also use pheromones to find food.** When an ant finds food, it takes a piece and returns to the nest[5]. Along the way, it releases a trail of pheromones. **Other ants follow the trail[6] to find the food.** If something blocks the trail, the ants look for a new way to reach the food. **When they find the shortest way, they produce a new trail of pheromones.** Ⓓ **In this way, pheromones help ants adapt to changes in their environment.**

❷ Ⓑ **When an ant is hurt or threatened[7], it produces an "alarm"[8] pheromone.** Ⓒ Other ants identify the alarm pheromone and immediately come to help. **The more serious the threat, the more alarm pheromones the ant produces.** In this way, ants can quickly organize to fight insects hundreds of times their size.

❷ Ⓑ **Some species of ants use "trick" pheromones to make trouble and confuse their enemies.** Ⓒ Fire ants, for

❶ Introduction
❷ Body paragraph
❸ Conclusion
Ⓐ Thesis statement
Ⓑ Topic sentence

[1] **to attract** to make someone like or feel interested in something

[2] **a moth** an insect like a butterfly that flies at night

[3] **a species** a group of animals or plants of the same kind who can produce young animals or plants of the same kind as them

[4] **to release** to let a substance flow out

[5] **a nest** a place where some small animals or insects live

[6] **a trail** a long line or a series of marks that has been left by someone or something

2 example, produce pheromones near the nests of other ants. Those ants become confused and begin to fight each other instead of attacking the fire ants.

2 (B) **Other insects use trick pheromones to imitate another species. In some cases, this protects them from becoming another insect's meal.** (C) An interesting example is the European blue butterfly. When the butterfly is a caterpillar[9], it releases a pheromone that is very similar to that of one species of ant. When the ants find a blue butterfly caterpillar in the forest, they think that it is one of their young. They then carry it back to their nest. There, instead of becoming a meal, the caterpillar is fed and protected for ten months. The ants do not suspect[10] that anything is wrong, even when the caterpillar starts to eat their young! **The caterpillar finally leaves the nest when it is about to turn into a butterfly.**

(B) **Yet another insect uses trick pheromones to attract its next meal.** (C) The bolas spider, a species common in South America and Africa, releases a pheromone similar to that produced by a female moth. The spider then waits for a male moth to arrive. Instead of finding a female, the unsuspecting[11] moth becomes a tasty meal for the spider. 2

(B) **Because of examples like these, many biologists now believe that pheromones are the true language of insects.** But pheromones are important not only to insects. They are important to plants and other animals as well. (D) Their importance in the natural world is undeniable[12]. (C) **Some scientists even believe that humans, like other living creatures, use pheromones to attract members of the opposite sex.** (E) If that turns out to be true, it might be more accurate to talk about "Love at first smell" than "Love at first sight!" 3

(C) Factual support
(D) Restatement of central idea
(E) Satisfactory ending
○ Cause and effect statement
○ Reference to authority

[7] **threatened** feeling afraid that someone or something will harm you
[8] **an alarm** a warning
[9] **a caterpillar** the young form of some insects, with a small round body and many legs
[10] **to suspect** to think that something bad is probably happening
[11] **unsuspecting** not knowing that something is about to happen
[12] **undeniable** definitely true or certain

Model Text 2: Cause and Effect (Social Studies)

SLEEPER HITS

❶ The 1999 horror movie *The Blair Witch Project* surprised audiences. It told a story about three students lost in a forest. At the time, no one had ever seen anything like it. The film also surprised movie companies. Ⓒ The expenses barely[1] reached $22,000, but the **income** from ticket and DVD sales was (and continues to be) **enormous**. *The Blair Witch Project* is an example of a sleeper. Ⓐ Sleepers are films that are made for very little money, but are enormously successful. Although it might seem that the makers of *The Blair Witch Project* just got lucky, there are actually some very specific reasons that certain movies become sleeper hits.

❷ Ⓑ **Marketing experts say that for a movie to become a sleeper, it has to appeal to college students.** College students are important **for two reasons**. First, they do not pay much attention to media reviews of movies. Instead, they listen to their friends' opinions. **And because of social networking sites such as Facebook, the average college student today has hundreds of "friends."** And those friends have hundreds of friends, and so on. **That is why college students play such an influential role in the success or failure of low-budget[2] films.** Ⓒ An example is the 1997 comedy *Austin Powers*. *Austin Powers* was a low-budget film. At first, ticket sales were low, and it made very little money. But after it came out on video, it became enormously popular on college campuses. In the end, *Austin Powers* made more money from video and DVD sales than it did in theaters.

❶ Introduction
❷ Body paragraph
❸ Conclusion
Ⓐ Thesis statement
Ⓑ Topic sentence

[1] **barely** only just

[2] **low-budget** something that does not cost a lot of money

Ⓑ **Another secret to sleepers is creative marketing.** This also **involves** the Internet. Internet marketing is cheap, and it can reach a **specific** audience. Ⓒ When director David Twohy filmed the science fiction[3] movie *Pitch Black* in the late 1990s, for example, he **needed an inexpensive way to promote the film, so he went on the Internet and visited science fiction chat rooms.** He had conversations with people about his movie. Slowly, science fiction fans became interested in the film. **"In the end, Internet buzz[4] helped make it a success," says Twohy.** ❷

Ⓑ **College students and Internet marketing were both important to the success of *The Blair Witch Project*.** Ⓒ The filmmakers designed a Web page for the movie. It said that *The Blair Witch Project* was a true story (it wasn't). It also said the three students in the film had disappeared (they hadn't). Soon, college students were talking about whether the movie was real or not. Many of them wanted to see for themselves. For the film's release, theaters were completely sold out. Today, many film studios follow the *Blair Witch Project* model when promoting their films. ❷

Ⓑ Of course, to make money, sleepers also need to be good films. The makers of *The Blair Witch Project* never saw themselves as marketing experts. **As Robin Cowie, who worked on *The Blair Witch Project*, says, "We never meant to change things … we set out to make a scary movie."** Similarly, the makers of *Austin Powers* set out to make a funny movie. Ⓓ And, as millions who have seen the films would agree, they succeeded. ❸

Ⓒ Factual support
Ⓓ Satisfactory ending
○ Cause and effect statement
○ Reference to authority

[3] **science fiction** stories about the future, for example about traveling in time and space

[4] **buzz** excitement

PRACTICE

Using the Thesaurus

A Read the model text *Sleeper Hits* again and pay attention to the words in boldface. In the exercise below, look at the key words from the *Longman Thesaurus* and write the boldfaced word that you think is a synonym for the key word next to it.

	KEY WORD IN THESAURUS	BOLDFACED WORD FROM TEXT
1	big	
2	interest (*verb*)	
3	particular	
4	important	
5	include	
6	advertise	
7	pay (*noun*)	

B Now check your answers to Exercise A by looking up the key words in the *Longman Thesaurus*. If you have matched the words correctly, you should find the boldfaced word from the text under the key word entry. Look carefully at the definition of the word from the text. Circle the parts of the definition that make the meaning more specific than the definition of the key word.

Linking Words

C Can you find the linking words that are used in the model texts? Circle them. Pay attention to how they are used.

Descriptive Writing: Poetry

In descriptive writing, writers use vivid, descriptive details to make sights, sounds, smells, tastes, textures, and feelings come alive for readers. Descriptive writing is used in many types of writing, including expository, narrative, and persuasive.

Poetry

Poets are writers that use a lot of description. There are many types of poetry and this unit covers two: *Haiku* and *Prose*. In all types of poetry, writers choose their words carefully, communicating a lot of meaning in very few words. A thesaurus can be particularly helpful when choosing words to communicate the exact meaning.

Haiku

Haiku is a traditional Japanese poetic form. Most haiku share certain characteristics. They are short—only three lines long. They describe a profound moment in a few simple, yet vivid words, and they mention nature in some way. They are very simple and direct. Haiku are often associated with the changing of the seasons. They also contrast something.

Basic Structure of Haiku

- Only three lines
- The three lines have only 17 syllables
    - The first line is 5 syllables
    - The second line is 7 syllables
    - The third line is 5 syllables
- Vivid yet simple language
- Often describe a profoundly peaceful moment
- Show a contrast
- Mention nature

Model Text 1: Descriptive Writing (Poem)

Here are two haiku by the 17th century Japanese poet Matsuo Kinsaku, better known as Basho. Please note that, because they have been translated, these haiku do not follow the 17-syllable structure.

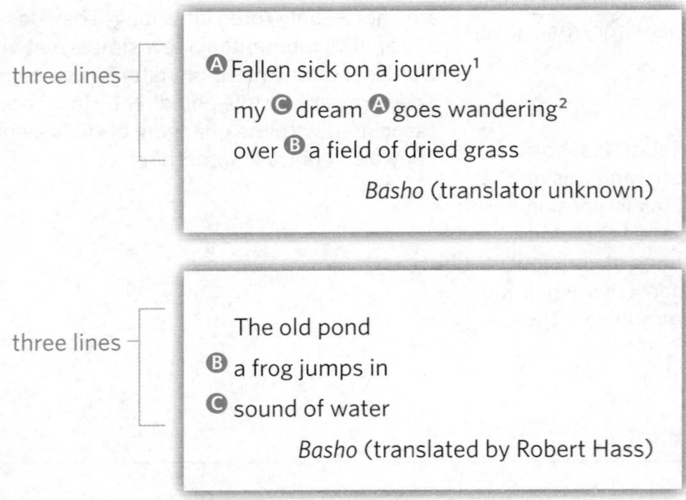

three lines

(A) Fallen sick on a journey[1]
my (C) dream (A) goes wandering[2]
over (B) a field of dried grass

Basho (translator unknown)

three lines

The old pond
(B) a frog jumps in
(C) sound of water

Basho (translated by Robert Hass)

(A) Vivid yet simple language
(B) Reference to nature; season implied
(C) Contrast

Notice how simple and direct the poems are. Other poets might write much more about frogs singing, but Basho simply describes the splash of a frog hitting the water. The poems clearly mention nature, and imply a season. They also contrast something—sickness and a dream wandering; the quiet of the pond with the noise of the frog. Finally, both haiku have a feeling of *sabi*, a Japanese word meaning "peaceful sadness." Basho's haiku create mental pictures. Readers can easily imagine feeling ill but dreaming that they are wandering in a field, or sitting alone by a pond, surrounded by the sounds of nature.

[1] **a journey** a trip from one place to another, especially over a large distance

[2] **to wander** to walk slowly around an area without having a clear idea of where you want to go

Writing a Haiku

Haiku can be a lot of fun to write. In this simple, short poetic form, writers can describe their environment, explain how they feel about something, or present a funny situation. To write your own haiku, just follow the steps below.

STEP 1 Choose a topic. Traditional haiku focus on nature, but they can be about anything. It is best if you have first-hand experience with the subject of your haiku. A lot of modern haiku discuss city life, work, or school. Others are about something the writer loves, hates, is thrilled by, is anxious about, or anything else that comes to mind.

Still in a meeting
boss talks, nightfall approaches
dreams of the weekend

Sandra Duque

STEP 2 Decide on the form of your haiku. In Japanese, a haiku must have exactly seventeen *on*, or segments of sound. To write haiku in English, writers count each syllable as one segment of sound and follow the 5-7-5 pattern.

Summer has arrived
see children running outside—
fresh smell of cut grass

Jessica Andrea

STEP 3 Include a contrast. The haiku that begins *Still in a meeting* contrasts work with dreams of the weekend. *Summer has arrived* contrasts something that you see (children running) with something that you smell (fresh cut grass). Some writers use special punctuation, such as a dash (—) or semicolon (;) to show the contrast in their poem.

STEP 4 Include a reference to the season, if possible. For example, if the haiku mentions "cherry blossoms," the reader knows it is spring. If the haiku mentions snow, the reader pictures winter. Depending on the topic you choose, you may want to eliminate this step.

STEP 5 Practice, practice, practice! The more haiku you write, the better you will get at it. It also helps to read a lot of haiku. Be sure to read a variety of types—traditional, contemporary, serious, sad, funny, and so on.

Prose Poems

Prose poems look like regular text (prose) that you might find in a story or essay. They have a theme—or main idea of what the writer is describing. They contain full sentences, but use poetic techniques—simile, metaphor, sensory descriptions, strongly evocative and vivid language, sound devices—to bring a person, place, thing, or event alive. They are usually short—one paragraph—although there is no exact limit on how long a prose poem can be. The topic or theme is usually set in the first sentence.

Model Text 2: Descriptive Writing (Prose Poem)

I LIE DOWN in the forest. Ⓐ Ⓔ The moss[1] against my cheek feels like another face. My ear Ⓑ cups the ground and I listen to my planet. I hear the sound of Ⓒ Ⓔ stones and bones, of Ⓓ marching feet and dancing feet, Ⓔ my father's voice ordering a beer, Ⓔ our first dog barking at the mailman, Ⓔ your laughter, Ⓔ a car horn and bells. It begins to snow and the flakes[2] Ⓔ melt on my face. I need to get up and go home, Ⓔ it's getting cold and Ⓔ soon the light will fade[3], but I'm not finished listening.

Lou Beach

Ⓔ THE COLD is most **intense** where my shoulders meet the water, Ⓐ Ⓔ a precise line as if a razor[4] had scored[5] my skin. I have Ⓔ no feeling at all in the submerged parts of my body and I wish my shoulders and head, above the dark green waves, would also be numb[6], for Ⓑ Ⓔ the bite of the air is **brutal**. But I know I need to feel pain to survive, sure that were I numb from head to foot I would sink into the sea, gone. I struggle toward the still unseen shore, hanging onto the life preserver[7] Ⓐ Ⓔ as tightly as I **cling** to the **vision** of my wife and children at home, Ⓔ the heat.

Lou Beach

Ⓐ Simile
Ⓑ Metaphor
Ⓒ Sound device: rhyming
Ⓓ Sound device: repetition
Ⓔ Sensory detail

[1] **moss** a soft green plant that grows on wet ground, trees, and rocks
[2] **a flake** a snowflake
[3] **to fade** to become less bright
[4] **a razor** a sharp tool for removing hair from your body
[5] **to score** to cut a mark into a surface with a sharp tool
[6] **numb** if a part of your body is numb, you are not able to feel anything, usually because you are very cold
[7] **a life preserver** something that can be worn in the water to prevent you from sinking

LANGUAGE BANK

Similes and Metaphors

Similes and metaphors describe someone or something by comparing it to someone or something else that seems quite different, but has some similarities.

Similes contain the words *like* or *as*:

*The moss against my cheek feels **like** another face.*

Metaphors do not contain the words *like* or *as*, so the comparison is implied rather than directly stated:

I hear the sound of stones and bones.

Sound Devices

Sound devices create a musical effect for the reader—for example, words like *hiss* that sound like the sound being described. Other types of sound devices include rhyming and repetition:

*I hear the **sound of stones and bones**, of **marching feet and dancing feet**.*

Sensory Details

Sensory details help the reader see, hear, smell, taste, or feel what the writer describes:

I have no feeling at all in the submerged parts of my body ...

PRACTICE

Using the Thesaurus

A Read the second model text on p.908 and pay attention to the words in boldface. In the exercise below, look at the key words from the *Longman Thesaurus* and write the boldfaced word that you think is a synonym for the key word next to it.

	KEY WORD IN THESAURUS	BOLDFACED WORD FROM TEXT
1	cruel	
2	hold (*verb*)	
3	strong	
4	illusion	

B Now check your answers to Exercise A by looking up the key words in the *Longman Thesaurus*. If you have matched the words correctly, you should find the boldfaced word from the text under the key word entry. Look carefully at the definition of the word from the text. Circle the parts of the definition that make the meaning more specific than the definition of the key word.

9 Creative Writing: Literary Analysis

A literary analysis is an essay in which the writer responds to a literary work—a poem, short story, or novel. In the response, the writer closely examines one or more literary elements, such as setting, theme, plot, character, or meter, as well as literary devices such as similes and metaphors. The writer also comments on the quality and significance of the work and provides his or her own interpretation of the meaning of the work.

Basic Structure of Literary Analysis

❶ Introduction

- Identification of the work or works being discussed (title and author)
- Writer's general opinion of the author
- Thesis statement (usually includes the general opinion of the work)

❷ Body

- Retelling of relevant parts of plot
- Interpretations of the work
- Support for the writer's interpretation through clear examples and quotations from the work (interpretations can come before or after the examples and quotations)
- Precise, descriptive language describing opinions or judgments, based on a close examination of one or more of the literary element(s) of setting, theme, plot, character, and meter (see Language Bank below)
- Clear and effective organization

❸ Conclusion

- Summary of the writer's overall opinion of the work and the author

LANGUAGE BANK

Words Related to Literary Analysis

analysis the careful examination of something in order to understand it better

conflict a situation in a book or play in which different characters or forces oppose each other in a way that causes or influences the action of the story

interpretation the way in which someone explains or understands what someone else has written

literary device the special use of words in literature to achieve an effect, for example an idiom, metaphor, or simile

metaphor a way of describing something by comparing it to something else that has similar qualities, without using the words *like* or *as*:
*She **was boiling** with anger.*

meter the way the words of a poem are arranged into a pattern of weak and strong beats

narrative the description of events in a story

perspective point of view

plot the events that form the main story of a book or play

protagonist the most important character in a book or play

setting the place or time that the action of a book or play happens

simile an expression in which you compare two things using the words *like* or *as*:
*He is **as clever as a fox**.*

theme the main subject or idea in a piece of writing, speech, or other work

Model Text 1: Short Story

Read the short story once. Try not to be distracted by unfamiliar vocabulary. Just try to get a "feel" for the story and the characters. You will look more carefully at the vocabulary later.

I See Him

BY LOU BEACH

I SEE HIM from the kitchen window. He is in the backyard standing beneath the maple tree, dirty and bearded, wearing a knit cap and the **grimy** uniform of the homeless. He is barefoot in the grass. I open the backdoor and yell "Hey, what are you doing here?" puffing up my chest and looking as **menacing** as I can in my plaid bathrobe and slippers, imbued with the **self-righteousness** of the homeowner, **indignant**. He **grins** and points at the birdhouse Tina and Josh made at camp, painted red and yellow. His eyes seem to work independently of each other, like a gecko's[1], and I **glance** at his fingers to see if the tips are flat and round. "I'm calling the cops," I shout and he continues to grin and **ambles** out the side gate. I put on jeans and a t-shirt, get the baseball bat from the hall closet and go out the front door. On the lawn, in the middle of the big pile of leaves that the kids had raked[2] together, he is asleep, curled like a lock[3] of Tina's hair, hands beneath his head near the worn shoes that hold a comb and socks, matches, a pack of cigarettes and a small mirror.

[1] **a gecko** a type of small lizard
[2] **to rake** to use a garden tool such as a rake for removing dead leaves from areas of grass
[3] **a lock of hair** a small amount of hair, often just one curl

Model Text 2: Literary Analysis

❶ Ⓐ**LOU BEACH** is a Ⓑtalented writer who has written a book of extremely short stories: Ⓐ*420 Characters: Short Stories*. Most of the stories are 300 words or fewer. ⒷIn the space that many of us would need for a shopping list, Beach is able to deliver everything that we expect from a well-told story: a conflict, strong characters and descriptions, and a satisfactory ending. Beach's stories do not have titles—he leaves those to the reader's imagination. ⒷⒸA story that I have titled "I See Him" demonstrates Beach's power as a masterful storyteller.

❷ ⒹThe story opens when a homeowner, looking through his kitchen window one morning, discovers a homeless man standing in his back yard. ⒺThe window serves to divide the characters and their very different worlds: Ⓔthe society insider—the homeowner—and the social outcast[1]—the homeless man. ⒼThe homeless man's outsider status is emphasized by a reference to the Ⓕ"birdhouse Tina and Josh made at camp;" Ⓖin this world, birds have houses, but human outsiders do not.

❷ The story is told from the homeowner's perspective. ⒼHis self-description reveals a man determined to protect his family and property, yet at the same time aware of his own vulnerability.[2] Ⓕ"I open the backdoor and yell 'Hey, what are you doing here?' puffing up my chest and looking as menacing as I can in my plaid bathrobe and slippers." ⒼHis choice of the words "puffing up my chest" is deliberately comical; we envision[3] a small bird trying to make itself look bigger and more threatening. The fact that he is dressed in a Ⓕ"plaid bathrobe and slippers" Ⓖis another comical element; how menacing can someone really be in one's pajamas? Both of these descriptions make it clear that Ⓖthe homeowner is vulnerable, perhaps frightened, but at the same time determined to chase away the outsider. Ⓕ"'I'm calling the cops,' I shout and he continues to grin and ambles out the side gate. I put on jeans and a t-shirt, get the baseball bat from the hall closet and go out the front door."

❶ Introduction
❷ Body paragraph
❸ Conclusion

Ⓐ Author/Title
Ⓑ Writer's opinion of the author
Ⓒ Thesis statement

[1] **a social outcast** someone who is not accepted by the people they live among

[2] **vulnerability** a state in which someone can be easily harmed or hurt emotionally, physically, or morally

[3] **to envision** to imagine something, especially as a future possibility

[4] **judgmental** too quick and willing to criticize other people

[5] **a reptile** an animal such as a snake or lizard

The other character in the story is the homeless man. (E) At first, his "otherness" is stressed. (F) "He is in the backyard standing beneath the maple tree, dirty and bearded, wearing a knit cap and the grimy uniform of the homeless. He is barefoot in the grass." (G) By describing the homeless man as being dressed in a "uniform," the protagonist shows his judgmental[4] attitude toward the homeless: that homelessness is somehow a choice—a job—rather than an unfortunate circumstance. In a sentence that is (G) deliberately strange, the homeowner further emphasizes the homeless character's otherness, by comparing him to a reptile[5]. (F) "His eyes seem to work independently of each other, like a gecko's, and I glance at his fingers to see if the tips are flat and round." ❷

(E) However, this sense of otherness quickly disappears (D) when the homeowner steps outside and truly "sees" the homeless man in the autumn leaves. (G) Beach accomplishes this transformation[6] by placing the stranger in an unprotected space created by the homeowner's children. (F) "On the lawn, in the middle of the big pile of leaves that the kids had raked together, he is asleep, curled like a lock of Tina's hair." ❷

(G) Comparing the stranger to a lock of the protagonist's daughter's hair strengthens the connection between the two men, while at the same time evoking[7] the image of a helpless, trusting creature[8]. (E) In this way, the stranger's vulnerability is revealed, and he is transformed from "the other" into a defenseless man/child in need of protection. ❷

(D) The narrative closes on a description of the homeless man's possessions: (F) "a comb and socks, matches, a pack of cigarettes and a small mirror". (G) In this short phrase, the writer communicates the stranger's dignity[9] as a human being, despite the difficult circumstances in which he finds himself. Thus the (E) shared humanity[10] of the characters comes into focus. In the end, (H) thanks to Beach's fine writing, we do indeed "see him." ❸

(D) Retelling of relevant parts of plot
(E) Analysis of theme
(F) Supporting quotation or example from the work
(G) Interpretation
(H) Writer's overall opinion of work

[6] **a transformation** a complete change in someone or something
[7] **to evoke** to produce a strong feeling or memory in someone
[8] **a creature** anything that is living, such as an animal, fish, or insect, but not a plant
[9] **dignity** your sense of your own value or importance
[10] **humanity** kindness and respect toward other people

GRAMMAR BANK

Verbs Forms

In a literary analysis, specific verbs are used to interpret the meaning of the text. The most common verb in this category is the verb *show*. To avoid repetition, the writer of the analysis will often use a variety of these verbs, in both the active and (where appropriate) passive form. These verbs do not all follow the same pattern, nor do they all mean exactly the same thing.

ACTIVE			PASSIVE	
the author/the text +	**show**	+ noun or noun clause	noun or noun clause +	**be shown**
	reveal			**be revealed**
	display			**be displayed**
	demonstrate			**be demonstrated**
	emphasize			**be emphasized**
	stress			**be stressed**

A story that I have titled "I See Him" ***demonstrates*** *Beach's power as a masterful storyteller.*
Beach's power as a masterful storyteller ***is demonstrated*** *by a story that I have titled "I See Him."*

ACTIVE			PASSIVE	
the author/the text +	**accomplish**	+ noun	noun +	**be accomplished**
	evoke an image of			

Beach accomplishes this transformation *by placing the stranger in an unprotected space ...*

This transformation is accomplished *by Beach by placing the stranger in an unprotected space ...*

ACTIVE			PASSIVE
the author/the text +	**serve**	+ infinitive form of verb	No passive form

The window ***serves to divide*** *the characters and their very different worlds.*

Verb Tenses

Simple present – used for reviewer's comments, opinions, interpretations, and recommendations.

Simple present and present progressive – used to talk about the action taking place in the work.

PRACTICE

Using the Thesaurus

A Read the model text *I See Him* again and pay attention to the words in boldface. In the exercise below, look at the key words from the *Longman Thesaurus* and write the boldfaced word that you think is a synonym for the key word next to it.

	KEY WORD IN THESAURUS	BOLDFACED WORD FROM TEXT
1	dirty	
2	threatening	
3	pride	
4	angry	
5	smile (*verb*)	
6	look (*verb*)	
7	walk (*verb*)	

B Now check your answers to Exercise A by looking up the key words in the *Longman Thesaurus*. If you have matched the words correctly, you should find the boldfaced word from the text under the key word entry. Look carefully at the definition of the word from the text. Circle the parts of the definition that make the meaning more specific than the definition of the key word.

Answer Key

UNIT 1 - Exercise A

1 tiny
2 promote
3 vast
4 reveal
5 maximum
6 prior to
7 truly
8 option
9 stuff
10 restore
11 assist

UNIT 2 - Exercise A

1 wealthy
2 fascinated
3 region
4 associated
5 exceptional
6 charming

UNIT 3 - Exercise A

1 intensify
2 solitary
3 convey
4 intriguing
5 purchase
6 privilege
7 charming
8 devoted

UNIT 5 - Exercise A

1 sufficient
2 costly
3 nutritious
4 drop
5 mandatory
6 startling
7 address

UNIT 5 - Exercise C

1 impact
2 fully
3 urge
4 foolish
5 first-hand
6 obtain

UNIT 6 - Exercise A

1 apply
2 masculine
3 trend
4 enhance
5 reject
6 pale
7 status
8 consequence
9 connotation.
10 elaborate
11 looks

UNIT 7 - Exercise A

1 enormous
2 appeal to
3 specific
4 influential
5 involve
6 promote
7 income

UNIT 8 - Exercise A

1 brutal
2 cling
3 intense
4 vision

UNIT 9 - Exercise A

1 grimy
2 menacing
3 self-righteousness
4 indignant
5 grin
6 glance
7 amble

The Academic Word List

Averil Coxhead, Victoria University, New Zealand

Averil Coxhead is a lecturer in English for Academic Purposes at Victoria University, New Zealand. She compiled the AWL in 2000. For further information on the AWL, go to http://www.victoria.ac.nz/lals/resources/academicwordlist/.

The Academic Word List (AWL) is a list of 570 word families that are commonly found in academic texts. This list was selected by examining a large corpus (or collection) of written academic texts and selecting the words that occurred:

1. In texts from all four academic faculty sections: Arts, Commerce, Law, and Science
2. Over 100 times in the corpus overall
3. At least 10 times in each academic faculty section
4. Outside the 2000 most frequent words on Michael West's *General Service List* (GSL). The GSL includes everyday words such as **I**, **house** and **do**.

These principles ensured that only words that occurred reasonably frequently in a variety of study areas were selected.

The AWL targets vocabulary that occurs most often in written academic texts. These words also occur in newspapers, but not as often as they do in textbooks. The AWL words appear even less in fiction. If your focus is learning academic vocabulary, you need to make sure you read academic textbooks so that you encounter these words in context.

The AWL is organized into Word Families. Word families are made up of the "parent word" and "family members." Take, for example, the word **maximize**. Its family members include inflections of the verb such as *maximized, maximizes* and *maximizing* as well as the nouns *maximum* and *maximization*.

If you learn the verb **maximize**, you will be able to recognise other family members such as *maximized* when you encounter them in your reading. These words are closely related, and the meaning is likely to be the same or similar. When you are looking for words in this dictionary, think about other word family members too.

In order to read and write successfully, you need to be able to recognize as many words as possible in your textbooks and use as many as possible in your writing. The bigger your vocabulary, the more you will be able to cope with the high reading and writing demands of your studies.

Not all the words from the AWL are included in the ***The Longman Thesaurus of American English***. The *Longman Thesaurus* is a special type of dictionary that helps find synonyms for common words, specifically for students who want to improve their writing. Academic synonyms or related academic words are included in the list of synonyms given for each common word, where appropriate. For example, synonyms for the adjective **certain** include the academic words *definite* and *inevitable*, which are also adjectives and have a similar meaning to *certain*.

Listed on pages 918–927 are the 570 word families on the Academic Word List. The words with an asterisk (*) are words that are included in ***The Longman Thesaurus of American English***, either as key words or as synonyms within a key word entry.

*abandon, *verb*
abandoned, *adjective*
*abnormal, *adjective*
abstract, *adjective*
abstract, *noun*
abstract, *verb*
abstraction, *noun*
*academic, *adjective*
academic, *noun*
*access, *noun*
*access, *verb*
accessible, *adjective*
accommodate, *verb*
*accommodations, *noun*
accompaniment, *noun*
*accompany, *verb*
*accumulate, *verb*
*accuracy, *noun*
*accurate, *adjective*
*achieve, *verb*
*achievement, *noun*
*acknowledge, *verb*
acknowledgement, *noun*
*acquire, *verb*
acquisition, *noun*
*adaptable, *adjective*
adaptation, *noun*
*adequate, *adjective*
adjacent, *adjective*
*adjust, *verb*
*adjustment, *noun*
*administration, *noun*
administrative, *adjective*
*adult, *noun*
*adult, *adjective*
advocacy, *noun*
advocate, *verb*
advocate, *noun*
*affect, *verb*
aggregate, *noun*
aggregate, *adjective*
aggregate, *verb*
*aid, *noun*
*aid, *verb*
albeit, *conjunction*
*allocate, *verb*
allocation, *noun*
*alter, *verb*
*alteration, *noun*
alternate, *adjective*
alternate, *verb*
*alternative, *adjective*
*alternative, *noun*
ambiguity, *noun*
*ambiguous, *adjective*
*amend, *verb*
*amendment, *noun*
analogous, *adjective*
*analogy, *noun*
*analyze, *verb*
*analysis, *noun*
analyst, *noun*
analytical, *adjective*
*annual, *adjective*
*anticipate, *verb*
anticipation, *noun*
apparent, *adjective*
append, *verb*
appendix, *noun*
appreciable, *adjective*
*appreciate, *verb*
*appreciation, *noun*
*approach, *verb*
*approach, *noun*
*appropriate, *adjective*
*approximate, *adjective*
approximate, *verb*
approximation, *noun*
*arbitrary, *adjective*
*area, *noun*
*aspect, *noun*
*assemble, *verb*
*assembly, *noun*
*assess, *verb*
*assessment, *noun*
*assign, *verb*
*assignment, *noun*
*assist, *verb*
*assistance, *noun*
*assume, *verb*
assuming, *conjunction*
*assumption, *noun*
*assurance, *noun*
*assure, *verb*
*attach, *verb*
*attachment, *noun*
*attain, *verb*
attainment, *noun*
*attitude, *noun*
attributable, *adjective*
attribute, *verb*
attribute, *noun*
*author, *noun*
author, *verb*
authoritative, *adjective*
*authority, *noun*
authorship, *noun*
automate, *verb*
*automated, *adjective*
*automatic, *adjective*
automatically, *adverb*
automation, *noun*
available, *adjective*
*aware, *adjective*
awareness, *noun*
behalf, *noun*
*beneficial, *adjective*
beneficiary, *noun*
*benefit, *noun*
benefit, *verb*
*bias, *noun*
bias, *verb*
*biased, *adjective*
*bond, *noun*
bond, *verb*
brevity, *noun*
*brief, *adjective*
brief, *noun*
brief, *verb*
briefing, *noun*
*briefly, *adverb*
*bulk, *noun*
*bulky, *adjective*
*capability, *noun*
*capable, *adjective*
*capacity, *noun*
*category, *noun*
*cease, *verb*
*challenge, *noun*
*challenge, *verb*
*challenging, *adjective*
*channel, *noun*
channel, *verb*
*chapter, *noun*
chart, *noun*
chart, *verb*
chemical, *noun*
chemical, *adjective*
circumstance, *noun*
*citation, *noun*

*cite, verb
*civil, adjective
*clarification, noun
*clarify, verb
clarity, noun
*classic, adjective
*classic, noun
classical, adjective
*clause, noun
code, verb
coded, adjective
coding, noun
coherence, noun
coherent, adjective
coincide, verb
coincident, adjective
coincidental, adjective
*collapse, verb
*collapse, noun
*colleague, noun
*commence, verb
commencement, noun
*comment, noun
*comment, verb
*commentary, noun
commentator, noun
commission, verb
communicable, adjective
*communicate, verb
communicative, adjective
compatibility, noun
compatible, adjective
*compensate, verb
*compensation, noun
compensatory, adjective
compilation, noun
compile, verb
complement, noun
complement, verb
complementary, adjective
*complex, adjective
complex, noun
complexity, noun
*component, noun
component, adjective
*compound, noun
compound, verb
compound, adjective
*comprehensive, adjective
*comprise, verb

computation, noun
compute, verb
*computer, noun
computing, noun
conceivable, adjective
*conceive, verb
*concentrate, verb
*concentration, noun
*concept, noun
*conception, noun
conceptual, adjective
*conclude, verb
*concluding, adjective
*conclusion, noun
conclusive, adjective
concurrent, adjective
*conduct, verb
*conduct, noun
*confer, verb
*conference, noun
confine, verb
confined, adjective
*confirm, verb
*confirmation, noun
*conflict, noun
*conflict, verb
conform, verb
conformation, noun
conformist, adjective
conformity, noun
*consensus, noun
*consent, noun
*consent, verb
consequence, noun
consequent, adjective
*consequently, adverb
*considerable, adjective
considerably, adverb
consist, verb
*consistency, noun
*consistent, adjective
constancy, noun
*constant, adjective
constant, noun
*constantly, adverb
constituency, noun
constituent, noun
constituent, adjective
*constitute, verb
constitution, noun

*constitutional, adjective
constrain, verb
constrained, adjective
constraint, noun
*construct, verb
construct, noun
*construction, noun
constructive, adjective
*consult, verb
consultancy, noun
consultant, noun
*consultation, noun
consultative, adjective
*consume, verb
*consumer, noun
*consumption, noun
*contact, noun
*contact, verb
contact, adjective
*contemporary, adjective
contemporary, noun
*context, noun
contextual, adjective
contextualize, verb
*contract, noun
contract, verb
contractor, noun
*contradict, verb
*contradiction, noun
*contradictory, adjective
*contrary, noun
contrary, adjective
*contrast, noun
*contrast, verb
*contrasting, adjective
*contribute, verb
contribution, noun
*contributor, noun
controversial, adjective
*controversy, noun
convene, verb
*convention, noun
*conventional, adjective
converse, adjective
conversely, adverb
*conversion, noun
*convert, verb
convertible, adjective
*convince, verb
*convinced, adjective

Academic Word List

*convincing, *adjective*
*cooperate, *verb*
*cooperation, *noun*
*cooperative, *adjective*
*coordinate, *verb*
coordinate, *noun*
coordinate, *adjective*
coordination, *noun*
coordinator, *noun*
*core, *noun*
*core, *adjective*
core, *verb*
corporate, *adjective*
*corporation, *noun*
*correspond, *verb*
*correspondence, *noun*
*corresponding, *adjective*
*couple, *noun*
couple, *verb*
*create, *verb*
*creation, *noun*
*creativity, *noun*
creator, *noun*
*credit, *noun*
credit, *verb*
creditor, *noun*
criterion, *noun*
*crucial, *adjective*
*cultural, *adjective*
culturally, *adverb*
*culture, *noun*
*currency, *noun*
cycle, *noun*
cycle, *verb*
cyclic, *adjective*
*data, *noun*
debatable, *adjective*
*debate, *noun*
*debate, *verb*
*decade, *noun*
*decline, *noun*
*decline, *verb*
*deduce, *verb*
*deduction, *noun*
*define, *verb*
*definite, *adjective*
*definitely, *adverb*
*definition, *noun*
definitive, *adjective*
demonstrable, *adjective*
*demonstrate, *verb*
*demonstration, *noun*
demonstrative, *adjective*
*demonstrator, *noun*
*denial, *noun*
denote, *verb*
*deny, *verb*
*depress, *verb*
*depression, *noun*
derivation, *noun*
derivative, *noun*
derive, *verb*
*design, *noun*
design, *verb*
*despite, *preposition*
*detect, *verb*
detection, *noun*
*detective, *noun*
detector, *noun*
deviate, *verb*
deviation, *noun*
*device, *noun*
*devote, *verb*
*devoted, *adjective*
*devotion, *noun*
*differentiate, *verb*
dimension, *noun*
*diminish, *verb*
diminution, *noun*
discrete, *adjective*
*discretion, *noun*
discretionary, *adjective*
discriminate, *verb*
disestablish, *verb*
displace, *verb*
displacement, *noun*
*display, *noun*
*display, *verb*
disposable, *adjective*
disposal, *noun*
dispose, *verb*
disproportion, *noun*
disproportionate, *adjective*
*dissimilar, *adjective*
*distinct, *adjective*
*distinction, *noun*
*distinctive, *adjective*
distinctly, *adverb*
distort, *verb*
*distribute, *verb*
distribution, *noun*
distributive, *adjective*
*diverse, *adjective*
diversify, *verb*
*diversity, *noun*
*document, *noun*
document, *verb*
*documentation, *noun*
domain, *noun*
*domestic, *adjective*
domesticate, *verb*
*domesticated, *adjective*
dominance, *noun*
*dominant, *adjective*
dominate, *verb*
*draft, *noun*
*draft, *verb*
draft, *adjective*
*drama, *noun*
*dramatic, *adjective*
dramatist, *noun*
dramatize, *verb*
duration, *noun*
*dynamic, *adjective*
dynamic, *noun*
economic, *adjective*
*economical, *adjective*
economically, *adverb*
economics, *noun*
economist, *noun*
economy, *noun*
edition, *noun*
editor, *noun*
editorial, *adjective*
editorial, *noun*
*element, *noun*
*eliminate, *verb*
elimination, *noun*
*emerge, *verb*
emergence, *noun*
emergent, *adjective*
emerging, *adjective*
*emphasis, *noun*
*emphasize, *verb*
emphatic, *adjective*
empirical, *adjective*
empiricism, *noun*
*enable, *verb*
enabling, *adjective*
encounter, *verb*

encounter, *noun*
*energetic, *adjective*
*energy, *noun*
enforce, *verb*
enforced, *adjective*
enforcement, *noun*
*enhance, *verb*
enhanced, *adjective*
enormity, *noun*
*enormous, *adjective*
*enormously, *adverb*
*ensure, *verb*
entity, *noun*
environment, *noun*
environmental, *adjective*
*environmentalist, *noun*
equate, *verb*
equation, *noun*
equip, *verb*
*equipment, *noun*
*equivalent, *adjective*
equivalent, *noun*
*erode, *verb*
*erosion, *noun*
erroneous, *adjective*
*error, *noun*
*establish, *verb*
established, *adjective*
*establishment, *noun*
estate, *noun*
*estimate, *noun*
*estimate, *verb*
estimation, *noun*
ethic, *noun*
*ethical, *adjective*
*ethnic, *adjective*
ethnic, *noun*
*evaluate, *verb*
*evaluation, *noun*
eventual, *adjective*
eventuality, *noun*
*eventually, *adverb*
*evidence, *noun*
evident, *adjective*
evidential, *adjective*
*evidently, *adverb*
*evolution, *noun*
evolutionary, *adjective*
*evolve, *verb*
*exceed, *verb*
*exclude, *verb*
excluding, *preposition*
exclusion, *noun*
exclusive, *adjective*
exclusively, *adverb*
*exhibit, *verb*
exhibit, *noun*
*exhibition, *noun*
*expand, *verb*
expansion, *noun*
expansionism, *noun*
expansive, *adjective*
*expert, *noun*
*expert, *adjective*
*expertise, *noun*
*explicit, *adjective*
*exploit, *verb*
exploitation, *noun*
*export, *noun*
*export, *verb*
exporter, *noun*
*expose, *verb*
exposed, *adjective*
exposure, *noun*
*external, *adjective*
externalize, *verb*
*extract, *verb*
extract, *noun*
*extraction, *noun*
facilitate, *verb*
facilitator, *noun*
facility, *noun*
*factor, *noun*
factor, *verb*
*feature, *noun*
feature, *verb*
*federal, *adjective*
federation, *noun*
*fee, *noun*
*file, *noun*
*file, *verb*
filing, *noun*
*final, *adjective*
*final, *noun*
finality, *noun*
*finalize, *verb*
*finally, *adverb*
finance, *noun*
*finance, *verb*
financial, *adjective*
financier, *noun*
*finite, *adjective*
flexibility, *noun*
*flexible, *adjective*
*fluctuate, *verb*
*fluctuation, *noun*
*focus, *verb*
*focus, *noun*
focused, *adjective*
*format, *noun*
format, *verb*
formula, *noun*
formulate, *verb*
*forthcoming, *adjective*
*found, *verb*
*foundation, *noun*
founder, *noun*
*framework, *noun*
*function, *noun*
*function, *verb*
functional, *adjective*
fund, *noun*
fund, *verb*
*fundamental, *adjective*
*fundamentally, *adverb*
funding, *noun*
*furthermore, *adverb*
*gender, *noun*
*generate, *verb*
generation, *noun*
globalization, *noun*
globe, *noun*
*goal, *noun*
*grade, *noun*
*grade, *verb*
graded, *adjective*
grant, *verb*
grant, *noun*
*guarantee, *verb*
*guarantee, *noun*
guideline, *noun*
hence, *adverb*
hierarchical, *adjective*
hierarchy, *noun*
*highlight, *verb*
*hypothesis, *noun*
hypothesize, *verb*
hypothetical, *adjective*
*identical, *adjective*
identifiable, *adjective*

identification, *noun*
*identify, *verb*
identity, *noun*
ideological, *adjective*
ideology, *noun*
ignorance, *noun*
*ignorant, *adjective*
*ignore, *verb*
*illegal, *adjective*
*illogical, *adjective*
*illustrate, *verb*
*illustration, *noun*
illustrative, *adjective*
*image, *noun*
*imagery, *noun*
*immature, *adjective*
*immigrant, *noun*
*immigrate, *verb*
*immigration, *noun*
*impact, *noun*
impact, *verb*
*implement, *verb*
*implement, *noun*
implicate, *verb*
implication, *noun*
*implicit, *adjective*
*imply, *verb*
impose, *verb*
imposition, *noun*
*imprecise, *adjective*
inaccessible, *adjective*
*inaccuracy, *noun*
*inaccurate, *adjective*
inadequacy, *noun*
*inadequate, *adjective*
*inappropriate, *adjective*
incapable, *adjective*
incapacitate, *verb*
*incentive, *noun*
incidence, *noun*
*incident, *noun*
incidentally, *adverb*
*inclination, *noun*
incline, *verb*
incline, *noun*
incoherent, *adjective*
*incompatible, *adjective*
inconceivable, *adjective*
inconclusive, *adjective*
inconsistency, *noun*
*inconsistent, *adjective*
*incorporate, *verb*
incorporated, *adjective*
indefinite, *adjective*
indefinitely, *adverb*
*index, *noun*
index, *verb*
*indicate, *verb*
*indication, *noun*
indicative, *noun*
indicative, *adjective*
indicator, *noun*
indiscretion, *noun*
indistinct, *adjective*
individual, *adjective*
*individual, *noun*
individualism, *noun*
individualist, *noun*
individuality, *noun*
individually, *adverb*
induce, *verb*
induction, *noun*
inevitability, *noun*
*inevitable, *adjective*
inevitably, *adverb*
*infer, *verb*
*inference, *noun*
*infinite, *adjective*
infinitely, *adverb*
inflexible, *adjective*
infrastructure, *noun*
*inherent, *adjective*
inhibit, *verb*
inhibition, *noun*
*initial, *adjective*
initially, *adverb*
*initiate, *verb*
initiation, *noun*
*initiative, *noun*
initiator, *noun*
*injure, *verb*
injured, *adjective*
*injury, *noun*
*innovate, *verb*
*innovation, *noun*
*innovative, *adjective*
innovator, *noun*
*input, *noun*
input, *verb*
insecure, *adjective*
*insert, *verb*
insertion, *noun*
insight, *noun*
insightful, *adjective*
*insignificant, *adjective*
*inspect, *verb*
*inspection, *noun*
inspector, *noun*
instability, *noun*
*instance, *noun*
instance, *verb*
institute, *noun*
institute, *verb*
*institution, *noun*
institutional, *adjective*
institutionalized, *adjective*
*instruct, *verb*
*instruction, *noun*
instructive, *adjective*
*instructor, *noun*
*insufficient, *adjective*
integral, *adjective*
*integrate, *verb*
integrated, *adjective*
integration, *noun*
*integrity, *noun*
*intelligence, *noun*
*intelligent, *adjective*
*intense, *adjective*
*intensify, *verb*
intensity, *noun*
intensive, *adjective*
interact, *verb*
interaction, *noun*
interactive, *adjective*
*intermediate, *adjective*
*internal, *adjective*
internalize, *verb*
*interpret, *verb*
interpretation, *noun*
interpretative, *adjective*
interpretive, *adjective*
*interval, *noun*
intervene, *verb*
intervening, *adjective*
intervention, *noun*
*intrinsic, *adjective*
invalidate, *verb*
invalidity, *noun*
invariable, *adjective*

*invariably, *adverb*
*invest, *verb*
*investigate, *verb*
*investigation, *noun*
investigative, *adjective*
investigator, *noun*
investment, *noun*
investor, *noun*
invisible, *adjective*
invoke, *verb*
*involve, *verb*
involvement, *noun*
*irrational, *adjective*
irrelevance, *noun*
*irrelevant, *adjective*
irreversible, *adjective*
*isolate, *verb*
*isolated, *adjective*
*isolation, *noun*
isolationism, *noun*
*issue, *verb*
*item, *noun*
*job, *noun*
*journal, *noun*
justifiable, *adjective*
*justification, *noun*
*justified, *adjective*
justify, *verb*
*label, *noun*
label, *verb*
*labor, *noun*
*labor, *verb*
labored, *adjective*
*layer, *noun*
layer, *verb*
lecture, *verb*
lecturer, *noun*
*legal, *adjective*
legality, *noun*
legally, *adverb*
legislate, *verb*
legislative, *adjective*
legislator, *noun*
legislature, *noun*
levy, *verb*
levy, *noun*
*liberal, *adjective*
liberal, *noun*
liberalism, *noun*
liberalize, *verb*

liberally, *adverb*
*liberate, *verb*
*liberated, *adjective*
license, *verb*
licensed, *adjective*
likewise, *adverb*
*link, *verb*
*link, *noun*
linkage, *noun*
*locate, *verb*
*location, *noun*
*logical, *adjective*
logician, *noun*
*maintain, *verb*
*maintenance, *noun*
*major, *adjective*
majority, *noun*
*manipulate, *verb*
manipulative, *adjective*
manual, *adjective*
*manual, *noun*
*margin, *noun*
marginal, *adjective*
marginally, *adverb*
maturation, *noun*
*mature, *adjective*
*mature, *verb*
maturity, *noun*
*maximize, *verb*
*maximum, *adjective*
*maximum, *noun*
*mechanism, *noun*
media, *noun*
mediate, *verb*
*medical, *adjective*
*medium, *adjective*
medium, *noun*
*mental, *adjective*
mentality, *noun*
*method, *noun*
*methodical, *adjective*
methodology, *noun*
*migrant, *noun*
*migrate, *verb*
migration, *noun*
migratory, *adjective*
military, *adjective*
*military, *noun*
minimal, *adjective*
*minimize, *verb*

*minimum, *adjective*
*minimum, *noun*
ministerial, *adjective*
ministry, *noun*
*minor, *adjective*
*minority, *noun*
*misinterpret, *verb*
mode, *noun*
*modification, *noun*
*modify, *verb*
*monitor, *verb*
motivated, *adjective*
motivation, *noun*
*motive, *noun*
motive, *adjective*
*mutual, *adjective*
mutually, *adverb*
negate, *verb*
*negative, *adjective*
negative, *noun*
*network, *noun*
network, *verb*
networking, *noun*
*neutral, *adjective*
neutrality, *noun*
neutralize, *verb*
*nevertheless, *adverb*
nonconformist, *noun*
nonetheless, *adverb*
norm, *noun*
*normal, *adjective*
normal, *noun*
normality, *noun*
normalize, *verb*
*normally, *adverb*
*notion, *noun*
notwithstanding, *preposition*
nuclear, *adjective*
*objective, *noun*
*objective, *adjective*
objectively, *adverb*
*obtain, *verb*
obtainable, *adjective*
*obvious, *adjective*
*obviously, *adverb*
occupancy, *noun*
*occupant, *noun*
*occupation, *noun*
occupational, *adjective*
occupier, *noun*

*occupy, *verb*
*occur, *verb*
*occurrence, *noun*
*odd, *adjective*
odds, *noun*
*offset, *verb*
*ongoing, *adjective*
*option, *noun*
*optional, *adjective*
orient, *verb*
orientate, *verb*
orientated, *adjective*
orientation, *noun*
oriented, *adjective*
*outcome, *noun*
*output, *noun*
output, *verb*
overall, *adjective*
overall, *adverb*
*overestimate, *verb*
overestimate, *noun*
overlap, *verb*
overlap, *noun*
*overseas, *adverb*
overseas, *adjective*
panel, *noun*
paradigm, *noun*
*paragraph, *noun*
*parallel, *noun*
parallel, *adjective*
parallel, *verb*
*parameter, *noun*
participant, *noun*
*participate, *verb*
participation, *noun*
participatory, *adjective*
*partner, *noun*
*partnership, *noun*
*passive, *adjective*
passive, *noun*
*perceive, *verb*
percent, *adjective*
percent, *noun*
*percentage, *noun*
*perception, *noun*
*period, *noun*
periodic, *adjective*
*periodical, *noun*
*persist, *verb*
*persistence, *noun*
*persistent, *adjective*
*perspective, *noun*
*phase, *noun*
phase, *verb*
*phenomenal, *adjective*
*phenomenon, *noun*
philosopher, *noun*
philosophical, *adjective*
philosophize, *verb*
philosophy, *noun*
*physical, *adjective*
physically, *adverb*
plus, *preposition*
plus, *noun*
plus, *adjective*
*policy, *noun*
*portion, *noun*
*pose, *verb*
*pose, *noun*
*positive, *adjective*
positively, *adverb*
*potential, *adjective*
*potential, *noun*
potentially, *adverb*
practitioner, *noun*
*precede, *verb*
precedence, *noun*
precedent, *noun*
*preceding, *adjective*
*precise, *adjective*
*precisely, *adverb*
*precision, *noun*
precision, *adjective*
*predict, *verb*
predictable, *adjective*
*prediction, *noun*
predominance, *noun*
*predominant, *adjective*
*predominantly, *adverb*
predominate, *verb*
*preliminary, *adjective*
preliminary, *noun*
presumably, *adverb*
*presume, *verb*
presumption, *noun*
*previous, *adjective*
*previously, *adverb*
primacy, *noun*
*primarily, *adverb*
*primary, *adjective*
*prime, *adjective*
*principal, *adjective*
*principally, *adverb*
*principle, *noun*
principled, *adjective*
prior, *adjective*
prioritize, *verb*
priority, *noun*
procedural, *adjective*
*procedure, *noun*
*proceed, *verb*
proceeding, *noun*
proceeds, *noun*
*process, *noun*
process, *verb*
processed, *adjective*
professional, *adjective*
professional, *noun*
professionalism, *noun*
professionally, *adverb*
*prohibit, *verb*
*prohibition, *noun*
prohibitive, *adjective*
*project, *noun*
*project, *verb*
projection, *noun*
*promote, *verb*
promoter, *noun*
promotion, *noun*
*proportion, *noun*
proportional, *adjective*
proportionate, *adjective*
*prospect, *noun*
*prospective, *adjective*
*protocol, *noun*
psychological, *adjective*
psychologist, *noun*
psychology, *noun*
*publication, *noun*
*publish, *verb*
publisher, *noun*
publishing, *noun*
*purchase, *verb*
purchase, *noun*
*pursue, *verb*
*pursuit, *noun*
qualitative, *adjective*
*quotation, *noun*
*quote, *verb*
*quote, *noun*

*__radical__, *adjective*
__radical__, *noun*
*__random__, *adjective*
*__range__, *noun*
__range__, *verb*
*__ratio__, *noun*
*__rational__, *adjective*
__rationalism__, *noun*
__rationalize__, *verb*
*__react__, *verb*
*__reaction__, *noun*
__reactionary__, *adjective*
__reactionary__, *noun*
__reactivate__, *verb*
__reactive__, *adjective*
__reactor__, *noun*
__readjust__, *verb*
__reassess__, *verb*
__reconstruct__, *verb*
__reconstruction__, *noun*
*__recover__, *verb*
*__recovery__, *noun*
__recreate__, *verb*
__redistribute__, *verb*
__redistribution__, *noun*
*__refine__, *verb*
__refined__, *adjective*
__refinement__, *noun*
*__regime__, *noun*
*__region__, *noun*
__regional__, *adjective*
*__register__, *noun*
__register__, *verb*
__registration__, *noun*
__regulate__, *verb*
*__regulation__, *noun*
__regulator__, *noun*
__regulatory__, *adjective*
*__reinforce__, *verb*
__reinforcement__, *noun*
__reinvest__, *verb*
*__reject__, *verb*
*__rejection__, *noun*
*__relax__, *verb*
*__relaxation__, *noun*
*__release__, *verb*
__release__, *noun*
*__relevant__, *adjective*
*__reliable__, *adjective*
*__reliance__, *noun*
__reliant__, *adjective*
*__relocate__, *verb*
__reluctance__, *noun*
*__reluctant__, *adjective*
__rely__, *verb*
__removable__, *adjective*
*__removal__, *noun*
*__remove__, *verb*
__remove__, *noun*
*__require__, *verb*
*__requirement__, *noun*
__reschedule__, *verb*
*__research__, *noun*
*__research__, *verb*
*__reside__, *verb*
*__residence__, *noun*
*__resident__, *noun*
__resident__, *adjective*
__residential__, *adjective*
*__resolution__, *noun*
*__resolve__, *verb*
__resolve__, *noun*
__resource__, *noun*
__resource__, *verb*
__resourceful__, *adjective*
*__respond__, *verb*
__respondent__, *noun*
*__response__, *noun*
__responsive__, *adjective*
__restoration__, *noun*
*__restore__, *verb*
__restored__, *adjective*
*__restrain__, *verb*
__restraint__, *noun*
*__restrict__, *verb*
*__restricted__, *adjective*
*__restriction__, *noun*
__restrictive__, *adjective*
__restructure__, *verb*
*__retain__, *verb*
__retainer__, *noun*
__retention__, *noun*
__retentive__, *adjective*
*__reveal__, *verb*
*__revealing__, *adjective*
*__revelation__, *noun*
*__revenue__, *noun*
__reversal__, *noun*
*__reverse__, *verb*
__reverse__, *noun*
__reverse__, *adjective*
__reversible__, *adjective*
*__revise__, *verb*
__revision__, *noun*
*__revolution__, *noun*
*__revolutionary__, *adjective*
*__revolutionary__, *noun*
*__revolutionize__, *verb*
*__rigid__, *adjective*
*__role__, *noun*
*__route__, *noun*
__route__, *verb*
*__scenario__, *noun*
*__schedule__, *noun*
__schedule__, *verb*
__schematic__, *adjective*
*__scheme__, *noun*
*__scheme__, *verb*
*__scope__, *noun*
*__section__, *noun*
__section__, *verb*
__sector__, *noun*
*__secure__, *adjective*
*__secure__, *verb*
*__securely__, *adverb*
*__security__, *noun*
*__seek__, *verb*
*__select__, *verb*
__select__, *adjective*
*__selection__, *noun*
*__selective__, *adjective*
__selector__, *noun*
*__sequence__, *noun*
__sequencing__, *noun*
__sequential__, *adjective*
*__series__, *noun*
*__sex__, *noun*
*__sexism__, *noun*
__sexual__, *adjective*
__sexuality__, *noun*
__shift__, *verb*
*__shift__, *noun*
*__significant__, *adjective*
__significantly__, *adverb*
*__signify__, *verb*
*__similar__, *adjective*
*__similarity__, *noun*
__similarly__, *adverb*
*__simulate__, *verb*
__simulated__, *adjective*

***simulation,** *noun*
***site,** *noun*
***sole,** *adjective*
solely, *adverb*
***somewhat,** *adverb*
***source,** *noun*
source, *verb*
***specific,** *adjective*
specific, *noun*
***specifically,** *adverb*
specification, *noun*
***specify,** *verb*
sphere, *noun*
***spherical,** *adjective*
stability, *noun*
stabilize, *verb*
***stable,** *adjective*
statistic, *noun*
statistician, *noun*
***status,** *noun*
***straightforward,** *adjective*
strategic, *adjective*
strategist, *noun*
***strategy,** *noun*
***stress,** *noun*
***stress,** *verb*
stressed, *adjective*
stressful, *adjective*
structural, *adjective*
***structure,** *noun*
***structure,** *verb*
structured, *adjective*
***style,** *noun*
style, *verb*
styling, *noun*
***stylish,** *adjective*
stylized, *adjective*
submission, *noun*
***submit,** *verb*
subordinate, *adjective*
subordinate, *noun*
subordinate, *verb*
***subsequent,** *adjective*
***subsequently,** *adverb*
subsidiary, *adjective*
subsidize, *verb*
subsidy, *noun*
***substitute,** *noun*
substitute, *verb*
substitution, *noun*
succession, *noun*
successive, *adjective*
***successor,** *noun*
sufficiency, *noun*
***sufficient,** *adjective*
***sum,** *noun*
sum, *verb*
***summarize,** *verb*
***summary,** *noun*
summary, *adjective*
summation, *noun*
***supplement,** *noun*
***supplement,** *verb*
supplementary, *adjective*
***survey,** *noun*
***survey,** *verb*
survival, *noun*
***survive,** *verb*
***survivor,** *noun*
***suspend,** *verb*
***suspension,** *noun*
***sustain,** *verb*
***sustainable,** *adjective*
sustained, *adjective*
sustenance, *noun*
***symbol,** *noun*
symbolic, *adjective*
symbolism, *noun*
***symbolize,** *verb*
tape, *noun*
***tape,** *verb*
***target,** *noun*
target, *verb*
task, *verb*
***team,** *noun*
team, *verb*
***technical,** *adjective*
technically, *adverb*
***technique,** *noun*
***technological,** *adjective*
***technology,** *noun*
***temporary,** *adjective*
***tense,** *adjective*
***tension,** *noun*
***terminal,** *adjective*
***terminal,** *noun*
***terminate,** *verb*
termination, *noun*
***text,** *noun*
textual, *adjective*
thematic, *adjective*
***theme,** *noun*
theoretical, *adjective*
theoretically, *adverb*
theorist, *noun*
***theory,** *noun*
***thereby,** *adverb*
***thesis,** *noun*
***topic,** *noun*
topical, *adjective*
***trace,** *verb*
***trace,** *noun*
tracing, *noun*
***traditional,** *adjective*
traditionalist, *noun*
***transfer,** *verb*
transfer, *noun*
transference, *noun*
***transform,** *verb*
***transformation,** *noun*
***transit,** *noun*
***transition,** *noun*
transitional, *adjective*
transitory, *adjective*
transmission, *noun*
***transmit,** *verb*
transport, *noun*
***transport,** *verb*
***transportation,** *noun*
transporter, *noun*
trigger, *noun*
***trigger,** *verb*
***ultimate,** *adjective*
ultimately, *adverb*
unaccompanied, *adjective*
unaffected, *adjective*
unaided, *adjective*
unalterable, *adjective*
***unambiguous,** *adjective*
unanticipated, *adjective*
unapproachable, *adjective*
unattached, *adjective*
unattainable, *adjective*
unavailable, *adjective*
***unaware,** *adjective*
***unbiased,** *adjective*
uncharted, *adjective*
***unconstitutional,** *adjective*
unconventional, *adjective*
undeniable, *adjective*

*underestimate, *verb*
underestimate, *noun*
*undergo, *verb*
underlie, *verb*
*underlying, *adjective*
undertake, *verb*
*undertaking, *noun*
undiminished, *adjective*
uneconomical, *adjective*
unethical, *adjective*
unfounded, *adjective*
unification, *noun*
unified, *adjective*
*uniform, *adjective*
uniformity, *noun*
*unify, *verb*
*unique, *adjective*
unjustified, *adjective*
unlicensed, *adjective*
unobtainable, *adjective*
unparalleled, *adjective*
unprecedented, *adjective*
*unpredictable, *adjective*
unprincipled, *adjective*
unpublished, *adjective*
unregulated, *adjective*
unreliable, *adjective*
unresolved, *adjective*
unresponsive, *adjective*
unrestrained, *adjective*
unrestricted, *adjective*
unscheduled, *adjective*
unspecified, *adjective*
*unstable, *adjective*
unstressed, *adjective*
unstructured, *adjective*
unsustainable, *adjective*
utility, *noun*
*utilize, *verb*
*valid, *adjective*
validate, *verb*
*variable, *adjective*
variable, *noun*
variance, *noun*
variant, *noun*
*variation, *noun*
*varied, *adjective*
*vary, *verb*
vehicle, *noun*
version, *noun*
via, *preposition*
*violate, *verb*
violation, *noun*
*virtual, *adjective*
*virtually, *adverb*
visibility, *noun*
visible, *adjective*
visibly, *adverb*
*vision, *noun*
visual, *adjective*
*visualize, *verb*
visually, *adverb*
*volume, *noun*
*voluntarily, *adverb*
*voluntary, *adjective*
volunteer, *noun*
*volunteer, *verb*
welfare, *noun*
*whereas, *conjunction*
whereby, *adverb*
*widespread, *adjective*

Irregular Verbs

This chart shows the verbs that have irregular forms for the **Past Tense**, **Past Participle**, or **Present Participle**. When a verb has more than one form that is used, the most common form is given first.

Verb	Past Tense	Past Participle	Present Participle
arise	arose	arisen	arising
awake	awoke	awoken	awaking
be	was/were	been	being
bear	bore	borne	bearing
beat	beat	beaten	beating
become	became	become	becoming
begin	began	begun	beginning
bend	bent	bent	bending
bet	bet	bet	betting
bid	bid	bid	bidding
bind	bound	bound	binding
bite	bit	bitten	biting
bleed	bled	bled	bleeding
blow	blew	blown	blowing
break	broke	broken	breaking
breed	bred	bred	breeding
bring	brought	brought	bringing
broadcast	broadcast *or* broadcasted	broadcast *or* broadcasted	broadcasting
build	built	built	building
burn	burned *or* burnt	burned *or* burnt	burning
burst	burst	burst	bursting
buy	bought	bought	buying
cast	cast	cast	casting
catch	caught	caught	catching
choose	chose	chosen	choosing
cling	clung	clung	clinging
come	came	come	coming
cost	cost	cost	costing
creep	crept	crept	creeping
cut	cut	cut	cutting
deal	dealt	dealt	dealing
dig	dug	dug	digging
dive	dived *or* dove	dived	diving
do	did	done	doing
draw	drew	drawn	drawing
dream	dreamed *or* dreamt	dreamed *or* dreamt	dreaming
drink	drank	drunk	drinking
drive	drove	driven	driving
dwell	dwelled *or* dwelt	dwelled *or* dwelt	dwelling
eat	ate	eaten	eating
fall	fell	fallen	falling
feed	fed	fed	feeding

Verb	Past Tense	Past Participle	Present Participle
feel	felt	felt	feeling
fight	fought	fought	fighting
find	found	found	finding
fit	fit *or* fitted	fit *or* fitted	fitting
flee	fled	fled	fleeing
fling	flung	flung	flinging
fly	flew	flown	flying
forbid	forbid *or* forbade	forbidden	forbidding
foresee	foresaw	foreseen	foreseeing
forget	forgot	forgotten	forgetting
forgive	forgave	forgiven	forgiving
freeze	froze	frozen	freezing
get	got	gotten	getting
give	gave	given	giving
go	went	gone	going
grind	ground	ground	grinding
grow	grew	grown	growing
hang	hung	hung	hanging
have	had	had	having
hear	heard	heard	hearing
hide	hid	hidden	hiding
hit	hit	hit	hitting
hold	held	held	holding
hurt	hurt	hurt	hurting
keep	kept	kept	keeping
kneel	knelt *or* kneeled	knelt *or* kneeled	kneeling
knit	knit *or* knitted	knit *or* knitted	knitting
know	knew	known	knowing
lay	laid	laid	laying
lead	led	led	leading
leap	leaped *or* leapt	leaped *or* leapt	leaping
leave	left	left	leaving
lend	lent	lent	lending
let	let	let	letting
lie[1]	lay	lain	lying
lie[2]	lied	lied	lying
light	lit *or* lighted	lit *or* lighted	lighting
lose	lost	lost	losing
make	made	made	making
mean	meant	meant	meaning
meet	met	met	meeting
mislead	misled	misled	misleading
mistake	mistook	mistaken	mistaking
misunderstand	misunderstood	misunderstood	misunderstanding
mow	mowed	mown *or* mowed	mowing
outdo	outdid	outdone	outdoing
outgrow	outgrew	outgrown	outgrowing
overcome	overcame	overcome	overcoming

Verb	Past Tense	Past Participle	Present Participle
overdo	overdid	overdone	overdoing
overhear	overheard	overheard	overhearing
oversleep	overslept	overslept	oversleeping
overthrow	overthrew	overthrown	overthrowing
pay	paid	paid	paying
prove	proved	proved *or* proven	proving
put	put	put	putting
quit	quit	quit	quitting
read	read	read	reading
redo	redid	redone	redoing
repay	repaid	repaid	repaying
rewind	rewound	rewound	rewinding
rewrite	rewrote	rewritten	rewriting
ride	rode	ridden	riding
ring	rang	rung	ringing
rise	rose	risen	rising
run	ran	run	running
saw	sawed	sawed *or* sawn	sawing
say	said	said	saying
see	saw	seen	seeing
seek	sought	sought	seeking
sell	sold	sold	selling
send	sent	sent	sending
set	set	set	setting
sew	sewed	sewn *or* sewed	sewing
shake	shook	shaken	shaking
shed	shed	shed	shedding
shine	shone	shone	shining
shoot	shot	shot	shooting
show	showed	shown	showing
shrink	shrank	shrunk	shrinking
shut	shut	shut	shutting
sing	sang	sung	singing
sink	sank *or* sunk	sunk	sinking
sit	sat	sat	sitting
sleep	slept	slept	sleeping
slide	slid	slid	sliding
slit	slit	slit	slitting
sneak	sneaked *or* snuck	sneaked *or* snuck	sneaking
sow	sowed	sown *or* sowed	sowing
speak	spoke	spoken	speaking
speed	sped *or* speeded	sped *or* speeded	speeding
spend	spent	spent	spending
spin	spun	spun	spinning
spit	spit *or* spat	spit *or* spat	spitting
split	split	split	splitting
spread	spread	spread	spreading
spring	sprang	sprung	springing

Verb	Past Tense	Past Participle	Present Participle
stand	stood	stood	standing
steal	stole	stolen	stealing
stick	stuck	stuck	sticking
sting	stung	stung	stinging
stink	stank *or* stunk	stunk	stinking
stride	strode	stridden	striding
strike	struck	struck *or* stricken	striking
string	strung	strung	stringing
strive	strove *or* strived	striven *or* strived	striving
swear	swore	sworn	swearing
sweep	swept	swept	sweeping
swell	swelled	swollen	swelling
swim	swam	swum	swimming
swing	swung	swung	swinging
take	took	taken	taking
teach	taught	taught	teaching
tear	tore	torn	tearing
tell	told	told	telling
think	thought	thought	thinking
throw	threw	thrown	throwing
thrust	thrust	thrust	thrusting
undergo	underwent	undergone	undergoing
understand	understood	understood	understanding
undo	undid	undone	undoing
unwind	unwound	unwound	unwinding
uphold	upheld	upheld	upholding
upset	upset	upset	upsetting
wake	woke	woken	waking
wear	wore	worn	wearing
weave	wove	woven	weaving
weep	wept	wept	weeping
wet	wet *or* wetted	wet *or* wetted	wetting
win	won	won	winning
wind	wound	wound	winding
withdraw	withdrew	withdrawn	withdrawing
withhold	withheld	withheld	withholding
withstand	withstood	withstood	withstanding
wring	wrung	wrung	wringing
write	wrote	written	writing

Picture Credits

The publisher would like to thank the following for their kind permission to reproduce their photographs:

(Key: b-bottom; c-centre; l-left; r-right; t-top)

Alamy Images: Tomas Abad 9tl, aldegonde le compte 487c, Davo Blair 358bl, Pat Canova 53cl, andrew chittock 438c, Cole Settle 380r, Corbis Bridge 852, Simon Curtis 481 (fragments), Sam Dao 514br, Chad Ehlers 34t, Fancy 365tl, PE Forsberg 67br, Richard Green 333tl, David Grossman 256bl, Steve Hamblin 395tl, i love images / city break 853, Independent Picture Service 305 (cottage), INSADCO Photography 588tl, itanistock 380l, Jaak Nilson 842, Juniors Bildarchiv 338cr, Krzysztof Szpil 297bl, Ruslan Kudrin 643b, Kuttig - People 365bl, Kuttig - RF - Kids 338cl, Lloyd Sutton 832b, Peter T Lovatt 425b, M.Sobreira 855, Monteverde 438b, ian nolan 481 (shard), Gabe Palmer 275tc, Ian Miles-Flashpoint Pictures 128bl, Profimedia.CZ a.s. 235br, Roswitha Reisinger 305 (apartments), Chris Schmid / Eyemage Media 274c, Alistair Scott 487b, Lana Sundman 305 (mobile homes), Nik Taylor 223tl, 514cr, Martin Thomas Photography 577tr, TongRo Images Inc. 850t, UpperCut Images 854, Visions of America, LLC 365br, Washington Stock Photo 599tr, Wavebreak Media ltd 487t, Janine Wiedel 9tr, Rob Wilkinson 244b, Richard Zanettacci 395br, 779 (scar), ZUMA Wire Service 438t; **Art Directors and TRIP Photo Library:** Helene Rogers 178br, 601c, 715t; **Corbis:** Franco Vogt 842t, Ocean 242cl, 403l, Randy Pench 9b, Lisa Pines / Fancy 338bl, Plattform / Johnér Images 492l, Patrick Strattner / fstop 256br, Dan Wozniak / ZUMA Press 708tc (left); **DK Images:** 606bl, Dorling Kindersley 55br, 143 (dice), 179br, Dave King 128tc (left), 143 (grate), Ian O'Leary 481 (wedge), Gary Ombler 452b, Tim Ridley 481 (slab), Mark Winwood 164tl; **Fotolia.com:** Actionpics 517b, Africa Studio 256tr, AGITA LEIMANE 256cr, albinoni 358tl, alephcomo1 365tr, Aaron Amat 456tr, 481 (bar), 481 (scrap), Andres Rodriguez 797l, 797r, Galyna Andrushko 558tr, Matthew Antonino 836b, Yuri Arcurs 372 (line), 708tr, 776 (ecstatic), 845, ArtHdesign 188tr, artincamera 739 (waddle), auremar 344tr, 776 (angry), Kitch Bain 456cr, balavan 779 (wrinkles), Andrey Bandurenko 601bl, 601br, marilyn barbone 140tr, Jana Behr 71cl, Alexei Bezborodov 372 (rut), BHARATHI RAMARAJU 599br, bloomua 771l, Bogdan Wankowicz 791tl, bonniemarie 52cl, Sinisa Botas 626bl, Irina Brinza 67tr, brusinarn 559tl, Monkey Business 180b, 773 (formal), 809r, CallallooAlexis 98bl, Carlson 372 (row), cat 396l, diego cervo 98br, 235bl, 403r, Eky Chan 642tr, chantal cecchetti 844l, CHILL 348br, christian42 809l, clearlens 82t, Coin 694 (crest), cosma 694 (kitchen utensils), Simon Coste 396r, Csaba Peterdi 289 (hard), 789 (hard), cynoclub 789 (fluffy), DAN 289 (stiff), 789 (stiff), dbvirago 53tr, denis_pc 65br, Denisa V 708tl, determined 559bl, dja65 39bl, dny3d 597tl, George Dolgikh 188bl, 345tr, dragon_fang 42 (milk), 514cl, drx 274l, duckman76 47 (handsome), Elenathewise 128tc (right), 514bl, Klaus Eppele 561br, ETIEN 606tr, FC Photography 289 (crisp), 791bl, filtv 825r, Stephen Finn 55tl, forcdan 183t, fotoeg 128tl, fotowebbox 55tr, FotoWorx 441b, francomonticomo 211r, gnohz 348tr, Warren Goldswain 626tr, goodluz 776 (scared), grekoff 39cr, Jörg Hackemann 181l, HandsomePictures 164b, irisphoto1 47 (magnificent), Mickael IRLES 275tr, Eric Isselée 280l, Dawid Jankowski 441t, Jgz 58 (gigantic trees), JJAVA 98tl, 481 (chunks), paulo Jorge cruz 586t, Joshua Resnick 789 (creamy), JPC-PROD 815l, Julián Rovagnati 791br, jwblinn 395cl, 779 (mole), karandaev 275tl, Irina Karlova 143 (chop), kazoka303030 52b, Kevan O'Meara 803r, Sergey Khamidulin 694 (tip), Sven Knie 441cl, koya79 65tl, Oleksandr Kramarenko 577tl, kropic 806l, Anna Kucherova 481 (slice), Oleg Kulakov 345bl, Chris leachman 347tl, Leonid & Anna Dedukh 47 (cute), Liaurinko 345br, Lidara 348bl, liping dong 58 (vast), lmel900 806r, Lucky Dragon USA 601t, lunamarina 193 (uninhabited), 822tr, Lyudmyla 179tr, Magalice 55bl, Franco Mantegani 275br, Maridav 773 (tailored), mariesacha 181r, Matti 557br, mayhemfreak 305 (hut), mearicon 694 (tools), meryll 803l, michaklootwijk 42 (apple), Warren Millar 242tr, Miroslawa Drozdowski 791tr, monstersparrow 832t, Ruud Morijn 661b, mykeyruna 344b, Nando Azevedo 785l, Igor Negovelov 642bl, neilovery 456tl, Netzer Johannes 841, Nik 72c, nn-fotografie 479tr, nyul 29t, oksun70 739 (crawl), Oleg-F 452t, Oleksandr 53cr, Popova Olga 643cr, Ruslan Olinchuk 561bl, Olyly 708br, Pat on stock 517tr, paylessimages 100t, Franz Pfluegl 71tl, GoodMood Photo 179tl, photoclicks 72t, Picture-Factory 456b, 776 (upset), Pixsooz 29b, Victor Potasyev 479bl, Gennadiy Poznyakov 608l, Anton Prado 183b, Prod. Numérik 47 (stunning), Scott Prokop 82c, 305 (cabin), Adam Radosavljevic 694 (dental instruments), Rafael Ramirez 305 (mansion), Ramses 597b, Silvano Rebai 358tr, Rido 773 (casual), Dmitry Rukhlenko 345c, Sabphoto 338tl, Julija Sapic 102tl, 102br, Mario Savoia 577b, Scanrail 708bl, Schlierner 98tr, Elena Schweitzer 634tr, Andrey Semenov 557t, Sergiy Serdyuk 128bc, Sergey Lukianov 831b, Sharpshot 425t, 785r, .shock 822br, shoot4u 689b, Andrey Sidey 375r, Sielemann 53tl, Viorel Sima 180tr, Rechitan Sorin 326 (interior car), soupstock 395bl, Subbotina Anna 844r, Sura Nualpradid 815r, SVLuma 372 (tracks), Ferenc Szelepcsenyi 561tl, taesmileland 140br, Tatty 441cr, teracreonte 347tr, terex 39br, 65bl, thanomphong 588tr, Tiler84 395tr, Harald Tjøstheim 256cl, Touch

235tr, Tomasz Trojanowski 344tl, valdis torms 597tr, Valua Vitaly 52cr, Jonathan Vasata 642br, Serghei Velusceac 235tl, 275bl, Vibe Images 338br, 606tl, 739 (hike), 825l, visuall2 47 (scenic), volff 326 (core), 492r, volkerladwig 42 (bread), vovan 193 (blank), Gary Whitton 300br, wngrider 58 (giant), yellowj 771r, yeti 694 (peak), Yong Hian Lim 242cr, Zacarias da Mata 58 (gigantic waves), alexandre zveiger 193 (empty restaurant), 326 (interior door), 326 (internal); **FotoLibra:** Philip Carr 178bl, 377tr, 377b, Janet Czekirda 223br, Mark Ferguson 71tr, 739 (tiptoe), Mark Goodwin 300cl, William Lee 242bl, Gordon Longmate 242br, Bernard O'Kane 274r, Richard Prud'homme 244t, Anthony A Rowe 689t, James Scrivener 256tl, Lana Sundman 297tl, 297tr, Harvey Wood 71b; **Getty Images:** Alistair Baker / Taxi 338bc, Tom Bean / Stone 557bl, bilderlounge 297br, David Clapp 193 (hollow), 326 (inside tree), CMSP 325br, Jeffrey Coolidge / The Image Bank 333tr, DTP / Stone+ 514t, F64 / Digital Vision 266t, Jon Feingersh / The Image Bank 52tr, Fotosearch 282b, Jeff Greenough / Blend Images 838, Bill Keefrey 164tr, LatitudeStock - Dennis Stone / Gallo Images 305 (shack), Nigel Pavitt / AWL Images 358br, Charles Peterson / Photographer's Choice 739 (wade), Lisa Pines / Taxi 517tl, PM Images 223bl, Frank Schwere 193 (deserted), Lisa Spindler 178tl, Stella 326 (inside pocket), Dimitri Vervitsiotis / Stone 708tc (right), Yellow Dog Productions 266b; **PhotoDisc:** 479br; **Press Association Images:** Nick Wass / AP 599bl; **Rex Features:** KPA / Zuma 223tr, London News Pictures 739 (march); **Science Photo Library Ltd:** DR P. MARAZZI 325tr; **Shutterstock.com:** 1125089601 282tr, Samuel Acosta 333b, adam. golabek 62, AISPIX by Image Source 65tr, Aletia 561tr, Stefan Petru Andronache 280r, Anneka 67tl, Walter G Arce 300bl, ARENA Creative 643tl, ayazad 375l, B Brown 300tr, Bashutskyy 65cr, Dan Breckwoldt 588b, Alexander Chaikin 606br, Paul Cowan 143 (carve), Jaimie Duplass 395cr, 779 (freckles), Daryl Dyck 608r, Elena Elisseeva 128tr, Johan W. Elzenga 275bc, Dirk Ercken 558tl, Frank F. Haub 128br, fotokik_dot_com 140bl, fotoluminate 835, Filip Fuxa 82b, FuzzBones 715b, gillmar 65c, Iwona Grodzka 558br, hans.slegers 634tl, Margo Harrison 13t, Damian Herde 325bl, Lim Yong Hian 39tr, hippo 188br, Home-lab 242tl, HomeStudio 65cl, terekhov igor 39cl, IgorXIII 372 (furrows), Tischenko Irina 193 (empty glass), itsmejust 71cr, Doctor Jools 61, Stepan Kapl 481 (chips), kedrov 39tl, Anne Kitzman 180tl, 773 (dressy), Fedor Kondratenko 325tl, Konstantin L 305 (town houses), l i g h t p o e t 102tr, Susan Law Cain 305 (duplex), vilena makarica 377tl, Aleksandr Markin 626tl, Karl R. Martin 837, Ilja Mašík 831t, Tyler Olson 850b, Papandreos 13b, Losevsky Pavel 52tl, 193tc (left), Jose Antonio Perez 661t, Thomas M Perkins 479tl, Picsfive 372 (groove), Pongphan.R 634b, Tatiana Popova 178tr, Pylypenko 558bl, redswept 140tl, ronstik 282tl, Henryk Sadura 300cr, jean schweitzer 586b, SeDmi 481 (lumps), Serg64 747, Iriana Shiyan 193 (bare), sweetok 642tl, Artur Synenko 188tl, Tony Campbell 836t, VasikO 456cl, Ieva Vincer 143 (peel), vlad_star 347b, Vaclav Volrab 211l, Piotr Wawrzyniuk 338tr, Wildheart 300tl, winnond 559r, Senol Yaman 345tl, Igor Zakowski cartooniz_com 179bl, Ron Zmiri 348tl, Zurijeta 143 (slice); **SuperStock:** BE&W 102bl, Francisco Cruz 67bl, F1 ONLINE 839, imagebroker. net 326 (inner), Cultura Limited 100b, Zen Shui 72b, Jeremy Woodhouse 34b, 822l

All other images © Pearson Education

Text

We are grateful to the following for permission to reproduce copyright material:

Poetry in Prose Poems (p. 908) from "I Lie Down", "The Cold" (Lou Beach, 2012) http://www.facebook. com/420Characters, copyright © Lou Beach. Reproduced by permission of Harvery Klinger, Inc.

Extract in Book Review (pp. 872-873) from 'The Girl with the Pearl Earring' by Tracy Chevalier. Reviewed by Erin Dempsey on 30 September 2003, www.bookreporter.com. Reproduced by permission of The Book Report Network.

Extract in Short Story (p. 911) from "I See Him" Short story (Lou Beach, 2012) http://www.facebook. com/420Characters, copyright © Lou Beach. Reproduced by permission of Harvery Klinger, Inc.

In some instances we have been unable to trace the owners of copyright material, and we would appreciate any information that would enable us to do so

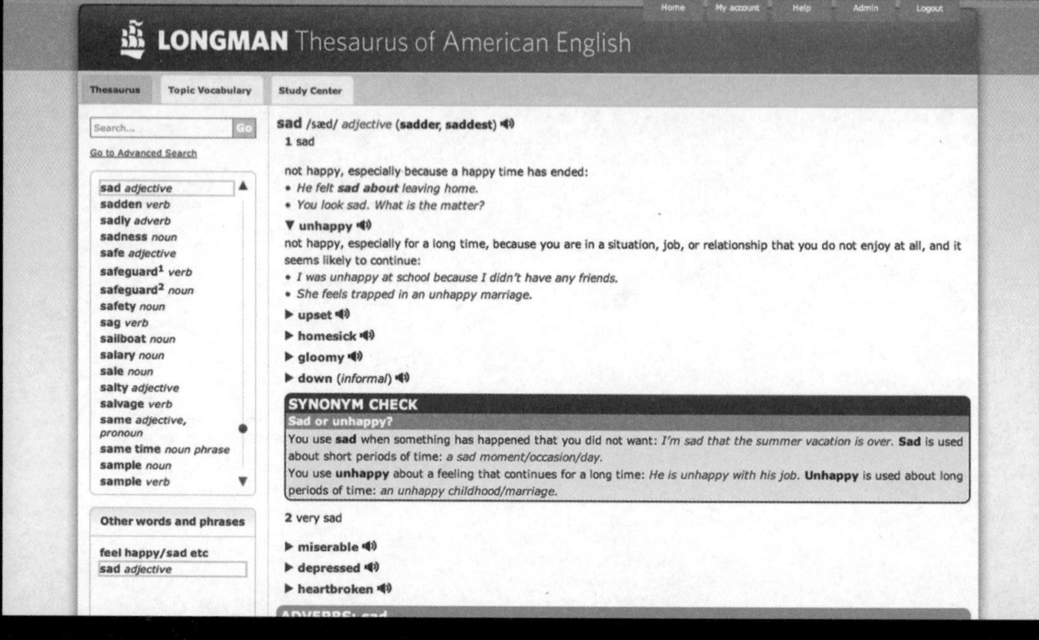

Online Thesaurus

Go to www.longmandictionariesusa.com

→ ***Longman Thesaurus of American English*** – with pronunciation of all the words

→ **Study Center** – interactive practice to help you learn synonyms, Academic Words, and Topic Vocabulary